RICHARD ASKWITH

Richard Askwith has been a journalist for more than 35 years, including 15 as Associate Editor of the *Independent*. A keen runner and a lifelong admirer of Emil Zátopek, he has written two previous books about running. His first, *Feet in the Clouds*, won Best New Writer at the British Sports Book Awards and the Bill Rollinson Prize for Landscape and Tradition. It was shortlisted for the William Hill and Boardman-Tasker prizes and was named by *Runner's World* as one of the three best running books of all time. His 2014 book, *Running Free*, was shortlisted for the Thwaites-Wainwright Prize.

ALSO BY RICHARD ASKWITH

Feet in the Clouds: A Tale of Fell-Running and Obsession

Running Free: A Runner's Journey Back to Nature

RICHARD ASKWITH

Today We Die a Little

Emil Zátopek,
Olympic Legend to Cold War Hero

YELLOW JERSEY PRESS
LONDON

1 3 5 7 9 10 8 6 4 2

Yellow Jersey Press, an imprint of Vintage,
20 Vauxhall Bridge Road,
London SW1V 2SA

Yellow Jersey Press is part of the Penguin Random House group of companies whose addresses can be found at global.penguinrandomhouse.com

First published in paperback by Yellow Jersey Press in 2017
First published in hardback by Yellow Jersey Press in 2016

www.vintage-books.co.uk

A CIP catalogue record for this book is available from the British Library

ISBN 9780224100359

Printed and bound in Great Britain by Clays Ltd, St Ives plc

Contents

Prologue

The curious incident

On a sun-scorched runway in Prague, a twin-engined Československé Aerolinie airliner is waiting for take-off from Ruzyně International Airport. More than a hundred young men and women, the finest athletes in the Communist state of Czechoslovakia, are bound for Helsinki, a seven-hour flight away, where the XVth Olympic Games will begin in nine days' time. But there is a problem. The brightest and best of them all, Emil Zátopek, is absent.

The greatest runner of his generation – perhaps of all time – is missing from the flight that is due to take him to the Games that will define his sporting life. He is at the height of his powers: twenty-nine years old, a world record holder, a reigning Olympic champion who has lost only one of his last seventy races at his specialist distances, with his sights set on an unprecedented and never-to-be-repeated clean sweep of endurance running events.

It is the most important journey of his life. And he is late.

At least, that is how it looks. Emil's wife, Dana, knows better. A javelin thrower with Olympic ambitions of her own, she is on the plane already, weeping. She knows the real reason why Emil is not beside her. She knows that he is engaged in a high-stakes game of 'chicken' that could not just end his career but quite plausibly see him sent to a labour camp.

It is Thursday, 10 July 1952. The Iron Curtain that fell across Europe at the end of the Second World War has grown more oppressive in recent years, especially in Czechoslovakia. The Communists seized power there in 1948; a ruthless secret service, the Státní bezpečnost (StB), has helped them keep it. By 1950, show trials had begun. The most notorious, the Slánský trial, is still being prepared, but already scores of enemies of the revolution, real and imagined, have been executed. Tens of thousands are under surveillance by the StB. And now, with the Soviet Union preparing to take part in its first ever Olympic Games, the shadow of Stalin looms ever larger over Czechoslovak life – literally so in central Prague, where the world's biggest statue of the Soviet dictator, eventually to be nearly thirty metres high (if you include the base), is under construction.

No one is immune from the obsessive and brutal enforcement of political conformity. Athletes of all kinds have been among those rounded up in the purges. You don't have to be guilty of anything: just out of favour. It is less than eight months since the entire national ice hockey team was arrested, on the evening of its departure to London to defend its world title. Twelve players were condemned to camps for, supposedly, contemplating defection (and, in some cases, singing disrespectful songs); the combined total of their sentences was seventy-seven years and eight months.

By those standards, the problem with Stanislav Jungwirth, Emil's teammate and a future 1,500m world record holder, is a trivial one. Stanislav himself is not in trouble. It is Emil's response to the problem that is potentially catastrophic. Stanislav's father is in prison for political offences – and that, the Party has decided, makes it inappropriate for Jungwirth junior to travel abroad, except to other Eastern Bloc countries. It is a modest restriction; unless, like Jungwirth, you are an Olympic athlete who has spent the past four years dreaming of Helsinki.

News of Jungwirth's exclusion emerged the evening before the athletes were due to fly, when they turned up at the Ministry of Sport to collect their travel documents. Jungwirth was devastated to find that there were none for him, but quickly accepted that making a scene would only make matters worse. But Emil was incandescent. 'No way,' he told the officials. 'If Standa does not go, nor will I.' Then he stormed out, leaving his paperwork behind him.

The next day, on the morning of the flight, Jungwirth implores Zátopek to calm down. Emil insists on standing his ground. He gives Jungwirth his team outfit and tells him to return it to the Ministry when he returns his own. Then he goes off to train alone at Prague's Strahov stadium.

The stand-off continues for days, by which time the plane has long since left without Zátopek. Dana is inconsolable: the stress causes her to lose her voice. It is barely a decade since her own father was taken away by the

Gestapo during the German occupation; he ended up in Dachau. Now her husband seems to have condemned himself to a comparable fate.

In Helsinki, Western journalists are told that Zátopek has tonsillitis.

* * *

More than seventy years later, on a wet Wednesday evening in January, I am sitting in an aeroplane on that same runway. It is a Wizz Air flight this time, delayed for well over an hour by one of those inscrutable problems to which budget flights are prey. Our destination is London Luton, and the passengers, far from being Olympic athletes, are mostly price-conscious tourists. But my head is full of thoughts of Olympic glory in Helsinki.

I have spent the past few days visiting Zátopek's old haunts and talking to people who knew him; the highlight was a long morning of memories, laughter and slivovice (plum brandy) with Dana herself. Now, on the homeward journey, I have just reached the end of my second Zátopek biography of the week and am wondering which one to begin afresh. They are all the reading matter I have, and today there have been many hours to kill.

The engine starts to hum with pre-take-off half-life. The air crew perform their safety drill, and I note with pleasure that I recognise several words. Maybe that teach-yourself-Czech audio programme is starting to work. Then I find myself thinking about the Jungwirth incident. I wonder if the puddled runway I can see through the window bears any resemblance to the view that Dana saw as she scanned the asphalt fretfully through an aeroplane window in the summer of 1952, wondering if Emil would appear.

Then a startling thought occurs to me. That incident with Jungwirth – where is it?

I check and double-check, but it isn't there: not in either of the biographies. As I write, they are the only lives of Zátopek available in the English language. Yet neither even mentions that stand-off on the eve of the Helsinki Games. Nowhere. Not a word.

The incident's absence is not just curious. It is revealing. In both cases, there are good reasons for the omission. One of the books was written in English; the other is a translation from Czech. One can be assumed to have left out the episode because it was not widely known in the West; the other because, under Communism, it was unmentionable. Yet it happened. Indeed, it is arguably one of the more significant episodes not just in Zátopek's life but in the history of sport. If that seems a bold claim, consider what it involved. First, the stature of the main protagonist: Emil Zátopek, a colossus of athletics who from the late 1940s to the mid-1950s bestrode his discipline as no other runner has ever done. Three of his Olympic golds were won at the same Games, in the space of eight days, in a distance-running grand slam that remains unique. He set eighteen world records, won five Olympic medals and, in the words of one otherwise staid official Olympic Games report, 'completely upset all previous notions of the limits of human endurance'. He did so by pioneering approaches to training that had hitherto been unthinkable, and that remain the basis of most serious distance-running training today. And he achieved all this with a grace and generosity of spirit that transcended sport.

For those too young to remember, this last point is easily overlooked. Zátopek was celebrated, globally, not just as an astounding athlete but as a shining ideal. This was a man from a small country, a simple soldier of austere habits, who achieved sporting heights few had dreamed of through a simple formula: the cheerful acceptance and mastery of pain. This was the man who, it was said, trained in army boots, in the snow, or jogged on the spot while on sentry duty, or ran carrying his wife on his back; a man whose training sessions were so intense that experts considered them all but suicidal. This was an athlete who was not just fast but heroically tough. A hard man, but also a man of infectious warmth and humour. A man who never gave up, never complained, and never forgot that, in words that will always be associated with his name: 'Great is the victory, but greater still is the friendship.'

His fellow Olympians worshipped him. The Englishman Gordon Pirie praised his 'magnificent character'; the Frenchman Alain Mimoun called him 'a saint'; Fred Wilt, the American, called him 'perhaps the most humble, friendly and popular athlete in modern times'; Ron Clarke, the Australian, said: 'There is not, and never was, a greater man than Emil Zátopek.'

Ordinary athletics fans were scarcely less enthusiastic. The Helsinki Olympics were supposed to be the Games of the Cold War, with two separate athletes' villages embodying humanity's bitter and terrifying ideological division. Zátopek did more than anyone to turn them, by sheer force of personality, into the Games of

Reconciliation, where athletes and spectators of all nations came together and celebrated their common humanity. They did so largely through celebrating him: his genius, his tenacity, his life-affirming exuberance.

Yet it almost never happened. Just over a week before the opening ceremony, after four years of unimaginably intense preparation, knowing that he was poised to make sporting history and would never get a better chance to do so, Emil Zátopek risked losing it all. He had worked all his life for this moment and now, for the sake of a friend, he was prepared to throw it all away.

I can think of only one other example of an athlete of such stature gambling so much – and, in doing so, showing moral greatness to match his physical gifts. That was when Muhammad Ali refused to be inducted into the US armed forces in 1967, during the Vietnam War. Like Zátopek, Ali was not just a talented athlete but one of breathtaking, sport-redefining genius – and huge personal charisma. Like Zátopek in 1952, Ali was at his physical peak when he took his stand. In taking it, he risked not just punishment and disgrace but also, most painfully, the loss of the best years of his sporting life. Ali took his gamble and, in sporting terms, lost. By the time he had won his appeal against his conviction for draft evasion and was allowed back into the ring, in 1971, his best years were behind him.

Zátopek's gamble came off; but it was no less a reckless one for that, and it is arguable that he paid a heavy price for it later, in 1968, when he, like Ali, defied a superpower and lost. If it hadn't worked – if the Communist authorities had called his bluff and condemned him to hard labour in the uranium mines instead of caving in at the last minute and sending him, with Jungwirth, to Helsinki – then he too would have forfeited his golden years: the years of miraculous achievement on which his claim to sporting immortality is founded. But whereas Ali's sacrifice is central to his legend, and is celebrated in countless books, films and documentaries, Zátopek's stand is forgotten; or, more accurately, lost – like the plan for 'exemplary punishment of Captain Zátopek' that was drawn up by officials as Zátopek and Jungwirth were taking off for Helsinki on a later plane, then hastily destroyed when news came back that Zátopek had just won his third gold medal.

How could that happen? As the Wizz Air plane finally heaves itself into the night sky, the riddle preys on my mind. How can a moment like that – a landmark in the history of sporting heroism – slip from collective memory?

In one sense, it hasn't. Most hard-core Zátopek fans are aware of it. But that just makes the paradox more perplexing. How can an event be both known and unknown? The answer, when I arrive at it, surprises me. Zátopek's whole life is both known and unknown, and for the same reason.

He was, for two decades in the mid-twentieth century, the most celebrated sportsman on earth. Even now, he remains exceptionally honoured, with his own statue (one of only four) outside the official Olympic museum in Lausanne. *Runner's World* named him the greatest runner of all time – over any distance – as recently as 2013. Yet the facts of his life as a human being are obscured, not just by barriers of time, language and ideology but, above all, by myth.

Every running enthusiast over a certain age knows something about Zátopek – or thinks they do. But much of it is no more than hearsay: legends and half-truths endlessly recycled and re-embroidered. Many of the most famous tales are simply false. Even those of us who idolise him – who see him, as I do, as a kind of patron saint of running – are liable to find, on closer inspection, that we know far less about him than we think.

Those who knew him best grow older and fewer in number each year. Old memories play tricks; as do the everyday habits of dissembling and concealment that four decades of Communist tyranny ingrained into most Czechoslovak lives, including Zátopek's. Primary sources, including official ones, cannot be assumed to be trustworthy; some tell outright lies. The rest is a sea of biographical confusion, in which solid facts can barely be discerned from the froth of rumour in which they float. So the truth dissolves, slowly. The legends persist: wonderful in their way but insubstantial, because they can be endlessly reinvented.

The bare facts of Zátopek's running are preserved in official archives. But the real worth of his victories is lost on all but his oldest admirers. As for his records: his fastest time for 10,000m would have earned him twenty-fourth place in the 2012 Olympics. Times and trophies quickly lose their power to excite. It is the human side of Zátopek's story that is still capable of brightening and energising lives, six decades after his prime and a decade and a half after his death. That is the story that matters. And that, despite all the millions of words that have been written about him, is slipping away.

Yet the reality of Emil Zátopek's life – the scarcely believable tale of his rise, fall and unfinished rehabilitation – is too important to be allowed to vanish. He was not just an Olympic immortal: he was a magnificent, if flawed, human being, who lit up the post-war world with the warmth of his personality during some of the chilliest chapters of modern history. His story was one of tragedy as well as glory, and his struggles were intricately interwoven with the troubled history of Europe itself. He was also, as the French writer Pierre Magnan pointed out, 'a man who ran like us' – an athlete who had to labour for his achievements as painfully as the rest of us do. In the words of the great coach Percy Cerutty, who considered him 'the most epoch-shattering athlete of this age', he 'earned, and won for himself, every inch of a very hard road'. Yet such was the greatness of Zátopek's heart that he found time even in the heat of his most agonising battles to relate to his rivals as fellow human beings; to make gestures of friendship and sportsmanship and playfulness that echo through the ages. He was magnificent in his running, but more magnificent still in his instinctive use of running as a medium for friendship. If ever an athlete's life was worthy of being preserved in print, it is his.

By the time I notice the orange lights of Luton through the aeroplane window, scattered like broken beads across the cold blackness below, I have made a resolution. I will not let his story dissolve any further. I will return to Emil Zátopek's homeland and try, as tirelessly as he used to train, to discover and record his true story. It is a daunting challenge. It was all a long time ago – in a faraway country of which I, like most Westerners, know little.

Much of the truth was concealed even then. But I must try, whatever the difficulties – because he deserves it.

Contemplating the task ahead, I feel an ache of apprehension deep in my stomach: the kind of fear you feel just before beginning a long-distance race. I feel, in short, a little like one of the forty-five men who stood with Emil Zátopek on the starting line of the Olympic marathon in Melbourne on 1 December 1956. It was one of those oven-hot days when marathon-running seems not just foolhardy but dangerous. Emil was past his best by then and, to make things worse, was not fully fit and was still recovering from injury. He looked around with a grim smile.

'Men,' he said, 'today we die a little.'

Then, still smiling, he began to run.

1

'Zá-to-pek! Zá-to-pek!'

Let us start at the summit: the golden minutes for which all his previous struggles can be seen as preparation, and from which all that followed might be seen as a descent. It is around 5.50 p.m., on 27 July 1952. The streets of Helsinki's Töölö district are buzzing, the pavements packed with excited spectators, chattering and cheering.

Some have been there all afternoon, revelling in the party atmosphere and the chance to see history made. The weather has been kind: still but not stifling. In the Olympic stadium, off Hammarskjöldintie, 68,700 people are buzzing too, their attention focused not on the track – where the 4 x 400m relay has recently finished – but on a huge electronic scoreboard which is providing periodic updates on the times and positions of the leading runners in the final event of the XVth Olympic Games: the marathon. The latest (and last) bulletin indicates that, with just over two kilometres to go, he is two and a quarter minutes ahead of his nearest rival.

For the next nine minutes or so, only those lucky enough to have good vantage points in the street really know what is going on. The rest fall back on rumour and imagination. But there does not seem to be a single person watching, in the stadium or out on the streets, who hopes for any outcome other than this: that Emil Zátopek should keep going for a few more minutes, all the way to the end.

The unanimity is startling. Sixty-nine different nations have sent athletes to the Games, and most have sent spectators too, although the majority of those watching are Finnish. Yet somehow everyone wants the Czechoslovak to win.

The unanimity is all the more startling when you consider the context. The world is divided, dangerously so, by an ideological iron curtain, still quite new, that stretches from the Baltic to the Adriatic. Two superpowers, one led by an increasingly deranged Josef Stalin, glower at one another across it. Helsinki has taken the unusual step of providing the 4,955 competing athletes with two distinct Olympic villages to reflect this divide: one for the Communist bloc and the other for the rest. George Orwell's line about sport being 'war minus the shooting' has rarely felt more apt.

Yet somehow, after two weeks of competition, it is ending with this: sports lovers of countless races, creeds and political convictions coming together in one joyous family, to celebrate the achievements and personality of a single extraordinary athlete.

It is not all Zátopek's doing. There have been gestures of goodwill from other athletes whose youthful instinct to fraternise has proved too strong for the ideological taboos that are supposed to restrain them. But somehow Zátopek has come to embody the idea that these Games are a celebration of our common humanity. Rumours about him have been slipping out all fortnight, not just about his sensational racing and insane training routines but also about his warmth, his sportsmanship, his spontaneous generosity. He is said to have given up his bed, the night before one of his big races, to a visiting Australian with nowhere to sleep. He gave his socks to his English rival Gordon Pirie. He shares his training secrets with anyone who cares to ask. His gregariousness has prompted him to learn half a dozen languages – some say more.

His public utterances have a wit that belies Western stereotypes of robotic Communist drones. On the track, he radiates decency and charm. He talks to rivals, offers pats of encouragement, takes his turn in the lead even when it is not in his interests to do so.

Yet somehow he has also found the steel not just to win but to win emphatically – some would say majestically. In the past eight days he has already won two Olympic golds, achieving the elusive distance-running double of winning both the 5,000 and the 10,000m. And now he is minutes away from completing a treble which everyone watching must realise will almost certainly never be achieved again – assuming that it can be achieved even once.

That is the history the crowds have come to witness. It is the biggest challenge of Zátopek's life, and it seems as though most of the world is holding its breath, willing him to succeed.

The odd thing is, the man who has elicited this unprecedented groundswell of goodwill is not some godlike being who skims over the ground with easy grace. He is small and a little ungainly. He has wide shoulders, a furrowed brow and an insect-like way of sticking out his elbows, especially the right one. A receding hairline makes him look older than his twenty-nine years.

As for his running style, he makes such a meal of it that people have been commenting on it for years: the way he grimaces as he runs, rolls his head, sticks out his tongue, claws at the air, clutches at his chest with his left hand, sometimes even seeming to swing his shoulders as he runs. Sportswriters love him for this, as it provides an excuse for some enjoyable phrase-making: 'He runs like a man who has just been stabbed in the heart'; '. . . as if there was a scorpion in each shoe'; '. . . as if tortured by internal demons'; '. . . as if he might be having a fit'; '. . . like a man wrestling with an octopus on a conveyor belt'. He is used to such criticisms, and has often laughed them off: 'I am not talented enough to run and smile at the same time.'

Those who understand such matters will point to the contrasting smoothness of his movements below the waist: the metronomic efficiency of his short, fast strides. None the less, it is hard to see how his upper writhings can be helping him. In fact, if appearances were all, he would be a laughing stock: an early precursor of such celebrated Olympic no-hopers as Eddie the Eagle and Eric the Eel.

But over the past week he has shown beyond all possible doubt that appearances are not everything. He is living, thrilling proof that what really matters is what is inside: the blazing spirit that allows a man, flesh and blood like the rest of us, to challenge the accepted limits of human aspiration.

This is, by the way, the first time he has ever run a marathon.

If that seems improbable now, it seemed improbable then. That's not to say no one expected him to be leading at this stage. His admirers believe that anything is possible where Emil is concerned. But there is something awe-inspiring about the fact that he is even trying. The audacity of the man: that is part of his greatness.

A flame of fresh information blows its way up Vauhtitie, and then round the corner into Hammarskjöldintie, gathering in intensity as it spreads. Zátopek is still leading; his lead is growing; he is almost in the stadium; he is coming.

Then, behind the flame, comes the roar of cheering – and, beyond that, the man himself.

Step by painful step, he drives himself forward to the stadium tunnel, vanishes, and then, to a longed-for fanfare of trumpets, emerges inside the arena, leaning almost forty-five degrees as he turns on to the track to minimise loss of momentum. The eruption of sound threatens to blow the skeletal runner off his feet. Nearly 70,000 people are standing, ecstatic, bellowing their approval; and the roar finally resolves itself into a chant in spine-chilling unison: 'Zá-to-pek! Zá-to-pek! Zá-to-pek!'

His grimacing face looks more agonised than ever. His sodden red vest clings to the outside of his shorts. His eyes seem glazed; his jaw is clenched. He looks tired: tired and empty as death. Every step seems a struggle – not in the sportswriters' sense but in a real, palpably excruciating way. You can almost feel the jarring in his battered legs as his thinly shod feet pound against the track. His whole body seems to be crying out: when will this stop? Yet not for one moment does he relax his rhythm.

The number of Czechoslovaks in the stadium can be counted in dozens. Yet each spectator is urging Emil Zátopek on with the fervour we usually reserve for our own most cherished national heroes. Among them is Hannes Kolehmainen, one of the great Finnish founding fathers of modern distance running, and – although perhaps cheering with a shade less enthusiasm than most – the British marathon world record holder and pre-race favourite, Jim Peters, who was brought back to the stadium in the press coach after dropping out with six miles to go.

'Zá-to-pek! Zá-to-pek!' Emil could not slow down his rhythm if he wanted to. There may never before have been a moment when people from so many different nations have come together in such a joyous celebration of sporting achievement. One of them, Juan Antonio Samaranch, a future president of the International Olympic Committee, will still be talking about it half a century later: 'At that moment, I understood what the Olympic spirit means.' But for a British journalist, J. Armour Milne, even that is not enough: 'All of us shared the common conviction that we were witnessing the greatest happening in athletics history.'

As he crosses the line, the gaunt runner can just manage a smile: curiously boyish in its transparent relief. He waves away the photographers, hobbles off the track, sits on the ground and removes his shoes from his bloodied feet. For a moment he seems overwhelmed, oblivious to the fact that he has not only achieved an all but impossible third gold but also slashed more than six minutes off the Olympic record – the third record he has broken in eight days. Then he is back on his feet, shuffling towards the stands to be kissed tenderly on the mouth by the gold medal winner in the women's javelin – who also happens to be his wife. Someone gives him an apple, which he gobbles greedily. Then he waits at the finishing line to offer congratulations and slices of orange to his fellow runners, the first of whom arrives more than two and a half minutes behind the winner – and five of whom have, like Zátopek, broken the previous Olympic record.

Minutes later, the Jamaican 4 x 400m relay team, who not long before set their own Olympic record, pick Zátopek up and chair him around the stadium on a lap of honour without parallel in Olympic history. And then, some time afterwards, Zátopek is standing on the winner's rostrum, listening to the Czechoslovak national anthem being played in his honour for the third time in eight days.

The final notes melt into applause. Zátopek congratulates his fellow medallists and then embarks on a weary, joyful lap of honour. He can hear tens of thousands of Finns calling him by their own special name for him, 'Satu-Pekka' – except that this time they are chanting '*Näkemiin, Satu-Pekka*'. He has taught himself enough Finnish to know what this means. They are saying goodbye.

And Emil Zátopek, basking in the world's adulation after pulling off the greatest feat in the history of distance running, feels suddenly overwhelmingly sad, because—

But to understand that, you need to know how Emil got there.

2

The Kopřivnice kid

Let us start again, at the beginning, in Kopřivnice, a small industrial town on what is now the eastern edge of the Czech Republic.

Back then, in 1922, it was Czechoslovakia – bang in the middle of it; four years earlier it had been part of the Austro-Hungarian Empire. Those who lived in the town thought of themselves as Moravians. They still do.

It's quieter today than it was then. Twentieth-century Kopřivnice was dominated by the factory of central Europe's premier car manufacturer, Tatra, which generated employment, pollution and noise in increasing measures as the century progressed (but has since declined).

František and Anežka Zátopek came here in 1922, drawn by the factory's magnetism from the nearby village of Zašová. They were in their early forties, with four children to feed – Jaroš, Marie, František junior (Franta) and Bohumil (Bohuš) – and barely enough money to do so. (Their eldest daughter, Ludmila – born out of wedlock and referred to, if at all, as an 'aunt' – was married and living in Brno; their first son, Josef, had died in an ice-skating accident at the age of ten.) František, a carpenter and cabinetmaker, was a founder member of a housing co-operative, with whom he built a semi-detached house on the northern edge of town: one of four such houses at the bottom of 1 Května Street ('1 May Street'). Each had a decent-sized patch of land for livestock and fruit trees.

Perhaps it seemed like a time for new beginnings. Czechoslovakia itself was new, created from the ruins of the First World War in a spirit of democratic idealism. Its founding fathers believed passionately in national self-determination and social inclusion. The economy seemed healthy, and if the hard-pressed Moravian working classes had yet to feel the benefits, there was at least hope for the future.

The Zátopek children had barely settled in when Anežka gave birth to her seventh child, Emil Ferdinand, on a bed in the corner of the kitchen that doubled up as František's workshop. It was 19 September 1922. An eighth, Jiří, would follow two years later.

The extra mouths strained the family finances. Anežka had long since given up her old job as a labourer in the brick factory. František earned what he could at the Tatra factory – wood was still an important component of cars' bodywork – and topped up his wages with private commissions, making furniture. This kept him busy but didn't make him rich. There was food on the table, but not always much, and Emil grew up with a yearning for a full stomach that never quite left him. Czech families traditionally celebrate Christmas by dining on carp. The Zátopeks made do with cheap smoked fish, while a present might be no more than a piece of fruit picked from the garden and wrapped.

Emil, writing about his childhood in later life, made light of the poverty. The way he told it, the overcrowded house was a place of cheerful chaos. Names were muddled up; children queued for breakfast 'like a factory canteen'; soap stung their eyes as they filed past their mother for the weekly wash. But he never entirely forgot the hunger and insecurity, and his adult worldview would reflect this.

As often happens in large families, not all the siblings were close, emotionally or in age. Jiří was Emil's nearest ally. But weight of numbers left the younger brothers little choice but to be, at least, gregarious. Emil grew used to living in a group, mostly among people bigger, stronger and more dominant than him.

Surviving grandchildren and friends remember the Zátopek household as a stable, loving, disciplined one. Anežka was known for her skill with herbal remedies, and for her compassion for the sick: 'limitlessly loving' was how one former neighbour remembered her. One grandchild – Jiří's daughter Dana – spoke fondly of the special hiding place where, when funds permitted, Anežka kept chocolate treats for small visitors. 'She was so kind,' Dana told me. 'She was always working, always smiling, always trying to look after her children.'

František was more intimidating: a man of firm principle whose efforts to instil discipline in his children once caused Anežka to burn the leather belt with which he had just thrashed one of them. (He subsequently used his wooden carpenter's ruler.) But he also had a kindly, twinkling side, tweaking noses in jest or inviting small children to light his long pipe and sip the froth on his beer. Emil was devoted to him. The grandchildren knew him as 'beardy grandpa' – even when his beard had become a mere moustache – so Anežka, logically, was 'beardy grandma'. The couple's greatest pleasure was to gather the whole family round to sing Moravian folk songs. Emil continued to sing them all his life.

The garden was scarcely less packed than the house, with goats, hens and geese jostling for space among trees and beehives. Children were expected to do their bit for animal husbandry, and would get into trouble for failing to do so. Emil once allowed the goats to get stuck in the clay of a nearby brick-making site ('It was Bohuš's idea' was his excuse), and he was beaten at least once for helping himself to fruit. But the world beyond was, or seemed, a benign place. There were streets and fields to play in; they could swim in the River Lubina (notwithstanding the raw sewage that flowed into it a mile upstream); and the foothills of the Beskyd Mountains were near enough for occasional hiking adventures.

The children were discouraged from taking part in sport, especially the new craze of football: the risk of wearing out shoes and clothes was too great, while any spare energy would be better spent, in Mr Zátopek's view, working in the smallholding. They played anyway – 'with more passion than those who were allowed to', according to Emil, who often played football barefoot. But they knew where their priorities were supposed to lie, and in one crunch match, against a tough team of older boys from the local German school, Emil deserted the team shortly after half-time when the sounding of the Tatra factory hooter reminded him that he had forgotten to feed the bees. His best friend, Jaromír Konůpka, who was captain of the team ('I owned the football,' Konůpka explained), didn't speak to him for a week.

But Mr Zátopek had a point. As the hopeful 1920s faded into the grim 1930s, home-grown food became a vital part of the family's subsistence. The Great Depression sucked the life from Europe's economy, and Kopřivnice did not escape. Tatra workers who kept their jobs faced lower wages, and less job security. For a long time, Emil's brother Jaroš couldn't find work at all. When he finally did, his clumsiness as a driver resulted in an accident and a ruinous damages claim; in despair, he took his own life. Emil was about seven at the time; and the terrible event became another subject that was never referred to in the Zátopek household. The family was no less scarred as a result. Anežka's response was to become even more solicitous – some would say fussy – about her surviving sons' welfare. František took the more practical step of joining Czechoslovakia's fledgling Communist Party.

This didn't prevent him from being an upstanding member of the community. The Party was more concerned with opposing fascism than with active subversion in those days, and most of its 60,000 members did no more than pay their subscriptions. František was secretary of the local federation of allotment holders and breeders of rabbits and small farm animals; later, he would be chairman of the Kopřivnice Beekeeping Association. Politically, he was more of a trade unionist than a revolutionary: he had been active in the bitter struggle to establish an eight-hour working day at Tatra but was otherwise best known for collecting union fees from fellow workers. He was not allowed to do this at the factory but had to tramp from home to home instead. Emil often accompanied him.

František also took his children to meetings of the Federation of Proletarian Education (FPT) – later superseded by the slightly less radical Workers' Association of Physical Education (DTJ). These offered opportunities for physical education for workers' children, usually in a specially kitted-out room in the Amerika pub, where Emil became adept at gymnastic tricks such as somersaults and headstands.

But that was about the limit of his early sporting prowess. He was energetic – 'the biggest fidget in the class', according to one schoolfriend – and enjoyed running around, a trait which at least one teacher exploited by using him as an errand boy. But he was puny and uncoordinated: by conventional measures of masculinity, he was a weakling – especially after a neglected bout of appendicitis, when he was eight, necessitated an extended stay in hospital. In football, he just ran around, enthusiastically but uselessly. He didn't get into fights, except occasionally with Jiří, while his tactic of screaming loud and early to escape his father's beatings earned him the nickname 'Emil the cry-baby'.

Early photographs show a small, plump-cheeked boy, with large ears and narrow shoulders combining to make his head look unusually wide. There is nothing athletic about his appearance: just an intent, curious, slightly anxious expression, as if he were trying to understand something. But one school picture, taken when Emil was six, has an interesting detail. Emil, sitting cross-legged in the front row, is the only child without shoes – although his friends have arranged their legs in such a way as to conceal, almost, Emil's bare feet.

You would never have put him down as a future Olympian. Yet somehow, even then, he seems to have had an air of being special. Jiří, speaking two years after Emil's death, claimed, without resentment, that Emil was his parents' favourite. 'Emil was the smartest one. If someone did something wrong, it had to be investigated. But if it turned out that it was Emil who did it, everything was all right.' Jiří's son – also called Jiří – proudly drew my attention to the family tradition that Emil was never stung by bees. 'When my grandfather wanted something taken out of a hive, he didn't need special clothing. He just got Emil to do it.'

Young Jiří – a big, moustachioed, bear-like man of middle age who lives in the neighbouring village of Štramberk – seemed to glow with affection when he talked about his uncle. It would not be the last time I would notice such animation in those who were sharing memories of Emil with me.

Milan Špaček, a classmate who became a champion skier, spoke laughingly about Emil's reckless streak. He once saw him rescued from drowning, after braving a water-filled gravel pit without having learnt to swim. Later, Emil proved better than anyone at swimming underwater: 'He could hold his breath longer, and he was not so afraid of drowning as the rest of us.'

Jaromír Konůpka, a retired draughtsman who remained close to Emil all his life, also laughed at the thought of his friend's recklessness. He particularly enjoyed the memory of a school expedition to the Beskyds when Emil was thirteen. The pupils stayed in a hostel on Bílý Kříž, but were kept awake by the snoring of a much older boy, Pepa Štefků. Around dawn, Emil decided to solve the problem by – for some reason – emptying an entire jar of salt into Pepa's mouth. Pepa woke up and leapt out of bed in fury. Emil, wearing only his underpants, jumped out of the window in the nick of time; Pepa pursued him via the door. 'He had found a big stick and was shouting that he would "kill that bastard". First they ran around the meadow, then we saw them in the forest . . .' Konůpka genuinely seemed to think that murder had been a possibility – but Emil had the stamina to escape unscathed.

Konůpka said that the key to Emil's youthful character could be found in a single statement: 'I don't want to do it, but if I have to, then I'm going to show you!' Passed over at the age of ten for a starring clown's role in the DTJ's Christmas play, *The Circus Comes to Town*, Emil stole the show by giving the gymnastics performance of a lifetime in his bit part as a monkey. Another time, forced to do algebra against his will ('Please, sir, why are we learning such drivel as $a+b$ squared when we are never going to need it in life?'), Emil saved face by swotting up furiously and confusing the teacher by coming top in a test for which he had originally refused to study.

Then there was the 'essay strike', which Emil organised at the municipal school, to which he had progressed at the age of eleven. The class were told to write on the theme: '*Komu se nelení, tomu se zelení*' (literally, 'He who is not lazy, gets the greens'). Emil declared the subject 'stupid' and, perhaps inspired by his father's political activities, persuaded around half the class to refuse to write it. The protest lasted several days. The inevitable climbdown was followed, ignominiously, by a Saturday spent writing the essay anyway. Emil exacted partial revenge by writing an enormously long one – five large pages of tiny script – which took his teacher the best part of Sunday to mark. Perhaps the last laugh was hers, though, because the proverb's message stayed with him for the rest of his life.

But there was more to the young Emil than mere stubbornness: there was also a startling independence of thought – a sense that things didn't necessarily have to be as they were. Notwithstanding the view of one of his teachers, Ladislav Buček, that: 'You'll never amount to anything in life', Emil seemed to feel that almost anything might be possible. Naturally left-handed, he taught himself to be right-handed – and if that could be changed, what couldn't? One much-repeated tale describes how he allowed a mosquito to bite him on the hand. Instead of brushing it off, he watched it closely, observing how it sucked up his blood. He wanted to learn. On another occasion, he is said to have stolen a wooden cup from a miserly stall-keeper at the market: not because he wanted it but because he wanted to see if he could evade the old man's obsessive security measures. Ota Pavel, the author and journalist who later became Emil's good friend, claimed that the young Zátopek's defining characteristic was that 'he tried everything differently'.

Emil's parents cherished hopes that he, perhaps alone among their children, might find a future beyond the Tatra factory. František thought that Emil could become a teacher, although it was far from clear how the fees for training college could be paid. Education had been in short supply when he and Anežka were growing up. Anežka had been taken out of school early so that she could be sent out to work. (The local priest was bribed to falsify her birth certificate.) But now, in the new Czechoslovakia, it was not unrealistic to dream that a bright, poor child might use education as an escape route to better things, and Kopřivnice was as good a place as any to do so.

Emil seems to have made the most of his nine years of free schooling. He was not particularly diligent, but he was bright, with unusual powers of memory. It was often noted by those who knew him in later life that he appeared to remember every single thing he was taught as a schoolboy.

When his class were told to memorise three verses from Karel Havlíček Borovský's poem, 'Král Lávra', Emil learnt all thirty-seven. He expected to be applauded when he recited them in front of his class. Instead, his classmates looked dubious – presumably fearing that he was making them look bad – while the teacher was simply stunned.

Emil would grow used to such dubious looks. They were the price to be paid for what would become a lifelong habit of doing things his own way. As a teenager, though, what he really craved (according to friends such as Ota Pavel) was the kind of peer approval that is given not to poetry reciters but to those who excel on the sports field; the only problem being that Emil didn't.

Yet there was one occasion when he did discover what it meant to bathe in sporting glory. A dozen local children decided to organise a race. It was an endurance race, or so they called it, around the block which included the Zátopeks' home. The rectangular circuit was about a kilometre in total; the idea was to go round it as many times as possible. They set off, old and young all jumbled up.

Most stopped after two or three laps; a few managed six or seven. But Emil, despite being by no means the eldest, just carried on running, lap after lap after lap.

The afternoon wore on, and still he kept padding along. The other boys applauded and then, as the number of laps reached double figures, grew bored. Some went home; others started a card game on the side of the road. Emil kept running, on and on as the afternoon faded to evening, until no one could keep track of how many laps he had run – thirty? forty? – and he could scarcely stand. Even his elder brothers joined in the congratulations. Emil considered this last detail so remarkable that he cherished the memory decades later.

The route is still there. Jog around it, as I did on a warm autumn afternoon, and you may share my sense that there is something mesmerising about the alternation of views from the quiet streets. In three directions, there are empty skies, with tree-topped hills occasionally appearing on the horizons between the low rooftops. But the south-western corner of the circuit is dominated by the railway and the giant chimneys – presumably belching smoke in Emil's day – of the Tatra factory.

It is fanciful to speculate that such views played any part in his deliberations about what to do when his schooling came to an end; yet they offer a neat analogy for the choice he faced. He could remain in Kopřivnice, work as a labourer for Tatra and accept the default fate that his family circumstances had prepared for him. Or he could set his sights on more distant, adventurous horizons.

Emil's brothers would all remain in Kopřivnice. But by the time Emil left municipal school, Tatra was laying off, not hiring. František, despite the financial obstacles, still hoped that Emil would become a teacher. Yet his son's application to the teacher training college in the neighbouring town of Příbor was rejected. He had achieved the necessary grades but, he was told, his ear for music wasn't good enough. This may have been a polite way of saying that the sons of impoverished carpenters were still unwelcome in the teaching profession; but it is also true that Emil's sense of pitch was less perfect than he liked to think. He was advised that, if he chose to stay on at school for another year and repeat the final grade, he would be allowed to apply again. Emil gave short shrift to the idea, saying that he wasn't stupid enough to repeat a class from which he had already graduated with honours.

Instead, following the example and advice of a friend's older brother, he took matters into his own hands. In the late summer of 1937, several weeks short of his fifteenth birthday, he caught a train to the city of Zlín, forty-five miles to the south-west, to seek his fortune.

3

Shoemaking

There was something miraculous about Zlín. For six centuries it had been just another anonymous central European town, on the bottom edge of Moravia, Then, in the four decades before Emil's arrival, it had been transformed by the crazed genius of one family: the Baťas.

A cobbler's son, Tomáš Baťa set up a small shoemaking company with his brother and sister when he was eighteen. It was 1894. Within a year the business was technically bankrupt. Tomáš's brother left to do military service, while Tomáš wrestled with the problem of not being able to afford to buy leather. Desperate, he started making shoes with canvas uppers instead. The innovation proved an instant bestseller. Tomáš Baťa built a small factory in Zlín. The business grew, and with it his ambition. He took time out to work in a factory in America, studying the production-line methods pioneered by Henry Ford. By 1912, back in Zlín, he had more than six hundred employees.

But mass production was just part of his vision. The same year, he began to build houses and flats for his workers. He believed that employees with a stake in a company's prosperity were more productive than those who were merely exploited. When the First World War broke out, he somehow obtained an exclusive contract to provide the Austro-Hungarian army with shoes. The company's size increased exponentially: by 1918 it employed 6,000 people. More or less the entire population of Zlín escaped conscription in order to meet demand.

By 1923 Tomáš Baťa was mayor of Zlín. There was a company library, a company kindergarten, a sports club, a cinema. Home-building expanded into town-planning, in conscious imitation of the British idea of the garden city. Cutting-edge architects such as František Gahura and Vladimír Karfík – and, later, Le Corbusier – were hired to ensure that this workers' utopia was created along the most rational lines. Everything was built in the same materials – mainly red brick and glass – and to similar, uniform dimensions, based on 6.15 x 6.15m modules.

In 1924, profit-sharing was introduced. In 1925, the Baťa School of Work was founded, initially as a shoemakers' apprentice school but before long as an establishment offering a secondary education to up to 1,500 students a year. The students financed themselves, working in the factory to cover the cost of their board and lodging before studying at night. The more they learnt, the more useful they were as employees. As Baťa put it: 'Every penny spent on our schools will pay back many times.'

Tomáš Baťa died in 1932. Thanks to his bold pricing policies, Baťa employees had escaped the worst of the Great Depression. The population of Zlín had increased tenfold in three decades – and well over half of the 26,350 inhabitants were Baťa employees. Tomáš's brother, Jan Antonín, continued the growth, and the all-encompassing – some would say overbearing – paternalism. When Emil arrived, the Baťa group employed 65,000 people worldwide, with dozens of factories and thousands of stores across Europe, America and Asia. A new headquarters, Building 21, was approaching completion in the centre of Zlín, with a tower – Czechoslovakia's tallest – whose most notable feature would be Jan Antonín Baťa's office-cum-elevator, which would allow him to keep watch on his staff on whichever of the sixteen floors he chose.

To capitalists, Baťa represented the ideal of private enterprise: utopian, innovative, constructive and as beneficial to workers as to investors. To the Communists who nationalised the company after the Second World War, the same facts had a different meaning. The company used its paternalism as a tool for exercising total control over workers' lives, turning them into units of productivity rather than autonomous human beings. Baťa's dominance of Zlín was unhealthy. It owned everything, including the police force, and anyone deemed subversive or insufficiently productive – including the old or unemployed – was liable to find themselves unwelcome in the city. The Baťa intelligence service, thinly disguised as the personnel department, pried shamelessly into everything. Zlín was, by one analysis, 'a totalitarian town'.

But two things were beyond debate. For young, poor Czechoslovaks seeking to make something of their lives from nothing, Zlín was an attractive proposition. And, if you did go to work in Zlín, you belonged to Baťa.

If Emil had been unaware of this last fact when his application to the School of Work was accepted in July 1937, it was rapidly made clear to him when he arrived that autumn. He was housed in a dormitory building on a hillside overlooking the town: the fourth of eight such buildings, which between them housed 6,000 students. The dormitory walls carried slogans such as 'The young eagles fly towards the sun' and 'Fight is the father of all'. There was a dormitory warden whose word was law. Morality was strictly enforced: bad language was punished with a fine, and young men were expected to sleep with their hands outside the bedclothes.

An alarm went off at 5.30 a.m., after which there were compulsory outdoor morning exercises. At 7 a.m., the apprentices began their shifts in the factory. These continued, barring a two-hour midday break, until 5 p.m. There was then an evening meal, followed by study until shortly before the 9 p.m. curfew. 'I always had to think for a while about where I was,' Emil claimed, 'because so many things in the boarding house were the same as in the factory.'

The first year's education was devoted to 'shoemaker's basic training'. More interesting subjects such as languages and science would come later. Meanwhile, there was the challenge of the factory work. Emil spent eight hours a day on the production line: initially 'ploughing' corrugations in crêpe soles but then, when he proved inept at this, putting lasts on to the conveyor belt: left, right, left, right, left, right, changing the sizes according to a strict plan. His workshop had to produce up to 2,400 pairs of shoes a day. If Emil faltered, the production line would falter too, and a red light would point the finger of blame. The midday break was often spent catching up.

For a fourteen-year-old boy, away from home for the first time, it must have been both overwhelming and disorienting. On one early visit home, Emil told his parents how exciting he found it all. Twenty years later he gave a starker account of the period: his new life seemed bleak, he wrote, and 'full of hustle and fear'. The camaraderie of the Kopřivnice streets had been replaced by adult anonymity, with thousands of ambitious students, steeped in Baťa's devil-take-the-hindmost ideology, and shouting overseers who were quick to remind grumblers that, for every student, there were ten unsuccessful applicants who would be only too pleased to take their place. 'I did not even have the courage to remember Kopřivnice, and the house and garden of my childhood, and my father's bees,' Emil wrote. And, like many an unhappy child away from home before and since, he kept the truth from his parents because 'I did not want . . . to make them grieve.'

On a wall of the factory, another of Tomáš Baťa's sayings was painted: 'There are 86,400 seconds in a day.' Perhaps little more need be said about Emil's first years in Zlín. Work, study, sleep; morning exercises and canteen meals: that was the sum of it. There was nothing for it but to conform. Emil did so, working unhappily but diligently; and learnt, if nothing else, some early lessons about the patient endurance of distress. Three times a year – Easter, summer and Christmas – he was allowed a brief visit home. The rest of the time he absorbed the Baťa philosophy that 'he who passes on to his coworker a piece of work unfit to be continued cannot be considered an honest man.' A sense that hard work was the key to success became central to his being.

His excellent memory served him well in exams, which meant that, after the obligatory two years at the School of Work, he was able to progress to the next level of Baťa education: the Higher Industrial School. He was doing his daily shifts in the chemical research institute by then. The air was noxious, but the daily grind was a fraction less mindless. His evening studies, too, were beginning to stretch him more. If there still wasn't a great deal of joy in his life, it was better than the alternatives.

In the wider world, terrible events were afoot. While Emil studied and worked, a series of unthinkable catastrophes had befallen his country. First, soon after his sixteenth birthday, Kopřivnice had ceased to be part of Czechoslovakia – ceased, in fact, to be Kopřivnice at all. The town lay just inside an eastern tentacle of the Sudetenland, which was ceded to Nazi Germany in September 1938 under the Munich Agreement – whereby Britain and France abandoned their Czechoslovak allies to Hitler. Zlín remained part of Czechoslovakia, but the Zátopeks' home town was now part of the Third Reich, and reverted to its old German name, Nesseldorf.

Five months later, in March 1939, Nazi Germany invaded what remained of Czechoslovakia. The loss of the Sudetenland had rendered the country indefensible, and Hitler was in Prague within days. Slovakia, by prior arrangement, declared independence. The rest of the country became the German Protectorate of Bohemia and Moravia. Perhaps this was marginally preferable to being totally absorbed into Germany, but it soon became clear that the SS was in charge, and Jews, Communists, trade unionists and non-compliant students and journalists quickly felt the effects. (Emil's father, however, was not victimised: he had temporarily left the Party a few years earlier after a row with a local official.) Six months later, the world was at war – and thousands of young Czech men began to be forcibly deported to Germany to supply slave labour for the Third Reich. The Baťa factory was as good a place as anywhere to try to sit out the storm.

All Czech factories were required to put their production at the disposal of the Wehrmacht – and thus Baťa, for the second world war in succession, found itself supplying footwear for the soldiers of the Central Powers. Jan Antonín Baťa had fled to America; his employees and students just had to make the best of things. Radomír Luža, a resistance activist who worked briefly for Baťa while on the run from the Gestapo in 1942, later described how he watched all the workers of Zlín going to work and 'wondered why they were so eager to get to work to make boots for German feet . . . didn't they realise that they were co-operating with the Nazis . . .?' Some may have felt guilty that their jobs at Baťa guaranteed them better rations than the bulk of the Czech population (who had a daily allowance of about 1,600 calories each), but most will have been preoccupied with getting from one day to the next without being arrested or shot.

Even Luža conceded that 'no one could refuse to work, and whoever worked, worked for the Reich'. The factory was 'purged' by the Gestapo at least once, in February 1941, and everyone knew that the country was scattered with labour camps for those who refused to co-operate. Dozens of workers in other factories had already been shot – in Brno, in Plzeň, in Ostrava – while many more had been arrested or beaten for falling behind with output. Overt resistance would have been suicidal. Instead, with as much foot-dragging as they dared, the Baťa employees and apprentices continued to churn out shoes, while those who could continued their studies as well, watching the months slip past and hoping for better days ahead.

Such was the background when, in May 1941, one of the wardens, a Mr Linhart, issued an order for all able-bodied fourth-year students under his charge to take part in the race through the streets of Zlín that took place each year in honour of Tomáš Baťa. (Zlín's annual May Day celebrations would not have looked out of place in Moscow or Nuremberg.) Any enthusiasm that the young men in question might ordinarily have felt for such a challenge was negated by a general reluctance to do more than was absolutely necessary to please the company bosses; and Emil, at this stage in his life, was in any case not keen on sport.

According to Emil: 'The warden said, "On Sunday there is a race across Zlín. I am an athlete, and everybody from my group will run. Only those who are sick do not have to run."' Emil raised his hand and said, 'My knee hurts.' The warden was contemptuous and insisted on an examination by the company doctor, who – quite reasonably – declared Emil a malingerer. He was ordered to run.

Even then, on the morning of 15 May, Emil had one last try at wriggling out of it. He retired to the reading room with a chemistry book, hoping that his absence would not be noticed. It was. He was tracked down and escorted to the starting line on Tomáš Baťa Avenue.

He was eighteen. The next five minutes would set the path of his adult life.

The course measured 1,400m. There were around a hundred young men competing. Most set off vigorously, although many eased off once they were out of sight of the start. Some had friends waiting with coats around the first corner. The crowd of runners spread out – and Emil, having vaguely resolved that, if he was to run, he might as well do his best, found himself towards the front.

'The desire to win took over me,' he recalled many years later, 'and I ran with all my strength.' He could hear people cheering him on, and he began to imagine the cheers that might greet him if he won. He made himself breathe faster than usual, reasoning that his lungs needed extra oxygen; this is unlikely to have helped. As the finish approached, he weakened, and an experienced athlete, Honza Krupička, drew away. Emil came second.

It barely mattered. 'He's my boy!' shouted Mr Linhart, the hostel warden. 'He's from my group!' Friends rushed to congratulate Emil. Krupička joined them, and suggested to Emil that he should try training with the regular athletes in the sports stadium: 'You will see how you will improve.' Emil laughed this off: he had no intention of running again, he said. Yet there was something potent about this post-race euphoria. Describing the moment half a lifetime later, he wrote: 'I felt something then that I had wanted since childhood.'

The feeling was strong enough to encourage him to spend a few sessions training with Krupička and others in the stadium beside the power station. Then, a few weeks later, he was persuaded to race again, for the Baťa team in the Silver Reed championships for high school students, organised by *Lidové noviny* newspaper, in Brno.

Emil came second in the 1,500m, beating Krupička this time, and helping his team to victory. He later described it as a 'great joy' to do well in such a competition, 'with an official starter and official timekeepers'. His time, 4 minutes 20 seconds, sounds slow by today's standards but was impressive for a novice in 1941.

Winter came, and the visits to the stadium stopped. Emil assumed that his running career was over; work and studies once again dominated his life. The employment was not pleasant: some of the workshops were known as 'devil's islands' because of their foul air. But the chemistry studies interested him: Baťa took research and development seriously.

In the spring, some friends organised an athletics competition between two halls of residence. Emil, now living in Hostel No. 3, was urged to do his bit for the Higher Industrial School. 'It was not difficult to talk me into it,' he admitted.

He won both his races, at 1,500m and 3,000m, and the embers of his ambition were rekindled. That, he said, was when 'it was decided that I would stick with athletics permanently.' Perhaps more significantly, he made an impression on some of the more serious runners, members of the local athletics club, who were in the stadium to train. One of them, the famous Jan Haluza, invited him to run with him the following evening. Popularly known as 'Ali', Haluza was one of Czechoslovakia's leading athletes, a champion at 1,500m and cross-country. He had recently moved to Zlín, where he ran for the SK Baťa club and was beginning to transfer his expertise into coaching. Even Emil had heard of him. He accepted the invitation eagerly.

The next evening, Haluza took Emil through his paces on Zlín's 453m track. The session went badly, or so Emil thought. He felt that he was tensing up under the star's gaze. He had no idea what times he ran and was embarrassed to ask.

The next morning he was summoned from his 'devil's island' workplace to answer the telephone. It was Haluza, calling to encourage him to train again – and, perhaps, to compete for the club. Haluza also enquired after Emil's diet, sleeping patterns and general lifestyle – all of which, he explained, played an important part in a serious athlete's preparation. By one account, Emil was close to tears: it had been so long since anyone had shown any interest in his wellbeing.

It is tempting to say that things now began to look up for Emil, but that would be an overstatement. These were miserable times. In September 1941, Hitler appointed the monstrous Reinhard Heydrich as Reichsprotektor of Bohemia and Moravia, with a brief to suppress dissent and to exploit Czech resources more ruthlessly. SS oversight of activities in factories was stepped up. Back in what used to be Kopřivnice, meanwhile, anything could have been going on. Most of the time, Emil couldn't even be sure that his family were still alive. Emil had been able to make occasional visits – returning to Zlín on at least one occasion with a large food parcel from his mother – and some correspondence got through. But the channels of communication would soon be blocked.

On 27 May 1942 (less than two weeks after Emil had quietly won his second Baťa 'Race Through Zlín'), Heydrich was attacked in Prague by a British-trained team of Czechoslovak paratroopers. He died a week later. Grotesque reprisals followed. Entire villages were obliterated; thousands of men, women and children were slaughtered or packed off to concentration camps. And in Zlín, the iron rule – of the Gestapo and the Gestapo-approved Baťa management – became even more oppressive. Reports of arrests and executions featured regularly in the newspapers; the athlete and resistance activist Evžen Rošický, executed on 25 June, was perhaps the most prominent victim.

In this terrifying climate, evening sessions on the athletics track – a permitted but largely unsupervised activity – began to seem like a precious release for Emil: the only time he felt free. According to Haluza, 'No one had to force him to go to training. He would even have slept at the stadium. As soon as his work in the factory ended, he would come immediately to the track. He was never visibly tired and never lost his humour and optimism.' By another account, 'his tracksuit transformed him into a boisterous young man.' The resulting friendships saw him spending more time with a group of fellow running enthusiasts at Baťa who occupied Room No. 19 in Hostel No. 2.

Occupants of the dormitory included Jindřich Roudný, a future Olympic steeplechaser, and Jaroslav Přeček, a leading sprinter. The friends would train together, eat together or simply hang out together; they kept a notebook in the room, in which they would leave each other messages. Another book kept a record of swearing fines: one crown per curse. According to Roudný, some people found it easier to indicate anger by simply slapping a crown down on the table. (Not that they had many: most of their earnings went automatically into compulsory savings accounts.)

Emil was nicknamed Badger – possibly in reference to his prematurely receding hairline, which, when he was barely twenty, had begun to give his upper forehead the vertically striped effect of a badger. He was also known as Sonny, in tribute to his habit of tricking the cook, Jarda, into giving him left-overs earmarked for the janitor's dog, Sonny.

The friends discovered girls together, too. Nothing serious: this was 1942, and morals were strictly policed in Zlín. But Emil found that women were not immune to his charms. According to Jaroslav Přeček, he favoured girls who were able to bring him gifts of food, such as apples or cakes. 'He was always on the lookout for a girl who was from the butcher,' Přeček told a Czech TV documentary more than half a century later.

Emil's most lasting romantic relationship was with a serious-faced young woman called Jarmila Švehláková, with whom he exchanged letters. He seems to have told her that he loved her. By 1943, however, the relationship would cool. Emil told her that, on his teacher's advice, he had to avoid all distractions before his final exams at the Higher Industrial School. This meant that he could not see her for two months – which she took to mean that he didn't want to see her again at all. She was probably right. They would not meet again until after the war.

Meanwhile, Emil had been becoming increasingly consumed by a rival passion: for running. He cannot possibly have imagined the importance it would eventually assume for him. In the short term, however, it filled a gap, giving him something thrilling and immediate to live for.

Jan Haluza led him gently, teaching him the basic techniques of warming up, breathing and structuring a training session but also nudging him – without pushing him – into setting his sights ever higher. The result, as Haluza may have intended, was that Emil developed his own voracious hunger to improve. 'Emil was very inquisitive and always asking about things,' Haluza recalled towards the end of his life. 'He wanted to know about everything – feet, legs, how to place them on the ground, how to work the arms, how to hold the torso.' He would also experiment – for example, by varying the ratio of steps to breaths he took. Haluza considered Emil 'very teachable – at first maybe too much so. I had to calm him down.'

In races, there was no stopping him. At first, Emil and his trainer used to compete in the same events. On 18 July 1942 they raced over 3,000m in Zlín. Haluza won; Emil came second. The report in the next day's *Zlínské noviny* newspaper mentioned 'a wonderful performance by Zátopek.' Emil read it again and again, and kept walking happily around Zlín with the newspaper in his hand. Two weeks later, he came second in another race, this time at 1,500m, and earned another accolade – 'wonderful performance by Zátopek' – in the paper. He was then selected for the Zlín team that travelled to Prague to take part in a national 4 x 1,500m relay contest. Zlín not only won but set a new national record.

It was a cheering note on which to end the season, and Emil embarked on his winter training with a greater sense of purpose than the previous year. Most days he would run to the neighbouring village of Malenovice and back after work – a round trip of about eight kilometres. In very cold weather, he wore up to three tracksuits, one on top of the other. Once, he and his companions were mistaken for partisans; they fled into the night without waiting to see if the shouts of alarm came from civilians or soldiers. But the possible dangers of keeping fit seemed less significant in Emil's eyes than the benefits. It was thrillingly simple. The harder he trained, the faster he could run. And he wanted to run faster.

He ran for fun as well. Some attempted visits to Kopřivnice got him no further than Frenštát, on the Protectorate's border; so he stayed there instead, with his old schoolfriend Milan Špaček. Sometimes they went running together, on the trails of the nearby Javorník Beskyds, near Radhošť. Emil remembered from geography lessons that this was the true 'spine of Europe': a watershed dividing the Continent more permanently than any line the Nazis could arbitrarily impose. Water on the northern side ultimately found its way to the Baltic Sea; that on the south to the Danube and thence to the Black Sea. He and Špaček took childish delight in stopping to urinate on this spine. 'We would start peeing into the Black Sea, but we wouldn't finish, and then we would dash across and pee into the Baltic,' remembers Špaček. 'We were so foolish – we were proud that no one else had peed, while running, into both seas.'

Increasingly, however, Emil was running with more conventional targets in mind. In the spring of 1943, he was narrowly defeated by the great Tomáš Šalé in the Vítkovice Road Race. He also lost to Šalé over 1,500m on the track, and achieved good times, but no victory, in a couple of 800m races. The near misses frustrated him. Then, as the season was drawing to a close, he took part in a match between Bohemia and Moravia, in Prague. His race was over 1,500m, and his opponents were focused on defeating his fellow Moravian, Šalé. Emil ran his own race, was third as the last lap began and noticed that none of his rivals was accelerating. He decided to overtake, and was surprised to find himself with a clear lead with 200m to go. 'Suddenly I realised I'm coming first. All I have to do is keep going . . .'

When he boarded the train for Zlín later that night, Emil was already clutching a copy of the next day's newspaper, and there his winning time was written: 4:01.4. 'I never had the brains for mathematics,' he said later, 'but that number enchanted me. I kept reading it for the whole night.' What made him happiest of all was the thought that this first victory in a 'proper race' had been won through the patient application of hard work. 'I had started as an average athlete – a normal boy. It took me three years to win a race. I was glad that I endured those three years – that I did not give up. I thought that, if I train more, I will run even better.'

But 'more' didn't just mean more miles. It meant more intensity, more speed, more focus – above all, more thought. Just running lap after lap at sub-racing speed, which was what most of his clubmates did, somehow didn't seem the best way to prepare for the rigours of a race. As Emil later put it: 'Why should I practise running slow? I already know how to run slow. I want to learn to run fast.' So Emil had begun to experiment with a different approach. He would run much faster, at something approaching full speed, and slow down only when he could no longer continue at that pace – after which he would revert to a jog even slower than his clubmates' 'normal' training pace. Then, when he had recovered, he would accelerate again. The experiment produced rapid improvements. Gradually, over the next couple of years, he began to systematise it.

It is hard to be certain precisely how much of the method Emil now developed was original and how much he was taught. Haluza had planted the seeds, emphasising the importance of not just practising running but practising running fast: 'Speed is the foundation of athletics,' he taught. And it seems likely that, through Haluza, Emil must have been at least vaguely aware of the rudimentary methods of interval training with which other European runners and trainers had been experimenting. Haluza knew of the enthusiasm of the great pre-war Scandinavian and Finnish champions – notably Paavo Nurmi – for *fartlek*, or 'speed play': that is, the practice of varying high speeds with more relaxed tempos in the course of an off-road training run. He probably knew about the German coach Woldemar Gerschler's use of short-distance speed sessions to improve spectacularly the performance of middle-distance runners such as Rudolf Harbig. He may even have heard reports that the Polish runner Janusz Kusocinski had incorporated such sessions into his training for longer distance races. If so, he may have passed some of this knowledge on to Emil. It is unlikely, however, that much detailed information about these pioneers had reached Zlín. Their examples may have informed Emil's thinking. The thinking was his own.

Emil summed this up well in an interview published in the *Observer* in Britain twenty years later. 'I didn't know much. It wasn't possible to buy a book about Nurmi, but I found out that in order to be faster over 10,000m he ran 5,000m many times in training. And to be better at 5,000m he ran 1,500m many times. And to be better at 1,500m he ran four times 400m in training. Maybe this isn't true because I never spoke to Paavo Nurmi, but running is easily understandable. You must be fast enough – you must have endurance. So you run fast for speed and repeat it many times for endurance.'

Such were Emil's influences; but the regime that he now began to develop would eventually go far beyond anything that anyone had tried before.

The principles were simple. As he later put it: 'I'm not interested in how long I can hold out, but in how fast I can reach the finishing line.' So, on the one hand, Emil would learn to run with sustained pace by running fast over distances of, typically, between 200m or 400m; and, on the other, he would develop endurance by repeating the process, again and again. Instead of resting between these semi-sprints, as other early interval trainers had done, he would allow himself only whatever recovery he could achieve while running slowly over a short distance – perhaps 200m – before taking off at speed again.

Speed, in this context, is an elusive concept. The most plausible estimates I have seen, for these early sessions, suggest that he typically ran each 400m lap in about sixty seconds: slower than his lifetime best for a 400m race (56.2 seconds, in 1943) but much faster than the sixty-four seconds a lap that he could sustain without interruption for a 1,500m race. The fast 200m repetitions would probably have been done at around twenty-six to twenty-eight seconds. A 200m recovery jog might take twice that. But these are just numbers. An athlete with more raw speed than Emil would have found such sessions easier, and thus less beneficial. They are also just estimates – of sessions that were rarely timed, in conditions that bear no comparison to those in which runners train today. It may be more helpful to focus on the thought that, once he had burnt through his anaerobic resources in the first lap or so of a session, Emil would have had to strive to achieve similar results aerobically, fuelling his muscles with whatever oxygen he could take in as he ran. Whatever his speed, he would have been struggling at the limits of physiology, trying to squeeze more power from a body that was growing emptier with each stride – just as he might in a frantic end-of-race surge for the line.

That's the thing about this kind of training. The figures aren't the point. It's keeping up the effort that matters. If you do so, the repetitions soon start to feel like flat-out, merciless, lung-bursting sprints, as the fatigue accumulates. Objectively, you are probably slowing down. Subjectively, you might just as well be trying to achieve your fastest-ever time for the distance every time, such is the degree of self-torture required. Keep repeating the torture, if you can, and the gains in performance can be spectacular.

Later, as his body and mind adapted to this hitherto unimagined challenge, Emil increased the volume. He began to focus more on 300m and 400m sections, mixing them up in different ways on different days, while reducing the recovery jog (the 'interval') to 150m. He tried sessions of 10 x 300m and 10 x 400m; or, more usually, 'ladders' or 'pyramids', whereby the lengths of the sections would progressively increase in length and then decrease again – so that a typical session might consist of 100m, 200m, 200m, 300m, 400m, 400m, 300m, 200m, 200m, 100m.

The details sound arcane, but, taken together, these represented the beginnings of a radical new approach. Previously, athletes had faced a choice between the the

'Long Slow Distance' method, which developed stamina, for long-distance running; and speed-focused interval training, usually for middle-distance runners. Emil was in the process of choosing both: high-quality repetitions, performed in such volumes as to build endurance as well as speed. And whereas Gerschler had taught his interval-training athletes to rest between repetitions for as long as it took to get their heartbeat back below 120 beats per minute, Emil was merciless in limiting his recovery intervals to the time it took to jog 150m. If his body couldn't squeeze enough recuperation out of those few moments, tough: it would just have to learn.

Different permutations produced different effects. Emil took careful note, observing, comparing and experimenting with the same rigour that he applied to his chemistry studies. But it wasn't a complicated formula. All it came down to was this: quantity plus intensity, multiplied by implacable persistence, equals steadily improving performance. And pain, endlessly repeated, becomes endurable. Tomáš Baťa would have understood: success came from hard, high-quality, consistent work. The rest was just detail.

Sometimes Emil's experimentation verged on the absurd. Walking down the poplar-lined avenue from his dormitory building towards the Higher Industrial School, he tried holding his breath for the time it took to get from the first tree to the fourth. The next day he did the same again, and then the day after that he kept going to the fifth tree – and so on. The exercise continued for over a week until, pushing double figures, he passed out in mid-stride. It seems unlikely that he gained much physiological advantage from this self-inflicted torture, but it was all useful experience in operating at the absolute extremes of endurance.

The further Emil explored the boundaries of possibility, the less relevant to his training his fellow athletes in Zlín became. 'The first year we trained together,' recalled Jindřich Roudný many decades later, 'but soon I was not good enough. There was no athlete who was able to keep up with Emil.' Some doubted Emil's wisdom; or even, at times, his sanity. They told him that he would damage himself – as he did in the winter of 1943–44, when the ill-fitting football boots in which he did his off-track training left him with some kind of abscess that required hospital treatment. But Emil was convinced that, notwithstanding setbacks, his new approach would work. As he put it later: 'This method of training brought me improvement in those basic characteristics a proper endurance runner should have. I was becoming faster, and more persistent.'

Some people made a different criticism, one which would dog him throughout his athletics career. He ran, they said, in an absurdly tortured way. Surely a smoother running style would be more economical – and less ridiculous? Emil shrugged off such jibes. 'I will run with perfect style when they start judging races for their beauty, like figure-skating,' he would say. 'For now, I just want to run as fast as possible.'

He also had to negotiate the more mundane challenge – familiar to runners of all standards – of fitting his running regime around his working life. In 1943, he had graduated from Baťa's Higher Industrial School and was moved to employment in the inorganic chemistry department. There he spent his days grinding silica into a fine dust. Most of this was used for shoes but much of it ended up in the air, on clothes, and in Emil's lungs. He had had more than one tuberculosis scare in his life, most recently the previous summer, and his growing athletic ambitions added to his anxiety about the damage he might be doing to himself. But his tentative request for a transfer was met with the threat of a labour camp.

He also worried about malnutrition, given the enormous amounts of energy he was expending and the limited calories he was able to take in. He countered this risk by gorging on potato goulash, which was off-ration. It was horrible, he said, and sometimes he ate so much of it that he was sick, but he kept at it. 'Maybe I was overdoing it,' he wrote later, 'but that never occurred to me, maybe because I overdid everything at the time.'

In January 1944 he attended a physical education course at which he met Josef Hron, Czechoslovakia's most famous trainer. This led to an invitation from Hron to a training camp in Toušeň in May. Hron seems to have bolstered Emil's confidence in his new approach to training, while also suggesting to him that he should consider competing at a longer distance, such as 5,000m.

Emil had his doubts. His best time for 5,000m was fifteen minutes thirty-eight seconds – getting on for a minute faster than the year before but still twenty-four seconds slower than the national record (which itself was more than a minute slower than the world record, 13:58.2, set in September 1942 by the Swede Gunder Hägg). But Hron persisted, even urging Emil to commit to an attempt on the Czechoslovak record before the year was over.

Another seed had been left to germinate. Emil ran 1,500m again at the 1944 national championships in July, coming second to Václav Čevona, and at a meeting in Přerov in September he broke four minutes at the distance for the first time. That still wasn't enough to beat Čevona, though. Maybe it was time to explore a longer distance.

Early in September, Emil asked a clubmate, Mirek Zdráhal, to time him in training as he ran 2,000m as fast as he could. The outcome astounded them both. 'Emil! Emil!' Zdráhal shouted. 'You've broken a record.' Emil was doubtful, but subsequently confirmed from a reference work that his time, five minutes thirty-six seconds, was two seconds faster than the Czechoslovak record. He urged Zdráhal not to tell anyone, but word leaked out. The following day, he received a call from the head of the SK Baťa club, telling him that a proper record attempt, with spectators and an official timekeeper, had been arranged for that weekend. 'You can't just break records in the evenings,' Emil was told. 'It needs to be done in front of people, officially. Otherwise it won't be valid.'

In fact, when Saturday came, there were only a few dozen spectators. The Third Reich was crumbling, and people were losing even the limited appetite they had had under the occupation for public events. Some Baťa dormitories had been requisitioned as hospitals for Luftwaffe pilots; other Baťa factories, such as Chelmek in Poland and Ottmuth in Germany, had become part of the Nazi concentration camp network. Not far to the east, the Slovak uprising was raging, while young Czech men and women were still being deported in thousands to Germany as forced labour: Franta, Emil's older brother, was among them. These were desperate times, and the possibility of a small line of sporting history being written in the city's stadium will have interested only the most hardcore athletics fans.

Emil was glad of it. The distance this time was 3,000m – a more frequently run distance than 2,000m and thus, he feared, unlikely to have such a 'soft' record. He hoped he would not humiliate himself.

He didn't. He was fitter than he had ever been, and, whatever his doubts, he had planned for success, working out how fast he needed to run each lap. He kept rigorously to his schedule – and his time of 8:38.8 knocked more than three seconds off the existing national best. It was 16 September 1944, and the name 'Emil Zátopek' had made its first appearance in the record books.

Emil enjoyed the triumph, not least because several people gave him presents of precious food – a slice of bread and butter; a couple of apples – as a reward; more than half a century later, he said he could still remember the taste. But news of his success was greeted with coolness in the national press – as if Prague-based sports editors doubted the validity of a record set in Zlín. Meanwhile, Josef Hron sent Emil a message reminding him of their discussions of the 5,000m record, and the management at SK Baťa decided to make the most of Emil's form. A new record attempt, this time at 5,000m, was announced for the following Saturday.

Emil spent the week focusing on speed-work: he did 10 x 200m on Tuesday, and the same again on Thursday. By Saturday he was raring to go and, undeterred by a significantly larger crowd of spectators, he proceeded to run 5,000m in 14:55 – forty-four seconds faster than he had ever run it before – knocking twenty seconds off the national record. Jindřich Roudný, in second place, was one minute and forty-six seconds behind.

The sporting heavyweights in Prague could no longer ignore this Moravian upstart. Never before had a Czechoslovak run 5,000m in less than fifteen minutes; some doubted that Emil could really have done so. Letters of congratulation found their way to Emil in Zlín, as did an urgent invitation to take part in yet another record attempt, this time in Prague.

And so, on Sunday, 1 October, Emil – three hours after gorging himself on plum dumplings made by Josef Hron's grandmother – lined up for his third record attempt in as many weeks: this time at 2,000m again. By some accounts, there were whisperings beforehand about 'Zlín time', and as the starter's gun fired there were many among the Prague spectators who wondered if an unknown athlete such as Emil could really have made such spectacular progress in such a short time. Five minutes and 33.4 seconds later they had their answer: Emil had broken his third national record in sixteen days – and the name Zátopek was becoming familiar to athletics fans right across the Protectorate.

Back in Zlín, there were even more letters of congratulation. Among them was one from Kopřivnice. The family had read about his triumphs in the papers, wrote Emil's father, and: 'We are worried about your health, and so we have decided that you will stop it. It is time to hang up your running shoes. And write to us straight away . . .'

Emil was not sure how to respond to this but decided that, since the racing season was now over, he could truthfully reply that he was no longer racing. But he had certainly not hung up his shoes. On the contrary, he felt hungrier for training than ever, ready to step up his workload and aim for higher things: 'Even when it was raining or it was cold, even when I didn't feel like it, I always found a moment to go to the stadium and to run at least ten laps with alternating pace,' he recalled. It was one of those precious moments in a young life when anything seems possible.

Then the bombs began to fall.

4

The soldier

Allied bombers had been marauding in the Protectorate's southern skies for weeks, heading from newly conquered bases in Italy to attack major Nazi transport hubs, such as Brno, and centres of oil production, such as Přerov, just twenty-five miles to the north. So Zlín was prepared for the worst. When the sirens sounded, at around midday on Monday, 20 November, most people had time to rush to the shelters they had dug in the surrounding countryside.

Bad weather had diverted the B-24s and B-17s from their original target further north, but the skies over Zlín were clear, and undefended. The Americans rained destruction on Baťa's factories until they had no more bombs to drop.

The first thing that Jindřich Roudný did when the all-clear was signalled was run back to the dormitory buildings. Room 19 was still there, but it had not been spared. But Roudný soon realised, as he inspected the damage, that Emil had beaten him to it. In a fresh entry in their shared notebook, Emil explained that he had rushed there in the hope of finding that the book recording swearing fines had been destroyed, and had been disappointed to find that it hadn't.

Altogether, 60 per cent of the factories in Zlín had been damaged. The human toll – forty-three dead and about ninety injured – was light by the standards of the time, but the blow to the morale of the Baťa management and their Nazi overseers was heavy. Everyone knew the Allies were coming. The border village of Kalinov, near the Dukla Pass, had already been liberated, by a Soviet-trained Czechoslovak regiment, two months earlier. Refugees, escaped prisoners and fleeing Germans were flooding across the eastern borders, and the Czech resistance, quiescent for so long, was becoming more active. It was now a question of when, not if, the occupation would end.

For Emil, as for most people, the main goal was simply to stay alive. Training seemed less important than avoiding the last-minute atrocities of an increasingly desperate army of occupation. With an evening curfew in force, much of his winter training was done indoors. He trained by running on the spot: five-minute bursts of fast, low steps alternating with five-minute bursts of high, powerful kicks – 'like when a horse digs something up with its hooves'. The intensity of the sessions made up for the fact that the hostel no longer had any heating. Eventually, however, they resulted in a tear to Emil's left quadricep, and a break in his training – much to his room-mates' relief.

When he recovered, he resumed his indoor sessions, this time in Room 19, all but one of whose occupants was an athlete. The exception, an architect called Solnes, used to watch and laugh as the others joined in Emil's rudimentary aerobics class. When the caretaker complained, he was told that they were practising a dance, which placated him because, in Emil's words, 'the only thing they would tolerate at the hostel was culture'.

By spring, the Germans and their collaborators were planning for post-war survival. Incriminating documents were destroyed, many of them in a bonfire in front of Hostel No. 1. By the end of April, Soviet artillery could be heard. There were none of the usual city-wide celebrations of May Day. Finally, on 2 May, the Red Army arrived.

Emil was at the stadium, training, when the sirens sounded. He ran three 200m sprints, with jogs in between, before they fell silent. Realising that this was no ordinary warning, he gathered up as much kit as he could carry and ran to find his friends. Shooting could be heard in the streets. Hurrying through the Zálešná neighbourhood, he realised that the soldiers he could see were not Germans but Soviets.

Several days of chaos ensued, about which all that can be said with confidence is that most of Zlín's inhabitants, including Emil, welcomed the Russians; that many – probably including Emil – offered various kinds of support, from food and drink to help in digging trenches; and that, after some resistance, the Germans and their supporters melted away. But that makes it sound less messy and terrifying than it must have been. The city's war memorial commemorates thirty Soviet soldiers who died in Zlín's liberation.

Within a week, the war had ended. On 5 May Prague rose up against the occupiers; on 8 May Germany surrendered. It would be many months – years, even – before central Europe could truly be said to be at peace; but the worst was over and the future at least offered hope.

Meanwhile, Emil was sufficiently enthusiastic about what he had seen of the Red Army to tell friends he was tempted to become a soldier himself. The athletes among them advised against it: it would, they said, be fatal to his development as a runner.

But working in Zlín no longer seemed such a good idea either. The Baťa management, struggling to come to terms with their second ideological U-turn in six years, seemed less sympathetic than before to Emil's racing ambitions. The Zlín running track was pocked with shell craters. And every medical check-up he underwent produced the same warnings about the job-related dangers of silicosis.

Not long after the liberation, Emil repeated his request to be redeployed. His manager, Mr Pumprla, didn't even pretend to care. You were willing to do that work for the Nazis, Emil was told, so we're certainly not going to let you stop doing it now.

This angered Emil, and perhaps also prompted the thought that being a Baťa man might not be a helpful tag to carry through life in post-war Czechoslovakia. Baťa had campaigned energetically against Nazism in the pre-war years, and had helped many of its Jewish employees to escape Europe altogether. But the company's subsequent co-operation with the occupation, no matter how unwilling, now made it an easy target for criticism from its left-wing enemies. The factory directors had already been arrested, and their deputies put to sweeping the city streets. There was an obvious risk for its employees of being tarred with the same brush.

So when Emil noticed a series of public announcements calling for recruits to the Czechoslovak army – which had been reconstituted along with Czechoslovakia itself – the opportunity seemed too good to refuse. The notices mentioned that there would be scope for cultural and sporting development. 'I liked that very much,' Emil explained later. He would probably have faced compulsory enlistment before long anyway. In the meantime, the army was arguably the safest place to be. Less than three weeks after the liberation, on 20 May 1945, he joined up.

He was not disappointed. On the one hand, the disciplined, regimented life was hardly a shock to someone who had spent eight years at Baťa. On the other, the physical side of the training, which many recruits found tough, was for Emil sheer pleasure. 'It was like training for long distances,' he explained in a radio programme a few years later. 'Marches, jumps, runs, with full combat gear. I thought to myself: this is good, this is a workout.'

His unit, in the 27th Infantry Regiment, was based in Uherské Hradiště, a small, rather beautiful old town about fifteen miles south-west of Zlín, and he embraced military life there with enthusiasm. There was no fighting to be done: just 'training from dawn to dusk'. Highlights included drills in the forest, morning gymnastics, assault courses, night exercises, and 'marching and running all the time'. Emil tackled them all with the same intensity that he had applied to his interval training, while also learning 'how to train my will, self-control and persistence'. His sense that running was his calling was growing stronger, and his world-view was increasingly coloured by a runner's priorities. He had to resist the urge to put fitness before military discipline, however. At one point he earned a reprimand for giving his comrades a head start in a run and then overtaking them.

It was a challenge finding opportunities to race, but his commanding officer proved surprisingly sympathetic, especially after Emil had won the 3,000m (setting a new Czechoslovak record) in the military championships in Prague on 1 June 1945. Not only did Colonel Ingr give Emil leave of absence for approved races: he even made sure that he was provided with rations to take with him. Emil repaid him with a string of superb results. 'After the war, we competed more joyfully, and some of that joy could be seen in my performances. Almost with every race I set a new record . . .'

In July, Emil was allowed to return to Prague for the Czechoslovak national championships. He won the 5,000m (setting another Czechoslovak record, this time of 14:50.8). The next day, back at barracks, he was surprised to hear Colonel Ingr congratulating him for his achievement in front of the whole regiment.

Emil had originally intended to finish his military service as soon as the rules permitted. Now he changed his mind. He had no desire to return to Zlín, whose inhabitants had been fleeing in thousands to escape the anti-Baťa backlash. Meanwhile, it was obvious that a soldier's life suited him. That autumn, the army reopened its officers' training academy, with a specific though as yet undeclared brief to train up officers from working-class backgrounds. Emil was among the first to apply. He was accepted, and in October he moved to Hranice, in Moravia's Přerov district, to begin a two-year course.

Once again, he thrived. The disciplines of military life felt like luxury: regular meals, somewhere to sleep, a uniform, laundry, challenging work, fresh air and endless opportunities to exercise.

Sometimes he had a training partner: a local youth called Milan Švajgr, who would later represent Czechoslovakia over distances from 800m to 10,000m, made contact with Emil and suggested that they run together. They used to meet outside the barracks once or twice a week, for runs together on the broad, sandy path beside the Bečva river. Švajgr sensed, however, that such excursions were frowned on by Academy officials; and Emil didn't seem especially keen either. Fitting in proper running around other duties required more flexibility than that.

But there was a good running track at the academy, which Emil used – and, for evenings when the weather was bad, an indoor riding school, where the combination of deep sand and heavy military boots lent a difficulty to his exercise that hugely increased the training value of each stride he took. (The legend that he also trained in the academy's 800m-long corridor is implausible: there were too many breaks and steps in it for this to have made any sense.) When the days grew short, Emil ran round and round the grounds of the barracks in the dark, torch in hand – although this is said to have provoked at least one potentially life-threatening confrontation with a sentry. Such misunderstandings may have encouraged him to seek more isolated training environments in the woods nearby, where he could pursue his repetitions untroubled by those who did not understand why they mattered.

One way or another, though, he managed to maintain, and increase, his training regime – even if the only way to do so was by jogging on the spot while on sentry duty. By some accounts, he even experimented with training in a gas mask, but his main gimmick was volume. He later claimed to have doubled his workload in the course of 1946. By the time he set yet another Czechoslovak 5,000m record in June – 14:36.6, at an international meeting in Prague – he was typically doing 10 x 200m and 10 x 400m every day, all fast, tapering off only in the week before a competition (with complete rest the day before).

It seems unlikely that it was part of anyone's plan that Emil should bring glory to the army through his running. The war was barely over, after all, and the army's overwhelming need was for competent officers, not prestige. Indeed, at one point Emil got into trouble at the Academy for having too many athletics trophies among his possessions – a reprimand that prompted him to give away the next one he won to Josef Hron's grandmother. He then discovered that this was one of those trophies that the winner is supposed to return so that it can be awarded again the next year.

But competence was not the only concern. The new army was being built under the supervision of a new defence minister, Ludvík Svoboda, a covert Communist whose overwhelming strategic priority was to make Czechoslovakia's armed forces ideologically sound. This required the gradual easing out of the old, conservative officer class and its replacement by a new generation of young, working-class, Soviet-friendly officers. And the idea seems to have taken root fairly soon that Emil, in addition to embodying this new ideal of the 'officer class', might also make a good advertisement for it. Emil's superiors clearly discussed his exceptional abilities: he was once ordered to run seven kilometres cross-country with a message, and the same distance back with the reply, simply to settle a bet between two superior officers as to whether or not he could cover the distance within an hour. Despite his duties, therefore, Emil was permitted to race half a dozen times in June and July of 1946; he won all but two of his races and set new Czechoslovak records for 5,000 and 2,000m. Then, in early August, he won the 5,000m in the national championships again, which led to an invitation to represent his country in the European Championships in Oslo later that month.

The experience was short but intimidating. The Czechoslovak team was full of novices. Emil, who had never been abroad before, was not the only one to go pale with fright when the elderly Junkers-52 took off. On arrival in Norway, they realised that they did not even have matching tracksuits; for the opening ceremony, they paraded around the track in vests and shorts instead. At the start of the 5,000m, Emil realised the size of the challenge he faced. The Bislett stadium was packed with fans, cheering loudly for their nations' heroes: Sydney Wooderson, British record holder for three miles; Viljo Heino, world record holder at 10,000m; Wim Slijkhuis, the 'flying Dutchman'; Evert Nyberg, the big Swede. Emil felt out of his depth – even after trying to reassure himself by touching Heino's leg for luck – and all four finished in front of him. The fact that Emil's time was yet another Czechoslovak record (14:25.8) did not prevent the odd pointed remark when he got home to the effect of 'Do you really need to go all the way to Norway to come fifth?'

Emil drew a more positive lesson: that 'what was enough for Czechoslovak standards would not be enough once I got to world competitions . . . so for me this meant that I should train more'. There was also the encouraging fact that, despite his failure to win, he had now run the 5,000m faster than Paavo Nurmi ever did.

'I still remember how elated I was,' he told a Slovak journalist forty-six years later.

In September Emil was selected to represent Czechoslovakia in the Allied Forces military championships in Berlin. Most of the competing nations had sent large teams. Emil was Czechoslovakia's sole representative. He left Hranice on a Friday, by train. By midnight, he was alone in the pitch-black ruins of Dresden – much of which had been reduced to rubble by Allied fire bombs eighteen months earlier. He slept briefly on a bench, caught another train at 3 a.m., and arrived in Berlin late on Saturday afternoon, terrified that he had missed his race. He was relieved to discover that the races he could see in progress were just qualifying events, and that the race proper was the following day.

Returning to the stadium on the Sunday after a few hours' sleep, he found it difficult to make anyone understand who he was. He knew barely any English, apart from 'I am from Czechoslovakia', but quickly recognised that people kept asking him the same question: 'Only one?' 'I understood the English word "one", so I deduced that they wanted to know if it was only me. So I enthusiastically replied: "Yes, only one!" And I was happy to have understood them.'

The organisers were less cheerful, as was the American soldier who had been deputed to carry the banner in front of the Czechoslovak team as the competitors marched around the track during the opening ceremony. 'He asked: "Only one?"', recalled Emil, 'and that I already knew. So I replied, "Yes, only one!" And I thought, see, boy, even with you I can make myself understood.' But the soldier was not happy; and when the one-man team behind the 'Czechoslovakia' banner provoked hoots of laughter from the crowd, Emil was not happy either. 'I was all red, ashamed. I thought to myself: I should have stayed at home.' Remarkably, a photograph of this moment has survived, and you can see him thinking it.

Emil almost missed the start of his race, because he could not understand what was being said on the public address system. But once the starting gun sounded he knew exactly what he was doing. The spectators watched in amazement as he surged into a huge and ever-increasing lead, unsure if this was great running or laughable misjudgement of pace. Eventually, as one runner after another was lapped, they began to cheer him, and there was a great roar when he lapped the man in second place. At the end, the organisers were bemused to find that Emil didn't seem particularly exhausted.

On the ceremonial lap that ended the championships, Emil's GI escort was the happiest banner-bearer on the track. And although Emil knew that the standards here were far below those of a top-level international meeting, the event seems to have provided a lasting boost to his confidence, both in his running ability and in his ability to thrive in the world beyond Czechoslovakia's borders.

That autumn he was transferred from Hranice to the tank training school in Milovice-Mladá, in central Bohemia, where he was attached for the remainder of his training to the 11th tank brigade. The upheaval may have been the final nail in the coffin of the romance he had been tentatively trying to rekindle, by post, with Jarmila Švehláková, who was still in Zlín. But he was re-united in Milovice with an old acquaintance. Ladislav Kořán, known to friends as Láďa, had been a promising competitive cyclist until the crackdown following Heydrich's assassination made cycling impossible. He had channelled his talents into running instead, and Emil had made friends with him when they raced in Prague. Shortly after Emil's arrival, they bumped into one another at the sports stadium near the barracks, and Kořán was able – with Emil's guidance – to unlock the potential that would turn him into an international athlete. Both were in the Czechoslovak team that travelled to London that autumn for the inter-services Britannia Shield. Emil won the cross-country, on Ascot racecourse, by 600m – despite the fact that many of those behind him took advantage of the thick fog to go around jumps rather than over them.

Soon afterwards, a winter of exceptional severity descended on central Europe. Emil decided to embrace the challenge and did most of his winter training outdoors. He had moved on from the sports stadium by now, having grown tired of the witticisms ('Who's chasing you?' etc.) of the footballers who shared it with him. Instead, he would run a couple of miles to some nearby woods and then do his training there. When the snow was too deep for normal running, he ran with great bounds instead. His army boots protected his ankles from unseen hazards; and the net effect was, of course, that his body was working even harder.

How hard? It is difficult to be precise. In his first forest excursions, Emil simply ran, exploring rather than training in a focused way; but he had soon grown tired of 'killing time without a goal'. So he found some grassy stretches on which to do his interval training. A typical session involved twenty sets of 'about 250m' and twenty of 'about 400m'. There was no accurate way of measuring the distances – but then he wasn't in the habit of timing himself. The units he was interested in were units of effort: hard to quantify but, for the runner with sufficiently ruthless honesty, unmistakably real. Muhammad Ali once remarked that, when he did sit-ups, he only started to count them when they began to hurt – 'because they're the only ones that count'. This seems to have been Emil's approach, too: he was raising his pain threshold. 'It's at the borders of pain and suffering,' he is supposed to have said, 'that the men are separated from the boys.' From now on, these would be the borders where he trained, every day of the year.

The fact that such sessions were often conducted in foul weather only added to the psychological benefits: there is a sense of empowerment that comes from facing down such discomforts (and in the days before weather-proof sportswear there was a lot of facing down required). Sometimes, when he got back late from training, his only means of washing was to pour cold water over himself in 'a bathroom hung with icicles'. He credited this for the fact that he never suffered from colds. But the benefits were not just physical. For Emil, it was all part of the same formula: load up the pain now, and you will be grateful later. In his words: 'There is great advantage in training under unfavourable conditions . . . for the difference then is a tremendous relief in a race.'

His subsequent performances bore this out. That Christmas, Emil beat the great Gaston Reiff in a cross-country race in Brussels, despite getting lost in mid-race. Conditions were so cold that Emil wore a copy of *Le Soir* as an improvised lining inside his vest. Afterwards, he made friends with some miners from Charleroi, undeterred by the fact that he knew barely a word of French.

One of the first things he did on returning home was obtain a French dictionary, which he proceeded to memorise, starting with 'A' and working his way towards 'Z'.

The Brussels trip was also notable for a rare ethical lapse on Emil's part. A Czechoslovak official upbraided him for charging too little for his travel expenses, and persuaded him to claim for a longer journey. When Emil did so, the official pocketed the extra money, and Emil was left feeling both ashamed and aggrieved. This appears to have been the last time he allowed himself to be tempted by the possibility of profiting financially from his running; it would not be the last time, however, that he allowed himself to be influenced in a way he would later regret.

For now, though, his main concern was bettering himself, continuing his exploration of the uncharted frontiers of human athletic possibility. It was a solo voyage, yet it was not lonely; in fact, the better Emil got, the more he relished the fact that running had a social side. The homesick youth who had come out of his shell on the running-track in Zlín would soon be forging friendships on running-tracks across Europe.

In the spring of 1947, he was part of a Czechoslovak cross-country team (Zátopek, Kořán, Roudný, Vomáčka, Zabloudil) that scored a resounding success over ten kilometres in the Allied Forces championships in Hanover. His abiding memory was of the post-race banquet, where he was congratulated by the wife of the garrison commander. She told him that, in all her years of watching racehorses, she had never seen a sight so beautiful as that of Emil, once again many hundreds of metres ahead of his rivals, running all alone back from the woods to the racecourse. The Czechoslovak athletes laughed at her infatuation. This was a notable departure from the prevailing view that Emil's running style was ugly.

But Láďa Kořán took away a different snapshot of that same trip. His memory was of Emil, before the race, mixing himself a drink consisting of lemon juice, water and the chalk used to mark lanes on the track. Emil explained that the lemon juice was to keep his vitamin C levels up, and the chalk was to boost his calcium levels to protect his teeth. The cheerful preference for logic over convention typified Emil's restlessly innovative approach. He never stopped asking 'What if?'; and as often as not he would try it for himself to find out. (Indeed, it seems likely that once, back in his Baťa days, he had even explored the effect on his running of amphetamine use, which was not then forbidden. If this is true (see note on p. 395), it was a one-off chemical experiment. But it would have been in keeping with his empirical spirit.)

A fortnight later, despite being exhausted from two successive nights of all-night tank exercises at Milovice, Emil achieved his best 5,000m time yet: 14:08.2 in the first Rošický Memorial Race (held in honour of the executed Resistance hero). He also made friends after the race with the Finns he had beaten, Väinö Koskela and Evert Heinström, and was invited to race in Finland a few days later. Emil ran at least twenty-five races that summer, at 5,000 and 3,000m. He won all but two and set three more Czechoslovak records. But none was so important to his development as the race in Helsinki.

It was, at one level, just an ordinary meeting, arranged in a spirit of international friendship. On the flight out, Emil enjoyed trying to speak to Koskela and Heinström in Finnish, despite not knowing any. By the time they landed he had ascertained (he thought) that Koskela was a farmer and Heinström an electrician. In athletic terms, however, he knew that he was taking a daunting step up. Finland was the home of his discipline: the land of Paavo Nurmi and of his great predecessors, Hannes Kolehmainen and Ville Ritola. It was also the home of that day's main opponent, Viljo Heino, Emil's conqueror in Oslo the previous year – European champion at 10,000m and the fastest 5,000m runner in the world for the current year.

As the starting gun was fired in the Helsinki stadium, Emil realised to his dismay that the capacity crowd was cheering unanimously for Finland. Panicked, he set off as quickly as possible, hoping to shake Heino off. Heino stuck to him, and they ran the first 1,500m in 4:08 – well inside world record pace for 5,000m. The next four laps were barely slower. This was suicidal. Then Heino struck properly, powering past Emil in the straight to loud applause. Emil felt helpless: it was 'a terrible uproar', he said later: 'not just applause – it comes from the belly.' Then he told himself: 'I will not give up so easily.' In the next straight, he took back the lead. In the straight after that, Heino overtook again. The crowd sensed a fight and roared even louder. Emil wrestled back the lead, then Heino took it back again. And so it continued, twice a lap, with the lead changing hands in each straight. The tactics were ludicrous – the two men were racing one another into oblivion, like two boxers slugging it out toe-to-toe – or, as one writer put it, 'like two foolish boys'.

By the final lap, Emil had nothing left. 'People were screaming,' he wrote later, 'and I felt desperate to think that I had travelled so far only to lose.' The pace had slipped but they were still running at the utmost extremes of their endurance. Heino was leading and Emil could only hang on behind. Still he refused to despair, even when he tried to attack with 200m to go, and nothing happened. Finally, fifty metres from the line, he made one last desperate effort – and felt himself draw level. This progress encouraged him, and that glimmer of encouragement somehow gave him the strength to push a little harder. He won the final sprint by half a stride.

Afterwards, the two men had to lean on one another to avoid collapsing. 'If I could have spoken his language,' said Emil, 'I would have said "Isn't it stupid. We are fighting for 5,000 metres and all that is between us is a few centimetres."' Their times were unspectacular – 14:15.2 for Emil and 14:15.4 for Heino – but the spectators knew that they had just witnessed an epic battle, and they applauded generously. They recognised in Emil a distance runner worthy of the Finnish tradition: someone with that most prized quality: fighting spirit, or '*sisu*'. They would not forget it.

The race had taken so much out of both men that Heino did not go to the medal ceremony. Emil went briefly, then walked down to the seafront and was sick on the beach. He barely slept, and was disturbed at dawn by Scandinavian journalists wanting to interview him. The media pestering continued throughout his homeward journey, by train and boat. After six years of running, he was an international celebrity.

But he also realised that he had come of age as a runner in a more important sense – and fifty years later, in an interview with *L'Équipe*, he would identify this as one of the races that had marked him most. If he could beat

Heino, in Finland, in a race that he had seemed to be losing, what race couldn't he win?

Returning briefly to Milovice, he felt ready to aim higher still. In just over a year's time, the Olympic Games would be held, the first for twelve years. Now, surely, it was realistic to dream of making a mark there as well?

It was a bold dream – more extravagant than hindsight makes it sound. Czechoslovakia's all-time tally of Olympic track and field glory consisted of a solitary medal: František Douda's shot-put bronze in 1932. The great Olympic nations would laugh at the idea that a runner from this obscure little country might snatch a medal in a major track event. Yet the results and the record books suggested that Emil must have a decent chance.

First, though, there were other things to attend to: an international meeting in Enschede, at which he defeated another of his great rivals, Slijkhuis, over 5,000m; the Czechoslovak national championships; matches in Prague against Italy and France. The France match saw Emil defeat the highly rated Alain Mimoun, a French, Algerian-born ex-soldier who would become Emil's great friend and rival over the next decade. This was their first meeting. Emil won by nearly a minute, but afterwards congratulated Mimoun on his performance, before sharing several glasses of Russian champagne with him – and practising his French – at the post-match celebration.

Two days later, Emil was back at the Academy he had started off in, in Hranice, to graduate as Lieutenant Zátopek, officer of the Czechoslovak army. On a fine, summery day, General Svoboda himself inspected the new officers, while Rudolf Slánský, the influential General Secretary of the Communist Party, was also present, and made a point of shaking Emil's hand.

Emil seems to have given remarkably little thought to his graduation, or to the significance it might hold for his poor, hard-working parents. It was at their initiative rather than his that they joined the other families who came to witness the passing-out parade, on 17 August 1947, and his joy at being able to share this moment with them was tempered with a certain awkwardness: the last time Emil had seen them, on a visit home the previous year, there had been a slight falling-out. He had sneaked out for a training run and – despite his practice of putting on his running shoes in the street, just round the corner – word had got back to his parents, who were still firmly opposed to the whole idea of running. They cannot have been entirely oblivious to Emil's success – he was the most famous runner in Czechoslovakia – but at home the fiction was maintained that he had obeyed their command to give up running. Somehow he had never quite found the right moment to resolve the issue.

To add to the awkwardness, he had no way of keeping from his parents the fact that, as a newly commissioned officer, he was now entitled to six weeks' holiday. He could hardly say that he had no time to visit them. So he returned home with them to Kopřivnice, wrestling privately with the question of what to do about the race in Brno in which he was due to be competing the following day.

He made his escape by announcing that he wanted to take some of his father's honey to his 'aunt' (presumably his sister) in Brno, promising to return straight away. But one thing led to another. Having delivered the honey – and set a Czechoslovak record for 3,000m – he was immediately invited to Bratislava, where he set a record for 2,000m three days later; and while he was there he was informed that arrangements had been made for him to fly to Paris to compete at 5,000m at the World Student Games (for which his time at military academy qualified him). So off to France he flew – and while waiting for his event there he entered and won the 1,500m as well.

He then had a few days off before his next race, in Ostrava, so he stopped off in Kopřivnice, sheepishly, on the way. His family were pleased to see him: they seemed to have resigned themselves to the incessant demands that racing put on his time. Then something curious happened. Some of his old schoolfriends insisted that he join in a race they had organised on the local playing field. To do so, Emil tried to make some minor repairs to his spiked running shoes. His father offered to lend him some suitable tools and, as he was looking for them, Emil noticed that he had a drawer full of newspaper clippings. He leafed through them and realised with a shiver what they were: a father's proud collection, meticulously ordered, chronicling Emil's achievements all the way back to Oslo and beyond.

Emil expressed his surprise. 'Do you collect the results of races?' he asked.

His father was embarrassed. 'Only the international ones,' he blustered.

Then, more remarkable still, when the time came to go to the race in Ostrava, Emil found his mother getting dressed up to go out. He asked her what she was doing. 'I would like to see you run at least once,' she explained.

The reconciliation must have heartened him. It did not, however, prevent him from continuing his exhausting globe-trotting lifestyle. There was another trip to the UK in September, for the Britannia Shield. Emil won the cross-country, at RAF Halton, by two minutes. Then there was a hastily arranged trip to Belgium, where Emil lost narrowly to Gaston Reiff over 3,000m. (The arrangements were so hasty that Emil did the entire trip without a passport, and had to show the Czechoslovak border guards race reports from the papers before they would let him back into the country.) October brought a quick trip to Poland, during which he won races in Warsaw, Gdansk and Katowice and was shocked by the freezing temperatures and war-ravaged cities.

Then he returned to Milovice, this time as commissioned officer. He was commander of a tank platoon, with three tank crews under him. It would be a short-lived posting. None the less, it marked the beginning of the next phase of his life.

5

Beginnings

It wasn't just Emil who was starting afresh. Czechoslovakia itself was changing. The final avalanche was still a few months away, but the creakings were unmistakable.

Some would say that revolution had been inevitable since the liberation; ever since Edvard Beneš, Czechoslovakia's pre-war president and leader of its wartime government-in-exile in London, had returned in July 1945 to form a new national government. His plan, a simple return to the pre-war status quo, had much to be said for it, but his hopes proved naïve. The country was too traumatised, the nationwide epidemic of post-war score settling had been too savage. People wanted something bolder. As the Catholic newspaper *Lidová demokracie* put it: 'It is impossible to return to the capitalist system which prevailed here during the first twenty years of our republic . . . We stand on the threshold of a new economic and social order.'

So it was that, while elections in 1946 had confirmed Beneš as president of the reconstituted nation, they had also confirmed that the most dynamic force in Czechoslovak politics was the Communist Party, which secured 38 per cent of the vote.

The Communists had had a good war, opposing the Nazis, supporting the Soviet liberators and having nothing to do with the Western powers that had betrayed Czechoslovakia to Hitler in 1938. In contrast to the Soviet-backed Communist parties in other Eastern European countries, who simply seized power in the late 1940s, the Communist Party of Czechoslovakia (KSČ) – though equally Soviet-backed – had genuine popular support. Yet that support was not quite enough to form a government.

The result had been eighteen months of stalemate and escalating political crisis, during which the democratic parties struggled to form a workable coalition with the Communists – and the Communists, who had insisted on control of the interior ministry as the price for any co-operation, busied themselves setting up a new police force from which non-Communist personnel were excluded with increasing brazenness. It is unlikely that Emil was too bothered by this: he himself, though not a Party member, was a beneficiary of the similar process that was taking place, less overtly, in the army. Yet he must have sensed that a crisis was imminent. Everyone did.

That December, in the last days of calm before the storm, Emil flew to Algiers. He and other leading European athletes had been invited by the *Journal d'Alger* to compete in both a 5,000m and, on Christmas Day, a ten-mile cross-country race. Emil won both, and turned down a prize worth 12,000 francs for fear of breaking the rules on amateurism. He persuaded officials to give most of the money to a Belgian friend who had no chance of winning anything himself. 'If he gets disqualified,' Emil argued, 'it will make him more famous.' Emil was also offered 'expenses' on his return trip, via Paris, but, again, refused them, saying only that, if the newspaper insisted, he would welcome a bag of oranges, 'as we cannot get them in Prague'.

What he did bring back with him were vivid memories of Algiers itself. He wrote later about the shocking contrast between the city's rich quarter and the shanty town beyond the kasbah (where he nearly had his jacket stolen); and about the beauty of the Atlas Mountains and the sea; and of the pleasure of meeting up again with his friend Alain Mimoun, who took Emil to Surcouf, where he had grown up, and introduced him to the delights of seafood. Emil also struck up a friendship with one of the Barbary apes that came to molest the athletes as they dined. Where others brushed the pests aside, Emil allowed one to climb all over him and spend a long time sitting on his head, picking at his thinning hair. With characteristic curiosity, he groomed the ape's head in return – and yet another bond was forged.

By the time Emil returned to Czechoslovakia, time had almost run out for democracy. With the government in paralysis, the Communists were losing public support and the party's paymasters in Moscow decided that, rather than wait to lose that spring's elections, they should act while they could. As 1948 began, the Ministry of the Interior stepped up its abuses of the democratic process, deliberately provoking the resignations of unsympathetic non-Communist ministers. A general strike was organised in February, to devastating effect. Armed 'workers' militias', later renamed People's Militias, roamed the streets, discouraging opposition. Ludvík Svoboda, the defence minister, confined the army to its barracks. President Beneš, whose health was failing, was bullied into accepting a new Communist-led government; he resigned in May after refusing to sign the new constitution. The last non-Communist minister, Jan Masaryk, died in suspicious circumstances in March. Czechoslovakia became, to all intents and purposes, a one-party state. The constitution took effect on 9 May, but for the next forty-one years the coup – or semi-coup – would be referred to as 'Victorious February'.

Emil, back in Milovice, would have been less affected than many by these events. True, the army was immediately purged of non-Communist officers – around 1,200 were reported to have been removed from their positions over the next four months, while the proportion of Party members in the officer corps would double over the next four years. But most of this ideological cleansing would have been above Emil's pay grade and perhaps even beyond his knowledge. He himself had nothing to fear: he was in the vanguard of General Svoboda's new cohort of officers from working class or peasant backgrounds who by 1952 would constitute two-thirds of the army's commissioned personnel. And the Communist takeover would have been presented to those in the barracks as a necessary emergency action, with huge popular support, to prevent Czechoslovakia from being dragged back to the bad old days by the forces of reaction.

Emil himself was not actively involved in politics at this stage of his life, but he would certainly have seen Communism as preferable to fascism. It was less than three years since he had seen the Red Army drive the Nazis out of Zlín – while his father, brothers and school-friends were among those who brought the Tatra factory in Kopřivnice to a complete standstill during the general strike. He remembered the hunger of his childhood. Not least, he remembered the tragic fate of his brother, Jaroš. If a struggle was going on between the Communists and forces hostile to Communism, Emil knew which side he was on.

And so the old order changed, and Emil, seeming to fit in his training around his new officer's duties without too much difficulty, carried on much as before. He stuck to the same self-created regime of interval training, ratcheting up the intensity and quantity of his training as steeply as his body would stand. Meanwhile, within weeks of the Communist takeover, sporting success was moved several places higher on the list of national priorities. The Sokol organisation – which might loosely be described as a mass participation sports movement with Boy Scout and nationalist overtones – was taken over by the state, and in March 1948 all sports clubs and associations across Czechoslovakia were forcibly brought under its control. (Later in the year, Sokol itself would be abolished – just as it had been by the Nazis a decade earlier – and replaced with a centralised sports federation.) The army was encouraged to increase the emphasis it placed on physical education.

Emil, while continuing to perform his more conventional military duties, made the most of the new climate. Over the next five months, he laid down the foundations not just of his own future success but also, arguably, of the future of elite running. He described his methods as 'simple and primitive', with a focus on 'speed and stamina, speed and recovery' and the golden rule: 'Run fast and try to recover during the movement itself.' But the way he applied these simple principles was revolutionary. It would be more than a decade before sports scientists first defined the physiological principles underlying Emil's approach – and yet, as Láďa Kořán pointed out sixty-five years later, 'within a few years there wouldn't be a single top athlete who wasn't doing interval training – and Emil was the first'.

A purist might argue that he wasn't. There had been interval trainers before; there had even been a few who, to some degree, recovered in motion. But no one had done with these methods what Emil did with them, turning them into tools for developing stamina and applying them in volumes that no one had contemplated before. That was his real innovation: to tear up every scrap of received wisdom about the load of intense work that an athlete's body could endure. As Fred Wilt would write in his 1959 'bible' of post-war athletic methodology, *How They Train*: 'Before Zátopek, nobody had realised it was humanly possible to train this hard.' By the spring of 1948, Emil was typically doing 5 x 200m, followed by 20 x 400m, followed by another 5 x 200m, every day – or, on alternate days, 5 x 150m, 20 x 250m and 5 x 150m – mostly in the woods with his boots on; with about five miles of extra jogging to get to and from the relevant parts of the forest.

But perhaps the most remarkable thing about these training sessions was not the volume but how solitary they were. He had no coach, partly because no coach worth his salt would have approved of Emil's outrageously unorthodox methods. As for training partners, there were other serious runners around, but none who could run at the levels to which Emil now aspired. Láďa

Kořán, for example, seems to have trained with Emil only on the track. In any case, there was something to be said for solitary sessions: just the runner and the runner's pain, repetition after repetition of lung-bursting, run-for-your-life intensity, endured and overcome day after day, week after week, month after month, until Emil understood with every nerve in his body a truth first expressed by Jan Haluza: 'Pain is a merciful thing. If it lasts without interruption, it dulls itself.'

As spring turned to summer, he upped the workload, until he was doing the longer sessions every day. There were interruptions. Some were significant. He ran four 5,000m races between early May and late June; his quickest was a victory over Slijkhuis in Prague in 14:10 – his second-fastest time ever. More important was a cross-country victory, in April, in Spa in Belgium. It was a tough, rough course – runners had to drag themselves up one wooded hillside by their hands – but Emil won by such a prodigious margin that he was besieged afterwards by athletes and journalists demanding that he tell them his secret. Yet what really excited him about this race was the distance: exactly 10,000m.

He had been thinking for several months about adding this longer distance to his track repertoire. The international competition seemed less dangerous, while Viljo Heino's 1944 world record – 29:35.4 – must have seemed eminently attainable, given Emil's 5,000m best of 14:08.2. His Spa victory confirmed Emil in his resolve to try himself out as a 10,000m runner.

He did so in Budapest, on 29 May. He won easily, in 30:28.4, and knocked well over two minutes off the fifteen-year-old Czechoslovak record. Three weeks later, in Prague, pacing himself more confidently this time, he sliced off another fifty-one seconds. His winning time, 29:37.0, was only 1.6 seconds outside Heino's world record. This was a stunning beginning, and a major landmark in Emil's athletics career. In terms of his life, however, it wasn't even the biggest landmark of the month.

On 11 June, there was an international match against Belgrade in Zlín. Emil ran – and won – at the unusual distance of 4,000m. Before he did so, the organisers asked him to present a congratulatory bouquet to another Zlín athlete: a javelin thrower called Dana Ingrová.

Dana was new to the sport. She had previously been a handball player. Her father – although Emil did not initially realise this – was Colonel Antonín Ingr, Emil's former commanding officer at Uherské Hradiště, where the family still had their home. Photographs from around that time show Dana as a dark-haired young woman, seemingly brimming with vitality, with a thoughtful face – slightly feline in its beauty – and a warm, humorous smile. She worked in Zlín at a girls' physical education college and had taken up the javelin in the same way that Emil had taken up running: reluctantly. At her first session, she completely failed to master the technique that the coaches were trying to teach. In frustration, she tossed away the final javelin, grasping it instinctively like a pen – and the coaches decided that they had a major talent on their hands.

They were right. Six days before the match against Belgrade, in the same stadium, Dana had set a new Czechoslovak record of 38.07m, in a match against Katowice. Hence the congratulatory bouquet when she returned to her home stadium. Dana accepted it from

Emil politely. 'I was quite cool with him,' she recalls. 'I turned away, so that he wouldn't think I was swept away.'

Emil then ran his 4,000m. He won, naturally, and set a new Czechoslovak record; and, more impressively, set a new Czechoslovak record for 3,000m in the process. So he, too, had to be given a congratulatory bouquet, and Dana was ordered to present it. 'And this time,' says Dana, 'we did talk a little bit.'

Emil was not unattached at the time. He had been seeing a young shot-putter, Adéla Macháčková: they used to meet when he went to Prague. They had even discussed marriage. But that first double-encounter with Dana – who was a friend of Adéla's – put an end to that relationship.

Five days later, the athletes of Zlín – including Emil – travelled to a match in Bratislava, in what is now Slovakia. For the return journey, Emil managed to secure the seat next to Dana on the bus. It was a long journey, everyone was in high spirits, and Moravian folk songs – Emil's speciality – were sung. It went down well. They were not, perhaps, an obvious couple: Dana's family were comfortably off and suspicious of Communism – which had already seen Colonel Ingr hustled into early retirement. But she and Emil shared a love of music and a sense of fun, and the journey passed happily.

Close to midnight, the bus passed through a small town called Lanžhot – still more than fifty miles from Zlín. The athletes noticed a pub that was still open and demanded a toilet break. ('Everyone shouted "Pee! Pee!"', according to Dana.) Inside the pub some kind of party was going on. Emil was recognised, and the revellers insisted that the athletes join the celebrations. Emil was nominated to do a 'solo' dance and chose Dana as his partner. By the time the bus reached Zlín, a much longer journey had begun.

Not long afterwards, Dana was at work in Zlín when word reached her that 'the runner' had left something for her. It was a huge bouquet of flowers – the biggest she had ever seen. Dana already knew Emil well enough to assume that he must have won them, but it secured him another meeting. Emil asked her to the cinema, but Dana said that she was going home to see her parents. Emil announced that he would accompany her.

Outside her home in Uherské Hradiště that day, Emil was startled to see his former commanding officer. 'This is my father,' said Dana. It is hard to say which of the two men was most shocked. Emil quickly inveigled his way into the kitchen, where his (unfeigned) interest in the pancakes Dana's mother was making seems to have worked the necessary charm. But Colonel Ingr had his doubts. He was a thoughtful man, who had spent much of the Second World War in Dachau and Buchenwald because of his associations with social democracy. He liked Emil. He had liked him even when he was just another soldier under his command. But he also loved his daughter. Think very carefully, he told her, before you decide to link your life to that of such a celebrated man. His fame will become your burden as well as his, and there will be no escaping it. He was right; but, like most fatherly advice, it fell on deaf ears.

A little later, Emil and Dana went out again – and discovered something surprising. It came up in conversation that Dana had been born on 19 September. 'But that's my birthday!' said Emil. Dana insisted: 19 September

1922 – that is, not just the same day but the same year. Much incredulity ensued: 'I though he was playing a trick on me,' says Dana. So they arranged another date. This time, each brought along identity papers. It was true, they really had been born on the same day. It felt like destiny. 'We could have our wedding on the same day too,' said Emil.

Dana laughed and said nothing. She had already noticed Emil's habit of speaking without thinking; no doubt this was just another amusing thing that had popped into his head. Then they paid another visit to Uherské Hradiště.

It was late June, the sun was shining, and the avenue of linden trees outside the Ingrs' house was bright with blossom. Emil suggested they go swimming in the river. Dana's mother begged them not to. A family tragedy long ago had given her a horror of swimming. She suggested instead that they should gather some linden blossom for her. So Emil and Dana went outside and climbed a tree, and while they were up there Emil, after the usual joking around, became solemn.

'Would you like to marry me?' he said.

Dana felt suddenly apprehensive. 'Couldn't we just go on having fun?' she asked.

'But we can carry on having fun when we're married,' countered Emil.

Dana smiled and then 'evaded the question' with a joke: 'How many other girls have you asked this already?' But it was obvious that the question would not go away.

In the short term, though, there was limited time for exploring the matter further. Emil had his army duties;

Dana had her job. Above all, each was anxiously aware that the Olympic Games were due to begin in July.

For Dana, the challenge was simply to take part. When her romance with Emil began, she had yet to throw the Olympic qualifying distance of forty metres. The prospect of sharing such an adventure with Emil inspired her to redouble her efforts. Finally, with less than four weeks to go, she got there. On 1 July, in Prague, she set a new Czechoslovak record of 40.06m – winning not just the national championships but also a precious place on the plane to London. 'I qualified by the ears,' was how she put it.

But Emil was thinking of medals – and so, it seems, was the army. The final weeks before the Games saw him moved yet again, to a villa set aside for army athletes at Stará Boleslav – not far from Prague and many miles from Milovice. There was accommodation (the villa had been confiscated from a chocolate millionaire), a running track, and woods, and, above all, unlimited time, which allowed Emil to focus on his running with an intensity that even he had barely contemplated before, training up to three times a day. For one ten-day period he upped his sessions to 60 x 400m each day. These would, of course, have been slower than the sixty seconds per lap quoted earlier. After the first few repetitions he would have been closer to the seventy-four-second laps that are more usually cited as Emil's training norm – and even that might have been a struggle. But these laps were something much more important than fast: they were flat-out. Emil ran each one at his limits.

It seems unlikely that anyone had ever prepared for an Olympic Games with a workload of such size and brutality. Yet there was no one coaching him, no one urging him on: just a solitary twenty-five-year-old, hurling himself through the woods time after time, in the unwavering, almost religious conviction that the sacrifice must ultimately bring its reward.

At the beginning of July, the Sokol movement held the last great *slet* in its history: a three-day festival of mass exercises and sporting demonstrations to celebrate its ideals of bringing fulfilment to the young through patriotism and sport. Emil and Dana were among tens of thousands of young people who went to Prague for the celebration – although not among those who took advantage of the occasion to chant anti-Communist slogans. Afterwards they wandered over Charles Bridge, and were enchanted by the view of Prague Castle over the River Vltava – a panorama they had previously known only through postcards.

And then, just over a fortnight later, they were in Prague again, boarding a plane together, Emil carrying a large kitbag while Dana carried Emil's guitar, on their way to London for the biggest adventure of their life so far.

6

The lights come on again

You didn't have to be young and in love to find something magical about the XIVth Olympic Games of the modern era. It was a moment of innocent hope such as the world has not often known. London, the host city, still bore the scars of the Blitz; most of those visiting for the Games will have seen worse damage at home. The phrase 'Austerity Olympics' meant little then, but from today's perspective it is hard to think of a better description.

Years of war had left Britain all but destitute. Rationing was still in force, although athletes selected for the Olympics were, like coal miners, allowed up to 5,467 calories a day – more than twice the general allowance. The total budget for the Games was £730,000: equivalent in real terms – that is, as a percentage of GDP – to one-seventieth of the budget for London 2012. Some thought even this was excessive – but it was generally felt that London had done the right thing by taking on the burden when there were no obvious alternatives. And now that summer was here, and the capital buzzed again with the make-do-and-mend spirit that had helped to get Britain through the war, it was hard not to feel that, as Vera Lynn had once sung, the lights were coming on again all over the world.

The BBC paid £1,000 for the television rights. The gold medals were made from oxidised silver. The running track at Wembley stadium was a former greyhound track that had been converted by having 80,000 tons of cinders dumped on it. The wood for the diving boards was donated by the Canadians. Sponsorship came from Craven A cigarettes, with a few hundred pairs of free Y-Fronts thrown in for the British athletes, 90 per cent of whom were men.

Three years earlier, the world had been at war. Now, young people representing fifty-nine nations – 4,104 athletes in all – were coming together to do nothing more lethal than see who could be fastest, highest or strongest. Rarely has the Olympic ideal seemed more life-affirming.

Even so, it probably did no harm to be young and in love as well – and perhaps that is why no one ever caught the spirit of London 1948 more poetically than Emil, in his much-quoted observation (made nearly two decades later) that: 'It was a liberation of spirit to be there in London. After those dark days of the war, the bombing, the killing and the starvation, the revival of the Olympics was as if the sun had come out. Suddenly, there were no frontiers, no more barriers, just people meeting together.'

For Dana, and for many others on the Czechoslovak team, there was an additional thrill. It was the first time she had been abroad. 'I was a country girl,' she remembers, 'from a small town. I had read about Big Ben and Westminster Abbey and Buckingham Palace, but now I was seeing them in real life. It was overwhelming – like a dream.'

The Czechoslovak team managers were anxious that no one – or at least, not Emil – should get carried away by the excitement. They knew that Emil had a strong chance of winning his nation's first ever Olympic gold in athletics – and that such a triumph would represent a huge propaganda coup for a regime still struggling to establish its legitimacy. British newspapers seemed more interested in events such as the defection earlier that month of General Antonín Hasal (the fourteenth Czechoslovak general to defect since February) or an alleged plot to murder General Svoboda than they were in any positive aspects of the new People's Republic. Emil had the chance to change the narrative. It was crucial that he should not be distracted.

The team arrived in London on 26 July, three days before the opening ceremony. There was no Olympic village in the modern sense: just a variety of military barracks and other units of improvised accommodation scattered across the city. The men were mostly in barracks in West Drayton; the Czechoslovak women were in a small boarding school, St Helen's, in Northwood, more than eleven miles away.

This was frustrating for Emil and Dana but a relief to their team managers, who were worried that romance would soften Emil's focus. (They had toyed with the idea of excluding Dana from the team but decided that this would be counter-productive.) As it was, Emil was able to devote the short period between arrival and the opening of the Games to training on the Uxbridge track with an intensity that prompted Paavo Nurmi, visiting with the Finnish team, to remark that only Zátopek understood what training really was.

There was a problem, however, when the day of the opening ceremony arrived. Thursday, 29 July was burningly hot – some said the hottest day of the year – and the team managers were afraid that Emil might succumb to heatstroke. He was told to remain at the barracks. He protested – 'People at home will ask me what the Olympics were like, and I will have to tell them that I don't know, because I was sitting in the shade' – but was overruled. He was allowed, however, to accompany his teammates as far as the stadium. After they had left him, supposedly safe beneath the stands, he made friends with the Danish team. ('Are you really from Denmark?' he asked them, momentarily lost for sensible words.) He got most of the way through the entrance tunnel concealed among red-coated Danes, then insinuated himself into the back of his own team just as they were emerging on to the track. His managers spotted him and were about to explode in fury when Emil whispered: 'The King is looking at us. How can I go off now?'

It was a foolhardy act of defiance, and could well have had serious disciplinary consequences for Emil. But the fact remains that he was right. What is the point of the Olympics, or even of sport, if all you care about is who wins? As giant letters proclaimed from the Wembley scoreboard, quoting Baron Pierre de Coubertin, 'The important thing in the Olympic Games is not winning but taking part. The essential thing in life is not conquering but fighting well.' (That said, it is only fair to record that Emil is also reported to have said: 'What? Not to win? Ah, but I wish to win.')

So it was that both Emil and Dana were there for what then passed as an opening ceremony. A military band played. The competitors paraded. Speeches were made. King George VI declared the Games open, the Olympic flag was raised, 2,500 pigeons were released, and a twenty-one-gun salute was fired. A young, unknown athlete – John Mark, chosen to symbolise youth and hope – ran into the stadium alone and lit the Olympic flame. 'God Save the King' was sung. And that was that.

Just over twenty-four hours later, at 6.40 p.m., Emil stood on the same cinder track, at the starting line for the first Olympic athletics final for twelve years: the 10,000m. There were twenty-seven runners. It was another stifling day, and Emil had agreed in a pre-race conversation with his main rival, Viljo Heino, that it would be foolish to set off at a blistering pace.

But the race had been delayed by nearly two hours – thanks to some confusion over the positioning of the hurdles for some earlier heats – and when the gun was eventually fired, Heino, whether from the build-up of nerves or because it was now a little cooler, set off at something close to a sprint. Others followed, and Emil was soon among the backmarkers.

The temptation to accelerate must have been strong, but Emil had a plan. He knew, and had agreed with Karel Kněnický (his notional 'coach' while he was with the team), that seventy-one-second laps should be enough to produce a winning time. If he could stick to that pace, victory would follow, irrespective of Heino. But he needed to get it right.

To help him, a signal had been agreed. If the pace was correct, Kněnický, watching from the stands with the other Czechoslovak athletes, would wave a pair of white shorts each time Emil passed; if Emil needed to go faster, a red vest would be waved – a task delegated to Dana. So Emil stuck to his pace, and each of the first seven laps provoked the white shorts. Emil found this alarming, as each lap saw his rivals extending their advantage: first Heino, then Heinstrom, and then fourteen others before Emil's struggling figure, apparently way off the pace.

The eighth lap saw yet another flutter of white. Emil was nearly eighty metres behind. Had he, or Kněnický, muddled up the signals? It took considerable willpower to resist the urge to go faster.

And then, to his relief, on the ninth lap Dana waved the red vest. Emil allowed himself to move up the field, progressing rapidly from seventeenth to fifth place. His sudden surge, made more conspicuous by the fact that many of the runners in front of him were starting to tire, caught the spectators' attention. The best-informed among them will have known that, with 1948's best 10,000m time to his credit, Emil was a contender for gold, but to most people he was just a clumsy Czechoslovak whose acceleration appeared to be costing him a superhuman amount of effort. As for Emil's fans back in Czechoslovakia, it was at around this point that radio coverage of the race was abruptly cut off: the delay to the start of the race meant that its allotted time was over, and no one wanted to risk their job by messing with the schedule.

Back at Wembley, there was a buzz among the spectators: as the ninth lap ended, Emil took the lead. It was an intriguing sight. Was this a genuine medal contender – or just a comical foreigner, out of his depth among serious athletes, flailing his way to the front through a sudden burst of misguided enthusiasm?

Such condescension may have been ill-informed, but it was not inexplicable. The post-war world did not lend itself to the rapid dissemination of sporting information, and Emil's running style did little to encourage the idea that he was a potential world-beater. He was, as usual, grimacing and writhing, eyes screwed up and tongue occasionally protruding. As one observer put it: 'He looked . . . as if he might be having a fit. At the very least, he seemed about to drop out.'

The positive side of these contortions was that they made Emil extraordinarily exciting to watch. When Pierre Magnan wrote that Zátopek was a man 'who ran like us', I am pretty sure that this was what he meant. You could see the effort, see the suffering, see the sacrifice and the struggle of the inner will. Anyone who has ever tried any kind of endurance running can recognise these concepts. They are metaphorical octopuses which we all have to wrestle. To watch a runner compete at the highest possible level, and to get an almost physical sense of what he is feeling, is to be very involved indeed in a race. It is thrilling theatre.

And this is what seems to have happened on that warm Friday evening at Wembley. People noticed Emil, wearing the number 203, hit the front. They noticed his clawing and straining; and they noticed the small Czechoslovak contingent in the crowd (mostly teammates) chanting with growing enthusiasm: 'Zá-to-pek! Zá-to-pek!' A few non-Czechoslovaks joined in. Suddenly, Emil had the wind of the crowd's excitement in his sails.

In the tenth lap, Heino seized back the lead. Emil let him keep it briefly; then, seeing the red vest again, put in another surge, opening up a thirty-metre lead. This brought him close to the tail-enders, a lap behind.

Soon he was actually lapping other runners. Spectators, officials, even athletes struggled to keep track. Emil pressed on confidently, but with one nagging doubt in his mind: he had no idea where Heino was. He decided to ask a trackside official – he and Dana had taught themselves a little English in preparation for the Games – but it took him a while to remember how to formulate the question. Eventually, he asked: 'Where is Heino?' – and received the answer 'Heino is out'. Exhausted by his excessive early pace, and demoralised by Emil's second seizure of the lead, Heino had left the track after sixteen laps.

The final nine laps were a glorious demonstration of fearless, rampant dominance. Runner after runner was lapped (including the future marathon world record holder, Jim Peters). Heinström, too, dropped out: reduced to an exhausted stagger, he was ushered off the track by a team-mate. Emil just kept on pressing. True, he found time to smile and pat Abdullah Ben Said gratefully on the shoulder when the French runner moved out of a lane to allow Emil to lap him more easily; but then he was off again, driving himself furiously forwards as if he were engaged in a desperate battle with an invisible rival just a pace or two behind.

In fact, he was so far ahead that the race officials became confused. The bell for the final lap was rung a lap early. Emil was composed enough to ignore it, and had enough in reserve to run a final lap of 66.6 seconds – the fastest of the race. He crossed the line in 29:59.6, lowering the Olympic record by twelve seconds. The runner-up, Alain Mimoun, was 47.8 seconds behind, with Sweden's Bertil Albertsson a further six seconds behind him. The irrelevance of the other placings was emphasised by the chaos of the official results. Positions were recorded for only the first eleven runners (two of which were later reversed) and times only for the first eight. Britain's Stan Cox, who came seventh, was later told that he should have come fifth as he had run an extra lap. Perhaps the most telling statistic was that all but two of the twenty-seven starters had either been lapped or failed to finish. Rarely has an Olympic victory been so crushing.

For the Czechoslovak team, the sound of their anthem being played as Emil stood on the winner's rostrum was overwhelmingly moving. 'We all had tears in our eyes,' according to Dana. Emil exchanged warm congratulations with Mimoun and Albertsson, then returned to the Uxbridge barracks feeling distinctly pleased with himself. Congratulatory telegrams were already arriving from Czechoslovakia. His insubordination at the opening ceremony was forgiven: as someone pointed out, Heino had stayed out of the sun, and look what it had done for him.

But there was limited time for self-congratulation. The Games had barely begun. The women's javelin final took place the following afternoon. Dana threw quite well: 39.64. It was not quite her best or the best she could have hoped for, but it earned her a respectable seventh place. Considering that a few weeks earlier she hadn't expected to go to the Olympics at all, and that on their arrival in London Emil had had to calm her nerves with the somewhat dispiriting words: 'Don't worry, not everyone who goes to the Olympics is a phenomenal athlete', this was a satisfactory outcome. She had not disgraced herself, or her country.

The Czechoslovak supporters were thus in good spirits when Emil lined up later that day for the 5,000m heats. Emil was in the second of the three heats, and had little to worry about. He and Erik Ahlden, the Swede, agreed that, since four of the twelve runners involved would go through, there was no point in overexerting themselves. They would save their best for the final.

For eleven and a half laps they did the bare minimum necessary. Then, with their nearest rivals 100m behind, Ahlden, perhaps seeking to steal a psychological advantage, powered into a dramatic lead. Emil, rashly, decided after a moment's thought that he was not going to allow this. The resulting last-lap battle was thrilling, reinforcing the previous day's impression that Emil was the most watchable athlete at the Games. Ahlden won – Emil had given him too much of a start – but only by 0.2 of a second, and Zátopek fever strengthened its grip on London. The Czechoslovak team management were less impressed. Emil had run his race nearly thirty seconds faster than most of the others who qualified – thirty seconds faster than he needed to. What on earth did he think he was doing?

The next day was a rest day. Emil and Dana went sightseeing, visiting the Houses of Parliament and St Paul's. And then came Bank Holiday Monday and the 5,000m final.

The golden summer weather changed abruptly. For much of the day, torrential rain pounded Wembley's cinder track. By the time of the final – just after 5 p.m. – it was little better than mud. Frenzied attempts to clear the puddles had little effect. Many spectators huddled beneath the stands for shelter until the last minute, then emerged into the downpour wearing makeshift hats of plastic or, in some cases, programmes. It is hard to imagine that many of the athletes were in high spirits as the cold rain lashed down on them on the starting line.

Väinö Mäkelä led for the first lap; then Emil took over, driving into the wind and rain while his rivals clustered behind him. He hoped that someone else might take on the burden of leading after a lap or two. No one did. So he pressed on, keeping the pace testing without ever really seeming to take it up to the next, destructive level. This was a high-risk strategy: Gaston Reiff and Wim Slijkhuis both had faster finishes than he did. If he wanted to beat them by front-running, he needed to stretch them to breaking point.

To most of the spectators it looked as though Emil was winning, and perhaps Emil, hearing the chants of 'Zá-to-pek!' ring out again, agreed with them. Later he confessed that his 10,000m triumph had left him 'puffed up like a frog'. Watching the old television footage, you wouldn't say that he looks complacent. The face still grimaces, while the miseries of the weather are obvious: every athlete's lower half is black with muddy cinders. Yet perhaps there is a lack of urgency about Emil's movements, and a lack of crispness to his foot placement. By his standards, he doesn't seem to be hurrying – and nor do those behind him.

With four laps to go, Reiff blasted Emil's comfort zone to pieces. The Belgian put on a dramatic spurt that became a 67.8-second lap: two seconds faster than the previous one. Soon he was thirty or forty metres ahead. Emil, demoralised, was unable to respond.

Sensing Emil's vulnerability, Slijkhuis passed him, too. With two laps to go, Slijkhuis was thirty metres ahead, with Reiff a further thirty metres ahead of him. Emil was clearly a beaten man. He was still clawing and flailing, but it felt as if he was going through the motions.

There were all sorts of possible explanation. He had tired himself out unnecessarily with that pointless sprint in his heat. His 10,000m gold had taken the edge off his desire. He was struggling with the slushy cinders. Or perhaps he simply didn't have the stomach for a fight when the weather was foul and the race wasn't going his way. Whatever the reason, he seemed to be running on treacle.

Then he woke up.

There is no other word for it. One moment Emil is asleep on his feet; the next, he isn't. Watching the old footage, I find myself imagining a small boy in Kopřivnice, running round and round the block in a kind of trance – and then suddenly thinking to himself: 'Right, now I'm going to run as fast as I possibly can . . .'

You can see him shaking himself into action, jerking his arms almost crossly, his eyes still screwed up as if he were in a world of his own. He later said that he asked himself at this point whether he had come to London just to run until he was tired, or whether he had come to win. He decided that, if nothing else, he would fight Slijkhuis for the silver. Closing in, he realised that Slijkhuis was tiring, and he began to suspect that Reiff, though still about fifty metres ahead, was tiring, too. And he realised that, as he put it, 'No one was wearing the gold medal yet.'

He began to sprint.

It was not, of course, a smooth, effortless glide. It was a Zátopek sprint: a thrashing, gesticulating life-or-death struggle – as if, to quote one sportswriter, he were 'possessed by devils'. By the time he had passed Slijkhuis, everyone in the stadium had noticed – everyone, that is, except Reiff.

Incredibly, Emil closed the gap. Forty metres, thirty metres, twenty metres – surely he wasn't actually going to do it? As with his previous races, there were only a few dozen Czechoslovaks in the stadium, but it felt like tens of thousands, most of them on their feet by now and shrieking with excitement. By the time Reiff was rounding the last bend, the screams were overwhelming. In the words of the BBC journalist Rex Alston: 'The roar of cheers from the crowd was almost deafening. Stride by stride he brought Reiff back to him.' Finally, Reiff looked around – and saw a whirling blur of red-vested Czechoslovak bearing down on him, scarcely ten metres behind. He roused himself into a desperate sprint, but Emil continued to close: nine metres, eight metres, seven . . . Harold Abrahams, Olympic gold medallist in 1924 and contributor to the official report of the 1948 London organising committee, described the spectacle as 'phenomenal'.

The line came too soon. Reiff was still a stride ahead as he crossed it. Another couple of metres and Emil must have overtaken. But a stride was enough. Reiff was Olympic champion, and Emil had to make do with silver. Their times, 14:17.6 and 14:17.8 respectively, were both inside the old Olympic record.

For most of those present, the result barely mattered, and the times even less. This was one of the gutsiest sporting performances most of them had ever seen. Shortly after the finish, Emil took off his shoes to relieve his sore feet. A few minutes later, he discovered that someone had stolen them – presumably as a souvenir of an unforgettable Olympic moment. It was a funny kind of consolation, but it did perhaps illustrate the extent to which Emil had fought his way into the hearts of thousands of spectators. His stubborn, never-say-die heroism appealed particularly to a British public for whom Churchill's speeches of wartime defiance were still fresh in the memory. In the Czechoslovak camp, however, it was a different matter. Everyone knew that Emil had messed up. How, they wondered (out loud), could he have been so stupid?

By any previous standards of Czechoslovak Olympic achievement, a gold and a silver medal was not a bad haul. But everyone knew that it could have been better. Especially Emil.

It was too late, though. Years later, Emil claimed to have consoled himself with the thought that he would do better next time – before realising that it would be four whole years before there was another Olympic Games. Then he turned his thoughts to Dana, and spent the remainder of their stay in London consoling himself with her company.

This wasn't always easy. What the athletes called the 'sharp eyes' were everywhere: Czechoslovak officials monitoring the athletes' movements to ensure that no one had any improper contact with decadent Westerners. But the 'sharp eyes' were sleeping when, two days later, Emil, still distraught and fretful, crept from his bed before dawn and slipped out of the Uxbridge barracks. Using a combination of bus, train, jogging and broken English, he found his way across west London to Northwood.

At about 6.30 a.m., he arrived at the gates of St Helen's. There was no one around. He whistled a pre-arranged signal: the opening bars of 'their' tune, the Moravian folk song '*V Zarazicách krajní dům*'. Dana looked out of the window and signalled that, if he climbed over the gate, she would meet him in the garden, by the swimming pool. They sat by the pool, talking in whispers. Dana said consoling things about the 5,000m – and Emil took the opportunity to show her his latest medal.

The medal was in its presentation case. 'When I opened the box,' says Dana, still aghast at the memory, 'it slipped from my hand – and fell into the pool.'

There was only one thing for it. Emil stripped to his underwear, dived in and retrieved it from the bottom. He was just trying to squeeze the water from his underpants, behind a tree, when the headmistress of St Helen's emerged – to see a naked Czechoslovak fumbling with his clothes while his girlfriend looked embarrassed nearby.

'She shouted something in English and pointed her finger,' said Dana, giggling like a teenager as she described the moment to me on her ninety-second birthday. 'We didn't understand, but we could tell what she meant. We felt so guilty. But we hadn't done anything.'

Emil tried clumsily to dress ('but you know how difficult it is to put your pants on when your backside is wet') before being chased out; tripped on the gate's bolt casing as he turned to wave goodbye; picked himself up; and left in ignominy. 'We were so embarrassed,' chuckles Dana.

Emil didn't dare show his face in Northwood again. Yet he and Dana were still able to snatch some moments alone – or more or less alone – in their remaining time in London. On one occasion, they spent much of a journey on the Underground trying to ruffle the composure of a respectable Englishwoman sitting opposite them by kissing passionately. They did eventually succeed in making her laugh.

Perhaps more significantly, there was a joint visit to a jeweller's in Piccadilly, where Emil bought two rings. Strictly speaking, they were not yet engaged, but the purchase left little room for ambiguity about their intentions. Characteristically, Emil did not think to ask if they could try the rings on. A few months later they realised that they did not fit, and the two rings were eventually melted down to make a single ring for Dana.

Bad weather dampened the appeal of sightseeing, but there were other distractions. On 3 August, Emil was among 300 competitors and officials who were guests of the King and Queen at an 'informal' party at Buckingham Palace. The King was effusive when Emil was presented to him: 'Czechoslovakia must have a remarkable army,' he is reported to have said, 'if its officers can run so fast.' Dr Karel Popel, manager of Czechoslovakia's canoe team, quipped back: 'Yes, and you should see how quickly our generals can run away.' This reference to the recent stream of military defections does not seem to have done much for Dr Popel's career back in Czechoslovakia, and he defected to the West himself a few years later.

And then, almost unnoticed, the end came. Like many teams, the Czechoslovaks did not stay for the closing ceremony, which was even more low key than the opening. Perhaps they were anxious about allowing their athletes to be exposed to more Western temptations than absolutely necessary. If so, they may have had a point. On the eve of their departure, Marie Provazníková, coach of

Czechoslovakia's gold medal-winning gymnastics team, announced that she would be remaining in London. Citing the 'lack of freedom' in her homeland, she became the modern Olympics' first political defector.

But Emil and Dana had other things on their mind: the magical fortnight behind them, the years that lay ahead; sport, love, and the possibilities of a new life together. Perhaps, too, there were echoes in their minds as they left Britain of the idea that Lord Burleigh, president of the British Olympic Association, had expressed in his speech at the opening ceremony: 'It is our firm belief that you are kindling a torch, the light from which will travel to the uttermost corners of the earth, a torch of that ageless and heartfelt prayer of mankind throughout the world, for peace and goodwill towards men.'

As the aeroplane carrying the athletes back to Czechoslovakia gained height over London, Dana looked out of the window. 'It was early in the morning. We were flying above yellow clouds. It was so beautiful. I was enchanted. I thought to myself that I had achieved a fat lot of good there. But I could try, I could really try. I told myself: now I will try to mean something in athletics.'

As for Emil, he wasn't even on the plane. He had already been sent off to Europe for his next race. Yet the resolution he took away from London with him cannot have been very different from the unspoken vow that Dana made as the plane soared away into the morning: 'If it is in my powers, I will do it.'

7

Love and death

Emil came home, by a roundabout route, trailing clouds of glory. Never before in its short history had Czechoslovakia won such global renown. If Emil had hoped to return to a normal military life, he was quickly disappointed: instead, he found himself committed to a whirlwind schedule of victory parades, public appearances and, not least, races.

There were press interviews; a sculpture to be sat for; a propaganda film to be made. There was a reception at Prague Castle, including an encounter with an effusive Klement Gottwald, Czechoslovakia's first Communist president. There was even indirect contact from the West, with a German shoemaker called Adolf Dassler (future founder of Adidas) reportedly making discreet enquiries about the possibility of supplying Emil with shoes.

Above all, there were autographs to be signed, thousands of them, and off-the-cuff speeches to be given: for example, when Emil was spotted visiting Kopřivnice on the weekend of its annual fair – and caused even more of a sensation than the 'headless woman'. He proved so good at public speaking, scripted or improvised, that

Party officials scrambled to recruit him to give morale-boosting addresses to workers' groups.

He was also promoted, to captain, and – after a brief extra tank course in Vyškov – moved to a job in Prague, as commander of a company in the newly created Army Sports Club (ATK). He worked mainly at the Strahov stadium, but struggled to fit his responsibilities around his travel commitments.

His post-Olympic victory tour took him to Brussels, Amsterdam, Ostend, Prague, Brno, Paris, Bucharest, Bologna and Milan, where he raced at distances from 3,000 to 10,000m. This twelve-race sequence included two defeats. Emil had a sore hip, and was struggling to cope with the endless media attention. Somehow among all this Emil and Dana found time to visit her parents in Uherské Hradiště. It was 19 September, their joint twenty-sixth birthday. In an ideal world this would have been their wedding day, but there had not been time. Instead, after a few celebratory drinks with friends, they returned to the house for Emil to ask Colonel Ingr formally for Dana's hand in marriage. Emil felt intimidated by this, especially when his former commanding officer asked him if he was sure he was sober. Emil attempted to prove him wrong by doing a handstand, but for some reason lacked his usual steadiness in the position. None the less, consent was granted, and the date was fixed for 24 October – a rare gap in the couple's hectic schedule.

Emil also had to get permission to marry from the army – and was shocked to have his request refused. The Ingrs, he was told, were not a suitable family. Dana's father – and, more importantly, her relative and godfather, the famous General Sergej Ingr – were associated with the democratic Beneš regime. It really wouldn't do for Czechoslovakia's new national hero to marry into such a family. But Emil was determined and said that, rather than give up Dana, he would give up the army. The army thought about this for a while and then – rather like Colonel Ingr – gave its assent, dubiously.

A month later, Emil and Dana returned to Uherské Hradiště for what can only be described as a celebrity wedding. They were slightly late, having gone cycling that morning and, while doing so, attempted to kiss. Valuable time had been lost patching up the resulting damage to Emil's uniform and Dana's knee. By the time they arrived, the square outside the church was so packed with people that Dana could barely fight her way through, despite an athletes' guard of honour forming an arch of javelins at the door. Inside, the crowds were so dense that people were standing on the pews. 'Everyone wanted to congratulate us,' according to Dana. 'My bridal bouquet disappeared in the crowd somewhere.' Several outfits were looking distinctly the worse for wear by the time all the guests had fought their way out again and joined the happy couple for the celebration dinner.

The only difficulty in Emil and Dana's immediate future was that there was no time for a honeymoon, and no immediate prospect of living together either. Dana was not yet able to leave her job in Zlín, while Emil was tied to Prague. The pain of separation was eased by the fact that, early in 1949, Emil was given an apartment: a two-bedroom flat at No. 8 U Půjčovny in central Prague. Perhaps this was less remarkable than it sounds to modern Western ears: it was owned via a housing co-operative, to which it would eventually be returned, and was a place to live rather than an asset. None the less, it was a handsome late wedding present. Western visitors to the first-floor apartment, which would remain the Zátopek home for nearly twenty-five years, tended to describe it as 'modest' or 'simple'. Yet for a poor boy from Kopřivnice who had never yet had so much as a room he could call his own and had been living in institutional accommodation since he was fifteen, it must have seemed like a palace.

This was, of course, part of the idea: part of a nationwide pattern whereby the Party rewarded those it favoured with privileges, positions and possessions. As one propaganda newsreel (showing Emil being driven past cheering crowds through the centre of Prague) put it: 'This is how the people reward those who are most faithful to them, who fight for society's glory.' It hardly needed spelling out that those whose attitudes or class backgrounds made them unsuitable for public employment were simultaneously losing their jobs and, in some cases, their accommodation. In the first few years of Communist rule, around 300,000 people were driven out of public life, including thousands of army officers.

Time for Emil to think about such matters was limited. If he wasn't travelling or racing, he was at his desk, trying to catch up with paperwork. By one account he was able to train only after dark, and had to climb a fence to get to the running track. Yet his appetite for self-improvement as a runner remained as voracious as ever. 'What you do when the stadium is full is important,' he said. 'But what you do when the stadium is empty is a thousand times more important.'

Medals or no medals, he still yearned to make himself faster, and he trained with obsessive persistence. 'When a person trains once, nothing happens,' he said. 'When a person forces himself to do a thing a hundred or a thousand times then he certainly develops in ways more than physical. Is it raining? That doesn't matter. Am I tired? That doesn't matter either. Willpower becomes no longer a problem.' That was part of his secret: he never spared himself.

But a 1949 article by the Prague-based Hungarian coach Klement Kerssenbrock also identified one other thing: the fact that, 'If Zátopek feels tired and has an idea that the speed is slowing down, he immediately tries to increase the pace.' This isn't rocket science; it's barely sports science; yet it may come close to explaining one of the most extraordinary adventures in sport. When the going got toughest, Emil got going: not just on the big occasions but every time, in repetition after repetition, day after day, month after month, until it became his instinctive reaction to the kind of pain that makes ordinary human beings give up. Emil even had a saying for it: 'When you can't keep going, go faster.' It was that simple, self-made instinct that raised him to a level beyond the mere elite. Everything else was detail.

In fact, it was not just ordinary human beings who were being left behind by Emil's relentless self-improvement. He and Dana were eventually allowed a quick honeymoon, in a hostel owned by the Czechoslovak Athletics Federation in the Vysočina region of the Bohemian-Moravian Highlands. It was comfortable, and offered a chance to rest and be together, but it wasn't especially private – in fact, they ended up inviting some friends from Brno to join them. There was also a German shepherd dog, owned by the woman who ran the hostel.

When the dog realised that Emil and Dana were going running every day, it agitated to go with them. So, each day, the three of them would head off on the mountain paths, jogging at first before Emil found somewhere to do more serious training. One day, the dog seemed to be lagging, distracted by its own agenda. Emil went back and chivvied it along. 'I don't know what he said to it,' laughs Dana, 'but suddenly the dog was in front and Emil was chasing it. It looked so confused!' The chase went on at full Zátopek speed, for mile after mile, culminating in a set of flat-out repetitions around a lake; and then, with more chasing, they all returned to the hostel.

That evening, the dog's owner was perplexed. 'I don't know what's wrong with this dog,' she said. It showed no inclination to eat or drink, let alone play. It just lay there, exhausted.

The next day, Emil came to fetch the dog for another excursion. When it realised who was there, it whimpered and crawled deep into the back of its kennel. It was a reaction with which a growing number of Emil's human rivals could identify.

When the new racing season arrived, Emil was pleased to find that his winter training had yielded dividends. There was a cross-country race in Horka u Jičína in April which he won narrowly after building up a huge lead, getting badly lost and then having to fight his way to the front from twenty-ninth position. He won a couple of 5,000m races, too, the second of which, in Warsaw on 9 May, yielded the impressive time of 14:10.2; and there was a 3,000m in Prešov three weeks later, which he also won. Then, on 11 June, he went to Ostrava to run the 10,000m in the Czech military championships.

Jaromír Konůpka, who had not seen Emil race before, made the short journey from Kopřivnice to watch him, and bumped into him beforehand at the Vítkovice stadium. 'I asked him how it was going to be. "Don't ask," he said. He said he had spent the morning being filmed in Zlín, and then had to stand all the way on the train. "I had two slices of bread and some cheese," he said. "And when the train stopped in Přerov I had a beer. So don't expect much . . ."'

But when the race started, Emil felt fine. There wasn't much competition, but, even so, he didn't hold back, and shortly after halfway he began to notice a certain excitement among the spectators. He wondered why: he was in no danger of being overtaken. Then the race announcer explained on the PA system that Emil had completed the first 6,000m faster than Heino had done at the equivalent stage of his 1944 world record of 29:35.4.

Spurred on by the crowd, Emil decided to go for it: his first world record. After 8,000m, he was still ahead of Heino's schedule. The cheering became hysterical. Czechoslovakia had never had a world record in men's running before. Emil, perhaps distracted, lost a little pace and found himself needing to run the final kilometre in less than three minutes. He could feel himself tiring – but his champion's instinct kicked in. He met the fatigue head-on with a fresh surge of effort which he maintained for two and a half laps. He crossed the line to rapturous applause, in 29:28.2. He had beaten Heino's record by seven seconds.

While officials hurried to telegraph the good news across the world, Emil made a gracious speech to those who had cheered him on, urging others to follow in his footsteps. Quite apart from the magnitude of his achievement, he seemed to be growing accustomed to his duties as a sporting figurehead, and he was handling his celebrity with a grace and ease that would soon become a central theme of the Zátopek legend.

Then there were more races, more travels; at times it must have seemed little more than a blur: a match against Romania in Ostrava; an international match in Stockholm; a four-race tour of Finland (including a 10,000m victory over Heino) in July; and a seven-race tour of Eastern Bloc nations that took in Moscow, Budapest, Sofia and Bucharest. Throw in a few races in Czechoslovakia and you have twenty-two track races from May to September, in eight countries, over distances from 1,500 to 10,000m. If war had broken out the Czechoslovak People's Army would have had to do its best without him.

It would be nice to dwell on all the races. Those who were there sometimes do. But all that really need saying here are three things. First: that's a lot of races. Mo Farah raced only eleven times in the whole of 2015 (and only five times at his specialist distances of 5,000 and 10,000m). The second is that Emil won all but one of them; and that, while most of the races were slow by his standards, he still managed three 5,000m times that were faster than the Olympic record-breaking 14:17.6 with which Gaston Reiff had snatched gold from him in London. And the third and most important thing is that, for Emil, it wasn't just about winning. He raced because he loved to race: to pit himself against the strongest opposition he could find and see who was best. And he did all this with a *joie de vivre* that brightened the process for all concerned. His growing mastery of foreign languages made him, in the words of British steeplechaser John Disley, a 'focal point' for conversation at international meetings. His warmth, good humour and interest in people made him more than an interpreter: he was a facilitator of friendship. Bill Nankeville, the British miler, considered him 'a wonderful man, terribly kind'. Unlike Disley, Nankeville didn't race against Emil, but he still appreciated the friendly glow of his personality.

Emil loved to talk: before, after and even during races. Perhaps he was making up for the solitude of his training. The chatter was largely inconsequential and often in a pidgin version of a half-learnt language; the details are mostly forgotten. But everyone remembered Emil's zest for human interaction: a witticism here, a word of encouragement there, a joke false start to entertain the crowd there. 'For me it was always about more than the victory,' said Emil later. 'I wanted to win, but not at all costs.'

His one defeat that summer was in the 1,500m in Přerov, a relatively obscure location in Moravia where he agreed to race as a personal favour to the organiser. Emil arrived at a railway station so packed with excited crowds that he could barely fight his way out of it, while the journey from station to stadium was such a struggle he almost gave up. Emil came third, behind Václav Čevona and Milan Švajgr – both specialists at the distance, unlike Emil. But the only person the crowd wanted to cheer was Emil, and local athletics fans still cherished the memory of his visit decades later.

It must have been tempting for Emil to bask in the same afterglow. In his past three months of racing, he had beaten Viljo Heino once and had beaten Väinö Koskela (world No. 2 at 5,000m) three times. He now had a sequence of fourteen consecutive victories at 10,000m – that is to say, every race he had ever run at the distance. Yet there was one small problem. In early September, news broke that Emil had ceased to be a world record holder. Running in Kouvola in Finland, Heino, who many people had assumed to be past his best, had shaved a whole second off Emil's time.

Emil professed himself unconcerned, suggesting that perhaps it was Heino's turn to hold the record for a while. His superiors felt differently. Later that month, there was a conversation with Colonel Václav Sábl, who was in charge of athletics at ATK Praha and may himself have been under some pressure from above, in which Emil was effectively ordered to bring the record 'back home'. Emil complained that he was too busy ('I was a company commander, so I can't train when I am supposed to be on duty'), and didn't have time to prepare. Colonel Sábl's response was a question: how much time do you need? The result was a three-week stretch in which Emil and two other athletes in his unit were excused all other duties. It was a rare privilege – some Westerners would say an unfair one – but also a huge responsibility. Colonel Sábl's intervention could be seen as support, or as something more threatening than that. Emil said at least once around this time that, when he raced in Czechoslovakia, he feared that, if he lost, he would be put in prison. Whether or not such fear was justified, there was an obvious implication that people in high places were disappointed that he had lost the record and would be still more disappointed if, now that these special arrangements had been made for him, he did not win it back.

The new record attempt was set for 22 October, in Ostrava. Emil's planned preparation involved two weeks of super-intense training, followed by a week's tapering off. For his first day of 'training leave' he did a modest 5 x 200m, 20 x 400m and 5 x 200m. For the second he increased the number of 400s to thirty, and thereafter he made it forty. His focus was primarily on pace; endurance wasn't really an issue by this stage of the season. Even so, it was a heavy load – and on the fourteenth day he developed bruising in his calf. He had no choice but to ease off more abruptly than he had planned, and rested altogether on the seventeenth and nineteenth days. By the twentieth day the calf seemed better, but it was, of course, too late for any more heavy training.

The record attempt was supposed to be unannounced, but news leaked out, and there were crowds awaiting him when he and his fellow ATK athletes arrived at Ostrava station. A car with a PA system accompanied them from the station to the barracks, drawing people's attention to the arrival of the great Zátopek. Emil, worried that the fanfare might undermine his hopes, spent the evening anxiously working out his schedule. He decided to aim for 70.5-second laps, which would yield a time of 29:23.0 – comfortably inside the record but more than five seconds inside his previous best.

The next day, a Saturday, was cold and blustery, but by 4 p.m. the wind had dropped. The Vítkovice stadium was packed with 20,000 people. Shortly before stepping on to the track, Emil was concerned to see a newspaper seller with a pack of posters pre-prepared to announce a 'special edition – Zátopek breaks world record'.

And then he was off. There were, of course, other runners, but there was no question of any pacemaking: no one else in ATK Praha was up to it. Yet the crowd's vociferous support provided a sense of urgency, and after a slow start Emil was able to stick fairly well to his 70.5-second laps – which he could monitor with the aid of a timekeeper who raised a flag at alternate seventy and seventy-one-second intervals. There was a minor crisis in the eighth kilometre, when he began to tire and, simultaneously, realised that he had slipped several seconds behind his own schedule, but the split times suggest that he was never in serious danger of falling behind Heino's pace. In any case, the spectators were not going to allow him to let the prize slip from his grasp, and their redoubled shouts helped to remind him to do what he did best – and respond to exhaustion by fighting back. Visibly gritting his teeth, he upped the pace. By the end of the ninth kilometre he had almost halved the deficit, and for the final laps he accelerated relentlessly. He finished with a near sprint for the final 300m, and crossed the line in 29:21.2 – six seconds faster than Heino's record.

The acclaim was huge, perhaps unlike anything he had experienced before. His Olympic medals had been won in London, before spectators who, however much they warmed to him, were not his countrymen. Here he was among his fellow army athletes, who hoisted him on to their shoulders, and among his fellow Moravians, including family and friends; and, not least, among tens of thousands of fans who had felt personally involved in the making of a new landmark in Czechoslovakia's sporting history. Once again, Emil made a dignified speech, reportedly praising 'the common struggle of all progressive human beings for peace and democracy'. There were more congratulatory messages and telegrams, too, including one from President Gottwald, while the approval of his military superiors was both obvious and gratifying.

The next morning, Emil visited Kopřivnice, where once again there were large crowds. He will have noted that building works were in progress for a new sports stadium named in his honour. Then he returned to Prague, where, according to Dana, he 'glowed like a meteor and couldn't fall asleep all night for excitement'.

Dana had been able to move to Prague by now, where she had found a job as a secretary for a sports magazine, *Ruch* (better known by its subsequent name, *Stadion*). She had struggled at first with the unaccustomed experience of living in a big city, and found it odd that, if she wanted to know what the weather was like, she had to go out on the balcony. But at least there was a balcony. There was also a maple tree outside, and a courtyard at the back, and friendly neighbours, including at least one fellow athlete, the discus thrower Jarmila Jamnická, with whom they socialised.

Inside, parts of the apartment came to look more like a gym than a home – one wall was lined with horizontal wooden exercise bars, which Emil had installed – reflecting the overwhelming priorities of the occupants. But it was, by all accounts, a happy home. After work, Emil and Dana used to train together at the Strahov stadium, at the top of the great hill that towers over Prague from the west bank of the Vltava. And afterwards, happily exhausted, they would jog home, down Strahov Hill, across Hradčany Square, through the grounds of Prague Castle – 'All the visitors had gone by then,' says Dana, 'and there were just the soldiers standing guard' – and then down the long, sloping, castle steps, chasing their shadows towards Klárov and the zigzagging alleys that would take them home. The hard cobbles cannot have been very comfortable for their plimsolled feet; none the less, says Dana, these twilight jogs were 'the most beautiful training I ever did'.

There were many such enchanted moments in those days. In November, there was another short holiday, this time in the Tatra Mountains. Much of it was taken up by the novelist František Kožík, who conducted interviews with Emil that would form the basis of a biography (published soon afterwards) that began life as *The Will to Victory* but was repeatedly adapted and expanded over the next five years to take into account Emil's multiplying achievements and fame. But there was also time for training, on wet roads in army boots, and for long walks with Dana which, according to Kožík, regularly degenerated into tree-climbing sessions and games of leapfrog. There was no dog to run with this time, but Emil did make friends with a flock of sheep, some of which seemed tempted to run with him but soon thought better of it.

Then, in spring, there was a trip to the Soviet resort of Sochi, on the Black Sea. It wasn't a holiday: like most things in their lives in this period, it was simply something they had been told to do. In effect, they were at a training camp, along with many other leading Soviet bloc athletes, and both took full advantage – for most of April – of the opportunities this offered. One report had Emil doing more than twenty-five kilometres' worth of fast 400m repetitions every day (which by June would increase to a staggering thirty-two kilometres' worth). The Soviet trainers watched and learnt, but Western experts were baffled by the reports that trickled back to them. 'I have yet to hear of any athlete who can manage anything approaching the Czech's programme,' wrote the editor of *Athletics Weekly* that spring. Yet Emil seemed to thrive on the workload, and he returned to Prague bearing tales not of hardship but of Sochi's unforgettable beauty, with the snowy mountain-tops of the Caucasus in one direction and, in the other, a shining sea in which it was warm enough to swim with dolphins. He was particularly enthused by the fact that the resort was populated not by 'millionaire drifters' but by factory workers and miners.

It is tempting to describe this phase of Emil's life as a golden one, but this would not be entirely true. Life was treating the Zátopeks kindly, but there were countless other Czechoslovaks for whom the years between the London Olympics of 1948 and the Helsinki Olympics of 1952 were anything but kind. The Communists' one-party state had quickly become a tyranny, in which the government's overwhelming priority was to eliminate threats to the Party's continuing dominance. By 1950, that policy had turned into what can only be described as a Terror. Those 300,000 'class enemies' driven out of public life were only the beginning. Less easily shrugged off are the tens of thousands – perhaps 200,000 in all by the end of the 1950s – convicted of political offences, of whom several hundred were executed and around 100,000 were sent to labour camps.

Few people knew the full extent of the Terror – perhaps not even all of its perpetrators. But it was hard for anyone to be totally unaware of it. Emil, for example, may not have heard of the execution of his fellow officer General Heliodor Píka, which took place on the day of Emil's first world record. But it would have been odd if the fate of his mentor, Jan Haluza, had passed him by. Haluza was arrested in Zlín in September 1948 for refusing to join the Communist Party and sent to a concentration camp at Jáchymov, where he would spend six years.

The Communists set up eighteen concentration camps in all. Those around Jáchymov were the most hellish, thanks to the mining town's deposits of uranium, for which the Soviet Union had an urgent appetite. Political prisoners offered a cheap solution to the challenge of getting the stuff out of the ground safely. It wasn't safe, but prisoners were expendable. They hacked out the radioactive rock with drills and pickaxes and loaded it on to trucks with their bare hands. Lung cancer was a common cause of death, as were bullets for would-be escapees. Life expectancy among prisoners was forty-two. But there were plenty more where they came from. The political prisoners were known as '*mukl*' – acronym-based slang for 'men marked for liquidation'.

It would be some years before the details of their ordeal became widely known, but most people must have had a notion that the camps existed, if only from the way that people kept disappearing. Ladislav Kořán was another one – Emil's friend from Zlín and Milovice and, in recent years, a fellow member of the Czechoslovak national team. Kořán combined his athletic gifts with a brilliant mind, which he applied to the field of electronics. In the late 1940s he developed a prototype for an instrument that would become one of the world's first electric guitars. (Later models of Blatenská Resonet guitars would be played by, among others, George Harrison of The Beatles and Led Zeppelin's Jimmy Page.) But the Communist coup put paid to Kořán's hopes of developing his own business, and so he tried to sell the company abroad. The next thing he knew, he was being tipped off about his imminent arrest for 'industrial espionage'. He fled the country in late 1949 but then, in April 1950, made the mistake of returning to fetch his family. He was picked up and sentenced to eighteen years. He would spend the next decade as a *mukl* in Jáchymov.

Information about specific cases circulated slowly: most people had learnt not to talk about them freely. But the wider shadows of totalitarianism were everywhere, from the city formerly known as Zlín (renamed Gottwaldov in 1949 in honour of the nation's slavishly Stalinist president) to the centre of Prague, where work was about to begin on that thirty-metre-high statue of Stalin, on the edge of the Letenské Gardens. You had only to look at a newspaper to realise that the press had long since ceased to be free – why else would there be all those gratuitous, sycophantic stories about the wonders of the Soviet Union? As for freedom of thought, you could be jailed for up to a decade simply for failing to tell the police about other people's disloyal intentions: this new offence was known as '*Věděl, nepověděl*' – that is, 'Knew, but didn't tell'.

And now, in case anyone was in any doubt, terror was brought to the top of the public agenda. The 'monster trials' of 1949–52 can be seen as a direct extension of the Stalinist purges in Russia. Soviet 'consultants' were sent to Czechoslovakia to oversee them. The idea was not just to eliminate opposition to the regime – although 178 victims were indeed executed as a result – but to cow the entire population. Special courts were set up for the purpose, and special crimes added to the legal code. Little attempt was made to disguise the fact that the accused had been tortured, physically and psychologically; or that nearly everyone involved in the trials – which were broadcast live – was reciting from a script.

The accused ranged from genuine dissidents to Party officials who had fallen from favour. The most shocking case, in June 1950, was that of Milada Horáková.

Horáková was a transparently decent politician. A democratic socialist and patriot, she had opposed the Nazi occupation and, as a result, had spent much of the Second World War in a concentration camp. Following the liberation, she had represented democratic socialism as an MP for the Česká strana národně sociální (which translates, misleadingly, as Czech National Socialist Party). She resigned in March 1948 but continued to campaign against the new post-democratic regime. She was arrested in September 1949, accused of plotting to overthrow the 'people's democracy' and tried, with twelve supposed co-conspirators, from 31 May to 8 June 1950.

The proceedings were broadcast not just on radio but on public address systems in the streets and in workplaces, so that everyone could hear Horáková condemned as a 'criminal mastermind' of a 'terrorist conspiracy'. At the same time, a vicious campaign of public condemnation was organised. The Central Committee of the Czechoslovak Communist Party organised public meetings at which people were urged to sign petitions calling for the harshest possible sentences for the 'traitors'. Those who refused soon realised that, in so doing, they were casting doubt on their own loyalty to the regime.

And so, like a grotesque precursor to the Ice Bucket Challenge, the campaign went viral. Hardly anyone dared refuse to join in: why would you, unless you were part of the conspiracy? Workers were asked to vote on motions calling for the death penalty. ('Somehow everyone's hand went up,' one former factory worker recalled.) Petitions were even taken into schools, and woe betide the parents of children who refused the invitation to sign. But the most visible manifestation of the campaign was a flood of letters, to newspapers and government offices, condemning the accused on behalf of individuals or groups. *Rudé právo*, the newspaper of the Communist Party, devoted entire pages to anti-Horáková correspondence.

Horáková, a politely spoken woman of forty-eight, conducted herself with courage and dignity, refusing to stick to her persecutors' script and insisting, 'I remain, on principle, firm in my convictions.' When, on 8 June, the inevitable death sentence came (for her and three others), Winston Churchill, Albert Einstein and Eleanor Roosevelt were among those who pleaded for clemency.

But the hate campaign continued, and the page that *Rudé právo* devoted to it two days later included the following letter:

> *The words used by the President when he spoke to ČSM Congress and quoted an old revolutionary song – 'Let the old, shameful world perish, so that a new life on Earth can begin' – are also our own thoughts, which lead us forward.*

After all, we are already building a new life. Yet monsters have been found, who wanted to destroy the road to socialism that we are building.

The behaviour of these spies and traitors is both shameful and foolish, because a people who have fought for better conditions in life will never give up their historical development and will never return to the old days. People are convinced of the benefits of socialism, of compliance and of cooperation, and will not ever allow their rights to be taken from them.

The subversives have condemned themselves by their actions – by their divisiveness and by their preparation of war against their own people.

This judgment is a warning to all who pursue nefarious goals within our Czechoslovak Republic. By working together we have built a better life, and anyone who wishes to disrupt our work together will meet the same fate as this group of spies and subversives.

This judgment was handed down by the entire Czechoslovak people.

As a member of the Czechoslovak army, I can see that the peaceful life that results from the hard work of all our workers and soldiers has been preserved by this judgment.

Captain Emil Zátopek

This is not something that one reads about very often in accounts of Emil Zátopek's life. When I first encountered it, I refused to believe it. I cannot imagine anything more out of tune with what I believe to have been his generous, gentle character. Yet it appeared. I have seen it in print in the *Rudé právo* archive, halfway down the left-hand column of page three of the issue of 10 June 1950.

Even now, I am not sure what to make of it. Did Emil write it? It is hard to believe. The voice is that of a party propagandist, not a playful-spirited sportsman. He certainly would not have written it spontaneously, or in isolation. Did he sign it, or agree to put his name to it? This is a different matter. The fact that it is mild compared with many of the letters *Rudé právo* published – it is not, for example, a call for the death penalty – raises the possibility that it might have been a negotiated compromise. I am not aware of Emil ever having been questioned about this, let alone having answered (although I have heard it said that he expressed approval when, nearly two decades later, a more humane Czechoslovak government retrospectively overturned the verdict against Horáková).

Asked about Emil's letter more than sixty years after it was published, Dana Zátopková insists that he never saw it, and may not even have been aware of it – although there was one time when, after President Gottwald had given a speech on the subject to which the Zátopeks and other athletes had been forced to listen, 'Someone ran up to Emil and asked him what he thought – and he said: "Don't ask me, ask Comrade Gottwald." But that was all.' Perhaps she is right, and that is all the authority he gave; we have no way of knowing. I suspect, however, that it is not quite so clear-cut as that. Dana also says: 'We had no idea that these defendants were being tortured, that the charges were made up – all the things we know about today.' This may be true, too. But I think it is also true that, then as now, many people will have known as much or as little as they chose to know. Even in Western democracies, most of us have some vague sense that certain things done by our governments – or perhaps by the corporations we work for – might be morally hard to defend. Most of us deal with such perceptions by keeping them vague. The less we know, the less we have to worry about, the less reason to disturb our otherwise comfortable lives. Respectable Germans did this in their millions during the Nazi era, but they were not unique. And if a little, nagging voice was whispering to Emil that perhaps the state's case against Horáková was a monstrous travesty – well, he would not have been the first person to ignore such a voice.

In Czechoslovakia there was an additional incentive not to inquire too deeply: fear. To allow the full obscenity of the situation to come to the front of one's mind would have been to invite catastrophe – to risk becoming a victim rather than a bystander. Six years of Nazi occupation had given the Czechoslovak people a brutal crash course on how to survive under a fanatical tyranny. Many were once again putting that lesson into practice.

'We did not live at that time,' a Czech archivist told me when I was beginning my research into Emil's life. 'So we cannot judge it.' She is right. But we can speculate – and in Emil's case the riddle is particularly perplexing. Just a few months earlier, an internal report in Emil's personal military service file had painted a picture of an officer of unusually independent spirit. Written in March 1950, it stated that, the previous March, Emil had refused point-blank to inform against his room-mate, Miloslav Ladýř. He told his superior officer directly that even if he knew that someone was speaking against the state, he would not report it – although he might intervene by 'explaining certain things' to him. He also stated that he was disillusioned with Communism, because of the violence the Party was now using, and because of the way it divided the country into two opposing groups, positive and negative. 'His honesty and directness, at times childish, are quite surprising,' wrote the scandalised reporting officer. 'He stated that he was himself aware that he could be locked up for many of his statements, but he thought it preferable to state them all rather than give the impression that he was pretending.'

That had been March 1949. Two months later, an education officer, Warrant Officer Vejvoda, had been entrusted with the political education of First Lieutenant Zátopek. In November, Emil had been sent on a six-week training course in Marxism at the Central Political School (ČSM), in Klecany, near Prague. We do not know what he learnt there, but we do know he developed a habit of cutting off his anti-Party grumblings with the words: 'I keep quiet, or else they would lock me up.'

In December 1949, Emil was reported to the military authorities for making 'adverse statements about the system of People's Democracy'; in May 1950, he was investigated for refusing to join the Federation of Czechoslovak Soviet Friendship; the same month, an informer accused him of being less enthusiastic about the USSR in private than he was in public. He was also under suspicion because, unusually for an officer (and unlike his father, brothers and father-in-law), he was not yet a member of the Communist Party: he claimed that his application had been held up. One informer's report in 1950 mentioned the notebook (possibly his training diary) that Emil kept in his tracksuit pocket and suggested that, if this could be stolen, it might reveal 'his true political opinions'. The fact that all this is preserved in his records (along with some pointed comments about Dana's reported lack of enthusiasm for the regime) reminds us how fanatically the army cared about conformity – and how much danger Emil was placing himself in by refusing to conform. Political attitudes were monitored, assessed, recorded and, if necessary, acted upon. In the words of the influential General Karel Procházka: 'He who does not have a positive attitude cannot serve as a commander.'

We can only guess how these circumstances affected Emil when the Horáková storm broke. Had his spirit been crushed by then? Was it put to him that, if he didn't co-operate, he could expect a similar fate himself? Was Dana mentioned? All we can say with certainty is that the letter appeared, with his name at the bottom.

Dr Libor Svoboda of the Institute for the Study of Totalitarian Regimes in Prague – an institution not known for its reluctance to condemn the crimes of Communism – was surprisingly sympathetic to Emil when I asked him about this. Dr Svoboda's aunt was at school when her head teacher and other functionaries came into class and told the pupils they had to sign a form requesting the death penalty for Horáková. No one volunteered, so the officials pointed to some students and told them to sign first. Such scenes were common throughout Czechoslovakia; and, Dr Svoboda argues, 'if inconsequential students had to sign, it wouldn't have been possible for an officer of the Czechoslovak Army to refuse.

'I imagine that they summoned him and political operatives "introduced him to the situation" and invited him to sign, as he had to be an example . . . I can't imagine what would have happened to him in that tense and hysterical atmosphere had he not signed. What would have awaited him was the fate of working in the mines or in agriculture and the end of any kind of career, not only in terms of athletics.

'I don't want to be an apologist for Zátopek – it was a failure on his part. An ideal hero would have refused and left the army. But Zátopek wasn't an ideal hero in this regard; he wanted to run and he sacrificed very much to achieve this end.'

In fact, Emil had found the backbone to defy his superiors more than once, not least in connection with marrying Dana. But perhaps he felt that he had used up his credit. Nine months later, in the more militantly Communist environments of ATK Praha and the Ministry of Defence, a doomed, heroic stand on behalf of Milada Horáková would have required an altogether more suicidal form of courage. Perhaps, in June 1950, Emil simply didn't have the stomach for a fight that would have ended his career and sporting dreams and risked his life and liberty as well.

So he signed – probably – whatever was put in front of him, with or without reading it; and then, presumably, put the whole matter to the back of his mind.

It would remain for ever a shadow on his past. But perhaps it also cast a shadow over his future, colouring his resolve to make nobler choices were similar situations to arise.

8

The Czech locomotive

Whatever Emil really felt about the purges, we can assume that he kept any dissenting thoughts largely to himself. Alexej Čepička, the new Minister of Defence, was a leading instigator of the persecution, and the army was expected to be beyond reproach in its orthodoxy. Yet it must have been around this time, or not long afterwards, that Emil admitted to his friend and fellow athlete Ivan Ullsperger that he 'had problems' with some of the things the Communists were doing.

He felt – according to Dana – that the movement he believed in had been hijacked by what he called 'quick brew Communists' who saw the ideology as a route to personal advancement rather than a recipe for universal happiness. But he avoided direct revolt, once saying that, rather than run in fear all the time, he preferred to 'bend' – without actually breaking. Sent for further political training later in the year, he veered between seeming 'politically mature' and making 'basic errors in Marxism-Leninism'; his supervisor was unable to decide if he was was 'cunning' or 'childish'. According to Ullsperger, Emil took the view that the world was divided into people who had 'the will to power', and made others conform to their views; and those who didn't. Emil considered himself to be in the latter camp and allowed himself – up to a point – to be pushed around. Perhaps this kind of outlook was inevitable for a soldier whose primary duty was obedience to his superiors; but it also tells us something about Emil's approach to life at the time. Another friend quoted him, later on, as saying that the key to happiness was to learn to behave as a domesticated animal rather than a wild one. Meanwhile, he did not allow the unpleasantness of the Terror to distract him from his relentless self-improvement as a runner. Perhaps it even encouraged it, in the same way that running had offered a form of escape from the Nazi occupation. On the running track, no one could tell him what to say or think.

On the day his letter appeared, Emil ran and won a 5,000m in Prague. His time, 14:17.2, was his best of the year so far. There was another 5,000m the following week, then a two-week break – during which he must have heard reports of Milada Horáková's execution, although perhaps not the ghastly details of her slow, cruel strangulation.

Five days later Emil was in Warsaw to win another 5,000m; the following weekend he was in Bratislava to win both a 5,000 and a 10,000m. Afterwards, there was a dinner in the nearby town of Modrá, where the wine flowed freely. 'Local people kept saying to him: "Drink a toast with me!", "Drink a toast with me!",' recalls Milan Švajgr. 'At the end of the evening, he couldn't stand up.' You can understand why someone might enjoy the release of alcohol in such tense, dangerous times. But it was perhaps not ideal preparation for his next big target: a crack at the Czechoslovak national record for 5,000m.

The plan was to make his bid in Ostrava, in the Army Championships at the beginning of August. His results in the preceding months – eight victories in eight races, seven of them at 5,000m – were almost incidental to his heavy, record-focused training, which he built up to a peak of thirty-two kilometres per day in early July. At the last minute, however, he was told that there had been a change of plan: an invitation had been accepted on his behalf to take part in a series of events in Finland, organised by the Finnish Workers' Sports Federation (TUL).

He could hardly object, given his publicly expressed enthusiasm for the centrally directed, politically guided state management of sport that the Communist regime had imposed on Czechoslovakia, but he cannot have been happy to have his athletics ambitions sacrificed so casually in the interest of diplomacy. Yet the trip offered chances to race as well as to meet and greet. The first of these came on 2 August, in Helsinki. The competition was minimal – his opponents were all TUL members – but the crowd was world-class. They already recognised Emil as a worthy visitor to the home of distance running, and they appreciated the fact that, despite effectively running alone, he appeared to be pushing himself to his limit from the start. With mounting enthusiasm, they urged him on – and he finished in 14:06.2. It was exactly two seconds faster than his previous Czechoslovak record, and the second fastest 5,000m time ever.

From there he went straight to Turku, Paavo Nurmi's birthplace, where he was due to race at 10,000m two days later. One of the first people he saw there was the Czechoslovak ambassador, who warned him that people in the town had hopes of a world record. Emil, notwithstanding his public speaking duties, was in the mood to oblige.

Once again, he had to all intents and purposes to run alone. Once again, he flung himself into the challenge; and, once again, the Finns were stirred by the sight. There is a nobility to running against the clock. For some aficionados, the truly great distance runner is the one who – as *Sports Illustrated*'s Kenny Moore later wrote of another giant of the discipline, Ron Clarke – accepts 'each of his races as a complete test, an obligation to run himself blind'. And Finnish athletics fans are nothing if not aficionados of distance running. They understood what Emil was trying to do, were excited by the thought that they were witnessing a historic piece of running, and cheered accordingly.

Emil was aiming for 29:15 – just over six seconds faster than his existing record – but in the second half of the race he began to step up the pace. The Finns roared him on. He ran the final lap flat out and finished in a scarcely believable 29:02.6 – nearly twenty seconds faster than his world record from the previous year. Afterwards, he warmed down outside the stadium, then returned to the centre of the track to retrieve his tracksuit. The spectators spotted him, and gave him a standing ovation that still brought tears to his eyes when he recalled it more than forty years later.

By the time he got back to Czechoslovakia, another victory parade had been organised for him in the streets of Prague. If monster trials were the stick with which the Communist regime beat its citizens into obedience, sporting glory was a carrot with which life in the new Czechoslovakia could be made to feel palatable. The fuss about Emil's achievements may seem excessive from today's perspective, but in those grim days a little triumphalism could go a long way. The message was simple. As František Kožík wrote, the record showed that: 'we have a supreme sportsman who is capable of anything if it is a question of winning the recognition of the whole world for his country.'

The acclaim for Emil was certainly becoming increasingly international. A Finnish newspaper hailed him as 'more than just a runner'. *The Times* of London, known for its sobriety, called him 'the fabulous Zátopek'. A few weeks later, a Belgian paper would call him 'a super-runner who enchants the whole world'.

There was additional justification for this last accolade, although the journalist who wrote it may not have known it. Emil's next major sporting engagement after returning from Finland was in Brussels, where he was due to be racing in the European Championships on 23–26 August. In the 5,000m he would get a chance to avenge his Olympic defeat by Gaston Reiff, who was back to his best form, so he stepped up his training to forty fast 400m laps a day. Then disaster struck.

Just over a week before the championships, Emil ate some cold Moravian duck that had been left for a little too long. The resulting acute food poisoning put him in hospital, where he had to have his stomach pumped. By Monday, 21 August he had stabilised but had lost five kilograms in weight. He would have lost more had he not taken advantage of the lack of medical staff at the weekend to sneak into the hospital kitchen and cook himself some sausages – washed down, he claimed, with beer – to give himself strength for a few desperate jogs around the hospital garden. On the morning of Tuesday 22nd the doctors finally gave way to his pleas to be discharged, which gave him just enough time to catch a plane to Belgium an hour later. Common sense suggested that it would be folly even to attempt to run, let alone try to win.

Even so, he ran – and it was as if he had winged feet. On the Wednesday, on a waterlogged track, scarcely twenty-four hours after leaving hospital, Emil ran the second-fastest 10,000m of all time, in 29:12.0. Alain Mimoun, who won the silver medal, was seventy-nine seconds behind.

On the Thursday, he won an easy 5,000m heat. Then, on Saturday, 26 August, came the showdown with Reiff, the local hero. There was a time when he would have been intimidated by the sound of 60,000 spectators chanting 'Gaston! Gaston!', but Emil was no more intimidated by the partisan atmosphere than he was by Reiff's coach telling him, shortly before the race, that Reiff would win in 14:03 – a time bettered only by Gunder Hägg's extraordinary 1942 record of 13:58.2. Reiff did indeed set off at something like world-record pace, but Emil was determined that, this time, he would not allow his rival to open up a lead.

This was easier resolved than achieved, but Emil stuck to his rule of keeping the gap between them to an absolute maximum of twenty metres and, where possible, less, no matter what the effort cost him. For the third and fourth laps he actually led; then Reiff overtook and, from that point on, led until the bell. Reiff was hoping that, as in London, he could simply burn Emil off, and it is possible that he assumed that he had opened up a decent lead. The loud support prevented him from hearing if anyone was close behind, and he did not want to offer the encouragement of a backward look. Then, as the last lap began, he did finally glance over his shoulder. Emil was right on his heels. The sight visibly punctured his morale – especially since Emil chose that very moment to launch his signature 400m finishing sprint. Reiff's stamina leaked away with his self-belief. Emil opened up a lead of more than 100m and won in 14:03. (Reiff's coach had been right about the winning time.) Reiff lost so much impetus that he finished twenty-three seconds behind, and Alain Mimoun just managed to overtake him for the silver – which the world was coming to regard as his customary position behind Emil.

It is hard to overstate the immensity of Emil's achievement in Brussels. For the second time in four days, fresh from hospital, he had run the second-fastest time ever for a distance, and had not just beaten but trounced the best endurance runners in Europe. His 10,000m victory had been another largely solo effort against the clock; for the 5,000m he had soaked up lap after lap of high-speed punishment from an Olympic champion before counter-punching with a devastating final lap. It was a dazzling display of the runner's art, and one can only assume that 'fresh from hospital' is the apposite phrase. Whatever the rest of his body had been going through, Emil's legs had had an unaccustomed rest.

But the truth was that, rest or no rest, Emil was now in a different league. He ended the year undefeated, after (by my count) thirty-two races – excluding relays. He had run the world's seven fastest times of the year at both 5,000 and 10,000m. The next fastest 10,000m-runner of the year, the Soviet Union's Ivan Semyonov, had a season's best more than a minute slower than Emil's.

It was around this time that the nickname 'the Czech locomotive' became popular, to convey the image of Emil leading every race, with the other runners stretched out behind him like a line of carriages – then dropping off one by one. (The nickname had appeared in *Rudé právo* as early as 31 July 1948, but took a couple of years to catch on in the West.) Other reporters deployed the idea of there being two races: one for Emil and one for everyone else. It was hard to disagree, when Emil was so far ahead. He won races by one lap, sometimes getting on for two laps – and no matter how far ahead he was, he would always finish with a flat-out final lap.

There had never been a runner like him.

Inevitably, people asked themselves how he did it. Was he a freak? Did he cheat? Or did he have some secret formula?

The answers are surprisingly mundane. Emil was not a freak: in most respects, he was a rather average physical specimen. He was 174.3cm tall, weighed just under 68kg and had well-developed thighs and calves – as one would expect, given his training regime. He had relatively long legs for his size, and his left thigh (circumference 52cm) was slightly smaller than his right (54.3cm), which might have had something to do with his ungraceful gait, either as cause or as effect. His resting pulse rate was at different times reported to be 68 beats per minute (which seems implausibly high), 56 and 52 (both more plausible, but still barely less than average – and high by the standards of today's elite endurance athletes). His VO2 max was estimated (later) at 76.2ml/min/kg – good, but, again, not as good as many modern athletes. He could hold his breath, after inhaling, for 127.6 seconds; after exhaling, for 11.4 seconds. His blood pressure was high when first measured, in 1944; but by 1945, after he set his first record, it had come down to 136/70mm Hg – that is, a little below 'normal'.

What made Emil exceptional physiologically were his powers of recovery: his heart rate would return to normal very rapidly, even after extreme exertion. In a test requiring him to get up and down off a chair fifty centimetres high 150 times in the space of five minutes, his pulse rate rose from a resting fifty-six beats per minute to a high of seventy-six beats per minute – but was back to fifty-six within a minute of finishing.

His muscles, too, seemed quick to revert to their relaxed state. One slow-motion analysis suggests that his fellow Olympic finalists' thigh muscles remained contracted in mid-stride for four times as long as Emil's did. But these are qualities that one might expect to result from years of intense training.

He had a relatively short, quick stride, averaging 170cm in length – although the physician who made that measurement, Dr Zdeněk Hornof, admitted that Emil had complicated the study in question by deliberately varying his stride length as a joke. He ran with a full ankle movement, landing on the balls of his feet but with the heel relatively low. As for the rest of his running style, there were those (notably the great Australian coach Percy Cerutty) who hypothesised that his agonised upper body movements were part of his secret, but there was never much evidence to support that theory: otherwise all elite runners would now run as though wrestling with an octopus. If Emil had a technical secret, it was that he ran with the utmost economy of effort below the waist.

But his real secret was less complicated than that. It was simply that, for five years now, he had been training harder, longer and more ferociously than anyone had ever trained before. He was not in the least secretive about his methods, and was happy to discuss them with anyone who asked. Ultimately, it could all be expressed in a simple equation: volume x intensity. Eventually, other athletes began to imitate him, and their times improved, too.

What nearly everyone agreed on was that Emil's success had nothing to do with tactical cunning. Ron Clarke, the future 10,000m world record holder, described his tactics in races as 'poor – or non-existent'. He tended to start slowly, partly because he had less basic speed than 5,000m rivals such as Gaston Reiff. (Reiff's best time over 1,500m was seven seconds faster than Emil's.) He tended to finish strongly for much the same reason: it was the only other option available.

If he had a tactical speciality, apart from his flat-out final laps, it was a tendency to put on surges, especially on bends. Generally, though, to revert to Ron Clarke's assessment, 'he ran too eagerly. He grabbed the lead and kept swopping it. He threatened his own resources.'

It was almost as if Emil saw tactics as unchivalrous. 'I am not particularly interested in beating my opponents,' he said. 'Above all I am interested in improving on my own performance. Why should I profit from my opponents' weaknesses?'

'A lot of journalists found that impossible to comprehend,' Clarke told me. 'For him it was competition for competition's sake, rather than the end result. He took the view that you're far better competing against someone at their best. It was the competition that was the exciting part, not the standing on the rostrum.'

Rather than try to outwit his fellow athletes, Emil liked to take advantage of their company, not just after the race but during it. He would chat away in mid-race as if he was in a pub. His growing command of languages allowed him to do this with most of his competitors, even in international meetings. Some welcomed it; others felt that he was trying to mess with their heads. I don't think he was, though: he was just a talker.

It could be argued – and a few in the West did argue – that Emil's role in the army was not a real job and thus, at a time when athletics was supposed to be strictly amateur, gave him an unfair advantage over those who had to fit their training in the small gaps around 'proper' work. It is hard to answer this definitively. The nature of Emil's military duties varied – in 1950 he was transferred to the Ministry of Defence, where he was made responsible for the physical training of troops – but all his jobs seem to have involved some combination of red tape, direct supervision of fitness training and testing, and absence from his post because of racing requirements. J. Armour Milne, the Prague-based British journalist and Communist who wrote for the *Morning Star* and *Athletics Weekly*, claimed that 'Zátopek is always to be found in his office or visiting an Army unit'; while Emil told his friend Jaromír Konůpka – who visited him at the track around this time and found him unavailable because he was at work – that he had to fit in his training around eight hours of other work each day. His service records suggest that he sometimes struggled to strike a suitable balance between his military duties and his running commitments. And the work must certainly have presented some kind of obstacle to his athletic training or the Ministry of Defence would not have decided, on certain specific occasions, to reduce his duties. In addition, Emil's status as a propaganda figurehead placed extra demands on his time that no Western runner had to worry about; and the regime expected him to perform social duties, too, such as providing fitness instruction at a hostel for miners' apprentices. (Not all of this was strictly compulsory, but Emil didn't like to refuse requests. 'If the decision is left to Captain Zátopek,' noted one superior officer wearily, 'he would say yes to everything.')

Having his workload reduced occasionally to allow him to train harder arguably constituted an advantage. Perhaps it was an unfair one. But he was not the only runner to receive such help. As Christopher Chataway, the British 5,000m runner (and future Conservative MP), admitted: 'There are certainly few top-class athletes in this country who would have difficulty in finding a firm to "carry" them for a few years.' Different societies support their athletes in different ways.

In any case, it was not just lack of time that prevented Emil's rivals from training as hard as he did. A lot of them simply didn't believe in it.

In Britain, for example, the prevailing orthodoxy was that athletes should train sparingly, resting several times a week and saving themselves for races. According to Gordon Pirie, one of the few Western runners to see Zátopek as a challenge rather than a freak, 'his training methods seemed quite fantastic. They were . . . derided by the take-it-easy British school.' Jimmy Green, editor of *Athletics Weekly*, spoke for many when he wrote: 'No athlete would be wise to emulate his colossal amount of severe work.' And Chataway, a runner with huge natural talent but a limited appetite for training, said, 'For me and many others, it is simply more than we could stand.' (Chataway, who like his friend Roger Bannister was Oxford-educated, admitted many years later that this was 'misplaced intellectual arrogance. I suspect that Zátopek, who was doing all this training that we disdained so much, was a great deal more intelligent than we were.')

The most important part of Emil's formula, in other words, was simply the effort he put in. Anyone could do interval sessions. The difficult thing was doing them as Emil did them: not just churning out the laps but doing each one to the genuine limits of one's endurance, without surrendering (as most runners do) to the instinct to keep a little bit in reserve. Sometimes, looking at the details of Emil's ruthless, obsessive self-punishment – the same drills again and again and again and again – you don't just wonder at his discipline: you wonder if there wasn't some kind of personality disorder that allowed him to tolerate it. Yet everything else we know about his character suggests the opposite. It wasn't his hard-won victories that made him a legend. It was his generosity of spirit. That was the special 'something' that made him unique.

How exactly? It is hard to pin it down. But countless friends and loved ones remembered him as, simply, a joy to be with. J. Armour Milne put it like this: 'His tremendous daily training has built him into a human powerhouse, power which he expends not only in breaking records but in making life agreeable for those around him.' More than sixty years later, Emil's nephew Jiří said something similar: 'He lightened people's lives.'

He was startlingly clever, in a slightly unworldly way, with a near-photographic memory. Years after they had taken place, he would discuss incidents and conversations in minute detail. His brain was full of poetry and songs.

He spoke many languages – eight, ultimately – but in childhood had learnt only Czech and a little German. The rest he taught himself from dictionaries. 'Learn enough words,' he said, 'and the grammar looks after itself.'

He was good-looking: not as a film star is but in the more intimate way of a man whose energy and good humour shine through his face. People remarked on his clear blue eyes and his engaging smile, while his receding hair and creased forehead gave him an air of thoughtful, confident maturity that women, especially, found attractive.

He was witty and playful; some would say incorrigibly facetious. He made mundane tasks into games, and loved to make people laugh.

He was a gifted mimic. 'He used to imitate the way different people ran,' says the British steeplechaser John Disley, who raced against Emil a few times and also knew him in later life. 'It's hard to explain, but he was terribly funny. It was the way he used his hands.' Another long-term friend, Olga Lišková, almost weeps with laughter as she tries to describe how 'he did this thing when we were having dinner once where he demonstrated how you clean a rifle – and we were laughing so much we were actually rolling on the floor. I wish someone could have filmed him.' Years later, someone did film him telling a story about a trip to Paris where a teammate tried to buy a bra for his girlfriend without knowing a word of French. The humour is indeed in the hand gestures, but the delight is in seeing Emil's listeners, initially stony-faced, creasing up in spite of themselves. His comic timing is perfect.

He had beautiful manners: not the grand kind, but the profound politeness that places great value on obligations of hospitality and courtesy. Nothing was too much effort for him. If there was a problem, Emil would make light of it and try to solve it himself.

A character assessment in his military service files for 1951 identified his defining characteristics as 'doggedness and humility' – but forgot to mention his frivolity. 'He would turn everything into fun,' said one friend; or, as Dana put it, 'He solved problems with jokes.'

If someone needed warmth or reassurance, he would offer it, unstintingly. Children and animals warmed to him. He made everyone feel special.

Neighbours and friends of many ages and nationalities have recalled the Zátopek home in U Půjčovny as a place of fun and friendship. Gordon Pirie called it 'the gayest and merriest home I ever visited'. 'His vitality shone,' said Ron Clarke, many years later. 'The man was pure joy.' Everything got caught up in the whirlwind of his cheerful energy. Jarmila Jamnická recalled Emil's habit of clowning around on the balcony, and the parties with wine and singing; another neighbour, Marie Hainová, would remember Emil's wonderful anecdotes, and the fact that he was always running, even when he went to the shop to buy milk.

Emil and Dana both believed that hospitality was one of the most important virtues. They enjoyed cooking, especially traditional Moravian dishes – although Emil (once he had grasped that there was more to gastronomy than the institutional food he was used to) had a tendency to insist that only he knew how to prepare them correctly. And they both loved to tell stories, during and after dinner, often interrupting and correcting one another as they burnished their anecdotes to new levels of hilarity.

They loved nature, and would escape to the countryside when they could. Emil enjoyed hunting for mushrooms, and cooking meals over campfires. Above all, both he and Dana seem to have had an insatiable appetite for mucking around. 'For the world's greatest runner,' wrote J. Armour Milne, 'he takes the craziest risks with his precious limbs. He seems to have no respect for them whatsoever.'

He was impulsive and restlessly energetic. Many people noticed something childlike about him. J. Armour Milne called him 'a boy in spirit and behaviour'. 'Physically he was more machine than man,' wrote Ron Clarke; 'in spirit, more boy than man.'

Claims in officially approved interviews that Emil never touched alcohol are contradicted by numerous accounts of celebrations at which wine and beer were drunk. Emil himself later joked that Dana came from south Moravia, where there were vineyards and wine, whereas he came from the rougher region to the east, where there was only beer. Dana, he said, believed that wine makes you sing, whereas beer merely makes you stupid. But Emil believed that beer was not only noble – the drink of the old Moravians – but positively beneficial for running. 'This gives me power,' he once said to Jaromír Konůpka, quaffing from the bottle on the day of a race.

Music played an important part in the Zátopeks' shared life. Both played the guitar, and both loved folk songs. Dana had the better ear but was less inclined to show it off. Emil's musical gifts were his memory, confidence and enthusiasm: 'I sing out of key, but I sing. Dana is a good singer, but she doesn't sing.' Dana insists today that she did like to sing, but didn't like songs that involved harmonising with Emil, because of his strange sense of pitch. On a less discordant note, Emil would often recite poetry as well. It helped that 'Král Lávra', which Emil had memorised as a child, was one of Dana's favourites.

Their mutual affection was palpable. Dana called Emil by the nickname 'Ťopek'. Emil used to call her Danuška, or 'Dušinko' ('my little soul') or, occasionally, 'Macku', roughly the same as 'sweetie'.

But the romance in their relationship was tempered by a playfulness that often spilled over into simple silliness. Emil, for example, encouraged Dana to think of household objects as living creatures – so that she would be less careless with them. 'It started when he saw me pull a plug out the wrong way, by its wire,' says Dana. 'He said: "You wouldn't pull a cat by its tail." He thought that if I felt an emotional connection with appliances, I would be more likely to look after them. He was right.' Soon all their devices had names, from Terka-Perka, the noisy washing machine, to Dáša, the bulky refrigerator, named after a big-bosomed friend. And then there was the concept of the Day of Complete Bliss, which either one of them was allowed to declare unilaterally. On such a day, no one was allowed to do any chores (especially washing) or anything else they didn't truly want to do. Such days happened very rarely, but their occasional occurrence – and constant potential occurrence – was one more thing to keep a smile on the young couple's faces.

They did argue, quite often. But when they did, according to Dana, they often ended up making one another laugh. Emil had two preferred techniques. 'Sometimes he would go quiet for a long time, and then, later on, he would say in a pathetic voice: "But you still love your Ťopek a little bit, don't you?"' On other occasions he would end the silence by adopting a mock military demeanour, calling Dana to attention and demanding to know her name ('Dana') and rank ('wife'), which they both found highly amusing – and which Dana, from the warmth of her laughter as she describes it, clearly still does.

Emil must have been maddening to live with at times; on the plus side, though, he was practical and happy to do his share of household duties. He had a cupboard that he called 'Paradise', in which he kept every possible kind of tool, nut and bolt, all carefully graded and organised. He was competent at DIY but not infallible. The kitchen table (a wedding present from the national sports federation) was unusually high in the early days of their marriage but ended up unusually low: Emil shortened the legs several times before he succeeded in getting rid of the wobble. Such mishaps were all part of the fun of living with Emil.

What do you miss about him most, I asked Dana, fifteen years after his death.

'The laughter,' she said.

In those early years of their marriage, it must have helped that they were both equally committed to the overwhelming importance of training. Their shared obsession may have seemed odd to Majda Štěrbová, a schoolfriend of Dana's who lived in their second bedroom for a while. It didn't seem odd to Emil and Dana. It helped, too, that they were both orderly: a career soldier married to a colonel's daughter. Gossip in military circles suggesting that Captain Zátopek paid too much attention to his training and not enough to his wife may tell us more about military circles than about the Zátopeks. They rarely quarrelled about misplaced priorities. Their main dissatisfaction was with the drudgery of endlessly washing sports clothes.

Sometimes, Emil and Dana used to train together, with Emil occasionally shouting advice about javelin-throwing technique that Dana dismissed as 'pathetic'. In the flat, they would round off their own training sessions by playing catch with a heavy medicine ball; the caretaker, who lived underneath, would bang on the ceiling furiously when they dropped it. And sometimes, too, at the track, they would play a game of high-risk catch with a javelin. According to Gordon Pirie, who witnessed it, this involved throwing it 'full tilt' and catching it, far across the stadium, above the head. The aim was to throw it back as quickly as possible.

Pirie believed that part of the secret of Emil's training was that he would never let himself get bored. His home-made gym included not only wooden wall bars (which he would use for endless leg raises) but, later, a system of weights and pulleys that allowed him to exercise his legs when work and weather prevented him from training outdoors. On at least one occasion he trained by running on the spot on the family washing in the bath, pounding the clothes with his feet ('soft and squishy, easy rhythm, thinking of other things') for two hours. Given Dana's reported horror at the resultant flood, it seems unlikely that he repeated this.

Sometimes he would alleviate the boredom of such indoor improvisations by reading a book or listening to the radio as he exercised. Usually, though, at least when running outdoors, he was too focused on doing his utmost to have need of (or be capable of enjoying) distraction.

Like many great athletes, he was keen on sleeping: he liked to sleep eight or nine hours a night. But he was not fussy about diet, his only rule being 'I eat when I am hungry'. Sometimes he would buy rolls, butter and a litre of milk on the way to work, and eat and drink his way through them in the course of the day. Yet he was always looking for ways to innovate, too. One friend, the pentathlete Karel Bártů, recalled seeing Emil emerge from the woods where he had been training near Stará Boleslav with dried salt on his tracksuit trousers (from sweat) and green stains around his mouth. Emil revealed that he had been eating the leaves of a young birch tree, on the grounds that deer are good at running and these were the deer's favourite food. This seems, however, to have been a short-lived fad – as were similar experiments involving dandelions and, on a separate occasion, vast quantities of garlic.

Another friend, Ludvík Liška, was among a group of athletes who, with Emil, contracted diarrhoea while at the Stará Boleslav training camp. Emil cured himself several days before the others by self-medicating with vodka, which he claimed helped him to sweat the illness out. It's probably best not to try this at home.

None of this squares remotely with the idea, popular among Western journalists of a certain kind, that Emil was some kind of robotic Marxist-Leninist machine, cranking out his victories as remorselessly and unfeelingly as a railway engine. Those who knew him testify to something far more mysterious: a paradoxical mixture of scientist, artist and dreamer. On the one hand, he would approach his running empirically, calculating lap-by-lap schedules, monitoring his speed and endurance, guarding against self-deception by keeping a training diary and modifiying his training according to his objective needs. On the other, he often ran his laps on the grass outside the track, to avoid hogging a lane that other athletes might want to use. He believed that training was a science, but he brought to it an intense subjectivity – focusing not on the stopwatch but on what it felt like at the limits of endurance, and learning how to manipulate those limits. (As he put it: 'You must listen to your body. You must feel hard, and you must feel easy.') And holding together those two contrasting sides of his character was a supercharged power of personality: dynamic, eccentric, intense and life-affirming.

Christopher Brasher, future founder of the London Marathon, interviewed Emil at length with the help of his fellow Olympic gold medallist Herb Elliott. Their conclusion is as good a summary of Emil's special spirit as I have read. He was, they wrote, 'not mad . . . just utterly absorbed, with every fibre of his explosive body, in what he is doing, and damn what the rest of the world thinks.

'It makes him the most refreshing, and the most exhausting, person to be with.'

9

Mission: invincible

He may have been made of tougher stuff than other athletes, but Emil was still human. Early in 1951, he crashed into a fir tree while skiing, tearing a ligament. He spent several weeks in plaster and could not train until April. Even then, he struggled with speed-work, and found himself focusing, by default, on endurance.

That summer, he raced less than usual, and, by his standards, less successfully. Between mid-May and mid-September, he ran nine races at 5,000 and three at 10,000m, mostly in Czechoslovakia. He won them all, but slowly. At 10,000m, he broke thirty minutes only once. At 5,000m, he was more often outside 14:30 than inside (and on two occasions he didn't even break fifteen minutes).

Emil also ran four 3,000m races, one of which, in Prague on 11 July, saw him beaten by Václav Čevona, the national champion at 1,500m.

It would be hard to interpret such results as a loss of form, yet the fact remained that Emil's rivals were closing in. Gaston Reiff looked suddenly dangerous again, recording a 5,000m time of 14:10.8. Herbert Schade, a German, had done 14:15.4 and was beginning to make an impression at 10,000m as well; as were Bertil Albertsson, of Sweden, and Alain Mimoun. It wasn't that Emil was past his peak: he had yet to reach his twenty-ninth birthday, and was much the same age as Reiff and Schade. But his best times over shorter distances were many years behind him, and, in the meantime, others had been raising their game. Perhaps it was premature to speculate – but could an end to Emil's period of invincibility already be approaching?

There were obvious explanations: the injury, the demands of work and the fact that Emil was giving up a lot of his time to the making of a propaganda film, which showed him meeting groups of workers and young people all over Czechoslovakia. None the less, Emil's superiors were worried – especially by the defeat to Čevona. Emil had pledged, at a meeting of the country's leading athletes at the end of 1950, that he would break a world record in the coming year. What if he was no longer capable of meeting that pledge?

Orders were given to suspend the filming, and Emil's military duties were rearranged again, so that he could train more easily – by day rather than at night. Emil was happy to take advantage. It is unlikely, however, that he was especially worried. He had already decided that he would adjust his aim this season.

By the end of the summer, his times were picking up. He ran 14:11.6 for the 5,000m in Berlin on 18 August and 29:29.8 for the 10,000m in Třebíč on 1 September. But those were just warm-ups, giving him the confidence that he was once again in good shape.

On 15 September, the world discovered just how good. The scene was the Strahov stadium in Prague, where the annual Army Championships were being held. Emil felt that this would be a good occasion to attack the world record for 20,000m, which had been set by Viljo Heino in 1949. The distance was so rarely run that it was hard to be certain how impressive Heino's time of 1:02:40 really was, but Emil reckoned that he could cut at least a minute off it, and set himself a schedule of seventy-five-second laps – fifty of them.

He ran the first twelve and a half with competitors in the army 5,000m event, whose start he shared; but he was a good 100m ahead of all of them by the 5,000m mark. The pace seemed slow to him, but he forced himself to stick to it, and passed 10,000m in 31:05.6. Then, bored of 'dawdling', he decided to run as fast as he could. He polished off the second 10,000m in 30:10.4 – giving him a 20,000m time nearly a minute and a half faster than the old record.

But Emil was dissatisfied. He had set his promised world record – two, in fact, for he had also beaten Heino's 1945 record for The Hour (that is, the greatest distance run in sixty minutes) by 219m. But he knew that he had been running within himself, and he wanted to know what he could have done if he had gone all out from the start. His time – one hour, one minute and sixteen seconds – was tantalisingly close to a nice round hour, while the distance he had run within sixty minutes – 19,558m – was tantalisingly close to a nice round twenty kilometres. And the thought that gnawed at him now was the same thought expressed by Heino when Finnish journalists asked him for his thoughts on Emil's achievement. 'Believe me,' said Heino, after passing on his congratulations, 'Zátopek could run 20 kilometres in one hour.'

Two weeks later, on the afternoon of 29 September 1951, Emil put that theory to the test. The scene was Houštka Spa, an idyllic track on the edge of the woods just outside Stará Boleslav, which – according to a helpful map in *Svět v obrazech* magazine showing how far Emil's Strahov stadium effort would have got him had he been running in a straight line – is twenty kilometres north-east of Prague. The roads were lined with people on the long walk from Stará Boleslav, and the little stadium itself was packed. Emil would eventually set eight world records here, but no attempt caused such excitement as this one.

Emil had set himself a schedule that would take him to twenty kilometres in one hour and twenty-four seconds; but it had certainly occurred to him that it might be possible to break the sixty-minute barrier, and he joked beforehand about which would be considered the 'real' record – the time or the distance – if he ran exactly twenty kilometres in exactly an hour. It was a still, warm afternoon, and the cinder track had been brushed smooth. As in Prague, there were other runners with him at the start: sixteen of them. But from the moment the gun was fired, at 4.23 p.m., there was only one runner who mattered.

Or perhaps there were two. In the words of František Kožík: 'The Emil Zátopek of 29 September was fighting the Emil Zátopek of 15 September.' The latter had shown what could be done comfortably. The former had to discover what could be achieved at the furthest extremes of pain and exhaustion.

The Emil Zátopek of 29 September didn't spare himself. After 1,000m, he was 6.7 seconds ahead of his previous pace; after 2,000m, 11.5 seconds. He passed 5,000m in 14:56 and 10,000m in 29:54 – faster than his winning time in the London Olympics. He was one minute and twelve seconds ahead of his time two weeks earlier, and a sub-sixty-minute twenty kilometres now seemed a distinct possibility.

But running for a whole hour at your fastest possible speed, round and round a track, can never be easy, even for a supreme athlete. It involves, almost by definition, sixty minutes of uninterrupted pain – or, at least, as much pain as you're prepared to go looking for. That's the agony of it. You have to keep asking yourself, can I keep this up? If the answer is no, you've blown it. If the answer is yes, you're not going fast enough. And while getting it just right may bring you glory, it won't bring you any less pain. Sir Bradley Wiggins, after setting a new world record for cycling's equivalent, The Hour, in June 2015, described it as 'the closest I'll ever come to knowing what it's like to have a baby'.

But an athlete whose training revolved around the mastery of pain was as well equipped as anyone to have a go. For more than three-quarters of an hour, Emil maintained the delicate balance, keeping the fatigue just within manageable levels while lapping runners with dizzying regularity. The track at Houštka Spa is unusually small – just 364m – and the spectators, around 6,000 of them, were exceptionally close to the runners. So Emil had plenty of encouragement, even without the timekeeper's regular announcements. He passed 16,090m, or ten miles, in 48:12 – more than a minute faster than the fifteen-year-old world record for that distance.

His work was not yet done, though. He still had another 4,000m to run, fast, and only a little more than ten minutes in which to cover the distance. He needed to be accelerating to the very limits of his ability. And now, just at that critical moment, he felt the agonising pangs of a stitch in his side.

If he gave any sign of it, it would have been difficult for the spectators to tell. Emil always looked agonised. As far as they were concerned, the locomotive was powering away at full steam, unstoppable as ever, as they roared their deafening support. But these grimaces were real. Emil – who had had a huge lunch barely three hours earlier – hardly felt able to continue. All he could do was grit his teeth and hang on, hoping the agony would subside.

It didn't. 'The continuous pain increased with every lap,' Emil recalled. 'It reached such a level that I lost track of things . . . I gritted my teeth, grimaced as I had never done before, and tried not to let up.' It was hardest when, having lost a few seconds, he no longer knew if he was on target for the record or not. He told himself to ignore everything he could feel above the waist. All that mattered were his legs.

Even they hardly bore thinking about. That's the trouble with The Hour: the mounting muscle fatigue resolves itself eventually into a continuous groan of distress. Jens Voigt, an earlier record holder for cycling's equivalent, had a simple formula for dealing with it: 'Shut up, legs!' But Emil was almost delirious by now: so overwhelmed that he could no longer keep track of his laps or his schedule. 'I really didn't know whether at that pace I would break the record or myself.'

The torture continued for four or five laps. Then, 'when I was feeling the very worst . . . something that I had never before experienced happened to me: that constant pain which grew with every lap reached such a limit that I stopped noticing it. The pain became duller.' He focused on the laps ahead – only four or five more now – and on the importance of keeping his legs, which he could now barely feel, moving at the same metronomic speed. The spectators kept urging him, with mounting excitement – and at Houštka, as Emil observed, it was a bit like having them screaming in your face. Eventually he was within a lap of the 20,000m mark – and the gunshot that would announce the final minute of his hour had not yet sounded. When it did so, he was well into the lap. He launched himself into a final semblance of a sprint with renewed hope. Or perhaps desperation would be a better word: the thought of failure was terrifying. To run all that way, through all that pain, without breaking sixty minutes would be too much to bear.

Listening at every stride for the second shot, which would mark the end of the hour, he sprinted towards the line – where the man with the gun crouched dramatically, pointing it skywards while a timekeeper, inches away, squinted at his stopwatch. Emil passed them before the gun had sounded. His surge had meant that his final kilometre was the fastest of the twenty (2:51.8). It also meant that he had to keep running, knowing that he ought to be hoping for the gunshot to be delayed as long as possible – but actually longing for it to come. 'What's going on?' he shouted to the timekeeper, when nothing came. 'Run! Run!' screamed the spectators. By the time the shot fired he had gone another fifty-two metres.

The acclaim was overwhelming: one report described the post-race ovation as 'indescribably cordial and enthusiastic'. Once again, Emil had redrawn the boundaries of the possible. His first thought, though, was: 'Today I really had more than enough.'

Having first had his pulse rate checked by Dr Zdeněk Hornof (it measured 168), he was carried on his fellow athletes' shoulders from the back-straight finish to the grandstand, where he made a short speech, broadcast on the PA system and on national radio, thanking the spectators and urging them to support youth athletics. Four minutes after the finish, his pulse rate was down to 108. Four minutes after that, the first of the runners who had started with him – remember them? – passed the 20,000m mark.

Three hours later, Emil's pulse was down to fifty-two beats per minute. The rest of the world found it harder to calm down. Only five other men had ever run 10,000m in less than thirty minutes. Emil had just done it twice, back-to-back, without a break. One newspaper hailed his performance as 'unique in the history of athletics'. *Rudé právo* took the exceptional step of reporting the record on its front page, hailing Emil's achievement as another success for the regime's centralised administration of sport.

But Emil knew that, already, that triumph was in the past; and it was not in his nature to dwell on achievements that were behind him. 'To boast of a performance which I cannot beat is merely stupid vanity,' he once said. 'And if I can beat it, that means it lies in my power to beat it, and therefore again there is nothing special about it. What has passed is already finished with. What I find more interesting is what is still to come.'

What was to come now was a more conventional challenge – but also a far more daunting one. The XVth

Olympic Games were due to begin in Helsinki in July 1952. Emil was expected to win at least two medals – both of them gold. Anything less would be considered a failure, or perhaps even a dereliction of duty. And the fact that he had, in the words of J. Armour Milne, just 'belted the living daylight out of two tremendous world records' did little to alter the fact that, at the less obscure distances of 5,000 and 10,000m, rivals – some of them starting to imitate Emil's training methods – were closing in. That gave him just over nine months in which, on the one hand, to work himself to still greater heights of fitness while, on the other, avoiding setbacks such as food poisoning and skiing accidents. It was, in its way, as hard a balancing act as The Hour. Yet Emil knew that he would never get a better chance to claim a place among the immortals of sport. Somehow, over the next nine months, he had to get it right. He needed to make himself invincible.

At Christmas, he and Dana took another winter holiday in the mountains. Emil avoided skiing this time, training instead by dabbling in speed skating and, more often, running through deep snowdrifts. Dana sometimes added a bombardment of snowballs, which Emil tried to dodge, adding to the intensity of the workout. There was also a notorious incident when, having agreed that they should give themselves a day off, Emil took them on a seemingly endless jog through the hills instead. Dana eventually rebelled and refused to go any further, flinging herself down in the snow. 'So he got an old washing-line out of his pocket and tied it around my waist,' she remembers. 'He said: "I thought this might happen." Then he dragged me all the way back like a sledge. I didn't move a muscle the whole way.'

In January 1952, at a meeting of Czechoslovakia's elite athletes, Emil renewed his commitment to win two golds. This was supposed to be a private commitment, but word of it leaked out. He might as well have been signing a contract. The imminent release of *One of the Relay*, an hour-long propaganda film devoted to his achievements and training methods, would soon add to the weight of public expectation on his shoulders. It was beautifully shot, as Czech propaganda films tended to be, and many of the iconic images of Emil that subsequently caught the world's imagination (training in the snow; running in his army boots, torch in hand; or striding through the sand of the indoor riding school) can be traced back to it. It would all look a bit silly, though, if Emil stopped winning. Somehow, he had to turn all that weight into a positive.

To do so, he retreated to Stará Boleslav, where he could combine the monastic existence of a military training camp with endless hours training alone in the birch forest that hid the Houštka Spa track from the outside world. This was one of his favourite places: an old wood with tall, well-spaced trees and mossy undergrowth; broad clearings in which to practise his repetitions; wide, silent plains to be glimpsed occasionally through gaps in the foliage; and, not least, a growing stock of memories of triumphs on the track. The sandy, yielding soil – a vestige of the days when this was a riverbed – was kinder to his legs than a cinder track or road; and when the light began to fail his army boots protected him from hidden mishaps. The uncomplicated asceticism can only have strengthened his conviction that, by sheer self-discipline, he could control his fate.

In mid-April, fate struck back.

Emil later blamed it on the fact that he had been persuaded to submit to a post-training massage, followed by an unplanned cold shower. Whatever the cause, he woke up the next day with a severe chill that became tonsillitis. The obvious solution was a few days in bed, but Emil was reluctant to follow the doctor's advice: partly because he had an athlete's aversion to missing a single training session but also because he was due to be racing in the national cross-country championships in Prešov that weekend. He was told to pull out, but he insisted. He had promised the organisers he would be there, and they had already printed the posters.

So he went, and, on a windy day, he ran, having fought his way through the usual crowds to get to the start; and he managed – just – to win. Afterwards, he was close to collapse – yet he still somehow managed to drag himself a few days later to Hradec Králové, where he won a slow 3,000m. Then he really did collapse.

It is hard to say with certainty what the problem was: the word 'angina' is ambiguous in Czech. But he seems to have entered that dangerous territory that is sometimes reached when a stubborn runner attempts to 'run off' a serious infection, viral or otherwise, and chest pains and fever result. He was confined to his bed and could not train for two weeks.

On 9 May he tried some tentative exercise, marching about four kilometres in full uniform from his workplace near Letná to the Strahov stadium. This is harder than it sounds: it is steeply uphill all the way. None the less, a would-be multiple Olympic champion would have hoped to be doing infinitely more, just two months before flying to the Games. Over the next few days he increased his workload: jogging, then running, wearing two tracksuits. The result, he claimed, was that he 'sweated' the illness out of himself – just as he had with vodka on a previous occasion.

Whatever the medical truth of the matter, by late May Emil reckoned that he was back to full health, which was something. But he had lost six problem-free weeks of super-intense training. He began to race again, and immediately resumed his winning habit, but his times were not impressive: 14:46.4 for a 5,000m in Prague on 21 May, 30:08.8 for a 10,000m in Leipzig in June; 14:33.6 for a 5,000m at the same venue the following day.

His rivals, meanwhile, were gathering in strength. Athletes with their eyes on the same Olympic medals as Emil included Herbert Schade, who had reduced his 5,000m time to 14:06.6, while Soviet runners such as Vladimir Kazantsev, Aleksandr Anufriev and Nikifor Popov (who had run 14:08.8, 14:12.2 and 14:16.0 respectively) also looked dangerously fast, as did the Englishmen Christopher Chataway and Gordon Pirie. At 10,000m, Anufriev, Mimoun, Pirie and Albertsson were all improving.

In mid-June, Emil, Dana and other members of the Czechoslovak Olympic team went to Kiev, where they competed and fraternised with other Soviet bloc athletes and underwent various measurements and tests. Emil's performances were unimpressive: on 11 June he came third in the 5,000m, behind Kazantsev and Popov; two days later, he just held off Anufriev to win the 10,000m. According to one report, he also did worse than any other athlete involved in a test to measure the force of runners' strides. His position wasn't quite hopeless, but, with a month to go, 'it was worth asking if I should even start the 5,000 metres in Helsinki at all'.

He didn't really have a choice. He had made a public vow: 'I will focus my training and performance for the Olympic Games in Helsinki to win two gold medals for our People's Democratic Republic.' Such undertakings were not to be made lightly: it was part of the Stalinist philosophy of sport that underachievers should face dire consequences. A few years later, for example, the celebrated Czechoslovak cyclist Jan Veselý would be accused of betraying the working class after giving up during the Karlovy Vary to Karl-Marx-Stadt stage of the Peace Race – and would be made to become a truck driver as a punishment. Emil had thrown away the chance of 5,000m gold in 1948; if he simply threw in the towel four years later, he risked bringing shame on himself and, worse, on his nation.

But what if he wasn't fast enough?

If the pressure didn't get to him, it might have been because, in the back of his mind, there was an escape clause: if he messed up one race, there might still be an opportunity to put things right. All he had to do was enter the marathon as well. This was an idea that had first come up the previous summer: his superior officer, Colonel Sábl, had suggested it, concerned at Emil's apparent loss of speed in the first half of 1951. Emil had never run a marathon, but, as Colonel Sábl pointed out, he was frequently running more than thirty kilometres a day, so it shouldn't be too great a shock to the system to do a race of 42.195km. Emil was non-committal, and they had left it as a tentative thought. But his successes with the twenty-kilometre and one-hour records had reassured them both that the idea of trying to win Olympic gold with his first attempt at the race was not quite as absurd as it sounded. Indeed, the idea had also been floated by Harold Abrahams, the British former Olympic 100m champion, who light-heartedly suggested in *World Sports* in September 1951 that 'that phenomenal runner, Zátopek' was 'quite capable of having another crack at both the 5,000 and 10,000 metres and then throwing in the Marathon on the last Sunday just for the fun of the thing'.

That's not to say that the idea wasn't far-fetched. A certain amount of pre-Games practice is generally considered essential for Olympic events; and a certain amount of rest – as opposed to two fiercely contested Olympic finals – is generally considered desirable in the days leading up to a marathon. But now – when the time came to send off the entry forms – it seemed to make sense to put Emil's name down for all three races, just in case. With a bit of luck he would have no need of his marathon entry, but it would be nice to have that little bit of insurance in his back pocket.

All that remained now was to survive the last few weeks before the Games without any further mishaps. In early July, the entire Czechoslovak Olympic team were summoned to Prague, where they were subjected to a series of last-minute checks, training sessions, political pep talks, lectures about Finland and, not least, a ceremonial parade, at Tyršův palace. Emil was chosen to make another public vow, this time on behalf of the whole team: 'We are aware of how greatly we are honoured by the confidence that the centralised sports department of the democratic people's republic of Czechoslovakia has placed in us. We solemnly promise our people, who have sent us to the Games, that we shall fulfil every task with which we will be faced . . . for the honour and glory of our beloved republic . . . This is our pledge.'

He was filmed as he spoke these words, for use in one of the weekly propaganda newsreels which usually preceded feature films in cinemas. (Television broadcasting would not begin in Czechoslovakia until 1953.) It all added to the burden of expectation. To many of Emil's fellow countrymen, it must have seemed as though his medals were already won.

He made the pledge on 8 July. The Games opened on the 19th. The first Czech athletes, including Emil, were due to fly to Finland on the 10th. After four long years, Emil's appointment with destiny had arrived: a chance to put right his lapse of concentration in London, and to put beyond all possible doubt his status as the greatest distance runner of his generation.

10

Fairy-tale Pete

And so we return to that curious incident in July 1952 with which we began, when Emil gambled everything he had worked for on the wildly optimistic hunch that, if he challenged the exclusion of Stanislav Jungwirth from the Czechoslovak Olympic team, the authorities would back down.

The more one thinks about this episode, the stranger it seems. What made Emil imagine that a regime implacable enough to destroy both its greatest sports stars (its world-beating ice hockey team, for example) and its own most senior officials (such as Rudolf Slánský) would make an exception in his case? What drove a man whose every waking moment for the past decade had been dominated by a yearning for athletics greatness to jeopardise his entire future as a runner? And what gave a man who two years earlier had allowed his name to be used against Milada Horáková the courage now to risk everything for the sake of a friend?

We can only speculate. The prospect of being sent to a concentration camp was both real and terrible, but it may have seemed less significant to Emil than the equally real danger of never being allowed to run competitively again. And that prospect was so obviously intolerable for him that, in an odd way, the Party officials may have been wrongfooted by it. Perhaps they simply did not believe that Emil would stick to his guns, and thus didn't bother to take further steps to intimidate or coerce him. When it began to seem that he really wouldn't back down, they panicked. (Imagine what would have happened to the official who had had to explain to his superiors that, actually, Emil Zátopek wasn't going to be at the Olympics after all.) As for Emil's lack of courage in the Horáková case, it seems entirely plausible that, if he felt ashamed of his behaviour then, that would have encouraged him to show more backbone this time.

He stood his ground. The authorities blinked first. Two officers found Emil at the Strahov stadium and drove him to the Ministry of Defence, where, to his surprise, he was not arrested but presented with his travel papers and a reinstated Jungwirth. The pair then flew to Helsinki on a later plane.

The precise timings are confused. Most accounts – including at least one of Emil's – have the stand-off lasting three days; some say that Emil and Standa flew in a third plane. But the official record shows them arriving in Finland just one day late, on Friday, 11 July, in a second aeroplane. It is by no means certain, however, that the official record is trustworthy; some say that he didn't arrive until Sunday 13th; and Dana, for whom it was a matter of life and death, insists that she cried for at least two days.

What can be stated confidently is that now, more than ever, Emil needed to return from Helsinki laden with gold and glory. As his friend Zdeněk Fator, the future manager of Sparta Praha athletics club, starkly expressed it to me: 'If Emil had sprained his ankle training, he would have been sent to the uranium mines.'

So it would have been understandable if the twenty-nine-year-old army officer and athlete who belatedly made his way to his quarters in the Olympic village had been a little preoccupied; perhaps even irritable and tense.

In fact, from the moment he set foot in Finland, Emil conducted himself with a good-humoured charm that was, in the circumstances, almost miraculous. Somehow, while engaged in the most soul-consuming physical struggles of his life, he found the time and energy to charm the world, with a generosity of spirit that shamed the distrustful orthodoxies of Cold War politics. If greatness is defined as showing grace under pressure, this was the eighteen-day period in which Emil most clearly demonstrated his greatness.

The world was glad of it. The Helsinki Games were perhaps the most politicised in Olympic history, dramatically embodying the frightening divisions of the post-war world. Nations competing for the first time included the Soviet Union, the People's Republic of China and Israel. Japan, barred in 1948, had just been re-admitted to the Olympic fold, as had Germany (although it would be another decade before the German Democratic Republic – East Germany – was recognised by the International Olympic Committee). The scope for ill feeling was considerable and obvious: the nation now known as Taiwan pulled out in protest at China's presence two days before the opening ceremony. And it did not bode well for international harmony that the Soviet Union had insisted on separate accommodation for athletes from Communist nations.

The main Olympic village was at Käpylä, on the western edge of Helsinki. But 1,360 athletes from the Eastern bloc nations (plus forty from China) were housed in a hastily constructed complex with a barbed-wire perimeter in the pine woods at Otaniemi, a couple of miles west, near the Soviet-owned naval base of Porkkala. The Soviet barracks there had a giant photograph of Stalin affixed to an outside wall. There was also a scoreboard to show how the Soviets were outstripping the Americans in the medals table – a new invention. (This was quietly removed when it became clear that they weren't.) If this was an international festival of friendship, it had a strained feel to it.

Emil was still in Prague when Erik von Franckell, president of the Finnish Olympic Committee, proclaimed 'Ekekheira' – the traditional Olympic truce between nations – on 10 July. By the time Emil arrived, however, there was an armed guard stationed at the entrance to Otaniemi.

But no one has ever succeeded in entirely suppressing the instinct of young people to make friends. Almost immediately, some US shot-putters struck up a cordial relationship with their counterparts from the USSR. Then Les Perry, the Australian 10,000m runner, made a tentative trip to Otaniemi, 'waltzed' past the guards, and was rewarded by seeing his idol, Emil Zátopek, training on a track by the woods on the edge of the site. He plucked up the courage to introduce himself. 'You come from the other village to see me?' said Emil. 'You honour me. Join me. We will run together.'

So they did, for twenty laps, chatting all the way (in English) about their lives at home. Afterwards, Emil invited Perry back to the Czechoslovakian accommodation in Otaniemi's Building No. 2. They ate with the Czechoslovak team, and then watched the entertainment that had been laid on for them: a performance by the Bolshoi Ballet. By the time Perry had jogged back to Käpylä, it was around midnight.

After that, the floodgates opened. Every Western runner wanted to meet Emil, or at least to see him train. The Otaniemi track that Emil used was on the edge of the village, and those who watched him running on it included the British journalist Norman Banks, who reported seeing Emil's tongue 'hanging out like a dog's' as he ran his fast laps, while his head 'rolled from side to side with every stride he took'.

There were plenty of laps to watch. Emil ran thirty fast 400m laps on his first day and forty a day thereafter, although he eased off as the competition drew near. But he still found time to seek out Bill Nankeville, who was unwell, and express his condolences; and to share his training secrets with everyone from John Disley, who found him 'a real gentleman' who was 'open and honest and willing to share his training ideas with anyone', to Australia's John Landy, the future world record holder for the mile, who quizzed Emil extensively and by one account went home with 'his notebooks crammed' with details of Emil's methods.

We can infer from this that Emil was now speaking English relatively fluently (or perhaps that John Landy had quite small notebooks). Nor was this the only example of Emil's proficiency as a linguist. The French writer Bénigno Cacérès enthused about the excellence with which Emil spoke to him in French, adding that Emil (whose second language was German) seemed equally confident in English, Russian and Polish. Even more impressively, he had taught himself Finnish (of sorts), and the accomplishment did wonders for the special relationship between the host nation and the Games' most celebrated distance runner – who had never lost a race in Finland. According to the relay runner František Brož, who was on the first Czechoslovak plane to touch down in Finland, thousands of Finnish fans had turned out in the hope of seeing Emil arrive on 10 July. As Emil told one American reporter (in English): 'I get a bigger welcome here than on Czech tracks.'

It is possible that Emil was grateful for the constant interruptions, which may have calmed his nerves. He was clearly pleased to see Gordon Pirie, inviting him to join him in training and, on noticing that (for some reason) he had no socks, insisting on giving him one of the pairs that he was wearing. (Emil often wore several, to keep his Achilles tendons warm.) He will have been touched, too, by a visit from Herbert Schade, his most dangerous rival in the 5,000m, who presented him with a gift of Solingen cutlery.

But it is hard to believe that Emil particularly appreciated the behaviour of Percy Cerutty, the eccentric Australian who coached Les Perry and John Landy. Hearing how his charges had been welcomed by Emil, Cerutty invited himself to Otaniemi, picked Emil's brains for hours and eventually stayed so late that it was no longer practical to return to Käpylä. Emil insisted on giving Cerutty his own bed, then retreated to a nearby shared room, where a member of the Czechoslovak rowing team nobly gave up his bed to Emil. Later still, an official came looking for Emil, found Cerutty instead, and made a scene. Cerutty was ejected, and Emil was later reprimanded for allowing a potential 'spy' into the camp. Cerutty was so taken with Emil's courtesy that he described the encounter in an effusive letter to a friend in Melbourne. The friend, in turn, was so impressed that he sent the letter to the Melbourne *Guardian*, whose readers thus learnt about Emil's desire to (in Cerutty's words): 'bring a cooperative understanding of the brotherhood of man, through sport, to peoples'. Cerutty summed up the meaning of Emil's chivalry thus: 'The willingness of athletes from all countries to meet on friendly terms makes it seem preposterous that we should ever be required to hate each other.' Emil's message had already reached the other side of the world – and he hadn't even started racing yet.

On Saturday, 19 July, the Games were opened. Heavy rain did not detract from the drama of seeing the great Paavo Nurmi bring the Olympic flame into the stadium and light the cauldron there, after which another immortal of Finnish distance running, Hannes Kolehmainen, lit the flame in the stadium tower. There were no arguments about Emil needing to keep out of the sun this time, but the 10,000m was, as in 1948, scheduled for the next day, and it is probable that, like most people present, Emil was too preoccupied to notice the scantily clad intruder (arguably sport's first ever streaker) who completed an unscripted lap of the track before she was hustled away by officials. His main concern was keeping dry – and hoping that he would not have to run the next day in the kind of deluge that had helped ruin his last Olympic race.

He didn't. By Sunday morning the rain had gone and the consensus was that, whatever his difficulties at

5,000m, Emil was the favourite for the 10,000m. He had a personal best nearly half a minute faster than Anufriev, the next fastest man in the race, while Schade, who at least one expert had tipped as an alternative winner, had decided to withdraw three days before the race to save himself for the 5,000m.

The thirty-three remaining runners gathered at the starting line for a race that would eventually begin at 6.13 p.m. Gordon Pirie had wished Emil luck as they were warming up, to which Emil deadpanned: 'I wish Anufriev to win.' But no one really expected such an upset. As the American competitor Fred Wilt had put it a few weeks earlier, 'The only thing we can hope for is that Zátopek breaks a leg.'

Emil later claimed that, even before the gun, people 'respectfully backed away' and 'gave me precedence' because of his reputation and his world record. But when the gun signalled the beginning of the first track final of the Games, Perry started off at an extravagant pace and led for a lap. Then Anufriev took the front and led for four. Emil coasted comfortably, mostly in tenth place, keeping an eye on the times on the giant electronic scoreboard that was the technological highlight of the Games. His time for the first lap was 68.9, and his time for the first kilometre was 2:52 – the second fastest of the ten. So it was not Emil who was running too slowly but the others who were going too fast.

After six laps, Emil moved smoothly into the lead. Gordon Pirie tried briefly to contest it with him, but Emil asserted himself, and from that point on he never looked back. Instead, with supreme self-confidence, he continued to churn out laps of around seventy-one seconds – knowing that none of the others could live with such a pace indefinitely.

The field was soon strung out: a line of carriages pulled along by the Czech locomotive and, one by one, falling off. One British commentator saw this as a reason to dismiss Emil, snootily, as a 'robot runner', and the race as one of 'inexorable monotony'. It wouldn't have felt like that to the athletes who were desperately struggling to keep in touch, and the 70,000 spectators showed no signs of being bored. Instead, the familiar rhythmic cries of 'Zá-to-pek! Zá-to-pek!' began to ring out; except that his Finnish admirers – thousands of them – had modified his name to 'Satu-Pekka', which sounds very similar but in Finnish means something like 'Fairy-tale Pete'.

Emil continued to justify their enthusiasm. He passed the halfway point in 14:43.4 – and then, mercilessly, turned the pace up a notch. If you looked at their faces, Emil was the only one who seemed to be suffering. The reality was quite different. Perry actually retired; the others merely gave up trying to keep in touch. Soon there were only Zátopek, Mimoun and Pirie in contention; and then, with about 3,500m to go, Pirie slipped back. The future 3,000m world record holder eventually finished seventh, forty-seven seconds behind Emil, in 'an oblivion of fatigue'.

Alain Mimoun, who had been imitating Emil's training methods for some time and was not afraid of pain, hung on grimly in his slipstream for several laps more. For a while it even looked as though he might pose a threat. But Emil kept injecting little bursts of acceleration, which he liked to apply on the bends. Once a lap, when the sun was behind them, he could see Mimoun's shadow, which allowed him to note that, gradually, Mimoun was becoming slower to respond to these bursts. A fast eighteenth lap may have been the killer blow. By the twenty-first lap Emil had opened up a big lead, and from then on he drew steadily away.

If the thought occurred to Emil that he could perhaps ease off, to save himself for the 5,000m, he dismissed it. Instead, he scorched round the final lap in sixty-four seconds, finishing in a new Olympic record of 29:17.0. Barely had he crossed the line than a Czechoslovak trainer came rushing to hug him and trod on his foot; but Emil had time to regain his composure before welcoming Mimoun, getting on for a hundred metres behind, as he came in second in 29:32.8. Anufriev was third in 29:48.2.

It had, despite the predictability of the result, been a remarkable race. Emil had run 42.6 seconds faster than the Olympic record he had set in London four years earlier. Mimoun had set a new French record, and Fred Sando, who came fifth, had set a new British one – an amazing achievement given that he had lost a shoe after barely a lap. Six men had run sub-thirty-minute times – still unusual – and sixteen had run times that would have won them silver in London four years earlier.

For those who knew what they were watching, it had been a compelling spectacle. One French journalist, Gaston Meyer, described it as 'a pitiless race of elimination', while another, Jacques Goddet, wrote of a 'battle conducted by Zátopekian fury'. *Rudé právo* (which seemed disproportionately excited by the bronze medal won for the Soviets by Anufriev) called it a 'dramatic fight'. *The Times* of London called it a 'rout'. But it was a front-page headline in *L'Équipe*, the French sports paper, that captured best the impression of total, ruthless dominance, dubbing Emil '*La brute magnifique*'.

After Emil had collected his medal – and the Czechoslovak anthem had once again been the first of the Games to be heard in the Olympic stadium – crowds of jubilant Finns accompanied him back to Otaniemi, where some of them had prepared a celebration dinner for him. He was presented with flowers and regaled with Finnish songs, while the Hungarian team gave him an enormous chocolate cake. He also received a morale-boosting visit from the great Gunder Hägg, the Swedish runner whose sub-fourteen-minute world record for 5,000m would soon be ten years old.

Later, Emil and Dana 'retreated into the Finnish solitude'. Emil had learnt his lesson from London and was determined to celebrate sparingly. Instead, they explored the woods around Otaniemi. The combination of pines, meadows, a lake and the long 'white nights' of the summer were profoundly calming to a couple who remained at heart mostly rural creatures. But even the peace of the forest was not quite enough to dispel the restless impatience that came from knowing that, for both of them, the biggest challenge was yet to come.

The 5,000m heats were held on Tuesday, 22 July, two days after the 10,000m final. They confirmed Emil's fears that his rivals were in the form of their lives. In the first heat, Alain Mimoun set a new French record of 14:19.0. Herbert Schade won the second in 14:15.4 – a new Olympic record – while Ernö Béres set a new Hungarian record of 14:19.66. Seventeen competitors finished in less than 14:30.

Yet Emil's own heat was a relaxed affair. He spent much of the early part of the race on the shoulder of the leader, Anufriev, whom he appeared to urge not to set too demanding a pace. Then, after about 2,000m, he spoke to Anufriev in Russian ('Sasha, come on, we must get a move on') to initiate a two-lap surge that left the five leaders – Emil, Anufriev, Albertsson, Chataway and Perry – with a fairly unassailable lead, whereupon they slowed down again, and Emil devoted the rest of the race to extravagant displays of friendly behaviour. He chatted away, in English, with Chataway. Then he dropped back to encourage the struggling American runner, Curtis Stone, with the words 'Come along, Stone, if you want to qualify', before speeding ahead to rejoin the leading group – whom he reminded, with five fingers, that all five of them would qualify and that there was thus no need for unnecessary effort. Anufriev – a big, long-sideburned young man who was reputed to hunt bears – none the less accelerated for the final lap, whereupon Emil waved him politely ahead. At least, that was what most people saw; Perry thought it was a wave of encouragement to him, and responded by kicking on to achieve fourth place, a personal best and a precious place in the final. Whatever the truth – and whether this behaviour constituted sportsmanship, showmanship or gamesmanship – the crowd loved it. Emil, meanwhile, could congratulate himself on having managed his resources infinitely better than in 1948, when he had exhausted himself with that unnecessary battle with Ahlden. Only three of the fifteen qualifiers were slower than him. (Emil came third in 14:26.) What mattered was Thursday's final.

The next day, Wednesday, was marred by the discovery that the women's javelin final was due to start just five minutes after the beginning of the men's 5,000m final.

Emil comforted Dana. 'We have been training together,' he reasoned, 'so we will compete together.' But Dana was concerned that she would not be able to concentrate if the stadium was echoing with screams that reminded her that Emil was in mid-race.

There was nothing to be done, though; and even if there had been it wouldn't have altered the size of the challenges they faced. Dana was up against three powerful Soviets, Aleksandra Chudina, Galina Zybina and Yelena Gorchakova, two of whom – Chudina and Zybina – had beaten her in Kiev barely a month earlier. She had set her heart on winning, but she would have to be at her best to get a medal of any kind.

As for Emil, the 5,000m was clearly going to be a far tougher challenge than the 10,000m. Talk of 'the race of the century' was perhaps an exaggeration – none of the contenders had seriously threatened Hägg's world record – but there was something about the balance of the field that suggested that something special might happen. On the one hand, you had Emil, the toughest endurance runner the world had ever seen. There was Mimoun, too, growing stronger with every race; not to mention Pirie, Perry, Albertsson and Anufriev, all of whom had run in the 10,000m final but might be better suited to the shorter distance. And then, from the other end of the spectrum, there were people like Reiff, the reigning champion; Schade, the new Olympic record holder; and the young Englishman Chataway, a future world record holder with a devastating final kick. All three of these speed specialists had fresh legs and might, on their day, simply burn the endurance runners away. The heats and the 10,000m final had confirmed that all fifteen finalists were in good shape. All that remained was the showdown.

Reiff had told *L'Équipe* that the final would be 'the atomic bomb of the Games', and the Finnish public seemed to agree. By late afternoon on Thursday, 24 July, 66,100 spectators were packed into the stadium. There were reports that people had been hanging on to the outsides of heaving trams in order to get there. Emil, who had spent the morning at Otaniemi fretting, uncharacteristically, that he might forget something crucial such as his shoes, was alarmed when the car from the Czechoslovak Embassy that was taking him to the stadium became stuck in a road blocked by crowds. The driver had to lean out of the window and shout 'Zátopek!' in order to clear the way.

Yet when the runners began to gather near the starting line at around 4.30 p.m., Emil seemed calmer than most. The afternoon was sunny and the stadium was buzzing. Emil spoke in German to Schade, who was clearly nervous, reassuring him that he was the favourite and advising him not to set off too fast; although it may not have helped Schade's nerves that, when he asked Emil who he was most worried about, Emil replied 'Reiff'. In fact, the consensus among commentators seemed to give Schade the best chance, marginally ahead of Reiff. Emil, remarkable as it seems now, was a relative outsider. The 10,000m/5,000m double had been accomplished only once before in Olympic history, by Hannes Kolehmainen in 1912. It would take a stupendous performance to replicate that feat, forty years later, against a field as competitive as this.

The starting gun sounded on time, at 4.40 p.m. The auburn-haired Chataway was the first leader, but the bespectacled Schade, who often forced the pace from the front, soon took over. Emil remained near the back, ignoring the cries of 'Zá-to-pek! Zá-to-pek!' (or, possibly, 'Satu-Pekka! Satu-Pekka!') that urged him on from, in particular, an area beneath the stadium tower. The first five laps passed quickly, with splits of 65.8, 67.6, 67.8, 68 and 68 seconds; Schade had completed the first kilometre in sub-world record pace. Then Emil moved forward, and led the field through another sixty-eight-second lap.

By Emil's account, he was concerned that Schade was being forced to do all the pacemaking and had taken the lead purely out of sportsmanship; Les Perry, who was close enough to see, was convinced that this was the case. Schade wasn't so sure and fought his way back into the lead. Emil then moved on to Schade's shoulder and shouted (in German): 'Herbert, come with me for two laps.' This time Schade allowed himself to be led, and the spectators, somehow managing to decipher what was going on, applauded warmly.

They passed 3,000m in 8:30.4 – fast but not blistering – at which point Schade, Chataway and Reiff moved smoothly into the lead. Emil began to wonder if this wasn't going to be his day; although Mimoun, who was once again in Emil's slipstream, clearly thought otherwise. Pirie made a brief attempt to take hold of the race, but his lead was short-lived and he lost touch with the leading five. Half a lap later, Schade took the lead again, and then, at 3,500m, Reiff detonated an explosive attack – 'like lightning', said Emil – much like the one that had won him gold in London four years earlier.

Emil responded immediately. There was an assertiveness to the way that he immediately took back the lead each time Reiff accelerated that Reiff found deeply disheartening.

With two laps to go Reiff had been neutralised as a threat – and with 600m to go he dropped out of the race altogether. But Schade, Mimoun and Chataway were looking as strong as ever, and it was clear that, unlike his rivals in the 10,000m, they were not prepared to step back politely and let the great Zátopek win. They wanted gold for themselves.

With so many people in contention, Emil – who one observer described as appearing to be 'on the verge of strangulation' – felt tempted to make his attack there and then. He resisted, however. He had a plan, one that he had been nurturing in his heart for four years: he would kick from the bell and break his rivals' will with one of those flat-out 400m bursts that were a staple of his daily training. Since the London Olympics he must have done at least 40,000 fast laps: each one had been fuelled by the thought that he would never again allow gold to slip from his grasp by mistiming his finishing sprint.

Now all he had to do was one more: one more flat-out lap to justify four years of self-torture. No matter what his rivals had to offer in terms of freshness, youth or raw speed, none of them would be able to match him when it came to soaking up the pain and maintaining the intensity to the very last stride. He had a fight on his hands, but he was ready to fight.

The bell tolled. The minute of his destiny had begun. He kicked. For a moment the whole stadium seemed to thrill to the prospect of another crushing Zátopek victory. Then, just as Emil was powering into the bend and wondering how big his lead was, Schade darted past him, followed closely by Chataway and, barely a pace behind, Mimoun. Coming out of the bend, Emil was fourth.

Despair overwhelmed him. He felt himself slipping backwards; a gap of several metres opened up between him and the third-placed Mimoun. 'You've messed it up,' he said to himself. 'You're going to come fourth.' And, as he often reminded people when he relived the race afterwards, 'There is no medal for fourth.' One journalist described him as looking like 'a tortured wreck' at this point. Yet he refused to succumb. That, in a nutshell, is what makes a champion a champion – that strange, irreducible lust for victory that dispels everything from fear to fatigue. It's the same instinct that allowed Muhammad Ali to walk into a storm of unexpectedly murderous punches from George Foreman in 1974 and think not of survival but of winning. The greatness lies in the split-second decision to fight back. The rest of us would be starting to think of excuses, of damage limitation; perhaps even of coming to terms with defeat. The champion seeks a new route to victory.

So it was with Emil. His plans in ruins, he was still thinking about gold. In the space of a few strides he considered the situation rationally and concluded that, in overtaking him so early, the other three must have been responding instinctively to the threat they perceived from him. They had, in other words, panicked, and sprinted earlier than they intended. Did it not follow, then, that they were likely to tire? In that case all was not lost.

Halfway down the back straight, Chataway, auburn hair flapping, sped past Schade, who responded by accelerating himself, as did Mimoun. With each flowing stride, Chataway looked more like a winner. But Emil, still in fourth, had persuaded himself that victory was, after all, in his grasp. The others were tiring. The others didn't have those 40,000 fast laps in their legs. The others could be beaten.

Going into the final bend, he had closed down the gap. Halfway round it, he launched a fresh attack, running wide past all three of his rivals in an agonised blur of flailing arms and pounding legs. Mimoun and Schade responded, pulling out to pass the tiring Chataway at the same time as Emil. For a tantalising fraction of a second, all four were abreast – and then . . .

What goes through a runner's mind at such a moment? Emil retold the story of this race many times, but at this point the narrative tended to peter out into generalities ('I ran like the wind') sometimes spiced with an expressive 'Grrrrrr'. Yet watch the footage today and you see beyond doubt that this – the final 150m – is the white-hot core of the race. Four men – three, if you exclude Chataway, who had run himself to exhaustion and tripped and fell shortly after being passed – each at his physical peak, each focused with every fibre of mind and body on the same prize, each giving the last possible drop of effort he can summon . . . and yet still it isn't over. Still there is another notch to be turned up. This is where words fail and all that remains is to imagine the boiling intensity of their struggle, in which the roar of the crowd and the roar of the bloodstream cease to be distinguishable. This is the lost zone, a place on the edge of death, in which only a handful of champions have ever set foot, and from which none has yet brought back a coherent account.

If you watch the footage, I urge you to find a version with a soundtrack that captures a little of the frenzied, spine-tingling excitement of the moment. The English newsreel commentary is cold and insular. ('Chataway falls. Oh dear, what a pity. Zátopek wins it.') The Czech version (actually a radio commentary) is barely comprehensible even to Czechs, but captures superbly the dizzying, table-thumping excitement as Schade fades and Emil and Mimoun match one another stride for stride on the bend, only for Emil – rejuvenated by the knowledge that victory is indeed still there for the taking – to find new reserves of strength and power madly forward. Somehow he thrashes his arms and legs with even more passion and conviction than before: not clinging on but driving, desperately seeking more intensity, more pain. His body seems to take on the shape and movements of a deranged insect: it is just like that crazy last-lap sprint in London four years ago – except that this time will be different. He believes now that he can win; that no one can endure this. ('The track seemed to be flying beneath me,' he said later. 'I could already see the gold medal.') Seventy thousand spectators are screaming with disbelieving excitement: it feels like an electrical storm. The commentator's inarticulacy (compounded by the yelling of a Slovak commentator right next to him) adds to the sense that something sensational and unprecedented is happening: '. . . Mimoun [*leads*] . . . But Zátopek finishes wonderfully . . . With a great burst he overtakes all three . . . Zátopek, you have four metres . . . five metres . . .'

Emil's winning time was 14:06.6 – a new Olympic record and his best time for two years. He had run the final lap in 58.1 seconds (within two seconds of his lifetime best for a single, one-lap 400m race); the final 200 took 28.3 seconds. It was, Emil thought, the fastest home straight he had ever run.

But times are just numbers. Afterwards, Emil and Mimoun embraced with the kind of warmth that you only see in sportsmen who know they have just taken part in something that no one who was not involved could ever fully understand. Schade, who understood well enough, was none the less distraught, and Emil spent some time comforting him, even going so far – according to one account – as to offer to give him his medal; an offer which, if it was made, was certainly not accepted. There could, in any case, be no question as to who had earned the glory.

The world was unanimous. *L'Équipe* hailed Emil's victory in 'the most terrific 5,000 of all'; *The Times* declared that Emil had 'established himself, beyond all argument, as the greatest long-distance runner of his period'; *Rudé právo* said that he had 'proved himself to be the best athlete in the world'. Australian readers could reflect on Percy Cerutty's verdict – 'Surely the deeds of the greatest generals pale before the deeds of athletes of the superhuman calibre of Zátopek' – while a Czechoslovak writer, the publisher Otakar Mašek, would go further still: 'The name Zátopek has become synonymous with the idea of speed, endurance, efficiency, reliability, fighting spirit and will-power. It would not surprise me if one day we should find his name in the dictionary as a common expression for all these terms.'

It was arguably the most extraordinary athletic achievement of Emil's extraordinary life. Yet others would say that it wasn't even the highlight of his week. And Emil claimed at the time that it wasn't even the highlight of his day.

One of the few people in the stadium unaware of the outcome was Dana. The women's javelin final had been delayed, apparently because of safety concerns.

(An English journalist, Guy Butler, had almost been hit by a javelin during qualifying that morning.) So Dana was waiting by the changing rooms in the bowels of the stadium, trying to stay warmed up and focused as she waited to be called for her own event. She could hear the roars and, later, saw officials rushing excitedly backwards and forwards. Eventually she managed to get a passing Soviet trainer to explain what had happened. He told her, and Dana squealed with delight. It was obvious from his face that he was thinking: 'What kind of wife doesn't watch her husband win a gold medal?' to which Dana thought in reply: 'The kind of wife who wants to win a gold medal of her own.'

Dana headed for the javelin ring immediately after the medal ceremony and met Emil just as she was emerging into the arena. They embraced quickly. Dana said: 'Ťopek, quick, give me the medal, for luck.' Before he could answer she had snatched it, put it into her bag and raced off to compete.

Emil, meanwhile, was hurried back to the changing rooms to shower. He was just emerging when he met the Czechoslovakian coach, Karel Kněnický, who told him excitedly: 'Dana just threw fifty metres.'

Emil refused to believe it. Fifty metres would mean not just beating her personal best (49.9m) but smashing the Olympic record. Kněnický was insistent: that was precisely what she had done. Stunned, Emil emerged into the stadium to watch the rest of the drama; but he had missed the highlight. Four other athletes threw further than the old Olympic record of 45.57m, but no one could match Dana's first, elated throw of 50.47m. Less than an hour after Emil's triumph, she had a gold medal of her own. She celebrated with a cartwheel – and earned a mention in the official report of the Helsinki Organising Committee as the 'happiest gold medallist' of the Games.

Emil later claimed that Dana's gold medal 'pleases me more than all the others', which was probably true. The couple finally caught up with one another by the team bus. 'I will never forget the way he looked at me,' Dana said many years later. 'It was as if he had never seen me before – as if I were a revelation.'

But Emil still had enough mischief in him to put into words, later, a thought that must have occurred to many people: that Dana's excitement at his 5,000m victory had 'inspired' her to make her best-ever throw. Dana memorably retorted: 'All right then, go and inspire some other girl to throw 50 metres.' As with much of the Zátopeks' banter, one could never be entirely sure how much of this was in jest.

Back in Otaniemi, the Czechoslovaks gathered for their daily team assessment. The political officer taking the session, Emanuel Bosák, congratulated Emil on his second gold medal but could not resist a reference to his insubordination in Prague: 'Comrade Zátopek runs well. If he could improve his behaviour, he could be a good example to our youth . . .' His teammates, few of whom yet knew of the Jungwirth incident, were baffled; some were later told that Emil was being too friendly with Westerners. The boxer Jula Torma, who had won a gold medal in London and thus had more liberty than many to speak his mind, made a pithy response that I'm told is best translated as: 'Ignore him, Emil. He's a prick.'

Late that night, in the women's quarters, Dana was too excited to sleep. Tiptoeing out of the room that she was sharing with a gymnast, she walked out of Building No. 8 – which the Czechoslovaks shared with six other Communist nations – and wandered through the silent woods to the lakeside. There she sat for two hours with her medal, marvelling at the midnight sun on the still water, and the wonder of her winning throw, and the sheer ridiculous beauty of everything.

But Emil was sleeping soundly, with the quiet confidence of a man with a hunch that his finest hour was yet to come.

11

The longest day

There were those in the Czechoslovak camp who felt that Emil should skip the marathon. He had reached his target. Why risk the loss of face that would come from a defeat? Emil later justified his insistence on going ahead with another famous piece of Zátopekian half-jest: 'I decided that the ratio of medals in the Zátopek household was insufficiently weighted in my favour.'

But there were other, more obvious motives. He had conquered the mountain that he had feared: the one that threatened to expose his weakness. Now he had a chance to make history: to show the world that what others considered impossible could in fact be done. This was the kind of challenge he lived for.

Even so, when the final day of the Games dawned on Sunday, 27 July 1952, it would have been odd if he hadn't been a little on edge. His body had enough experience of running very long distances to suspect that it was about to be put through the wringer. As for his mind: by defying those who urged him to avoid this final test he had once again stuck his neck out. If he was going to be in it, he needed to win it.

He spent much of the morning trying to learn to run slowly. He had calculated that the Olympic record for the marathon was equivalent to eighty-five-second laps of a 400m track. Assuming the record was likely to be improved a bit, he decided to aim for eighty-three-second-lap pace. But when his teammate Jaroslav Šourek (the Czechoslovak marathon champion) timed him, he kept running too fast. Even keeping over eighty seconds seemed beyond him.

Finally, he came up with a different strategy. The Englishman Jim Peters was the strong favourite. He had set a new world record, 2:20:42.2, just weeks earlier, and, said the newspapers, he would be wearing the number 187. If Emil stuck with him, he would be unlikely to go far wrong.

When the athletes assembled that afternoon at the starting line, Emil approached the tall, dour, pale-skinned man wearing 187. He did not want to discover later on that the papers had made a mistake.

'How do you do?' he said. 'Are you Peters?' Peters confirmed it. 'I am Zátopek,' said Emil. It barely needed saying. Half the world now knew that Zátopek wore 903 on his red shirt. In any case, Peters had raced against Emil before. Four years earlier, in London, he had been so demoralised by being lapped by Emil in the 10,000m final that he had given up running altogether for a while, before returning at the longer distance. It is unlikely that he relished the prospect of having a talkative, world-beating Czechoslovak for company for the next two hours or so.

None the less, polite words were exchanged. Then, at 3.28 p.m., the race began. The sixty-six runners, who had lined up in four rows, began by running three and a half laps of the track. Aslam, the barefooted Pakistani, was first to show in front, but Peters soon forced his way to the front, and by the time the first runners emerged from the stadium he was over a hundred metres ahead of a group that included the Englishman Stan Cox; the Swede Gustaf Jansson; and Emil.

Emil was unsure how to respond to Peters's aggressive start. He was wary of burning himself out: those laps felt much faster than eighty-three seconds. Behind him, all sorts of dangerous, experienced runners were lurking: notably the Argentinians Delfo Cabrera and Reinaldo Gorno, the Korean Choi Yun-chil, and a third Englishman, Geoff Iden. But what if Peters just kept on drawing ahead? Emil discussed the problem with Jansson – which was strange, since they had no language in common – and they concluded that Peters must at all costs be prevented from increasing his lead to 200m.

As they made their way northwards and eastwards through Helsinki's tree-lined streets, with a slight breeze behind them and thousands of spectators on either side, Emil, Jansson and Cox established themselves as the second-placed group. It was a straightforward out-and-back course: 42.195km in non-imperial reckoning. The weather was pleasant – 18°C – and the pace, though exceptionally fast by marathon standards, was still nothing special by Emil's. The difficulty was to run sensibly while keeping Peters in sight.

By the time they had passed the main Olympic village at Käpylä, Peters had a nineteen-second lead. He had run the first five kilometres in 15:43, equivalent to a track pace of seventy-five seconds a lap. After Emil's group, the nearest challengers, a further eighteen seconds behind, were Gorno, Yakov Moskachenkov (of the

Soviet Union), and Doroteo Flores (of Guatemala). As they headed out into the countryside on highway number 137, the field was strung out. Anyone with aspirations to a medal already had a fight on his hands.

The roadside was still lined with Finns, often two deep. Many had bicycles and picnics. They clapped politely as each runner passed. A bus just behind the leaders carried selected journalists, with a separate open car for photographers; sometimes one or other drew alongside, and Emil was seen to exchange pleasantries with those on board. Everyone agreed that he looked relaxed and strong.

The landmarks rolled by: Pakinkylä, Tuomarinkylä, the Vantaa river and its bridge. By ten kilometres (Malmi), Peters had slowed very slightly. Jansson was sixteen seconds behind him, with Emil just a second back in third.

The city suburbs thinned; buildings gave way to green fields of newly mown hay; but still the road was lined with applauding Finns. By the time runners were approaching Helsinki parish church (fourteen kilometres), Emil and Jansson had made significant inroads on Peters's lead; by fifteen kilometres Jansson had caught up. Soon afterwards Emil, too, was running alongside him. Emil, inevitably, started talking. His exchange with Peters is one of the most famous in sporting history, but it has been repeated in so many variations that it is hard to say authoritatively precisely what was said. Peters gave one version, which he admitted might have been clouded by exhaustion; Emil, characteristically, gave several. Jansson, the only other witness, did not speak English.

The most plausible sequence is this:

Emil: 'The pace, Jim – is it too fast?'

Peters (irritably): 'No, it has to be like this.'

(Pause.)

Emil: 'Are you sure it is not too fast?'

Peters (with what he later described as Cockney defiance): 'Actually, it's too slow.'

Soon afterwards, Peters moved to the other side of the road, the implication being that he would not welcome further questioning. Emil took this as a sign of weakness; he had noticed, in any case, that Peters looked more haggard than he had at the start ('like a boxer after the third round'), and he sensed, correctly, that he was struggling.

Emil did not – as legend suggests – immediately go speeding over the horizon, but he did accelerate enough to leave Peters nearly ten metres behind, and thereafter he felt emboldened to keep pushing the pace. Just as Peters was ready to ease off, Emil made sure that he couldn't. The next five kilometres offered a classic demonstration of a distance runner being tortured by a pace that is just a tiny bit too fast for him.

By the twenty-kilometre mark, at Ruotskylä, Peters was ten seconds behind, although he had made back three by the time they turned at Mätäkivi. Emil and Jansson began the homeward journey side by side. No one was talking now. Even the wide-eyed Finns who watched them from the roadside seemed to do so largely in silence. There is something dreamlike about the black and white footage that survives, with pale skies, still pine forests and a straight, featureless, seemingly endless road. Perhaps it seemed dreamlike to Emil, too; he was, at the very least, in unknown territory. He had been running for longer than he had ever run in a competitive race before, and he was barely past the halfway mark. He had no real idea of what the rest would feel like; no idea what ordeal awaited him; no idea how best to manage his failing strength.

He later claimed that, around this point, he felt an almost irresistible urge to give up, and was deterred only by the thought that he had no money in his pocket with which to get back to Helsinki. If that seems unconvincing, it is almost certainly true that he was in pain. The easy chatting of the early kilometres had given way to dogged endurance (although he still exchanged the odd word with the accompanying press pack). Like every marathon runner, he found himself appreciating, from the gut, what a monstrous, unnatural distance 26.2 miles really is for running. His mouth was dry. His feet felt sore. He had bought some new shoes specially for the race – some say Karhu (a Finnish brand), others Adidas (disguised for political reasons) – and although he had followed the advice of the American 10,000m runner Fred Wilt to soften them in advance with cooking grease, they were still basically just track shoes with the spikes removed. There was none of the cushioning that modern road runners take for granted. To make matters worse, Emil had made a marathon runner's rookie mistake – of checking his socks for irregularities with insufficient paranoia. First one foot, then the other, developed a blister. He was still running within himself in terms of aerobic exertion, yet his body was taking a beating.

As they passed the refreshment station at twenty-five kilometres, Emil and Jansson were offered half a lemon each. They had ignored all the previous refreshment stations, not wishing to lose precious time, but Jansson's supporters seemed to feel that their man could do with a boost. Jansson took the proffered fruit, but Emil, who had no experience of eating while racing, felt it would be too much of a risk to try it for the first time now. Instead (he claimed later), he decided to see what happened to Jansson. If the lemon appeared to help him, at the next station Emil would take one, or perhaps several.

The self-denial hurt. Shortly afterwards, however, they came to an uphill stretch (one of several on the middle part of the course). By the time he reached the top Emil realised that Jansson had slipped behind – and appeared to have a stitch. Emil kicked on, his thirst to some extent offset by the satisfaction of having made the right decision. And then . . . well, after that, all that remained was to keep going.

To the sportswriters on the bus – none of whom, as far as I am aware, had ever run a marathon – perhaps it looked easy. It wasn't. No marathon is easy. Those final seven or eight miles are an ordeal – a test of pain management. No matter what your speed, your preparation or your talent, one screamingly obvious fact never goes away: you would feel better if you stopped. But Emil faced an additional trial: he was alone.

By thirty kilometres he was twenty-six seconds in front of Jansson, and more than a minute ahead of Peters. Cox had dropped out by now, collapsing at around twenty-five kilometres and having to be taken to hospital. But Emil had no way of knowing this, or of knowing what other threats – Gorno, Cabrera, Choi – might be gaining in strength and speed. An experienced marathon runner might have felt confident enough to coast. Emil had no experience, but he did know that at the previous

Olympics the eventual winner, Cabrera, had not taken the lead until he entered the stadium for the final lap. He dared not do anything but run as fast as he could, fighting the urge to take it easy, telling himself that each step taken meant one step less to go; and perhaps also reminding himself that, as Tomáš Baťa had taught, 'There are 86,400 seconds in a day' – from which it must follow that there are 8,700 seconds in a 2:25 marathon and, no less certainly, that running the final ten kilometres of a marathon at that pace would take 2,062 seconds.

Just over 2,000 seconds: that was all that stood between him and sporting immortality.

In fact, for all his efforts, he was losing speed – lots of it. His ten-kilometre split times for the race were 32:12, 32:15, 34:15 and 36:38. He admitted later that he had felt 'terribly tired' from around thirty kilometres. 'The finish line was a long way off. I was alone, and my strength had gone.' But his spirit hadn't – not quite.

As he passed back through Pakinkylä at thirty-five kilometres, Emil was still only sixty-five seconds ahead – a significant lead, but not unassailable. There were still nearly five miles to go. This was where he needed to find his unbreakable core of champion's stubbornness. If you look at his face in the brief, surviving footage of this stage of the race, you see a man who is no longer enjoying himself. There is something trance-like about him. His eyes are glazed; his face has settled into a fixed, almost peaceful mask, like a man close to death. He has rolled up his vest, bikini-like, to expose his dehydrated body to the breeze. His hands claw the air feebly. If he were wrestling an octopus, the octopus would win. 'If you want to enjoy something,' he said later, 'run 100 metres. If you want to experience something, run a marathon.' These are the words of a man who knows what it really costs to keep going for 26.2 miles.

But the price was worth paying. The fast early pace had taken even more out of Emil's rivals than out of him. Peters had dropped out at thirty-two kilometres, slumping to the pavement in an agony of cramp and heat exhaustion. As for Jansson, he was struggling desperately to keep in touch. Gorno was gaining on him, while Emil, without realising it, was now increasing his lead.

By forty kilometres Emil led by more than two minutes. The tower of the Olympic stadium was visible by now, with the Olympic flame blazing from it. The roadside support was growing denser and louder. He must have known that victory was within his grasp, yet the pain never stopped. The bounce had been hammered out of his calves and thighs: the next day, he had to hobble downstairs backwards, and it would be a week before he could walk normally. 'My legs were hurting up to my neck,' he said later. Yet still he kept pounding on, fixing his eyes on the flame, refusing to yield.

Not far from the stadium, he heard a 'Bravo, Emil!' among the Finnish cries of '*Hyvä,* Satu-Pekka!', and was boosted by the sight of several of the athletes who had been battling with him for medals earlier in the week – Mimoun, Reiff, Pirie – cheering him on from the roadside.

The final uphill slope before the stadium seemed, as such stretches do, to go on for ever. Somehow he reached the top. He was in the stadium tunnel. He could see the track. He later claimed that, even now, he was afraid that he might collapse before the line, but he cannot seriously have doubted that the 'impossible' third gold was now his.

A trumpet fanfare greeted his entry. Nearly 70,000 people rose to their feet and erupted into ecstatic applause. According to the official report of the Games' organising committee, he arrived at the stadium 'in extremely good condition', with 'no sign now of that look of agony to which the public had become used in the 5,000 and 10,000 metres'. According to Emil, this was the first moment in the race when he felt happy.

The final 300m could hardly have been more different from that dramatic last half-minute of his battle with Mimoun, Schade and Chataway three days earlier. Yet they were equally unforgettable. The acclamation was deafening: 'Zá-to-pek! Zá-to-pek! Zá-to-pek!' – a pulsating, spine-tingling thunderclap of celebration and goodwill. The Czechoslovak radio commentator struggled to make himself heard as he proclaimed: 'We declare to the republic, at these, the fifteenth Summer Olympics in Helsinki, Staff Captain Emil Zátopek is approaching the finishing line in first place . . .'

The applause prompted Emil to think about a final sprint on the home straight, to please the crowd, 'but my legs would not listen.' Instead, 'I tried to balance my steps and started to smile, so that no one would see how tired I was.' At last, his wet chest touched the longed-for tape. The attempted smile finally became visible, weak but radiant, the smile of a man who knows, blissfully, that he has just taken the last step of a 26.2-mile race; and that, as a bonus, his wildest dream has just come true.

He limped off the track. As soon as he could, he sat. He took off his shoes. His feet were bleeding. Someone offered him a blanket. He refused, but asked for a fresh vest instead. He ate an apple. Then he looked for Dana, and jogged happily over for the most famous kiss in Olympic history.

Gradually, over the next thirty-six minutes, the other fifty-two finishers struggled over the line. Emil greeted several, offering Gorno, who had overtaken Jansson towards the end, an orange and a consolatory hug. To Jansson he gave a blanket. It was striking how wrecked the runners-up looked – a reminder that, simply in physical terms, this had been no ordinary race. It was the first time that every finisher in an Olympic marathon had broken the three-hour barrier. The first fifteen finishers had run personal bests; the first nine had broken the old Olympic record; the first twenty had run fast enough to have won gold at the previous Games. Cabrera, who finished sixth, was more than eight minutes faster than he had been when winning gold in London in 1948. Emil, the novice in the field, had spurred everyone else to surpass themselves. That was one of the things his fellow athletes loved him for.

You know the rest. There was the chairing by the Jamaican relay team, the lap of honour, the third medal ceremony in the space of eight days, broadcast to well over a hundred nations on radio and, in a few cases, television. The young man who just eleven years earlier had feigned injury to avoid running less than a mile through the streets of Zlín had, in the words of the *New York Times*, forced 'the once-peerless Paavo Nurmi . . . to yield his pedestal as the greatest distance runner in history'. In the space of eight days he had done thirty-eight and a half miles of racing, in 3 hours 20 minutes 52.8

seconds (less time than it takes many good recreational runners to do just a marathon), at an average speed of 11.5mph; and, in the process, he had rewritten sporting history. All over the world, people who a month before had never heard of Czechoslovakia listened to its anthem with a growing sense of familiarity, and chattered excitedly about 'Zátopek'. This latest triumph meant that only twenty of the sixty-nine nations competing at Helsinki had won more gold medals than Emil and Dana; if you limited the medals table to athletics, they had come second, behind the United States but ahead of all the other great powers of East and West.

In Czechoslovakia itself, Emil's parents were among the millions who listened to his achievements live (although the much reproduced photograph of them stooped anxiously by the wireless in Kopřivnice was taken some time before the Games). Word even reached the men-to-be-eliminated in the concentration camps in Jáchymov. Ladislav Kořán, Emil's old training partner, was given the news as an example of what a 'decent socialist' could achieve. Jan Haluza, Emil's old trainer, was told by a non-political prisoner – a common criminal – who came swaggering across the yard shouting: 'Emil Zátopek won three gold medals! Emil Zátopek won three gold medals!' Seeing Haluza, he upbraided him for appearing insufficiently delighted. Haluza told him: 'If you knew the relationship between me and him, you would not talk to me like that.' He rejoiced at his protégé's triumph; yet the joy was inseparable from sharp grief at being prevented from sharing it with him.

But the moment was a bittersweet one for Emil, too. As he embarked on his final slow lap of honour, and the cries of 'Farewell, Fairy-tale Pete' echoed around him, the sheer perfection of the moment made him feel suddenly sad. 'I was sorry that, already, it belonged to the past – like when a man is reading a book and turns the last page. It has happened, and now it cannot happen again.'

Strictly speaking, he was right. But if he imagined that this marked the end – or even the high point – of the drama of his life, he could not have been more mistaken.

12

The people's champion

If Emil was not the most famous person on the planet at the end of July 1952, he would certainly have been in most people's top ten. In Czechoslovakia, he was beyond famous. He returned to a blitz of parades, presentations and fawning dignitaries that might have left even a twenty-first-century celebrity dizzy.

The adulation seemed endless. An event in honour of the returning athletes in the giant Strahov stadium, with Emil as the star attraction, was packed out. Politicians and senior military officers rushed to congratulate him. Two leading poets, Miloslav Bureš and František Branislav, wrote epics in his praise. Two senior figures in the world of sport, Emanuel Bosák and Josef Pondělík, embarked on a new, hagiographic mini-biography. There were fresh editions of František Kožík's biography, too, rebranded as *Zátopek: The Marathon Victor* and, in one case, lavishly illustrated with photographs. Many of these images were stills from the filming of *One of the Relay*, which itself acquired a new momentum; some were almost certainly staged rather than genuine. But the image of Emil and Dana kissing after his marathon victory was not just authentic but, for a while, the most famous news photograph in the world.

Emil was on the covers of magazines everywhere; his achievements were front-page news in serious as well as popular newspapers. In the Czechoslovak press he was hailed as an example of a new 'unique breed of conscientious athlete, tireless in training and able to fight for the honour and glory of our people's democratic republic'. Even *Rudé právo*, not given to the hero-worship of anyone but Stalin, joined in the excited chorus: 'Staff Captain Emil Zátopek's name flew around the world, and with it the name of our country . . . In capitalist countries, where workers still live under the yoke of the exploiters, the workers, peasants and other labourers rejoice at the success of our athlete . . .'

Scarcely less dizzying, from Emil's point of view, was the fact that the caretaker at 8 U Půjčovny, who had been hostile to Emil for years because of his habit of treating the apartment as a gym, organised a party to celebrate his homecoming. Emil later cited this startling volte face as his greatest achievement.

There were other, more tangible rewards. Emil was promoted again, this time to the rank of major. Alexej Čepička, the defence minister, personally announced the promotion, saying that it was 'for services to sport'. He also announced that Emil had been given the Order of Work (Řád práce). What he didn't say was that while the Olympics were still going on and he was on holiday, a document proposing 'the exemplary punishment of Staff Captain Emil Zátopek' had found its way to his in-tray. General Jan Kratochvíl, the chief of staff standing in for him, looked at the plan, then at the headlines in that day's newspapers, celebrating the extraordinary achievements of Emil Zátopek, hero of Helsinki. He called in his secretary and asked: 'Tell me – I'm not very well up on sport – are there two Emil Zátopeks?' The secretary (who Emil claimed later told him about this) assured him that there were not; whereupon General Kratochvíl looked again at the recommendation for punishment, dismissed it as 'nonsense' and tore it up.

There is (obviously) no documentary evidence to corroborate this story. But Emil repeatedly told it, once it was safe to do so; numerous friends, fellow athletes and family members have assured me that it is true; and although it has been widely published in Czech I have never heard it disputed. Meanwhile, it certainly seems fair to say that, a month after his outrageous insubordination over Stanislav Jungwirth, Emil showed no sign of being out of favour with the regime.

No doubt it helped that he was finally in the process of becoming a member of the Communist Party. It was remarkable for such a senior army officer not to be one already. But what really assured him of official favour was the fact that, thanks to his fame and achievements, he was an irresistible instrument of Party propaganda: a one-man solution to the problem of national morale.

Emil had been doing his bit for the regime – making speeches, visiting factories, encouraging grass-roots sport – ever since his first gold medal, but his triumphs at Helsinki took this aspect of his life to a new level. Proclaiming the Party line – often in speeches that had been written for him – became as crucial a part of his duties as winning races. Mostly he was supposed to proselytise about the virtues of sporting participation, but sometimes he was expected to deliver more specific messages. The Olympics were still technically in progress when, on 3 August (the morning of the closing ceremony), Emil addressed an audience of 2,500 at a peace rally, organised by the Finnish Communist Party, at Alppilava in one of the parks outside Helsinki's Olympic stadium. Emil spoke – rapidly rather than passionately, according to one witness – about the evils of American foreign policy. He would address a similar theme later in the year at the World Peace Congress in Vienna.

Where possible, however, Emil spoke about matters closer to his heart: the rewards of working systematically towards a sporting (or other) objective; the pleasures of forming friendships with athletes from foreign countries; and the endlessly re-told tale of his hard road to Olympic glory, fuelled by self-belief, self-discipline and unlimited hard work.

From the Party's point of view, this was useful enough, allowing them to present Emil's values as Communist values, and to promote the narrative that Emil's triumphs represented a triumph for the entire Communist system. Large parts of the Czechoslovak public still seemed perplexingly unenthusiastic about Stalinism. Emil's popularity could be exploited to rectify this. Some senior figures also saw it as an opportunity to boost the productivity of the workforce. According to apologists for the regime, workers all over Czechoslovakia were inspired by Emil's achievements to increase their output. As František Kožík put it, 'The workers followed his example and set a higher pace for their work, in order to hasten the building of socialism in their country.'

It hardly needs saying that reports of a surge of spontaneous mass enthusiasm for hard, Zátopek-style work should be taken with fistfuls of salt. It may well be true that the miners at the General Yeremenko mine in Ostrava achieved their highest rate of coal extraction since 1945 in the aftermath of Emil's Helsinki triumphs, or that a tinplate-making factory in Prague increased its output by 218 per cent. What is open to question is the degree to which this 'Zátopkovite' movement (consciously modelled on the Russian Stakhanovite movement) was spontaneous. In later life, Emil met workers who reproached him for having caused unwanted increases in their compulsory workload.

Emil's own, supposedly voluntary workload was not exactly light. Public appearances became as regular a feature of his life as racing – often more regular. Ota Pavel claimed that he had up to twenty-five public engagements a week; whatever the truth, it was heavy enough for Emil to find it tiresome – and, indeed, his exploitation for these purposes became so notorious that Věra Čáslavská, the gymnast, would speak half a century later of Emil being 'chased like a bloated goat . . . from one forum to another'. At one point, in the course of yet another excursion to address a 'forum', Emil made his Party minder laugh with a joke to the effect that he would probably be addressing a forum on the day he died. He was later reprimanded for his disrespectful words, which the minder had reported. Meanwhile, no matter how much he grumbled, he had little choice but to comply. As his friend Jaromír Konůpka points out: 'He was a soldier. He had to obey orders.'

There is footage of Emil engaged in this kind of work in *One of the Relay*. In one sequence, in a factory, he listens with a glazed grin that will be familiar to British royal-watchers, while a spokesman for the workers tells him: 'I promise you that, taking your performances as an example, we at the factory will work with the same zeal and enthusiasm with which you win your races.'

Unspontaneous as such encounters feel, it is clear that Emil had a talent for them. He was smart enough to know what was required of him, and what he needed to say to keep out of trouble. But he was also charming and humorous and enjoyed engaging with ordinary people – who, in turn, were genuinely excited to have any kind of contact with the greatest sporting hero the world had ever seen. His life-lessons-drawn-from-sport felt (and still feel) relevant to ordinary people: 'You cannot jump to the second floor from the pavement – step by step, though, a man will come to the fifth floor'; 'What a man wants, he can achieve'; 'One's willpower increases with every task fulfilled'. Compared with some of the politically edifying addresses that Czechoslovaks were expected to listen to, an event involving Emil must have seemed thrilling.

It is also likely that Emil believed at least some of the messages he was delivering. He had clearly begun to have his doubts about the fanaticism, cruelty and stupidity of the Communist regime. But it is unlikely that much arm-twisting was required to persuade Emil to assert that, at Helsinki, the friendship that developed between athletes of most of the world's nations 'was so beautiful that it could only arise among people who want to live in peace'. As for the regime's wider political message, Emil had been brought up as a Communist, had been bombarded with Communist ideology since joining the army in 1945, and had experienced both the evils of fascism and the poverty of the 'have-nots' under capitalism. He once said (much later in life) that he would prefer to live on bread and water under Communism than in luxury under capitalism, and this was probably true. He had his reservations about the Party's authoritarianism, but the system had improved his own life immeasurably, while rescuing his family from the gnawing insecurities it had known before 1948. He knew, too, what life had been like for Czechoslovak athletes before the Communist era: Koščák, Emil liked to point out, had laid paving stones in Wenceslas Square in between his records, while Černý had slept rough during a period of unemployment. If Communism offered something better than this, he was in favour.

Emil cannot have been unaffected, either, by constant exposure to crowds of adoring members of the public, or to the idealistic messages he was expected to share with them. Sometimes he longed for it all to stop: 'If such hell should last a lifetime,' he wrote later, 'I'd rather not live.' Yet if people were inspired by his preaching of Communism's nobler ideals, how could he scorn them? So it was that, when Dana complained about the adulation she was experiencing, Emil told her: 'The people love us, Dana. We have to love them back.' For the cult of Zátopek to thrive, Emil had to believe in it, too.

There were believers in the West, as well: not just among the ideologues who – like the Communist *L'Humanité* newspaper in France – saw him as 'the new man: Socialist Man', but also among the wider, non-Communist public. Wonder at his achievements fed an appetite for his back story, which Party propagandists had been polishing for years. In a world still scarred by the Second World War and chilled by fears of a Third, there was something compelling about this socialist with a human face – this working-class hero who, no matter how dubious the regime he lived under, seemed to embody universal values of human decency. He was a soldier – an occupation with which millions could identify – but there seemed to be no hint of brutality about him. Instead, he was courteous, charming, humorous, with an extravagant sense of sportsmanship that recalled the noblest ideals of chivalry. He owed his achievements not to privilege but to unremitting hard work which was evident both from his agonised style and, no less memorably, from the photographs and film footage that were now becoming more widely available, showing a lone, indomitable soldier bounding uncomplainingly through the snow at night.

'As a good soldier, he must obey. As a true champion, he must surpass himself. And, behind him, the youth of the nation follows . . .' You didn't have to share the pro-Soviet sympathies of J. Armour Milne to find the message stirring. Friends who sang Emil's praises in the West, such as Les Perry (who had left Helsinki with Emil's red vest and white shorts) and Gordon Pirie were anything but pro-Soviet. They loved Emil for his human qualities, not his politics. 'I am sure that for very many years yet he will be an inspiration to new generations,' wrote Pirie. 'Above all he is . . . the greatest sportsman I have ever met.'

Meanwhile, ideology or no ideology, Emil still had to find time to perform at least a semblance of his military duties. These would become easier in November 1952, when Emil was made a desk officer at ATK – a simple, unexciting role that, without affecting his seniority, allowed him to train without the stress of worrying about how to get his job done. The racing, however, must sometimes have felt more like performing in a circus. On 17 September 1952, for example, more than 20,000 fans crowded into the little stadium in Ústí nad Labem, to watch Emil run the 5,000m in a club match. Many workers were reported to have refused to work their afternoon shifts, so that they could be sure of seeing him, and reports of forged tickets led to a police investigation.

Two weeks earlier, in the little Moravian town of Znojmo, Emil had won a fiercely contested 5,000m against Milan Švajgr – the local runner who had trained with Emil for a while in Hranice. The ferocity may have had something to do with the fact that Švajgr had been dropped from the Olympic team for Helsinki at the last minute, despite having the world's fastest time of the year for 3,000m. According to Švajgr, who had been selected to run 5,000 and 10,000m, this was because of something Emil said to one of the personnel commissars in charge of vetting the team for political reliability. Švajgr claims to have been in the room with Emil and the commissar when Emil said that he considered Švajgr a defection risk – or, at least, refused to guarantee that he was not. When Švajgr protested, Emil withdrew the remark. None the less, this supposed risk was cited as the reason for Švajgr's sudden omission from the team, despite protests from his home town of Opava. If this is true, it may tell us something about Emil's ambiguous relationship with the regime. He was, after all, a major: it would have been difficult to hold down such a job without buying into the Party's programme to some degree. Perhaps he felt that Švajgr was dispensable; there was no great bond between them. Or perhaps he really did have doubts about Švajgr's loyalty. Under the 'knew, but didn't tell' law, standing up for the wrong person could have disastrous consequences. With Jungwirth, by contrast, Emil's efforts to keep him in the team included an undertaking that he would vouch for his loyalty – one he would have been foolish to give had he mistrusted Jungwirth. One reason for his success in that battle may have been that he appeared to accept in principle the Party's right to enforce ideological conformity. He engaged with the idea that defection had to be guarded against – and evidence from his later life suggests that he genuinely felt it was a form of treason.

None of that was of any comfort to Švajgr, who may have felt that Emil had been trying to safeguard his own medal chances at his expense. But the contest in Znojmo made a nonsense of that imputation. Emil ended up a convincing winner, while Švajgr, for all his motivation, was twenty-five seconds outside Herbert Schade's bronze medal-winning time in Helsinki. Afterwards, there was a dinner at some wine cellars in Jaroslavice, where they all got drunk. Švajgr berated Emil, who held out his hands and said: 'OK, so beat me! Beat me!' The two men later resumed a friendship, of sorts; but when I met Švajgr more than six decades later it was clear that he had not forgiven him.

Emil, meanwhile, whatever his true beliefs, continued to add to his credentials as a Party loyalist. He joined the Central Committee of the Czechoslovak Union of Youth – a kind of Young Communists organisation – and when Stalin died, in March 1953, Emil was among those who put their names to tributes in the daily newspaper *Mladá fronta*, mourning, in his case, 'a great teacher of Soviet sport'. Did he really believe that? It seems unlikely, but it is impossible to tell. Part of the tragedy of Czechoslovakia's decades of Communist tyranny is that all but the most simplistically fanatical learnt to keep their real motives to themselves. Dissimulation became the norm.

But one thing that remained unambiguous was Emil's passion for running. On the track, if nowhere else, he could be himself. And if he carried on torturing himself in training as obsessively as if he had never won a medal in his life, well, perhaps it didn't always feel like torture. Perhaps it felt like release.

If further incentive was needed, it probably came from the knowledge that most other leading distance runners were now imitating Emil's methods. This was particularly noticeable among his fellow athletes in Prague and in Stará Boleslav, where young men such as Ivan Ullsperger and Stanislav Jungwirth were beginning to get impressive results by attempting to do their own versions of Emil's training sessions. Even beyond the specific discipline of endurance running, the general Zátopkovite principles of hard work and systematic progress towards supposedly unthinkable goals were gaining currency among athletes generally. No doubt Emil found all this flattering. It also served to remind him that, where he had pushed back the frontiers, others, including rivals, could now follow.

On 4 October, in Opava, Emil made an unsuccessful attempt on Gunder Hägg's 5,000m world record; he failed by more than eight seconds, but even that produced a time – 14:06.4 – that suggested that he was still in excellent shape. Three weeks later, at Houštka Spa, he set a world record for thirty kilometres (1:35:23.8) and, in the process, world records for twenty-five kilometres and fifteen miles as well. The next finisher was fifteen minutes behind.

The following year started badly, however. Emil began to be troubled by sciatica, which occasionally caused him agonies in his legs. He had to have his tonsils removed, and some teeth. And there was an unfortunate incident in the spring when, messing about, he wrecked Dana's hopes for the season.

Dana had been in brilliant form – so much so that her coach rewarded her with a Sunday off. Emil suggested an excursion to the countryside, with a swim in the River Sázava as a highlight. 'So in the morning we ran up to this place where Emil knew there was a pool,' says Dana, apparently relishing the memory. 'When we got there, there was a young man lying there, reading a newspaper. We never even found out his name. Emil said, "OK, let's go for a swim." But the man said: "There's not enough water here."

'So Emil said, "OK, we'll throw her a little bit further, into the deep bit." So he and the young man grabbed me by the hands and legs, swung me, and threw me into the water, as far as they could. The riverbed was sandy, but when I fell in I got my foot stuck under a rock.' She broke her right leg – the one that matters most for javelin throwing – just above the ankle.

All things considered, Dana took this well – at least, she laughs as she describes it now. Emil's punishment was to carry her on his shoulders all the way back to the cottage they were staying at: a journey of just a few miles that gave birth to the enduring legend, which Dana denies, that Emil regularly ran while carrying her. Meanwhile, the accident was a salutary reminder to Emil that things wouldn't automatically work out perfectly just because he was Emil Zátopek.

This was no time for complacency. Rivals were rising in the east who threatened his dominance. In early June, Aleksandr Anufriev achieved an impressive double, running 13:58.8 for 5,000m in Moscow and then 29:23.2 for 10,000m the following day. In July, Vladimir Kuts, a young Soviet who had been developing his own version of Emil's methods and would soon become a byword for implacable dominance on the track, ran 14:14.6 for 5,000m; while József Kovács, of Hungary, ran 14:07.4. The higher echelons of distance running were starting to feel a bit crowded.

In August, Emil confronted Kuts and Kovács over 5,000m at the International World Youth Games in Bucharest and was forced to produce a stunning final kick of fully 800m to hold them off. The 10,000m, four days later, yielded a rather easier victory for Emil. The races were also memorable for Emil's visible gestures of sportsmanship: carefully guiding Dave Stephens, during the 10,000m, to the best ever 5,000m time by an Australian, or stooping to tie Kovács's loose shoelace for him just before they began to race. You would never have guessed, from Emil's manner, that he was under any pressure. Stephens, who collapsed in the second half of the 10,000m, joined the growing band of overseas athletes who considered Emil a lifelong friend. He later spent two weeks training with Emil, studying his methods; Emil, in return, received a boomerang and lessons in how to use it.

In the course of the next six weeks, however, Kuts, Pirie and Kovács all produced sub-14:03 5,000m performances. Emil was now fifth in the all-time list of 5,000m runners. He managed to put Kovács in his place by beating him in a head-to-head at the Strahov stadium in October, but even that was a struggle – Emil had to overcome a twenty-metre deficit in the final lap before sprinting away to win by a similar distance. Was he starting to rely more on desperate willpower and less on superior fitness and talent? It was hard to tell. Meanwhile, it had not escaped the attention of the management of ATK that Emil ranked no better than fourth – behind Pirie, Kovács and Anufriev – in the list of the best times of the year for 10,000m.

This prompted a late attempt to put things right. On 1 November, on a damp, windy day at Houštka Spa, Emil knocked a second off his 10,000m world record, which he reduced to 29:01.6. In the process, he also beat Gordon Pirie's world record for six miles; a congratulatory telegram from Pirie arrived shortly afterwards.

The result was also gratifying for the Melichar family, who lived next door to the athletes' retreat on the edge of Stará Boleslav, and who were among the spectators for Emil's record-breaking run. They had first encountered Emil when one of his shoes, left outside the athletes' villa to dry, was snaffled by their dog, Arko. Emil eventually tracked it down, only lightly chewed, and, in the process, met and made friends with the family.

Over the next few months, he dropped in regularly, sometimes with fellow athletes in tow; and on one visit the conversation turned to Emil's growing interest in using resistance training to build up strength. Various examples were discussed: running in army boots, or wearing a heavy rucksack. All you needed was a worthwhile amount of extra weight, arranged in such a way that you could run with it. Someone asked if it was feasible to run with a person on your back. There was only one way to find out, and the Melichars' six-year-old daughter, Iva, was produced as a guinea pig. Emil put her on his shoulders, and off they went.

The details are a bit of blur today, but Iva – now called Iva Kazda and living in the USA – remembers that 'he went very fast. It was cool. We ran down the hill to the woods, and then ran around the woods for a long time.' She doesn't know if he was doing his usual repetitions, or just messing around; she remembers only the speed, and the fact that he was funny and kind and didn't seem bothered by the load. Iva became a keen marathon runner. Now nearly seventy, she still loves running in the woods – and still marvels at the fact that, once, she saw with eyes just a few inches above Emil's what the woods of Stará Boleslav looked like to the great Zátopek as he bounded tirelessly through them.

The new world records at 10,000m and six miles were pleasing proof that this exercise had done Emil no harm, and that his shoes had not been too badly damaged by Arko's attentions. But if reports of Emil's decline were premature, the problem of his ever-more dangerous rivals remained; as did the inconvenient truth that, no matter what he did to boost his strength, his basic speed was – at the age of thirty-one – unlikely to improve. In an interview with J. Armour Milne for *Athletics Weekly* at the end of the year, Emil warned: 'You must not expect too much from me in the future . . . I shall be able to compete in the shorter of the long distances only as a sort of 'guest artist'. I feel that my true distances are from 10,000 metres upwards.'

To most of the world, Zátopek remained simply Zátopek: a man of unique sporting genius and charisma whose powers verged on the supernatural. At the end of the year Emil was allowed to travel to Brazil, where he had been invited to take part in the famous Saint Sylvester New Year's Eve road race in São Paulo. Between 800,000 and a million spectators turned out to watch the event, which began shortly before midnight. Shrugging off the humid conditions, Emil easily defeated 2,139 rivals over the 7,300m course. He remained in the city for nearly a week and, despite catching a chill and having to be treated with penicillin, rounded off his visit with an impressive 10,000m victory.

Overseas visits by Czechoslovak athletes were frowned upon by the Communist authorities, who feared defections and the corrupting effect of contact with the West. But Emil was becoming a special case. He had already travelled widely and had, on the whole, proved himself reliable. Each visit had to be cleared in advance with the security services and observed by an accompanying representative of the 'sharp eyes'. Travellers would then be expected to report back on what they had seen: whom they had spoken to; what they had noticed about the customs and condition of the host country; and, if relevant, the behaviour of those who had travelled with them. Emil, whose gifts as a linguist far outstripped those of most professional spies, seems to have reported back regularly, although not necessarily reliably. No transcripts of his debriefings survive in the archives of the security services, but indirect evidence implies that, initially at least, his brief was to bring back something comparable to travel journalism: general impressions, not without telling detail, gathered by looking around and talking to people. I am not aware of his ever having commented on the behaviour of a fellow athlete.

What made Emil valuable to the regime was not the information he provided but his gifts as a diplomat. His track triumphs had done wonders for Czechoslovakia's international profile, but one day those triumphs would dry up. His charm, on the other hand, was capable of being exploited for years. An age of Zátopek diplomacy beckoned.

But Emil had other priorities. He was still bubbling with energy, still hooked on the buzz of competition ('To stand on the starting line, to look my rivals over, and tell myself: "Well, boys, let's get going and see who's best . . ."'). And his appetite for sporting glory remained unsated.

The winter of 1953–4 saw him subjecting himself to his toughest workload yet, much of it away from home at the camp in Stará Boleslav. His training diary recorded that, in a twelve-day period in mid-February, training in the woods twice a day, he accumulated the following daily totals (with 150m recovery jogs in between each approximate lap):

Monday 15th: 70 x 400m
Tuesday 16th: 40 x 400m
Wednesday 17th: 40 x 400m
Thursday 18th: 80 x 400m
Friday 19th: 80 x 400m
Saturday 20th: 70 x 400m

Sunday 21st: 40 x 400m
Monday 22nd: 80 x 400m
Tuesday 23rd: 80 x 400m
Wednesday 24th: 80 x 400m
Thursday 25th: 80 x 400m
Friday 26th: 50 x 400m

By the end of the month (from 29 February to 2 March), he was doing 100 laps a day. The speed varied. A giant session might be done largely at racing speed, or as near as Emil could get to it. But somewhere in the middle would be a sequence of fifteen or more flat-out, frenzied, catch-Reiff-or-die sprints. Given the volumes involved, the will-power required was superhuman.

To help his focus, he took the radical step of shaving his head – temporarily dampening the interest of the photographers, film-makers and sculptors who were constantly asking him to pose for them. The fact that his hairline was continuing to recede may have played a part in this, but it is also a characteristic expression of his belief in the empowering effects of asceticism. He ran 1,845km in February and March alone – getting on for three-quarters of it flat-out; and that's not counting the hours of extra exercising he did indoors (back at home), jogging on the spot on a rubber mat for up to two hours at a time when the weather was so severe that even he couldn't train outdoors.

His clear priority for the year was to defend his two titles at the European Championships, to be held in Berne in July. But he was also committed to improving his world record for 10,000m and his national record for 5,000m, and to achieving a classification of 'outstanding' in 'party political education'. We know this because by early 1954 the 'Zátopek movement' had been more or less formally enshrined in the administration of Czechoslovak sport. Leading athletes were expected to make specific, public pledges about their goals for the year. The Ministerial Council for Physical Education and Sport announced the most prominent in a poster displayed in a shop window in Wenceslas Square. (Dana was committed to a new national record in javelin throwing and 'active participation in sport education of youth'; others had targets including 'mastery of the Russian language' and a 'thorough study of the history of the Bolshevik party'.)

The 1954 season began with Emil in scintillating athletic form; as a diplomat, however, he was initially not at his best. His first event was a cross-country race in Paris organised by *L'Humanité*. Several top athletes from Soviet bloc countries had been invited, but Emil was the star attraction. The French athletics federation (FFA) disapproved of the event – partly for bureaucratic reasons and partly for ideological ones – and had forbidden French athletes to take part. The race that Emil won in the Bois de Vincennes on 21 March – the first day of spring – was therefore an unofficial one.

This minor irritation may have had something to do with some uncharacteristically blunt comments that Emil gave to the journalists who welcomed him on his return to Prague – some of which were published in *Svobodné slovo*. Asked about the impression that Paris had made on him, Emil replied that he had been disappointed. Apart from the notorious Pigalle district, there wasn't much to see, and he saw little to enthuse about in 'the Paris of junk literature, the Paris of pornographic revues and magazines', in which everything seemed to be subservient to a hunger for commercial gain. The journalists may have polished his quotes a little. None the less, they were enough to form the combustible raw material for '*l'affaire de Colombes*'.

It took time to ignite. For a few weeks more, Emil simply trained and raced. The training was merciless: at times he was doing 100 x 400m, sometimes seven days a week; 'horse dosage, every day' was how he described it. Then, as a race approached, he would reduce the quantity – to 30, 20, even 10 – and increase the speed accordingly. The combination was irresistible. On 25 April he won an eleven-kilometre cross-country race in Nové Město na Moravě, in the scarcely credible time of 31:12. On 14 May he won a 5,000m at Houštka Spa, in 14:04.0; two days later he won another one, in Kladno, in 14:19.2. He was, in short, ferociously fit: so much so that his weight had dropped to sixty-two kilograms – five or six kilograms less than normal. The last time he had weighed so little was when he left hospital on the eve of the last European Championships, in August 1950, following that famous bout of food poisoning. Given his stupendous performances on that occasion, he and Dana joked that perhaps another world record was on the cards; and the conversation somehow ended with Dana vowing to bow down to him, literally and publicly, if he succeeded in breaking Gunder Hägg's seemingly unbreakable record for 5,000m.

There was an obvious opportunity to do so. On 30 May Emil was due to return to Paris, to race in an international match in the northern suburb of Colombes. But that was when the trouble began. The exact chain of cause and effect remains confused, but there is no dispute about the component parts. The French athletics authorities may have been ruffled by reports that Emil, having committed to the match, might race in Hungary instead. There were elements in the French establishment who objected to a Communist figurehead such as Emil being an honoured guest in their country. And then, shortly before he was due to arrive, Emil's comments about his earlier visit found their way back to France.

This was the final straw. The Czechoslovak team arrived in Brussels on 26 May. From there they were due to travel to France – but the journalists who greeted them had already heard the news: Emil was not going to be granted a visa. A three-day diplomatic storm followed. The Czechoslovaks were outraged; the French stood upon their dignity; others weighed in according to politics and prejudice. French commentators were divided between those who found their foreign office's stance embarrassing and those who suggested that Emil was a 'Communist fanatic' who should make a public apology. Even in the era of McCarthyism, it was a bizarre spat – and a bizarre stance for a Western government to take in relation to the world's most famous sportsman.

Emil tried to focus on his training, while frantic phone calls were exchanged in the background. Finally, late on Saturday, 29 May, the French foreign office authorised its consulate in Brussels to grant Emil a visa. Emil rushed to the consulate shortly before midnight, and just had time to catch a flight that arrived in Paris at 6 a.m. on Sunday, 30 May. The race was to take place that evening.

The Stade Olympique Yves-du-Manoir was filled to overflowing. Emil, tired and grumpy, lined up for the 5,000m against a weak field of just four others – and proceed to run one of the most astonishing races of his life. There was no one to pace him; nothing to pull or push him on apart from several days' worth of accumulated frustration and a desire to provide something special for the ordinary French athletics fans who had turned out to see him. But that was enough. Running alone for all but the first half-lap, he pushed himself as even he had rarely pushed himself before, simultaneously driven and liberated, upping the tempo as the fans responded to what they could sense was a historic effort.

His final kilometre was sensational. Encouraged by rhythmic applause, Emil ran it in 2:43.8, overturning a four-second deficit on the world record schedule to finish in 13:57.2 – an improvement of an entire second on Gunder Hägg's twelve-year-old time. The second finisher, Yugoslavia's Drago Štritof, was forty-six seconds behind. Afterwards, Emil was mobbed by autograph hunters, and eventually had to be escorted from the track by gendarmes – whose own requests for autographs confirmed to Emil that he had made his peace with the French people. The next day's headlines confirmed this: Emil was praised for his '*admirable réponse*' to the rudeness of the French government, which, in turn, was condemned for its '*incroyable stupidité*'. Emil had won the diplomatic battle as resoundingly as he had won the race.

The day after that, Emil was back in Brussels, where he raced at 10,000m in the Stade Trois Tillauts. Despite forty-eight hours of rain and little serious opposition, Emil once again ran as if his life depended on it – and was rewarded with a time of 28:54.2. Less than a month after Roger Bannister had made global headlines by running the first sub-four-minute mile, Emil had reclaimed his position as the most noteworthy athlete in the world by becoming not only the world record holder at 5,000m but also the first man to run 10,000m in less than twenty-nine minutes.

The fact that the diplomatic stakes had been so high gave extra weight to Emil's triumphs when he returned to Prague. His immediate reward was to be greeted at the airport by Dana, who presented him with a bouquet and, at Emil's insistence, made a low(ish) bow to him. But the Czechoslovak state was even more enthusiastic, seizing hungrily on this fresh propaganda fodder. A new wave of Zátopkovism was reported: some miners in Příbram were said to have broken a world record for fast coal cutting. The message was simple. As Otakar Mašek wrote: 'The delight in work, the conscientiousness, the courage, the feeling of responsibility of a Zátopek should run throughout our whole lives.'

Emil, meanwhile, was promoted yet again, this time to lieutenant colonel, which in military terms was farcical. Emil had barely more experience now than he did when he graduated from military academy. None the less, it was a relatively decorous way of bestowing on Emil some arguably legitimate material reward. In addition to a generous salary, there were perks: a car, for example (Klára the Saab – although technically this belonged to the Ministry of Defence and some of Emil's colleagues had access to it, too). Athletes also received a 'nutrition allowance', which was not supposed to be spent on items other than food but often was. Even if rumours of cash bonuses for Olympic medallists weren't true (and Dana insists that they weren't, in those days), the Zátopeks were becoming steadily more entrenched in Communism's elite: the new ruling class, whose privileges – however justifiable they seemed from within – insulated them from the hardships and frustrations the system inflicted upon ordinary people.

Somehow, though, the privilege didn't stick to Emil. When people saw him driving Klára, they forgave him the (relative) ostentation. They knew how hard he worked, and they knew that he always had time for ordinary people and cared about their welfare. When Emil saw that Ivan Ullsperger didn't have a watch, for example, he not only asked him why but took note of the answer – Ullsperger had been been planning to buy a watch but had, like many Czechoslovaks, lost all his savings in the great currency reform of 1953. A few days after explaining this, Ullsperger was stunned to receive a watch from Emil as a gift. Much later, he learnt that it was the watch awarded to participants in the Helsinki Olympics.

To say that Emil was entirely indifferent to material things would be an exaggeration. No one who has known poverty ever is. But apart from good food and drink, which he relished, and freedom from financial anxiety, which he appreciated, he does not seem to have been interested in luxury. Rather, he cared about people, and about running. Running was not a means to an end: it was an end in itself. And his accumulated medals and glory counted for little compared with that gnawing anxiety that every runner knows – the fear that the slightest loss of willpower and focus will see the accumulated fitness of the years haemorrhaging away, irrecoverably.

13

'Today we die a little'

On 3 July 1954 there was a sporting earthquake in Hungary. In an international match in Budapest, Emil was beaten over 10,000m. It was his thirty-ninth race at the distance, and the first he had ever lost.

He took the end of his six-year winning streak in his stride. There was only an eighth of a second in it; he had not been well that day; his conqueror, József Kovács, was an athlete he admired; and the winning time, 29:09, was respectable. It would have been silly to overreact.

Even so, he must have worried. No champion likes losing, or, worse, feeling his powers ebb away. Emil responded, inevitably, by training harder. In August, he got his revenge, beating Kovács by nearly twenty-eight seconds to win in 28:58 in the European Championships in Berne. But third place in the 5,000m at the same meeting, behind Kuts and Chataway, spelled out the dispiriting underlying message: there were runners out there who were faster than him. And speed, as Jan Haluza had taught, is the foundation of everything.

Nothing Emil could do would rectify this shortfall. He could redouble his efforts, but only with respect to those areas that were within his control: endurance; strength; resilience; and, not least, the ability to function and thrive on the borderline between tolerable and intolerable agony. But with his thirty-second birthday approaching there was no more raw speed lying latent in his body, waiting to be unlocked by training.

The clock was ticking. He had nine successive victories at 10,000m before losing again: to Kovács in Bratislava in September 1955 and to Pirie in London three weeks later. But his times were worsening, while at 5,000m he was losing almost as often as he won. In fifteen races between the 1954 European Championships and the end of 1955, he won eight and lost seven, and ran faster than 14:10 only four times. Even Ivan Ullsperger, Emil's protégé at ATK Praha, managed to beat him twice.

As far as the general public was concerned, Emil's pre-eminence remained beyond doubt. When the first Spartakiáda mass gymnastic display was held in Prague in July 1955 – the Communist alternative to the now suppressed Sokol *slets* – nothing could have been more natural than that Emil should address the packed Strahov stadium, urging everyone to join him in contributing to 'the glory of our physical education'. That autumn, at Čelákovice on 29 October, he added some extra glory of his own, setting new world records – his seventeenth and eighteenth – for fifteen miles and twenty-five kilometres. But these would be his last, and, meanwhile, the world's athletics journalists had been following a different narrative. In the words of *Athletics Weekly*'s Jimmy Green, 'the great Czech master has reached the point where he is capable of being beaten by younger, speedier runners.'

In October, Emil conceded the obvious. 'I am not fast enough for the 5,000 metres,' he said in a television interview in London. He would not, he announced, be defending his Olympic title at the distance.

That Christmas saw Emil, Dana and other athletes from ATK (soon to be renamed Dukla) sent to India, where they visited Bombay, Delhi and Calcutta. Emil made such an impact that he was later said to have single-handedly started an Indian running boom. Emil beat the Indian champion, Gulzara Singh, over 5,000m in Calcutta. Singh was so overwhelmed that he touched Emil's shoes and sprinkled dust from them on to his head. Emil responded by giving Singh his shoes.

The trip was also notable for the heat, for the welcoming crowds, and for at least one spectacular marital row between Emil and Dana, which was written up with ill-concealed relish for the Czechoslovak secret service by an agent who appears to have been eavesdropping. They seem, however, to have been on relatively good terms on returning to Czechoslovakia, and according to some reports early 1956 saw Emil incorporating wife-carrying into his training regime as a regular feature. If true, this would be consistent both with Emil's character and with his preoccupations at the time – and with the fact that, around the same time, he suffered a painful hernia in his groin.

There is, however, a difficulty. Dana insists that the only time she remembers Emil carrying her was after he broke her leg, in 1953. This is the problem with writing about Emil: myths and legends swirl around his name, and many evaporate when you try to grasp them. In this case, as in many, the legend seems to originate with him. He told at least two writers that his problems in 1956 began when he went running in the woods carrying Dana on his shoulders. Others have recorded that it took place in the snow; that Dana complained about Emil's bony shoulders; and that at one point Emil tripped on a tree root. J. Armour Milne, in a book published in 1956, described Emil attempting 'to jog trot for several hundred yards along a forest path' with Dana 'astride his shoulders'. Does any of this make it true? Not necessarily. Emil liked few things better than to entertain people with anecdotes that would become more amusing each time he retold them; and he seems to have adopted a similar approach when it came to those who sought to set his own story down in words. He knew a good tale when he saw one, knew how to improve it, and wasn't too fussed if journalists – or publishers, or Party officials – did a bit of extra polishing of their own, just so long as they got what they wanted and stopped bothering him. 'Do anything they ask of you,' was his media strategy, 'because there's no other way of getting rid of them.' So he helped package his story into anecdotes – the medal in the swimming pool, the running in the bath tub, the sausages and beer from the hospital kitchens – and the anecdotes crop up again and again, with variations, in contemporary and subsequent writings about him, without necessarily becoming any truer as they mature.

And the wife-carrying? We can only guess. Perhaps Emil was exaggerating; perhaps Dana has forgotten; perhaps he had a different passenger (a child?), and the journalists misunderstood. But at some point in early 1956 Emil became aware that, probably as a result of some kind of running with a heavy load, he had injured himself.

Like countless lesser athletes after him, he had tried too hard to halt time's depredations. Like them, too, he responded at first by trying to shrug off the injury. By June, however, after coming a dispirited fifth in the Rošický memorial 5,000m in Prague, he faced facts. He had surgery in early July, and he spent a fretful summer reading reports about his world records being broken: by Pirie (13:36.8 for 5,000m); by Hungary's Sándor Iharos (28:42.8 for 10,000m); and by Kuts (28:30.4 for 10,000m).

A short spell in Moscow, advising Soviet marathon runners such as Ivan Filin and Albert Ivanov, did little to restore his equanimity. He made a tentative comeback on 26 August, winning a low-grade 5,000m in Kladno in a spectacularly slow 15:18.6 – his worst time since 1944. In late September, less than two months before the Olympics, he was forced to take a break from heavy training. He returned to run 10,000m, at a military meeting in Prague on 7 October, and won, against modest opposition, in 29:33.4. Then he ran out of time.

The Czechoslovak team touched down in Australia on 9 November. Emil, desperate for fitness, had trained incessantly during the four stopovers; he had even tried training in mid-flight, but the rest of the team forced him to stop, terrified that he would cause the plane to crash.

They reached Melbourne on the 10th. Six days earlier, Soviet tanks had rolled into Budapest to crush the Hungarian uprising – Eastern Europe's first significant revolt against the Kremlin's dominion. Tens of thousands would die by the time the rebellion was extinguished. Emil admitted to journalists that the events cast a shadow over the Games. 'It's a pity . . . To have this sudden shadow of strife and misery cast over the whole

Zátopek in action: he lack of challengers does nothing to soften the agonised body language.

mil leads the Olympic eld in a rain-drenched 10,000 metres in London 1948; Gaston Reiff is second.

His finest hour

Emil on the point of breaking the world records for both 20,000km and The Hour at Houštka Spa, 29 September 1951.

His finest moment?

Emil takes the lead coming out of the final bend in the Olympic 5,000 metres final in Helsinki, 1952. Alain Mimoun is second, Herbert Schade third; Christopher Chataway is on the ground behind them.

Crossing the line at the end of his first marathon, Emil claims his third gold medal at the Helsinki Olympics.

Bounding through the snow in the woods at Stará Boleslav.

Above left: Dana throws for gold at the Helsinki Olympics in 1952 and, right, celebrates her victory.

Below: the most famous kiss in Olympic history, moments after Emil had finished the Helsinki marathon.

Above left: Uherské Hradiště, 24 October 1948: fellow athletes pay their respects at Emil and Dana's wedding.

Above right: Emil and Dana in their hillside garden in Troja.

Below: towards the end of Emil's life, sharing a glass of wine in the house they built there.

Emil, in and around Wenceslas Square, denouncing the Warsaw Pact invasion that crushed the Prague Spring in August 1968.

'Great is the victory, but greater still is the friendship.'

Emil congratulates Alain Mimoun after the 1956 Olympic marathon in Melbourne, and the two friends relive their old rivalry in 1988.

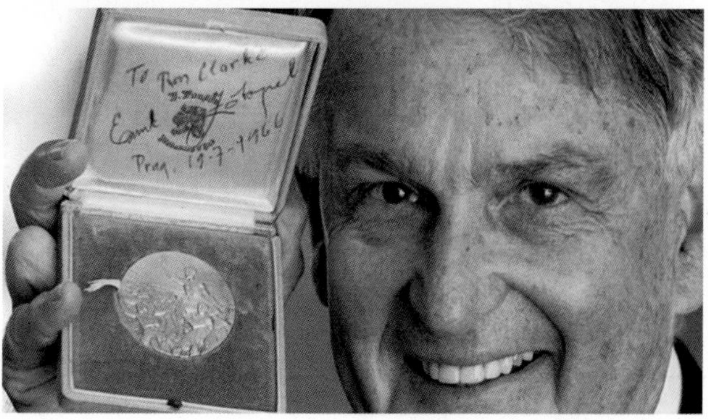

'Because you deserve it...'

Ron Clarke with the Olympic gold medal that Emil gave him in 1966.

affair so late in the day is a great disappointment. Many of us feel it has spoilt the Games before they have begun.' He stopped short, however, of apportioning blame for the events; or of invoking the 'Olympic truce'. Instead, he announced that he would compete only in the 10,000m, adding: 'And I've no chance of winning that because I'm too old.' Asked who was likely to beat him, he said, 'Probably the whole field.'

In the Olympic village, however, he seemed to be in good shape, and in good spirits. He had brought a case of Pilsner Urquell beer with him, for 'medicinal' purposes – he believed that nothing replaced a runner's lost body fluids so well. But he found himself sharing rather more of it with his teammates than he had intended. Despite the shadow of Hungary, and the ubiquitous 'sharp eyes', it was impossible not to feel thrilled at being at the Olympics, in such a strange, distant land.

Athletes from all nations were housed in the same complex this time, and Emil was once again the focal point for fraternisation between athletes from East and West. One hour-long track session saw him giving encouragement and advice in a variety of languages to athletes from several nations, with barely an interruption or a pause for breath. This prompted the *Melbourne Argus* to observe that 'the true Olympic spirit burned brighter than ever at the Village yesterday. And – fittingly – it was the "grand old man" of modern Olympiads, Emil Zátopek, who gave the lead.'

One of the runners who took advantage of Emil's generosity was a young American marathon runner called John J. Kelley. The US distance runners were initially nervous about approaching Emil: they felt that it would be presumptuous. But Nick Costes, the eldest of their party, eventually went over to say hello, and before long Kelley had been introduced, too. He ended up training with Emil most afternoons. He noticed that his hero was now running with a very slight limp. His main recollection, however, was that: 'He was a wonderful, affable fellow. He put me at ease instantly, and I marvelled at all the languages he spoke.' They remained friends for years afterwards, and would send one another cards. Kelley thought so highly of Emil that he named his first daughter Emily in his honour. Emil marked her birth by sending the Kelleys 'a beautiful cut glass bowl'.

But no number of friendly laps could alter the fact that Emil was way short of the kind of fitness he would need to be a medal contender for any of the track events. He tried to avoid journalists, and claimed that there was a special cupboard in the Czechoslovak team's quarters where he would hide whenever he heard unfamiliar footsteps in the corridor. By the time of the opening ceremony – where Emil raised eyebrows by high-spiritedly throwing his hat in the air as he passed the Duke of Edinburgh's box – he had conceded that he would not defend his 10,000m title either. He would save himself for the marathon instead, just over a week later.

On the first day of competition (23 November), he watched the 10,000m final from the stands, using a towel and a stick to signal to his Australian friend Dave Stephens whether or not he was on schedule for his target time of twenty-nine minutes. The ruse proved futile. Stephens couldn't keep the pace up, while Vladimir Kuts stormed irresistibly to gold in 28:45.6; all three medallists beat Emil's Olympic record from Helsinki. Five days later, Kuts knocked forty-seven seconds off Emil's Olympic record to win the 5,000m as well, destroying Gordon Pirie in the process, and causing several commentators to make observations to the effect that (as the *Canberra Times* put it): 'Kuts has proved conclusively that he has taken over the mantle of the great Zátopek as the outstanding stayer of world athletes.'

Emil hardly needed to read these reports: the observation made itself. He will not have welcomed it, no matter how sincere his congratulations to Kuts, with whom he was on friendly if not especially intimate terms. (Kuts was a more abrasive character than Emil, and was never likely to take over his mantle in terms of charm.) The fact that Dana managed only fourth place in the javelin final that same afternoon cannot have improved spirits in the Zátopek household. The marathon was three days later. It would be gratifying if Emil could win it.

But it was a palpably less confident Emil Zátopek who stood at the Olympic marathon starting line shortly after 3 p.m. on 1 December than the effortlessly invincible superman who had introduced himself to Jim Peters in Helsinki four years earlier.

True, he was among friends rather than strangers this time: Alain Mimoun, for example, who had belatedly decided to try the marathon after finishing a disappointing twelfth in the 10,000m; Les Perry; John J. Kelley; or the Soviets, Ivan Filin and Albert Ivanov, whom he had been advising in Moscow. But he must have sensed that, for all the reverence and affection in which he was held, he no longer instilled fear. He was a hero, but he was beatable.

To spectators who were close enough, it was obvious that Emil had aged. He wore a cap to protect his increasingly bald head from the sun, but the face beneath had the tired, stretched look of an athlete in the twilight of his career. There were even those who felt that he had 'allowed himself to be persuaded against his better judgement to run'.

Emil also had the disadvantage from which all but first-time marathon runners suffer: he knew what it would be like. He knew what he had been through the last time. The conscious mind forgets; deep down, though, the body remembers the ordeal, and dreads repeating it.

This time it would be worse. The temperature was officially reported at 30°C – 12° hotter than in Helsinki – and some measured it at nearer 35°C. Several runners had coated their shoulders in Vaseline to protect them against the sun; many wore hats. Few could doubt that, as the race headed out into the open road and the afternoon's heat accumulated, the torture would come from the conditions as much as the pace. This was the kind of weather that did for Pheidippides.

This must have been what Emil had in mind when he – allegedly – uttered the famous words: 'Men, today we die a little.' I say 'allegedly' because, despite the large number of reputable works in which this remark is quoted, I have not been able to identify a primary source in which it is reported in this precise form. Even if the accepted phrasing is apocryphal, however, I make no apology for celebrating it. Emil certainly said something along those lines; and it is hard to think of a neater encapsulation of his spirit: his cheerful camaraderie; his dry humour; and his slightly bonkers bravado in the face of the agonies of his sport. It was also, in context, a starkly accurate prognosis.

The race began oddly, with the Olympic marathon's only ever false start. They set off correctly at the second attempt, at 3.13 p.m.; circled the track two and a half times; and headed off into the hot afternoon. There were forty-six runners from twenty-three nations. A broken green line – an Olympic first – had been painted on to the tarmac to guide them. Paavo Kotila of Finland and Arap Sum Kanuti of Kenya were the early leaders. Emil was content to hang back, conserving his energy and hoping that the fast starters would eventually come back to him. But when Mimoun hung back with him, Emil revealed what he really felt about his chances: 'Alain,' he told him, 'I am not good. Don't stay with me.' Mimoun hesitated: sticking with Emil, or trying to, had for so long proved the best way of making sure he was in with a chance of a medal at the end of a big race. But Emil insisted – and, in so doing, proved beyond doubt that friendship in sport mattered more to him than stealing a march over a rival.

They ran past palm trees and parked cars, along wide, prosperous streets. Some runners varied the side of the road they ran on to take advantage of the occasional scraps of shelter; others stuck to the shortest route. The crowds were perhaps a little thinner than in Helsinki; no doubt the heat deterred a few. But Emil was as warmly applauded as anyone.

After 8.6km they passed a railway bridge and joined Dandenong Road. It was a thoroughfare that few of them were ever likely to forget.

The first 1,500m or so were uphill. By then, Kotila was leading by two seconds from Mimoun, Filin and Ivanov. Emil was seventeen seconds back in eleventh place. One television commentator was already describing him as 'in trouble', but he was in contention.

After 12.2km they left Dandenong Road – but not for long. A mile and a half later they were back on it, once again heading uphill. The straight single-carriageway road seemed to go on for ever, bare and largely featureless. The only shadow came from the sporadic groups of spectators on the roadside. The sun beat down viciously, the heat rebounding from the hot tarmac, and still the slope continued upwards.

At fifteen kilometres, Mimoun was just ahead; Emil was still eleventh but now only five seconds behind. He could see that others were struggling with the heat, pausing to douse themselves with water at the drinks stations, and the sight may have encouraged him. But he, too, was struggling – with, among other things, his shoes. The heat of the asphalt was melting the glue that stuck the crêpe soles to the leather uppers, causing the crêpe to disintegrate into little pellets. The agony, stretched out over the best part of two hours, must have been unspeakable: Emil's room-mate, the triple-jumper Martin Řehák, was horrified when he saw Emil's raw, bloodied feet afterwards. For Emil, the memory of gluing so many thousands of soles and uppers together himself can only have made the experience more frustrating.

There was nothing for it but to continue, rolling and slipping slightly with every step. It was too hot to go much faster anyway. This was a contest of resilience rather than speed. But Alain Mimoun, the veteran war hero who had won so many silver medals as Emil's 'shadow', was resilient, too, and around the halfway point he sensed his chance. First to reach the short downhill stretch before the turnaround, he put on a sudden spurt, turned, powered back up to the crest of the hill and then strode out confidently on the long downhill return journey while his rivals were still negotiating the turn. His lead was soon unassailable: by twenty-five kilometres he was fifty seconds ahead.

Emil had nothing to keep him going but pride, and perhaps the odd scrap of hope. He had seen the demoralising sight of Mimoun speeding homewards while he was still heading outwards, but he could not be sure that the Frenchman was keeping it up. Meanwhile, he was moving up the field: to sixth place at twenty-five kilometres and fifth at thirty. Nine runners had already dropped out, while others were going backwards. But as for the kind of sustained attack that he would need to make a dent in Mimoun's lead – you had only to look at him to see that the strength was not there.

Marathon runners can imagine for themselves the remainder of the ordeal: an hour or so of constant struggle, teetering on the edge of despair without ever quite succumbing, that niggling hint of old injury becoming steadily harder to ignore. From the outside there is nothing to see but a glassy-eyed runner, banging out the same monotonous pattern of largely identical strides. Inside it is an epic drama of suffering, courage and endurance; even if, from a competitive point of view, it is a failure. At thirty kilometres, Emil was two minutes twenty-two seconds behind Mimoun; by the end, that gap had almost doubled. The lowest point, from Emil's perspective, was being overtaken with a couple of kilometres to go. He tried to respond as Korea's Lee Chang-hoon passed him, but he was no longer able to accelerate even a little bit.

By the time Emil reached the stadium, at 5.41 p.m., Mimoun had been waiting at the finish for several minutes, applauding each new arrival in turn: Mihalič, Karvonen, Lee, Kawashima. But everyone could see that he was still looking for someone. Then Emil appeared on the track – and was cheered as deafeningly as if he had won. Stubbornly keeping up his rhythm, he completed his final Olympic lap, perhaps more dead than alive; then crossed the line, stepped off the track, gratefully accepted the officials' proferred blanket, took off his cap and sank heavily to the ground. The fact that, at the age of thirty-four, he had beaten all but five of the world's forty-five top marathon runners (thirteen of whom failed to finish) – or that his Olympic record for this event, at least, remained intact – meant nothing. This was a man who had had enough.

Mimoun rushed over to him. 'Emil, congratulate me,' he said. 'I am an Olympic champion.' After all those years as Emil's shadow, he was now the hero in his own right. 'Emil turned and looked at me,' Mimoun recalled in later life, 'as if he were waking from a dream.' He got to his feet, took two steps backward, 'snapped to attention', took off his cap and saluted him. Then he embraced him. 'For me,' said Mimoun, 'that was better than a medal.'

If you like Olympic moments that make your eyes prick with tears, seek this one out. You will see from the brief footage that Emil really does look as delighted as if he had won himself. 'Great is the victory,' he is supposed to have said, 'but the friendship of all is greater.' I'm not sure that he really did. But if you see the two old warriors smiling and embracing, suffused with joy in Mimoun's triumph and in their long bond of respect, love and shared suffering, you will understand what that old Olympic saying means.

Later on there were questions from journalists. Emil's face was etched with weariness and defeat; it was hard to believe that he had crossed the Helsinki finishing line with that radiant, boyish smile only four years earlier. When he told journalists, 'It was too much for an old man,' he said what many were thinking.

Later still, he was more specific: 'I realised I was licked at the halfway point. I started confident that I could make a good race of it, but I suddenly realised about all that was left was to go out like a champion. That was when I decided it was no use breaking my neck with any more speed and risk collapse . . .

'This was my last race.'

14

The ambassador

It wasn't, of course. No champion surrenders his greatness so lightly. But it was the beginning of the end.

In the short term there was plenty of time for Emil to reconsider his position: not just in the final days of the Games, when Percy Cerutty enjoyed showing him round the local zoological and botanical gardens, but on the journey home. A bizarre outburst of Cold War paranoia meant that, instead of flying home as planned on a French aeroplane, the Czechoslovak team, supposedly fearing sabotage, travelled instead by sea. They shared the ship, the *Gruzia*, with the Soviet team and a large cargo of live sheep. The extra mouths to feed were bad news for the sheep – lamb dominated the menu – and the overcrowding caused ill feeling among both Czechoslovaks and Soviets. An angry Vladimir Kuts got drunk three days in a row and, when reprimanded for his behaviour by a political officer, suggested that they resolve the matter with their fists. Emil took a more placid approach. He spent an hour a day running around the deck, and suggested to Dana that they treat the voyage as a second honeymoon.

It was hardly idyllic. The toilet paper ran out halfway through the three-week journey: everyone was made to contribute diaries and notebooks to meet the common need. There were typhoons when they passed Japan, and when they landed at Vladivostok the temperature was -32°C. By the time they got home, via the Trans-Siberian Express and Moscow, Prague was in the grip of a severe winter as well, and Emil, several pounds heavier, could certainly be said to have cooled off.

He announced in March that in future he would compete only domestically. In fact, in the course of 1957 he ran nine times at 5,000m and ten at 10,000m, with a couple of cross-country races thrown in for good measure; the venues included Oslo, Stockholm, Athens, Krakow, Moscow and Berlin. But these appearances were very much a coda to Emil's career. There were no big international meetings, no showdowns with the new giants of his disciplines. He won just over half his races, in times that were respectable rather than world-beating. It kept him in shape, though, and the cross-countries, in November, helped set him up for his final famous victory.

This took place just over a year after his agonies in Melbourne. Patxi Alcorta, a Spanish journalist, race organiser and bar owner, persuaded the Czechoslovak sports federation (now called the Československý svaz tělesné výchovy and referred to from now on as the ČSTV) to send a couple of athletes to Spain for the prestigious cross-country race in San Sebastián, in the Basque region close to the French border. Emil was sent with the young Miroslav Jurek, escorted by an official called Jan Jirka, an old friend. They flew to Paris, then caught a train. From the moment they crossed the Spanish border, they were mobbed by fans; even the customs officials were interested only in securing Emil's autograph. The fact that the visiting Czechoslovaks were Communists, while Spain was still ruled by the Fascist General Franco, does not seem to have bothered anyone. The Basques felt that Emil was one of them.

When the party reached San Sebastián, the rocky coastal town was in the grip of Zátopek-mania. An estimated 50,000 spectators – getting on for half the population – turned out to see the race, over a hilly twelve-kilometre course on a cold, windy day.

It was a world-class field. Britain's George Knight – the fastest man in the world over 10,000m in 1957 – was favourite, with France's Hahmoud Ameur also fancied, along with the promising Jurek. Emil responded to the threat by running aggressively from the start, as if he were still in his prime. There were five big laps to run, and for part of each one the wind gusted directly into the runners' faces. Emil, whose preparations had included hundreds of 200m uphill repetitions in heavy boots, chose those sections to crank up the pace mercilessly, turning the race into a test of physical and mental toughness. One by one, his rivals dropped off, until only Ameur and Jurek were still in contention. With 2,000m to go Ameur took the lead, but Emil responded imperiously. In the words of the next day's report in *The Times*: 'The old master produced a relentless burst of speed in the final straight.'

His emphatic victory was met with celebrations that even Emil may have found disconcerting. The rejoicing Basques chaired him on their shoulders, threw him gourds of wine, kitted him out with a beret and took him to Alcorta's bar, the Iru Txuli, where, in keeping with tradition, he was made to do a stint as a barman before being invited to celebrate long into the night.

At some point – the accounts are a little confused – someone tried to present Emil with a puppy. (Alcorta was also a dog breeder.) Emil demurred, partly because it would have been illegal to transport a dog into France. But when, the next day, the train carrying the exhausted Czechoslovaks crossed back over the Pyrenees, there at Hendaye station on the French side of the border was an old Basque woman with a basket which she presented to Emil. Inside was the little white puppy.

Emil didn't have the heart to refuse a second time, and so his new companion, whom he christened Pedro, accompanied him for the rest of the journey, hidden in his kitbag. Jirka, who was supposed to be keeping a sharp eye on the athletes' behaviour, turned a blind eye instead, even during the awkward moment when they were approaching Czechoslovak customs and Emil kept whispering to Pedro to keep quiet. 'But,' Jirka objected later, 'the dog didn't even speak Czech.'

He soon learnt what it sounded like, though, becoming a valued if anarchic member of the Zátopek household who was particularly devoted to Dana. An Andalusian terrier, he was bred to hunt waterfowl, and would often leap in uninvited when he saw someone taking a bath. Years later, travel commitments forced Emil and Dana to give Pedro away to friends, the Rašíns, but by then they were firm dog-lovers, and they subsequently obtained several other puppies from Alcorta, for themselves and their friends.

The gift of Pedro may have had more significance than the Basques realised. The visit to Spain seems to have coincided with – or been preceded by – another rocky patch in the Zátopek marriage, and Emil was reported to be reluctant to go back to Czechoslovakia: not for political reasons but because Spain somehow felt less complicated. Talked out of this, he was said to have asked if, on their return, he could be taken straight to the training retreat at Stará Boleslav instead of going home. But Pedro, of course, made such a plan impossible; and, like many a puppy before and since, he seems to have been a healing influence.

The fact that such an influence was needed may come as a surprise to some. Emil and Dana's relationship is generally presented as an idyllic love story. In fact, it had more ups and downs than is usually suggested; and the decade that followed Emil's last Olympic race may have been one of the more troubled periods. One obvious source of tension was the fact that, while Emil's competitive career was all but over, Dana's emphatically wasn't. She felt stronger than ever, had her eye on the 1960 Olympics in Rome, and was living and training – and travelling – accordingly.

Another issue, which would manifest itself more clearly as the next decade unfolded, was the couple's inability to have children. The problem may have originated with a bout of peritonitis suffered by Dana during a trip to Poland in 1945. They both adored children, and would have loved to have had their own; and Dana, in particular, was distraught to find that they could not. Emil tried to comfort her, telling her: 'Do you think that the human race will die out, just because we do not have children?' But such sorrows are not so easily dispelled, and it seems likely that the issue contributed for a long time to a niggling sense of dissatisfaction with their lives. In the long run, perhaps the shared pain brought them together; in the short term it may have done the opposite.

Eventually, according to Dana, their relationship became 'more like a friendship'; I suspect that this long transition was more painful for Emil than for Dana. There were intimate outside relationships, and distressing jealousies, on both sides. Dana is reluctant to discuss the details – and it would be wrong for me to invade her privacy further. But she concedes that 'of course there were incidents. It happens in life, once in a while, that someone finds themselves liking somebody. Things like that happen.'

Yet the special bond between them – that peculiar shared outlook based on playfulness, warmth and a sense of infinite possibility – always brought them back together. And, 'as time went on, our relationship grew. We went through hard moments as well as good moments, and the experience made us stronger.'

Meanwhile, there was nothing that either Dana or Pedro could do to alter the fact that, as a competitive runner, Emil had nowhere left to go. Five weeks after his San Sebastián triumph, on 6 March, he announced his retirement. 'I can't run until my death,' he said. 'I want to stop racing and devote myself entirely to the Army.' The world believed him this time, and marked his departure from the competitive stage with a fanfare of praise. In the words of the *Manchester Guardian*, 'He departs once more a winner and can rest as one of the immortals of his sport.' There would be no better time to go; and if he had any sense at all there would be no coming back.

You have only to think for a moment about the enormity of Emil's commitment to his sport – the years of demented, all-consuming dedication – to see what a gap this must have left in his life. In eighteen years he had run more than 50,000 miles – the equivalent of twice round the earth – and at least half of that had been at fast racing speed. His life had been a blur of championships, records, medals – and now all that was over. His fellow athletes, including his wife, were making plans for the European Championships in Stockholm that summer, but he could only look back, not forward. In fact, there had been voices in the ČSTV suggesting that he should make one final appearance in Stockholm, but he was wise enough to resist. To symbolise the finality of his decision, he hung a pair of his running shoes from a nail in the wall of his living room. He knew that his body could not cope with the required degree of intensity of training any more. The question was, could his mind cope without it?

It is hard to believe that he really relished the prospect of focusing on his military career; at one point shortly after his retirement he talked about becoming an adventurer instead, joining the celebrated writers Jiří Hanzelka and Miroslav Zikmund on their travels around the world. Following a brief spell after the Olympics as a trainer at the Miroslav Tyrš military school, Emil was moved in 1958 to the Ministry of Defence, where, once again, he was supposed to oversee the promotion of physical fitness in the army. This was a pleasant and comfortable place to work, in Prague's prestigious Dejvice district and within jogging distance of the Strahov stadium, with regular excursions to pursue his brief in military installations across the country. It was hardly an adventure, though, and sometimes Emil's continuing public duties as a propaganda icon must have felt like a welcome diversion.

He seems to have been well-liked by his colleagues, and he clearly enjoyed the physical disciplines of a soldier's life: he once said that 'to be in the military in peacetime is heaven on earth'. From now on, however, he would be largely desk-bound. His San Sebastián victory had earned him yet another promotion: this time to full colonel. He does not seem to have taken naturally to the dignity of the role. He once went swimming in the Vltava in Prague, in defiance of regulations, and was ordered out at gunpoint by some soldiers. He retrieved his uniform from behind a bush, dressed hastily, and was amused to see the expression on the soldiers' faces when they realised that they had threatened a senior officer.

On another occasion, in 1959, arriving for a spell overseeing army athletes in Lipník nad Bečvou, he was escorted into a room full of conscripts who were watching one of their number demonstrate his ability to walk on his hands. The escorting officer called them sharply to attention, and the hand-stander responded by standing to attention upside down. Then he realised the seniority of the visitor and hastily righted himself. Emil put him at his ease by saying: 'I can do that too' – and proceeded to demonstrate.

Some years later, on a similar assignment at the Higher Training Institution of Artillery in Martin (in what is now Slovakia), Colonel Zátopek allowed himself to be diverted from his fitness inspection duties into a trip to the shops, a mile and a half away. A liaison officer, Václav Bednář, escorted him. Emil insisted that they go on foot – but soon said: 'I can't walk this slowly. Let's jog.' They bought a huge, eighty-litre jar for Dana to make jam in. Bednář, already sweating heavily in his uniform, tried to summon an official car; but, he recalls: 'Emil flatly refused: "Don't call any car – we'll walk." I took one handle of the pot, but that was a serious mistake. Zátopek immediately ordered: "Captain, at the double, jog." I had no choice but to obey.' When they were close enough to the artillery school for soldiers to be watching, the order was revised. 'He said: "Come on, we will show these gawkers how we can sprint." I had to use the last part of my strength and join him. My colleagues teased me about it for years.'

Generally, Emil seemed more comfortable as a doer than as a giver of orders. Coaching athletes, he liked to jog along the track with them. Supervising marches, he was known to ask someone else to take over so that he could enjoy marching himself; supervising artillery exercises, he insisted at least once on having a go at firing a gun. Such eccentricities were harmless. But it seems reasonable to infer from them that, had it not been for his genius on the track, he might not have progressed so far in his military career. As one (early) internal report on his exercise of command observed: 'He is kind-hearted, has a soft nature, and is humble, talkative, sometimes childish, which is perhaps what makes him popular with his subordinates. But his command authority suffers as a result.'

There was also the question of politics. The armed forces were a stronghold of Communist orthodoxy. Most commanders had sworn oaths of loyalty to socialism and the Soviet Union, and officers were regularly assessed for ideological soundness. The annual reports on Emil preserved in his military service record painstakingly log his supposed views. He tends to score better on Marxist philosophy than on the workings of the Communist Party – but it is the tone of scrutiny that is most revealing: 'In political terms he is quite mature, applies his theoretical knowledge in practice, and can discuss his opinions. He is capable of being directed by and promoting the policy of the Party and government . . .' You half expect them to add that Emil has been learning to cut out basic shapes with scissors.

In such an environment Emil had no choice but to go through the motions of being an enthusiast for the regime. His tireless public speaking helped bolster that impression. Yet he unquestionably had doubts by now – and it is striking that, as the 1960s unfold, those official assessments of him take on a more critical tone: 'Sometimes he discusses questions which he has not yet understood completely. Sometimes he adopts the wrong opinion on a certain matter, which he finds difficult to drop . . .' Years of travelling had opened his eyes to the fact that life beyond the Iron Curtain was not all bad, while life in the Soviet empire was not all good; he could see, as he put it later, 'the progress in the world – and return home to a country where time has stopped'. He knew better than to express dissent openly, but like many young men who had felt passionate about Communism at the outset he was no longer an uncritical admirer. He had learnt, however, like most Czechoslovaks, to adjust his expansiveness according to the company he was in.

What he couldn't adjust was his individualism. He watched his words, and avoided direct challenges to authority, but he was still a maverick – a one-off. He had, in the words of one StB informer's report, 'peculiar' views on a range of subjects. And for all his efforts to conform, the fact remained that he thought – knew – that he was special. How could he have felt otherwise? Everywhere he went, people clamoured to see him, to talk to him, to touch him. It was like being a one-man forerunner to

The Beatles; and, as he had grown used to it, so he had developed a sense that, where he was concerned, otherwise inflexible rules could be bent.

One famous example of this took place in the aftermath of the Melbourne Olympics. Olga Fikotová, who had won gold for Czechoslovakia in the discus, had begun a romance at the Games with the US hammer thrower Harold Connolly, also a gold medallist. There were those in the Party, and perhaps even in the Olympic team, who saw this as little short of treason. Others, including Emil and Dana, saw it as a charming expression of the Olympic ideal.

After the Games, Connolly came to Prague to seek Fikotová's hand in marriage. He stayed at a hotel but Emil and Dana lent Fikotová the keys to their flat, so that they had a safe place to meet. The obstacles to this unprecedented cross-Curtain union seemed insuperable, even when Connolly wrote personally to Antonín Zápotocký (Klement Gottwald's successor as president). Then Emil interceded. He saw the president at a conference on sports administration in the Smetana Concert Hall in Prague's Municipal House and took the opportunity to ask him to give the marriage his blessing. President Zápotocký insisted that it was not his business; none the less, it seemed to make a difference. The next day Fikotová was invited to an audience at which the president agreed to 'put in a kind word', and shortly afterwards a licence was issued. Tens of thousands of people turned out to see the couple married in Prague in March 1957. There were three separate ceremonies, in the Old Town Hall, in a Catholic church and in a Protestant church; Emil and Dana were witnesses at all three.

A more daring example of this independent spirit took place in 1962. Two years earlier, Ladislav Kořán, Emil's old training partner, had been released from concentration camp under a general amnesty. Unable to find work, and shunned by many former friends and associates, he continued to work at Jáchymov in a private capacity, as an electrical engineer. Sometimes, though, he visited Prague, and on this occasion, in early August, he went to see the European Rowing Championships taking place on the Vltava. He noticed Emil among the spectators on the starting line but stood well away for fear of embarrassing him. (Just a few weeks earlier, an old friend had run away from him at an athletics meeting in Brno.) 'I was maybe thirty, forty metres away. But Emil saw me, and he ran over. He embraced me and said: "Láďa, I am so pleased to see you. We were all afraid you wouldn't make it." It was not very smart of him – there were StB people everywhere.' It seems hard to believe that such small actions can once have had such large significance, but they did; and when Kořán told me about it more than fifty years later, there was still a catch in his voice.

It is possible that Emil was bolder than most because he missed the thrills of competition – including the satisfaction of taking those risks under pressure that separate the champions from the also-rans. His legs might be worn out, but his spirit was not. He was not yet ready to sink into obscurity.

Yet that is the role that life seemed to have lined up for him. In 1960, for example, the Zátopeks travelled again to the Olympic Games, this time in Rome. Dana, three weeks short of her thirty-eighth birthday, threw magnificently to win an unexpected silver. Emil – despite training in the Olympic village with Western athletes such as Bruce Tulloh, Ron Laird and Colin Young – was only a spectator. A few weeks later, the Zátopeks were guests of honour at a reception in Zlín, where Dana had many friends. When the master of ceremonies presented them, he raised a big laugh with an introduction that reversed the order of priorities that Dana had grown all too used to over the years. He began: 'Welcome, Merited Master of Sport Dana Zátopková, world record holder, winner of two Olympic medals' – and continued, slowly and at great length, to list all of Dana's achievements. Emil, meanwhile, sat smiling in his chair, fidgeting and looking increasingly awkward as the list continued. Finally, as if as an afterthought, the speaker added: 'And I welcome her husband too.'

It was the kind of leg-pulling that was bread and butter to the Zátopeks' bantering relationship, but I doubt that Emil enjoyed it quite as much as Dana. He knew that it would be many years before his existing fame really began to subside – but how would he ever earn fresh renown? After rising to so many impossible challenges, he needed fresh worlds to conquer.

He found one, of sorts, in an unlikely place. On a sunny Saturday afternoon early in 1961, he and Dana decided to go for a walk. The area they chose was what is now the wealthy Prague suburb of Troja. In those days it was countryside, beyond the final tram stop at Pelc-Tyrolka, with little in the way of development apart from a zoo and a grand estate (the Kazanka). They walked for a while along the riverside, then turned northwards until they found themselves on a lane that was little more than a track. It was called Nad Kazankou. There were a few houses on the southern side; the steep slopes on the northern side were divided into plots and gardens but were largely overgrown.

The sun was shining, and the hill was bright with bloom; the yellow forsythias were particularly brilliant. Emil stopped suddenly and said: 'It would be great to have a plot like this here. I can see a fire, sausages, and a group of friends . . .' Then they carried on walking.

But the thought wouldn't go away. By Monday, it had become a plan. Emil went to the municipal council office in Holešovice and made tentative enquiries. Some time later, news came back of someone – a Mr Brejcha from Břevnov – who had inherited a plot at Nad Kazankou from his grandmother and was so fed up with the resulting red tape that he wanted to sell it. Emil and Dana went to see him – and in due course they found themselves the owners of an acre or so of impenetrable wasteland on a steep slope five miles from the centre of Prague.

They were soon doubting the wisdom of their purchase. But they were not short of strength and stamina, and for Emil, in particular, hacking and digging away at their patch of sloping jungle became as all-consuming a passion as his interval training had once been.

They had no plans at first beyond making a nice garden for themselves, but a week or so of frenetic excavation produced an interesting discovery: a tiny garden house or shed, buried beneath the bushes; it even had a small cellar. Emil attached a board to the door, with the words 'Santa Puelo Pub' painted on it in red. Clearing the wilderness became a social as well as a physical activity. Friends from near and far were quick to lend a hand, and to bring gifts for the garden. Half a century later you could still see a blue spruce smuggled from her homeland by the Austrian athlete Erika Strasser; and the pines brought from Wallachia by the Tempír brothers (then leading athletics coaches); and the walnut planted by Jarda Kovář, the high-jumper; and, biggest of all, the cedar of Lebanon given by Herbert Schade.

It would be more than a decade before the project was finished, partly because the mission expanded, and partly because there were regular interruptions. Dana continued to travel to sporting events even after retiring from international competition in 1962. (She had left her magazine job after the Helsinki Olympics and was now employed by the ČSTV, training young athletes at the Strahov stadium. Unlike Emil, she turned out to have a talent as a coach.) As for Emil, the fact that he was no longer competing had done little to diminish his perceived value as a diplomatic pawn.

His later years as a competitor had been increasingly marked by what could almost be described as state visits, and these continued after his retirement: sometimes initiated by the nation in question or, sometimes, set up by the Czechoslovak government. Emil and Dana spent the last three months of 1958 on a Far Eastern tour that took them, via Moscow, to China (where Emil ran a post-retirement 10,000m), Korea and Vietnam (where he ran a 5,000m). Other such trips would follow: to Egypt, Tunisia, Syria, Cuba – seemingly any part of the world with which the regime wished to establish or maintain good relations. Some people joked that Emil's hosts confused him with President Zápotocký. It is not inconceivable that this was true.

The most disruptive of all these missions began in October 1963, when Emil and Dana were dispatched to Indonesia for a whole year. It was a pleasant enough experience, with light coaching duties and a comfortable expatriate lifestyle, and Emil, characteristically, learnt the language. He would get up at 4 a.m. to learn words from a dictionary. But neither Emil nor Dana seems to have been particularly inspired by the adventure, and Emil was later scathing about the folly of Czechoslovakia giving aid to such regimes. Emil, tormented by mosquitoes when he sat out on the balcony in the evenings, even tried taking up smoking, briefly, to deter them. The experiment was not a success; but the fact that he even thought of it suggests a certain mental restlessness.

No one could accuse Emil – or Dana – of being incurious about foreign cultures. But the place that enthused them most was that patch of hillside in Troja. On returning to Czechoslovakia, they set about improving it with renewed enthusiasm. Not only that: they expanded their mission. Rather than contenting themselves with a garden and a shed, they decided, they would build themselves a house – just as Emil's father had done forty years earlier.

This was an enormous undertaking: a huge amount of clearance and levelling was required before they could begin; and they intended to do it all without professional help. But there was no hurry, and the difficulty of the challenge was what made it enjoyable. Emil held the record for shifting forty barrel-loads of earth in a day, whereas Dana could manage only twenty-eight. Later on, Dana would come into her own, with an unmatchable performance throwing pebbledash on to the walls. 'Now, at last, Dana's javelin training is paying off,' joked Emil.

The author Ota Pavel, one of many friends who were persuaded to lend a hand, wrote a memorable account of running to the plot with Emil from his workplace in Dejvice, before struggling to keep up with Emil's astonishing work rate. 'After two hours,' he reported, 'I had flickering in front of my eyes . . .' Emil was way past his physical best by now. An army test in 1963, shortly before his forty-first birthday, recorded surprisingly ordinary figures: he could run 100m in 13.9 seconds, throw a grenade forty metres, and run a 3,000m cross-country course in eleven minutes thirty seconds. But he could still bring a breathtaking intensity to everyday tasks – and, no less characteristically, a slightly crazed creativity. Many uproarious evenings were spent arguing over their plans around the campfire with friends. As it grew, the building acquired, like most of Emil and Dana's possessions, a name: 'Domeček' ('little house'); and, in due course, its own distinctive character. When the time came to think about insulation, the Zátopeks opted for a new material of their own invention. They called it *Warmflaschenizolation*; a more prosaic description would be empty wine bottles set in concrete. Later still, Emil took great pride in a particularly complicated (and temperamental) stove that he had installed; other oddities included an old ship's bell, attached to the side of the house as a doorbell, which was a gift from František Šťastný, the motorcycling champion.

Of course, this was just one facet of the Zátopeks' life. They still had their jobs; and, not least, their busy social lives, being in demand not just among old friends but also, increasingly, in the fashionable Prague circles of intellectuals, artists, journalists and politicians. There were regular visits from former rivals from abroad, too; on one memorable occasion, in 1966, Herbert Schade, Gaston Reiff and Alain Mimoun all arrived simultaneously. Emil also kept in touch by letter with sporting friends around the world. There was something special about the friendship of athletes, he thought: 'You honour opponents in a different way than the friends in the street,' he explained once. The shared experience of 'a fight about who was better' remained 'deeper in the soul' than the everyday friendship of those 'who have not been through anything together'.

Emil and Dana had families and friends to keep in touch with in Moravia, too, although Emil's parents were both dead by now. Anežka had died in 1962 and František a year later. He was, according to one granddaughter, 'too sad to live without her'. But Emil continued to make regular visits to Kopřivnice, for school reunions and get-togethers with his surviving siblings. There were always excited crowds when he did so. 'People would come out on to their balconies,' says Jiří, Emil's nephew. 'He used to come down by train, all the way from Prague,' says Marie Vlachová, a former neighbour who was in the ninth grade with Emil, 'and he would be so tired, because everyone on the train wanted to talk to him, and he would find time for them all.' And then, in Kopřivnice, it would start all over again.

The globally celebrated superstar must have seemed a slightly unreal figure to the brothers and sister who had stayed behind. But Jiří (the brother), who had done a spell in the air force before returning to Kopřivnice to join Bohuš and Franta at Tatra, was certainly devoted to Emil, and the siblings' reunions appear to have been warm, usually culminating with all the brothers singing folk songs. 'They stayed close,' remembers Jiří's daughter, Dana. 'And they sang from the heart.'

Often, on such visits, Emil would stay with his old schoolfriend Jaromír Konůpka. Occasionally they would even retreat into the countryside together, with no more comforts than they had had when they were two hard-up schoolboys three decades earlier. It was a far cry from chatting with the president in Prague, but I think we can guess which Emil preferred. 'He always thought of himself as a Kopřivnice person,' says Konůpka. 'He remembered how we used to play in the woods together as children.' Such moments were the exception, though, and not the rule. No matter how much he might sometimes yearn for a simple, down-to-earth life, Emil could not erase his celebrity. He was a member of the privileged elite, and – it seemed – would always remain one.

His public speaking duties tailed off only slightly as the memory of his golden moments faded and younger athletes from far-off lands began to chip away at his dominance of the record books. His nephew remembers an address to the young people of Kopřivnice, in which Emil hammed up his Olympic adventures for their amusement. 'When he talked about the marathon,' says Jiří, 'he made it sound funny: "The Swede, Jansson, he was a giant, two heads taller than me, with legs as long as a toilet spider. I had to take three steps for each one of his . . ."' Jiří rocks with laughter as he imitates Emil's mock-scary voice.

Emil also had a regular but not-too-onerous slot as a speaker at the ROH Leningrad, a luxury hotel owned by the national trade union federation (Revoluční odborové hnutí) in Mariánské Lázně – Europe's most luxurious spa town. It was here that, in 1966, Emil heard that a local athlete, Hana Trejbalová, was seriously ill. Not yet nineteen, she was the national junior hurdling champion, but had suddenly developed cancer in her neck. (It has recently been suggested that she was a victim of early, reckless experiments by the Czechoslovak sporting establishment with anabolic steroids.) Emil and Dana repeatedly visited her in hospital in Plzeň; and attempted to ensure that she received the best possible specialist treatment. Emil left her a gift, a teddy bear, which she kept in her bed until her death later that year.

It is hard not to sense, somewhere below the surface of this period of relative calm in Emil's life, a faint but persistent throb of longing. 'It was my dream to give a good example to children and get them started,' Emil told an American journalist shortly before his seventieth birthday, 'but it was only a dream.' In the mid-1960s, that dream was still fresh, and it is possible that, while Dana came to terms with their lack of children, Emil began to feel it more keenly. 'He loved children very much,' said his friend Zdeněk Fator. 'He loved my son, and Jiří loved seeing him.' 'Our boys used to ask: "When is Mr Zátopek coming? We have so much fun with him,"' said another friend, Olga Lišková. Jaromír Konůpka said much the same about his children, and both he and his son (also Jaromír) reminisced delightedly about the time when they visited Emil in Prague, and Emil spent half the afternoon racing young Jaromír and his sister up Prague's first escalator, off Wenceslas Square. They used the up escalator while Emil used the downward one, and Emil in any case let them win; so, naturally, they insisted on repeating it again and again, until a large crowd had gathered to watch.

Others spoke of Emil exasperating his relatives, and countless Kopřivnice mothers, by disrupting his visits to the town with endless games of street football with the children who followed him around; and of his strange habit, when driving with children on board, of using his feet to steer – just to entertain them. 'It made the boys crazy with happiness,' said Olga Lišková. Emil's nephew Jiří has a comparable memory of being taken for a drive in Emil's smart Saab when he was six or seven years old. Emil let Jiří sit on his lap as he drove and then, to make things more fun, let Jiří drive. Half a century later, Jiří's jaw still drops at the memory of executing a left turn across a street full of traffic, with Emil apparently exercising no control at all.

'Perhaps it was just as well that we never had children,' Dana laughed, when we talked about such matters once. 'We would have argued all the time about how to bring them up. I would have wanted to give them rules about how to behave, while Emil would have wanted them to have no rules at all.'

She was speaking in the tone that she often uses about Emil: that kind of affectionate exasperation that develops through the decades of a long, mostly happy marriage. For a spouse, the habitual flouting of convention that the rest of us find so charming in Emil could be maddening – and yet still be charming. One day, for example, Dana decided to sweep the floor and noticed something odd – and familiar. Closer investigation revealed that Emil had been using his DIY skills. The old broom handle had broken; so, rather than buy a new broom, he had improvised a new handle by using the wooden javelin with which Dana had won her Olympic gold medal in 1952. She still has it today, and brings it out proudly, surprisingly small and light compared with a modern javelin: a permanent memento of her greatest sporting moment, and of her husband's restless, slightly deranged ingenuity.

Ota Pavel, the writer who knew Emil best, thought his great gift was his ability 'to think how to do it differently. He uses the word "if" . . .' There were some rules he respected: those of hospitality, for example, or fair play. But the limiting rules of unthinking convention were, as he saw it, there to be challenged and, if appropriate, ignored.

There are obvious drawbacks to such an outlook if you are, say, an army officer, or if you live in a society where ideological conformity is rigidly enforced. But Emil – who since January 1967 had been deputy to the head of the physical educational unit of the Defence Ministry's Operative and Combat Readiness department – had convinced himself that, where he was concerned, the drawbacks could be overcome. He was right, for now; and the habit of doing things as he saw fit became an ingrained feature of his life. In March 1967, the British sports journalist Neil Allen met Emil at a reception at the British Embassy in Prague. Emil took him for a drive around the city afterwards, reminiscing happily (in English) about times gone by. The encounter resulted in a much-quoted article by Allen in *The Times*, including Emil's famous remark about the 1948 Olympics being 'as if the sun had come out'. Emil also talked about how stupid he had been in the 5,000m at that Games, and about how much more competitive distance running had since become; and about how he would still try to be a champion if he were young again. 'You have something inside you which makes you always try, however hard it may seem.' Strictly speaking, Emil should have given a report of this encounter to the secret police; but I can find no record of his having done so. Luckily, Allen was not so negligent, and wrote it up for *Times* readers.

Let us end this chapter, and this phase of Emil's life, with perhaps the most revealing snapshot of all, in which the restless nobility of his spirit finally found the gesture that it craved. It was the summer of 1966. At the request of the ČSTV, Emil wrote to the great Australian runner Ron Clarke, inviting him to compete in a meeting in Prague. Clarke had by then redrawn the boundaries of distance running scarcely less dramatically than Emil had in his prime. He had set fifteen of his eventual total of seventeen world records – twelve of them in a forty-four-day period the previous summer – and had obliterated most of Emil's in the process. He had just lowered his 5,000m time to 13:16.6 – more than forty seconds faster than Emil's best. As for his 10,000m record, set the previous summer, it was 27:39.4 – a minute and a quarter faster than Emil's supposedly superhuman 28:54.2 in 1954. Clarke had, however, never won a gold medal, either at the Olympics or at the Commonwealth Games. For an athlete who towered so spectacularly over his sport, it was a startling and rankling omission.

Clarke cancelled some engagements to come to Prague – 'I wasn't going to miss that opportunity' – and from the moment he landed Emil was the perfect host. 'He met me on the steps of the plane,' said Clarke, still enthusing about the experience when I spoke to him a few months before his death in 2015. 'He just waved us straight through customs and drove me to his home rather than the hotel. We had a great chat, then he took me to the hotel, by the track.' Clarke won his race, over 3,000m, cheered on by Emil. Then, at six o'clock the next morning, Emil picked him up from his hotel and drove him to Stará Boleslav.

'It was a beautiful forest, and we did a huge workout, talking and chatting, and he showed me all the training things he did.' There was a television cameraman there to record the event, but he left his lens cap on: the few images that survive were taken on a camera borrowed from Ludvík Liška, caretaker of the athletes' villa. But Clarke wasn't interested in the visual record: he was absorbed in the moment, and the thrill of running with Emil Zátopek. 'We just clicked – I felt very comfortable with him.' Emil was eight years into his retirement, but Clarke later wrote that it had been one of the most demanding sessions he had done for a long time.

Later on, Emil took him shopping, to buy a souvenir of Prague crystal for his wife. 'It was the middle of the day by then, and in the centre of town it was very busy. Emil drove to this big store and just parked right outside it. This traffic policeman stormed over – and as soon as he got within recognition distance his face transformed: "Emil! Emil!" Emil signed his book for him, and we left the car and went in.'

They couldn't find what they wanted, so they came out – to where the policeman was guarding the car. Emil did a highly improper U-turn, and they repeated the process at another store – complete with another traffic policeman, initially angry and then starstruck. This time, when they came out, the car had gone – but Emil just whistled and the policeman brought it back. 'Any sportsman who can do that,' said Clarke, 'anywhere in the world, has made it.'

Finally, it was time to leave. Emil drove Clarke to the airport, shepherded him through customs and passport control and accompanied him all the way up the steps to the plane. As he said goodbye, he pressed a small package, roughly wrapped in brown paper and string, into Clarke's hand, and said words to the effect of: 'Look after this, because you deserve it.'

Clarke said nothing, thinking that perhaps he was being asked to smuggle something out to the West. He kept a close grip on the package until they were well outside Czech airspace. Even then, he wasn't sure what to do. Should he declare it at customs in London, where he was changing flights? He resolved not to open it. Then, at last, with the plane taxiing on the runway just after landing at Heathrow, 'curiosity overcame me'.

At this point, the accounts get blurred. The way Clarke told it to me, forty-eight years later, he was sitting in the front of the plane. In an account given much nearer the event, he retreated to the toilet. Either way, he was sitting alone and unobserved as he unwrapped a small box. Inside was an Olympic gold medal – one of the three that Emil had won in Helsinki. Emil had signed the inside of the lid, adding (in the limited space available): 'To Ron Clarke, Prag. 19-7-1966'.

For a moment, realising what it was, he felt 'overwhelming excitement'. And then (reverting here to the earlier account) he understood what it meant – and: 'I sat on that lavatory seat and wept.'

Like all the best Zátopek stories, this one has been endlessly retold and 'improved'. The most widely repeated revision places the story two years later, in late 1968. This is impossible, for all sorts of reasons, and, as it happens, not true. But you can see the attraction. The 1968 version finds Clarke – who almost killed himself making one last desperate bid to win a gold of his own, at altitude, at the Mexico City Olympics – at the lowest point in his life, and Emil (as we will see) at his own moment of desperate crisis; and the gift thus becomes an act of magnificent selflessness and compassion. It is a neater story this way.

Yet the true story carries its own, stranger message. By 1966, Clarke had missed out on an Olympic medal only once. He was not in desperate need of Emil's generosity. If there was such a need, it must have been Emil's. Perhaps he felt his spirit smothered by middle-aged normality; perhaps he craved a gesture with which he could once again express his generosity of soul, and affirm that, if he chose, he was still capable of greatness. Or perhaps – in keeping with a world view that his nephew Jiří summarised with the sentence 'If you are happy, I am happy' – he just wanted to lighten Clarke's life. The gesture was no less great for that.

Clarke became a permanent convert to the Zátopekian ideal of sporting friendship, and spent the best part of a half-century thereafter 'trying to tell people what a good man Emil Zátopek was'. He rarely did so more eloquently than in an article he wrote for *Athletics Weekly* in 1987. Describing the moment when he opened Emil's gift, Clarke wrote: 'I thought back to the words he said as he passed it across to me, which at the time I did not understand. "Because you deserved it," he said. I wish I had.'

Then he added: 'I do know that no one cherishes any gift more than I do, my only Olympic gold medal, and not because of what it is but because of the man whose spirit it represents.'

After a brief spell in a museum on Australia's Gold Coast, the medal is now back in the hands of Clarke's family. Contrary to popular belief, there is no identifying inscription on the medal itself. You cannot even tell which race Emil won it for.

None the less, it is the noblest Olympic medal of them all.

15

Spring fever

Unlike the Arab Spring of 2011, which spread like a series of summer wildfires, the Prague Spring of 1968 really was spring-like in its dynamics. It began imperceptibly, as a thaw does. By the time most people realised that it was happening, it had been in progress for ages.

Some historians trace its beginnings to the adoption, in 1960, of a new constitution, which declared the 'building of socialism' complete and proclaimed a new mission to create an 'advanced socialist society'. Others point to the final abolition of the concentration camp network, in 1961; or to the destruction, in 1962, of that giant statue of Stalin, five-and-a-half years in the making, that had towered over central Prague from Letná since 1955. Antonín Novotný, who succeeded Antonín Zápotocký as president in 1957, was a hardliner in most respects, but he lacked the almost comically slavish pro-Soviet tendencies of President Gottwald. And then there was the intervention of Professor Ota Šik, the economist, who in 1966 persuaded the Party leadership that, without some kind of radical decentralisation, economic catastrophe loomed. His reforms were introduced in 1967, and green shoots of private enterprise began to appear.

That same year, a group of writers led by the novelist Ludvík Vaculík called for a relaxation of censorship. Vaculík's address to the Fourth Congress of the Union of Writers, in July 1967, was one of the bravest and most inflammatory acts of defiance of the Communist age. His audience that day included such prominent figures as Milan Kundera, Pavel Kohout and Václav Havel. The fact that he escaped jail shows how far the thaw had already progressed.

One underlying theme of the 'spring' was that, in purely economic terms, the existing system clearly wasn't working. Another was that the generation who had risen to prominence as young, enthusiastic Party members in the early days of Communism – including Kundera, Kohout, Vaculík and, not least, Emil – had come of age and, at around the same time, acquired both perspective and influence. The idea that things could be different, and better, ceased to be totally heretical. And when Alexander Dubček replaced President Novotný as First Secretary of the Communist Party in January 1968, the advocates of reform acquired a political figurehead who was actually in a position to instigate change. Dubček was initially a compromise candidate, acceptable to conservatives as well as reformers. Once he took charge, however, it was clear that the reformers were taking over. A new kind of Communism seemed possible. Dubček called it 'socialism with a human face'.

For those who had spent the previous two decades buttoning their lips, the spring and summer of 1968 were a glorious time to be alive. Students, intellectuals, artists, celebrities – everyone seemed to be excited, talkative, optimistic; almost anything seemed possible. 'A time of sunshine, great music, great theatre, beautiful women' was how one Prague-dweller evoked it for me. It can't really have been that good, but there was no denying the excitement. Reformers, including those who had fallen from favour in the 1950s, were appointed to other key positions: General Ludvík Svoboda became president in March, while Josef Smrkovský became chairman of parliament. Hundreds of victims of Stalinist persecution – even Milada Horáková – were partially (though often posthumously) rehabilitated. In June, censorship was abolished. Programmes made by Radio Prague began to discuss what was going on – and were suddenly deemed unsuitable for retransmission in the Soviet Union; the circulation of the Writers' Union's journal, *Literární listy*, soared to 300,000 copies.

Around the same time, a young woman called Marta Kubišová recorded a song – based on a prayer by the seventeenth-century Moravian philosopher Comenius and initially broadcast in a children's television series about the defeat of a cruel tyrant – which became the accidental soundtrack of Czechoslovakia's awakening. 'May peace settle across all of this land,' it began. 'Anger, envy and resentment, fear and strife, may they all be banished . . .' And then, in a spine-tingling but almost untranslatable final line: 'Now your rule over the things that are yours, which was taken from you, is coming back to you – people, it is coming back to you!' By the time the remaining hardliners had realised how subversive it was, the song that became known as 'A Prayer for Marta' had gone viral, and the Prague Spring had long since turned into a Czechoslovak Summer of Love.

It was not all sunshine, of course; partly because of the menacing rumbles that kept emerging from the Soviet

Union about 'threatening the foundations of socialism'. But the taste of freedom was too intoxicating to be surrendered lightly. To stiffen the reformers' resolve, Vaculík wrote a manifesto, called 'Two Thousand Words that Belong to Workers, Farmers, Officials, Scientists, Artists, and Everybody' but more generally known as 'The Two Thousand Words'. With remarkable frankness, it spelled out the failings of the old system: 'Most of the nation welcomed the socialist programme with high hopes. But it fell into the hands of the wrong people . . .' It praised the 'regenerative process of democratisation' that had been taking place since the beginning of the year and called on the public to take direct action – from public criticism of discredited officials to demonstrations and strikes – to keep the momentum going. Published simultaneously in three national newspapers on 27 June, it enraged the hardliners and their Soviet backers, but was endorsed by nearly seventy public figures: authors, journalists, scientists, academics – and, not least, Czechoslovakia's most famous sporting couple, Emil and Dana Zátopek. In the weeks that followed, thousands of ordinary people spontaneously added their signatures.

A month and a half later, in the third week of August, two young American students, George Fenigsohn and Ron Kephart, found themselves in Prague at the tail-end of a backpacking tour of Europe. Being keen runners, and being young, and it being 1968, they decided to see if they could find Emil Zátopek. They looked him up in the phone book and called. Kephart, who knew a few words of Russian, tried to explain who they were and what they wanted. 'Let's talk in English,' said the voice at the other end of the phone. The next thing they knew, Fenigsohn and Kephart had been invited to 8 U Půjčovny, and were being fed, entertained, shown memorabilia and regaled with Olympic reminiscences.

'He was just so kind,' remembers Fenigsohn, nearly fifty years on. 'We just showed up, these American *studenti*, and he looked after us for a day and a half. He showed us round Prague, and people kept stopping him, because they all recognised him. He was incredibly gracious. We had meals with him. Then he drove us to the woods where he used to train [i.e. Stará Boleslav], and the three of us jogged around together on the paths there. It was beautiful.'

They were not the first strangers to be welcomed so warmly to 8 U Půjčovny, or the last. But the timing of their visit was poignant. The picture of Emil preserved in their memories – and in Fenigsohn's photo album – is a snapshot of his life as it was in the final, deceptively idyllic moments before everything changed utterly. Straight afterwards, the students took a train to the West. Disembarking in Amsterdam, they bought a newspaper, and realised that, unwittingly, they had visited at a historic time.

On the evening of 20 August, Emil and Dana were asked to a party in Prague but decided not to go. Dana went to bed early. Then the hosts rang up and Emil was persuaded to run over and join them. He was still there at 2 a.m., when someone turned on the radio – to hear a breathless newscaster trying to explain that a huge Soviet-led army of Warsaw Pact forces (including twelve tank divisions, thirteen motorised rifle divisions and two parachute divisions) had begun to invade Czechoslovakia twenty minutes before midnight. Czechoslovakia's army was confined to barracks, just as it had been in 1938 and 1948.

Emil's first thought – oddly – was of the house at Troja: nearing completion, unguarded and, in his view, irresistibly tempting to invading soldiers. He drove straight there, turned on the lights, locked the doors and windows and generally tried to make it secure and inhabited-looking. Then he attempted to drive home through roads that by then were blocked with tanks. He asked them politely in Russian to get out of his way, but it didn't always achieve the desired effect. He ended up abandoning the car in a backstreet and completing the journey on foot.

By the time he got home, Dana had been awake for some time. A friend had phoned with the shocking news. 'I realised that Emil was gone. I looked out of the window and saw that Klára was gone. Where was he? Had he been arrested already? Would I be next? I was so frightened. It was the worst hour of my life; or two hours – I don't know how long it was. Then I heard footsteps coming up the stairs . . .' When they stopped outside the door of the flat, she could hardly breathe: 'I was so wound up.' Then the door opened. When she saw Emil's face, she slapped it.

They calmed down. Dana apologised. Emil justified his actions with the assertion that 'Domeček was there all alone, crying'. ('I understood what he meant,' says Dana.) Then they decided to go out and see what was happening.

There were tanks and people everywhere. A low growling sound, mechanical and human, filled the air. Slowly, Emil and Dana made their way to Wenceslas Square, where the crowds were thickest. Some people were shouting, some hitting the tanks with their fists. 'Then people started to notice Emil,' says Dana. 'They asked him what he thought. He was quite mad. He said the Russians should not be allowed to go to the Olympics.'

Some people were speaking directly to the soldiers, asking them in Russian what they were doing; Emil joined in. A few soldiers replied to the effect that they had come to help the Czechoslovaks to deal with the counter-revolution that was threatening them; others said that they didn't know. 'Some of them didn't even know what country they were in,' says Dana.

It is difficult to imagine the sense of shock and violation that Czechoslovaks must have felt at the invasion. Europe had been at peace for more than twenty years. The Soviets were supposed to be their best friends. Yet here were Soviet tanks on the streets, soldiers with machine guns and live ammunition. Was this mere political theatre? Or was it all-out war? Were people actually going to get killed? The answer, tragically, was yes: at least nineteen people were killed in Prague alone on the first day; by the end of the year, the civilian death toll had reached at least 108.

For the most part, the invaders tried to avoid violence, firing machine guns in the air or driving vehicles towards crowds at high speeds only to halt at the last second. But the angry thousands who poured out on to the streets refused to be intimidated. Much of the resistance was passive: road signs were vandalised with remarkable speed, to make it harder for the invaders to find their way around. But there were also young men who not only threw stones at tanks but found ingenious ways to set fire to them.

The invaders moved ruthlessly to assert themselves, seizing Dubček and key supporters from Party headquarters and attempting to take control of the media. The staff at Radio Prague, which had been broadcasting protests against the invasion since the small hours of the morning, were driven out at gunpoint. The national news agency, ČTK, was among the last to fall, releasing its last bulletins at eight minutes before midnight: 'Russian troops are entering the ČTK building' and – before a KGB man in civilian clothes ripped off the ticker tape – 'This is the last item of the free ČTK news agency. All further statements will not be issued by—'

But the reformers were quick, too. As one Western news report put it: 'No sooner had the great mailed fist clanged down on the land than the Czechs everywhere were scrambling out from underneath it, standing on top of it in voluble and hostile crowds.' Many gathered outside the national public radio headquarters in Vinohradská Street, trying to defend their precious uncensored radio. When that battle was lost, they massed around the corner in Wenceslas Square. It was a remarkable display of popular unity and defiance. And the most visible symbol of that defiance was a balding man in a rumpled jacket, standing on a pedestal by the statue of St Wenceslas, furiously denouncing the invasion.

It was Emil.

According to his fellow reformer Luděk Pachman, the chess grandmaster, on that first evening, 'Emil was clearly the dominant figure'. With his champion's instinct for recognising the moment that really mattered and seizing it, he was throwing every ounce of his energy into the battle. He had already been on the radio, with Dana, calling for the invading nations to be barred from the Olympic Games, which were due to begin in Mexico City on 3 October.

Now Emil was making the same point in person – and from time to time expanding it by addressing the invaders directly, invoking the idea of the Olympic truce.

Given the chaos, anger and fear, it is hard to set down with absolute confidence what was said when and to whom. According to Pachman, however, at one point Emil 'quite literally rushed towards a group of Soviet soldiers, he announced his name and sporting titles, and then straight away said (in Russian), "Come on, let's talk."' Other accounts spoke of Emil moving from tank to tank, talking to individual soldiers in turn.

'They didn't want to listen,' he told *Sports Illustrated*'s Leigh Montville two decades later, 'but the people kept saying, "Hear him out. Do you know your Olympic champions? He is our Olympic champion."' Eventually an officer came over, and Emil told him how upset everyone was by the invasion, and how harmful it was to the Communist movement. 'He said nothing, but at the end, he shook my hand. That told me that maybe he felt not right about what he was doing.'

Over the next few days, Emil would talk to many more Russian soldiers. Most were given the same twofold message. First: the Czechoslovak people didn't ask for this invasion, no matter what you may have been told at home about our requests for 'help' against counterrevolutionaries. And, secondly: speaking as an Olympic champion, I tell you that you should be ashamed of taking part in this military operation, and invading a friendly neighbour, at a time when the Olympic Games are imminent, and all nations are supposed to observe a truce.

There is no evidence that Emil persuaded anyone with this argument, although he may have sown seeds of doubt. Nor, of course, was he the only figure around whom protesters rallied. But his presence and active involvement were hugely encouraging. Even after a decade of retirement, Emil remained his country's most instantly recognisable hero. It was like seeing the barricades manned by David Beckham.

It was also astonishingly brave of him. Not only was there a very real risk of being shot; there was also a secondary danger – and motivation – that had been eloquently spelled out in 'The Two Thousand Words': 'We have spoken out and come so far out into the open that we can only complete our intention of humanising this regime. Otherwise the revenge of the old guard would be cruel . . .' Large parts of the military establishment had been bitterly opposed to reform, and many actively supported the Soviet invasion. For Emil to oppose it so publicly and passionately was to risk a major disciplinary backlash.

The first six days of the occupation were later described by Milan Kundera as 'the most beautiful week that we have ever lived through'. At a political level, the reformist leaders, several of whom were now in Moscow, haggled with the Soviets in search of a compromise. On the streets, what one historian later called 'the most dramatic case of non-violent action against foreign aggressors that the world has ever known' continued.

On Thursday, 22 August, the second day, Emil – wearing military uniform this time – could once again be seen haranguing the crowds in Wenceslas Square, and round the corner in Na Příkopě as well. According to one report, he 'addressed the crowd under the muzzles of Soviet cannon and called for Russia to be banned from the Olympic

Games'; according to another, he 'called on the Russians to leave and accused them of violating the sovereignty of a friendly socialist state'. In snatches of sound recording, he mentions 'the internment of our representatives' and 'the raid on radio and television'.

Employees of Radio Prague, meanwhile, had continued to broadcast, calling themselves Free Radio and using a network of underground studios that had been set up in case of war. There were also several days of clandestine television broadcasts, using small parabolic FM transmitters from locations around the capital. Emil lent his voice and his prescence to both enterprises, and possibly his professional expertise as well. (This recent knowledge of Operational and Combat Readiness would have been an asset.)

The broadcasts appealed for defiance, but also for caution: 'We must develop a new citizen tactic, continuing normal life peacefully, completely ignoring the invaders.' Emil echoed the cautious message: 'Do not give them a provocation,' he implored. The 20,000 people protesting in Prague appeared unconvinced.

Friday saw the first of a series of general strikes. In the morning, Emil was seen outside the offices of *Mladá fronta*, once again addressing a large crowd; his words were broadcast shortly afterwards on Free Radio. Emil's public speaking skills had been developed through years of involuntary practice at the Party's behest, and now he had found a fitting use for them. It is unlikely that many in the Party enjoyed the irony. Later that day, Free Radio broadcast an urgent warning, telling Emil and Dana not to go home, because 'our good friends' – that is, the Russians – were waiting for them. They spent three days with friends in the suburb of Spořilov, but eventually decided that the danger had been exaggerated.

Emil, in any case, had been out on the streets again the next day. According to Pachman, Emil was seen putting up a poster 'without even noticing that just a couple of steps away from him was a soldier with an assault rifle'. When the soldier approached and poked his gun into Emil's back, Emil just turned round, offered his hand and said (in Russian): 'Everything is OK, comrade.' Then he went round the corner and stuck up the poster there instead.

Each day, Emil struck another blow in the PR battle against the invader. On the 24th a statement from him appeared in *Svobodný svět*, spelling out his demand that the Soviet Union be barred from the Olympics. On the 25th, speaking on Free Radio, he went further: 'We made a big mistake, collaborating with the Russians these past 20 years. This collaboration has cost us dearly.' On the 26th he made a similar point (in French) in the television interview with France's INA channel, adding: 'The young, the old, workers, intellectuals, students – the whole nation shares the view that we have the right to live according to our dreams and our sovereignty . . . The Russian people desire the same liberty.'

By then, however, the politics had moved on. Seeking to salvage something from a hopeless situation, President Svoboda and his fellow delegates had given in to overwhelming Soviet pressure and signed the Moscow Protocol – a compromise agreement that they hoped might offer a way out of the emergency. Censorship was to be reintroduced, and the 'leading role' of the Communist Party was to be reinforced; but Dubček would be allowed to continue as First Secretary, and the occupying forces would, with some exceptions, be gradually withdrawn from cities and confined to (Czechoslovak) barracks.

Some saw this as a betrayal: all that risk and loss of life, only for the 'spring' to be smothered on the Soviets' say-so. Others saw it as the least bad option: a compromise that offered some hope for the future, with many of the good guys still in place. Emil, speaking from the branches of one of the large lime trees that used to line Wenceslas Square, urged protesters to contain their anger, 'because anger leads to bloodshed. We must be united in the future,' he added, 'for that is our only salvation'.

He was right, but it was a futile hope. A crack had appeared in the reform movement that could never be entirely mended; the hardliners would have ample opportunity to exploit it in the months ahead. The next day, Dubček, Svoboda and Smrkovský attempted to justify their compromise to the nation in a series of emotional and occasionally tearful addresses. Some believed them, and many more sympathised. But the fact remained that, in Emil's words: 'It's over.'

All that remained was to defy the inevitable as bravely as possible – and wait for the backlash.

In the West, Emil's friends feared the worst – and tried to do what they could to help. On 31 August, athletes competing in a meeting at White City signed a petition, organised by Gordon Pirie, expressing their 'grave concern' for Emil and Dana's personal safety and calling on the Soviet authorities to 'guarantee the safety of this great and courageous athlete and his wife'.

Prudence suggested that Emil should quieten down a bit. He struggled to do so – despite an anonymous note pushed through the door at 8 U Půjčovny, denouncing him as a CIA agent bent on counter-revolution and warning that punishment would follow. Journalists from many nations remained keen to hear his views, and he still had plenty to say. Sometimes he said it discreetly. An interview with Jaroslav Dietl for *Stadion* magazine, ostensibly about the role of fear in sport, discussed the need to keep going in a long, hard marathon – in terms that could easily have referred to a different kind of struggle. 'Every race has its finish line,' said Emil pointedly. But an article in the Swedish newspaper *Arbetet* included some less guarded comments about, among other things, the way that Emil and Dana's overseas travels had turned them into reformers: 'In West Germany we saw new homes and free people. In East Germany, we saw mostly desolation, decay and poverty.' This was not the kind of remark that was calculated to keep him out of trouble; and trouble was closing in.

The second week of September saw Emil at the spa of Teplice, presumably for a pre-arranged visit. Instead of his usual talk, he spoke out against the Soviet Union. Then, on the night of 12–13 September, he caused the watching 'sharp eyes' great concern by disappearing. Subsequent investigation – including a four-hour interrogation by the security services in Prague on 20 September – suggested that he thought he was being watched by the Soviet KGB as well as the Czechoslovak StB, and was afraid for his own safety. He had spent the night at the apartment of the spa manager, before taking a car back to Prague. The StB were not sure whether to believe this; one of their three different reports on the incident concluded that, if Emil could not learn to respect the law, some action might have to be taken – action relating to his personal freedom.

It's possible that a demonstration on 23 September outside the Soviet Embassy in London by athletes bearing 'Zátopek in danger' banners may have helped to persuade Emil's enemies to exercise restraint. It seems more likely that, for the time being, Emil was still considered 'too big to jail'. The Olympic Games were just three weeks away, and he and Dana had been invited as honoured guests. As Emil later put it: 'If they punish me, they will discredit themselves in the eyes of the world.'

The Czechoslovak security services agonised about the possibility of the trip backfiring, but it was felt unlikely that Emil would defect – he had had plenty of opportunities to do so in the past – while Dana promised that they would not discuss politics with Westerners. Meanwhile, colleagues at Dukla and athletes in the Olympic team undertook to try to influence Emil 'positively'. The couple flew to Mexico City with the rest of the Czechoslovakian team, and the politicians in Prague kept their fingers crossed that they would not do anything provocative.

In fact, the Games passed quietly as far as the Zátopeks were concerned. The eyes of the world were upon them, but they kept their heads down and confined themselves to watching the sport and meeting up with old friends. There was a brief, warm reunion with Ron Clarke – before he collapsed at the finish of the 10,000m on the first day of athletics competition, his heart permanently damaged by the effects of the altitude. Emil was also seen jogging with Gaston Reiff, and had lunch with the Swiss middle-distance runner Paul Martin, who may have made veiled enquiries about Emil and Dana's interest in defection. Emil reportedly responded, 'We love our country too much to live anywhere else.'

There were also discreet offers of overseas coaching work in Sweden and Finland – but, as Emil later explained: 'If I had left my country at that time, our people would have thought the situation was hopeless for all of us . . . I did not want to leave my country like a rat abandoning a sinking ship.'

No amount of discretion on Emil's part could disguise the warmth of the world's concern for his and his country's wellbeing. Applause and encouragement followed him, just as they had when he was electrifying earlier Olympics with his running. This time, though, Emil responded with diplomatic diffidence. There were others who could make patriotic gestures – notably the gymnast Věra Čáslavská, another signatory of 'The Two Thousand Words', who won four golds and two silvers and, on the two occasions when she was on the medallists' rostrum while the Soviet anthem was being played, made plain her displeasure by pointedly looking downwards and away. Her homeland would reward her with years of persecution.

But three weeks was a long time for Emil to keep quiet. Eventually, he got into an animated discussion about the invasion with Will Grimsley of the Associated Press. 'The Russians . . . were acting out of fear,' he told him. 'They were afraid their political system might fall under the weight of freedom and social progress.' As he talked, Dana could be seen walking past repeatedly, gesturing with her hands. It wasn't that she disagreed: it was just that she could see where such comments might lead. Emil laughed. 'Dana wants me to shut up,' he said. 'She thinks I talk too much.' Christopher Brasher had a similar experience, chatting with Emil in a café while Dana said: 'Hush, Emil. They'll hear you, and then it will be bad.' In both cases, she was right.

The most difficult moment was the encounter with Vladimir Kuts. Emil bumped into him in the hotel they were both staying at, and their angry discussion grew into a shouting match in which Dana, too, became involved. Kuts, now a hard-drinking trainer, considered Emil a traitor to the Communist cause, and said so; Emil and Dana were appalled by Kuts's unapologetic support for the killing of Czechoslovak civilians. By the end of the confrontation, Dana was in tears. They would never exchange a friendly word again.

Shortly afterwards, the Games came to an end. The Olympic flame was extinguished, and the athletes began to return to their 112 different nations. There was a brief last hurrah, in the form of a flamboyant, chaotically crowded wedding in Mexico City Cathedral between Věra Čáslavská and the runner Josef Odložil. Then the Czechoslovaks, too, headed for the airport, and Emil and Dana returned to Prague to face the music.

16

Disgrace

The hardliners took their revenge slowly. There was no hurry. In the short term, the reformers could be left to calm things down. So when students occupied Charles University in November 1968 to protest against the compromises of the Moscow Protocol, it was Emil who went to the campus to talk to them, sympathising with their anger yet urging restraint.

But not everyone wanted to be restrained. Notwithstanding Dubček's undertaking in October that attacks on the Soviet Union in the Czechoslovak press would now stop, the weekly magazines *Politika* and *Reportér* continued to criticise both the Soviets and the undertaking. In November, both were banned (*Reportér* temporarily). For many reformers, including Emil, this was too much to bear. Emil, Dana and Luděk Pachman put their names to a 300-word 'proclamation to defend press freedom', copies of which ended up in, among other places, the Dukla sports club. It was hard-hitting stuff, denouncing 'foreign despotism' and warning of 'a new dark age' in which 'insincerity will become a virtue, lies will become truth and silence will become an existential necessity'.

Emil also read this out publicly, at a rowdy meeting at the Alcron hotel on 13 November. An agent of the secret services attempted, with limited success, to eavesdrop on this gathering, which seems to have been organised by the Belgian journalist Hugo Claes. There was much drinking and singing of patriotic songs – and little doubt that Emil, who arrived late, was the star attraction. It seems inconceivable that he could have imagined that such behaviour would go unnoticed or unpunished. If he did, he was wrong. Two days later, he was called into the Ministry of Defence, told to restrain himself and warned that there would be consequences if he failed to comply strictly with the army's rules and regulations. But that was just a faint foreshadowing of what was to come. The approaching new year would be as bleak as the old one had been full of hope.

First came the personal attacks. An editorial in *Sovietsky sport* on 1 January 1969 was devoted to denouncing Emil as a 'traitor'. A few days later, Friedrich Janke, the East German distance runner, observed acidly that 'Zátopek changes his convictions the way he changes his shirts'. But that was just mood music. What followed was real. On the morning of 16 January, Jan Palach, a twenty-year-old student at Charles University, doused himself in petrol in Wenceslas Square and set fire to himself. He died of his injuries three days later. A letter found in his briefcase indicated that his self-immolation had been a political protest: not so much against the Soviet invasion as against the reformers' subsequent 'demoralisation'. Alarmingly, it suggested that, unless the reformers reasserted their independence, if necessary encouraged by a general strike, then other 'human torches' would follow.

Much controversy surrounds the details of Palach's death and motivation, and of the authorities' response. Other self-immolations did follow; some may have been copy-cat acts by disturbed young people unconnected with Palach; it is possible that the clandestine movement implied by his letter never existed. It can be said with confidence, however, that most Czechoslovaks, reformers and hardliners alike, were horrified – not least by the fear that other young lives, perhaps closer to home, would be thrown away, terribly, in the same cause.

Emil's reaction was mixed. He was overheard speaking animatedly about Palach's suicide, praising the moral qualities of his action. Yet he spent a day in Wenceslas Square a few days later, talking to students and, once again, urging calm. It was an awkward position for reformers to find themselves in, caught between the threats of Soviet retribution and student self-harm. Even Luděk Pachman, one of the most reckless champions of reform, agreed to appear on television to discourage other young people from following Palach's example.

But Emil had other things on his mind as well. On 19 January he was summoned to the Ministry of Defence, reprimanded for his behaviour – and dismissed from his post as the army's Director of Sport. He was given a revised role at Dukla instead: as youth coach and deputy to the chief coach.

Emil and Dana were still digesting this news – which Dana, in particular, took badly – when a new cloud appeared. On 20 February, at a public meeting in the Merkur hotel in Česká Lípa, Vilém Nový, a hardline member of the Central Committee of the Communist Party, made an astonishing claim about Jan Palach's death. Palach, he said, had not intended to kill himself: he had been tricked into it by a group of liberal conspirators who had persuaded him that he would be using a conjuror's substance called 'cold fire' that would not actually burn him. Then Nový named the five alleged conspirators: the authors, Vladimír Škutina and Pavel Kohout; Lubomír Holeček, the student leader; Luděk Pachman; and Emil Zátopek.

The claim was so preposterous that it was barely worth responding to. (You can hear the audience's hoots of disgust in the recording of Nový's address that has, remarkably, survived.) Yet there was something chilling about being singled out and named. Nový's main aim was, presumably, to undermine the 'human torch' movement by spreading doubt as to Palach's motives, while simultaneously smearing some leading liberals. But there may have been another message: we're coming for you.

Four weeks later, the five named men lodged a defamation suit against Nový. It is not clear who instigated this; what is clear is that it was rash. It would, however, be well over a year before the case came to court.

Meanwhile, the hopes of the Prague Spring continued to recede. Those who had supported liberalisation were steadily disempowered – and, in some cases, eased out of their jobs. Emil, talking to fellow reformers in the offices of *Svobodné slovo* at the beginning of April, said that it felt like a 'time of darkness'. Ten days later, at a district conference of the ČSTV in Tachov, he gave a slightly rambling address in which, having said that he would not discuss politics, he talked about little else.

He made derogatory jokes about the Soviet Union and East Germany and talked, among other things, about the billions of crowns' worth of aid – including tanks smuggled in oil tankers – that the Czechoslovaks had given, on Soviet instructions, to North Korea and Hungary. The message seemed to be that this was wasteful, or possibly corrupt; it certainly wasn't the sort of thing that his military superiors would have wanted him to talk about. Answering questions afterwards, Emil said that the army was 'a pile of shit' and that officers just took money for doing nothing.

He returned to the theme of the army's deficiencies two days later, on 14 April, in a discussion with students at the law school at Charles University. The theme was 'post-January politics'. Speaking dressed in uniform, Emil was again in loose-cannon mode. He suggested that the money spent on the army might more usefully be spent on education. He discussed gossip he had heard about alleged plans for a military coup – presumably before the invasion – and implicated, among others, the defence minister, Martin Dzúr. And he revealed that he had been ordered to report on the morale and attitude to the Soviet Union of the athletes under his charge at Dukla – but had resolved the matter in a characteristically maverick fashion, telling the commander that 'everything was all right' without having asked the athletes to do anything more than indicate a broad sympathy for socialism and democracy. With hindsight, it seems astonishing that Emil could have expected to get away with such behaviour. But he had, over the years, grown used to the idea that he could be a law unto himself. Those days were coming to an end.

Disorder following demonstrations that celebrated Czechoslovakia's victory over the USSR in the world ice-hockey championships at the end of March had provided the Soviets with the excuse they needed for piling on the pressure, and the reformers in the higher echelons of the Czechoslovak Communist Party could hold on no longer. On 17 April, Dubček was forced to resign as First Secretary of the Party. He was a broken man, and the movement he had led was as good as broken, too. He was replaced by Gustáv Husák, a former political prisoner who was now thoroughly committed to a pro-Soviet agenda that he called 'normalisation'. Dubček's supporters knew what to expect.

On 21 April, Emil was suspended from his coaching role at Dukla, pending investigation of 'reasonable suspicion' that he had spread 'false news' and for 'conduct at variance with the relevant orders of the Minister of Defence'. He was questioned by military investigators about some of his public statements, and there was talk that he would soon appear before a military tribunal. The official transcript of the interrogation shows Emil in typically baffling mood, alternately submissive, evasive and insolent. ('Question: "As an officer, you should not talk about certain things, and yet you do talk about them. Why?" Answer: "It's mostly like this: people ask me, and I answer them . . ."') At the end he says helpfully that he will 'happily accept any solution' to the conflict between his need to speak freely and the army's need for him to conform. If he is bluffing, he will soon regret it.

In public, meanwhile, he remained cheerfully defiant. He told an Associated Press reporter that he didn't care if he went to prison: 'It would be quiet, and I could write without being disturbed.' The Ministry of Defence, which received a large number of concerned letters from Emil's friends and supporters abroad, felt it necessary to reassure the world that his case would be 'dealt with entirely in harmony with the prevailing legal provisions' and that 'his merits will be taken fully into account'.

Later that week, an article appeared in the Swedish publication *Aftonbladet*, in which Emil admitted that he and Dana had been offered coaching jobs in Sweden and would like to take them up – if the ČSTV would give them permission to do so. Emil revealed that the offer had first been made in Mexico, but he had not wanted to admit defeat at that point. 'It is better to be beaten in a fair game than to win an unfair one.'

The following week, Emil announced that he was unable to take up the Swedish offer. 'Under normal conditions I would accept, but when people are leaving the country I do not want to leave . . . I belong here.' The implication now was that, if he did leave, he would not be allowed back.

He was, however, in need of new employment. The news would not be made public until December – but on 22 April Emil had effectively been dismissed from the army as well. In an interview published in *L'Express* in Austria on 18 August, he explained that he had 'received a letter firing me from the Army. After 1 October 1969, I will no longer belong to the military.' The extended notice period may reflect the friendly feelings that many of Emil's colleagues still had towards him, and their regret that twenty-two years of military service should end like this. It also meant that he could be summoned to account for his behaviour in giving the interview, in which he had also expressed the view that, following Dubček's resignation, 'people came to power in our country again who think of nothing else but a good job and a good salary for themselves but don't care about the people'. Emil's excuse was that two young Austrians had visited him at his flat, and he had thought they were just talking about sport. 'I am not a politician,' he told the head of Dukla, 'and I don't know why so many people visit me day in day out, and everyone wants to hear my opinion.' Dana, he added, was now sending all visitors away.

Emil was still physically spending much of his time at Dukla, despite his earlier suspension. Presumably it was felt that he could do less damage here than inside the Ministry of Defence – or out on the streets. A secret service report on 19 August noted approvingly that he had not been saying anything provocative while at work; but six days later a different Dukla informer reported a conversation in which Emil had said that the 1950s were making a comeback in Czechoslovakia, and that the best outcome might be for him to be sent to prison, where he would work honestly and at least have a break from everything.

Prison was looking increasingly likely. On 21 August, Emil and others marked the anniversary of the invasion by signing the 'Ten Points', an uncompromising condemnation of foreign interference, censorship and the one-party state. Unlike 'The Two Thousand Words', which struck fear into the Soviet empire and temporarily rallied a nation, the 'Ten Points' seems to have had little impact beyond getting its signatories into trouble. Pachman, one of its main instigators, was arrested the next day; Emil spent a long time comforting his wife, Evženka, on the phone.

But these were not the 1950s. The hardliners imposing 'normalisation' were not war-hardened fanatics but the Eastern bloc equivalent of baby-boomers – led, in Husák, by a former victim of totalitarian repression who hoped to achieve his ends with rather less brutality than he had suffered. In any case, it had been agreed at the highest level that celebrity martyrs should not be created. The notorious Law 99, which came into effect in December, gave the state more or less unlimited powers to jail people for political offences; but its victims could be counted in hundreds, not thousands. Normalisation deployed a different weapon: freezing out.

All over Czechoslovakia, the purge was enforced. People were asked to renounce reform or lose their jobs; the most active reformers often lost their jobs anyway. By the mid-1970s, more than 300,000 people would have lost their employment for ideological reasons; they included around 11,000 army officers and 30,000 NCOs judged to be politically unsound.

Many, especially the more vociferous liberals, found it all but impossible to get alternative work – they had to all intents and purposes been blacklisted. Those who had signed 'The Two Thousand Words' were particularly visible among the victims. The academic Milan Hübl, formerly Dubček's chief ideologist, spent a year unemployed before getting work on a building site; Jaroslav Kladiva, former dean of the Charles University philosophy department, became an undertaker's apprentice; Karel Pecka, the author, became a sewer-worker; Miloslav Vlk, a future cardinal, became a window-cleaner. Others were unable to get their work published or performed. Some writers, such as Stanislav Neumann, Jiří Pištora and Jan Alda, committed suicide. Marta Kubišová – whose only offences had been to make an extra recording of 'A Prayer for Marta' for Free Radio to broadcast in the aftermath of the Warsaw Pact invasion; and, subsequently, to have become Czechoslovakia's most popular singer – was hounded out of the music business and ended up (after a divorce, a miscarriage, a physical breakdown and a court case involving faked pornographic photographs of her) doing menial work for a doll-making co-operative, attaching the legs to plastic bears.

It was an almost invisible form of persecution, and horribly effective. As the film director Pavel Juráček put it, the normalisers were 'counting on starving us out so that finally we come to them and humbly do whatever they want of us'. Most people, of course, had no desire to starve, and preferred to go through the motions of obedience to Husák's regime – even if this meant dissociating themselves from the dissenters. Being a troublemaker began to be a lonely business.

Even Emil found that – in Dana's words – 'people who had been friends became less than friends', with some literally crossing the street to avoid him. There was also the worry that those who didn't avoid him might get into trouble on his account. Václav Bednář, Emil's liaison officer in Martin, remembers bumping into him in Prague around this time. He greeted him warmly; but Emil, who was wearing a tracksuit, backed away. 'He didn't want to talk to me. He said, "Vašek, don't stop, so you won't get into trouble because of me. I am being watched by the counter guys [i.e. military counter-intelligence].' I said I didn't give a damn, but he ran off. I never saw him again.'

Emil was used to being spied on. A less familiar but increasingly pressing issue was the need to find a job. He was not poor: the royalties from his books provided some income, and he was getting a military pension of sorts, although almost certainly reduced. In the short term, Dana could support him – assuming that she did not lose her job, too. (She didn't. Her fellow javelin trainers closed ranks around her – a kindness she never forgot.) But they had ploughed their accumulated savings into Troja: Emil later reckoned that, by the time it was finished, it had cost them 180,000 crowns.

In any case, Emil was only forty-six, and to be jobless was a criminal offence. He had to find something – but one option after another melted away. In August, he had talked of joining a sporting goods firm near Prague – or perhaps (in a rhetorical flourish) becoming a garbage collector. That came to nothing, as did another prospective job in Vlašim, where the town committee of the Communist Party did not agree with his being taken on. By September he was talking of finding a job in chemistry in Karviná, or as a storeman for the state railway company. But those came to nothing, too. By October he was simply on holiday, working on the house at Troja, having promised to inform Dukla if he left Prague. Even if he wasn't formally blacklisted, no one who knew what was good for them would have anything to do with Emil Zátopek.

At the end of October, he finally left the army. When he went to collect his belongings from Dukla, he was devastated to find that no one came to say goodbye to him.

Meanwhile, a threatening new mood music had been building in the freshly tamed media. In September, an article in *Květy*, the Party central committee's weekly magazine, raised the prospect of trials for Dubček, Smrkovský, Pachman, Šik and Zátopek. 'I heard the word treason used in connection with their activities,' wrote Bořivoj Horák. 'One cannot avoid using it.'

In October, an article in *Rudé právo* both revealed and justified the fact that Emil had been expelled from the Communist Party. (The expulsion had actually taken place the previous month.) Emil had committed 'a number of acts at variance not only with the duties of a Communist but also with the law and the statutes of our state,' wrote Jiří Hečko, a member of the army's military administration. Among other things, Emil had 'betrayed a number of internal measures of the Czechoslovak Army contained in secret documents of the Ministry of National Defence. Every young lieutenant knows how to deal with secret documents. It would not seem to be asking too much if one demands the same from a colonel with more than twenty years of service.'

On 30 October, the governments of Czechoslovakia and the Soviet Union issued a joint declaration confirming that the invasion of August 1968 had been a welcome act of solidarity to block the progress of counter-revolutionary forces. A month later, on 28 November, the Czechoslovak Olympic Committee formally withdrew its request, made with Emil's encouragement a year earlier, that the invading nations be barred from the Olympics. It also confirmed that Emil had resigned from the Committee. Dr František Kroutil, its secretary general, told reporters that Emil was fine, working on his house in Troja, drawing a full pension and receiving royalties from his books. 'He can,' he added, 'do everything – except controlling himself in press interviews.'

The same day, *Obrana lidu* published a justification of Emil's expulsion – hitherto unreported – from the army. It was, wrote the army weekly, 'naturally unprecedented that a colonel, worker of the defence ministry, was speaking in such a way . . . No wonder the army eventually had to part company with Emil Zátopek in spite of all his merits.'

Then, in early December, a Ministry of Defence statement applied the final seal of disapproval. Emil had been dismissed from the army, it confirmed: for 'violating legal norms', according to General Dzúr, by 'making serious revelations' about Czechoslovak leaders.

There was no avoiding the message. Emil had fallen, spectacularly, from grace. He was no longer a national hero – and if he knew what was good for him he would keep his head down for a very long time.

But while that was clear enough, there was one question that was exercising a growing number of people: where *was* Emil?

He had been seen at the annual *Rudé právo* run on 28 September, where he had acted as official starter. (The race organiser was Emil's close friend, Zdeněk Fator, the athletics manager of Dukla's civilian rival, Sparta Prague; this small act of defiance deserves acknowledgement.) For a few weeks after that, he was occasionally glimpsed by passers-by in Troja, working on his house and garden. Since late October, however, even those sightings had stopped.

There had been rumours. Some said that he had been working as a garbage collector, only for the process to be disrupted by members of the public insisting on doing his work for him. This rumour has been widely repeated, but I have never heard of anyone who actually saw it, while Dana and others insist that it was not true. Other reports had him driving a water-sprinkler lorry for Prague's sanitation department, provoking demonstrations by passers-by that were deemed a 'threat to public order'. But that, too, was almost certainly mere rumour.

But the fact remained that Emil appeared to have vanished – in which case, where was he?

17

Exile

It depended on who you asked – and when. Some said that Emil had been seen in the Slavkov Forest region, in the remote north-west, or in the grand spa town of Mariánské Lázně. Others spoke of sightings in the Bohemian–Moravian highlands, in the south. There were even suggestions, later on, that he was working in the mines of Jáchymov, up by the German border. Each of these reports was, in its own way, accurate. Emil was on the move, usually in obscure, sparsely inhabited areas. He was not, however, on the run.

This was his new life: yet another re-imagining of what it meant to be Emil Zátopek. With the help of Zdeněk Fator and other friends, he had been found a menial job with one of the few companies that was not discouraged from employing out-of-favour citizens. It was called Stavební geologie ('Structural Geology') and prospected for underground resources, mainly on behalf of the state, throughout the region of Bohemia (roughly the western two-thirds of what is now the Czech Republic). Its 1,200-odd employees included a dozen or so other dissidents, mostly intellectuals; they were generally assigned the least demanding work, measuring water-surface levels with the pumping crews. Jaromír Malák, the regional manager who was made responsible for Emil when he arrived in November 1969, initially assigned Emil to this. But Emil kept demanding a 'real job'. Within a few weeks he got one, as part of a small drilling team.

The team's work ranged from boring new wells to maintaining existing ones and could take place pretty much anywhere where there was or might be water. There were usually just three or four in a drilling team, including the foreman. Being itinerant, they all lived together in a *maringotka* – a traditional caravan not unlike an old wheeled shepherd's hut – where they shared their leisure hours just as they shared the working hours in between. The same three or four might live in this kind of proximity for months at a time – and one was usually an StB informer. Every two or three weeks, they were allowed a couple of days off to visit their families.

The work, from dawn to dusk, could be hard. Much of it involved digging – making ditches, or excavating ground for drilling – and much of the rest involved carrying. According to Emil, his fellow workers 'could have made things quite nasty for me, as I had been a "brass hat". But they were OK.' Some of his friends weren't convinced. 'I fear that they humiliated him,' Zdeněk Fator told me. There certainly seems to have been an early incident when Emil hurt his arm trying to lift a 50kg bag of cement – and was mocked by a foreman who said, in effect, 'What's the point of being an Olympic champion if you can't even lift a bag of cement?' There is little doubt that Emil, who for as long as he could remember had been fitter and stronger than anyone, felt the frustration deeply. 'He had worked so hard for his achievements, and he was used to being among people who appreciated them,' says Dana. 'Now they counted for nothing. It was very hard for him.'

But he buckled down without complaint, and he seems to have won a tolerable amount of respect. His workmates welcomed his willingness to run and fetch items of kit; and he could also be persuaded to run to the nearest pub with a backpack to fetch supplies of beer. He enjoyed the escape and the exercise – which was all the more beneficial because it had to be done in heavy rubber work-boots – and the team, one imagines, enjoyed sending him. But Zdeněk Fator's assessment, that Emil spent his time being bullied by 'drunkards', seems pessimistic. Emil insisted that his workmates 'taught me to drink beer from the bottle and I taught them Moravian folk songs', and claimed that he won their special respect when he showed them his training diaries and they realised how hard he had worked for his glory. Some refused to believe that anyone could have worked so hard.

If there was friction, it may have related to the way that Emil's celebrity sometimes attracted intolerable amounts of public attention. One early assignment, in Mariánské Lázně itself, seems to have been brought to an early conclusion because unacceptable numbers of visitors to the spa, including foreigners, were recognising Emil and taking photographs of him. There was also the problem of women. According to one former Stavební geologie employee, Richard Händl, 'Emil could be a little bit crazy. Often in the morning he would come out of the *maringotka*, naked, and pour two buckets of freezing cold water over himself. But of course he was very famous, and he was attractive, so women from all the local farms would come and watch him doing it. And because word travels quickly, within a few days women from neighbouring villages would want to watch as well.'

But none of this seems to have caused serious resentment. Emil was never the kind to give himself airs, and it is hard to believe that even the most enviously disposed could have envied him for long. Unlike some public figures who had been forced to become menial workers, he was at home among the working classes; and, of course, he had no fear of hard physical work. When friends expressed concern he said: 'I have already got to know the world from on high. Now I am getting to know it from down below.'

For a while this was literally true. One relatively early job during Emil's time with the team took them to Jáchymov, to repair a well deep in the Svornost mine shaft. This gave rise to the much repeated rumour that Emil had been 'sent to the uranium mines' like Jan Haluza and Ladislav Kořán. In fact, the concentration camps had been long closed, as had the mines, the last of which ceased operating in 1964. Svornost remained open so that radioactive water could be pumped down to the Radon Palace in Jáchymov itself. (The 'palace' had begun life as a general health spa – one of many in north-west Bohemia. When the lethal effects on clients' health became apparent, it was rebranded as a source of specialist treatment for clients who actually needed radiotherapy. But the well still needed to work.)

Emil spent most of his time in Jáchymov 150m underground, moving barrowloads of earth. According to Petr Loukota, a mining electrician who still works at

Svornost today: 'He was a good worker. He didn't complain. He just got on with it. We all used to sit in the same hut for our breaks, and he used to entertain people with tales about his experiences in life.' Sometimes these tales were punctuated by complaints about Luděk Pachman, although the details of the gripe went over Loukota's head. Emil also spent many evenings in a Jáchymov pub – drinking not with his co-workers but with a local policeman. Perhaps a proper policeman felt more comfortable as company than a bunch of colleagues who probably included a secret informer.

The team also spent a long time based in the desolate, depopulated Slavkov Forest area, near the tiny village of Nová Ves, where many key springs were drilled. Even today, it feels like a godforsaken area, on the western edge of the Sudetenland. Hundreds of thousands of ethnic Germans were deported from these parts after the Second World War. (Czechoslovakia expelled three million altogether.) They left behind a highland wilderness of ungrazed pastures, untamed woods, derelict houses and, in places, abandoned villages. If you wanted to make a public figure disappear, it would be hard to think of a better place to send him.

Emil passed many months here. He was in a more congenial crew by now, with a sympathetic foreman who had at least some sense of what Emil had achieved in life, and what he had sacrificed to achieve it. But sympathy couldn't alter the loneliness of exile, and the knowledge that the familiar comforts of Mariánské Lázně were down in the valley below can only have served to remind Emil how overwhelmingly the world he had once conquered had now turned against him.

The physical demands of the work here were exacerbated by the environment – bitter cold in winter, tormenting midges the rest of the year – and by the lifestyle: beer, slivovice, more beer, and little else. It must have taken its toll, but Emil bore it with the same stoicism with which he had endured all the other hardships of his life.

According to Alžběta Vlasáková, a Slovakian-born former farm-worker who says that she is the last remaining inhabitant of Nová Ves to remember those days, Emil fitted in well with what was then a reasonably close-knit rural community. 'No one had a problem with him. There was nothing grand about him. He worked hard, and would talk to anybody. There was no "*I'm Zátopek*" about him' – which she accompanies with a gesture indicating a turned-up nose.

Sometimes Alžběta would see Emil on a bicycle, but more often he would be running. 'He used to run to Bečov [Bečov nad Teplou, more than seven hilly miles there and back] or Mnichov [nearly ten], just by himself, on the roads. He wasn't racing then. But he kept running – because if you're running, you're alive.'

There was a pub in the village, and the drilling team were familiar faces there. There was a dance floor on the first floor, and Saturday nights involved marathon sessions of ground-floor drinking and first-floor dancing. Emil was an enthusiastic participant.

It is hard to know if he was happy, but it is clear that he had found a way of adapting to his exile. He was earning good money (more than he earned in the army, he later claimed); he was keeping fit; and at least there was a point to the work. In some ways it was like making the garden in Troja. You put in the physical effort, and the land obeyed. Emil certainly felt he was doing something useful, and took pride in working hard with his hands. By the time the team left Nová Ves for the last time (probably in 1972) there were several new well-heads in the area. One was named the '*Zátopkův vrt*', or Zátopek's spring – although when I looked for it in 2015 it appeared to have vanished under a small lake.

But even Emil had to concede that working on the drills 'was not seventh heaven'. It was not the life he had won for himself with all those years of effort and sacrifice. For most of the past two decades he had been courted by presidents, sports stars, intellectuals – the great and good of the land. Now he was a nobody, in the middle of nowhere. He must have felt the difference. And if he didn't, others did.

Once, on a team working near Jihlava – about eighty miles south-east of Prague – Emil received a surprise visit. Dana had driven down with Patxi Alcorta, the Spanish sports official who organised the San Sebastián cross-country race. Alcorta was a colourful character who could charm his way anywhere; he was visiting Prague en route to Moscow. The old friends embraced – Emil still in the overalls in which he often slept as well as worked. On the journey back to Prague, Alcorta wept. 'Is this how they treat their hero?'

Perhaps he was overreacting. It was not as if Emil couldn't cope – with the work or the lifestyle. Yet I suspect that there was something heartbreaking about the sight of him. According to the Czech author Pavel Kosatík, there was one occasion when a boy from a village near Litomyšl knocked on the *maringotka* door to offer Emil a present – a piece of smoked meat – from his mother. The shambling figure who greeted him looked tired and had a bottle in his hand. He thanked the boy, but added: 'I am not the Zátopek who you used to know.' I got much the same impression from a fleeting clip of film footage that I have seen of Emil during this phase. He looks tired and, for the first time in his life, defensive. He does not appear to be suffering, but the relaxed confidence has gone. He seems to be holding himself in check. It is like seeing a lion in a circus.

Forced dislocations such as Emil's did not occur in isolation, and it was often the context, not the discomfort, that hurt. It is easy to imagine how Emil, with his physical energy and natural grace and empathy, found ways to bond with his new companions. It is much harder to imagine how he reconciled this new life with his old, lost life with Dana in Prague. This – even more than the long winter nights in the crowded *maringotka* when even the slivovice wasn't enough to keep out the cold – must have gnawed away at him, just as family memories have always gnawed at those kept away from home by war, prison, education or work. You can adapt yourself: humans always adapt. But what do you do with the part of you that you have left, unchanged, behind?

Every few weeks, Emil would return to Prague for a day or two. It was not enough, for either of them. 'Emil changed during that time,' Dana recalls sadly. It hardly matters how. The visits were largely taken up by doing his washing. There was no time to get to know one another again. She, like him, was adapting, keeping herself going through her work as a coach, through other friends, and through feverish needlework, to which she applied herself with the same discipline she had brought to her athletics training. 'People thought I must be doing a lot of shopping,' she says, 'because I kept appearing in new clothes. But I was just making them.'

Attempts to keep in touch by post were handicapped by Emil's lack of a fixed address. He wrote when he could, usually discussing details of work to be done at Troja; but Dana rarely knew where to send her replies. She addressed one to 'Emil Zatopek, Maringotka, Vendolí, somewhere near the cemetery'.

For Emil, meanwhile, there was no guarantee that his punishments were at an end. One evening, visiting Troja on his way back from the *maringotka*, he was beaten up by a group of men who appeared to be soldiers. He shrugged off the injuries with difficulty – several of his ribs were damaged – and took home the message that this was 'a warning'.

Harder to shake off was the pain of his distance from Dana, and the growing divergence in their experiences and outlooks. Emil, in Dana's view, had become 'wild'; while Emil, as far as we can tell, felt misunderstood. This, I suspect, was what bothered him most: not the discomfort or the humiliation, but the sense that he was losing his marriage.

In the spring of 1970, reports given by the informers of eastern Bohemia to the security services paint a picture of a man trying to avoid controversy. In February, in Osík, near Litomyšl, some young people recognised him and asked him to sign autographs, but Emil, uncharacteristically, refused; he also turned down an invitation to speak at a village function. In March, in the villages around Polička, Emil is quoted as saying that he liked the quietness of the place. In Prague there had been too many parties and public events and it hadn't been good for him. In Vendolí, in April, local people kept inviting Emil to their parties, but Emil didn't like this: he would prefer to be alone – and he didn't want to talk about politics. In Svitavy, in May, he declined an opportunity to officiate at a sports event: he knew the security services followed him everywhere and he didn't want to risk doing anything to make the situation worse.

It is possible that Emil expected that what he said and did would be reported, and adapted accordingly. But even that is revealing. The Emil of 1968 or even 1969 had seemed indifferent to what the authorities made of his pronouncements. Now he seemed to be sending a message: that he was going to behave himself.

We cannot be sure why. No doubt loneliness and despair played their part, but there may have been a more pressing reason. Emil's joint defamation lawsuit against Vilém Nový was getting closer to its long-delayed hearing, and it seems likely that pressure was being put on Emil to back down. Much of it was 'soft' pressure: people in high places trying to persuade him that, in bringing the case, he was damaging a cause – socialism – in which he believed. At some point, too, someone seems to have persuaded him that at least one of his co-plaintiffs, Luděk Pachman, had double-crossed him and was about to flee the country. But there were probably 'bad cops' on his case as well as 'good' ones. One informer's report, from Agent 'Saša', said that Emil was 'afraid of being sent to jail for 20 years' – and some of Emil's closest friends are convinced that he was being explicitly threatened with prison (although Dana doubts this). At the very least, Emil's resolve was cracking. And when, on 30 July 1970, the case was finally heard, it – or he – broke.

The hearing took place at the ward court for Prague 7. Emil sat with his co-plaintiffs, Lubomír Holeček, Pavel Kohout, Luděk Pachman and Vladimír Škutina. The judge read the indictment. Emil got up, approached the judge and asked if he could apologise to Nový and withdraw from the action. He said that he did not want to be perceived as an enemy of socialism, having always supported socialism, and that he regretted that the court case had happened. The judge gave her consent, whereupon Emil approached Nový and asked his forgiveness.

According to Pachman, who later dismissed the hearing as 'a farce', Emil 'went over to Nový, his hand extended – it looked as if they were about to hug each other in a "double Khrushchev", but they merely shook hands'. Pavel Kohout compared it to seeing 'a grown man collapse like a house hit by a bomb'. Emil spent the rest of the case sitting in the public gallery.

On a practical level, Emil's U-turn made little difference. The judge, after a peremptory hearing, threw out the case anyway, claiming (preposterously) that Nový had not said the words complained of and, in any case, had been acting within his rights. Kohout later claimed that Emil's climbdown was 'an example of surrender which meant the end to the solidarity of Czech society'. That seems an overstatement: the solidarity of 1968 had dissipated long ago. On a personal level, however, for Emil, the difference was huge. He had avoided the threat of further punishment by the regime – but at what price? No one could read the report of the proceedings in *Rudé právo* without a degree of sympathy for various witnesses who had clearly been bullied into undermining the case. (For example, the sound engineer who had recorded Nový's speech testified that the recording might not have been an accurate representation of what Nový had said.) But sympathy is a vague and shifting thing. The solid fact was that Emil had failed conspicuously to live up to his image as a hero of the liberal cause.

That was not all. It would emerge much later (although few people noticed) that, at some point, Emil had withdrawn his signature from the 'Ten Points' manifesto that he, Pachman and others had signed the previous August. It is not clear how or when this happened, let alone why, but there is no shortage of possible reasons. Signatories faced trial and imprisonment: Pachman was already in jail; others would follow. Backing down got Emil off the hook (although he would later be called as a witness), and he was not the only signatory to withdraw. But he may also have been motivated by a desire to dissociate himself from Pachman. He seems to have felt that he had been hustled into getting into more trouble, and adopting a more anti-Communist position, than he had intended. There were probably more personal issues, too. Pachman was a difficult personality – a womaniser with a huge ego – and it was easy to fall out with him.

Emil later told friends, referring to the Nový trial: 'I was prepared to go to the edge of the abyss but not to jump into it.' It is unlikely that he was left undamaged by the choice. For two decades his identity had been bound up with his heroism: he was the man with the strength and willpower to hang on while others succumbed to despair. Now he too had succumbed – and presumably learnt the great drawback of such shame-faced surrenders. It's like quitting in mid-race. The longed-for relief soon fades; the regret doesn't.

Just a few months earlier, Christopher Brasher had written of Emil in the *Observer*: 'He is as great a human being as he was an athlete . . . Those who have dismissed him have demeaned themselves. Zátopek himself will never be demeaned; he will never be defeated.' Now his greatness seemed to have deserted him.

It got worse. In May 1971, a British journalist named Brian Freemantle tracked Emil down during one of his breaks from drilling. Their conversation resulted in an article in the *Daily Mail*. 'Zátopek . . . The will to win is crushed' said the headline. Emil was portrayed as a broken man, who described himself as 'reconciled' to the state of his nation and yet plainly wasn't: 'Once I was unhappy, but not now. There seems little point. I exist.' Emil added that he had been stripped of his army rank and pension, and was quoted as confirming the rumour that he had been working as a dustman. This may have been a misunderstanding, or a mistranslation, or perhaps just Emil getting carried away – but the Czechoslovak authorities were furious. This was precisely the kind of bad publicity that the Husák regime was trying to avoid. It was also the kind of loose-cannon behaviour that Emil was supposed to have had bullied out of him.

A month or so later, Emil came back from his drilling shift to Prague. He was exhausted and a little frightened: he was being harassed by the police about a small car accident in which he had been involved and a problem with a stolen tractor at work for which he seemed to be being made the scapegoat. It was hard to know if he was becoming paranoid or if, as was common security service practice, a deliberate effort was being made to soften him up. Either way, he was vulnerable. Dana was away for the weekend. He had not been home long when the phone rang. A friend with close connections to the Party was inviting him to dinner. Emil knew that she wished him well, despite their recent political differences, so he went over – and found that his fellow guests were two *Rudé právo* journalists, Zdeněk Hoření and Václav Švadlena. 'Perhaps Emil's friend was trying to help,' says Dana today. 'But these things were "organised" . . .'

There was a lot of talking and plenty of wine; there appears to have been a tape-recorder; and by the time Emil left, Hoření and Švadlena had a scoop. According to Dana, Emil realised that he had got carried away. He rang Hoření later that weekend and asked him not to publish anything without showing him the article first; he also sent the paper a short letter, clarifying a particular point about his *Daily Mail* interview. Then he went back to his drilling.

On 20 July 1971 *Rudé právo* published precisely what the Party had been hoping for: a 3,000-word interview under the heading 'Emil Zátopek answers the *Rudé právo* editorial board concerning matters of the past and the present', in which Emil recanted pretty much everything he had fought for in 1968.

Among other things, Emil was quoted as saying that he was still a reserve colonel and still receiving a military pension of 1,160 Czech crowns (just over half of the average male wage). He denied that he had been persecuted for his opinions and distanced himself from 'The Two Thousand Words' and its authors, expressing regret that 'I was one of the wild ones who poured fuel on the fire that might have grown into an inferno which could truly endanger the socialist world.' Far from being an enemy of the regime, he added, he would 'consider it shameful to be an enemy of the socialist regime'. The article ended by quoting in full Emil's short letter of clarification.

The interview took up most of a broadsheet page, and the main illustration was a giant reproduction of Emil's signature. Close inspection of the image reveals that the signature is taken from Emil's letter of clarification, but the average reader will have assumed that it referred to the article as a whole. There could be no doubt about the message: this was a signed, public retraction – one of the most prominent since Galileo's.

According to Dana, Emil 'got what for' when she found out. 'Emil did not talk to me before . . . If he had, I don't think he would have done it.' Perhaps this was a little unfair. Remembering her father being dragged off in the night to Buchenwald by the Gestapo, and fearing that something similar would happen to Emil, Dana had told him many times not to be a hero. Well, now he hadn't been.

He could reasonably have argued that he hadn't been especially cowardly, either. He had just been manipulated – as he had been in the Nový case. Such protestations were useless. You can't uneat your words. Word of the 'retraction' soon reached the West (in contrast to the Nový case), and Emil's admirers on both sides of the Iron Curtain struggled to reconcile the news with their long-cherished ideas of Emil. Had his heroism been an illusion?

Emil was not the first or the last famous dissident to retract in the face of normalisation. Most people who came across such statements gave them little thought, knowing the circumstances in which they must have been extracted. But Zátopek – Zátopek, who could endure everything . . . could they really have got to him, too? For anyone who had ever been inspired by Emil's character and achievements, it was a bitter disappointment.

It must have been bitter for Emil, too. He had built his life around the idea that pain could be endured – and now, publicly and irrevocably, he had capitulated in the middle of his biggest test of all. It is understandable that he did so: what choice did he have, with the entire might of the Czechoslovak state against him and, behind that, the might of the Soviet Union? No one who has not lived and behaved heroically in a totalitarian society has a right to judge him. That will not have made Emil feel any better about it. Waking up on the morning after he first saw the *Rudé právo* article in print, Emil must have felt what Robert Browning expressed with the line: 'Never glad confident morning again . . .'

What must have made it even harder was Emil's awareness that he had already been cast off by many of his former friends: the Party hardliners at home and abroad who felt that he had betrayed the Communist cause; and less committed types who none the less felt that it was no longer wise to be associated with him. Now he was scorned by the other camp, too: the reformers – henceforth to be known as dissidents – who had briefly seen him as an ally and a figurehead.

In practice, the general public seem to have judged him less harshly than he may have feared. They had loved him for so long; it was hard to get over the habit just like that. But Emil's self-esteem may be assumed to have taken a battering, and at times he seems to have sought refuge in, among other things, the bottle. It was not an unusual response. A popular joke of the period suggested that the Marxist-Leninist theory of historical development had been revised, with a new intermediate stage now appearing in the progression from socialism to Communism: alcoholism.

I don't think Emil was an alcoholic, but it is clear that, with no thoughts of heroism to sustain him, he drank heavily and often. With the drilling team, it was hard not to – Emil is supposed to have complained to friends that, in addition to struggling with those 50kg bags of cement, he couldn't keep up with his workmates in the pub either. Now he began to spend more of his Prague evenings out drinking as well – in wine bars where everyone who saw him either cut him dead or insisted on buying him a drink. This, of course, was part of the problem: Emil's glory followed him wherever he went. But he must have realised that, no matter what people said to his face, they knew as well as he did that he was running away – from the fact that he had let both himself and his admirers down.

One kindred spirit he found in this period was a young actor called Ladislav Županič, who would later become director of the Karlín Musical Theatre but was then struggling to make progress in his career because of his refusal to declare to his superiors at the National Theatre that he approved of the Soviet invasion in 1968. (Such declarations were becoming an increasingly widespread workplace requirement.) Županič and Emil drowned their sorrows together several times, often in a wine bar called Malokarpatská, where they could talk uninterrupted. Sometimes Emil talked about his frustrations. 'He used to say how he envied the Czechoslovak pilots who went abroad to fight Hitler during the Second World War. "At least they could fight," he'd say. "I just sleep in a *maringotka* and look at the forest."' At other times, conversation would turn to 'the sort of matters that men discuss only when they're drunk'. From the context of our discussion, I took this to include Emil's marriage – but the details are lost in drink and discretion.

One evening, Županič invited Emil to the opening night of a production of *The Vagabond King* at the National Theatre. Afterwards, they went backstage, and Emil, predictably, stole the show. No one wanted to talk about the production; everyone wanted to talk to Emil, and be seen with him – and, not least, buy him a drink. As the cast headed for the bar, the departing audience noticed Emil too – and they, too, wanted to join in the adulation. The theatre's director, a hardline Communist, glowered impotently. Emil was the star of the evening, and there was nothing he could do about it without risking a public order incident.

Such moments must have been exhilarating for Emil: fleeting reminders of the charmed life he once led. 'But it ended badly,' Županič added, 'because we didn't get home until six in the morning.'

Županič smiles at the memory, yet there is something sad about it, too: a life forged in the unsparing realism of the running track, melting away in a blur of greasepaint and wine-drenched self-pity.

But Emil was not wholly broken. Nor had he lost his lifelong habit of believing that he could, through his own efforts, improve things. He sought comfort not just in alcohol but also, more helpfully, in his marriage. The home at Troja was almost finished. He and Dana resolved to complete the work. The shared objective helped bring them back together. Breeze-block by breeze-block and fitting by fitting, the slightly ramshackle structure edged closer to completion.

Progress was slow. Materials and skilled assistance were harder to obtain than they had once been. Those who knew what was good for them kept their distance. But by mid-1972, Emil and Dana were making serious plans for moving in – and, as a result, for moving out of 8 U Půjčovny. Emil took advantage of this impending change to attempt another wild act of kindness. His friends the Fators had been struggling to fit into their cramped one-bedroom flat since the birth of their son. So Emil proposed they swap homes. The Fators would get a nice, centrally located two-bedroom flat in 8 U Půjčovny with plenty of space for a young family; while the flat that the Zátopeks eventually vacated would be somewhat smaller than the one they had been living in.

The scheme came to nothing, but Emil and Zdeněk Fator did get as far as signing a formal application (dated 2 August 1972) and delivering it to Prague's City Hall. Whatever else had happened to crush his spirit, Emil had retained his taste for extravagant generosity.

Afterwards, he and Fator went to the restaurant at the Zoological Gardens in Troja, but decided that they didn't like the look of the food. 'Emil took one look at it and went: "*Jesus!*"' remembers Fator. 'So we simply got drunk. And much later, we went from the restaurant to their place [at Nad Kazankou]. It was about five hundred metres, and we were singing "Communists, go fuck yourselves" at the top of our voices. Dana was furious.'

The curious thing about this is that it took place only a few weeks after Emil had appeared in court (on 5 May 1972) for the trial of Luděk Pachman. The proceedings were closed to the public, but the charges were thought to include subversion, slandering the Republic, incitement and preparing a felony. Emil is assumed to have been called as a witness. Pachman later claimed that Emil's evidence related to a conversation in which Pachman and the Soviet chess player Paul Keres jokingly discussed emigration. As with the Nový case, what Emil did made little practical difference. Pachman was found guilty – that had never been in doubt – but was immediately released: the two years he had spent in prison on remand cancelled out his sentence. He emigrated to the West soon afterwards.

Was Emil just saving his own skin? Was he motivated by malice? Or did he genuinely consider it his duty (as one informer's report in the StB archives suggests) to give evidence against a 'reactionary' who wanted to undermine Communism? I suspect it was the latter, at least in part: he never stopped believing in the core ideology. Yet it is hard to reconcile this with the attitude he drunkenly expressed in Fator's company. No doubt he was confused; or, more accurately, conflicted. His attempts to behave as a dutiful Communist citizen were forcing him into stances and actions that he must have known were unheroic. I cannot believe that he felt comfortable about this. Maybe his discomfort occasionally expressed itself in alcohol-fuelled fury at what the Communists had done to him.

Luckily for Emil, the Communists didn't hear his song – because this was almost exactly the time that they were deciding a delicate question about his future. The Olympic Games were due to begin in Munich on 26 August and the West Germans had put the Czechoslovak authorities on the spot by inviting Emil to be guest of honour at the Olympic Games in Munich, daring them to embarrass themselves by saying that he was unavailable – their usual approach to enquiries about Emil from overseas – or, worse, that they did not even know where he was.

They did not dare: apart from anything else, a diplomatic push for better relations with West Germany was in progress. Emil had to be made available, and made to behave. An invitation arrived in west Bohemia, via the Sports Ministry in Prague. Emil requested leave of absence to go to the Olympic Games. 'No way,' said the foreman. 'Where am I going to get someone to replace you for three weeks?' So Emil wrote back, politely declining.

Frantic behind-the-scenes activity followed. Eventually, in mid-August, it was announced that Emil was available to go to the Games after all. There could, however, be no question of Dana going as well. 'Normalised' Czechoslovakia was a land that only one half of a married couple could leave at once – just in case anyone felt tempted not to return.

Emil arrived back from the drills the night before departure. 'Quick,' he said to Dana, 'mobilise!' They dug out some respectable clothes, and spent hours frantically trying to scrub the black ingrained dirt from Emil's fingers. Twenty-four hours later he was being escorted into Munich's most luxurious hotel, with a brief that could not have been clearer: to look happy and keep his mouth shut.

There were plenty of old friends to catch up with. One of the first people he met there was the former 1,500m world record holder, László Tábori, a Hungarian who had defected to the US after failing to return from the Melbourne Olympics. Later, Emil sat near Jesse Owens in the VIP section of the stands during the opening ceremony, and spoke briefly to the West German Chancellor, Willie Brandt. He generally avoided journalists, but he did give one interview to *Spiegel*. He talked mainly about sport, discussing the increasing prominence of Third World athletes. Asked about what he was doing now, he said: 'I am a simple worker and drill outside Prague for mineral water. But, please, I am very reluctant to talk about politics.'

But the eyes of the world weren't really on Emil, or on Czechoslovakia – and especially not after 5 September, when members of the Black September Palestinian terrorists broke into the Olympic village and took eleven Israelis hostage – all of whom were subsequently killed. Controversially, the Games then resumed, but no one was taking much pleasure from them after that. At the ceremony for the victims, held in the stadium on 6 September, Emil was seen wiping away tears. For a man who believed so warmly in the power of the Olympic ideal to heal divisions between nations and ideologies, the tragedy must have felt heartbreakingly grotesque.

A week later, Emil was at the airport waiting to go home, at the same time as a party of *Runner's World* readers. One of them, Joe Henderson, plucked up the courage to approach him. He was rewarded with twenty minutes of Emil's time and autographs for most of his party.

Emil was happy to talk about running – in English – but avoided politics. He did say, however, that it was odd to receive so much attention. 'In my country I am just a common man – a nobody.'

Then he flew home, to assume the workman's clothes in which he would work and sleep for the next two weeks – or, for all he knew, the next ten years. He was still a decade short of retirement age, and had no reason to believe that the rest of his working life would be any different. Very slowly, however, an end to his exile was approaching.

18

In the drawer

On 24 August 1973, Arthur I. Wortzel, chargé d'affaires at the US Embassy in Prague, sent a cable to the US State Department assessing the state of Czechoslovakia five years after the Soviet-led invasion. The anniversary itself, he reported, had passed 'almost without notice', although there had been extra police on the streets and special fencing had prevented access to Jan Palach's grave. 'Normalcy', he concluded, had been restored to such a degree that it was almost as if 'this upheaval had never occurred'.

Not everyone had forgotten, though. 'Former Olympic champion Emil Zátopek,' reported Wortzel, 'was seen August 20 muttering into beer "Five years, five years . . ."'

Five years is a long time to spend in limbo, half living as a kind of outlaw, watched and warned, cut off from your dreams and from the love of your life. Emil was far from the only Czechoslovak to endure such frustrations in the Husák era. But few can have experienced such a soul-sapping contrast. Once, his refusal to accept limits had thrilled the world; now, almost nothing was possible.

He was comfortable on the drilling team – comfortable enough to annoy his colleagues, sometimes, with his incessant talking; or by challenging them, once, to race him to the work site they were heading for, with them going forwards while he ran backwards. And they, too, had accepted him for who he was. Once, seeing Emil struggle with a heavy load, his foreman said to him: 'Emil, relax. You've already earned your oats.' But acceptance, and endurance, are not the same as happiness. Emil was still caged.

Yet that visit to Munich had loosened the lock. Enquiries from the outside world about his availability – to present the prizes, to be guest of honour – kept coming in, and the ČSTV grew weary of lying in response to each one. In October 1973, Paavo Nurmi died. The Finns organised a race to honour the memory of their greatest distance runner. Emil was invited to be starter. Once again, he was given permission.

The visit passed quietly, and the authorities decided that Emil no longer posed a threat to the re-established order. It was time to end the awkwardness of having to track Emil down in the wilderness. All that remained was to find him a job where he couldn't do any damage.

Wheels were set in motion. While they turned, Emil and Dana continued their strange, disjointed existence. Dana developed her gift for coaching. The work became both fulfilling and demanding of her time; sometimes, when Emil came home, she was away. Any positive feelings Emil had developed towards his itinerant, outdoor existence were offset by the thought that, unless he could return to Prague permanently, he would barely see Dana at all – when what they really needed most was time together.

But at least, when they were both at home, they could, if they chose, be left to themselves. Being out of favour politically meant being less in demand socially. This left space in which to rediscover one another. Dana says that she took to heart her mother's advice: to 'hold each other's hands while you still have one another'. She knew what the regime required. 'They wanted,' she says, illustrating the point with an opening and closing gesture, 'to put us in a drawer.' She and Emil decided to turn this into a positive, saying to themselves (as Dana puts it): 'Life is the most precious thing we have, and even though it just treated us badly, we live on; and we can find a corner where we will feel comfortable even in a table drawer.'

You could think of it as a kind of twilight: a grey no-man's-land somewhere between celebrity, notoriety and anonymity that was, in their case, the price of peace. Other heroes of the Prague Spring ended up in prison, in exile or, in a few cases, in suspiciously premature graves. Emil and Dana still had enough friends in high places for an exception to be made in their case – if they would just refrain from making a nuisance of themselves.

It wasn't always easy. Emil was troubled, in a way that he never had been before. 'What happened after 1968 wounded his soul,' says Dana, without quite being able to put her finger on how. 'It was hard for him. He had been a star, and all of a sudden he was unknown. Books about him disappeared. He stopped being invited to schools to talk. There was an emptiness. Most people didn't see it, but it left a scar.' Sometimes he would be his old self, urging Dana not to be hurt by the friends who had deserted them – because 'at least we know that those who stayed are really worth something'. At other times a shadow would fall on him: a new pessimism that could manifest itself in anything from drinking to uncharacteristic grumpiness.

Yet life 'in the drawer' was less alien to his temperament than some might have imagined. Even with a smaller audience than he was used to, Emil never lost his instinct to brighten the lives around him. He would still make everyday matters into jokes, still exercise his restless mind; occasionally, he would indulge his romantic side. Some of Dana's happier memories of this period are of sitting under the walnut tree at Troja, drinking wine while Emil recited poetry to her from memory. Happiest of all were his performances of 'Král Lávra', which often degenerated into wild hilarity as he got carried away with the characters' different voices.

At other times, they focused their still considerable energies on caring for their home and garden. Dana grew flowers but left the vegetables to Emil. And, as she points out: 'One good thing about the invitations for public speaking drying up was that it left us with a lot of time.' Between them, she says: 'We made an environment of our own.'

Yet it was not always a particularly private environment, especially when Emil began to indulge his lifelong taste for offering hospitality to strangers on the spur of the moment. He had always liked the idea that he had a sacred duty to put his home comforts at other people's disposal: Les Perry and Percy Cerutty were among the beneficiaries in Helsinki, just as Olga Fikotová and Harold Connolly were in Prague when seeking permission to marry. If a friend needed somewhere to live, as Ivan Ullsperger did for a while, Emil and Dana would be quick to offer their spare room. As Dana put it: 'Our door was never really closed.' Sometimes there were strangers-in-need, too, such as the German tourists, lost in Prague late one rainy night in the mid-1960s, whom Emil invited back to U Půjčovny. 'When they saw Emil's colonel's uniform hanging up inside, they were terrified,' laughs Dana.

Now, however, in Troja, Emil began to invite so many strangers to dine and to stay, so regularly, that Dana – who usually ended up doing the catering – found herself dreading coming home from work. She would scan the windows for signs of unexpected guests before deciding whether to come in or not.

You can see her point of view; yet you can see Emil's, too. Maybe he was motivated by loneliness. Maybe he wanted an excuse for the familiar comforts of wine, anecdotes and song. Or maybe he just felt a restless desire for something – anything – beyond his new tamed normality. Whatever the truth, it is hard not see something noble in his compulsion to share what he had with strangers. When the world fell in love with the idea of Zátopek in the days of his athletic prime, it was partly because, in contrast to other athletes who competed only for themselves, Emil seemed to see himself as part of a wider human family, and behaved accordingly. Now he was doing the same, in the privacy of his own drawer.

Some of the guests turned into lifelong friends. But the sheer volume of visitors drove Dana nuts, especially when she discovered, in 1975 or 1976, that many of these guests were coming from a campsite down the road whose owners would direct them to the Zátopeks' house when their site was full. 'At that point,' she says, 'I declared the Tourist Hotel closed.' Even then, there were quite a few who slipped through security over the next couple of decades, as dozens of grateful admirers from around the world will testify.

Back in the early 1970s, however, perhaps there was one additional attraction to the company of strangers: there was no risk that they would get into trouble from being seen to associate with the Zátopeks. Emil took this concern seriously, and for that reason was relatively relaxed about those who chose to keep their distance. But a few friends insisted on standing by them. Their loyalty meant a lot. One example was Emil's former teammate Ludvík Liška, who since leaving the army had been caretaker at the Stará Boleslav training retreat, and his wife Olga. Emil and Dana were regularly guests of the Liškas for Saturday night village dances in Slapy, just outside Prague. It was a modest form of entertainment for such a fêted couple, and quite a big risk for the Liškas. But it formed an important part of what Dana calls a 'process of renewal'.

It must have been around this time that Emil first raised the question, which he and Dana discussed many times, of whether there were more good people in the world than bad – or vice versa. Dana felt that the good were in the majority; Emil disagreed. They also talked about the possibility of starting a club – perhaps even a worldwide organisation – whose members would all be good people. 'The trouble was, we couldn't agree on the criteria for membership,' says Dana. They had fun discussing it, though: sometimes at dinners where other loyal friends – Jan Veselý, the cyclist; František Šťastný, the motorcyclist; Zdeněk Ujčík, the ice hockey player; and their spouses – would gather with the Zátopeks and the Liškas and, instead of trying to change the world, quietly celebrate their shared humanity. They drank wine, told jokes and stories, sometimes sang songs: did, in short, the things that people who love life have always enjoyed doing, in tyrannies as in democracies. After a while, they began to talk of themselves as the Old Guard. They carried on meeting for decades, until (quite recently) the gang became too depleted by ill health and death to be viable.

'This table has so many memories,' says Dana, reliving some of them for me over slivovice on a cold winter's morning in Prague. Seeing how her face brightens as she dips into that pool of remembered friendship, I begin to sense what Emil must have meant by his observation, mentioned earlier, that the key to happiness is to learn to behave as a domesticated animal rather than a wild one. Luděk Pachman, who reported it, clearly felt that it was discreditable to his erstwhile friend. I am not so sure. Learning to live well, irrespective of who controls the levers of worldly power, has much to be said for it; the Christian injunction to 'render unto Caesar the things that are Caesar's' expresses much the same view. Not everyone who lives under a tyranny can fight it head-on, all of the time; someone has to keep the flame of ordinary humanity alive as well.

Emil was an atheist. But he was also a humanist, and there was something almost sacramental about his insistence on the basic human virtues of courtesy, consideration and hospitality. If this part of his life now became more important to him than his public profile, that does not seem inappropriate.

Even then, however, Emil's life was not yet permanently settled. In 1974 he was told that a job had been found for him with the ČSTV. There was probably little option other than to accept, and at least it meant working in Prague. The job involved monitoring foreign publications for the latest developments in sports science and training techniques, taking advantage of Emil's proficiency as a linguist. 'I became a sports spy' was how he described it.

He handed in his notice at Stavební geologie in June and began work in July, in the ČSTV's documentation centre, in a little office underneath the Strahov stadium. It was a pretty lowly job, shuffling papers in a way that seemed significantly less worthwhile – and perhaps even more humiliating – than what he had been doing before. He endured it because there was no alternative. To speak of it as a liberation would be overstating it. None the less, that was how it appeared in the West, and perhaps how it was intended by the Czechoslovak regime. As Neil Allen wrote in *The Times* on hearing the news: 'Emil Zatopek has been welcomed back into the fold of Czechoslovak sport.'

In fact, he was on the outermost edge of the fold. The 'sports spy' label made the job sound more interesting than it was. Emil was just providing a not particularly important cuttings service. He could use his language skills but little else. It was tolerable but dull.

His old friend Jaromír Konůpka visited Emil one day at work and found him delighted with the distraction – and apparently indifferent to his employers' approval. 'After we had been chatting for a while,' recalls Konůpka, 'his manager came in and summoned him to the daily "ten-minute meeting", which was about to start.' (Such collective political pep-talks were a daily occurrence in

Czechoslovak workplaces.) 'Emil said he'd be along in a minute, then carried on chatting. Five minutes later, the manager came back: "Come on, Emil, it will look bad if you're not there." "Yes, yes," said Emil, and waved him away. Then, after he'd gone, he turned to me and said: "I'm glad you're here today. It means I don't have to go."'

In some ways, the documentation centre was more soul-destroying than the *maringotka*. At least with drilling wells he had been outside, exerting himself and doing productive work. 'Emil always wanted to be useful,' says Dana, 'and he didn't feel that this work was useful.'

But his half-rehabilitation brought one big benefit: he could travel again. The invitations took time to start coming in, but he appreciated them all. In 1975, for example, he was allowed to travel to Paris, to receive a UNESCO Pierre de Coubertin Fair Play medal. This may have been the trip from which he returned by train, laden with gifts, including a signed, limited edition print by Pablo Picasso. Emil pronounced this 'sort of OK' before giving it away to the photographer with whom he was sharing a compartment.

But the freebies weren't what mattered. Emil was the first Czechoslovak sportsperson to receive such a prestigious international award. Even the most hardline normaliser could see that there was a diplomatic benefit to such honours. Bit by bit, the shackles loosened.

There was still a price to be paid, though. On 6 and 7 January 1977, a group of Czechoslovakia's most stubborn remaining dissidents (including Václav Havel, Pavel Kohout and Ludvík Vaculík) published the 'Manifesto of Charter 1977', urging the government to allow its citizens the basic human rights to which it had supposedly committed itself in the 1975 Helsinki Accords. The manifesto was instantly suppressed, but was widely published abroad, and many of the 242 signatories were in due course arrested. Meanwhile, the regime launched a ferocious counter-attack of propaganda-based intimidation that recalled the hate campaign against Milada Horáková in the 1950s, though without the threat of death. *Rudé právo* kicked it off on 12 January, with an issue denouncing the charter as Goebbels-esque anti-socialist propaganda and its authors as 'remnants of bourgeois reaction'. Then came the supposedly spontaneous attacks from ordinary people; and then public figures were 'invited' to join in. Singers, writers, actors, artists and musicians were encouraged to sign an 'anti-charter' promising 'new creative acts in the name of socialism and peace', on the unstated but clear understanding that, if they didn't, they would find it impossible to get work in future. There was little resistance; most Czechoslovaks had long since succumbed to what Pavel Kohout called 'the great surrender' (which he blamed Emil for starting). For two weeks, *Rudé právo* printed the names of compliant celebrities, filling page after page with well over seven thousand signatories.

Emil was not among them. He did, however, take part in television's precursor to the campaign, appearing on ČST on 15 January to express his condemnation of 'political adventurers who with this Charter have tried to stick a knife into our collective work'. I don't suppose he gave it much thought; nor would he have read the manifesto that he had been told to denounce (it was impossible to get hold of). He had made enough speeches in defence of socialism in the past: what difference did one more soundbite make, when his reputation as a liberal was ruined anyway?

No one's life was at stake, in contrast to 1950; while in contrast to 1968 the prospect of regime change seemed infinitesimal. Why risk wrecking his life again? In any case, he really was opposed to the undermining of socialism – and *Rudé právo*'s description of the Charter, which he probably had read, made it sound like a blueprint for precisely that.

None the less, it was one more gesture of submission to the Stalinist forces that Emil had once defied. A few more former admirers found themselves thinking a little bit less of him; and no doubt Emil did, too. Once he had preached that 'one's willpower increases with every task fulfilled'. Now he was discovering the dispiriting opposite: that each surrender makes it easier to surrender again in future.

From this point on, however, the burden of official disapproval lightened. That autumn, Emil was allowed to attend the dinner following the annual *Rudé právo* road race. The Finnish runner Lasse Viren – double gold medallist at the previous year's Montreal Olympics – was the star guest, and Emil, Viren and Zdeněk Fator drank many toasts together (one of which was 'Death to all Bolsheviks'). Emil 'sang English songs extremely loudly', by one account.

The following year, Emil attended a ceremony to mark the fiftieth anniversary of the stadium at Mikkeli, in Finland. Dana was allowed to travel with him. The world would hardly have noticed had they not been there, so it seems fair to see this as an act of trust – or perhaps a test – on the regime's part. Huge numbers of Finns turned out to see Emil, and were rewarded by hearing him give a seven-minute speech in what his (superfluous) interpreter called 'beautiful' Finnish.

That year also saw the European athletics championships held in Prague. Emil kept a low profile, but one British journalist bumped into him at the stadium and was delighted to obtain his autograph, which he then showed proudly to a nineteen-year-old member of the British team. 'Who's Emil Zátopek?' was the response.

Some people remembered, though. The following year, George A. Hirsch, chairman of the New York Road Runners and founder of *The Runner* magazine, invited him to the USA to serve as grand marshal for the New York City Marathon. Emil spent several happy days being shown around the city, where, according to Hirsch, 'he captivated everyone with his engaging manner, bubbling storytelling, and absolutely unassuming demeanour'. At one point, he was taken to a meal in a Chinese restaurant, and impressed both waiters and guests by ordering in Chinese; at another, he sang songs to the secretaries in the offices of *The Runner*.

The race itself, Emil later said, 'was like a miracle for me – all those people jogging'. But a scarcely less memorable moment occurred the day before, when Hirsch took Emil to Central Park for some photographs, along with Bill Rodgers, the leading US marathon runner of the day. The photographer asked the driver of a passing parks department cart if he could stand on the cart's back step to photograph the three men as they jogged. The driver turned out to be from Prague, and, on realising who Emil was, rushed to embrace him. 'Zátopek!' he shouted, and was overcome by tears.

The subsequent photograph, of Hirsch, Rodgers and Emil jogging, sticks in the mind for three reasons. Emil, in shorts and T-shirt, looks strikingly fit. Rodgers and Hirsch, no underachievers themselves, are visibly thrilled to be running with him. Most memorably of all, Emil looks radiantly joyful, with an ear-to-ear grin and laughing eyes. This was him in his element: making people happy by sprinkling a bit of Zátopek magic into their lives.

The air miles began to accumulate. In June 1980, Emil and Dana spent two days in Zurich, where Emil had been invited to present the prizes at the West-athletic Cup by the Indian spiritual leader and running enthusiast Sri Chinmoy. At the airport, Chinmoy made to shake hands with him, but Emil folded his hands in the Indian way and said 'Namaskar' and continued to talk in Hindi until he ran out of remembered phrases (which related largely to drinking tea).

Then there were trips to Japan, to meet Kohei Murakoso, the great Japanese marathon champion; to Germany, to be official starter of the 1982 Frankfurt Marathon; and to Finland, in 1981 and 1983. For the latter trip, Emil was supposed to help promote sales of Czechoslovak tractors. He found himself having to demonstrate the alleged manoeuvrability of an enormous tractor and trailer combination, and credited his tank-driving experience for the fact that he did not make a mess of it.

Emil had retired by then. He and Dana both had, on the first day they were eligible to do so: 19 September 1982. Emil was not sorry to leave the documentation centre behind, although his final year had been enlivened by sharing the office with another sports star who had vanished under normalisation: Věra Čáslavská. She, too, was being grudgingly edged towards rehabilitation, and although she was even less enthusiastic about the work than Emil, their shared sense of humour helped pass the time. Sometimes, she told her biographer, 'work with him didn't even feel like working'.

Dana found that her annual pension was just 1,427 crowns: barely half what she had been expecting. When she enquired, she was told that it was because of 1968. She complained, pointing to her lifetime of service to her country as athlete, trainer and ambassador. She was told: 'Yes, but you signed the "Two Thousand Words". You will get no more.'

In fact, they were not too badly off. Emil had a pension, too, and they had saved enough over the years. Later on, a retainer to Emil from Adidas would add financial security – while further still into the future the house and garden in Troja would become a valuable piece of real estate. Yet it must have been dispiriting to realise that, getting on for quarter of a century later, and despite having lost all credibility as liberal reformers, they had still not been forgiven for their support for socialism with a human face.

Dana shrugged off her disappointment and continued to mentor young athletes in a less formal capacity for many years more. Emil responded, characteristically, by setting himself a new challenge, creating a large wine cellar, in the Moravian style, beneath a walnut tree in the garden. He put a considerable amount of effort into this, and in due course filled it with a considerable amount of wine, which might not have been a brilliant idea for a man who now had so much time on his hands but did help keep alive the Zátopeks' reputation for warm hospitality.

Around the same time, Ludvík and Olga Lišková invited Emil and Dana to a special celebration at Houštka Spa. Their friends wore Moravian costumes and welcomed them, in the traditional way, with bread and salt. It was a brave, poignant, heartfelt tribute – only slightly marred by the fact that the coaches who were using the track at the time hurriedly ushered their young athletes from the track, forbidding them even to go near the clubhouse window while the Zátopeks were present. It is possible that they would not have recognised him anyway: his name had long since been removed from school textbooks – just as it had been removed from the sports stadium in Kopřivnice, which had been renamed (and remains) the Summer stadium.

Yet the message must have sunk in eventually that Emil and Dana were no longer as toxic as they had once been. In 1983, the first World Athletics Championships were held in Helsinki. Emil was an honoured guest – and saw Grete Waitz win the women's marathon in a time only five minutes slower than his own victory on the same course in 1952. Back in Prague, there were enquiries from Juan Antonio Samaranch, president of the International Olympic Committee, about the possibility of meeting both Emil and Věra Čáslavská, so that he could honour them on behalf of the IOC. He was told that Emil was ill and Věra was unable to meet him because of family problems. He persisted, and eventually, in November 1984, he came to Prague and presented them both with the golden insignias of the IOC's Olympic Order.

By then, another Olympic Games had taken place: in Los Angeles. Emil did not go; nor did anyone from Czechoslovakia. Like the rest of the Warsaw Pact countries, they were boycotting the Games, in retaliation for the US boycott of the Moscow Olympics four years earlier. Asked for his views on the matter, Emil had been diplomatic but lukewarm. He gave his broad backing to the boycott but also expressed his sorrow for 'all athletes who have conscientiously trained for the Games and can't go now'. He said nothing about his own sorrow – although US sources suggested that, a few months earlier, he had been invited to be the torch-bearer at the Games. But he did observe pointedly that 'our [Czechoslovak] functionaries see their role model in the Soviet Union and follow every counsel the Soviets give them'.

He had learnt his lesson, though. Pressed to say more, he talked instead about his sincere distaste for the creeping commercialisation of the sport he loved. 'The modern Olympics should not be subject to commercial exploitation, but should glorify the ideals of the Olympics.'

Emil was reminded of what those ideals had once meant to him when, the following year, Les Perry arranged to fly him to Australia for the Jubilee running of the Zátopek race, which he, Percy Cerutty and Reg Prentice had set up in Melbourne in Emil's honour in 1961. According to the *Sydney Morning Herald*, 'The generosity, charm and charisma that so impressed John Landy, Les Perry and the other Australians who met him at the 1952 Helsinki Olympics were on display throughout his stay.' Emil not only attended the main race but also insisted on supporting all the lesser events, cheering, helping to officiate and presenting prizes. 'He had a word for each of the hundreds who met him,' the *SMH* continued. 'His presence transformed an otherwise mundane occasion into one to remember.'

It was an occasion to remember for Emil, too. 'I think he was genuinely touched to see a far-off country had recognised his achievements,' said Les Perry. But, of course, it was not just his achievements that were being honoured. All those years of kindness and charm, all those small courtesies and words of encouragement – that was what people were really trying to repay.

Whether they succeeded in soothing the scars on Emil's soul is a different matter. He still tended, sometimes, to drink too much – to such an extent that, if Dana was away, the Liškas would ring him up every now and then to see if he was all right. Olga used to challenge him to recite a tongue-twister, 'and if he couldn't say it we'd know that things were bad'. Sometimes, if they sounded really bad, or if there was no answer, they would drive over and check. On one such visit, in 1986, they found him on the floor. He had had a heart seizure.

Emil was out of hospital soon enough, but the episode brought a temporary halt to his travels. It also brought an end to his running. He had not been doing much anyway, despite regular encouragement from Dana, who seemed untouched by age, to go jogging with her. But it was still a huge, unwelcome landmark in a life that had been defined by running.

Age had not treated him kindly. Perhaps it was the years of self-torture on the track; or perhaps the more recent years of unhealthy living. More probably it was coming from a family with a history of cardiovascular problems. It was no less cruel for that. There would be other invitations, and other visits: for example, to London in September 1987 to be starter for the *Sunday Times* National Fun Run in Hyde Park, where, according to John Disley (who arranged it), 'He was a delight. He didn't need entertaining. He just disappeared into the crowd and started talking to people. He didn't hold himself aloof at all.'

There was, however, a difference. There could be no question of Emil joining in the running, as he had originally intended to do. And no matter how many other races he started in future, that single, crushing reality would not change. From now on the guest of honour would not be Emil the tamed but unbroken hero.

Instead, it would be Zátopek: the old man.

19

'Say it ain't so, Emil'

In the autumn of 1989, following months of unrest across Eastern Europe, the Berlin Wall came down. Czechoslovakia's Communist tyranny evaporated soon afterwards, abruptly as morning mist.

It was over in weeks. The Wall fell on 9 November. On 17 November, a student demonstration in Prague was broken up violently by police; days of wider protests followed, swelling in numbers until the crowds could be counted in hundreds of thousands; the police abandoned the streets. A wave of strikes began, culminating in the first general strike since 'victorious February' in 1948. A new pro-democracy movement, Civic Forum, came to the fore, and half-forgotten icons of the dissident movement began to be seen in public. More than 200,000 people packed Wenceslas Square on 24 November to cheer Václav Havel, the dissident playwright who had spent five of the past twelve years in jail, as he waved and spoke briefly from the balcony of the Melantrich building; then they listened in dumbstruck silence, hands raised in V-for-victory signs and tears streaming down careworn cheeks, as Marta Kubišová emerged from two decades of obscurity to sing 'A Prayer for Marta' from the same balcony.

The popular unity was irresistible. The despised First Secretary of the Communist Party, Miloš Jakeš, recognised that the game was up and resigned. The rest of the Party leadership followed suit. On 30 November, the Communist Party relinquished its monopoly on power. Free elections – the first since 1946 – were announced. By the end of the year, unthinkably, Václav Havel would be president and Alexander Dubček would be speaker of the federal parliament.

Emil and Dana spent that first crucial fortnight of protest at home.

Then, on the day after the Party leadership's resignation, between 800,000 and a million people gathered on Letná plain – the park overlooking the city from which Stalin's statue had once loomed. It was a miraculous, haunting occasion; as if an entire people had emerged blinking into the daylight, still scarcely able to believe that now, perhaps, the land that had been theirs truly was coming back to them.

Emil and Dana joined them. Songs were sung and speeches were made and solidarity was expressed. Someone spotted Emil and suggested that he say something, too. He shook his head. 'This revolution belongs to other people,' he said. 'It is their world now.'

But Emil and Dana had to live in it, too, and they soon noticed the difference. There was no more fear of arbitrary disgrace and exile; no more looking over the shoulder for eavesdroppers. Censorship was abolished; borders were opened. On 11 March 1990, Emil was formally rehabilitated. Just ten weeks into Václav Havel's presidency, the new defence minister, Miroslav Vacek, publicly apologised for Emil's dismissal from the army.

In Troja, the phone began to ring. For a long time, it rarely stopped. Friends, admirers and curious journalists from around the world all wanted to know what their lost hero had been up to. One of the first to call was the Australian journalist Hedley Thomas, to whom Emil spoke with unaccustomed frankness about politics. He had not, he explained, been against the old regime: 'They gave me the chance to compete in the Olympic Games . . . Maybe on the one hand I was very keen to protest, but as Olympic champion I had more than other people.' The telephone interview was punctuated by angry shouts from Dana, trying to get him to shut up, but Emil would not be silenced. 'I am a Communist,' he insisted. 'But the problem with Communism is that people at the top become egotists . . . They had to have two or three houses, an account in a Swiss bank. This is not real Communism.'

There had, Emil admitted, been other drawbacks with the old regime. 'It was not possible to protest . . . This telephone was controlled . . . I was very careful not to say anything bad.'

Now, by contrast, the only control came from Dana, shouting in the background each time he said something positive about the old regime. 'In our house there is democracy,' Emil continued. 'We have different views.' To him, 'Communist ideology means to work and to give to society so nobody will die of hunger.'

Shortly afterwards, the call was cut off, possibly by Dana. The hard-learnt lesson that careless talk about politics can land you in bad trouble was not easily forgotten. For more than a decade, the Zátopeks had found a tolerable existence by disciplining themselves to live 'in the drawer'. Why risk coming out?

'Our hope is that all will be quiet and that we can live the last years of our life in a democracy,' Dana told another journalist, *Sports Illustrated*'s Leigh Montville, who visited them in Troja. 'We hope for peace and good health.'

For a while, that wish was granted. The quiet currents of their late lives flowed on: the meetings of the Old Guard; the birthdays and reunions; the pottering in the garden. There was much-loved new dog, a spaniel–terrier cross called Kuba (a diminutive of Jakub, not a tribute to the socialist state). Old friendships were rekindled. Ladislav Kořán – who had emigrated in 1968, arrived in the US with $5 in his pocket and used his electronics expertise to become a very successful businessman – took the opportunity to start making regular visits to his homeland. The Zátopek home was usually his first stop. Emil's trips abroad continued, too: to Spain, where he received the city of San Sebastián's Tambor de Oro award and met the family of his late friend Patxi Alcorta; to Argentina, where he was reunited with Reynaldo Gorno, runner-up in the 1952 Olympic marathon; even to California, where a group of physicians at Stanford University – who had paid for the trip – tried unsuccessfully to help with the sciatica in his left leg and Olga Fikotová-Connolly and her daughter showed him the opulence of Los Angeles. 'To live in such a place – how is it possible?' marvelled Emil.

The following year he went to Barcelona, for the Olympics, and at one point appeared on the track – to be applauded so warmly that it must have brought back memories of his days as a fairy-tale hero.

At times, it must have seemed reasonable to think in terms of living happily ever after. But no new dawn lasts for ever; or even, usually, for long. As the spectre of Communism receded, recriminations began. In December 1990, the secret service that had underpinned the Communist Party's dominance was dismantled. Inevitably, people began to ask what secrets were stored in its archives. Names of supposedly 'compromised' politicians began to be circulated. The government moved quickly to limit access. It has been estimated that during the Communist period one Czechoslovak in four assisted the secret services to some extent. The potential was obvious for an orgy of destructive finger-pointing – the last thing the country's delicate young democracy needed. In May 1992 the government drafted a law, enacted that summer, to restrict publication of the names of StB agents. Not until 1996 was the public given partial access to the archive. Even then, individuals were allowed to see only their own files, or those of dead family members, or to authorise others to do so; alternatively, they could inspect the general index. That was all. Many people decided not to exercise even that limited right, for fear of what they might find.

It would be several years before stories began to emerge about this or that public figure being mentioned in the archives (as many were) and thus being implicated as – perhaps – an StB informer or agent. And it was not until 1998 that word began to spread that Emil might be compromised. The claims were vague at first. President Havel had decided to award the Order of the White Lion – the country's most senior honour – to around ninety public figures, to mark the eightieth anniversary of Czechoslovakia's founding. Emil was to be one of them. The German newspaper *Süddeutsche Zeitung* complained that another proposed recipient, Helmut Zilk, the formerly Prague-based mayor of Vienna, was named in the archives as an StB informer. During the furore that followed, the right-wing politician Václav Benda, a former dissident who had briefly been head of the Office for the Documentation and Investigation of Crimes of Communism, announced that he had doubts about the integrity of several other of the candidates. It wasn't long before a television channel, Nova, was suggesting that one of those under suspicion was Emil Zátopek.

The charge didn't get much further at the time. Emil wasn't paying attention, and, in any case, had never been that worried about what people said about him. Yet the claim planted a seed of doubt that has been bothering Emil's admirers ever since – especially after it emerged that Emil's name could indeed be found in the general index of the StB archive.

In itself, that information implied little: you could be in the archives as an agent, an informant or a 'person of interest' – or, in many cases, as some combination of the three. That did not prevent gossip that 'Zátopek worked for the StB'. There had always been those who could not forgive Emil for his closeness to the regime; and a few who envied him his years of glory. His public climbdowns in the 1970s had tarnished his reputation further. Why not go all the way and mark him down as a Communist snitch?

What made the whisperings worse was that this was not the first time that suspicion had been attached to Emil. In November 1975, Josef Frolík, a senior StB officer who had defected to the US in 1969, gave evidence to a hearing on 'Communist Bloc Intelligence Activities in the United States' to the Senate's Committee on the Judiciary. His testimony included denunciations of prominent Czechoslovaks in most walks of life: politicians, entertainers, authors, diplomats and sportspeople, all of whom, he claimed, had been in the pay of the Czechoslovak intelligence service.

It included this:

> Emil Zátopek, the multiple Olympic victor in the 5-km, 10-km, marathon and endurance run events, has been an agent from the early fifties. He is one of the most cynical of agents who was even informing on his own wife Dana. During the period of the 'Prague Spring' he was being used as an agent-provocateur who, through his own activities and through participation in other operations, was supposed to help compromise the regime of A. Dubček and his supporters. He comes across like an anticommunist and as being very liberal.

For one reason or another, this sensational claim made no ripple in the media, even when a printed record of the testimony was made publicly available in 1976. Perhaps Emil's fame had faded so much by then that the handful of intelligence wonks who monitored such things didn't recognise his name, buried as it was among a series of sensational claims about the sex lives of famous cultural figures and the allegedly subversive activities of British politicians. In Czechoslovakia, meanwhile, the press was scarcely going to report the fact that a senior spy had defected and was pouring out secrets to the West.

But it was only a matter of time before Frolík's claim resurfaced – not least via his book, *Špión vypovídá*, which became available in Czechoslovakia in 1990. Emil's enemies were quick to repeat the allegations – although generally in whispers rather than in public. The rumours don't seem to have intruded much on Emil's existence. Today, however, with Emil no longer around to defend himself, you will find plenty of places on the internet where the allegations are repeated as fact.

And are they fact? Was Emil really working for the secret police, as informer, agent or both?

For a long time, even when I had secured Dana Zátopková's authorisation to inspect the security services' files on Emil, I simply didn't want to know the answer. It is one thing discovering, as I have while researching this book, that your hero was a flawed human being who sometimes did things that he should have been and probably was ashamed of. That's life. But Frolík's suggestion is that everything – the whole Zátopek legend of friendship, chivalry and shared humanity – was just one monstrous fraud. Can it possibly be true?

'Say it ain't so, Joe,' a young fan is supposed to have begged baseball hero Joe 'Shoeless' Jackson when Jackson was implicated in the fixing of the 1919 World Series. I feel much the same about Emil. Please, Emil, you have meant too much, for too long, to me and to so many others. Please don't let this be true.

Eventually, I looked. Frustratingly, even that didn't entirely resolve the matter. Once you enter the world of the spooks, it is hard to be 100 per cent sure of anything. Even gut feeling pulls in two directions. Who do you trust? Frolík – a man who lied for a living and was known to be a dirty tricks specialist? Or Emil, a warm, charming, kind, visibly decent man who made friends easily and inspired trust in nearly everyone he met? The question should answer itself – except that, when you think about it, all those qualities of charm and apparent decency would be precisely what a master of deception would need.

It's the same with the papers in the archive. There are, by my count, twenty-two surviving files relating to Emil in the archives of the StB and the ZS GŠ (Zpravodajská správa generálního štábu), its military counterintelligence sub-section. The former refer to him by the code name ATLET and the latter by the code name MACEK. Between them they contain some 320 pages of often abstruse records. Most are typed; some are handwritten; many are hard to decipher. It would be easy to miss something. Yet certain conclusions leap out at me. Emil is in these files as a 'person of interest', not an agent. He does seem to have reported back from some foreign trips, at least early in his career, but the reports have not been preserved – although at least one such report seems to have been considered unacceptably thin. And I can find no reference anywhere to Emil's having been an agent provocateur, or to his having informed on Dana, or, for that matter, to his having informed on anyone else.

Some of the reports are mind-numbingly mundane; many refer to Emil only in passing. As for the rest, the overwhelming impression is of a security service that sees Emil as an object of suspicion. The raw material comes largely from informers – Agent Vaško, Agent Saša, Agent Marie – who may or may not be reliable and who no doubt have agendas of their own. But there is no mistaking the agenda of the officers for whom the reports are written: they want to know what Emil is up to, where he is, who he is talking to, and what he is likely to do next.

Does that prove his innocence? More or less. But what if the day-to-day agents of the StB and the ZS GŠ weren't in on the plot? What if the reality involved some deep, John le Carré-style game of smoke, mirrors and triple-bluff? What if the archives don't tell the full story? There are gaps in the record: big ones. Some files have been destroyed – many, for some reason, in 1980. The Institute for the Study of Totalitarian Regimes assures me that this would probably have been a routine rationalisation of the records. Yet I can't help feeling uncomfortable about the fact that, where Emil is concerned, most of the 1950s and the first half of the 1960s are a complete blank. The fact that tens of thousands of other files in the archive have been destroyed doesn't really reassure me; nor does the fact that all sorts of people other than Emil (informers, for example, or agents) might have benefited from the destruction of his files. Suspicion poisons everything.

At this point, the only sane approach is to fall back on known facts and common sense. These suggest three things. First: if Emil really was a secret agent, he doesn't seem to have been a very successful one. He was active in the anti-invasion protests at a time when agents provocateurs weren't needed (everyone was protesting anyway) and then went quiet just when a bit of stirring up could conceivably have been useful. His anti-Soviet 'act', supposedly performed for their ultimate benefit, projected worldwide the idea that, in his unforgettable words, they 'have been shown up as the gangsters of the world'. Wouldn't they have been better off without him? His supposed services to the StB and their Soviet overseers did not save him from four and a half years of internal exile – and if he informed on Dana, how come she didn't get into trouble? If it comes to that, what about all those countless kindnesses, large and small, that he showed to so many friends and strangers over so many years? If they were performed with an ulterior motive, why does no trace of those betrayals survive? It just doesn't make sense.

Secondly: other evidence argues against Emil's having been an StB agent. Close friends who lived and worked with him are adamant he was one of 'us' rather than 'them' – Ivan Ullsperger, for example, who actually lived at U Půjčovny for several months; or Ludvík Liška, who insists that 'we knew who they [the informers] all were' and says that Emil used to pull the wool over their eyes on foreign trips by deliberately mistranslating for them. There were clearly doubts in high places about Emil's political reliability. He didn't even become a member of the Communist Party until December 1953, and he was sent on at least one course of political education. In 1956, he and Dana were reportedly reprimanded shortly before leaving for Melbourne, after indiscreetly telling a Swiss journalist how much they hated being followed around by 'sharp eyes'. And Ladislav Kořán, while in Jáchymov, was interrogated more than once about Emil by the secret police, being asked specifically about the possibility that Emil might defect. Emil's military service records show that, throughout the 1950s and 1960s – and especially after 1968 – he was constantly being monitored by his army superiors for signs of ideological unreliability. If he was actually secretly working *for* the security services, there must have been so few people in on the plot that it is hard to see what purpose it could have served. As for his dealings with Westerners, one of the reasons given for his dismissal from the army, in a three-page internal report dated 21 April 1969, was that he 'doesn't report his contacts with foreign agents and citizens'. None of this seems consistent with Emil being a master agent.

Thirdly: there is no evidence of guilt in the archives; just Frolík's assertion and his enemies' suspicions. The fact that Emil is in the archive proves nothing. In the words of Dr Libor Svoboda, 'It would have been more suspicious if he hadn't had a file.' As for the missing files, Emil would hardly have been in a position to order their destruction, especially in 1980. Nor would he have had a motive: everyone assumed, then, that Communism would last for ever. As for Frolík: it is a fact, and not just a suspicion, that the StB were masters of disinformation, including the trick of smearing enemies as their own informers. They had a whole section – Department D – devoted to such practices. It makes more sense to doubt their version of events than Emil's. According to the British espionage expert James Rusbridger, 'It is now generally accepted that Frolík was a plant designed to waste MI5's resources while important spies remained undetected and to sow seeds of distrust between MI5 and the CIA.' I must admit to being both convinced and relieved by Rusbridger's judgement. I cannot categorically prove that Emil was not an agent of some kind – how do you prove a negative? – but in the absence of plausible evidence that he was it seems foolish to consider him anything but innocent. Or, at least, relatively innocent.

These allegations do not come completely out of the blue. Over the years, Emil was repeatedly tainted by his perceived closeness to the Communist tyranny. He may not have been an agent, but his record is far from perfect. He allowed his name to be used in the denunciation of Milada Horáková in 1950; was unsupportive, to put it mildly, towards his fellow runner Milan Švajgr in 1952; turned his back, in 1970 and 1972, on those who had stood beside him in calling for liberty and denouncing the Soviet invasion; condemned Charter 77; and those are just the instances we know about.

A series of critics have excoriated him for this, from Milan Švajgr, who called him a 'snitch', to the historian Stanislav Berton (another Moravian former athlete who failed to achieve lasting glory on the track), who wrote in 2009 that Emil 'sold his soul to the Communist regime'. Luděk Pachman, too, was scathing about him in his autobiographical *Checkmate in Prague* (although others have been equally scathing about Pachman's reliability).

To fail to address such attacks would do Emil an injustice; but I do not think they are fair. Yes, Emil made compromises with one of Communism's nastier regimes. These do him no credit, and one or two were to his lasting shame. But to suggest that his support for the regime was some kind of guilty secret is absurd. It was public: that was the point of it.

As for the StB, Emil clearly spent a lot of time in their company. Most athletes did. 'They tried to keep themselves secret, but we always recognised them,' says Dana. Some kept their distance more successfully than others. There was one, Dana adds, a Mr Lala, with whom 'we all used to discuss what he should put in his reports about us and what he should leave out'; and another who they persuaded to help out with training by retrieving shots and javelins for the throwers – 'because he might as well do something useful'. With Emil, there were certainly some 'sharp eyes' who took pride in being attached to such a great man – just as that American soldier did, escorting his one-man Czechoslovak team around the track in Berlin in 1946. It would have been out of character for Emil not to talk to them at all (although Pavel Kosatík claims that if he ever talked *about* them, 'it was always as about people whom he feared'). No doubt he was sometimes indiscreet.

Dana is dismissive of the darker charges against Emil, including Frolík's. 'People say all sorts of things. Once you're famous, people start saying anything about you. If you let yourself be bothered by it all, you would never do anything.' She reckons that Emil would have been a hopeless spy. 'They wouldn't have wanted him, because he was so talkative. He would have given away every secret.' Indeed, she claims that one of her 'tame' 'sharp eyes' told her that the StB agreed with this diagnosis.

She also argues that some things that might look like 'collaboration' on paper were actually more trivial than they sound – and perhaps were even close to subversion. Once, before going to race in Paris, Emil was instructed to report back on how many aeroplanes he saw there. He shared this mission with his fellow athletes: 'Quick, everyone, help me. How many planes can you see?' It became the running joke of the trip: 'Look, Emil – a plane!' Presumably at some point the StB were presented with a number. It may not have been of much use.

I feel sure that Emil was not working for the security services in or after 1968: the evidence seems overwhelming that he was their target, not their collaborator. I wouldn't be entirely surprised, though, if the StB archives once contained reports of some kind relating to Emil's foreign trips – or even, conceivably, to his visits to military units around Czechoslovakia. (One of the most persistent rumours is that he worked for military counter-intelligence.) That does not make him a monster or a fraud – and not just because there was so much kindness and decency to set against his moments of weakness. Everyone who lived in Czechoslovakia between 1948 and 1989 faced choices that most of us can barely imagine. Zdeněk Fator, for example, was once called in for interrogation by the StB because he had been associating with an unsuitable friend. He was subsequently put under pressure to become an informer. When he refused, he was told: 'You have a very intelligent son, Mr Fator. Do you really want to ruin his life before he even has a chance to go to university?'

Fator was lucky. He escaped from this trap by having a word with a friend in the sporting world who was also a senior member of the security services. The pressure stopped. But that, too, sheds light on Emil's case. Everyone involved in the tragedy of Czechoslovak Communism was a human being. Some were evil; most were just trying to make the best of things. People compromised; threw the security services scraps of information to keep them off their backs; or did what they had to do but tried to do so in a humane way, bending or even breaking rules to minimise suffering.

And Emil? I think he conformed where he felt he had to, filled in the questionnaires he was supposed to fill in for foreign trips, perhaps shared some additional impressions and gossip about the countries he had visited – and then got on with living. I don't think he collaborated with the StB in a cynical or ill-intentioned way. No doubt his fame and his public support for Communism will have earned him an easier ride than many citizens, and it is likely that he escaped harsher retribution after 1968 because there were people in high places who liked him. Does that make him an agent, or an intelligence officer?

It is possible that Emil's garrulous nature may sometimes have got people into trouble. Once, he earned his dear friend Olga Lišková a reprimand by absent-mindedly revealing that she had lent him an ideologically unsound book. She knew it was he who blabbed because he told her – and was surprised to be told that he had done something wrong. 'But why would I not say it,' he asked, 'when it's true?' This reminds us that his working life was spent in the army, in the Ministry of Defence and at Dukla Praha – three of the most dogmatically pro-regime institutions in the country. He did not have to be a secret informer for word of what he said and did to get back to the security services.

I think Emil knew this, and sometimes led the StB on – just as he led most of the Communist establishment on. He probably believed much of what he said in his pro-regime speeches, but he later confessed that at the end of at least one of them, delivered to him in triplicate in advance from the Ministry of Defence, he felt like weeping. Yet I'm not aware of his ever having dug his heels in and refused to deliver them. Perhaps he should have done. Even Ivan Ullsperger, a close friend to whom Emil often confided his political misgivings, concedes that 'only on a few occasions would he step up against it' – 'it' being the regime.

Even in free societies, few of us speak our minds all the time. You can call it dissembling if you like, but it is how we get by, and it is how most people got by under Communism, too – the only difference being that, under Communism, the quality of your dissembling could make the difference between freedom and imprisonment, even life and death. And with Emil, remember, it wasn't just dissembling. He believed in Communism. Unlike some of his subsequent critics (such as Luděk Pachman and Pavel Kohout, before they became liberals), he was never an aggressive Communist. He just believed that Communism was preferable to capitalism. And – who knows? – perhaps, if everyone had been like Emil, Communism might have worked.

Emil was, Ullsperger believes, 'too trusting', and people in the regime 'took advantage of him'; Dana says much the same, as does Ludvík Liška. They all use the same expression: 'took advantage'. People didn't just bully him into supporting 'it': they persuaded and manipulated him, using his socialist beliefs to convince him that giving in to their demands was not just the easy thing to do but the right thing. Emil had a habit, according to Ullsperger, of starting an argument believing one thing but ending it believing the opposite. It is clear from the StB archives that Ullsperger was not the only person to notice this susceptibility.

To paint Emil as the villain in Czechoslovakia's tragedy is to misunderstand both it and him. He was a victim: not a blameless one, but a victim none the less. He spent most of his adult life being bullied and ordered around: by the Baťa management, by the Nazis, by his superiors in the army, by the ČSTV, by the StB, by the Czechoslovak Communist Party; by the Soviet Union (indirectly); and, not least, by some of the more forceful personalities in the reform movement. Amazingly, he preserved his inimitable character largely intact, with all its childlike kindness, eccentricity and spontaneity. Sometimes – in 1952, in 1968 – he took a stand, and in each case showed immense personal courage by doing so. But if he lacked the strength to defy them all head-on, all of the time, that isn't entirely surprising. Ultimately, there was only one sphere in which he had the self-belief to be certain that he was right, even when the clamour of voices telling him he was wrong was deafening, and that was running.

Czech history is littered with the charred remains of heroes who refused to compromise in the face of irresistible force. Czech geography, too: just look at all the streets and squares named after Jan Hus – forefather of European Protestantism – or, more recently, Milada Horáková or Jan Palach. Emil was well aware of the eternal battle in his nation's soul between pragmatism and principle, unpalatable surrender and suicidal defiance. The Czechoslovak army, which played such an important part in his life, could have fought Hitler in 1939 – and been utterly destroyed. It chose instead to survive. By contrast, the 'Orphan' or Taborite army that refused to compromise in the Hussite Wars was annihilated more or less in its entirety at the Battle of Lipany in 1434. I mention this obscure detail because Emil himself raised it, in one of his addresses on Wenceslas Square in 1968, to illustrate the futility of doomed defiance. History mattered to Czechoslovaks. They were caught in the middle of it.

Defiance looks good on paper. In real life, it comes at a price that many cannot bring themselves to pay. As Dana once put it: 'What good is it if someone says five or ten years after you are dead that you are a hero? Maybe don't be such a big hero. Maybe be alive, instead.'

Ivan Ullsperger cites the contrasting examples of Jan Hus and Galileo Galilei. Hus, who had publicly defied the then irresistible Roman Catholic Church, refused repeated opportunities to recant in 1415 – and was burnt at the stake. Two centuries later, Galileo defied the same church over his claim that the Earth moved round the Sun – but then, threatened with the stake, recanted. He lived, and is supposed to have muttered later: 'Yet it does move.' 'Emil,' says Ullsperger, 'was of the same view as Galileo.'

It is a good comparison. Yet perhaps an even more helpful one comes not from history but from literature, in the person of the most famous of all Czech fictional characters: Josef Švejk. Jaroslav Hašek's comic creation – hero of his 1921 masterpiece, *The Good Soldier Švejk* – drinks and shirks his way through the First World War with unfailing cheerfulness thanks to his simple yet subtle tactic of feigning obedience. His superiors have a nagging suspicion that he is taking them for a ride, yet they can never quite put their finger on it. Švejk, meanwhile, gets on with enjoying life as best he can.

Some say that 'Švejking' has become a Czech national characteristic: a technique by which the powerless individual can maintain a degree of independence in the face of irresistible state power. If this is true, then I suspect Emil was a Švejker.

There are worse things to be guilty of; just as there are worse failings than imitating Galileo. Given what I at one point feared, I am happy to leave these faults on the debit side of Emil's life. There is plenty on the other side to balance them.

20

The last lap

On the first day of 1993, Czechoslovakia was dissolved. Its seventy-four-year life story had been almost contemporaneous with Emil's. Like him, it had known peace and war; poverty and prosperity; social democracy, Nazi occupation and Communist tyranny; and now, finally, another attempt at democracy. At this point, it quit while it was ahead, divorcing itself, painlessly but a little sadly, into the Czech Republic and Slovakia.

Emil outlived the land to which he had brought such glory. He was frail now, but he had not given up. As the world remade itself around him, he settled into the quiet endgame of his life: a kind of lap of honour in which the great currents of history were no longer his concern, and his gaze was more likely to be drawn to the familiar horizons of the past than to seek out new, unexplored ones.

That August, Emil and Dana spent a week on holiday in Finland, in Kuopio, in the north. Láďa Kořán and his American wife, Vaneesa, joined them. Once again, the Finnish atmosphere worked its magic: the round-the-clock daylight made the holiday feel like a happy dream. But Emil was conscious that he was just another tourist, heavy-footed and thick-waisted. He was no longer the unmistakable, charismatic hero he had been four decades earlier, and the absence of adoring fans may have troubled him. At one point on the trip, the friends decided that their evening would benefit if they went out and bought a bottle of wine. Emil asked a passer-by for directions. The man complimented Emil on his Finnish, and, noticing his accent, asked him where he was from. Emil told him. 'Ah,' said the stranger, 'the land of Zátopek.'

'I am Zátopek,' said Emil.

The stranger stared incredulously, then flung his arms round him. 'Zátopek! Zátopek!' he exclaimed. Or perhaps it was 'Satu-Pekka!'

Emil wept.

So it continued: alternate obscurity and acclaim, at home and abroad. As time went by, the foreign trips became rarer; news of the deaths of friends more frequent. But the reunions with long lost figures from the past grew, if anything, warmer. Emil caught up, for example, with Jan Haluza, his first trainer, who, like Láďa Kořán, had somehow survived Jáchymov. They had kept in touch, sporadically, after his release, but had disagreed about the significance of Haluza's contribution to Emil's success. A blurred but vivid photograph of the two old friends hugging, wreathed in smiles, at Haluza's ninetieth birthday party in July 1994 is a vivid reminder that the friendships forged on the athletics track endure better, and perhaps mean more, than the glory won there.

Later that summer, Emil and Dana returned yet again to Finland, this time to Helsinki, for the European athletics championships. At one point, Emil was spotted in the background at a medal ceremony and was warmly applauded. Yet perhaps it was the place itself that meant most to them: 'Our golden town', Dana called it – the scene of those miraculous days all those decades ago, when everything went right for both of them, and the world shared their joy, and it seemed as though the daylight would never fade.

This time, the midnight sun obscured the fact that, high in the night skies above them, among all those constellations named after the heroes and heroines of Greek myth, a tiny asteroid was glittering, somewhere between Mars and Jupiter, that had just had its name changed from '1989 WH4' to 'Zátopek' – a fitting tribute to a man whose legend must surely have inspired more people in the twentieth century than Perseus and Andromeda combined.

Back on earth, however, time was running out. In 1995 Emil was invited to Athens for an event relating to the impending centenary of the modern Olympic marathon. The morning after he left Prague, Dana was surprised to receive a telephone call from the organisers, asking where Emil was. After several hours of frantic enquiry, it emerged that he had collapsed on arrival at Athens airport – having had a small stroke. He was rushed to hospital, where no one knew who he was. Only when Emil had recovered his senses sufficiently to say (since he knew no Greek) the words 'Olympic Committee' was he tracked down.

By the time he came home, a few days later, 'You wouldn't have noticed there was anything wrong with him,' says Dana. Understandably, though, it shook him badly. It was another grim landmark in a journey whose destination was all too obvious.

He became depressed. All his siblings were dead now, apart from Jiří; most had died from cardiovascular illness. His friends were slipping away, too, with the great rivals of the past seemingly the most susceptible: Gordon Pirie had died in 1991, Gaston Reiff in 1992, Reynaldo Gorno in 1994. Others, such as Alain Mimoun, increasingly kept in touch by telephone rather than in the flesh.

Yet there always seemed to be something that brought him back from despair. Sometimes it was an unexpected visitor; sometimes it was a chat with his next door neighbour; sometimes it was his work as a figurehead for the Foundation of the Czech Sports Representation; sometimes it was another ripple of glory from the past.

In June he was guest starter for the first Prague International Marathon. Then there was a cameo appearance in a high-profile Adidas TV advertisement that linked the brand explicitly to Emil's story. It never quite spelled out the claim that Emil won his medals in Adidas shoes, but few who viewed it will have noticed. For Emil, the association was more important for offering a useful strand of extra income that he might reasonably hope would help keep him secure during a long, contented retirement.

He was not rich, considering all that he had achieved. But he never wanted much. Sport continued to reward him, periodically, with comforts of a certain kind: dinners, hotels, flights. Possessions didn't interest him. Dana kept their remaining medals and trophies locked away in a drawer, so that Emil wouldn't give any more away. She only found out about Ron Clarke's one years after the event.

He would have liked children. That ache never went away, and perhaps in old age it was more noticeable, like the ache in his left leg. But he had Dana, and Kuba, and the house and garden; a steady stream of friends, dignitaries and strangers eager to share his memories; and just enough public duties to reassure him that his achievements had not been entirely forgotten.

But memories were fading. On a trip to Berlin, to be guest of honour at an ISTAF Grand Prix meeting in September 1995, Emil was seen sitting unrecognised and awkward in the stands. The organisers appeared to have forgotten to introduce him to the spectators; one official even seemed to hustle him away from the medal ceremony. The stars of the event, Haile Gebrselassie and Moses Kiptanui, admitted afterwards that they had little or no idea who he was.

The German film-maker Hagen Bossdorf followed Emil on this trip; the resulting documentary is sometimes harrowingly poignant. Emil is just another old man: harmless and perhaps a little afraid; still the person he used to be, but made invisible by ill health and age. It ends with Emil's arrival back in Prague. Dana and Kuba are there to meet him at the station. His tired face lights up when he sees them, and there is something about the way that he and Dana hug each other that make your eyes prick with tears. There is so much tenderness, so much trust – it reminds me of something that Jaromír Konůpka said about Emil and Dana: 'Those two: they had been looking for one another.'

She takes him gently by the hand and leads him home.

By 1996, Emil was finding it difficult to walk and usually did so with a stick. The old energy had gone: left to himself he would sit in a chair, reading newspapers or dozing. It was frustrating for Dana, who remained fit and cheerful. She felt that he had become pessimistic and, by his standards, 'lazy'. Yet in a curious way it was the closest they had been for years; and sometimes, even then, Emil's cheerful, life-affirming self could be goaded back into life. Dana used to urge him to cut wood for the stove – less because they needed it than to keep him active. It probably helped; as it did when friends came round, and the old instincts to entertain and to welcome would kick in.

By 1997, however, there were crueller challenges to deal with. Two photographs of Emil and Dana, one taken on their seventieth birthday and one on their seventy-fifth, tell the story with harsh clarity. Dana has hardly changed from one to the other: still handsome, smiling, animated. Emil is barely recognisable. In 1992 he seems confident and robust. Five years later he looks shrunken, puffy-faced and stooped, with an unaccustomed hint of confusion in his eyes. He could be a decade older than the soulmate who was born within a few hours of him.

His facial expression is particularly haunting. Anyone who has had any kind of contact with dementia will recognise the fixed mask of bewilderment that can seize even the most animated among us. It was never overwhelming, in Emil's case, and it was disguised by the ease with which, once he was in the groove of a much-told story, he could tell it as joyfully as ever. But there was no getting away from the fact that, by the second half of the 1990s, bouts of forgetfulness or confusion were sometimes muddying the flow of his thoughts. For a man whose greatness had so much to do with the burning clarity of his mind, it was a particularly cruel affliction.

In 1997 Emil Zatopek was elected Czech 'Athlete of the Century', which seems an understatement. His world records had long since been broken – the last fell in 1965 – but no one, Czech or otherwise, had come close to challenging his breathtaking dominance as an Olympian and a sporting figurehead. By the time President Havel presented Emil with the Order of the White Lion in 1998 – and the whisperings about being a collaborator began – he may not have known much about it. Perhaps it wouldn't have meant much to him anyway – he had, after all, received so many trophies, medals and honours before; and the award came only four days after an arguably more momentous occasion: his fiftieth wedding anniversary. But attempts to mark that landmark with a special radio celebration were hampered by Emil's health: the programme makers were shocked at how tired and confused he seemed. Still, at least his countrymen – or some of them – were trying to make some kind of amends before it was too late.

They were only just in time. Not long afterwards, Emil had a second stroke, from which he awoke speaking only English. Not until Dana took him home was he persuaded to speak Czech again. 'Me and Kuba nursed him back to health,' she says. But she sensed that he was losing the will to live. 'At this age,' he told Dana, 'there is no shame in dying.'

Yet his spirit had not quite surrendered; nor had he forgotten one of his guiding principles: that 'the people love us, Dana – we have to love them back'. Whatever else happened, he still liked to make people feel special. Vaneesa Kořán remembers a car journey through Moravia, with Dana, Emil and Láďa. Emil, in poor health, seemed largely oblivious to what was going on. Then they slowed down in a small village. 'I know a good restaurant here,' declared Emil. Before they knew it he was out of the car, asking for directions and, once someone had worked out who he was, happily trying to sign autographs – it was no longer easy for him – for the crowd of young people who mobbed him.

In 1999, the British journalist Alasdair Reid visited Emil in Troja in connection with a feature he was writing. Knowing that Emil's health was poor, Reid took an interpreter with him, but Emil insisted on speaking in English. It was clear, however, that he was finding it hard work retrieving the words he wanted, so Reid suggested, several times, that they speak in Czech. Emil raised his hand and said, very firmly: 'You are a guest in my house, so we will speak in your language.' As Reid later wrote in the *Sunday Herald*, following Emil's death: 'The obituaries recorded the victories of one of the greatest sportsmen ever, but the memory I treasured was of the character revealed in that simple moment of courtesy, and of the human decency he still held dear towards the end of a life of towering achievements and adversities overcome.'

But even the greatest champion cannot overcome adversities for ever. A third stroke, towards the end of that year, damaged Emil still further. The doctor overseeing his treatment revealed that, after the immediate crisis, Emil spent a 'tough week full of deep depression, hardly communicating, sometimes delirious, hardly recognising anyone and not wanting to live. Sometimes he refused to open his eyes.' Eventually, Emil started calling for someone, but no one could recognise the name. Then they realised what he was saying: 'Kuba.'

Dana and Kuba nursed him again, but his final months were dominated by medical mishaps. A fall in October 1999 left him with a broken hip from which he never fully recovered; when he did come home from hospital he spent most of his time sleeping. He joked that he was 'practising for eternal sleep – we endurance runners like to practise a lot'. A bout of pneumonia in September 2000 put him in hospital for a week that included his seventy-eighth birthday; and then, finally, on 30 October he had a stroke from which he would not recover.

For three weeks, the nation and the world of sport hung on the daily news bulletins. He was in a 'serious condition'; he was 'tired'; he had a 'high fever'; his condition was 'sad and very critical'; he was 'on artificial ventilation'. Anxious visitors began to appear. When the Liškas visited, Emil seemed vaguely aware of them. Asked who Ludvík was, he said, 'He's a nice man.' When the Kořáns visited, he seemed to recognise that Vaneesa was there and muttered something that might have been English.

As the end approached, Dana telephoned Emil's closest friends and advised them to come and say goodbye. 'When I came out of that room,' recalls Zdeněk Fator, 'I cried for half an hour. When I went home, my eyes were red like a rabbit's. My wife asked me what had happened to me. I said, "I was saying goodbye to the idol of my life."'

On 22 November, Emil died. The greatest of all endurance runners could not hold on for ever; and, indeed, Dana felt that he had chosen not to hold on. He knew his race was run.

The world, which had ignored him for so long, woke up abruptly to what it had lost. Obituarists retold his story in more languages than even he could have understood; his face gazed out of front pages as well as back; not since Helsinki had he had such global acclaim. In Britain he was 'Zatopek the great'; in France an 'Olympic legend'; in China he was 'Champion of the People'. 'As an athlete he is unequalled and never will be equalled,' wrote Chris Brasher in the *Daily Mail*. The *Sydney Morning Herald* mourned 'the passing of his golden ideals' and quoted Ron Clarke's tribute to 'probably the greatest track athlete of all time'. Clarke added the crucial point that: 'It wasn't just what he did but how he did it.'

'This is a sad day not only for sports people, who saw embodied in Zátopek all the virtues of a champion,' said Lamine Diack, president of the International Amateur Athletics Federation, 'but also for the common people who recognised in Zátopek an honest and intransigent defender of the fundamental principles of dignity and freedom of the individual. Emil Zátopek knew the greatest triumphs and the greatest suffering and that is what will keep him as an eternal symbol of athletics . . .'

Milan Jirásek, head of the Czech Olympic Committee, said something similar: 'With his death, the legend does not disappear. Everywhere in the world, even young generations know him and his achievements.' President Havel, who wrote personally to Dana, added a small but obvious point that many of Emil's compatriots had, by then, forgotten: 'His results made our country famous.'

But for Alain Mimoun, and for many others, the loss was more personal. 'I am losing a brother, not an adversary,' he said sadly. 'It was fate that brought me together with such a gentleman.'

The funeral was held on 6 December, at the National Theatre in Prague. There had been talk of a state funeral, but Dana asked for it to be kept simple. It was; but every seat in the large theatre was filled, and thousands of people queued outside as Emil's coffin was carried in, wrapped in the Czech flag and borne by leading athletes of the day. Inside, a small folk orchestra played on a stage radiant with bouquets, to an auditorium packed with statesmen, athletes, diplomats and friends, including Czech Prime Minister Miloš Zeman. President Havel was ill but was represented by his wife. Old friends and rivals who had come from around the world included Alain Mimoun, John Disley and Lasse Viren, and the Portuguese marathon champion Rosa Mota. Jindřich Roudný spoke briefly, in a voice fragile with emotion: 'You always fought with all your heart,' he said to Emil's coffin. 'You never let your fans down.'

'It was a lovely service,' says Olga Lišková – although, as someone pointed out on the day, Emil used to say, 'Better an ugly wedding than a lovely funeral.' 'It was a moving experience,' says John Disley. 'The theatre was packed. And I think Dana was glad that we took the trouble to come.'

Juan Antonio Samaranch took the opportunity to award Emil, posthumously, the Pierre de Coubertin medal, the IOC's highest honour; Lamine Diack awarded him the IAAF's Golden Order of Merit. There was something slightly futile about the gestures: what use did Emil have for two more medals that he would never see and couldn't even give away? But Samaranch spoke words that bear repeating, fifteen years later. 'Emil was a living legend,' he said. 'And a legend never dies.'

Outside, as the coffin was taken away for cremation, members of the army from which Emil had once been summarily dismissed fired a salute in his honour under a cold, grey sky. Traffic halted; onlookers stood silently. Then, quite by chance, the bells of nearby St Ursula's church began to ring. Someone clapped, and a great wave of applause – Emil's last – swept along the pavements. Dana watched, supported by friends on both sides, her face hollowed out by horror and grief. It was as if all that miraculously preserved youth and optimism had leaked out in an instant, leaving only an agonised mask of bereavement – white skin, red mouth, red eyes, like a thin parody of a clown.

They had been born on the same day, married on the same day, won Olympic gold on the same day. It would have been too much to hope to die on the same day as well.

Epilogue

Gold dust

I am sitting on the low doorstep of an old wooden church, running my fingers through dry Moravian earth. I can feel the glow of autumn sun through high, deciduous trees; my skin is sticky with evaporating sweat. Out of sight, some children are squealing. I am thinking about dust and ashes.

There is a line of graves in front of me. One is bright with flowers. It always is at this time of year: 19 September. His birthday. Her birthday.

I am sitting because I am too tired to stand. I have just run, with 184 other people, the half-marathon distance from Kopřivnice, Emil's birthplace, to Rožnov pod Radhoštěm, his last resting place. Dana brought his ashes here six months after the big National Theatre funeral and buried them in a separate ceremony – or most of them, anyway. Shortly after his cremation, unable to bear the thought of being parted from her soulmate for ever, she removed some and took them back to Troja. She keeps them in her apartment there (she sold the house a few years after Emil's death), in a blue and white Moravian jug which she brings down from the windowsill on special occasions, so that old friends can toast him.

The rest of his remains are here, in Rožnov, beneath a pair of big, grey, lichen-smeared boulders. One of them is blank: waiting, according to Dana, 'for me'. On the other, the carved bas-relief of a runner seems to struggle restlessly, like a sleeper caught in a dream of immobility. The plot looks small and bald, despite the flowers. All that life, all that energy, all that world-enhancing human warmth – all reduced to this: to ashes and to dry, Moravian dust.

It seems an apt image for a thought that has recently been preying on my mind: the thought that something similar has happened to my hopes as Emil's biographer. I set out, barely a year ago, to celebrate the life and soul of one of sport's noblest heroes. Somehow I seem to have spent much of my time since then probing his alleged shortcomings.

It has been hard to resist. Czechs have been picking at Emil's faults since the day he died; sometimes mercilessly. Within a month of his death, he had been denounced on the radio as a 'decadent' or 'fallen' character by the director of the National Gallery, while Josef Frolík's allegations had been raised on television, on the *Katovna* talk show. The internet, just getting into its stride then, has been catching up ever since. The exiled poet Jiřina Fuchsová wrote a blog describing Emil as an 'StB colonel' on the day of his funeral. Some time later, someone dug up his letter about Milada Horáková. The narrative of 'Zátopek the Communist stooge' took root: the last time I looked at Emil's Czech Wikipedia page it stated without qualification that he was a secret collaborator of military counter-intelligence.

It is not as if Emil went un-judged in his lifetime, either: by the Communists who thought he had betrayed them and by the anti-Communists who thought he had betrayed *them*. We in the West could afford to ignore such squabbles; but many Czechs, understandably, cared. The glory he brought to his nation and the honour he brought to his sport were often submerged beneath the claims and counter-claims. Perhaps that is what Emil's brother Jiří had in mind when he said, in 2002: 'He travelled around the world and was welcomed everywhere. But in our country they scorned him.'

Sitting in judgement over our fellow human beings is both easy and habit-forming. It's not just a Czech thing. But that's not what keeps the happier parts of the internet abuzz with Zátopek. Go to any runners' website – any blog, forum or chat-room – and before long you will come across a corner where Emil's memory is celebrated. Most are joyous, energising jumbles of truths and half-truths, memories, motifs and myths. So many of us have felt our lives brightened by Emil's story; naturally, we want to spread the good news. Not all the news is 100 per cent accurate, but who has it broadly right? The finger-pointers? Or the running enthusiasts who look at Emil's life and see cause for awe and rejoicing?

Emil may not have been, as Alain Mimoun claimed, 'a saint', but he had saintly qualities: an innocent, great-hearted spirit that prompted another Olympic great, Herb Elliott, to describe him as 'sophisticated because he is so simple'. There is certainly something saintlike about the cult that surrounds him: the way that stories are repeated and embroidered and cherished and enthusiastically passed on. To throw a cold bucket of investigative water over such a cult seems mean-spirited – and risks missing the point. It's as fruitless as worrying about what kind of person the real, historical St Francis was. So what if the flesh and blood man once kicked a cat on a bad day? The St Francis who matters – simple, compassionate and miraculously attuned to his fellow creatures – is the semi-mythical figure of Christian tradition.

Is it stretching my hero-worship too far to suggest that something similar applies to Emil? It matters little how much of the Emil legend was real and how much mere pretence or aspiration – not least because, if an illusion is wonderful enough, even the illusionist can be changed by it. As the journalist Caitlin Moran once observed, albeit in a different context, 'constantly pretending to be a decent person, and actually being one, are basically the same thing.'

Emil wasn't perfect – but he had a pretty good stab at it. Like millions of other Czechoslovaks, he had the misfortune to live under a regime that trapped all who lived under it in the same cruel dilemma: submit to the Party – or be (at best) a second-class citizen. Failing to emerge from such a tragedy with a spotlessly white paper trail isn't just forgivable: it doesn't need forgiving. What Emil did emerge with was decades' worth of evidence that, at every stage of his life, he retained his humanity, his childlike idealism and his belief that, through his own energy and kindness, he could make other people's lives brighter. Officialdom never stopped being exasperated by him. Ordinary people never stopped feeling empowered and inspired by him. It is hard to imagine a less appropriate response to such achievements than finger-pointing.

Emil's magic mattered partly because the times he lived in were so dark and dangerous. It worked because the kind of hero he aspired to be, or to impersonate, was the kind of hero the divided world needed. Like a shining knight in the Dark Ages, he seemed to offer hope simply by virtue of his perceived character: strong, brave, confident, selfless, magnanimous, tireless, light-spirited, chivalrous. How much of this perception was real and how much invented is of secondary importance.

In his 1967 book, *Běží Zátopek* ('Zátopek runs'), Emil describes sitting on a train, travelling from Hulín to Staré Město in south Moravia, and watching a little boy with his nose pressed to the window. The boy suddenly points to a passing runner and shouts: 'Look, Mum! Zátopek!'

'How do you know it was Zátopek?' asks his mother.

'He was running,' says the boy.

His mother explains that not everyone who runs is necessarily Zátopek, but the boy refuses to be persuaded. 'Zátopek can run best of all,' he adds.

Emil, all the time, is sitting opposite, unrecognised in his officer's uniform.

It is possible that this actually happened. It is also possible that Emil 'borrowed' the incident from Ladislav Kořán; or that it was pure invention. Yet the core message is rock-solid truth: Emil inspired people. Young, old, talented, ordinary; Czech, Slovak, foreign; Communist and capitalist. All through my Czech travels, I have been meeting them: from Zdeněk Fator, who was inspired to take up running as a ten-year-old boy after seeing Emil win the Rošický Memorial Race in Prague in 1947 ('We asked him for his autograph and he talked to us, and from that moment I wanted to be like him'), to Miloš Škorpil, the Czech Republic's most famous ultra-runner, who was inspired to take up serious running after Emil paid a visit to his school in 1967 ('After that, I started running in winter, through the snow, in heavy shoes').

Even now, the name of Zátopek casts its spell over countless young lives by introducing them to the great adventure of running. Dana, who fired the starting gun for today's race and will shortly be presenting the prizes, has spent much of the past forty-eight hours visiting schools in and around Kopřivnice. She does this every year, as part of a birthday ritual that also takes in this Emil Zátopek memorial race through the countryside. The Emil Zátopek elementary school and the nearby Milada Horáková elementary school are just two of the places where she has watched children running 'mini-Zátopek' races. They are clearly thrilled by Dana's beaming presence, and scream with excitement as they run – first for victory and then, with scarcely less fervour, for the extra prize of touching Dana or being photographed with her. Lack of enthusiasm among young people for vigorous exercise, as widespread in the Czech Republic as anywhere else, doesn't seem to be a problem in Emil's birthplace. And, who knows, maybe as they run their laps of their small tracks, some of these children feel an awakening sense of the possibilities of the world beyond Kopřivnice, just as Emil did when he was their age. One former pupil of the Emil Zátopek school, Lenka Masná, now competes at World Championship level in the 800m.

Here in Rožnov pod Radhoštěm, I stand up to bring my stiffening legs back to life. As I do so, I notice that other runners are strolling, singly and in pairs, among the graves. Some are already showered and changed. You can still recognise them: the thin frames, the glow of post-race satisfaction; and the way they glance from grave to grave before pausing when they find the one they were looking for. What draws them to the tomb of Emil Zátopek? What draws them, if it comes to that, to this annual race in his memory – from Prague, from Germany, Hungary, France, the UK; even from Africa and America?

It is, of course, the same thing that draws me: the legend of the Good Soldier Zátopek, a man who started with nothing – not even exceptional talent – and through the sheer quality of his spirit became the greatest sportsman of his age; a man who, in the words of J. Armour Milne, 'proved that the ordinary man is capable of feats previously considered impossible'; and who did all this with grace, kindness, warmth and humour that made an even deeper impression on his contemporaries than his unprecedented haul of records and medals.

We have come here to honour him, just as Les Perry came to honour him in Helsinki; and we hope, too, just as Perry did, that, as we do so, a little of Emil's great spirit will somehow seep into ours. I have met one person after another who is still thrilled – fifty, sixty, seventy years later – by that small moment when Emil touched their existence. One individual described an afternoon in the pub with Emil as 'one of the most important days of my life'.

Many people add an extra detail: 'He not only signed his autograph for me – he drew a special cartoon for me. I still have it; I can show it to you if you like . . .' Further enquiry invariably reveals the same cartoon: a stick-man Emil being pursued by a javelin-wielding stick-woman Dana. He and she must have drawn tens of thousands of them, and every single recipient – rightly – feels special.

'The people love us, Dana – we have to love them back' – that was at the heart of it. But there is a flip-side. Emil put real love into creating his legend for us. Perhaps it would be a fitting response for us to love him back a little more, and to judge him a little less harshly.

Somewhere during the race from Kopřivnice to Rožnov, we crossed the Javorník Mountains – perhaps at the very point where Emil and Milan Špaček once urinated on to both sides of the central European watershed at once. I should have stopped to do the same myself, in his honour; but I was too busy thinking other, more pressing Zátopekian thoughts: 'Pain is merciful'; 'Am I tired? That doesn't matter'; 'An athlete cannot run with money in his pocket – he must run with hope in his heart and dreams in his head'; 'When you can't keep going, go faster'; and, not least: 'Today we die a little.' The thoughts gave me strength. I found courage, belief and renewed motivation from contemplating Emil's legendary approach to life and sport; countless thousands of other runners, fast and slow, have done the same – and not just while running. That, surely, is reality: a reality at least as solid as any gap between the man Emil aspired to be and the man he really was. Even if the magic was partly an illusion – and Emil, like the Wizard of Oz, was in fact just an ordinary man hiding behind an elaborate machinery of image-making – so what? Grand illusions have a power of their own. The Wizard of Oz made the Cowardly Lion brave and the brainless Scarecrow clever, simply because they believed in his magic.

Some people will never forgive Emil for not being the flawless hero he aspired to be; some consider it inexcusable that he allowed himself to be used as a poster boy for Communism. Their criticisms should not blind us to the huge weight of love that others felt and feel for him – as a legend and as a human being. It is not only Dana who comes here each September to honour Emil's memory. (The race, the Běh rodným krajem Emila Zátopka, has been run in his memory every year since 2002.) Friends and admirers gather, too, from all over the Czech Republic and beyond. In a hotel in Rožnov, Dana celebrates her shared birthday. This year, a dinner was held the night before the race. Wine and slivovice were drunk; favourite folk songs were sung; old friends relived golden moments from years gone by. It takes a special kind of person – a special kind of couple – to generate this kind of enduring love.

The ranks of those who shared Emil's golden years grow thinner each year. Jindřich Roudný and Ladislav Kořán were both in Moravia to pay their respects in 2014; neither survived to do so again in 2015. One day, like the Old Guard, these reunions will cease to be viable. But something will – or should – live on.

'All that really matter,' Dana once said, 'are the traces you leave after you.' Emil left many. The athletics world tends to focus on his achievements on the track: the records – eighteen world, four Olympic, fifty national – and the medals. But Emil knew as well as anyone that records and medals are there to be broken, lost and forgotten. The first person to run 10,000m in under twenty-nine minutes? Today's champions are inching their way towards twenty-six and a quarter minutes; Emil would not even have qualified for the event in the 2016 Olympics. One day – who knows? – even that three-gold miracle in Helsinki may be matched. As for Emil's training methods, they have been accepted, absorbed and developed so widely that his role as innovator and pioneer barely warrants a footnote in the training manuals.

But some traces that Emil left are more enduring. Rousing myself to do some half-hearted stretching, I realise that fragments from conversations with Emil's friends and family are drifting through my mind, like leaves in a September breeze: 'He was a simple man – a good boy . . .'; 'He was a gentleman – he never stood aloof from anyone . . .'; 'He lightened people's lives . . .'; 'He was too honest for his own good . . .'; 'I cannot imagine Emil ever doing anything to hurt someone . . .'; 'He was a pure being – he saw the human being inside everyone . . .'; 'He was so beloved . . .'; 'He always had compassion for the simple people . . .' 'There was so much love and friendship inside him . . .'

'He used to see the good in people,' said Dana, 'even when it wasn't there. I could never have been so happy with any other man.'

Nothing I have learnt while researching this book alters that special quality of Emil's soul; or, for that matter, the essential contours of his life. There really was a poor boy from Kopřivnice who built himself up through his own efforts and ingenuity, step by painful step, to be the most famous athlete the world had seen. There really was a man who discovered that, by loading himself up with pain (boots, sand, snow, burdens), he could learn to shrug it off. There really was a runner who reached such summits of achievement that he redefined the boundaries of his sport – and yet maintained throughout his journey a lightness of heart and warmth of spirit that brightened the lives of those whose paths crossed his. And there really was a sportsman whose gift for friendship brought a divided world a little closer together; who shared himself and his success with every ordinary person who asked; who shared his home and his medals as gladly as he shared his time and expertise; and whose charisma, for a while, helped to stop a superpower's invasion in its tracks.

In the end, they broke him. There's no point denying that; and broken lives are rarely pretty. Even then, though, enough of Emil's great spirit remained for more or less everyone who came into contact with him to feel privileged to have done so. That was his great strength: he could shrug off his own pain and make others feel stronger – and make them laugh, too. His great weakness, as a potential political hero in a totalitarian age, was that he loved life too much: not just being alive, but love and laughter and friendship and wine and song. He lacked the cold indifference of the unhesitating martyr, bubbling instead with enthusiasm for the warm things that make life worth living.

Those of us who never knew him tend to feel privileged to have come into contact with him indirectly: to have seen footage of his races, to have heard his stories and sayings, to have met the friends and family who loved him. I am sure I am not alone in feeling this. And I am sure that I have rarely felt it so strongly as I do now, walking tentatively from the graveyard and through the old, wooden Wallachian village, towards the prize-giving area.

When I get there, I bump into Dana, ninety-three the previous day and glowing with energy. Hospitable as always, she checks that I am taking advantage of the hot food that is being distributed to finishers. I tell her that I'm not sure my stomach is quite ready for a meal. 'Have beer,' she says. 'Emil always said beer is best, after a race.'

It is tempting, but I will have to drive soon, back to the airport at Ostrava to catch yet another budget flight (Ryanair this time). So I refresh myself instead by immersing myself in the peaceful spirit of the place. It is Emil's spirit: the spirit of friendship through sport. In the clearing nearby, a couple of hundred people from a dozen or more countries – most either badly washed or still caked, like me, in the long run's grime – are sharing the post-race buzz. You don't have to speak their languages to get the gist of many of the conversations. People are enthusiastically exchanging times, targets, positions, mishaps, injuries and embarrassing chafing – all the minutiae of the latest shared adventure in their life as runners. I can think of few places in the world I would rather be.

Much later, washed and changed, I wander back past the chattering runners, trying to shake a little more circulation into my trashed legs. Maybe I did die a little today, I reflect, but now I am feeling more full of joy and life with each passing minute. Why leave now? Common sense prevails, though, and I head, reluctantly, for my hire car.

I glance again into the graveyard as I pass. The flowers on Emil's grave look brighter: lush and fresh with life. Even the runner in the stone doesn't seem to be struggling any more. He is already free, speeding joyfully towards an unseen destination.

I drive northwards towards the airport, but by a roundabout route, via the nearby villages of Zubří, where

Emil's mother came from, and Zašová, his father's birthplace. These, like Rožnov pod Radhoštěm, are at the very heart of the mountainous sub-pocket of Moravia known as Moravian Wallachia. František and Anežka took great pride in their Wallachian roots, as Emil did in his. He was especially fond of songs from these parts.

The autumn afternoon is losing its brightness; and, I imagine, its warmth. In Emil's honour, I listen as I drive to a recently purchased recording of Moravian folk songs. They are easy to like – although nothing will ever make me see the point of the traditional Wallachian costumes that singers of such songs like to wear. A few tracks in, a frisson of recognition makes the hairs on the back of my neck stand up. That song! I realise that I have heard it before: not once but many times. It is what the folk singers were singing last night, at Dana's birthday party, and before that in Zlín, a year ago, at a ceremony to unveil a life-size statue of Emil in the sports stadium by the power station. They sang it at his funeral, too. It is their song: '*V Zarazicách krajní dům*', the one that Emil whistled to her in London in 1948 to signal that he was outside.

Perhaps it is the combination of exhaustion and endorphins, but the song suddenly seems to embody for me the essence of Emil Zátopek.

There is nothing sophisticated about the words. Strip out the repetitions and you're left with this:

V Zarazicách krajní dům,
měl jsem já tam frajárečku, bože můj

Dyby ně ju chceli dat,
vědel bych ju, ach můj bože, milovat.

Ve dně bych ju šanoval,
ale v noci, ach můj bože, miloval.

. . . which translates (roughly) as:

In Zarazice, in the house on the edge,
I had a girlfriend there, my God!

If they wanted to give her to me,
oh my God!, I would know how to love her.

By day I would look after her,
but by night, oh my God!, I would love her.

If the English set such words to music, it would be a drinking song, with sniggers and lewd gestures. In Moravian hands, it is a song of aching romance, with delicate layers of harmony, swaying between sorrow and bliss with a slow, lazy rhythm like a calm sea's slap on shingle. It is the timeless song of the ordinary man yearning for his lover, echoing across borders and across history, melancholy and life-affirming, melting the physical and the spiritual into a pool of deep, elegiac longing.

That was the thing about Emil. He was a romantic: the most romantic of all runners. He looked for romance not just in love, but in friendship; and not just in friendship but in sport. He took something mundane – 'putting one foot in front of the other, as fast as possible, for as long as possible' was how Ron Clarke liked to describe it – and made it into a thrilling adventure, a daring exploration, in which all were welcome to join him, of just how far a human being could reach. He could have just been a runner who won races. Instead, he was a runner who loved life.

A few miles further on, not far from Kopřivnice, I notice some children playing in a rough field. It strikes me that I may have seen them already today. Every village we passed through during the race seemed to have a whole village's worth of children out on the roadside, trying to touch our hands as we ran while their parents clapped encouragement. (For Emil's second funeral, those same roadsides were lined with people in Wallachian costume.) I am not sure if these ones are playing an organised game or just messing around, but there seems to be a lot of running – and one of them is sprinting away from the main group.

He seems smaller than the rest. Two or three set off in half-hearted pursuit, but he is far ahead and, at the edge of the field, turns up a dusty track. He kicks up a cloud of the stuff: it hangs in the air behind him like the contrail of a jet.

As I pass, there is a moment when I can see straight up the path, which slopes up towards a wooded hillside. The sinking sun shines straight back down from the skyline, and I find myself looking into a golden explosion of light. The boy is a silhouette, elbows flailing, running faster and faster as he shrinks into the distance. He trails glory as he does so, in the gold dust that swirls from his shoes.

'Look,' I say to myself. 'Zátopek.'

Sources

Given the passage of time since the main events of Emil Zátopek's life, it has not been possible or even desirable to rely exclusively on the spoken testimony of eyewitnesses. I have also drawn on a variety of printed, recorded and filmed sources – especially when directly quoting Emil himself.

Most of the non-printed sources I have used are cited in the relevant page-by-page notes that begin on p. 387. However, I must make particular acknowledgement of *Pohádkový Péťa*, a superb television documentary by Miroslav Kačor, shown on Česká televize (ČT2) in 2002, in which I first heard the voices of many of the eyewitnesses quoted in this book. I have also benefited from watching: *Sláva vítězům: Emil Zátopek*, dir. Simona Oktábcová, Theodor Mojžíš, a Česká televize documentary first broadcast in 2001; *Z televizniho alba Emila Zátopka*, a Česká televize documentary by Karel Hynie, Zdeněk Patočka, Vojtěch Peták and Pavel Taussig, first broadcast in 2003; *Život atleta Emila Zátopka*, an Inventura Febia TV documentary, dir. M. Mináč and O. Sommerová, broadcast (as part of an *Emil Zátopek a*

Věra Čáslavská programme) on Česká televize in 2011; *Nejen zlaté vzpomínky*, Česká televize, October 2014; *Slavné olympijské osmičky Podruhé v Londýně* (2008); *Emil Zátopek: Olympic Highlights, 1948–1952*, Phoenix, 1980; and *Emil Zátopek: Die Lauflokomotive*, a documentary by Hagen Bossdorf for ARTE television, first broadcast 3 October 1995. None of these, unfortunately, is available in English.

I have been helped by a number of radio programmes, including *Životopisy: Emil Zátopek*, a radio series directed by Pavel Krejčí for Český rozhlas and first broadcast on 1 May 2012; *Emil Zátopek Vyprávění o životě a sportování* (probably recorded for Česk' rozhlas in *c.*1953–5 – and abbreviated as *EZVžs*); and *Neznámý Emil Zátopek*, by Karel Tejkal (ČRo 2, 2009). And I have made extensive use of online television archives such as those of Pathé News (at britishpathe.com) and Česká televize (at Archiv ČT24: ceskatelevize.cz) – especially the weekly propaganda newsreels known as Československý filmový týdeník.

As far as printed sources are concerned, I have repeatedly referred to, and quoted from, Emil's own writings: *Dana a Emil Zátopkovi vypravují* (first published 1960; my edition is STN, 1962), in which Emil's words alternate with Dana's; *Běží Zátopek* (Olympia, 1967), in which Emil recycles many of the anecdotes from *Dana a Emil Zátopkovi vypravují;* and *Můj Tréning a Závodění* (ČSTV, 1956). The books' titles can be roughly translated as, respectively, 'Dana and Emil Zátopek tell their stories', 'Zátopek runs' and 'My training and races' (and are abbreviated in the Notes as *DEZ*, *BZ* and *MTZ*). None is currently available in English.

I have also made use of two existing biographies. *Zátopek, the Marathon Victor*, by František Kožík, was first published in Czech as *Vítězství vůle* (NČOS, 1949) but extensively revised to become *Zátopek, vítěz maratónský* (Artia, 1952). Kožík also did a different version of the text for *Zátopek in Photographs* (Artia, 1954). The English translation I have used was published as *Zátopek, the Marathon Victor* by Artia in 1954. Kožík interviewed Emil at length for the book but was not above distorting facts for propaganda purposes, sometimes grotesquely.

Zá-to-pek! Zá-to-pek! Zá-to-pek!, by Bob Phillips (Parrs Wood Press, 2002; revised 2004) is more reliable, but focuses far more on Emil's races and training than on other aspects of his life.

Other useful biographical works – none, so far as I am aware, available in English – include *Emil Běžec*, by Pavel Kosatík (Český olympijský výbor, 2015), a short, rigorous historical biography which covers some of the same ground as this book but with less focus on Emil's running; and *Zátopek: Le Terrassier de Prague*, by Pierre Naudin (Le Légendaire, 1972), a colourful but sometimes highly speculative life which runs into a brick wall after 1968. Some extra details can be found in: *Emil Zátopek: olympijská legenda*, by František Macák, Alexandr Žurman, Milan Jirásek (Olympia, 2002); *Emil Zátopek a sport objektivem Emila Fafka a jiných,* with words by Zdeněk Hrabica and Marie Šusterová-Fafková (Vytiski Akcent, 2001); *Zátopek: la locomotiva umana,* by Marco Franzelli (Biancoenero Edizioni, 2011); and *Emil Zátopek*, by Emanuel Bosák and Josef Pondělík (Orbis, 1953).

Many enjoyable accounts have been written of specific periods or aspects of Emil's life. The best are the

Zátopek chapter in *The Kings of Distance*, by Pete Lovesey (Eyre & Spottiswoode, 1968), and 'Jak to tenkrát běžel Zátopek', by Ota Pavel, in his collection *Plná bedna šampaňského* (Naše vojsko, 1967; the edition I have used is Olympia, 1977). Both are excellent on the minutiae of Emil's races. Sadly, Lovesey's book has long been out of print, while Pavel's has never been translated into English.

Most of my other printed sources are either self-evident from the text or specifically cited below. However, I should acknowledge a broader debt to (among others): *Stars of Czechoslovak Sport*, by J. Armour Milne (Orbis, Prague, 1956); *Track and Field: The Great Ones*, by Cordner Nelson (Pelham Books, 1970); *Tracking Heroes*, by Robert J. Corrigan (Winston-Derek, 1990); *Fast Tracks: the History of Distance Running*, by Raymond Krise and Bill Squires (The Stephen Greene Press, 1982); *Running Through the Ages*, by Edward S. Sears (McFarland, 2001); *The Ten Greatest Races*, by Derrick Young (Gemini Books, 1972); *The Lore of Running*, by Tim Noakes (Leisure Press, 3rd edition, 1991); *The Complete Book of the Olympics*, by David Wallechinsky and Jaime Loucky (Aurum Press, 2008 edition); *Olympic Marathon: the History and Drama of Sport's Most Challenging Event*, by David E. Martin & Roger W. H. Gynn (Human Kinetics Publishers, 2001); *Olympic Marathon: A Centennial History of the Games' Most Storied Race*, by Charlie Lovett (Praeger, 1997); *The Austerity Olympics: When the Games Came to London in 1948*, by Janie Hampton (Aurum Press, 2008).

I have both enjoyed and gleaned valuable information from: *Running with the Legends*, by Michael Sandrock

(Human Kinetics Publishing, 1996); *How they Train*, by Fred Wilt (Track & Field, 1959); *Trénoval jsem Emila*, by Oldřich Koudelka (written in close collaboration with Jan Haluza; Lanškroun, 2007); *3:59.4*, by John Bryant (Hutchinson, 2004); *The Perfect Mile*, by Neal Bascomb (CollinsWillow, 2004); *Why Die? The Extraordinary Percy Cerutty, Maker of Champions*, by Graem Sims (Lothian, 2003); *Running Wild*, by Gordon Pirie (WH Allen, 1961); *The Unforgiving Minute*, by Ron Clarke (with Alan Trengrove; Pelham Books, 1966); *The Lonely Breed*, by Ron Clarke and Norman Harris (Pelham Books, 1967); *The Rings of Destiny*, by Olga Connolly (David McKay Company, 1968); *The Destiny of Ali Mimoun*, by Pat Butcher (Globe Runner, 2011); *Pitch Invasion: Adidas, Puma and the Making of Modern Sport*, by Barbara Smit (Allen Lane, 2006); and *Marathon-training*, by Manfred Steffny (Schmidt Hermann Verlag, 2001).

Of the countless available printed sources on the broader history of Czechoslovakia, I owe particular acknowledgement to the following: *The Prague Spring and its Aftermath*, by Kieran Williams (Cambridge University Press, 1997); *Nightfrost in Prague*, by Zdeněk Mlynář (Karz, 1980); *Reform Rule in Czechoslovakia: the Dubček Era, 1968–1969*, by Galia Golen (Cambridge University Press, 1973); *Prague Spring*, by Z.A.B. Zeman (Penguin, 1969); *Fools and Heroes: the Changing Role of Communist Intellectuals in Czechoslovakia*, by Peter Hruby (Pergamon Press, 1980); *The Greengrocer and His TV: The Culture of Communism After the 1968 Prague Spring*, by Paulina Bren (Cornell University Press, 2010); *Srpen 1968: Vzpomínka Stále Živá* (Několik Osobnich Ohlédnutí, Kopřivnice 2006); *August 21st: The Rape of Czechoslovakia*, by Colin

Chapman (Littlehampton, 1968); *The Deception Game*, by Ladislav Bittman (Ballantine Books, 1972); *The Frolík Defection*, by Josef Frolík (Leo Cooper, 1975); *Spymaster*, by Ted Shackley (Potomac Books, 2006); *The Intelligence Game*, by James Rusbridger (Bodley Head, 1989); *The Soviet Union and the Czechoslovak Army, 1948–1983*, by Condoleezza Rice (Princeton University Press, 1984); *Prague in Black: Nazi Rule and Czech Nationalism*, by Chad Bryant (Harvard University Press, 2007); *The Hitler Kiss: A Memoir of the Czech Resistance*, by Radomír Luža with Christina Vella (Louisiana State University Press, 2002); *World of Dissent: Charter 77, The Plastic People of the Universe and Czech Culture under Communism*, by Jonathan Bolton (Harvard University Press, 2012). I have also made extensive use of more general historical works such as *Iron Curtain: the Crushing of Eastern Europe*, by Anne Applebaum (Allen Lane, 2012); *Savage Continent: Europe in the Aftermath of World War II*, by Keith Lowe (Viking, 2012); *The Establishment of Communist Regimes in Eastern Europe, 1944–1949*, ed. Norman Naimark and Leonid Gibianskii (Westview Press, 1997); and *Revolution and Resistance in Eastern Europe*, ed. Kevin McDermott and Matthew Stibbe (Berg, 2006). And I both acknowledge and enthusiastically recommend Mariusz Szczygiel's wonderfully entertaining *Gottland: Mostly True Stories from Half of Czechoslovakia* (translated by Antonia Lloyd-Jones; Melville House Publishing, 2014).

I have also benefited enormously from the impending publication, of Dana Zátopková's own memoirs – eventually published by Academica in June 2016 under the title *Náš život pod pěti kruhy* ('Our Life Under the Five Rings'). At the time of going to press. I had seen no more than a few sentences from Dana's manuscript, but I know that the hard work she put into marshalling and authenticating her memories was of great value for my book as well as hers. Once again, I thank her for the generosity with which she has shared her life with me.

Source notes for material that I have taken from closed archives, such as those of the security services and the Army, are indicated only in general terms (e.g., 'Archiv bezpečnostních složek' for the security services, or, for Emil's military service records: 'Ministerstvo národní obrany – Osobní spis, 24503: Zátopek, Emil'). The Zátopek-related archive of the Czechoslovakian Olympic Committee can be found in the Czech National Archives (NAČR, fond ČSVO, č. 625, karton 42, Karty sportovců a funkcionářů S-Ž, Zátopek Emil, list I). Other printed records can be found at the Emil and Dana Zátopek exhibition in the Technical Museum Tatra, and in the Muzeum Fojtství – both in Kopřivnice. Many of the most important contemporary documents relating to the events of 1968 and 1969 can be easily accessed in *The Prague Spring 1968: A National Security Archive Documents Reader*, by Jaromír Navrátil (Central European University Press, 2006).

It would have been perverse not to have made use of the vast quantities of source material available online – although I have tended to treat such material with a degree of scepticism. For Czech-speakers, Dav Schovánek's Zátopek-related blog at www.bezeckaskola.cz is among the most useful resources. I have also made use, gratefully, of the ourCollectiveMemory project.

In the citations that follow, I have acknowledged only those sources which are not evident from the text itself.

I apologise in advance for any accidental omissions and will gladly correct any that are brought to my attention. Titles and references that have not been officially translated into English I have left in their original languages: partly to minimise the risk of confusing readers who wish to follow them up – but mainly because I lack the skill to translate them.

Notes

p. vii: **lost only one of his last seventy races at his specialist distances**

A much higher figure is sometimes quoted for Emil's winning streak: for example, that he had won all but one of his past ninety-six races. I can't make those numbers add up. After his two defeats to Reiff in 1948, Emil lost at 3,000m to Čevona on 11 July 1951, and at 5,000m to Kazantsev on 11 June 1952. See *Můj Tréning a Závodění,* by Emil Zátopek, ČSTV, 1956, pp. 87–90.

p. viii: **the entire national ice hockey team was arrested**

For detailed accounts of this bizarre, complex story, see 'A life on ice: Bohumil Modrý and Jáchymov', by Michael Stein, Česká pozice, May 2012; and the interview with Augustin Bubník by Tomáš Bouška at politicalprisoners.eu. See also *Fifty Years of Czech Sport in Totalitarian Society*, published by The Institute for the Study of Totalitarian Regimes and the Magistrate of the Capital City of Prague in cooperation with the Czech Olympic Committee and the National Museum, 2014. The arrests clearly owed something to the outspoken nature of the team's drunken protests when they were prevented from travelling to London. The longest sentence was 15 years.

p. ix: **the problem with Stanislav Jungwirth**

There have been many accounts of this incident, none official and some contradictory. The story was first told publicly by Ota Pavel, in 'Jak to tenkrát běžel Zátopek' in 1967. Emil repeated it in an interview with the temporarily uncensored *Rudé právo* on 3 April 1968. In later life, he spoke about it many times, as did Dana. In addition to discussing the matter with Dana, with Jiří Zátopek, and with team-mates such as Ludvík Liška and Ivan Ullsperger, I have taken into account versions of events given by Emil in, for example, *Život atleta Emila Zátopka*, *Z televizního alba Emila Zátopka* (from which the 'If Standa does not go . . .' quote is taken) and *Životopisy: Emil Zátopek*; given by Dana in interviews with Radio Prague, on 19 July 2012, and with *Zátopek* magazine, No 2, April/June 2007, pp. 62–65; and given by former team-mates, now dead, such as František Brož (quoted by Adam B. Ellick in an excellent obituary of Emil in *Running Times*, 1 March 2001). See also notes to pp. 159 and 196.

p. x: **Western journalists are told that Zátopek has tonsillitis**
AP report, 10 July 1952, published in the *Chicago Daily Tribune*, 11 July 1952 (Part 3; p. 2).

p. xi: **not in either of the biographies**
Zátopek the Marathon Victor, by František Kožík (Artia Praha, 1954); *Zá-to-pek! Zá-to-pek! Zá-to-pek!*, by Bob Phillips (The Parrs Wood Press, 2002).

p. xi **One otherwise staid official Olympic Games report**
Official Report of XV Olympiad Helsinki 1952, p. 248.

p. xii: **'Great is the victory, but greater still is the friendship'**
Kožík, p. 8; note, however, that the words are not actually attributed to Emil.

p. xii: **His fellow Olympians worshipped him**
Running Wild, by Gordon Pirie, p. 137; *The Destiny of Ali Mimoun*, by Pat Butcher, p. 26; *How They Train*, by Fred Wilt, p. 87; *The Lonely Breed*, by Ron Clarke with Norman Harris, p. 103.

p. xv: **would have earned him twenty-fourth place**
Zátopek's best, 28:54.2, would have left him well behind the 23rd placed Ayad Lamdessam, who finished in 28:49.85, but would still have put him ahead of six other finalists. In 2016, on the other hand, his career-best times would not even have won him qualification for the Rio Olympics, at either 5,000m or 10,000m.

p. xvi: **'a man who ran like us'**
Unsourced quote from 1948, quoted by Kožík (p. 84), Pavel (p. 31) and Kosatík (p.110). Magnan's many distinctions included being

born on the very same day in 1922 as Emil and Dana; but much of his *oeuvre* is now hard to track down.

p. xvi: **'most epoch-shattering athlete of his age'**
Middle Distance Running, by Percy Wells Cerutty, p. 21.

p. xvii: **'Men . . . today we die a little'**
See note to p. 226.

p. 4: **some enjoyable phrase-making**
The first of these quotes, much repeated, is reported to come from a European coach whom I have not been able to identify. The other phrases were coined by, respectively: William Johnson; Kenny Moore; Cordner Nelson; and Red Smith. Some post-date the Helsinki marathon.

p. 6: **'At that moment, I understood what the Olympic spirit means'**
Address by Juan Antonio Samaranch at Emil's funeral at the National Theatre, Prague, 6 December 2000.

p. 6: **'the greatest happening in athletics history'**
Cover note written by J. Armour Milne for the English edition of Kožík.

p. 7: **feels suddenly overwhelmingly sad**
See *DEZ* (p. 109); Pavel (p. 49); as well as Emil talking in (among other places): *Pohádkový Péťa*; and in *EZVžs*.

p. 8: **but has since declined**
Tatra seemed likely to be wound up in 2012, and when I first visited Kopřivnice, in 2014, I assumed that it was closed. It has since undergone something of a revival under new ownership, and in 2015 it sold 850 trucks to India. Production is expected to double by 2020.

p. 8: **the nearby village of Zašová**
Some sources identify Valašské Meziříčí – the nearest town to Zašová – as the Zátopeks' former home. However, both Dana Zátopková (with whom I discussed this in January 2016) and Emil's brother Jiří, talking in *Pohádkový Péťa* in 2002, insist that Emil's siblings were born in Zašová.

p. 9: **in the corner of the kitchen that doubled up as František's workshop**

Jiří Zátopek mentions this in *Pohádkový Péťa*, in which the corner in question is shown.

p. 10: **'limitlessly loving'**

The neighbour was Emil's friend and former classmate, Marie Vlachová.

p. 11: **'with more passion than those who were allowed to'**

This and other direct quotes from Emil in this chapter are, unless otherwise indicated, taken from *DEZ*, pp. 19–30.

p. 12: **The family was no less scarred as a result**

According to Dana, Emil would always point out 'the tree where my brother hanged himself' when they passed it on the journey between Kopřivnice and Štramberk.

p. 12: **Politically, he was more of a trade unionist than a revolutionary**

According to Emil's military service files, František joined the Communist Party when it was founded, in 1929, but left in 1932 after a row with a local official, Mr Urx. He then joined the Social Democratic party – only to join the Communists again in 1948. Jaromír Konůpka, whose father was active with František in the trade union, thought of František as a social democrat.

p. 13: **'the biggest fidget in the class'**

The schoolfriend in question, Jaromír Konůpka, in addition to speaking to me at length in Kopřivnice in May and July 2015, was also kind enough to share with me some of his written recollections, published and unpublished, of his and Emil's childhood – including Emil's various acts of defiance at school.

p. 13: **'Emil the cry-baby'**

Pavel (p. 28); Emil describes his screaming policy in *DEZ* (pp. 24–25).

p. 13: **Emil's bare feet**

A copy of this school photograph, from 1928–29, is in Kopřivnice's Folk Museum.

p. 14: **'If it turned out that it was Emil who did it, everything was all right'**

Jiří was talking in *Pohádkový Péťa*.

p. 14: **'He could hold his breath longer . . .'**
Špaček also described Emil's swimming exploits in *Pohádkový Péťa.*

p. 16: **observing how it sucked up his blood . . . stolen a wooden cup**
Pavel, pp. 28–9.

p. 18: **Emil's brothers would all remain in Kopřivnice**
Franta worked for a while as treasurer at the post office but later became test driver at Tatra. Bohouš worked at Tatra, rising to the post of head company inspector. Jiří left for a while to join the air force but then returned to work at Tatra, where he worked his way up to become head planner. Jaroš, as we have seen, struggled to find work during the Great Depression, at one point even attempting to move to the Soviet Union to find a job; he eventually found employment as a labourer and driver in Kopřivnice, only to run over a horse, with tragic consequences. The horse was killed, its owner demanded compensation, and Jaroš, facing ruin, took his own life.

p. 19: **he wasn't stupid enough to repeat a class**
Emil's brother Jiří, talking in *Pohádkový Péťa.*

p. 20: **There was something miraculous about Zlín . . .**
Of the many published studies of the Baťa phenomenon, the most readable is Mariusz Szczygiel's *Gottland,* from which many of the details in this chapter are taken.

p. 21: **'Every penny spent on our schools will pay back many times.'**
Quoted in the official company history at tomasbata.com. Baťa is now based in Canada.

p. 22: **'a totalitarian town'**
Life and Death in the Kingdom of Shoes: Zlín, Baťa, and Czechoslovakia, 1923–1941, by Zachary Austin Doleshal (University of Texas at Austin, 2012).

p. 23: **'I always had to think for a while about where I was . . .'**
DEZ (p. 31). Much of this chapter relies on Emil's own accounts. (Of the eyewitnesses from this period whom I have met, the only one who was actually at Baťa with Emil was Jindřich Roudný, who sadly died in 2015 before I could interview him at greater length.) Direct

quotations come from *DEZ* unless otherwise indicated – although many can also be found in *BZ* and in the *EZVžs.*

p. 24: **Emil told his parents how exciting he found it all**
Jiří Zátopek describes this, and Emil's subsequent disillusionment, in *Pohádkový Péťa*; and Jaromír Konůpka confirmed to me that this was the sequence of Emil's reactions. The honeymoon period appears to have been short – while Emil's reflections on the subject in *DEZ* feel very much like homesickness written from the heart.

p. 24: **'he who passes on to his co-worker a piece of work unfit to be continued . . .'**
Knowledge in Action: The Baťa System of Management, by Tomáš Baťa, translated by Otilia M. Kabesova (Fordham University, New York, 1992).

p. 26: **Radomír Luža . . . 'wondered why they were so eager to get to work to make boots for German feet . . .'**
See *The Hitler Kiss: A Memoir of the Czech Resistance*, by Radomír Luža & Christina Vella, pp. 46–7.

p. 29: **when 'it was decided that I would stick with athletics permanently'**
Emil speaking in *EZVžs.*

p. 30: **By one account, Emil was close to tears**
See Kožík, p. 20.

p. 31: **No one had to force him to go to training**
Haluza described his training with Emil at some length in *Trénoval jsem Emila*, by Oldřich Koudelka, from which a number of details in this chapter are taken – although I understand from Dana and others that Emil felt that Haluza (who died in 2011) exaggerated his importance in Emil's development.

p. 31: **'his tracksuit transformed him into a boisterous young man'**
See Kožík, pp. 22–3.

p. 31: **Room No. 19 in Hostel No. 2**
Many of the details I have included here were evocatively described by Jindřich Roudný in *Pohádkový Péťa*. But Emil also wrote about it, in *DEZ*, and discussed his eating excesses with Jaromír Konůpka – who even witnessed an encounter between Emil and Jarda the cook

towards the end of Emil's life. Jarda felt that he could claim some of the credit for Emil's subsequent success.

p. 32: **'He was always on the lookout for a girl who was from the butcher'**
Jaroslav Přeček, talking in *Pohádkový Péťa.*

p. 32: **a serious-faced young woman called Jarmila Švehláková**
The most detailed interview I have seen with Jarmila Švehláková is in *Pohádkový Péťa.* Milan Švajgr told me that there were those in Zlín who felt that Emil had treated her badly.

p. 33: **'Emil was very inquisitive . . .'**
Haluza's comments are taken from *Trénoval jsem Emila* and *Pohádkový Péťa.*

p. 35: **'Suddenly I realised I'm coming first . . .'**
Emil reflected on this race in *EZVžs.*

p. 35: **Emil had begun to experiment with a different approach**
J. Armour Milne gives a good account of Emil's first tentative forays into interval training in *Czechoslovak Sport 1945–1955* (Orbis, Prague, 1955), p. 47. Writing in *Athletics Weekly* ('Emil Zátopek', 12 May 1951, pp. 8–12), Milne implies that he began doing systematic interval sessions in April 1944.

p. 36: **It is hard to be certain precisely how much of the method the Emil now developed was original**
Lovesey, Bryant and Phillips are all good on the historical precursors of Emil's methods.

p. 36: **an interview published in the *Observer* in Britain twenty years later**
'Zátopek: athlete on the track', by Christopher Brasher and Herb Elliott, *Observer*, 27 September 1964, p. 18.

p. 37: **Speed, in this context, is an elusive concept.**
Sources that estimate Emil's early lap times as 60 seconds include *How They Train*, by Fred Wilt, p. 87; *Fast Tracks: the History of Distance Running*, by Raymond Krise and Bill Squires (The Stephen Greene Press, 1982) and *The Ten Greatest Races*, by Derrick Young (Gemini Books, 1972). Elsewhere, figures as high as 70–75 seconds (with around 34–35 seconds for the fast 200m repetitions) are often

cited: for example, in *Running Through the Ages*, by Edward S. Sears (2nd edition), p. 196; *The Lore of Running*, by Tim Noakes, p. 277. This seems implausibly slow – especially for these first sessions, when the number of repetitions was small. But I assume that the higher figures would have been accurate for the vast sessions that Emil performed later in his career. Fred Wilt, who knew Emil better than the others, quoted 70–75 seconds as the likely range for the last laps of the kind of sessions Emil was doing in 1948. The fact that the laps were slower would not have meant that they were any easier: just that he was testing his body even closer to destruction.

p. 40: **'There was no athlete who was able to keep up with Emil'**
Address at Emil's funeral, National Theatre, Prague, 6 December 2000.

p. 40: **'This method of training . . .'**
Zátopek, Emil – Vyprávění o životě a sportování.

p. 40: **'I will run with perfect style when they start judging races for their beauty . . .'**
Kožík, p. 93.

p. 42: **Franta, Emil's older brother, was among them**
I found this rather startling detail in Emil's personal military service records (Ministerstvo národní obrany, Osobní spis: Zátopek, Emil – 2-29/2008, 1. část). He was sent to Berlin but seems to have returned home unharmed after the war.

p. 43: **more than half a century later, he said he could still remember the taste**
Interview by Christophe Wyrzykowski in *L'Équipe*, 4 August 1998.

p. 44: **three hours after gorging himself on plum dumplings**
Emil mentions this in *DEZ*, p. 44; J. Armour Milne, writing in *Athletics Weekly* (19 May 1951, pp. 8–12) adds that Emil's hosts – presumably the Hron family – begged him not to eat them so soon before the race, but Emil couldn't resist.

p. 46: **The first thing that Jindřich Roudný did**
Roudný describes this episode in *Pohádkový Péťa.*

p. 47: **'like when a horse digs something up . . .'**
See *DEZ*, pp. 44–7 – where Emil's quote about culture can also be found. Emil also discussed this phase of his life in *BZ* and (on radio)

in *EZVžs*, and some of his quotes can be found in more than one of these sources.

p. 49: **their deputies put to sweeping the city streets**
Szczygiel, p. 38.

p. 51: **'competed more joyfully'**
EZVžs.

p. 51: **whose inhabitants had been fleeing in thousands**
Szczygiel (p. 38) says that 13,000 fled within two months of liberation.

p. 52: **the academy's 800m-long corridor**
I am grateful to Petr Cimala for demonstrating, during a long tour of Hranice military academy in July 2015, why this would have been impossible.

p. 54: **touching Heino's leg for luck**
The Great Ones, by Cordner Nelson, p. 57.

p. 55: **'I still remember how elated I was'**
Interview with Ladislav Krnáč, 1992, quoted in Phillips, p. 129.

p. 56: **the romance he had been tentatively trying to rekindle**
'Emil Zátopek – porážka je taky škola', by Dav Schovánek, 16 January 2013, at bezeckaskola.cz.

p. 57: **'Who's chasing you?'**
Kožík p. 47. See *MTZ* for Emil's most detailed descriptions of his training in the woods, including his thoughts on 'killing time without a goal'.

p. 58: **'a bathroom hung with icicles'**
Pavel, p. 32; see *DEZ*, p. 9, for Emil's views on washing in icy water.

p. 58: **'There is great advantage in training under unfavourable conditions . . .'**
Kožík p. 48.

p. 60: **explored the effects on his running of amphetamine use**
I have mentioned this detail only tentatively and in passing, because I have not been able to verify it with as much confidence as I would like. All I know is that, towards the end of his life, Emil told an interviewer that, while still based in Zlín, he briefly experimented with the amphetamine benzedrine, but concluded that it was a bad idea, because it 'did not agree with him'. The interview

appears in *Ano* magazine ('O Daně a Emilovi', by Vašek Vašak, *c.* 1998). Emil says that he used the drug at a meeting at the Strahov stadium in 1944. It made him feel invincible for two laps, after which his legs gave out and he finished fifth. He never tried it again. Kosatík, who mentions this (p. 162), told me in 2016 that Ladislav Kořán confirmed the story to him. Sadly Kořán was dead by then, as was another possible witness, Jindřich Roudný; so I could not check. Nor could I find any official record of a race that corresponds to Emil's description. Assuming that the story is true, however, should Emil's admirers worry? Is it conceivable that Emil's real significance in the history of athletics might have been as the chemically-trained pioneer of a system of training that could be sustained only with pharmacological assistance (which was not banned in Olympics athletics until 1968)? I don't think they should, and I don't think it is. Kosatík is also confident that Emil's flirtation with benzedrine was no more than that: a fleeting experiment. In any case, if Emil's amazing powers of recovery suggest any kind of drug use, it would surely be steroids – yet anabolic steroids were not even invented until 1958. Systematic doping in Czechoslovakia did not begin until the 1970s, although there have been rumours of early experiments in the 1960s. I am convinced that, had Emil's success been owed to such practices, it would have left both a paper trail and witnesses.

p. 61: **'not just applause – it comes from the belly'**
Quoted in Brasher and Elliott, *Observer*, 27 September 1964.

p. 61: **'like two foolish boys'**
Pavel, p. 33.

p. 62: **'I would have said "Isn't it stupid . . ."'**
Brasher and Elliott, *Observer*, 27 September 1964; Pavel, p. 34.

p. 62: **fighting spirit, or '*sisu*'**
Phillips, p. 29.

p. 62: **Heino did not go to the medal ceremony**
Dav Schovánek, 'Heino v Helsinkách poprvé prohráváý.

p. 62: **was sick on the beach**
Pavel, p. 34.

p. 63: **one of the races that had marked him most**
Interview by Christophe Wyrzykowski, in *L'Équipe*, 4 August 1998

p. 63: **congratulated Mimoun on his performance, before sharing several glasses of Russian champagne**
The Destiny of Ali Mimoun, by Pat Butcher, p. 12.

p. 64: **his practice of putting on his running shoes in the street**
Marie Vlachová said he normally did so outside her family's house, a few doors away.

p. 65: **'Do you collect the results of races? . . .'**
DEZ p. 64.

p. 67: **As the Catholic newspaper, *Lidová demokracie* put it**
23 May 1945.

p. 68: **'If he gets disqualified . . . it will make him more famous.'**
Account by Emil quoted in *Running with the Legends*, by Michael Sandrock, p. 27.

p. 69: **he would welcome a bag of oranges**
Pierre Naudin, citing Gaston Meyer and Pierre Lewden as witnesses, in *Zátopek: Le Terrassier de Prague*, pp. 203–4.

p. 69: **introduced him to the delights of seafood**
Butcher, p. 11.

pp. 70–1: **brought the Tatra factory in Kopřivnice to a complete standstill**
Vítězný únor 1948 (Komunistický svaz mládeže, Praha 2008), p. 18.

p. 71: **'simple and primitive'; 'speed and stamina, speed and recovery'; 'Run fast and try to recover . . .'**
Emil gave the first quote to Michael Sandrock (*Running with Legends*, p. 6) and the other two to Julie Cart ('Back Into the Light', interview in the *Los Angeles Times*, 29 April 1991).

p. 72: **more than a decade before the sports scientists first defined the physiological principles**
Reindell and Roskamm (1959) are often cited as the theoretical pioneers; see: 'High-Intensity Intermittent Exercise: Methodological and Physiological Aspects', by Gerhard Tschakert and Peter Hofmann,

International Journal of Sports Physiology and Performance, 2013, 8, pp. 600–10; *et al.*

p. 72: **Emil was typically doing 5 x 200m . . . etc**
MTZ, p. 21. Emil says that it was 2km to the clearing where he did his 200m repetitions, and a further 2km to the clearing where he did the 400ms; all of which subsequently had to be retraced.

p. 73: **'Pain is a merciful thing . . .'**
Pavel, p. 30.

p. 74: **grasping it instinctively like a pen**
Phillips, p. 131.

p. 76: **'His fame will become your burden . . .'**
Conversation with Dana Zátopková, January 2015; also 'V Emilově Stínu', in *Zátopek a ti druzí*, by Zvonimír Šupich, pp. 70–6.

p. 77: **'We could have our wedding on the same day too'**
DEZ p. 75.

p. 78: **For one ten day period he upped his sessions to 60 x 400m each day**
See 'Emil Zátopek', by J. Armour Milne, *Athletics Weekly*, 12 May 1951, pp. 8–12. The Hungarian coach Klement Kerssenbrock – or possibly František Kožík (see note to p. 101) – also claimed to have 'personally witnessed' these sessions.

p. 80: **athletes selected for the Olympics were, like coal miners, allowed up to 5,467 calories**
'1948 Olympics: We had much more fun and a greater sense of achievement than modern athletes do", by Mike Rowbottom, *Independent*, 7 July 2005.

p. 80: **equivalent . . . to one-seventieth of the budget for London 2012**
Calculation by Larry Elliott, economics editor of the *Guardian*, considering the budget as percentage of GDP; see: 'London's 1948 Olympics: the real austerity Games', by Larry Elliott, *Guardian*, 30 March 2012.

p. 81: **The BBC paid £1,000 for the television rights . . . Sponsorship came from Craven A cigarettes . . . etc.**
These and other minutiae about the organisation of the Games, in this paragraph and elsewhere in this chapter, are largely gleaned

from Janie Hampton's delightful *The Austerity Olympics: When the Games Came to London in 1948* (especially chapter 3).

p. 81: **'It was a liberation of spirit to be there in London . . .'**
Interview with Neil Allen in *The Times*, 24 March 1967; this charming, endlessly quoted article, by one of our finest sportswriters, also features in chapter 14.

p. 82: **the defection earlier that month of General Antonín Hasal . . . or an alleged plot to murder General Svoboda**
See *The Times*, 19 July 1948, p. 3; and 22 July 1948, p. 3.

p. 82: **They had toyed with the idea of excluding Dana**
Dana discussed this in an interview with Mark Eben on *Na plovárně*, Česká televize, 5 March 2006.

p. 82: **only Zátopek understood what training really was**
Lovesey p. 119; Kožík p. 72.

p. 83: **'People at home will ask me what the Olympics were like . . .'**
BZ, pp. 40–1.

p. 83: **'The King is looking at us. How can I go off now?'**
Allen, *The Times*, 24 March 1967.

p. 84: **a red vest would be waved**
Countless different versions of this signal have been reported over the years, not least by those involved, including: white vest (or shirt) and red shorts, red vest and white socks, red shorts and white socks, red scarf and white scarf, even red-and-white scarf and yellow scarf. I believe this version is correct – partly on the basis of Emil Zátopek's own writings (e.g., *DEZ*, p. 78, and *BZ*, p. 42) and sayings (e.g., *EZVžs*), and partly on the basis of a long conversation in May 2015 with Dana Zátopková, who was in charge of the red vest. František Kožík (who opts for white socks rather than shorts) adds that the items were Emil's spare clothes. I have also seen film footage (in *Jeden ze štafety*, dir. Jaroslav Mach, Československo, 1952), which may or may not be authentic, which appears to confirm my version.

p. 86: **'He looked . . . as if he might be having a fit'**
Nelson, p. 55.

p. 87: **he had no idea where Heino was. He decided to ask**
Emil mentions trying to remember how to ask the question in *EZVžs*. See also *DEZ*, pp. 78–9.

p. 87: **ushered off the track by a team-mate**
The team-mate in question, the high-jumper Kuuno Houkonen, persuaded Heinström to stop only by telling him that he had finished the race.

p. 87: **the race officials became confused**
See *The Olympics' Strangest Moments*, by Geoff Tibballs, p. 100; Phillips p. 36; and Mike Rowbottom's article, '1948 Olympics: "We had much more fun and a greater sense of achievement than modern athletes do"' in the *Independent*, 7 July 2005. Fourth place was originally awarded to Sweden's Severt Dennolf and fifth to Norway's Martin Stokken, but the runners corrected the error. Belgium's Robert Everaert was awarded sixth place, until he pointed out that he had dropped out five laps before the end.

p. 88: **'Don't worry, not everyone who goes to the Olympics is a phenomenal athlete'**
Dana Zátopková speaking in *Slavné olympijské osmičky: Podruhé v Londýně vstupuje Emil Zátopek* (2008).

p. 90: **'puffed up like a frog'**
DEZ, p. 79.

p. 91: **'No one was wearing the gold medal yet'**
BZ, p. 44.

p. 91: **'possessed by devils'**
Lovesey, p. 130.

p. 92: **'The roar of cheers from the crowd was almost deafening . . .'**
Quoted in Hampton, chapter 11.

p. 92: **someone had stolen them**
The shoes are rumoured to have ended up in a museum in France. The Musée National du Sport in Nice, which has a pair (with Emil's name on) that looks rather like them, has not responded to my request for information about their provenance.

p. 94: **to show her his latest medal**
The medal in this incident is generally assumed to have been the 10,000m gold, but the last time I discussed it with Dana she told

me that she thought it was the silver – which would be more logical, given the timing of Emil's visit. Then again, different accounts give different versions of that, too. My interpretation of the timing is taken from Dana, both in person and in *DEZ*, p. 81.

p. 95: **'you should see how quickly our generals can run away'**
Quoted in 'Když utíkali generálové', by Jiří Jakoubek, *Lidové noviny*, 16 February 2007.

p. 97: **a German shoemaker called Adolf Dassler**
See *Pitch Invasion*, by Barbara Smit. My repeated requests to Adidas to clarify the details of the company's relationship with Emil have failed to elicit a response; but I have discussed the matter with Smit, who is probably the greatest expert on the company's history. Smit is confident that Dassler did make contact with Emil and that, at some point, he began to supply Emil with shoes. She thinks it unlikely, however, that there was any financial aspect to the relationship. It was simply about the shoes – which, she adds, really were very good. Enquiries at the IOC's Olympic Museum confirm that the two Adidas shoes exhibited there – a spiked track shoe and a spikeless 'marathon shoe' – are just shoes once worn by Emil; the information displayed with the shoes makes no further claim than that, and nor do the loan documents from Adidas. Since Emil only ever ran two marathons, however, it seems probable that the marathon shoe, at least, was used in an Olympic race. It is likeliest that this was in 1956 in Melbourne, when Adi Dassler's son, Horst, spent much of the games distributing his company's shoes to athletes. Dana Zátopková thinks that the first time Emil wore Adidas shoes (with the stripes removed) may have been in 1953, in a championship event in Bucharest; before that, he usually ran in shoes made specially for him, out of goat-skin, in Zlín. Later still, Adidas began to supply kit in bulk to the ČSTV and were, I am told, 'very generous'.

p. 97: **spotted visiting Kopřivnice**
Práce, 31 August 1948; see also records in the Kopřivnice Folk Museum of the creation of what used to be the Zátopek Stadium but is now the Summer Stadium.

p. 98: **attempted to prove him wrong by doing a handstand**
I initially found this detail in an interview with Dana Zátopková by Guillaume Narguet published in *Zátopek* magazine, January 2007.

p. 100: **'This is how the people reward those who are most faithful to them . . .'**
The footage is in the archive of Krátký Film Praha; it also appears in *Jeden ze štafety*. I do not know if that is what it was originally shot for.

p. 100: **around 300,000 people were driven out public life, including thousands of army officers**
The Prague Spring and its Aftermath: Czech Politics 1968–1970, by Kieran Williams, p. 5; *The Soviet Union and the Czechoslovak Army, 1948–1983*, by Condoleezza Rice, pp. 62–76.

p. 100: **'What you do when the stadium is full . . .'**
Quoted in *Stars of Czechoslovak Sport*, p. 15.

p. 101: **'When a person trains once . . .'**
Quoted in *Zátopek in Photographs*, p. 38; and Bryant, p. 210.

p. 101: **Klement Kerssenbrock**
Kerssenbrock's article in *Leichtathletik* was translated for *Athletics* magazine by Jim Alford in October 1949 (and quoted in Phillips, pp. 43–5) – the curious thing being that the article appears to be identical to a chapter in František Kožík's *Zátopek, the Marathon Victor*, where it appears (in my edition) with no reference to Kerssenbrock. I am not sure if Kerssenbrock omitted to credit Kožík or if, more probably, Kožík forgot to credit Kerssenbrock (who translated *Zátopek, the Marathon Victor* into German). But the appearance of Alford's translation can at least be taken as a reliable date marker.

p. 101: **'When you can't keep going, go faster'**
Quoted in Kosatík (p. 1). Readers who can come up with a better translation of *'Když nemůžeš, přidej'* are welcome to have a go.

p. 102: **crawled deep into the back of its kennel**
This incident is also described, more colourfully, in Pavel, p. 26. I assume that Dana's eyewitness account is more reliable.

p. 105: **a word of encouragement there, a joke false start . . . there**
For example, Gordon Pirie, in *Running Wild* (p. 137), describes how Emil entertained the crowd with a mock false start in Prague in 1955; and how, in Manchester later that year, Emil, who was struggling, none the less found the strength to catch up with Pirie halfway through the

5,000m and urge him: 'Faster, faster – it is getting too slow.' To Pirie, both incidents were evidence of Emil's 'magnificent character'.

p. 105: **'For me it was always about more than the victory . . .'**
Quoted in *Životopisy: Emil Zátopek*, a radio series directed by Pavel Krejčí for Český rozhlas and first broadcast on 1 May 2012, part 4.

p. 106: **'I can't train when I am supposed to be on duty'**
Quoted by Brasher and Elliott, *Observer*, 27 September 1964

p. 106: **Emil and two other athletes in his unit were excused all other duties.**
Interview with Emil Zátopek in *Slovo*, by Jiří Jakoubek ('Slavný vytrvalec splnil rozkaz a vytvořil světový rekord'), 29 May 1997; *et al.*

p. 106: **feared that . . . he would be put in prison**
Informer's report in Emil's military service records (Ministerstvo národní obrany – Osobní spis, 24503: Zátopek Emil, 1. Část).

p. 109: **The discus thrower Jarmila Jamnická**
Jamnická is interviewed in *Pohádkový Péťa.*

p. 111: **twenty-five kilometres' worth of fast 400m repetitions every day**
See: Phillips, p. 48.

p. 111: **'I have yet to hear of any athlete . . .'**
Jimmy Green, *Athletics Weekly*, 4 March 1950; quoted in Phillips p. 48

p. 112: **acronym-based slang**
'*Mukl*' stands for '*muž určeny k likvidaci*'.

p. 117: **'I am not aware of Emil ever having been questioned . . .'**
Richard Kozohorský, in his 2016 book, *Zatracenej Zátopek*, says that Emil denied having written the letter. He gives no further details, however.

p. 119: **'I keep quiet, or else they would lock me up.'**
Quoted (disapprovingly) in Emil's military service records (1. Část, pp. 15–18) – in which the reported misdemeanours that follow are also recorded. Most of this information presumably came from StB informers but it has not been preserved in the StB archives. The secret service reports on Emil's political behaviour and attitudes in this chapter all come from his personal file in his military service

records. The StB eventually developed a formidable filing system, but record-keeping in its earliest years was more haphazard.

p. 119: **he claimed that his application had been held up**
This explanation appears more than once in his service records. Emil claimed that he had applied to join the party in Stará Boleslav in June 1948 but was told to apply again when he had a permanent posting; and that by the time that happened new members were not being accepted. He finally applied on 11 October 1951 – after an interval during which it seems to have been generally assumed that he must already be a member – and was accepted on 10 December 1953. The revealing thing is Emil felt obliged to explain all this to his military superiors. It was highly unusual for an officer not to be a Party member. Even Colonel Antonín Ingr had joined by 1948.

p. 120: **'He who does not have a positive attitude cannot serve as a commander.'**
Quoted in *The Soviet Union and the Czechoslovak Army, 1948–1983*, by Condoleezza Rice, p. 75.

p. 122: **he preferred to 'bend'**
Quoted in Emil's military service records (Ministerstvo národní obrany – Osobní spis, 24503: Zátopek Emil, 1. Část, p. 22).

p. 123: **Emil considered himself to be in the latter camp**
Quoted in Kosatík, p. 218.

p. 123: **to learn to behave as a domesticated animal**
Jak to bylo, by Luděk Pachman (1974), p. 282.

p. 125: **accepts 'each of his races as a complete test . . .'**
'But only on Sunday', by Kenny Moore, *Sports Illustrated*, February 1973.

p. 125: **that still brought tears to his eyes**
Running with the Legends, by Michael Sandrock, p. 13.

p. 126: **A Finnish newspaper hailed him**
The Finnish and Belgian newspapers are quoted in Kožík, p. 133; the other quotation is from *The Times*, 22 August 1950, p. 2.

p. 128: **the nickname 'the Czech locomotive'**
For an exhaustive study of contemporary media coverage of Emil, see: *Hrdina v totalitních médiích: srovnávací analýza olympijských*

vítězství Emila Zátopka (1948, 1952), by Petr Dušek (Univerzita Karlova v Praze, 2010).

p. 129: **a rather average physical specimen**
Details of Emil's physiology in this and the following paragraphs are taken from, among other places, 'Emil Zátopek from a Medical Point of View', by Dr Zděnek Hornof, published in *Zátopek in Photographs*, by František Kožík, pp. 69–70; 'Emil Zátopek', by J. Armour Milne, *Athletics Weekly*, 12 May 1951, pp. 8–12; 'O největším vytrvalci všech dob – Emilu Zátopkovi', by Dr Ladislav Fišer (a trainer at Dukla Praha), *Práce*, 6 June 1954, p. 10; Phillips, pp. 57–8; and 'L'apport de la science dans l' entraînement sportif: exemple de la course de fond', Véronique Billat, Université Lille 2, *STAPS 2001*, p. 36. The slow-motion analysis can be found at: https://archive.org/details/Emil_Zatopek, with comment by Dr Nicholas Romanov of Pose-Tech (also at https://www.youtube.com/watch?v=XdYHCSAMDr4).

p. 131: **'poor – or non-existent'**
The Lonely Breed, by Ron Clarke and Norman Harris, pp. 107–8 – also the source of the 'ran too eagerly' quote. Clarke's subsequent comments come directly from him, in a telephone interview in September 2014. Fred Wilt's 1956 book, *How They Train*, supports Clarke's analysis.

p. 131: **'I am not particularly interested in beating my opponents'**
Kožík, p. 125.

p. 132: **'Zátopek is always to be found in his office or visiting an Army unit'**
Armour Milne, writing in *Athletics Weekly* in early 1955; quoted in Phillips, p. 108. See also *Stars of Czechoslovak Sport*, by J. Armour Milne (Orbis, Prague, 1956), p. 24; Kosatík, pp. 113–15; and *MTZ*, p. 33.

p. 133: **'There are certainly few top-class athletes in this country who would have difficulty in finding a firm to "carry" them for a few years.'**
'The stresses of international competition', by Christopher Chataway, in *Modern Athletics*, ed. H.A. Meyer (OUP, 1964), p. 98.

p. 133: **'his training methods seemed quite fantastic'**
Pirie, pp. 49–50.

p. 133: **'No athlete would be wise . . .'**
Athletics Weekly, 4 March 1950; quoted in Phillips, p. 49.

p. 134: **'it is simply more than we could stand'**
Quoted in *The Perfect Mile*, by Neal Bascomb, p. 168.

p. 134: **'misplaced intellectual arrogance'**
Quoted in Bryant, p. 214.

p. 134: **'making life agreeable for those around him'**
Stars of Czechoslovak Sport, by J. Armour Milne (Orbis, Prague, 1956), p. 21.

p. 135: **He spoke many languages – eight, ultimately**
With Dana's help I compiled the following list: Czech, German, Russian, English, French, Spanish, Finnish, Indonesian. There were others (e.g., Hindi, and perhaps Polish) in which he was happy to have a go. This can-do attitude was clearly part of his secret.

p. 135: **'a story about a trip to Paris'**
The footage appears in *Z televizního alba Emila Zátopka*, Česká televize (2003).

p. 136: **'the gayest and merriest home I ever visited . . .'**
Quotes from Pirie and Clarke are taken from, respectively, *Running Wild* (p. 50) and 'All-Time Greats', an article by Clarke in *Athletics Weekly*, 5 November 1987, p. 19. Jamnická and Hainová both gave their accounts in *Pohádkový Péťa* (2002).

p. 137: **'he takes the craziest risks with his precious limbs'**
Milne (*SCS*), p. 21.

p. 137: **'Physically he was more machine than man'**
Clarke & Harris, p. 108.

p. 137: **'I sing out of key, but I sing . . .'**
Quoted in an interview broadcast posthumously in the Česká televize documentary, *Nejen zlaté vzpomínky*, 3 October 2014.

p. 140: **'soft and squishy, easy rhythm, thinking of other things'**
Quoted by Kenny Moore in his foreword to *Running with Legends*, by Michael Sandrock, p. viii. Other authors – including Pirie (p. 50), Nelson (p. 61) and Corrigan (p. 40) – suggest that this was a regular occurrence. But this seems improbable, given the horror with which

Dana greeted the resulting flood. In a later interview with Sandrock, Emil seemed to imply again that it had been a one-off (*Running with Legends*, p. 12). On balance, I would advise not trying this at home.

p. 141: **'I eat when I am hungry'**

Emil, talking in *Jeden ze štafety*, dir. Jaroslav Mach (Československo, 1952).

p. 141: **he would buy rolls, butter and a litre of milk on the way to work**

'Emil Zátopek', by J. Armour Milne, *Athletics Weekly*, 19 May 1951, pp. 8–12.

p. 141: **Emil revealed that he had been eating the leaves of a young birch tree**

Karel Bártů, speaking in *Pohádkový Péťa*.

p. 141: **similar experiments involving dandelions and . . . vast quantities of garlic**

Kosatík, pp. 89–90.

p. 141: **self-medicating with vodka**

Ludvík Liška, speaking in *Pohádkový Péťa*.

p. 142: **often ran his laps on the grass outside the track**

'Emil Zátopek', by J. Armour Milne, *Athletics Weekly*, 19 May 1951, p. 9.

p. 142: **'You must listen to your body. You must feel hard, and you must feel easy.'**

Sears, p. 217.

p. 142: **'not mad . . . just utterly absorbed, with every fibre of his explosive body'**

Brasher & Elliott, *Observer*, 27 September 1964.

p. 144: **his best times over shorter distances were many years behind him**

Emil's career-best middle-distance times were set as follows: 1:58.7 for 800m in 1943, 3:52.8 for 1,500m in 1947, 8:07.8 for 3,000m in 1948.

p. 145: **'Zátopek could run twenty kilometres in one hour'**

Quoted in Nelson, p. 61; Kožík, p. 143.

p. 146: **twenty kilometres north-east of Prague**

Svět v obrazech, September 1951. The cutting is in the Zátopek archive at the Technical Museum Tatra in Kopřivnice.

p. 146: **Emil would eventually set eight world records here**
The eight were: at 6 miles (1 November 1953), 10,000m (1 November 1953), 10 miles (29 September 1951), 20,000m (29 September 1951), 15 miles (26 October 1952), 25,000m (26 October 1952), 30,000m (26 October 1952) and One Hour (29 September 1951).

p. 147: **'the closest I'll ever come to knowing what it's like to have a baby'**
Sir Bradley Wiggins, quoted on telegraph.co.uk, 7 June 2015.

p. 148: **'The continuous pain increased with every lap . . .'**
Emil's descriptions are taken from *BZ*, pp. 53–6.

p. 149: **'indescribably cordial and enthusiastic'**
Rudé právo, 30 September 1951, p. 1.

p. 150: **'Today I really had more than enough'**
Quoted in Kožík, p. 146.

p. 150: **fifty-two beats per minute**
Phillips, p. 61.

p. 150: **'To boast of a performance which I cannot beat is merely stupid vanity'**
Kožík, p. 121.

p. 151: **'belted the living daylight out of two tremendous world records'**
Quoted in Phillips, p. 60.

p. 152: ***One of the Relay*, an hour-long propaganda film**
Jeden ze štafety had its première on 25 April 1952.

pp. 154–5: **did worse than any other athlete involved in a test to measure the force of runners' strides**
Pavel, p. 27.

p. 155: **'it was worth asking if I should even start the 5,000 metres'**
DEZ, pp. 102–3.

p. 155: **'I will focus my training and performance . . . to win two gold medals'**
Quoted in 'Emil Zátopek: Osamělost přespolního běžce', by Pavel Malík, published in *Lidové noviny*, 28 July 2012.

p. 155: **made to become a truck driver as a punishment**
See 'Jan Veselý's Perič bicycle' at www.sterba-bike.cz.

pp. 156–7: **'We are aware of how greatly we are honoured by the confidence . . .'**
Rudé právo, 9 July 1952, p. 4. See also: Kožík, p. 152.

p. 157: **He was filmed as he spoke these words**
I have not seen the footage, but you can see him being filmed in *Zátopek in Photographs.*

p. 159: **where, to his surprise, he was not arrested**
I have based these details on Emil's account, quoted in Macák, Žurman & Jirásek, p. 21; Emil also described the incident in much the same terms in, among other places, an interview with František Bouc, 'The legend lives on', *Prague Post*, 29 December 1999.

p. 159: **The pair then flew to Helsinki on a later plane**
Readers wishing to do their own detective work may wish to consult versions given by the following: *Rudé právo*, 12 July 1952, p. 4; *Kdo byl kdo v České atletice*, by Jan Jirka *et al.* (Praha Olympia 2004); 'The legend lives on', by František Bouc, *Prague Post*, 29 December 1999; the interview with Emil Zátopek shown in the Inventura Febia TV documentary *Emil Zátopek a Věra Čáslavská,* (dir. M. Mináč a O. Sommerová), Česká televize, 20–22 September 2011; and Part 1 of *Životopisy: Emil Zátopek*, Pavel Krejčí's radio series for Český rozhlas (first broadcast on 1 May 2012). Dana Zátopková spoke to me of a three-day delay, as she did when interviewed by Daniela Lazarová for Radio Prague, on 19 July 2012; in an interview with Karel Tejkal for vitalplus.org, 21 June 2010, she insisted that she cried for two days. Emil, talking in the Česká televize documentary 'Z televizniho alba Emila Zátopka', also describes a three-day stand-off. Zdeněk Fator told me that Emil and Standa flew in a third plane. Naudin (p. 136) says that the plane didn't arrive until Sunday, 13 July.

p. 161: **plus forty from China**
Only one of the Chinese athletes actually competed.

p. 161: **Les Perry . . . 'waltzed' past the guards**
For the fullest account of Perry's visit, see *Why Die? The Extraordinary Percy Cerutty, Maker of Champions*, by Graem Sims, p. 124, where

the quotes used in this paragraph originally appeared. See also *The Perfect Mile*, by Neal Bascomb, p. 64.

p. 162: **Emil's tongue 'hanging out like a dog's'**
The World in My Diary, by Norman Banks, p. 61.

p. 162: **'open and honest and willing to share his training ideas with anyone'**
Quoted in *3:59.4*, by John Bryant, pp. 212–13, where you will also find the statement that John Landy left with his 'notebooks crammed' with details of Emil's methods.

p. 162: **Bénigno Cacérès enthused about the excellence with which Emil spoke to him in French**
La XVième Olympiade, by Bénigno Cacérès (ed. du Seuil), quoted in Naudin, p. 135. It is possible that Emil was actually speaking to the Poles in Czech: the two languages are said to be mutually intelligible.

p. 163: **thousands of Finnish fans had turned out in the hope of seeing Emil arrive**
František Brož, quoted by Adam B. Ellick in his obituary of Emil in *Running Times*, 1 March 2001.

p. 163: **'I get a bigger welcome here than on Czech tracks'**
Quoted in *Miami News*, 25 July 1952.

p. 163: **an official came looking for Emil, found Cerutty instead, and made a scene**
Some accounts suggest that Emil retreated into the woods with a sleeping bag. Emil, in his 3 April 1968 interview with *Rudé právo*, makes it clear that it was an unnamed rower who resorted to the sleeping bag. See also Sims, p. 125; Macák, Žurman & Jirásek, p. 24; *DEZ*, p. 110.

p. 164: **Cerutty . . . described the encounter in an effusive letter to a friend in Melbourne**
Cerutty's letter, dated 17 July 1952, was not only reproduced in the *Melbourne Guardian* but also quoted at length in the Sydney *Tribune* (6 August 1952, p. 5; and 20 August 1952, p. 6). I suspect that its publication was what gave rise to the much-repeated tale that Emil gave his bed to an Australian journalist the night before the 10,000m final – a story for which I have yet to track down a primary source or even an alleged subject.

Roger Bannister shared the 'journalist' version with his team-mates while in Helsinki (see *The First Four Minutes,* p. 131), but Bannister was merely passing on a story he had heard. It is possible that this was a garbled version of the Cerutty incident. Or perhaps I am doing Emil an injustice, and he gave his bed up to an Australian not once but twice in the run-up to the Games; in which case all I can say is that, for an athlete who placed considerable value on getting a good night's sleep, this was generosity taken to almost lunatic extremes.

p. 165: **'The only thing we can hope for is that Zátopek breaks a leg'**
Fred Wilt, quoted in the *Sarasota Herald-Tribune*, 29 June 1952, p. 13.

p. 166: **One British commentator saw this as a reason to dismiss Emil, snootily, as a 'robot runner'**
Olympic Games 1952: Official Report of the British Olympic Association (published by World Sport), p. 23.

p. 166: **his Finnish admirers . . . had modified his name to 'Satu-Pekka'**
The play on words works better for Finns, for whom 'Pekka' is the name of a character in many folk tales – perhaps roughly comparable to the British 'Puck'. But the Czech equivalent is 'Péťa' – with Emil's full Finnish nickname thus translating into Czech as 'Pohádkový Péťa' – and the English equivalent of 'Péťa' is 'Pete'. So 'Satu-Pekka' translates into English as 'Fairy-tale Pete'.

p. 166: **'an oblivion of fatigue'**
Pirie, p. 93.

p. 167: **'a pitiless race of elimination' . . . a 'battle conducted by Zátopekian fury'**
Gaston Meyer is quoted in Phillips, p. 67; Jacques Goddet is quoted in Naudin, p. 139.

p. 169: **'Sasha, come on, we must get a move on'**
Quoted in Nelson, p. 63.

p. 169: **'Come along, Stone, if you want to qualify'**
Quoted in Nelson, p. 63. Others, such as Krise and Squires, give the quote as 'Come along, Stone, or you'll miss the bus' – which wouldn't be out of character for Emil. It seems sensible, however,

to prefer Nelson's version, which was published twelve years earlier.

p. 169: **Perry thought it was a wave of encouragement to him**
See: Sims, p. 129.

p. 170: **Talk of 'the race of the century'**
Kožík, p. 161.

p. 171: **'the atomic bomb of the Games'**
Gaston Reiff, quoted in *L'Équipe*, No. 1,957, 23 July 1952, p. 1.

p. 171: **reports that people had been hanging on to the outside of heaving trams**
Lovesey, p. 141.

p. 171: **the consensus among commentators**
Based on surveys by *Athletics Weekly* and an unnamed Swedish newspaper quoted in, respectively, Phillips, p. 65, and Kožík, p. 161.

p. 172: **had taken the lead purely out of sportsmanship**
See *BZ*, p. 59; and Pavel, p. 40. Pavel gives this account of Emil's thinking: 'Better not to win at all than to win like this' (i.e., unsportingly allowing Schade to do all the work). Les Perry's interpretation was quoted by Ron Clarke in an article in the 'All-time Greats' series in *Athletics Weekly*, 5 November 1987 (p. 19).

p. 172: **at 3,500m, Reiff detonated an explosive attack**
See Kožík, p. 164; *et al.* The *Official Report of the Organising Committee for the Games of the XV Olympiad, Helsinki 1952* (p. 252) seems to be alone in suggesting that Reiff's move didn't come until 4,400m – which would be hard to reconcile with Reiff dropping out with 600m to go. See also: Macák, Žurman & Jirásek, p. 69.

p. 173: **fuelled by the thought that he would never again allow gold to slip from his grasp . . .**
Emil is fairly explicit about this motivation in *EZVžs*; he reckoned that he could have won the Olympic 5,000m in 1948, if he had only started his final sprint a bit earlier.

p. 174: **'There is no medal for fourth'**
Quoted in Macák, Žurman & Jirásek, p. 70; *et al.*

p. 174: **One journalist described him as looking like 'a tortured wreck'**
'Czech and Double Czech', by Red Smith, *New York Herald Tribune*, 24 July 1952; collected in *Views of Sport* (1954).

p. 174: **Did it not follow, then, that they were likely to tire?**
In chapter 31 of *The Official History of the Olympic Games and the IOC – Part II: The Post War Years (1948–1980)*, by David Miller, Emil said: 'I was experienced enough to know that the sprint by the other three . . . would produce quick fatigue.'

p. 175: **'I ran like the wind'**
Quoted in Macák, Žurman & Jirásek, p. 70.

p. 175: **sometimes spiced with an expressive 'Grrrrrr'**
Quoted in Macák, Žurman & Jirásek, p. 21. See also a charming account on YouTube by Michael Sandrock, in which he describes turning up uninvited on Emil's doorstep and being welcomed, invited in and entertained for hours with accounts of triumphs gone by.

p. 176: **'The track seemed to be flying past beneath me . . .'**
Emil's account in *EZVžs*; the 'I could already see the gold medal' remark is quoted in Macák, Žurman & Jirásek, p. 70.

p. 176: **'Mimoun . . . But Zátopek finishes wonderfully . . .'**
You can hear parts of the commentary at Radio Praha (http://rebel.radio.cz/mp3/podcast/en/archives/111126-emil-zatopek-a-czech-sporting-hero.mp3); or in the first part of Pavel Krejčí's radio series, *Životopisy: Emil Zátopek*. But the best place to listen is in Kopřivnice, at the Expozice Emila a Dany Zátopkových in the Technické muzeum Tatra – where the radio commentary has been synchronised with (non-Czechoslovak) film footage. I have made it sound more coherent than it is.

p. 177: **even going so far – according to one account – as to offer to give him his medal**
Pavel, p. 42; *Zátopek a ti druzí*, by Zvonimír Šupich, p. 72.

p. 177: **Percy Cerutty's verdict**
See note to p. 164; the letter was subsequently republished at least once.

p. 177: **'The name Zátopek has become synonymous with the idea of speed . . .'**
Otakar Mašek, quoted in Kožík, pp. 167; I have not been able to track down where these words were originally published.

p. 178: **An English journalist, Guy Butler, had almost been hit by a javelin**
See: 'Czech and Double Czech', by Red Smith.

p. 178: **Eventually she managed to get a passing Soviet trainer**
Dana has given many accounts of this episode, including a detailed one in an interview with Daniela Lazarová for Radio Prague on 19 July 2012. The trainer is sometimes identified as Markov and sometimes as Romanov. See also: 'A Bridge to Long Ago', by Leigh Montville, *Sports Illustrated*, 26 March 1990; and Šupich, p. 72.

p. 179: **'pleases me more than all the others'**
Kožík, p. 167.

p. 179: **'I will never forget the way he looked at me'**
Dana Zátopková, interviewed by Daniela Lazarová on Radio Prague, 19 July 2012.

p. 179: **'If he could improve his behaviour, he could be a good example to our youth . . .'**
Emil spoke of this incident in, among other places, his interview with *Rudé právo* on 3 April 1968. Ludvík Liška, who was present, also described it to me. I have taken the wording of Jula Torma's quote from an interview with Dana Zátopková by Karel Tejkel for vitalplus.org, 21 June 2010. Torma's words are given thus: '*Kašli na něj, Emilku, veď je to kokot*.'

p. 185: **with what he later described as Cockney defiance**
Quoted in Sears, p. 198.

p. 185: **'like a boxer after the third round'**
Emil Zátopek, talking in *Pohádkový Péťa*.

p. 186: **He had bought some new shoes specially for the race – some say Karhu (a Finnish brand), others Adidas (disguised for political reasons)**
I find the Adidas theory unconvincing. (See note to p. 97.) However, it does seem plausible that, when Emil did eventually start competing

in Adidas shoes, he would have removed or disguised the stripes, so that his use of a Western product would be less conspicuous.

p. 186: **to soften them in advance with cooking grease**
Lovett, pp. 57–62.

p. 188: **'The finish line was a long way off. I was alone, and my strength had gone'**
Quoted in Macák, Žurman & Jirásek, p. 70.

pp. 188–9: **'If you want to enjoy something,' he said later, 'run 100 metres. If you want to experience something, run a marathon.'**
This quotation has been repeated many times, in many forms. Dana insists that the most common form – typically along the lines of 'If you want to win something, run 100 metres. If you want to experience another life, run a marathon' – is a mistranslation. Emil's aphorism depends on the play between the Czech words 'užít' ('enjoy') and 'zažít' ('experience'). My wording reflects this advice.

p. 189: **the next day, he had to hobble downstairs backwards**
Macák, Žurman & Jirásek, p. 24.

p. 189: **'My legs were hurting up to my neck'**
Emil talking in *Sláva vítězům: Emil Zátopek*, dir. Simona Oktábcová, Theodor Mojžíš, first broadcast on C2 and C1 on 10 December 2001.

p. 189: **Mimoun, Reiff, Pirie – cheering him on from the roadside**
See Pavel, p. 47; *BZ*, p. 65; *Zátopek in Photographs*, p. 56; *et al.*

p. 190: **the first moment in the race when he felt happy**
Emil talking in *Pohádkový Péťa*.

p. 190: **'but my legs would not listen'**
Personal communication from Emil's former colleague, Václav Bednář, to whom he told this, August 2015.

p. 190: **'I tried to balance my steps and started to smile . . .'**
Macák, Žurman & Jirásek, p. 70.

p. 192: **an example of what a 'decent socialist' could achieve**
Ladislav Kořán, interviewed by Karel Tejkal for vitalplus.org, 21 June 2010.

p. 192: **'If you knew the relationship between me and him . . .'**
Jan Haluza, talking in *Pohádkový Péťa.*

p. 193: **'I was sorry that, already, it belonged to the past . . .'**
Emil Zátopek, talking in *Pohádkový Péťa*; Emil makes a similar point in *BZ*, p. 65.

p. 194: **Two leading poets . . . wrote epics in his praise**
'Píseň o marathonském vítězi', by Miloslav Bureš; 'Tvé jméno rodnou naši zemi . . .', by František Branislav.

p. 194: **a new, hagiographic mini-biography**
Emil Zátopek, by Emanuel Bosák & Josef Pondělík (Artia Prague, 1953). This was the same Bosák who had criticised Emil's behaviour at that team meeting in Helsinki.

p. 194: **almost certainly staged**
According to the Czech National Film Archive of the Czech Republic, *Jeden ze štafety* is part-documentary and partly dramatised. It is often, but not always, obvious which scenes are which.

p. 195: **'unique breed of conscientious athlete . . .'**
Květy, 7 August 1952, p. 2; the *Rudé právo* quote is from 28 July 1952.

p. 195: **the Order of Work**
Other honours received by Emil over the years included the Order of the Republic, the Medal for Services to the Nation, the Order of Merit for the Defence of the Homeland, the title Merited Master of Sport, the Czechoslovak Peace Prize and, at the end of his life, the Order of the White Lion.

p. 196: **General Kratochvíl looked again at the recommendation for punishment, dismissed it as 'nonsense' and tore it up**
Emil told this story many times. The fullest version I have seen is in *Sláva vítězům: Emil Zátopek*. Emil is also quoted at length on the subject in Macák, Žurman & Jirásek, p. 24.

p. 197: **Emil addressed an audience of 2,500 at a peace rally**
See: 'Letter from Helsinki', by A.J. Liebling, in *The New Yorker*, 23 August 1952. Emil is quoted as saying: 'The burden that is hanging over this year's Olympics is like a heavy shadow – the fact that the war adventure carried on for more than two years by

foreign-intervention troops under the command of American generals against the Korean people has not been terminated, or even suspended, for the duration of these Games . . .'

p. 197: **According to apologists for the regime**
See: *Czechoslovak Sport: 1945-1955*, by J. Armour Milne, p. 57. Milne, who lived in Prague, was a committed Communist.

p. 198: **their highest rate of coal extraction**
See: Bosák & Pondelik, pp. 12–13; and Naudin, p. 124.

p. 198: **'chased like a bloated goat'**
Věra Čáslavská: život na Olympu, by Pavel Kosatík, p. 43. My thanks to Anna Kudmová for explaining that farm animals with colic were traditionally forced to keep walking or running to get rid of the bloating.

p. 199: **life-lessons-drawn-from-sport**
See Kožík, p. 93 and p. 124.

p. 200: **Koščák . . . while Černý**
See: *DEZ*, p. 72.

p. 200: **'If such hell should last a lifetime . . .'**
Letter written to Dana during Emil's '*maringotka*' years in the early 1970s, quoted in *Náš život pod pěti kruny* (p. 449).

p. 200: **'the new man: Socialist Man'**
L'Humanité, 28 February 1953 ('C'est cela l'homme nouveau, l'homme du socialisme').

p. 201: **'As a good soldier, he must obey . . .'**
Czechoslovak Sport: 1945–1955, p. 20.

p. 201: **' . . . the greatest sportsman I have ever met'**
Pirie, p. 51.

p. 202: **reports of forged tickets led to a police investigation**
'Lidé utíkali z práce, přijel Zátopek', iDNES.cz, 12 April 2006.

p. 203: **evidence from his later life**
See, for example, Emil's remarks about his own possible defection after 1968, and his falling-out with Luděk Pachman (chapters 15–17).

pp. 203-4: **mourning . . . 'a great teacher of Soviet sport'**
'Učíme se z myšlenek a díla soudruha Stalina', by Emil Zátopek, in *Mladá fronta: Deník československého svazu mládeže*, 1953, r. 9, č. 58, s. 3.

p. 205: **The next finisher was fifteen minutes behind**
Phillips, p. 77.

p. 205: **'OK, we'll throw her a little bit further . . .'**
Kožík implies that Dana jumped in of her own accord – presumably to avoid the suggestion that a Communist hero such as Emil could have been so reckless and stupiavd.

p. 206: **the best ever 5,000m time by an Australian**
The Australian authorities refused to ratify it as an Australian record, because of the circumstances in which it was run.

p. 208: **'You must not expect too much of me in future . . .'**
Quoted in Phillips, p. 88–9.

p. 209: **No transcripts of his debriefings survive**
A summary in the StB archive suggests that Emil's trip to Algiers for Christmas 1947 produced some eight pages of debriefing in January 1948. (The StB was founded in 1945 and, like the Ministry of the Interior from 1946, was controlled by the Communists. It is not hugely surprising that Emil, as a soldier as well as an athlete, was ordered to give debriefings even before 'victorious February' in 1948; in *Běží Zátopek* he reports that the Czechoslovak team were accompanied by a 'sharp eye' to the European Championships in Oslo in 1946 – and tampered with her notebook as a joke.) Emil's debriefing is said to have included his accounts of 'interviews' with visiting and local athletes, an account of a visit to the Baťa factory in Algiers, four pages of his own 'observations' – and the excuse that he could not do more because there was not enough time. It is possible that some of those he spoke to would have been surprised to have their encounters written up in this way – but perhaps no more than Emil would have been by many Western journalists' write-ups of their meetings with him. I suspect that Emil may have recycled some of his observations for his published writings, in which foreign trips, including this one, are described at length. (See: Archiv bezpečnostních složek, ZS GŠ, č. 37843; and *DEZ*, pp. 69–70).

p. 210: **'To stand on the starting line . . .'**
Quoted in 'Zatopek now runs with pupils', AP (Prague), 10 April 1962 (printed in the Milwaukee Sentinel, part 2, p. 5, 11 April 1962).

pp. 210–11: **His training diary recorded . . . 100 laps a day**
See: *MTZ*, pp. 56–7; see also Sandrock, p. 25. The 1,845km figure is calculated from figures recorded by J. Armour Milne in *Athletics Weekly*, quoted in Phillips, p. 106.

p. 211: **catch-Reiff-or-die sprints**
See: Steffny, pp. 54–5. It is not absolutely clear which year Steffny has in mind, but his suggestion seems to be that, in these later years, Emil might do a set of fast 200s (30–35 seconds), some sub-racing-pace 400s (80–90 seconds), some fast-as-possible-in-the-circumstances 400s (70 seconds), some more sub-racing-pace 400s (80–90 seconds) and some more fast 200s (30–35 seconds). My own view is that it would be a mistake, from this distance in time, to get too hung up about the numbers: we cannot even be certain that the distances quoted were exact.

p. 212: **specific, public pledges . . . displayed in a shop window in Wenceslas Square**
Described in the *Guardian*, 8 April 1954.

p. 212: **The French athletics federation . . . had forbidden French athletes to take part**
For this and other details of *l'affaire de Colombe*, see: 'Emil Zátopek dans la Guerre Froide: de la soumission à la rébellion (1948–1968)', by Yohann Fortune, in *Sciences Sociales et Sport, 2012/1 (No.5)*, pp. 264ff.; '1954: l'indésirable Zatopek triomphe à Colombes', by Jocelyn Lermusieaux, *L'Équipe*, 20 May 2014; Naudin, pp. 179ff.; Phillips, pp. 92–5; and Christophe Wyrzykowski's interview with Emil in *L'Équipe*, 4 August 1998.

p. 212: **'the Paris of junk literature, the Paris of pornographic revues and magazines'**
Quoted in *Figaro*, 29 and 30 May 1954.

p. 213: **'horse dosage, every day'**
Quoted in part 4 of Pavel Krejčí's radio series, *Životopisy: Emil Zátopek.*

p. 214: **those who found their foreign office's stance embarrassing and those who suggested that Emil was a 'Communist fanatic'**
See: *L'Équipe*, 29 May 1954; *Figaro*, 29 May 1954; and *L'Aurore*, 31 May 1954.

p. 215: ***'admirable réponse' . . . 'incroyable stupidité'***
Respectively from *L'Équipe*, 31 May 1954; and *L'Aurore*, 31 May 1954 (both quoted in Naudin, pp. 184–6).

p. 216: **made a low(ish) bow to him**
Československý filmový týdeník, Archiv ČT24. The footage makes a nonsense of Kožík's claim that this was a 'deep' bow.

p. 216: **'The delight in work, the conscientiousness, the courage, the feeling of responsibility of a Zátopek'**
Quoted in Kožík, p. 167.

p. 216: **Athletes also received a 'nutrition allowance' . . . rumours of cash bonuses for Olympic medallists**
See: *The Rings of Destiny*, by Olga Connolly, p. 102.

p. 219: **'capable of being beaten by younger, speedier runners'**
Jimmy Green, writing in *Athletics Weekly*, October 1955 (quoted in Phillips, p. 112).

p. 219: **'I am not fast enough for the 5,000 metres'**
Reported in the *Manchester Guardian*, 12 October 1955.

p. 220: **single-handedly started an Indian running boom**
See: 'The Haves and the Have-Nots', by Ashwini Kumar and Ashwani Kumar, *India International Centre Quarterly, Vol. 9, No. 2: Sports through the looking glass* (June 1982), p. 122. For more details of this trip, see: *The Illustrated Weekly of India*, Volume 107, Issues 1–13, p. 52; and *Emil Zátopek: earth's tearing cry and Heaven's beaming smile*, by Sri Chinmoy (Agnes Press, 1980).

p. 220: **incorporating wife-carrying into his training regime as a regular feature**
Reputable sources in which this assertion can be found include: *Olympic Marathon: A Centennial History of the Games' Most Storied Race*, p. 64; Macák, Žurman & Jirásek, p. 25; 'A Bridge to Long Ago', by Leigh Montville, *Sports Illustrated*, 26 March 1990; *The Lonely Breed*, by Ron Clarke and Norman Harris, p. 106 (where the wife-carrying is supposed to have happened in the snow); *Velké osudy: Emil Zátopek*, a radio programme by Karel Tejkal for Český rozhlas, first broadcast on 27 October 2009 (which mentions the bony shoulders and the tree-root). J. Armour Milne's description appears

in *Stars of Czechoslovak Sport* (pp. 22–3). Pat Butcher, in his 2016 book, *Quicksilver* (p. 112) suggests that the injury occurred when Emil briefly carried Dana for the benefit of a photographer.

p. 221: **'Do anything they ask of you . . .'**
Connolly, p. 16. Connolly (who in those days was Olga Fikotová) adds that, nonetheless, Emil would often skip on the spot during interviews, so that the time wouldn't be entirely wasted.

pp. 222–3: **'To have this sudden shadow of strife and misery cast over the whole affair . . .'**
Quoted in *The Argus* (Melbourne), 10 November 1956, p. 24; the 'probably the whole field' quote at the end of the paragraph is from the *Manchester Guardian*, 10 November 1956, p. 3.

p. 223: **a case of Pilsner Urquell beer**
Yet another colourful detail that appears in *The Rings of Destiny* – which is worth reading in its own right for its compelling account of Olga Fikotová's romance with Harold Connolly.

p. 224: **'He was a wonderful, affable fellow . . .'**
Quoted in 'The Man Who Taught Me Everything', a tribute to Kelley by Amby Burfoot, published in *Runner's World*, May 2007.

p. 226: **'against his better judgement'**
Leading article marking Emil's retirement in the *Manchester Guardian*, 8 March 1958.

p. 226: **'Men, today we die a little'**
The words have been endlessly quoted, nearly always with a confident attribution to the starting line of the Melbourne Olympic marathon. A random selection of reputable sources from around the world might include the following: Ian O'Riordan's interview with Olympic marathon runner Frank Murphy in the *Irish Times*, 29 November 2014; the *Troy Messenger*'s obituary of Nicholas Costes (to whom the remark was allegedly addressed), 13 April 2003; *Modern Training for Running*, by Ken Doherty (Prentice Hall, 1964), reporting Dean Thackery's version of the remark; 'Profiles: Emil Zátopek' at runningpast.com; *László Tábori: a Biography*, by András Kő, chapter 15; *The Gigantic Book of Running Quotations*, by Hal Higdon (2008); *Zátopek* magazine, No 26, May/June/July

2013, p. 42; *et al.* But I confess to being slightly perplexed as to who first reported the remark in this form. The nearest I have seen to a primary source is a letter from John J. Kelley to the director Benjamin Rassat, written more than half a century later (and published in 2011 by Pat Butcher on his website, globerunner.org), in which Kelley remembers a 'playful' Emil saying 'Today we die' on the starting line. It is possible that the other three words are a later invention – but I can't quite bring myself to discard them. They seem a strange piece of embroidery for someone simply to make up.

p. 227: **'Alain . . . I am not good. Don't stay with me.'**
Emil's account, quoted in Sandrock, p. 28.

pp. 227: **One television commentator was already describing him as 'in trouble'**
Unidentified American footage, viewed here: https://www.youtube.com/watch?v=NSQPWA915-c.

p. 228: **causing the crêpe to disintegrate into little pellets**
See: *BZ*, p. 86. Martin Řehák's comments were reported to me by Dana Zátopková. See note to p. 97.

p. 229: **no longer able to accelerate even a little bit**
See *DEZ*, p. 151 – although Emil confuses Lee with Kawashima of Japan.

p. 230: **'as if he were waking from a dream'**
Mimoun described these moments when interviewed in William Johnson's article, 'After the Golden Moment', in *Sports Illustrated*, 17 July 1972. Ron Clarke, who was watching close to the finishing line, gave a very similar account to me in a telephone conversation in September 2014. See also: *The Legend of Alain Mimoun*, dir. Benjamin Rassat, TV5 MONDE; Butcher, p. 26; 'Alain Mimoun: Athlete who ran in the shadow of Emil Zátopek', by Emily Langer, *Washington Post*, 9 July 2013. Emil gives a slightly different account in *DEZ* and *BZ* – focusing more on the detail that Mimoun passed on the news, of which he had just been made aware, that he had just become a father.

p. 230: **'Great is the victory . . . but the friendship of all is greater'**
Quoted in Kožík, p. 183. This appears to be the original source for the endlessly recycled quote. It is not attributed to Emil.

p. 231: **'It was too much for an old man . . .'**
The Argus (Melbourne), 3 December 1956, p. 20.

p. 232: **They shared the ship, the *Gruzia*, with the Soviet team**
The voyage is described in *DEZ*, but the most colourful details in this and the next paragraph come from *The Rings of Destiny*. Olga Connolly was on board. There is also a good description of the voyage in 'Emil Zátopek na cestě domů z Melbourne – část první: plavba lodi 'Hrůzia'', by Dav Schovánek, at bezeckaskola.cz.

p. 233: **in times that were respectable rather than world-beating**
At 5,000m Emil's times in 1957 ranged from 14:06.4 to 14:36.2, at 10,000m from 29:23.8 to 30:31.0.

p. 233: **escorted by an official called Jan Jirka, an old friend**
Jirka – who worked in broadcasting but should presumably be thought of, in this context, as a 'sharp eye' – described the trip in 'Olympijští vítězové Emil Zátopek a Dana Zátopková a jejich vztah k Přerovu', *Sborník Státního okresního archivu Přerov 2006* (p. 137), from which several details in my description are taken. Other sources I have used include 'Zátopek Brillante Vencedor del III Gran Premio Internacional', by Miguel Vidaurre, first published in *La Voz De España*, 28 January 1958, and collected in *Retazos de la vida de Lasarte y Orla del siglo XX a través de la prensa*, pp. 192–9; and Adam B. Ellick's obituary, 'Emil Zátopek, 1922–2000', published in *Runner's World*, 1 March 2001 – in which Jirka is interviewed. Emil's own account (in *DEZ*, pp. 153–4) is tame by comparison.

p. 234: **made to do a stint as a barman**
See: 'Veía boinas por todas partes', a blog by Ander Izagirre, Patxi Alcorta's nephew, 16 May 2009 (see: http://www.gentedigital.es/blogs/anderiza/22/blog-post/1695/veia-boinas-por-todas-partes/).

p. 235: **'But . . . the dog didn't even speak Czech'**
Quoted in Adam B. Ellick's *Runner's World* obituary – which also features a delightful picture of Emil, Jirka and Jurek standing at the airport in Paris alongside a bulging kit-bag that looks very much as though it contains a puppy.

p. 236: **asked if, on their return, he could be taken straight to the training retreat at Stará Boleslav**
An informer's report in the StB archive (č: 648808 MV) describes this episode at length.

p. 236: **The problem may have originated with a bout of peritonitis**
13. komnata Dany Zátopkové, interview by Zuzana Burešová, Česká televize documentary first broadcast in 2011.

pp. 237–8: **'I can't run until my death' . . . one final appearance**
Manchester Guardian, 8 March 1958, p. 7.

p. 238: **joining the celebrated writers Jiří Hanzelka and Miroslav Zikmund on their travels**
Informer's report in the StB archive (č: 648808 MV). Hanzelka was from Štramberk, just a few miles outside Kopřivnice, and was related to the Zátopeks, via Emil's mother. Emil's father had helped Hanzelka create Kopřivnice's folk museum, which Emil also supported. This would not be the last time that Emil fantasised about joining Hanzelka and Zikmund on their travels.

p. 239: **'to be in the military in peacetime is heaven on earth'**
Süddeutsche Zeitung, 24 November 2000.

p. 239: **ordered out at gunpoint by some soldiers**
Pirie, p. 133.

p. 239: **Emil put him at his ease by saying: 'I can do that too'**
One of the conscripts, Milan Středa, described this episode to the ourCollective Memory Project, March 2009.

p. 240: **Coaching athletes, he liked to jog along**
'Emil Zátopek only chugs now', AAP report, printed in *Miami News*, 8 April 1962, p. 13.

p. 240: **Supervising marches . . . supervising artillery exercises . . .**
Milan Středa, talking to the ourCollective Memory Project, March 2009.

p. 241: **'and return home to a country where time has stopped'**
Emil, interviewed by Frank Csongos for Radio Free Europe/Radio Liberty, 9 June 1996.

p. 242: **'put in a kind word'**

The best source for this episode is Olga Connolly's own account, *The Rings of Destiny*, which includes a detailed account of her audience with Zápotocký. However, I have also drawn from an interview with Connolly by Ian Willoughby for Radio Prague, 1 May 2008; an interview with Dana Zátopková quoted in 'Olympic gold medalist Olga Fikotová-Connolly celebrates eighty' in *Sport iDnes*, 13 November 2012; an extensive obituary of Harold Connolly, by Frank Litsky, in the *New York Times*, 19 August 2000; and an account by Denzil Batchelor, 'Two gold medals and a gold ring', *Picture Post*, 8 April 1957, pp. 12ff.

p. 244: **On a sunny Saturday afternoon early in 1961**

Much of the detail in my account of Emil and Dana's creation of their Troja home is taken from 'Danešek, Ťopek and Zadní Ovenec', an article by their close friend Karel Engel for the journal of the Czech Olympic Committee, August 2009. Karel has been almost as tireless and tolerant as Dana in indulging my insatiable curiosity about Emil's life.

p. 246: **a post-retirement 10,000m . . . 5,000m**

See: Phillips, p. 125; *DEZ*, pp. 161–84.

p. 247: **even tried taking up smoking**

Emil made this startling admission when interviewed for *Emil Zátopek: Die Lauflokomotive*, a television documentary by Hagen Bossdorf for ARTE television, first broadcast 3 October 1995.

p. 247: **'Dana's javelin training is paying off'**

Quoted in 'Emil und die Detektive', *Der Spiegel*, 23 September 1968.

p. 248: **'After two hours . . . I had flickering in front of my eyes'**

Pavel, p. 26.

p. 248: ***Warmflaschenizolation***

Interviewed about this in *Mozaika* in February 1995 (p. 6), Emil and Dana even supplied the magazine with an architectural diagram, which explained in a marginal note that the bottles were 'unfortunately empty'.

p. 249: **'You honour opponents in a different way than the friends in the street'**

Emil talking in *Emil Zátopek: Die Lauflokomotive*.

p. 249: **'too sad to live without her'**
This comment came from Dana Zátopková, Emil's niece.

p. 251: **Hana Trejbalová**
See: 'Medvídek Emila Zátopka', by Leoš Pernica, in *Kulturní přehled*, 7/1968, pp. 16–17 (quoted at hamelika.cz/?cz_emil-zatopek-(1922-2000),313). See also: 'Steroids linked to early deaths of athletes', by Maggie Lawson, *Prague Post*, 31 July 1996; 'Československý doping: Byl to podvod, přestože nevraždil', by Václav Pacina, in *Mladá fronta/Dnes* (undated; published on svet.czsk.net/clanky/publicistika/csdoping.html).

p. 251: **'It was my dream to give a good example to children and get them started'**
Quoted by Cart, *Los Angeles Times*, 29 April 1991.

p. 254: **Luckily, Allen was not so negligent, and wrote it up for *Times* readers**
The Times, 24 March 1967.

p. 256: **'Look after this, because you deserve it . . .'**
I am tentative about the phrasing because no one really knows. Clarke, writing more than twenty years after the event, phrased it as 'because you deserved it'; but much earlier accounts (for example, by Neil Allen and Kenny Moore), based on conversations with Clarke, use 'deserve' – which was also how Clarke phrased it when I spoke to him in 2014. It is hard to imagine Emil saying 'deserved' in the context. Similar confusion applies to the precise time and place of Clarke's opening of the gift. See: 'A witness to change – 40 years of Olympic reporting', by Neil Allen, 20 June 1997 (published in *Society's Watchdog – or Showbiz' Pet? Inspiration to Better Sports Journalism*, Danish Gymnastics and Sports Associations 1998). For other relatively contemporary accounts, see 'But only on Sunday', by Kenny Moore, first published in *Sports Illustrated* in February 1973 and collected in *Best Efforts* (Doubleday, 1982); and 'A gold medal to Ron Clarke', *Sydney Morning Herald*, 18 July 1976, p. 60. Clarke's own account was published in *Athletics Weekly*, as part of the 'All-time greats' series, on 5 November 1987, p. 19.

p. 258: **After a brief spell in a museum**
Clarke lent the medal for a while to the Gold Coast Sporting Hall of Fame in Southport.

p. 260: **Vaculík's address to the Fourth Congress of the Union of Writers**
Published as *The Relations Between Citizen and Power*, by Ludvík Vaculík (Liberal International British Group, 1968).

p. 261: **It can't really have been that good**
A Czech academic who very kindly read my manuscript before publication made a marginal note at this point: 'It really was that good.'

p. 262: **'threatening the foundations of socialism'**
The idea was used most pointedly in the notorious 'Warsaw letter', sent to the Central Committee of the Communist Party of Czechoslovakia on 15 July 1968, drafted under Soviet guidance by the leaders and senior Party members of the USSR, Bulgaria, the Germany Democratic Republic, Poland and Hungary in the course of a two-day conference in Warsaw. 'We are convinced,' said the letter, 'that a situation has arisen in which the threat to the foundations of socialism in Czechoslovakia also threatens the common vital interests of the other socialist states.'

p. 265: **by the end of the year, the civilian death toll had reached at least 108**
Victims of the Occupation: the Warsaw Pact Invasion of Czechoslovakia: 21 August – 31 December 1968, by Milan Bárta, Lukáš Cvrček, Patrik Košický and Vitězslav Sommer (Ústav pro studium totalitnich režimů), itemises the deaths.

p. 266: **'All further statements will not be issued by—'**
Some English language reports phrase the bulletins differently; I have relied for the wording on Jan Krčmář, who actually wrote and issued them.

p. 266: **'No sooner had the great mailed fist clanged down . . .'**
'How the coup went wrong', by Cyril Dunn, Laurence Marks and Andrew Wilson, *Observer*, 25 August 1968, p. 2.

p. 266: **'Emil was clearly the dominant figure'**
Checkmate in Prague, by Luděk Pachman (Faber & Faber, 1975), p. 91.

p. 267: **'They didn't want to listen . . .'**
Montville, *Sports Illustrated*, 26 March 1990.

p. 268: **'the most dramatic case of non-violent action against foreign aggressors that the world has ever known'**
'Civilian Resistance as a National Defence: Non-Violent Action Against Aggression', ed. Adam Roberts (Penguin, 1969) p. 7 (quoted in *The Prague Spring and its Aftermath: Czech Politics 1968–1970*, by Kieran Williams, p. 42).

p. 268: **'addressed the crowd under the muzzles of Soviet cannon . . .'**
'Olympic ban demand by Zátopek', by Neil Allen, *The Times*, 23 August 1968, p. 5.

p. 269: **'called on the Russians to leave . . .'**
Untitled report by Reginald Peck, *Daily Telegraph*, 23 August 1968.

p. 269: **Emil lent his voice and his presence to both enterprise**
Emil told Murray Sayle, who reported on the invasion for the *Sunday Times*, that he had been spirited away by Czech soldiers on the morning after the invasion and kept in hiding for four days to assist with the broadcasting. It was, he said, 'a hell of a lot of bloody fun'. I find this impossible to reconcile with all the photographic, film and eyewitness evidence showing Emil out on the streets on 21 and 22 August. Perhaps Emil exaggerated, or something was lost in translation – Sayle described Emil's English as 'rapid but inaccurate'. I have more confidence in Dana's detailed hour-by-hour description, on which my account is based. See Chapman and Sayle, pp. 58–60. See also: Kosatík, p. 233; *Televize v srpnu 1968*, by Václav Kolář and Ladislav Kejha (ČT, 2001); *External Affairs Review* , Volume 18, p. 29.

p. 269: **'Do not give them a provocation'**
UPI report (New York), printed in *The Argus* (Fremont-Newark, California), 23 August 1968, p. 1.

p. 269: **'our good friends' . . . were waiting for them**
Mit blossen Händen, by Erich Bertleff, p. 152.

p. 270: **'without even noticing that just a couple of steps away from him was a soldier with an assault rifle'**
Pachman, p. 94.

p. 271: **'anger leads to bloodshed'**
'Shots as crowds taunt soldiers', by David Leitch, *The Times*, 28 August 1968, p. 1.

p. 271: **'It's over'**
Prague, l'été des tanks, by Vaclav Byk (Paris, 1968); quoted in Fortune, pp. 53–86.

p. 272: **'Every race has its finish line . . .'**
Stadión, September 1968, quoted in 'Osamělost přespolního běžce', by Pavel Malík, *Lidové noviny*, 28 July 2012.

p. 273: **'If they punish me, they will discredit themselves'**
Interview with Johan Struye in *Express* (Austria), August 1969; quoted in Naudin, p. 196.

p. 274: **'We love our country too much to live anywhere else'**
Naudin, p. 194.

p. 274: **'If I had left my country at that time . . . I did not want to leave my country like a rat . . .'**
AP reports from Prague (23 April) and Stockholm (27 April) (printed in the *Bridgeport Post*, 24 April, and the *Danville Register*, 27 April, respectively); the latter draws from an interview published in *Aftonbladet* on 26 April 1969.

p. 274: **'The Russians . . . were acting out of fear . . .'**
'Zátopek recalls invasion', by Will Grimsley, Associated Press report, 9 October 1968.

p. 275: **'Hush, Emil. They'll hear you . . .'**
'Golden legacy of a great man', by Chris Brasher, *Daily Mail*, 23 November 2000.

p. 277: **An editorial . . . denouncing Emil as a 'traitor'**
Sovietsky sport, 1 January 1969 (quoted in Naudin, pp. 194–5).

p. 277: **'changes his convictions the way he changes his shirts'**
Friedrich Janke, quoted in Naudin, p. 195.

p. 279: **an astonishing claim about Jan Palach's death**
The claim had already been circulated in leaflets around Prague, and Nový had said something similar in a newspaper interview a few weeks earlier, but this was the fuller, more aggressive version. To hear the recording, search for 'Vilém Nový O Janu Palachovi - lež o studeném ohni'. The audience reception prompted Nový's wife to observe: 'They don't seem to like Vilém here.'

p. 281: **'conduct at variance with the relevant orders'**
See: 'Zátopek seiner Funktion enthoben', *Neues Deutschland*, 22 April 1969, section 3; Naudin, p. 195.

pp. 281–2: **'It would be quiet, and I could write without being disturbed'**
AP report, 23 April 1969 (printed in the *Bridgeport Post*, 24 April 1969).

p. 282: **'his merits will be taken fully into account'**
'"Expel dissidents" call at Czech party rally', by Michael Hornsby, *The Times*, 22 April 1969.

p. 282: **'It is better to be beaten in a fair game than to win an unfair one'**
Quoted in an AP report, 27 April 1969, printed in the *Fresno Bee* (p. 30) and the *Danville Register*, 27 April 1969.

p. 282: **'when people are leaving the country I do not want to leave'**
UPI report, 1 May 1969 (printed in the *Times Recorder*, 2 May 1969, p. 9).

p. 282: **'received a letter firing me from the Army . . .'**
Interview by Johan Struye, *L'Express*, 18 August 1969, quoted in AP (Vienna) reports, 18 August 1969; and in Naudin, p. 198.

p. 283: **'I am not a politician . . .'**
Informer's report, StB archive (č: 648808 MV).

p. 283: **The 'Ten Points'**
'Deset bodů adresovaných federální vládě, Federálnímu shromáždění ČSSR, České národní radě, vládě České socialistické republiky a ÚV KSČ', Václav Havel Library.

p. 285: **doing menial work for a doll-making co-operative**
See Szczygiel, pp. 166ff., for a haunting account of Kubišová's ordeal.

p. 285: **'counting on starving us out'**
Pavel Juráček, quoted in *The Greengrocer and His TV: The Culture of Communism After the 1968 Prague Spring*, by Paulina Bren, pp. 56–8.

p. 286: **it had cost them 180,000 crowns**
Interview in *Mozaika*, February 1995.

p. 286: **to be jobless was a criminal offence**

Under Section 188a of Czechoslovakia's Penal Code, anyone who 'avoided honest work' could be jailed for up to three years for 'parasitism'.

p. 286: **one option after another melted away**
The examples come mainly from informers' reports in the StB archives (č: 648808 MV), although Emil raised the first two in his interview with Johan Struye in *L'Express* (18 August 1969).

p. 286: **no one came to say goodbye to him**
Kosatík, p. 245.

p. 287: **'I heard the word treason used . . .'**
Květy, 6 September 1969 (quoted by UPI, 11 September 1969, and printed in *The Daily Notes*, 12 September 1969, p. 10).

p. 287: **an article in *Rudé právo***
'I pro Emila Zátopka platí stanovy strany', by Jiří Hečko, *Rudé právo*, 24 October 1969, p. 8; also reported by AP and printed in *Santa Cruz Sentinel*, 25 October 1969.

p. 287: **'He can . . . do everything – except controlling himself in press interviews'**
AP report, printed in *Kansas City Times*, 29 November 1969.

p. 288: **'No wonder the army eventually had to part company with Emil Zátopek'**
Obrana lidu, 28 November 1969; reported by AP and printed in *Kansas City Times*, 29 November 1969.

p. 288: **'violating legal norms . . .'**
ČTK news agency report, 5 December 1969, reported by AP (Vienna) and New York News Service.

p. 288: **working as a garbage collector**
The garbage collector story has been circulating since the early 1970s. Pierre Naudin repeated it (*Zátopek: Le Terrassier de Prague*, p. 19), quoting anonymous Prague-dwellers; and Brian Freemantle, quoting Emil himself, included it in his *Daily Mail* article in May 1971. But Dana denies it, as (less convincingly) did the Czechoslovak government. There is no mention of it in the archives of the StB – who were watching Emil's every move in late 1969 and early 1970. And Emil himself denied it, not just in his 'retraction' interview in *Rudé*

právo, 20 July 1971 but also in an interview with Hedley Thomas, published in the Queensland *Sunday Mail* on 15 April 1990, in which he was quoted as saying: 'Was I forced to be a garbage man? No, no. I once helped a garbage man, that's all.' The sanitation department story was reported by the New York News Service, 6 December 1969 (and printed on the front page of the *Ottawa Journal*, 6 December 1969). But Dana denies it, and, again, I can find no mention of it in the archives of the security services. I suspect it was a garbled account of his actual employment, which began in early November and may well have been misinterpreted by, for example, foreign visitors in Mariánské Lázně.

pp. 290–1: **Jaromír Malák . . . Emil kept demanding a 'real job'**
Jaromír Malák was talking in *Pohádkový Péťa*, 2002; if he is still alive, I have been unable to trace him. I am grateful to Oldřich Stehlík, Stanislav Šula and Richard Händl for helping me to understand the practical details of Emil's employment at Stavební geologie, based on their own experience.

p. 291: **one was usually an StB informer**
Kosatík (p. 255) implies that this was a matter of policy; given the number of informers' reports from this period in the StB archive, this is easy to believe.

p. 291: **'could have made things quite nasty for me'**
Quoted, along with Emil's words in the two paragraphs that follow, in part 4 of *Životopisy: Emil Zátopek*, directed by Pavel Krejčí for Český rozhlas (first broadcast 1–5 May 2012).

p. 295: **more than he earned in the army**
Quoted by Zdeněk Hrabica in *Emil Zátopek a sport objektivem – Emila Fafka a jiných*, p. 12.

p. 296: **'not seventh heaven'**
Quoted in *Životopisy: Emil Zátopek.*

p. 296: **'Is this how they treat their hero?'**
I first came across this in 'Šest let hloubil studně', by Jiří Jakoubek, *LUCIE*, September 2009; Dana and others confirm it.

p. 297: **'I am not the Zátopek who you used to know'**
Kosatík, p. 255.

p. 297: **a fleeting clip of film footage**

The short clip appears in *Pohádkový Péťa.* Emil is not actually working, but appears to be in drill-worker mode. I have spent many months trying unsuccessfully to follow up a rumour that there was once a public information newsreel that included footage of Emil and his team at work. I suspect that the footage once existed (an StB informer reported that some filming took place in early 1970), but it does not appear to have survived.

p. 298: **'Maringotka, Vendolí, somewhere near one cemetery'**

Náš život pod pěti kruhy (p. 449).

p. 299: **Pachman . . . was about to flee the country**

This was what Dana remembered, and reports in the StB files (č: 648808 MV) appear to bear it out – as does Pachman's account of the evidence Emil is supposed to have given in May 1972 (see notes to p. 309).

p. 299: **'afraid of being sent to jail for 20 years'**

Close friends who believe this to have been the case include Karel Tejkal, the journalist, and Zdeněk Fator. The StB files seem to support this. Kosatík suggests that Emil was afraid for his liberty from late 1968 onwards.

p. 300: **'as if they were about to hug each other in a "double Khrushchev"'**

Pachman, pp. 132–3.

p. 300: **'a grown man collapse like a house hit by a bomb'**

Speech by Pavel Kohout for a 'Palach evening' commemorating Jan Palach's death at the Nová scéna at the National Theatre in Prague, 16 January 2015.

p. 300: **'an example of surrender which meant the end to the solidarity of Czech society'**

'O druhém upálení Jana Palacha', by Pavel Kohout (3 March 2012), published in Kohout's collection, *Zánik trilobitů v Čechách*, pp. 121–3.

p. 301: **others would follow**

For example: Rudolf Battěk, the sociologist, and Jan Tesař, the historian.

p. 301: **not the only signatory to withdraw**
Josef Wagner, deputy president of the council of youth associations, also withdrew; see: 'Osudy a smysl petice "Deset bodů" ze srpna 1969', ed. Michal Lakatoš, Luděk Pachman, Ludvík Vaculík – in *Proměny Pražského jara 1968–1969* (Doplněk, 1993), pp. 218–310.

pp. 301–2: **'He is as great a human being as he was an athlete'**
'Why quarrel with the Prime Minister?', by Christopher Brasher, *Observer*, 28 December 1969, p. 19.

p. 302: **an article in the *Daily Mail***
'Zátopek, the will to win is crushed', by Brian Freemantle, *Daily Mail*, 31 May 1971.

p. 303: **a 3,000-word interview . . . in which Emil recanted pretty much everything he had fought for in 1968**
Rudé právo, 20 July 1971, p. 3 ('Emil Zátopek odpovídá redakci rudého práva o věcech včerejších i dnešních').

p. 304: **Emil 'got what for' . . . 'I don't think he would have done it'**
See also: 'Šest let hloubil studně', by Jiří Jakoubek *LUCIE*, September 2009; Montville, *Sports Illustrated*, 26 March 1990.

p. 305: **'Never glad confident morning again . . .'**
'The Lost Leader', by Robert Browning (1845).

p. 306: **he couldn't keep up with his workmates in the pub either**
Praha Velké osudy: Emil Zátopek, a radio programme by Emil's friend Karel Tejkal, first broadcast 27 October 2009, Český rozhlas.

p. 309: **thought to include subversion, slandering the Republic, incitement and preparing a felony**
It is hard to say with absolute certainty exactly what took place. The proceedings were closed to the public, while the relevant court records were dispersed in the floods that overwhelmed the Prague city archives in 2002, and are now partly contained within the StB archive. This summary is based on Reuters reports printed in *The Times* ('Prague trial of former chess grand master', p. 7, 5 May 1972; 'Czech court frees Ludek Pachman after giving him a jail term', p. 5, 6 May 1972) and the Amnesty International Newsletter (Vol. 2, No. 7, July 1972). The order for his immediate release was interpreted as an attempt to prevent him from becoming an international *cause célèbre*.

p. 309: **Emil is assumed to have been called as a witness**
A Reuters bulletin reported that Emil was 'seen leaving the court . . . apparently after having given evidence at the trial'; see: 'Czech on trial for radio talk', printed in *New Nation*, 5 May 1972, p. 7. Emil's appearance is also discussed in an informer's report in the StB archives.

p. 309: **a conversation in which Pachman and the Soviet chess player Paul Keres jokingly discussed emigration**
Pachman, pp. 128–9.

p. 310: **'Where am I going to get someone to replace you for three weeks?'**
Emil's account, quoted in part 4 of *Životopisy: Emil Zátopek.*

p. 310: **a brief . . . to look happy and keep his mouth shut**
According to a report in Emil's file in the StB archive, Antonín Himl, president of the ČSTV, personally briefed Emil in July on the importance of not discussing politics in Munich.

p. 311: **'I am a simple worker and drill outside Prague for mineral water'**
'Laufen wie die Vögel fliegen: Interview mit dem Olympia-Gast Emil Zátopek', *Der Spiegel*, 4 September 1972.

p. 312: **'In my country I am just a common man – a nobody'**
The episode is described in chapter 31 of *Going Far*, by Joe Henderson (Create Space, 2012).

p. 313: **'Former Olympic champion Emil Zátopek,' reported Wortzel**
Diplomatic cable, courtesy of Wikileaks (https://www.wikileaks.org/plusd/cables/1973PRAGUE02002_b.html).

p. 315: **'Life is the most precious thing we have . . .'**
From Dana Zátopková's 2016 memoir, unpublished when this book went to press, *Náš život pod pěti kruhy* (Our Life Under the Five Rings).

p. 315: **'at least we know that those who stayed are really worth something'**
Quoted by Zdeněk Hrabica in *Emil Zátopek a sport objektivem – Emila Fafka a jiných*, p. 12.

p. 316: **often degenerated into wild hilarity**
'Chtěla bych ještě jednou posedět s Ťopkem', Jiří Jakoubek, *Lidové noviny*, 16 September 2002.

p. 319: **'render unto Caesar the things that are Caesar's'**
Matthew 22:15–22; Mark 12:13–17; Luke 20:20–26.

p. 320: **'I became a sports spy'**
Montville, *Sports Illustrated*, 26 March 1990.

p. 320: **'Emil Zátopek has been welcomed back into the fold . . .'**
'Hoffman's staying power to be tested', by Neil Allen, *The Times*, 26 July 1974, p. 9.

p. 321: **a signed, limited edition print by Pablo Picasso**
I have been trying, so far without success, to contact the alleged recipient; and as a result have been unable to determine which print it was, beyond the fact that it was some kind of dove. (Picasso did several.)

p. 322: **'the great surrender'**
"Neumírat předčasně!", by Pavel Kohout (18 January 2014), collected in *Zánik trilobitů v Čechách*, pp. 278–80.

p. 322: **'political adventurers who with this Charter have tried to stick a knife into our collective work'**
Quoted in 'Anticharta, 1. mimořádné číslo' for *Revolver Revue*, by Viktor Karlík and Terezie Pokorná (eds), p. 21; and *Charta 77 v dobovém mediálním a sociálním kontextu*, by Jakub Železný (Charles University, Prague, 2010), p. 49. The footage has not survived: ČST routinely re-used old film in those days.

p. 323: **which he probably had read**
Emil said on television that he had been upset when he read *Rudé právo*'s account of the Charter – published under the headline 'Ztroskotanci a samozvanci' ('losers and usurpers') on 12 January 1977.

p. 323: **'sang English songs extremely loudly'**
'Winning is the only thing that matters', by Rob Hughes, *The Times*, 16 August 1997.

p. 324: **'beautiful' Finnish**
Pirkko Järvinen, who was supposed to be acting as Emil's interpreter, quoted in *Pohádkový Péťa*. See also Macák, Žurman & Jirásek, p. 28.

p. 324: **'Who's Zátopek?'**
Cliff Temple described this incident in his 'Sports Diary', *The Times*, 2 September 1978, p. 12.

p. 324: **George A. Hirsch . . . invited him to the USA**
Hirsch wrote two evocative descriptions of this episode: 'Zátopek should carry torch', *New York Times*, 22 April 1984, Section 5, p. 2; and, more fully, '60 Years Ago, an Olympic Trifecta of Endurance', *New York Times*, 23 June 2012, p. 11. Marc Bloom, who was editor of *The Runner* at the time, also described it to me. See also: 'Zátopek lasts the political distance', an Associated Press interview with Emil, printed in *The Times*, 23 April 1982, p. 29. *The Runner* merged with *Runner's World* in 1986.

p. 325: **At the airport, Chinmoy made to shake hands with him . . .**
Salutations, numbers 1–4, by Sri Chinmoy (Agni Press, 1981; srichinmoylibrary.com/slt-2).

p. 326: **'work with him didn't even feel like working'**
Věra Čáslavská: Život na Olympu, by Pavel Kosatík, p. 149.

p. 326: **'Yes, but you signed the "Two Thousand Words". You will get no more.'**
Montville, *Sports Illustrated*, 26 March 1990.

p. 327: **a special celebration at Houštka Spa**
Dana described this occasion in detail in an interview with Karel Tejkal for vitalplus.org, 21 June 2010.

p. 328: **gave his broad backing to the boycott**
Rudé právo, 14 May 1984, p. 7.

p. 328: **'all athletes who have conscientiously trained . . .'**
Quoted in a report by United Press International (Prague), 10 May 1984.

p. 328: **invited to be torch-bearer**
United Press International, 13 October 1983; *New York Times*, Section A; p. 27, 14 October 1983. See also George A. Hirsch's article, 'Zátopek should carry torch', *New York Times*, April 22, 1984.

p. 328: **'The generosity, charm and charisma that so impressed John Landy, Les Perry and the other Australians . . .'**
'50 Years of the Emil Zátopek Race', by Len Johnson, *Sydney Morning Herald*, 4 December 2011.

p. 329: **'I think he was genuinely touched . . .'**
Quoted in *The Age* (Melbourne), 13 December 1993, p. 28.

p. 333: **One of the first to call was the Australian journalist Hedley Thomas**
'Emil!', by Hedley Thomas, *Queensland Sunday Mail*, 15 April 1990. The full interview is much more entertaining than my brief extract suggests.

p. 334: **'Our hope is that all will be quiet . . .'**
Montville, *Sports Illustrated*, 26 March 1990.

p. 334: **'To live in such a place – how is it possible?'**
Cart, *Los Angeles Times*, April 29, 1991.

p. 336: **During the furore that followed . . . suggesting that one of those under suspicion was Emil Zátopek**
See: Radio Prague report, 2 November 1998; 'Spy backlash hits president', by René Jakl, 'Prague Post', 4 November 1998; 'Benda: Vyznamenáno bylo více agentů StB', *ČTK - Z domova* (str.02), 2 November 1998; 'Jak viděla StB dění na severu', by Antonín Viktora, *Severní Čechy* (str. 03), 15 November 2006; *et al.*

pp. 336–7: **Josef Frolík . . . gave evidence to a hearing**
United States Congress Senate Committee on the Judiciary, Subcommittee to Investigate the Administration of the Internal Security Act and other Internal Security Laws. *Communist Bloc Intelligence Activities in the United States: Hearing, 94th Cong., 1st–2nd Sess. November 18, 1975 [and April 12, 1976]* (Washington: U.S. GPO, 1975–1976, p. 22; LC Catalog Record http://lccn.loc.gov/76600952. LC Call Number: KF26 .J832 1975b).

p. 338: **not least in his book, *Špión vypovídá***
Frolík also published an English version of his memoirs, *The Frolík Defection* (Leo Cooper, 1975). His allegations about Emil do not appear in it, however.

p. 340: **'gangsters of the world'**
Quoted by Michael Knife in 'Prague students clean Wenceslas statue', *The Times*, 29 August 1968, p. 5.

p. 341: **reprimanded shortly before leaving for Melbourne**
Kosatík, p. 204.

p. 341: **Ladislav Kořán . . . was interrogated more than once about Emil by the secret police**

See: Kosatík, p.76.

p. 342: **Department D**

The department's activities are described in jaw-dropping detail in *The Deception Game*, by Ladislav Bittman.

p. 342: **'It is now generally accepted that Frolík was a plant . . .'**

The Intelligence Game: The Illusions and Delusions of International Espionage, by James Rusbridger (I.B. Tauris, 1991; first published by The Bodley Head, 1989), pp. 58–9.

p. 343: **'sold his soul to the Communist regime'**

'Setkávání s Emilem Zátopkem', by Stanislav Berton, *CS-Magazín*, 3 May 2009 (cs-magazin.com/index.php?a=a2009061008).

p. 343: **although others have been equally scathing about Pachman's reliability**

Several of Emil's friends spoke disparagingly of Pachman to me. Ludvík Liška, Emil's former team-mate, described him as 'a crooked man'. See also: *The Miracle Game*, a novel by Pachman's US publisher, the Czech exile Josef Škvorecký, in which a Pachman-like character, Bukavec, admits to the invention of malicious lies about people. Informers' reports in the StB files confirm the view that the eventual animosity between Emil and Pachman was personal as well as ideological; Emil particularly disapproved of the way Pachman cheated on his wife.

p. 344: **some 'sharp eyes' who took pride in being attached to such a great man**

Examples include Jan Jirka (see pp. 233–5); and, according to Ludvík Liška, a regular 'sharp eye' called Nikolaj Hrib.

p. 344: **'always as about people whom he feared'**

Kosatík, p.97.

p. 346: **people in high places who liked him**

Dana is sure that Emil's former colleagues in the Army 'tried to protect him'.

p. 346: **he felt like weeping**
Informer's report in the StB archive.

p. 347: **Luděk Pachman and Pavel Kohout, before they became liberals**
See: *Fools and heroes: the changing role of Communist intellectuals in Czechoslovakia*, by Peter Hruby, chapters 2 and 4, for a detailed account of Pachman and Kohout's pre-liberal activities.

p. 347: **starting an argument believing one thing but ending it believing the opposite**
See: Kosatík, p. 218.

p. 349: **'What good is it if someone says five or ten years after you are dead that you are a hero?'**
Quoted in Montville, *Sports Illustrated*, 26 March 1990.

p. 352: **Haluza's contribution to Emil's success**
Haluza's account of the relationship can be found, along with the blurred photograph, in *Trénoval jsem Emila*. But Dana and others insist that Haluza was less crucial to Emil's development than he claimed – and that Emil exaggerated his influence in order help him back on his feet after Jáchymov.

p. 353: **a tiny asteroid**
I understand that Zátopek, asteroid serial number 5910, can be found at these coordinates: 2.28, 0.14, 5.0. See: *Dictionary of Minor Planet Names*, by Lutz D. Schmadel, p. 473.

p. 356: **Two photographs**
Emil Zátopek a sport objektivem Emila Fafka a jiných, p. 95.

p. 357: **the last fell in 1965**
The last records to go were those for 15 miles and 25,000m, broken by Ron Hill in Bolton on 21 July 1965.

p. 357: **But attempts to mark that landmark with a special radio celebration were hampered by Emil's health**
Kosatík, p. 270.

p. 357: **'At this age . . . there is no shame in dying'**
Quoted in 'Die tschechische Lokomotive', by Karl-Heinz Bergmann, *Berliner-Zeitung*, 23 November 2000.

p. 358: **'You are a guest in my house, so we will speak in your language . . .'**
'Radcliffe has many miles to run to match true legend', by Alasdair Reid, *Sunday Herald*, 2 August 2005.

pp. 358–9: **a 'tough week full of deep depression . . .'**
Petr Krejčí, head of the department of functional diagnostics and sports medicine, Prague Central Military Hospital, quoted in PA report in *iDNES*, December 7, 1999.

p. 359: **'practising for eternal sleep . . .'**
Quoted in Kosatík, p. 270.

p. 360: **'Zátopek the great' . . .**
Headlines from, respectively, *Mirror*, 23 November 2000; Agence France Press, 22 November 2000; Xinhua General News Service, 22 November 2000.

pp. 360–1: **'I am losing a brother, not an adversary . . .'**
Quoted in *L'humanité*, 23 November 2000.

p. 361: **Dana asked for it to be kept simple**
It was Emil and Dana's great friend Karel Engel, a former Olympic wrestler and now a prominent member of the Czech Olympic Committee, who arranged for the National Theatre to be made available. He knew the director's father and decided to call in a favour.

p. 361: **'Better an ugly wedding than a lovely funeral'**
See: 'Tisíce lidí se poklonily legendárnímu atletovi', by Jiří Jakoubek, *Lidové noviny*, 7 December 2000.

p. 364: **denounced on the radio . . . allegations had been raised on television**
The director of the National Gallery was Milan Knížák; the allegations were made on Katovna by Jan Rejžek; at the time of going to press Jiřina Fuchsová's blog could still be found at http://www.britskelisty.cz/0012/20001218l.html. See: *Emil Zátopek a sport objektivem – Emila Fafka a jiných*, p. 13.

p. 365: **' . . . in our country they scorned him'**
Jiří was talking in *Pohádkový Péťa.*

p. 365: **'sophisticated because he is so simple'**
Quoted in the *Melbourne Age*, 2 August 1992, p. 3.

p. 366: **'constantly pretending to be a decent person . . .'**
'How famous am I? Not very', by Caitlin Moran, *The Times* (magazine), 2 August 2014. Moran had unexpectedly found herself a role model for troubled young women, following the success of her book *How to be a Woman*, and felt obliged not to disappoint them.

p. 367: **possible that Emil 'borrowed' the incident from Ladislav Kořán**
Karel Tejkal's 2009 radio programme, *Praha Velké osudy: Emil Zátopek*, suggests that this may have been the case.

p. 369: **'proved that the ordinary man is capable of feats previously considered impossible'**
Stars of Czechoslovak Sport, p. 12.

p. 370: **'An athlete cannot run with money in his pocket . . .'**
Emil wrote these words in a hand-written message (complete with cartoon runner) to the British athlete and orienteer, Ted Norrish, after they sat next to one another at a dinner in Coventry on 27 May 1966. I get the impression that he wrote or said them elsewhere as well.

p. 372: **'He was a simple man – a good boy . . .'**
The speakers are, respectively: Jaromír Konůpka, John Disley, Jiří Zátopek (Emil's nephew), Ludvík Liška, Olga Lišková, Marie Vlachová, Vaneesa Kořán, Zdeněk Fator; Dana Zátopková (Emil's niece).

Acknowledgements

This book could not have been written without the kindness and enthusiasm of many people. I am especially indebted to the Zátopek family, particularly (and obviously) Emil's widow, Dana Zátopková but also (less visibly) to his nephew and niece, Jiří Zátopek and Dana Zátopková.

Nor could it have been written without the tireless, patient and at times inspired support of Petr Bráník, Radka Brahová and Lewis Paines.

I am also very grateful for the support of (in no particular order): Karel Engel of the Czech Olympic Committee; Michaela Bortlová (historian and curator of the permanent Emil and Dana Zátopek exhibition in the Technical Museum Tatra in Kopřivnice); Kateřina Mikulcová; Ondřej Šalek at Kopřivnice's Muzeum Fojtství; Petr Cimala at the Hranice military academy; Šárka Kárpátiová; Radomir Michálková; Rudolf Braha, Oldřich Stehlík, Stanislav Šula and Richard Händl; Jiří Pihera and Petr Loukota; Vojtěch Franta; Dr Libor Svoboda of the Institute for the Study of Totalitarian Regimes; Steve Riley of the Faculty of Management at Prague's University of Economics; Judita Matyášová; Stephen Weeks; Jaroslav Šonka; Olga Šílová; Barbara Smit; Emily Howard; Vaneesa Kořán; Ondrej Kohout; Kateřina Moravcová; Tomáš Luňák; Jan Dufek; Petr Hájek at Krátký Film Praha; Tomáš Mrva; Jan Havlíček; Zuzana Štefunková and Eva Pavlíková at the Czech National Film Archive; Libuše Pekárková at the Archiv

ČT Praha; Ivana Roháčková at ASC Dukla; Stanislav Berton; Ian Robilliard; Glynis Nunn-Cearns; Claire Sanjuan; Alice Laurent; Alan Hubbard; Filip Paulus at the National Archive of the Czech Republic; the staff of the Czech National Library in Prague, the Archiv bezpečnostních složek, the military archive in Olomouc, the Jáchymov museum and (not least) the British Library Reading Room. I am grateful to Supraphon A.S. for permission to quote, in my own rough translation, the lines from 'A Prayer for Marta' ('Modlitba pro Martu', words by Petr Roda and music by Jindřich Brabec) on p. 261. I also owe warm thanks to Tomáš Dimter at Mlada fronta (for helping me find my feet in Prague); Alexandr Kohák (for repeatedly looking after me there); three generations of the Konůpka family; my colleagues at the (now only digital) *Independent*; and, almost certainly, several other people whose names I have forgotten to list, but to whom I am no less grateful.

I owe additional and special debts to Jon Waldron, Jon Henderson, Anna Kudrnová, Jan Krčmář and Dr Jan Čulík (senior lecturer in Czech Studies at the University of Glasgow), all of whom have encouraged me and advised me with extraordinary generosity and saved me from countless embarrassing mistakes. The embarrassing mistakes that remain are exclusively mine.

Finally, nearer home, I thank Robin Harvie, who first encouraged me to write about Zátopek; Brie Burkeman and Meg Davis, my past and current agents; Matt Phillips and Frances Jessop at Yellow Jersey, who kept faith in this book when it would have been easier not to – and cajoled me into making a far better job of it than I would ever have done unaided; and, above all, my family (Clare, Isobel, Edward, Anne), who have been patient and encouraging beyond the call of duty while I have been immersed in the world of Emil Zátopek. I hope they will forgive me for occasionally seeming reluctant to emerge from it.

I do not know what I have done to deserve so much kindness, but I suspect that much of it was initially directed at Emil: a great man in his life who continues to inspire us to find our better selves long after his death.

List of Illustrations

Index

September 4, 1880.
New Moon.

THE WITCHES OF NEW YORK

Robert Bryndza is the author of the international #1 bestselling Detective Erika Foster series and the Kate Marshall series. Robert's books have sold over 3 million copies and have been translated into 28 languages. He is British and lives in Slovakia.

ALSO BY ROBERT BRYNDZA

The Detective Erika Foster crime thriller series

The Girl in the Ice

The Night Stalker

Dark Water

Last Breath

Cold Blood

Deadly Secrets

The Kate Marshall crime thriller series

Nine Elms

Shadow Sands

The Coco Pinchard romantic comedy series

The Not So Secret Emails of Coco Pinchard

Coco Pinchard's Big Fat Tipsy Wedding

Coco Pinchard, the Consequences of Love and Sex

A Very Coco Christmas

Coco Pinchard's Must-Have Toy Story

Standalone Romantic Comedy Novels

Miss Wrong and Mr Right

Lost In Crazytown

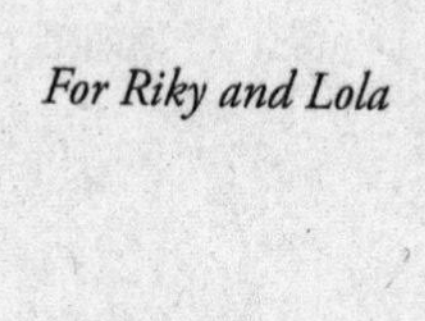

For Riky and Lola

Man is least himself when he talks in his own person.
Give him a mask, and he will tell you the truth.

Oscar Wilde

CHAPTER ONE

It was late on Christmas Eve when Marissa Lewis stepped off the train onto the platform at Brockley, moving with the drunken crowds to the footbridge. The first flakes of snow twirled lazily in the air, and the crowds were full of warmth and alcohol, eager to get home and start the festivities.

Marissa was a beautiful woman with blue-black hair, violet-coloured eyes, and an hourglass figure. She took pride in being the kind of girl your mother warns you about. She was coming home from the club in London where she performed as a burlesque dancer, and wore a long black vintage coat with an elaborate fur trim, heavy pale make-up, false lashes and a slash of scarlet on her lips. As she reached the steps up to the footbridge, a couple of young men up ahead turned back, greedily checking her out. She followed their eyes down and saw that the bottom half of her long coat had come undone, revealing, as she climbed the steps, a flash of the stockings and suspenders she wore for her act. She stopped to fasten the large brass buttons, and the crowds surged around her.

'I hope that's fake fur,' muttered a voice behind. Marissa glanced back to a bony young woman with her equally bony boyfriend. They both wore scruffy winter coats and the woman had long greasy hair.

'Yes, it's fake,' Marissa insisted, a dazzling smile masking the lie.

'Looks like real fur to me,' said the young woman. Her boyfriend stood staring with his mouth slightly open at the flash of lace and suspender as Marissa finished arranging her coat.

'Frank!' she barked, dragging him away and off up the stairs.

The fur trim on Marissa's coat *was* real. It had been a bargain from a second hand vintage shop in Soho. She'd bought it, along with the vanity case hooked over her arm.

Marissa climbed the remaining stairs and crossed the footbridge. The train tracks below gleamed in the moonlight, and a thin dusting of snow was starting to lay on the rooftops. As she neared the end, she saw the two young men had dropped back, and were waiting at the top of the stairs. Her heart began to beat faster.

'Can I help you?' asked the tallest, offering his arm. He was handsome, with red hair, and a smooth ruddy face. He wore a three-piece suit, a long tan winter coat, and his tan leather shoes gleamed. His friend was shorter, and dressed almost identically, but wasn't quite as blessed in the looks department.

'I'm fine,' she said.

'It's slippery,' he insisted, thrusting his arm up under hers. They were now blocking one half of the stairs down. She eyed him for a moment, and decided it might be easier to accept help.

'Thank you,' she said, and took his arm. His shorter friend wanted to take her vanity case, but she shook her head and smiled. The salt crunched underfoot as they climbed down, keeping Marissa sandwiched between them. They reeked of beer and cigarettes.

'Are you a model?' asked the tall guy.

'No.'

'What does M.L. stand for?' asked his shorter friend, indicating the letters printed on the vanity case.

'My initials.'

'And? What's your name?'

'I'm Sid, this is Paul,' said the taller guy. Paul grinned, showing large yellow teeth. They reached the bottom of the steps, and she thanked them, unhooking her arm. 'You fancy a drink?'

'Thanks, but I'm due home,' said Marissa. The guys were still blocking one half of the stairs, and a stream of people moved past beside them. They stood for a moment, waiting, weighing things up.

'Come on, it's Christmas,' said Sid. Marissa stepped away, putting the other commuters between them. 'Or we can give you a lift?' he added, pushing through them to join her. Paul followed, shoving a young lad out of the way. His beady eyes were both piercing and unfocused.

'No. Really. I must get home, but thank you, guys. Have a Merry Christmas.'

'You sure?' said Paul.

'I am, thank you.'

'Can we have a picture with you?' asked Sid.

'What?'

'Just a selfie with us; we like a pretty girl and it gives us something to look at when we're cold and lonely in our beds at night.'

The way they stared at her made Marissa think of wolves. Hungry wolves. They came either side of her and leaned in. She felt a hand on her backside as Sid held out his iPhone, and took a selfie, and then another. His fingers began to work their way between her buttocks.

'Great,' she said, pulling away. They showed her the photo. She looked wide-eyed, but not as scared as she'd felt inside.

'You are really fit,' said Sid, 'are you sure we can't persuade you to come for a drink?'

'We've got vodka, Malibu, wine,' said Paul. Marissa looked back at the bridge, and saw there were still a few passengers crossing. She looked back at them and forced another smile.

'Sorry, guys. Not tonight.'

She looked up at one of the CCTV cameras above them, encased in its plastic dome. They followed her gaze. Then finally seemed to take the hint, and moved off.

'What a stuck-up bitch,' she heard Paul say. She hung back, relieved, watching as they went to a car by the kerb, but averting her eyes as they glanced back. She heard laughter, doors slamming, and then the engine starting up. Marissa only realised she had been holding her breath when their car pulled away and left the station approach.

She exhaled, and saw the last few passengers were coming down the stairs. At the top was a tall, handsome man in his early fifties, with his wife, who was very pale.

'Shit,' she said under her breath. She hurried over to the row of self-service ticket machines and busied herself looking at one of the screens.

'Marissa! I see you!' said the woman's voice, thick with booze. 'I see you, whore!' There was a clatter on the stairs as the woman hurried towards her.

'Jeanette!' shouted the man.

'You leave us alone,' shouted the woman, reaching Marissa, but stopping short of making contact. She brandished a long finger, an inch from Marissa's face. 'You stay away from him!'

Her eyes were bloodshot and her face was red and puffy, and her scarlet lipstick had bled out into the smoker's lines around her mouth.

'Jeanette!' hissed the man, catching up and pulling her away. Although the couple were about the same age, he had a rugged, handsome face. It was a reminder to Marissa that time can be kinder to men.

'I do my best to keep out of your way, but we live on the same street. Our paths are bound to cross,' said Marissa, smiling sweetly.

'You're a bitch!'

'Been to the pub, Jeanette?'

'Yes!' she snarled. 'With *my* husband.'

'You look sober, Don. I would have thought you're the one who needs the beer goggles.'

Jeanette raised a hand to slap Marissa around the face, but Don grabbed it.

'That's enough. Why can't you keep your mouth shut, Marissa? You can see she's not well,' he said.

'Don't you fucking talk as if I'm not here,' slurred Jeanette.

'Come on, we're going,' he said. He led her away, almost like an invalid.

'Fucking prostitute,' muttered Jeanette.

'No one's ever paid me for sex!' shouted Marissa. 'Ask Don!'

He turned back with a look of sadness. She wasn't sure if he was sad for his alcoholic wife, or himself. He helped Jeanette to a car by the kerb, easing her into the passenger seat. As they drove away, Marissa closed her eyes at the memory of him. The times when he knocked on her door late at night, when her mother was asleep, and they stole up to her bedroom. The feel of his warm body against her skin as they made love...

When she opened her eyes again, she saw the last of the passengers had dispersed into the surrounding streets, and she was alone. Snow was falling heavily, and it caught in the arcs of the bright lights around the station concourse. Marissa emerged onto the station approach, and took a right down Foxberry Road. Christmas trees glowed in the windows of the houses, and the crunch of her feet on snow broke the thick silence.

The end of the road turned sharply to the right, and became Howson Road. She hesitated. It stretched away in darkness. Several of the streetlights were out, leaving just two to illuminate a five-hundred-yard stretch lined on each side with terraced houses. She had wanted to walk this with the other commuters from the last train; there were always at least a couple of people who took the

same route, and it made the walk feel safer. However, Jeanette and the two creeps at the station had put paid to that.

Marissa hurried past shadowy alleyways and dark empty windows, speeding up to each pool of light. She was relieved when Coniston Road came out of the darkness, it was brightly lit thanks to the school at the end. She turned left, and walked past the playground, before crossing the road to her front gate. It creaked as she opened it. The windows were all dark, and the tiny front garden was bathed in shadows. She had her keys ready, and was about to put them in the lock, when she heard a soft thud behind her.

'Jeez! You scared me, Beaker,' she said, seeing the sleek, dark body of the cat sitting on top of the wheelie bin beside the gate. She went over and scooped him up. 'Come on. It's too cold for us both to be out roaming.' Beaker purred and looked up at her with intense green eyes. She put her face against his warm fur. The cat seemed to give her a moment's grace, then squirmed in her arms. 'Alright, you little crap bag.' He jumped down and darted off through the hedge to the next garden.

Marissa reached up to put her key in the lock, but the gate creaked behind her. She froze. There was a faint scrape, and then a crunch of feet on the snow. She slowly turned.

A figure in a long black trench coat stood behind her. Its face covered in a gas mask, with a hood made of shiny black leather, tightly enveloping the skull. Two large round glass eyeholes stared blankly, and the drum, or breathing apparatus, elongated the face down to where it hung just above the chest. The figure wore black gloves, and in its left hand was a long, thin knife.

Marissa scrabbled to get the key in the lock, but the figure rushed at her, grabbing her shoulder, and slamming her back against the front door. There was a flash of silver, and blood sprayed across the glass eyeholes of the mask.

Her vanity case fell to the ground, and she reached up to her neck, only then feeling the terrible pain of the deep slash across her throat. Marissa tried to scream but there was only a gurgling sound and her mouth filled with blood. She put her hands up as the figure staggered and swung the knife, slicing through two of her fingers and the material of her coat into her forearms. She was unable to breathe and gasped for air, gurgling and spraying blood. The figure grabbed the back of her head and dragged her along the path, slamming her face first into the brick gate post. Pain exploded in her face, and she heard a crack of bone.

Marissa heaved and retched, no longer able to breathe air into her flooded lungs. She watched, almost detached, as this strange figure struggled to drag her across the ground, away from the gate post to the middle of the tiny garden. The figure tottered, and looked as if it was about to fall, but kept balance. With both hands, it brought the knife back down, slicing and stabbing at her throat and neck. As her blood pumped out over the blanket of snow, and the life left her body, Marissa thought she recognised the face through the large glass eye holes of the gas mask.

CHAPTER TWO

Detective Chief Inspector Erika Foster's alarm went off at 7 a.m., and from the depths of her bedcovers and blankets, a thin pale arm emerged and switched it off. Her bedroom was dark and chilly, and the streetlights shone through the paper-thin blinds that she'd been meaning to change since she moved in, but had never got around to asking her landlord about. She rolled over and pulled the covers off, then padded through to the bathroom, where she took a shower and brushed her teeth.

It was only when she had pulled on her clothes, pocketed her phone, wallet and warrant card that she remembered it was Christmas Day, and she was invited for Christmas lunch at Commander Paul Marsh's house.

'Shit,' she said, sitting down on the bed. She ran a hand through her short blonde hair. 'Shit.'

Most police officers would have seen this as a coup, an invite to spend Christmas lunch with the borough commander and his family, but for Erika, her relationship with Marsh was… *complicated.*

Erika had just completed work on a harrowing case, involving a young couple who had committed a string of murders. As part of their sick game, they had abducted Commander Marsh's two small girls, and Marsh's wife, Marcie, had been attacked during the abduction. It had led to a fully fledged man-hunt. Erika had been responsible for rescuing the girls, and she understood that Marsh and Marcie had invited her to say thank you, but she just wanted to move on.

Erika got up and opened her wardrobe, staring at the sparse rack of clothes, of which almost all were for work. Rooting through the neatly hung black trousers, sweaters and white blouses, she dug out a blue sleeveless dress. Turning to the mirror above her dressing table, she held the hanger up under her chin. Erika stood six feet tall in bare feet. She had strong, high cheekbones, large green eyes, and short blond hair which stuck up in wet tufts. 'Jeez, I'm scrawny,' she said, moulding the dress to her body, where once she'd had curves. She looked at the photo of her late husband, Mark, on the dresser. 'Who needs Lean Cuisine, eh? Being a widow does wonders for your waistline…' The bleakness of her humour shocked her. 'Sorry,' she added.

Mark had also been a police officer. Erika, Marsh and Mark had all trained together, but Mark had been killed over two years previously, during a drugs raid. The photo of Mark was taken in the living room of the house that he and Erika had shared for fifteen years in Manchester. The sun streamed through the window, catching in his close-cropped dark hair to create a halo of gold. His face was handsome, his smile warm and infectious.

'I don't know what to say to Marsh and Marcie… I just want to turn the page and move on, without any fuss.'

Mark grinned back.

'Bah, humbug, eh? Is it too late to think up an excuse?'

Yes, his grin seemed to say. *Come on, Erika, play nice.*

'You're right, I can't cancel… Happy Christmas.' She put a finger to her lips and pressed it against the glass.

Erika went through to the small kitchen/living room, sparsely furnished with a little sofa, a television, and a half-empty bookshelf. Perched on top of the microwave was a tiny plastic Christmas tree. It sat on top of the telly in years gone by, but since the advent of the flat screen, the top of the microwave was the only place it could go without looking ridiculous. She switched on the coffee

machine, and opened the curtains. The car park and the road beyond were under a deep carpet of snow, glowing orange under the street lights. There were no people or cars, and she felt like the only person in the world. A gust of wind blew across the ground, skimming a dusting of snow across the surface to join the banked-up drift by the car park wall.

The landline rang as she poured her coffee, and she hurried through to the hallway and answered, hoping for a miracle and that lunch was cancelled. It was Mark's father, Edward.

'Did I wake you up, love?' he said, in his warm Yorkshire accent.

'No, I'm up. Merry Christmas.'

'Merry Christmas to you, too. Is it cold down there in London?'

'We've got snow,' she said. 'It's ankle deep, admittedly, but it'll be enough to make news headlines.'

'We've got four feet here. And over in Beverley, it's even deeper.' His voice sounded frail and strained.

'Are you keeping warm?'

'Yes, love. I've got the fire on, and I'm feeling a bit rakish, so I'll keep it on all day… It's a pity I won't be seeing you.'

Erika felt a twinge of guilt.

'I'll come up in the New Year. I've got holiday saved up.'

'Have they got you working today?'

'Not today. I'm invited for lunch at Paul Marsh's place with his family… After everything that happened to them, I felt I couldn't say no.'

'Who's that, love?'

'Paul; Paul Marsh…'

There was a pause on the line.

'Yes, of course. Young Paul. Has he had any luck selling that Ford Cortina?'

'What?'

'I doubt he'll get much for it. It's such a rust bucket. You can poke your finger through the body work.'

'Edward, what are you talking about?' said Erika. Marsh had owned a red Ford Cortina, but that was years ago, back in the early nineties.

'Oh, course. I'm being daft… I didn't get a very good night's sleep. How are things with them, after what happened?'

Erika didn't know what to say. She twisted the phone wire in her fingers. Edward was almost eighty, but always so sharp and on the ball.

'It's early days. I haven't seen them since…'

She heard the kettle whistle in the background.

'You give them my best, will you?'

'Of course.'

'I'll be off, love. I just need my morning cuppa, and to wake up. And open my presents. You take care, and happy Christmas.'

'Edward, are you sure everything's okay?' she started, but he'd hung up.

She stared at the phone for a moment, then went to the window. The Victorian manor house opposite was large and ornate, and like the rest of the houses on the street had been converted into flats. Several lights were now on, and she could see in one of the windows a couple with two small children opening their presents around a large Christmas tree. A woman in a thick coat struggled past on the pavement, her head down against the driving snow, pulling along a small black dog behind her. Erika went back to the phone and picked it up, then put it down again.

*

Erika got ready, and left the flat just before eleven. The snow was coming down thick, and there was a sleepy quality to the day, with

all the shops closed, and she saw a few children playing outside, having a snowball fight.

As she drove past the row of shops by Crofton Park train station, the traffic began to thicken and slow, and then things ground to a halt. The windscreen wipers squealed as they cleared the dry snow. Up ahead she could see the flash of blue police lights. This cheered her a little; it made her think of work. The traffic crept forward, and just past Crofton Park School, one of the roads on the left was blocked by two squad cars and a line of police tape. Detective Constable John McGorry was talking to two officers by the fluttering tape. As Erika drew level, she honked her horn and they looked over.

'What's going on?' shouted Erika, winding down her window. A flurry of snow poured in, but she took no notice. McGorry pulled up the lapels of his long black coat and hurried over. He was a handsome young man in his mid-twenties, with dark hair which fell over his face with a floppy fringe. His skin was smooth and pale, and his cheeks flushed from the cold. When he reached her window, he swept back his hair with a gloved hand.

'Merry Christmas, Boss. Going somewhere nice?' he asked, noting that she was wearing make-up and earrings.

'Lunch… What's going on?'

'A young woman, found stabbed to death on her doorstep. Whoever did it went crazy on her, blood everywhere,' he said, shaking his head. The traffic in front started moving, and he stepped back onto the pavement, expecting Erika to drive off. 'Have a nice lunch. I was hoping to be off duty by now. You on tomorrow?'

'Who's the DCI on call today?'

'Peter Farley, but he's out at a triple stabbing in Catford. People don't seem to stop killing each other just because it's Christmas.'

The car in front pulled away, and a van behind sounded its horn. Erika thought how much more appealing a brutal murder

scene was than Christmas lunch with Marsh. The van behind honked again. She put the car in gear and pulled up onto the pavement, causing McGorry to jump back. She grabbed her warrant card and coat and got out.

'Show me the crime scene,' she said.

CHAPTER THREE

Erika flashed her warrant card, and she and McGorry ducked under the police cordon. They started along the street, passing the rundown houses where neighbours watched from their doorsteps in various states of early morning dress, gawping at the police tape at the end of the road, and craning up the street to where uniformed officers milled around another police tape cordon.

Erika struggled to keep up with McGorry, finding the heels she'd put on for Christmas lunch had no grip on the icy pavement. She wished the weather was warm so she could take her shoes off and go barefoot.

'It's the worst day to close off the road; we've already had to turn people away who are coming to visit relatives…' He glanced back and saw Erika gripping a nearby wall as she carefully picked her way along.

'What?' she said, when she'd caught up, noticing McGorry staring at her.

'Nothing. You're wearing heels,' he said.

'Great work, detective.'

'No, you look great. I mean smart, really good…'

Erika scowled and went to move off, but slipped. McGorry grabbed her just as she was about to fall.

'Do you want to take my arm?' he asked. 'The house is a little way down the end.'

'Not really, but it might be quicker. And I don't want to go arse over tit in front of uniform.'

She grabbed his arm and they moved off at a slower pace.

'I wore heels, once,' said McGorry.

'You did?'

'Six-inch stilettos. When I was at Hendon, we did a charity Christmas show. I played Lady Bracknell in *The Importance of Being Earnest*.'

Despite her annoyance, Erika smiled as she picked her way through the ice.

'Six-inch stilettos? Isn't Lady Bracknell meant to be a staid and stuffy elderly Victorian lady?'

'I'm a size twelve. They were the only heels I could get for my feet,' he said, indicating his large shoes.

'How much did you raise for charity?'

'Four hundred and seventy-three pounds fifty…'

'Go on then, give me a bit of Lady Bracknell,' said Erika.

'*A handbag?*' he said, affecting an upper-class old lady vibrato.

Erika shook her head and smiled, 'I'm glad you didn't give up your day job.'

She let go of his arm as they reached another police cordon ballooning out in front of a terraced house near the end of the street. A low wall and a tall snow-topped hedge obscured the front garden, and through the open gate they could see a crowd of forensics officers in their blue paper Tyvek suits. The officer at the cordon peered at Erika's warrant card.

'A DCI has already been called. He's delayed, triple stabbing in Cat…' she started.

'Well, he's not here, and I am,' said Erika. The officer nodded and lifted the cordon. They went to the forensics van parked up on the pavement. Another uniformed officer, a stern middle-aged woman with a nose stud and cropped grey hair, handed them each a Tyvek suit. They took off their coats, draping them over the top of the van.

'Bloody hell, it's freezing,' said McGorry, quickly stepping into the legs and pulling it up over his thin suit.

'It got down to minus twelve last night,' said the officer. Erika held on to the van, balanced on one foot, and pulled on the paper suit, but her left heel caught in the fabric and tore the leg as she pulled it up.

'Shit!'

'I'll bag that up; here's another one,' said the officer, handing her a fresh suit. Erika took it and pulled it on, but the same thing happened again. 'You should be in flats, especially on a day like this,' the officer said.

Erika shot her a look, and McGorry looked away politely as she took a third suit, and successfully managed to get it on over her heels. She zipped it up, and they both pulled up the hoods. They put on shoe covers which, again, Erika found tricky, but once they were ready they moved to the front gate and entered the tiny, cramped front garden.

Isaac Strong, the forensic pathologist, was working in the small space with two assistants. He was a tall, thin man in his early forties. The widow's peak of his dark brown hair poked out from under the hood of his Tyvek suit. He had long, thin eyebrows, which made him look constantly quizzical.

The blood-spattered body of a young woman was on her back under the bay window. Her long black coat lay open. The plummeting temperature during the night had frozen her spilled blood to the consistency of a ruby-red sorbet. Her throat had been sliced open, and this was where there was the most concentration of blood, stretching out in a pool underneath her. It saturated her thin green strapless dress, split up the left leg to reveal black stockings and suspenders, and it covered the bay window and sill above in a fine frosted spray.

'Morning, Merry Christmas,' said Isaac, shaking his head. His greeting hung awkwardly in the air. Erika looked back at the face of the young girl. Her face was frozen, figuratively and literally,

in fear. Her lips were drawn back, and one of her front teeth was broken off close to the gum. Her eyes, though cloudy, were violet, and they were strikingly beautiful, even in death.

'Do we know who she is?' asked Erika.

'Marissa Lewis, twenty-two years old,' replied Isaac.

'Is that a formal ID?'

'Her mother discovered her body this morning, and there's a driving licence in her wallet.'

Erika crouched down and took a closer look. A square vanity case with the initials 'M.L.' was half-buried in snow by the hedge, and beside it was a black high-heeled shoe. They were both marked up with plastic numbers.

'Anyone touched the body?'

'No,' said McGorry. 'I was first on the scene with uniform. The mother found her and said she didn't touch anything.'

'Do you have a time of death?'

'The extreme cold is going to make it difficult,' said Isaac. 'Her throat was slashed with a very sharp blade, resulting in deep cuts and severing both carotid arteries on each side of the neck. You can see this led to rapid blood loss, and she would have bled out very quickly. On her right hand, the index finger is almost severed, and there are lacerations to the thumb, middle finger and arms, which indicates she put up her hands to defend herself.'

'There's no way out of the garden, apart from the gate, or through the front door,' said McGorry. Erika saw that in addition to the window, the front door had a fine spray of frozen blood on its faded blue paintwork.

'Are those her keys?' she said, noticing a bunch of keys with a heart-shaped keyring.

'Yes,' said McGorry.

Erika closed her eyes for a moment, imagining what it must have been like, overpowered by a knife-wielding maniac in this

small enclosed space. She opened them again, and looked at Marissa's face.

'Her nose is broken,' she said.

'Yes. And her left cheek. We also found her front tooth, embedded in the gate post,' said Isaac.

Erika and McGorry turned to look at the gate post, where a numbered marker was fixed halfway up. Clumps of snow clung to the brickwork. Next to it was a wheelie bin, and a recycling box stuffed with empty vodka bottles. Erika turned back to look at the house. The curtains were drawn, no lights were on.

'Where's the mother?'

'At the neighbour's house,' said McGorry, indicating a terraced house diagonally across the street.

'And we're sure the victim lives here? She wasn't visiting her mum for Christmas?'

'We need to check that.'

'We're going to have difficulties moving her,' said one of Isaac's assistants, who had finished clearing the snow from the blood-spattered legs.

'Why?' asked Erika.

He looked up at her – a small man with large, intense brown eyes. He indicated the vast pool of frozen blood spreading out from under the body.

'The blood. She's frozen solid to the soil underneath.'

CHAPTER FOUR

Isaac came to the gate with Erika. He looked up at the cloud hanging low and grey.

'I need to move her before the weather turns; there's more snow on the way,' he said. She looked back at the body, where Isaac's assistants worked carefully to dig her out of the frozen blood-soaked soil. Erika felt the same pang of horror and excitement she always experienced at the scene of a murder. So much in her life was out of her control, but she had the power to track down whoever had done this. And she would.

'When do you think you can do the post-mortem?'

Isaac blew out his cheeks. 'Sorry. Couple of days. I have a backlog; this is a busy time of year for suspicious deaths. And did I tell you? I've been moved. I'm working out of the morgue at Lewisham Hospital.'

'Since when?'

'Since the morgue in Penge has been sold to a developer. A big sign went up for Parkside Peninsula Apartments a few weeks ago, and we moved last week. It's causing all sorts of delays.'

'Parkside Peninsula Apartments, Penge,' repeated Erika, raising an eyebrow. Isaac raised one in return.

'Oh, and another thing,' he said. 'Blood spatter. The person who did this would have been covered in blood and carrying a weapon, but the drops of blood end abruptly at the gate.'

'You think they wiped the knife? Or had a vehicle parked by the gate?' asked Erika.

'That's for you to find out,' said Isaac. 'I'll keep you in the loop with the post-mortem.' He went back into the front garden.

Erika and McGorry changed out of their Tyvek suits, handed them in, then ducked under the police tape into the road. They buttoned up their coats against the cold. A large police support van had just arrived, and was attempting to park against the kerb. One of the police cars pulled out to make extra room, and it got stuck in the snow, its wheels spinning and squealing.

'So, we're looking at someone who had a car, potentially,' said Erika. 'They got in and drove away. But where?' Erika looked up and down the street. The house was on the end of the terrace, with an alleyway running along the side. It was overlooked by the back gardens of the houses in Howson Road, which ran parallel to Coniston Road. 'I want to get the house-to-house going ASAP. There should be plenty of people home on Christmas Day. I want to know if anyone saw anything, and I need the details of persons of interest in the area: violent offenders, anyone with previous or ongoing convictions.'

Two uniformed officers had come to help the squad car, and were giving it a push. The engine roared and the wheels spun.

'There's a railway bridge at the end of the next road, which leads over to the Fitzwilliam Estate,' said McGorry.

Erika nodded. 'Worth including in our H2H, but whoever goes in there needs to go easy.' She knew that the Fitzwilliam Estate, like many high-rise council buildings in poor areas, was known for trouble. She peered down the long alleyways running along each side of the terraces. 'And we need to check out if any garden gates back onto these alleyways…'

They stepped out of the way as the squad car broke free from the snow. It shot past, took a right at the end of the street, and parked outside the school opposite. The support van pulled into the gap by the kerb and turned off its engine. In the sudden silence came the click of a camera shutter. Erika turned to McGorry.

'Did you hear that?' she murmured. He nodded. They looked up at the surrounding windows, but couldn't see anything. There was a rustle directly behind. Erika turned and looked up into the branches of a tall oak tree across the road, next to the railings of the school playground. A young man who looked to be in his early twenties was slithering down the branches. He stepped onto the top of the metal railing lining the playground, and dropped down into the alleyway. He was scruffy, with long blond hair, and had a long-lens camera around his neck on a strap. He glanced at Erika and McGorry, then bolted for it down the snowy alleyway.

'Hey! Stop!' shouted Erika. McGorry headed off in pursuit down the alleyway, and Erika followed. The young man wore a long coat, which flowed out behind him as he ran. He jumped up onto the lid of a wheelie bin, and vaulted up and over a high wall with tall trees behind it. Seconds later, McGorry reached the wheelie bin, hitched up his coat and heaved himself up shakily. Erika tottered unsteadily along and reached the bin as McGorry grabbed hold of a branch of one of the thick, snow-covered evergreens and climbed up onto the lip of the wall.

'What's over there…?' she started, but he jumped off, and landed on the other side with a thud and a yell. The branches above the wall swayed, dislodging the snow, and then they were still. Erika heard more yelling, and instinctively reached for her radio in her pocket, but it wasn't there. She looked back down the alleyway, but the road with the crime scene appeared a long way off.

'Shit, if he's broken something…' she muttered, thinking how much paperwork there would be to fill in. Shaking the guilty thought away, she took off her heels and shoved them into the pockets of her long coat, before hitching the coat up to climb up onto the wheelie bin. The plastic lid creased and bent downwards with her weight. She hooked her leg up onto the brick wall, and

grabbed a branch of one of the evergreens to steady herself, dislodging more snow on top of her head in the process. The ground was higher on the opposite side, and Erika dropped down softly onto a bed of soil and leaves between the wall and the thick row of trees. She slipped her shoes back on and walked out of the trees into a large, snow-covered garden. A gap in the middle was churned up with two sets of footprints, and there were two large sheds, a greenhouse, and a long polythene tunnel beyond. The garden's high walls muffled the sounds of traffic from surrounding streets.

McGorry was moving slowly towards the sheds. He turned to Erika and put a finger to his lips, pointing to the second shed in the row of two, closest to the house. She nodded. The house was large and crumbling. The sash windows were grimy, with peeling paint. A tall gate in one corner was blocked by overflowing rubbish bins. The back door to the house had a small roofed porch with steps down to the garden, which were covered in plant pots.

As Erika reached McGorry, from inside the house came a cacophony of clocks chiming the hour. The blond-haired lad appeared from behind the shed, and ran back to the wall. McGorry moved faster, tackling him to the ground. Erika hurried over to them, but lost one of her shoes in the process, and fell back into the snow.

'Calm down!' said McGorry as the lad fought, throwing punches and landing one in McGorry's face.

'Get off me!' cried the young man. He was wiry with a thin, feral face and bright blue eyes a little too far apart. Erika got up, losing her other shoe in the snow. McGorry was churning up the snow, struggling to keep hold of the young man, who kicked and flailed, and then got the upper hand, pushed McGorry's face into the snow. McGorry flailed and reached around, managing to get hold of the camera, and tightened the strap around the boy's

neck. The boy released his grip on the back of McGorry's head, and grabbed at the strap tightening around his neck.

'Get back!' shouted a voice. 'Let him go!' A large, elderly woman in an orange onesie was at the top of the porch steps, holding a shotgun. Her grey hair hung past her shoulders, and she wore huge glasses that magnified her eyes. She aimed a shotgun at them, and advanced towards them through the snow.

Erika put up her hands. The elderly woman's eyes looked crazed, and she felt this situation had suddenly escalated to red alert. McGorry coughed and spat out snow, still holding the strap tight. The young man was scrabbling frantically at his throat.

'John. Let him go!' shouted Erika. McGorry let go of the camera strap, and the lad fell onto the snow, coughing. 'I'm Detective Chief Inspector Erika Foster of the London Metropolitan Police, and this is Detective Constable John McGorry. We can show you our warrant cards, but you need to put the weapon down… Now.'

The woman looked anxiously between Erika and McGorry, but she didn't lower the gun.

'That is *my* son you are attacking, and you are trespassing on *my* property!'

'We are police, and your son was trespassing and photographing a crime scene,' said Erika. She wondered what the woman was capable of.

'Joseph! Come away from them!' the woman shrilled, still training the gun at them. Joseph coughed, and staggered over, his coat covered in snow.

'Elspeth!' shouted another voice. An elderly man emerged behind her from the back door. He looked like an eccentric university professor, and was wearing a long blue cape and a tatty skull cap dotted with sequins. He had a magnifying lens fixed to

his head with a band, giving him one huge, staring eye. 'Elspeth, put that down at once!'

'Sir, we are police and we can show you identification,' said Erika, her heart beginning to race. She felt stupid for blundering into this situation, and she was aware she wasn't wearing any shoes. Her feet were numb from the cold. The man gently took the shotgun from Elspeth, and opened the barrel.

'It's not loaded,' he said, hooking it over his arm in the manner of a gamekeeper. 'And we have a firearms certificate.'

'My boy, my boy!' said Elspeth, who had gathered Joseph into her arms and was checking him over, running her hands over his neck and peering into his eyes. 'Did they hurt you? Are you okay?'

Joseph looked a little bewildered and shell-shocked.

'Why was that gun so easily to hand?' asked Erika. McGorry leaned breathlessly on his knees and spat out snow.

'If you join us inside, officers, you can all get dry, and we can sort this out,' said the man.

CHAPTER FIVE

Erika and McGorry stamped their feet in the porch and brushed the snow off their coats. Then they were shown through to a warm, cosy kitchen. Elspeth fussed over Joseph like he was a small child, guiding him to one of the chairs at a long wooden table. McGorry moved to stand close to a blazing fire in the corner. The room was decorated like a country farmhouse kitchen, with a Welsh dresser, and a large green Aga from which a delicious smell of turkey was filling the room.

'There's a welt coming up already!' cried Elspeth, tilting Joseph's head to one side. He kept hold of his camera, and scowled at Erika and McGorry.

'Do take a seat, officers,' said the man, pulling out more chairs at the table.

'Can I see the certificate for your firearm?' said Erika, ignoring the chair.

'Certainly,' he said, leaning the shotgun by the fireplace and moving to a drawer in the Welsh dresser.

'It's a legal firearm,' insisted Elspeth, helping Joseph out of his wet coat and draping a towel around his shoulders. Erika noted he didn't want to let go of the camera, even when she was trying to get his arms out of the coat.

'What's your full name?'

'Family name is Pitkin. I'm David, this is Elspeth and Joseph. I take it you weren't expecting to be on duty today?' he said, looking up from rummaging in the drawer. He indicated Erika's soaked, misshapen shoes.

'No.'

'Were you headed anywhere nice?'

Erika realised she still had to tell Marsh she wouldn't be coming for lunch. She ignored him and pushed the thought to the back of her head.

'What do you do for a living?'

'I'm a horologist,' he said, tapping the magnifying lens strapped to his head by a leather band. 'I repair clocks and watches, although, to be honest, it's more of a hobby since I retired from the bar. Ah, here we are,' he said, pulling out a folded piece of paper.

'You were a barrister?' Erika said, her heart sinking.

'Yes. Thirty years.'

Erika took the licence and scanned the details.

'It's Elspeth's gun. I have my own. We like to shoot. It's a hobby, of course.'

'That seems in order,' said Erika, passing the licence back to him. 'But if it's a hobby, why was the gun so easily to hand?'

Elspeth looked up from peering at Joseph's neck. 'I have it in a locked cabinet in the back office! I saw you in the garden, creeping about. This isn't the nice area it used to be. There's drugs, and burglaries almost every other day… Look what you did to him! He's going to have a nasty bruise.'

'I'll also remind you, DCI Foster, of the law in Britain regarding self-defence, based on the principles of reasonable force being used?' said David.

'Does she brandish a double-barrelled shotgun, in broad daylight, to anyone she finds in the garden? Seems a bit excessive,' said Erika.

'Excuse me, I'm not going to be called "she" in my own house,' snapped Elspeth. 'I was going to offer you a piece of my coffee and walnut cake, to show no hard feelings, but I'm not going to now.'

McGorry turned away, suppressing a grin, but Erika didn't find the situation funny. What she wanted to do was to get hold of the camera Joseph was still clutching tightly, and return to the crime scene.

'A court will usually take into account the fact that being threatened in or at one's home is a frightening situation,' said David. 'The spirit of the law being that someone should have the right to defend themselves, their possessions, and those they are responsible for…'

'At no point was your son's or your wife's life in danger,' interrupted McGorry.

'Really? What's your name, young man?'

'John McGorry, Detective Constable.'

'Detective Constable John McGorry, why were you attempting an illegal chokehold on my son?'

'I wasn't…'

'Please don't lie. You were using Joseph's camera strap to restrain him about the neck. It's illegal to use chokeholds on suspects or members of the public. In years gone by, the police were trained in chokeholds, but I would think you're a little young and inexperienced…'

'I was merely…' started McGorry, his cheeks flushing with annoyance. Erika shot him a look to stay quiet.

'And your superior officer should know this too,' added David.

'I do know this,' said Erika. 'I can also tell you that if a police officer *does* use a chokehold, the officer may be able to present a justification for the use of force based on the circumstances. And based on the fact your son was attempting to suffocate my officer, by pushing his face into the snow, a chokehold in self-defence could be considered reasonable or necessary. Check online, this was detailed in a recent freedom of information act to West Mercia police.'

David tried, but failed to hide his annoyance.

'This still doesn't explain why you were pursuing my son?'

'Your son was trespassing at a crime scene.'

'Which isn't a criminal offence,' said David.

'He was taking photos of the crime scene…'

'Again, not a criminal offence.'

Erika paused and gave him a thin smile.

'He was evading a police officer.'

'Yes, and now we are all here and he will cooperate, within reason.'

'Your son may have information on his camera which could help our investigation,' said Erika. She felt foolish for giving chase, and now she was having to defend herself and McGorry to this retired barrister who was threatening to get the better of her.

'Where is the crime scene?' asked David.

'I can't comment on that.'

'They've found a body, up on Coniston Road,' said Joseph. He had a soft, cultured voice, almost speaking with received pronunciation.

'You found a body?' said Elspeth, who was still patting at his hair with the towel.

'No, mother,' he said, batting her away. 'The *police* found the body.'

'We're not at liberty to speak about an ongoing murder case,' said McGorry.

'You believe it's murder?' said David.

'Murder?' said Elspeth.

'It was Marissa Lewis; someone stabbed her to death on her doorstep,' said Joseph.

'That's speculating…' started Erika.

'No. I was there when her body was discovered.' Joseph pulled the camera into his lap protectively.

'Did you call the police?' asked Erika.

'I didn't have my phone.'

'But you took photos of the crime scene, before the police arrived?'

'You don't have to answer that, Joseph. We bought him a new lens for his camera, as a Christmas gift,' said David.

'If anyone round here was going to come a cropper, it would be Marissa Lewis,' said Elspeth, shaking her head.

'My wife is also speculating,' said David. 'Which is legal, is it not?' He was infuriatingly calm, and Erika took a deep breath.

'Of course it's legal, but could she – could you – explain?'

Elspeth draped the towel over the back of a free chair, crossed herself, and turned to Erika.

'Marissa Lewis has – *had* – a certain reputation, if you get my drift. A promiscuous reputation. She worked as a stripper.'

'You've seen her at work?' asked McGorry.

'Of course I haven't seen her at work! None of us have!' She glanced at David and Joseph, who shook their heads and looked at the floor. 'My hairdresser told me.'

Erika's eyes strayed to the loose, greasy grey hair hanging around Elspeth's shoulders, and wondered exactly what a hairdresser did for her.

'Who is your hairdresser?'

'Marissa Lewis's best friend, Sharon-Louise Braithwaite, is my hairdresser. At the Goldilocks Hair Studio by Crofton Park station. Marissa asked Sharon to put up a poster for one of her… *performances*, in the salon. It was a picture of her wearing nothing but stockings, suspenders and a bra!' Elspeth shook her head at the memory. 'I also heard from Sharon that Marissa had an affair with a married man who lived a few doors down, and she had several other blokes on the go.'

'Do you have the name of the married man?'

'Don Walpole. He has a wife, Jeanette. They're still together, despite it all.'

Erika turned her focus back to Joseph.

'So, you were in the tree opposite Marissa Lewis's house early this morning, and you took photos? What did you take photos of?'

'The sunrise,' he said, with a smarmy smile.

'You were up in the tree to capture the sunrise, but you remained in the tree after you saw there was a dead body in the garden opposite, and the road was closed off by police officers?'

'I only saw the body when I heard Marissa's mother scream.'

'What time was this?'

'I dunno.'

'We opened our Christmas presents at ten to seven,' said David. 'We had breakfast, and Joseph left around seven-twenty. Sunrise today was at 8.05 a.m.'

'It had just got light, so it was around that time when Marissa's mum came out of their house,' said Joseph. 'I don't wear a watch.'

'Do you know why Marissa's mother came to the front door?'

'No.'

'She probably had more bottles to put in the recycling bin; she's a drinker,' said Elspeth. 'It's not the nicest street.'

'There's been snow and thick cloud for the past few days. How would you expect to see the sun rise?' asked McGorry.

'If all photographers thought like that, they wouldn't take any photos,' said Joseph.

'You're a professional photographer?'

'The word *professional* is rather redundant. Would you say you are a professional police officer? Did you act professionally when you pinned me down in a chokehold?'

'Listen, you little sh…' started McGorry, taking a step towards him. Erika held up her hand.

'Joseph, stop wasting time, and answer our questions.'

'He doesn't have to answer any of your questions!' cried Elspeth.

'A young woman has been brutally attacked and murdered on her doorstep. She should be with her family this morning, but instead she's lying in the snow with her throat hacked open. The bones are broken in her face, and she may or may not have been sexually assaulted,' said Erika. 'Joseph doesn't have to answer any of my questions, but he could have information that helps our investigation.'

Joseph looked uncomfortable for the first time, and shifted in his seat.

'Okay, I did watch stuff for a bit, then the police arrived really fast. Then they closed off the road. I didn't know what to do. When I climbed up that tree, it wasn't a crime scene, but by the time I stepped back down, it was.'

'Did you photograph the body?'

'No.'

'Can I look through the photos on your camera?'

'No. It's a film camera,' he said, holding it up. Erika moved over to him and saw that it was a vintage model, and had no digital screen. She went to take it, but before she could, Joseph flipped it over, opened the back and whipped out the roll of film. He pulled out the negative, and dumped it on the table.

'There. No photos to process. All gone.'

Erika stared at him. He had an odd face, both vulnerable and hard. He stared at her, defiantly.

'I think we've been more than cooperative, officers,' said David. 'Now if that is all, we'd like to get on with celebrating Christmas.'

*

Erika and McGorry left through the front door. It had stopped snowing and the road was busy with cars. When they turned and looked back, the house looked oddly out of place: a crumbling,

sagging structure, sandwiched in a gap between the smart, upright row of terraces.

'It's like it's been dropped from above,' said McGorry.

Erika put her hands in her pockets and hunched down against the cold, as they started back down the alleyway towards Coniston Road.

'I'm going to have to write all this up,' she said.

'What about the chokehold?'

'They haven't said they're going to complain, but that doesn't mean they won't. You're a bloody idiot, John. Why the hell did you let it go that far?'

'He was lashing out, I was trying to… calm him down, stop being hit. It was instinctive. And you said all about that freedom of information request, that I can justify a chokehold.'

'He could still complain, and cause problems. You need to be on the ball. You have to always think about the consequences of your actions.'

'That's impossible.'

'Of course it's bloody impossible, but that's part of being a police officer. You can't let yourself get into a situation where you are using unnecessary force.'

'I'm sorry,' said McGorry, his face flushing.

'It's okay. We live in a shitty time, John. Everyone takes offence at everything, and you're presumed guilty, at all times. Be smart. Think. I'll do my best to steer my report away from it…'

They were now back in the alleyway and level with the high wall leading back over to the Pitkins's garden. Erika spied something behind the wheelie bin and stopped.

'What?' asked McGorry.

She crouched down, and using a small, clear plastic evidence bag from her pocket, she picked up a small, black plastic cylinder. She stood and held it to the light. She fiddled with the bag and

managed to get the small lid of the plastic tube to come off inside the bag.

'A camera film,' she said, smiling at him.

'Used?'

'I hope so. I saw his camera before he yanked out the film. He'd only taken one photo on it.'

'You think he used a whole film when he was up in the tree, then changed it?' said McGorry hopefully.

'We'll know for sure when we get it developed, and the tube tested for prints,' said Erika.

CHAPTER SIX

When Erika and McGorry arrived back at Coniston Road, the house-to-house was underway. Uniformed officers were moving up and down the street, knocking on doors, and several were talking to neighbours on their doorsteps. It had started to snow again, and despite the early hour, just before 3 p.m., the light was starting to fade. The police presence was at odds with the Christmas lights in the windows.

They stopped off at the support van, where Erika asked McGorry to get the roll of film fast-tracked through forensics and developed. She left him to work on it, and when she emerged from the van, a small black body bag was being wheeled through the narrow gate posts on the post-mortem trolley. There was a brief pause as everyone stopped and watched. Erika thought how small it looked. Isaac nodded to her as it was loaded into the van, and the doors closed. She felt a wave of exhaustion and depression approaching, but she forced herself to keep it at bay. She took a deep breath and welcomed the distraction of an officer with a short blonde bob of hair, wearing a long blue winter coat, who had just arrived on the scene.

'I'm Detective Constable Tania Hill, I'm the family liaison officer,' she said, offering her hand.

'What do you know about the case so far?' asked Erika.

'I just saw the body of the young girl. I've never seen so much frozen blood,' she said, pulling the lapels of her coat around her face. 'The mother is, apparently, very vulnerable. Low income, serious health issues with alcohol.'

'She's with the neighbour; I'm glad you're here. I'd like to talk to her,' said Erika.

They crossed the road to a smart house with brand new uPVC windows and a small square of concreted-over front garden. Erika rang the bell. The door was opened by a small, middle-aged lady wearing a red velvet tracksuit and gold slippers. Her snow-white hair was neatly clipped in a pixie cut, which looked at odds with her lined face. In her left hand, she held a cigarette.

Erika made the introductions and they held up their warrant cards. 'What's your name?'

'Who's asking?' said the woman, with almost comedic defensiveness. Her voice had a deep smoker's growl.

'I am,' said Erika.

'The name's Joan Field.'

'Can we please come in?'

Joan stood to one side. The dark blue carpet in the hallway was immaculate. 'Shoes off,' she added.

'Can I call you Joan?' asked Tania.

'No, I'd prefer Mrs Field.'

'I'm the family liaison officer,' said Tania, placing her shoes by the bannister. 'I'm here in a support capacity, to bridge the gap between Mandy and the police investigation.'

Joan looked her up and down. 'Bridge the gap? Isn't that fancy talk for answering the phone?'

Tania ignored the dig.

'Where is Mandy?'

'In the kitchen.'

They followed her, passing a living room which contained a heavy red velvet three-piece suite and a small silver Christmas tree, but which was otherwise devoid of any ornaments or photographs and didn't looked lived-in. At the back of the house was a small kitchen, looking out over the snowy garden. It was clean, but

cramped. The ceiling and the walls were yellow from nicotine. A frozen turkey, still wrapped in plastic, floated in the sink.

Marissa Lewis's mother, Mandy, was a huge woman, her vast frame swathed in a grubby pink tracksuit. She sat at the table, her enormous buttocks spilling over either side of a wooden chair. Erika's eyes strayed to the old trainers Mandy was wearing, which had been cut up the middle to accommodate her swollen feet. Her face was pale, and her eyes bloodshot and watery.

'Mandy Trent?' she asked.

'Marissa weren't adopted. We're blood,' said Mandy, seeing Erika's surprise at her appearance. 'She got her father's name, and I changed mine back when he fucked off… Marissa got the slim genes from him.' Her voice was loaded with bitterness.

'I take it you both want tea?' said Joan, moving to the kettle.

'Please,' said Erika. Tania nodded and they each pulled up a chair.

'Mandy, I'm here as your family liaison officer,' said Tania, placing a hand on her arm. 'This will be a very hard time for you, and I'm here to help, and to explain what happens next.'

Mandy lit up a cigarette and blew the smoke in Tania's face.

'What happens next? You want to take me to see her body? It was her.'

'Are you up to answering some questions?' asked Erika.

'I found her outside the front door, this morning, when I took out the rubbish. Just lying there, quiet and still, but the blood. There was so much of it.'

'Can you remember what time?'

'Eight-ish.'

'Marissa lived with you?' asked Erika.

'Yeah. She's paid me housekeeping since she was sixteen.'

'Do you know where Marissa had been last night?'

'She had a dancing gig, don't ask me where. She has – had – a lot of them. She was a burlesque dancer, worked in clubs all around the West End. A few nights a week.'

'And you heard nothing last night; you didn't hear her return home?'

'No.'

'Did you expect her home at a certain time?'

Mandy shook her head. 'I've done my job rearing her, she's an adult…'

'What time did you go to bed?'

'I nodded off about ten-ish, I think.'

'You didn't hear anything?'

'Like what?'

'Screaming, sounds from the front garden. A vehicle?'

'No.'

'Marissa's front door key was still in the lock outside when you found her?'

'Yeah. I told the police that.'

'Were you in the living room until 10 p.m.?'

'Yeah, I was watching telly. It was shit. They used to show decent stuff on Christmas Eve.'

'How long had Marissa been working as a burlesque dancer?' asked Tania.

'Three or four years. She's been doing well for herself, always had bookings. Though she don't make much money from it – didn't. She'd pay me housekeeping and then borrow it back three days later.'

'The gear costs a packet,' said Joan, as she took cups from the cupboard. 'Props, costumes she used for dancing. Big feather fans, head dresses. Mandy even moved to the back bedroom, so she'd have more room to store it all, didn't you?'

'The back bedroom's nearer the loo, and I put her housekeeping up,' clarified Mandy, as if she didn't want it on record that it was a nice gesture. Erika couldn't work out what was going on. Mandy seemed so matter-of-fact about Marissa's death. Joan came over with mugs of tea.

'Did Marissa have a serious boyfriend?' Erika asked.

Mandy exhaled cigarette smoke with a long, silent chuckle.

'They never seemed to hang around long enough to get serious. A lot of the local lads used to sniff around, and she had a few admirers who'd watch her dance, buy her presents...' Erika and Tania exchanged a look. 'I don't want to speak ill of the dead, but my daughter was a right slag. She slept with two blokes on this road, both married. And there were all sorts of lads coming and going, and those were the ones I knew of.'

'Who were the married men?' asked Erika.

'Don Walpole, lives at number 46 with his wife. Marissa was shagging him a few years back, when she was sixteen...'

'The rumour is, he was sleeping with her before her sixteenth birthday,' interjected Joan, with a knowing nod.

'Don Walpole ain't no kiddy fiddler, Joan. He just did what any bloke would do when it's offered up on a plate. Marissa was an early developer, by the time she was fourteen she looked twenty,' said Mandy, lighting another cigarette with the stub of the old one.

'And the other married man?'

'Ivan... Whatsisface...'

'Stowalski,' said Joan.

'Yeah. He's Polish. Got a few quid in the bank, so I think that's why she liked him. He's certainly not good-looking. Pale and washed-out as anything, he is. He's been around for a few months.'

'Do you know when she last saw him?'

'No. He rang the bell a few weeks ago, but he didn't come in.'

'Marissa worked full-time as a burlesque dancer?'

Mandy shook her head. 'No. She also did a few hours a week as a carer for an old lady, in Hilly Fields over the way.'

'What's her name?'

'Elsa Fryatt,' said Joan. 'She's ninety-seven. Very posh, despite the name Elsa. Lives in one of the big houses overlooking the fields.'

'Marissa was onto a nice number there,' said Mandy. 'All she did was took her shopping; she got herself insured on the old girl's car. It wasn't proper caring work. I think she liked having Marissa around, much like a woman likes a bit of rough in a bloke. I think she finds common people quite entertaining.'

'What about her friends?' asked Erika.

'I would think most of her friends are dead, didn't you hear? She's ninety-seven.'

'No, I meant Marissa,' said Erika.

Mandy exhaled smoke and took a big gulp of tea. 'The girls she works with on the burlesque circuit are a bunch of bitches, that's what Marissa used to say, but she's got a friend she's had since school. Works up the hairdresser, Sharon-Louise Braithwaite.'

'The Goldilocks Hair Studio?'

'Yes, that's it.'

'Could I ask you to make a list of the clubs where Marissa worked?'

Mandy's bottom lip trembled and she wiped at her eyes.

'Bloody hell, I can't think straight to make lists, and all this talking in the past tense: worked, lived…'

'We can get to that later,' said Tania, touching Mandy's arm.

'When can I go back to my house?' she said, pulling it away.

'The forensics officers are inside to make sure there isn't any other evidence that can help. We will let you know as soon as we've completed our investigation,' said Erika. 'Would you like Tania to find you somewhere to stay?'

'No, I'll stay here, with Joan,' said Mandy. Joan nodded, but she didn't look too thrilled.

CHAPTER SEVEN

'What did you make of that?' asked Erika, pulling up the collar of her coat, as she and Tania left Joan's house.

'Grief displays itself in different ways,' said Tania.

Erika frowned.

'Leave it out, don't give me hot air. You see a lot of grieving relatives. There was real hostility there.'

'From both of them, although I think Joan was being led by Mandy. Mandy wears the trousers, and had the most dislike for her daughter.'

'Not everyone that gets murdered is loved by their relatives.'

'You think the mother is a suspect?'

'Everyone is a suspect. I want forensics to take a look at her clothes, and I'd like swabs taken from under her fingernails…' Erika beckoned to a young uniformed officer, who looked worried as she crossed the street to the front gate. 'What's your name?'

'Kay Hornby, PC Kay Hornby, ma'am,' she said.

'I need you to grab one of the CSIs and bag up the clothes and get fingernail swabs from the victim's mother, Mandy Trent.'

'Yes, ma'am… Erm, I have a spare pair of trainers in my car,' she said, noticing Erika's heels, which were soaked and on the verge of disintegrating. Erika looked down at the young woman's feet, clad in black shoes.

'What size shoe are you?'

'A six. They're not stinking gym shoes. I use them for driving. It was just a thought, ma'am.' She looked worried, as if she'd overstepped the mark.

'Thank you. I'd appreciate that,' said Erika.

'Absolutely, ma'am. I'll just run and get them.'

Erika's phone buzzed in her pocket. She pulled it out and moved off along the street.

'Where the hell are you?' said Marsh. 'It's almost four o'clock!'

'Sorry. I was called to a crime scene. A young woman killed on her doorstep on Coniston Road, near Crofton Park.'

'You weren't on call today.'

'I'm helping out, loads of officers have taken leave over Christmas…'

'I know that!'

'I'm just explaining to you why I'm here.'

'I was expecting you for lunch.'

'I know, I'm sorry. I won't be coming. I've got presents for the girls, so I'll arrange to drop them round later…'

'I said: I was expecting you for lunch.'

'That's an order, is it?'

'No. I just wanted to see you; Marcie and the girls wanted to see you…'

Marsh paused. The silence went on, and then Erika realised he had hung up on her. She put the phone back in her pocket, feeling guilty. She crossed the road to the support van, where Kay was waiting with a pair of pink and white running shoes.

'Thank you,' said Erika.

'There's socks too, in the shoes.'

Erika took off her ruined high heels and Kay held onto her arm as she pulled on the socks and trainers. 'Ahh, that's so much better. Thank you.'

McGorry came out of the van. He noticed Kay and smiled and raised an eyebrow.

'I'll get the shoes back to you later today,' said Erika.

'That's okay, take as long as you need with them,' said Kay, and she went off to the forensics van, giving McGorry a curt nod.

'Haven't you got a girlfriend?' asked Erika, seeing McGorry glance after her.

'Yeah,' he said, seeming a little annoyed.

'You know, not every young female officer has to fall for your charms.'

'I dunno what you're talking about.'

Erika rolled her eyes. 'Come on, let's get to it.'

A police officer was stationed at the front door. The body of Marissa Lewis had now been removed from the front garden, leaving a vast pool of frozen blood. Snow had been cleared from the path, and the course of the blood spatter was marked with small yellow numbers.

The house was messy inside, with dated furniture and overpowering smells of damp and fried food. There was a tiny Christmas tree in the living room, and the kitchen was overflowing with dishes and grime. Stairs led up to a dingy landing, where the ceiling sagged. Doors led off to a bathroom and two bedrooms. Erika and John pulled on latex gloves. The bedroom at the front had a bay window looking out over the road, busy with police activity. The room looked freshly painted, and was neat and tidy with new furniture and a beautiful flowered bedspread. Three tailor's mannequins lined one of the walls, and they were dressed in feathered costumes, one with a black corset. A set of shelves on the opposite wall contained seven wigs on polystyrene heads, and a dressing table under the window was covered in make-up. A row of high-heeled shoes in different colours were neatly lined up in front of a fitted wardrobe.

'Does she toast marshmallows on the gas fire?' asked McGorry, moving to a small fireplace and picking up one of several thin metal rods with blackened marshmallow shapes on the end, which were leaning up against the grate.

'I think they are used for fire eating,' said Erika, peering at them. There were a couple of framed photos on the wall. In the first, Marissa lay in a huge champagne glass, wearing see-through pink lingerie. In another she wore black stockings, suspenders and nipple tassels, and held one of the flaming rods close to her mouth. The final framed photo was a publicity poster, where Marissa lay on a chaise in a silver bodice, surrounded by muscled young men in underwear. A huge header read:

A NIGHT WITH MISS HONEY DIAMOND
JULY 4TH 2017
BETHNAL GREEN WORKING MEN'S CLUB

'That must be the name she performs under, Miss Honey Diamond,' said McGorry.

Erika noticed a diamond shape embroidered in gold on the bodice of the black corset on the second tailor's mannequin. 'This diamond logo is the same as it is on the poster. It's also embroidered on the other two costumes,' she said, looking at the other two mannequins.

'A diamond for Miss Honey Diamond,' said McGorry, coming over to run his finger over the stitching.

'We need to check if this is a brand of clothing, or if it's been stitched on afterwards. And our first port of call – along with phone records – should be her social media.'

'Forensics said there wasn't a laptop or a PC in the house,' said McGorry. 'There wasn't a mobile phone, and they didn't find one on her body.'

'So her phone is missing.'

Erika went to the wardrobe and opened it, seeing more of Marissa's burlesque clothes. Two additional bras were embroidered with the diamond logo. There was also some civilian gear: jeans, jumpers, a few 'conventional' dresses and shoes. Tacked to one of the wardrobe doors were several pictures of Dita Von Teese performing burlesque, and one of her lying in a giant martini glass.

They moved back out along the landing, past a grotty little bathroom, to a small bedroom at the back of the house. It was nothing more than a box room, sparsely furnished with a single bed and a wardrobe. The bed was covered in bin bags full of clothes and towels. Perched on the windowsill was a hairbrush and some face cream. On the radiator was an enormous pair of greying knickers.

'Jeez,' said McGorry, holding them up. Erika gave him a look, but didn't say anything. 'She gave up the best bedroom for Marissa and her stuff?'

'She said she charged her extra housekeeping.'

'Doesn't look like she sleeps in here.'

Erika saw that the plastic bags had a layer of dust.

'She said she was in bed around 10 p.m.'

'Did she mean she slept on the sofa?' asked McGorry. They came back downstairs and went into the living room. The sofa under the bay window was covered in a creased duvet and a pillow. On the floor was an empty litre bottle of cheap own-brand vodka and two empty tubes of Pringles.

'She didn't say that she sleeps on the sofa,' said Erika. She went to the window. It was grimy with dirt and condensation, and the spray of Marissa's blood. There was a single pane of glass, and a freezing draught was blowing through the rotten window frame, and they could hear very clearly the noise from the road outside.

'Maybe she was too pissed to remember,' said McGorry, indicating the empty bottle of vodka.

Erika heard the door of the support van slam, and the crunch of snow as someone walked past on the road behind the hedge. She wondered if the killer had been lying in wait.

'I wonder if Marissa had the chance to scream,' said Erika, more to herself than to McGorry.

CHAPTER EIGHT

Erika and McGorry came back to the police support van, where a group of six officers were taking a quick break. They had been chatting away, but fell silent when they saw Erika.

'Don't mind me,' she said.

'Refreshments have arrived, ma'am,' said one of the officers, indicating the table in the corner with an urn and a cluster of pre-packaged sandwiches.

'Thanks. What's your name?' she asked.

'PC Rich Skevington, ma'am.'

Erika and McGorry grabbed a sandwich each and filled paper cups with steaming coffee. The sound of the coffee hitting the paper cup was loud in the silence. Erika looked around. She didn't recognise most of them; they all seemed so young.

'Who can give me an update on the house-to-house?' she asked, ripping the plastic off her sandwich and taking a bite.

'We haven't been able to get an answer from Don Walpole and Ivan Stowalski. We're waiting on their mobile phone numbers,' said Kay, the young officer who'd lent Erika her shoes.

'What about the rest of the street? Are people being helpful?' asked Erika, washing down a mouthful of the dry sandwich with a gulp of coffee.

'Half the houses are empty, but the locals who knew Marissa Lewis also knew about the affair she had with Don Walpole and that she was sleeping with Ivan Stowalski behind his wife's back.'

'The jury's out as to whether or not Ivan Stowalski's wife has left him,' said Rich. 'Their next-door neighbour, a beady-eyed old girl, says they're both up north for Christmas visiting his family. We've also been on the lookout in gardens and dustbins for the victim's mobile phone, in case it's been dumped, but nothing so far.'

'How are the team getting on over at the Estate?'

'I've just come back,' said another young male officer. 'We spoke to the usual suspects. A couple of lads said they'd heard of Marissa Lewis.'

'How do you mean, "heard of"?' asked Erika.

'They said she's had a reputation in the past for being the local bike – their words, not mine. One of them has a record, did three years for rape. The other has a record for assault, GBH. Both of them say they have an alibi, they were out until 6 a.m. this morning at a club in New Cross Gate, H20. They told us to check the club's CCTV.'

Erika rolled her eyes.

'*Haitch 20*. I know it. I've lost count of the times we've requested CCTV from them. Okay, get someone on it…' She took another bite of the sandwich. 'What the hell is in these sandwiches?' she said, through a mouthful.

'"Festive Christmas dinner sandwiches", that's all they had at the petrol station,' said Rich.

Erika spat a mouthful out into the packet. 'I can see the appeal in turkey and cranberry, even some stuffing, but who puts roast potato in a bloody sandwich?'

Erika dumped the rest of the packet in the bin. She looked around at the team, who had averted their eyes, not wanting to risk her wrath. Every other officer her age had taken leave to be with their family or other halves. She missed the continuity of the officers she regularly worked with. Detective Inspectors Moss and Peterson, and Sergeant Crane. She wondered fleetingly if they were

having a good Christmas. She was pleased that McGorry was with her, but he was still a relative newbie – and even he had volunteered to stay, risking the wrath of his girlfriend waiting at home.

Her phone rang. It was a number she didn't recognise, so she came out of the van. It was now dark, and the cold air caught at the back of her throat.

'Hey Erika, this is Lee Graham.'

'Hi, Merry Christmas,' she said.

'Merry Christmas to you too. I've drawn the short straw today, and I'm in the lab.'

Erika liked Lee. He was a forensics and computer expert in the Met police, and they had worked together on a few cases. There had been a frisson of flirtation between them, but nothing more. She wondered now if he was single, and if that was the reason he had decided to work on Christmas Day.

'To what do I owe the pleasure?' she asked.

'Unfortunately, this isn't a personal call. I saw your name on an urgent request for developing a camera film.'

'Yes. How soon can you get it done?'

'It's already done. I've scanned them in, and I'm just emailing the photos over to your work email. I'll get the hard copies over by snail mail.'

'Thank you. I should buy you a drink sometime.'

'Here's hoping,' he said.

Erika heard her phone beep. 'I think I just got your email.'

'Okay, I'll let you go. Merry Christmas,' he said and rang off.

She opened his email and scrolled through the attached photos. They were mostly taken from the tree opposite Marissa's bedroom. There was a series of photos taken at night through Marissa's bedroom window, where she was fresh out of the shower and wearing a towel, then naked and pulling on her underwear. There were also three photos, taken from above, of Marissa's body lying in

the snow. And three more at a lower angle, which looked like they were taken at ground level, close to, or inside, the front garden.

'Joseph Pitkin, you lying little shit,' said Erika. She walked over to the front gate of Marissa's house, where the frozen blood in the front garden was rapidly being covered by fresh snow. She could see up into the tree, with its thick bare branches. 'Was that your regular spot, to spy on her, Joseph?' Erika looked at the photos again, and saw that Lee had included a message at the bottom of the email:

The owner of this camera uses ILFORD DELTA 100 Professional 35mm film. They could be using a darkroom to process photos. Lee.

She was about to return to the van, when she caught an acrid smell of burning plastic. She looked around, and saw that at the end of the alleyway leading down to Joseph Pitkin's house, smoke was rising into the sky.

Erika hurried down the alley towards it, the smell growing stronger. By the time she reached the back wall of the Pitkins's house, thick black smoke was billowing into the air from behind the line of evergreens. She climbed up onto the wheelie bin, finding it much easier in the borrowed trainers, and pulled herself up onto the wall. Through the trees, she could see Joseph in his long coat, huddled over a burning oil drum. On the snowy ground beside him was a box of papers. He picked up a handful and dumped them into the drum, a shower of sparks and flames floating up into the dark sky. The windows in the house behind him were dark, and he was only lit by the glow of the flames.

Erika dropped down softly onto the strip of earth between the wall and the line of trees and stepped through. Joseph heard her feet crunch on the snow as she came towards him.

'Stop what you're doing. Right now,' she said. He grabbed at a spade propped up against the oil drum, but she moved faster and grabbed it from him. She thought he would attempt to run, but he sank back onto the snow with his head between his hands as she put in a call to McGorry.

CHAPTER NINE

'Loads of these photos are of Marissa,' said Erika, sifting through the box of photos on the snow beside the oil drum. She held up a black-and-white shot of Marissa performing in a burlesque gig. McGorry was picking up several which had dropped onto the snow. The fire inside the drum had died down, but it still beat out warmth into the cold evening.

'Talk about a Kodak moment!' said McGorry, holding up a photo of Marissa striking a pose on a stage wearing knickers and nipple tassels, and removing a long black glove with her teeth.

'I don't need silly comments. Just bag them up,' said Erika. She looked back at the house. The lights were now on in the kitchen, and two uniformed officers were standing over Joseph, who was sitting in a chair. One was talking to him, the other was taking notes, and Joseph was crying. 'Do you think those tears are real?'

'He is a mummy's boy,' said McGorry.

Joseph had now lost his cool, and was pulling at his hair. He stood up, shouting at the officers. One of them pushed him roughly down into the chair, which almost toppled over, and started shouting back. Erika pulled off her latex gloves and lit up a cigarette. They weren't able to salvage anything from the fire, and inside the drum was a blackened lump. She needed to move fast, and make up her mind whether or not she wanted to bring Joseph in for questioning. He had told them his parents had gone round the corner to visit their friends for a quick Christmas drink. She checked the time. It was coming up to 8 p.m. She took a deep drag

on her cigarette, and her phone rang. She moved down to the end of the garden, and saw it was Marsh. As she silenced the ringing phone and put it back in her pocket, she accidentally dropped the lit cigarette. It rolled across the snow and under the line of trees. She pulled her phone back out and activated the torch, training it under the trees. She found the cigarette, tucked under one of the evergreens, still lit. She also saw that a small square of soil had been disturbed towards the end of the row of evergreens. It hadn't been like that earlier in the day. She called back to McGorry to bring the spade propped up against the oil drum.

'Look,' she said, when he joined her. 'The ground wasn't disturbed when we came over the wall this morning. Get digging.'

She trained the light on the ground as McGorry began scraping at the soil. He only had to dig down a few feet before he uncovered something small and grubby, wrapped in plastic. Erika pulled on a fresh pair of latex gloves and squatted down beside the hole. She shook off the soil, and gently started to unwrap several layers of plastic bags, thinking she was going to find a block of cannabis resin. The final layer of plastic uncovered an iPhone with a pink bejewelled case. Written across the back in clear Swarovski crystals was the name, '*Marissa*'.

'Bloody hell,' said McGorry.

'Indeed. Let's bring him in for questioning,' said Erika. She checked the iPhone was switched off, and slipped it into a clear evidence bag.

They went back to the house and into the kitchen. David and Elspeth Pitkin had just arrived home.

'What is the meaning of this intrusion?' said David, still wearing his thick winter coat and grey bobble hat. Elspeth went to Joseph and started to examine his tear-streaked face.

'What did they do to you?' she said. He stared blankly at her.

'Mr and Mrs Pitkin. Did you have a nice evening?' asked Erika, smiling sweetly.

David turned to her. 'What is this?'

'Your son was burning photos of the murder victim in your garden.'

Elspeth shot a look at her husband, but he ignored her.

'It is not illegal to take photographs; we've already been over this, DCI Foster.'

'It is illegal to steal a mobile phone from a dead body and then bury it in the garden.' Erika held up the mobile phone in the evidence bag. 'It's called withholding evidence.'

'How do we know you didn't plant it there!' cried Elspeth, her voice cracking with emotion.

Erika nodded at the two uniformed officers. 'Joseph Pitkin, I am arresting you on suspicion of withholding evidence…'

'NO, NO, NOT MY BOY!' cried Elspeth, moving to block the two officers.

'…Withholding evidence pertaining to a murder enquiry. You do not have to say anything; but it may harm your defence if you do not mention when questioned something which you later rely on in court. Anything you do say may be given in evidence.'

'He was with us all last night! He didn't go out!' insisted Elspeth, reaching to grab at Joseph. One of the uniformed officers moved her to one side and handcuffed Joseph with his hands behind his back. 'Don't you touch me! Don't you assault me!' she screamed. David looked on, his face ashen.

'Please, officers, my son is very vulnerable,' he said.

'Get his phone,' said Erika. One of the officers reached into Joseph's coat and pulled out a smartphone. She handed it to Erika, who switched it off and put it in a clear evidence bag. 'I want this house searched, top to bottom. And as you are aware of the law,

Mr Pitkin, you'll agree that your son has given me enough cause to search without a warrant.'

'Please! Don't lock him away. Please!' cried Elspeth. David had to hold her back, as Joseph was led away.

CHAPTER TEN

The custody suite at Lewisham Row police station was down in the basement, and separated from the rest of the offices in the station by a thick steel door. Erika had been a police officer long enough to remember that it used to be called 'the cells'. However, the fancy term didn't hide the fact that this was a dank and depressing part of the station: a thin corridor lined with big steel doors with hatches, painted a deep pea-green colour.

Ray Newton was the custody sergeant who was on duty. He was a small, rotund, balding officer with a thick moustache, and he was waiting for them when Joseph was led up to the desk by two uniformed officers.

'He's had a full body search,' said Erika. 'And we're waiting on word about a solicitor.'

'Right, young man,' said Ray, pulling out a clipboard and handing him a pen attached to the desk with a thick piece of string. 'We have to fill out some paperwork, so the officers are going to remove your handcuffs. I don't want any funny business. You treat me well, and I reciprocate.'

Joseph's mood flipped, and he started thrashing about with his arms still cuffed behind him.

'You! You're fucking cunts!' he screamed, trying to turn around and see Erika and McGorry.

'That's enough!' said Ray.

'They stitched me up! I've done nothing! NOTHING!'

'We'll leave him with you,' said Erika, indicating to McGorry that they should go.

They came up the stairs, through the thick doors, and into the main part of the station. They stopped at the vending machines by the stairs.

'That's a first, being called the C-word on Christmas Day,' said McGorry.

'Makes you feel all cosy and festive, doesn't it? Like you're beside the fire with a glass of something warm.'

'You want to let him sweat in the cells overnight?' said McGorry.

'I want to wait till morning to question him,' corrected Erika. 'Kay is working on unlocking the phones upstairs.'

Her phone rang and she had a brief conversation with one of the officers at the Pitkin house.

'They found an improvised darkroom upstairs, in a small cupboard in Joseph's bedroom, but there were no photos,' she said when she came off the phone.

'Burned them before we got to him,' said McGorry.

'Kay is trained to forensically examine electronic devices. I want to know what's on his phone and Marissa's, before we question him. Let's hope there's something.'

'They're a bit of a weird family, aren't they? The posh ones always are a bit odd. Is he really stupid enough to have buried that phone, with Marissa's personalised case still on it?'

'Don't underestimate how stupid people can be. I also want to run his prints against the ones we found on the plastic film holder in the alleyway.'

'What about all those photos of Marissa? Do you think she knew he took them?' asked McGorry.

'He probably bought a ticket to her show.'

'Then why burn them?'

Erika shook her head, feeling exhausted.

'We need to confirm the phone was registered to Marissa, and see if we can get any more information about Joseph. Has he got a record? Etc.' She selected her coffee, and they were silent as the cup dropped out and it began to fill and steam. 'Mandy Trent was pretty open about who Marissa associated with. She didn't mention Joseph. I'll get Tania, the FLO, to ask her again.' She took her cup from the dispenser.

'We don't have enough to charge him with her murder. And he has an alibi,' said McGorry.

'From his mother.'

'We've got nothing that places him at the scene last night.'

'Yet. Nothing *yet*. Post-mortem, forensics, everything is still left to play.'

McGorry yawned as he put money in the machine and selected coffee. Erika studied his tired face as the machine filled his cup. 'You should go home and get some rest. I want you here when I question him tomorrow morning.'

They both sipped their drinks, then spat them back in the cup.

'What the bloody hell is that?'

'Oxtail soup,' he grimaced.

'Did you press the coffee button?'

'Yeah.'

They dropped their cups into the small bin by the machine. Erika pushed more change in, and selected a white coffee. When it was done she put the cup to her nose.

'That's bloody oxtail soup as well. They close down the canteen, and leave us with nothing but oxtail soup!'

'They must have filled the machine up wrong,' said McGorry.

Erika rolled her eyes and dropped the second cup in the bin. 'What is it with this country? Potato sandwiches, and oxtail bloody soup! I've never met anyone who actually eats oxtail soup,

yet in the world of second-rate vending machines that's the third option after tea and coffee!'

'You can buy it in tins…'

'What?'

'Oxtail soup. My Nan has a cupboard full of tins of oxtail soup. She loves it.'

Erika looked at him and grinned.

'Go on, bugger off home, have your Christmas dinner. I'll see you tomorrow,' she said.

Erika went up to her office on the fourth floor. It was tiny, with barely enough room for a small desk, a chair, and a bookshelf. Kay was working at a laptop with Joseph's smartphone plugged into it.

'Sorry, the coffee machine is buggered, and there's nothing in the staff kitchen,' said Erika. 'How are you getting on?'

'The iPhone is password protected. You'll have to get it sent to the Cyber Crime Unit, and even then, they probably won't have any luck. It's virtually impossible to hack into an iPhone. I can also see from the IMEI number that this was a pay as you go phone.'

'Which will make the phone records harder to track down. Shit.'

'The good news is that Joseph Pitkin's smartphone isn't password protected.' Kay indicated a window on the screen with all the downloaded files. 'I've just pulled off a load of video files.'

Erika's mood brightened and she pulled up a chair. Kay started to click down the list of image and video files; some were very short, of a tabby cat on a summer's day stretching on the windowsill outside Joseph's bedroom, another of Elspeth, red-faced and taking a huge plaited loaf of bread on a tray out of the Aga, another of the tabby cat in the garden, amongst the flower pots,

chasing after a red admiral butterfly in that playful-yet-lethal way cats enjoy.

'All very charming,' said Erika. When Kay clicked on the next video, the sound blared out from the computer, making them jump. Distorted music played, and the video was a blur of colour until it came into focus. Marissa Lewis was on a small stage in a crowded club. Behind her was a red velvet curtain. The video was taken a little further back in the audience, and some people's heads were visible. Marissa's dark hair was set in pin curls, and she wore bright red lipstick and huge lashes. She was slowly unbuttoning a long black coat, and then she let it drop to the floor. Underneath she wore a 1950s-style pink silk satin corset, stockings, suspenders and towering heels. The video seemed to tremble as she went through her act, stripping down to underwear and nipple tassels. Marissa took a bow to applause and sashayed off the stage.

'Blimey, she was good,' said Kay.

'I thought her act would be sleazy, but this is – well, professional burlesque,' said Erika. They clicked through photos of the same evening, of Joseph standing with Marissa among the tables in the club. They were posing for the camera; someone else must have taken the pictures.

'Do you think it looks like Marissa knows him?' asked Erika, as Kay clicked through six almost identical shots: Joseph with his arm slung around Marissa's waist.

'He looks like the creepy fan you want rid of. Why did he need six photos? By the sixth she looks like she wants to get away,' said Kay.

'When are these dated?'

'Almost a year ago. Last January.'

Kay clicked through more photos of the same evening, of Marissa talking to other guests and posing for photos, then a couple of blurred ones as she went to the bar. Then the background

changed. The next few photos were dark, and illuminated with a flash.

'When is this?' asked Erika.

'The time stamp shows the same day, same time.'

'Looks like backstage.' There were photos of what looked like a dressing room. It was empty, with a large mirror surrounded by lights. There were close-ups of a rack of burlesque clothes; a pair of lacy black knickers discarded on the floor. A hand holding them up to the camera. There was a diamond symbol sewn into the fabric.

'Honey Diamond,' said Erika. 'That diamond symbol was embroidered on Marissa's burlesque costumes.'

Abruptly, the photos then changed to a video of Marissa Lewis's house. It was taken high up, at night, looking down into the window of Marissa's bedroom. It started off shakily, and they could hear wind distorting the phone's microphone. Marissa came into focus, walking around the bedroom in a towel. She went to the dressing table and picked up a brush, dragging it through her wet hair. Then Marissa dropped her towel, and was naked. The video zoomed in closer and lost focus. When it came back into focus, Marissa was staring out of the window, directly at the camera.

'Shit,' came Joseph's voice, above the wind distorting the microphone. He kept the camera trained on her. She stood, very still, watching. Then she cupped her breasts, and ran her hands down the front of her body. She stopped above her pubic hair, and waggled a finger and pulled the curtains together. The camera stayed on the glowing curtains for a moment, then the video ended.

'She knew Joseph was watching her?' said Kay.

'She knew someone was watching her,' said Erika. Kay clicked on another video, which showed the same view, at night. This time, Marissa's bedroom was brightly lit, and she entered the room with a tall, older man. Marissa made sure they both came close to the window, and the camera caught his face. Kay ran the video

forward, as they moved to the bed, starting to kiss and undress each other. The video was the longest on the phone, ten minutes in total, and it zoomed in as the couple had sex on Marissa's bed. 'We need to get a clear image of that man's face, and find out who he is. When was this taken?'

'December 14th, this year. Do you think she knew they were being filmed?'

'Or she asked Joseph to film,' said Erika. She rubbed her tired eyes and sat back in her chair. 'What did you make of him?'

'In the short space of time I was there? He seemed scared, but clingy with his mother.'

'He's ticking all the boxes so far. He was obsessed with Marissa. He stalked her, and spied on her. He stole Marissa's mobile phone, and photographed her dead body. But I need forensics. I need DNA if I want to really nail him and make an arrest.'

*

In the basement of Lewisham Row, all was quiet in the custody suite. The long line of cell doors was propped open, ready and waiting for any offenders Christmas night had yet to offer. Only the cell door at the far end was closed. Ray, the custody sergeant, got up from his desk, and went to do his fifteen-minute check, his polished shoes squeaking on the floor. He opened the metal hatch on the closed door, and shone his torch inside. Joseph Pitkin lay on a bed in the corner.

'You alright, lad?' he said.

Joseph shrank away, and turned to the wall.

'Yeah, great,' he murmured. He flinched as the metal hatch slammed shut. He shifted on the bare bed in the darkness, trying to get comfortable, silent tears rolling down his cheeks.

CHAPTER ELEVEN

Four miles away in Sydenham, a cold wind screamed down Walpole Road, pushing the snow in drifts up against the walls of the terraced houses. Diana Crow left her friend Fiona's house just after 11 p.m., wincing at the cold. She'd stayed longer than she'd intended, but Fiona had insisted that she saw the end of the Christmas film.

Diana put her head down, and hurried along the dark snowy street to the main road. Despite the cold, her face felt hot after four glasses of sweet sherry. She waited for a small Fiat to drive past before she crossed. Snow had been falling heavily all day, and the pavement and road had merged into one. She carefully picked her way across, and slowed, feeling around in the snow for where the kerb began on the other side. She stepped up onto the pavement and shivered. It was so quiet. Every window was lit, but the curtains were clamped shut. It was only a few minutes' walk home. Fiona had told her to call a taxi, but Diana thought it a ridiculous extravagance to pay good money for a thirty-second taxi ride, three streets away.

As she passed by the train station, the streetlight was out, and the short station approach was shrouded in darkness. There were no cars on the road now, and she picked up the pace as she approached the railway underpass. The air was damp, with a nasty smell of urine. She pulled the lapels of her coat up over her mouth. The pavement was dry in the underpass, and her footsteps echoed, breaking the silence. The pavement on the other side, lit up by the

orange streetlight, seemed far away. She hurried on, and had almost reached the light, when one of the dark walls seemed to bulge out. A tall figure moved out from the shadows and blocked her path.

She stopped, and couldn't move. Afterwards, she would ask herself why she hadn't turned and run – she had been less than sixty seconds away from her front door – and why she hadn't fought back, or shouted out for help? Instead, she stood there, paralysed with fear as the tall figure came closer. Loomed over her. He moved with a soft creaking sound, and as her eyes adjusted a little to the dark, she saw he wore a gas mask. The two large eyeholes were blank, and rubber material stretched up and over his head like a hood. Vapour streamed out from the large breathing drum hanging down. White squares were painted on the drum, and it looked like a grotesque smiling mouth. There was a faint chemical smell about him as his breathing quickened, and she saw that his coat was open and he was exposing himself, masturbating with a gloved hand.

Diana opened her mouth to scream, but it was cut short when he grabbed her by the throat and pinned her to the cold bricks, his powerful leather-gloved hand tightening around her neck. It was all so quiet, and she gagged and choked, wishing she would pass out. Just as the edges of her vision started to go black, he loosened his grip enough for her to take a breath, then his hand tightened again.

Outside the underpass, the road remained empty. The snow fell. Everything was quiet and still.

CHAPTER TWELVE

Erika arrived home late to a cold flat. In the two years she'd lived there, she hadn't got around to figuring out how the timer on the boiler worked. The first thing she did when she got in was flick on the heating, and she kept her coat on until it started to warm up.

She then ran a bath, with the water boiling hot, almost too hot to bear. The scalding water helped her to block things out, and made her forget about work, but despite the hot water, she couldn't shake off the image of Marissa Lewis's body lying in the snow. A crime scene always tells a story, and the small front garden in Coniston Road told of a violent struggle. The sheer volume of blood, caking Marissa's body and the surrounding snow. Her shoe, left lying close by; her vanity case, broken on its side, the contents spilling out into the snow. Her keys still dangling in the lock of the front door. If Marissa had reached her door a few seconds earlier, would she have been able to turn the key and get safely inside?

Erika found it a struggle, the balance between feeling sorrow for a murder victim, and shutting it out. To stay sane, it was easier to dehumanise a dead body, and think of the person as an object: a thing, or a piece of evidence. Erika could never do that, though, any more than she could come home from work and live a normal life. She didn't have anyone to come home to. Since Mark's death, she had been involved in a relationship with her colleague, Detective Inspector James Peterson, and for a time he had been someone she could come home to – or more precisely, she would

go to his place and they would watch television and eat takeaway and laugh. Then Peterson had been badly injured in the line of duty: shot in the stomach, on Erika's watch, at the climax of an abduction and murder case. His subsequent battle to recover and return to work had driven a wedge between them. It had been a messy end to a promising relationship. And she was left alone again, for endless evenings with her thoughts.

The image of Marissa Lewis's tooth embedded in the brickwork of the gate post swam into her head. She closed her eyes, but it was still there: broken off, close to the gum, and daubed with a smudge of red lipstick. Erika opened her eyes and added fresh hot water to the bath. Her usually pale legs were an angry red from the heat. In her mind's eye, she saw Marissa's blood-spattered legs in the picture taken from high in the tree. The folds of her long winter coat, open in the snow. Then she saw the crime scene, and Isaac crouching down beside the body. The thin material of the dress hitched up to expose Marissa's underwear. The underwear had been spotless. There had been no blood, and a neat strip of pubic hair had shown through the sheer material.

Erika yanked out the plug, and stepped out, wrapping herself in a towel. She hurried through to the living room, where she had her laptop and the case file laid out on the coffee table. The lights were off, and the curtains were still open. Snow was falling again. It made a dry rustling sound as it hit the glass. She went to her computer and clicked through the photos taken by Joseph. First, the ones high up in the tree, and then the close-ups.

'You sick little shit,' she murmured, flicking between the two different perspectives and zooming in. 'You lifted up her skirt when you came down from the tree…'

Erika's phone rang, making her jump. She checked the time and saw it was just after 11 p.m. It was Edward, asking if she had enjoyed lunch.

'I didn't go in the end. I was called out to a crime scene,' she said. 'Very sad. A young girl, murdered on her doorstep.'

'Oh. Do you want to talk about it?'

'Not really. It's too dark and gruesome for Christmas. Did you have a good day?'

'I had a bit of a party, as it turns out,' he laughed. 'Kelly from down the road popped over with her mother, Shirley. They brought over a big lasagne and Monopoly. It was Manchester Monopoly. Guess where the most expensive street is?'

'Coronation Street?'

'No. I thought the same. It's the Lowry on Salford Quays. It's the same price as Park Lane on the London version. I don't think you can win Monopoly unless you fork out for the best real estate.'

'Listen to you, saying things like "real estate".'

'And that's why I won. I was a proper little tycoon!'

He sounded normal, nothing like the confused old man from that morning. In the background, she could hear the television.

'I'm glad you had a nice day,' she said.

'I've just been over to the graveyard. And it was snowing, but over on the hills it was clear and the moon was up. Is it right that I thought it was beautiful?'

'It is.'

'I didn't want Mark to be on his own on Christmas Day…' His voice trembled and broke on the end of the phone. 'It's so hard, him not being here.'

'I know,' she said, wiping her eyes.

'There's 'owt we can do about it, is there?'

'No.'

There was a long silence, interrupted by tinny laughter from Edward's television in the background.

'Oh well, I just wanted to check on you, lass, and wish you goodnight.'

'Thank you.'

'Merry Christmas. I'll phone you soon.'

'Merry Christmas,' she said. The laughter on his television cut out, and Erika was back in the silence of her flat, the snow against the windows. She closed the curtains and flicked on the lights. Her phone rang again. This time it was Kay.

'Sorry it's late, ma'am, but I found something on Joseph Pitkin's phone, amongst the files.'

'That's okay. You're still working?' asked Erika, impressed.

'I was just going over the downloaded files, and I found some files on the hard drive which had been deleted. I managed to recover some of them. They're troubling.'

'Pornography?'

'No. Pictures and video of Joseph. I'm sending them over now.'

Erika came off the phone and opened the email. There were six photos. Joseph was naked, lying on his back, and fastened with leather straps to a wooden table, by his neck, arms and thighs. His eyes were bloodshot and wide with fear. The hand of an unknown man gripped him by the throat, making the tendons on his neck strain. Erika clicked on the video file. It showed the same scene as the photos, and looked like it was filmed with a mobile phone.

'Please, please! Let me go. I won't say anything. I won't tell!' Joseph pleaded, wincing up at the bright light on the phone camera.

'You won't tell. Do you want this video sent to all the people you know?' said a voice. It had been electronically distorted. The hand appeared and grasped Joseph's genitals, and he screamed out as the hand twisted them. 'I have your address,' said the voice. 'I have your phone. You say anything, I send this to everyone in your contacts… Friends. Family. Everyone.'

The camera angle jolted, and moved to show a table with a row of sex toys. The disembodied hand picked up the largest, and went

back to Joseph, who tried to close his legs, but they were spread and strapped to the table.

'NO!' he screamed. 'NO!'

Erika muted the sound, and had to force herself to watch the rest of the video.

CHAPTER THIRTEEN

Erika arrived at Lewisham Row police station just after 8 a.m. The construction work around the centre of Lewisham, which had started when Erika was first assigned to South London, was almost complete. Several high-rise blocks of luxury apartments now dwarfed the eight-storey police station. The cranes were still on the snowy morning, and on one there was a Christmas tree, lit up.

It had been a sleepless night. The images of Joseph had haunted her dreams. In the photos, he appeared to be a victim, but she needed to question him about his role in Marissa Lewis's murder, and there was still so much information she didn't have: post-mortem results; DNA; the murder weapon hadn't been found. Erika felt uncomfortable about it, but the photos of Joseph could be used as leverage.

At 9 a.m., Joseph was brought into Interview Room 1 by two uniformed officers. He wasn't cuffed. He looked pale, and had dark circles under his eyes. A bleary-eyed solicitor in an expensive pinstripe suit filed in with him. He didn't seem happy that he'd been called in to work on Boxing Day. He introduced himself as Henry Chevalier, and sat next to Joseph.

Erika sat on the opposite side of the table with an equally tired-looking McGorry, who Joseph eyeballed with hatred.

'It's 9.04 a.m. on December 26th, 2017,' said Erika. 'Present for the interview is DCI Erika Foster, DC John McGorry, Joseph Pitkin and his legal representation, Henry Chevalier.'

Henry leaned over and whispered something in Joseph's ear. He didn't react, but nodded. Erika opened one of the grey cardboard files she had stacked on the table and took out hard copies of the photos which had been developed from the roll of film.

'Joseph. Can you tell me if you took these photos?' She spread them out across the table. For a split second, Joseph's eyes registered shock, then he sat back and folded his arms.

'My client has chosen not to answer this,' said Henry.

Erika went on, 'This is from a roll of undeveloped film in a small plastic tube we found in the alleyway behind your parents' garden. I believe it fell out of your pocket when you climbed over the wall.' Joseph scrunched up his face in a scowl. 'We lifted prints from it. A thumb and forefinger, and they match yours. I'll ask you again. Did you take these photos?'

Joseph looked at Henry, who nodded.

'Yeah, I took them.'

'Photos of a dead body,' said Erika.

'We can see the photos,' said Henry. Erika picked up one, a close-up of Marissa's blood-spattered face, her eyes wide. Frozen with fear.

'This photo is taken from high up, in the tree opposite Marissa's house.' Erika held it up to Joseph and he looked away. 'You'll see her skirt is down over her thighs.' She picked up another. 'But in this photo, taken up close, her dress has been lifted to expose her underwear. Did you touch the body, Joseph?' He shook his head. 'We've also recovered videos from your mobile phone, which show you had quite an unhealthy obsession with Marissa Lewis. You filmed her covertly when she was in her bedroom, and on one occasion when she had sex with another man.'

Joseph was now shaking, and his face had drained of blood. 'I didn't kill her.'

'What did you do, then?' asked McGorry, sitting back and folding his arms. 'Have a fiddle with her as she lay dead? You took the opportunity to dip your fingers into her knickers when she wasn't able to object?'

'Officers, I would appreciate a more respectful line of questioning,' said Henry.

Erika gathered up the photos and put them away. She opened another cardboard file. 'I have your PNC record. You served six weeks in a youth detention centre when you were fourteen. You attacked a boy at school with a broken bottle. The surgeon managed to save his eye.'

Erika held up the photo of a young, dark-haired boy from the file. An ugly purple line of stitches ran from his left eyebrow and across his eyelid.

'I was defending myself. He hit me,' said Joseph.

'Then why not hit him back? Instead, you smashed a glass bottle and ground it into his face. Bit of a psycho thing to do,' said McGorry.

'Can I ask if you are planning to charge my client?' said Henry. 'And if so, what are you planning to charge him with? He served his time for what he did. He also has an alibi for the time when Marissa Lewis was killed.'

'From his mum and dad,' said Erika.

'My client's father is a former Queen's Counsel with an impeccable reputation. He states that Joseph was at home all night and didn't leave the house until the next morning.'

'Do they all sleep in the same bedroom?'

'That's a ridiculous question.'

'Is it? The murder scene was less than two minutes from Joseph's house. He's already shown that he likes to hop over the

back wall. He could have made it there and back in a very short space of time.'

'*Could* being the operative word. Detectives, do you have any concrete evidence?'

'We have taken DNA samples from the victim's body. I also have officers searching the Pitkin house. It's just a matter of time,' said Erika.

'Yes, eleven hours and counting.'

'I have the right to extend custody for another two days.'

'I would advise against that,' said Henry softly, with a steely sense of finality. His eyes bore down at her from across the table.

'Is that a threat?'

'Of course not,' he said, with a fake smile. 'Do you think I would threaten you, in a room full of cameras, where a transcript of our conversation is being recorded? Are you, DCI Foster, feeling paranoid?'

'No. It's probably just caffeine withdrawal.' She smiled.

'Our coffee machine is on the blink,' said McGorry. 'Whatever button you press, oxtail soup comes out.'

Henry rolled his eyes. 'How is this relevant?'

They ignored him. McGorry looked at Erika. She pulled the third and final cardboard folder from the pile, and took out the photos of Joseph, naked and strapped to the table, and a still image from the video file. She lay them out on the table and they both sat back.

They weren't prepared for the reaction. What little colour Joseph had left drained from his face, and his hands started to shake uncontrollably.

'Hang on. Why weren't these photos disclosed to me?' said Henry.

'We recovered these photos and an explicit video file from your mobile phone, Joseph,' said Erika. 'Who is the person who did this to you? Did he send you the files?'

Joseph shook his head and stood up, his chair crashing back onto the floor. He vomited spectacularly across the table. Erika just managed to pull two of the folders out of the way, and they all leapt back.

'Christ!' shouted Henry, recoiling at the pile of saturated paperwork he held, before dropping it onto the floor.

Joseph stood very still, and hunched forward, a long line of drool hanging from his mouth. They all stood in shocked silence. Suddenly, he lunged at Erika, screaming with bared teeth.

'You fucking bitch!' he spat as McGorry held him back, pinning his arms to his sides. 'Where did you get them? How? How did you get them? He's nothing to do with this! NOTHING! He'll kill me!'

'Who? Who will kill you?' said Erika, pivoting out of the way as Joseph kicked out at her. 'We need some help in here!' she shouted, turning to the camera mounted in the corner of the interview room. Seconds later, two uniformed officers came rushing in, and they helped to pull Joseph towards the door. 'Who? Who will kill you? Give me his name and all this will be over.' Joseph was dragged out of the interview room, kicking and shouting. 'Give me his name, I can protect you!' The door slammed.

'Boss,' said McGorry, putting a hand on her arm. 'The interview's over.'

Erika looked at McGorry and the solicitor, and the mess across the table, and she came back to her senses.

'Yes.'

'Jesus Christ,' said Henry, picking up his bag from the corner of the room, and seeing where he'd been caught with vomit on the sleeve of his jacket. 'Jesus fucking Christ!' And he left. Erika and McGorry stood in shock.

'We know one thing for sure. He had a big Christmas lunch,' said McGorry, wrinkling his nose.

CHAPTER FOURTEEN

Erika and McGorry were joined in the corridor outside the interview room by Kay, who had been watching from the observation suite next door. She had with her a bunch of paper towels.

'What the hell just happened in there?' asked McGorry, taking one and dabbing at the sleeve of his suit. 'Yuck, this is all I need today.' He gingerly took off his jacket.

'I got to him. I hit a nerve,' said Erika. She absently took the offered paper towels, and saw she had managed to remain unscathed.

'We don't know that those photos and the video have anything to do with the Marissa Lewis case. This looks like revenge porn,' said Kay.

'I've got to get rid of this jacket, I won't be a sec, Boss,' said McGorry, holding his jacket between thumb and finger and hurrying off.

'Revenge porn is about scorned lovers, and exposing. No. Whoever it is on that video is blackmailing him not to talk,' said Erika.

'We can't use past trauma as leverage.'

'I was so bloody close.'

'How? How can we be close to something completely in the dark to us, ma'am?'

Erika turned to her. 'You need to make sure that interview room is cleaned properly,' she said, handing back the paper towel. 'And don't call me ma'am.'

*

Erika came back up to her office. She put in calls to Isaac, and forensics, but they both told her they wouldn't be able to come back with anything until the next day. She then called the officer who was following up on the house-to-house in Coniston Road, and he told her that the two men who had been involved with Marissa, Don Walpole and Ivan Stowalski, had still not been made contact with. He did, however, have the contact details for Marissa's friend, Sharon-Louise Braithwaite, who worked at the hair salon. Erika thanked him and wrote down the number. She was about to call her when there was a knock at her door.

'What?'

It opened and McGorry stuck his head round.

'Alright, Boss. The doc has examined Pitkin. There's nothing wrong with him physically. Blood pressure okay, temperature okay, no infection, but he's recommended to the custody sergeant that Pitkin gets a couple of hours' rest and the chance to calm down before we attempt to interview him again. He's still in quite a state.'

Erika looked at her watch. It was coming up to midday.

'I've got five hours before I have to decide whether or not to keep him in custody for another couple of days. I'm no closer to being able to charge him… You know you can come into my office; you don't have to hang around in the doorway!' she snapped. McGorry came inside and shut the door behind him. 'Okay, direct question. Do you think he did it?'

McGorry shrugged. 'I dunno if he's got it in him. The person who did it went batshit crazy. Hacking at her with a knife. They would have been covered in blood. And what about the trail of blood from the crime scene? He doesn't have a car. We haven't found a murder weapon.'

'Who do you think is blackmailing him with the photos?'

'Could be a man or a woman. Judging from his reaction, I think it's a man. You can see in the photos that he's not a willing participant, or if he was at the beginning, he wasn't by the time he was strapped in and naked. He was being overpowered physically. He looks terrified. And of course, he yakked all over the interview room when he saw we had the photos and video.'

'He could have been working as a rent boy,' said Erika. 'No, the family is well off.'

'He was signing on at the Jobcentre.'

'There's too many questions surrounding him, and you're right, he did look frightened in the video. We should tread carefully. Whoever this person is, they have the power to terrify him.'

CHAPTER FIFTEEN

Four floors down, in the custody suite, Joseph lay on the single bunk in the harsh light of the cell, staring at the tiny window. His face was ashen, and he was almost catatonic with fear. He had been checked over by a doctor, cleaned up, and put back in his cell. He wore dark jeans, ripped at each knee, and a thick dark sweater. His belt and shoes had been taken from him.

He could hear voices echoing in the corridor. A group of young lads had been arrested and brought in, and were making a noise, shouting and swearing at the custody sergeant.

How did they get those photos? he thought. *I deleted them. He told me if I kept my mouth shut, no one would see them.*

Joseph saw the face of the man he knew as 'T': a wide, handsome face with a high forehead. Piercing eyes. He had thought they were friends, and T had trusted him enough to show him what he kept in the basement.

'This is where I play,' he'd said.

The basement was dark, with a low ceiling and bare, stained concrete floors. The air was hot and stank of sweat. There were wooden stocks, a cage and leather restraints. Pornography, cut out from magazines, covered the walls. Joseph wasn't shocked by the nudity or sex. What chilled him were the faces of the women and men in the pictures who were being dominated. There was genuine fear in their eyes, and some of them were bleeding.

'Are they real?' he'd asked.

T had nodded, smoothing his hands over his crotch, and he came towards Joseph.

'I have to go,' Joseph had said, making a dash for the door.

'Stay for one more drink,' said T, reaching out and grabbing the back of Joseph's shirt, catching the material in a powerful grip. Joseph, eager not to appear scared, and to diffuse the situation, said yes. That last drink had been spiked, and he'd woken up naked, and tied up. Unable to move.

He didn't know how long it had lasted. The fear that he was going to die had been bad enough, but looking into the eyes of a person who ignored your screams, who seemed to get excited by your pain, was terrifying. The final image that burned into his mind was of the gas mask. He could still smell it, the filthy sweat mingled in with rubber and amyl nitrate.

He was strangled to the point of unconsciousness several times and woke up as T was reviving him with mouth-to-mouth. He didn't remember the photos being taken, but he remembered the video… The bright light from the phone camera. He'd got them in an email a day later, with a note:

I have these photos and the video file locked away. So long as you keep your mouth shut, they'll stay that way.
T.

And now the police knew, and if the police knew they would follow it up. Did they have the note too? Would they tell his parents, and who else would find out? Joseph put his hands between his thighs and began to sob and rock himself. Blind terror flashed through his body again and he retched, but there was nothing left to come up, just bile. He reached up to wipe his mouth and his fingers caught on the rip in the left knee of his jeans.

He jumped as the hatch opened and the noise at the end of the corridor became clearer. The lads were still shouting, but now from inside their cells.

'You alright, lad?' came the custody sergeant's voice. Joseph turned on the bed and looked over, making himself nod. The hatch slammed shut again, and the shouting receded a little. Joseph set to work with his fingers, widening the tear in the knee of his trousers and tearing off a long strip of the material.

*

The commotion had died down outside the cells, and all the men in custody were locked up when the custody sergeant did his next check on Joseph Pitkin fifteen minutes later. When he opened the hatch, he couldn't see where he had gone, as the single bed was empty.

'Son, you alright?' he asked, shining the torch over the steel toilet and sink in the far corner. The hatch was high up on the door, so when he saw the piece of material hooked into the tiny joint which made up the hinge of the hatch, he panicked. He reached a hand inside and felt the thin line of taut material and then the top of Joseph Pitkin's head. 'Shit! Shit!' he cried. He ran back down the corridor to the desk, and hit the emergency alarm. It rang out, echoing along the corridor as he grabbed the keys and ran back to the door. Once he had it unlocked, he had to push against the weight of the body against it. His colleague, a female officer in her mid-fifties, came running down to help him as he got the door open, then pulled it back. Joseph hung from the back of the door, a couple of feet off the floor, suspended by his neck with a strip of denim. His face was bright purple, and his eyes were wide open and bloodshot. 'Get him down, quick, get him down!' he cried. The female officer had thought to grab a pair of scissors, and she cut the improvised noose. The custody sergeant

lay Joseph down and loosened the strip of material. His colleague didn't say anything as he started to perform CPR, continuing for several minutes, pumping Joseph's chest and blowing into his mouth at intervals.

She knew that he was dead. She had seen it so many times before.

CHAPTER SIXTEEN

Superintendent Melanie Hudson stood at just over five feet, with short blonde hair and soft grey eyes, but her eyes and elfin frame belied a steely determination.

She was settling down for an afternoon of television and a box of chocolates with her husband and young son when the call came through that a young man had died in custody at her police station.

She drove straight to Lewisham Row, and was able to attend the scene as Joseph Pitkin's body was taken out. She heard statements from the two custody officers, and then she came up to her office. When she rounded the corner into the corridor, she found Erika waiting on the chair outside.

'Have you been sitting here in the dark?' she said, reaching up and flicking on the lights with her elbow.

'It helps me think.'

She put down her bag and unlocked the office door. Erika followed her inside.

'Start from the beginning, and tell me everything,' she said, indicating the seat opposite her desk.

Erika outlined everything that had happened with Joseph, from when she was first on the scene at Coniston Road, discovering him watching the crime scene, and the subsequent arrest when they found the photos and video.

'I'll need to review all video that you have from formal interviews. I also want a full written report from you. And from McGorry. Is there anything you want to tell me?'

Erika looked at the floor.

'Joseph's father is a retired barrister… When we chased him, at the end of the chase, McGorry got involved in a tussle – well, a fight – with him. He was trying to stop him getting away… He held him by the strap that was around his neck.'

'Define "held"?' said Melanie.

'The father, David Pitkin, said that he thought it was a chokehold.'

'Was it a chokehold?'

'It was in the heat of the moment. Joseph was throwing punches, he was on top of McGorry. John was acting in self-defence.'

'But was it a chokehold?'

Erika scratched her head. 'Yes. Bloody hell, yes.'

'For how long?'

'I don't know. A few seconds, ten seconds.'

'You understand that there will be a full investigation as to why Joseph Pitkin hanged himself. He was on suicide watch.'

'Why are suicide watch checks every fifteen minutes? A lot can be achieved in fifteen minutes. He tore off strips of his jeans, for God's sake!' Erika wiped tears away from her cheeks. She sat up and took a tissue. 'I want to inform the parents.'

'No. That's not a good idea.'

'He was in custody because of me.'

'He was in custody because you had compelling evidence to arrest and question him. You have also had conflict with the family; they need someone impartial. I will go and inform them with a family liaison officer.'

'I wasn't aware he had any mental health issues. I don't have his medical records, but he was examined by a doctor after our first, explosive interview, and the doctor was satisfied that he could be interviewed again, after a break. We didn't get that far. He was a key part of my investigation…'

'Okay. I need you to take the rest of the day off,' said Melanie.

'I'm off the case?'

'No. I need to look over the interview footage, and I need to talk to the custody sergeant, and the arresting officers. I also need a written statement from you with all the details. I also want to talk to McGorry.'

Erika got up. 'Okay.'

'Just hold on, sit down.'

Erika sat back in her seat.

'What?'

'I'm going to say something you're not going to like, but I want you to hear me out.'

'Yes?'

'You've been through a lot this year, Erika. It's barely a week since you came off the murder-kidnap case.'

'It's ten days…' Erika closed her eyes. It had been a harrowing case, involving a young couple, Nina Hargreaves and Max Kirkham, who had committed a string of murders and robberies across the country. The press, inevitably, had made a Bonnie and Clyde-style story out of it, and then Commander Marsh had made a fateful statement to the press, denouncing the two killers.

Marsh had thought he had been smart, giving them an ultimatum, but what he'd given them instead was a face and a name. It hadn't taken long for Nina and Max to dig around in his personal life, and discover that Marsh's wife came from a wealthy family, and that they had two young daughters.

They'd attacked Marcie when she was at home alone, and Nina Hargreaves had duped the nursery into thinking that she was the girls' new nanny. This was when the case escalated to a full-blown kidnapping. Against all advice, Marsh and Marcie had paid a ransom of £200,000 – but it had only ended when Erika had managed to track Nina and Max down to where the twins

were being held in a remote location on Dartmoor, in the south of England.

The subsequent bloodbath, where Max and Nina had turned on each other, was still imprinted on Erika's mind. She'd rescued the twins, who were physically unhurt, but the emotional scars would take a long time to heal.

'Erika! Erika!'

She opened her eyes. Melanie was looking at her with concern. 'What happened there?'

'Sorry. I'm tired, and still a bit shocked. Not only is it tragic when someone so young takes his own life – he was a key witness.'

Melanie took out her wallet and removed a card, handing it to Erika.

'Dr G Priestley. Clinical Psychologist,' she read, looking up at Melanie. 'Is this for me?'

'Yes.'

'You think I'm crazy? Unbalanced?'

Melanie put up her hand. 'No, I don't. And before we go any further, I want to add that Dr Priestley is my doctor. I see him once a week.'

'Therapy?'

'Yes.'

Erika didn't know what to say, and she looked down at the card again.

'What is this? A referral? I come off another successful case and stop two multiple murderers and rescue the daughters of the borough commander, and I'm not congratulated, I'm put in therapy?'

'Erika. No. This is me talking to you as a friend, or a colleague, privately. This is nothing to do with the Met, or any case, or the suicide of Joseph Pitkin. You are one of my finest officers, and I am confident that you will be back shortly and continuing work

on this murder case, but this is what I want from you. It's my duty to report if any of my officers are struggling with the pressures of work.'

'You're going to report me?'

'No! Listen to what I'm saying, you bloody idiot!'

Erika looked up at her and smiled.

'Sorry…' started Melanie.

'No, it's okay. I'll take being called a bloody idiot over bullshit corporate language…' She held up the card. 'This is your therapist?'

'Yeah.'

'Do you mind me asking why you…?'

Melanie took a deep breath and sat back.

'My first pregnancy was twins. I carried them to full term, had the baby shower, had the excited family and husband waiting in the delivery room to hold our babies… They were both stillborn.' She took a deep breath and wiped a tear from her eye. 'The doctors didn't know why. I have no family history of stillbirth. It was a textbook pregnancy. The lack of reasons why it happened were devastating. I lost my faith, and I almost lost everything else. It almost destroyed me.'

'I'm so sorry. When was this?'

'Ten years ago, but it was a long journey to come back to normality. Of course, I never think I'll come fully back from that place, but life is good now. So, I'm talking to you as a friend, with no judgement. Don't crash and burn, Erika. The job isn't worth that much. I don't want to tell you how to live your life, but I am not against you. As I said, you are one of my best officers and I want you to stay that way. I want you to go on and keep doing what you're doing, but you need to make sure you are in the right frame of mind.'

Erika looked down at the card again. 'Can I think about it?'

'Sure, just don't think about it for too long. In the meantime, go home and get some sleep. I'll call you. And send in McGorry.'

Erika came out of the office, and closed the door. McGorry and the custody sergeant were both waiting on chairs in the corridor. They both looked in shock.

'How did it go?' asked McGorry, blowing out his cheeks.

'OK. Just tell the truth, as it happened. I had to mention the chokehold on Joseph. I said it was in self-defence. I'll be putting it all in my report.'

'Jeans, his jeans,' muttered the custody sergeant, shaking his head in disbelief.

'You did your job,' said Erika.

'It's not enough, though,' he replied.

She briefly put her hand on his arm, and nodding goodbye, she left the station. When she got into her car, she saw that the Christmas presents for the twins were still on the back seat. She started the car and headed for Commander Marsh's house.

CHAPTER SEVENTEEN

Marsh lived on a smart road of large detached houses near Hilly Fields, which had a stunning view of the London skyline. The sun came out just as Erika found a parking spot outside, and it gave the snowy streets a golden hue. She hoped the Marshes were out, so she could leave the presents on the porch, but she took a deep breath and grasped the large iron door knocker. It crashed loudly against the wood.

A moment later, Marsh opened the door. He was a handsome man in his mid-forties with short-cropped blond hair. He looked pale and drawn, and like he'd lost a lot of weight.

'Erika,' he said, surprised. She held up the presents.

'I know I'm a day late, but I wanted to give these to the girls, and apologise for my no-show.'

Marsh went to say something, but Marcie appeared in the hall behind.

'You made it. Merry Christmas,' she said, giving Erika a hug. 'How are you?'

Marcie was a beautiful woman, but she too had lost too much weight. Her usually glossy black hair was long and lank, and she wore heavy pale make-up, which didn't quite disguise the two black eyes and swelling from the broken nose, still healing after the attack.

'I'm fine,' said Erika, feeling awkward. She and Marcie went back a long way. They'd never had an easy relationship, until Erika had rescued her two small daughters.

'Come on, inside, out of the cold,' Marcie said, rubbing Erika's shoulders. 'That coat isn't very thick; you need more than a leather jacket in this weather!'

They took her through to the living room, which was stiflingly hot. An open fire was blazing, and next to it was a huge Christmas tree. Marcie's father, Leonard, was snoozing in an armchair in one corner, and Marsh's father, Alan, was asleep in another armchair by the tree.

'Do sit down,' said Marcie. 'I'm just putting out a buffet lunch. I've got cold meats and cheeses, and some broccoli and stilton soup.'

'Lovely,' said Erika.

'Can we get you a drink? Champagne?' said Marsh.

'Paul, keep your voice down. They're sleeping!' scolded Marcie in a stage whisper.

'My voice is the same level as yours,' he hissed.

'No, you were bloody loud… Come and help with the food. Do excuse us, Erika.'

They left the room. Erika looked over at the two old men, red-faced and snoozing. Marcie's dad, Leonard, was tanned and well-dressed in casual blue slacks and a checked shirt with a cravat. Alan was scruffier, in old jeans and a yellow woollen jumper. Leonard shifted in his chair, coughed, and sat up, taking a moment to get his bearings. With an almost comic double take he noticed Erika.

'Hello.'

'Hello.'

'I know you, don't I? You're that lady police officer,' he said. His voice was posh and plummy. 'Ulrika, isn't it?'

'Erika Foster, Detective Chief Inspector.'

He got up awkwardly and came over and held out his hand, smiling. His false teeth looked unnaturally white against his tanned

skin. She took it and they shook, and then he swooped in and kissed her on both cheeks.

'We're very grateful for what you did, for Paul and Marcie, and the twins. Thank you,' he said, continuing to pump her hand.

'I was just doing my job.'

'Bloody awful business. I saw the news report; they had to blur out the pictures of Max Kirkham's body.'

'Yes…'

Leonard was still shaking her hand.

'Paul tells me the girl fired a distress flare at him – blew his whole head open, brains all over the place? Do you think the twins saw it?'

'Yes, I do think so.'

'My grandfather survived the trenches during the First World War. He had shell shock, of course. He remembered young lads having the backs of their heads blown off by shrapnel fire… Course, these days we're all encouraged to have therapy; back then they suffered in silence…'

Alan woke up. He took a moment to come around, and smacked his lips and rubbed his eyes. He was an older version of Marsh, with a craggy face and full head of short-cropped grey hair.

'Alan, this is Ulrika, the police officer who caught those murdering bastards!'

'Hello, it's Erika,' she said, pulling her hand away from Leonard's grip.

'Ulrika… That's a Swedish name. Did you used to do the weather?' asked Alan, with dead-pan seriousness.

'The weather?'

'Poor old git is losing his marbles,' murmured Leonard, tapping the side of his head.

'I heard that!' said Alan. 'Is she the district nurse?'

Thankfully, Marsh came back into the room with a tray of champagne.

'Dad, this is Erika. Erika Foster. We trained together in Manchester,' he said. Alan nodded, but looked none the wiser.

'Were you at lunch? Was she at lunch, Paul?'

'No, Dad, Erika has just arrived,' said Marsh, speaking slowly and loudly. There was an awkward silence. Leonard picked up the remote and switched on the TV. There was a cacophony of noise as *The Sound of Music* came on the screen. The von Trapp children were marching down the stairs. 'Let's go through to the kitchen,' Marsh added in a low voice. Erika smiled at the two old men, now engrossed in the film.

'Sorry about that. Dad's getting a bit confused. It's been quite a frustrating Christmas. I keep having to repeat everything,' said Marsh as they went along the hall and into the kitchen. 'Leonard's fine, he just doesn't listen. He's in his own world.'

'Who doesn't listen?' asked Marcie as they came into the kitchen. She was laying out a beautiful buffet on the long kitchen table.

'Your father.'

'At least my father knows what day it is.'

'That's a bit harsh,' snapped Marsh.

'It's an observation. He should be in a home. It's been very stressful having him here. There's nothing wrong with my father. If you remember, he won Trivial Pursuit yesterday.'

Erika looked down at her champagne glass, wanting to be out of the firing line.

'I'm not saying he's going the same way as mine. I'm saying he's bull-headed, and the way he talks to your mother…'

'My mother can be just as bad.'

'Why else did she go out today? I wish I'd gone out!'

Marcie looked at him. She had tears in her eyes.

'Maybe I should go,' said Erika.

'No, please stay,' said Marcie, dabbing at her eyes with tissue. Marsh stood beside her, trying to control his anger.

Sophie and Mia came into the kitchen, breaking the mood. They were two tiny, identical four-year-olds, dressed in matching purple velvet dresses with thick cream tights and pink hairbands in their long dark hair. They saw Erika and wordlessly came to her and gave her a hug. Erika put her glass down and crouched to hug the two little girls, smelling their hair against her cheek. In the warm, bright kitchen, what had happened all seemed surreal, and so long ago.

'We're so pleased to see you,' said Sophie, taking the lead.

'I'm pleased to see you, too,' said Erika. They all looked at each other. Mia nodded solemnly; her big brown eyes were so expressive. Erika felt rotten that she had missed coming for lunch the day before.

'I brought you both presents. They're a bit late, but Merry Christmas.' She gave the two bags to the girls, and they pulled out the wrapped gifts and tore off the paper excitedly. The first was a Blingles Glimmer Studio Sticker Maker set, and the second was a Fashion Headbands set, with options to make your own hairbands in different colours and with flowers and glitter. 'I got two different things, but I remembered how much you two like to share,' said Erika.

Both girls had genuine faces of wonderment and excitement.

'Oh. Girls, what do you say to Erika?' said Marcie.

'Thank you, Erika!' they both said.

'You didn't already get them for Christmas? My niece and nephew are around your age, and they said these were really good presents.'

'No, we haven't got them, and they are the best presents, EVER!' cried Mia, giving her another hug.

The girls looked up at Marcie. 'Mummy, get the thing,' said Sophie. Marcie went to the kitchen counter and picked up a small gift-wrapped box. She handed it to Sophie, then Mia grabbed the corner and they both handed it to Erika.

'We got this for you,' said Mia.

Erika pulled the paper off a small jewellery box. When she opened it, inside there was a necklace with a small silver cross. Marcie took the box and undid the necklace, and Mia lifted the short hair at the back of Erika's head so that they could put it on.

'This is a beautiful gift,' said Erika to the girls, then looking up at Marcie and Marsh. They smiled. The twins then pulled out two new iPhones from the pockets of their dresses, and with their tiny hands they expertly swiped through their screens.

'These were presents from Mummy and Daddy,' said Sophie. 'They want us to be in contact with them, always, because of what happened.'

They held their phones up to Erika and showed her the picture they'd taken of her in the necklace. She looked gaunt and almost translucent; against the white fridge, she was so pale.

'You look pretty,' said Sophie.

'But you look like you could do with some food,' said Mia. Luckily, this broke the atmosphere and they all laughed.

'Girls, go and wash your hands,' said Marcie.

Erika waited until the girls had left the room. 'How are they doing?' she asked.

Marcie and Marsh looked at each other. 'Surprisingly good, all things considering,' said Marcie. 'Sophie is much stronger. She's been the one who looks after Mia.'

'They keep disappearing off into corners to talk to each other in their own made-up language,' said Marsh.

'There's no manual for what to do. I'm taking them to see a therapist in the new year,' said Marcie.

'How are you both doing?' asked Erika. They looked at each other, as if seeing that they were a couple for the first time. They hesitated.

'Taking each day as it comes,' said Marsh, and he patted Marcie on the leg. She twisted out of his way.

'Come on, let's eat,' she said.

*

Erika drove home later that evening. The gift from the girls brought her great comfort, and she kept reaching up to touch it on her neck. For once, she was relieved to come home to an empty flat. The atmosphere at Marsh's had been so hostile, and despite the size of the house, it had seemed claustrophobic with all their guests.

Erika was just pouring herself a vodka over ice when her phone rang. It was Melanie.

'I've been through everything to do with Joseph Pitkin, and at this stage, I can only say it was a tragic accident.'

'Okay. Did you tell his parents?'

'Yes. As expected, they were devastated.'

'Do they blame me?'

Melanie sighed. 'I'm not going to answer that. But they obviously see this whole situation very differently.'

'Did you ask them about the photos and the note?'

'No, Erika. I didn't…' Melanie was silent on the end of the phone for a moment. 'I do need you back at work tomorrow, though. I'm giving you a bigger team for the Marissa Lewis murder case. Get a good night's sleep.'

When Melanie had hung up, Erika went to the living room window. The lights were out, and she stared at the dark snowy street. A fox moved into the glare of the orange streetlight, pausing with its feet in the snow, its sleek body rippling under the light.

It was waiting, checking out her building and whether it could ransack the dustbins. Erika watched from the shadows.

'Come on. It's safe, make a dash for it,' she said. The fox crept forward slowly into the car park, past the white humps of the snow-covered cars, towards the rubbish bins, which were no doubt groaning with leftover food. 'That's it.'

There was a creak from upstairs and a light went on in the window, illuminating a large square of the dark car park. The fox turned and dashed off, disappearing into the shadows.

CHAPTER EIGHTEEN

Dark winter nights in the suburbs of London were always exciting for the man who liked to call himself 'T'. He would leave the house under cover of darkness, dressed in black, with the leather gas mask stowed in one of the large pockets of his long coat.

The sprawl of South London stretched for miles, and every time he felt lucky to find an area he had never seen before amongst the rows upon rows of terraced houses, dark alleyways, small tucked-away parks and scrubland. The suburban areas of South London were mostly free of CCTV cameras. The train stations only had them in the lit areas.

He believed his face was the true mask. It was an ordinary face, not quite the guy next door, but acceptable enough. In all the months he had been doing this, the only mug shot the police had was of the gas mask.

It always struck him how little people noticed in plain sight. Commuters were experts at not seeing. They just wanted to get to work and were eager to return home. They rarely engaged. Eyes blinkered. Almost afraid that they might have to get involved with the world around them. The unemployed, the drunkards, and the homeless were the ones you had to watch out for. They were differently tuned to their surroundings, and not just passing through from A to B. They were stuck in plain sight, forced to conjure the tools for their survival from a barren landscape. They were the expert watchers, instantly aware of who they could squeeze some change or a spare cigarette out of, and who wanted drugs.

The good news for T was that no one took any notice of the homeless. No one who mattered. It would have been far easier to pick off a homeless person. Offer them a few quid to follow him into a dark corner. For a fiver, he could do almost anything he wanted, depending on how desperate they were.

But that would be no fun. It was fear that he enjoyed, finding someone clean and upwardly mobile. Finding a nice, well-dressed, tax-paying pillar of society and ripping them out of their nice little bubble. There was always a look in their faces when he cornered them, as if to say: *This kind of thing doesn't happen to me. It happens to other people. Bad people. I'm good.*

The gas mask had its practical purpose, but it also added a sensory wow. The feel of the tight leather hood, the goaty smell of his own stale sweat, mixed with the smell of animal hide. The way the thick glass eyeholes distorted his vision, and slightly magnified the faces of his victims.

Tonight, he would just be a spectator. The snow added an extra layer of protection. Muffling sounds. He would watch and wait. He never knew their names, but he did like to crack their routines. That was another thrill. To work out when they left the house. What time they left for work, what time they came home. People could be such creatures of routine. Even at Christmas.

Learn their routine, and the rest was easy.

CHAPTER NINETEEN

The next morning, Erika arrived early at Lewisham Row, and went down to the tiny kitchenette on the ground floor, next to the cloakrooms used by uniform officers. She was staring at an open cupboard full of mugs when two young officers came in still wearing their stab vests.

'Morning, ma'am,' they said in unison. They looked surprised to see her.

'Morning. What's the cup situation? Do these belong to anyone?'

The young man, who was shorter than Erika, reached up and took out two mugs, handing one to the young woman, who seemed embarrassed to make eye contact.

'No one uses the flowery ones, ma'am,' he said. Erika took one out of the cupboard, and there was an awkward silence as the kettle came to the boil then clicked off. No one moved.

'Go on, go first; you've earned it,' she said. The young man spooned coffee from a large catering tin and filled their mugs. 'Was it a rough night?'

He nodded. 'The usual nightmare around kicking-out time from the pubs. The young teenagers seem to get more drunk and abusive around holidays.'

'And we were called out three times by people who thought they'd seen the gas mask attacker,' said the woman.

'Gas mask attacker?' said Erika.

'Yeah. It's been in the local news in the past few weeks. You haven't heard?'

'No, I was preoccupied with another case.'

'A guy wearing a gas mask has been assaulting women and men. He likes to target train stations, early in the morning, or late, after the last train has gone.'

'How many victims?'

'Five, going back to the middle of November.'

'Does he rape them?'

'Not all of them. His first two victims were strangled until they passed out, and when they woke up he was gone. The local news put out an appeal for information yesterday morning, after a woman was attacked on Christmas Day, next to Sydenham train station.'

'She was less than a minute from her front door,' the man said.

'So we've had call-outs all night from people who think they've seen or heard something. They were all false alarms,' the woman added.

They took their tea and left. Detective Inspector Moss then came into the kitchen, wearing a huge winter coat. She was a short, solid woman. Her flame-red hair was dotted with melting snow, and her pale face was covered in a sea of freckles.

'Morning, Boss. How was your Christmas?' Moss undid the buttons on her coat and took out a mug.

'It was…'

'You worked, didn't you?'

Erika nodded. 'On the murder case I'm about to brief you about.'

'Did you get a nice lunch?'

Erika shook her head. 'I had my first, and last "Christmas dinner" sandwich.'

Moss pulled a face. 'I had my first and last Christmas pudding smoothie. And my brother Gary came to stay with his wife and kids.'

'How many?'

'He's just got the one wife.'

'Very funny.'

'Three kids.'

'Do they get on with Jacob?'

Moss rubbed her eyes and filled her cup with boiling water.

'Yeah, they just don't get on with each other, and they're at that age: Seven, eight and nine. It was pandemonium. Our house is too small. And during Christmas lunch, the kids asked about the L-word.'

'Lapland?' said Erika.

Moss grinned and stirred milk into her coffee. 'Ha, ha. No. Lesbians. Namely, me and Celia, why we are married, how we are married, and how we managed to give birth to Jacob. Celia managed that of course, but there were a million questions. We didn't even get around to telling the jokes inside the Christmas crackers. It was all fine, but not the conversation I expected to have.'

Erika went to say more, when a tall, handsome black officer came into the kitchen. He stopped when he saw Erika and Moss.

'Alright. Morning,' he said, recovering his composure. It was Detective Inspector Peterson.

Moss looked between Erika and Peterson, trying to work out what to say. 'Bloody hell. He's finally back at work!'

He nodded and flashed his warrant card, giving them a big grin which made his serious face goofy.

'You're looking much better,' said Erika. It was a surprise to see him. A nice surprise, she realised. 'Did you have a good Christmas break?'

'It wasn't a break really; it was more of a countdown so I could get back to work… It turned out to be… Well, it was one of the best Christmases ever.'

'Care to elaborate?' asked Erika, wondering if he had met someone else, and then wishing she hadn't asked.

'This is officially my first day back at work,' he said, changing the subject. There was an awkward silence.

'You've picked a good day. I'm briefing in five minutes down in the main incident room. Don't be late.' Erika picked up her mug and left.

*

Moss and Peterson stood in silence for a moment. Moss went to the door and checked Erika was out of earshot.

'Did you see her over Christmas?' she asked.

'No.'

'Are things going to be okay with you two? I can't be stuck in the middle of two of my favourite people.'

'Am I one of your favourite people?' he grinned.

'Sometimes. Depends. You should have called her on Christmas Day. I know you two have broken up, but she ended up working. She was meant to take the day off… You know she's a lonely old bird, and I mean that in the nicest sense. I invited her over to mine, but she didn't want to intrude.'

'I was going to go over and see her, and then something… happened,' said Peterson. 'I'm still trying to process it.' He smiled and shook his head.

'I can see by your face that it was something good?' said Moss.

He went to the door and closed it. 'Make me a cup of coffee, and I'll tell you,' he said.

CHAPTER TWENTY

The meeting was held in the largest incident room on the ground floor of the station.

Erika stood in front of a huge map of London, which was three metres square, the maze of roads blending under the North and South Circular and the M25 forming increasing circles around central London, and the thick blue lines of the River Thames snaking across the centre. Twenty officers and civilian support staff had been called to work on the Marissa Lewis case, and it was the first time since Christmas Day that they had all been called back to one place.

The team included officers Erika had worked with before: Sergeant Crane, a pleasant-faced officer with thinning sandy hair; Moss and Peterson, who she noted were still getting coffee; McGorry and Kay, who were sorting out their desks – they both nodded and smiled at Erika as she passed. Detectives Knight and Temple were working with PC Singh, a small and fiercely intelligent officer, to collate the information about the case onto the whiteboard.

Superintendent Hudson slipped into the briefing and closed the door, taking a position perching on a desk at the back. She nodded and smiled.

'Good morning, everyone,' started Erika. 'I hope you all had a good Christmas, and sadly it's over all too quickly…' She went to an ID picture of Marissa Lewis, taken from her passport. 'Twenty-two-year-old Marissa Lewis was murdered on the doorstep of her

house on Coniston Road in South London. I'm still waiting on details of the post-mortem, but time of death has been estimated as late on Christmas Eve...' The door opened, and Moss and Peterson filed in, carrying their mugs of coffee. Moss mouthed an apology to Erika, so did Peterson, and they took their seats next to a photocopier underneath the long line of windows looking out over the corridor. 'Thanks for joining us. I didn't know it took that long for instant coffee to brew.'

'Sorry, Boss,' said Moss, looking mortified. Peterson stared down guiltily at his mug.

Erika went on, 'Marissa Lewis was slashed repeatedly with a sharp serrated blade.' Erika indicated the pictures on the whiteboard, the close-up photos taken of the injuries on the dead body. 'At this stage, we don't have a murder weapon. But we do know from early forensic reports from inside the house that the crime scene was confined to the area in the small front garden. There is no evidence of blood spatter, or Marissa's blood inside the house. We're also waiting on more detailed results from forensics, and on the post-mortem...'

'Does that rule out Marissa's mother being involved?' asked McGorry.

'No. It just means if she did kill Marissa, she would have cleaned herself up, and disposed of whatever she was wearing before going back into the house. No one is being ruled out this early in our investigations. Everyone is a suspect.'

Erika went on to explain everything that had happened with Joseph Pitkin, and his suicide the day before in custody. There was a moment of silence. Suicides in custody were a terrible reminder of how vulnerable prisoners could be.

'At this stage, we are still treating Joseph Pitkin as a person of interest to this case. I feel that we need to arm ourselves with more evidence before we ask his family for any more informa-

tion. We have video and photo evidence, taken from his mobile phone, that he had some kind of relationship with the victim. On several occasions, mostly at night, he filmed her covertly, when she was at home, in her bedroom. I believe that at some point she became aware he was filming her. We need to establish if this was something she encouraged, or if there was a reason why she allowed him to film her. There is a video of Marissa having sexual intercourse with a man who matches the description of a neighbour called Don Walpole.'

Erika indicated some stills taken from the video, which were being pinned up to the board.

'Don Walpole is married, in his early fifties, and is believed to have had a relationship with Marissa when she was a teenager. He also lives on Coniston Road. Another neighbour, again from the same street, is Ivan Stowalski. He also was involved with Marissa in a sexual relationship. He is in his mid-thirties, Polish, but lives in the UK with his wife. Marissa was a burlesque dancer who performed in clubs around London. She was also a carer for an elderly lady, who lives in Hilly Fields, just around the corner…'

As Erika was talking, Detectives Knight and Temple were working with PC Singh to put up photos from the case files.

'Marissa's mother is also someone I would like us to look at closely. She told us that she sleeps upstairs in the back bedroom, and that this was where she slept on Christmas Eve. But when we looked round the house, we saw that the back bedroom hasn't been inhabited for some time. The bed was covered with old clothes and a layer of dust. We found bedding on the living room sofa, which is on the other side of the single-glazed and poorly insulated window where Marissa was stabbed and killed.'

Erika paused and let everyone digest this. She went on, 'Christmas and Boxing Day have slowed things down, hampering our ability to do a house-to-house. Thank you to everyone here

who talked to neighbours, but we are going to have to go back and do it all again. I'd like backgrounds on Marissa Lewis and the neighbours I've mentioned, and anyone else you discover who was part of her life. Friends, family, colleagues, burlesque clubs. We are still working on getting into her iPhone to access emails and social media. We've requested her phone records. A request was also put in yesterday for any CCTV footage covering the area around Coniston Road, and from Brockley train station. We need to know if she took the train home after her burlesque gig on Christmas Eve, which is the normal mode of transport she used. Sergeant Crane will now be tasked with delegating tasks. We need to go back to the beginning and we're playing catch up from the Christmas break.'

The room sprang to life, and Erika went over to Moss and Peterson.

'Sorry, again, Boss,' said Moss.

'Welcome back, James,' said Erika. She seemed to take him off-guard.

'Thanks,' he said, standing up.

Several other officers and support staff came and patted him on the back, and welcomed him back before they dispersed around the incident room.

'You look good. I mean, you've put a lot of weight back on,' Erika said, correcting herself. 'You look like your old self again.'

'I still need to put on a few more pounds,' he said, opening his jacket and hitching up his trousers. 'But I'm feeling back to normal.' He slapped his flat stomach.

'Leave it out, you're putting us all to shame!' grinned Crane, slapping his own beer belly.

'Speak for yourself!' said Moss, grabbing at her ample stomach. 'I'm just big boned.'

'Okay, okay you lot, let's focus. I figured that as you've only just returned to work, you'd want to stay desk-bound and ease yourself in?'

Peterson nodded. 'I'll need a new login for Holmes; I'm told mine is no longer active, cos I've been off for so long.'

'OK. Get Crane to put in a call about your login.' Erika smiled at him and he smiled back, their eyes locking for a moment. Then he looked away. 'Moss, I want you with me; James, I want you to work on building us a profile of Marissa Lewis, and work to untangle her life.'

He nodded and went off, leaving Erika with Moss, who had been watching her.

'What?'

'Nothing. Things seem cool between you, which is… Cool. Where are we going?'

'I want to talk to Marissa's best friend.'

CHAPTER TWENTY-ONE

Erika arranged to meet Sharon-Louise at the Brockley Jack pub, a little way down from the hair salon where she worked – which was still closed on the 27th of December. It was snowing again as they drove through Crofton Park, but the temperature had warmed up a bit, turning it to slush on the road. They passed the train station, a Co-Op and some shops, before seeing the sign for the Goldilocks Hair Salon.

'Why do hair salons always go for pun-tastic names?' asked Moss, peering in at the garish white-and-gold interior decor as they passed. 'When I was growing up, I used to go to "Herr Kutz", but the owner wasn't German. And during my training at Hendon, there was a "Curl up and Dye".'

'Is that relevant?'

'Don't you have that in Slovakia? Hairdresser names with puns?'

'No.'

'The clientele is often working class – nothing wrong with that, of course – but they're ladies who like to look after themselves. I bet it has lots of regulars who like a gossip, not like a central London stuck-up place.'

'You think this Sharon-Louise likes a gossip?'

'Hairdressers hear everything,' Moss said. 'Don't you end up saying far too much when you get your hair cut? I know I feel obliged to chat.'

'When I get my hair cut, which is not that often, I ask them not to talk to me,' said Erika.

'I bet you do,' muttered Moss with a grin.

Erika only noticed an old lady step off the pavement at the last minute and had to slam on the brakes, throwing them both forward. The car came to a screeching halt, less than a foot from the old lady, who, unfazed, continued to push her battered old shopping bag across the road. She had long grey hair, and for a moment Erika's heart quickened, thinking it was Elspeth Pitkin, but when the old lady turned she saw she was much older, with the compressed mouth of someone with no teeth.

'Jeez that was close,' said Moss.

The old lady reached the pavement on the other side, and stepped up. For a moment Erika saw Joseph, hanging in his cell, the noose tight around his neck. His face waxy and swollen. There was a honk from behind.

'You okay?'

Erika nodded. They pulled into the car park of the Brockley Jack. At just after 10 a.m. it was empty, apart from a couple of cars.

It was quiet and warm inside the pub, apart from an old man seated at the bar, watching the TV with a pint on the go. A large young girl sat tucked away in a corner booth. She waved, and they went over.

'Hi. I'm Sharon-Louise, but you can call me Sharon,' she said, getting up and shaking hands with them. She had long, sleek honey-blonde hair with streaks of pink, and wore a wraparound dress with a flower pattern. Her face was round and wide, and she wore a pair of large glasses with thick lenses. She had an orange juice on the table.

'You alright for a drink?' asked Moss.

'Yeah. I could murder some crisps… I don't mean… Oh shit, not murder.'

'It's okay,' said Moss. 'What flavour?'

'Tomato sauce or prawn cocktail,' she said. Erika asked for a juice and Moss went off.

'I didn't sleep last night, after hearing about Marissa.' Sharon took out a tissue and lifted up her glasses, dabbing delicately at her eyes.

Erika took the chair opposite. Moss returned a few minutes later with orange juices and crisps, and took the seat next to Sharon.

'Who told you about Marissa?' asked Erika.

'My mum got a phone call from someone she knows on Coniston Road… It's bad enough that I had to say goodbye to her, but I thought I'd see her again one day…'

She broke down, pulling out a scruffy ball of used tissue, lifting her glasses again to dab at her eyes.

'Sorry. It's just too much to believe… And look, everything is going on as normal. The Christmas decorations are still up, happy music is playing. Makes you think that no one cares… But that's life.'

'Why did you have to say goodbye to Marissa?'

Sharon reached forward and tore open the packet of crisps, spreading it out between them so they could share.

'She was going off to America.'

Erika and Moss exchanged a glance.

'When?'

'Tomorrow, it was supposed to be.' Her eyes welled up again and she pulled out the tissue.

'Where in America?' asked Moss.

'New York.'

'Why?'

'She was sick of it here. The weather. The way things work. "I'll always be scum," she used to say. She thought the odds stacked against her, not going to the right school or having money. She

had dreams of being the next Dita Von Teese, and the burlesque scene in New York is huge. There's more opportunity in America. Hard work can actually get you somewhere over there. She wanted a new start.'

'Did she have a work permit?' asked Erika.

'No, she got a six-month tourist visa. Obviously, she was planning to work there, but gigs are often cash in hand. And she had Ivan.'

'Ivan Stowalski?'

Sharon nodded.

'What was Ivan going to do?'

'He was going with her. He works in pharmaceuticals, and he'd got a job out there.'

'This is the same Ivan Stowalski who's married and lives in Coniston Road?' asked Moss.

'Their marriage was over years ago. Ezra was living a separate life from him.'

'Did Ezra know?'

'He'd managed to keep a lot of it from her, according to Marissa. He's a bit wet. Spineless. I don't know how he holds down such a well-paid job managing loads of people, because in his personal life he's hopeless. They drove up north, late on Christmas Eve, to see Ezra's parents who now live in the UK. According to Marissa, he was going to tell Ezra when he was there, and then drive back… Well, today.'

Erika frowned.

'I know. Fucked up, isn't it?'

'How long was Marissa involved with Ivan?'

'A year. He'd been paying for lots of stuff for her: costumes, props. A lot of money. He got quite obsessed with her, and was needy.'

'How was he needy and obsessed?' asked Erika.

'He got very jealous about her doing her act. He always wanted to know if any blokes had spoken to her after the shows, and he would go and see her often, and sit on the front row, policing her show… Marissa was going to bin him, and then he told her about the New York thing and she saw it as an opportunity. He paid for everything.'

'What did her mother think?' asked Erika.

'Mandy. I don't know if Marissa even told her. They really don't get on. Didn't. Mandy's a mess. She's never had a proper job, and when Marissa was little she was always shacking up with random guys, getting drunk and doing drugs. Marissa had a pretty horrible childhood. She was taken into care twice, when she was ten and then twelve.'

'Why did Marissa stay living with her as an adult?'

Sharon shrugged.

'It's complicated. They had a bond. And they both claimed all the benefits they could. Mandy claims attendance allowance, disabled; Marissa was paid as her carer, and was signing on and getting housing and council tax…' Sharon furrowed her brow. 'Shit. I've just put Mandy in it.'

Erika waved it away.

'We're not investigating benefit fraud. How did they manage that, though? Living under the same roof, mother and daughter?'

'Marissa has her father's surname. Her mum is Mandy Trent.'

'Yes. Where is Marissa's father?'

'Long gone, when she was little. He was a builder working on something in the local area.' Sharon's eyes started to well up and she pulled out the tissue. 'I'm going to miss her so much.'

She had eaten all the crisps, and now was reduced to picking up the crumbs. Moss went to fetch more drinks and crisps, and Erika waited until she was back for Sharon to compose herself.

'What do you know about Joseph Pitkin?' asked Erika.

Sharon shook her head dismissively. 'He's had life handed to him on a plate, and he's just a waste of space.'

'Why?'

'His parents are minted. They sent him to the best schools and he was expelled. He could be anything, and he chooses to be a creepy little loser. He was obsessed with her, showing up at her gigs.' Sharon shook her head distastefully. 'Skinny little runt, with a weird mother complex. His mum comes in for a haircut every now and again. Her hair is always filthy and she smells of B.O. She's not the type of person we like to encourage, but she's a good tipper.'

'Did Marissa ever ask him to take photos of her?'

'What kind of photos?'

'He was an amateur photographer.'

'Was he now? By that, I take it his parents bought him all the gear. She never mentioned him doing that… Hang on, what do you mean, "was"?'

Erika told her, without going into too much detail.

'Bloody hell,' Sharon said, shoving more crisps in her mouth. 'I'm not surprised. They were a weird family, and he always seemed like a messed-up kid. Rumour is that Elspeth breastfed him until he was nine. Marissa used to joke that the only person his mother wanted him to lose his virginity to was her.'

Moss creased her forehead. 'The boy killed himself.'

'I know. Very sad, but what? You want me to lie and pretend to be upset? I didn't like him.'

'What did he do to you?'

'Nothing, but he wouldn't leave Marissa alone. He was odd and creepy. She told me that a few times she came home late from a gig and he would be waiting to talk to her on her doorstep.'

'Did she ever report him?'

'No. I don't think she felt… like… threatened. I think he weighed less than she did, which wasn't much.'

Erika sat back and ran her hands through her hair. 'Okay. What do you know about Don Walpole?'

Sharon sighed. 'Is this all you want to talk about? The men in her life? This is the year 2017. People screw. She liked him. She had a thing for older guys. Marissa wouldn't shut up about his big cock, and how he knew how to use it…' She screwed up her face in disdain.

'Did Marissa sleep with other older men? Random men?'

'Yes. She had no qualms about going into detail. Guys she'd picked up on the train home. Classy. A couple of lads from the Fitzwilliam Estate. Don, Ivan. It was just sex. She only used men for sex. Her friendships were much deeper. I was her only true friend. I knew the real Marissa.'

'And what was the real Marissa?'

'Under all that armour, she was kind. We met at school. I was being bullied and she was the only one who would talk to me.'

'Did she stick up for you?' asked Moss.

'Yes, and she gave me tips on how to diet and she offered to give me a makeover, so I wouldn't get bullied. She encouraged me to train as a hairdresser. She also said she would come with me if I got laser eye surgery. You, know, hold my hand and then drive me home from the clinic.'

'Were you planning on getting it done?'

'Yes… Sometime. Although, who will I have to hold my hand now?'

They gave her a moment to compose herself.

'Was Ivan the only man she was serious about?'

'I told you she wasn't in love with him! He had money. He could take her places.'

'What about the old lady Marissa cared for?' asked Erika.

'Elsa Fryatt? That was another case of Marissa landing on her feet. Mrs Fryatt's son was getting funny about her living on her

own, she had a fall or something, and he wanted to pack her off into a home. The compromise was that she got a carer. She turned up her nose at all the official carers, you know, the ones who are screened and trained. Mrs Fryatt put up a note in the café on Brockley High Road, the arty one. She paid fifteen quid an hour! I think she found Marissa interesting. And Marissa would milk it for all it was worth. She got lunch, and they'd go out to garden centres. Mrs Fryatt even insured Marissa on her Porsche. Marissa was going to borrow it for my eye surgery.'

'How many hours a week did she work for Mrs Fryatt?'

'Ten, fifteen. It was a great job. Round the corner. The old girl paid cash.'

'It seems Marissa was quite a complex person,' said Erika. Sharon stared at her. 'Sorry I should frame that more as a question than an observation.'

'No. It's okay. I'm just trying to think of how to comment on that. I don't think she was complex. She had an effect on people around her. She wasn't, like, academic, but she was smart, and so beautiful.'

Sharon burst into tears again, and pulled out a tissue, which she clamped over her face to muffle the sobs. 'She… She pushed people's buttons,' she said, between sobs. 'But who would want to kill her? She was always honest about who she was. And for that I… I liked her very much. Can I see her body? I'm going to ask Mandy if I can be the one who styles her hair. I don't want them to make her look like an old lady at the funeral home…'

*

'Bloody hell. What do you make of all that?' asked Erika when she and Moss were back in the car. They watched as Sharon walked away from them down Crofton Park Road. She had a slow gait, and she was still clutching tissues to her face.

'She told us a lot,' said Erika. 'Do you think she told us everything?'

'I don't know. She didn't seem to hold back. Although, if Marissa used people, what was she using Sharon for?'

'A free haircut?'

Moss pulled a face. 'Really? London is full of great hairdressers, and you can easily get a trainee to practise on you. No, there's got to be something else.'

Erika's phone rang.

'Oh, this is McGorry,' she said, before answering. 'Yeah?' She listened for a moment, thanked him and hung up. 'Ivan Stowalski drove back to London late last night. Alone. Let's go and find out his side of the story.'

CHAPTER TWENTY-TWO

Ivan Stowalski's house was on the top end of Coniston Road, close to Crofton Park Road. It was sandwiched in the terrace between a house on the left, which was wrapped in plastic and undergoing renovation, and a house on the right, which was crumbling and in need of renovation.

There was no answer at the door, but the curtains were all closed. Erika rang again, and a bell echoed loudly through the house.

'The curtains weren't closed on Christmas Day. In the door-to-door it says that there is a tree in the front room,' said Erika. Moss peered through the letter box.

'Jesus,' she coughed. 'Smell this.'

Erika came to the letter box, put her nose to the gap, and recoiled, coughing.

'Shit. That's gas.'

They came back to the front gate and looked up at the house. All the windows were closed, and the curtains were drawn. It looked like the edges of the windows in one room were stuffed with blankets. She pulled out her radio, and called in the address for backup. Then she went back to the front door, leant down and shouted through the letter box.

'This is the police. Is anyone in there?' She coughed. 'It's really strong.'

'If the concentration of gas is that strong inside, the whole row of terraces could blow. And so many people are home,' said Moss, indicating the lights on in many of the surrounding windows.

Erika nodded. She charged the door, bouncing off it painfully the first time. On the second attempt, it cracked and swung inwards with a crash, and she landed on the carpet in the hallway. The strong smell of gas flooded out, and she covered her nose with her sleeve.

'We need to get the windows and doors open and find the source,' she said, coming back to the doorway to grab fresh air. Moss took a deep breath, covered her mouth and nose, and they rushed into the house. It was smartly furnished inside, but dark. The curtains were drawn in the living room. Erika pulled them open and saw that the double-glazed sash windows looked strong: they were made of thick wood and were all taped shut. At the bottom, along the sill, the windows were packed with blankets. Erika signalled to Moss, feeling her lungs starting to burst. They ran back out onto the front path. Their eyes were streaming and they gasped and coughed.

'We need… to get the windows and doors open inside,' said Erika. Moss nodded. They took deep breaths, then charged back inside, going back into the living room.

Erika picked up a heavy chair by a bookshelf, and Moss looked around the room, finding a pair of scissors on the desk under the window. Her eyes were streaming, and she wiped them with her sleeve, then holding the scissors like a dagger, she stabbed in the corner of one of the double-glazing panes. It took a couple of attempts but she pierced the glass. She then did the same with the other two panes. She stepped back and nodded to Erika, who charged at the windows with the legs of the chair. She bashed all three open. The glass exploded outwards, and fresh air began to flood in.

They came back out to the front path, to get some gulps of fresh air.

'Hey! You! What are you doing?' shouted an older man from across the road. He had glasses around his neck on a chain, and was holding a newspaper.

'Get back inside!' shouted Moss.

'Not until you tell me what you are doing!'

'Police, get back inside!' they both shouted.

'Kitchen, at the back,' said Erika. They took deep breaths and ran back inside, down the hallway, past the stairs, where the smell of gas intensified. A smart modern kitchen looked out over a garden. The oven door was open, and the gas hobs were all hissing. Moss turned everything off. There was a huge glass sliding door, but no key. Erika couldn't see any scissors, but there was a large stone doorstop. She picked it up and flung it at the glass. It bounced off and she had to jump back.

They were now both coughing and choking. Erika picked the doorstop up again and lobbed it at the glass. A sea of cracks burst outwards, almost frosting the glass, but it still didn't break. Erika's lungs were bursting and Moss had now fallen to her knees. On the third attempt, the doorstop smashed through the huge pane of glass. They staggered out to the snow-covered back garden and took more deep breaths, loving the cold, clean air.

'Upstairs; we need to check upstairs,' coughed Erika. They took deep breaths and dived back inside, through the kitchen, feeling that the gas was dispersing.

They heard the sound of a siren as a fire engine pulled up outside. The house upstairs had the same layout as Marissa's, with a bedroom front and back, and a bathroom on the opposite side to the staircase. The small back bedroom and bathroom doors were open. They got the windows open, then ran to the master bedroom door, which was locked. They could feel a breeze as the air was now being sucked out from downstairs,

and the toxic air was clearing. They heard feet on the stairs, and voices.

'Up here!' shouted Erika. Three firefighters appeared at the top of the landing. 'We need to get this door open.'

They took an axe to the door, and it splintered and then swung open. Gas flooded out, and the firefighters rushed in and got the curtains and windows open.

On the neatly made bed lay a tall, thin man. He was pale, with thin sandy hair. Erika recognised him as Ivan from the photos they had of him in the incident room. Two paramedics entered the bedroom, carrying medical gear. Erika and Moss stood back as they examined him.

'He's got a faint pulse,' said the female paramedic. Together with the male paramedic, she got him strapped to the stretcher they had brought with them, and once he was on it, they lifted him down to the floor.

'His name's Ivan Stowalski,' said Erika.

'Ivan, can you hear me?' asked the woman. She slapped his face, and he gave a low moan, his eyelids fluttering.

'His blood is flooded with carbon monoxide. Let's get an IV in and oxygenate him.' She opened the first aid box.

Erika then saw what was on the bed. She'd thought, at first, it was a brightly patterned bedspread, but now she saw it was covered with photos of Marissa Lewis, all printed off on paper. There were photos of her performing in her burlesque shows, several of her naked in bed, and wet in the shower. There were scores of snapshots taken of Marissa and Ivan in parks and at famous London landmarks, smiling into the camera. Amongst the pictures, were also a couple of her burlesque outfits, a black corset and a red silk bra.

Erika looked back at the paramedics, who had now hooked up an IV to Ivan's arm and were pumping in air through a large air bag and mask.

'What's that in his hand?' asked one of the firefighters. Erika reached over and gently took it from him.

'Underwear,' she said, seeing it was a small pair of red knickers with a gold embroidered diamond in one corner. 'They belong to Marissa. That's her branding.'

CHAPTER TWENTY-THREE

Ivan Stowalski was stabilised by the paramedics. He was breathing, but hadn't regained consciousness.

Erika and Moss watched from the pavement as the ambulance sped away to hospital.

'There goes another suspect, dying on us,' said Moss.

'He's not dead yet,' replied Erika.

The firefighters then moved through the house, checking the gas connections, and searched the attic. When they gave the all-clear, a forensics team arrived to go through the contents of the house.

Erika ducked under the police tape to join Moss, who was sitting in the car, drinking from a bottle of water.

'You okay?' she asked.

'Yeah. Bit of a sore throat.'

'Me too, and I smoke twenty a day.'

'They've taken Ivan Stowalski to University College Hospital. As soon as he gains consciousness, I've said we want to talk to him. We've got his car leaving the congestion zone and going northbound at 11.30 p.m. on Christmas Eve.'

'Is that late to go and see relations?'

'They would have arrived very late, if they were driving up north.'

'Four or five a.m. Why would you leave so late? We need to find out what time Marissa got back from her burlesque gig. If it was earlier, he could have had time.' Erika coughed, a little of

the residue still in her lungs, and she squinted up at the sky, at the bright grey cloud. Several neighbours were looking out of their windows or had come to their front doorsteps, including the man with the glasses who still had his newspaper clutched in his hand. Erika looked back at the mess of glass over the front garden of Ivan's house. Then she looked at Moss, who was downing more water.

'You okay to keep going?'

'You bet.'

'I want to talk to Don Walpole and Marissa's mother.'

Moss got out of the car, and they started up the street. Two doors down from Ivan's house, a large elderly black man with salt and pepper hair was smoking a cigarette.

'Did Ivan try to kill himself?' he asked. He spoke with a warm Jamaican accent, and wore large, billowing grey trousers and a thick orange fleece dotted with cigarette burns. He tilted his head back and squinted at Erika and Moss, as if they were about to do something unexpected. They stopped by his gate.

'We can't talk about a case,' said Erika.

'Bad business, that girl being murdered. I've been watching that Ivan make a fool of himself with that girl for a long time. She was always going to be out of his league. I saw him being stretchered out. Tried to kill himself, didn't he?' He came close and put his hand on Erika's shoulder, the tip of his cigarette glowing. 'You see that car there, opposite?' he said, pointing to a white Alfa Romeo with a huge dent in the bumper. The rear lights on the right-hand side were broken and the plastic littered the filthy snow below. Erika felt the man's hand grip her shoulder. The smell of his breath was a mixture of cough sweets and cigarettes. She delicately unhooked her shoulder and stepped away.

'Yes.'

'That's his car. He arrived back early this morning, drove straight into that car opposite, and crushed the front lights. Didn't

hang about, didn't knock on the door to get insurance details.' He put the cigarette back in his mouth and folded his arms across his chest.

'What time was this?' asked Moss.

'Seven o'clock this morning or thereabouts.'

'Why were you up?'

'I'm old,' he chuckled, with a stream of smoke. 'And my wife doesn't let me smoke in the house.'

'And you're sure it was Ivan Stowalski?'

'I don't know his second name, but I'm not blind! It was the Polish man.' Erika and Moss contemplated that for a moment. The man went on. 'He must have heard she died, the girl he was carrying on with.'

'How do you know he was having an affair with her?' asked Erika.

'You call yourself a detective? I know because I'm out here most of the day. I see a lot, although people don't take no notice of an old man… She used to come and go a lot from his house. After his wife had gone to work.'

'When?'

'Over the summer. Since the weather got cold she hasn't been there as much. Last time I saw her was Christmas Eve…' Abruptly, he walked back up the path and opened his front door.

'Hey!' started Erika, but he only reached inside and returned with an ashtray.

'My wife. She never puts it back out here after she's emptied it,' he said, balancing it on the gate post. He stubbed out the cigarette and lit another.

'What time did you see Marissa?'

'I saw her twice on Christmas Eve. Once in the afternoon. It was just getting dark, so just before four. She came out of Ivan's house with a face like thunder. He came out after her, pleading

with her to come back… Oh lordy, he looked pathetic, just in his jeans and T-shirt and no shoes. He got down on his knees, cried and begged, and the ground was covered in snow. That really brought it home, what a knockout she is. Do you know she was a stripper? A stripper with stuff up here,' he said, tapping his head. 'That's a real combination.'

'Did you know what they were arguing about?' asked Moss.

'No. She shouted at him, expletives, to go away and leave her alone. He followed her up the road like a dog, but she told him to keep away from her or she'd call the police.'

'She said that, "call the police"?' said Erika.

'I'm not deaf, woman. It's what I heard.'

'Did he come back to his house?'

'He did, a little while later, tail between his legs.'

'When did you see her for the second time?'

'About 10 p.m., she just walked past on the way to her house.'

'She was alone?'

'Yes.'

'Do you know if Ivan was home?'

The old man thought for a moment.

'The lights were on, I think.'

Erika and Moss chewed that over.

'Has anyone been to talk to you?' asked Erika.

'Like who?'

'The police. There was a door-to-door over Christmas, and I would have expected you to have told one of my officers this.'

The man raised his hand and shook a finger at Erika.

'Hold your horses, Juliet Bravo. I wasn't here at Christmas. We was with my daughter and grandkids – she lives in Brent Cross. We drove over early on Christmas morning.'

'What time?'

'We set off around seven. Terrible, the roads were.'

'Did you see anything else on Christmas morning?'

He shook his head.

'Okay. Thank you. Can I send one of my officers over to take all of this down officially?'

'If I'm here, I'm happy to.' He gave her a broad smile with yellow teeth.

They carried on walking up the road.

'So, she rowed with Ivan the day she was killed,' said Moss. 'He was home when she came back from her gig at 10 p.m.'

'The plot thickens,' said Erika.

CHAPTER TWENTY-FOUR

Don Walpole's house was a few doors further down, six doors up from Marissa's house. It was smart and nondescript. Erika realised just how many terraced houses there were in South London, and how they would all often blend into one. Back in her native Slovakia, there were very few, if any, terraces. Pre-fabricated blocks of flats were the equivalent, which were equally claustrophobic.

The Walpoles's front garden was open, with just a low wall and no hedge. The red hats of a couple of garden gnomes poked up out of the snow, and there wasn't a number on the house. Beside the door, on the brickwork, was a sign which said '*Summerdown*' in curly black iron writing. There was a television on in the living room.

Erika rang the bell, and a moment later the door was opened by a large woman in a grubby red fleece. She had bloodshot eyes.

'Yes?' she said, placing a hand on the wall to steady herself.

'Are you Jeanette Walpole?'

'Who's asking?' she said, tottering a little on her feet. Erika could tell she was drunk.

They introduced themselves and showed their warrant cards.

'Is your husband home?'

She threw back her head and shouted, 'Don! The police want to talk to you about your whore!'

There was a clattering on the stairs and Don appeared, wearing jeans and a polo neck jumper. He looked so much younger and more vital than his wife. He was handsome, in a geeky sort of way.

His wife took pleasure in his embarrassment. 'He's shitting himself, can you see?' She looked him up and down with a sneer. 'He hasn't got the balls to have killed that little bitch… He hasn't got much in the way of balls.' She reached out to grab his crotch, but Don caught her hand in his grip.

'That's enough, Jeanette,' he said.

'Ow! He's hurting me,' she whined. He let go instantly.

'I wasn't hurting her,' he said, apologetically.

'We'd like to talk to you, Mr Walpole,' said Erika. 'Maybe it would be better to meet you somewhere outside the house?'

'It's fine. Go through to the kitchen; I'll join you in a second.'

They walked through the hallway, which was immaculate, past the stairs to the kitchen at the back. It was comfortable, with an ageing wooden fitted kitchen. A television mounted on the wall was on low, showing an old black-and-white film, and there was a mug of coffee on the kitchen table. A copy of the *Guardian* was spread out and opened at the sports page.

There were no photos on the fridge, just a small magnet from Barcelona. In one corner was a flat-screen PC computer on a stand. Erika went over to it and moved the mouse. A screensaver appeared of Don and Jeanette in the gardens at some stately home. He had his arm awkwardly around her shoulders, but she was standing apart from him. Neither of them were smiling.

Beside the fridge were boxes of Pinot Grigio piled high. Moss went to the window overlooking the garden.

'Blimey, look at those empties,' she said. Erika moved to join her and saw them piled up and spilling over a small recycling box.

'You think that's a week's worth?' asked Erika.

'It's just over a week's worth,' said a voice. They turned and saw Don in the doorway. He gently closed the door. 'I managed to get her to lie down.' He said this in the tone of someone who has just managed to get a baby down for its afternoon nap. 'My

wife has had problems with alcohol for many years… But I take it that's not why you're here?'

'We're here about your relationship with Marissa Lewis,' said Erika.

Don nodded. He was a large, imposing man, very trim and fit with broad, muscular arms.

'Would you like coffee?'

'No, thank you.'

They sat down at the table and he cleared away the newspaper.

'We've heard that you and Marissa were involved in a relationship?' asked Erika.

'Lots of people knew about it. About six years ago, she knocked on the door asking if we needed any cleaning done. She was going around the street trying to get work. Her mother had just had her benefits stopped, and they were short of money. I gave her work, as I was aware that her mother drank. Jeanette was getting worse with the booze. I thought, at least I'm an adult with a job, and I can deal with it better. She was only just sixteen.'

'How did it start?' asked Moss.

'I don't know, just having her around. She started giving me looks and then one day, we ended up in bed when Jeanette was asleep.'

'How long did it go on for?'

'A couple of years. Jeanette found Marissa's hair in her brush one day, after she'd taken a shower here.'

'And what happened?'

'She went mad, threatened to divorce me. Slapped Marissa about, gave her a bloody nose. Marissa went home and then Mandy comes round, and there's a huge fight between her and Jeanette. Out in the street, shouting, screaming. My nose got broken and I lost a tooth trying to break them up…'

'And did it end then, you and Marissa?'

'Yeah,' he said, sitting back and folding his arms.

'You didn't see her again?'

'No. Well, I saw her, she only lived a few doors down, but I didn't have anything to do with her.'

'You didn't meet her or have sex with her again?' asked Moss.

'No. I told you. No.'

There was a pause. Erika pulled out her phone. She scrolled through and found a video and then placed the phone between them on the table. On the screen, the video from Joseph Pitkin's phone began to play. Marissa in her bedroom, the man who looked like Don coming into the room, looking around shiftily. They kissed by the front window. Marissa began to unbuckle his trousers.

'Stop, I don't need to see any more,' he said. He got up from the table and went to the window, looking out into the garden. Erika stopped the video and tucked the phone back in her pocket. 'Do you ever feel like, jeez, how did I end up here?'

Erika and Moss remained silent.

'I wanted to do so much. I trained with the under-fourteens squad at Millwall. They said I could have gone professional, and I thought I would, but I broke my leg in a car accident.'

'What does this have to do with you lying to us about seeing Marissa?' asked Erika.

'She was exciting. She was… sexy and… she made me feel alive.'

'She flattered you?'

He paused and nodded, wiping tears from his eyes. 'She wanted to hook up again, a few months ago.'

'This video is dated last September.'

He nodded. 'We had sex, as you've probably seen. It was great.'

'Did she initiate it, or you?'

'She did. She sent me a text message, out of the blue one night. Jeanette was out of it. She's been getting worse, drinking all day,

getting abusive and then throwing up everywhere. Her health is getting worse. It's like having a kid. I realised a few months ago, I'm pretty much her carer, and when I'm not at work, that's what I do. I take the shit, I cook and clean, I feed her, I clear up the sick. So, when this text message came from a beautiful young woman who wanted to screw my brains out, I went. I'm not ashamed of that.'

'Why was it only the one time?' asked Erika.

'She told me afterwards that when we first slept together she was fifteen…' He put his head in his hands.

'And let me guess, she was going to report you?'

He nodded. 'She told me that historical abuse cases get lots of press attention, and that she would be believed.'

'Did you abuse her?'

'NO! It was consensual, you have to believe me, and I thought she was sixteen. She was a woman. She had the body of a woman. I'm not into… I would never…' He started to sob now; big fat tears rolled down his cheeks. Erika took out a packet of tissues and passed him one. He took it and wiped at his face, embarrassed. 'She told me that she wanted five grand, or she would go to the police and report me.'

'Did you believe her?'

'Yeah.'

'How did you react?' asked Moss.

'She was clever about it. She asked me to meet her in central London, at a coffee place. It was busy and she told me how it was going to go down.'

'Did you give her the money?' asked Erika.

He nodded and rubbed at his face.

'I thought it would be a one-off but she blackmailed me for another five grand.'

'How did you give it to her?'

'Bank transfer.'

'Was she fifteen when you first had sex with her?'

'Is this on record…'

'Was she fifteen?' repeated Erika, raising her voice.

'Yes! Alright. YES! She was two days away from her sixteenth birthday. I didn't know at the time, she told me in September, but it was just two days!' he said, holding up two fingers. 'If it had been after the weekend, it would have been legal. How does that work? On Friday I'm a paedophile, but the following Monday I'm not? If I'm done for sex offences, do you know what they would do? I'd lose my job. We have a mortgage. My wife can't look after herself. You know what things are like right now. It would make headlines.'

Erika rubbed her face, and Moss shook her head.

'When did you last see Marissa, Don?' said Erika.

'Christmas Eve. At the train station.'

'What time?'

'Around 9.45 p.m. Jeanette saw her by the ticket machines and had a few words to say to her.'

'What did she say?'

'Nothing different to all the other times: "you bitch, you whore".'

'Does Jeanette know about the blackmail?'

'No.'

'And where were you for the rest of Christmas Eve?' asked Erika.

'I was here,' he said, looking up at her, staring her directly in the eye. 'Working.'

'What do you do?'

'I'm a graphic designer. I work from home.'

'Do you have a home office?' asked Moss.

'I use the kitchen table.'

'You don't use your spare room?'

He sighed. 'No. That's where I sleep.'

'And Jeanette?'

'She has the front bedroom. Is it necessary to ask these questions? I don't know what it's to do with?'

'Your wife is your alibi for Christmas Eve, but you sleep in separate bedrooms, and she is often drunk in the evenings,' said Erika.

'I didn't kill Marissa,' he said, his hands starting to shake.

'Why weren't you here for the door-to-door to answer questions on Christmas Day?'

'We drove over to see Jeanette's sister on Christmas morning; she lives in Greenwich and she cooked lunch. She can confirm this.'

'What time did you leave?'

'Around eight. We wanted to be there for when they opened presents. She's got kids and grandkids.'

'Do you have any kids?'

'No. We tried, but Jeanette couldn't. She carried two babies to full term, but they didn't make it… I wish people knew that when they saw her. There's a reason why she drinks. I suppose you're going to arrest me?'

'No. I would like to send an officer round to get all of this in an official statement. I also want you to provide us with a DNA sample. This is of course voluntary, but it will be taken into account if you decline.'

'Can I think about it?'

Erika and Moss exchanged a glance.

'You have twenty-four hours. I'd also like to search your house; I will apply for a warrant if needs be.'

'Search it. I don't have much dignity left. I'm honest about who I am. I don't have anything to hide.'

CHAPTER TWENTY-FIVE

'Jesus, Marissa had guts to tap him for money like that,' said Moss as they left Don Walpole's house.

'The police would have taken her accusation seriously,' said Erika. 'I'm also concerned that he doesn't want to give us a DNA sample.'

'What are you going to do about it?'

'We need to look into him a bit more. I don't see how it would serve anyone to prosecute him for having underage sex with Marissa, now she's dead, but we could use the threat of it for leverage if he doesn't agree to give us a DNA sample in connection with our murder enquiry. I also want to check in with Marissa's mother and see if she knew anything about America.'

Erika put in a quick call to Tania, the family liaison officer. 'Mandy is still over at the neighbour's house,' she said when she came off the phone.

They crossed the road diagonally, and went to Joan's front door. She answered the door wearing another brushed velvet tracksuit, this time in royal blue. She looked tired and harassed.

'We've come to check in with Mandy,' said Erika.

Joan made them remove their shoes, then took them through to the living room. Mandy sat in one of the high-backed armchairs, next to Tania, on the sofa. Tania muted the volume on the television, which was showing *This Morning*. There were cups on the vast polished coffee table, and a half-eaten packet of Mr Kipling's French Fancies. Mandy looked up at them from craggy eyes with dark circles underneath.

'Any news?' she asked hopefully.

'We're still working on things,' said Erika. 'Can we sit down with you?'

'Yes,' she said.

'Mandy wanted me to ask when she can arrange the funeral?' asked Tania.

'I can give you more news about that in the next day or so,' said Erika, taking the seat by the window. Moss perched on the sofa beside Tania. 'There are still things we need to do for Marissa.'

'What things?'

'We need to make sure we have all the information regarding cause of death – forensics. Your daughter's remains are being cared for.'

There was a long silence. Joan hovered in the doorway, anxiously.

'Are you finished with those teacups?' she said.

'Yes, thank you,' said Tania.

Joan started to stack the crockery onto the tray, and noticed a mark on the table. 'What's this?' she said accusingly. They all peered at a tiny drop of tea which had landed on the polished table. She scrubbed at it with her finger and then pulled out a tissue, tutting, 'It's a tea stain! This table has only just had a French polish!'

Mandy looked up at Joan.

'It wasn't me. I used a coaster!'

'Sorry, it must have been me,' said Tania. Joan took the tray and stomped off to the kitchen. Moments later, there was a crashing, as it was loaded up in the dishwasher.

'I think she's getting sick of me being here,' said Mandy in a low voice. 'But I can't face going back to the house. I keep seeing her lying out the front on her back. Her eyes wide open.'

'Tania. Would you go and help Joan out in the kitchen?' asked Erika, giving her a nod.

'Of course,' she said, giving Erika an amused look. She left, closing the door.

Mandy seemed to relax now that the angry sound of Joan crashing about in the kitchen was gone. 'She's a nice girl, that Tania,' said Mandy. She took her phone from the pocket of her hoodie. 'I keep looking at the pictures I have of Marissa. I'm worried I'll forget what she looks like.' She scrolled through and found a picture of Marissa, dressed up in full burlesque gear but standing in the dull confines of the kitchen, in front of the pedal bin and a cupboard door where the carpet sweeper was propped up.

'She was very beautiful,' said Moss.

'Yeah. I don't know where she got her looks from. Look at me. I'm no oil painting, and her father, well, he could have eaten an apple through a picket fence.' She laughed and then the laughter turned to tears. 'We'll never be a family again. We weren't much of one in the first place.'

'Mandy, there's something crucial to our investigation. It's the time when Marissa was attacked in the front garden. What time did you say you went to bed?'

'I dunno, what did I say? Just before ten?'

'Okay, well we've got two witnesses who saw Marissa get off the train at Brockley around quarter to ten, and another who saw her walk past his house on Coniston Road around 10 p.m.'

'Who?'

'Don Walpole and his wife Jeanette were on the same train; they saw her by the ticket machines at the station around 9.45, and a man at number 37 was outside having a cigarette when she went past around 10 p.m.'

Mandy half closed her eyes.

'He's not got the best eyesight.'

'This timing would fit with Marissa getting off the train; the station is less than ten minutes' walk away. If you were still

up around ten, or getting ready for bed, you may have heard something?'

Mandy went to say something, but was cut off by Joan, who bustled in with a cloth and polish, followed by Tania.

'Please, I'm trying to talk to Mandy,' snapped Erika.

'You need to get to water marks fast or they're a bugger to shift!'

'Joan, please can you do this later,' said Tania.

'This is my house! I can do whatever the bloody hell I like!' shouted Joan. Her lip curled up in anger, reminding Erika of a small, mealy-mouthed dog.

'Sorry, Joan,' said Mandy. 'I think I'm gonna to try and spend the night back over at my place. The officers only want a few minutes, then you can help me?'

Joan's mood changed and she became overly sympathetic.

'Oh, are you sure, dear? You can stay here as long as you like, it's really no trouble…'

'No. I'd best head home.'

'Maybe it's for the best. I'll pack your sponge bag for you,' said Joan, already half out of the living room and up the stairs. Tania left with her, closing the door.

'Mandy, I was asking you about Christmas Eve. Did you hear anything when Marissa arrived home?'

'Officers, you must know, I have a problem with alcohol,' Mandy said, rubbing her hands together in her lap. 'I was embarrassed to say before, but I had a blackout. I drank more than normal on Christmas Eve. It's the time of year, when it's cold and dark and… I can remember making myself some cheese on toast in the early evening, and then nothing until I woke up the next morning.'

'What time?'

'Early. I had to use the loo.'

'And did you sleep downstairs on the sofa?'

'Yeah.'

'You said before that you didn't...'

'I was in a blackout; I think it was downstairs. I just remember being up on the loo, then I heard the cat.'

'You have a cat?'

'Beaker. Well, he was a stray who hit us up for food. I was up on the loo when he was scratching at the door, so I went down, and that's when I found her.' Mandy put a large pudgy hand to her face as she started to cry. 'I'm sorry, officers, I really can't remember anything. I really can't.'

'Did you know that Marissa was planning to leave, and go and live in New York?'

'On her own?'

'No, with Ivan. He'd been asked to transfer there with work and he was going to take Marissa with him.'

'Instead of his wife?' asked Mandy.

'Yes.'

Erika and Moss watched as her face creased with confusion.

'She knew I needed her housekeeping money...' She scrubbed at the table with a stubby finger, her eyes filling with tears. 'That sounds about right. She was going to bugger off without telling me.' She wiped her face with the back of her hand. 'I know you shouldn't speak ill of the dead, but she was a selfish little bitch.'

'I'm sorry to have to tell you, but we want to keep you up to date with all the information,' said Erika.

'I still want you to catch who did it, mind. Marissa might have been a bitch, but she was my flesh and blood,' said Mandy, looking Erika straight in the eye, and fixing her with a cold stare.

CHAPTER TWENTY-SIX

Erika and Moss made their way over to Mrs Fryatt's house.

'Bloody hell. We've now spoken to three people who have completely different experiences of Marissa,' said Erika. 'Was she a different person to everyone in her life? Was she nice; was she a bitch? Was she honest; was she a liar? She gave plenty of people reason to want her dead.'

'You think Mandy did it?'

'I think everyone is a suspect. Although, there's no evidence to back it up. No trace evidence of Marissa's blood was found inside the house. Mandy would have had to get back inside, covered in blood, and clean herself off without leaving any trace evidence. And the house is in a state, she hadn't even done some hurried clean up. It looks like the place hasn't been cleaned in weeks.'

'And what's her motive? The weekly housekeeping she received from Marissa was a lot of money for her. With Marissa dead, that's stopped,' said Moss.

Mrs Fryatt lived on the opposite side of the large Crofton Park cemetery, on Newton Avenue, in Hilly Fields – near where Marsh lived. The houses on the avenue were large and grand and set back from the road, with huge front gardens. The avenue was close to Coniston Road, but at the same time another world away from the grubby, tightly packed terraced houses.

'She must be posh: she's got a boot scraper,' said Moss when they reached the front door, indicating the elaborate iron boot scraper embedded in the white marble step next to the front door. Erika pulled an iron handle, and a bell rang out deep in the house. A few minutes later, the door was opened by a tall, broad, older man with thinning, wispy black hair. He eyed them beadily. They showed their ID and introduced themselves.

'We understand that Elsa Fryatt, who lives here, was cared for by Marissa Lewis?' asked Erika.

'We heard the news,' he said, his beady gaze running over Erika and Moss. Sweat glistened on the top of his head. 'I'm Charles Fryatt, Elsa Fryatt's son.'

'Where did you hear the news?' asked Moss.

'Her mother phoned. Said she'd been brutally murdered, so she wouldn't be coming to work any more.'

He seemed old, in his late sixties.

'Could we talk to your mother?'

He stood to one side and invited them in. The hallway opened out to a grand staircase and double height ceiling.

'She's in the drawing room,' he said. They passed a large grandfather clock by the base of the staircase, under a huge crystal chandelier. Charles Fryatt had an odd loping gait, and a hunched-over neck. They passed the front room, which was dominated by bookshelves, and contained a huge Christmas tree, tastefully decorated with white lights. At the back of the house was a large sitting room, which looked over the snow-covered garden. This room looked more lived-in, with a big television, lots of armchairs and a coffee table littered with magazines and books. On the largest sofa sat an old lady. Erika had been expecting a wizened invalid, but instead, a small woman with a strong jaw and steely eyes sat bolt upright on the edge of the sofa. She was dressed in a woollen skirt and a tweed jacket, and her only concession to the

cold was a large pair of sheepskin-lined slippers. Her ash-blonde hair was short and fashionably styled. Her face, however, showed her years and was deeply lined.

'Good morning, officers, I'm Elsa Fryatt,' she said, standing and shaking their hands. 'The hearing aid picks up everything,' she added, indicating the two aids in her ears. She moved with fluidity, more so than her son. She also had a faint metallic crispness to her accent, which Erika couldn't quite put her finger on. Erika and Moss introduced themselves again and showed their warrants.

'Would you care for some coffee, and perhaps a mince pie?' Elsa asked. 'Charles, you know how to use the coffee machine?'

'Yes, of course.'

'Warm up the Marks and Spencer mince pies… And throw away the ones we bought at the Christmas Fayre.'

Charles nodded. Erika watched as he left the room and wondered if he was ill. He was sweating profusely.

'I much prefer the bought ones to home-made, don't you?' Elsa said.

'I'm happy with a mince pie, wherever it comes from,' said Moss. There was a fire burning in the grate. They sat down on the sofa opposite the old lady. She clasped her hands in her lap and fixed them with startlingly blue eyes.

'You've asked to speak to us regarding Marissa?' She tutted and shook her head. 'Terrible business. Who would do that, and to someone so young?' She put one of her gnarled hands to her mouth and shook her head, but stopped herself from breaking down in tears.

'Can I just confirm that Marissa was your carer?' asked Erika.

Mrs Fryatt waved the word away.

'She was more of a companion. She did my shopping, she would manage my diary. I trusted her to do the things that one wouldn't ask of a general domestic servant.'

'Can I ask… Do you have a large staff?'

She laughed. 'No, I make myself sound more glamorous than I am. I have a cleaner who comes in every day for a few hours; she also cooks me a meal. There is a gardener who doubles as a handy man. Charles is in a lot. Marissa was in charge of washing my clothes and helping me with shopping and all the other personal things.'

'How long did she work for you?'

'Just over a year. I had advertised in the local café, as well as on the internet – well, Charles, he did all that. I wanted someone who lived locally.'

'Were you aware that Marissa also worked as a burlesque dancer?' asked Erika.

'Of course. I went to see her perform on several occasions.'

'In the strip clubs?' asked Moss.

Mrs Fryatt turned her attention onto Moss, almost for the first time.

'Strip clubs!? I have never been to a *strip club*. I saw Marissa perform at the *Café de Paris* just off Leicester Square, and she had a regular weekly show in Soho – I forget the name of the club, but it was smaller, and much more fun… Stripping it was not. Burlesque is an art form, and she was very good at it…' She bit her lip and looked as if she was about to break down again. 'I'm sorry. She was just so vital. She made things so much fun here.'

'Can I ask how much Marissa earned in your employment?'

'I don't talk about money,' she said, turning up her nose at the thought. 'I paid her very well, and she worked three or four hours every day during the week.'

'Mrs Fryatt, I'm trying to place your accent,' said Erika.

'Are you now…'

Erika paused, and when Mrs Fryatt wasn't forthcoming, she went on, 'Can I ask where you're from?'

'I'm originally from Austria. How is that relevant?'

Erika looked surprised.

'It's not. I just detected something there. I'm from Slovakia.'

'Yes, I wondered about you, too, but you flatten your vowels. You say "ask" instead of "aaask".'

'I learnt English in Manchester, where I lived when I first came to the UK.'

'Oh dear,' Mrs Fryatt replied. She tipped her head to one side and gave Erika a chilly smile.

'So where did you learn your… charm… with the English language?' asked Erika icily.

'My family came to England when the war broke out; my father was a diplomat.'

Charles came loping back into the room with a large tray covered in an elegant china tea set: cups, saucers and a milk jug and sugar bowl, with another plate laden with warm mince pies. Mrs Fryatt eyed him as he struggled with where to put the tray, balancing it on his knee, but she didn't help him move the piles of books and magazines on the table. Then the cups and the cafetière of coffee started to slide. Luckily, Moss leapt up and took the tray from him.

'Christ! Put the tray down first, and then move things,' Mrs Fryatt snapped. 'Men are incapable of thinking more than one step ahead…'

Charles eyed her murderously, scooping up a pile of books and magazines to make space for the tray.

'Charles is an expert jeweller, with an encyclopaedic knowledge of gemstones, precious metals and antique jewellery, but he is hopeless at everyday tasks.'

Charles took the tray and set it down on the table.

'There we are, mother.' He sloped off out of the room and Mrs Fryatt sat forward and poured them coffee.

'He doesn't know what to do with himself when the shop is shut.'

'Shop?' asked Erika.

'He's a jeweller, in Hatton Garden,' she said, proudly. 'Married a lovely Jewish girl and they inherited the shop. Of course, he's become the linchpin. His knowledge is so broad. He's become accepted in that community, and it's tough, if you know what I mean.'

They sat back and sipped their coffee.

'Do you have any suspects?' Mrs Fryatt asked.

'We've found that Marissa lived quite a colourful life. Did she tell you much about her private life?'

'Not a great deal. I got the impression she was professional. She seemed to be getting lots of acclaim for her burlesque work, and she wanted to go places. I met a few of the girls she danced with. They seemed to have great camaraderie. I wasn't too impressed with this – what was her name? – dreadful, lumpen creature she was, with thick glasses. She had one of those situation comedy names…'

'Sharon,' said Moss.

'Yes. That was her. Marissa said she was a bit of a pain, always hanging around. She said this Sharon was constantly pestering her to be the "face" of the hairdresser's she runs on the high street…' Mrs Fryatt pulled a face.

'I take it you're not a client?' asked Erika.

'No, I am not. I go to Charles and Charles in Chelsea and it's worth every penny to travel that far.'

'So you didn't get the impression Marissa had any enemies?' asked Moss.

'Well, as much as I knew her. Don't forget, dear, she was… Well, I know it's not a fashionable way of putting it any more, but she was *the help*. I thought she was a lovely girl, but the chasm of our age difference and our social difference meant we weren't on

intimate terms. Well, I wasn't; she seemed to have no qualms in telling me all about her awful mother, however. Alcoholic, obese, and a nasty piece of work by all regards.'

Mrs Fryatt leant forward and offered them a top up, which Erika accepted.

'Marissa did recount something to me, which was upsetting… This was a few weeks ago. She was coming home from a gig, and left the train at Crofton Park station. It was late and rather dark. When she passed the cemetery, she was approached by a very tall man wearing a gas mask.'

Erika put her cup down.

'What?'

'Yes, she was walking back late from the station on her own – which was madness in my mind – and he appeared out from the cemetery, and pulled her into the shadows by the tall iron gates. Luckily, she fought him off and got free.'

Erika and Moss exchanged a glance.

'Did she tell the police?'

'I don't know. She was almost flippant about it, chalking it up as another crazy creep. But it seems more serious than that. I've seen the news reports. The man in a gas mask, attacking people late at night on their way home from the train stations. He attacked a woman and a young man a few weeks back, and then there was that poor woman on Christmas night. Have you any idea who it can be?'

Erika ignored the question. She thought back to the conversation that morning with the two officers at the station. The case suddenly moved from her peripheral vision, and it had her full attention.

'Do you know exactly when and where this was?' asked Erika.

'I don't know the exact date, perhaps early November. She told me she'd got the last train home, so the station was quiet. It was

after midnight. She walked home from Crofton Park station, and just by the entrance to the cemetery on Brockley Road a tall, dark figure appeared from nowhere. He was dressed all in black – a long black coat, black gloves – and he wore a gas mask. Terrifying, it was, she said. He tried to pull her into the cemetery.'

'Did he assault her?' asked Moss.

'Yes. He tried to, but she managed to escape. A car came along, and the headlights scared him off. She ran for it, all the way home. She was very, very lucky, but that was Marissa. I always thought she had a guardian angel,' said Mrs Fryatt. 'Well,' she added, her face clouding over. 'Until now.'

CHAPTER TWENTY-SEVEN

Erika and Moss grabbed some lunch on the way back to the station. It had been a morning of revelations: Sharon telling them that Marissa had planned to leave the country, Ivan's suicide attempt, Marissa blackmailing Don, and now Mrs Fryatt saying that Marissa was attacked by a man in a gas mask.

Along with all of these thoughts and questions running through her mind, Erika could feel a headache looming ominously at the back of her head. When they arrived back at Lewisham Row, they went down to the incident room. A large poster of Marissa Lewis in her burlesque gear had been added to the whiteboard. McGorry, Peterson and a couple of other male officers were grouped in front of it next to the desk.

'I really fancy some of that,' Peterson was saying.

'What's going on?' snapped Erika, feeling anger rise in her. Peterson went to speak, but she cut him off: 'I get that Marissa was a sexy burlesque dancer, but she's a murder victim. Do you all need to hang around photos of her dressed provocatively in her underwear?'

There was an awkward silence.

'The reason that's up there is because the poster shows the brand name on her costume, and the embroidery work which has been added,' said Peterson. 'You see the pink corset with the embroidered diamond?'

'Yes. I'm aware of that. Her stage name was Honey Diamond,' said Erika. The bright lights in the incident room had sharpened the dull thumping at the back of her head.

'We've been in touch with the shop where the costume was bought. It's called Stand Up and Tease, and based in Soho. I found out they also offer an alteration and embroidery service, and they've given us the name of the man who did this embroidery work on her costumes…'

'Okay, so why are you standing around making comments?'

'We're standing around because lunch just arrived,' said McGorry, indicating a box of Pret sandwiches on the table in front of the whiteboard.

'I was just saying I really fancy some of that cheese and pickle,' said Peterson. He stared at her. The other officers looked away, and Moss looked uncomfortable.

'Okay. Good work. I'd like a print-out of all the shows Marissa has been performing in over the past month. And send me the contact for this person who does the customisation of the costumes.'

'Of course,' said Peterson.

'Moss, can you fill everyone in on what happened this morning, and update the whiteboard?'

'Sure thing, Boss.'

Erika left the incident room. Moss reached over and grabbed a sandwich.

'What's up with her?' asked McGorry.

'It's been an eventful morning,' she said.

'No need to take it out on us,' said Peterson. Moss gave him a look and then she started to tell them what had happened.

*

Erika left the incident room feeling foolish. She saw how the other officers had looked at her while she ticked Peterson off. Did they know the two of them used to be together?

She stopped at the coffee machine, seeing it was now fixed, and grabbed herself an espresso. She thought of Peterson being

back, and how they would have to work together. He was a good officer, and a valuable part of the team, but if it was going to be like this, perhaps she would have to have him reassigned.

'You should never shit where you eat, stupid idiot,' she muttered as she waited for the machine to fill her cup. She took the stairs up to her office. Sitting at her desk, she booted her computer up and logged into Holmes. She input the phrase 'gas mask attack' and a list of results came up.

In the past three months, there had been four cases – two women and two men – assaulted by a large male wearing a gas mask. The assaults had all taken place around train stations late at night or early in the morning. The first victim was a twenty-year-old woman called Rachel Elder, who had been walking to Gipsy Hill station to work as a nurse at Lewisham Hospital. She was pulled into an alleyway, where a male exposed himself and then grabbed her by the throat. The attack went on for a long time, as she was asphyxiated to the point of passing out, then allowed to breathe for a moment, before being asphyxiated again. She reported passing out, and when she came back to consciousness the attacker was gone.

The second incident happened close to East Dulwich station. This time the victim was a Kelvin Price aged twenty-three – an actor who was appearing in a West End play. He'd been for drinks after work and got the last train home. Just after midnight he had been pulled into an alleyway close to the station by a man wearing a long flowing black coat and a gas mask with glass eye holes. Again, he had been asphyxiated to the point of unconsciousness several times. He said that the man had been masturbating, and had exposed himself.

'Oh my god,' said Erika as she read the words on the screen. The third attack happened to a Jenny Thorndike, close to Penge East station. She had been walking to get the train early one morning, when a person in black wearing a gas mask had 'appeared from nowhere'. She'd attempted to fight him off, but he'd punched her

in the face and pulled her into a small area of parkland close to the station, where she was badly beaten and asphyxiated.

The most recently reported case had occurred on Christmas Day in Sydenham. A woman in her late fifties called Diana Crow had been returning home from her friend's house, when she was grabbed in the railway underpass next to the train station. Again, she was asphyxiated and had been punched in the face, resulting in a fractured cheek. She hadn't, however, reported the incident until the following day.

'Marissa, you had a lucky escape, but why didn't you report it?' said Erika, taking a sip of her espresso. She found the name of the SIO on the gas mask attacker case, DCI Peter Farley, and sent him an email, asking for the case file, and informing him that they could have a crossover with their cases. Her inbox beeped with a new email:

Hi Erika, the Cyber Crime Unit recovered this deleted image file from Joseph Pitkin's phone.
KAY

Erika opened the attachment.

I have these photos and the video file locked away.
So long as you keep your mouth shut, they'll stay that way.
T.

'Jesus…' she said, sitting back. It was an eerie drawing, done with what looked like a black biro on yellowing paper.

There was a knock at her door, which made her jump.

'What?'

It was Peterson. He poked his head round the door.

'Is this a good time?'

'Why?'

'I just had Isaac Strong on the phone. He's completed the post-mortem on Marissa Lewis. Wants to know if you've got time to meet him?'

'Okay, thanks. I can call him back,' she said, rubbing her temples.

Peterson came into the office and closed the door.

'What the hell is that?' he asked.

'Another image recovered from Joseph Pitkin's phone. He'd deleted it, along with the pornographic photos and video.'

'A gas mask? You think it's this guy's signature, to send notes with a drawing?'

'I don't know. I just got the bloody thing. I need you to circulate this to the guys downstairs, get it up on the whiteboards. See if any of the other victims received anything like this, either through the post or via email. Also see if we can match this gas mask drawing with any of the e-fits from the victims.'

'Yes…' Peterson looked awkward. 'Can I have a word?'

'I've got one minute,' she said, picking up her coat off the back of the chair. 'Why?'

'I just need to talk to you about something.'

'Work-related?'

'Erm, well…'

'Can it wait? Can we catch up when I'm back?'

He nodded. Erika grabbed her phone and car keys and left.

Peterson came back down the stairs and met Moss at the coffee machine.

'That was quick. How did she take it?'

He shook his head.

'She went off to the morgue. I didn't get the chance to tell her.'

'James! You need to let her know.'

'I know I do. It's just bloody hard when we're in the middle of a case.'

'You need to grow a pair, and make time,' Moss said, sipping her coffee and heading back into the incident room.

CHAPTER TWENTY-EIGHT

The car park was busy when Erika arrived at Lewisham Hospital, and she had to wait to take a ticket before the barriers would let her enter. She got lost, twice taking a wrong turn, and she had to ask a hospital porter where the parking was for the morgue. Finally, she found it and parked the car next to a short, squat building, with a huge chimney pumping out black smoke into the grey sky.

She had to sign in at a front desk, then she passed a doorway to the hospital incinerator, before finding the morgue at the end of a long corridor, where Isaac buzzed her in.

'You found us,' he said.

'Yes, it's not as easy as it was in Penge…'

'And we have to pay for the privilege of coming to work.'

Isaac took her into the large post-mortem room, and she blinked at the bright lights. Six steel post-mortem tables lay in a row, with steel guttering.

'Keep your coat on if I were you,' he said. 'I've got a fleece on under my medical scrubs… Sorry that this has taken longer than I would have liked.'

Marissa's body lay on the first post-mortem table. She was covered to the neck with a white sheet. Isaac pulled it back. Her skin had a sallow yellow appearance. A long line of coarse stitches ran from her navel, spreading out in a Y shape between her breasts and across her sternum. Her body was washed clean of blood, and the repeated slashes across her throat made Erika think of fish gills. Her eyes moved down.

'She has a diamond tattoo just above her knicker line,' she said, pointing above the slim line of pubic hair. 'It's also embroidered on all of her clothes – the clothes she wore to perform.'

Isaac nodded. 'She had a small amount of alcohol in her blood when she died, but this should be expected if she was out partying on Christmas Eve. There were no other drugs, illegal or legal, in her bloodstream.'

Erika looked back at the scar running along Marissa's sternum, and then at her face, which, scrubbed of make-up, was so youthful. She didn't look much more than a child herself. Erika took a deep breath and felt her headache come hammering to the front of her skull. She felt strange, as if she was being pressed down and lifted up at the same time.

'She was healthy. All organs in good health.' Isaac moved to her head. 'The blade used was about eight inches. There are three long slits in the throat, one of which severed the main arteries. Which meant she bled out very quickly. The top of the knife had a serrated edge. Some older knives for paring fruit have this feature on the blade.'

'So it could have been a knife that someone has owned for some time?'

He nodded. 'We weren't able to lift any DNA samples from the body.'

'Nothing?'

'No. No bodily fluids, hair samples. She wasn't sexually assaulted.'

One of Isaac's colleagues came in and went to one of the large stainless steel doors along the back wall. She opened it with a click and the drawer slid smoothly out. Erika did a double take. It was the body of Joseph Pitkin.

'What is it?' asked Isaac.

'This young lad, he killed himself in custody on Boxing Day… May I?'

Isaac's colleague nodded and Erika and Isaac moved over to the body. Joseph seemed smaller in death, and his body was so thin. Angry red wheals surrounded his neck, and a deep purple line showed where the noose had cut into the skin under his chin, crushing his Adam's apple.

'I wanted to check his body again,' said the colleague, a small woman with soft grey eyes. 'I wanted to run something by you, Isaac.' He moved round and she lifted up Joseph's hands. 'He has this pigmentation on the skin, very white spots peppering the backs of his hands and moving up the wrists. I've been back over medical records and there is no mention of skin disorders such as vitiligo in the family.'

Isaac peered at it. 'Yes. I don't think this is disease-related. It looks to be chemical bleaching rather than natural pigmentation.'

'He was an amateur photographer, and he had a dark room,' said Erika.

'Right, that answers my question,' said the woman.

'Dark room chemicals used in processing photographs can often cause pigmentation of the skin, if gloves aren't used. Was there any scarring in the lungs?'

'No,' said the woman. 'Very healthy. Like his organs.'

The woman's words began to echo arounds Erika's head: *'Very healthy. Like his organs.'* She saw the drawing of the gas mask, and then the video of Joseph, the disembodied hand reaching into the shot and gripping his throat. His face turning red, then purple; the tendons on his neck straining… Erika saw the note again in her mind; the blank eyeholes of the gas mask bored into her head.

The dull pain intensified, and blazed through her skull. The room began to spin, and she had to grip the edge of the post-mortem table.

'Erika?' asked Isaac, as she felt the room start to fade out, and her vision fill with stars. Then everything went black.

CHAPTER TWENTY-NINE

When Erika opened her eyes, she was lying on a small sofa in an office. It was warm and filled with packing boxes. Isaac knelt beside her with a look of concern on his face.

'Here, drink some water,' he said. She took the cup from him and drank. It was deliciously cold, and it washed away the nasty dry taste in the back of her mouth. 'Can I take your blood pressure?' he asked, pulling out a blood pressure cuff. She nodded and he pulled up her sleeve, slipping it over her arm.

'What's in the boxes?' she asked.

'Books.'

She watched as he pumped the pressure cuff and it tightened around her arm.

'Did you eat today?'

'I had some lunch.'

He let it go, and placed the end of a stethoscope on her wrist and counted on his watch, listening as she felt her pulse beat through her arm. Then he released the pressure. 'Blood pressure is a little low: a hundred over sixty-five.' He pulled out a tiny torch and shone the light in her eyes. She winced.

'Since when do you have a little torch to do that? Surely all the patients you deal with can't dilate their eyes?'

'I got this in a Christmas cracker. I swapped a pink hair clip for it.'

Erika grinned. Her head was still banging, but the pain had eased a little.

'You were out for several minutes. Can I take some blood?'

'If you must,' she said. Isaac left the room, and returned moments later with a syringe and sample tube wrapped in sterile plastic. He pulled on a fresh pair of latex gloves. Erika turned away whilst he took the blood from her arm, grimacing at the pricking sensation.

'Okay, that's one sample,' he said, removing the little bottle and screwing another onto the end of the needle. 'Have you had any other fainting episodes lately?'

'No.'

'Been to see a doctor?'

'No… I was called out to a house, earlier today… A guy tried to top himself, turned on all the gas and sealed up the doors and windows…' She explained what had happened.

'You didn't hang around to get checked out by the paramedics?'

'No.'

'Jesus, Erika. You were exposed to high levels of natural gas. What have you drunk today?'

'An espresso.'

'You need to flush the toxins out; you should be drinking gallons of water.'

'Okay, okay.'

He went away and came back with a huge pint glass of water and a Mars bar. He watched as she took a drink and a bite of the chocolate.

'Finish what you were telling me about the post-mortem.'

'That was everything. Oh, there was something else. She had paraffin residue on the inside of her mouth. I can't work out why it would be there. I've only ever seen this with people who commit suicide, or truly desperate alcoholics who try to get a high in the strangest places.'

'She did fire-eating in her burlesque act,' said Erika.

'Ah,' said Isaac. 'Mystery solved.'

'I'm going tonight to The Matrix Club where Marissa worked. I want to talk to some of the girls who she performed with. You wouldn't want to come along?'

'That sounds like a very weird date,' he grinned. 'Sadly, I have to work.'

'Ah, okay.'

'Although you need to take it easy.'

'I'm going to chill at home for an hour, and get some food,' she said. She downed the last of the water and got up.

'I'll run your bloods through all the usual tests. Save you a trip to the doctor,' he said.

'Thanks.'

'I'm sorry about that lad, the one who killed himself in custody.'

'I am too,' she said.

Erika left the morgue and came out into the dark. The car park was busy, and there was a long queue waiting to leave at the barriers. She hunted around for her wallet in the folds of her coat and went to validate her parking ticket. As usual, she pushed down all her feelings about Joseph and Marissa and all the dead she had seen during her long career, brushing them under the carpet, just like she'd been doing for years.

CHAPTER THIRTY

Erika came back to her flat, took a shower, and ate a huge portion of fish and chips that she'd picked up on the way home in front of her laptop. Peterson sent over an email with the details of the tailor who had worked on Marissa's costumes, adding that he would be working that evening at the Matrix Club on Wardour Street in Soho.

Erika had just finished getting tastefully dressed up for an evening of burlesque, and was in front of the mirror, debating if she looked too severe, when the doorbell rang.

'Evening,' said Peterson when she opened the door. He was dressed in a fresh black suit with a navy-blue tie, and a long smart black winter coat.

'What are you doing here?' she asked.

'I'm coming with you, to the Matrix Club,' he smiled.

'Why didn't you call me? Or say in your email?'

'Because you'd probably have told me to piss off.'

'I would have said something more professional. As it was work-related.'

They both smiled.

'You look great,' he said.

'I don't look like an undercover copper trying to be glam?' she asked, looking down at the smart blue tailored trousers and white sleeveless blouse. She touched her hair, which was rock solid. She had blow-dried it, then doused it in hairspray, trying to copy what

they had done the last time she had been to the hairdresser's, but it had ended up a little severe.

'No. You don't,' he said.

'Good. And you look great; I mean, smart.'

'Thank you. Are you happy for me to come along? It is police business, and I did find you the info about this tailor who worked for Marissa.'

'Okay, I could use another pair of eyes.'

Despite the snow, Soho was buzzing, with people surging down Old Compton Street, making good use of the lull between Christmas and New Year. Snow fell lazily, and the white pavements were dappled with coloured light from the surrounding bars. Erika and Peterson joined the crowds walking up the centre of the road. They had talked about the case during the train journey from Forest Hill to Charing Cross. Erika told him about her visit to the morgue, where she'd seen Joseph Pitkin's body. She left out the bit about her collapsing. Peterson updated her on Ivan Stowalski, who was still in hospital, and hadn't regained consciousness. His wife had appeared at his bedside late afternoon.

'They still don't know if he has brain damage, from oxygen deprivation,' said Peterson. 'We also ran a background on Don Walpole. He extended his mortgage by eleven grand in the autumn, and sent ten grand to Marissa's bank account... He doesn't have a record, not even a parking ticket, poor bastard.'

'That doesn't mean he didn't kill her,' said Erika.

They hadn't had much of a chance to talk about anything other than work by the time they got off the train and walked up to Soho, through the crowds in Leicester Square. The Christmas decorations were magical, and Erika felt sad at the way things had turned out between herself and Peterson. She held a little hope

that they might be able to salvage their relationship, but she put it to the back of her mind.

The Matrix Club was on the corner of Wardour Street and Old Compton Street. The entrance was a small black door with a neon sign above. A small strip of the pavement was roped off, and a tall, thin black man stood at the door, behind a podium. He was dressed in a long, thick winter coat, wore bright blue eyeshadow and had a tiny pink fascinator stuck to the side of his shaved head.

'Two tickets, please,' said Erika as they approached him.

'What's the name?' he asked, giving them the once-over.

'Erika and James,' she said, looking back at Peterson. Somehow, saying their first names made it feel like a date.

'Your *full* names? I'm not just making conversation,' he said, rolling his eyes and pointing to a clipboard. His nails were painted bright pink.

'I didn't book,' said Erika, feeling stupid.

'Then sorry. You are the Weakest Link, goodbye.' He waved them away, and beckoned to another couple arriving behind them.

'Cheeky fucker,' said Peterson, getting out his warrant card.

'Shit. I wanted us to go in like Joe Public, without them knowing we're coppers.' She pulled out her warrant card, feeling inept. It wasn't like her to make mistakes. The couple who had been behind them were on the guest list, and the rope was unclipped for them with a flourish.

They went back to the podium. The guy on the door eyed Peterson.

'Have you got any Caribbean in you?'

'No.'

'Would you like some?'

Erika had to suppress a smile.

'I don't need this,' muttered Peterson.

'What do you need?' said the guy, suggestively leaning forward and feigning comedy desire. Erika stepped forward.

'I'm Detective Chief Inspector Erika Foster; this is my colleague, Detective Inspector James Peterson. This is an informal visit, but I would appreciate your cooperation. One of the women who worked here, died a few days ago. She worked as…'

'Honey Diamond,' finished the doorman. The bitchy veneer dropped away. 'Terrible tragedy. We're putting together a benefit show. Do you think someone here did it?'

'No, we'd like to speak to some of the people she worked with. I understand Martin Fisher works here?'

'Yes. He's the dresser.'

'He worked for Honey Diamond, Marissa. We'd like to talk to him, just to get some background.'

'Right, okay, follow me.'

He unclipped the rope and ushered them through the door. The club inside was beautiful, with black polished tables and chairs, dotted around a small stage with a red curtain. He took them to a table near the front.

'What's your name?' asked Erika.

'Mistress Ebony. By day, I'm Dwayne Morris,' he said, pulling out a chair for Erika and using a cigarette lighter to light the small candle on the table. 'It's table service, and feel free to vape.'

He went off and a waitress came and took their order. They stuck to orange juice and Coke.

The club soon filled up, and then the show began. Whilst there was no full nudity, Erika felt awkward being there with Peterson. The acts were women and men of all different shapes and sizes. Some did traditional striptease, but there was a stripping Adolf Hitler, a Star Wars stormtrooper, and then there was a woman who came on dressed as a suicide bomber. She slowly stripped off her clothes whilst a ticking noise got louder, to reveal wires and sticks

of dynamite covering her modesty. Then the lights went out, there was the sound of a huge explosion and when they came back up again, she wore a sheer body stocking, embroidered with dazzling red and gold sequins to represent flames and fire.

And that was the end of the show.

'Blimey,' said Peterson. 'The last show I saw was *Riverdance* with my mum before Christmas.'

'Yes, that was much more than an Irish jig,' said Erika.

Dwayne appeared through the members of the audience who were moving towards the bar.

'Martin wants to talk to you,' he said. They picked up their coats and followed him up to the stage and through the velvet curtain. It came out into a chaotic little backstage area filled with stacking chairs, racks of costumes, and old takeaway containers. The door to a small office was open, where a large middle-aged man with a balding head and glasses was working behind a sewing machine. There were racks of costumes along one wall and behind him was a desk with a phone and computer. A huge poster of the original Broadway production of *Mame* was up on the wall behind him, and the remaining wall was covered by a huge mirror.

'This is Detective Chief Inspector Erika Foster, and her colleague, Detective Inspector James Peterson,' said Dwayne, and he left, closing the door.

'Did you see the show?' Martin asked, pressing the pedal of the sewing machine and pushing a large panel of blue fabric past the needle.

'Yes,' said Erika.

'What did you think of the suicide bomber?'

'It was very clever.'

He gave a smirk and adjusted his glasses. He lifted the needle off the fabric and examined the seam. 'You want to know about Honey Diamond? AKA Marissa Lewis?'

'You did alterations for her, and you designed the diamond emblem she had sewn on her costumes?' asked Peterson.

'Yes. Although, she was always late paying… I'm not going to sugar-coat it. She was a little bitch. I'm very sorry that she's dead, but that doesn't change things for me.'

'Why didn't you like her?'

Martin put down the piece of fabric and gave them his full attention.

'She was devoid of grace, without warmth, with a hideous drive and ambition. She'd tread on anyone to get where she wanted to go.'

'Where did she want to go?' asked Erika.

'God knows, she just wanted to be famous. She wanted to be the next Dita Von Teese. What she didn't realise is that she also needed to work on her craft. Anyone can go off and be a Kardashian, or at least they can try. We had some American footballer, don't ask me who, come in last summer. She made no bones about trying to bed him; she even said she would try and make a sex tape with him.'

'Did she?' asked Erika.

'No. He went with one of the blonde girls, Jenna Minx, who has a little more class than Marissa. Although, that's not saying much.'

'How long had Marissa performed here?' asked Erika.

'Since January.' He picked up a pair of scissors and started to cut a bright yellow piece of fabric. 'To be fair to her, despite all her failings, she has real stage presence and she became one of the most popular dancers. Although there have been rumours that she's done more than dance for some of the punters.'

'Prostitution?'

He nodded. 'A few times, rich types have taken her out afterwards, and she's had no shame about saying what she did and how much she got for it.'

'She told you?'

'Yes, me, whoever else was in the room, and the kitchen sink.'

'Did she ever talk about neighbours, friends, any relationships close to home?'

'There's a drippy Polish guy, Ivan, who she's been bleeding dry for a long time. Poor bugger. Used to come often to see the show. Sat on the front row and kept his anorak on. All goggle-eyed, and crossing his legs over his erection. There was a girl here who had a boyfriend who works in TV, commissioning reality shows. Marissa went after him, but he wasn't interested. There was a fight between the two girls just moments before curtain up. I was frantically trying to mend their costumes during the show.'

'Did Marissa go into much detail about her relationship with Ivan?'

'She used to joke that she kept him in the cupboard… on account of how pale he was. And she'd often ring him up to ask for more money, or a new frock, and she'd put him on speakerphone, for us all to laugh at. Poor bastard.'

'Did Marissa ever say if he hit her, or if she was scared of him?' asked Peterson.

'No. Marissa wore the trousers. She was in control of him and his wallet.'

'Did Marissa ever talk about her other work?' asked Erika.

Martin pushed his glasses up his nose and snorted.

'Yes. She was multi-talented, it seems. She was also a carer. Although, to me that's a bit like King Herod getting a job in the antenatal unit… She stole from that old woman. Food and toiletries at first. The old woman…'

'Mrs Fryatt,' said Erika.

'Yes, she came here one night to watch Marissa as Honey Diamond. All dressed up like Joan Collins in furs and diamonds. That's when we realised why Marissa was her carer…'

'What did you mean, "at first", when you said Marissa was stealing from Mrs Fryatt?'

'Marissa stole a pair of diamond earrings from her.'

'When was this?' asked Peterson.

Martin put down the piece of material. 'Must have been a couple of weeks before Christmas. I thought it was bullshit, and that she'd concocted some story to make a pair of costume jewellery earrings into something more than they were – that was a very Marissa thing to do, she liked to lie – but she took one of the girls up to Hatton Garden, and had them valued. They were the real deal, worth ten grand.'

Erika glanced at Peterson. Mrs Fryatt hadn't said anything about a pair of earrings.

'Did Marissa mention anything about an attack?' asked Peterson.

Martin looked surprised. 'Marissa attacked someone?'

'No, she was attacked, about a month ago, on her way back from the train station where she lives. A man grabbed her.'

Martin shook his head. 'Not that I heard. And I used to hear everything about that girl's life, whether I wanted to or not.'

'You do understand that this is a murder investigation, and you aren't speaking about Marissa Lewis in favourable terms?' said Peterson.

'Do you want me to lie?'

'No,' said Erika.

'I know it's not right to speak ill of the dead, and no one deserves to be cut down on their own front step. Awful,' he said, taking off his glasses and crossing himself. He let them hang down over his large belly on a gold chain.

'Did you know she was planning to move to New York?'

'Yes. She talked about it.'

'No specifics?'

'No, but I did ask her how she would fund herself. It's not cheap, and there are visa costs and all sorts. She did say something

which stuck in my mind. She said the diamond would bring her good fortune and a new start in life.'

'The diamond on her costume?'

'No, she was thinking of changing that, and her burlesque name.'

'Was she going to sell the diamond earrings?' asked Peterson.

'I know she wasn't the brightest star in the firmament, but she knew the difference between singular and plural. She meant one diamond, and this was before the earrings appeared,' said Martin. 'She was either being cryptic, or talking shit. Sadly, with Marissa, it was often the latter.'

'Were you here when she did her last gig on Christmas Eve?'

'Yes. And she wore the diamond earrings on that night.'

'Can you be sure?' asked Peterson.

'Yes, 'cos she came in here stark naked, asking me to fix her suspender belt. I kept my eyes above her neck. I'm not too keen on the female anatomy,' he said, pursing his lips. 'Especially when it's shoved in my face with no warning.'

'Who is the woman Marissa took with her to the jeweller in Hatton Garden?' asked Peterson.

'She was performing tonight, I'll just give her a tinkle…' He pulled a phone out, removing one of the clip-on earrings he was wearing to make the call.

'Wench! Are you still here? The police want to talk to you… Nothing bad, just a couple of questions.'

A door outside creaked, and a small woman in jeans and a purple woollen jumper appeared at the door. Erika recognised her as the stripping stormtrooper.

'You wanted to see me?'

'Come in, Ella, don't skulk by the door jamb,' said Martin, putting his earring back on. 'This is Ella Bartlett.'

She smiled at Erika and ran an appraising glance over Peterson.

'You went with Marissa to have her earrings valued?' asked Erika.

'Yeah. The guy estimated they were worth ten and a half grand. He offered to buy them as they had *exceptional* purity, he said.'

'And Marissa didn't take him up on it?'

'Not when I was with her; she seemed pretty chuffed to have such a shit-hot pair of earrings. Like she didn't want to part with them.'

'When did you go with her?'

'A week or so ago.'

'Were you and Marissa good friends?'

'Not really. I was just as intrigued as everyone else to see if they were real, and I was going up that way to my gym, so I thought I'd go with her.'

'Can you remember which jeweller it was?'

'No. It was close to the Gym Box where I work out, the one in Farringdon, like, two roads away…' Erika looked at Peterson. That only slightly narrowed it down from the hundreds of jeweller's in Hatton Garden.

'Can I give you my number, and if you remember, let me know? It's very important,' said Erika, handing over her card. The girl nodded and was about to go.

'Ooh, Ella, that reminds me. I got you some Febreze for your stormtrooper helmet. I know it gets very hot in there,' said Martin, handing her a bottle. Ella looked at Peterson, embarrassed, and grabbed it from Martin. 'And you owe me five ninety-nine,' he shouted after her. 'Officer, are there any more questions? I've got to run up six G-strings from scratch and I can't miss the last train home.'

'Thank you,' said Erika.

CHAPTER THIRTY-ONE

'Oh my lord, this case,' said Erika, as she and Peterson walked back to Charing Cross station. They took the quieter back streets so they could talk over what they had discovered.

'And what is this diamond thing?' said Peterson.

'It was Marissa's trademark. Perhaps she thought that she, Honey Diamond, would be the one to make a fortune from her career. Dita Von Teese has made millions, and she wanted to be the next Dita Von Teese.'

'There just seems to be more and more layers of…'

'Intrigue? Deception?' asked Erika.

'Shit. The word is shit. This case is a quagmire. Everyone hated her.'

Erika nodded. 'Marissa had a big mouth and was indiscreet, but as far as I can tell, she only told Mrs Fryatt about being attacked by the guy in the gas mask.'

'Just because Marissa was a fantasist and not well-liked by people, doesn't mean she didn't have fears and secrets. So many people are too scared to report when they are attacked or assaulted. And the most confident people can often be bluffers, and feign confidence,' said Peterson.

Erika nodded. They had been so deep in discussion that they hadn't noticed where they were walking, and they emerged from a side street out into Regent Street. Sleet had started to fall.

'Do you fancy a coffee?' asked Peterson, seeing a Starbucks still open on the corner. 'At least until this sleet stops.'

'Okay.'

They waited for a couple of red buses and then crossed the street, hurrying out of the snow and into the brightly lit coffee house. Erika found a seat by the window and Peterson returned with two coffees. Erika could see the Christmas displays in the shop windows opposite, and the canopy of Christmas lights strung above Regent Street. They took a sip of the hot coffee and watched the busy street.

'So, we've got Joseph Pitkin, who stalked and photographed Marissa on several occasions and then filmed her, we think at her request, to blackmail Don Walpole?' started Erika.

'We have Ivan Stowalski, who was obsessed with her, willing to leave his wife at Christmas and go off with her to New York, and he tried to kill himself,' said Peterson.

'There's Don Walpole, who she slept with when she was fifteen, and then blackmailed him, saying he would go on the sex offenders register if he told… She also allegedly stole a pair of diamond earrings from Mrs Fryatt, but Mrs Fryatt didn't mention it, and she seemed sharp as a tack when we spoke to her.'

'Do you think her son knew about it? Isn't he a jeweller in Hatton Garden?' asked Peterson.

'Possibly… But Mrs Fryatt was the only person who Marissa told she was attacked,' said Erika.

'By a man in a gas mask, who it seems is somehow linked back to Joseph Pitkin. He topped himself because of those photos you showed him during the interview… Well, what I mean is that he was scared.'

'It pushed him over the edge,' she said, wearily. 'If only we had been able to recover the note with the drawing of the gas mask at the same time. I might have been able to get more out of him before he died… Or, stop him… I don't know.'

'You weren't to know,' said Peterson, putting a hand on her arm. She gave him a weak smile.

'And Mandy is being evasive about the night Marissa died. She must have heard something.'

'Isn't she an alcoholic?'

'Yes. She could have been blotto on the sofa as Marissa was stabbed on the other side of the window. What we need to do tomorrow is to work backwards and establish who has an alibi and who doesn't. I also want to pay Mrs Fryatt another visit, and ask her about those earrings.'

They took a sip of their coffees, and for a moment they were silent. Peterson shifted awkwardly on his stool.

'Erika, there's something I need to talk to you about…' he started. She pulled her phone out of her bag.

She checked her watch and saw it was almost eleven-thirty.

'Shit. I'm going to miss the last train, and I need to finish up writing a report tonight.'

Erika downed the rest of her coffee, and picked up her phone again.

'I'm going to get an Uber,' she said, swiping the screen. 'Ah, there's a car close by that can be here in one minute. Brill. Do you want to share?'

'Nah, I'm going to get the train,' he said.

'Do you think you'll make it?'

'Yeah. I fancy the walk. The Christmas lights are cool.'

Erika looked at him for a moment.

'Are you okay? What were you going to say before?'

'I don't know if there's time.'

Her phone pinged, and a car pulled up outside.

'No. That's my car. It was close.'

'It was nothing, you go on ahead.'

'Okay. Thanks for the coffee. I'll see you tomorrow, bright and early.' She grabbed her coat and swung it over her shoulder, and with a wave she was out of the door, dashing through the sleet to the car.

*

Peterson watched her get in and it drive away. He took another gulp of his coffee, and a text message came through on his phone. He took it out and quickly made a call.

'I know, I'm sorry. I thought I would be done by now… Yes, I did see her, but we ended up doing some work on a murder case… Yes, it's a twenty-four-hour job… No, I didn't tell her, but I will. I promise… I love you, too.'

He hung up the phone and stared out of the window for a moment. Guilt and regret flooded through him. Guilt that he was happy, and regret that Erika wouldn't be a part of it. He downed the last of his coffee, and started back towards Charing Cross station, walking under the canopy of Christmas lights and reflecting on how life can often take a turn and shock you. In a good way.

CHAPTER THIRTY-TWO

It was hot inside the Uber car as Erika sped through Piccadilly Circus. The driver looked at her in the rear-view mirror.

'You want a copy of the *Evening Standard*?' she asked. Erika said she did, and the driver passed it back.

She settled back and started to read, preferring to concentrate on gossip articles as she flicked through. They were just crossing the river at Vauxhall when Erika turned the page, and let out a loud, 'Fuck.'

'Everything okay?' asked the driver.

'Sorry. I just forgot something,' she lied. There was a huge single-page article about the previous case she'd worked on: the murders, and the kidnap of Marsh's twins by Max Kirkham and Nina Hargreaves. The newspaper had run several sensationalised articles about the case, focusing on Nina and Max as a modern-day Bonnie and Clyde, or Myra Hindley and Ian Brady. This article said that no one had claimed the body of Max Kirkham. The *Evening Standard* had contacted his mother, who said she didn't want to have anything to do with him, and was quoted saying, 'Take him to the landfill, he's no son of mine.' This was the same mother who was on bail for perverting the course of justice.

There was a picture of Erika at the bottom of the article. She was used to the papers portraying her as a trouble-making, scrappy senior police detective. What pissed her off now was that they'd used a photo of her coming out of the front entrance of her block of flats. The road sign, 'Manor Mount SE23' was

clear in the corner of the photo, and they hadn't pixelated her car number plate.

She pulled out her phone and searched through for a number. It rang a few times, and then a bleary voice answered.

'Hello?' said Colleen Scanlan, the Met's media liaison officer.

'Colleen, this is Erika Foster.'

'Erika. It's very late.'

'I've just seen a piece in the *Evening Standard* about the Max Kirkham and Nina Hargreaves case. They've printed a picture of me coming out of my house, next to the road sign, and you can see my number plate.'

There was a long pause.

'I can't control what they run in the press.'

Erika put her hand over the phone, and took several deep breaths. She loathed Colleen, who was, in her opinion, a lazy jobsworth who did just about enough to keep her job, but never wanted to go that extra mile to help.

'I know you can't do anything about the print edition, but what you can do, please, is check if the online edition has this picture, and if so, get it taken down. NOW.'

Colleen sighed. 'I doubt the office is open, but I can leave a word. I can do that for you,' she said stiffly.

'Thank you,' said Erika and she ended the call.

They rode the rest of the journey in silence. Erika kept checking her phone to see if Colleen had messaged or emailed, but there was nothing. Shortly before midnight, they approached Forest Hill, and the Uber dropped her outside her building.

When Erika got indoors, she flicked on the heating, took a shower and then came back into the living room in her pyjamas. She poured herself a large glass of vodka and settled down on the sofa with her laptop, opening the report she had started writing for Melanie. The floorboards upstairs creaked as Allison, her

neighbour, moved around. She clicked on Internet Explorer and opened the *Evening Standard* website. The same article was online with her photo.

'Shit,' she said. She got up and closed her curtains, suddenly feeling paranoid, knowing that information about her and where she lived was online. She told herself not to be ridiculous. It wasn't as if they had published her full address. She checked her emails, but there wasn't one from Colleen. She tried calling her again, but it went to voicemail. She took a large gulp of vodka, and started to work on the report.

Erika woke with a start. Her laptop was upended beside her on the sofa, and the phone was ringing. She turned to the clock in the kitchen. It was shortly before two in the morning. She sat up as the phone continued to ring. She put her laptop on the coffee table and heaved herself up, her first thought being that Colleen was ringing her back. Then the answerphone clicked in. After the recorded message, a breathless, ragged voice said:

'Erika…'

'Erika…'

'Erikaaaaa…'

She stopped in her tracks in the doorway to the hall. Her name faded out into a breath, and then there was a strange scratching sound. The message carried on, with a discordant, ragged breathing.

'Erikaaaaaa… Erikaaaaaa…'

The voice was hoarse and deep, with a malevolent rumble. There was a distorted sound, a ragged wheeze and an almost inhuman retching which made her cry out with fear.

Erika grabbed at the answerphone machine cord and pulled it out of the wall. Then she did the same with the phone. She hurried to the front door and checked that it was locked, and then

worked through the flat, turning on all the lights and checking the windows were locked. She sat back on the sofa, shaking, and tried to control her breathing.

For the first time in her long career, she wished she had a gun.

CHAPTER THIRTY-THREE

Jason Bates's alarm woke him at six. Shortly afterwards, there was a soft knock on the door. It was one of the council carers, arriving to take over, so he could go to work.

'How's she been?' asked the kind woman with the lined face. In his bleary state, it took him a moment to remember which one she was… *Dawn*… Her name was Dawn.

'She had a good night,' he said. A good night for his mother meant that he had only been woken three times. Dawn took off her coat and warmed her hands over the radiator, as Jason busied himself making breakfast and getting ready for work.

The plastics factory was a fifteen-minute train journey away. It was still dark when he stepped out of the house. He looked back to where his mother had been put in her chair and wheeled to the window to watch him leave. He waved back at her, and she lifted a hand. The anger and frustration he felt towards her melted away. He wondered if her carers did this every morning, to remind him that she was a person. He could only see this from outside the house, looking in.

The streets were dark with a freezing fog, which made him feel like he was wading through wet sheets. The small coffee shop outside Gipsy Hill train station wasn't open at such an early hour, and he hurried past, through the open barriers, just making it onto the train as the doors closed. The one good thing about working further out of London was that the morning trains going in the opposite direction from the city were less crowded, even less so

between Christmas and New Year. The carriage was almost empty, and he sat in a window seat, the heater by his legs pumping out warm air. He slipped on his headphones and put on an audiobook, which he planned on listening to for the rest of the morning while he drove the forklift – just one headphone, the other ear would be free for safety.

He left the train at West Norwood. Again, he was the only one on the platform. It was a fifteen-minute walk to the warehouse, and there was a long industrial slip road leading up from the station, lined with derelict buildings and overgrown hedges. He put up his hood and trudged through the snow, his footsteps crunching through the silence. The streetlights couldn't penetrate the fog, creating a tunnel of light. The sky in the far distance was only just starting to turn from black to a dark blue. As he passed the gates to an old office block, a dark shape bulged out from the shadows, and a tall figure stepped into the light. It was dressed in a long black coat, and stretched over its head was the dark shiny hood of a gas mask. Vapour streamed out from the large breathing drum which hung down to its chest, and there was a line of small white squares on the breathing drum, which gave the impression of wide smiling teeth.

Jason stopped, and at first he didn't feel scared. It was so unexpected. He heard the clack of a train on the tracks as it sped past. The figure watched for a moment and then advanced towards him.

'Hey, hey!' he shouted as the figure steamed towards him, bearing down, then punched him hard in the face.

*

Jason came to a little while later. He could feel snow under his back. He could see the outline of the sky above, now a palette of light blues. His hands were fastened behind him, and he was lying painfully on his wrists. His legs were cold, and then he realised that he was naked from the waist down. There was something in

his mouth, material or cloth. He looked around, moaning, hearing the sound coming out in a feeble murmur. A train whooshed past on the tracks behind a high wall to his left, to his right was the main entrance of the vast decaying edifice of the office block. Rows and rows of broken windows stared down at him, and in a few, birds fluttered. He felt sick when he saw that in the doorway of the building, about five metres away, the figure in the gas mask was watching him. His coat was open and he was masturbating, his black gloved hand working quickly back and forth. Streams of vapour poured from the breathing drum of the mask.

It felt at once insane and terrifying. Jason could see a few shapes poking up out of the melting snow: a burnt-out car and some disused gas bottles. Suddenly, he heard voices on the slip road from the station, and he looked over to the tall hedges. The road was obscured.

People walking past. Commuters! he thought. He cried out, but it sounded nothing more than a muffled moan. The voices carried on past. The figure abruptly stopped, fastening his trousers, and started towards him. He picked up Jason's feet, and dragged him through the melting snow. Jason tried to kick, but felt stones and sharp pain as he was dragged up three steps, and onto the bare concrete of the doorway. There wasn't much space on the top step leading into the building. The figure stood directly over him, looking down through the blank eye holes. Then he knelt down.

Jason kicked out, and his foot connected with the gas mask, knocking it to the side. The man gave a muffled yell and fell back through the broken glass door. A shard of glass scraped across the side of his neck, and he tottered over, landing on his backside on the other side of the door. The gas mask almost came off, sliding up at a drunken angle to reveal his mouth and nose.

Jason panicked and stared. The figure's loss of control was somehow more terrifying. Jason scrambled to get up, but his

trousers were around his ankles, and his feet tangled. The figure slowly sat up and took off his glove, putting a hand to the scrape on the side of his neck, which was bleeding. He turned away and lifted the mask to inspect his hand. Apparently satisfied that it wasn't a deep cut, he pulled the mask back down and turned, pulling on his gloves again.

Then he walked towards Jason, and dragged him back to the top of the steps.

CHAPTER THIRTY-FOUR

Erika had switched on breakfast TV at six, after a sleepless night spent on the sofa. She prided herself on her stoicism, and even though the call had terrified her, she refused to let that terror overtake her. The sound of her neighbours stirring, and water running through the pipes, started to bring her back to normality. At seven-thirty she made coffee and took a shower, and then as it got light she opened the curtains and felt her fears fade with the pale blue dawn.

Just before she left the house, she plugged her phone back in and played back the message of the rasping voice. The person who'd called hadn't withheld their number. It was a mobile number which she didn't recognise, but which she made a note of. She wound up the cable and took the answering machine with her.

Once she was in her car, and driving amongst the busy morning traffic, she felt reality settle over her. There was still nothing from Colleen Scanlan, no voicemail or text on her phone.

She'd thought a lot about the case during her sleepless night, and the question about the diamond earrings kept coming back to her. Why hadn't Mrs Fryatt mentioned them? She checked the time and saw it was just past 8 a.m. She took a detour from her usual route, and went through Honor Oak Park and down to Hilly Fields. As she approached Mrs Fryatt's house, she peered through the window, and saw the old lady was rugged up against the cold, and waiting outside her house, leaning on a walking stick. When Erika pulled into the parking spot by the kerb, Mrs Fryatt started

waving her stick in the air, shouting, 'Go on, you can't park there, I am reserving this space!'

Erika wound down her window.

'Morning. Can I give you a lift anywhere?' she asked.

'I'm waiting for my son; he's taking me to the doctor's surgery. He said he'd be here…' She looked past Erika and up the empty street, leaning painfully on the stick.

'Is everything okay?'

'It's my leg. I've been waiting four days to see someone; you know what it's like trying to get an appointment… Where is he? I'm going to miss my appointment! Please, move your car.'

Her nose was dripping from the cold, and she juggled her stick to pull out a tissue and wipe it.

'I have some more questions,' said Erika.

'More? You asked me a plethora of questions yesterday.'

'Did Marissa steal a pair of diamond earrings from you?'

'No.'

Erika kept her eyes on Mrs Fryatt as she looked past her distractedly.

'Are you sure?'

'Of course I'm sure. I'm in perfect health, both physically and mentally.'

'Yes, you said that yesterday, but now you're off to the doctor's.'

'What is this? I've done nothing wrong. I will cooperate with you, but I don't like your tone.'

A car appeared at the top of the road, and Mrs Fryatt looked hopeful, until she saw it wasn't her son and it sped past.

'I spoke to a colleague of Marissa's; he did the alterations for her costumes. He said that Marissa was showing off a pair of diamond earrings, and she boasted that she took them from you.'

Mrs Fryatt turned to Erika. Her composure regained.

'Really? How strange. That's not true.'

'I don't know why he would make it up,' said Erika, searching the old lady's face, but she was still distracted by the top of the road.

'Well, if you don't know, how the heck should I? Did you find a pair of diamond earrings on Marissa's person, or in her house?'

'I can't share that with you.'

'That's a "no" then,' said Mrs Fryatt dismissively.

'Marissa went with another of the girls and had them valued in a jeweller's in Hatton Garden.'

'Ah, here he is! About bloody time!' she said, whirling her walking stick around her head. A sleek white car pulled up next to Erika's. 'Officer, is that all? I don't know what Marissa could have been talking about. She was probably winding this person up. She was like that.'

Mrs Fryatt's son, Charles, got out of the car and came up to the pavement.

'You're late!' she shouted. He looked flustered and he eyeballed Erika.

'The traffic was bad,' he said. 'Hello, Officer. Is everything okay?'

'Marissa never said anything to you about stealing a pair of your mother's earrings?' Erika asked him.

Mrs Fryatt rolled her eyes and started to make her way to the car. 'He wouldn't know. I'm the only one who opens my safe, and all my jewellery is accounted for! Now come on! I can't miss this appointment!'

Charles gave Erika an awkward smile. She noticed that he had a large sticking plaster on the side of his neck, and a little blood had soaked through.

'How did you cut yourself?'

'Shaving, the razor slipped… A symptom of not wanting to be late for my mother,' he said, giving her a smile. It was an odd smile, showing wide crooked teeth, but it didn't reach his eyes.

He hurried off to help his mother, who was now at the passenger door. Another car pulled up behind and honked its horn. Mrs Fryatt started to shake her stick at it.

'Can you wait for ONE MINUTE!' she cried. Charles helped her into the passenger seat and did up her belt. He nodded at Erika, the serious expression back on his face, and then he drove away.

There was something that wasn't quite right, but Erika couldn't put her finger on it.

'Well, I did ambush her,' she said. She took out her phone and dialled McGorry.

'Alright, Boss,' he said. 'I'll be there in a sec, I just got off the DLR at Lewisham.'

'It's okay. Just a question. You've been going over everything in Marissa Lewis's house, all her belongings. There weren't any diamond earrings?'

'Erm, there was jewellery… But I dunno. I don't know if I would know the difference between a real diamond and costume jewellery. I can look back over the photos taken by forensics. Do you remember seeing anything when we looked round her bedroom?'

'No. Can you have a look for me?'

'Sure.'

Erika came off the phone. She thought of all the people who could have taken the earrings. Joseph Pitkin touched Marissa's body before the police arrived… Mandy found her daughter's body. Could Ivan have taken them? When had been the last time Don Walpole saw her alive?

'He saw her on Christmas Eve, at the station!' she said triumphantly. She started the engine and did a U-turn, driving over to Coniston Road.

CHAPTER THIRTY-FIVE

Don Walpole opened his front door, and wasn't pleased to see Erika again.

'Is this a good time?' she asked. He was wearing an apron, and Erika could smell bacon frying, which made her stomach rumble.

'Does it matter if it is?' he said.

'I just need a few minutes of your time.'

He stood to one side and she came indoors. He took her through to the kitchen, and she saw Jeanette staggering down the stairs, wrapped in a huge purple towelling robe with a towel over her wet hair. She looked dreadful.

'Who's that?' Jeanette said, through half-closed eyes. Erika introduced herself, but Jeanette didn't seem to remember her from the day before. They carried on through to the kitchen.

'I need to ask you a question, about Marissa,' said Erika in a low voice. Don rushed back to the hob and quickly flipped the eggs over in the pan. He wore dark jeans and a thick brown knitted rollneck. Jeanette shuffled in, oblivious of Erika, and took a large bottle of orange juice from the fridge.

'Do you need me?' she asked.

'No. This is just…' started Erika, but Jeanette was already shuffling off out of the room.

'Do you want eggs?' asked Don.

'No!' she said. Erika watched as she shuffled down the hall and into the living room. She closed the door, and moments later the television came on. Don sighed and stood over the eggs, pushing

them around in the oil. Bread popped up in the toaster and he pulled it out, dropping it onto plates.

'Do you want her eggs? I'll only chuck them,' he said.

Erika hesitated. She was suddenly ravenous, but she stopped herself from accepting. 'No, thank you. I just came to ask you a couple of questions…'

'I try to get her to eat, but she gets most of her calories from alcohol. It's given her this huge belly, and these two tiny stick legs.'

'My mother was an alcoholic,' said Erika.

'Is she?'

'No, was. She died, a long time ago. She was never violent, but she was belligerent and she made life difficult.'

Don nodded. His eyes were sad and dark, and he had black circles under them. He started to butter the toast.

'What do you want to ask me?'

'You said you saw Marissa on Christmas Eve, at Brockley station?'

'Yeah. When Jeanette… had words with her, shall we say.'

'Do you remember if Marissa was wearing earrings? They would have stood out, they were real diamond earrings.'

Don scooped the eggs out of the pan and placed two on his toast.

'Real diamonds? Where would she get real diamond earrings from?'

'I can't go into details. Was she wearing earrings on Christmas Eve?'

'She had no shortage of admirers. I'm sure she was able to convince some poor mug to buy her expensive jewellery.'

'Don. Please, really think. What was she wearing when you saw her at the station? Break it down.'

'All I can remember is that she wore a long black coat.'

'What about her hair and make-up?'

'She was done up. Er, she had those false eyelashes on… I can't remember if she wore any earrings.'

'Can I ask Jeanette?'

'I doubt she'll remember.'

'It's important to my case.'

Don put the plate down on the table. Erika followed him into the living room. Jeanette was lying on the sofa. Her wet hair hung limply down, half over her face. She was watching morning TV, with the sound up high.

'Jeanette. She wants to talk to you,' said Don, raising his voice. He went back to the kitchen and left them alone.

Jeanette eyeballed Erika from behind her wet hair. 'What?'

'I need to ask you a question?'

'Go on then.'

'Can you turn down the TV?' Jeanette made a sulky show of muting it. 'Thank you. You and Don saw Marissa Lewis on Christmas Eve.'

'That whore,' she spat.

'Can you remember if she wore any jewellery?'

'I couldn't see her tits – for once – she had a thick coat buttoned up over her cleavage. But she was wearing earrings.'

'What kind?'

She shrugged. 'White gemstones, little studs.'

'Are you sure?'

'Completely sure,' she said, her eyes not leaving the TV.

'How can you be so sure?' asked Erika.

Jeanette turned to her. 'Cos I was thinking about ripping them out of her ears, and how much it would hurt,' she said.

Erika wished she had a photo of the diamond earrings to show her.

'Would you say the earrings were real diamonds?'

'I doubt they were real.'

'But would you know real diamonds if you saw them?'

'Do I look like the kind of woman who knows real diamonds?' she said, bitterly.

Erika didn't need to answer. She looked around the room and noticed a long black coat spread over a clothes airer. It was in front of the lit gas fire, and steaming lightly.

'Is that Don's coat?'

'Who else's coat did you think it was?'

'Has he been out today?'

'I dunno. Probably went to get milk. Are you done with your questions?'

'Yes. Thank you.'

Jeanette unmuted the TV, and the sound boomed out again.

When Erika left the house, she sat in her car for a few minutes, trying to organise the facts of the case. She drove back up the road and came to a stop outside Marissa's house. The front garden was covered in a fresh layer of melting snow. There were two alleyways, one running alongside the house and one on the opposite side of the road. There was also a junction, just past the school, at the end of the road, which led off to a railway bridge, and a housing estate.

The killer had used a car, according to the blood spatter analysis. Whoever did it would have been covered in blood, and carrying a dripping murder weapon, which left blood up the path and onto the pavement, but it stopped there. Erika inched her car up to the alleyway, and very slowly she turned it in and looked at the bonnet. The alleyway was too narrow for it to fit down.

Her phone rang, making her jump. It was McGorry.

'Boss, you need to get to the station fast, we've had a major breakthrough,' he said.

CHAPTER THIRTY-SIX

Erika parked outside the station, grabbed her bag and the answering machine and hurried down to the incident room. Moss, Peterson, Kay and the rest of the team were gathered around McGorry's desk.

'What is it?' asked Erika, seeing the excited faces looking at her.

'I've been working on all the statements with regard to Marissa Lewis's death, and I've been putting together a timeline of the events on Christmas Eve,' said McGorry. 'She was working at the Matrix Club until eight-thirty. They had an early Christmas Eve show. She had a very quick drink after the show, and then headed off for home. She took the 9.10 p.m. train from Charing Cross…' He maximised a window on his computer monitor. 'Here she is, running for the train, and just making it before the doors close.' He played the short clip of Marissa Lewis running along in towering heels, her long coat flowing behind her. 'She was alone when she got on the train.'

'Okay,' said Erika. 'Does all this have a point?'

'Oh yes,' said McGorry with a grin. Peterson grinned and nodded too.

'Well, get on with it!'

'I also got footage from the train, when she changed at London Bridge. It's a newer carriage and equipped with CCTV.' They saw a crowded train carriage from the viewpoint of a camera mounted in the ceiling above the doors, looking down the carriage. 'There she is, crushed in beside these two guys. Gay, I'm guessing, as they don't seem to be paying any attention to her.'

'Okay, okay, less of the personal comments.'

'I'm just saying that there are no creeps who seem to be interested in her,' he clarified, as he ran through the footage on the screen, showing the ten-minute train journey. 'Okay, here we are at 9.42 p.m., and the carriage empties out at Brockley.'

'Is there any footage from TFL of the station?' asked Erika.

'No. Nothing apart from the platform, and Marissa getting off with the rest of the crowds,' he said, moving to another short clip.

'Okay, what else do you have for me?'

'This is the best. The school opposite Marissa Lewis's house on Coniston Road has CCTV on two sides of the playground. One of them shows a view of Marissa Lewis's front gate.'

The last video showed half of Marissa's house, from the gate past the alleyway, and a portion of the street leading up to the junction.

'What's the time stamp on this?' asked Erika.

'This video is from 9.40 p.m.'

He scrolled through the black and white video, showing the empty snow-covered street, and the gate.

'What's that?' asked Erika, when there was a flash of black at 9.51 p.m.

'A cat jumping up on the gate,' said McGorry.

'Marissa had a cat,' said Kay. 'Beaker, its name is.'

'Did you interview it?' asked one of the uniformed officers.

'Piss off,' said Kay.

'Quiet!' said Erika.

'Here we go,' said McGorry. A figure in black, wearing a gas mask, walked into shot by the gate, moving carefully and purposefully along in the snow, almost staggering against the slippery surface. It reached the gate and looked up at the house. Then it carried on walking past the house, and stepped into the shadows of the alleyway.

'Jesus,' said Erika.

'Okay, we run this forward for seven minutes,' said McGorry, as the time stamp on the video whirred past. 'There, you can just see Marissa Lewis arriving home.'

Marissa appeared at the gate. The room fell silent. Most of them had already seen the video, but the impact of it was just as striking the second time. Marissa opened the gate and went through, vanishing in the shadows of the front garden. Ten seconds later, the figure in the gas mask moved out of the shadows and approached the gate, carrying a long knife. It moved quickly through the front gate and was swallowed up by the darkness.

'The camera doesn't pick up anything that happened in the front garden,' said McGorry. 'Four minutes later, he comes back out.'

'Are you sure there's nothing?' asked Erika.

'I've watched it several times, slowed down. There's nothing; the camera doesn't pick up anything.'

He moved the video forward, as the figure came out, carrying the dripping knife. It stopped in the gate and looked back into the shadows.

'He wipes it with a cloth, conveniently taken from his pocket. He stashes the knife in the pocket with the cloth, and then immediately turns to his right, leaving the shot.' The team around Erika was silent. 'I've lost him after that; there's no CCTV in the residential area. He could have got in a car out of shot, or gone into a house; we don't know.'

'Run it back again,' said Erika. She paused the video where the man in the gas mask emerged from the gate, and for a moment there was a clear view of the mask. She got up and went over to her desk, where she had a copy of the note sent to Joseph Pitkin. She held it up against the screen, looking at the hand-drawn gas mask in black biro ink.

'Does this look like a similar kind of gas mask?' she said.

'I don't know, it's perhaps an old military gas mask,' said McGorry.

'We need to go back over the e-fit images given by the people who were attacked. And if there aren't any, we need to go back and get them to work with an e-fit artist. Also, now we have this CCTV with the date and time stamp we could concentrate on a new door-to-door in the houses overlooking Marissa's, in case anyone saw anything. This is great work.'

'I was working with Kay,' he said, grinning at her. One of the phones started ringing in the background and Moss hurried over to answer it.

'This is good work, both of you.'

'Boss,' said Moss, holding her hand over her phone. 'There's been another attack by the man in the gas mask, in West Norwood, early this morning. A young lad on his way to work.'

CHAPTER THIRTY-SEVEN

Jason Bates had been taken by police to the SARC, the Sexual Assault Referral Centre in Camberwell. Erika drove alone to the centre, and arrived there late afternoon. It was a small, nondescript building off the main road. Erika was met by a big burly police officer with a thick beard at an unmarked door at the side of the building.

'Have you managed to take any evidence?' asked Erika.

'Yes, he's already been examined; we've taken swabs and samples.'

'Did you manage to get anything workable?'

'Blood.'

Erika nodded; she couldn't let her enthusiasm show.

'Can I talk to him?'

'The SIO of this case is with him now; he's been through a terrible ordeal. He's deeply traumatised.'

'I know, but the murder case I'm working on has just crossed over with this.'

He nodded. 'Wait here a moment, please.'

Erika took a seat on a small bench in the long corridor. The officer went through a door marked 'Initial Room', which was a forensically safe examination room: a sterile space with wipe-clean plastic surfaces so that there could be no possible contamination of evidence.

Erika looked around the corridor. There were pictures of a sunny meadow and of a few sacks of brightly coloured oriental spices that had been hung in an attempt to dilute the clinical

atmosphere. The door opened and the police officer emerged with DCI Peter Farley, a middle-aged man with greying hair. Erika showed her warrant card.

'Hi, Erika, good to meet you,' he said. She followed him into the small room, which again had been unsuccessfully disguised with posters and pot plants.

A nurse sat with a young lad who had a blanket wrapped around his shoulders. His bare feet poked out of the bottom of a long paper gown. There was an untouched cup of tea beside him. He was slight, with strawberry-blond hair and pale eyebrows. His left eye bloomed with red where a blood vessel had burst. His lip was cut and his nose was crusted with blood. His eyes had black bruises. He shifted in his seat painfully.

'This is Erika; she's my colleague,' said Peter.

Jason stared ahead and nodded.

'What can you tell me about the person who did this?' asked Erika.

Jason swallowed with difficulty and winced. 'He was tall. I'm five nine. I think he was taller than me. He wore a gas mask.'

'Can you describe it?'

He did. He went on to describe what had happened, how the attacker's mask had almost come off his head and how he'd cut himself on the glass in the door frame.

'This is where we got the DNA blood swab,' said Peter.

Jason went on, 'He, he forced himself on… He…' A tear formed in his bloodshot eyes and ran down his cheek. Erika went to take his hand but he pulled it away. 'He put his, the mask, close to my face. I saw his eyes, they were dark and small, and the whites… I could really see the whites around his eyes. He then… He raped me.' He started to gag and retch and bent over and gripped his stomach. The nurse pulled out a tissue and gave it to him to wipe his mouth.

'We should stop there,' she said to Erika.

'No,' said Jason, wiping his mouth and scrunching the tissue up into a ball. 'I want to talk to her.'

The nurse nodded.

'Thank you, Jason. I can understand this is hard for you,' said Erika.

'You don't understand... The sick bastard put on a condom.' He wiped his eyes. 'He was well-built, strong.' He looked up at the ceiling and shook his head, not believing that this was happening.

Erika looked over at Peter. She wanted to know if they had been able to get any semen swabs, but he shook his head.

'Is there anything else? Anything, however small?' asked Erika.

'He was dressed all in black. A long winter jacket. He had on black boots, the mask. Thick leather gloves... When he took one of the gloves off, he touched me.'

'Where?'

'My throat. He touched my neck to feel my pulse...'

'What about the gas mask, how would you describe it?' asked Erika.

'It was a gas mask. I dunno, like the ones you see people wore in the war. There were these white squares on the breathing bit, the round bit where his breath was coming out...' Jason shook his head and scrunched up his eyes. 'It was only just getting light. But there was this smell, his breath when he got close. It was like a chemical smell, like industrial, or nail polish. I don't know.'

'It's okay. Thank you, Jason.'

*

When Erika came back outside, she put in a call to Moss, who was back in the incident room. She relayed the information, and that they had a DNA sample from blood on a piece of glass.

'I want a DNA sample taken from Don Walpole. Send an officer round with a DNA kit to get a mouth swab.'

'You checked out the Matrix club with Peterson last night. How did that go?' asked Moss.

Erika briefly outlined what had happened and that she'd gone to see Mrs Fryatt and Don about the earrings.

'I've just been checking over everything from forensics, and what the police recovered from Marissa Lewis's house, and there are no earrings. I also had Tania ask Mandy Trent, but she wasn't aware of Marissa having a hugely expensive pair of diamond earrings,' said Moss.

'Okay. Oh, if you check out my desk, there's my answering machine.'

'Okay, not sure I understand why you brought that to work?'

Erika explained what had happened with the *Evening Standard* and then the strange message late at night.

'There are more than enough weirdos in the world who probably have my number and want to give me a fright. Can you just run the number? It's from a mobile; I've left it on my desk.'

'Sure. One more thing, Boss. University College Hospital called. Ivan Stowalski is still unconscious. His wife, Ezra, arrived this morning and she's there with him.'

'Okay, I'm halfway there. I'll go over and see what I can get out of her. It will be interesting to hear her side of things. Keep me posted.'

CHAPTER THIRTY-EIGHT

Ezra Stowalski was a small woman with short fair hair, and a kind, careworn face. Ivan had been given a room on the top floor of the hospital, and when Erika arrived, a nurse was taking some blood from his arm. Erika waited until she was finished and then produced her warrant card and introduced herself.

'I'm so sorry for everything that's happened,' said Erika.

'Why didn't you leave him?' Ezra said, becoming angry. 'Why did you have to break the door down and save him?' She had a slight accent, but pronounced every word correctly.

'I'm trained to save lives.'

Ezra looked down at Ivan. His skin was grey, and he was hooked up to so many machines, tubes and wires. His chest rose and fell with a hiss of a ventilator. Ezra looked away from him and closed her eyes, her face registering pain.

'I didn't know anything. About him leaving with her. How stupid am I?'

'You're not stupid.'

'Are you trained to humour people, too?'

'I'm not usually very good at it. Something must be going wrong today.'

Ezra smiled.

'Did you know he was having an affair?'

'Yes.'

'How did things start?'

'She put a leaflet through the letter box, asking if anyone wanted any cleaning or ironing done. Her mother has never looked after her. I felt sorry for her. I thought it was admirable that she wanted to work her way out of her situation. I asked if she'd like to come and do some ironing…' She looked over at Ivan. 'I never thought that he would go for a young girl.'

'When was this?'

'A year ago, maybe more.'

'Did you confront them?'

'No. I was scared to, and I was happy he wasn't… that he didn't want anything from me. We'd been sleeping in separate bedrooms for some time. I just buried my head in the sand. Although, I never thought he would leave me, or plan to leave me so callously. The cheating I could deal with; it was the lies and the lack of respect for our life together that hurts me.'

'Why did you come back?'

'My wedding vows,' she said, looking back at him. Although, she didn't sound too convinced.

'What was your husband doing on Christmas Eve, after 8 p.m.?'

'He was upstairs in his office, going over paperwork. I was packing.'

'Why did you leave so late to drive up north to your parents? You left around 11 p.m.'

'How do you know what time we left?'

'We have your car on CCTV, at 11.30 p.m. leaving the congestion charge zone, and heading up north.'

'You think he killed her?' asked Ezra, her eyes wide. Erika didn't answer.

'Where was Ivan between 8 p.m. and 10.30 p.m.?'

'He told me he had to do some work.'

'On Christmas Eve?'

'His job, his work, it never stops. He's always having to work in the evenings and at weekends.'

'Where were you packing?'

'Upstairs in our bedroom.'

'And where does Ivan work, when he's at home?'

'In the kitchen.'

'Were you up and down the stairs as you were packing?' asked Erika.

'No. I finished what I had to do by nine. I stayed upstairs and watched TV in our bedroom.'

'Did you see Ivan working in the kitchen between 9 p.m. and 10.30 p.m.?'

'No. I just waited upstairs… I might have fallen asleep, I was dozing. That's around the time she was killed, isn't it?'

'Yes, we think so. Was there anything out of the ordinary about Ivan that night? And is there anything else you want to tell me. Was he a jealous type? Was he obsessive about who you were friends with, who you spoke to?'

'No. Not with me, anyway… I thought it was just a silly affair. I didn't know he was so serious about her. That he wanted a future with her. That he loved her. Perhaps he did kill her. It just goes to show, you don't really know the people who you share your life with.' She put out her hand and touched the blankets, pulling them up around Ivan's chin. 'He doesn't deserve to wake up. Is that bad, that I think that?' she said. Again, Erika didn't answer.

CHAPTER THIRTY-NINE

McGorry rang the bell of Don Walpole's house just after 5 p.m. He was flanked by two uniformed officers, one of whom carried a portable DNA kit. The road was quiet, and the snow was melting, leaving the road with a grey slush. He leaned up and rang the bell again, hearing it chime from inside the house. He stepped back and went to the window, peering through the curtain.

'No one in,' he said. The two officers shifted on their feet in the cold. McGorry took out his mobile phone and tried the number they had for Don. It went straight to the answer machine. McGorry noticed an old man standing at the end of his front path a few doors down, smoking, with an ashtray balanced on the gate post. McGorry came out of Don Walpole's front garden and approached him.

'Do you know the person who lives here?' he asked. The old man took a drag of his cigarette, his whispering lips making a small 'O', then he exhaled, nodding.

'That's Don and Jeanette.'

'Have you seen them today?'

'They left this afternoon, about an hour or so ago. In a hurry, they were.'

'How can you tell if someone is in a hurry? What do you mean?'

'They was moving fast… And have you seen Jeanette? She's a big woman. She don't move fast.'

'Did they say when they were coming back?'

'What do you think this is? People don't talk to each other. I saw them leave.'

'Did they drive?'

He nodded.

'Did they have any bags?'

'No.'

'Shit,' said McGorry. 'Thanks.'

As he went off, the old man lit up another cigarette, and McGorry overheard him mutter, 'Useless bloody police; takes three of them to knock on a door.'

CHAPTER FORTY

It was gone six when Erika left the hospital, and she realised, again, that she hadn't eaten or drunk anything all day. She walked to the Starbucks across the road, and joined a long line to grab a sandwich and a cappuccino. It was very busy, and she thought about taking it back to the car, but she felt so exhausted, and it was so cold outside. She just needed ten minutes to sit down and think about the case and all the new developments. Did Ivan have motive to kill Marissa? He certainly felt guilty enough to try and top himself.

The seats were all full, mostly with kids in their twenties sitting and chatting on their phones, or working away at their computers. At the back, she found a small table, with three big easy chairs dotted around it. A young couple in their teens occupied two of the chairs, and they were holding hands and leaning across to nuzzle and kiss. Shopping bags were piled up on the third chair.

'Excuse me,' said Erika. 'Can I sit here?'

The young guy was kissing the girl. He opened an eye to look at her, but carried on.

'Hey. I'm talking to you! Could you please move your bags,' said Erika, showing that her hands were full.

The couple broke apart and the girl said, in an infuriatingly ironic tone, 'Um, sorry, but we've got, like, a friend coming.' She turned back to kiss the young guy.

'When is your friend coming?'

'I don't know. Soon.'

'Well, until he does show up, can I please sit here?'

The girl sat back and her eyes widened in shock.

'Look, lady, I've just told you my friend is coming, okay? You're making me feel uncomfortable.'

Her condescending tone made something snap in Erika. She slammed her coffee cup and sandwich down on the table. She picked up the shopping bags and dropped them on the floor.

'Hey! That's so rude. And there's, like, expensive stuff in those bags. Can't you see they're from the Apple Shop!' said the guy.

Erika sat down, tore into the wrapping on her sandwich and took a bite.

'Excuse me,' said the girl, attracting the attention of a barista carrying a plastic tub filled with used coffee cups. 'This woman has just been rude and abusive and she's damaged my shopping. She threw my bags on the floor!'

The young male barista seemed to be taken in by the girl's doe-eyed stare, and he turned to Erika, who looked dishevelled in her coat and mucky shoes, cramming the sandwich into her mouth.

'I'm sorry, ma'am. If that's the case, I'm going to have to ask you to leave.'

Erika chewed her sandwich and looked up at the young barista, who was bearing down on her with a firm, condescending smile. She chewed the last mouthful and swallowed.

'No.'

'I'm sorry?'

'No. I'm not leaving.'

'He just, like, told you to leave,' said the girl indignantly. 'You do realise that coffee shops invite you to be in them until they say otherwise? It's, like, the law.' The boyfriend nodded solemnly.

Erika took another bite of her sandwich and then a sip of her coffee.

'Do I have to go and get my manager?' asked the barista.

Erika reached in her pocket and pulled out her warrant card. 'I'm Detective Chief Inspector Erika Foster. I suggest you go back to clearing cups. Have you seen what a mess it is in here? And you? You need to learn some bloody manners.'

'What? You can't talk to me like that!' said the girl.

'We can all talk to each other however we want. This is a democracy. Of course, as a police officer, I have the power to stop and search. I can detain you if it really takes my fancy. Now, you could've just given up the spare seat, but no, you're part of this entitled young generation who think you can do exactly what you want. You reap what you sow. You were rude to me, and in turn I could make life very difficult for you. Or you can all fuck off, let me sit in this chair for ten minutes, and leave me to eat my sandwich in peace.'

The young girl and guy got up and picked up their shopping bags, watched by the surrounding tables. The barista eyed her, but he seemed unsure if she was in the right as a police officer. He went off to the cash desk.

Erika ate the rest of her sandwich quickly, under the gaze of the other customers, then grabbed her coffee cup and left, before anyone in charge came to talk to her.

CHAPTER FORTY-ONE

Erika walked back to the NCP car park where she had left her car, her blood still pumping after the encounter in the coffee shop. She got in and put the heater on, rubbing her hands to warm up. The snow was whirling past outside the car park, and the warm air and the comfy seat made the tiredness wash over her even more. She sat back and closed her eyes.

It seemed like seconds later that her phone rang. She had fallen asleep, and was soaking with sweat under her coat. It was coming up to 8 p.m. She pulled out her phone and groggily answered.

'Boss, you okay?' asked Moss.

'Yeah,' she said clearing her throat.

'We just got a call from UCL. Ivan Stowalski died half an hour ago.'

'Shit… I was just there.'

'Do you think he was a viable suspect? From everything we've heard he was a bit wet, and was dominated by Marissa.'

'He was obsessed with her,' said Erika. 'And the quiet timid ones can flip out just as much as the hotheads.'

There was silence for a moment.

'You still there?' asked Moss.

'Yeah. It's just been a long day, and hearing one of our suspects has kicked the bucket is never good news.'

'Yeah, it's less satisfying when you have to prove the dead guy did it,' said Moss.

Erika wound down the window and let some fresh air inside the stuffy car.

'Okay. Thanks for letting me know. Let's catch up tomorrow.'

Erika hung up, and was still staring at the phone in her hand when it rang again.

'Hello, is this Erika Foster?' asked a woman's voice.

'Yeah. Who is this?'

'I'm calling from the NHS Health Centre at St. Thomas's Hospital. For data protection, can I just take your date of birth?'

Erika's head was still reeling from hearing that Ivan was dead. 'Hang on, what are you calling about?'

'I need your date of birth before I can talk any more about your medical records.'

'Fourteenth of August, 1972.'

'And your postcode?'

'SE23 3PZ.'

'Thank you. I'm calling with results of your blood tests. Dr Isaac Strong sent samples over yesterday, and asked us to contact you with the results…'

The tone of the nurse's voice induced a mild panic in Erika. She thought back to when she had last had any kind of blood test. There had been an incident when she was working on the Andrea Douglas-Brown murder case, when a young boy had bitten her. She'd had blood tests three months later, which were thankfully negative for anything untoward. She turned off the heater.

'Are you still there, Erika?'

'Yes.'

'You'll be pleased to hear that there's nothing nasty or untoward showing in your blood after you were exposed to the high levels of carbon monoxide. The tests all came back clear. However, the levels of oestrogen in your blood are very low. Can I ask if you are still having regular periods?'

Erika switched off the car engine and racked her brains to think when she'd had her last period.

'Six, eight weeks ago?'

'Right. Have you had sex in the last month?'

'No.'

'Okay. I'd recommend a check-up with your doctor. You may well be pre-menopausal, but all signs are showing that you may have started the menopause.'

'Menopause?'

'Yes,' said the nurse, with a kinder tone. 'You are in the age range. We would expect your oestrogen levels to drop as you advance into your forties. Have you had any other symptoms? Thinning hair, dryness of the skin and the vagina, hot flushes, night sweats, irregular changes in mood… You mentioned irregular periods?'

Erika put a hand to her head and opened the car door a little. Cold air came flooding in.

'Look, I'm at work. Can I call you back?'

'There's no cause for alarm, Erika. I just wanted to inform you of this; everything in your blood shows that you are perfectly healthy. Iron levels good. Unfortunately, the menopause comes to all of us.'

Erika thanked her and put the phone down. The shock of what she had heard hit her hard. She had spent so long working, and focusing on her career, and getting through each day, and now this was full stop, a dead end. Her body would no longer be able to give her children.

She started the engine and drove back to South London. She thought long and hard about her life, and about the evening she'd had with Peterson. She didn't want to have a child with him, but she'd felt happy with him, and despite the fact that their outing last night had been work-related, she'd enjoyed his company. She

tried to call him, but his phone rang out and went to voicemail. Then she tried the station and got Crane, who said that Peterson had headed home for the night. It suddenly felt imperative to Erika that she sort things out with him, to stop this strange limbo – to maybe even rekindle their relationship.

She knocked on Peterson's front door just before 9 p.m. He lived in a small block of flats in Ladywell, a little way from her flat in Forest Hill. A moment later, he opened the door. He was dressed in jeans and a T-shirt and was carrying a little mixed-race boy, who must have been about six or seven.

'Hello,' Erika said, looking confusedly between him and the little boy, who gave her a toothy grin. He was very cute, and wore Spiderman pyjamas.

'Erika, hi,' Peterson said. There was a look of shock on his face, but then his eyes narrowed in concern when he saw how pale and upset she was.

'Daddy, the bath will run over,' said the little boy. A blonde-haired woman in her late thirties appeared behind them.

'James, who is it?' the woman asked, eyeing Erika suspiciously.

'Why did he just call you "Daddy"?' asked Erika, holding on to the doorframe.

'Because he's my daddy,' said the little boy.

There was a horrible pause.

'Fran, can you just take Kyle and turn off the water in the bathroom?' said Peterson.

Fran glanced nervously at him, and took the little boy in her arms. 'Is this…?' she asked.

'"This"? What do you mean, "this"?' started Erika.

'Okay, okay, okay, let's talk about this outside,' said Peterson. He ushered her out into the corridor. Erika stared at him.

'You have a son?'

He nodded.

'How old is he?'

'He's five.'

'How? What?' She was lost for words.

'Erika. I only found out two weeks ago.'

'And that woman, that's his mother? Who is she?'

'Fran was my girlfriend; we broke up in 2012, a couple of months before the Olympics.'

'What have the fucking Olympics got to do with it?' she shouted.

'I'm saying that it was a long time ago! We broke up, and she went to work in Germany. She's a graphic designer, and she found out she was pregnant very late.'

'She didn't tell you?'

'No.'

'And now she's in your flat, and you're running baths for her kid? And you've brought me out into the fucking hallway to tell me!'

'Erika, I didn't know how you'd react.'

'This isn't helping!' she cried. She stared at him and her eyes began to fill with tears.

'I've been trying to tell you. I tried at work and then I tried to tell you the other night when I came over, and then we went out and it was for work, and then we had coffee, but you had to go.'

'You should have tried harder, you fucking wimp! And now I have to find out like this, just as I drop by your flat!'

'Who just drops by these days? What do you expect?'

'I called your phone, James.'

'What about my landline?'

'I don't know your landline number.'

'If you didn't bother to learn my bloody landline, that's not my problem.'

Erika slapped him around the face. They both froze. A door further along opened, and a little old lady's face peered through the gap where the chain was on.

'James, is everything alright?'

He turned to her. 'Yes, sorry, Doris, everything is fine. We're just…'

He heard the communal door close and saw Erika walking away towards her car. He ran outside after her.

'Erika!'

But she started the engine and drove away, swerving dangerously in the snow. He watched as her car vanished over the top of the hill. 'Shit,' he said, looking down at his bare feet in the snow.

CHAPTER FORTY-TWO

Isaac Strong loved to make bread. There was something deeply soothing about rolling up his sleeves and kneading dough. He loved his kitchen, tastefully decorated all in white: white cupboards, floor, walls, and surfaces. The absolute deal-breaker was the large white Butler sink, which had cost a fortune. He couldn't have dealt with any stainless steel; he saw enough of that at work. As he kneaded, he listened to *Gardeners' Question Time*, and to a very serious young woman who was having a terrible time with her indoor plants, which were suffering from mealybugs. He was listening to the radio through the BBC iPlayer app on his phone, and the programme abruptly cut out as his phone started to ring. He saw it was Erika and answered with his elbow, carrying on kneading.

'Are you home?' she asked. Her voice sounded bleary and odd.

'Yes, of course.'

'I'm outside.'

When he opened the door, he saw an Erika he had never seen before. Her eyes were red and streaming with tears. She looked broken. He didn't say anything, and reached out and gave her a hug. She came inside and they went through to the kitchen.

'Drink?' he asked, reaching for a bottle of whisky.

'Please.'

She sat down at the table.

'It's James Peterson. He has a son…'

'What?'

She launched into the story. Isaac listened, poured her another drink, and listened some more.

'I never thought we would have children together,' she finished. 'And I knew from him, and from the times I've met his mother that he wanted kids… But there was this selfish part of me that thought we might end up as this childless couple… You know, happy and content.'

Isaac raised an eyebrow. 'For someone as intelligent as you, Erika, that is the stupidest thing I've heard you say.'

She burst out laughing and wiped her eyes. 'When he opened the door, he looked so happy. He was a father. It suited him. And there's a little boy who now has a father. I could never take that away.'

'Nor should you.'

Erika nodded and took another sip of whisky. She grimaced. 'That's disgusting.'

'You didn't say that about the first two glasses. *That* is a twenty-five-year-old Chivas Regal.'

'It tastes like Benadryl.'

'You fancy a beer?'

'Yes, please.'

He went to the fridge and got her one and popped it open.

'Thanks,' she said, as he set it down in front of her. She took a long pull on it and wiped her mouth. 'Oh god, this is such a mess. I have to work with James. He must have told Moss, because she was asking if we'd managed to have a "chat" the other night. God knows how long she's known for? And what about everyone else on the team? Did they know, and I'm the only one, stomping about in the dark?'

'Come on, this is Moss, I don't think she would keep this from you out of malice. She's loyal. Straight down the line… What's Peterson's son called?'

'Kyle. He looked very sweet.'

'And the girlfriend, or mother?'

'I've forgotten her name...' Erika took another deep pull on the beer. 'She's pretty, and she looks sorted.'

'How does someone *look* sorted?'

'She had a pullover slung over her shoulders, catalogue style, and her hair was sleek and straightened.'

'What if she's a catalogue model?'

Erika looked at him.

'What if she was rehearsing for a job?'

'A catalogue bitch,' said Erika darkly, picking at the beer bottle label.

'Don't go down that road, Erika. You're better than that. And the name Catalogue Bitch will stick in your mind, and you'll end up calling her that at the wrong moment.'

Erika stared gloomily ahead and rubbed her eyes. 'You're right.'

Isaac went back to his dough and dumped it in the bin, then he started to wipe down the counter. 'How is the case going?'

'Impenetrable,' she said, draining the last of her beer. Isaac went to the fridge and got her another.

'You're not going to join me?' she said.

'I'm on antibiotics. I had a chest infection.'

'Two cases have merged. The murder case, and now another case concerning a man in a gas mask who attacks his victims close to public transport late at night, or early in the morning. I am clueless on both counts.' Her phone began to ring and she saw it was Crane. 'Sorry, I have to take this. Hello?'

'Boss, sorry to call so late. I got back the information about that number that called your house in the early hours of the morning. It's a pay-as-you-go mobile, registered to an Edward Foster? Is this someone you know?'

Erika felt her blood run cold.

'Oh my god, yes. That's my father-in-law.'

CHAPTER FORTY-THREE

Erika made some calls, and discovered that Edward had been admitted to the Manchester Royal Infirmary Hospital in the early hours of the morning. He'd had a fall, and had to have an emergency hip replacement operation. There had been complications, and he had been placed in intensive care.

It was late, but Isaac offered to drive her up from London to Manchester, reminding her she was far over the limit. He had thrown some things for himself into an overnight bag, but she didn't want to waste any more time driving back her to her flat, so they set off straight away.

The snow was falling steadily, and Erika was quiet in the car. When they reached the top of the M25 motorway, a huge sign appeared up ahead for 'THE NORTH'. As it passed above them on the dark motorway, she felt fear and trepidation. This would be the first time she'd returned to Manchester since Mark's death.

'What are we going to do when we reach the hospital?' asked Isaac, looking at the GPS on the dashboard.

'I'm going to ask to see Edward, of course.'

'The GPS is saying we'll get there just after three in the morning. They won't let you in to see him.'

'What do you think we should do?'

'Where does Edward live?' asked Isaac, flicking on the windscreen wipers.

'Slaithwaite; it's a small town in Yorkshire, about an hour from Manchester.'

Isaac tapped in the details and waited as the GPS recalculated the route.

'It's saying we can get to Slaithwaite a little earlier than we would get to Manchester…'

'Edward talked about snow in the village,' said Erika, peering out as the headlights lit up the whirling snow outside.

'Do you want to stay near the hospital in a hotel, then?'

Erika thought of how close Manchester Royal Infirmary was to the house she owned – the house she'd lived in with Mark, which was now rented out. It was less than three miles away. She hadn't been back there since the day Mark died. Friends of theirs still lived close by, people she hadn't seen since then. The windscreen wipers dragged rhythmically across the windscreen and the leather heated seats in Isaac's Jeep Cherokee made her feel sleepy.

'No, let's head for Slaithwaite,' she said.

Isaac switched on the radio very low, and a news reporter started to murmur. Erika thought of their house. She'd left that morning, the morning of the raid on the drug den in outer Manchester. A mass shoot-out had killed Mark and four other officers in her team – officers she had called friends. She'd known their wives. One of their wives had been a civilian support officer on the same team.

The news report on the radio moved to a story about fighting in the Middle East, and faint gunshots could be heard. Isaac reached over and changed to a music station.

Erika had been shot during the raid: a bullet had passed through her neck, narrowly missing major arteries. She'd been airlifted to hospital, and had spent two weeks recovering in intensive care, only emerging to attend Mark's funeral. She'd never gone back to their house. She'd arranged for a removal company to take out all their things and put them in storage.

It had shocked Erika, how easy it had been to pack up her former life. A few phone calls and a large chunk of cash had meant

that she had never had to deal with any of it. The house was now rented to people she had never met.

The car ploughed on through the snow, lulling her into an exhausted sleep.

It had been early when she'd left the house on the day of the drug raid – before seven – but it had been summer, and the sun had been streaming through the windows in the kitchen. She'd grabbed her phone off the kitchen table. There had been fruit in the bowl, an apple and a banana, and there had been two tickets on the kitchen counter for them to go and see a Woody Allen film that night: 'Magic in the Moonlight.'

Erika had had the opportunity to offload the case to another team, but she'd held onto it, like a dog with a bone. She had been tracking the drug dealer Jerome Goodman for the past two years, and she'd wanted to nail the bastard.

But where had that got her? She'd taken the risk and lost her husband, her four colleagues, and nearly lost her life. Although, the life she'd been left with wasn't anything to write home about. And to top it all, Jerome Goodman had vanished. He was still at large. Still out there.

In her fitful sleep, her thoughts moved to Edward. Why hadn't she been more vigilant? Why hadn't she spent more time with him, or made more of an effort to see him? Why didn't she know his mobile phone number? She saw him lying on the floor at the bottom of the stairs. A bone sticking out of his leg, pushing through the material of the old towelling pyjamas he wore… But in her dream, it was snowing inside… And behind the stairs there was no wall… She moved to help Edward, but he had changed. It was Marissa lying there, but there were no stairs, she was lying on the path outside the front of the house, half-covered in snow and frozen blood… Erika crouched down

and Marissa opened her eyes; blood started to pour from her mouth and she reached up to grab at Erika…

'Erika? Erika?'

Her eyes snapped open and the dark interior of the car came back. It was warm, and on the radio, 'Do They Know It's Christmas?' was playing. Isaac was looking over at her. 'You okay?'

'How long was I asleep?'

'A couple of minutes… You were shouting out names: Edward, Mark and Marissa.'

Erika rubbed her eyes.

'Just a dream,' she said.

'Do you want to stay at Edward's place? We'll get some sleep, and then go over to the hospital for visiting?'

'Yeah. Are you still okay to drive?' She peered outside, but there was darkness all around. Only the snow-covered motorway was visible.

Isaac nodded. 'We've got another couple of hours at least. Get some sleep, if you want.'

'No. Let's talk, about anything. Anything but work.'

CHAPTER FORTY-FOUR

Moss and her wife, Celia, were eating their breakfast in the kitchen early the next morning when Moss's phone rang. It was Erika, who started to explain that Edward had been in an accident, and that she would be taking a few days' leave.

'I'm up North,' said Erika. 'In Slaithwaite, the village where Edward lives. Isaac is with me.'

'Isaac Strong?' said Moss, swallowing a mouthful of cereal.

'Yeah…' Erika clearly didn't want to elaborate, so Moss didn't press her.

'Are you okay?' she asked.

'I'm fine.'

'What about Edward?'

'He fell and broke his hip. They've operated, but he's on a high-dependency ward.'

Moss and Celia's son, Jacob, came crashing into the room with his toy electric guitar. He skidded across the floor on his knees, the guitar blaring out a tinny squealing. Moss waved her free hand at Celia, who jumped up from the table and grabbed Jacob, switching the guitar off.

'Mummy's on the phone,' she whispered.

Jacob stopped and watched his other mother as her face creased, listening to the call.

'What's the snow like up there?' Moss asked.

'A foot or so,' said Erika, on the end of the phone. 'Luckily, the roads were cleared and we're in Isaac's four-wheel drive. I'm

going to be here for at least a couple of days. I've just phoned Superintendent Hudson and made her aware of the situation.'

'Okay, I can brief whoever covers for you…'

'I'd like you to cover for me. I've already discussed it with Melanie, and she's in agreement that you are acting Detective Chief Inspector and SIO on the case.'

For a second, Moss was lost for words. 'But… It's a complex case; we've got so many strands and now we're taking over the assaults from the gas mask attacker…'

'Don't you want to take over?'

'Yes! Of course I do,' she said quickly. Celia was watching her, dying to know what was going on, and what had made Moss's face flush with excitement. 'So this is for a few days?'

'It could be longer. I need some time to make sure that Edward's okay. My life seems a little unbalanced; it has been for some time.'

'Okay,' said Moss, the enormity of the case starting to dawn on her.

'This is now your investigation. I wouldn't trust anyone else to take this on. I'm here if you need me. Melanie is already working on giving you clearance as a DCI. You do know that overtime doesn't exist for my rank. We're always on duty.'

'Sure,' said Moss, looking over at Celia and Jacob.

'Phone me if you need anything,' said Erika, and then she was gone.

'What is it? You look like someone just died!' said Celia. Then, seeing Moss's serious face: 'Did someone die?'

'No. Erika's had a family emergency, her father-in-law is sick. She's promoted me to acting DCI on this case.' Moss sat down heavily. She pushed her bowl of cereal away, no longer hungry.

'But that's great, babe – not the father-in-law part, but that she trusts you,' said Celia.

'Yeah, that's really great, babe,' said Jacob, imitating her voice. Moss grabbed his feet and gave them a good tickle. He screamed and squirmed.

'Stop the tickles; you know I detest the tickles!'

'He *detests* the tickles. Good vocabulary for a five-year-old,' said Celia, with a knowing smile. 'I hope they're paying you more?' She put Jacob down.

'Of course… There's so much to sort out. I'll have to do the briefing this morning. Perhaps I should get everyone on the team a coffee.'

'You'll be great. Everyone likes you,' said Celia, gripping Moss's shoulder and giving her a kiss. 'Just don't become as obsessed as Erika.'

'She's not obsessed; she's bloody good at her job. And it's not about being liked. I now have to lead everyone.'

'I think the two things go hand-in-hand. Be yourself. How's Peterson doing? I take it she didn't put him in charge because of their history. Has he told her yet, about his long-lost son?'

Moss shrugged. 'I don't know. I told him to do it fast, but he chickened out.'

'Do you think it's a bit weird that this woman phones him suddenly, just before Christmas, and announces that he has a son?'

'Yes.'

'What do you think her motivation was?' asked Celia.

'She wanted him to be part of Kyle's life… Maybe she wanted some security. He told me she's been living in Germany, and she was made redundant.'

'But she actively withheld the information from him for six years.'

'He almost died earlier this year. And he's wanted kids for so long.'

'Do you think she wanted kids? Erika?' asked Celia, smoothing a strand of her long blonde hair behind her ear and starting to clear away the breakfast things.

'She probably still wants them.'

'I don't mean to be horrible, but hasn't that boat sailed for her?'

'I don't know, and I don't like talking about this.'

'What? She's not here.'

'It feels disloyal. She's a private person, and a good friend.'

'I know that, but you can talk to me. It's not going to go any further.'

Moss leant in and gave her a kiss. From the corner of her eye, she saw Jacob staring up at them.

'We have a little spy,' she said. 'It seems that he needs another good tickling.'

Jacob shrieked in delight and ran away as Moss and Celia chased him around the kitchen table and into the living room, where they collapsed on the sofa and tickled him until he shrieked again.

*

When Erika came off the phone with Moss, she looked around at the gloom in Edward's upstairs bedroom. It was just getting light outside, and through the window, the view of the snowy hills was just appearing in the blue haze of dawn. The room was a shocking mess, with filthy sheets on the bed. A cracked sash window was letting in freezing gusts of air. The floor was filthy with dirt, and there were tablets scattered over the carpet beside the bed. The power was also off. She came back out onto the landing, where Isaac was just coming out of the bathroom.

'It's a complete mess,' he said. 'Damp up the walls, black mould, and it hasn't been cleaned in a long time.' He held up a clear plastic bag filled with prescription pills. 'He's got a whole medicine cabinet filled with old antibiotics, heart pills, blood thinners, statins, and there are antidepressants. It looks like he's not been finishing the course, or not taking them regularly, because there are several half-full bottles, all repeat prescriptions.'

Erika pulled her coat around her and tried to block out the musty smell. The cottage had always been so warm and cosy. What had happened?

They had arrived late, in the darkness. They had managed to get the wood-burning stove lit, and took a sofa each for a restless night's sleep.

'The heating is gas-powered,' said Erika. 'I need to find out if the bill hasn't been paid, or if it's the boiler.' They came down the small flight of stairs to the living room. It was a little cleaner here, but there were still dirty dishes over the coffee table. There was a small Christmas tree in the living room, but it was only half-decorated. They went through to the kitchen and found that the sink was overflowing with dirty dishes, and the counter littered with crumbs and scraps of food. The fridge was almost empty, with half a mouldering white loaf, and some blackening carrots in the salad drawer. They jumped as a cockroach crawled out from underneath an upturned saucepan on the draining board and scuttled along the counter.

'Christ almighty!' Erika cried, grabbing an old newspaper and whacking the cockroach. They both stared at the squashed body.

'If there's one, there could be more,' said Isaac softly. His thin eyebrows knitted together with concern. Erika threw the newspaper down, went to the phone on the wall, and lifted the receiver.

'Disconnected,' she said, looking down at the plug. She put her head down and wiped her eyes. 'He phoned me over Christmas; he said he was with neighbours and I presumed they were here. I didn't know he had a mobile phone. I just didn't know. When I spoke to him on Christmas morning he was confused about a few things, but he seemed fine other than that. I should have asked if he was able to look after himself.'

Isaac reached out and squeezed her hand. 'You're here now. We're here now. Focus on that.'

She nodded. 'Are you as cold as me?'

'Colder,' he said. 'Let's get some breakfast and a cup of hot tea. We'll be able to make plans with some hot food inside us…' He checked his watch. 'It's eight o'clock; visiting won't start for a couple of hours. We can make plans.'

'We need to get this place cleaned up, and I need to check his bills… and…'

'Food, and hot tea,' said Isaac. 'Then we'll make a plan.'

CHAPTER FORTY-FIVE

Moss could see through the glass that the incident room was busy, and she took a deep breath before she went inside. Superintendent Hudson was with her, and when the officers saw Hudson enter with Moss, the room fell silent.

'Good morning, everyone,' said Melanie.

'Morning, ma'am,' the officers replied, almost in unison.

'Erika – DCI Foster – has been called away on an urgent family matter. Her father-in-law is ill, and she has had to go to Manchester to be with him. Detective Inspector Moss will be taking over as the Senior Investigating Officer; she will be acting Detective Chief Inspector. I ask you to show her the same respect and courtesy that you show Erika. It's very straightforward, but does anyone have any questions?'

The officers all looked at Moss standing beside Hudson, who looked a little uncomfortable, and no one said anything.

'Good. Then I'll let you take over, Moss.'

The moment Melanie left the room, and was out of earshot, everyone started to ask Moss questions about Erika, and when she would be back.

'I know as much as the Superintendent,' she said, putting her hands up to quiet them down. 'Nothing has changed from yesterday. We are still hunting this bastard.' She went to the whiteboard and pointed at the e-fit of the gas mask, and then moved to the line drawing of the gas mask that had been in the note sent to Joseph Pitkin. 'We need to start finding links and unlocking information.

We no longer have the luxury of questioning Joseph Pitkin, but I want to talk to his parents and see if we can find out more about this note. We also need to work on unlocking Marissa's iPhone. She didn't have a laptop or a PC, so all of her online activity on the iPhone could be crucial to this case.'

She moved along the whiteboard, to the photos of the other victims who had been attacked by the man in the gas mask.

'We need to look for a link between the victims, if there is one. Something that the attacker zones in on. Now, the link has to be something deeper than just physical. The victims were different ages and sexes, ranging from twenties to late fifties, men and women. Of the two men who were attacked, one was straight and one was gay. There is only one murder. Marissa Lewis. All the victims were targeted either close to their homes or close to their place of work, near train stations. Marissa had arrived back on the late train and she got the furthest away from the train station of all the victims. Did the attacker slip up? In the most recent attack, the victim kicked out and dislodged the gas mask on the attacker's face. Was Marissa killed because she saw the identity of the attacker? Or did she know the attacker?'

Moss moved along to the crime scene photos of Marissa. 'In Isaac Strong's post-mortem report, he says that the weapon was a long knife with a serrated edge. We still have no murder weapon, and time is moving fast. Perhaps now is the time for extreme measures. Perhaps we need to knock on every door in Coniston Road and check people's cutlery drawers.'

There were a few smiles and laughter from the team. Moss held up her hand.

'Okay, okay. I know I like a laugh, but I'm being serious here. What is it the boss says? There are no stupid questions. Well, I want to add to that: there are no stupid lines of enquiry.'

'But you're the boss now,' said Kay.

'Yes, I am.'

Moss went on, moving to the photos of the suspects and persons of interest.

'Our list of suspects is dwindling. Joseph Pitkin, now dead – but there was a new gas mask attack yesterday, which seems to rule him out. The same applies to Ivan Stowalski, he died in hospital yesterday evening after being exposed to the gas leak at his house. It was self inflicted, and we are ruling it as suicide. We do, however, have Don Walpole: no record, cares for his alcoholic wife, but cheated on her with Marissa when Marissa was underage. Marissa then tried to blackmail him, saying she would go to the police about the underage sex. We attempted to get a voluntary DNA swab from him yesterday, but he wasn't at home, and he wasn't answering his phone. I am going to attempt this again today. Also, Marissa alleges that she stole a pair of diamond earrings from Mrs Fryatt. Another dancer from the Matrix Club states that she went to Hatton Garden with Marissa, and saw the earrings being valued, but Mrs Fryatt denies any jewellery was stolen from her, and no earrings have been found. Charles Fryatt runs a successful jeweller's in Hatton Garden. There's a bit of a question mark there.'

'Could Marissa have got the earrings from an admirer?' asked McGorry. 'The boss… I mean, the other boss' report, says that the girls in the clubs had a lot of admirers – rich guys, hanging around after shows in the hope that they'd get a bit more than a dance?'

'Yes, but we need to rule all of this out. I want one of you to get back in contact with the girl who went with Marissa to the jeweller, and if needs be, one of us should take her back to Hatton Garden to see if she can remember which jeweller it was.'

There was a pause, and Moss looked around at the despondent faces. She felt the same inside, but was determined not to show it.

'Okay. Let's get to work and we'll reconvene back here at 4 p.m.'

When the team dispersed and started to work, Peterson came over to Moss, and asked if they could speak privately.

'You need to make it quick.'

'Well done, by the way.'

'Thanks. Although I thought she might ask you instead.'

He shook his head, and pulled her over to the back of the incident room, next to the line of photocopiers.

'She found out last night, about Kyle and Fran,' he said in a low voice.

'Found out?'

'She dropped round, late, at bath time. Kyle's bath time, I mean.'

'Obviously…'

'I opened the door holding Kyle; he called me Daddy. Fran was there too.'

'Shit.'

'I tried to talk to her, but she drove off in her car, swerving up the road. I didn't know if I should follow, but I didn't, and now she's gone off sick.'

Moss saw how worried he looked.

'James, it's nothing to do with you. It's true that Mark's dad had a fall and was rushed to hospital. He had to have an emergency hip replacement and there were complications. That's why she's gone.'

'Oh, shit. She didn't say anything to you about me?' he said.

'Her mind was on other things… As is mine.'

He nodded. 'Okay. And well done, I'm made up for you taking over.'

'Thanks. I need you and Crane to keep things moving here.'

'Sure.'

Moss went over to Kay, who was sitting at her computer.

'You're with me today; I want to go and see the Pitkin family and ask some questions about Joseph.'

CHAPTER FORTY-SIX

The snow was melting when Moss and Kay arrived at Coniston Road, and they tried Don Walpole's front door. Kay was ready with the portable DNA kit, but there was no answer.

'Shit,' said Moss. She pulled out her radio, and called into the station. 'Crane, I need you to do a search for Don Walpole…' Moss looked up and saw the old man in his usual spot, smoking a cigarette. 'Hang on, I need to call you back.'

They came out of the front gate and went over to the old man.

'You looking for Don?'

'Yes, we are,' said Moss, showing him her warrant card. 'My colleague said that you saw him and his wife leaving yesterday afternoon. Have you seen them today?'

The man shook his head. 'I'm out here a lot; the wife don't let me smoke indoors. I was out just before six and again at seven-thirty and eight… And again at nine.'

'So, you're quite a heavy smoker?' asked Kay.

'You will go far as a detective,' he said, pointing his cigarette at her and grinning with a set of yellow teeth.

'You didn't see any lights on, any movement?' asked Moss.

'Nope.'

They came back to the car and Moss called back in to Crane at the station, telling him to keep trying Don's phone and to put out a search on his number plate against the national database. They then drove the short way around the corner to David and Elspeth Pitkin's house.

David Pitkin opened the door; he was dressed in black, and had deep, dark circles under his eyes. They showed their ID and asked if they could come inside to talk.

'Haven't you people done enough?' he said imperiously.

'We have some more questions about Joseph, about his friendship with Marissa Lewis,' said Moss, trying to be tactful.

'I'm sorry, no. My wife is in a terrible state. She hasn't left her bed since...'

'I'm so sorry about what happened to your son,' said Kay. 'We just don't want his death to be in vain. We think he may have known things about this case. He may have been able to help us with our investigations.'

David looked down at them from the step, chewing over what they were saying. 'Where is she?'

'Who?' asked Moss.

'That bloody awful detective with the blonde hair.'

'She is on leave. I have taken over the case,' said Moss.

'Is this because of my formal complaint? I wrote to the assistant commissioner, asking for a full enquiry and that she be removed from duty.'

'Yes, that's in process. That's why I am now on the case,' said Moss. She was sure Erika would understand her playing along with David Pitkin.

He took them through to the kitchen. 'Would you like tea?' Kay looked at Moss for guidance.

'We wouldn't want to impose,' said Moss. 'We just need to ask you a few questions.'

'Have some bloody tea!' he snapped. 'I need to keep busy.'

They nodded and sat at the long table. Moss noticed that all the clocks, of which there were many on the walls, had stopped at 1.25 p.m. The room was silent.

'It's something I wanted to do,' he said, noting her gaze. 'That's the time the doctor pronounced Joseph…' He didn't finish the sentence. They waited in silence as he made three cups of tea and then came to join them.

'How long had Joseph been involved in photography?' asked Moss. David Pitkin looked surprised at the question.

'I don't know, four or five years.'

'And you bought him supplies?'

'At school, his art teacher did a project where students made a pinhole camera out of lavatory rolls, tinfoil and photo paper. He found it fascinating, and pestered me to buy supplies so he could make his own pinhole camera.'

'And he needed a dark room to process the photos?'

'Yes.'

'Where did you buy the chemicals?'

'I got them locally from a camera shop in Greenwich. Detectives, I'm not sure how relevant this line of questioning is, unless you are planning to start doing photography as a hobby?'

'We are trying to establish where Joseph went in connection with his hobby.'

'It's wasn't a hobby. He wanted to do it as a career.'

'When did Joseph graduate to having his own camera, buying his own materials?'

'I don't know. As I said, a few years. I was still practising as a barrister back then and I rather neglected my home life. I wouldn't see my family for days on end…' David looked wistfully out of the window and sipped his tea. 'Makes me think it wasn't all worth it, my job. The law… It's just a huge chess game.'

Moss didn't press him.

'Was Joseph a member of any camera or photography clubs?'

'Again. I don't know.'

'Could we speak to your wife?' asked Kay.

'No, you may not. The doctor had to come early this morning to give her something to sleep.'

'Did Joseph get paid for any of his photos?'

David gave a bemused smile.

'No. He was signing on, for a long period. You must know this, officers.'

'Did Marissa Lewis ever come to your house?' said Moss. 'I'm asking in particular about the past year?'

'No. Not that I know of. We were always rather worried about him; he never seemed to have any interest in either sex.'

Moss looked at Kay. They had exhausted all of their questions, and there was just one other thing they had to ask about.

'Mr Pitkin. I need to show you some photos we found on Joseph's mobile phone. They may be upsetting, but I only ask you to look at them because they are vital to our investigation.'

David's eyes narrowed as Moss pulled out a cardboard file. She opened it on the table and took out the photos of Joseph tied up in the restraints. She also took out the note with the gas mask drawing.

David looked through the photos, attempting to stop his emotions from showing. Finally, he looked up, and his eyes were full of anger.

'Who the hell do you think you are, to come into my house and show me these?'

'Mr Pitkin. Did Joseph ever mention a friend, or that he was scared for his life?'

'Did anyone mention to you that Joseph looked at risk of taking his own life?' he shot back.

'No.'

'But you must have seen that he was distressed when he was being interviewed? Did no one at your station think to call a doctor, or think that he shouldn't have been put back in that cell,

BY HIMSELF!?' David swept the photos off the table. 'NOW GET OUT OF MY HOUSE!'

Kay hurriedly picked up the photos from the floor and stuffed them back in the file.

'Mr Pitkin, please, do you have any idea who might have sent Joseph a note like this?'

'DID YOU HEAR ME?' he bellowed. He grabbed Moss by the back of her coat and dragged her up out of her chair and into the hallway.

'Sir. Please, stop this,' said Kay, moving after them as David dragged Moss to the front door.

David let go of Moss, leaned across, turned the handle and pulled it open. Moss put up her hand when he tried to grab her again.

'That's enough,' she said, stepping outside. Kay was no sooner out of the door behind her than it was slammed shut. They walked out onto the pavement.

'You okay, ma'am?'

'Yes, and please don't call me "ma'am". I'm not a member of the royal family,' said Moss. She straightened her jumper under her jacket. 'What else were we expecting? I just thought it was worth a shot, in case he knew something.'

'Do you think he knows anything?' asked Kay.

'No, I don't. But I'm not much good with my gut instinct. That's Erika's speciality.'

CHAPTER FORTY-SEVEN

McGorry had been tasked with following up on Ella Bartlett, the burlesque dancer who had been to the jeweller's with Marissa. Earlier in the morning, he'd spoken to an extremely camp man called Martin, who had given him Ella's number. She had agreed to meet him after her workout, but she was now late. He had been waiting for her outside the Gym Box in Farringdon for twenty minutes. It had stopped snowing, but the air was damp, and his feet were starting to go numb. The Gym Box was on a busy road on the edge of the Hatton Garden jewellery district in central London, and as he'd drunk his coffee next to an old-fashioned red phone box, he'd seen six security vans move past.

'Hi, are you John?' said a voice. He turned to see a petite blonde woman in her early twenties. She was breathtakingly beautiful, with long honey-coloured hair, and big blue eyes.

'Yes, I'm Detective Constable John McGorry. I take it you're Ms Bartlett?' He realised how ridiculously formal he sounded.

'Call me Ella. Can I call you John?' she said. 'And can I see your ID? You know you can't be too sure, these days.'

He pulled out his warrant card and passed it to her.

'You're much cuter in real life,' she said, handing it back.

'Let's get started,' said McGorry.

'Do you have a gun?'

'No. Detectives don't carry guns.'

'Cuffs? Pepper spray?' she asked, her eyes wide and innocent.

'Sometimes. In my car.'

'How did you get here?' she asked, looking around.

'I came on the tube; I travelled on the tube…' McGorry suddenly felt flustered and stupid.

'So you're unarmed? Vulnerable? Sorry, I'm kidding.'

'I need you to help me find this jeweller's shop. It's very important to our investigation. It's not a big laugh.'

'Sorry… I thought she was alright, Marissa. I've thought about jacking it all in and going to L.A or New York. I haven't got the guts. She had guts.'

They started walking down the road, and then turned right onto Hatton Garden, where the first jeweller's windows looked out over the street. They glowed brightly against the cold grey day, showing fabulous displays of gold and silver. The two of them walked for a few minutes. Ella kept stopping at intervals to peer into windows and look down the street.

'We were talking loads, and we were coming from the other direction; I wasn't paying attention,' she said. 'They all look quite similar after a while.'

They went a little further, and then she stopped at a red post box.

'I think it was here,' she said, pointing at a door opposite.

'What makes you think it's this one?' asked McGorry.

'The post box. It's a really old one.'

McGorry looked up at the frontage. It said: 'R.D. LITMAN & SONS FINE JEWELLERS EST. 1884.'

They went inside, where a comfortingly old-fashioned bell rang above the door. There was a hushed elegance to the interior, and a long glass counter, which gleamed. An elderly balding man with a slightly hunched back came out from a door at the rear of the shop. He sized them up with a practised glance, but waited for them to speak first.

McGorry showed his warrant card and explained why they were there. Ella didn't seem to recognise the man, but he recognised her.

'Yes. You came in with another young lady with dark hair. Diamond earrings, princess cut: 1.62 carats of exceptional purity, set in 24 carat gold.'

'You can be sure of all that?' asked McGorry.

'It's my job to remember,' said the man, sniffily. 'And of course, I always remember a pair of beautiful ladies. Did your friend reconsider selling? What was her name?'

'Marissa? No. She died,' said Ella.

'I see. I'm sorry,' he said. 'Do you wish to sell?'

'No, we don't want to sell,' said McGorry. 'I need to verify that they existed. Is there any chance you could be mistaken about their value?'

The look on the old man's face told him in the negative.

'I valued them at… The exact figure escapes me… Ten…'

'Ten and a half thousand,' finished Ella.

'Yes.'

'What's your name?' asked McGorry.

'Peter Litman.'

'Do you have much contact with the other jewellers' shops around?'

'Contact?'

'Yes.'

'This is a tight-knit community of traders which goes back a long way. Family businesses – but we remain businesses. With business relationships.'

'Can I give you my card, in case you remember anything else?' said McGorry.

'Yes.' He took the offered card. McGorry thanked him, and they left.

*

Peter Litman watched McGorry and Ella from the window, with his hands neatly behind his back. When they had receded from view, he went out back to an office, where there was a huge walk-in safe.

'Charles, that was a police officer, Detective Constable McGorry. He was asking about the princess-cut earrings belonging to the dead girl.'

Charles Fryatt looked up from where he was working at a computer and a desk piled high with paperwork.

'I heard everything.'

'You would have also *heard* that I told them the truth. I won't lie to the police. I'll ask you again. Are you involved with the death of that young woman?'

'No,' said Charles, shifting in the seat. 'It's to do with the earrings. Nothing more.'

'They were your mother's earrings?'

'Yes.' Charles kept working at the computer and didn't look up.

'Charles, as your father-in-law, you have my loyalty, but only to a point. If anything comes back to me that embarrasses me or my daughter…'

'It's nothing!' said Charles, raising his voice. 'And you didn't lie, and it's fine.'

Peter looked at his son-in-law for a long moment, and then went back out to the shop front to rearrange the displays, a deep feeling of unease rolling over him.

CHAPTER FORTY-EIGHT

It was early afternoon when the man who called himself 'T' left work. The shop he worked in had been quiet all day, apart from a man and woman who had come in with some enquiries.

He felt lucky that he worked for a private family business; he was able to come and go as he pleased when business was quiet. He took the short train journey into central London.

As he walked up Rupert Street and into Soho, the derelict facade of the Raymond Revue Bar rose up in front of him. His heart began to hammer in his chest, and he felt his penis grow hard. There was always a frisson of excitement when he entered the sex district, with its garishly lit bars and sex shops. It was a place where one could be both anonymous and covert, and in this small quadrant of streets, all vestiges of polite British upper-class reserve fell away. The gays felt they could hold hands; people could express themselves. As he passed the Prowler store a couple of young guys emerged and did a double take, admiring his height. He waited for a council road sweeping machine to rumble past, the brushes working frantically on the filthy street. He crossed the road, heading past the sex shop on the corner and along Walker's Court. It was a narrow, pedestrianised street made dingy by the tall buildings rising up either side. Sex shops and lap dancing clubs packed each side, with gaudy neon lights illuminating the gloom.

Meltwater from the rooftops ran into a broken gutter and then spattered the floor next to a sex shop with blacked-out windows. A neon teacher's cane with the word 'SPANKING' repeated in

flashing rows, advertised the shop's specialist sex gear and porno vids. T felt his excitement grow, and almost without noticing, put his hand down to his groin, feeling the leather through the thin material of his dark trousers. He always imagined that the street had looked pretty much the same two hundred years ago, just without the garish lights and blacked-out windows. Back then, young men or women could go missing, and little would be said about it. Life was cheap.

A small girl in a thick silver puffa jacket hung around outside one of the small lap dancing clubs, where music blared out. T felt the booming bass fizzing on his teeth and rumbling through his chest. He slowed as the girl made eye contact, and she opened her coat. Underneath she wore a skin-tight mini skirt and a cut-off black top which showed her emaciated ribcage. Her eyes were a piercing green, but dead, and her plump lips were dotted with cold sores.

'You want some fun?' she said, raising her voice enough to be heard at close range.

'I want someone to model for me,' said T, leaning down to her, his lips almost touching her ear. She moved back, looking from side to side, green eyes scanning the narrow street for police. A short, dark-skinned man with heavy stubble glanced over from his spot by the sex shop at the end.

'Yeah? How much?' she said.

'Private work. Very private.'

'A hundred quid for an hour. You have a hotel?' said the girl, her eyes remaining dead throughout. Like an animated corpse. The loud music cut out, and then another track started, trance music, starting off with a low beat. The short man at the end was tilting his head towards the girl. T felt nerves growl in his stomach: this was both thrilling and worrying. This girl would give him consent, but he wanted to go far, and he didn't want too many people to see her with him. The short guy at the end was her pimp, he was sure.

'I'm going shopping,' said T, tipping his head towards a sex shop further down. 'I need a girl who's not afraid to bleed, but I would make it worth your while. You also need to travel. My place is a little far out.'

'It's a hundred and fifty an hour if I have to travel, minimum three hours up front...' The girl was so nonchalant. There was no fear or trepidation. She had the look of someone who was deep in drugs, perhaps in hock to a dealer or the short pimp.

She suddenly bolted away and down towards Rupert Street. T looked for the pimp, but he was gone. A couple of community support officers had entered Walker's Court at the other end. They were deep in conversation, as community support officers always seemed to be, but their eyes scanned the street, which was clearing out. Shadows vanished into doorways.

T felt relief and picked up the pace, moving like a commuter, fast and in a rush. He breezed past the two community support officers and out into the fresh air at the other end, into a fruit market and away from temptation and excitement.

CHAPTER FORTY-NINE

Erika and Isaac couldn't get in and see Edward until early afternoon. Isaac said he would wait for her to go and see him first, and he hung back and grabbed a cup of coffee in the cafeteria downstairs.

The ward was on the fifth floor. Erika was buzzed in through a set of double doors and directed to a row of beds at the end. As she approached the row of beds, she couldn't work out which old man was Edward. So many of them were asleep, lying on their sides, with identical grey hair.

She found him at the end of the ward, by a window overlooking the car park. He was tucked up under blankets. His face lit up when he saw her.

'Erika, love,' he said, lifting a bruised hand with a drip coming from it. The cabinet beside him was empty. She saw lots of the other old men had cards and fruit, and she wished she'd brought him something.

'Hello,' she said, reaching out and taking his hand. It was very dry. She pulled up a chair and sat close to the bed. 'What happened?'

'I had a fall. I got up in the night, and I don't remember much else. The postman heard me shouting the next morning.'

'You tried to call me, didn't you?'

'I can't remember.'

'I didn't know you had a mobile phone.'

'I don't usually use it, but me phone was cut off a couple of days after Christmas, and I couldn't find out why. I always pay my bills...' He sat up, agitated.

'I know you do.'

'And then the heating broke. I tried to get by with the fire. The 'lectric went. I always pay the bills, Erika. You know that, don't you?'

She nodded.

'I'm here now, and I'm going to make sure that everything is fixed,' she said.

'You're a good lass.'

She shook her head. 'You've had a hip replacement?'

'Yes. They put some pins in there too, the doctor said…' He swallowed and started to cough. Erika took a cup from the cupboard by the bed and poured him some water from a jug. 'Thanks, love.' He drank the whole cup and passed it back to her. 'I'll be on the mend before you know it. Although, I'm not sure if I'll have a bit of a problem in the shops.'

'Why the shops?'

'Won't the pins beep when I go through the security barriers? It's right embarrassing when it happens in Tesco.'

'No, it's not a metal detector in the shops, that's only in airports.'

'Oh,' he chuckled. 'I'm not planning on going anywhere, so that doesn't matter. It's so lovely to see you. Are you staying long?'

'I'll stay as long as you need me.'

He waved it away. Isaac appeared at the top of the ward, and Erika nodded and beckoned him over.

'This is my friend – colleague – Isaac Strong,' said Erika. Edward looked up and took his hand, and they shook.

'Very nice to meet you, Mr Foster. Erika's told me a lot about you.'

'Bet you think I'm a right fool though.'

Isaac shook his head and smiled.

'You're a big lad… Tall.'

'Er, yes. No good at sports though.'

Edward squinted up at him. 'Shame, I bet you would have made a cracking high jumper.'

'Isaac is a doctor, a forensic pathologist.'

'Is that dead people?'

Isaac smiled. 'Yes.'

Edward chuckled. 'I nearly needed your services. Thankfully the postman saw me.'

'No!' said Isaac, his eyebrows shooting up in alarm.

'I'm just kidding, lad, nice to meet you. Any friend of Erika's is a friend of mine.'

A doctor appeared at the top of the ward and asked to speak to Erika. She left Isaac with Edward, and followed the doctor to the nurses' station.

'It was a fairly straightforward operation,' he said. 'We've already had him up and about. Recovery time is fast.'

'Good.'

The doctor's face clouded over. 'We are, however, concerned by the situation at home. Edward is underweight, and has a vitamin deficiency. He also came in with a nasty urinary tract infection. Normally we wouldn't risk operating on a man in his condition, but the break was very bad. Luckily, the infection is starting to respond to antibiotics. We can't discharge him until we know he has a care plan in place. Are you local?'

Erika explained that she lived in London. She recounted the conversation she'd had with Edward on Christmas Day, and how he had been confused. The doctor nodded and listened.

'Often, one of the symptoms of a urinary tract infection is confusion – or even hallucinations,' he said, regarding Erika gravely. 'This doesn't solve our problem with him living on his own and being vulnerable, though. I'm going to recommend social services pay his house a visit, to see what his living situation is like.'

He left Erika and went off on his rounds, and she stood for a moment in the corridor. Trying to work out how it had come to this. How fast the time had gone. It had come too soon for her to be facing middle age with an elderly father-in-law to look after.

This was why she buried herself in work. Work made her feel alive, and young. Work was constant. There were always bad guys out there to catch. Evil had no age limit. She shook the thought away.

'That's fucked up,' she said to herself. She smoothed down her hair and went back into the ward.

CHAPTER FIFTY

Moss felt the Marissa Lewis murder case, complicated by the gas mask attacks, was spinning out of her control – and as the acting SIO, she was still playing catch up. She was used to being a cog; in fact, she prided herself on being a cog in the overall machine: keeping things oiled, providing support and cracking jokes when things seemed to get tense.

Now she was the boss, she felt the pressure of scrutiny, and despite only being the temporary SIO, she felt the shift in the team and the way they behaved towards her. She was called 'ma'am'. The first time Sergeant Crane had called her 'ma'am', she'd thought it a joke – something along the lines of it rhyming with 'Spam'. But she'd stopped herself, realising she needed to be serious.

The other thing that was hampering her progress was the way Erika worked as an SIO. She didn't write much down, preferring to work in her head, so Moss had spent most of the day playing catch up. The superintendent had asked her if anyone had re-interviewed Marissa's mother, Mandy, about her sleeping arrangements, and Moss had been clueless, racking her brains and trying to think back to the reports she'd read: did the superintendent mean Mandy's sleeping arrangements as in the men she shared her bed with, or where she slept? Moss remembered at the last minute Mandy had been sleeping downstairs when Marissa was murdered, but drawing a blank had shaken her up. She couldn't bear the thought of being demoted back to a Detective Inspector before the case was solved, but she had no clue as to how she was going to solve

it, and even whether she could. Erika solved the cases, and she was always there ready to execute orders. Moss realised now how much she enjoyed following orders.

After talking to the superintendent, Moss had gone to the rarely used toilets on the top floor by the conference rooms, locked herself in a cubicle and phoned Celia, biting back tears as she poured out her woes.

'This is the first time you've been given a case,' said Celia. 'You have to be kind on yourself… And you're taking over in the middle of a complex case. You're a popular member of the team. You should crack some jokes to lighten the mood; is there anyone new who doesn't know your first name is Kate?'

Moss laughed and blotted her cheeks with a scrunched-up ball of loo roll.

'I'm now the boss; I can't make Kate Moss jokes, people are looking up to me to provide them with guidance and wisdom and strategy. And I have to solve the bloody thing whilst jugging case files and…' Her voice tailed off.

'Lists,' said Celia. 'You're bloody good at lists. You've always got a pile of Post-its by the fridge, and we work through them and we always solve problems, and we get things done. You should always break problems and tasks down, instead of trying to tackle them head on in one.'

'You're right,' Moss said. 'It's not a murder case, it's a series of to-do lists.'

It was now late afternoon, and Moss was back in the incident room, working at her cluttered desk in the corner. She had been offered the use of an office, but there hadn't been any time to move her computer access and the vast amount of paperwork on her desk. On Celia's advice, she now had a terrifyingly long to-do

list, but she felt better about it. One good thing about being the boss was that you got to delegate.

'Any news on Don Walpole's location?' she shouted.

'We're still waiting on the national ANPR data centre,' said Crane. ANPR stood for the Automatic Number Plate Recognition database. 'If he crossed the congestion charge zone, that will be the bullseye.'

'Can you chivvy them along, and tell them we're not asking for our health!' she said, scanning her list. 'We should also put out a check on his passports and his credit cards at this stage. He is the closest we have to a suspect.'

Crane nodded and picked up his phone.

'What about the diamond earrings? Where is McGorry?' Just as Moss asked, McGorry came back into the incident room. 'You went this morning to find the jeweller's in Hatton Garden, yes?'

'Yes, Moss, I mean, boss.'

'Stick with Moss.'

'Okay. The guy in the jeweller's, Mr Litman, remembered Ella coming in with Marissa to have the earrings valued. He said they were genuine and worth ten and a half grand. I then went back to see Mrs Fryatt at her house, to ask her again about the earrings… I even had a description. They were princess-cut diamonds in twenty-four carat gold.' He blew his cheeks out. 'She's a nasty old cow, she accused me of being in the wrong, saying that all her jeweller's is accounted for and up in her safe.'

'Did you ask to see the safe?'

'I did, and she said it was in her bedroom, and that she didn't invite young men into her bedroom without a warrant.'

Peterson and Crane laughed, and Moss had to keep a straight face. It was on the tip of her tongue to crack a joke that no one ever needed a warrant to get in her knickers, that all it usually

took was a slap-up meal at Nando's, but she reminded herself she was now acting SIO.

'Did you think Mrs Fryatt was lying?'

'I'm confused, because I also asked her to confirm the name of the jeweller where her son works,' said McGorry. 'It's the same jeweller, R.D. Litman & Sons. Charles Fryatt is married to Mr Litman's daughter, Lara… She's a retired schoolteacher and they have three children who are all grown up. It's quite a big family business. Mr Litman's other two sons also work there.' He paused for everyone to take in the link. 'Charles Fryatt wasn't at work when I went in. We only saw Mr Litman. I asked Ella if there had been anyone else in the jeweller when she and Marissa went in to have the earrings valued, and she said they had only seen Mr Litman.'

'There's a chance that Charles Fryatt *didn't* know?' asked Crane.

'That's one hell of a fishy chance, but you say Mrs Fryatt offered up the information about where Charles worked?' said Moss.

'Yeah, with no qualms, she didn't seem worried. She seemed proud that he had such a good job,' said McGorry.

'Have you spoken to Charles Fryatt?'

'No. I couldn't get hold of him. When I called the shop back, Mr Litman said that Charles wasn't at work. He wasn't answering his phone either, and his wife didn't know where he was.'

'What if Marissa was lying about where she got the earrings?' said Peterson.

'Why lie that you stole them from someone? Wouldn't it be easier to say that she got them from an admirer who came to see her dance at the club?' said Moss.

'What if it was something more sinister?' said McGorry. 'I don't know what, but Marissa Lewis was a woman with a million secrets.'

'That's all this case needs, is to get more sinister,' said Moss, looking down her list, and once again, feeling overwhelmed.

CHAPTER FIFTY-ONE

Erika and Isaac stayed at the hospital until late in the afternoon.

'He seems very stoic,' said Isaac, as they drove back to Slaithwaite.

'It's a northern thing. People are much nicer than in London, and they have a much more sensible way of looking at life.'

'What did the doctor say?'

'They won't let Edward back home until they can see he's able to look after himself, or it's a nursing home.'

'Shit.'

'I need to clean his house, and try and get things working again. I can't have him being discharged to the place in that state, and what would social services say about it?'

They stopped at the supermarket on the way home, and stocked up on food and cleaning products. It was dark when they approached the village, and it looked cosy, with the lights from the houses twinkling off the snow.

'I'll see if I can get the fire going,' said Isaac when they came inside. 'I think it's warmer outdoors.' He started working on the stove, emptying it out and cleaning the grate.

'Mystery solved about the gas,' said Erika, finding and opening a pile of mail. 'Looks like Edward changed over his provider, and they don't have the right bank details…'

Isaac was holding a match to a pile of paper and logs, but nothing was happening.

'And the same with his phone. It looks like one of those comparison companies persuaded him to switch over *all* of his utilities, but they've got the wrong address, the wrong bank details… Bastards,' she said, picking up her phone. Isaac watched in amusement as Erika tore into the utilities companies, registering a complaint and getting Edward reconnected.

They spent the rest of the evening scrubbing and cleaning Edward's house. An engineer came out very quickly, and the gas supply was back on around 8 p.m., so they were able to get the central heating working, and more importantly they were able to wash. Isaac took a shower, and then Erika ran a bath in the newly clean bathroom. As she eased into the hot water, she felt her aching body relax, and the cold which had dogged her for the last few days started to ease away. She'd lit candles, and they gave the bathroom a homely, cave-like feel. Edward's bathroom had been the same for years, with its lavender-coloured tiles. There was a set of shelves above the toilet, with a stack of boxed Pears soap, a knitted Spanish señorita toilet roll holder, boxes of talcum powder, and hair dye in 'conker', the shade Mark's mother used to use. Erika hadn't dared throw anything away on the shelves when she'd cleaned. They seemed sacred; they were the remnants of Edward's life with Mark's mother, Kath. Erika thought back to Mark's mother, and how kind and innocent she had been. She'd lived in her own little world, wrapped in the protection of Edward and Mark, in this cosy little village.

As she shifted in the hot water, there was something about that shelf – a memory that niggled at the back of her mind, but she couldn't quite access it. The steam floated up to the ceiling and made the candle flames flicker and fizz. She tipped her head back against the cool tiles, and her eyes began to lull shut in the warm water.

*

Erika found herself back in Forest Hill, on Foxberry Road. It was late at night, and the road, which was usually busy with rows of parked cars, was empty. Snow was falling, but it felt hot, like she was breathing in steam. She crouched down, and scraped away the snow: there wasn't tarmac underneath the snow, there were tiles. Lavender bathroom tiles with white grouting. She scraped more of the snow away and saw the road was laid with tiles as far as she could see. The silence was broken by a crunching sound, footsteps on snow. She turned. A tall man dressed in black was walking towards her. He was wearing a gas mask. The slick, shiny leather of the hood reflected the streetlights above. He slowed and stopped a few feet from her. He lifted his head and sniffed the air, the long breathing drum of the gas mask reminding her of a dog's snout. He seemed to stare around her, but not see her, like she was invisible. She moved closer, so close that she could hear his breathing, and see the reflection of the streetlight on the hood as his head moved. She looked into the glass eyeholes, but couldn't make out a face, it was a swirl of black. As the vapour streamed out from the breathing drum, she caught a strong chemical smell, intoxicating and metallic…

Erika jolted awake as her mouth and nose hit the cool water. The steam had cleared, and her fingers had started to prune. She got out of the bath, and wrapped a thin towel around her. Standing on the mat, she stared at the shelf above the toilet. The Pears soap and the hair dye… Just after she and Mark had got married, they'd come to visit Edward and Kath, and Mark had gone up to use the bathroom. The rest of them were having tea in the front room, when Mark had come back down holding a small black bottle, with the words 'RELAX-FUN' written on it in red.

'Mum, why have you got poppers in the bathroom?' Mark said. Kath looked up from rearranging Eccles cakes on her best cake plate.

'What's that, love?'

'You've got an open bottle of poppers in the bathroom. I started to get high just having a wee.'

'That's a room deodoriser,' said Kath. 'I got it down the market. It's for keeping rooms nice and deodorised. Only cost a quid. There were quite a few young lads there. One of them mentioned he was having a party… I suppose he wanted his house to smell nice for his guests. Although, I'm not sure about the smell.'

Erika had choked on her tea, laughing.

'Mum, this isn't a room deodoriser. It's amyl nitrate,' said Mark.

'What?' she said, putting on her reading glasses and going over to him. 'No, look. It says on the label that it's a room deodoriser.'

Mark had explained to his mother that people inhaled poppers for the 'high' or 'rush' that the drug could create.

'Is this true, Erika, love?' Kath had asked, turning to her.

Erika had tried to keep a straight face. 'Yes. It's classed as a drug, though not illegal… Some people do use it for a high. It's popular in the gay community, as it relaxes…'

Mark had shot her a look to make her stop.

'Oh my word, what must they have thought of me?' Kath had exclaimed, clutching at her chest.

'You weren't to know,' said Erika.

'But I told them I was getting it for my husband, for when he visits the bathroom,' she said in horror.

*

Erika smiled at the memory, but it then hit her. She rushed downstairs in her towel and grabbed her phone. She called Moss, but it went to her answering machine.

'Moss, it's me. I told the team to focus in on the guy in the gas mask, and look for someone who could be a collector of old masks from the war. Go back and look at the statements from all the people who were attacked. Jason said he smelt something weird and metallic, see if any of the other victims mentioned this. Whoever it is could have had the breathing apparatus packed with tissue or cotton soaked in amyl nitrate, for a sexual high. You should also be looking at S&M gear. If you can get a clear idea of the exact design of the mask then you can start working on suppliers… I don't know how it fits in with Marissa Lewis, but it could unlock who this person is… Anyway… I hope things are going well.'

Erika hung up her phone, feeling very far away from the investigation.

CHAPTER FIFTY-TWO

Moss sat bleary-eyed at the kitchen table the next morning, eating her cereal. Jacob came in with his guitar and started to play a new song he'd made up. As he strummed at the guitar and started to sing, Moss shouted at him to cut it out. Jacob looked up at her with shock on his little face, and his eyes started to run. She never shouted.

'Mummy's got a headache this morning. Why don't you go and put the guitar away, get dressed, and then I'll make you some hot chocolate,' said Celia.

'I thought you wanted me to make up a song for you. That's what you said yesterday, you said for me to make up a song and now I've made one up…'

'I just need some peace and quiet this morning,' snapped Moss. Celia took Jacob out of the kitchen and returned a few minutes later. 'You don't want to get him into the habit of having hot chocolate every morning,' Moss added.

'He's only having it over Christmas…' said Celia.

'Yeah, well tomorrow is New Year's Eve; he's been having it every morning for the past ten days!'

'Is this really about Jacob having hot chocolate? Or are you taking stuff out on him, and me, because things are bad at work?'

'Things are not bad at work!' said Moss, getting up and dumping her half-full bowl of cereal in the sink. 'I just need time to think! You have no idea how complicated this case is… And there's all this noise here.'

'That's called having a five-year-old. You made a big deal last night about him writing you a song, when what you were really doing was fobbing him off!'

Moss's phone started to ring, and she pulled it out. It was Peterson.

'We've tracked down Don Walpole. His wife was taken ill the other day, and he's been staying at her bedside in hospital. University College London. The ANPR came back with details of his car crossing the congestion charge zone.'

'Good work. Can you get me there?'

She hung up and left the kitchen. Seconds later, Celia heard the front door slam.

'Charming. She becomes an acting DCI and I'm just the help… No goodbye or kiss on the cheek.'

'I'll kiss you on the cheek, Mummy,' said Jacob, appearing at the door, still holding his little guitar.

Moss and Peterson arrived at UCL hospital just after nine. Jeanette Walpole had been admitted to the renal department, and they had to get directions from the front desk.

'Renal is kidneys, yeah?' said Peterson as they travelled up in the lift.

Moss nodded. 'You've got everything ready. The paperwork? Spit kit?'

He nodded, holding up a thick folder. The 'spit kit' was shorthand for the Forensic DNA Evidence Collection Kit. 'You okay?' he asked, seeing her tense face.

'Had a row with Celia this morning, and I shouted at Jacob for being noisy.'

'I'm liking the noise, having a kid around…' Peterson got out his phone and swiped through, holding up the screen to Moss. It was

a video of Kyle playing on pots and pans. He was crouched on the kitchen floor with a sheet around his shoulders like a superhero cape, and he was banging on a line of upturned pots with a wooden spoon.

'Very tuneful,' Moss said, her eyes flicking to the digital display. The lift stopped and a porter wheeled in a long metal box, which both she and Peterson knew to contain a dead body. 'How is it all going?'

'Good, really good. They're living with me on a temporary basis, until we work out what we're going to do,' he said.

'I can see that you want them to stay.'

'Yeah.'

'Did you talk to Erika?'

'I figured she's got a lot going on with her father-in-law, and I'd rather do it face-to-face, when she's back.'

'Don't let it fester. Although, I think she's the one who'll be doing the festering.'

'I've got another video of Kyle singing,' said Peterson, swiping through his phone, his face beaming with pride.

'James, later. We need to concentrate.'

The lift doors opened, and they inched past the long box destined for the morgue. They came to a set of double doors for the renal ward, but they were locked. Moss peered through the glass windows.

'Can't see anybody. And there's no buzzer or bell.' She hammered on the glass with the flat of her hand. 'Hey… HEY!'

'Jeez, Moss, take it easy,' said Peterson.

'We could be here for bloody hours.'

A nurse appeared at the top of the corridor and came towards them.

'Or, we chill out and everything is going to be okay,' he said.

She took deep breaths and nodded. 'I'll be happier if his DNA is a match. Don Walpole is our man. I can close this case and move back to a happier pay grade.'

The nurse opened the door and they showed her their warrant cards. She took them to a side room at the end of the corridor.

'Mrs Walpole is in here,' she said, opening the door. Jeanette was sitting up in bed, hooked up to a dialysis machine. Her skin was bright yellow, and her breathing laboured.

Don was sitting beside her, and he eyed Moss and Peterson. 'Yes?'

'Can we have a word, please? Best outside,' said Moss. Don kissed the back of Jeanette's hand and came outside. Moss and Peterson showed him their warrant cards.

'We've been trying to get in contact with you, Mr Walpole,' said Moss.

'You can see, my wife is very sick.'

'We need to take a DNA swab from you,' said Peterson. Don looked him up and down.

'Are you arresting me?'

'No.'

'Then I have to volunteer my DNA, and I'm not prepared to do that.'

'Mr Walpole. Legally, we are able to take a DNA sample if we have grounds to suspect you have been involved in a crime. Now, we can find a place and do this here, or we can go to the station,' said Moss.

Don looked between them.

'I have here a document detailing your rights,' said Peterson. 'We can give you time to read it.'

Don stared through the strip of glass in the window at Jeanette, who now lay back on the bed with her eyes closed. 'Okay,' he said.

Peterson saw there was a small kitchen next to Jeanette's room. They went inside and closed the door. Don sat at a small table. Peterson pulled on a pair of gloves and then took out a plastic tube with a long cotton wool swab.

'I need a sample of your cells from the back of your throat,' he said. Don opened his mouth and Peterson swabbed the back of his throat and the inside of his cheek. Then he placed it back in the tube and sealed it up.

'Thank you,' said Moss, handing Don a form to fill in. He scanned down the page and then signed.

'She's dying,' he said. 'Her body is giving up on her.'

'I'm sorry to hear that,' said Moss. 'We expect the DNA results in the next twenty-four hours.'

The sun was fighting to come out from behind the clouds when they left the hospital.

'I'm going to head over to the lab in Vauxhall with the sample,' said Peterson.

'Good. I'm going over to speak to Mrs Fryatt. I need to solve the mystery around the earrings. I want to get a DNA sample from Charles Fryatt, too.'

'You want me to swing by Hatton Garden? I have another kit.'

'No. Get that in for testing. I need to ask her a few more questions, I want more than just a suspicious coincidence before we go after her son.'

CHAPTER FIFTY-THREE

There was no answer at Mrs Fryatt's house. Moss rang the bell several times, and peered in through the window. She came back out onto the pavement and looked up at the large house. The polished windows reflected the grey sky and stared back blankly.

Moss leaned on the railing and felt a wave of fear and anxiety roll over her. This was not an emotion she was used to. She thought of how she'd left that morning, forgetting to say goodbye to Celia and Jacob. As she took out her phone to call them, it started to ring. She didn't recognise the number.

'Hi, this is Lisa Hawthorne. I'm an advisor at Jobcentre Plus in Forest Hill. One of your police officers asked me to come back to you with details of Joseph Pitkin's past employment.'

'Oh, yes, but…'

'Sorry for the delay, we're snowed under here with work. Joseph Pitkin was claiming benefits for the past four years. He's only been claiming Jobseeker's Allowance off and on. He's had four periods of employment. On three occasions, he was working in a pub in Honor Oak Park – seasonal work over December in 2014, 2015 and 2016.'

'I'm sorry, could you call one of my colleagues at…' said Moss, trying to get her off the phone, but she went on:

'The fourth period of work was for a photographic studio in New Cross, called Camera Obscura. He was there for six weeks during early 2016…' There was something about the photography link which made Moss listen. She put the phone under her chin

and pulled out her notebook and pen. Lisa went on, 'It's run by a man called Taro Williams. It's an old-fashioned photographic portrait studio.'

'Do you know why the job ended?'

'No. Joseph's records show that this was meant to be a full-time position as a photographic assistant, but after six weeks he unexpectedly quit. Which was odd, as we worked hard to get him into the job, and he was very enthusiastic about it.'

'There was nothing else? No complaint from the employer?'

'No. It's such a shame Joseph didn't get the chance to pursue his passion for photography.'

'How well did you know Joseph?'

'I worked on his case, and used to see him twice a week when he signed on.'

'I'm afraid to say that Joseph recently took his own life.'

'I'm sorry to hear that,' she said, wearily. It sounded like she often heard this kind of news about her claimants. Moss thanked the woman, and came off the phone. She looked back at Mrs Fryatt's dark house, weighing up her options. New Cross was only a short drive away.

CHAPTER FIFTY-FOUR

Taro Williams was a tall, broad man in his late thirties, with a thick wide forehead and large features. He'd inherited Camera Obscura, and the living quarters above it, from his father, who had started the business during the 1960s. It was on Amersham Road, a residential street of large crumbling terraced houses, a few minutes' walk from New Cross station. In years gone by, these grand four-storey structures had been built by merchants who had found their fortune during the industrial revolution. They'd boasted well-to-do families and quarters for live-in staff. As well as three storeys rising above the street, each house had a large basement. The shop front of Camera Obscura, with a plate glass picture window, was set back from the road, and partly shrouded by a huge hawthorn bush by the front wall.

The photography shop had functioned for many years as a studio, but over the past few years, with the advent of digital cameras and smartphones, business had slowed. This didn't worry Taro. He was independently wealthy, and he liked to have time to himself. When it took his fancy, he worked as a wedding photographer. He only opened the shop a couple of times a week to take portraits, mostly of young couples who'd got engaged, and couples with small children who wanted to document their little darlings in an official capacity.

It depressed him that most of the parents with small children shunned the solid silver-gilt frames he had on offer, and instead

wanted their photos printed on cushions or jigsaws, or even worse, baseball caps and mugs.

Taro was just breaking down the lights and backdrop from a photoshoot that morning. A young Japanese couple had been to have pictures produced for their engagement invitations. It always struck him how tiny the Japanese were. They'd seemed quite intimidated by his huge frame and his serious face, but he'd broken the atmosphere with a joke and a broad smile, which transformed him into a jovial bear of a man. They had both giggled along with him during the shoot, but hadn't noticed that the smile never quite reached his eyes.

He was just packing away the last lighting softbox when a short red-haired woman came up the path to the front door. She tried to open it, and when she found it locked she knocked on the glass.

He strode over and pointed at the sign propped up at the bottom of the window: PLEASE RING FOR ASSISTANCE.

His face broke into a smile and he indicated that she should ring. She rolled her eyes and pressed the bell by the door. He smiled and gave her the thumbs up, then unbolted the door.

'Hello, I'm Detective Chief Inspector Moss,' she said, holding up her warrant card. 'Can I have a few minutes of your time?'

'Of course.' He smiled. He stood to one side and she came through the doorway.

CHAPTER FIFTY-FIVE

'How can I help you?' asked Taro, as he invited Moss to sit down in one of the oversized chairs he used for photo shoots. There was a camera on a tripod, a huge sheet of white reflective paper hanging along a square of the wall, and several lights dotted around on stands.

Moss sat down and pulled out a file from her bag. 'I'm here to ask a few questions about a former employee of yours. Joseph Pitkin. He worked here for six weeks in early 2016.'

'Yes, that's correct.'

'Can I ask why he left?'

Taro nodded regretfully. 'I'm afraid I had to fire him.'

'Why?'

'He was… dishonest. He stole from me…'

Moss nodded. 'How much did he steal?'

'Nothing vast. I think it was fifty pounds.'

Moss looked around at the cash register, which was alongside the wall, towards the plate glass window.

'Did you inform the police?'

'No.'

'What about the Jobcentre?'

'I can't say I remember. It was almost two years ago.'

'He was signing on, and his advisor found him the job. Did anyone get in contact with you to find out why the job had ended so fast?'

'Yes, I think someone did…' His voice trailed off. He smiled again, and came closer, perching on the arm of the chair in front

of her. He wore a tailored chocolate brown three-piece suit. A gold watch chain hung from one of the pockets.

'Can I ask what kind of photography you do?'

'Portraits, mainly. Young couples, bouncing bundles of joy...' He indicated a display of portraits on the back wall. 'Nine times out of ten, you put a baby in front of a camera and it screams its head off. Although, I do tend to scare children.'

'Do you take any other kinds of photos?'

'Weddings, but I tend to go along on the day.'

'Any erotic work?'

'Are you asking on a personal level?' he said, grinning the wide grin again.

'No,' she said. He was a handsome man, but there was something about him that made Moss uncomfortable.

'Sorry, bad joke.'

She waved it away.

'How would you rate Joseph as a photographer?'

'I can't say I got much of a chance, he was here for such a short time.'

'Did he take photos for you?'

'Yes.'

'Photos of what?'

'I let him do a session with a young couple who'd got engaged.'

'Did he show an interest in photographing nudes, or anything more... I don't know how to put it.'

'Explicit? No. I'm not that kind of business... Look, I'm parched after a long morning, are you sure I can't get you a cup? I can also look out my employment records to check if I made any other notes about Joseph and the contact I had with the Jobcentre.'

'Okay, thank you,' said Moss. Taro got up and went off through a door in the back, closing it behind him.

Moss had a look around the photographic studio. There was a large machine at the back used for processing pictures. It was covered in dust and junk, and had a 'one-hour photo' sticker on the front. Above it was a cabinet, displaying all of the options for having your photos produced: cups, jigsaws, magnets, hats and cushions. Each one had a stock image of a young girl holding a yellow balloon. On another wall were the examples of past shoots that Taro had indicated earlier: mostly baby photos.

Moss went over to the counter with the till. Behind it were shelves containing a trophy, and several plaques from 1991, when Camera Obscura won South London's Business of the Year. An older version of Taro, presumably his father, was pictured with his wife and children, out the front of the shop.

'You've found the embarrassing family photos,' said a voice behind her.

Moss jumped, and turned to see Taro standing directly behind her. She forced herself to smile.

'I've just put the kettle on,' he said. She could see there was a storm coming: the cloud outside was heavy and dark. The lights inside reflected the interior of the studio back at them from the shop window. 'I've found my records about Joseph.'

Moss came back to her chair, and Taro took the one opposite. He took a pair of glasses from his top pocket and put them on, then opened a folder. 'I don't have many people who come to work for me, but there have been a couple of assistants over the years. This is Joseph? I knew him as Joe,' he said, holding up a passport photo of Joseph, taken in an instant photo booth.

'Yes, that's him,' said Moss. Joseph stared up blankly, as most people do in ID photos, going through the motions. 'I wanted to ask about your experience of employing him. Did he borrow any equipment? Did you meet anyone he was friends with or associated with?'

'Is he under investigation?' asked Taro, looking up from the folder, his face amiable and placid.

'I'm afraid he's dead.'

'Oh, how awful. How?'

'Suicide.'

Taro took off his glasses and chewed one arm.

'That really is terrible. When?'

'Boxing Day.'

'So recent… And over Christmas, too.' Taro started to leaf through the folder. He found another photo, this time printed in 10 x 8 format.

'I did take photos of him.'

'I thought he worked for you?'

'He did. Joseph posed for me when I decided to transfer over to digital, and I needed to test the new cameras. I think I hung on for too long to the old technology and processing methods.'

The photograph was a full-length shot of Joseph, standing against the pale backdrop, wearing just a pair of jeans. He looked uncomfortable.

'Why is he shirtless?'

'He wanted some photos to give to a girl he was interested in,' chuckled Taro. 'Here's another.' He handed her a photo of Joseph standing in a crinkled pair of briefs. He was flexing his puny arms in what was supposed to be a macho pose, but it was the blank look in his eyes which bothered Moss. She'd seen that look before, a long time ago when she'd been fresh out of training college and had been assigned to work on sexual abuse cases. She'd seen that look on victims who had zoned out, and taken themselves to another place.

'You say he asked for these photos to be taken?' said Moss. She jumped as a kettle began to whistle out the back.

'Yes. This is a photographic studio,' said Taro, getting up. 'I'm often asked to take strange pictures, although I always draw the

line at photographing nudity.' He looked at her for a moment, as the kettle continued to scream. 'I won't be a moment.'

As soon as he'd vanished through the door. Moss took her phone out of her coat pocket. She had dialled Peterson's number when Taro popped his head around the door.

'Milk and sugar?'

'Yes.'

'This road has a bit of a black spot when it comes to mobile phone coverage. Perhaps it's the trees.'

Moss had the phone against her head as she heard the no signal tone. Taro smiled at her again, so amiably, and disappeared off to the screaming kettle. Moss was completely thrown by his behaviour. She moved to see through the door and noted that behind it was a long corridor. She heard the clank of the kettle and a spoon in a saucer at the end of the hall. She moved to the till and picked up the landline. It was dead. She then moved to the door and found it was locked. There was no key. Had Taro locked it when she came in? Hadn't she noticed?

This is ridiculous, she thought, trying to calm herself. She had been so concerned about doing her best, about being in charge of the investigation. She moved around the room with her phone held high, trying to get a signal.

As she crossed behind the two chairs where they'd been sitting, she noticed that Taro's folder lay open on his seat. There was a form inside from the Jobcentre, neatly filled in with spidery blue handwriting. Then there was a blank page of handwritten notes, and rows of figures. In the bottom right hand corner, in the same ink, there was a drawing. With shaking hands, Moss picked up the folder. It was a sketch of a face wearing a gas mask, intricately done and shaded using a black biro.

Moss had her phone in her other hand, and she scrolled through to the image of the gas mask, drawn above the note to

Joseph. Both the handwriting and the image matched: they had been drawn by the same hand.

There was a faint rattle. Moss turned. Taro was standing behind her, holding two china tea cups.

'Did you draw this?' asked Moss, turning and taking a step back. The folder shook in her hand.

'Yes. Yes, I did,' Taro said softly. The tea cups rattled again as he gently placed them down on the small table.

Moss opened her mouth to speak, but Taro moved swiftly to the door and flicked off the lights, plunging the room into a murky gloom. Moss hurried towards the front door, where a dim light came through the huge plate glass window, but she felt something hard hit her on the back of her head, and then everything went black.

CHAPTER FIFTY-SIX

Erika and Isaac had been to visit Edward again, and he had shown great signs of improvement. The nurse had got him up and walking, and he said his leg felt brand new, after years of having dealt with a twinge of pain in his hip. He'd said goodbye to Isaac, who had to return to London for work the next morning.

On the way back to Slaithwaite, Erika asked Isaac to take a detour through a series of pleasant avenues with detached houses.

'Can you stop just here,' she said. He pulled the car to a halt outside a detached two-storey house. The front lawn was covered in snow, and a snowman sat close to the front door with a carrot nose, two black eyes and a red scarf. Christmas lights were strung around the eaves, and through the front window they could see a Christmas tree.

'This is nice,' said Isaac. 'Why have we stopped here?'

'It's my house,' Erika said, staring up at it sadly. 'It's the house Mark and I lived in for fifteen years.'

'Oh.'

Erika stared at it. A tear formed in her eye and she wiped it away.

'I haven't been back since the day he died. I had all my stuff packed up and put in storage, and I had an agency rent it out.'

'Do you know the people renting it? Do you want to get out and knock on the door?'

'No.'

Isaac nodded. 'How long are you planning to stay up here?'

'I need to get Edward settled back in at his home. Find him a carer.'

Her phone rang. She didn't recognise the London number, but answered.

'Erika?' asked a woman's voice, sounding worried.

'Yes.'

'It's Celia, Kate's wife. Moss's wife.'

'Hi, Celia, sorry. I don't have your number in my phone, I didn't recognise it.'

'Have you heard from Kate?'

'No. I left her a message a while back but she hasn't replied.'

'It's just that she usually calls me in the day. We had a silly row this morning, nothing serious, but she's the kind of person who'll ring and smooth things over. I phoned James and John McGorry, but they don't know where she is. I've left her six messages.'

'She's now running a huge case. Believe me, it can make you lose track of everything.'

'I know. Kate's been very stressed out about taking over this case from you…'

'She's probably picked up bad habits from me. I tend to lose track of time working on an investigation…' Erika's voice tailed off. She only lost track of time because she never had anyone waiting for her to call. 'She's probably been called into a briefing meeting. She'll have to be attending them now she's acting DCI, and they can go on and on.'

'Okay,' said Celia. 'Sorry, you must think I'm weird.'

'No. I think Moss is very lucky. When I have rows with people, they often never speak to me again! If she calls, I'll tell her to ring you.'

'Yes.'

'And here's the direct number for Superintendent Hudson,' said Erika. She gave Celia the number and then rang off.

'Everything okay?' asked Isaac. Erika dialled Moss's number, but it went straight to answerphone.

'Celia says Moss hasn't been in contact since this morning.'

'And that's unusual?'

'For them, yes.'

'I miss having someone who expects me to ring them,' said Isaac.

'Me too,' said Erika, staring up at the house. 'The wisteria, it's grown so fast,' she added, pointing at the high, thick branch which curled up the side of the house and snaked its way along the eaves at the top. 'I bought that in a tiny pot, the day we moved in. We'd stopped to get some paint at B&Q and it was on this discount table. It was 70p. Mark said, don't waste money on that little stick, it looks dead.'

'I bet it's pretty when it flowers,' said Isaac.

Erika nodded and wiped her eyes. 'Come on. Let's go. I just wanted to see it, but it's just a place, a house. What made it a home was the people inside it, and we're not there any more. There's another family in there now.'

CHAPTER FIFTY-SEVEN

Taro, or 'T' as he liked to call himself for short, hit Moss hard over the back of the head with a leather sap. He kept it in the kitchen drawer, and he'd pushed it into his back pocket as he was making the tea in the kitchen. His mind was whirring, but he wasn't scared and he wasn't panicking. She hit the floor hard, but it was away from the window and in the shadows, with the lights out.

He listened to the clock ticking. A car trundled past on the road. He crouched down, holding the sap in his right hand in case she still had some fight left in her. He took her wrist with his free hand, and felt her pulse. It was beating slowly, rhythmically. He held his finger there. Feeling the life beating through her, moving it over the firm, pulsing nodule deep in her skin. He moved his hand around to the back of her head. Her hair was slick with blood. He stood and placed the sap back in his pocket. He stepped over her and moved to the window. The road outside was quiet. Retreating back into the shadows, he rolled her over.

'Big girl,' he muttered as he patted her down, kneading her breasts and running his hands between her legs. He held them there for a moment, savouring the warmth, then he switched his attention to her pockets. He took out her car keys, phone, wallet and warrant card. He placed them on the counter, by the till, then came back to her. With considerable strength, he bent down and picked her up in one fluid move, throwing her over his shoulder. He carried her limp body through the doorway, disappearing for a few minutes, then came back.

He flicked on the lights. The carpet where she had fallen was clean and there was no sign of blood. He would be thorough, though, and give it a clean. He came back to the counter and retrieved her phone and car keys. Unbolting the front door, he came outside and walked down to the pavement. A smattering of cars was parked up in the permit spaces. He pushed the key fob and looked to the right. Nothing happened. When he looked to the left and pushed the button, the lights flashed on a dark Rover fifty yards away.

T stopped for a moment. Thinking. He was surprised how calm he was. His heart was beating faster, and he could feel the blood pumping through his legs and wrists, but he was in control. He wasn't panicking.

He didn't know if she'd told anyone she was coming. It was early afternoon. Police officers weren't always the most sociable creatures; Moss might not be missed until the next morning, but when the alarm was raised, someone would eventually come and question him. He would need to acknowledge that she had dropped by, but he would tell anyone who asked that she'd left. He looked down at the keys and wallet. How would he make it look as if she'd left?

A van from Lewisham Council's gardening department rounded the corner up ahead. It was one of the ones with an open flat-back truck, used to transport grass cuttings and plants. He moved round to the driver's side of Moss's car and fiddled with the door, then quickly wiped the phone on his jacket. As the van drove past, he dropped Moss's mobile phone onto the flat bed, amongst a pile of branches and dead leaves. He climbed into her car, and watched as the van paused at the traffic lights at the end, then drove on. Hopefully to the South Circular.

Taro started the engine and drove the car two miles away, working rhythmically up and down the residential streets to avoid

any CCTV cameras. He parked the car up at the end of Tresillian Road, a quiet residential street. He locked the car, then, after wiping the key off, he dropped it down a drain.

He walked back to the photography studio, the light fading as he passed, unhurried, through the streets. The lull between Christmas and New Year was the perfect cover for his movements. He didn't see anyone. He almost wished he'd brought his gas mask with him, to have some fun. But he knew he had to get back to his studio and deal with the policewoman.

CHAPTER FIFTY-EIGHT

Mrs Fryatt was sitting by the fire, drinking tea from her favourite bone china tea set, when the doorbell rang. It took her a moment to remember that there was no one else in the house to answer, so she heaved herself up out of her favourite armchair.

It took her a while to get there, the size of the house and the stiffness of her legs from sitting for several hours impeding her speed. She opened the first door and went into the cold porch. Through the glass in the door she could see a black man in a suit, flanked by five police officers in uniform.

A black man, she thought disapprovingly as she unlocked the door and opened it. He held up his warrant card.

'Mrs Elsa Fryatt? I'm Detective Inspector James Peterson.'

'What do you want?' she answered imperiously. Despite her small height, the front door was raised up, so she was able to see most of them at eye level.

'We have a warrant to search these premises in connection with the murder of Marissa Lewis,' he said, handing it over.

'This is no use to me; I haven't got my glasses,' she said.

'I'm not waiting for you to read it,' said Peterson. He stepped up into the porch, suddenly towering above her. She put out her arms to stop him, and he gently lifted them away, and moved into the house.

'You get your black hands off me!' she cried. The police officers surged around her and into the house, and started pulling on latex gloves. 'What are you doing? Why are you coming into my home?'

A young policewoman started opening the small drawers in one of the occasional tables in the hall, and Mrs Fryatt tried to close them.

'Ma'am, you need to step back, or we will arrest you.'

'On what grounds?'

'Obstructing a police officer with a warrant.'

She moved to the banister and watched as the police fanned out and started searching through her house. She went to the phone, and with shaking hands, she dialled her son's mobile phone.

'Charles? The police are here!' she shrilled, her voice climbing a register. 'They say they've got a search warrant… They're going through everything…' She listened as her son fired questions at her, watching through the doorway to the front room where books were being taken down from the shelves, upended, shaken and dumped on the floor. 'I don't know. I haven't got my reading glasses. They won't tell me what they are doing. One of them manhandled me on the front doorstep… Okay, come quickly!'

She put the phone down and tried to find a spot in the house where she could wait, but the police seemed to be everywhere. There seemed to be more than the six officers who had initially been on the front doorstep. She went back out to the freezing porch and sat on the small chair she used for putting on her shoes. Her hands were shaking, and it wasn't just from the cold.

An hour later, Charles Fryatt appeared through the glass outside the front door.

'Why the hell did it take you so bloody long!' she hissed when she opened the front door.

'Where's the warrant?' Charles said. He took it from her, scanning the writing on the page and the signature. They moved into the hallway as Peterson was just coming down the stairs.

'Are you Charles Fryatt?' he asked.

'Yes. I think this is quite ridiculous, what could my mother have to do with the murder of Marissa?' Charles said. 'Look at her, she's ninety-seven years old!'

Peterson ignored him. 'Is the front bedroom yours, Mrs Fryatt?'

'Yes! You've been in there? You?' she cried.

'Yes.'

'I would expect a *lady* police officer to have been assigned to do that. No doubt you've had those hands all over my personal items!'

Charles shot his mother a look. 'Mum. You need to watch it,' he warned.

'I can say whatever the hell I like in my house. There's freedom of speech for a reason!'

'We need you to open the safe in the wardrobe,' said Peterson. Charles looked at his mother; his eyes were wide and fearful.

'I take it I don't have a choice?' she said.

'No, you don't. Either you open it, or we drill it open.'

They followed him up two flights of stairs to the front bedroom, which held her huge four poster bed, a heavy wooden dressing table in front of the bay window, and a large fitted wardrobe lining one wall. The middle door was open, showing a heavy metal safe with a combination dial.

'I'm the only person who knows the combination,' said Mrs Fryatt imperiously.

'What if you can't remember it?' asked Charles. There was something about the way he said this that suggested to Mrs Fryatt that her son was giving her some kind of cue to forget, but she tottered over to the safe and slowly knelt down.

'I need you all to turn away,' she said. Peterson, Charles and two of the uniformed officers also in the room looked away. There were some soft clicks and then the safe's lock opened. Charles tried to catch his mother's eye, but she refused to look at him. 'There,' she said.

Peterson went to the safe, and crouched down to peer inside. There were three shelves. The first had a stack of twenty-pound notes and some old-fashioned bank bonds. The second was packed with velvet-lined jewellery boxes. The two uniformed officers joined him, and pulled on fresh latex gloves to take these out, placing them on the carpet. The first box was wide and flat and contained a dazzling diamond necklace; the second and third contained a Cartier diamond watch and two bracelets. Peterson sorted through the other boxes laid out on the carpet, which contained a diamond brooch, gold earrings, and another necklace with a six-ounce block of gold pendant. The final two boxes contained a pair of huge round-cut diamonds in gold, and the second a pair of square princess-cut diamonds.

The bottom shelf of the safe was empty.

'Do you own any other princess-cut diamonds?' asked Peterson.

'No,' said Mrs Fryatt. 'You will see underneath the bond certificates on the top shelf that I have all the insurance paperwork for my jewellery. It was made up at the end of last August. You will find everything there, present and correct.'

Peterson spent several minutes checking through it all. Then he got up and went to Charles, who was watching from in front of the window. His grey skin glistened with sweat, despite the cool temperature.

'Can you confirm that Marissa Lewis came to the jeweller's where you work, with a pair of princess-cut diamond earrings, exactly the same as these?' he asked, holding up the box.

'Er. Yes… apparently, she did,' Charles said. Mrs Fryatt stared at her son coldly.

'Why didn't you tell my colleagues this when they visited you before to talk about Marissa's murder?'

'Because I didn't know she had been in to the shop, until one of your colleagues came in and spoke to my father-in-law. I'm

one of four in the family who work there,' said Charles. His eyes darted between Peterson and his mother's steely gaze.

'This is your wife's family business?'

'Yes, I work there along with two of her brothers.'

'I need to take these earrings away for testing,' said Peterson.

'What do you propose you test for?' asked Mrs Fryatt.

'DNA.'

'Well, you'll find my DNA, and no doubt there might even be some from my daughter-in-law, who's borrowed them on a couple of occasions. And of course, you'll find Marissa's DNA on them.'

Peterson stared at her. 'Why do you say that?'

'Because I let her try them on, officer. If you care to wait, I could even dig out a picture of her wearing them. She did a photoshoot here for her burlesque portfolio. Her friend Sharon came and helped out.' She held out her hand for the earrings.

'I would still like to take these earrings for testing and analysis.'

'Is that all you'd like to take? Do you want a blood or urine sample? Or perhaps you want to dust every surface for prints?'

'Just the earrings,' said Peterson, locking eyes with her, refusing to look away.

'Fine. Test them, but you're wasting your time, and I warn you, if there is any damage to them, however minor, I will sue you, and the police force. I have the money to do it.'

*

Peterson bagged up the earrings. He left the room, followed by the five officers. No one spoke until they came out onto the street to the waiting cars.

'Shit,' said Peterson, banging his fist on the bonnet. 'Fuck!'

CHAPTER FIFTY-NINE

Moss slowly regained consciousness, but everything was black. She could see nothing. She lay on her back, on a hard surface, and her head was throbbing. She breathed in. There was a strong goaty smell of body odour, and sour sweat. Strong feelings of nausea flooded over her; she thought she was going to throw up. Panic shot through her as she realised that her mouth was taped up. As she came fully awake, she felt that her hands were fastened tightly in front of her, bound at the wrists, and her ankles were bound too. She swallowed and tried to stay calm. She listened. There was a faint hiss, and then a *whoomph* and a tiny blue square appeared in the corner of her vision. It stayed on for a few seconds and then vanished.

Moss swallowed again. Her throat was so dry and sticky. She slid from side to side, feeling around on the floor. She moved her bound arms to the right and felt a metal grille, and the same on the left. She shuffled up and down, feeling bars above her head and below her feet. Her heart began to beat again and panic rose in her. It threatened to overwhelm her. She was in some kind of cage.

Keep calm, keep calm, calm, calm, came the voice in her head. She thought of the mindfulness techniques that Celia had started to do, to try and control her worry. She'd taken the piss out of Celia for carrying the mindfulness book around with her. Now she wished she'd read it. She tried to remember what it was about, what Celia had said. It was about concentrating on what was actually happening, and not letting your emotions get the better of you.

She concentrated on the cold floor underneath her back. She felt around and was pretty sure it was wood.

What was that blue light? It was a flame; the little flame behind the square hole in a central heating boiler. She had to see if she could sit up, and see what it illuminated, if it came back on again.

Moss slowly breathed in and out. Her nose didn't seem to pull in enough air. She started to sit up, but she had to stop halfway, because the blood beating through her veins seemed to push the pain up to her head, like it was going to explode. She felt nausea roll over her. If she threw up, she would choke.

She slowly lay back down, and took deep breaths, tilting her head to put her cheek against the cold floor. She thought back to what had happened. She thought of the gas mask drawing, the moment when it had all fallen into place – and of course, he'd seen it too.

Panic rose in her again. He was going to kill her. The flame was from a boiler, which probably meant she was in the basement. Tied up. Gagged. In a cage. Fear and hopelessness came over her again. Then Jacob's face came into her mind. His beautiful eyes and his innocent smile. How good he smelt. How he loved to put his arms around her ever-expanding waist, and stand on her feet as she walked around the room, giving him a ride. And Celia, with her honey-blonde hair and her beautiful kind face. Why hadn't she hugged them and told them she loved them before she'd left the house?

Tears filled her eyes, and this gave her energy to fight. She took deep breaths and slowly inched herself up to a sitting position, trying to remember which side of her the blue flame had appeared. She put her head against the bars on the left, and inched herself up. The pain beat through her head, almost overwhelming her. She sucked in more air, deep breaths. He had taken off her jacket, and her hands were bound in front of her from above the wrist

and forearm, down to her knuckles. She could feel it was duct tape, by the way it stuck to the fine hairs on her arms.

Something clicked in a far corner on the right, and the blue flame appeared again. Her vision was blurred, but she managed to adjust her eyes and see the outline of a few shapes. The box shape of the boiler high up on the wall. There were several shapes between it and her, and she could see that the cage was on the floor. The flame went out and she was plunged into darkness again.

She felt the nausea return and her back muscles started to cramp painfully, as well as the muscles in the back of her legs. Having her legs bound was bad enough, but the way her arms were bound in front of her, with her hands pointing forward, made it impossible to sit up straight. The cramp got worse and she winced in pain.

Breathe, breathe, breathe. The pain will pass. She gave a muffled cry as the cramps became unbearable. Her shoulders were hunched over, her elbows locked together. She remembered a video she had seen online, some American self-defence dude who had explained what to do if your hands were bound with duct tape. This was another of Celia's hobbies, going to self-defence classes. She'd wanted Moss to go with her, but it always seemed to clash with work. Celia had shown her this YouTube video… A guy had raised his bound arms above his head, and brought them down so that they hit his stomach, snapping them apart. It was something to do with the tensile strength of duct tape; if you try and pull it one way it just stretches like the strongest chewing gum, but if you use force on it another way it will break cleanly along the ridges.

Moss took a deep breath and went to lift her arms up, but in the darkness, she misjudged the angle and her tightly bound wrists bashed her on the bridge of the nose. She gave a muffled sob, and then began to panic as her nose was flooded with blood. She bent forward, but her wrists were still tightly bound, and she couldn't breathe. In the darkness, she started to choke on her own blood.

CHAPTER SIXTY

T enjoyed the slow walk back through the houses. It gave him time to think. He thought of his life as light and dark. His work with the family portraits was so quaint and down to earth, that he thought of this as the light. Then when he closed the shop and he was alone, he would move through to the darkness.

He had been introduced to the darkness by a girl he'd met fifteen years ago – no, that wasn't quite right. The darkness had always been there, but Tabitha had teased it out of him, brought it to the fore. He had always thought he was the only person in the world who had violent fantasies, but Tabitha, a young, precocious student had encouraged him to experiment with sex toys and role play. She had encouraged him to tell her his secrets in the darkness.

Tabitha loved being tied up, and they would act out a fantasy where he kidnapped and raped her. At the time, it had felt shocking and daring, but looking back now he knew it was kids' stuff. Tabitha had been acting. It was only role play. And her acting wasn't quite good enough. Her fear was wooden and hollow. She was a stepping stone to darker places.

One night, they'd gone to an underground bondage club in Soho. This was where he'd discovered hoods, and breath control, and it also saw the end of his relationship with Tabitha. That night, he'd almost suffocated her. He'd seen real fear in her eyes and he hadn't been able to stop. He'd managed to dissuade her from going to the police.

Over the next few years, he'd indulged in visits to Amsterdam, where he would go to bondage clubs and buy extreme porn, but he'd quickly found that even the hardest type of porn wouldn't satisfy him. Then he discovered gas masks, and in particular engaging in sex acts whilst wearing a gas mask, with the breathing drum closed for breath control, or packed with cotton wool soaked in amyl nitrate.

He couldn't quite remember when the idea came to him to stalk the streets late at night. He'd got high with a guy who he'd invited round to the sex dungeon he had built in his basement. They had somehow ended up in the garden, and then he'd staggered out through the back gate and into the street, where he'd crouched in a dark corner, watching people, hidden from view. The power it had given him was bigger than anything that had come before. He'd got bolder, at first exposing himself to men and women, and then, his first attack.

T slowed as he approached Camera Obscura. He needed time to think. The fact it was a policewoman gave it an extra frisson. After all of the attacks over the years, he had never been caught. He had no police record, they didn't have his DNA, and he had never even had a parking ticket or points on his licence.

She was there in the basement. She had seen him. If he let her go, it would all be over.

He was a risk-taker. He had already thrown them off the scent. He would have to think about how to dispose of her body. She was a big girl. He doubled back and decided to circle the block again. He needed to think and plan.

CHAPTER SIXTY-ONE

Moss raised her arms in the darkness and brought them down, her wrists hitting her chest. She repeated it again. Her nose was pouring with blood and she was fighting to breathe. On the third attempt, her wrists snapped apart and her elbows slammed into the bars. She didn't care about the pain and reached up with her numb fingers, ripping off the piece of duct tape covering her mouth. She gagged and spat and managed to pull huge gulps of air into her lungs.

'Oh my god, oh my god!' she cried, relieved by the sensation of being able to use her hands and breathe through her mouth. She started to work quickly, ripping and pulling at the tape around her ankles until they were free. She rolled her shoulders, and shifted around in the cage into a crouching position. She started to feel around inside the cage. Above her head were thick bars, and she couldn't stand and straighten her legs. There was a padlock on one side of the cage, and it was fastened securely.

'Shit,' she said. It was like a cage for a large dog. There was a click, and the flame lit up the small room. Her eyes had adjusted to the dark now and she could see there was a series of posts mounted on the back wall. She could see shapes and outlines: something long and thin coiled up, and there was a hood with eye holes, and a breathing drum. It was a gas mask. She felt around again. The cage bars were solid, thick metal, but underneath, the base of the cage was wood. Now she had taken off the duct tape, she was able to move more freely around. She swallowed and wiped

her nose, feeling the blood starting to clot. She braced herself in the crouching position and put her back against the top of the cage. She rocked from side to side and felt it shift across the floor a couple of centimetres. It wasn't fixed to the floor. She started to rock it harder, so that it skidded along, away from the brick wall. It took a huge amount of effort and she had to stop a couple of times to catch her breath. She reached through the bars and couldn't feel the brick wall any more, so she was satisfied she had enough room either side. Moss braced her back against the bars, and rocked the cage from side to side, exploiting its low centre of gravity. The sides of the base started to lift off the floor as she rocked harder. Suddenly, it tipped over and landed with a loud clattering crash which echoed around the basement. Moss cried out as she landed painfully on the left side bars, which now were the floor of the cage.

She took a moment to catch her breath and then she started to kick at the base board of the cage.

'You. Should. Have. Taken. My. Boots. Off. You. Dumb. Fuck!' she hissed, punctuating each word with a kick, rhythmically slamming her boots into the base. With each kick, pain jangled in her bones and the metal bars dug into her back and shoulders, but she kept on. Finally, as her feet felt like they were going to explode, the wood cracked – and then her leg went through it. The splinters scraped at her leg and she cried out with pain, but nothing would stop her. She pulled out her leg and started to work on the hole, kicking and pushing and peeling the thick chip board away. It seemed to take forever, but she finally tore her way through, hands and legs filled with splinters. She was free. She scrabbled around in the darkness, managed to find a light switch, and turned it on.

CHAPTER SIXTY-TWO

Moss had barely caught her breath, when she saw the full horror of where she was. There was another, taller cage in one corner of the room, a set of stocks, and table with leather restraints. There were blood stains soaked into the concrete floor. Pornography was pinned up all over the walls: extreme images of nudity and torture. And there was a large-screen TV with rows and rows of DVDs neatly stacked up on a shelf.

Hung on pegs along the wall were whips and chains, a harness, two full-body latex suits, and at the end was a black gas mask with large glass eye holes and an elongated breathing drum; a series of white squares made it look like a face with teeth.

Moss froze when she heard footsteps outside the door. A bolt shot back in the door, and it opened.

Taro stood in the doorway, shaking and white-faced. In one hand, he held a large syringe filled with a dark blue liquid, and in the other he had a pile of black plastic sheeting. He had come to kill her in the neatest and cleanest way possible, but she had complicated things. She was sure he had wanted to poke the syringe though the bars and inject her. It made her think of a terrible film she had seen, about animals being tested on. The way they shrank away from the bars as a needle was poked through and into their skin.

'How did you get out?' he said. His voice was low and even.

'You can see how I got out,' she said. He kept his eyes on her and stepped into the room, closing the door behind him with one of his feet. He took another step towards her.

'Stay back,' she said.

'You shouldn't have come here. I was going to stop. I was going to stop and just melt away… Now I have to deal with you. NOW I HAVE TO DEAL WITH YOU!'

Moss tried not to show her fear. She moved back, putting the cage, lying on its side, between them. He moved closer. She grabbed the top of the cage and tried to slide it towards him as a battering ram, but it didn't slide smoothly on the floor, inching forward, and she lost her footing and fell forward.

Instantly he was on her, moving quickly around the cage, and grabbing her from behind. She fought and struggled, and saw him switch the grip on the syringe, so he had it in his fist with his thumb on the plunger. He held it up, preparing to bring it down on her.

She bent forward and then threw her head back. The back of her skull struck his mouth, shattering his top teeth and breaking his nose. He cried out and staggered back. Moss ran for the door, but it wouldn't open. She yanked at the handle, but it wouldn't budge.

She turned to see Taro staggering around, blood pouring from his nose. He spat out two of his teeth onto the floor, and looked up at her. His face was now crazed. She looked around for something and she saw a table by the door with a large open padlock, next to a chain. Quick as lightning, she grabbed the padlock, and using everything she had, she hurled it at him, aiming high. Time seemed to slow down and it turned in the air, once, twice, before striking him on the temple. He gave her a look of shock and surprise and then crumpled to the floor, his head hitting the concrete with a nasty crack.

Moss made for the door again. It was stiff, but she managed to turn the handle and get it open. She came out into a brightly lit hallway, and slammed the door behind her.

She could see the hallway had old-fashioned wooden panelling, and that she had exited through a secret door. When it was closed,

it blended into the wall. There was an old Singer sewing machine table in the hall, covered in books, plants, plus a bowl for keys. Moss dragged it, squealing, across the stone floor, keeping her eye on the door, thinking that it would open. She pulled it across the door, hoping that it would do for now.

Then she ran for it, down the corridor and into the front of the photographic studio. It was now dark outside and the door was still locked, but she picked up one of the tripods for the photography lights, and with almost hysterical fear, hurled it through the plate glass window. The window exploded outwards. She kicked aside the glass with her foot, climbed through and ran for it, down the path and out into the street.

Her car was gone, and she didn't have a phone. She staggered down the street, the adrenalin pumping, feeling the blood pouring from the back of her head. She tried to find a phone box, but there was nothing on the road.

Moss ran to the end of the road, where it curved around to New Cross station. The road was busy with young teenagers piling out of the station, all dressed up for a night out. The noise was deafening. She pushed her way through the crowds, and saw an old phone box next to the station. She grabbed the receiver and her first impulse was to speak to Celia. She dialled 100, for the operator, and then she asked to make a reverse-charge call.

CHAPTER SIXTY-THREE

Erika was sad to see Isaac leave. He had set off back to London and she hoped that he wouldn't hit any more snow storms. She lit a fresh fire in the stove and checked her phone, but there was nothing about Moss. She felt restless, and so far away from everything. She thought back to her visit to the old house. In the past few years, she had thought of London as temporary, a place she was exiled to after what had happened in Manchester, but she realised now that London was now home to her. Life up north was in the past. She no longer belonged here.

She flicked through the TV channels, but there was nothing she fancied watching. She pulled on her coat, an old hat and a pair of gloves, and set off to the graveyard, which was a short walk across the fields. It was a clear, starry night, and as she climbed the hill, she could see the houses in the village spread out below, their lights glowing in the windows. The moon sailed out from behind the clouds as she reached the entrance to the graveyard, meaning she was able to see as she picked her way through the rows of graves to find Mark's.

His headstone was made of polished black granite, and it glittered in the moonlight:

IN MEMORY OF
MARK FOSTER
1ST AUGUST 1970 – 8TH JULY 2014
LOVED AND REMEMBERED ALWAYS

Erika took a Jack Daniel's whisky miniature from her pocket, undid the cap, took a small sip, and then poured the rest into the soil.

'I never thought this was how we'd end up,' she said. 'I miss you every day…' She wiped a tear away with her gloved hand. 'I've told you this so many times before, but I have to live my life, and go on living my life. If it were me, I wouldn't want you to stay here on earth and be miserable… I've decided I'm going to sell the house. I went back today, and it's not the place I remember any more. It's not our home. I'm going to buy a new place, and make it my home…' Erika swallowed back the tears. 'Because you're not here, and I can't carry on living my life with a space beside me that needs to be filled. You're never going to be forgotten, and I will always love you, but I can't carry on being half a person.'

Clouds slid across the moon, plunging her into darkness.

'I sometimes check on Jerome Goodman. I wonder where he is. If he even thinks about all of us. I run his name through the computers at work, but he's vanished. If I ever got the chance to spend time in a room alone with him… I'd kill him, slowly, for what he did to you, and me, and…'

A freezing cold chill blew along the path, and she felt the cold seeping into her shoes and gloves, and on the small of her back. 'I'm going to look after your dad. I'm getting a carer to come in, and I'm going to keep more of an eye on things, and visit more.' She pressed her fingers to her lips and put them against the gold letters spelling out his name.

*

When Erika arrived back at the cottage, the fire had died down. She raked the ash in the stove and put another couple of logs on. Just as she closed the stove, her phone rang. It was Melanie.

'Erika, there's been an incident with Moss,' she said, without preamble. Erika listened as Melanie explained what had happened with Moss, and that she had been found, barely conscious, in a phone box in New Cross.

'Is she okay?'

'I hope so. She's just in the A&E, having a scan. She has bad concussion. We've arrested a thirty-five-year-old man called Taro Williams, who runs a photography studio in New Cross. Moss had been to talk to him, based on a lead she'd got from the Forest Hill Jobcentre. Apparently, Joseph Pitkin worked as his assistant in early 2016.'

Erika felt exhilarated, and then frustrated that she wasn't there. 'I'm up north; I can't leave my father-in-law.'

'I know, and please, stay. Everything is in hand here. Williams is a man of means and he has already hired a top-notch solicitor, so we're going to have to move very carefully and make sure we do everything by the book.'

'Moss should have called in where she was going; she put herself in danger,' said Erika.

'Are you kidding me? How many times have you put yourself in danger? You've been beaten up more times than Jackie Chan. You're like the bionic woman!'

'Very funny.'

'Sorry. I'm just delighted we could have this case sewn up so quickly.'

'Pending DNA tests,' said Erika.

'Of course… Now, take as long as you need with your father-in-law.'

Erika went to say something else, but Melanie had hung up.

Erika sat up for a long time, watching the fire burn down through the window of the stove, feeling a long way away from it all.

CHAPTER SIXTY-FOUR

It was three o'clock in the morning, but the atmosphere at Lewisham Row station was one of intense excitement. Peterson, McGorry, Crane and Superintendent Hudson had all been called back to work when the news had come in about Moss. After calling Celia, she'd phoned for police backup, and then, finally, about to lose consciousness, she had phoned Peterson.

Uniformed officers had sped round to Camera Obscura, where they found Taro Williams in the basement. He had regained consciousness, and after being checked over by a paramedic, he had been arrested and brought to Lewisham Row. His fingerprints and a sample of his DNA had been taken, and rushed over to the lab.

McGorry and Crane were with Superintendent Hudson in the observation suite at Lewisham Row. They watched as Taro Williams was being questioned by Peterson.

'He's not saying a word,' said McGorry, as they stared at the screen showing the live feed.

'He's a big bastard, isn't he?' said Crane.

'A big hairy bastard. His eyes creeped me out,' said McGorry. 'When they brought him in and booked him, took his fingerprints and DNA, he was completely impassive. Like none of it bothered him.'

On the screen, Peterson asked Taro to confirm that he was the owner of Camera Obscura and the building, and if he worked full-time as a photographer.

Taro leaned forward amiably. 'Yes. I inherited the business from my father when he died twelve years ago,' he said. His voice was soft and he was well-spoken.

Superintendent Hudson's phone rang.

'This is forensics,' she said. The guys watched as she answered the phone, and McGorry crossed his fingers.

'It's a match! The DNA sample taken from blood on the broken glass at the office block doors in West Norwood matches the sample we took from him in the custody suite. We've got him!' cried Melanie. They punched the air with their fists.

'What a sicko,' said McGorry.

'It's enough to charge him for all six of the sexual assaults, and the murder of Marissa Lewis?' asked Crane.

'Yes, especially the murder of Marissa. I don't want him back out on the streets. He has no record, and I don't want to give his slimy solicitor the opportunity to wangle him bail by not making a murder charge,' said Melanie. She leaned over to the microphone. 'Peterson, I need you to suspend the interview for a sec. We have the DNA results back.'

Peterson came out. Melanie gave him the results and the go-ahead to charge Taro Williams.

They watched from the observation suite as Peterson went back in and formally arrested Williams for the sexual assault of Rachel Elder, Kelvin Price, Jenny Thorndike, Diana Crow and Jason Bates, and the murder of Marissa Lewis.

Taro remained impassive, going so far as to pick a speck of lint from his jacket as the charges were read out. He then looked up at the camera, and the officers in the observation suite felt a chill run through them. It was as if he could see them. He smiled. It was a broad toothy grin, but it didn't reach his eyes.

CHAPTER SIXTY-FIVE

Erika stayed up north for two weeks. In between visiting Edward every day, she had had a stair lift put into his cottage. She'd also done some decorating, and registered all his utilities online so that she could check that his bills were being paid.

During one of the last hospital visits, before he was due to be discharged, Edward had been enthusiastic about these ideas and changes. That is until she told him she had hired a carer to come in and visit him three times a week.

'I'm not having some stranger let themselves in to wipe my backside!' he'd said. By now he was sitting up in bed, and well on the road to recovery.

'Edward. It won't be like that. She'll be there to help with whatever you need doing.'

'She?' he'd said, narrowing his eyes.

'Do you want a bloke?'

'Good Lord, no.'

'She'll help with the washing, cleaning, making a meal, or she can ring up about something, like a doctor's appointment. She'll be company. I promise you there will be no backsides being wiped.'

'I'm too young for a carer!'

'Okay. How about we call her your PA?'

He'd laughed. 'Who is she? I can't have a Tory in the house. And I don't want some youngster, glued to their mobile phone the whole time.'

'Of course not.'

'And I want a northerner. I don't mind southerners, but having one in the house three times a week would be too much.'

'She's sort of a northerner... North Slovakia. Her name's Lydia. She's twenty-five, speaks excellent English and she's been caring, sorry, working part-time as a PA, for a lady in the next village.'

'Do you have a photo of her?'

'No. You'll meet her when you come home, which I hope, is tomorrow.'

Edward was discharged from hospital the next day, and Erika was waiting at home with Lydia. He liked her, and they instantly struck up a rapport, and Erika felt like the last piece in the puzzle had been slotted into place.

Erika spent the rest of the day and the next with Edward. On Sunday January 14th, she left to drive back to London. He came to the taxi with her, now walking with the aid of one stick, and they hugged.

'Now, you'll keep doing your exercises,' said Erika.

'Yes, love.'

'And keep eating well. Lydia is bringing over goulash tomorrow.'

'I'm looking forward to it.'

'And use the stair lift. No showing off to her that you can climb them on your own.'

He nodded.

'I've told Lydia to make sure you keep those compression stockings on for another two weeks. They prevent…'

'Yes, blood clots,' he said, lifting up the bottom of his trousers to show the green support stockings. 'And you won't be a stranger?'

'No, of course not,' she said.

Erika felt she was going to cry, so she hugged him again, and got into the taxi. The journey down to London by train was smooth and fast. The snow had all melted, and despite having been busy

for the past two and a half weeks, she felt rested. The break had done her good.

When she got into the flat, it was freezing cold and there was a huge pile of post on the mat.

The next morning, she woke early and drove into work at Lewisham Row. She went through the reception, and greeted Desk Sergeant Woolf, a large, red-faced officer who was a few weeks away from retirement.

'Happy New Year,' she said.

'Bloody hell, you're a bit late,' he replied. 'New Year seems in the mists of time. There's already Easter Eggs in the shops!'

Erika grabbed some coffee and went up to her office on the fourth floor, starting to work through all the post and emails which had banked up over the past couple of weeks. Around mid-morning, there was a knock on her door, and Superintendent Hudson poked her head around.

'Alright stranger, welcome back. How's the father-in-law?'

'Well on the way to recovery… I'm just catching up on everything,' she replied, indicating a pile of folders on the desk beside her.

'I sent you an email yesterday, and I didn't want it to get lost amongst everything else in your inbox. We've been putting together the evidence and casefiles to go over to the CPS and defence team involved in the Taro Williams case. We've got the official DNA match, linking him to two of the attacks, with enough circumstantial evidence to implicate him in the other attacks. The CCTV footage will be submitted along with a statement from Mrs Fryatt with regards to the murder of Marissa Lewis.'

'Statement from Mrs Fryatt?'

'Yes, she's gone on record to say that Taro Williams attacked Marissa a few weeks before he killed her.'

'Surely that's a bit vague, she said that Marissa said…'

'The case is a slam dunk. We have him on CCTV following Marissa into her front garden. I want you to check through everything and submit your report before we sign off. Moss and Peterson have been working on it whilst you've been away, as I'm sure you know.'

'Are you confident of a conviction for Marissa's murder?'

'Confident as you can be with CCTV evidence, a DNA sample, a past history of violence... You're not going to tell me that you think there's a copycat killer out there?'

'No. Just asking the questions. No stupid questions when it comes to a murder investigation,' said Erika. Melanie nodded.

'Taro Williams has money, and he has the best of the best working on his behalf, and you know how good they can be at sniffing out a minor error in procedure. The hard copy file is there on top.'

'I'll look at it now.'

Melanie's phone rang and she excused herself. Erika pulled the file off the pile, and started to look through it. There were statements from all the attack victims, from Marissa's mother, Mrs Fryatt, and some of Marissa's colleagues. What upset Erika was seeing Moss's statement, where she described her ordeal of having been captured against her will.

Erika pored over the custody photos taken of Taro Williams. He was a big man, with a wide face and large features. He seemed so impassive in the shots, with dead eyes. She logged in to Holmes, and accessed the police interviews which were being submitted on a disk to the prosecution. He had been interviewed three times in the space of two days. In the first interview, Taro Williams sat impassive opposite Peterson, and in the other interviews, Peterson

was joined by McGorry. Taro remained in handcuffs throughout all three interviews, despite his solicitor requesting that they be removed. Taro was gangly, and sat hunched over the table. The T-shirt and tracksuit bottoms he wore looked too small. Like he had been stuffed into his clothes. Erika ran the second interview forward to the end, and then watched as Taro stood to leave. He towered over the solicitor, McGorry, and Peterson, who was himself six feet tall.

Erika then went back to the CCTV footage taken from the school opposite Marissa Lewis's house on the night she was killed. She watched as Taro Williams arrived at the house ahead of Marissa. The figure dressed in black, wearing a gas mask, walked into shot by the gate, moving carefully and purposefully along in the snow, almost staggering against the slippery surface. He reached the front gate and looked through into the front garden, and up at the house. Then he moved into the alleyway beside the house, to wait in the shadows.

She glanced down at the attached notes with the time stamp, and she ran the footage forward. Marissa appeared at the gate. She was such a beautiful girl, thought Erika, as she watched her move gracefully in her long coat, with her vanity case hooked over her arm. Marissa opened the gate and went through, vanishing in the shadows of the front garden. Ten seconds later, the figure in black, wearing the gas mask, moved out of the shadows in the alleyway and approached the gate, carrying a long knife.

'There you are, Taro,' murmured Erika. On the screen, he moved through the front gate and was swallowed up by the darkness.

Erika peered at the footage and felt panic rise in her chest. She ran it back to when the figure in the gas mask reached the gate post, and played it again, and then again. With shaking hands she went back to the footage from the third custody interview with

Taro Williams, when Peterson led him into the interview room. She paused it, and compared it with the figure standing by the gate post. She picked up her phone and called Melanie.

'You need to get up here, now,' she said.

CHAPTER SIXTY-SIX

'How tall is Taro Williams?' asked Erika. Melanie was sitting beside her, as she played back the CCTV footage from outside Marissa's house on Christmas Eve.

'I don't know. He's tall …' Melanie started.

'He's six feet four, or 193 cm,' said Erika, holding up the report from the custody suite when Taro had been arrested and brought to the station. 'Look at the footage again.' She dragged the time stamp underneath the video window to just before Marissa Lewis appeared in shot, arriving back at her house. Erika paused the video as she reached the gate post. 'Marissa Lewis was five feet two, that's about 157 cm. You can see she is only a little taller than the gate post.'

'Okay,' said Melanie, sounding uneasy at where this was going. Erika took a small sticker and where the video was paused, she placed the sticker so it touched the top of Marissa's head. 'OK, moving the CCTV footage on,' said Erika. 'Bearing in mind the marker on the screen…' The figure in the gas mask came moving through the snow with difficulty, head bent down. Erika paused the video when he reached the gate post. 'You can see here that the person in the gas mask…'

'Taro Williams,' insisted Melanie.

'The person in the gas mask is only fractionally taller than Marissa.' She placed another sticker on the screen, which was only slightly higher than the first. 'Taro Williams is thirty-six centimetres taller than Marissa Lewis. That person in the gas mask

is not Taro Williams. Unless he's the incredible shrinking man.' Melanie leaned in and ran the footage back and then forward, her face clouding over. 'We have two people here to compare against one fixed object, the gate post,' said Erika.

'Shit.'

'And this would be leapt on by the defence team. I've seen cases where it's come down to a height difference on CCTV of a few centimetres. They would ask for the footage to be examined, and they would apply more rigorous tests than a couple of stickers on the screen.'

'Fuck!' said Melanie, slamming her hand down on the desk. 'Our case is screwed. We have no case.'

'Yes, we do have a case!' said Erika. 'Taro Williams assaulted five people, and we can link him with DNA, but I'm more concerned as to who the hell killed Marissa wearing the gas mask. It's not Taro Williams.'

CHAPTER SIXTY-SEVEN

Early next morning, Erika pulled up outside Moss's house in Ladywell. She was going to get out, but Moss appeared at the gate and got in the car.

'Morning. It's good to see you're in one piece,' she said, giving Moss an unexpected hug.

'Oh, you know me. I don't fall down, I bounce,' Moss said, her cheeks flushing red. Erika started the engine, and they rode in silence for a minute. She gave Moss a sideways glance. Her silence was unusual. She was always upbeat and chatty.

'Are you crying?' asked Erika.

'No,' said Moss, wiping tears away angrily.

'It's too early for allergies.'

'I missed the height thing on the CCTV. It's such a rookie mistake. I'm fucking embarrassed…'

'Whose fault is it?'

'Mine.'

Erika nodded.

'You win brownie points for taking responsibility. I'd be annoyed if you tried to blame someone else.'

'Not my style, Boss.'

'I know.'

'When we caught Taro Williams we went into evidence gathering mode. Most of the team was re-assigned so I lost manpower. Again, that's not an excuse. I'm not cut out to be SIO. I've realised I prefer playing second fiddle.'

'But you caught Taro Williams.'

Moss shook her head. 'I feel like I just blundered into it. And then nearly got myself killed in the process.'

'But you didn't,' said Erika. 'And he would have carried on attacking people, and now he's off the streets.'

'Off the streets, and still refusing to talk.'

'That's nothing new. He can talk or he can keep his mouth shut. Either way, we've got DNA.'

'You're a poet, and you don't even know it.'

Erika grinned. 'As I said. You did a great job.'

Moss waved it away, her cheeks flushing again. 'Enough about me. How were things up north?'

'Edward is doing good. For so many years he's been the responsible adult, and me the youngster. It made me aware of how old I am, now I'm caring for him.'

'You're not old! What's the saying? You're only as old as the man or woman you feel.'

'There's nothing happening in that department, unless I count the old geezer in Sainsbury's who rubbed up against me at the till.'

Moss grinned. 'Good to have you back, Erika.'

'Thanks,' she said, smiling in return. 'It's good to be back. Now, onwards and upwards. Let's hope today gives us a breakthrough.'

Erika indicated and they turned into Coniston Road, and drove towards Mandy Trent's house.

They parked a few doors down from Mandy's house. The snow was long melted, and it was break time at the school opposite. The playground was full of kids, their loud playing and chatter filling the street. Erika and Moss got out of the car, and joined a small team of four forensic height analysts who were setting up their equipment outside the front gate of the house. Half of the

playground opposite had been cordoned off, giving a clear view to conduct the test using the CCTV camera mounted on the wall at the end of the school building. One of the guys was positioning an oblong of plastic, like a giant ruler, next to the gate post outside the house. It reached up to two metres tall, and 5 cm increments were marked out on it with red lines. Another woman was unpacking a tripod and camera, and setting it up at the same height and angle further along the pavement towards the top of Coniston Road. Some of the more curious children who weren't running around and playing were lined up at the railings, watching.

Erika and Moss introduced themselves to the team, and then went through the front gate. The hedge had been chopped down, leaving just the low wall surrounding the tiny garden, which without snow was just a patch of flattened earth. Marissa's mother, Mandy, was also watching the proceedings from her front doorstep. She was dishevelled, and smoking a cigarette. They said hello, and asked how she was doing. She said she was making the preparations for Marissa's funeral, which would be taking place in a few days.

'I want to have "All Things Bright and Beautiful" play, 'cos I loved singing that hymn when I was at school,' she said, sucking on the butt of her cigarette. 'Do you think that's nice?'

'Yes, I love that hymn,' said Moss.

'And with all the flowers. I'm gonna have lilies. Marissa liked lilies. Joan's ex-husband runs the florist down in Honor Oak Park… He's gonna do me a good deal, get some nice ones which are open. I hate lilies on bunches when they're closed,' she said. 'I went to Joseph Pitkin's funeral the other day, I sat at the back, mind. They got lilies for the top of his coffin, and they was all closed up. It was a burial, and all I could think was that they would never open, what with the cold weather we've been having. They would just die, before they had the chance to bloom… And then

it made me think of Marissa. She was killed before she got the chance to bloom. What do you call it?'

A look passed between Erika and Moss.

'It was a tragedy,' said Erika.

'No,' said Mandy, impatiently flicking the cigarette butt into the hedge. 'It's what you call it? A metaphor. The lily not opening, that's a metaphor for Marissa, and for Joseph.'

Erika and Moss nodded in agreement.

'So why are you all measuring my gate post?' she added.

'It's for the CCTV evidence. Standard procedure. It helps give us more detail in court.'

'Does it matter that I had the hedge cut down? I just didn't feel safe with it there. There's nowhere for anyone to hide.'

'It's fine,' said Erika. They could now see up and down the street, and Don Walpole emerged from his front door with a bag of rubbish. He noticed them, and nodded his head, and then went back indoors. Mandy lit another cigarette.

'Jeanette's home from hospital. They put an implant in her stomach, to stop her drinking. One sip of anything alcoholic and she pukes it back up… I just hope he's stocked up on carpet cleaner.'

'Have you packed away any of Marissa's belongings yet?' asked Erika.

'No. I can't bring myself to do it. Not until she's buried. Joan's good with cleaning; she said she'd come and help me, we can work out what to keep and what to give to charity. A lot of her costumes can go on eBay,' said Mandy.

'You take your time, there's never any rush with these things.'

'I'm glad you've got the bastard who done this to her… I'd seen the stuff on the news about him, skulking around the streets at night. I know this is a rough area, but you never expect this kind of thing to happen, literally on your own doorstep.'

'Would you mind if we took one last look in Marissa's bedroom, just to make absolutely sure we have everything for the court case?' asked Erika.

'Yes, go on up. Of course, you know where it is,' said Mandy. The sun came out, and she rested her head against the brick wall, closing her eyes and tilting her pale lined face upwards.

They came inside and went up the stairs to the front bedroom. It looked just as it had when Erika had come to look at it with McGorry. The same posters were on the wall, and all of the burlesque gear was untouched. She went to the window and looked down at the street below. Several of the neighbours had come out to gawp at the team of forensic height analysts. A bell rang opposite, signalling the end of break time, and the children all started to run to line up at the top end of the playground. Mandy had crossed the road, still in her slippers, nightie and thick winter coat, and she was talking to Joan, who was smoking a cigarette on her front step.

'The diamond earrings are still bugging me,' said Erika. 'They feel like they are the key to this. Why did Marissa go to the jeweller's where Charles Fryatt worked? And did he know she was there? I've read the reports, and he says he only knew when McGorry went back with Marissa's friend, Ella. And they deny that the earrings were even the same ones belonging to Mrs Fryatt.'

'Charles Fryatt has an alibi, his wife, and he's also a very tall man,' said Moss, picking up a fire-eating rod from in front of the tiny fireplace and examining the tip.

'According to Martin, the costume guy at the Matrix Club, and Ella, one of the dancers, Marissa said she took the diamond earrings from Mrs Fryatt, but who is telling the truth? We don't know where those earrings came from, or where they are now.'

'Could Mandy have taken them off the dead body?' asked Moss, joining her at the window. Joan and Mandy were lighting up fresh cigarettes.

'There's still a question mark where Mandy was sleeping on the night Marissa died. She told us that she was sleeping upstairs in the back bedroom, but there was evidence that she slept downstairs on the sofa.'

'There was a duvet on the downstairs sofa,' said Erika. 'But that's hardly evidence. She could have just been napping.'

'Erika. This case comes down to the height of whoever did it. It's not all about diamonds, or should I say, the diamond earrings.'

'What did you just say?'

'This case is about the height of the person who killed her, we know it's not Taro Williams…'

'No, after that.'

'It's not all about the earrings. At least, I don't think it is.'

Erika was now pacing up and down the room.

'When me and Peterson went to the Matrix Club, the guy who does the costumes told us Marissa kept saying it was all about "the diamond" not "diamonds". That it would be "the diamond" that would make her fortune… He said something along the lines, like, "I know Marissa was stupid, but she did know the difference between the singular and plural." If she wasn't talking about the diamond earrings, then what was she talking about?'

'Now I'm getting confused,' said Moss. 'There's a diamond embroidered on her costumes.' She went over to the three mannequins, which were lined up along the wall and wearing some of Marissa's costumes, embroidered with the diamond logo. 'She was planning to go off to New York, and perform as Honey Diamond. Maybe she thought she was going to make her fortune there?'

Erika shook her head, and looked out of the window. Mandy and Joan were still deep in conversation. Joan said something out of the corner of her mouth, and Mandy hooted with laughter, expelling a long stream of cigarette smoke. The last of the kids were filing back into the school building, and one of the forensic guys was shouting at a group of the neighbours.

'Please get back!' he said, waving his gloved hands at them. They were walking backwards – two old ladies, and a young lad – much like sheep do when they are being herded.

Erika looked back at the bedroom, and spied a large framed photo on the wall, amongst the framed publicity shots of Marissa. It was of a huge diamond, mounted on a ring, sparkling with clarity. She crossed to the picture and carefully lifted it off the wall. She started to examine it. There was a thick paper backing on the frame.

'Do you have any latex gloves?' she said. Moss rummaged in her pockets and handed her a pair.

CHAPTER SIXTY-EIGHT

Erika placed the framed print face-down on the bed, and they stared at the thick backing paper.

'The frame is pretty old and crappy,' said Erika. 'And the diamond image is faded, like it's been on the wall and caught the sun, but this backing paper looks brand new.'

Erika took a pair of nail scissors from a pot on the desk by the window, and Moss held the frame as she neatly scored the thin backing paper, and then carefully peeled it away. They stood back and stared. There was nothing inside but the print, which was on a piece of card. Erika lifted it gently away from the frame. It felt thick, and she held it up to the light.

'It's faded yellow on one side, but the back is white,' said Moss. 'But then again, only the side facing the window would fade.'

Erika examined the edges of the card. 'There's a slight overlap here, look, with this white side, and the other which has the yellower shade.'

'It's two pieces, they've been stuck together,' said Moss. Erika gently moved her gloved fingers over the diamond print. Her fingers stopped in the centre.

'There's a slight ridge, here; it feels like there's something inside. Oblong: could be folded paper, or an envelope which has been glued in between the two pieces of card.'

*

Erika and Moss bagged up the print and rushed it over to Lewisham Row station, where they took it into one of the sterile

medical examining rooms. They donned gloves and masks, and using a scalpel Erika carefully cut between the two sheets of glued-together card.

'Careful,' said Moss, watching as Erika slowly pushed the knife up through the seam between the two pieces of card. Erika finally got the two pieces to part.

Inside lay a small brown envelope.

'We should take this to forensics,' said Moss.

'I know,' said Erika. 'I won't touch where the envelope is stuck down. Forensics will have to test for saliva… If it is anything that needs testing.'

She carefully slit along the top of the envelope with the scalpel, and she pulled out two pieces of folded paper. The first was a scanned image of a set of German identity papers, dating back to October 1942. They were of a young woman called Elsa Neubukov. The woman in the sepia photo was twenty-two, having been born in January 1920. There were three fingerprints in the identity papers: a thumb, and a right and left index finger. What chilled Erika was the stamp of the Third Reich, Nazi Germany: the eagle with wings spread, and underneath, the swastika. The woman in the sepia photo had short fair hair, a high forehead and a handsome face, staring almost defiantly at the camera.

'This Elsa was born in 1920. She would be ninety-seven, almost ninety-eight, now,' said Moss quietly. They turned their attention to the second piece of paper. It was another scanned-in image, this time of an Austrian passport. It was dated six years later, three years after the end of the Second World War. The photo was different, but it was the same woman. This time the name said Elsa Becher. It had the same date of birth and a set of fingerprints.

Moss and Erika looked at each other.

'What is Elsa Fryatt's date of birth and maiden name?'

'We can soon find out,' said Erika. She took out her phone and called up Elsa Fryatt's address, and the council tax records. 'Date of birth is the same. We'll need to check out her maiden name.'

'Elsa Fryatt has been living under another identity?' started Moss.

'But these are scans, where are the originals?' asked Erika. She turned over the first German identity papers scan, and she saw that on the back was a phone number written in pen. It was long, and Erika didn't recognise the code. There was also an obscure web address ending in the .de German domain.

'You think this is Marissa's handwriting?' said Moss.

'We'll soon find out,' said Erika, already dialling the number.

CHAPTER SIXTY-NINE

Two days later, after following up several leads, Erika and Moss arrived at Elsa Fryatt's house. It was a grey morning, and the street outside was empty and quiet. Moss glanced nervously at Erika as they opened the gate and started up the path to the front door. They were about to ring the bell when Mrs Fryatt appeared at the gate behind them, carrying bags of shopping.

'Good morning, officers. Can I help you?' she asked, taking a key from her coat pocket. As she walked toward them, Erika thought how sprightly she was for a woman of ninety-seven.

'Morning, Mrs Fryatt. We've come to return the diamond earrings my colleague took away for forensic examination,' said Erika, holding up a small evidence bag containing the small velvet box.

'And it takes two of you to do this?' said Mrs Fryatt, putting the bags of shopping down and opening the front door.

Erika gave her a disarming smile. 'We understand they are very valuable, and we just need you to sign a couple of forms to confirm that we are returning your property, and everything is in order.' There was a moment when she thought Mrs Fryatt wouldn't invite them in, but she relented.

'Very well,' she said. Moss went to pick up the shopping bags for her, but Mrs Fryatt batted her away. 'I can manage.'

They followed her into the house and down the long hallway to the kitchen. Charles was filling the kettle, and he went very pale when he saw Erika and Moss.

'Charles, would you make these officers some tea? They are here to return my earrings.' She gave him a look and he nodded. She took off her coat and hung it over a chair. 'And put my shopping away.'

They left Charles in the kitchen and followed her through to the large living room. Mrs Fryatt showed them to a sofa, and took the armchair opposite.

'Okay. Here are your earrings,' said Erika, placing the small clear evidence bag on the polished coffee table in front of her. 'Please can you check them over.'

Mrs Fryatt put on a pair of glasses, took the box from the bag and opened it. The earrings nestled, sparkling on the small blue cushion.

'Yes, my babies,' she said, peering at them and holding them up to the light.

'We also need you to sign a form, which states that your property has been returned to you,' said Erika. 'If you could make sure everything is in order and that they are in fact your earrings.'

There was a rattling sound as Charles brought in a stack of teacups on a tray. His hands shook as he took them off and placed them on the table.

'Charles, I need you to cast your expert eye over these,' said Mrs Fryatt, handing him the earrings in the box. 'I have to sign that they are mine. I can tell the difference between a diamond and a zircon, but I need to be sure these officers aren't taking me for a ride.' She smiled across at Erika and Moss, but the smile didn't quite make it to her eyes. Charles took a jeweller's eyepiece from his pocket, and peered through it at the earrings.

'He always comes prepared.' Mrs Fryatt grinned indulgently. Charles peered at them, breathing heavily, and then went to the window to catch them in the light. The clock ticked.

'Everything okay?' asked Erika.

'Yes,' he said coming back and placing the box on the table. Moss opened the folder she was carrying and took out a pre-filled form, and put it in front of Mrs Fryatt.

'Check we have your name and address correct, and sign underneath,' she said.

Mrs Fryatt took a pen from a corner of the table and scanned the form, then signed her name at the bottom.

Erika leaned over and placed the scanned identity papers for Elsa Neubukov on top of the form. Mrs Fryatt stared at the sepia photograph and the swastika stamp of the Third Reich for a long moment, frozen in shock. Then she looked up at Erika. Her eyes moved to Moss, and then to Charles, whose mouth was also agape. She sat back and put a shaking hand to her mouth.

'We found these papers concealed in a print on the wall of Marissa Lewis's bedroom,' said Erika. 'Along with these…' She placed a copy of the Austrian passport for Elsa Becher, dated six years later, beside the identity papers. Then she produced a copy of a marriage certificate, for Elsa Becher and Arnold Fryatt, and placed it beside the Austrian passport. 'You can see we have a paper trail from Elsa Neubukov, to Elsa Becher and then Elsa Fryatt. All of them are you.'

'This is absurd,' Mrs Fryatt said. All the colour had drained from her face, and her hands shook. She leant forward and took the scan of the German identity papers. 'This isn't an original. This is a sick joke. That girl was a liar, and you can do all sorts of things on computers these days…'

'You'll see there's a phone number written on the back,' said Erika. 'Marissa's mother has confirmed that is Marissa's handwriting. It's the phone number for a Dr Arnold Schmidt, who works in Hamburg at an office responsible for investigating historical Nazi war crimes.'

Charles had slumped against the wall by the door, and he looked pale and ill.

'You should sit down, Charles,' said Erika. He moved to the sofa and sat at the opposite end to his mother. 'Dr Schmidt wasn't aware of your identity, Mrs Fryatt, but Marissa was. Or she put two and two together when she found these identity papers. She called him a few weeks before Christmas, making some vague enquiries. She said she had seen an article in one of the tabloid newspapers that said these so-called Nazi hunters were offering a reward for information about anyone who worked in concentrations camps during the war. He says he told her that the reward was two thousand euros… I think Marissa realised that she could make much more money from blackmailing you.'

'Lies!' she hissed. 'That little bitch; she made this up. Where are the originals? Tell me? Where?'

Moss opened the file again and gave Erika a sheet of paper.

'Mrs Fryatt, or can I call you Elsa Neubukov? Elsa, you worked at the Mauthausen-Gusen concentration camp in upper Austria.'

'Lies! Austria was *never* a willing participant in the war. We were annexed into the German Third Reich. The people didn't have a choice, we just became part of it all, on the whims of politicians.'

'Dr Schmidt was able, very quickly, to access records from the Mauthausen-Gusen camp. You worked there, Elsa,' said Erika.

'Don't call me that,' she cried, putting her hands to her ears.

'You took part in the extermination of people, based purely on the race they were born. They were used for slave labour, experimented on, tortured.'

Elsa slammed a hand down on the coffee table. 'You think we were responsible for this? You think the Austrian people wanted this? We had no choice!' she cried, her eyes blazing.

'Mauthausen was one of the biggest concentration camp complexes in the German-controlled part of Europe,' said Erika.

'I don't need a fucking history lesson!' cried Elsa. Charles was staring blankly at the paperwork on the table.

Erika went on, 'Prisoners at Mauthausen-Gusen were forced to work building arms, quarrying stone. The conditions were horrific. What did you do, exactly? The records state that you were a guard, which is very broad, but it was your job to control the prisoners, yes? To move them from place to place, to dole out discipline and order, to carry out orders. And what were those orders? They were from Hitler and the Third Reich. Orders to reshape Europe to their Aryan ideals. Do you see yourself as part of a superior race? What do you think of me, Elsa? I'm Slavic, and we were thought of by the Third Reich as a subhuman inferior race.'

'Officers, this is too much. My mother is an old lady, look at her!' said Charles.

'Too much?' said Erika, starting to lose it. 'Just because she's an old lady, we should just forget? Or perhaps I'm being too political? Or am I trying to force my liberal agenda onto you?' Charles was shaking his head. 'It makes me sick that people think anything to do with the Holocaust and concentration camps is somehow diminished by time. The systematic slaughter of millions of people based on their genetic make-up or the colour of their skin is something which should never be forgotten or excused. It's still going on today. Your mother is as guilty today as she was all those years ago.' She stared at Elsa, and looked around at the opulent house, at Elsa's fine clothes and at the diamond earrings lying in their open box next to the tea cups.

'Dr Schmidt, Dr Schmidt,' muttered Elsa. 'How old is he?'

'I don't know,' said Erika.

'Is he the same age as me?' she said, thumping her chest with her fingers.

'He's of working age. In his fifties.'

'Then how can he possibly know what it was like?' Elsa spat.

'You were a guard at a concentration camp, Elsa. It wasn't a holiday camp!' said Moss.

'And if I had refused the job, they would have put me in that camp!' insisted Elsa, her voice low, her eyes blazing. 'The German soldiers, they came knocking around the farms… Where we lived it was farmland, we had a farm. My father was one of the best farmers for miles around, and they went to the farms, demanding that the young adults came to work at the camps. They told us if we didn't, then we'd be put there with our families. You people never lived through it; you can't imagine what it was like!'

'And yet you lived through it, and you must have watched hundreds die, even thousands,' said Erika.

'Do you have family?' snapped Elsa.

'No.'

'You?' She pointed at Moss.

'Yes,' said Moss.

'You have children?'

'I have a small son.'

'Then if the Germany army knocked on your door and told you that if you didn't go and work in the camp, your little boy would be gassed? What would you do?'

'I would fight. I would fight for my boy, and I would fight them,' said Moss, red-faced and shaking.

'Everyone has morals until it matters.'

Erika resisted the urge to punch the old woman in the face, and when she looked across, she could see Moss fighting the same impulse.

'So, you trotted off every day to work and brutalised prisoners, sent people to their death, and played your part in the extermination of millions. Did you whistle on your way to work, thinking that you were safe?'

'Of course not!'

'The concentration camp where you were a guard was labelled grade three, which were the toughest camps for the "incorrigible

political enemies of the Reich." It was also one of the most profitable.'

'How many times do I have to tell you. I didn't agree with Hitler! I worked there because I had to!'

They were silent for a moment, and Erika could hear the clock ticking again.

'Elsa. Your son married a Jewish woman,' said Erika. 'I just don't understand.'

'We didn't know,' said Charles, speaking for the first time. 'My father went to his grave not knowing. My mother, she changed her details when she immigrated to England. She forged her papers. Dad knew she was Austrian, and that she was the daughter of a farmer. He knew that Austria had been occupied, but none of us knew…' He buried his head in his hands.

'When did Marissa find out your identity?' asked Erika.

'A few weeks before Christmas. I have kept this secret for years, and all it took was for the safe to not be locked properly.' Elsa shook her head. 'One mistake, one small mistake and it all… It all comes crashing down.'

'You kept the paperwork in that safe, and your husband didn't know?'

'I had a safety deposit box in a bank in London… I opened it when I first came to the UK in the 1950s. I kept hold of that paperwork, because that was who I was. My family name wasn't anything to do with the Nazi party. It was a good name. I should have burned the papers, but I couldn't. Then, the bank was moving premises, and they contacted me a few years ago, just after my husband died, and I put them in my safe here at home.' Elsa sat back and closed her eyes.

'When did Marissa start to blackmail you?' asked Moss.

'When I let her have those diamond earrings, to begin with. I thought it would be enough to keep her quiet, but it wasn't. She

realised what the consequences would be for my family, for Charles and his family, if people found out. The Litmans' have a lucrative jewellery business in Hatton Garden, which is historically a Jewish place of business. Think what would happen if it was made public that his mother…' her voice trailed off. She looked weary now, resigned to her fate.

'You told us that Marissa had been grabbed by a man wearing a gas mask, a few weeks before Christmas,' said Erika.

'Yes.'

'You wanted to make us think that she had been targeted by him before?'

'It was the perfect opportunity. He was making headlines, the man in the gas mask; the public were afraid… It was around the same time that I heard people in our local shop talking about a young woman who he had attacked, late at night, on her way home from the train station.'

'It was feasible that he could have attacked Marissa,' said Moss. Elsa nodded.

'To commit the perfect murder, you need the perfect cover,' said Erika. 'And Taro Williams was your perfect cover.'

'It's taken us some time to access Marissa's mobile phone records. We now know she phoned you, Charles, shortly before she boarded the train to Brockley on Christmas Eve.'

He looked up from where he was slumped on the sofa. 'She phoned me to say she wanted more money, or jewellery, whatever was quicker,' said Charles, putting his head in his hands. 'She said she was going away, she needed it fast... We had already given her the earrings and money. I didn't have a choice. It would never have stopped; she would have gone on blackmailing us and threatening us.'

'Where did you get the gas mask?' asked Erika.

'It was from a second-hand shop in Soho,' said Charles. He hung his head and started to cry.

'The only problem, Charles, is that you have an alibi for Christmas Eve,' said Erika. He looked up at her. 'We have CCTV footage of you on a petrol station forecourt in North London, eleven minutes before the CCTV images we have of Marissa's murder. There is no way you could have been here.'

They looked back at Elsa.

'No one will believe that a ninety-seven-year-old woman had it in her to kill a strong, young twenty-two-year-old,' Elsa said, giving them a nasty, sly smile. A chill descended over the room.

'Are you admitting you did it?' asked Erika.

Elsa shook her head, still smiling.

'The post-mortem showed that Marissa was killed by a particular kind of paring knife. An eight-inch blade, with a serrated edge at the top,' said Erika. 'When the police searched your house with the warrant, one of my officers took away an identical knife… It wasn't classed as valuable, so you weren't informed. I'm sure you washed it, but you'd be shocked to discover what tiny amounts modern forensics can work with. We found microscopic amounts of Marissa Lewis's bone and blood on that knife…'

The smile had now been wiped from Elsa's face and her mouth was agape in horror. Erika went on, 'Not only that, we were also able to match the knife to the cuts and slashes on Marissa's body. Your knife is the murder weapon. We've also used the latest technology to study the CCTV camera opposite Marissa's house, which caught the murder. We can match your height with the height of the figure in the gas mask.'

'No… No!' cried Elsa.

'And the last piece of the puzzle, well, it's the best yet. On Christmas Eve, when Marissa got off the train at Brockley, she was wearing those diamond earrings,' said Erika, indicating the box which was still open on the table. 'Jeanette Walpole has confirmed Marissa was wearing them, and we also saw, again, on CCTV at

Brockley station, that Marissa spoke to two drunken young men at the bottom of the footbridge. They were sleaze bags, and were trying to chat her up, and they asked her for a selfie, no doubt to show their mates.'

Moss took another photo from the folder. It was the selfie, in very high quality, of Marissa with the two young men. Marissa could be clearly seen wearing the earrings.

'It was taken around fifteen minutes before she died,' said Erika. 'We tested the earrings for DNA. As well as small amounts of sweat and oil, they were covered in blood. They had been wiped clean to the naked eye, but we used a chemical called Luminol, which shows traces of blood on objects. You have probably seen it on police TV shows. It glows blue under the right light. We found that both earrings were saturated with blood. Far too much for it to have been from a simple cut. You killed Marissa, Elsa. You slashed her throat with your paring knife, and then as she lay dying, you removed the diamond earrings.'

The front door bell rang, and then it opened. Peterson came into the living room with McGorry and three uniformed officers. Erika looked over to them and nodded. Elsa sat back in the chair. Her face had sunken in on itself and she looked ashen. 'No… No…' she croaked, but all her bravado and confidence had evaporated.

'Elsa Fryatt, I'm arresting you for the murder of Marissa Lewis. You do not have to say anything, but it may harm your defence if you do not mention when questioned something which you later rely on in court. Anything you do say may be given in evidence against you. I'm also informing you that a lawyer from the international war crimes court, and the German government, have requested to speak to you under caution regarding your time working as a guard at the Mauthausen-Gusen concentration camp, and the crimes you committed against humanity during the Second World War.'

Mrs Fryatt stared up at her. Then she grabbed a gold letter opener from the coffee table and lunged across at Erika, holding it in her fist. Peterson ran forward and caught her wrist, the tip of the blade inches from Erika's face.

'Black hands. Get those filthy black hands away from me,' hissed Elsa, her eyes glittering with hatred. Peterson prised the letter opener out of her grip. He pinned her arms to her side, and McGorry handcuffed her hands behind her back. Elsa stared up at Erika. 'You people will never understand. If I had my time again, I would do the same.'

'Take her away,' said Erika. Peterson led Elsa from the living room and out to the waiting police car.

EPILOGUE

Erika, Moss, Peterson and McGorry watched as Elsa and Charles were loaded separately into waiting police cars. As the car containing Elsa pulled away, she sat upright, with her head held high, looking straight ahead. As the second car followed, Charles was slumped with his head down, and he was weeping.

Across the street, the neighbours had come to their gates and front doors, and others were peering through net curtains.

'I wonder what they'd think if they knew they'd been living beside a murderer and a Nazi war criminal,' said McGorry.

'They'll be shocked, I'm sure. She was always dressed head to toe in Marks and Spencer,' said Moss. 'Covers a multitude of sins.'

Erika smiled.

'What's going to happen to her now?' added McGorry.

'Even though she's old, we'll push to go to trial for Marissa's murder,' said Erika. 'And Charles will be charged with conspiracy to murder. I'm just concerned about the other charges. The historical war crimes. I want her to live long enough to pay for what she did during the war.'

'Let's hope she lives for a long time, and gets to rot in prison,' said Peterson.

A black van pulled up at the kerb, and a team of forensic officers got out and went to work on the house. Erika took out a cigarette and lit up. Peterson gave Moss a look.

'Come on, John,' Erika said. 'Let's go get some coffee.'

'I've already had two coffees…' he started, but Moss gave him a look and he followed her through the gateway.

Peterson shifted on his feet and looked at Erika.

'You okay?' she asked.

'What?'

'Elsa, and what she said.'

'You never get used to racism. It's always there. Every day, in some shape or form…'

Erika nodded, and didn't know what to say.

'I wanted to talk to you, about something different. Not work,' he said.

'What?'

'I should have told you straight away about Kyle and Fran… I tried to tell you the night we went to the club, but… I wimped out.'

'After all these revelations. The fact you're a father doesn't seem so shocking now.'

'If you put it like that…' he said.

'I can't say I'm over the moon for you, James, but I'll get there,' said Erika.

'Okay.'

'You always wanted kids, and you've been able to miss out on all the nappy changing…'

He shook his head.

'Sorry, that came out wrong,' she added.

'It's okay. I know what you mean.' He smiled at her. 'Are we cool? Can we be cool?'

'Yeah. We can,' she said. She was glad when his phone rang, and he indicated he had to take it. 'Shall I meet you in the coffee shop?'

She nodded and watched him go off and answer the phone, a big smile on his face.

*

She stayed at the gate, smoking. The feeling of relief and elation washing over her that she had nailed a case. She wasn't sure how long she was there, until she looked down and saw four cigarette butts on the ground.

'Screw it,' she said to herself. 'It's not every day you catch a murderer and a Nazi war criminal before lunch.' She took out her packet of cigarettes and lit another. One of the uniformed officers came out of the house towards her.

'Sorry to interrupt, ma'am. We think we've discovered the coat the murderer wore, stuffed under some floorboards. And there's a gas mask. Both look to be encrusted with blood.'

'I'll be there in a second,' she said. The officer went back in the house, and Erika took a moment to savour her success. A bird was singing, high in one of the surrounding trees, and she looked up at the bright sky, savouring the soft sound. She took a drag on the freshly lit cigarette, before stubbing it out on the bottom of her shoe and slipping it back in the packet.

Then she made her way back into the house.

She [illegible] the ground [illegible] [illegible] and [illegible] walking [illegible] than [illegible] [illegible] [illegible] [illegible] long [illegible] minute [illegible] [illegible] [illegible] [illegible] [illegible] on the ground.

[illegible] she [illegible] to [illegible]. [illegible] [illegible] and [illegible] [illegible]. She took [illegible] [illegible] of [illegible] of the [illegible] [illegible] of the [illegible] [illegible].

[illegible] her arm. [illegible] the [illegible] [illegible] [illegible] [illegible] [illegible] [illegible] with blood.

[illegible] [illegible] back [illegible] [illegible] [illegible] [illegible] [illegible] [illegible] in [illegible] of the [illegible] trees and she looked up [illegible] [illegible]. She took a [illegible] [illegible] from the bottom of her [illegible] back to the [illegible].

Then she made her way back into the hut.

A LETTER FROM ROB

First of all, I want to say a big thank you to you for choosing to read *Deadly Secrets*. If you are picking up one of my books for the first time, or if you are back again for more Erika Foster, I would be very grateful if you would consider writing a short review. It needn't be long, just a few words, but it makes such a difference and helps readers to discover one of my books for the first time.

I love hearing all your thoughts, and reading your messages. Thank you to all those readers who have been in touch, I read and appreciate every message. You can get in touch on my Facebook page, through Twitter, Goodreads or my website, which you'll find at www.robertbryndza.com. There are lots more books to come, so I hope you'll stay with me for the ride!

Robert Bryndza

ACKNOWLEDGEMENTS

Thank you to Oliver Rhodes, Claire Bord and the wonderful team at Bookouture. Thanks also to Rebecca Bradley for your feedback and advice on police procedure. Any liberties taken with fact are mine.

Thank you to my amazing agent, Amy Tannenbaum Gottlieb, for guiding me through the last few months with such grace and wit. Thank you also to the equally amazing Danielle Sickles, and all at The Jane Rotrosen Agency. Thank you to Jan Cramer, for your wonderful audiobook narration of the Erika Foster series.

Thank you to my mother-in-law, Vierka for all your love and support, and for the line drawing of the gas mask. You did me proud, and came up with something chilling. A massive thank you to my husband, Ján for reading endless drafts, and putting up with my crazy writer behaviour. If there was a literary awards category for writer's spouses, you would win it every year. And thanks to Riky and Lola for the unconditional love, and for making our days so bright and full of fun.

And lastly, to all my wonderful readers, all the wonderful book groups, book bloggers and reviewers worldwide. A writer is nothing without his readers. Thank you.

Read on for the pulse-pounding beginning of Robert Bryndza's Kate Marshall series, *Nine Elms*

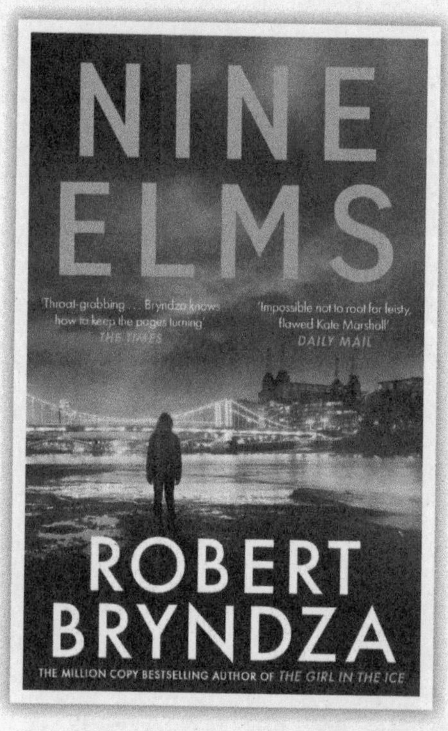

AUTUMN
1995

CHAPTER 1

Detective Constable Kate Marshall was on the train home when her phone rang. It took a moment of searching the folds of her long winter coat before she found it in the inside pocket. She heaved out the huge brick-like handset, pulled up the aerial and answered. It was her boss, Detective Chief Inspector Peter Conway.

'Sir. Hello.'

'Finally. She picks up!' he snapped, without preamble. 'I've been calling you. What's the bloody point in having one of these new mobile phones if you don't answer?'

'Sorry. I've been in court all day for the Travis Jones sentencing. He got three years, which is more than I—'

'A dog walker found the body of a young girl dumped in Crystal Palace Park,' he said, cutting her off. 'Naked. Bite marks on her body, a plastic bag tied over her head.'

'The Nine Elms Cannibal . . . '

'Operation Hemlock. You know I don't like that name.'

Kate wanted to reply that the name had now stuck and was bedded in for life, but he wasn't the kind of boss who encouraged banter. The press had coined the epithet two years earlier, when seventeen-year-old Shelley Norris had been found in a wrecker's yard in the Nine Elms area of south-west London, close to the Thames. Technically, the killer only bit his victims, but the press didn't let this get in the way of a good serial killer moniker. Over the past two years, another two teenage girls had been abducted, each in the early evening, on their way home from school. Their

bodies had shown up several days after their disappearances, dumped in parks around London. Nothing sold newspapers more than a cannibal on the loose.

'Kate. Where are you?'

It was dark outside the train window. She looked up at the electronic display in the carriage.

'On the DLR. Almost home, sir.'

'I'll pick you up outside the station, our usual spot.' He hung up without waiting for a response.

Twenty minutes later, Kate was waiting on a small stretch of pavement between the station underpass and the busy South Circular where a line of cars ground slowly past. Much of the area around the station was under development, and Kate's route home to her small flat took her through a long road of empty building sites. It wasn't somewhere to linger after dark. The passengers she'd left the train with had crossed the road and dispersed into the dark streets. She glanced back over her shoulder at the dank empty underpass bathed in shadows and shifted on her heels. A small bag of groceries she'd bought for dinner sat between her feet.

A spot of water hit her neck, and another, and then it started to rain. She turned up the collar of her coat and hunched down, moving closer to the bright headlights in the line of traffic.

Kate had been assigned to Operation Hemlock sixteen months previously, when the Nine Elms Cannibal body count stood at three. It had been a coup to join a high-profile case, along with promotion to the rank of plain-clothes detective.

In the eight months since the third victim's body was found – a seventeen-year-old schoolgirl called Carla Martin – the case had gone cold. Operation Hemlock had been scaled back, and Kate

had been re-assigned to the drug squad, along with several other junior officers.

Kate squinted through the rain, down the long line of traffic. Bright headlights appeared around a sharp bend in the road, but there were no police sirens in the distance. She checked her watch and stepped back out of the glare.

She hadn't seen Peter for two months. Shortly before she was reassigned, she had slept with him. He rarely socialised with his team, and during a rare night of after-work drinks they'd wound up talking, and she'd found his company and his intelligence stimulating. They had stayed late in the pub, after the rest of the team went home, and ended up back at her flat. And then the next night he had invited her over to his place. Kate's dalliance with her boss, on not one but two occasions, was something that burned inside her with regret. It was a moment of madness – two moments – before they both came to their senses. She had a strong moral compass. She was a good police officer.

I'll pick you up at our usual spot.

It bothered her that Peter said this on the phone. He'd given her a lift to work twice, and both times he had also picked up her colleague, Detective Cameron Rose, who lived close by. Would he have said *our usual spot* to Cam?

The cold was starting to creep up the back of her long coat, and the rain had seeped in through the holes in the bottom of the 'good shoes' she wore for court. Kate adjusted her collar and huddled into her coat, turning her attention to the line of traffic. Almost all the drivers were men, white, in their mid- to late thirties. The perfect serial killer demographic.

A grimy white van slid past, the driver's face distorted by the rainwater on the windscreen. The police believed the Nine Elms Cannibal was using a van to abduct his victims. Carpet fibres matching a 1994 Citroën Dispatch white van, of which there were

over a hundred thousand registered in and around London, had been found on two of the victims. Kate wondered if the officers who'd been retained for Operation Hemlock were still working through that list of Citroën Dispatch white van owners. And who was this new victim? There had been nothing in the newspapers about a missing person.

The lights up ahead turned red, and a small blue Ford stopped in the line of traffic a few feet away. The man inside was a City type: overweight, in his mid-fifties and wearing a pinstriped suit and glasses. He saw Kate, raised his eyebrows suggestively and flashed his headlights. Kate looked away. The blue Ford inched closer, closing the gap in the line of cars until his passenger window was almost level with her. It slid down, and the man leaned across.

'Hello. You look cold. I can make you warm . . . ' He patted the seat beside him and stuck out his tongue which was thin and pointed. Kate froze. Panic rose in her chest. She forgot she had her warrant card, and that she was a police officer. It all went out of the window and fear took over. '*Come on*. Hop inside. Let's warm you up,' he said. He patted the seat again, impatient.

Kate stepped away from the kerb. The underpass behind her was dark and empty. The other vehicles in the line had male drivers, and they seemed oblivious, cocooned in their cars. The lights ahead remained red. The rain thrummed lazily on the car roofs. The man leaned farther over and the passenger door popped open a few inches. Kate took another step back, but felt trapped. What if he got out of his car and pushed her into the underpass?

'Don't fuck me around. How much?' he said. His smile was gone, and she could see his trousers were undone. His underpants were faded and dingy. He hooked his finger under the waistband and exposed his penis and a thatch of greying pubic hair.

Kate was still rooted to the spot, willing the lights to change.

A police siren blared out suddenly, cutting through the silence, and the cars and the arch of the underpass were lit up with blue flashing lights. The man hurriedly rearranged himself, fastened his trousers and pulled the door shut, activating the central locking. His face returned to an impassive stare. Kate fumbled in her bag and pulled out her warrant card. She went to the blue Ford and slapped it against the passenger window, annoyed that she hadn't done it earlier.

Peter's unmarked police car, with its revolving blue light on the roof, came shooting down the outside of the row of traffic, half up on the grass verge. The traffic light changed to green. The car in front drove away, and Peter pulled into the gap. The man inside the Ford was now panicking, smoothing down his hair and tie. Kate fixed him with a stare, put her warrant card back in her bag and went to the passenger door of Peter's car.

CHAPTER 2

'Sorry to keep you waiting. Traffic,' said Peter, giving her a brisk smile. He picked up a pile of paperwork from the passenger seat and put it behind his seat. He was a good-looking man in his late thirties, broad-shouldered with thick dark wavy hair, high cheekbones and soft brown eyes. He wore an expensive tailored black suit.

'Of course,' she said, feeling relief as she stashed her handbag and groceries in the footwell and dropped into the seat. As soon as she closed the door, Peter accelerated and flicked on the sirens.

The sunshade was down on the passenger side, and she caught her reflection in the mirror as she folded it back up. She wasn't wearing any make-up, or dressed provocatively, and Kate always thought herself a little plain. She wasn't delicate. She had strong features. Her shoulder-length hair was tied back off her face, tucked away under the neck of her long winter coat, almost as an afterthought. The only distinguishing features were her unusual eyes, which were a startling cornflower blue with a burst of burnt orange flooding out from the pupils. It was caused by sectoral heterochromia, a rare condition where the eyes have two colours. The other, less permanent mark on her face was a split lip, just starting to scab over, which had been caused by an irate drunk resisting arrest a few days before. She'd felt no fear when dealing with the drunk, and didn't feel ashamed that he'd hit her. It was part of the job. Why did she feel shame after being hit on by the sleazy businessman? He was the one with the sad, saggy grey underwear and the stubby little manhood.

'What was that? With the car behind?' asked Peter.

'Oh, one of his brake lights was out,' she said. It was easier to lie. She felt embarrassed. She pushed the man and his blue Ford to the back of her mind. 'Have you called the whole team to the crime scene?'

'Of course,' said Peter, glancing over. 'After we spoke, I got a call from the assistant commissioner, Anthony Asher. He says if this murder is linked to Operation Hemlock, I only have to ask and I'll have all the resources I need at my disposal.'

He sped around a roundabout in fourth gear, and took the exit to Crystal Palace Park. Peter Conway was a career police officer, and Kate had no doubt that solving this case would result in a promotion to superintendent or even chief superintendent. Peter had been the youngest officer in the history of the Met Police to be promoted to detective chief inspector.

The windows were starting to fog up, and he turned up the heater. The arc of condensation on the windscreen rippled and receded. Between a group of terraced houses Kate caught a glimpse of the London skyline lit up. There were millions of lights, pinpricks in the black fabric of the sky, symbolising the homes and offices of millions. Kate wondered which light belonged to the Nine Elms Cannibal. *What if we never find him?* she thought. *The police never found Jack the Ripper, and back then London was tiny in comparison.*

'Have you had any more leads from the white van database?' she asked.

'We brought in another six men for questioning, but their DNA didn't match our man.'

'The fact he leaves his DNA on the victims, it's not just carelessness or lack of control. It's as if he's marking his territory. Like a dog.'

'You think he wants us to catch him?'

'Yes . . . No . . . Possibly.'

'He's behaving like he's invincible.'

'He *thinks* he's invincible. But he'll slip up. They always do,' said Kate.

They turned off into the north entrance to Crystal Palace Park. A police car was waiting, and the officer waved them through. They drove down a long straight avenue of gravel, usually reserved for people on foot. It was lined with large oak trees shedding leaves, and they hit the windshield with a wet flapping sound, clogging up the wipers. In the far distance the huge Crystal Palace radio transmitter poked up above the trees like a slender Eiffel Tower. The road banked down and ended in a small car park beside a long flat expanse of grass, which backed onto a wooded area. A police tape cordon ringed the entire expanse of grass. In the centre was a second, smaller cordon around a white forensics tent, glowing in the darkness. Next to the second cordon sat the pathologist's van, four squad cars and a large white police support vehicle.

Where the tarmac met the grass, the tape of the first police cordon flapped in the breeze. Kate and Peter were met by two uniformed police officers – a middle-aged man whose belly hung over his belt and a tall, thin young man who still looked like a teenager. Kate and Peter showed their identification to the older officer. His eyes were hooded with loose skin, and as he glanced between their warrant cards, he reminded Kate of a chameleon. He handed them back, and went to lift the police tape, but hesitated, looking over at the glowing tent.

'In all my years, I ain't never seen nothing like it,' he said.

'You were the first on the scene?' asked Peter, impatient for him to lift the tape, but not willing to do it himself.

'Yes. PC Stanley Gresham, sir. This is PC Will Stokes.' He said gesturing to the young officer, who suddenly grimaced, turned away from them and threw up over the police tape. 'It's

his first day on the job,' he added, shaking his head. Kate gave the young officer a look of pity as he heaved and threw up again, thin strings of spittle dangling from his mouth. Peter took a clean white handkerchief from his inside pocket, and Kate thought he was going to offer it up to the young officer, but he pressed it to his nose and mouth.

'I want this crime scene locked down. Not a word to anyone,' said Peter.

'Of course, sir.'

Peter fluttered his fingers at the police tape. Stanley lifted it and they ducked under. The grass sloped down to the second police cordon where Detective Cameron Rose and Detective Inspector Marsha Lewis were waiting. Cameron, like Kate, was in his mid-twenties, and Marsha was older than all of them, a thickset woman in her fifties, wearing a smart black trouser suit and long black coat. Her silver hair was cropped short and she had a gravelly smoker's voice.

'Sir,' they both said in unison.

'What's going on, Marsha?' asked Peter.

'All exits in and out of the park are sealed, and I've got local plod being bussed in for a fingertip search and house to house. Forensic pathologist is in there already, and she's ready to talk to us.'

Cameron was tall and gangly, towering above them all. He hadn't had time to change, and looked more like a louche teenager than a detective in his jeans, trainers and a green winter jacket. Kate wondered fleetingly what he had been doing when he got the call to come to the crime scene. She presumed he'd arrived with Marsha.

'Who's our forensic pathologist?' asked Peter.

'Leodora Graves,' said Marsha.

*

It was hot inside the glowing tent, where the lights were almost painfully bright. Forensic pathologist Leodora Graves, a small dark-skinned woman with penetrating green eyes, worked with two assistants. A naked young girl lay face down in a muddy depression in the grass. Her head was covered by a clear plastic bag, tied tightly around her neck. Her pale skin was streaked with dirt and blood and numerous cuts and scratches. The backs of her thighs and buttocks had several deep bite marks.

Kate stood beside the body, already sweating underneath the hood and face mask of her thick white forensics suit. The rain hammered down on the tight skin of the tent, forcing Leodora to raise her voice.

'The victim is posed, lying on her right side, her right arm under her head. The left arm lies flat and reaching out. There are six bites on her lower back, buttocks and thighs.' She indicated the deepest bites where the flesh had been removed, so deep as to expose the girl's spine. She moved to the victim's head and gently lifted it. The length of thin rope was tied tight around the neck, biting into the now bloated flesh. 'You'll note the specific knot.'

'The monkey's fist knot,' said Cameron, speaking for the first time. He sounded shaken. Everyone's face was obscured by the mask of their forensic suit, but Kate could read the looks of alarm in their eyes.

'Yes,' said Leodora, holding the knot in her gloved hand. What made it unusual was the series of intersecting turns, like a tiny ball of wool, almost impossible to replicate with a machine.

'It's him. The Nine Elms Cannibal,' said Kate. The words came out of her mouth before she could stop them.

'I'll need to conclude more from my post-mortem, but . . . yes,' said Leodora. The rain fell harder, intensifying the thundering thrum on the roof of the tent. She let go of the young girl's head, placing it gently back where it lay on her arm. 'There is evidence

that she was raped. There are bodily fluids present, and she's been tortured, cut with a sharp object and burned. You see the burn marks on her arms and outer thighs? They look to be caused by the cigarette lighter from a car.'

'Or a white van,' said Kate. Peter gave her a hard stare. He didn't like being corrected.

'Cause of death?' he asked.

'I need to do the post-mortem, but off the record, at this stage I would say asphyxiation with the plastic bag. There are signs of petechial haemorrhaging on her face and neck.'

'Thank you, Leodora. I look forward to the results of your post-mortem. I hope that we can quickly identify this poor young woman.'

Leodora nodded to her assistants, who brought in a pop-up stretcher with a shiny new black body bag. They placed it beside the body, and gently turned the young woman over onto the stretcher. The front of her naked body was marked with small circular burns and scratches. It was impossible to tell what she looked like – her face was grotesque and distorted under the plastic. She had large pale-blue eyes, milky in death, and frozen in a stare. The look in her eyes made Kate shiver. It was devoid of hope, as if frozen in her eyes was that last thought. She knew she was going to die.

City of Wonders.

In the dusky haze of evening a ruddy-cheeked newsboy strode along Fifth Avenue proclaiming the future. "The great Egyptian obelisk is about to land on our shores! The Brooklyn Bridge set to become the Eighth Wonder of the World! Broadway soon to glow with electric light!" In his wake, a crippled man shuffled, spouting prophecies of his own. "God's judgement is upon us! The end of the world is nigh!"

New York had become a city of astonishments. Wonders and marvels came so frequent and fast, a day without spectacle was cause for concern.

Men involved themselves with the business of making miracles. Men in starched collars and suits, men in wool caps and dirty boots. From courtrooms to boardrooms to the newsrooms of Park Row; from dockyards to scaffolds to Mr. Roebling's Great Bridge—every man to a one had a head full of schemes: to erect a monument to genius, to become a wizard of invention, to discover the unknown. They set their sights on greatness while setting their watches to the drop of the Western Union Time Ball. Their dreams no longer came to them via stardust and angel's wings, but by tug, train and telegraph. Sleep lost all meaning now that Time was in man's grasp.

In the building beneath the tower that held the time ball, a mindful order of women sat—side by side, row on row, storey upon storey, one hundred young ladies in all, working round the clock to translate the wishes of men to dots and dashes. Transfixed by the steady *click-clack* of their task, the ghost of Mr. Samuel Morse hovered near. He'd tried to get to Heaven on numerous occasions, but could never seem to find his way past the tangled canopy of telegraph lines that criss-crossed the skies above Manhattan. What he needed was an angel, or better yet, a witch. Someone to translate the knocks and rappings of his soul, to convey all the things he'd left unsaid. Where could one be found? Were there any left?

In a halo of lamplight near the Western Union Building, a prostitute leaned her aching back against the bricks. Lips rouged, eyes rimmed with charcoal, she was waiting for a man. Puffing on a cigarette she'd begged off a stranger, she blew a steady stream of smoke rings in the air. At the edge of her sight, a shadowy figure in the shape of a fine-dressed gentleman appeared—five feet off the ground, coattails flapping in the breeze. Rubbing her eyes, the girl shook her head, thinking she'd had too much to drink. She swore, hand to God, she'd get off the booze one day, not now, of course, maybe in the spring.

As the ghost dissolved from her view, the girl flicked the stub of her cigarette to the ground and crushed it with the heel of her boot. Hand in her pocket she reached for a trinket she'd been given by her last john. "A lucky rabbit's foot," he'd said, "blessed by a bona fide witch." "Liar," the girl had complained when he'd offered her the charm along with half of what he was supposed to pay. "No, no, no," the john had insisted. "I tell you, she was *real* . . . a real witch with a very fine ass." With that, the girl had grabbed the trinket and sent the john on his way. Something was better than nothing. She needed all the help she could get.

Stroking the soft fur of the rabbit's foot, the girl thought of all she lacked. She was tired, she needed sleep, but she wanted more booze. When she glanced at the spot where she'd snuffed out the butt, there was a shiny new dime in its place. Picking the coin off the ground, she wondered if maybe the john had been right after all. Maybe the damn foot was lucky. Maybe the witch was real. Maybe her luck had changed because the john had dipped his willy in a witch and then dipped it in her, leaving behind some strange magic. There were worse things she could catch, she guessed.

In the shadow of the Great Bridge, a young widow knelt to plead with the river. Just after supper she'd spied something terrible in the soapy murk of her dishwater, a vision she'd seen once before, and she'd just as soon forget. Each time she closed her eyes, it came to her again—a man's face, bloated and blue, gasping for air. The last time she'd seen it, it'd been her husband's. This time it was a stranger's.

"I understand," the woman said to the river, touching the surface of the water with a finger. "I know how it feels to be slighted." She also understood that the river required payment from those who wished to cross it. Blood, flesh and bone were what it liked best. The widow didn't have much of anything to give as an offering—a few pennies, a splash of whiskey, the cheerful tune of an ancient song—but she hoped that if she were gentle, persuasive and kind, the river might change its mind. Was it witchcraft she was plying? She didn't care so long as it worked. Something had to be done. Something was better than nothing.

In the cellar of a modest house on the edge of the Tenderloin, a weary housekeeper lit a candle and said a prayer. Taper in one hand, glass jar in the other, she poured wax around the edge of the jar's lid to seal it shut. The jar—filled with stale urine, old needles, shards of mirror, brass buttons, bent nails and thirteen drops of blood from her left thumb—was what her wise grandmother had called a "witch's bottle." While others might call it humbug, the housekeeper saw the jar and its contents as her last hope to dispel the strange darkness that'd settled in her midst. What else could explain all that'd happened since the master of the house had passed? For weeks she'd been plagued by what she thought was a ghost or, perhaps, a demon, lurking in her room, stealing her sight, shaking her bed, night after night. What did it want? Where had it come from? Why wouldn't it leave her alone? Prayers, hymns and a desperate stint of almsgiving hadn't driven it away. She feared the terrible thing wouldn't rest until it saw her dead. Had she been cursed? Something had to be done. As her grandmother would say, *Wo gibt es Hexen, gibt es Geister.* Where there are witches there are ghosts.

In a quiet corner of a cozy teashop just shy of Madison Square Park, a magnificent raven sat on a perch, preening its feathers. As the bird tugged and fussed at its wing, three women conversed around a nearby table—one, a lady of considerable wealth, the others a pair of witches, keepers of the bird and the shop.

"Can you help?" the lady inquired, worry catching in her throat. "I'm at my wit's end. Something must be done."

One witch answered with a confident, "Of course."

The other humbly replied, "Leave it with us."

The raven cast an indifferent eye upon them. He'd witnessed this sort of thing before—the woman, unable to manage her affairs, needed a witch (or two) to make things right. That was all fine and good, but he was more interested in a faint sound coming from overhead, an enchanting jangle akin to when prisms on a chandelier touch. But how could that be when there was no chandelier to be found in the shop? He was certain unexpected magic was afoot.

Tea was poured, complaints and concerns heard, sympathy given. Crystal ball and grimoire consulted. Palms and tea leaves read. How pleased the bird was when he noticed the tray of teacakes in the centre of the table had barely been touched. How pleased the lady was when the witches presented her with a small package tied with red string.

The lady was sure she felt something move within the parcel. A tiny tremor of mystical vibration, perhaps? A sign of things to come? She'd heard rumours from a friend of a friend that these women could work miracles. She prayed it was true. She wanted to believe. Lowering her voice, she said, "You swear this thing has been touched by witchcraft?"

One of the women gave a polite nod and said, "Of course, my dear, of course."

The other replied with a smile and a shrug. "Call it what you like."

The raven simply cocked its head. It was all he could do not to laugh.

By Knot of One.

THIRTY-SIX MILES UP the Hudson as the crow flies, a young woman stood atop the widow's walk of a grand house in Stony Point. To the east lay the silhouettes of ships' masts and church towers beneath the first stars of night. The girl was looking for signs of change—in the skies, in the weather, in her heart.

"Starry. Crisp. Clear," she pencilled in a small notebook. Licking the tip of her finger, she raised it above her head to check the direction of the wind. *Nothing unusual*, she thought. *Nothing unusual ever happens here*. "NW wind," she wrote beside her other observations. "No sign of rain."

Bright and bored at seventeen, Beatrice Dunn longed for her life to take an extraordinary turn. She had no reason to think such a thing would ever happen—still, she hoped, she prayed, she wished.

She knew, from reading yellowed copies of *Scientific American* and *The Old Farmer's Almanac*, that the slightest shift in chemistry, in temperature, in the atmosphere, in the stars, could bring about tremendous transformation. An avalanche begins with a sound or a misplaced step. Gunpowder explodes with the tiniest of sparks. One flaw in a steam boiler can lead to catastrophe. Lightning can be conjured inside a jar. From time to time Beatrice made lightning of her own by scuffing her feet on the rug in her room and touching her finger to one of her iron bedposts. A sharp charge of static would run through her hand as her nightgown clung to her skin, and the tiny hairs along the back of her neck rose to attention. Occasionally the taste of metal fizzled in her mouth. It was a childish act, she supposed, but it thrilled her nonetheless. If only she could find a spark to set the tinder of her days ablaze.

She'd read in the *New York Herald* that great changes were set to sweep the world in the coming days.

> Strange, malefic times (whatever cynical people may say to the contrary) are soon to begin, due to the presence of an immense planetary influence not seen on the Earth for two thousand years. The vitality of every living thing will be subjected to extraordinary pressures. Surely miracles and mayhem will arise in its wake.

To prepare for whatever might come her way, Beatrice had begun keeping track of things that couldn't be explained. Charting every instance of the miraculous that appeared in the news, she faithfully logged them in her notebook as she did the weather, noting the hour of their occurrence, as well as the phase of the moon. She aimed to measure the rate of the inexplicable, the temperature of strange.

According to her records thus far, instances of unnatural phenomena had risen substantially in the last month. Most notably within the city of New York.

AUGUST 1—*Woman Has Premonitions of Death.*
AUGUST 5—*Doppelgänger Seen on Delancey Street.*
AUGUST 10—*Girl Thrives Without Food or Drink.*
AUGUST 15—*Ghosts Haunt the Fifth Avenue Hotel.*
AUGUST 20—*Accusations of Witchcraft Abound.*

To Beatrice, such accounts were deliciously compelling—not only for the fantastic stories they held, but for the many questions they raised.

What is the weight of a soul? Where does it go when we die?
Are there such things as ghosts?
Can they speak to the living?
What of spirits, demons, fairies and angels?
Can dreams hold portents, visions, foretellings?
Are witches real?
Does magic exist?

Night after night, kitchen shears in hand, she'd sit at her desk clipping squares and columns of newsprint to pin to the walls of her room. Printed matter from *Vennor's Almanac*, *Scientific American*, *The Ladies' Companion*, *Frank Leslie's Illustrated Newspaper*, *New York* Saturday *Journal*, *The Fireside Library* and *Madam Morrow's Strange Tales of Gotham* soon crept across the rose-patterned wallpaper, replacing blossoms and stems with headlines, illustrations and odd bits of news.

Even the advertisements intrigued her. *Find God! Find your match! Find your fortune in the west! Become an expert in calligraphy, telegraphy, engraving, pottery, telepathy, mesmerism, clairvoyance, embroidery, pianoforte, violin. Charm lessons, five cents! Discover the ancient art of getting what you wish!* The back pages of every newspaper were peppered with the calling cards of mediums, clairvoyants, seers and mind readers, boasting the ability to converse with spirits, predict the future, find lost treasures, conjure true love. *Madam Morrow the Astonisher. Miss Fortuna the Lucky. Mrs. Seymour. Madame Prewster. Miss Adelaide Thom.* Was it possible for one city to contain so many mystics? Beatrice was counting the days until she could discover the truth for herself. Twelve days, thirteen sleeps.

RESPECTABLE LADY SEEKS
DEPENDABLE SHOP GIRL.

Must be well versed in sums, etiquette,
tea making and the language of flowers.
Room and Board provided.
Candidates will be considered on one day ONLY
September 17, 1880 One to five o'clock

TEA AND SYMPATHY.
933 Broadway, New York, New York.
Those averse to magic need not apply.

Beatrice had spied the notice while combing through the latest issue of *Harper's Weekly*. As soon as she'd seen it, she'd felt it was meant for her. Even though she guessed there'd be other girls who'd feel much the same, she couldn't imagine that any of them were half as qualified as she was. Had they read *Flowers and Flower-lore* by Reverend H. Friend, cover to cover? Did they have an aunt who was as staunch about the proper preparation of tea as her aunt Lydia? She doubted it, especially when it came to the latter. Her proficiency with sums was excellent, her appetite for wonder insatiable. She'd need to brush up on her etiquette, but she could do that quite easily with a quick re-reading of *How to Behave.*

If she didn't get the job, then she'd simply march down Third Avenue to the Cooper Union and enroll in their women's course on telegraphy. She'd already committed Mr. Morse's code to memory by practicing the longs and shorts of it on the end of a ruler she'd rigged with elastic to the edge of her desk. If her quest to become a telegrapher failed, then she'd return to her aunt's house in Stony Point, the place she'd called home for the last seven years, and resign herself to a safe, secure and predictable life.

Was she nervous?

-.-- . ... (Yes.)

Was she frightened?

-. --- (No.)

She'd travelled to New York first as a child, holding fast to her mother's hand and then, after her parents' passing, once a year in the spring with Aunt Lydia by her side. This time, however, there'd be no frantic rush to find the perfect hat, no fretting over fumes from the train aggravating her aunt's lungs, no worry about getting there and back in a day. This time she was going alone, and she was going to stay. Although she cared for her aunt and would miss her dearly, she relished the thought of being someplace Lydia wasn't.

Their relationship had been brought about by a vigorous strain of smallpox that'd swept through Albany in the summer of 1873. Beatrice, just shy of her tenth birthday, was the only person in her house to survive. Not long after her parents had died, the court had appointed her mother's sister, Lydia Floss, to serve as Beatrice's guardian "until such time as Miss Dunn is legally wed, or turns nineteen." With quiet composure, Lydia had collected Beatrice's belongings, then whisked the girl away to the Floss family homestead in Stony Point. "Nothing here but blue skies, green pastures and hard-working folk," Lydia had told the girl. "I can't remember the last time someone fell ill or came to any harm." They'd lived there, just the two of them, in a house so large that even their shadows occasionally got lost.

Beatrice was given proper clothes to wear, healthful food to eat, a roof over her head. Aunt Lydia, the beneficiary of her family's estate, and a spinster by choice, had always shown Beatrice a great deal of interest and respect, and, when occasion called for it (on birthdays, at Christmastime, on the anniversary of her parents' deaths), an appropriate amount of affection. Lydia had raised Beatrice in the way she wished she had been raised, by teaching the girl to pick up books because of a love of learning (rather than a desire for praise), to do good deeds because of an enduring belief in kindness (rather than a fear of God's wrath). While the other girls in Stony Point were braiding one another's hair and spreading schoolyard gossip, Beatrice had preferred to sit by the fire (or in summer, under a willow tree in the back garden), reading and making figures between her fingers with a loop of string—cat's whiskers, cup-and-saucer, owl's eyes, the witch's broom. When girls her age began pairing off with young men at dances and church socials, Lydia had encouraged Beatrice to look beyond the altar by handing her tracts from teacher's colleges and nursing schools, with words of encouragement scrawled in the margins.

Fortune favours the prepared mind.

Beauty seeks attention. Intelligence commands it.

As an ardent follower of Miss Susan B. Anthony, Lydia believed the only path to a woman's betterment was through making her own way. If that path led Beatrice away from Stony Point, then so be it.

With that in mind, Beatrice had told Lydia of her plans over her aunt's favourite breakfast (poached eggs, rosehip tea and toast with blackberry jam). Much to the girl's surprise, Lydia hadn't balked in the slightest. She hadn't lectured her about the dangers of the city, or warned her about seducers and swindlers lurking around every corner. If Beatrice hadn't known better, she might've thought Lydia was happy to see her go. In the end, her aunt had given her blessing in the best way she knew how. "According to Miss Anthony," she'd said, "'the girl who is able to earn her own living and pay her own way should be as happy as anybody on earth.' There's no match for the sweetness independence brings. Nothing would make me happier than to see you succeed."

Staring at the sky, Beatrice thought, *Thirteen sleeps before my departure. How lucky am I?* "Luck," of course, according to her aunt, "is what happens when preparation and opportunity collide." What then of magic, Beatrice wondered, of destiny, of kismet?

She'd recently read an account of a strange charm being found by a farmhand in the rafters of a run-down cottage outside of Tarrytown where a witch was supposed to have lived. It'd been fashioned from the simplest of things—a length of string, a few ratty feathers and six stray hairs (probably from the witch's head). Nine knots had been tied along it, to secure the feathers and hair. When a farmer's wife from the next house over had been asked by a newspaper reporter if she'd ever seen the likes of such a thing before, she'd eagerly replied, "Yes, indeed I have! 'Tis a witch's ladder, for healin' the sick, protectin' loved ones, cursin' yer enemies or gettin' what you wish. It contains some of the strongest magic there is. Once the spell's complete, its magic will be stored in the charm forever. So long as the ladder remains whole, so too will the magic. There's a rhyme that goes along with it, to help the spell set. Would ye like to hear it?"

Taking three black feathers, a length of string and six strands of red hair from her own head, Beatrice began tying knots to secure her wish, reciting the farmwoman's verse as she went.

By knot of one, my spell's begun.
By knot of two, it will come true.
By knot of three, so may it be.
By knot of four, this power I store.
By knot of five, my spell is alive.
By knot of six, the spell I fix.
By knot of seven, the future I'll leaven.
By knot of eight, my will be fate.
By knot of nine, what's done is mine!

She hoped the farmer's wife was right. She hoped the magic would prove true. She wanted to believe—in miracles, in fate and in witches too.

Twelve days. (Thirteen sleeps.)

Those averse to magic need not apply.

September 17, 1880.
Full Moon.

The time between first and second sleep is neither slumber nor waking. Too much dark and your mind will stay at rest, too much light and your dreams will surely flee. Use this time wisely—for writing spells, summoning spirits, and most importantly, remembering your dreams. Queens have been crowned, schemes hatched, fortunes gained, demons defeated, lovers found—all from visions born in the stillness of the night. In dreams, our souls are given the eyes of Fate. **Dreams must be encouraged by all possible means.**

—*From the grimoire of Eleanor St. Clair*

Between Sleeps.

ELEANOR ST. CLAIR was fast asleep—a pair of silver scissors tucked under her pillow, a sprig of lavender tied to the post of her bed. The scissors were for protection against curses and other dark magic; the lavender, to foster sweet dreams. As the clock in the shop below her moved through its hourly dance, gears clicking, pendulum ticking, hammer poised to strike, Eleanor stirred, but didn't wake. The clock, as if it meant to take pity on the tired woman, slowed to a stop just shy of two. Adelaide Thom, Eleanor's partner and friend, had forgotten to wind it again.

Moonlight shone in the windows of the building where Eleanor slept. Nestled between Markowitz's Bakery and the ticket office for the Erie Railroad, the unassuming storefront was easy to miss. The awning was faded, its crank frozen with rust. The door was in need of a fresh coat of paint. The sign above it, a simple placard with modest letters painted in cerulean, read: ST. CLAIR AND THOM, TEA AND SYMPATHY. EST. 1879. To most passersby, the place was neither remarkable nor inviting. To a select society of ladies who spoke the right words and asked the right questions, it was a place of whispered confessions and secret cures—a refuge run by women they could trust.

The crippled awning and peeling paint were of no consequence to Eleanor, who saw no need to attract undue attention from zealots, skeptics or the law. Assisting women through their difficulties carried certain risks. A young female doctor from the Women's Infirmary had been thrown in the Tombs by Anthony Comstock and his Society for the Suppression of Vice for fashioning pessaries from bits of sea sponge and silk floss (Distribution of Contraceptive Devices). A bookseller, who'd sold copies of *Fruits of Philosophy: The Private Companion of Young Married People* from behind his counter, had met a similar fate (Distribution of Obscene Literature). The abortionist Madame Restell, considered by some to be a saviour, by others a sinful hag, had slit her own throat to avoid two years of hard labour. Apothecaries no longer carried French safes or "preventative powders" for fear that Comstock would shutter their shops.

Women who found themselves in trouble were left to their own devices, or worse yet, to quackery. Mail-order medicines under the guise of vegetable compounds, regulating elixirs and an assortment of pills (renovating, periodical, Catholic and lunar) promised to "restore female regularity, remove weakness of the stomach, dissolve unwanted uterine growths." While clever language allowed their makers to avoid the long arm of Comstock, the packages in which their remedies were delivered could easily be intercepted and destroyed. Even when the item arrived safely and was used accordingly, there was no assurance a product would make good on its boasts. "Desperate times make for desperate women," Adelaide had quipped. "And desperate women with rich husbands mean more money for us."

But Eleanor hadn't gone into business with Adelaide for the money. In her eyes, their venture was more about duty than due. While Adelaide had been born a creature of the city, Eleanor had been born in a humble cottage on the banks of the Bronx River. Her mother, Madame Delphine St. Clair, was a keeper of spells, a *gardien de sorts,* so Eleanor had spent her childhood learning to embrace the traditions of her ancestors: growing herbs, keeping bees and mixing potions. She'd come from a long line of wise women that stretched back to the shores of Normandy and to the woman after whom she'd been named—who, in her mother's words, "had been twice a queen as well as a witch." Eleanor's mother had also taught her to carefully guard her gifts. "Always needed, ever hunted," was her motto—spoken each day before rising, written in the margins of her grimoire, carved into the wood of her daughter's cradle beneath the family crest. She told Eleanor, "A shepherdess sees to the care and feeding of her flock, a seamstress sees to the cut of a lady's dress. Witches see to things best sorted by magic—sorrows of the heart, troubles of the mind, regrets of the flesh. This is what we do. That is who you are."

Delphine had left Paris for New York in the spring of 1848 after yet another revolution had rocked France. Newly pregnant and alone, she'd settled in the cottage on the edge of her brother's farm and waited for her husband (and her baby) to arrive. Eleanor was born late that December, but Madame St. Clair never saw her husband again. Her brother had kept her and her new baby fed by sharing any surplus he had from the farm, and she'd provided the rest of whatever she needed for herself and Eleanor by offering her services to the women of the surrounding countryside, dubbing her little home "l'Hermitage."

Once a month, she'd bundle Eleanor in blankets and paddle a little rowboat down the river to deliver bottles and jars of her concoctions to a handful of apothecaries in the city. Over the years Eleanor became as much apprentice as daughter, happy to learn all she could about tinctures, elixirs and the traditions of the "cunning folk."

For a time, she'd abandoned those ways, choosing to leave home and study at the Women's Medical College in Manhattan, but when her mother had taken ill not quite a year into her studies, Eleanor had returned to l'Hermitage to care for her in her dying days. In the two years since Madame St. Clair's passing, Eleanor hadn't once considered going back to school. What she'd learned of modern medicine had only made it clear to her that the lessons her mother had taught her were the ones she held most dear. Honey infused with saffron, cinnamon and horny goat weed makes an effective aphrodisiac. A tonic of valerian, mugwort and poppy heads promises deep sleep and sweet dreams. A pastille containing liquorice, skullcap and chasteberry tames an aggressive lover's lust. A mix of rose petals, lavender, lemon balm and hawthorn berries soothes a broken heart. Red clover, oatstraw, nettle and red raspberry ready a woman's womb for child bearing. Tea brewed from tansy keeps a woman's blood on course. Tansy failing, there are other herbs that can bring things around: black cohosh, milkweed, pennyroyal, oarweed, Queen Anne's lace. Or, as her mother liked to sing, "Parsley, sage, rosemary and thyme . . ." Whenever Eleanor was concocting a batch of this or that, Adelaide preferred to sing a different sort of tune: "Buds, berries, leaves and roots . . . keep a girl healthy, wealthy and loose!"

Eleanor could only wish her task was as simple as that. For every woman who sidled up to the shop counter wishing to have her heart mended, her beauty increased, her lover made true, her courses stayed or started, there was a host of enchantments, incantations and charms for Eleanor to keep in mind. "Of all the creatures under Heaven," her mother used to say, "women are, by far, the most perplexing. It stands to reason that the path to solving their troubles is just as convoluted. Travel it with care, my dear. No matter a lady's concerns or burdens, be they heavy as a millstone or light as a feather, every word she speaks must be heard, every tear she sheds considered."

Over the years, Eleanor kept track of the lessons she'd learned by recording them in a large leather-bound book she'd been given by her mother, a grimoire grown so thick, the binding was split. The first time she'd brought the thing out in Adelaide's presence, her friend had cringed at the sight of it.

"It won't bite," Eleanor had teased, caressing the book's cover. "Cross my heart, hope to die."

Sheepishly, Adelaide had replied, "I've seen it, it's seen me, that should be enough."

Adelaide was young yet, twenty-one to Eleanor's thirty-two, and she'd already suffered more than her share of sorrow. Still, the young woman's quick wit, sense of style, head for business and keen intuition made her the ideal partner—the perfect complement to Eleanor's unkempt braids, stained apothecary's apron and brilliantly cluttered mind. Eleanor's only quibble with the girl was that she hadn't yet accepted the truth of who she was—a seer filled with untold promise, a wise-woman in the making. If only Adelaide would stop hiding behind the ratty deck of fortune-telling cards she kept in her pocket, and embrace the gifts that so clearly had been passed on to her in her blood. In all her life, Eleanor had never met anyone who could peer so thoroughly into the minds and hearts of others as Adelaide could, yet remain so oblivious to the truth in her own.

"Don't be so hasty to dismiss true magic," Eleanor had advised after Adelaide had recoiled from her grimoire. "Your gifts are stronger than you think."

"Stop plying me with your hocus-pocus," Adelaide had said. "I'm not like you, and my mother was most certainly not like yours. I'm just a girl from the wrong side of Chrystie Street, born to a slum-house mystic who lived on petty schemes and poppy juice. The only thing my mother ever gave me was reason to doubt her."

"You shouldn't speak ill of the dead."

"She never spoke well of me, unless you count the night she sold me away."

"Don't talk like that . . ."

"Fine," Adelaide had said. "I wouldn't want to give you the morbs."

"Honestly, Adelaide, you should take these things seriously."

"Oh, but I do," Adelaide had said, giving the grimoire a sideways look.

"I could teach you how to use it," Eleanor had offered. "I'm sure you'd be a quick study."

Adelaide had flatly refused. "Women come to me when they wish to hear what they already know. They come to you when they want a miracle. I'll stick with turning cards, if it's all the same to you. It's easier that way."

"Someday what's easy might not be enough," Eleanor had warned.

With a smile and a shrug Adelaide had replied, "When that day comes, you'll be the first to know."

They bickered sometimes but they were fast friends; two strong-willed women who refused to conform to society's expectations. Just after New Year's 1879, Eleanor had received a letter from a former medical school colleague. *I thought this might be of interest to you,* the last line of her note had read. Attached was an advertisement for a private nurse's position in the city. Thinking a change might do her good, she'd shuttered her mother's cottage and headed for the city with a bag full of tinctures and her pet raven. Adelaide Thom would prove to be the most exasperating patient she'd ever cared for, and, next to her raven, her most loyal friend.

Resting on a bamboo perch near the head of Eleanor's bed, the witch's pet raven ruffled his feathers and peered into the darkness. Squinting at his mistress, the bird wondered when she might wake. He recalled a time in the not so distant past when she'd wake in the middle of each night without fail to light a candle, sit by his side and tell him her dreams. The bird remembered every last one of her visions, no matter how odd or insignificant they'd seemed. How long had it been since she'd last risen in the night? Was she ill? Had she been cursed? Or perhaps, the raven wondered, had man's misguided ambition made the city around them shine too bright? How distracting the sparkle of their false lights was at night, their world barely fit for anything, most especially dreaming.

He'd been opposed to leaving the countryside, but it hadn't been his choice to make. He'd promised her mother that he'd stay by Eleanor's side, no matter what. The great sorceress was dead, so the promise was no longer negotiable. He often wondered if Eleanor, too, missed the mossy banks of the river, the sound of frog song in the evening, the sweet buzzy chorus of cicadas rising and falling in the dark.

He tried to rouse her by tapping at the gold band that rested around his leg, an ancient ring that bore the inscription, "Alle my trvst." *Tap, tap, tap,* he rapped persistently. *Tap, tap, tap.*

Pulling her pillow over her head, Eleanor gave the bird a gentle scolding. "Perdu!" she grumbled. "Let me sleep!"

Perdu, from the French, meaning stray or lost, generally reserved for things such as dogs, husbands and hope. If the bird ever had another name, he couldn't remember what it was.

"Wake up," he chortled, soft and low. "Wake up, wake up, wake up . . ."

Eleanor did not obey.

Poor thing, thought the bird. *How tired she must be. The world is too much with her.*

The raven was not alone in his concern.

As Perdu sat and wished for the company of his mistress,

two shadowy beings stood at the foot of her bed. They, however, wished for Eleanor to remain asleep.

At first blush, the strange creatures might've been mistaken for a pair of guardian angels. Made from equal parts memory, mischief, goodwill and longing, they belonged to an ancient order of Fay who involved themselves exclusively with the fashioning of dreams. Eleanor, who'd never seen one face to face, had been taught to refer to them collectively as the Dearlies, a name her mother had assigned to them in hopes that her daughter might take kindly to the peculiar creatures and their work.

"Is that truly what they're called?" Eleanor had asked, when she was nose-high to her mother's hip.

"No," Madame St. Clair had answered, "but they must keep their true name a secret from the dreamers they assist. A person may read or write the name, but if they speak it, they'll never dream again."

Flitting to Eleanor's side, one Dearly took hold of the edge of her blanket with its nimble fingers. Then stealing under her covers, it laid its head on her chest.

"What are you doing?" the second Dearly asked, following close behind.

"Hush!" the first Dearly scolded. "I'm measuring the space between her heartbeats."

"Why for?"

"To calculate her willingness, to see when the time is right."

"To give her the dream?" the second Dearly inquired. To this point in his life (short by Dearly standards, yet biblical by mankind's), he'd only been allowed to tend to the dreams of dogs. He'd been terribly good at it, though, earning himself the name Twitch, on account of his ability to inspire a great deal of tail thumping, whimpering and muffled yelps in the canines under his care.

"Yes, of course, to give her the dream," the first Dearly replied. "We've only got one chance to get it right." This Dearly was called Bright, due to her vast intelligence, and because whenever demons were about, she glowed with a vibrant blue light.

Plucking a whorl of lavender from the stems tied to Eleanor's bed, Twitch went about the business of preparing the air so the woman's dream might take. Chewing on the flower's buds until his breath was laced with their scent, he readied himself to send the aroma through a tiny clay pipe pointed in Eleanor's direction.

"Move closer," Bright instructed with an impatient wave of her hand. "She hasn't got the nose of a Chien de Saint-Hubert." Always aware that a person's surroundings are what prepare the mind for dreaming, Bright used every trick she held in her practical, sturdy rucksack of a brain to assist her in her work—from casting bits of spider's silk on Eleanor's eyelashes to clipping the wings off a fly that buzzed too near. Just as a master mason takes great pains in constructing a wondrous cathedral, so too did Bright take the utmost care in crafting Eleanor St. Clair's dream. She checked the loft of Eleanor's pillow and cooled its surface by fanning it with her wings, determined that this night, above all others, her charge's sleep would be held together with flying buttresses of stone, rather than wattle and daub.

"How will we know if it's worked?" Twitch interrupted, now sitting cross-legged atop a bedpost, puffing away on his pipe.

"We won't," Bright answered, shaking her head, "not until we do."

"In a second, in a minute, in an hour, in the morning?"

"Not until we do."

"All will be well," Twitch announced, in an effort to bolster his wavering confidence. "This will be good, my friend, you'll see."

"You shouldn't say such things," Bright said with a sigh. "And don't count yourself my friend just yet. A wise Dearly never speaks of success."

Rolling his eyes, Twitch teeter-tottered his head. "What's the harm, I say. It's never hurt me yet."

"There are other forces at work besides ours," Bright warned. "Don't forget that."

Like Perdu, Bright had been with Eleanor since the day she was born, and she, too, was worried that something had come between the wise-woman and her dreams. What else could explain Eleanor being stuck in her sleep, night after night? Bright figured the trouble might have been caused by the grief that still lingered in Eleanor's heart over a love affair that'd gone wrong, not to mention the overall harried nature of her life. Recently she'd started talking in her sleep, sighing over holding too many secrets and mumbling complaints against the landlord. Whatever the cause of Eleanor's distress, Bright was determined to carry on as best she could. If only she could speak to Eleanor directly, she'd tell her that she was truly sorry for her troubles. Grief, regret and demons were among the most difficult problems to banish, as they had a terrible tendency to hover between a dreamer and her Dearlies. Madame St. Clair had always blamed such troubles on the Devil, claiming, "Satan never sleeps. He stays awake so he can order his demons to mix more straw into the wheat." Bright didn't know much about the Devil, and believed him to be more invented than real, but she understood quite a lot about demons. They were evil, occasionally smart and always happy to interfere with people's dreams.

"Will she remember the dream when she wakes?" Twitch asked.

"If we've done it right," Bright replied.

"Do you think she'll tell the bird?"

"Perhaps."

"Is that good?"

"Yes."

"Will it do what needs to be done?"

"Dreams aren't bound by wants or needs. Dreams do as they please."

The vision Bright tucked inside Eleanor's mind was simple, elegant and brief. Meaning to transport the woman far from her cares, Bright conjured a hill in the dark of night, surrounded by an ancient landscape that Eleanor had never seen, yet knew in her blood. At the top of the hill a great bonfire burned, built from an enormous scaffold of twisted sticks and branches. Its flames climbed high into the night sky, hissing and crackling, and sending up sparks. Overhead the moon looked helplessly on as moths dove and spun and sizzled to their deaths.

Perdu was there, too, perched in a craggy yew tree, just steps from the fire. Spreading his wings and opening his beak, he let out a surly *caw*. The glow of the fire shone in his eyes, and smoke curled from his tongue.

Before long, a young woman entered the dream, approaching from the shadows. Circling the fire, she sang a tune under her breath, much like a child who wished to banish her fears.

May you rise with the sun, ready to make hay.
May the rains come at night to wash your cares away.

May you sleep with the angels sittin' on your bed.
May you be an hour in Heaven a' fore the Devil
knows you're dead.

Bending low, she crouched in front of the fire, her pale skin and copper-coloured hair illuminated by its flickering light. With a curious sense of calm she reached out her hand and plucked an ember from the centre of the flames. Cradling it in her palm, she turned and held it out to Eleanor.

"You must help her," Bright whispered in Eleanor's ear, mimicking her mother's voice. "Two is good, but three is better. She is the first of many."

Before Eleanor could act, the girl was consumed in a tumult of flames. When the fire threatened to devour Eleanor as well, Perdu flew from the tree and covered her eyes with his wings. With that, the vision was gone.

"Is it done?" Twitch asked, hovering over Bright's shoulder.

"Yes," Bright answered, "it's done."

Twitch snuck behind Perdu, steadied himself on the raven's tail and yanked hard on one of the raven's feathers. "Ready or not, it's begun!"

Flapping and spitting, Perdu let out a loud squawk.

Eleanor woke with a start. In her confusion she thought she smelled smoke, but soon realized a gust of wind had whistled down the chimney pipe, kicking up a sudden whirl of cold ashes in the room's iron stove. Sitting up, she struck a match, lit a candle and tried to hold on to what was left of her dream. To her dismay, all that remained was the sensation of feathers brushing against her cheek, a fleeting glimpse of the girl's face, and the overwhelming sense that no matter how hard she tried, she'd always be too late to save her.

"Douce?" Perdu said with a gentle coo. *Douce*, his name for her, from the French meaning soft, gentle and sweet (generally reserved for things such as melodies, candies, animals, cakes and sometimes little girls).

Eleanor beckoned to the bird and said, "Come here, old friend."

Perdu cooed again, and hopped to her side.

Tenderly stroking the tiny feathers that graced the top of the raven's head, she asked the bird a question she'd often asked her mother in her youth. "How old is Perdu?"

"Older than you," the bird replied with a throaty chuckle.

Her mother had sworn a thousand times over that it was Perdu who'd taught Eleanor to speak. "He's older and wiser than you and me and all our mothers." Eleanor had never imagined her mother's words could be true, even though she'd always wished them to be.

"Was that you?" she asked her pet. "In my dream?"

Perdu gave a solemn nod.

"Did you see the girl clearly?"

He nodded again.

"Don't forget her," Eleanor said. "Remember the girl."

Cocking his head, Perdu repeated her instruction. "Remember the girl."

As Eleanor returned Perdu to his perch, the Dearlies looked on from behind a coal scuttle, waiting for their chance to leave.

"You should apologize to Perdu," Bright said, wagging her finger at Twitch. "Tell him you meant no foul."

Twitch gave her a confused scowl. "Why should I?" he asked. "He's just a harmless bird."

"He's not harmless," Bright warned, her cheeks turning blue. "And he's no bird."

The Girl Who Knows.

ADELAIDE THOM BEGAN the day by readying herself to read the minds of others. Dressed in an elegant day suit of blue watered-silk (bustle high, waist cinched, lace cuffs buttoned around her wrists), she seated herself at a small dressing table near the window in her room. She recited no incantations, cast no summoning spell. The only rituals the young seer performed were pinching colour into her cheeks, tugging a comb through her hair, patting rouge onto her lips.

Gone were the trappings of her days as a sideshow sweetheart on the Bowery—the wild, unruly Circassian curls, the fine embroidered robes from "the Orient," her image and the moniker ZULA MOTH printed on countless posters and cartes-de-visite. *Easy come, easy go*, she thought as she stared at a faded photograph pinned above her looking glass. *I'll never see that girl again.*

Her work at the Palace of Illusions had been a clever deception, invented by the theatre's owner, Mr. Thaddeus Dink. Each night before Adelaide would come out on stage, the impresario had rapped his cane on the boards and exclaimed, "From the depths of a squalid slave market in the dark heart of Constantinople comes a girl so alluring, so mysterious, you'll wonder if she's real. I implore you, dear friends, to pinch yourselves—you're not dreaming. Once she's in your presence, who knows what might occur!"

Adelaide's enormous halo of curls had been achieved by washing her hair with stale beer. The costumes she'd worn had been fashioned by a seamstress who'd dressed wax figures at the dime museum next door—General Washington crossing the Delaware, President Lincoln at his moment of death, Bloody Mary seated on her throne, Joan of Arc tied to the stake. Even Adelaide's stage name was only half hers—and that half had questionable origins as well, supposedly whispered to her father by a mythical pear tree that'd once stood at the corner of Thirteenth and Third. *Call the child Moth*, the twisted tree had said to him, its branches bending low, leaves brushing against his ear. The tree was long gone, as was her father, so she couldn't query either of them. Had she ever believed the tale to be real? Yes, when she was little (and sometimes still, whenever a rare south wind rustled through the leaves of the locust trees in Madison Square Park). Whether the tale was true or not didn't matter much anymore. Adelaide was simply glad to have one pleasant childhood memory to call her own.

By the age of thirteen she'd been sold three times over—first, by her mother as a lady's maid, then by a brothel madam as a child whore, then by Mr. Dink as a Circassian Beauty—all in the space of a year.

She'd fought hard to make her way from the run-down tenement where she'd been born to the rooms of a well-appointed suite on Gramercy Park, but her struggles hadn't ended there. On New Year's Day 1879, her life had taken a devastating and tragic turn, leading her to move house and change her name again. She'd chosen *Adelaide*, because she'd thought it to be a more respectable form of "Ada" (the name her mother had wanted to give her at birth), and *Thom*, because she'd wanted a name that would remind her of who she'd been without giving herself away.

Surveying her reflection in the mirror she said her name aloud as if it were an invocation to a prayer. "Adelaide Thom," she whispered, savouring the sound of it as it tumbled off her tongue.

Miss Adelaide Thom

MIND READER. SEERESS. WITCH.

Daily consultations at St. Clair & Thom — Tea & Sympathy
Evenings by appointment

Adelaide next rehearsed her smile. Eye soft, lips together. Yes, that looks best. Something that'd once come so naturally now required effort. Putting her hand to her face, she traced the taut, wormy borders of her misfortune, a sinewy web of scars that ran from nose to ear, brow to chin, down the left side of her face. Where her left eye had been was a hollowed wink, a gruesome puckered dimple. With the tip of her finger she gave her cheek a gentle nudge in an attempt to return it to its proper shape. This was to remind herself of how she wished to appear—less crooked, more sincere.

"Half past eight and all is well!" Eleanor's voice echoed up the stairs. This was her not-so-subtle way of letting Adelaide know she was about to open the shop. On this particular morning, however, the cheerful greeting was swiftly followed by the din of shattering crockery.

"*Merde*!" she heard Eleanor exclaim, followed by the sound of a stomping foot.

"Everything all right?" Adelaide called.

"No worries," Eleanor replied. "I'm fine. All's well."

With that, Perdu let out a shrill whistle. "Top off the pot!" he cried. "Top off the pot!"

"Quiet, you insufferable heap of feathers!" Eleanor scolded. "This is your fault, for not letting me sleep."

The bird gave a penitent coo.

Adelaide stayed put listening as Eleanor took up her broom and swept the remains of a broken teapot into a metal dustpan. With each rattle and scrape, the left side of Adelaide's mouth quivered, eventually finding its way into an uncontrollable frown. Would the day ever come when she'd no longer be unnerved by the sound of something shattering? Even when a clumsy child dropped her penny-lick on the pavers, or a young rough tossed an empty bottle to the gutter, she could not curb her reaction. Worst of all were the times when the sound occurred only in her mind. Holding her breath, she waited for the memories that came along with the sound to pass, knowing they wouldn't leave until she'd relived them.

She'd been standing on the sidewalk in front of her house on Gramercy Park, waiting for a hansom cab. Normally, she would've waited inside until the driver called at the door, but she'd been invited to a New Year's soiree at Delmonico's and she didn't want to be late. Pulling her wrap around her shoulders, she'd bowed her head against the brisk wind. She hadn't noticed the young woman in the hooded cloak coming at her, clutching a bottle.

"Fucking witch!" the woman had cried, throwing vitriol in Adelaide's face.

In the next instant Adelaide felt the acid burning her flesh, she heard the bottle breaking. The last thing she remembered was the woman's figure slipping out of sight.

If she believed in God, then she might've also believed that what happened was punishment for her sins. How many transgressions had she committed in her short life? God only knew. Lusting, thieving, lying—she'd done more than a bit of each. Or maybe what she'd been punished for was living an unconventional life. She was a New York woman through and through, rather than a lady. She did as she pleased, went where she wanted. She laughed immoderately, adored the music of Offenbach and shunned the Women's Christian Temperance Union. She rode by herself on streetcars and elevated trains. She went to the theatre, the opera house, the concert hall—alone. She took strolls through the fashionable (and unfashionable) parts of town, unattended. She'd had her share of rivals, but she'd done her best to ignore them—sideshow performers who'd resented the fact that she'd been "made" a freak (and a beautiful one at that) rather than born one, soothsayers and skeptics who'd tried (and failed) to uncover the secrets of her trade, jealous wives who'd resented her failure to share their addiction to domesticity.

Thank heavens her attacker had been caught and promptly shuttled off to Blackwell's Island. The cruel madwoman turned out to be someone she knew, but barely—a magician's assistant who'd briefly been part of the sideshow and then was cut loose. Adelaide couldn't say what she'd done to incur the girl's wrath. She couldn't remember ever getting in her way.

If not for the kind soul who'd promptly come to her aid—washing her face with snow, helping her to her feet, getting her swiftly and safely to Bellevue and into a surgeon's hands—who knows what might've been her fate? She'd been told that as she lay on the table of the operating theatre, a wondrous, inexplicable thing had occurred. After the morphia, ether and iodine, after the skillful plucking of her eye and the careful stitching of what little eyelid remained, after the tidying of the remaining flesh of her cheek, she'd died on the table. Evidently the shock of it all had done her in, and the surgeon, finding no pulse, had instructed his assistant to note the time. No sooner had the young man reached into his pocket to retrieve his watch than Adelaide had gasped and jerked back to life, causing the doctors assembled around her to startle and scratch their heads. She'd laughed when she'd first learned of it, relished the thought of their puzzled faces. How perfect that she should give her greatest performance on such a stage, with her blood weeping into the sawdust strewn about the floor.

Flowers and well wishes arrived in the days after the incident, first at the hospital and then at Adelaide's home as she lay sequestered in her bed. Her dearest, oldest friend, Dr. Sadie Fonda-Hetherington, came all the way from Ocean Grove to see to her every need. But as soon as Adelaide had been able to dress herself and make a cup of tea, she'd turned to her friend and said, "It's time for you to leave."

"Come stay with me," Sadie had urged. "James and I will take good care of you. There's plenty of room to spare."

"Heavens no," Adelaide had replied. "I'll frighten your children out of their wits."

"Are you sure?" Sadie had asked, shaking her head. "I've no doubt you can look after yourself, but won't you be lonely?"

"Pity doesn't sit well with me. It causes too much commotion. It makes me a nervous wreck. There's only so much mending I can do in the company of friends."

Within a week of Sadie's departure, a knock came at the door, and Adelaide had answered it to discover a woman standing on her stoop with a leather gripsack full of tinctures in one hand, and a birdcage with a sulking raven in the other.

"I'm Eleanor St. Clair. I'm here in response to the ad in the *Evening Star*," she had announced.

"What ad?" Adelaide had asked.

"This one," Eleanor had replied, handing over a feathery bit of newsprint.

PRIVATE NURSE DESIRED.

Knowledge of wound care,
nervous ailments and the
pharmacopoeia required.
Reply to: PO Box 314 Ocean Grove, New Jersey
Room and board provided.

"I didn't place this," Adelaide had said, returning the paper to its owner.

"No," Eleanor had replied, brushing past Adelaide and into the house's foyer, "but the woman who did said you'd say precisely that. She also said that I should tell you, 'There's no sense arguing, the deed is done.'"

It'd never occurred to Adelaide to flee the city after the destruction of her beauty. Even if she had, New York would've refused to let her go. She felt now, more than ever, that the city wasn't done with her, or she with it. If there ever was a place where one could start again, it was Manhattan. Move a block, and your enemies become your friends. Move ten blocks and you might never see anyone you knew again. She'd gained a new costume, as it were, complete with a mask that could never be removed, and she'd soon learned there were advantages to that sort of thing as well as to calling herself a witch. In their gawking and their pity, people made themselves quite vulnerable. She saw more clearly now with one eye than she ever had with two—people's desires, fears, hopes, dreams and sins were laid bare before her, plain as day. With that in mind she'd come up with the notion of opening the teashop. Eleanor had resisted the plan at first, but after some persuading she'd finally agreed to it. "You'll be the Tea," Adelaide had said, "I'll be the Sympathy." They'd started their venture the previous autumn selling tea, potions, advice and fortunes to the women who shopped on Ladies' Mile.

She could hear Eleanor still shuffling about downstairs, muttering under her breath. Adelaide couldn't tell if it was in response to Perdu, or just a symptom of being overworked. More and more she'd noticed that Eleanor was exhausted at the end of the day—that her shoulders slumped and her eyes looked tired. Seeing her that way had made her wonder what she would have done without Eleanor. She owed so much to the woman and their friendship. That's why she'd decided to take a page from Dr. Sadie and placed an ad of her own for a shop assistant in *Harper's Weekly*, the *Evening Star* and the *New York Times*. As Eleanor went about her morning ritual of sprinkling salt and tea leaves across the threshold to keep the ghosts at bay, Adelaide hoped that what she'd done might serve as a bit of magic to help lighten Eleanor's load.

Placing her hat on her head, she tilted the brim slightly forward and to the left. *Less crooked, more sincere.* Gingerly draping the hat's scalloped veil in front of her face, she took a deep breath and set her mind on the task ahead. The prospective shop girls would be arriving just after noon. How many? God only knew. Surely one of them would suit. She'd know the right one when she saw her, she was sure of that. Someone with spark. Someone they could trust. Someone to help Eleanor in her work, without being a pest.

Just as she was about to make her way downstairs, the familiar scent of cherry liqueur filled the room. Pungent and sweet, it was a scent that Adelaide had always associated with her mother. This sort of thing had happened from time to time since the attack (coming out of the blue, like the mysterious sounds she heard in her head), but it'd never been this strong or seemed so close, and it'd never occurred in the shop. Perhaps Eleanor's magic couldn't keep the ghosts away after all.

"Is that you, Mama?" Adelaide asked, not really expecting an answer. "If it's you, give me a sign."

As quickly as the scent had come, it vanished.

Go on with you then, Adelaide thought. *You won't like what I have to say*. In death, as in life, Adelaide's mother was largely absent. Whenever Adelaide had tried to address her spirit—out of grief, out of anger, out of curiosity, out of desperation—she'd never gotten so much as a boo from the other side. All she wanted from her was the answer to one question: *Did you ever regret selling me away?* Once, in her frustration she'd asked Eleanor if she'd be willing to help her contact her mother's ghost, but Eleanor had firmly replied, "I can't help you with that."

"You can't, or you *won't*?"

"Those who can properly converse with the dead are rare. Anyone who dares to dabble in such matters without proper knowledge is dreadfully misguided. The laws that govern the dead are not the same as ours."

"Have you tried? I'm sure you could do it."

"That's not how it works."

"How do you know?"

"I just do."

After that, Adelaide had chosen to pursue the matter on her own. She'd read many articles, attended countless lectures, even sought out mediums she'd read of in the paper in hopes that she might find at least one of them to be real. She hadn't been home last night to wind the clock because she'd gone to Washington Square to visit Mrs. Seymour, a woman who reportedly acted as a conduit for spirit. But when she'd gotten there, the woman's husband had said she was gone. "Good riddance, too!" he'd roared. "I was about to ship her off to the lunatic asylum on Blackwell's Island." Disappointed, Adelaide had put off going home, choosing instead to wander the city in pursuit of other, more pleasurable, spirits.

"Will you be coming down anytime soon?" Eleanor called up the stairs. "Your tea is getting cold."

"Be right there," Adelaide replied.

Opening the top drawer of her dressing table, Adelaide brought out a delicate, heart-shaped bottle. Where it once had contained a generous dose of fine French brandy, it now held the glistening, floating orb of her left eye. Putting her lips to the glass, she kissed it and made a wish, "May the right girl appear, today."

"Careful what you wish for," her mother's ghost chirped from behind the eye in its watery little chamber, silent to Adelaide's ears.

The Great Obelisk

The Egyptian monument commonly known as "Cleopatra's Needle" is due to make landfall in Manhattan today. In anticipation of the next leg of the three-thousand-year-old obelisk's journey, it was moved yesterday evening up the Hudson to a dockyard at Ninety-Sixth Street via a pair of sturdy pontoons. Although the Needle, a seven-storey, two-hundred-ton piece of granite, arrived from Alexandria aboard the SS *Dessoug* in late July, the obelisk was left in the ship's hold at the dock at Staten Island until such time as the tide might conspire to carry it ashore.

Cleopatra's Guard

Even while the obelisk was settled in the ship's hold, eager curiosity seekers came in great numbers to see it. Unable to delay their enthusiasm, the visitors balanced upon a series of planks supported on dinghies in order to board the vessel. Upon reaching their destination, the visitors were greeted by a solemn-faced, smartly dressed watchman holding a lighted candle who led them into the dark region of the ship where the obelisk lay. "What a strange fellow!" one visitor remarked. "He never spoke a word the entire time I was aboard the ship." Rumour has it the watchman was first spotted standing among the ruins when archeologists unearthed the Needle's pedestal and insisted on accompanying the obelisk all the way to

New York. Some say he's not a man at all but rather a mystical *jinni* sent to guard the monument who will vanish when it no longer requires his protection.

A True Survivor

The obelisk has survived many hardships and journeys through the ages—the storming of Heliopolis, an arduous trip down the Nile, an earthquake at Alexandria, and last but not least, a perilous voyage across the Atlantic. Still, there are naysayers who question whether Cleopatra's Needle will ever reach its final resting place in Central Park. If and when it does, will anyone pay it any mind "way up there" on Greywacke Knoll, among the shantytowns and the sparse constellation of mansions that surround the park? Commodore Henry Honeychurch Gorringe, the man in charge of moving the Needle, says they will. So, too, do the multitudes of Freemasons that populate this country, including Mr. William Vanderbilt, who paid a pretty sum to fund the Needle's trip. No doubt these men are especially enamoured with the object, as they believe certain markings found upon it hold great symbolic ties to their order.

The Obelisk Speaks

What significance, if any, does the obelisk hold for the rest of us? What secrets are hidden in the many hieroglyphs carved into the Needle's faces? An expert in translations has confided to the *Daily Messenger* that he believes the glyphs foretell the future of America. Whatever meaning the ancient markings hold, the obelisk has certainly got New Yorkers under its spell.

Beatrice Dunn Takes Flight.

"One ticket for the nine-thirty train to New York, please."

"Sorry, miss, the last passenger train left at half past seven."

"The last train for the day? How can that be? Don't they usually run every two hours?"

"They do, but not today. There's an interruption on the tracks."

"What sort of interruption?"

"Don't know."

"Are you sure there won't be any more trains?"

"Well, miss, all I've heard from the head office is that our passenger service is disrupted until further notice. For all I know that could mean today, tomorrow or next week. You can wait here if you like, but I can't make any promises."

Picking up her bag, Beatrice turned from the station agent and looked for a bench where she could sit to sort her thoughts. For weeks she'd had the day mapped out, down to the minute. Was this roadblock a sign that she should turn back? Reaching inside her pocket, she felt for the witch's ladder she'd fashioned from her hair, feathers, string and wishes. Shaking her head over the faith she'd put in the crude little charm, she wadded it up and tucked it deep inside her bag. *Serves me right for believing I could perform even the simplest bit of magic*, she thought. Still, until now, everything had gone right.

8:00–8:40 Breakfast with Aunt Lydia. Oatmeal with stewed apples, tea with honey and milk. Lydia had insisted on it. "Such hearty fare will keep you sated and help to deter motion sickness on the train." Their conversation had been cordial and kind—not too anxious on Beatrice's part, not too sentimental on Lydia's.

"Will you be coming to visit me in the city?" Beatrice had asked, more out of obligation than desire. She knew that Lydia didn't like to travel, that she'd made the annual trip to New York solely on her account, that the speed of the train caused her to fret and that the fumes aggravated her lungs (the faintest hint of smoke in the air could set her wheezing). Still, Beatrice had thought she should extend an invitation to let her aunt know that she'd be missed. "Perhaps you could travel by steamboat instead of train," she'd suggested. "It might do you good to take in the fresh air along the river."

"I've got all the fresh air I need right here," Lydia had countered. "If it's all the same to you, I'd rather stay put. I'm sure you'll get back to Stony Point for holidays."

"Of course I will," Beatrice had assured her. "And I'll write each and every day with all the details of my adventures."

Saying this had made Beatrice feel incredibly guilty, for she knew she'd just told her aunt a terrible lie. There might well be things she'd see or do or say while she was away that she wouldn't wish to share with Lydia. It wasn't that she didn't love and trust her aunt, it was just that she'd reached the point where she believed she should keep certain things private if she was ever truly going to belong to herself. "Those adventures of yours had better be plenty grand," Lydia had teased, bringing a handkerchief to the corner of her eye. Her words had been in jest, but the tears were real.

"Oh they will be," Beatrice had said, kissing her finger and crossing her heart. "I promise." And then she, too, required the aid of a handkerchief. Although she knew Lydia would be fine on her own, she still worried about her. Over the years certain women in Stony Point had been awfully pointed in their opinions about the way Lydia had chosen to raise her. In recent days they'd been quick to play Cassandra, predicting all manner of misfortunes for Beatrice—seduction, illness, injury and so on—all stemming from Lydia's liberal attitudes and her consent to letting her niece go. Beatrice couldn't wait to prove them wrong.

8:40–8:45 Goodbyes. "I'm not one for lengthy farewells," Lydia had announced as she stood next to Beatrice on the wide front porch. Slipping her hand in her pocket, she'd pulled out a lovely silver brooch and pinned it to the collar of Beatrice's coat.

"What's this?" Beatrice had asked, turning the edge of her lapel so she could examine the trinket—a beautiful striped feather encased in a delicate oval of glass.

"It's a wren's feather," Lydia had answered, "for protection and luck. Your father gave it to your mother on the occasion of your birth, but she thought it so precious, she rarely wore it. She gave it to me before she died and asked that I give it to you on a special occasion—such as your wedding or the birth of your first child."

"Maybe we should wait until then," Beatrice had said. "Maybe you should hang onto it for me a little while longer?"

"No," Lydia had responded. "Today's the day."

Fearing she might cry, Beatrice bowed her head and turned

away, thinking helplessly that even proper goodbyes were hard. Lydia had taken great pains to keep her away from her parents in their last days, and although Beatrice no longer harboured any hard feelings towards her aunt over the matter, losing the chance to say goodbye to them had left a mark on Beatrice's heart. Within that mark, dark and deep, lay Beatrice's biggest fear—that one day, when the balance of the life she'd lived with her parents inevitably tipped in favour of her life without them, all her memories of their time together, precious and irreplaceable, would be lost. "Thank you," she'd whispered to Lydia as she'd given the woman's hand a gentle squeeze. "I'll cherish it, always."

8:45–9:00 Stagecoach to Stony Point Station. The stage had been on time, the ride uneventful. Beatrice hadn't brought any trunks to stow and they'd made no stops for other passengers. Lydia had kindly offered to send along anything she might need from home once she was settled, and with that in mind Beatrice had packed only an extra dress (blue calico with velvet trim), a dressing gown, a pair of felt slippers, a cotton chemise, three hair ribbons (red, yellow and blue), a hair brush, a light shawl, an assortment of unmentionables, five handkerchiefs (two lace, three cotton), needles and thread, a bar of lavender soap, a tin of pins, pen and ink, pencils and paper, her book of observations, and the latest issue of *Madam Morrow's Strange Tales of Gotham* for reading on the train. She'd tucked everything neatly inside a sturdy carpetbag that Lydia had given her.

In preparation for the day's travel, Beatrice had pulled her hair into a long braid, and donned a practical dress of dark green broadcloth. Along with black patent leather boots, a light plaid ulsterette and her favourite straw hat, she'd felt her ensemble accentuated her youth without seeming too naïve. The last thing she'd wanted was to appear fresh off the boat. She'd read enough of Madam Morrow's tales to know what happens to girls like that.

As an extra precaution, she'd sewn most of the money she'd saved for the trip into the hem of her petticoat. It wasn't much—enough for a couple nights lodging, and a ticket back to Stony Point—but she couldn't afford to lose it. When the stage had reached the station, she'd carefully handed over what she owed the driver, including a modest tip, and then proceeded to the ticket booth with plenty of time to spare, or so she'd thought.

Sitting on the bench now, she considered her next step. Should she wait for a train that might never come? Should she call it a day and go home? If only she'd come to the station earlier! She'd barely slept all night and had been ready to leave by sunrise. Still, she'd wanted to give Lydia a last morning together. She'd figured that by taking the 9:30 train she'd still be able to get to the teashop before the appointed hour and maybe even be the first in line. How many applicants could there be? She had no idea. All she knew was that the closer she was to the front of the line, the sooner the shopkeeper's search could end, and the sooner her life in the city would start.

"Perhaps we could take the steamboat?" a gentleman's voice suggested. "There's one that leaves at noon from Grassy Point."

Beatrice turned to find that he wasn't speaking to her, but to a woman dressed in a red silk dress whose bonnet was adorned with a matching spray of ostrich feathers.

"I guess it will have to do," the lady sighed, the plumes on her bonnet trembling.

Figuring the steamboat might have to do for her as well, Beatrice rose to follow them.

As they made their way off the platform, a train whistle sounded in the distance. Stopping short, Beatrice waited for it to sound again. The next time the whistle blew it was somewhat closer, and when she looked down the tracks she could see a train approaching the station. Rushing to the ticket window, she rapped on the counter to get the station agent's attention. "What's that train?" she demanded.

"The New York Central."

"When's it set to leave?"

"Ten a.m., but it's freight only."

"Why's it running when the passenger trains aren't?"

"Milk, hay and potatoes don't give a fig if they're on time."

Smoke belching from its engine, the train pulled into the station with a string of boxcars hitched behind it.

Beatrice picked up her bag and turned to leave, walking past groups of farmhands loading heavy cans of milk and barrels of apples. Just as she was about to exit the station, she recognized a young man who was hefting sacks of potatoes, one after another into the dark hold of a boxcar. It was Joseph Wheeler, the eldest son of the owner of one of the largest farms in Stony Point. She and Joseph had gone to school together and their families had held adjacent pews at the Stony Point Presbyterian Church. Beatrice watched as the young man loaded the last of his sacks into the car, then hopped up and stowed a sturdy handcart. When he didn't reappear, she realized he meant to go along for the ride.

"Joe!" Beatrice called. "Joseph Wheeler!" she tried again, feeling like a fool. As she hurried towards the car, she prayed she hadn't been mistaken, that it truly was Joseph she'd seen.

"Beatrice Dunn?" Joseph said when she arrived at the car's door. "What on earth brings you here?"

"I'm going to the city, or at least I was."

As he wiped his brow with his handkerchief, Joseph asked, "Miss your train?"

"Not exactly. The station agent says my train's not running. I couldn't even get a ticket."

"That's a shame," he said with a shrug. "Guess I'll get there before you." He always did like to tease.

"You and your potatoes," Beatrice said.

Joseph let out a laugh.

"Think I might join you and your russets?" Beatrice ventured to ask.

"Oh, I don't know," Joseph replied, actually scuffing the toe of his boot on the boxcar's dusty floor.

Beatrice didn't know what else to say.

"I wouldn't mind the company, of course," Joseph said at last, grinning at her. "You're welcome to come along, but I have to warn you—you're in for a pretty bumpy ride."

The train's whistle sounded a sharp toot, announcing its departure.

"I don't care about a few bumps," Beatrice said, holding out her bag. "Mind taking this for me?"

"Happy to," Joseph replied, pulling the carpetbag into the hold. Then offering his hand to Beatrice, he exclaimed, "All aboard!"

She spent much of the journey perched atop a heap of burlap sacks that Joseph had arranged for her. "It's this," he'd said, "or get that pretty-looking getup of yours covered in god-knows-what."

"Thanks," she'd said, blushing. "How thoughtful of you."

She was glad when Joseph turned his back to sit in the open doorway of the car, legs dangling over the edge.

When they were younger, he'd often leaned forward on the edge of the church pew behind Beatrice to flick the frayed end of a goose feather at the back of her neck. Time and again she'd ignored his pestering, guessing he was only doing it to get her in trouble. Once, when they were older, he'd asked her if he could walk her home from school, but she'd thought the invitation was another one of his pranks. She'd replied by snorting out an awkward laugh, which Joseph had promptly taken as a "no." *All the girls like Joseph Wheeler*, she'd thought. *What would he want with me?* When he'd made the same request the following week, this time loud enough so every girl within ten feet could hear, Beatrice had turned tail and run, hot tears of embarrassment streaking down her face, chased by the titters of the other girls and the disbelief in their jealous eyes.

Carefully shifting on her sacks, Beatrice turned the collar of her coat up and held it around her neck to shield herself from the raw nip of wind coming through the car's door. She found herself longing for warmth and solid ground under her feet. Determined not to succumb to regret, she stared past Joseph in the open door, and became transfixed by the ever-changing view. Moss-green pastureland skirted the tracks as they rolled past, and beyond that, she could see the Hudson River. Haystacks dotted the land, and a lone dairy cow made its way along a winding path to the water. Had the gentle beast managed to break through the barnyard fence? One could hope. One could pray. One could wish.

Closing her eyes, Beatrice remembered a farm she used to visit with her parents when she was a child. Why they'd gone there she couldn't remember, but she did recall the farmer's wife allowing her to feed the chickens, and milk their favourite cow. How pleasant it'd felt to rest her head against the velvety warmth of the Holstein's flank as she went about the steady grasp and tug of emptying its udders. What she wouldn't give to be back there again, to feel her mother's gentle hand on her shoulder, to hear the farmer's wife sing in time with her work.

May you rise with the sun, ready to make hay.
May the rains come at night to wash your cares away.
May you sleep with the angels sittin' on your bed.
May you be an hour in Heaven a' fore the Devil knows you're dead.

She guessed they'd been travelling for well past an hour. How much longer would it take to get to New York? By passenger train the trip usually took a little over two hours. Was it the same for freight? By the way her belly was rumbling, Beatrice guessed it must be getting close to noon. *Click-clack, click-clack, click-clack.* Fingering the coins in her pocket, she wondered if she should offer to pay Joseph for her passage. She hadn't had to buy a ticket at the station, so she had more than enough to share.

Holding out a quarter, she called to him over the noise of the train. "Here," she said, "this is for you."

"Why for?" Joseph asked, getting up and coming to sit by Beatrice's side.

"For letting me come along with you and your potatoes."

The young man waved the offer away. "There's no need for that. I'm happy for the company." Then taking an apple and a knife from his knapsack, he sliced a wedge from the ripe red fruit and offered it to Beatrice.

Grateful, she took the slice and bit into its crisp, sweet flesh. Now he was next to her she couldn't help feeling that she needed to fill the space between them with whatever thoughts came into her head. Mouth half full, she nervously sputtered, "Did you know the trains in the city are elevated? Three storeys off the ground. Every three minutes a string of train cars atop one of those tracks rattles from one end of the city to the other. For a nickel you can ride from Battery Park to the Harlem River. Of course there's noise and smoke and showers of hot cinders that get spewed to the streets below, and there's always a risk of falling from the platform, or getting pushed by the crowds, but five cents is a small price to pay for turning hours to minutes, don't you think?"

Joseph smiled at her, then pointed to the sacks of potatoes piled all around them. "Me and the russets go to the city most every week, you know."

"Right," Beatrice said, feeling stupid. "Of course. I'm sorry. I should've known."

How ridiculous it was for her to think that she could understand all that was worth knowing about a place simply from reading newspapers and guidebooks, and from a yearly jaunt with Aunt Lydia to the tamest parts of the city. Had she ever stayed in New York overnight? If she had, she couldn't remember it. But it was too late to turn back now. All she could do was try her best not to look as uncomfortable and scared as she felt. "Shouldn't be long now," Joseph said, checking his watch. "Know where you're goin' when we get there?"

Beatrice said, "Madison Square Park, or thereabouts."

"Nice spot," Joseph replied. "Be sure to visit Lady Liberty's torch while you're there. Even without the rest of her attached, it's truly something else."

"You've seen it?"

Beatrice had begged Lydia many times over to take her to the park to see it, but her aunt had insisted they wait until the statue was whole and in place on Bedloe's Island.

"Just last week. Even climbed to the top to have a look around. You get a great view of the Fifth Avenue Hotel from up there."

"Have you been to the hotel as well?" Beatrice asked, now thinking that anything might be possible when it came to Joseph Wheeler.

"Yes," he said, "but only in the lobby. To tell you the truth, the place is far too fussy for my taste. All that velvet and crystal and marble makes me anxious."

The thought of Joseph standing amongst the hotel's elite clientele made Beatrice smile. "Do you stay over in the city on these trips?"

"Sometimes. I've got cousins who run a saloon near the Bowery. I stay with them on occasion."

"The Bowery," Beatrice repeated. She'd read of it in *Madam Morrow's Strange Tales of Gotham*, which had described the street as having pits dug into the floors of every beer hall for cock fights and rat-catching matches, and prostitutes plying their trade on every corner. Biting her lip, she said, "Sounds nice."

Joseph shrugged. "It's not, but they're good people and it's a place to rest my head." Pitching his apple core out the door, Joseph turned so he could meet Beatrice's eyes.

"What is it?" she asked, wiping her face with a handkerchief, hoping to brush away the smudge of dirt she imagined must be there.

"Nothing," Joseph said, his cheeks turning pink.

"Joseph, be honest. I've an important appointment ahead. I can't afford to look shabby."

"Your face is fine," Joseph said.

"What is it then?"

Sunlight shone through the slats of the boxcar and across his face. "I always figured you'd go away someday," he said. "To New York, or out west, or maybe London or Paris."

"Whatever made you think that?"

"Because you aren't like any of the other girls in Stony Point."

Just then the train's wheels began to squeal on the tracks, and they came to a stop.

"Are we there?" Beatrice asked.

Sticking his head out the door and looking both ways, Joseph answered, "We're close, but we're not at the station."

They could both hear a great commotion building outside as a man shouted, "Stand back! Everyone, stand back!"

"Come on," Joseph said, "let's go see what all the fuss is about."

"Are you sure it's safe?"

Joseph took her hand in his, helping her up. "We'll find out."

Climbing out of the car, they picked their way down a steep rocky grade to a scrubby patch of grass. A crowd had gathered around the engine, which had stopped just shy of a curious contraption that'd been laid over the tracks. Made from massive wood beams that supported a set of iron rails with cannonballs for bearings, it held an enormous wooden box at one end and a bright red steam engine at the other. A sturdy chain attached the engine to the box, presumably to haul the box across the tracks. Beatrice recognized the odd shape at once. "That's Cleopatra's Needle," she whispered to Joseph. "It has to be." Glancing around she saw that, indeed, they were stopped next to the dockyard on the Hudson where the pontoons were moored after carrying the Needle up the river.

One by one the other farmhands who'd been riding along with their goods got off the train to join them, and they all moved to get a better view.

"Clear the area!" a red-faced man began to shout. His was the same voice that earlier had instructed the crowd to stand back.

Beatrice couldn't see past the sack-coated men who now surrounded her, their hats cocked to the backs of their heads, their weathered hands on their hips. When one of the men spat to the side without thinking, his spittle landed on the toe of her boot. He stared at Beatrice and grinned.

Dragging her boot across a clump of grass, she thought, *Welcome to city life.*

"Why are we standing around looking at a box?" the rude man groused.

"'Cause Vanderbilt paid for it," the man next to him answered.

"How much?"

"A hundred thousand smackers."

"You lie."

"I don't."

"You do! You told me there'd be something to see—that there's just a box."

Beatrice and Joseph found their way past the men to a less crowded spot where the sound of the steam engine drowned out the men's chatter. The grind of the chain winding on its spool along with the growling churn of cannonballs tumbling in their channels caused the ground to shake as the obelisk inched forward. Soon the terrible sound of metal scraping against metal squealed through the air. Holding her hands over her ears, Beatrice looked on as a man standing atop the obelisk waved a white flag and signalled for the engine to be brought to a stop.

A chorus of whoops and hollers erupted from the contraption's crew to celebrate the safe delivery of the Needle across the tracks.

Atop the roof of a warehouse nearby, two men were observing the proceedings. One was a photographer hired by Mr. Vanderbilt to document this important moment in the obelisk's journey. The other was Gideon Palsham, a master architect who had a great interest in ancient stone structures and anything said to have been touched by magic. While the photographer stood hunched behind his camera, cloaked in a heavy black cloth, Palsham caught sight of Beatrice. He watched the girl intently, never taking his eyes off her. She was the only female in the crowd, the only one of her kind. As the photographer drew the cover over his lens, the train's whistle sounded, calling its passengers back.

Beatrice held fast to Joseph's arm. Who could've imagined that she'd arrive in New York at the same time as this magnificent wonder? Perhaps there was magic in the world after all. Everything she'd read about the obelisk had pointed to it being an object of untold mystical powers.

Tugging at Joseph's sleeve, she hoped she might convince him to stop so she could get a better look at the obelisk.

Although it was dressed in wood planking and laid on its side, she couldn't help but feel that she should pause to honour it. "Joseph, wait," she said. "I'll just be a moment."

Looking up to make sure he'd heard her, she discovered that the sleeve she'd gotten a grip on wasn't his: a stranger now stood in his place. Flustered and confused she pulled away from the gentleman. "I'm so sorry," she said. "I thought you were someone else."

"It's quite all right," he said, turning to protect her from the jostling crowd. "I'd like to help you, if I might."

His skin was the colour of nutmeg, and his face was lined with wrinkles as if he'd spent most of his life turned towards the sun. He wore no hat, but his greying hair was neatly combed and his beard came to a jaunty point. Dressed in pinstriped trousers and a double-breasted waistcoat, he held his jacket over his arm. The sleeves of his linen shirt were loosely rolled to his elbows, but the blue silk ascot he wore around his neck was properly tied and fixed with a silver pin in the shape of a scarab. When he smiled, a gold-capped tooth glinted in the corner of his grin and his dark eyes shone with steadfastness. Although Beatrice hadn't any reason to trust him, she was certain he didn't mean her harm.

"Thank you," Beatrice found herself saying as the crowd continued to push on around them.

"This way," the gentleman said, leading her to a platform of wooden skids, directly beside the obelisk. "Just until those barbarians pass."

From where she stood, Beatrice could see a team of men going about the business of dismantling the portion of the contraption that still obstructed the tracks. They were making quick work of it, and she was sure the train's conductor wouldn't waste any time once the tracks were clear. "I should be getting back on the train," she said.

"Have you come a long way?"

"Not nearly as far as the obelisk," Beatrice answered him with a smile.

Patting the side of the box the man said, "It has been a long journey."

"Have you travelled with it the entire way?" Beatrice asked.

"I have indeed," he replied with a solemn nod. Pointing to a brass handle on the side of the box, he asked, "Would you like to see it?"

Glancing back at the train, Beatrice shook her head. "I'd love to, but I really must go."

"I won't let them leave without you. I promise." Gently sliding the wooden panel to the left, he revealed a space just large enough for Beatrice to peer through. "Go on," he urged. "It misses being seen."

Beatrice stuck her head inside the box. The space was filled with the smell of damp stone, reminding her of the smooth rocks she'd collected along the Hudson as a child. Standing on tiptoe, she shifted slightly to one side to allow a bit of sunlight to pass into the box. All at once she could see the rosy, mottled surface of the obelisk; the graceful curve of a glyph was within her reach. She traced it with her fingers. The stone was cool and damp, and when she held her palm against it, she could feel a low, steady pulse. Was it the obelisk? Was it the train's engine preparing to depart? Or was it just her heart, racing with excitement? Giddy with wonder, she let out a soft laugh, which to her surprise echoed quite freely inside the dark space. It carried on long after it should have, fading into an eerie, undulating whisper. Closing her eyes, Beatrice leaned forward and said, "Hello?" half thinking if she waited long enough, she might receive an answer.

"Beatrice!" a voice shouted behind her. "Beatrice Dunn!"

Withdrawing her head, Beatrice turned to see Joseph approaching, wringing his cap in his hands. "Come away from there, we'll miss the train!"

The gentleman who'd opened the box for her was gone.

Not waiting for Joseph to reach her, Beatrice climbed down from the platform on her own. Misjudging the distance, she stumbled and tripped on the hem of her skirts, and landed in a heap on the ground. Her world went sideways, then black. The last thing she heard was the sound of coins tumbling out of her petticoat, cheerily ringing as they lost themselves among the planks and stones.

The Known World is filled with mystical messages. Signs, portents and foretellings come in many guises—smoke on the wind, sparks from a fire, ripples on the water, lines in the sand. If you wish to master magic, pay attention. If you wish to master love, do the same.

—From the grimoire of Eleanor St. Clair

Shop Talk (and Secrets).

ELEANOR LIT THE WICK on a small kerosene stove and watched the flame flicker and bloom in the heater's isinglass window. Filling a copper kettle, she placed it on the stove's iron rest, and waited for the water to boil—and for the three women who were standing at her counter to make up their minds.

"I quite like the hibiscus," the youngest woman remarked. "Doesn't it smell divine?"

"Orange pekoe is my favourite," said the woman on her right.

"You must try the Darjeeling," urged the woman to her left.

Each of them had paid a recent visit to the shop, albeit alone and for very different reasons. Mrs. Orange Pekoe had been in search of a tonic to help her sleep, Madame Darjeeling had requested an elixir to foster desire, and Lady Hibiscus had required a tincture of Queen Anne's lace to clear the womb and restore peace of mind. This pretty young woman had also been responsible for Eleanor's broken heart. For a few blissful weeks in the spring they'd carried on an affair, quietly hidden from the rest of the world, even Adelaide. All through the month of May it'd been flesh against flesh—honey sucked off fingers and breasts, silk sashes wrapped around wrists, feathers plucked from bonnets for tickling thighs and ribs. "This must remain a secret," Lady Hibiscus had insisted, "just between us two." She was promised to a gentleman of great social prominence and had no intention of breaking their engagement. Eleanor thought she could stay levelheaded, but being dismissed by the young woman had hurt more than she'd imagined. Once the wedding was over and done, the girl's affection had turned to calculated indifference. Still, she insisted on coming into the shop for this and that, never giving so much as a nod to her former place in Eleanor's life. *If that's what she wants,* Eleanor had vowed to herself, *so be it.*

As the trio took turns sniffing at open tea tins, Eleanor covered her mouth to stifle a yawn. Her sleep had been fitful and brief, especially after her dream, and before she'd known it the sun had risen and it was time to drag her tired body out of bed.

There'd been books to balance, and remedies to concoct, linens to press and honey pots to fill. There'd been blessings to recite, spells to consider, and a pleasant exchange with Mr. Markowitz's son, a bright-natured boy named Isaac, who'd come to the door bearing a basket of baked goods to sell. Feeling generous, Eleanor had chosen to buy the whole lot—three glazed lemon tarts, one loaf of scalded rye, and an assortment of teacakes, fritters and biscuits (honey, apple and buttermilk).

Despite her exhaustion, Eleanor quite liked waking when most of the city's inhabitants (including Adelaide) were still half asleep, and the only sounds on the sidewalk were the yappy bickering of newsboys and the cheerful swell of the milkman's voice singing a ditty as his wagon rolled by. This morning she'd even taken a few moments to sit on the roof amidst the maze of potted herbs that surrounded her two small beehives and collect her thoughts.

Everything in the humble potager had had its beginnings in her mother's garden, from lemon balm to lavender, from mugwort to mint. As the sun hit the rooftop, a few keen bees had straggled forth from their hives. Soon, Eleanor thought, all her golden beauties would be taking to the air to nuzzle among the late summer blooms of Madison Square—the last of the daylilies that surrounded the fountain in the park, the bright asters and pot marigolds that graced every flower box on Fifth Avenue, the hardy roses that climbed the trellises of the grand houses on Marble Row. Soon, their sisters would commence their preparations for autumn's chill by capping their stores for winter and ridding themselves of anything that got in their way—failed eggs, lost wings, and every last one of their brothers, whose usefulness had come to an end. Crouching near a hive, Eleanor had listened in on the glorious steady hum of their work. This, and the heady scent of their honey, never failed to make her worries disappear.

Carrying this sense of contentment in her heart, she'd gone about her daily tasks with ease until the teapot had crashed to the floor. Oddly enough, she hadn't been standing anywhere near the pot when it fell. Only the lid had survived, sitting safe and untouched in the centre of the counter. Perdu's startled cries of "Top off the pot!" had caused her mother's voice to sound in her head. *Top off the pot means a stranger's coming to call.*

Madame St. Clair had always put great faith in the happenstances that occurred while making, serving and drinking tea: *two spoons placed on the same saucer mean a wedding will soon follow; two women pouring from the same pot means one will soon carry a child; tea spilled from the spout of a carried pot means a secret will soon be revealed; tea stirred while in the pot will surely stir up a quarrel.*

Sometimes Eleanor wondered if her mother's sayings mattered anymore. The world was changing at an alarming pace and the city right along with it. Perhaps all these changes called for a new sort of magic, one divined not from teacups and spoons, but from the *rickety-tick* of the elevated trains as they roared past, or the flickering haloes cast by the street lamps that stood outside her window. Something strange was in the air, she was sure of it, but she couldn't put her finger on exactly what it was. How was she supposed to understand what the city was trying to tell her when she couldn't properly remember her dreams? Closing her eyes, she tried once more to catch a glimpse of her most recent vision, but she only felt off-balance and dizzy, as if she were about to fall from a great height. Had some dark spectre come into the shop without her knowing? A ghost, a ghoul, a demon, the Devil in disguise? She'd always been so careful to keep the place protected and safe. "Mother, help me," she'd whispered. Then, "*Mère, aide-moi.*"

"I can't decide," Madame Darjeeling said shaking her head.

"Neither can I," Mrs. Orange Pekoe seconded.

"Nor can I," said Lady Hibiscus.

Can't you? Eleanor thought. She really wanted to hate the girl but couldn't. She watched as the young woman nervously turned her wedding ring around her finger. Was something bothering her? Was something wrong? "Why don't I brew a pot of each so you can sample them all?" she suggested. "My treat."

"That would be lovely," said Madame Darjeeling.

"Simply splendid," remarked Mrs. Orange Pekoe.

"If it's not any trouble," Lady Hibiscus added.

As Eleanor set the tea to steep, a single honeybee clung fast to a fold in her sleeve. Perdu, watching intently from his perch, spotted the bee before his mistress. Flapping his wings, he bobbed his head and exclaimed, "Treat, treat, treat!"

Mrs. Orange Pekoe's eyes went wide with disbelief. "Was that the bird?" she asked.

Lady Hibiscus smiled and nodded. "I've heard him speak before."

"What a clever trick!" exclaimed Madame Darjeeling.

Holding a bit of teacake in the palm of her hand, Eleanor offered it to Perdu. "What's gotten into you?" she whispered. "You're acting like a spoiled brat."

The bird refused to take the sweet.

Eleanor ignored her pet's antics and resumed the work of preparing the tea. "Why don't you ladies take a seat? I'll only be a minute."

Perdu hopped to the counter and took hold of her sleeve with his beak. He knew what he wanted, even if she didn't.

The bee, enticed by a pitcher of honey Eleanor had placed on the counter, crawled out of hiding, and moved towards her hand.

"Well hello, m'dear," Eleanor said, spotting the object of Perdu's desire.

"Treat!" Perdu demanded again.

"She's not for you," Eleanor scolded, moving out of his reach.

Had it been a drone, she might well have handed the doomed creature over to the raven to gobble up, but this bee was no drone. She was a healthy female, meant to be rushing from flower to flower in the last days of harvest. Knowing the ruckus the little darling would cause if she happened to get tangled in Madame Darjeeling's curls, Eleanor poured a single drop of honey onto a saucer, gently transferred the bee alongside it, and covered them both with an empty, upturned cup. For a moment, the bee bumped and buzzed against the porcelain in protest, but as soon as Eleanor bent near the cup and whispered, "Patience, my dear, you'll soon be free," she stopped.

Perdu returned to his perch to sulk.

Amidst a collection of Moroccan lanterns, tasselled pillows and tufted furniture, Adelaide Thom was sitting in the back corner of the shop, taking advantage of a brief lull in her morning. She'd been holding court since half past nine, turning cards and entertaining questions from a steady stream of clients.

Miss Edith Jones. A dear, bright girl, always on time. She came in blushing, fidgeting, heart aflutter. Crossed her legs at the ankles, once, twice, three times over. So keen to fall in love.

Her question: *Is he the one?*

Her cards: Courtship. Jealousy. Disappointment.

Adelaide's answer: *He thinks he is, but his mother does not.*

The mother of the "he" in question was Mrs. Marietta Stevens—socialite, widow, owner of the Fifth Avenue Hotel. She'd visited Adelaide the previous day for her own consultation, during which she'd heartily complained of Miss Jones's pursuit of her son and repeatedly asked if she might eventually find success in breaking up the pair. All signs had pointed to yes. (*What a pity*, Adelaide had thought. *Edith is such a lovely girl.*)

Mrs. Violet Pritchett. Newlywed. Face aglow. Dress hugging her figure. Downed two cups of peppermint tea in quick succession. Complained of shoes feeling tight, and of stiff, swollen fingers.

Her question: *When shall I get with child?*

Her cards: Fortune. Plenty. Home.

Adelaide's answer: *Congratulations, my dear, you already are.*

Mrs. Rose Blanchard. Nervous. Quiet. Eyes downcast. Every time she moved, the right cuff of her dress shifted, revealing a ring of dark bruises on her wrist.

Her question: *When will it end?*

Her cards: Deceit. Ruin. Death.

Adelaide's answer: *Not until you leave him, or he's dead.*

Mrs. Blanchard's response: *It's easier to kill a man than to divorce him, I'd guess.*

Adelaide thought that she'd like to kill the woman's husband herself, if she could get away with it. Perhaps she could pose as a housemaid and slip the powder of some noxious root from Eleanor's cupboard into his coffee. Until she could think of a better plan, poor Mrs. Blanchard would have to go it alone.

Checking her watch Adelaide saw it was five past noon. The prospective shop girls would be arriving in less than an hour. She knew that she should inform Eleanor since her partner hated surprises, even when they were good.

Shuffling her cards, Adelaide posed a question of her own, in hopes the answer might direct her to do what she wished, rather than what she should.

Miss Adelaide Thom. Hopeful. Confident. Impeccably dressed. Holds her impatience in check with the steady tap of her left foot.

Her question: *What will Eleanor think of me if I don't tell her?*

Her cards: Falsehood. Treachery. The Judge.

Her answer: *Nothing good.*

Picking up the cards, Adelaide shuffled them back into the deck as quickly as she could. As with her sitters, they had served to remind her of what she'd already supposed. She didn't need them to discern the truth, but having them near certainly didn't hurt. By turns, they gave her courage to say what needed to be said, or admonished her to stay quiet when she might've been inclined to speak too freely. Frayed and worn at the edges, they'd come from another era, each card holding a simple, crude illustration skirted by a word or two of description written by a shaky hand in English, German, Italian and French. The reverse of each card had been decorated with a curious symbol, a flaming heart entwined in the grip of two snakes. When Eleanor had first seen the cards, she'd asked all sorts of questions. *Where did they come from? Has anyone blessed them? Are they enchanted? If so, by what order of magic?* All Adelaide could say was that they'd been left for her long ago at the ticket booth of Mr. Dink's sideshow with a note that had simply read, "From an admirer." Since the loss of her eye, she'd been especially grateful to have them, as they gave her sitters something to gaze upon other than her face. (Not a day went by without someone trying to get a better look at what sat beneath her veil.) Slipping the cards inside her pocket, she checked her watch again—twenty after twelve. *Time's a wastin', Adelaide. Tick-tock. Tick-tock. Tick-tock.*

Approaching Eleanor, she sweetly said, "Sorry, I forgot to wind the clock."

"I would've done it myself," Eleanor replied, "but I couldn't find the key."

"You couldn't?" Adelaide asked. "That's strange. I left it where I always do, inside your favourite teapot."

"The pot is no more."

With a nod, Adelaide said, "So that was the crash I heard. I'm sorry for that too."

"Did you leave it out on the counter?"

"The clock key?"

"No, the teapot."

"Why would I? What are you getting at?"

"You were out so late . . . Where were you, by the way?"

"Here and there. No place special."

"I see."

"I wasn't drunk, and I didn't touch your teapot."

"I didn't say that—"

"You didn't have to."

"It's just you look a little worse for wear."

"I do?"

"Only in the way that I can see. No one else can tell."

Staring at her reflection in the mirror behind the counter, Adelaide turned first to the right and then to the left. As she leaned forward to get a better look, she felt a sharp, nagging twinge of pain. Over time, she'd come to accept her scars, but she often wondered if she'd ever get used to the pain. If only she had some way of predicting when it was coming, and how long it would last. It'd been a week since her last bout and she'd even begun to hope that perhaps she might be rid of it at last. If it had to persist, why couldn't it be of some use? Why couldn't it warn her of impending danger or of the presence of insufferable company, at the very least? "Give it time," Eleanor had advised. "It may prove useful yet." One could hope. One could pray. One could wish.

"Cup of tea?" Eleanor asked, staring at Adelaide with concern.

"Thank you, yes."

"Willow bark?"

"That would be good."

Eleanor could always tell when the pain was with her. As she turned to her herbs, Adelaide took a deep breath. *It's now or never*, she thought. "There's something I've been meaning to tell you."

"What's that?" Eleanor asked.

"Promise you won't get angry?"

Eleanor sighed. "It *was* you who misplaced the pot, wasn't it? Honestly, Adelaide, I wouldn't be half so displeased if you'd just confessed it from the start."

Just then the bells above the door jangled, announcing the arrival of another customer. Perdu glanced up from his perch, and then resumed his sulking over the loss of the bee. The three ladies sitting in the window seat turned to stare, taking a brief nosy pause before continuing their discussion of the impending resurgence of the bustle.

When Adelaide turned and spied the woman standing in

the doorway, she abandoned her conversation with Eleanor.

"Mrs. Dashley," she said, advancing on her with open arms.

"Miss Thom!" Judith Dashley replied, enthusiastically kissing the air on either side of Adelaide's cheeks. Lace parasol in hand, pearls at her bosom, she was a perfect specimen of a Fifth Avenue *Femme*, a true New York Lady.

She was also Adelaide's best customer, coming to the shop for tea and divinations every day of the week except Sundays throughout the season. This was her first visit since she'd gotten back to town after her summer in the country, and Adelaide had high hopes that they'd resume their previous schedule. If the lady wished to consult the cards on a regular basis, who was she to say no?

"I trust your holiday agreed with you," Adelaide said. "You look radiant."

"You flatter me," Judith replied with a blush.

"I only speak the truth," Adelaide said. "It's my gift as well as my curse."

"Trust me, my dear, it's the city that's put a spring in my step. That, and getting away from the damnable scenic riverfront at Tarrytown. The place was simply crawling with catch-penny girls come by steamboat from the city hoping to land themselves a rich lad. Oh, to be young and free and taut and firm, and to have more life ahead, than not!" Jutting out her chin ever so slightly, she forced a small pucker of crepey wrinkles to disappear from her neck.

"I'm sure when they caught sight of you, they were sick with envy."

"I'm sure they didn't give me a second thought."

"You underestimate the impression that earned beauty can make."

"Whether or not, I'm thrilled to be in your company. Alden returned two weeks ago, so I was stuck playing whist with a tiresome circle of Tarrytown hens. The cottage was starting to feel more like a barnyard than a retreat."

"You must be glad to be back on Marble Row."

"I'm back, yes, but not exactly at home. The house is being refurbished and won't be finished until the New Year. Alden and I are staying in a suite at the Fifth Avenue Hotel for the duration. Some say the hotel's decor is passé, but I don't mind it one bit. Call me old-fashioned, but I feel it fits the history of the place." Lowering her voice she gleefully added, "You know, they say it's haunted . . ."

"Do they really?" Adelaide replied, knowing full well the hotel's reputation for ghosts.

"That they do."

"Care to sit?" Adelaide suggested.

"Oh, yes please," Judith replied.

Leading Judith to her secluded corner in the back of the room, Adelaide said, "Make yourself comfortable. I'll fetch the tea. I can't wait to hear about the socialites and spectres you've encountered at the hotel so far."

Aside from liking Judith's money, Adelaide had grown quite fond of the woman herself. They'd met at a psychic demonstration featuring a medium who called herself Mrs. Saunders and her spirit guide, Little Moon. As Mrs. Saunders had prattled on, eyes rolling back in her head (supposedly possessed by her guide), Adelaide had noticed that the woman seated next to her in the darkened theatre was holding back tears. In an attempt to comfort her, Adelaide had leaned close and whispered, "None of this is real."

The stricken woman had whispered back, "Don't you believe?"

"In ghosts, yes. In this dog-and-pony show, no."

"Have you ever seen a ghost?"

"Possibly, yes. Have you?"

"Once, I think. It was the spirit of my dear son, Billy, staring up at me from the bottom of a silver fruit bowl. He died when he was only seven."

Placing her hand on the woman's arm, Adelaide had said, "I'm sorry for your loss."

"Have you lost someone too? Is that why you're here?"

"My mother, when I was just a girl."

"Oh, heavens, that's awful," the woman had remarked, putting her hand to her mouth.

Adelaide hadn't been sure if the woman was reacting to her loss or the scars on her face. Still, she'd handed the woman her calling card and said, "Perhaps we'll meet again someday."

The next morning Judith Dashley had come to the tea-shop and requested a meeting with Adelaide. "I think I need a little respite from chasing the dead," she'd said. "I'd like to turn my attention to the business of living. Can you give me any advice on how to do that?"

"What shall it be today?" Adelaide asked as she poured tea into Judith's cup. "Your usual consultation?"

Judith stirred in a splash of milk. "Actually," she said, biting her lip, "I'm here to give you some news."

"Colour me curious."

Leaning forward, Judith said, "I've someone who wishes to meet you."

"Any friend of yours is a friend of mine. Tell her to come to the shop and to mention your name. I'll be sure to put her at the top of my list."

Lowering her eyes, Judith shook her head and said, "I can't."

"Whyever not?" Adelaide asked.

Blushing, Judith answered, "Because it's not a she, but a he."

Now it all made sense. Judith's hemming and hawing, her schoolgirl blush. Whoever he was, Judith Dashley was smitten with him. Had she been unfaithful to her husband? No, not yet. She showed no signs of that—none of the excuse-laden talk that accompanies guilt, or the all-too-upright posture of infidelity. With a teasing laugh Adelaide asked, "He's quite handsome, yes?"

Eyes darting to the side, Judith measured the memory of him from shoes to hat. "Oh, yes."

"And tall, too," Adelaide pressed, "and not of your family."

"Why do I bother thinking anything could come as a surprise to you!" Judith exclaimed. "What a gift you have. I wish I could do that."

"Careful what you wish," Adelaide said with a smile. "Now why don't you tell me why this mystery man wishes to meet me, or do I have to guess that as well? You know I don't suffer salesmen, preachers or politicians, so if he's one of those, you needn't bother."

"He's a doctor," Judith said, "and highly regarded."

Resisting the urge to touch her scars, Adelaide asked, "What kind of doctor?" Handsome or not, she'd been poked and prodded and examined enough.

"He's an 'alienist,'" Judith explained, "a doctor of the mind. He's keenly interested in studying the way women think and something he calls 'intuitive inclination.' Alden's been a long-time acquaintance of his father's, but I only met him when we dined together last night. He's been away in Paris, furthering his studies, but he recently came back to the city to settle his father's estate. Alden's asked him to speak at the annual conference of the Fraternal Order of the Unknown Philosophers. Isn't that exciting?"

"Just," Adelaide said.

"When I told him of your gifts, he begged me to arrange a meeting as soon as possible. He's such a charming fellow, I simply couldn't say no. Will you meet with him?"

"Only if you tell me his name," Adelaide replied.

"Oh yes, I suppose I should do that. It's Dr. Quinn Brody."

"Shall we try for tomorrow morning, then, say half past ten, at the hotel?"

"Half past ten it is," Judith replied with a smile. Raising her teacup she added, "Here's to intuitive inclination."

Shortly after Judith's departure, the three ladies in the window seat also took their leave. As Eleanor cleared their table, she discovered that each of them had tucked a calling card, on which they'd written a note, beneath their saucers.

Mrs. Orange Pekoe's card read, "More of the same, please, sent to this address."

Madame Darjeeling's card simply said, "Success!"

Lady Hibiscus's note was more pressing. "I must speak with you soon, in private."

Eleanor upended her former lover's cup on its saucer and turned it three times. Righting it, she peered into the bowl to inspect the leaves. Her mother would never have done such a thing without the tea drinker's consent, but in light of their past and the urgent tone of the young woman's note, Eleanor felt she was in the right. Eyes half closed, she gazed at the shape of the leaves until they formed a series of images in her mind. First an apple, then a snake, then a broken quill. *An affair of the heart gone wrong. A couple divided.* Running out the door, Eleanor stared down the street in the direction Lady Hibiscus had turned, hoping the woman might still be nearby. Sadly, she was out of sight.

As she turned to go back inside, she saw that a long line of young women had formed outside the shop.

The girl at the head of the line stepped forward and asked, "Excuse me, ma'am, is it time?"

"Time for what?" Eleanor replied.

"For considerin' a new girl to work in your shop?"

"Whatever gave you that idea? You must have the wrong address."

Pointing to the sign above the door the girl asked, "Ain't this St. Clair and Thom's teashop?"

"It is, but we're not looking to hire anyone."

The girl stepped forward to press a square of newsprint into Eleanor's hand. "The paper said you is . . ."

Without even a look at the paper, Eleanor said, "I'm sorry, but it's a mistake." Staring pointedly at the ever-growing queue, she gave the girl a curt nod and said, "Pass it on."

Back inside the shop, Eleanor locked the door and turned the sign in the window to Closed. "Adelaide," she said, folding her arms across her chest, "what was it you wanted to tell me?"

As Adelaide came towards her, struggling to find the right words, Perdu threw back his feathered head and squawked, "Top off the pot! Top off the pot!"

Adelaide laughed.

Eleanor did not.

Adelaide looked out the window in time to see the last of the prospective shop girls disperse. Hand on the doorknob, she thought she might chase after them so the day wouldn't be a complete bust.

"Don't," Eleanor said, eyes narrowed.

Adelaide threw up her hands. "I was only trying to help."

"You were only thinking of yourself."

"How is hiring an assistant for *you*, thinking of myself?"

Eleanor was tired, fragile, fed up, and worried about what she'd seen in the cup. "You act on every whim that pops into your head without thinking of the consequences. Did it ever occur to you that I might like a say in the matter?"

Adelaide bit her lip. She couldn't recall ever seeing her friend react quite like this.

Eleanor pressed on. "I'm sure it didn't because it never does."

"What's that supposed to mean?"

"Just look around this place," Eleanor said, gesturing towards Adelaide's corner. As of late her taste in decor had begun to spill over into the rest of the shop—a gilded mirror here, a pair of velvet curtains there. "It's starting to look more like a bordello than a teashop."

The remark stung, but Adelaide didn't take the bait. She sensed that Eleanor's words, though pointed and somewhat true, were hiding a deeper anger, she hoped meant for someone else. Arguing with her would only make matters worse. Shrugging into a wrap, she announced, "I'm going out."

"Of course you are," Eleanor muttered, fetching her grip-sack from behind the counter. Then, as Adelaide went through the door, she said, "I hope you have your key, because I'm going out as well. I can't say when I'll be back."

The two witches went their separate ways—Adelaide storming off towards the park, Eleanor marching, with grip-sack in hand, to search for Lady Hibiscus.

Knocks and Rappings.

Beatrice arrived at Tea and Sympathy to find the shades drawn and the door locked. Twisting the bell, she waited for someone to answer. When no one came, she gave three loud raps on the window. She was late, she knew, but it was only two o'clock. Why was the shop closed? Had the owners already found their girl and called it a day? Just as she was about to walk away, she heard a sound on the other side of the door. "Hello?" she called. "Is anyone there?"

When no one responded, she began to wonder if perhaps she'd been hearing things. The spill she'd taken at the dockyard had left her terribly unsettled, and she hadn't felt right since. A small, aching bump had formed where she'd hit her head and she could only recall bits and pieces of how she'd gotten back to the train. Had Joseph led her safely across the tracks or had he scooped her up and carried her? In any event, he'd been incredibly kind, arranging the burlap bags in a comfortable nest, offering her a drink from a flask he'd squirrelled away in his knapsack. Of course he'd forgotten to tell her that the flask contained whiskey, and she'd wound up spitting half the stuff out. Still, the shock of the alcohol burning down her throat had caused her to sit upright and see straight, so in that sense it'd done the trick.

As soon as they'd arrived at the station, Joseph had placed a pile of silver coins in the hand of a carriage driver and instructed the man to deliver Beatrice to her destination. Helping her inside the carriage he'd asked, "Are you sure you'll be all right?"

"Yes, of course," she'd lied. "I'm perfectly fine, I swear it. Thanks for all your help, and best of luck with your russets."

Now her head was throbbing as she stood outside the shop. The sounds of the city seemed to echo around her—voices crowding in her ears from all directions, strangely more within than without. She felt as if she'd been run over by a train rather than riding on one. She'd so wanted to make a good first impression, and now she was late, and so unwell. Not ready to give up just yet, she rang the bell again.

A loud thump sounded on the other side of the door, followed by silence.

Leaning to peer through the keyhole, Beatrice discovered an eye staring back at her. It was dark and shiny and definitely not human.

"Hello," she called again, unsure as to whether or not she wanted an answer.

"Who's there?" a voice responded, soft and sweet.

Before Beatrice could reply, the lock clicked, the knob turned, and the door opened wide. No one was there to greet her. Choosing curiosity over fear, she entered the shop.

The place was dimly lit, yet welcoming and warm. The scents of tea, dried herbs and honey filled the air. It reminded her of the chapel of the Stony Point Presbyterian Church on

Christmas Eve, all close with beeswax candles, cedar boughs and age-old mysteries. To her great relief, the cacophony that'd been ringing in her ears was suddenly silenced.

"Hello?" she quietly called, hoping to find a friendly face at last.

"Hello," a voice, eerily like her own, replied from overhead.

Looking up, Beatrice discovered a large raven perched atop the open door. "Heavens!" she exclaimed, dropping her bag to the floor.

Flapping to Beatrice's feet, Perdu hopped in a wide circle around the girl then waddled towards her bag to peck and pull at its clasp.

Amazed by the creature's antics, Beatrice bent down to the bird and asked, "Was it you who let me in?"

With a hearty *caw*, Perdu vigorously nodded.

Beatrice laughed, feeling as if she were Alice, gone through the looking glass.

In the back of the room someone seconded her laughter.

"Who's there?" Beatrice asked, taken by surprise.

No sooner had the girl posed the question than the shop's door slammed shut, and the air in the room turned cold.

Perdu lit on the counter and began to hiss. The feathers around his neck puffed into a menacing mane.

Beatrice wasn't sure if she should stay or run.

"Care to have your palm read?" a voice asked from the shadows. "Your future revealed?"

Slowly walking towards the voice, Beatrice came upon a beautiful woman seated at a small, round table. Silver hoops dangling from her ears, silk scarf tied around her head, bangles clanging on her wrists, she looked every bit like the woman whose image graced the back covers of *Madam Morrow's*

Strange Tales of Gotham, a woman who Beatrice had always assumed was Madam Morrow herself.

"I've come to inquire about the position that was advertised in the paper," Beatrice replied. "Are you the shop's owner?"

Silver hoops swinging as she shook her head, the woman said, "No one's here."

"Perhaps I'll come back another time," Beatrice faltered.

"Come, sit!" the woman ordered. "Give me your hand."

Those averse to magic need not apply.

Remembering the words that had appeared at the bottom of the newspaper notice, Beatrice wondered if the fortune teller's invitation might be some sort of test. Seating herself across from the woman she extended her hand.

As the Gypsy turned Beatrice's hand palm up, her own fingers turned pale and withered and her face went blue with death. When the Gypsy opened her mouth, no words came out, just the stink of dank river water, fishy and thick with rot. Gasping, the woman began to choke as if she had something caught in her throat. Before Beatrice could move to help her, the fortune teller stuck her crooked finger between her teeth to retrieve the thing that was causing her distress. With a violent tug and a terrible retch, she brought up a long length of old fishing net tangled with seaweed and oyster shells.

Beatrice hid her face in her hands and made a wish, *Let this be a dream. Let this all be a terrible dream.*

When she opened her eyes the Gypsy had vanished. Sighing with relief, Beatrice tried to stand, but found she was trapped in her seat. Her wish might have caused the woman to disappear, but it hadn't set her free. Her own dress was now dark and heavy and wet—water dripping from her sleeves and skirts, and pooling on the floor at her feet. From the murky puddles a nest of eels emerged, slithering around her ankles. Struggling to escape, she let out a terrible scream and fainted.

Eleanor returned to the shop to find the girl lying in a heap on the floor, and Perdu pacing frantically beside her. Racing to her side, she listened for her breathing, wrapped her fingers around her wrist. "Hello, miss?" she said in her ear. "Please wake up."

Fanning the air in front of the girl's face, she implored again, "Miss . . . wake up."

Perdu stayed close, tilting his head with concern.

Taking a phial of smelling salts from a chatelaine at her waist, Eleanor removed the lid and waved it under Beatrice's nose.

With a terrible grimace, Beatrice opened her eyes.

"Are you all right?" Eleanor asked. The girl had a bump on her head that looked angry and fresh, but at least it wasn't bleeding.

"I think so," Beatrice answered, trying to make sense of her surroundings.

Eleanor helped her to her feet and then to a nearby couch. "I'll get you some water," she said, "or would you prefer tea?"

"Tea," she answered, then remembering her manners, she added, "please."

As Eleanor busied herself behind the counter, Beatrice struggled to collect her thoughts. Was the woman who'd just offered her tea the same woman who'd offered to read her palm? Surely not. Unless, of course, her brain had taken her on some bizarre flight of fancy. Perhaps the bump on her head was worse than she'd thought.

"Here you are," Eleanor said, handing Beatrice a cup. "This should help."

"Thank you," Beatrice said, inhaling the tea's sweet scent.

"Chamomile, lemon balm, lavender and St. John's wort," Eleanor said. "To soothe your nerves."

Closing her eyes, Beatrice took a sip.

Eleanor asked, "When was your last meal?" The poor thing really did seem unwell.

"Breakfast," Beatrice answered, "although I did have a bite or two of apple on the train."

Fetching a plate of teacakes, Eleanor placed it in front of her.

"Thank you," Beatrice said, pinching a small, sticky sweet between her fingers. "They look delicious."

Eleanor smiled as Beatrice gobbled down the cake. Now that the girl was awake and alert, she began to wonder where she'd appeared from. Likely she was just a straggler, a latecomer from the horde of young women she'd turned away outside the shop. But that didn't explain how she'd gotten inside the place—Eleanor was sure she'd locked the door—or why she'd found the young woman in a dead faint on the floor. Weirdly, the girl seemed familiar to her, yet she couldn't place her face. "How exactly did you get in here?" she asked at last.

Beatrice nervously cleared her throat. "The door was open," she stammered. "Well, it was locked at first, but then it was open." Sheepishly pointing to Perdu, she added, "I know this might sound impossible, but I think the bird let me in."

Eleanor looked at Perdu for confirmation.

Puffing out his chest, Perdu gave Eleanor a defiant stare.

Eleanor wondered if she should be interrogating him, not the girl.

At least I didn't imagine the bird, Beatrice thought. *At least he's really here. I saw him before, I see him now. That's a good sign.* "I'm very sorry for causing such a fuss," she said to Eleanor. "As I said to the woman when I first came in, I was hoping to apply for a position in the shop."

"What woman?" Eleanor asked with a scowl. Had Adelaide enlisted this girl?

"There was a woman sitting at a table in the back when I arrived," Beatrice said, "at least I think there was." The table where the Gypsy had sat was no longer there.

"What did she look like?" Eleanor asked, thinking her suspicions were about to be confirmed.

"She was a fortune teller," Beatrice replied.

"In a blue silk dress with a matching hat and veil?"

"No, not at all like that," Beatrice said. "She was a Gypsy, with scarves and bangles and big silver hoops in her ears. She seemed friendly enough at first, but then she changed, or perhaps I was just falling ill, but I swear it looked to me as if she turned into a ghost."

Eleanor bit her lip, knowing exactly who and what she'd seen.

Pacing up and down the length of the counter Perdu squawked, "Top off the pot! Top off the pot!"

"Perdu!" Eleanor scolded. "Hush!"

Sulking, the raven settled down next to Beatrice's bag and again began to peck at its clasp.

Hands trembling, cup rattling in its saucer, Beatrice set her tea aside. She wasn't sure if she was suffering from exhaustion or fear. Perhaps both. "Please don't think me mad," she said, wringing her hands. "I believe I might have train brain, or railway spine, or whatever they call it. The passenger train wasn't running from Stony Point, so I rode the freight train instead. Then we stopped and I fell and by the time I got here, my mind was a complete mess. After that I began hearing things, and quite possibly seeing things too. I don't know what's come over me. I usually travel quite well."

Reaching for Beatrice's cup, Eleanor filled it to the rim. "Here," she said, "have more tea, Miss—"

"Dunn," Beatrice said, realizing she hadn't given the woman her name. "But you can call me Beatrice."

"I'm Eleanor St. Clair, half of St. Clair and Thom."

"Thank you for your kindness, Miss St. Clair," Beatrice said reaching again for her cup.

Eleanor nodded. "You said you fell?" she asked. "Care to tell me about it?" She couldn't help but feel there was more to this than a bumpy train ride or a knock on the head. She didn't think the young woman had it in her to lie, so her talk of ghosts was quite concerning. *First the teapot, now this? What was next?*

"Yes. I fell when the train got stopped outside the city so the great obelisk could pass."

"Cleopatra's Needle? That must've been quite something."

Beatrice nodded. "I got off the train so I could see them move it across the tracks."

"And that's when you fell?"

"No," Beatrice answered. "I fell after it got moved. Right after I touched it."

"I see," Eleanor said, gooseflesh blooming up the length of her arms. She'd heard rumours that the obelisk was imbued with ancient magic. As she continued to regard Beatrice, Perdu finally managed to open the girl's bag. Fishing out a long, knotted string from inside it, he hopped to Eleanor's side and dropped the thing in her lap. “Remember the girl,” he softly cooed. “Remember the girl.”

“Where did you get this?” Eleanor said, examining the hair and feathers that were tied along the length of it. She recognized it at once for what it was.

“I made it,” Beatrice confessed with a nervous chuckle. “It’s nothing, really, just a childish plaything.”

“I wouldn’t say that.” As Eleanor turned the string between her fingers, the fiery strands of Beatrice’s hair that’d been twisted into the charm glinted in the sun. Eleanor smelled smoke, tasted ash on the tip of her tongue. *Remember the girl.*

Blushing, Beatrice insisted, “Truly, it’s only a silly charm. They call it a witch’s ladder, or some such thing.”

“I know what it is,” Eleanor replied, her breath catching as she recognized Beatrice for who she was.

“I only wanted to make a wish come true,” Beatrice whispered, embarrassed and ashamed.

With a smile Eleanor placed the charm in Beatrice’s hands. “I think it worked.”

Vinegar Hill, Brooklyn. If there is any person in New York (man, woman, white or black) who can drive out a witch and her affiliated ghosts, let them come and do their best. **Complete success or no pay.**

Mr. Robert Beadle.

A Moth Seeks the Light.

NOT WANTING TO go back to the teashop while it was still light—she'd had enough of Eleanor for one day—Adelaide had taken a train to the Fulton Ferry and made her way to Vinegar Hill. As the ferry cut across the East River, passing alongside the Great (yet unfinished) Bridge, Adelaide had stared at the magnificent structure, amazed at the way the labourers skittered like spiders along the network of steel suspension wires attached to the bridge's main cables. Oh to be so fearless! The last time she'd visited the bridge, they'd barely begun the work of winding the wire cables. She'd stood on the banks of the river that day, still whole and even happy, her hand tucked in the arm of a man who'd insisted upon reciting poetry to her. He was a good person, lovely in every way, which is why she'd cut him loose. She hoped that he'd found happiness, and that he hadn't used up all his poetry on her. Love had never been in her cards.

Just as on the night she'd met Judith Dashley, today

Adelaide was on a search for a true medium. She'd visited countless sideshows, dime museums, lecture halls, theatres and séances only to be met with disappointment. Vinegar Hill was a departure from the usual places she looked, but once she'd read the newspaper notice, she couldn't resist the chance to seek out Mr. Beadle and his witch. Just in case.

Standing across the street from the Beadle house, Adelaide wondered if she should bother knocking on the door. *Perhaps he isn't home*, she thought. From the outside, it didn't look much like a place a witch or her affiliated ghosts might dwell. The storey-and-a-half cottage was modest, and recently whitewashed. At the end of a side street off a side street, the house was older by far than the many brick buildings that crowded it. As Adelaide walked up the steps to the door, she hoped that Mr. Beadle would be as welcoming as his home appeared. "Here goes nothing," she said taking hold of the door's knocker and giving it a loud rap.

A few moments later, an elderly man in a wool sack-coat answered the door. He stared at Adelaide with bloodshot eyes.

"Mr. Beadle?" she asked.

"I'm he," the man replied, squinting in an effort to see past her veil. "Why do you ask?"

"I'd like to speak with you about the notice you placed in the *Times*."

Mr. Beadle wiped his nose with a limp handkerchief and came closer to his visitor. Taking a deep sniff as though to breathe in the scent of Adelaide's perfume, he fixed his gaze on her décolletage. He smiled a queasy-making smile, and said, "Lilac parfum's my favourite."

Adelaide took a step back. "Are you receiving visitors?"

"I can be seen," he answered.

"Thank you," Adelaide said, "I won't take too much of your time."

Mr. Beadle turned and led Adelaide down a long, narrow hallway. As she followed him, she wondered if he really did have a witch, or if he'd simply placed the ad in order to bring strangers into his lonely little life. In her experience, people who had no one to care for but themselves were either mad, sad or guilty of some unspeakable crime. Her hatpin was quite sharp and could be used to pierce the papery skin of his neck if need be. She'd use the ivory-handled stiletto she kept tucked in a leather sheath on her right boot only as a last resort.

"Here we are," Mr. Beadle said, opening the door to a small parlour.

Its trappings were as sparse as the hairs on Mr. Beadle's head. A single tin candlestick, a stub of tallow listing in its well, sat on a table between two windows. A rocking chair had been placed to one side of the table, and a small three-legged stool to the other. In the corner, a pot-belly stove was ticking with heat, a kettle humming on its top, spitting drops of water. Mr. Beadle pulled the windows' faded paper shades halfway down against the late afternoon sun. Without offering Adelaide a seat, he settled himself in an armchair close to the stove. "So," he said, rubbing his hands together then holding them out to the heat, "you've come to inquire about my witch, have you?"

"Yes," Adelaide answered, choosing the rocking chair. The room had suddenly taken on the smell of scorched wool, and she hoped that Mr. Beadle wasn't about to go up in flames.

"Tell me, miss," Mr. Beadle said, "have you ever been bewitched?"

"Not to my knowledge."

Taking a pipe and a pouch of tobacco from his pocket, Mr. Beadle went about the tuck, tamp and puff of preparing a smoke. "Well," he said, when the stem was clenched between his teeth, "it's a very hard thing to suffer. This witch of mine, she got me good. She has me right hexed. Some days I can barely speak nor eat. Every time I put my head down to sleep, I wonder if I'll wake. I haven't worked a lick in weeks."

"How do you make your living?" Adelaide asked, unable to imagine that there was any work he was fit enough to do.

"I'm a carpenter," Mr. Beadle said. "A coffin maker as of late. I expect to get back to it soon, God willing."

From the way the man's pipe was shaking in his hand, Adelaide doubted that Mr. Beadle could hold a hammer, let alone swing one. "How did you come to encounter this witch?"

"How does anyone come to know a witch?" Mr. Beadle replied, shaking his head. "It's not like I went looking for one. Only a fool would do that."

"Yes," Adelaide said. "Only a fool. So she came to you, unbidden?"

"No, no, no," Mr. Beadle replied. "A witch can't enter your house unless you invite her in, and that there was my mistake. My wife passed on several months ago, God bless her soul, and I needed someone to do the things she done—cooking, cleaning, fetching things—so I asked around, looking for a maid. Not long after, a young woman came to my door, fresh-faced and sweet, staring at me with the prettiest blue eyes you ever did see." Taking a puff on his pipe he added, "That's important, so don't forget."

"What's that?" Adelaide asked, wishing Mr. Beadle's witch might show up and put an end to the man's prattling.

"Her pretty blue eyes," Mr. Beadle replied. "The prettiest shade of blue."

"So you said."

"That girl and I," Mr. Beadle went on, "we talked a good spell, and in the end, I agreed to let her live here in exchange for her service. There's nine rooms and that's plenty to spare, so she moved in and took the big room upstairs. She also asked if she might use the cellar from time to time for this and that, and I didn't see any harm in it. I never had reason to go down there, so why should I care? She said she'd been married to a sailor, but shortly after they were wed, he'd taken a job on that godforsaken bridge and fallen to his death. With her husband gone she'd had to fend for herself. She had no one in the city and no means to get back home to her family in Scotland. She was a Scotch lass, you see. That's important too."

"So she was Scotch," Adelaide said, tapping her foot in time with the ticking of the stove.

After a hacking cough, Mr. Beadle carried on with his tale. "The first strange thing I noticed was the noises. Her room was directly over mine and every night I heard great rackets up there—voices, wails and whispers, along with footsteps that thudded across the floorboards as if someone was being chased around and around and around. One morning when she was out, I went and tried the door so I could see what she'd been up to, but the door was locked. When I looked through the keyhole, I saw she'd traced a great circle on the floor in a white powder what looked like chalk. In the very centre of the circle was a little black book and next to it, a long, twisted stick. Seeing that was too much for me! Witches use circles to commune with demons and ghosts, you know, and I'm certain that was her intent." Eyes wide, Mr. Beadle added, "I always knew there was witches in the world, but I never thought I'd have one in my house!"

Adelaide guessed it wasn't the first time he'd looked through that keyhole. "Did you confront her with what you'd found?"

"Of course I did!" Mr. Beadle exclaimed. "And no sooner had I put it to her, than she said to me, says she, 'Mr. Beadle, I didn't do it.' 'You did,' says I, holding my ground. 'I saw it with my own two eyes.' 'Mr. Beadle,' says she, 'I didn't. I'll get my Bible and swear to it.' Then I says to her, says I, 'If you swore to it on a thousand Bibles I wouldn't believe you.' After that she started crying and talking gibberish about how she'd heard a voice calling to her from the river. The next time she looked at me, I saw that one of her eyes was turning black. If you've ever seen a witch, you'll know that they always have one black eye. No matter what colour their eyes was before, when they get to be witches, one eye goes black. That's when I knew it wouldn't be long before she'd be trying to take one of my good eyes from me." Pointing at Adelaide's face he asked, "Is that what happened to you? Did a witch get your eye?"

"Not quite," Adelaide replied. If only she had her bottled treasure with her to show Mr. Beadle. Imagine what he'd have to say about that.

"Count yourself lucky," Mr. Beadle said with a nod. "This witch tried all she could to do me in. She thought I'd believed her, but the next time she went out to do the shopping, I figured I'd better check the cellar. So I went in very careful, walking on tiptoe, clear to the back of the chimbley. It was there I found a bundle of rags, tied around a bunch of bones, no doubt belonging to a black cat. There was a bigger bundle beside it, so I opened that one, too, and found it was a pair of men's pantaloons. They was covered with a fine white powder, just like you'd find on a person that's bewitched. I got some of the stuff on me by accident and everywhere it touched my skin it made little spots like pinheads with little circles around them. They itched like crazy when the sun went down. They nearly drove me mad."

"I can imagine," Adelaide said, guessing it was more likely that Mr. Beadle had a nest of bed bugs in his mattress than a witch in his house.

Scratching at his wrist, Mr. Beadle added, "And that wasn't all I discovered down there."

"No?" Adelaide asked.

"Just yesterday I found a little bunch of black hair all wadded up and half buried in the cellar floor. It looked as if it was a piece cut off of the witch's own plait. No sooner had I brought it up and laid it on the table, than it began to wiggle around, rising in the air before my eyes! It frightened me so much that I threw it in the fire. If I hadn't done it, I don't think I'd be alive now. I've heard tell that's the way witches work with hair. To bewitch a person they'll take a bunch of their own hair and bury it, and as soon as it rots, the person dies. But I burned that hair, so it can't rot. Thanks be to heaven, I'm still alive."

"Thanks be," Adelaide said. She thought this man was ridiculous, but her mother had believed in a similar sort of magic. "Never let a stranger get hold of your hair," she'd warned young Moth. "Powerful magic can be done against you by the person who has it." Every night she'd collected the hair from their brushes along with any stray hairs she found on the floor. She kept the hair tucked inside a cloth bag she used as a pincushion, and when the bag got full, she'd cast the hair into the fire while reciting a prayer. Then she'd tell her daughter once again the tale of poor Mrs. Deery, who'd had her hair stolen by an angry sister and then given away to a bird. "The bird wove it into its nest, round and round, back and forth, between sticks and spider webs, causing Mrs. Deery to go mad. The woman walked the streets of the city, afraid of everyone and everything, turning about in circles until she ran right into a delivery wagon and her brains got smashed to bits." The lady who'd bought Adelaide from her mother had cut off her braid with one terrible snip of her scissors, though eventually Adelaide had gone free and the woman had gotten what she deserved. "So where is your witch now?" Adelaide asked, half expecting Mr. Beadle to say she'd flown away on a broomstick.

"A gentleman came three days ago to take her."

"What kind of gentleman?"

"A reverend," Mr. Beadle answered. "He said it's his speciality to look after such business. When I told him I was certain there'd be trouble in it for him, he said not to worry. Then he asked for me to direct him to the witch so he could take care of the rest. It was going on half past ten, so I told him that I guessed she was down at her usual spot by the river. She went there most every day to mark the time and place of her husband's passing. Before the reverend left, I gathered up the girl's things, including what I found in the cellar, and gave it all over to him. He said the only way to be rid of her and her magic was to leave no trace of her in the house. I haven't heard from either of them since."

"What do you suppose he did with her?" Adelaide couldn't help but imagine the worst.

"I don't really care now that my problem's solved," Mr. Beadle answered. "Maybe he'll put the screws to her, or dunk her in the river. I think a witch is worse than a murderer, don't you? A murderer kills you all at once and it's over, but a witch kills you by inches. I think witches ought to be killed themselves. They used to kill them in this country and I hear they still kill them over in Scotland. Send her back, I say."

"Did the gentleman happen to give you his name?"

"I was so pleased to get rid of the girl, I didn't ask. He was well spoken and finely dressed. When I offered to pay him for his services, he refused to accept one penny. I told him he was either a saint or gone mad. I'm sure he'd make a killing if he charged for this sort of thing. They say they got rid of all the witches long ago, but I say they're wrong. Witches are like rats. Where there's one, there's a hundred."

Rising from her chair, Adelaide moved to take her leave. "Thank you for your time, Mr. Beadle. I hope no other witches ever cross your path." *For their sake, not yours*, she thought.

"Thank you kindly, miss," Mr. Beadle said, puffing on his pipe. "You wouldn't happen to know of any girls who might be looking for a housekeeping position, would you? A God-fearing American-born girl, of course."

"I'm afraid I don't," Adelaide said, shaking her head.

Mr. Beadle didn't get up to see her out, so she showed herself to the door. Pausing at the threshold, she spat on it to place a curse on Mr. Beadle's head. She'd seen her mother give such curses to anyone who'd done her wrong. "That," Adelaide said, "is for the blue-eyed maid. Wherever she may be."

Good Citizens of New York

Beware the Lure *of* WITCHCRAFT!

Do not let yourselves be fooled by those who say that witches are a thing of the past. WITCHCRAFT is alive and well in America, thanks to a NEW order of WITCHES who are eager to pull the unwitting, the curious and the weak into their web of deceit. These are worrisome times, dear friends. Do not let the renewed workings of the DEVIL take away what our forefathers fought so hard to secure.

Sly in her approach, the NEW WITCH targets men and women alike. Whether dressed in the garb of the "Old Country" or in the fashion of everyday women, she is EVIL in disguise. GENTLEMEN, do not let yourselves be enchanted by her flattering words! By the time you realize the destructive nature of your association, it will be too late! LADIES, do not be tempted to admire these foul creatures, for YOU are her most valued prey! It is a witch's greatest triumph to lure God's daughters away from family, hearth and home.

HOW does she do it? By touting intelligence over righteousness, books of black magic over the Bible, superstition over faith, fashion over modesty, politics over prayer. Crafty in her dealings, she takes on many forms—the healer, the fortune teller, the academic, the suffragist, the spiritualist—all in an effort to lead others astray. TRUE women of GOD do not trouble themselves with such matters. TRUE women of GOD know and obey HIS laws.

 TIMOTHY 2:11 **But I suffer not a woman to teach nor to usurp authority over the man, but to be in silence.** 

The WITCHES that plague our city must be rebuked and cast out!

COME to **The Church of the Good Shepherd** to hear HIS word.
LEARN of Satan's ways so we might prove victorious over him.
SHARE your knowledge of EVIL DOERS so we may bring them into the LIGHT. Do not be afraid. The power of the LORD is on our side.

All are welcome who seek the light. —Rev. Francis Townsend

Mr. Beadle's Witch.

LENA MCLEOD HAD been locked in a cold dark cellar for three days. She'd barely had any food to eat except for a hunk of stale bread she'd been given the first night. It'd been so salty she hadn't been able to keep it down. After gagging it up she'd begged her captor for water. "Please," she'd cried, "take pity on me. My thirst is terribly strong."

"Salt is the bane of witches," Reverend Townsend had said, seeming to take pleasure in her pain. "God will soothe your thirst if you repent of your sins."

Lena had not known what to say to that, and was too afraid to speak.

The next day he'd come at her with questions and accusations, threatening to hit her with a thick wooden rod he liked to smack against the palm of his hand. It was carved with primitive markings—circles, crosses, daisy wheels and double Vs—much like those that'd been scratched into the willow tree that stood outside the stone wall of the churchyard in Lena's village in Scotland. Her great-great-grandmother Mrs. Davina Hale had been hanged there, found guilty of witchcraft long before Lena was born.

"State your name," Reverend Townsend had said, prodding her with the rod.

Breath stuttering, Lena answered, "Mrs. Lena McLeod."

"Do you know where you are, Mrs. McLeod?"

"In a house of God?"

"And do you know why you're here?"

"I've done nothing wrong," she insisted. "Please let me go."

"I'm afraid I can't do that," the Reverend replied.

"I'll do whatever you want," Lena pleaded.

Leaning close, the Reverend whispered in her ear, "I'll keep that in mind." As he straightened up he asked, "Is your husband living, Mrs. McLeod?"

"No sir, he's dead."

"How long ago did he die?"

"One year ago this December."

"And how did he come to pass?"

"He fell from the Great Bridge."

"And you had nothing to do with it? You did nothing to cause it?"

"No, nothing," Lena answered honestly, yet feeling sick with guilt. Not a day had gone by since Johnny's death that she hadn't blamed herself for it. She should've believed the signs when she first saw them and not let him walk out the door. There'd been talk in her family of other women having similar visions, that Davina's gifts had been passed down through her blood, but Lena's mother, a God-fearing woman, had told her it was best not to pay any attention to such tales. The foretelling had seemed so strong . . . but, still, she'd been afraid that if she told Johnny what she'd seen, he'd think she'd gone mad. (For a time, she'd thought maybe she had.) She'd seen his face in the washbasin the morning of his death, staring up at her through the soap flakes, then rising to the surface, gasping for air. But she'd let him go to the bridge. Then she'd grown frantic and decided to warn him. She'd been ready to climb the wobbly footbridge made of planks and wire that stretched to the top of the caissons, but the foreman hadn't let her pass.

Instead she'd knelt at the water's edge. "What if I gave you my life for his?" she'd asked the River in her desperation.

"That's not how it works," the River had answered. "The choice is made."

Within the hour, Johnny was dead.

"And you came to live with the good Mr. Beadle sometime after that?" the Reverend asked.

"I did," Lena answered.

Cradling her chin in his hand, the Reverend tipped her face so her eyes met his and said, "And you seduced him into taking you on."

"I did not!" Lena cried.

"But you had no means to support yourself and no place to go." Taking a little chapbook from his pocket the preacher laid it in Lena's lap. The title on the cover read, *Madam Morrow's Book of Potions, Hexes and Spells.* "Is this yours?" he asked.

"Yes."

"So you don't deny it?"

"No sir," she said.

"What was the purpose of your having it?"

"A woman at the market offered it to me after my husband died. She said there was a spell in there for talking to the dead. I was mad with grief, so I took it. I was curious and desperate. I wanted to be sure he was all right."

"And what of the things Mr. Beadle found in his cellar?"

"I was only trying to scare him a little. He was awfully mean to me."

The Reverend hadn't stopped heaping abuse upon her since then. No matter how hard she begged, he hadn't relented. He'd said it was God's will for him to test her and if she came through clean he'd let her go. He'd taken her clothes and burned them. He'd cut her hair and burned it too. He'd collected her urine for God knows what purpose. He'd pricked her arms, her thighs, her breasts and every freckle she had with a hot needle. He'd asked her to recite the Lord's Prayer, but when she'd done so in her native tongue, he'd beaten her with the rod and told her "those are the Devil's words."

She was never sure when he was going to torment her. She could hear his footsteps overhead, pacing, at all hours of the day and night. She was free to move about the room but there was no escape. The furnishings were sparse, the floor was dirt, the walls stone and the door always locked.

To pass the time she sat and looked at a single small window, high on the back wall. It was bricked over on the outside, braced by thick bars sunk deep into the stone on the inside. For a short while each day, a scant beam of light shone through a crack between the bricks. This morning, while she lay on her straw mattress, the light had heralded a vision that floated and danced before her eyes. She was hanging by a noose from the willow tree, her body swinging next to Davina's.

Shrugging out of her cotton shift, she tore it into long, ragged strips. She sang the Lord's Prayer as she braided the strands together, even laughed as her sadness turned to elation.

Ar n-Athair a tha air nèamh,
Gu naomhaichear d'ainm.

Standing on a rickety stool, she tied one end of the rope to one of the bars in the window.

Thigeadh do rìoghachd.
Dèanar do thoil air an talamh,
mar a nìthear air nèamh.

She fashioned the other end into a hangman's knot and slipped it over her head.

Tabhair dhuinn an-diugh ar n-aran làitheil.
Agus maith dhuinn ar fiachan,
amhail a mhaitheas sinne dar luchd-fiach.
Agus na leig ann am buaireadh sinn;
ach saor sinn o olc:

Stepping off the stool she let God do the rest.

oir is leatsa an rìoghachd,
agus an cumhachd,
agus a' glòir,
gu sìorraidh. Amen

Reverend Townsend found her body not long after, limp with death, her flesh still warm. Hand lingering on her calf, he was disappointed, then relieved, then deliciously satisfied.

There was immense beauty in the demise of evil. Falling to his knees he uttered a prayer of thanksgiving.

Before he'd finished, before he'd even begun to consider what he might do to get rid of the young woman's body, two strangers entered the room from the cellar doorway. Like a pair of funeral mutes, wearing long frock coats and wide-brimmed hats, the men moved with an air of quiet, unshakable purpose.

Startled, Reverend Townsend feared he was caught. "She did herself in," he stammered. "There was nothing I could do."

One of the men approached him and placed a steady hand on his shoulder. "Go to your bedchamber," he ordered. "Fast and pray until first light."

Pointing to the open door the other man said, "Leave us now. All will be well."

September 17, 1880, Evening.
St. Clair and Thom,
Tea and Sympathy,
933 Broadway,
New York, New York

Dear Aunt Lydia,
I am well. I am safe.
Please send my winter coat, my second pair of shoes, my other day dress, and my Sunday best to the above address at your earliest convenience.
As you may have guessed, the position is mine!
More soon, when I am properly settled.

With affection,
Beatrice.

Messages From Abroad.

ELEANOR SAT IN the window of the teashop that night, waiting for Adelaide to return. Feet propped on a low wooden stool, she nursed a cup of blackberry tea and wondered where the day had gone. So much had happened, yet it felt as though the day had passed in a blink. She hated days that ended with more questions than answers.

Beatrice had retired upstairs, and Eleanor hoped the girl would soon be nodding off to sleep with Perdu on his perch at her side. Seeing the toll the day had taken on the girl, Eleanor had offered up her own bed for the night. They'd make a cozy place for her in the garret tomorrow. Besides, Eleanor had so much on her mind, she wasn't sure she could sleep. Her head was still swimming with the day's events—her argument with Adelaide (which she was sorry for now), the strange circumstances of Beatrice's arrival, and the unsolved puzzle as to what was troubling Lady Hibiscus (she never had caught up with her old lover). If she did need some shuteye, she could always curl up on the couch, or lie down next to Adelaide for a spell. That was, if Adelaide ever decided to come home. She could use her friend's advice in sizing up their new girl.

"You say you're from Stony Point?" she'd asked Beatrice over dinner.

"Yes, Miss St. Clair," Beatrice had answered. She was so polite, so sweet!

"Please, call me Eleanor."

"Yes, ma'am . . . I mean, Eleanor."

"Stony Point is on the Hudson, up past Sleepy Hollow?"

"Yes," the girl had answered. "Just across the river from Verplanck."

Eleanor wondered if Stony Point, like Sleepy Hollow, was a place of covered bridges, haunted burial grounds and headless horsemen. Had Beatrice really spotted a ghost in the shop or had she brought it with her? She'd come to the city with so little in hand, had she really planned to win the job and stay here? And what of the witch's ladder Perdu had found in her bag? Well done, dear bird. His nose for magic was as keen as ever.

The charm was far more than the simple plaything Beatrice had made it out to be. Did the girl truly not know what she'd done? How could she not see the perfection in her handiwork, feel the magic bound in every knot? Was the girl being fully honest? Had she run away from someone, or from some terrible deed? "And no one's missing you?" she'd asked, hoping to get to the bottom of the matter.

"My aunt Lydia, I suppose," Beatrice had answered. "But I'm here with her blessing, if that's what you're wondering."

"Yes," Eleanor had said with a laugh, "I suppose it is." What would Adelaide do faced with such a situation? *Confess a little, learn a lot.* "I come from an out-of-the-way place as well," Eleanor had confided. "I know how tempting it can be to leave the past behind."

"Where was that?" Beatrice had asked.

"On the Bronx River," Eleanor had replied.

"Was it anywhere near Fordham Village?" Beatrice asked. "I hear it's lovely there."

"No," Eleanor had said, shaking her head. "It's far too small to have a name. There isn't even a road leading to it. You can only get there by water."

"Sounds idyllic," Beatrice had said with a smile.

"It was," Eleanor replied.

Taking another sip of tea, Eleanor wondered how her mother's cottage was faring. Her uncle had promised to keep an eye on it, but she guessed he was too busy with farm and family to give it much attention. She hoped it hadn't gotten terribly overgrown or broken down. She hadn't been there since early spring when she'd gone to collect fiddleheads from the forest. She'd like to see the place again, someday soon, perhaps—to pick apples from the craggy trees that surrounded the garden, to collect hips from the wild roses that grew along the hedgerows, to raid the cellar for a bottle or two of elderberry wine.

In the last days of her life, Madame St. Clair had ordered Eleanor to sit by her side so she might confess all her secrets. In those sad, beautiful, drawn-out hours, Eleanor had sat quietly with pen in hand as her mother recited a number of stories she'd often told her in her youth. The lively tales of peasants and princes, witches and queens, came to life again in her mother's ailing voice—her advice peppered with laughter, her warnings accompanied by tears. The last story she'd recited was "The Princess Who Wished to Be a Witch," an eerie tale filled with magic and wonder and a raven who bore a striking resemblance to her dear Perdu.

The Princess Who Wished to Be a Witch

Long ago, a beautiful princess named Odoline wanted to become a witch. Her mother, the Queen, had died when she was born and aside from the Queen's jewels and robes, all Odoline had left of the woman were the precious books she'd collected in her library. Whenever she grew tired of listening to her five quarrelsome brothers bicker (which was quite often), she'd steal away to the library to sit and read and ponder.

Among the volumes were a handful of books devoted to tales about sorceresses, seers and witches. As a young girl, Odoline's nurse had told her that the women in the tales were her kin, connected to her by her mother's blood. When Odoline had asked her father, the King, if what her nurse had said was true, he'd laughed and said, "Those are nothing but fairy tales, dear daughter." Sure enough the stories were populated by fairies (and trolls and ghosts and demons, too), but Odoline found more truth in the pages of those books than in her daily life. It wasn't long before she was able to read the magic that lived between the stories' lines.

When the time came for her to choose a suitor, her father called forth the brightest and strongest princes and knights of the land. One after another Odoline rejected them, sometimes dancing only one dance at a ball or watching one jousting match, so she could return to her studies in the library.

The King, at his wit's end, sought the counsel of a sage, hoping he might have a solution to the problem. After a brief conversation with Odoline (where she barely looked at him over the top of a book), the sage had returned to the King. "Leave it with me," he said, "I'll take care of it."

Not long after, a handsome young prince named Sev came to the castle and presented a gift to Odoline—a book of tattered parchment, bound in chains and fixed with a heart-shaped lock. "'Tis a book of spells," he said, "the most powerful known to man. I give it to you along with the key, but you must promise never to open it."

Sev, of course, was the sage in disguise, and he'd hatched a terrible plan. He knew that the princess had witchery in her blood and desired to become a great sorceress. Seeing her powers as a threat to his own, he sought to deny them to her. The book was indeed as powerful as he claimed, but he was willing to part with it to secure his place in the kingdom. He'd charmed the book to tempt the princess so the minute she gave in to its powers, she'd feel the wrath of its curse. The book contained spells of all sorts—including precise instructions on how to summon demons. Those who understand magic know that demons have their uses, but only when tempered by the company of angels. The book contained the names of forty angels. The number of demons it named was forty-one.

Odoline did indeed choose Sev for her suitor. In return for his gift she gave him a gold ring inscribed with the words, "All my trust." The book sat for one hundred days unopened on her desk while the pair danced and sang and made love in the corridors and gardens of the castle. The key to the lock on the chains that bound the book was tied safely on a scarlet ribbon around Odoline's neck.

When the day of her wedding arrived, Odoline snuck away from her attendants to sit alone in her library. She wished to find a verse to read to her new husband on their wedding night. Spying the book of spells on the desk, she went to it. When she touched it, the chains around the book began to rattle, the lock began to shake. "Who is Sev to forbid *me* to open it?" she thought. "It belongs to me and I'll do with it as I see fit." Removing the key from around her neck, she opened the lock and shook the chains free from the book.

Instantly, a cloud of darkness swirled around the princess and a terrible howling sounded in the air. An enormous demon appeared before her, growling, snorting and gnashing his teeth.

"Heaven assist me!" Odoline cried, but no angel came to her aid.

The demon stared at Odoline with hungry yellow eyes, then opened its gaping, ragged mouth. "When the balance of good and evil is tipped towards hell, nothing can save you," it said.

Odoline was sure this wasn't true. She'd read about angels as well as demons and knew that each one had their strengths and weaknesses. "State your name," she demanded, knowing the demon would be compelled to answer by the witch's blood that flowed in her veins.

"Malphas," the demon hissed, foaming at the mouth.

It was a name that Odoline knew well. Malphas was the mighty prince of Hell with forty legions of demons under his command, second only to Satan. Malphas, builder of towers, strongholds and monuments. Malphas, destroyer of desires and dreams. Malphas was also known as "the giver," because when conjured by a witch, he was bound by her magic to spare her life and present her with a familiar. "Bring me a companion," Odoline said, making the sign of the horns with her fingers. "And then be gone."

The demon threw his head back and roared. "Because of you," he said, "all witches will suffer! They'll be forever cursed to hide their gifts from the light." Then he vanished from the room leaving behind the stench of sulphur and a heap of black feathers at Odoline's feet.

When Odoline bent to inspect what Malphas had given her, she discovered a handsome, bright-eyed raven with a gold ring around its leg.

That was the day Odoline declared herself a witch.

It was also the day the hunts began.

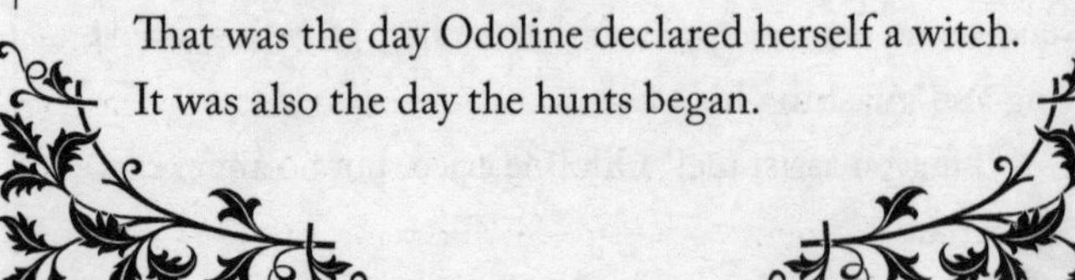

After Madame St. Clair had recited Odoline's tale one last time, she'd tugged at something around her neck. To Eleanor's surprise, it was a scarlet ribbon. She was sure she'd never noticed her mother wearing it in the past. "Take the key," her mother had whispered, "to remind you of our past. Demons may cross your path, but you have the power to beat them."

As Eleanor had dropped the ribbon around her own neck, her mother had struggled on, her words catching on every breath. "The time will soon come when witches won't be born, but made. The first will come to you. She'll need to learn. You must teach her."

"How will I know who she is?" Eleanor had asked, desperate to make sense of her mother's words.

"Perdu knows," her mother had answered. "He's always known."

Within hours of her mother's passing, two men had come to the door wearing the dark frowns and wide-brimmed hats of undertakers. "May we assist you in your time of sorrow?" they'd asked. Eleanor hadn't the faintest notion of how they'd gotten there, or how they'd found out about her mother's death. In her grief, she'd considered letting them in, thinking her mother might have summoned them without her knowing, but Perdu had kicked up a terrible fuss. Flying to the peak of the roof he'd cried out as if he were in agony. In an instant, a flock of ravens had appeared, darkening the sky overhead. In the midst of their cacophony, Eleanor had sworn she'd heard the words, "All my trust." She'd told the men, "Thank you for your offer, but there's nothing for you here."

She herself had dug a grave under a hawthorn tree and laid her mother to rest. Then she'd gone to the bees to tell them their mistress had died. Perdu had grieved alongside her as she'd wept among the hives, and followed at her heels as she'd cast spells of protection over every inch of the land and every corner of the house.

"Here's to you, Maman," Eleanor said, finishing her tea and holding her cup to the air. Then upending the cup on its saucer, she turned it three times round. If ever she needed the counsel of the leaves, it was now. When she turned the cup and saucer over again, she heard a loud clang. Setting the saucer aside, she discovered that the key her mother had given her was resting inside the teacup's bowl, its scarlet ribbon spilling over the rim.

"What witchery is this?" Eleanor whispered, staring at the key in disbelief. She hadn't worn the thing in ages, hadn't looked at it in months. She'd kept it hidden in her room, safe from any chance of losing it. Placing the key around her neck, she rushed to the counter to fetch a jar of salt. Spreading a thick line of grains in a wide circle around herself, she chanted a spell of protection.

Thrice around, the circle's bound.

Sink all evil to the ground.

O goddess good, of day and night,
Protect this place with all your might.
By the magic power of three,

Summon the angels to accompany me.
So may it be, so may it be, so may it be!

As Eleanor spoke the last words of the spell, Adelaide came through the door, wobbling to and fro and smelling of absinthe. Standing outside the circle, she shook her head. "I don't want to know."

"Quiet," Eleanor shushed her, reaching out to Adelaide, inviting her to cross the line.

Adelaide immediately saw the fear in Eleanor's eyes. "What's happened?"

Clutching Adelaide's hand, Eleanor answered, "I'm not sure."

As Beatrice slept, Twitch lay on her pillow, propped on his elbow, chin in hand. With a lovesick sigh he stared at the girl, then reached out to tuck a curl behind her ear. "You're beautiful," he whispered. "If only I could tell you to your face."

"Stop it," Bright scolded, cuffing Twitch on the back of his head. "You know it's against the rules. Besides, it won't do her any good. Flattery does nothing but cloud a girl's judgement."

"Humph," Twitch said, before resuming his adoration of Beatrice.

Although she wasn't about to admit it, Bright was enjoying watching the girl sleep as much as Twitch was. It was a relief not to have anything to do outside of observing the sweet-faced creature. Twitch was right, she was a beautiful thing—so full of new-found magic that Bright could taste it in the air. It was fresh, like morning dew on rose petals, delicious as the nectar in a honeysuckle blossom. Still, Bright wasn't about to encourage Twitch's silly notions. When it came to Beatrice Dunn, they couldn't afford to make mistakes. That's why they wouldn't be building her any dreams—not yet.

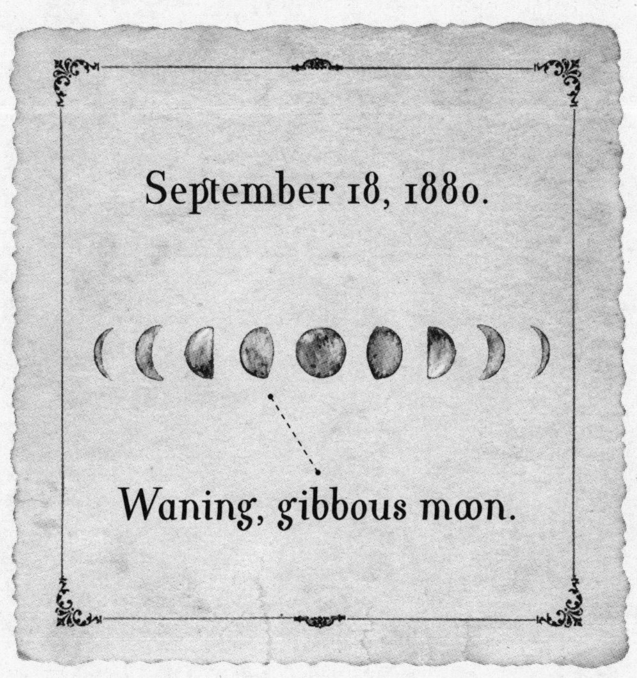
September 18, 1880.
Waning, gibbous moon.

A NOTE on WAYWARD GHOSTS.

Most witches needn't bother with ghosts. There's magic enough to be found among the living. Still, it's important to know how best to deal with stray spirits, if and when they should cross your path.

The likelihood of this happening is great. Spirits of a confused, uneasy nature often clamour after magic and those who practice it (especially newborn babes with witchery in their blood, and young, inexperienced witches). For the most part, they mean no harm. Do not confuse their activities with the work of various otherworldly folk—demons, goblins, imps, elementals, shadow beings, angels, fairies, nymphs, gnomes, elves and so on.

Most hauntings are brief affairs marked by the typical signs—strange shadows on the wall, odd reflections in mirrors, scents lingering in the room, draughts of cold air, bumps in the night. Should these signs persist or increase, they may indicate an infestation. Poltergeists are often the most troublesome of the lot. They can move objects with ease—within a room, about the house, and in rare cases, from one time or place to another. Should these things happen, be wary but not afraid. Do your best to allow the spirit to pass through, unchecked. It's likely they have important business to which they must attend, just as you have yours.

. . . continued

If wayward ghosts insist upon disrupting your life or your dwelling place, look first to yourself for the reason why. Have you done something to encourage their presence? Did you leave your house or yourself unprotected? Have you moved a sacred object from its proper place? Did you bring a relic of unknown origins into your home? Has a person of questionable motives crossed your threshold in the recent past? Have you disturbed sacred ground, either knowingly or unwittingly? Have you undertaken mundane tasks during sacred hours? Did you trifle with magic to call upon the dead? (There are proper ways to go about this. Rules must be obeyed.)

Whenever possible, make amends without directly addressing the deceased. Endeavouring to make contact without taking proper precautions is a recipe for disaster. Such activities should only be carried out by experienced witches skilled in the art of necromancy.

—From the grimoire of Eleanor St. Clair

Mirror, Mirror on the Wall.

"WHERE'S PERDU?" ADELAIDE asked, hands on her hips. She'd come downstairs that morning and the bird hadn't announced her arrival. He always made a point of it, especially when she'd slept in: she swore the bird liked to stir up trouble.

"He's with Beatrice," Eleanor answered, pouring tea into a pair of cups—one for Adelaide, one for herself.

Adelaide pondered the name "Beatrice," but found she couldn't place it.

Placing a small pitcher of honey on the counter, Eleanor prompted, "Our new girl—"

"Oh yes, that's right," Adelaide said. "I almost forgot."

She'd been dreadfully tipsy when she'd come home for the night so the memory of her conversation with Eleanor was sketchy at best. Squinting against the sunlight that was streaming through the shop windows, she tried to think if there was anything important (other than the girl, of course) that she might've forgotten.

After her fruitless trip to see Mr. Beadle's witch, she'd stopped by the Fifth Avenue Hotel for a late supper. She'd hoped she might run into Judith Dashley ahead of their scheduled meeting with the mysterious Dr. Brody.

Although she hadn't had any luck spotting Judith, the soup du jour had been clam chowder, which she loved. The hotel kitchen served it beer-garden style, with brown bread and a side of baked beans drowned in syrupy molasses sauce. The dining room had bustled with the usual evening crowd—ladies gossiping after a long day of shopping, businessmen courting out-of-town clients, and politicos embroiled in a heated discussion about the best way to get their man into the White House. The election was less than two months away, and Senator Roscoe Conkling and his merry band of Republicans had set up shop at the hotel for the duration. He and two of his Conklingites were at the next table going back and forth about what would win more votes: promising to back the struggling economy with the gold standard, or reminding the public that theirs was the party that'd preserved the Union by winning the war.

Conkling stood firm on his views. "Men want to be assured that the money they make, however much or little that might be, is as good as gold."

The man to his left shook his head. "Times are tough for the average Joe. Best not get them thinking about money. Heaven knows Garfield's business record doesn't instill much confidence." The portly fellow had a line of beer foam clinging to his moustache.

"Hear, Hear!" the man to Conkling's right bellowed. "I say let's not make this about Garfield at all. Who cares about a farm boy from Ohio? The only way he's going to win is if we point the finger in the other direction. Blame the Dems for everything that's gone wrong—secession, the war, hard times . . . need I go on?" He was long-necked and gangly, the Jack Spratt to his foamy-faced companion.

Conkling looked as if he'd smelled something rotten. "Do you really think we can play the war card again? How long can we get away with waving the bloody shirt?"

"It worked for Hayes," the portly one replied.

"Barely," the gangly one sighed.

"Barely's good enough," Conkling said. "So long as you're the winner."

Adelaide didn't know much about Conkling's political leanings, and she didn't much care to, but she knew quite a lot about his reputation among women. The greying yet virile statesman had been known to go a round or two in the boxing ring as well as between the sheets with several of his colleagues' wives. The previous summer he'd been caught with his pants down while tending to Mrs. Kate Sprague at her summer home in Rhode Island. Her husband, the Governor of the Smallest State, had reportedly held a shotgun in his hand while showing Conkling the door.

After waving away the dessert cart, Adelaide had treated herself to a glass or three (or had it been four?) of absinthe. Each time the waiter dutifully poured her more, she'd squinted at the dose line and pronounced, "It looks a little short." Balancing a slotted silver spoon across the rim of her glass, she'd gotten on with the artful task of preparing her drink. First came a sugar cube, carefully set on top of the spoon. Then came a measure of cold, clear water, meted out in drips. When done correctly, it created a beautiful, cloudy mixture. To Adelaide the stuff looked as inviting as the tall, refreshing glasses of milk they served at the Central Park Dairy on hot summer days. *Here's to life's short play and all that*, she'd thought, as she'd raised her glass to her lips. *Here's to Anthony Comstock and all the fine ladies in the WCTU! Here's to the green fairy and to making mischief! Here's to the Fifth Avenue Hotel and its resident ghosts!* (Thinking back, there was a distinct possibility that she'd said those things out loud.)

As the anise-flavoured liquor had wriggled its way through her senses, she'd turned her attention from the obstreperous politicos to the hotel's owner, Mrs. Marietta Stevens, who was making her evening rounds through the dining room, stopping at every table to hand out compliments and gather whatever morsels of information her patrons cared to offer. Each time she'd said her goodnights and farewells, she'd ended the conversation by saying, "It's by my guests' happiness that I prevail." It was an effortless performance that Adelaide greatly admired.

Time and again the press had referred to the widowed Mrs. Stevens as "a woman of lowly beginnings," but Adelaide regarded her as a woman to be revered. What's more, she thought that if she hadn't married Mr. Paran Stevens, the famous hotelier, she would've made one hell of a mind reader. Marietta had the knack for knowing what people needed before they knew they needed it, and the forethought to commit a person's secrets to memory until such time as they might be of use. Adelaide prided herself on the fact that she and Marietta were more alike than different, and that a woman of such influence chose to come to her for advice. While she wasn't sure there was anything in particular she could do about the romance that'd blossomed between the widow's son and Edith Jones, she figured she should at least ask if there'd been any progress one way or another. When Marietta had reached her table, Adelaide had asked, "How goes the disenchantment of Miss Jones?"

"Slow," Marietta had replied, settling down next to Adelaide.

Adelaide wished she didn't have to choose sides in the matter. Edith Jones was a lovely young woman, keen and bright and observant. Adelaide was convinced that if no one got in her way she'd go quite far in life. "You said the girl has an active mind, no?"

"It never stops."

"Not to worry, then. She'll think herself out of her passion for your son, eventually. I say let the affair run its course."

"I suppose that's all I can do, for now," Marietta replied. "I've more pressing matters at hand."

"Anything I can help you with?"

Marietta had stared across the room, thoughts clearly

turning in her head. Fingers steepled, she'd finally looked at Adelaide and said, "Perhaps."

Waving to the waiter for another dose of absinthe, Adelaide leaned close to Marietta and said, "Go on."

"I hate to admit it," Marietta whispered, "but it's the ghosts."

Shaking her head, Adelaide said, "I thought you believed they weren't real."

"Let's just say they've been rather convincing as of late."

"How so?" Adelaide asked, intrigued by Marietta's words.

"Extinguishing gaslights in the corridors, knocking over chairs with abandon, showing their ghoulish faces to the help. The chambermaids are beside themselves and my poor housekeeper, Mrs. Fisher, can barely keep up with their wild tales and silly superstitions."

Adelaide gave a sympathetic nod. "Perhaps you should consider that such occurrences might be reason to rejoice. I've heard encounters with wayward spirits are all the rage among certain circles."

Marietta rolled her eyes. "Be that as it may, for every spook-loving Judy that thrills at the mention of ghosts, there's a shrinking violet who'll pack her bags and head somewhere else."

"Your ghosts may be less trouble than you think," Adelaide suggested. "You just need to persuade them to follow your command."

"The trouble is they're not on my payroll. I haven't any clout when it comes to making them behave. You wouldn't happen to know anyone who can reason with spirits, would you? I don't want some sideshow charlatan, mind you, but the genuine article."

The sideshow remark wounded Adelaide, but she'd let it slide since Marietta had no inkling of her past. "I might," she'd answered. Eleanor had never said she couldn't talk to ghosts. She'd only said she wouldn't.

"Well if you come across such a person, please send her straight to me. Imagine the business I'd pull in if I could get those sneaky little ghouls to do my bidding!"

After another round of absinthe, Adelaide had finally made her way back to the shop, her limbs numb and heavy, her head feeling as if it might float away on the cool autumn breeze. Aside from the brief moment of confusion she'd suffered when she'd first come through the door, it'd seemed a positive sign to find Eleanor off her nut and circled by a line of salt sprinkled on the floor. Perhaps she could talk to ghosts after all! Waiting for her chance to broach the subject, Adelaide had only half-listened as Eleanor went on about Perdu and a late train and some girl who'd fainted in the shop. When Eleanor had gotten to the part where she'd announced that she'd taken the girl on as hired help, all Adelaide had been able to think was that it didn't seem quite fair that she hadn't gotten any say in the decision, especially after it'd been her idea to put the notice in the paper in the first place.

Remembering she was still slightly sore over the matter, Adelaide glowered at Eleanor. "So where is this Beatrice now?"

Pointing to the ceiling, Eleanor whispered, "She's asleep."

"Asleep?" Adelaide exclaimed, hoping to make enough noise to rouse the girl. She didn't appreciate having to tiptoe around someone she'd never met.

"Hush," Eleanor scolded. "She won't be any good to me if she's under the weather. I told you of the state she was in . . . don't you remember?"

"Right, right," Adelaide said, not wanting their discussion to turn to the state *she'd* been in last night. Better that Beatrice be on the receiving end of Eleanor's bedside manner. A vague memory of Eleanor slipping into bed beside her sometime in the night led her to ask, "Were you up late?"

"Not too late." Eleanor clutched a key that was hanging around her neck then slipped it under the collar of her dress. Adelaide didn't think to make anything of it. Eleanor had any number of amulets she wore to assist her with her magic—a bone trinket carved in the shape of a hand, a locket containing the whiskers of a black cat. Adelaide had stopped keeping track of them all. "Let's hope Sleeping Beauty wakes up soon or I'm afraid you'll regret giving her your bed."

Eleanor shook her head. "Did anyone ever tell you that you talk in your sleep?"

"I do not," Adelaide replied.

"Yes, you do."

"Tell me then, what did I say? Anything good? Did any burning confessions fall from my lips?"

"Nothing worth repeating."

The ghost of Adelaide's mother looked on while the two women bickered. She remembered what it had been like to share a bed with her daughter, how the child's wiry little legs had kicked about under the thin covers, and how, yes indeed, she'd had a tendency to blather in her sleep. *I was "Mama" then*, she thought. *And you were my little "Moth." Who am I now? What have we become?*

She didn't like this business of Moth calling herself "Adelaide," which sounded snobbish to her ears. But who was she to judge? She hadn't held her child enough, she knew that now. She'd never been able to give the girl a decent life. She hadn't wanted to raise her with things that would make her weak—hugs, lullabies, kisses, hope, dreams, love—so she'd replaced comfort with disinterest and hard knocks. She'd only done what she'd thought was best. How could she have known that she wouldn't be able to protect her—not in life, not in death?

It haunted her still. That's why she was chasing after Adelaide. She wanted to tell her daughter everything she'd left unsaid, and more importantly, of the things she'd witnessed since she'd gone beyond the veil. If only she hadn't spent all her time with her daughter feeding her sorrow! She might've saved them both from so many terrible things. Now she was being punished for it, bound by chains of regret—for how she'd lived and how she'd died—sentenced to stand at her daughter's side during every bad thing that'd happened to the girl since. She'd watched helplessly on that terrible day when her dear girl had been attacked, her screams of warning unable to reach Adelaide's ears.

"Moth!" the spirit cried. "Do you hear me? Listen to me, Moth!"

Upstairs, the bottle in Adelaide's desk rolled from side to side.

Scowling, Adelaide waved her hand in the air. "Damn flies. Always buzzing in my ear."

The spirit gave up her pestering and hid between two teapots. *She'll hear me soon enough,* she thought. *That damned know-it-all fairy promised me as much.* The scheming pixie had brokered a deal with her, allowing her to slip through a crack unprotected by Eleanor's spells in exchange for her agreeing to do the fairy's bidding—break a teapot, move a key, show herself to the girl.

Oh, maybe it hadn't gone the way the fairy had instructed, but she was only having a bit of fun. She hadn't meant to scare the poor child. How was she to know she'd be so delicate? In the end she'd done as she was told. She'd enticed the girl to come into the shop and the girl had stayed. In the dark of night as the pixie had fluttered near the girl's bed, the cranky spirit had tipped her over, wing over ass, and asked, "Why can *she* see me when my own daughter can't?"

"She's special," the fairy had answered before turning her back.

Humph, the spirit thought. *We'll see about that.*

At ten o'clock, Beatrice came downstairs with Perdu hopping at her heels. "Good morning, Miss St. Clair," she said. "I hope I'm not too late."

"You're right on time," Eleanor said, pouring a cup of tea for her. Offering her a plate filled with sliced cheese and sugared pastries, she asked, "How are you faring this morning? I trust you had a good sleep?" Pulling a saucer of raw stew meat from behind the counter, she set it on the floor for Perdu.

The bird sank his clawed foot into the largest chunk to hold it steady. Tugging it into stringy bits with his beak, one by one he flipped each morsel into the air, then gobbled it down.

Adelaide stared at Beatrice over the rim of her teacup.

"I'm feeling much better, thank you," Beatrice replied. "It was awfully generous of you to lend me your bed." Then reaching for a piece of cheese she said, "I hope you'll see fit to put me to work today. Otherwise I'll feel awfully spoiled."

Adelaide smiled and said, "Perhaps Miss St. Clair's only fattening you up so she can boil you like a ham hock and eat you with a side of cabbage."

Beatrice let out a nervous laugh.

"Adelaide!" Eleanor scolded. "Behave yourself." Turning to Beatrice she said, "Beatrice Dunn, meet Adelaide Thom."

Grinning, Adelaide looked to Beatrice. Lifting her veil away from her face she said, "You know I'm teasing, don't you, dear?"

Beatrice's eyes went wide. "Yes, of course, Miss Thom," she stammered, offering Adelaide her hand. "It's nice to meet you."

Adelaide gave the girl's hand a firm squeeze. *We'll see about that*, she thought. "So lovely to meet you too, Beatrice."

Perdu chortled, then tapped at his plate. All that was left was a runny puddle of blood.

"Here," Eleanor said, setting a bowl of water in its place. "Drink up."

Dipping his beak, the raven slurped the liquid into his mouth, then tipped it down his throat.

Adelaide nicked a pastry from Beatrice's plate, tore a sizable chunk from it and stuck it in her mouth. Returning the remainder of the sweet, she said, "You don't mind, do you? I couldn't resist."

Beatrice gave Adelaide a kind smile. "Not at all," she said. "Help yourself to the rest of it if you like. I'm not really one for sweets. My aunt Lydia says they make the senses sluggish."

Licking the sugar off her fingers Adelaide said, "How sad."

Eleanor squinted at Adelaide. A warning-shot across the bow. Adelaide kept her sights fixed on Beatrice. "How old are you?" She reached for the wounded pastry. (*And why shouldn't she? The girl didn't want it.*)

"Seventeen, this past summer."

"Seventeen!" Adelaide exclaimed. "I can barely remember it."

"Ha!" Perdu squawked, with a violent shake of his head.

Eleanor smiled at her pet.

Ignoring the bird, Adelaide studied Beatrice—the sweet timbre of her voice, the casual confidence in her posture, the sincere interest in her dewy eyes. Eleanor hadn't bothered to mention she was a beauty. Save for the small scrape on her forehead (which the poor girl had tried to hide with one of her shiny curls), everything about her was measured and neat, near perfect. Even the bright blue ribbon tied at the end of her braid was crisp and clean. The girl's face was much the same—not a trace of ill will or disappointment was discernible on it. *And oh, what a searching gaze! She's waiting for me to like her. How frustratingly endearing! If she expects my approval today, she'll have to wait.* Spying the clock on the shelf behind the counter, Adelaide turned to Eleanor and said, "Oh my, look at the time. I must fly. I'm off to breakfast with Judith at the Fifth."

"When will you be back?" Eleanor asked, wiping the powdery trail of sugar Adelaide had left on the counter. "What am I to tell your sitters?"

"Tell them they should've made an appointment," Adelaide said with an indifferent shrug. Walking to her table in the back of the shop, she hung an elegantly lettered sign on her chair: THE SEER IS OUT.

"Wait," her mother's ghost called, flying out from her hiding spot. She desperately wanted to follow her daughter but was afraid to leave the shop in case she might not be able to get back in.

"Ta-ta," Adelaide said, as she headed out the door. Bells jangled in her wake.

"I don't think she likes me," Beatrice whispered to Eleanor.

"Give it time," Eleanor said. "She'll come around."

Clearing away the dishes, Beatrice glanced at the mirror behind the counter and caught sight of Adelaide's mother's ghost. She stifled a scream.

Silver hoops glinting in the looking glass, the Gypsy woman put her finger to her lips.

Flapping to the counter, Perdu stared sideways at the mirror. "Ta-ta," he squawked. "Ta-ta, ta-ta, ta-ta!"

"Ta-ta," the ghost whispered as she faded from sight.

A Preponderance of Marys.

THE FIFTH AVENUE HOTEL stood on a bed of bones—lacy, worm-etched remains of the poor, finding their way to dust. Skull by jaw by rib by spine, they were nestled as tight as cordwood in a maze of pauper's pits that stretched out from below the building, under the streets of Madison Square and beneath the walkways of its pleasant, manicured park. Time and progress had caused these unfortunate souls to be forgotten, but their restless echoes had lived on, rising up through the cobblestones and pavers, acting as ghostly ether, provoking fear and dark thoughts. This is what happens when the dead don't get their due. This is what happens when the past is ignored.

In the hotel's grand, marble-tiled lobby, the ghost of Mr. Paran Stevens sat waiting for his wife, Marietta. The impatient spirit's preferred seat was neither comfortable nor fancy, just a well-worn spot at the end of the long wooden bench nearest the Twenty-Third Street entrance. Above the doorway was a large sign that read LADIES ONLY, marking it as a special entrance for unaccompanied women who wished to be discreet on their visits here. It was a change Marietta had insisted they make when they'd first taken over the lease, just one of the many savvy schemes she'd hatched in the early days of their May–December marriage. Back then, everything

Marietta had done had seemed (at least in Paran's eyes) to be inspired by some greater, all-knowing force of fiscal intuition. Who could've guessed that placing a single square of chocolate on a patron's pillow would stir such feelings of goodwill? Or that offering late supper to both the patrons and the public would result in the dining hall being filled to the rafters every night? Oh, what a terrific team they'd been! He'd never have been half so successful if he hadn't married his darling wife.

The ladies of Mrs. Astor's 400 had relished making a scandal of their union—"She's a chiseller." "She's a grubber." "She's a climber." "She's his daughter's age, for heaven's sake!" In the end, his dear Marietta had risen above all the chatter, proving herself equal to (in his eyes, better than) the lot. Best of all, she'd forced New York society to accept her on her own terms. No, she hadn't come from money or the upper crust; and yes, her words sometimes could be cutting, hurtful and rough, but anyone fortunate enough to find themselves in her good graces knew the truth—there never was a truer friend than his wife.

Paran had quietly expired in his own bed one bright April day in 1872. For a short time, he'd haunted the parlour of their home on Marble Row, but he'd soon grown tired of listening to the laments and platitudes of those who came to pay their respects. "How can we go on without him?" they'd cried. "What a tragic loss," they'd said. The words were nothing but hollow kindnesses, meant to fill the uncomfortable silences of mourning—the daylight hours when the company of others is inescapable, the days between death and burial, the parade of firsts without the deceased marked by holidays, anniversaries, birthdays and so on. He'd hovered near his family for as long as he could stand it, hardly able to bear the disparity between Marietta's sorrow and the brave face she put on for their two children. Each night, after she'd fallen asleep, he'd kissed her weary brow and blessed her dreams. Soon, he'd decamped to the hotel, feeling it was the best place for him to be.

Tapping a foot, Paran watched out the window, on the lookout for his wife. Forty-six was far too young for her to be a widow, to be draped head to toe in Henrietta cloth. Why did she insist on continuing to wear the dreadful uniform of mourning, day after day? He wished he could tell her, "Enough already." He also wished he knew when she was going to arrive! What day was it again? Spotting a gentleman with a copy of *Frank Leslie's Illustrated Newspaper*, Paran guessed it must be Saturday. He hated the way time moved on the other side—there was no sensible ebb and flow to it. Days dragged on at a snail's pace or flew past like a hawk diving after its prey. In a blink, a whole month could be gone and he'd be left wondering what he'd been doing while it'd passed. Eight years into it and he still hadn't mastered the best way to go about the business of being dead.

At least he'd figured out this—just as a child learns reading, writing and arithmetic, the dead had to tackle their three Rs as well: revenge, regret and reconciliation. Luckily, he'd lived his life in such a way that there was little revenge to exact, especially since the other two Rs kept him working round the clock. Currently he was involved with a task of the heart, getting Marietta to reconcile her differences with their dear son, Harry, over the matter of Miss Edith Jones. Time was of the essence. He'd seen the Reaper hovering over Harry, on account of a sickness settled in the boy's lungs that had no cure. The reprieve Harry had gotten this past summer from breathing the fresh air along the shores of Bar Harbor wasn't going to last. Was Marietta aware of their son's ill health? If she was, she wasn't letting it show. *Let him be happy, my dear*, Paran thought. *He isn't long for this world. Let him have at least a taste of what we once had!*

He'd been diligently trying to communicate with the living—getting up the nerve to pass through a body, rather than simply brushing near; knocking over progressively heavier objects, a hat, a wine glass, a coat rack—in hopes of getting through to Marietta. Last week he'd pestered a beggar woman who liked to feed birds in the park because he'd been told by another spirit that she'd been known (on rare occasion) to speak the words of the dead. The woman hadn't entered into a conversation with him, or even looked as if she'd known he was there, but he'd felt a great sense of accomplishment when she'd flapped her arms and yelled, "Paran Stevens is here!"

"Good morning, Mr. Stevens," a spirit said to him now as she passed by. (The same spirit who'd told him of the woman in the park.)

"Good morning, Mary," he replied, with a tip of his hat.

He'd been sitting in this same spot near the Ladies' Entrance eight months after he'd passed on the fateful cold December night when she'd met her death, horribly, in this very hotel. He watched the little spectre as she glided through walls and wafted past patrons on her way to scrub the marble steps of the hotel's grand staircase. He wondered why, in his ghostly form, he still bothered to wear a hat, and why the girl held fast to the handle of her bucket as it sloshed with the memory of hot, sudsy water. Why were they still here? Was this all there was to death? Had St. Peter become so choosy he wouldn't grant them entrance into Heaven? *That might be true for me*, Paran Stevens thought, *but surely not for this spectre and the ten other hard-working, kind-hearted girls who'd died with her in the fire*. They were the girls who'd scrubbed the hotel floors, the woodwork, the dishes, the laundry. None of them had done anything to deserve such a terrible lot.

They'd been young, hopeful immigrants, mostly of Irish descent, who'd never seemed bothered by the fact that their pretty, freckled cheeks were covered with smudges by day's end. He hadn't paid much attention to them while they'd been alive, something he regretted in his present state. They'd all known him by sight, addressed him by name, but he'd not taken the time to learn theirs. Whenever Marietta had scolded him for his lack of interest in the staff, he'd complained that there were too many Marys among the help, from the chambermaids to the scrubbing girls, from the cooks to the calligraphers. How was he supposed to remember who was who?

After the girls had died, though, he'd come across their spirits circled around the smouldering ashes of the fire. Hands clasped, they'd been reciting the rosary, calling for Mother Mary to bless them in their time of need. *Holy Mary, Mother of God, pray for us sinners, now and at the hour of our death.* In the years that'd passed since then, he'd tried asking them their names, but they'd always refused to answer. At first, he'd thought it might be a small punishment for his indifference to them when he'd been alive, but over time they'd kept refusing, all the while growing more alike than different in movement and appearance. Eventually he'd stopped asking.

Sometimes late at night he saw them floating about in the corridors, wailing like banshees as they made their way to the attic. They'd changed in the afterlife, their sweet natures now prone to turn spiteful and angry at the slightest provocation. Afraid of what they might become when there was no one among the living who remembered who they once had been, Paran Stevens prayed for them, fervently and often. "God bless the Marys," he whispered, before resuming his wait for his wife. "Keep them whole. Give them peace."

Mary Corday, Margaret Connor, Delia Cummings, Mary McCabe, Lizzie Moran, Margaret Campbell, Margaret Fagan, Mary Donnelly, Hannah Ward, Mary J. Heavey, Kate Cushing.

The hotel's head housekeeper, Mrs. Fisher, was conducting her Saturday morning inspection. She recited the scrubber girls' names twice a day—each morning after making the daily roll call, each night after calling for lights out. Once a week she visited Old St. Patrick's Cathedral on Mulberry Street to light candles in their memory. Her girls were never far from her thoughts, and always in her heart. How could she forget them or the terrible way they'd died?

By the time she'd been alerted to the fire, the entire west wing of the attic was engulfed in flames, the streams of water from the pumper wagons failing to staunch the raging blaze. She'd stood outside, tears freezing on her cheeks as a chorus of screams howled from above. Firemen, mere shadows on the roof, dragged hoses this way and that as a group of brave porters pulled as many girls as they could through broken windows and skylights. Carriages rushed from all directions to take in the sight—liveried vehicles with ladies and gents inside, as well as a string of wobbly hacks crowded with fast women and their gallants, half drunk with the night's dissipation. Pacing the ground floor of the hotel, Mrs. Fisher helped wherever she could—bringing hot tea to half-dressed ladies sitting on their trunks, shutting the door to the reading room so the laughter and cigar smoke of the businessmen crowded inside wouldn't seep into the lobby. When the rescued maids began to scurry through the front door, she'd ushered them into a private parlour so she could count their heads. "Oh Mrs. Fisher," they'd cried, sobbing and shivering while wringing their hands. "It's a terrible calamity. The worst thing I ever saw!" Between curses and prayers, the trembling young things had taken turns recounting the horror they'd escaped and guessing what might've caused it.

"The fire shot right up the stairwell—we had no way out."

"Do you suppose someone dropped a candle on her way up to bed?"

"More likely Mary McConnell's lover dropped his lantern on his way back down."

"The windows were shut tight, the bars fixed fast to the frames. If the boys hadn't torn them out, we would've cooked in our beds."

"The gas jet in a laundry closet was missing its guard. It was only a matter of time before a pile of linens caught light."

"I hope they can get everyone out before it's too late."

"Where's Mary Katherine?"

"Where's Mary Margaret?"

"I'll bet Mary Grove forgot to turn down her lamp again."

"The smoke was black as pitch. We could barely find our way through it."

Nine girls had gotten trapped in the last two rooms on the corridor. Before the porters could reach their window, the timbers of the roof fell in, sealing their fate. The best anyone could hope was that they were already dead when it happened. Six were found in a heap by the window. Two more were huddled under a bed. One was in the middle of the room, her knees bent in prayer, a crucifix in her hands. Two others managed to escape through a skylight only to die at Bellevue later that night. Half of the girls were burned beyond recognition. There was only one staircase that led to their quarters, with no other way out. Hadn't anyone ever thought of what might happen if a fire broke out? The wall between the men's and women's rooms was built like a fortress, and solid bars covered the windows—they'd been put there by the proprietors to protect the girls' honour. Instead they'd served as a death sentence. *Isn't that always the way,* Mrs. Fisher had thought, *man's fears causing him to do things that lead to far greater sins.*

In the dark of the night, the coroner had asked Mrs. Fisher to view the corpses, hoping she might tell him who was who. At the time she'd been in such a state, she hadn't been able to bring herself to do it, but when first light had come, she'd made the daily roll call, noted which girls were missing, and found her way to the morgue. The sight she'd seen when she'd gotten to Bellevue was as alarming as the fire itself. The line for those who wished to have a look at the dead snaked down Twenty-Sixth Street and around the block. For every person who thought they might've lost a dear one, a hundred more were there to gawk. Visitors entered from the left and exited to the right, slowly moving past the dead as if dancing a strange, macabre reel. The girls' bodies were hideous to behold—flesh burned off their faces and limbs, bones exposed and charred black. When it was Mrs. Fisher's turn, she'd covered her face with her handkerchief and held her breath, not because of the stench, but because she was afraid the Reaper might be standing guard, waiting to choose who'd be next. Straight off she'd identified three of the girls—one by a ring on a finger, one by a cross around the neck, and one by what little remained of a face. The coroner had quickly drawn sheets over their bodies and set three wooden lids in place. Mrs. Fisher had never imagined she'd feel such relief in hearing a coffin nailed shut.

Nearly eight years on, the fearful, living maids who worked under her supervision would come to her in the middle of the night, scared and begging not to be sent back to their beds in the attic. "Oh Mrs. Fisher, don't make me go back there. One of the Marys is floatin' over my bed, ready to wrap her sooty fingers around my neck!" On any given night, a handful of frightened chambermaids or scrubber girls might smell smoke when there weren't any fires lit, see handprints on frosty windowpanes, or hear voices wailing in the stairwell.

Truth be told, Mrs. Fisher had had her fair share of run-ins with the spirits as well. She'd felt their presence wax and wane over time, their powers growing greater as daylight grew shorter and winter drew near. During the recent full moon they'd seemed especially restless, rattling the doors of her linen closet, and sending the pitcher next to her wash-basin crashing to the floor. The mere thought of it raised the hairs on the back of her neck. She tried her best not to speak of these things to anyone, especially not the guests. She'd given the maids strict orders to follow suit. Still, from time to time, one or more of them would try to make contact with the ghosts, by asking them to blow out a candle or to play with a needle tied to the end of a string. Whenever she caught wind of such activities, the housekeeper would pull the guilty maids aside and say, “I don’t want to hear of you doing that again. Never trouble trouble until trouble troubles you.”

As Mr. Stevens’ ghost resumed his watch for his wife, and Mrs. Fisher went about her business of checking for dirt and dust, a steady stream of guests came and went from the lobby. A parade of maids (some living, some dead) scurried down the corridors, arms laden with baskets of roses and fruit. A trio of men from Mr. Knox’s hat shop appeared with tape measures in hand, ready to fit top hats and derbies (silk, felt or beaver) to the crowns of eager heads. A bevy of well-dressed ladies gathered in the main entryway, keen to begin their morning promenade through Madison Square Park. A boisterous throng of gentlemen poured into the reading room, their brows waggling with speculation and wagers concerning bears, bulls and horses—new and old, lame or dark. They’d embraced Friday night with open eyes, ears, arms, legs, thighs, lips, tongues, mouths. They’d seen the sights. They’d eaten rich food. They’d met interesting strangers. They’d drunk too much. They’d witnessed a theft, a threat, a pursuit, a fight. When Saturday morning came, they’d woken up (with or without companionship), unaware that the hotel was filled with ghosts.

Scientific Gossip

Turin, Italy. Neuro-Scientist Dr. Angelo Mosso has announced that he is currently constructing a machine to weigh the soul. Based on a principle he calls the "human circulation balance," he hopes to document his findings within the year.

Paris, France. During a course this Winter at Salpêtrière, M. Charcot is to produce new instances of cases like those troubles regarded in the Dark Ages as caused by demonical agency or cured by witchcraft.

The Amazing Dr. Brody.

Dr. Quinn Brody copied the items from the morning edition of the *Times Gazette* into a small leather-bound journal. Clean-shaven and bespectacled, he sported a Newmarket coat because he didn't wish to bother with the numerous buttons of a double-breasted Albert. Holding the journal steady against a tottery table in the corner of the gentlemen's reading room of the Fifth Avenue Hotel, he whispered to himself as he wrote, his one hand made of wood, the other of flesh. It'd been seventeen years since he'd lost his right hand and forearm in the war, yet he still wasn't quite comfortable writing with his left. He could've saved himself time and effort by tearing the notice from the paper and shoving it in his pocket, but the newspaper didn't belong to him, so he felt he had no right to it. Even though he'd already paid the room's attendant for two cups of coffee, he wasn't a paying guest.

Most men wouldn't have given a second thought to committing the trivial crime of ripping a small article from the paper. In fact most men wouldn't have thought it a crime at all, but they weren't Quinn Brody. The middle-aged doctor was far from being without sin, but he liked (no, he needed) to feel that the things he did and said and thought served to subtract from the overall chaos of the world. There was enough nonsense to go around these days without him adding to it. Besides, who wanted to open the morning paper and find a hole torn out of its middle?

His fellow alienists liked to explain men's foibles, rants and rages as "occasional surges of masculinity." Nothing was wrong, per se, nothing a bit of cattle roping, rough-riding and hunting out West couldn't fix. If those prescribed activities couldn't be arranged, then just about any strenuous activity would do. The male mind was, after all, resilient, bold, daring, quick, meant to be taxed. It was built to be elastic and forgiving, especially during the most difficult of times, in the most trying places—from the examination halls of Yale and Harvard, to the battlefields of Gettysburg and Antietam. Still, if Quinn Brody had learned anything during the War Between the States, it was that men's minds, even those of the strongest, brightest and most even-tempered, could come unhinged when faced with unspeakable horrors. A few of the soldiers he'd known had gotten past their tribulations, but many had remained irreparably damaged by what they'd experienced, their hearts and minds changed forever. Still others, unable to put their demons to rest, had—by rope, pistol, knife or poison—taken their own lives.

With the loss of his arm in that war, Brody had been forced to grapple with demons of his own—memories, hallucinations, nightmares. Lying in the Stump Hospital day after day, he'd sworn he could feel a variety of strange sensations in the limb that was no longer there—the pain of his wound, the curling of his fingers, the touch of a gentle hand. One morning during rounds, the famed neurologist Dr. Silas Weir Mitchell had diagnosed him with "phantom limb," a common ailment among soldiers who'd lived through an amputation. What the doctor hadn't mentioned was whether there was a cure for the condition or how long it might last. His only advice had been, "Don't let it make you less of a man."

Mitchell's words had served as little comfort to Brody, who until then had served admirably as an assistant surgeon in New York's Fighting 69th. One minute he'd been tightening a tourniquet around the leg of a wounded soldier in preparation for amputation, and the next he'd been reeling from a deep nick in his arm caused by the head surgeon's overreaching scalpel. Three days later, when gangrene set in, the surgeon had amputated Brody's limb too. Everything that'd come after had led him to his current occupation.

Although he'd lost the ability to slice and saw and cut, he'd gained an intense fascination for deciphering the human mind. Like the mountains and canyons of the Wild West, the lobes and folds of the brain provided vast spans of uncharted territory to explore. What wondrous secrets the mind held within it! What curious, inexplicable tasks it could perform! Closing his eyes, he put his own brain to the test, contemplating the limb he'd lost. In an instant he was overwhelmed with the feeling that his arm had been restored, so solid and perfect, he was sure he could reach out and grasp anything he wanted—a ripe red apple, a tankard of beer, a beautiful woman's breast. It was maddening and miraculous all at once. How could something that had disappeared so long ago still persist?

"Hallo there, Brody!" a gentleman's voice boomed, breaking the doctor's reverie. "Old friend, is that you?" Dressed in a brown checkered suit, the man limped towards the doctor's table, aided by a silver-handled walking stick: Bartholomew Andersen, formerly Private Bart Andersen of the 20th New York Infantry. The two men had spent several months together at the Stump, in adjacent iron cots amidst the rows that stretched down the length of the recovery ward. Andersen had saved a dozen of his fellow soldiers from certain death at Fredericksburg, then taken a Minie ball to the left shin. The men had all lived, but Andersen's leg hadn't stood a chance.

Brody replied, "Andersen, my good man. You look to be in fine fettle." For obvious reasons, he did not offer the hearty handshake and clap on the back customary between veterans.

Andersen exclaimed, "I knew it was you!" Pulling up a chair he added, "How goes the fight, St. Nick?"

Andersen had made a point of assigning ridiculous yet apt monikers to every man he'd encountered at the Stump. He had branded a young soldier from Cincinnati who'd been fitted with a glass eye, Buckeye Jones, and Brody, St. Nick. How long had it been since they'd last seen each other? More than a decade, Brody guessed. He'd lost everyone he loved since then—his wife, his mother, his brother, and most recently, his father. Not wishing to recount past miseries, he only replied, "I can't complain."

"Good, good," Andersen said with a smile. "So what brings you to the Fifth on this fine morning, business or pleasure?"

"Business," Brody answered, figuring "pleasure" would lead to more questions. "And you?"

Tugging a large gold watch from his pocket, Andersen made a show of checking the time. "Business, like you."

"Your business is clearly more profitable than mine," Brody teased, responding to Andersen's obvious cue.

"Can't complain," Andersen said, flashing a toothy grin. Polishing his watch on his lapel, he asked, "Are you living in the city, or just passing through?"

Brody wasn't quite sure what to say to that. He'd returned to New York at the start of the summer after being away in Paris, and found his father was gravely ill. Much of that season had been spent in a daze, the hours alternately racing or crawling past as he tried his best to help the frail man navigate the passage from this life to the next. There'd been hands to hold, sheets to change, names to remember. Then letters to write, arrangements to be made and promises to keep. The funeral had been a lovely affair (as far as those things go), attended by two hundred upstanding citizens from New York and beyond, chief among them the members of the Fraternal Order of the Unknown Philosophers.

The dozen or so members of the group had been of great comfort to Brody, congregating every Wednesday evening in his father's optician's shop to carry on with the work of the order—the pursuit of the unknown. Brody had closed the shop to business, but had left the sign hanging over the door: MR. TOBIAS BRODY, OPTICIAN. IMPORTER AND MAKER OF PHILOSOPHICAL INSTRUMENTS, SINCE 1834. He hadn't given much thought as to what he was going to do with the place, or whether or not he was going to stay. The Philosophers were so happily consumed with planning their upcoming symposium; he hadn't had the heart to turn them away. He'd actually grown quite fond of them these past few weeks, especially Mr. Alden Dashley, a man who wasn't afraid to admit he didn't know everything about everything. Brody had been surrounded by arrogance (intellectual and otherwise) while in Paris and he'd almost forgotten what it was like to move among forthright peers and good friends.

"I'm living here," Brody finally answered, thinking it might be time he made up his mind to stay.

"Same here," Andersen said, nodding. "I've got a little place over on Twenty-Sixth. How about we team up tonight, for old times' sake? We can play some Faro, take in a boxing match, paint the town red. I hear there's a house in the Tenderloin with girls who cater to stumpies. You keen to pay it a visit? Excepting the gambling, I'll happily foot the bill. It's been a good week."

Shaking his head, Brody replied, "I'm sorry, but I've got other plans." He'd been looking forward to spending a quiet evening in front of the fire—browsing through old issues of *Scientific American* and reading a novel he'd picked up at Brentano's Books called *Dr. Heidenhoff's Process*, about a doctor who develops a mechanical method of eradicating painful memories from his subjects' brains.

Andersen persisted. "Send your regrets and come out with me instead. I promise it'll prove more entertaining than whatever you've got planned." Leaning forward on his elbows he lowered his voice and said, "How about I take you out to Blackwell's Island to dance with the lady lunatics."

Brody stared at Andersen. "Surely you jest."

"Not in the least," Andersen replied, raising an eyebrow. "The place boasts several inmates who are young and fair and not too far out of their heads. It's Manhattan's best-kept secret. Whole parties of gents take a ferry out there on Saturday nights to have a waltz or two and tour the asylum. The musicians that play for the dances are some of the finest in the city, on par with the little orchestra that plays at Delmonico's."

"Sounds like quite the outing," Brody said, attempting to hide his disgust.

"Remember the nurse who used to look after us at the Stump?" Andersen asked.

"Nurse Fitch," Brody said, the haggard woman's face looming in his mind. Most of the men had been terribly unkind to her, so foul he'd wondered why she hadn't poisoned their pabulum.

"Fitch the Bitch!" Andersen said with a laugh. "Hand to God, one of the loonies at the asylum is the spitting image of her. You gotta see it to believe it."

"Perhaps another time," Brody offered.

Handing Brody his card, Andersen said, "God, it's great to see you. Let's get together soon, eh St. Nick?"

"Soon," Brody replied, tucking the card away. Rising from his seat he gave Andersen a polite bow. "Be well," he said as he headed for the door.

Andersen bellowed after him, "You too, you old stumpy!"

In the lobby, Brody stopped to check his watch—twenty after ten. His breakfast with Alden's wife and her interesting friend, Miss Thom, was almost upon him. He'd hoped to have time to conduct a brief experiment of psychical research before their arrival. "Damn Andersen," he mumbled under his breath. How could one person talk so much without saying anything of interest? *Never mind all that now*, he thought. He needed to make the most of the minutes he still had.

Taking a small brass compass from his pocket, he held the instrument in the palm of his hand. Walking towards the Ladies' Entrance, he kept his eyes fixed on the compass's needle. Judith Dashley had told him that every time she got to the end of that corridor, she felt as if she was surrounded by beings she couldn't see: "The air grows cold, even when the door's shut, and I get gooseflesh up and down my arms." Surprisingly, she hadn't seemed the least bit troubled by it. On the contrary, she'd been downright giddy when she'd explained that she suspected the beings were the ghosts said to inhabit the hotel.

Like her, Brody was intensely interested in what remained after someone (or something) had been lost. If a phantom of his arm remained after his limb was taken, it stood to reason that a shadowy figure of a whole person might be left behind after death. If he could sense his missing arm, then why wasn't it possible for Mrs. Dashley to sense the presence of beings who'd passed? Sensing the spirits of the dead wasn't enough to prove they existed, of course, but surely such sensations shouldn't be dismissed. What was needed was measurable evidence. He liked Alden's wife well enough, but she wasn't, by any stretch of the imagination, well versed in the scientific method or, for that matter, true mediumship.

Dr. Brody paused at the end of the corridor. No sooner

had he stopped than the needle on his compass began to spin with wild abandon, moving so erratically he thought the instrument might break. Oh, ho! This was better than he'd hoped! He'd guessed that if there were any ghosts near, the compass would register an electromagnetic disturbance, but he'd never imagined the sign would be so blatant. Smiling broadly, the doctor stared at the whirling needle and whispered, "Would you look at that!"

Mr. Stevens' ghost flew to the doctor's side and peered over his shoulder.

The spirits of three scrubber girls raced down the corridor towards them pursuing a smaller, younger ghost—that of a little boy. He was new to the hotel, but not to the afterlife. "Master Dashley!" they sang in unison. "Get back here you little imp! If you don't do as we say, we'll put you in the dumbwaiter and send you through the wash!"

Scampering like a scared rabbit, Billy Dashley's spirit slipped between Dr. Brody's legs and ran towards his mother who was coming down the corridor from the main staircase.

Judith Dashley felt a chill rush up her spine. "Dr. Brody," she said, pulling her shawl around her shoulders. "Weren't we supposed to meet in the dining hall?"

Quickly stowing his compass, Dr. Brody said, "You're quite right, Mrs. Dashley. I hope I haven't kept you waiting."

Placing her hand on the doctor's arm, she whispered, "You can't fool me. I saw what you were up to."

"You did?" Brody answered. He couldn't recall discussing his theory of ghostly energies and electromagnetic forces with her the other night at dinner. In fact he was positive they hadn't. Was she as much of a mind reader as she claimed her friend to be?

"Of course I did," she replied with a wink. "You were hoping to catch a glimpse of Miss Thom upon her arrival. I knew I shouldn't have pointed her out to you through the teashop window. It doesn't seem fair that you can recognize her when she knows next to nothing about you."

"It seems perfectly fair to me," Brody teased. "How else am I to believe in her abilities as a seer? I put my trust in you, Mrs. Dashley. I hope you haven't deceived me."

Cheeks turning pink, Judith stammered, "I assure you, I haven't!"

"And I can assure you that I wasn't attempting to ambush poor Miss Thom. If you must know, I was hoping to cross paths with a ghost."

Judith's eyes lit up. "So you believe what I told you about my encounters here?"

"I believe you felt something, yes."

"Am I to take it that you believe in ghosts?"

"I neither believe nor disbelieve, but I hope to settle the matter for myself very soon. I envy your confidence when it comes to detecting spirits."

"You shouldn't," she said, shaking her head. "While it might be fashionable for a lady to attend a public lecture on the afterlife, or participate in a séance from time to time, claiming to have seen a ghost yourself does not go down well in polite circles. I confess I'm rather envious of you and Alden and the rest of the Philosophers. You men of science, you *possibilitists*, as my dear husband would say, can engage yourselves in the pursuit of the unknown around the clock and no one bats an eye. If a woman of social standing dares to speak of what can be felt but not seen, or unwittingly mutters to herself under her breath, why, it's off to the doctor to have her head examined! I suppose by confessing my experiences to you I've given you my trust, dear doctor. I hope you're the man I think you to be."

"What sort of man is that?" Dr. Brody asked.

"A man who believes women."

Quinn Brody had certainly encountered plenty of men who didn't, Dr. Mitchell being foremost among them. After the war, he'd studied with Mitchell at the Infirmary for Nervous Diseases, and as a result he'd quickly discovered the full measure of the man. In nearly every case that involved a female patient, he'd witnessed Mitchell chastising them (often quite severely) for "thinking, day-dreaming and fretting, too readily and too much." He'd diagnosed every woman who had a stray feeling, craving, desire, wish, interest, worry, affection, inkling, suspicion, knowing, predilection or ability, with nervous exhaustion. In an attempt to cure these "poor creatures" he'd ordered them to be shuttered away at home, or committed to an asylum. There was no strenuous activity prescribed, no adventure-filled trips to the West—only bed rest and boredom leading to loneliness and desperation.

When Brody had tried to discuss the matter, the cranky neurologist had insisted, "They've got no one to blame but themselves. They've taxed their minds into a state of nervous exhaustion. Someone needs to tell them enough is enough. Women's minds are weak and fragile, invariably prone to shock, disorder, delusion and hysteria." Finding Mitchell's methodology woefully lacking, Brody had chosen to go to Paris in search of more progressive thought. He'd had no idea that once he got there, he'd discover something far worse.

As the chimes in the lobby announced the half hour, Judith said, "Miss Thom will be here any minute. Shall we head to the dining hall and wait for her there?"

"After you," Dr. Brody replied.

Adelaide arrived ten minutes late, wearing a scarlet promenade dress trimmed with jet buttons, swirling soutache, and a fluted silk flounce elegantly circling the hem of her skirt. Her matching veiled bonnet was topped with a cluster of crepe roses, and a single black ostrich plume poised like a jaunty question mark atop her head. Her tardiness had been calculated so she might catch sight of Dr. Brody before they met face to face. Pausing behind a potted palm inside the dining hall entrance, she scanned the room for Judith.

She spotted her friend at a secluded corner table a few yards away, giving her full attention to a gentleman Adelaide assumed was the doctor. Taking a long look at him, she decided that perhaps he did warrant the blushing Judith had done when she'd mentioned his name in the shop. His dark hair was swept to the side and slightly unkempt, yet his face was freshly shaven. This said to Adelaide that although he wasn't one to fuss over his looks, he liked the feel of hot towels on his neck and the scrape of the barber's blade against his chin. Looking on in some amazement, she watched as Judith gestured enthusiastically (no doubt telling the poor man every last detail of the ongoing renovations at Marble Row) while Dr. Brody nodded and smiled, and barely spoke. How refreshing it was to see a man sit contentedly, free from the urge to dominate the conversation. Each time he took a drink from his cup, his movements were thoughtful, refined, exact.

Before she could appraise him any further, she caught Judith glancing impatiently towards the door. *Better get moving*, Adelaide thought, straightening her skirts. There was a fine line between running late and being rude, and when it came to Judith Dashley, it was best not to cross it.

Gliding past three Boston ferns, a cluttered teacart and a handful of waiters, Adelaide approached the table with a friendly smile. "Good morning," she said.

"My dear Adelaide!" Judith turned in her seat, the wires of her bustle softly creaking in protest. "So lovely to see you at last." (Judith's way of saying, "You're late, but you're forgiven.")

Dr. Brody had risen from his chair and was waiting to be introduced.

Adelaide stared at him, biting her lip.

Commanding. Proper. Shoulders back. A military man.

Eyes, blue. Long lashes. Faded handkerchief, monogrammed.

Nose freckled, shoes dusty. He likes a good walk.

Crow's feet. Dimple in the chin (the Devil is within).

"Miss Adelaide Thom," Judith announced, "allow me to introduce Dr. Quinn Brody."

"A pleasure to meet you, Dr. Brody," Adelaide said, ready to extend her hand in greeting should the gentleman offer his.

"The pleasure is mine," Brody replied, keeping his hand at his side.

Adelaide drew her hand back as if she were a cat with an injured paw. *How stupid am I?* she thought. *Why didn't I notice the slight tick in his right shoulder, the stiff false fingers at his cuff? Why didn't Judith share this important detail instead of leaving it as a surprise?* Flushed with embarrassment, she stumbled slightly as a waiter offered her the chair next to Brody's. "Thank you," she said, relieved to take her seat. It wasn't the doctor's lack of an arm that had unsettled her, it was being caught unawares. She was the one who was supposed to take people by surprise. She was supposed to have, as it were, the upper hand.

The waiter stood at attention, pressed towel draped over his arm.

"Are we ready to order?" Judith asked, breaking the awkward silence.

Brody handed Adelaide the menu card. "I've already made up my mind," he said.

Adelaide gave the card a cursory glance. "Shirred eggs, and tea, please," she said, before passing the card to Judith.

Judith handed it to the waiter. "Just toast and tea for me."

"I'll have the shirred eggs as well," Brody said, "and another cup of coffee."

Adelaide lifted the dark swath of her lace veil and pinned it to the top of her hat. *No need to hide*, she thought. *Let's see what other secrets Judith may or may not have kept.*

There was no moment of shock when Brody looked at her face, no revulsion, no wide-eyed stare, no uncomfortable downward gaze. Only a warm, kindly smile, as if he were seeing an old friend.

Adelaide knew this had to mean that Judith had somehow arranged for the doctor to catch sight of her before their meeting. Perplexed, she wondered, *Dear Judith, what are you playing at?*

Judith was watching her with smug satisfaction. Giving her friend a sideways glance, Adelaide got a sly, encouraging wink in return. *Ah ha!* she thought. Judith means to make a match. All that blushing, all that talk about the handsome Dr. Brody wasn't meant to be a confession, but an enticement.

How many times had Judith boasted of her talent for matchmaking—describing in great detail the joy she'd felt in swapping place cards at this or that soirée in order to kindle the flames of desire? Adelaide had never dreamed she'd be on the receiving end of one of Judith's romantic schemes. What nerve! Step right up and see the one-armed man converse with the one-eyed girl! *Well Mrs. Dashley, if it's a show you want, you're about to get one.*

"Would you like me to pour your tea for you?" the waiter asked, returning to the table with breakfast.

"Yes," Judith answered with a polite nod.

"No," Adelaide said, shaking her head. Staring at Judith she added, "I can help myself."

Judith frowned and spooned a generous helping of orange marmalade on her toast.

Dr. Brody stirred sugar into his coffee, one lump at a time. Turning to Adelaide, he gamely said, "Mrs. Dashley tells me you're a mind reader by profession. A seer of sorts."

"I am," Adelaide answered.

"Fascinating," Brody said, taking a sip. "I'm curious to know, what exactly does that entail?"

"A little of this, a little of that."

Judith wiped a few stray crumbs from the corner of her mouth. "Come now, Adelaide, that's not much of an answer."

Adelaide pierced the quivering yolk of one of her eggs with her fork. "It wasn't much of a question."

Judith forced a laugh. "Why be so coy? Dr. Brody won't give your secrets away."

"He can do whatever he likes with my secrets. I'll happily tell them to him right now." Staring at Brody she said, "One: I don't play tricks. Two: I don't entertain skeptics."

At that, Judith dropped her cup, spilling tea down the front of her dress. "Oh dear!" she exclaimed, dabbing at her skirt with her napkin. "If I don't see to this right away, the stains will never come out. You'll excuse me, won't you?"

"I'll come with you," Adelaide offered.

"No, no," Judith protested. "You stay and enjoy your breakfast. It wouldn't be right to abandon the good doctor."

Looking puzzled, Brody said, "If you both must go, I'll be fine alone—"

"Nonsense," Judith said, standing. "Adelaide will stay. I insist."

Dr. Brody stood, as per good manners.

Adelaide stood, too, wishing she could give Judith a piece of her mind. "We'll catch up later, then? Perhaps at the shop?"

"Yes," Judith answered, "at the shop." Then moving close to Adelaide she gave her a kiss on the cheek. In a soft whisper she said, "Stop making everything so difficult. He's really a lovely man."

Pulling away from her friend, Adelaide said, "Good day to you, Judith."

After Judith had made her farewells, Adelaide and the doctor sat down and ate their eggs in silence.

Once Adelaide had thought things through, she realized that Brody had been as much in the dark as she as to Judith's scheme. Furthermore, it had been quite a long time since she'd shared a meal with a polite and handsome man. Before the attack, she'd had no trouble making small talk with any gentleman she met; in fact, she'd prided herself in being a flirt. That part of her now felt distant and foreign, but she supposed she could make an attempt at being interesting, at least. There was nothing left to do then but be herself. Saying the first thing that came to mind, she asked, "Did you keep it?"

"Hmm?" Dr. Brody asked, looking around as if there was something he might've missed.

"Your arm?" Adelaide said. "Did you keep it? Maybe give it a proper burial?" She wanted to see how far she could take things before the gentleman flinched. "I once met a man who paid to have the bones of his left leg extracted after his limb was taken. He keeps them on display in his house."

"Interesting," Dr. Brody replied. "But no, I lost it in the war. It was too . . . well never mind what it was. Suffice to say, there wasn't much left to keep."

Adelaide poured herself another cup of tea. Maybe this wouldn't be a complete wash after all. "As you may have gathered, I'm not squeamish," she said, pointing to her scars.

"Ah, well then," Brody replied. "I'll put the same question to you. Did you keep it?"

Laughing, Adelaide answered, "Yes. It resides in a lovely little bottle beside my bed."

Dr. Brody laughed, too, then held up his cup to show the waiter he wanted more coffee. Turning back to Adelaide he said, "I'd like you to know that I'm not a skeptic."

"What are you then, Dr. Brody?"

"A man of science."

"Aren't they the same?"

He shook his head. "A skeptic is only interested in being right. I'm only interested in finding truth."

"Even if there's a chance your theories are wrong?"

"Especially then, because it means I might be on my way to discovering something new."

All Adelaide could think was that the doctor's eyes were a beautiful shade of blue. (And, if she wasn't mistaken, there was a shade of interest in them, too, keen and real and the slightest bit improper.) Maybe Judith's matchmaking powers were greater than she'd guessed. There was only one way to find out. "Scientists occupy themselves with theories, tests and demonstrations, do they not?" she asked.

"Largely, yes."

"Then why bother discussing my occupation when I can treat you to a demonstration."

"Here?"

"Why not?" Adelaide said. "I'm willing if you are. The proof will be in the doing."

"If you like," Dr. Brody said, "although I'm not quite sure how you wish to go about it."

Moving her chair so close her knee brushed against his, she said, "Give me your hand."

Brody did as he was told.

Elbows resting on the table, Adelaide cradled the doctor's hand in hers. Tracing the lines on his palm with her finger she asked, "Past, present or future—which would you like me to see?"

"Past," the doctor quickly answered, as if he'd made the choice ahead of time.

"All right," Adelaide said. "Past it is. Shall we begin?"

"I suppose so," Dr. Brody replied, then gave her a more assured "Yes."

Ignoring the chatter and clinking of cutlery on plates all around them, Adelaide closed her eyes. She took a deep breath and inhaled a scent that was medicinal and clean. It reminded her of waking up in the operating theatre at Bellevue with a dozen surgeons gathered around her. "Carbolic soap," she said, opening her eyes again. "A tool of Listerism. You used it then, as you use it now, because you believe in things that can't be seen." Examining the doctor's graceful yet strong fingers, she added, "And it reminds you of who you used to be."

Glancing at the handkerchief folded in the breast pocket of his coat, Adelaide saw that the monogram, though elegantly stitched, was faded. It wasn't something he'd gotten for himself. It was a gift from long ago, from someone he'd loved, so he hadn't the heart to replace it. "You live alone," she said, "but that wasn't always the case. You had a wife, but she's been gone for several years."

Brody looked towards Heaven, then lowered his gaze and closed his eyes.

"She believed in God," Adelaide said, pushing forward, "but you're not sure He exists. She promised she'd send you a sign, but you've never received it." Fingers resting on his wrist, Adelaide felt the doctor's heartbeat begin to race. Leaning close, she whispered, "You're starting to wonder if you ever will."

Dr. Brody could barely breathe—not because she'd laid bare his past, but because she'd exposed his heart. How could this lilac-scented bohemian know so much about him? She'd spoken of things he'd never shared with anyone. What a gift she had. What a beautiful mind she'd been given. When Judith had pointed her out to him, he hadn't been able to take his eyes off her scars, couldn't help but think of how he might've done things differently if he'd been the one to put the scalpel to her skin. Now that he was in her presence, those thoughts, along with her scars, had faded away. All he could think of was how rare she was, this woman who could see into a heart he'd thought was no longer even there.

"Thank you, Miss Thom," he said, wondering if she knew how right she'd been. Oh how he'd like to spend hour after hour in pursuit of how her brain worked!

"You're welcome," Adelaide replied, her palms moist, her face flushing. "It was my pleasure." She wondered if she shouldn't be thanking him instead. She'd almost forgotten how it felt to blush.

My Dearest Eleanor,
Please meet me at Lady Liberty's Torch at eleven a.m. I must speak with you today. It's urgent.
Come alone to the usual spot.
This is a private matter.
Yours,
L.N.

Seeing Is Believing.

THE NOTE WAS slipped under the shop door by an anonymous hand.

Perdu, first to see it, pinched the letter in his beak and delivered it to Eleanor.

"Good bird," Eleanor said, rewarding the raven with a hunk of stale bread.

While the bird pecked at the treat, Eleanor read the brief missive and thought, *Something's gone wrong*. The clock on the shelf read quarter to eleven. Was that right or had the infernal thing wound down again? Leaning close, Eleanor listened for the steady click of its works. Everything seemed to be in order.

She tucked the note inside a small leather satchel at her waist. She'd owned the bag since she was young, had carried it with her everywhere—through the meadow behind her mother's cottage, into the woods at the edge of the meadow, along the banks of the river that would one day lead her away from the place she'd called home. Each time she opened the little bag she was reminded of her childhood, of days spent gathering roots and blossoms for her mother and muddy worms to present to Perdu as treats. These days she used the purse for holding things she needed in her daily doings—pencil and paper, a phial of salt, a ball of beeswax pierced with pins and needles, a trio of engraved measuring spoons (*pinch, dash, smidgen*), a few coins to give to the needy, and a packet of parchment envelopes for collecting botanical specimens in the park. Opening a small wooden cabinet under the counter, she brought out a few other items she thought she might need—among them, mandrake root for protection and a tangle of dried oarweed stalks (as she suspected the young woman might be late with her courses).

She wished she knew when Adelaide would be back from breakfast. She really didn't like the thought of leaving Beatrice alone on her first day on the job. Ten minutes to eleven. No time left to fret. Slipping beneath the counter again, she fetched three paper-wrapped parcels and placed them on the shelf. One was labelled "Mrs. Anna Stewart," another "Miss Lorna Gowan" and the third "Mrs. Judith Dashley." Thank heavens she'd already filled the orders. At least that much had gone according to plan.

Beatrice was across the room, washing the front window, with Perdu overseeing her efforts. The shop was free from customers, but Eleanor had no idea how long the lull might last. Saturday mornings were unpredictable, as women tended to come through the door in fits and starts. She suspected their ebb and flow was dependent on things like the phase of the moon, the latest play at Booth's Theatre, the season of the year, the sales at Macy's, the state of the weather.

With any luck the shop would stay quiet at least until after noon and surely she wouldn't be gone any longer than that. Walking over to Beatrice, Eleanor gave the girl's shoulder a soft tap.

Beatrice dropped the rag she was holding into a wash bucket at her feet. The air around her was scented with vinegar and lemon. "Let me know if I've missed any spots. I'll happily go after them again."

Eleanor found the girl's enthusiasm endearing. Had she ever been that eager? "You're doing a fine job," she said, giving Beatrice's arm a reassuring squeeze. "In fact, I was wondering if you might be up to the task of looking after the shop while I run a quick errand?"

Beatrice crinkled her brow. She didn't want to seem unwilling. She wanted to do her best, but she wasn't sure she wanted that much responsibility just yet. "I could run the errand for you," she volunteered. "I studied several maps of the city before I came. I'm sure I can find my way around, given a few landmarks."

"It's very kind of you to offer," Eleanor said, "but I'm afraid the task is mine alone."

"In that case," Beatrice said, "I'd be glad to look after the shop." She hoped she appeared more confident than she felt.

"Are you sure you're all right with this?" Eleanor asked. "If not, I can close up until I get back."

"Please don't do that on my account," Beatrice said. "I promise if I feel the slightest bit uneasy, I'll turn the sign in the window and lock the door."

"All right then," Eleanor replied. "Here are the things you'll need to remember."

Wiping her hands on her apron, Beatrice gave an eager nod.

"First," Eleanor said, pointing to the shelves behind the counter, "don't trouble yourself with every jar and tin. Orange pekoe, Darjeeling and jasmine are the most popular choices among the fashionable set, so if you offer them as 'our preferred teas,' chances are you won't need to bother with anything else. They're kept in those three large containers to the right of the stove."

"I see them," Beatrice said, pointing to a trio of squat, wide-mouthed crocks.

Realizing she hadn't bothered to label the jars, Eleanor asked, "And you know how to tell the teas apart?"

"Yes," Beatrice answered. "They're among my aunt Lydia's favourites."

"Excellent."

"But suppose someone isn't content to choose one of those three?" Beatrice asked.

"Explain to them that you're new and that those are the teas you brew best. If they seem put out, offer a sweet on the house."

"Right," Beatrice said. "On the house."

"And if a customer presents you with a question you can't answer, don't guess or make up some silly story. Just admit that you don't know and tell them they're welcome to wait until I come back. Whatever you do, don't lie."

"No," Beatrice said, shaking her head. "I mean yes. I won't guess. I won't lie."

"Good."

As Eleanor started for the door, Beatrice spotted the parcels on the counter. "Miss St. Clair," she called, "what are those?"

"Oh, heavens," Eleanor said, rushing back. "Well noticed, dear girl. They're orders waiting to be picked up—special requests."

"Do you get many of those?"

"Yes indeed. If a lady tells you there's something out of the ordinary she'd like me to make, then write it down and place it in the shop's ledger. The book is under the counter."

The clock's chimes sounded eleven times, chiding Eleanor. "I'm sorry, but I really must go. You're sure you'll be all right?"

"Don't worry about me. I'll manage until you return," Beatrice answered.

Perdu waddled behind his mistress and tugged at her skirt.

"I'll be back soon," Eleanor said, bending down to speak to her pet. "Be good," she whispered. "No magic while I'm gone."

Once Eleanor was out the door, Beatrice spread her arms wide in the middle of the shop floor and twirled.

Perdu whistled with approval.

Although she was nervous, Beatrice couldn't help but feel she'd been given the perfect opportunity to prove her worth. Yesterday things had been so topsy-turvy she'd wondered if she'd ever feel right again. Today, aside from the brief vision that had appeared in the mirror during breakfast, things seemed better, maybe even fortuitous. There were so many questions she had for Miss St. Clair (and Miss Thom, too, if she could penetrate her reserve), but they'd have to wait. Curtsying to the raven, Beatrice rehearsed her best greeting in anticipation of her first customer: "Welcome to St. Clair and Thom's Tea and Sympathy. How may I serve you today?"

Upstairs, a window that overlooked the street rattled in its sash.

Perdu hopped to the counter and tilted his head towards the ceiling. "Hush!" he warned. "She's coming."

No sooner had the bird spoken, than a woman came through the door dressed in a long black cloak.

"Welcome to Tea and Sympathy," Beatrice said, hands folded at her waist. "How may I serve you?"

"Is the seer here?" the woman asked, looking past Beatrice to the back of the shop. "Is she available for consultation?"

"I'm afraid Miss Thom is out," Beatrice replied. "But I imagine she'll return soon, if you'd like to wait."

"How long will that take?"

"I can't say for certain."

The cloak the woman was wearing nearly swallowed her whole. Beatrice could tell by the tone of her voice that she wasn't pleased. The only bright spot on the woman's person was a small brass bell that dangled around her neck, its jangle as impatient and tinny as its owner's words.

Pointing to the clock behind the counter the woman asked, "Is that the right time?"

"I believe so," Beatrice answered.

"Then no, I wouldn't like to wait."

Thinking fast, Beatrice asked, "Would you like to leave your name? Or a message for Miss Thom?"

With a sneer the woman replied, "Tell her God sees who she is and what she does." Looking Beatrice up and down she clicked her tongue. "Caught in Satan's web at such a tender age. Don't you know this place is designed to lead women astray? God bless you, my child. May you soon see the light." And with that, she exited the shop.

Leaning on the counter Beatrice looked at Perdu. "Was it something I said?"

Perdu hissed and ruffled his feathers, looking as if he'd sprouted a sooty lion's mane.

Beatrice shrugged off the woman's words, and wondered how she should pass the time. She'd spent much of the morning washing cups, saucers and windowpanes, and filling honey pots. What was left to be done? Everything seemed to be in order. Lighting the stove, she put a kettle on, thinking she might as well brew herself a cup of tea. As she waited for the water to boil, she turned to the crocks of tea near the stove and said, "Orange pekoe for me, please." Fetching a cup, saucer and teaspoon, she made a half pirouette, cut short when the toe of her left shoe got caught in a gap between the floorboards. The cup went airborne, but Beatrice caught it in one graceful swoop before it crashed, sacrificing the teaspoon for the china. When she bent to retrieve the spoon, she spied a large book sitting on the shelf beneath the counter, overflowing with scraps of paper and coloured ribbons that stuck like snake's tongues from between its pages. Was this the ledger Miss St. Clair had mentioned that was meant for special orders? Lifting the heavy volume to the counter, Beatrice decided it might be in her best interest to inspect it. After all, as Aunt Lydia would say, fortune favours the prepared mind.

Perdu watched from his perch, not the least bit surprised.

Beatrice opened the book's cover and found the following verse.

This book belongs to none but me,
For there's my name inside to see.
To steal this book, if you should try,
It's by the throat you'll hang high.
And ravens then will gather 'bout,

To find your eyes and pull them out.
And when you're screaming 'oh, oh, oh!'
Remember, you deserved this woe.

Beatrice looked to Perdu for direction. "I'm not stealing it," she said. "I'm only looking."

The raven chortled and croaked, "Only looking."

Taking his response as permission, Beatrice turned the pages one by one. Botanical sketches gave way to herbal remedies, which in turn led to recipes for everything from "dream tea" to "angel water." In and amongst these entries were other, more intriguing accounts of fairy rings, demon banishing and dream interpretation. Curious symbols and diagrams were annotated with instructions such as "charm against thieves," "talisman against the stupidities of wine" and "incantations for luck, love, and the dispelling of spirits." Eyes fixed on a page titled "Wish Magic," Beatrice spotted an illustration that looked remarkably like the charm she'd made for herself in Stony Point. "A Witch's Ladder" was written beneath the diagram in red ink.

Between a section called "The Oration of the Salamanders" and another called "Against Maladies and Accidents" was an entry that made Beatrice's blood run cold.

A VERSE *for* MAKING ONESELF OBLIVIOUS *to* TORTURE.

To avoid suffering under the question of a malevolent being, or when put to the stake, rope, rock, rack, pricking, scolding, dunking or screws—swallow a note on which the following words have been written in your own blood.

Before she could read any further, the shop's door opened again to admit a pleasant-looking woman with a sweet-faced boy clinging to her skirts. The woman, who was carrying a large bouquet of flowers, was having great difficulty getting through the door.

Coming to the rescue, Beatrice held the door for her, and gave the boy a friendly wink. "I've got it," she said. "Please come inside. Watch your step."

As the woman fussed with her skirts, the boy leapt over the threshold. Running to the back of the store he hid under Adelaide's fortune-telling table, peeking at them from beneath the fringe of the tablecloth.

"Welcome to Tea and Sympathy," Beatrice announced. "How may I serve you?"

"Well you can start," the woman replied, "by telling me who you are."

Beatrice's cheeks flushed. "Miss Beatrice Dunn," she stammered, "the newly hired help."

Circling around Beatrice, the woman scrutinized her carefully, then nodded with approval. "Lovely to make your acquaintance, Miss Dunn. I'm Mrs. Judith Dashley, friend of the proprietors."

"Mrs. Dashley!" Beatrice exclaimed, recognizing the name from one of the parcels that was waiting on the counter. "So pleased to meet you."

Judith smiled with the satisfaction of someone who enjoyed being known. Clutching the bouquet, she asked, "Would Miss Thom happen to be about? I've brought her a present."

"I'm afraid not," Beatrice replied, shaking her head.

"Oh dear," Judith said. "I'm not quite sure what to make of that."

"I beg your pardon?" Beatrice asked.

With a sigh, Judith plucked a wilted petal from an otherwise unblemished white rose. "It's nothing," she said. "Or it could be something . . . and that could be a good thing, I guess. Yes, let's hope for that."

In addition to the rose, the pretty bouquet contained geranium, heather, white chrysanthemum and ivy. Beatrice guessed that if she had the floriography right (and she was sure that she had), the flowers were meant to be a peace offering. Holding her hands out to Mrs. Dashley, she asked, "Would you like me to put those in some water?"

Judith happily surrendered the bouquet. "Yes, please," she said. "How very thoughtful of you."

Beatrice took the flowers and set them inside a water pitcher. "Miss Thom should be back soon. I'd be happy to make you some tea if you'd like to wait for her return."

Nodding, Judith settled herself in the window seat at the front of the shop.

"What kind of tea would you prefer—Darjeeling, orange pekoe, jasmine?"

"Hmm . . ." Judith pondered, finger to her chin. "Darjeeling, I think . . . no, wait, orange pekoe. No, begging your pardon, it's Saturday isn't it—so let's make it jasmine. Saturday mornings and jasmine tea go together nicely, wouldn't you agree?"

"Jasmine it is," Beatrice said, relieved.

As she prepared the tea, Beatrice heard laughter waft from under Adelaide's table. She wondered if she should offer to make something for the little boy as well—warm milk, toast with honey, a slice of lemon tart? No, wait, on second thought, perhaps she shouldn't. Mothers had hard and fast rules about indulging their children, and she didn't wish to do anything that might offend Mrs. Dashley. For the time being, she'd leave well enough alone.

Perdu, however, couldn't resist the urge to meddle with the lad. Hopping to the floor, he waddled towards the table and stuck his head under the tablecloth. In a low, throaty whisper he said, "Boo."

The boy let out a gleeful squeal.

Beatrice stifled a laugh.

As she delivered the tea to Mrs. Dashley, she was amazed to find the woman staring at the street, seemingly deaf to her child's excitement. Such calm, she thought. Such nonchalance. "This tea smells divine," Judith said, sniffing at the ribbon of steam that was whirling from the pot's spout.

"Would you like me to pour?" Beatrice asked, at the ready with honey and milk.

Motioning to the seat across from her, Judith suggested, "How about you fetch another cup and join me? Drinking tea should never be a solitary endeavour."

"That's very kind of you, Mrs. Dashley," Beatrice said, "but I'm not sure Miss St. Clair would approve."

"Miss St. Clair isn't here," Judith argued, "and I insist."

"All right then," Beatrice replied. "If you insist."

On her way back to the counter, Beatrice spotted a shiny marble rolling towards her along a groove between two floorboards. Catching it, she picked up the sweet blue orb and stared at the tiny constellation of bubbles trapped within it. This must belong to Mrs. Dashley's boy, she thought. Did he know he'd lost it? Walking to Adelaide's table, Beatrice lifted the edge of the tablecloth expecting to find him there. Much to her surprise, he was gone.

"Everything all right?" Judith called from across the room.

"Yes," Beatrice replied as she glanced around the shop to see where he might've got to. "I'll be right there." The last thing she wanted was to get him in trouble. Tucking the marble in her pocket, she fetched a cup along with the parcel Eleanor had set aside for Mrs. Dashley.

"Ah yes," Judith said, giving the parcel an affectionate pat. "Eleanor's Sweet Dreams Tea—have you had the pleasure of trying it?"

"No," Beatrice answered, wondering if it was the same tea that was mentioned in the book she'd found.

Holding the package to her nose, Judith inhaled deeply. "It works like a charm. I'd been having the most terrible time falling asleep, but this tea fixed all that. Just one cup an hour before bed and I drift off like a baby. Miss St. Clair has given it a fitting name—I've been having the most wonderful dreams since I started drinking it."

"Really?" Beatrice asked as she poured tea into Mrs. Dashley's cup.

"Beyond belief," Judith said, offering, passing, accepting, honey, sugar, milk. "Just last night I dreamt of a secret room, hidden from everyone in the world except me. It looked identical to the parlour in my house on Marble Row, only everything was white—the furniture, the draperies, the fixtures, the flowers. There was no clock, no mirror, no letter tray, no doorbell. Nothing was expected of me, and no one came to call except for one delightful visitor, my dear little Billy."

"Your son?" Beatrice asked, puzzled as to why Mrs. Dashley would consider her child a visitor in her own house.

"That's right," Judith replied. "Did Eleanor tell you about him?"

"No," Beatrice said, remembering that Eleanor had instructed her not to lie. "She didn't."

Judith took a sip of tea and smiled. "He was such a beautiful child, so full of joy and life. I can't believe it's been five years since he's been gone."

Gooseflesh blossomed on Beatrice's arms as the sound of a child's footsteps seemed to race in circles around the shop.

Perdu ruffled his feathers and nervously sidestepped on his perch.

Oblivious, Judith closed her eyes in wistful thought.

Beatrice tried to make sense of it. Hand in her pocket, she felt for the marble she'd found on the floor. It was solid, round and real, even if nothing else was.

In an instant, the boy appeared again, this time from behind his mother's chair. He stared at Beatrice with sunken eyes, his pale face shining with the sweat of sickness. Despite the form he'd now taken, his clothes were tidy, his countenance keen, and from the way he looked at his mother, Beatrice sensed that he loved her with all his heart and that he desperately wanted her to know it.

Unlike the frightful Gypsy woman, the boy's spirit didn't scare her. Perhaps it was because he was only a child, or because his mother was so incredibly kind, but any uneasiness she felt was soon replaced by an overwhelming sense of duty and care. Turning to Mrs. Dashley she quietly said, "He's here."

"Who?" Judith asked with a confused stare.

"Your son."

"Didn't you hear me? He's been gone for years."

Unable to take her eyes off the boy, Beatrice said, "I believe his spirit remains."

The colour drained from Mrs. Dashley's face. "My dear girl," she said. "I want to think well of you, I really do, so please don't toy with me. Did Miss Thom tell you to do this?"

"No," Beatrice said, shaking her head. "She did no such thing."

"Are you a medium?" Judith asked. "Some sort of spiritualist?"

"No," Beatrice said, regretting her impulse to help. "Please believe me when I say that I don't want to frighten you, or upset you in any way. I wish I could explain exactly what it is I'm seeing, but I'm not sure I can."

"Try," Judith said, desperately. "I'm listening."

The boy remained at his mother's side, as if he too were waiting for Beatrice to speak.

Taking a sip of tea to calm herself, Beatrice considered how to begin. Should she steer clear of mentioning the darker details of Billy's appearance? Yes, she thought, that would be best. His mother remembered the toll the boy's illness had taken on his body—no need to revisit those horrors. She cleared her throat and said, "There's a young boy here with a round face and dark curls. He came in with you when you entered the shop. He's all of six years old, maybe seven. He's missing a front tooth."

"Billy—" Judith cried, looking around in all directions. "Is it really you?"

Turning to the ghost, Beatrice asked, "Is that your name?"

The boy nodded.

"He's a fine lad," Beatrice said. "A real charmer."

Looming in front of Beatrice, Billy put his face to hers, nose to nose.

"A little too curious for his own good," Beatrice said, leaning back in her seat. "He's got a small, crescent-shaped scar on his left cheek. A souvenir from a nasty spill."

Billy gestured for Beatrice to gaze into his eyes. When she did, she caught a glimpse of a lovely parlour with large windows and flocked wallpaper. "He was playing too close to the edge of the mantel," she said. "He slipped and fell."

Judith gasped.

"Good thing the stove wasn't hot," Beatrice went on, rubbing her hands together as if to warm them by a fire. "He only suffered a nick, no stitches required. You'd told him a hundred times not to chase the dog through the house. He knows, Ma. He knows."

"Yes," Judith said, caught between laughter and tears, "that's right. I did."

Sticking his hand inside his coat pocket, Billy brought out a crumpled paper bag.

"What've you got there?" Beatrice asked.

"Peanuts," the boy answered with a grin. Then, holding the sack next to Beatrice's ear, he shook it and teased, "Get 'em while they're hot!"

Beatrice's mouth went dry. Parched with thirst she licked her lips, tasted salt on the tip of her tongue.

Perdu bobbed his head and let out a hungry squawk.

Billy took up the greasy, rumpled bag again, this time holding it out to his mother.

Imitating the boy's actions, Beatrice said, "He's clutching a sack of roasted peanuts like a prize and saying 'Get 'em while they're hot!'"

Judith's hands went to her face as she began to sob.

Tugging at Beatrice's sleeve, Billy begged, "Please tell my ma I'm sorry. I don't want her to be sad."

"It's all right," Beatrice said attempting to comfort mother and son, "all will be well."

Billy moved to his mother's side and placed his hand on her shoulder.

Through her tears, Judith instinctively reached to touch her hand to his.

Moved by the sweetness of their bond, Beatrice felt as if she, too, might cry. Clutching the marble tight in her fist she closed her eyes. In her mind she saw the parlour again, now with a Christmas tree in the window, decorated top to bottom with candles, beads and bows. Underneath the tree sat several toys all bearing tags that read "For Billy"—a hobby horse, a tin soldier, a pair of skates, a wooden puzzle, an India rubber ball. Bells and carols sounded in her ears, heralding a vision of mother and son. Holding hands, the pair twirled in uneven circles like a wobbly wooden top before skittering into a happy heap on the floor.

Judith attempted to recover from her tears. "Please forgive me," she said, "I didn't mean to make a fuss."

"I'm the one who should apologize. I never meant to cause you heartache."

"You didn't," Judith insisted. "You've only brought me happiness, I swear it."

She leaned towards Beatrice. "Every minute of every day since my dear boy's passing, I've tried to imagine what had become of him, and I just couldn't figure it out. Was he in Heaven? Was he lost? Nothing anyone said has brought me peace. I fretted over Billy after his death more than I did when he was alive. I've never felt such worry in my life! It's weighed on me something fierce . . . right up to the moment you mentioned those silly peanuts. They were his favourite treat. He used to beg for pennies to give the vendor whenever we visited the park, pulling at my sleeve until I gave in. Bless you, my dear girl! Bless you again and again and again. Bless you and my darling Billy and those wondrous peanuts!"

Beatrice sat trembling, not knowing what to say. The woman was staring at her with such reverence and awe. Looking at the boy, she noticed his form was growing less distinct, his presence waning. "He's leaving now," she said. "He's fading away."

Judith begged, "Can't you make him stay?"

"I'm afraid I don't know how."

"Quick then," Judith said, "ask him something for me before he leaves?"

"Of course," Beatrice replied. "What is it?"

Hand to her heart, Judith asked, "Is he safe?"

Looking to the boy, Beatrice waited for an answer.

With a solemn nod, Billy kissed his finger and crossed his heart.

"Yes," Beatrice said, "he's safe."

May my mind be free from worry, my eyes clear of tears.
May my heart be filled with calm instead of fear.
In times of darkest turmoil, may the light of hope shine bright,
Fuelled by the knowledge that all will soon be right.

Lady Hibiscus.

ELEANOR STOOD ON the balcony of Liberty's torch waiting for Lucy Newland to arrive. It was Lucy with whom she'd had the affair, whom she'd chased the day before (but never found), who'd left a cryptic note under the door requesting they meet in the park. Yesterday, Lucy had needed to speak with her "soon." This morning, whatever was on her mind had become "urgent." Eleanor wished the young woman had given at least some small clue as to what was troubling her.

Holding fast to the railing, Eleanor kept watch on the pathway that led to the base of the popular attraction. Couples were walking arm in arm while nurses pushed baby buggies around the block. Two girls were making a game of bouncing a ball, chanting their progress as they played. "Twenty-one, twenty-two, twenty-three, twenty-four . . ." When a gangly boy scampered between the pair and interrupted their fun, the girls shouted curses at his back. "May you sprout a dog's tail! May your papa go to jail! May you step on a crack and break your mama's back!" Eleanor saw no sign of Lucy. Had she already been here and left? Reading the note again she checked to make certain she'd gotten the place and time correct. *Meet me at Lady Liberty's Torch at eleven a.m.* Yes and yes. It was just like Lucy to make her wait.

They'd met in early May when Lucy's aunt Mrs. Ida Scrope had brought her to the shop. Lucy had been a month away from marrying Cecil Newland, a successful real-estate magnate determined to leave his mark on every square inch of Manhattan. "The poor girl is beside herself with nerves," Mrs. Scrope had explained. "Have you anything to soothe her jitters?"

Taking a bottle of nerve tonic from the shelf, Eleanor had placed it on the counter in front of the fidgety flaxen-haired bride-to-be. "This should do the trick. Take one teaspoon in the morning, another at noon, and one more before bed—no more, no less. There's a verse on the back of the bottle designed to give comfort in times of distress. Don't hesitate to recite it whenever you feel tested."

The following day, Lucy had returned to the shop, this time without her aunt. With her hands behind her back, she approached the counter.

Fearing the tonic hadn't agreed with her, Eleanor had asked, "Is there anything else I can assist you with?"

"Yes and yes," Lucy had replied, giving her a smile. "Would you mind closing your eyes?"

Taken aback, Eleanor had said, "Why would I do that?"

"Indulge me," Lucy had urged. "You'll be glad you did."

Feeling foolish, Eleanor had followed Lucy's orders. After some shuffling about, Lucy had announced, "All right, Miss St. Clair. You can look."

A marble mortar and pestle, tied with a bright red bow, sat on the counter. "Is this for me?" Eleanor had asked, cupping the mortar's beautiful bowl in her hands.

"A token of my appreciation."

"That's not necessary," Eleanor had said, ready to return the gift.

"Yes, it is," Lucy had insisted.

"Why?" Eleanor had asked.

"Because I woke up this morning feeling more myself than I have my whole life."

Eleanor had had enough companions over the years (the most notable, a dark-eyed nurse named Florence with a predilection for ether) that she understood when certain cues were being given. A lick of the lips here, a well-timed compliment there, could get the point across nicely, efficiently. Sensing the young beauty's gesture was meant to test the waters, Eleanor had placed the mortar and pestle front and centre on the shelf and said, "Yes, it does seem to agree with you."

Two days later, Lucy had paid Eleanor another visit, this time with an errand boy trailing close behind carrying a large rosemary plant in a pretty brass pot. After Lucy had paid the boy for his help, she'd turned to Eleanor and asked, "Care to take a stroll with me through the park after you close shop? It's a lovely evening and it would be a shame not to take advantage of it. Please say you'll come."

The invitation had made Eleanor feel as if she was being courted, and she'd quite liked it. Her other affairs had been more accidental in nature—brief, enjoyable encounters that had filled a need. She'd never been the sort to seek out opportunities for love or lust. She'd thought herself to be more like Princess Odoline, happy to reject romantic overtures in favour of keeping company with books. Her mother had been right. Women were complicated creatures. Still, if Lucy, with her confident gaze and winning smile, insisted upon pursuing her, she wasn't going to turn her away. Impending nuptials be damned, it was spring.

They'd stopped for ice cream (Lucy's treat), then strolled along the garden paths until it was near dark, eventually finding their way to the top of the torch. The structure itself was a wonder to behold, a magnificent marriage of glass and copper metalwork. Lucy, with the last rays of the day's sunlight shining on her rosy cheeks, had leaned into Eleanor and said, "You're not like anyone I've ever known. Will you dine with me tonight?" Then she'd dared to caress Eleanor's hand. "My parents have gone to Boston, and except for the cook and maid, I'm quite alone in the house."

"Yes," Eleanor had replied, "I'd like that."

Eleanor hadn't planned on keeping the affair from Adelaide, but when things with Lucy had felt tantalizing and fresh, she'd chosen to follow her lover's lead and not say a word. The last thing she'd wanted was to unleash the barrage of questions Adelaide would be sure to heap upon her. Adelaide had always been quite free in her talk of her own exploits, but Eleanor had found it easier to play the stoic than confess to things she wasn't sure Adelaide would understand.

In a moment of weakness on their last night together before Lucy's wedding, she'd turned to her lover and asked, "Why didn't you choose to lie with your future husband instead?"

"Why would I? It's my last chance to make him wait."

Eleanor had hoped Lucy might make him wait forever.

On the sixth of June, as Lucy was becoming Mrs. Newland in an orange-blossom-bedecked affair at Trinity Church, Eleanor had stood near the shop window for much of the day, half expecting her to come running through the door.

"What's the matter with you?" Adelaide had asked. "Who are you waiting for?"

The day slipped by without a word from Lucy. A week passed and the only news Eleanor received was by way of a wedding announcement torn from the society page and delivered by Ida Scrope. "It was an astounding success!" she had reported. "Not a petal or pearl out of place. Whatever magic you performed on behalf of our dear Lucy, it certainly worked."

After reading the glowing account of bouquets, topiaries, tulle and lace, Eleanor had crumpled the paper in her hands and sighed. *The dashing groom and his radiant bride will be touring Europe for the summer. They intend to welcome visitors to their Manhattan residence in September.* Tossing it into the fire, she'd thought, *Lucy's made her choice.*

In August the bride had reappeared, once more seeking Eleanor's help. "I need something to keep my womb clear," she'd said, nervously turning her wedding ring around her finger. "I've run out of the regulating powders I purchased while abroad." She'd offered Eleanor no apology, expressed no regrets, shown no sign of being a reluctant wife other than not wanting to be a mother.

Swallowing her hurt, Eleanor had handed her a tin of tansy tea. "Drink a cup of this once a day for a full week before your courses are due. So long as you've kept proper track of things, it should provide all the help you need."

"Is there no verse to recite this time to soften my trials and woes?"

Was the young woman teasing her? Eleanor had been tempted to write something cruel on the receipt (*you've made your bed, now you must lie in it* came to mind), but she chose to take the high road instead. "The tea should suffice."

After that, Lucy had returned to the shop at least once a week—sometimes alone, sometimes with her aunt—never showing a hint of regret or longing on her lovely face. Last week when she'd asked for something stronger than the tea, Eleanor had given her a tincture of Queen Anne's lace along with instructions on how to use it.

This morning, when Eleanor had read the note that Lucy had slipped under the door, she'd assumed it could only mean one thing—she was pregnant. Why hadn't the tincture worked? And why leave a note rather than come back to the shop? If it was so important they meet at eleven in the park, why wasn't she here? Did she ever think of anyone but herself?

Just as Eleanor was about to leave, she heard footsteps on the stairs that led to the balcony. Turning, she caught sight of Lucy, decked out in a lavender walking suit and feather-laden hat. Making an attempt to smooth the wrinkles from her plain linen dress, Eleanor only said, "You're late."

"In more ways than one," Lucy replied, moving to Eleanor's side.

"I was afraid that might be the case. Did you take the tincture as I instructed?"

"You never mentioned how horrible it tastes. I couldn't stand it so I stopped."

Eleanor shook her head. "No wonder you're in a bind. How many days are you past due?"

"It doesn't matter," Lucy said, dismissing Eleanor's concern.

"It most certainly does," Eleanor chided. "I need to know how late you are, so I can decide how best to help you."

Lucy sighed. “What if I don’t want your help?”

“Then why are we here?” Eleanor asked.

Lucy didn’t reply.

“Do you want a child?” Eleanor asked, wishing she knew whether or not Lucy even wished to be married.

“I don’t know what I want anymore,” Lucy said. “I’m tired of thinking. Please tell me what to do.”

It was all Eleanor could do not to leave her there. “Why don’t you ask your aunt for advice, or better yet, your husband. I’m sure Mr. Newland would have something to say about the matter.”

“That’s not fair.”

“Life’s not fair.”

Tears in her eyes, Lucy leaned close and whispered, “He found the bottle and threw it out. I tried to explain it away as best I could, but I’m sure he didn’t believe me.”

“He knows what it’s for?”

“He seems to, yes.”

“Does he know where you got it?”

“I don’t think so,” Lucy replied, “but it’s hard to say what he does and doesn’t know, or just what he’s thinking. He gets so terribly angry sometimes. He said it’s only a matter of time until he uncovers all my secrets. I can’t imagine what he might do if he found out about us.”

Eleanor placed a hand on Lucy’s arm. “For what it’s worth,” she said, “you’re always welcome to stay with me.”

“What a scandal that would be!” Lucy said with a forced laugh.

Eleanor frowned. “I’m concerned for your welfare.”

“You might consider your own before making such an offer. The consequences could be devastating.”

"I'm not afraid of the consequences," Eleanor said. Despite the girl's fickleness, she still cared for her. If Lucy was in danger, she had to take a stand.

"Perhaps you should be," Lucy replied. "We'd both be ruined and I've no doubt that your fate would be far worse than mine. Society would turn its back on me, that's a given, but I can always run off to Paris or London to ride out the storm. You, my dear, would be tossed in the Tombs once the police got wind of the services you provide to the women of the Ladies' Mile. We were so careful to never speak of love! Why must you insist on being so self-sacrificing now?"

"This isn't about love," Eleanor retorted. "It's about liberty."

"But I'm not the one who would be thrown in a cell." Lucy shook her head in disbelief. "I don't know why I came to you about this. I quite like the way I live—my house, my parties, my dresses, my friends."

"But is that life really yours?"

Lucy's face softened. "If this is about what we shared together, please know I've no regrets. If we were living in another time or place—if I'd been your dark-eyed nurse, or you were my distant cousin, we could walk hand in hand down sidewalks or through ballrooms and no one would say a word. But you being who you are and me being who I am, our friendship was fated to end."

"My offer stands," Eleanor said. Her mother had never turned away a woman in need. *That is who we are. This is what we do.*

"I can't afford to take such a risk," Lucy said. "I've too much to lose."

"They're only losses if you perceive them to be," Eleanor insisted. "Think of what you might gain."

"By that same logic, I'm only a prisoner if I think myself one. I'm not like you, dear Eleanor. I'm weak and spoiled and afraid. It's simply not in me to be brave."

Those were the truest words Eleanor had ever heard Lucy speak.

"Here," Eleanor said, fishing in her satchel for another bottle of the tincture she'd brought with her just in case. "Ten drops beneath your tongue each morning for five days straight. It's sure to bring on your blood so long as you're less than two weeks past due. If you're any further along than that, you'll need something stronger and I'd need to look after you."

Lucy took the bottle. "This time I'll be more careful with it."

"Careful or not, it won't do you any good unless you take what's in it." Eleanor sensed that Lucy had no intention of using the tincture. There was a dullness in her eyes that said she was resigned to be more child than woman, more possession than partner in her marriage. "Send word if you need anything else," she said, reaching out to touch Lucy's hand.

Nodding, Lucy gave a weak smile. "I'll have Aunt Ida bring me something from time to time to remember you by."

"Hibiscus tea?" Eleanor asked, knowing it was her favourite.

Delivering a kiss to Eleanor's cheek, Lucy said, "Yes. I always liked hibiscus best."

Eleanor stayed awhile at the torch after Lucy left. In the gardens below, she spotted an old woman sitting by the fountain feeding the birds. The woman had once told her that the web of footpaths within the park had been arranged in such a way that anyone who visited more than once would rarely walk the same path. She'd claimed this was because the place was enchanted, guarded by the spirits of those buried far beneath the tea roses and locust trees. "Take care that you never tell a lie here," she'd warned, "or the spirits will follow you home."

Tossing the last of her crumbs, the old woman rose to trail after a group of pamphleteers making their rounds through the park. Two ladies dressed in white led the ragtag parade, carrying the standard of the National Woman Suffrage Association. Every so often the Bird Lady would bend down to collect a stray notice or bit of debris. Eleanor had seen her follow other groups in the past—the Daughters of Light, who were raising funds to build a proper base for Lady Liberty; Congregationalists from the Church of the Good Shepherd, who wished to rid the world of sin; the gentleman members of the Fraternal Order of the Unknown Philosophers, who had a question for every answer. After she'd collected all she wanted, the Bird Lady would sit on a bench with needle and thread and sew her precious scraps into paper stars and give them away to any passerby who bothered to approach her. To most, the shabby tokens were nothing more than trash, but to those who looked upon the woman's offerings with kindness, they were delicate artifacts shaped by skilled hands. Eleanor had kept every star the Bird Lady had ever given her. She planned to string them in a garland and hang them in the shop window come Christmas. Every fold, every stitch the woman made was filled with care and thought; somehow the Bird Lady found meaning in what the rest of the world tossed away. Although she didn't often speak to Eleanor, on the occasions when she did, the lilt in her voice reminded Eleanor of her mother.

She wondered if the wise Madame St. Clair could've convinced Lucy to flee her situation. As a child Eleanor had watched in awe as her mother had said whatever she thought whenever she wanted to whomever she pleased, mostly to great success.

"When do I get to do that, Maman?" she'd asked. "When do I get to say whatever I wish?"

"When it pains you not to," her mother had replied.

"What if I'm too scared?"

"All the more reason to speak your mind."

Known for its beautiful fountain, lovely trees and pleasant walking paths, Madison Square Garden is equally inviting at night. Every evening after sunset, spectators gather there to witness a great sight atop the Erie ticket building just opposite the park. It's there that the enterprising Mr. Eno has installed an enormous stereopticon (or Magic Lantern) along with a presentation screen three storeys high. Scenes of the world (Niagara Falls, the Grand Canyon, the Amazon River) are intermingled with advertisements, bible verses and the news of the day, each image dissolving into the next at a steady pace in the skilled hands of the lanternist. Although most observers come with an understanding of how the contraption works, they are still inclined to marvel whenever the screen is lit. The days of witchcraft and sorcery may be happily past, but man is not above believing in magic when science is so convincingly turned to spectacle.

—*Sights and Wonders of the City: A Guide to New York, 1880*

Phantasmagoria.

Adelaide loved nightfall in the park, the way the glimmer of lights—from windows, street lamps, lanterns on carriages—made it seem as if there were stars twinkling on the ground. When she was a child she'd stay out all day and not go home until well after dark. (It was that or catch her mother accommodating the landlord while drinking herself into a sordid mess.)

She hadn't returned to the shop that afternoon, hadn't gone back to the hotel either, all in an effort to avoid Judith Dashley. After window-shopping up and down the length of Ladies' Mile, she'd decided to end the day in the park. She felt quite at home watching the buskers and beggars find their places, as if they were about to perform a pantomime of her past.

Let the lady stew, she thought, as she settled on her favourite bench. I'll mend whatever needs fixing tomorrow.

She knew Judith had meant well by introducing her to Dr. Brody, so why had her kindness felt so intrusive? If anything she should thank the woman for her efforts, because for a fleeting moment that morning, with Dr. Brody's hand in hers, she'd felt the excitement of having someone new to figure out. But then she'd bungled that up as well—she'd been too forward too fast, too revealing with her words. In her experience, most men became unbearably squeamish when faced with hard truths. It'd been a long time since she'd read a man's palm, and even longer since she'd felt a man's hand on the small of her back. Was she interested in the good doctor? Yes. Did she wish to fall in love? Absolutely not. And there lay the root of her problem. She hated to disappoint Judith, but she highly doubted that whatever might happen between her and Dr. Brody (or any man) would ever last. While her encounter with him had served to reinforce the notion that she was in dire need of something new to pursue, she was quite convinced that any involvement with him would wind up being a limited engagement.

What then should I focus my energies upon? she wondered. Things were going well enough at the teashop, but they could always go better. She wasn't like Eleanor, who was perfectly content with paying the bills and getting by. She dreamed of a larger clientele, of greater success, of enough money to buy out the landlord, Mr. Withrow, who was always belittling their role as businesswomen and threatening to raise the rent.

When they'd first opened the shop, all Adelaide had wanted was to repay Eleanor for her kindness, and make a fresh start for herself. With the heady early days of starting their business now behind them, she'd begun to feel restless and bored. Any new ideas that sparked in her brain never seemed to catch fire. She'd thought that reading cards for the ladies of Fifth Avenue would hold her interest for a good long while, but their problems were far too much alike for her taste. She felt that something was about to change (it simply had to), but she wasn't sure if she should run to or from it.

Considering her options, Adelaide wondered if the new girl, Beatrice, might hold the key to attracting more business to the shop. With her alabaster skin, shiny hair and homespun charm, she might pull even the most reluctant passerby into their orbit. In the sideshow, they'd called her kind "a draw." Adelaide had been one herself. Maybe she could teach the girl how to tell fortunes. If Beatrice's mind was as keen as her attitude, then it wouldn't be too difficult a task. Her looks could certainly make up for any intuitive inclination she lacked. Eleanor, of course, would be sure to say that she was taking advantage of the girl's eager nature, and there'd be some of that, yes. But it would all be for the greater good of their venture. In any event, she'd need to observe the girl, spend time with her, which also might help her shake her own malaise. In the meantime, she had Mrs. Stevens' proposition to consider. If only she could get Eleanor to see the benefit of using her craft to wrangle at least a few of the hotel's wayward ghosts.

Evening chimes sounded from the bells of a nearby church. *One, two, three, four, five, six, seven, eight, nine.*

As spectators gathered to watch the latest round of images featured in the magic lantern show, a young girl wearing a shabby gingham dress passed through the crowd and stopped in front of Adelaide. Wisps of dark hair dangling in her face, she splayed a handful of playing cards like a fan. With a shy smile she said, "Tell your fortune, ma'am?"

"How much?" Adelaide asked. There was something about her hungry eyes and sunken cheeks that made her feel as if she were being shown a vision of her younger self.

"Three pennies a card," the girl replied. "A nickel if you like what you hear."

"All right then," Adelaide said, reaching for a card. "Let's see what I get."

"Choose carefully," the girl instructed. "Take your time."

Running her finger across the top edges of the cards, Adelaide studied the girl's eyes. When her lashes fluttered ever so slightly, Adelaide plucked a card from her hand. "Nine of Hearts," she announced, presenting it to the girl for evaluation.

"Excellent choice, ma'am," the girl cooed. "The best one in the deck. That's no lie."

Adelaide gave the girl a smile. Not because she felt lucky in her choice, but because the little soothsayer had just proved her worth. The Nine of Hearts was universally acknowledged among Gypsy fortune tellers to be the luckiest card of all. "What does it mean?" Adelaide asked, feigning ignorance.

"It means you get to make a wish," the girl replied. "And by and by, it'll come true."

Just then, a group of women in velvet-trimmed cloaks came towards them on the footpath, singing hymns and distributing religious tracts.

Sowing in the morning, sowing seeds of kindness
Sowing in the noontide and the dewy eve;
Waiting for the harvest, and the time of reaping,
We shall come rejoicing, bringing in the sheaves.

One of the women stared at the girl like a cat in want of prey. She reminded Adelaide of the Christian ladies who went slumming down on Chrystie Street when she was a child. They came from parish halls and ladies' societies to peer into the windows and lives of the less fortunate, one hand holding a skirt out of the muck, the other a peppermint-scented handkerchief to the nose. "Poor dear," they'd say while dropping pennies into her hand, taking care not to touch her. Then they'd invite her to their Bible study meetings so they could tell her she was nothing but a sack of sin. As soon as all those wretched *r*'s started coming from between their lips—*refuge*, *reform*, *religion*—she'd grab one of their biscuits and race out the door.

"Tell me more about my card," Adelaide said, motioning for the girl to sit next to her on the bench. She wasn't about to let this child get swept up in the Christian ladies' fervour.

"It's like I said," the girl replied, lighting on the bench's edge. "A wish come true."

"Wishes are serious business," Adelaide said.

"I'd say so," the girl replied with a wink.

Reaching inside her pocket, Adelaide pulled out a shiny dime and handed it over. "This is for you."

"Thank you, ma'am." The girl stared at the coin as if she couldn't believe her own luck. "That's awfully generous of you."

"There's more where that came from next time I see you," Adelaide promised.

"I hope it's soon then," the girl said, already looking for her next mark.

Watching the girl slip back into the crowd, Adelaide made her wish. *May she always find a way to survive.*

Bringing in the sheaves, bringing in the sheaves.
We shall come rejoicing, bringing in the sheaves.

The women's voices faded as they moved through the park. In their wake another voice sounded, off-key and broken by time. The Bird Lady was spouting profanities as she picked up dropped copies of the women's pamphlet: "God's Wishes for Women."

"Burn in Hell!" she shouted. "God damn you all!" Spotting Adelaide, she stopped in her tracks.

"Hello," Adelaide said, greeting her as sweetly as she could. She knew how much Eleanor revered the woman.

The Bird Lady sidled near, so close that Adelaide could smell the rot in her teeth, and asked, "Sit with you?" She reached out to touch the scars on Adelaide's face. "Sit with you?"

"All right," Adelaide said, and when the woman sat, she took her grubby hand in hers and held it in her lap. "Sit with me awhile."

The Bird Lady laid her head on Adelaide's shoulder and heaved a pitiful sigh that shuddered and creaked through her tired body.

"He's coming," the Bird Lady whispered. "He's coming for her."

On the other side of the park, Reverend Townsend waited for Sister Piddock and the rest of the women from his congregation to finish their rounds. He'd promised that he'd escort them (and any other they'd found) back to the church for refreshments and prayers afterwards. Their clucking chatter annoyed him no end, but their devotion was a sure sign that he was winning the fight against sin.

Bringing in the sheaves, bringing in the sheaves.
We shall come rejoicing, bringing in the sheaves.

The Reverend turned his attention to a young girl who was making her way towards him (the same waif who'd read Adelaide's cards). As she passed into the glow of the street lamp nearest to where he stood, he could've sworn for a moment the dishevelled child looked more otherworldly than human. Was she a demon? An angel in disguise? Another witch? Blinking away the vision, he figured he was seeing things. After all, he hadn't slept last night. He'd stayed on his knees in fervent prayer just as the two men in black had instructed him to do. And at first light Lena McLeod's body was gone. A miracle! A sign that all he'd done was right. Perhaps the girl standing before him was another test of his faith. *Thy will be done*, he thought, smiling down at her.

"Tell your fortune, sir?" the little soothsayer asked, staring up at the Reverend.

"Oh child," Townsend replied, "that's the Devil's work." Putting his hand on her shoulder he asked, "Why do you indulge in his deceptions?"

With a cheeky grin the girl replied, "I need to eat."

"Come with us then," Townsend said, guiding her towards the sisters. "The ladies of my church will give you food and rest."

"And what will *you* give me?" the girl asked.

"All that you deserve," Reverend Townsend replied.

With a lively skip the girl fell in line behind the women. As she did, a single card fluttered from her pocket and stuck between two pavers. The Ace of Spades, foretelling misfortune, difficulty and a treacherous path.

If you wish to upset the law that all crows are black, it is enough if you prove that one crow is white.

—William James

Dr. Brody's Ghosts.

Quinn Brody began the evening just as he'd hoped—snifter of brandy in his hand, new book on the table, fire crackling before him as he sat in a worn leather chair in his father's study. Even as a boy, he'd preferred the dusky, book-filled room above all others in the house. Back then, his mother had held sway over what did and didn't make its way inside the Brody residence, except for the study. It was there that Quinn had first witnessed the wonder of electricity inside a Leyden jar, watched Pepper's ghost get conjured via magic lantern, climbed the spiral staircase to the roof to view the moon through a refracting telescope. It was there that he had learned to love science.

After his mother died, Quinn's father spread the tools of his trade throughout the house. The conservatory became a laboratory, the downstairs cloakroom a makeshift *Wunderkammer*. Before long there was little discernible difference between the dining-room table and a mad scientist's workbench. Saturday mornings the lonely widower visited estate sales in the countryside to rescue vast caches of philosophical equipment from abandoned barns and tumbledown shacks.

Crucibles, notebooks and leather-bound tomes were strewn on every surface. The smell of coal, sulphur and molten metal belched from every chimney, wafting up from the alchemist's cauldrons that Mr. Brody kept bubbling over roaring fires throughout the year.

As the elder Brody's obsessions grew, the world around him changed. The house, an exceptional example of the Italianate style just west of Madison Square, was suddenly on the edge of the Tenderloin, bordered by saloons, theatres, dance halls, clip joints, gambling dens and bordellos. To protect his possessions from questionable elements, Mr. Brody had affixed ironwork grates and bars to all accessible windows and doors, causing the house and his place of business to appear like a pair of giant birdcages.

During the last year of his life, the only people the old man trusted to cross the threshold were his son, his long-time housekeeper, Mabel Stutt, and the gentlemen members of the Unknown Philosophers. Identical signs placed on the front of the house and shop read, NO ADMITTANCE SHALL BE GIVEN TO PREACHERS, TAX COLLECTORS OR T.A. EDISON.

After his father's death, Quinn conducted a meticulous inventory of the many items that cluttered the place, precipitated in part by the upcoming symposium of the Unknown Philosophers to be held at the Fifth Avenue Hotel. As a tribute to his father, they'd asked him to deliver the opening evening's lecture and he'd agreed, figuring it was also a good place to share the latest findings of his own research: the finer points of his theories on spirit detection and communication with the afterlife (so long as he could gather satisfactory proof). With the symposium less than a month away, he'd turned the study into a space devoted to his work, adding to his father's kit a working model of Holtz's electrostatic influence machine, a Bennet gold-plate electroscope and a collection of various and sundry pendulums and planchettes. The greatest and perhaps most important item in the study, however, was something Quinn's father had directed him to unearth from the back of the shop before he'd died—a strange-looking contraption he'd simply called a "spiritoscope."

Made to be attached to the top of a table, it featured a wooden board fitted with casters that could roll freely under the hands of the operator and a "spiritual telegraph dial" (patterned after the cast-iron dials used on early telegraph machines). Letters of the alphabet were arranged around the circumference of the dial, which was a little larger than the face of a grandfather clock, with the numbers one through ten inside that ring. At the one, three, five, six, seven, nine and eleven o'clock positions the following words and phrases appeared: YES, NO, DON'T KNOW, THINK SO, SPELL OVER, MUST GO, MISTAKE.

"It's for testing spiritual mediumship," Mr. Brody had explained. "Any and all who claim they can speak with the dead are welcome to try it. The dial is positioned so the operator can't see it. Any messages received from the Great Beyond are therefore free from bias."

"Have you ever had any luck with it?" Quinn had asked, wondering why his father had never spoken of the machine before.

"Only in exposing frauds," his father had answered. "It's terribly accurate when it comes to detecting liars. Perhaps you'll have better luck. I've placed a message in a bottle and stashed it in the rafters. Once I'm gone, see if you can get the machine to work. If the message comes through word for word, then you'll know you've heard from the other side."

Not long after his father's passing, Quinn had sat himself down at the machine and waited to see if the board might move beneath his fingers, but nothing happened. He'd also taken a turn sitting opposite the dial with pen and paper, and invited his father's spirit to move the needle on his own. On that occasion, the pointer had twitched ever so slightly to the left, and then gone still. That twitch may have been all his father could manage, but it'd been more than enough encouragement for Quinn. Now all he needed to do was find a medium through whom his father's spirit might freely act. It couldn't be just anyone, of course, but someone preternaturally sensitive to ghostly transmissions. Perhaps Miss Thom, with her uncanny knack for discerning the past, would be willing to give it a try?

Flustered by their breakfast conversation, he'd had an awkward parting with the soothsayer and they'd made no further plans to meet. Even when Quinn had been married, he'd never been quite clear on what it was women wanted from men (or to be more precise, from *him*). In fact, he'd often thought that his wife's acceptance of his proposal had been an accident. Not that it mattered anymore. She'd been gone so long he barely remembered what their life had been like. Did he wish to be paired with anyone ever again? Maybe yes. Likely no. Who would take him in his current state—without youth, ambition or a right arm? Still, he had to admit he wanted to see Miss Thom again. Before he let himself be discouraged from the attempt, he sat down at his desk with pen and notepaper.

Dear Miss Thom,

~~*I appreciated*~~ (No, that wasn't quite right.)

Dear Miss Thom,

~~*I greatly enjoyed our conversation*~~ (Too boring? Too trite?)

Dear Miss Thom,

I greatly enjoyed our enlightened exchange this morning at the Fifth Avenue Hotel.

May I converse with you again, at your convenience?

You name the time and place, and I shall obey.

Sincerely,

Dr. Quinn Brody

Laying his pen aside, Quinn sensed a presence in the doorway, the weight of a familiar, pressing gaze.

"May I help you, Mrs. Stutt?" The housekeeper had a terrible habit of standing in the shadows, as if she meant to catch him doing something he shouldn't.

"*Nein*," she said. "If you're not needing me for anything, I'm off to bed."

The grey-haired woman had been a fixture in Quinn's life since his youth, and it seemed his father's passing had affected her nearly as much as it had him. Earlier in the day, he'd caught her crying, hunched over a stray button she'd found in the bottom of her sewing kit. She'd meant to reattach it to his father's favourite frock coat before he died, but hadn't gotten the chance.

"Perhaps you'd like some time away?" Quinn had offered, wanting to make things better for her. "With pay, of course. I'd be more than happy to make all the necessary arrangements."

"*Nein*," Mrs. Stutt had replied, drying her tears. "What I'd like is for you to tell me what you want for supper."

Unlike his father, who'd often invited Mrs. Stutt to sit with him to discuss knackwurst or the weather, Quinn preferred to dine alone, to think alone, without interruption. Mrs. Stutt could cook whatever she wanted, he didn't care. He'd happily live on bread, cheese and cold cuts, day in and day out, if she'd allow it. He knew he was a disappointment to her.

Still standing in the doorway, Mrs. Stutt waited to be dismissed.

"You're free to do as you wish," Quinn said. "I've got a new book that wants to be read. I'll be awake a while yet."

"Very well then," Mrs. Stutt said. "*Guten nacht*, Dr. Brody."

"Goodnight, Mrs. Stutt. Pleasant dreams."

As the housekeeper took her leave she muttered under her breath, "*Geister zeugen Träume*." Ghosts beget dreams.

The novel Quinn had chosen for his evening's entertainment turned out to be a bust. More romance than adventure, much of *Dr. Heidenhoff's Process* concerned itself with a pair of young lovers who were, by turns, brooding, flippant, arrogant and insufferable. By the time Dr. Heidenhoff arrived on the scene, it was very near the end, and the character's scientific reasoning, intriguing as it was, was highly flawed and unconvincing.

As he placed the book on the shelf, he felt a nasty pinch between his shoulder blades. The leather straps that fastened his false arm to his body never stopped chafing his back. He'd tried wrapping the straps in muslin, but no matter what he did, the buckles and fittings found new and cruel ways to dig into whatever soft flesh he had left. His father had planned to replace the arm with a more comfortable and useful limb, but had never gotten around to completing the project. Taking his watch from his pocket, he placed it on his father's desk, then set about the task of unbuttoning his waistcoat, collar and shirt.

Tick-tick-tick-tick, the watch nagged.

He could hardly wait to be free of the weighty, wooden albatross tethered to his body. He would've removed the bothersome thing hours ago, but he knew it troubled Mrs. Stutt to see his sleeve limp without it. *Tick-tick-tick-tick.*

Thump!

His government-issued limb made a sickening thud as it dropped to the floor, causing Quinn's heart to pound and race. In an instant he was overcome with a sense of dread, his thoughts descending into the chaos of the war. The desk turned into an operating table made from two barrels and a plank. The flames of the fire became a distant battlefield lit with flashes of orange and red. Rows of furrows lay before him, dotted with blue jackets soaked in blood. In a blink, a heap of sawed-off legs, arms, hands and feet appeared at his side. The smell of gunpowder and chloroform filled the air. The soldiers at the Stump Hospital circled around him—one with no legs, one with no eyes, one with a copper nose; a dozen more falling into fits and convulsions at his feet. Then he was staring at his own body, naked and writhing under the knife of a surgeon who was sawing, cutting and slicing him to pieces. Bit by bit, hunks of his flesh got tossed aside until there was nothing left.

Trembling and drenched in sweat, Quinn went to his father's desk and tripped a lock on a hidden drawer. Why should he continue to be haunted when relief was so close at hand?

Tick-tick-tick-tick.

Stump propped on a tufted pillow, Quinn reclined on a woven mat and meditated on the opium pipe that sat on a tray beside him. *Yen tshung* was what the Chinese called the sleek, silver-saddled length of bamboo. *Yen hop*, the lacquered opium box. *Sui pow*, the sponge to cool the bowl. *Yen dong*, the small lamp that cast a friendly yellow gloom upon his face, reminiscent of the light from a waning campfire. *Yen hock*, the needle he used to tease and pull at the balled-up pill of *chandoo* until it turned soft. The substance reminded him of molasses taffy, yet its pleasures weren't nearly so innocent. He made sure he was precise with the dosage, because he didn't want to get hooked. He'd promised himself that he wouldn't fall too far under the poppy's spell. Still, he thought it a better choice than swilling a bottle of laudanum or getting piss drunk.

As he inhaled the nutty and sweet-tasting smoke, he did his best to allow the opium to ease his mind. The weight of him melted into the floor, his worries sinking down, down, down, along with it. Dancing skeletons and floating burial shrouds soon turned into a trio of rouge-lipped can-can girls in frilly skirts. *Tick-tick-tick-tick.*

One of the dancers broke away from her sisters to sit on the edge of the stage.

"Charlotte," Quinn said, recognizing her at once. "My dearest wife."

Her auburn hair fell to the small of her back, free from ribbons or pins. Leaning forward, Quinn tried to kiss her, but she averted her face.

He'd spent a blur of days keeping vigil at her bedside while she lay dying. Time and again he'd wondered, why couldn't she have been blessed with a better end?

"Kiss me," he begged, "I miss you."

She shook her head and disappeared.

Tick-tick-tick-tick-tick-tick-tick.

"Dr. Brody . . ." a second woman called. Another can-can girl come to taunt him.

"Dr. Brody," she called again, this time from the corridors of the Salpêtrière, the asylum in Paris where he'd studied under Jean-Martin Charcot. "*Aidez-moi!*"

She was young, full of figure and far more affectionate towards him than she should've been.

"Nadine," he whispered. "You got out again."

Her mother had tied Nadine to the gates of the asylum with a note pinned to her dress: *La fille de Lucifer.* Professor Charcot was more than happy to take her into his care.

"*Aidez-moi!*" she'd cried as Charcot and his students poked and prodded, pricked and scratched her as she lay strapped fast to an examining table. Not Brody, never Brody.

"*Elle est hystérique!*"

"*Elle est délirante!*"

"*Elle est une sorcière!*"

On Tuesdays she'd been brought to the lecture hall to be hypnotized and observed by the public transfixed by Charcot's *musée pathologique vivant.* The heat in the room was unbearable, the size of the crowd absurd. Hypnotized, she'd spoken of a handsome prince who'd fed her sweets, given her jewels and then repeatedly raped her. (On the ward, she wrote him lengthy letters filled with curses, and signed them "*du diable*.")

"*Aidez-moi*, Dr. Brody!" she'd wailed. "Help me!"

Quinn had watched as the young woman's ruffled skirts fell from her body, leaving her naked. Embarrassed, he'd given her his jacket.

In it, Nadine had slipped through the asylum gates unnoticed.

Tick-tick-tick-tick.

The last can-can girl gracefully straddled Quinn's lap. Wrapping her legs around him, the pretty one-eyed dancer gave him a crooked smile and said, "Giddy-up."

Quinn slipped his ghostly hand beneath her skirts and stroked her bare thigh.

Lips grazing his ear, Adelaide whispered, "How long has it been since you've been loved?"

Before Quinn could answer she was gone.

The little oil lamp twinkled before him, urging him back to his pipe. Another bowl would bring about another sweet release, followed by a pleasant stupor.

Then again, he could resist. He could pull on his coat and hat and go for a walk. The fresh air might do him good.

Before he could make up his mind, his belly lurched. Thank heavens there was a bucket nearby, waiting for the slippery lump that'd gathered in his throat. Those new to the pipe, like him, often suffered from surges of the fiend's remorse.

Tick . . . tick.

Retching until his stomach was empty, he thrust his hand in his pocket to search for a handkerchief. Clutching the keepsake Charlotte had given him all those years ago, he wiped his nose and mouth on his sleeve instead. As he settled on his pillow, he thought of Adelaide Thom. Would she be the one to bring him proof of the afterlife? Would she be the one to ease his longing?

Taking the pipe in hand, Dr. Brody made his choice. The day would end with more forgetting.

MAY 16, 1879 *The New York Times*

The lunatics were told that there was to be a dance in the Amusement Hall, a building in which concerts and balls are given to the inmates of the asylum. A merry air was played on the piano, and in a few minutes the lunatics were dancing and capering about in high glee.

The Lunatics' Ball.

THE AMUSEMENT HALL at the lunatic asylum on Blackwell's Island was a clean, open room sparsely furnished with an upright piano and half a dozen chairs lined up against the far wall. The light was dim but festive, twinkling from strings of brightly coloured lanterns hanging from the rafters. Several gentlemen who'd come by ferry from Manhattan were milling about the space, waiting for the female inmates to arrive. A small band played in the far corner of the room led by a fiddler who held his ensemble together with great flare, dancing a spirited jig as the viol, bass, guitar and banjo accompanied him.

The women—around thirty altogether, varied in age, race and education—were brought to the hall by a pair of orderlies. Some of them were quite eager to dance, practically running to take their places on the floor. Others reluctantly shuffled into the room, heads bowed. Hand-picked to attend the ball because of their good behaviour during the week, the inmates had been scrubbed and dressed for the occasion, their faces still red from rough rags and harsh soap, their hair tucked into neat braids or buns, their calico gowns unadorned and out of date. They looked like farm girls out to a country dance.

Among them was Sophie Miles—tall and lean, with large hazel eyes and honey-coloured curls. She'd been at the asylum for a year and nine months, and in that time she'd gone from being considered a danger to others to a shining example of recovery. The doctors were impressed with her progress, the nurses were coming around, and her sister inmates (who either feared or adored her) believed her to be a witch. What was the truth? All of it, she guessed. She was willing to do whatever it took to gain her freedom.

She'd been sent to the madhouse for throwing vitriol in a woman's face. The judge had told her she should be grateful—it was better than being locked up in the Tombs. Neither the cops nor the judge had believed her when she'd told them that she was right to do what she'd done. That smug bitch of a soothsayer had snubbed her, laughed behind her back. Miss Zula Moth had no idea of the kind of witch she'd wronged. The judge had described Miss Moth's injuries in detail: the agonizing pain; the gruesome scars on her face; the loss of her eye. "Lucky for you the young woman didn't die," the judge had grumbled. "Yes sir," Sophie had replied. *Pity she didn't*, she'd thought.

Tonight was Sophie's third time attending the ball and she had grand plans for the evening, hanging her hopes in the old saying, *Three times a charm*. Last week she'd spotted a man who'd seemed an ideal candidate to help her get out of the asylum. She'd smiled at him from across the room and she was sure she'd caught his eye, but he'd left before she'd had the chance to speak with him. Tonight he would not get away.

When she spotted him coming in at last, she clutched a small poppet she'd stuck in her pocket, one which she'd fashioned in his likeness, and whispered, "Come to me."

The well-dressed gentleman looked right at her and she gave him a shy smile and a wave. She'd chosen him because beneath his confident-looking exterior was a man who harboured a fair amount of self-doubt. She could see it in the way he'd taught himself to swagger even though he required the use of a cane. He was afflicted by things that couldn't be mended, and not just his wooden leg. Even within the walls of a madhouse he was the odd man out. He didn't possess the agility required for dancing a polka or reel. Hooking arms with a partner to swing her around was completely out of the question. He was a wounded animal. Easy prey.

The man made his way across the room and stopped in front of Sophie. "Mr. Bartholomew Andersen," he said, holding out his hand.

"Sophie Miles," she replied, with a soft Southern lilt, taking his hand briefly in return.

"Wonderful music," Andersen remarked.

"Yes," Sophie replied. "I like it very much."

"And where do you hail from, Sophie?" he asked, as if they were at a cotillion rather than an asylum.

"New Orleans, originally. It's where I was born."

"I'm from Baltimore myself."

Sophie swayed a little in time to the music and longingly looked at the dance floor.

"I'd ask you to dance," Mr. Andersen said at last, raising the cuff of his trouser, "but I'm afraid I wouldn't be much of a partner."

Sophie glanced at the wooden leg and shrugged. "I wouldn't say that." Daintily picking up her skirt, she dosey-doed around him for the rest of the song, occasionally brushing up against him, shoulder-to-shoulder, elbow-to-elbow.

When the song was over, Sophie took Mr. Andersen's hand in hers. Pointing to different women in the room, she listed why they had been consigned to the asylum, in an effort to show him that she, too, was out of place. "Intemperance. Hysteria. Jealousy. Nymphomania. Immoral life. Self-abuse. Preventing conception. Religious obsession. Setting fires. Kicked in the head by a horse. Mental excitement. Opium habit. Domestic affliction. Grief. Desertion of husband. Bloody flux. Brain fever. Death of child. Quackery. Uterine derangement. Vicious vices. Over-action of the mind. Syphilis. Greed. Parents were cousins. Rumour that she murdered her husband. Seduction and disappointment."

"And you?" he asked, just as she'd hoped.

"Superstition," she said with downcast eyes.

"That certainly doesn't seem reason enough to be locked away in a madhouse. What sort are you talking of?"

"Belief in witchcraft," Sophie answered, "and its practices."

Just then, the bandleader raised his bow and called for quiet. In a booming voice, he announced, "Grab your partners, gents, 'tis the Sweetheart Waltz!"

Another gentleman who'd been eying Sophie from across the room approached. "May I have this dance?"

Blushing, Sophie looked at Andersen. "I believe it's spoken for."

Leaning his cane against the wall, Andersen placed an arm around Sophie's waist and took her hand in his. Together they swayed to the music, their eyes locked. As the last chorus swelled, the former soldier felt as if the leg he'd lost was suddenly whole and perfectly steady. Turning Sophie around with ease he exclaimed, "I do believe you've bewitched me!"

Smiling, Sophie said, "Perhaps I have."

The Dumb Supper is the most respectful way to summon the dead. Although traditionally held on All Hallows' Eve (the time of year when the veil is thinnest), it can be performed at other times, in other seasons, should the need arise. The rules of the ritual must be strictly obeyed, lest unintended consequences follow. Reverence and respect are required throughout.

—From the grimoire of Eleanor St. Clair

The Song of the Sibyl.

BEATRICE HAD NEARLY paced a hole in the teashop floor while waiting for Eleanor to return. Everything with Mrs. Dashley had ended well, all things considered, but the episode had left the girl terribly unsettled. Worst of all, while Beatrice was still trying to make sense of what had happened with the boy's ghost, Mrs. Dashley had made it clear that she was eager to try to contact him again as soon as possible. As she was leaving, she'd squeezed Beatrice's hand and exclaimed, "What an angel! What a gift! You're the answer to my prayers."

She didn't want to be the answer to Mrs. Dashley's prayers. What she wanted was for someone to answer the questions that were racing around in her brain. How had this come to pass, and why? Was the book she'd found under the counter what she guessed it to be? Did it have anything to do with what was happening to her? Should she pack her things and catch the next train to Stony Point? After her spill at the pier, did she even have enough money to do so?

As soon as Eleanor walked through the door, Beatrice rushed to her. "Might I have a word with you, Miss St. Clair. May we sit?" Perdu waddled behind Beatrice, feathers puffed, chest thrust out, displaying all the confidence the girl lacked.

Eleanor could see the worry in her eyes. "Did everything go all right while I was out?" Taking a seat at the table by the window she asked, "What is it? What's the matter?"

Beatrice sank into the opposite chair. "I'm not quite sure, but something strange happened while you were away."

Perdu flew to perch on the back of Beatrice's chair.

Eleanor could swear he meant to protect the girl.

With her encouragement, Beatrice described all that had gone on as best she could, from Billy's footsteps running across the shop floor, to his greasy bag of peanuts, to the marble she still clutched in her hand. Presenting it to Eleanor she said, "I need you to know this is no game. The things I've been seeing—the Gypsy woman from yesterday and Judith's son—they're real to me, in some ways more real than you or Miss Thom. Their thoughts come into my awareness unbidden, without my permission. They aren't like anything I've ever seen. As a child I used to stay awake at night, staring at images of ghosts, ghouls, devils and witches in a book of spectropia until my eyes were so tired they saw things that weren't there. I can assure you, these encounters were nothing like that. I've either gone mad or I'm seeing ghosts, or both."

"You're not mad," Eleanor said. "But I do believe that you can see spirits."

"How can you be sure?" Beatrice whispered, her hands trembling.

"About which?" Eleanor asked. "The madness or the ghosts?"

"Both."

Eleanor reached out to the girl and clasped her hand. "Do you trust me?"

Beatrice nodded. Eleanor got up and slipped behind the counter to fetch her grimoire. She carried the heavy book across the room and set it on the table in front of the girl.

"Are you a witch?" Beatrice blurted, unable to hold the question back any longer.

"Yes," Eleanor answered, placing her palms on top of the book.

Perdu hid behind Beatrice and gently tugged at her braid.

Eyes closed, Eleanor said, "I see you've opened the grimoire."

Beatrice tried to think of an acceptable excuse. Could she blame the bird? Certainly not. Why would she? It wasn't his fault. "Yes," she admitted, praying Eleanor didn't have plans to turn her into a toad or boil her in a cauldron. "But I didn't mean to."

Eleanor opened her eyes and smiled. "I'm glad you found it. It'll make things easier from here on in."

Remembering her run-in with Adelaide during breakfast Beatrice asked, "Is Miss Thom a witch too?"

"Yes," Eleanor answered, "I suppose she is." Staring into Beatrice's eyes she added, "As are you."

"Me, a witch?" Beatrice asked. "I'm afraid you're mistaken."

"No," Eleanor said. "You're just afraid."

Perdu leaned his head against Beatrice's and made a noise in her ear that sounded for all the world like a purring cat. None of this seemed real. "How can I be a witch?" Beatrice asked. "So far as I know, I haven't any in my family. I've never heard of one in Stony Point. There's one rumoured to live in Sleepy Hollow, but I've never even caught a glimpse of the woman. I crossed the covered bridge near her house once, on a dare, when I was little. I held my breath and walked backwards the whole way. Could that be what caused this?"

"No," Eleanor laughed. "I don't believe so."

Beatrice shook her head in disbelief. "Beg your pardon, but until today, for me witches were the stuff of fairy tales. How can I be one if I don't believe they're real?"

"It's complicated."

"I was afraid of that."

Perdu hopped into Beatrice's lap.

"No doubt your thoughts are jumbled," Eleanor said. "Don't bother trying to untangle them. That's not how this works. This isn't like sums or telegraphy or scientific equations. It isn't something you can easily figure out."

Picturing herself with a wart-ridden face and wearing a pointy hat, Beatrice stroked Perdu's feathers to calm herself. "Why is this happening to me?"

"I believe you opened yourself to magic when you tied your knots and made your wish."

"Does this happen to everyone who makes a witch's ladder?"

"No," Eleanor said. "The magic working within you is more powerful than most. Your desire to discover if magic truly exists in the world is what allowed it to find you."

"What if I don't want to be a witch?"

"I suppose you could reject it," Eleanor replied, "but it can't be undone without great effort, and I wouldn't want you to come to any harm."

Beatrice's mind was reeling. "How do you know all this? Have I been bewitched?—by you, or Miss Thom, or someone else?"

"I saw you in a dream before you arrived," Eleanor admitted.

"A good dream?"

"From what I can remember, yes."

"Tell it to me."

Eleanor sighed. "Most of it left me the minute I opened my eyes. All I recall is that you and the girl in my dream are one and the same."

"And she's a witch?"

"Yes."

"And that led you to believe that I'm one too?"

"The dream and many other things, including what you experienced today. But if you'd like, I can perform a test to confirm it."

Visions of dunkings and hangings and burnings at the stake filled Beatrice's mind. The passage she'd read in Eleanor's spell book suddenly seemed painfully prescient. "What kind of test?"

"We'll need to speak with my mother."

"She's also a witch?"

"Yes."

"Is it far for her to come?" Beatrice asked.

"She's never far," Eleanor answered. (At least that's what she'd promised Eleanor when she'd died.)

"How long will it take her to get here?"

Looking to the clock, Eleanor considered the hour, the moon, the day of the week, the direction of the wind, the time of year. "Until tonight," she said. "Unless she can't be disturbed." She opened the grimoire to a page near the middle and said, "Read this. We've much to do if we want to be ready by midnight."

RULES *of the* DUMB SUPPER

1. Preparations shall be carried out in an orderly fashion—ingredients for dishes gathered, linens set aside, serving utensils and dishes cleaned, candles anointed, the room blessed. Instructions shall be made clear to all participants.

2. The table shall be set backwards—forks on the right, knife and spoon on the left, and so on.

3. A place must be set and a candle lit for each spirit you wish to contact. Their chair shall be shrouded in black. Personal items or tokens may also be included so the spirit feels welcome and at home.

4. All dishes served are meant to honour the dead as well as feed the living, so choose the menu wisely with consideration for the spirit's preferences and appetites.

5. The meal itself is to be served backwards—tea and sweets first, wine (or spirits) last.

6. A scrying mirror may be set before the place of the spirit.

7. Each participant may choose to bring an offering or write a message for the deceased to bring with them to the dinner.

8. Participants shall enter the room facing backwards, eldest to youngest.

9. A bell shall be rung to begin the rite, and then again to end it.

10. Once the rite begins, the living must remain silent until the rite has ended.

11. The rite shall begin at Midnight.

The two women spent the rest of the day preparing for the ritual. For the sweets, they baked soul cakes filled with honey, spices, raisins and currants. For the tea, Eleanor sent Beatrice back and forth to the pantry to gather the ingredients for "seer's steep"—star anise, calamus root, wormwood, mugwort, rose petals, lavender, peppermint and chervil. The rest of the meal would consist of her mother's favourite autumn foods: mashed turnips, sautéed mushrooms, pickled beets, cheese curds, black grapes, stewed apples, pumpkin soup with fresh cream, and noggins of mead.

Eleanor had been pleasantly surprised at how well the girl had taken the news that they were about to call upon another spirit. She'd grown up holding yearly dumb suppers with her mother at l'Hermitage, but she'd never had to organize one herself.

After sunset, Eleanor directed Beatrice to walk down the block, past the park, to the monument where General William Jenkins Worth was buried. "Scrape off a few bits of the lichen clinging to the tomb. I need it to make the incense I'll use to bless the room. Be sure to leave an offering in exchange for what you take." Giving Beatrice a handful of pennies, she said, "This should be more than enough."

As she approached the tomb, Beatrice looked all around, hoping she wouldn't get caught. Lifting her skirts, she stepped over the decorative border and slipped behind the grave, crouching near the edge of the towering obelisk that marked the site. Decorated with symbols and inscriptions lauding the General's heroics, it wasn't nearly so large or magnificent as Cleopatra's Needle. Still, it occurred to Beatrice, as she scraped her knife along the granite, that this was the second such object she'd touched in as many days. Tucking the lichen into a small purse, she carefully placed the pennies along the top edge of the plaque that bore the General's name.

Eleanor sang a tune under her breath as she ground the lichen in her mortar, mixing the powdery orange flakes with bits of sage, yew, cedar, myrrh and a sprinkling of henbane seeds. She'd given Beatrice the task of making hag's tapers—mullein stalks dipped in melted beeswax. "The smoke from the tapers will help to guide Maman from beyond the veil," she explained.

Beatrice nodded, then asked, "What's that song you were singing?"

"'J'ai vu le loup,'" Eleanor answered. "'I Saw the Wolf.' My mother used to whistle it while clacking a pair of sheep's ribs to keep time. Before the burnings, witches sang it as they danced at their Sabbaths."

"I can see why," Beatrice said. "It's lovely."

Smiling, Eleanor thought of her mother. *We'll make a witch of her yet, Maman.*

When it came time to set the places around the table Beatrice asked, "Will Miss Thom be joining us for the supper?"

"I hope so," Eleanor replied wondering what was keeping Adelaide out so late, again. "It would be a shame for her to miss it."

"And what about the place for our ghost?"

"Our *guest*," Eleanor corrected. "Leave that to me."

Climbing the stairs, she went to her room to fetch several items from an old wooden trunk—a dagger, a chalice, a mirror, a bell and a cloak. The dagger, worn with age, had a handle made of antler. The chalice, though tarnished, was made from the finest silver. The mirror, meant for scrying, was of polished obsidian, stowed inside a leather case to protect it from damage and demons. The brass bell, no bigger than an egg, was inscribed with angelic script. Holding it upside down in her palm Eleanor silenced the clapper with a small rag, to ensure it wouldn't sound prematurely. Last but not least, she scrutinized the cloak that was waiting in the bottom of the trunk. Simple in design yet exquisitely made, the cloak, with its pointed hood and crescent-shaped clasp, was a beautiful shade of blue, akin to the wash of azure that paints the sky as twilight turns to night. Her mother had told her its origins. "The woman who was first to wear this cloak was also the one who made it. She tended the sheep to get the wool. She grew the woad to dye it. She spun the wool into yarn. She wove the yarn on her loom. She poured the silver to make the clasp. She sewed each stitch by the light of the moon. Every fibre of the garment contains her determination, her sweat, her blood."

Eleanor hugged the cloak, burying her face in its folds. It smelled of woodsmoke, sweet grass and beeswax. "I need you,

Maman," she whispered. "Please come." The key Eleanor was wearing around her neck grew hot against her skin, prompting her heart to open and her tears to fall.

The opening of the trunk brought Bright out of hiding. The minute the Dearly saw what Eleanor was up to, she knew what was in store. "Twitch," she hissed, after Eleanor had left the room. "Come here!"

"Why for?" Twitch asked, yawning and stretching his spindly arms above his head.

"We need to move a ghost."

"Again?" Twitch complained.

Tugging on Twitch's arm, Bright pulled him into the air and guided him towards Adelaide's room. She hovered over Adelaide's mother's ghost (who was curled up in a washbowl, snoring). "We need to oust her now. I don't want her to interfere with the supper."

"Where to this time?" Twitch asked.

Forcing the chimney's flue wide open, she said, "Up and out!"

The Gypsy woman snorted and turned in her porcelain bed.

"I don't have a good feeling about this."

"Don't you care about the girl?" Bright needled.

"Beatrice?" Twitch asked, eyes gleaming.

"Who else?"

Twitch couldn't deny that the beautiful young woman had stolen his heart. "Well, all right then, let's put her out. How do you want to do it?"

"By hook or by crook," Bright replied with a grin. Then she roused the dead Gypsy from her sleep so she could tell her something between the truth and a lie.

"You're sure she needs me?" the befuddled ghost asked, unsure as to why the fairy was in such a rush.

"Your daughter's not home yet. Who knows why."

"Who knows why she does anything," the Gypsy replied.

"She should be here asleep in her bed. Don't you wonder where she's got to?"

The ghost knew her daughter could take care of herself. But it'd been a long time since she'd seen the whole of the night sky, or given a fright to gaily-dressed ladies who'd had too much to drink. If the fairy was willing to let her out, then who was she to argue? "You'll let me back in?" she asked, just to be sure.

"Of course," Bright replied, nudging Twitch with her elbow.

"Of course," Twitch parroted. "Of course."

Had the Dearlies made the ghost a promise they didn't intend to keep? Not quite. Bright would gladly let the wayward spirit in, *if* she could find her way back. Flying up the chimney, the eager ghost swallowed great gulps of soot and smoke, savouring the dirty air.

Bright quickly threw a handful of graveyard dust on the fire, then watched it spark and hiss. "That should keep her from coming back any time soon."

"She's going to be angry," Twitch warned, shaking his head.

"She's always angry," Bright said. "It had to be done."

It was quarter to midnight when Adelaide finally appeared. She'd fallen asleep on the park bench with the Bird Lady at her side. When a policeman had poked her with his stick, she'd woken with a start and found the old woman was gone. She was hungry, thirsty and tired. She wanted her bed.

Finding the shop with the table set, blinds drawn, strewn with lit candles, she wondered if she might already be asleep and dreaming. "What's all this?" she asked while reaching to pinch a grape off a plate that was overflowing with fruit.

"Don't," Eleanor said, rushing to push Adelaide's hand away from the offering. "If you've ever considered yourself my friend, you'll listen carefully and do as I say."

Adelaide stopped where she stood. Not because she was offended, but because there was something in Eleanor's voice that said there was more at stake than their friendship. Taking hold of her partner's hand she said, "Tell me what to do."

Beatrice stood near as Eleanor explained the strange things that'd been happening in the shop and everything that was about to take place. She could tell from the expression on Adelaide's face that she, too, had never participated in such a rite.

"What if I forget something?" Adelaide asked.

"You won't," Eleanor said. "You're the girl who sees everything, remember? Watch, observe, listen. Use your gift. It's what you do best."

At one minute to midnight, everything was in place—food and drink on the table alongside the sacred tokens of Madame St. Clair's past. A small cauldron served as a centrepiece, sending curling billows of smoke wafting through the air. Beeswax candles anointed with oil of myrrh burned bright about the room. A single taper glowed before Madame St. Clair's chair.

Bright and Twitch sat on the stairs, waiting for the proceedings to begin.

"Join hands," Eleanor said to Adelaide and Beatrice. "It's time." Closing her eyes, she began the rite.

Earth, air, wind, fire,
In a circle we conspire,
To make ourselves dumb so we might see,
Across the veil to summon thee.
As we are, so you once were
As you are, so we shall be.
So may it be
So may it be
So may it be

The hands on the clock touched twelve, but the chimes did not strike.

Eleanor took the bell in hand and rang it three times.

One by one, each of the women moved through the room, their backs towards the table—first Eleanor, then Adelaide, then Beatrice. Once they were seated, Perdu made a graceful swoop and landed on the back of Madame St. Clair's chair.

They ate the first course in silence.

Eleanor savoured her share, allowing each bite to conjure memories of her mother.

Adelaide fought the urge to devour the sweet in one go.

Beatrice wondered if she'd be able to finish everything on her plate. Her nervousness had returned with a vengeance, and she could hardly swallow.

Thankfully, as the meal progressed, their nerves were soothed by feelings of sisterhood and friendship. When the soup was gone and the last course over, Eleanor reached for her cup of mead and held it aloft, making a voiceless toast to her mother. Adelaide followed suit, as did Beatrice (as did Bright and Twitch with thimbles full of May dew).

The flame of the candle that'd been placed at Madame St. Clair's seat began to dance and flicker. A rhythmic clacking sounded in the room, seeming to come from all directions.

Throwing his head back, Perdu imitated the sound in his throat. *Click-clack, click-clack, click-clack, click-clack.*

Beatrice stifled a laugh.

Adelaide tapped her teaspoon on the edge of her plate, keeping time with the raven.

Eleanor did nothing to stop her.

Between the clicks and clacks someone began to whistle "J'ai vu le loup."

The cloak draped on Madame St. Clair's chair began to move, undulating to the music. As the tune grew to a frenzied pitch, the wise-woman's spirit appeared, inhabiting the garment. Her skin was wrinkled, her bones gnarled, but her eyes shone bright as the full moon on a clear night. "Hush!" she said, then gave a roaring laugh.

Adelaide dropped her spoon, sending it tinkling to the floor.

Madame St. Clair turned to her. "As you are, I once was. As I am, so you shall be."

No sooner had she uttered those words than the ceiling above the table turned into a night sky dotted with stars. The walls of the shop disappeared, giving way to a dark forest. Wind rustled through trees, punctuated by the hoot of an owl and the distant howl of a wolf. The scents of moss, pine needles, leaf litter and smoke filled the air.

Eleanor kissed her finger and held it out to her mother.

Adelaide pinched the fleshy part of her forearm to make certain she was awake and not dreaming.

Beatrice bit her lip in fear, tasted blood on her tongue before it trickled down her throat.

Perdu took hold of the hood of Madame St. Clair's cloak with his beak and gave it an impatient tug.

The spirit laughed as she addressed the raven. "Old friend," she said, "you've tricked us all, haven't you? Now that I'm on the other side, I can see who you are. Do not forget the Mothers are watching you. So long as you behave yourself, your secret will be safe."

The raven cocked his head and nodded.

"Dear Eleanor," Madame St. Clair said, turning to her daughter. "You're wondering how I'm feeling, being called here this night? I will tell you I'm disturbed but not surprised. But it matters not. That is the way of all spirits. I wait for the past. I remember the future. Time means nothing." She caressed the objects before her—the dagger, the chalice, the mirror. Cradling the mirror in her hands, she gazed across its black surface searching for signs. "For you, my child," she said, "I see blessings from beyond, from all the Mothers who have ever lived and all the Mothers yet to come. You are as strong and wise as the Bright Ones who came before you, from Heidr to the Queen. Your strength comes from on high, but you needn't be a nun."

Adelaide looked at Eleanor and gave her a wink.

"And you," Madame St. Clair said, turning to Adelaide. "Why have you chosen to forget your name? The tree has not forgotten you, Moth. Do not ignore the magic it gave you." Holding her hand in front of her face, she blew on her fingertips until a perfect golden pear appeared in her palm.

"Eat of its fruit," she commanded. "It will help you remember."

Adelaide reached for the pear and took it. She sank her teeth into the fruit's ripe flesh, and felt its juice run down her chin. It was the sweetest, most delicious thing she'd ever tasted.

"Beatrice!" Madame St. Clair exclaimed, now clutching the girl's witch's ladder in her fist. "You tied these knots to make your wish and by so doing bound your fate. Do you deny it?"

Eyes wide, Beatrice shook her head. She thought she might be sick.

Wriggling in Madame St. Clair's hand, the charm slowly changed from a tangled length of string to a writhing, hissing snake. Holding fast to the serpent, Madame St. Clair opened her mouth again to speak, only this time it was unclear as to whether it was her voice or the snake's. "This realm of the living is a palace of forgetting. Birth gives us life, but leaves us blind to all other worlds. We witches, we wise-women seek to touch all that's been forgotten. Isn't that the stuff of your dreams, dear girl?

"Your wish was your choosing and now you have been chosen—to remember the worlds before the present, to see those who've passed beyond the veil, to hear the whispers of the Fay, to learn the sacred order of nature, to speak the language of dreams. The world has need of more witches. Sibyl, oracle, seer, prophetess, hag—it is their hearts that wish to beat within you, their souls you see in the face of the Moon. The Mothers are always watching. They've seen you cross paths with a sacred stone and confer with an ancient jinni. They've watched you sleep in the house of witches, and heard you speak with spirits. They are here with us now, come to bring you a message. *The first witch not born but made shall renew the work of the Mothers. She shall lead her sisters through the fire.*"

Madame St. Clair slumped in her seat, her spirit fading fast.

In the forest an animal drew near, snarling and breaking branches underfoot.

Disappearing into the darkness, Madame St. Clair cried, "Le Loup!"

With that, every candle in the room went out.

Twitch bolted upright and looked at Bright, who took his hand and held it tight.

Ringing the bell three times, Eleanor whispered, "Don't be afraid."

Beatrice sighed.

Adelaide smiled.

The clock struck midnight at last.

September 25, 1880.

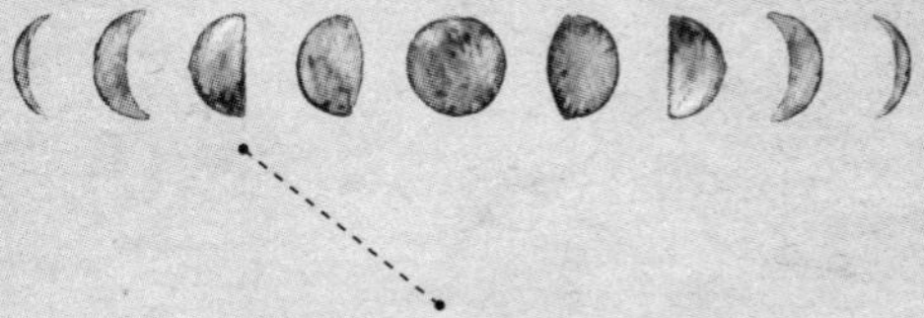

Waning, third quarter moon.

Neptune, Saturn and Jupiter, aligned.

THE MORNING SUN *Saturday, September 25, 1880*

Cleopatra's Needle Stuck

Engineering woes, lack of personnel and a spate of rainy weather have conspired to bring the Great Obelisk's journey through our fair city to a temporary halt. In the week since the ancient monument's landfall at the 96th Street Pier, its movement has stalled, largely due to what Chief Engineer Lieutenant-Commander Henry Honeychurch Gorringe calls "unforeseeable delays."

The ascent up Ninety-Sixth Street has proved more troublesome than originally anticipated, causing Gorringe and his fellow engineers to re-think their approach. The method initially devised for moving the obelisk through New York's streets lasted just long enough to get its precious cargo across the Hudson River Railroad line. Shortly thereafter, the tremendous weight of the stone caused it to fail. The former method has now been abandoned in favour of a modified "marine railroad," which should, according to Gorringe, easily accommodate the load. This revised plan will require more manpower for the duration of the obelisk's trek—to grade the ground ahead of the caravan, reposition the track beams, move timber and other materials and sink anchors to stabilize the device. Able-bodied men with experience in railroad construction are encouraged to apply for immediate employment. Work should resume as soon as there is a break in the weather.

EGYPTOMANIA TAKES HOLD.

The delays in the movement of the monument haven't quashed Manhattanites' excitement over the Needle. Visitors have been steadily making their way to see it, despite the stone being clad in a protective sheath of wood planking. Crafty treasure hunters have also been caught with chisels in hand, hoping to steal a bit of granite for themselves. "Who can blame them?" one bystander said. "Everyone who's seen the obelisk for themselves has walked away in a wild state of excitement. Ladies swooned, lovers made wishes, and an elderly gentleman prayed he'd be sent another wife—all in the short time I was near it."

A-B-R-A-C-A-D-A-B-R-A
A-B-R-A-C-A-D-A-B-R
A-B-R-A-C-A-D-A-B
A-B-R-A-C-A-D-A
A-B-R-A-C-A-D
A-B-R-A-C-A
A-B-R-A-C
A-B-R-A
A-B-R
A-B
A

The Witches of New York.

IT RAINED EVERY day for a week after the dumb supper, and the three witches did their fair share of thinking and worrying and scheming about the best way to proceed. When Saturday arrived with more rain rolling down the windows, Eleanor rose early from her bed, slipped on a dress and snuck downstairs before Adelaide and Beatrice were stirring.

For the past six mornings she'd performed six different spells to keep the shop protected and safe. What had happened the night of the supper had been astounding (even to her), but it had worried her as well. She could still hear her mother's panicked cry of *Le Loup!* She had no idea who or what "the wolf" might be, but she knew the sound of fear in her mother's voice. The words had clearly been meant as a warning, much like those of her family's motto, *Always needed, ever hunted.* Even if Eleanor couldn't say for certain why her mother had sounded the alarm, she figured that being more vigilant couldn't hurt. After all, she wasn't alone in this. She had Adelaide and Beatrice to consider and protect.

On Sunday she'd spread salt and tea leaves between the floorboards to keep all evil at bay. Monday she'd hung a mirror facing the shop door to reflect all negativity back to its source. Tuesday she'd placed an old shoe filled with bent nails beneath the threshold, to dispel whatever dark magic might be cast upon this place. Wednesday she'd dipped her finger in water in which a mandrake root had been bathed, and traced pentagrams on the windows, doors and mirrors to seal every portal from any dark forces that might wish to enter. Thursday she'd burned bay, juniper and sage in a large brass censer and wafted the smoke through every room, swinging the thing floor to ceiling, front to back and kitty-corner. Friday she'd swept the shop top to bottom with a crooked-handled hickory broom, collecting bits of lint and dust. Tossing the litter out the door she'd recited the following verse, *Under the watch of a waning moon, I sweep out the old to make room for the new.*

This morning she planned to pin a piece of parchment over the entryway, inscribed with an ancient charm spelled out in a magical cypher to invoke the aid of beneficent spirits against disease and misfortune. Her mother had made use of it time and again at their little cottage, swearing by its power to protect and heal. Whenever Eleanor was feverish or ill, her mother would write the charm on a scrap of paper then hang it with linen string around her neck to rid her body of all sickness and evil.

Perdu watched from his perch as Eleanor stood on a chair and fixed the charm in place with three brass tacks.

Sensing the bird's gaze, Eleanor finished her task, then set the chair aside and fetched a hunk of cheese for him.

Ruffling his feathers, the raven stretched out his neck and pinched the treat in his beak.

Eleanor couldn't stop wondering what her mother had meant when she'd told the bird, "You've tricked us all." What did her mother's ghost know about Perdu that she didn't? "Tell me who you are," she urged as she watched her pet gobble down the morsel.

The raven replied with a stubborn chortle, shaking his head. She'd asked him the same question every day since the dumb supper, and each time he'd refused to answer. She'd try again tomorrow.

It bothered Eleanor to think Perdu might be keeping something from her. The raven had been a constant companion, following her through meadow and forest, sleeping by her bedside every night of her life. Together they'd heard knockings, rattlings and voices from the ether; seen feathers, goblets and flaming cauldrons float and dance above the kitchen table.

On one occasion Perdu had had the misfortune of being (briefly) possessed, his feathered body inhabited by a strange spirit who spoke in a bullying, unearthly voice. "Skip through the graveyard! Ring the coffin bell! Dance beneath the full moon, then follow me to Hell!" Madame St. Clair had chased the entity out of Perdu by spitting in the bird's face and reciting a series of banishing spells from the *Petit Albert*. Later she'd explained the incident away, saying, "There's nothing to worry about, my dear. Perdu's the same sweet bird as always. One of Old Scratch's minions just thought he could steal his feathered cloak and not get caught. The pesky imp should've known better. When it comes to demons, witches always have the last laugh!" Contrary to her reassuring talk, Madame St. Clair had insisted the bird drink nothing but holy water for nine days straight. Perdu had then proceeded to hack up nine balls of lead shot, one for each day.

By and large, the other ghostly beings who'd visited their home had come in the form of harmless apparitions—gauzy and transparent, prone to take their leave shortly after they'd appeared. Seeing her mother's spirit take on such a magnificent form had caused Eleanor to wonder if what she'd witnessed was real. When the dumb supper was over and the gaslights lit, she'd turned to Adelaide and Beatrice and said, "Tell me everything you saw." In short order the three witches realized that they'd seen and heard much the same things, and pledged not to speak of what'd taken place to anyone outside themselves. Pricking their thumbs with the tip of Madame St. Clair's dagger, they'd sealed the promise in blood.

To Eleanor it'd been abundantly clear what should happen next. She and Adelaide were to assist Beatrice in gaining her full powers as a witch. Surprisingly, Adelaide had agreed. "How do we begin?" she'd asked, her eagerness causing Eleanor to wonder exactly which spell had been cast upon the magical pear she'd consumed (and how she might go about learning it). Beatrice, still reeling, was understandably reticent. "I'd like some time to think on it, if it's all the same to you."

"Right," Adelaide had replied.

"That's very wise," Eleanor had said. "Take as long as you need." The last thing she wanted was for the girl to feel pressured in any way. If everything her mother had said was true, then she wasn't about to do anything that might keep

Beatrice from fulfilling her promise. In the meantime, she'd set Adelaide the task of holding Judith Dashley off until things had settled.

After a quick visit to the Fifth Avenue Hotel, Adelaide had returned to the shop to report, "I've got good news and bad news."

"Out with it," Eleanor said.

"The good news is that Judith has promised she'll not breathe a word about Beatrice's gift to anyone without our permission."

"And the bad?"

"The cat's already out of the bag."

"Who did she tell?"

"Mr. Dashley."

"That's to be expected," Eleanor said. "Anyone else?"

"Quinn Brody."

"Who?" Eleanor asked, unable to place the name.

"He's a mind doctor, an alienist who also dabbles in chasing ghosts."

That last remark gave Eleanor pause. "You know him?"

Cheeks turning pink, Adelaide replied, "We've met."

"And?"

"Leave him to me."

Eleanor tried to keep her mind on daily business at the shop. Her regular customers came and went, buying tea and sweets and making their usual special requests. Beatrice donned her apron and moved about the store, happy to pretend she hadn't a care in the world. For the first few nights after the dumb supper, she'd stayed up late re-reading *Strange Tales of Gotham* and writing letters to Lydia, most of which she didn't intend to send. On Wednesday, at quarter to midnight, she'd finally gone to Eleanor and said, "I'm ready to learn. I'd like you to teach me all you know."

Since then, Beatrice had spent her evenings studying Eleanor's grimoire while absent-mindedly feeding Perdu hunks of bread. Eleanor had made herself available for any questions the young novice might have, watching with a fair bit of pride as Beatrice wrote page upon page of notes in a small notebook of her own. She'd never thought she'd have someone to teach her craft to, and she only hoped that she'd be able to do everything right. Her mother had been extremely patient and thorough in her teaching, never scolding her for being distracted, or for wandering off to paddle along the river with Perdu, or for sitting for hours in the crook of a weeping willow tree, daydreaming. If she hadn't learned all she needed to know in order to be a good tutor, she had no one to blame but herself.

For Beatrice's first lesson, Eleanor had given the girl a small gift, a witch's purse to carry in her pocket or to wear around her neck. She told her, "It's a place to store sacred herbs, stones and amulets to assist you in your work." Guiding the girl through choosing the proper herbs to place inside it, she'd explained how different roots, leaves and flowers have the power to enhance certain spells. "There are herbs for luck, herbs for love, herbs for divination, and so on."

"Which herbs do you think I should start with?" Beatrice had asked, giving the purse's strings a nervous tug.

"Those for protection," Eleanor had answered straight away. "Horehound, to guard against demons, sorcery and fascination. Caraway for protection against malevolent entities. Toadflax to keep the evil eye at bay. Thistle for strength, and to confuse your enemies."

Following Eleanor's instructions, Beatrice had placed each of the herbs inside the bag, then tucked the purse inside her pocket. She was glad for any help she could get.

In her effort to discern what, if anything, Dr. Brody had made of Judith's talk of her encounter with Beatrice, Adelaide had boldly tracked him to where he lived so she might address the subject head on. After an evening's worth of conversation with the doctor (which she'd quite enjoyed), she'd come to Eleanor with a surprising plan. "I propose Beatrice meet with Dr. Brody."

Eleanor asked, "Why on earth would she do that?"

"He's already aware of her talent for speaking with ghosts. What harm could it do?"

"I thought you said you'd take care of things with him."

"I have, I swear it. This will only lead to good things, I can feel it. Don't you trust my good sense?"

"I do," Eleanor replied, "but that doesn't mean you're not up to something."

Adelaide folded her arms. "I say we let Beatrice decide for herself."

Eleanor sighed. "I hope for her sake you know what you're doing."

Beatrice had decided to say yes to Adelaide's plan. Although the dumb supper had led her to be more inclined to believe in magic and less inclined to feel she was out of her mind, she was still left wondering how everything that'd happened to her had transpired. If a man of science wished to try and shed some light on her situation, then she was willing to give him a few hours of her time. Adelaide had spoken well of Dr. Brody, so she had high hopes for her visit with him. In short order a date and time was set— Saturday, September 25 at ten a.m.

When the day of her appointment arrived, Beatrice began the morning trying to decide which dress to wear.

"The red calico," Adelaide urged.

"Whichever you like," Eleanor said with a shrug. "It should be your choice."

Reaching for the dress she'd worn her first day in the city, Beatrice inspected the place where the skirt had ripped when she'd fallen near the obelisk. To her surprise, the tear was no longer noticeable. She'd never made such fine, even stitches in her life! It was as if nothing had happened. Had Eleanor repaired it? Pleased, she pulled the dress over her head and buttoned it up the front. She hoped that when the day was done she'd feel just as satisfied about her decision to meet Dr. Brody.

The previous morning a steamer trunk had arrived with the rest of the things she'd requested from her aunt. Upon receiving it, Beatrice had penned Lydia a note of thanks, making sure to include all the news she thought she'd be expecting—a description of the teashop ("quaint, cheerful, bustling"), a glowing review of her employers ("wise, amiable, independent") and a light-hearted complaint about the relentless rain ("if it goes on much longer, some enterprising gentleman will have to erect an ark in Central Park"). As she'd done with her previous missive, she'd omitted any and all details of the magic that'd befallen her. Sealing the envelope, Beatrice glued a three-cent stamp to the upper right-hand corner, one that bore the image of George Washington in stately profile.

Gazing at the envelope, she could swear that General Washington had turned his head ever so slightly to give her a disapproving scowl. ("Why haven't you told your aunt the truth?") He was right to question her, of course, but where would he have her begin?

Whenever something odd had happened in Stony Point (a rare thing indeed), the townsfolk were quick to try to put things into a shape they could understand. One spring, after one of Mr. Wheeler's nanny goats gave birth to a two-headed kid, the town square soon filled with people exclaiming, "My heavens!" "What a sight!" "Have you seen it?" "What could be the cause?" "Have you ever heard of such a thing in all your life?" By the end of the day, a half-deaf grandmother, a travelling salesman and Mr. Walter Rose, the town apothecary, had come forward with stories that made Mr. Wheeler's goat seem not so special after all (of a two-headed calf, a six-legged sow, and a dog that could whistle "Dixie" through its teeth). The poor kid died early Easter morning, and the talk between the pews at the First United Presbyterian Church turned more towards sympathy than sensation. "I guess it wasn't meant to live." "I suppose it's just as well."

What on earth would the people of Stony Point make of Beatrice now? The closest thing she could think of to match her own odd experiences were the occurrences she'd read about in Lydia's copy of *A Compendium of Miracles*. She'd especially enjoyed the accounts of young girls who'd had miraculous visions, and had often imagined herself in their place—something akin to being a mouse caught in a lion's maw and living to tell the tale. How sad she'd been to discover that more often than not, the girls hadn't found a happy ending. It's a risky thing for a girl to admit she's witnessed a miracle.

Joan of Arc, witch. Also known as the Maid of Orleans. Burnt at the stake for heresy and witchcraft, at Rouen, in 1431. Joan had her first vision at the age of thirteen while sitting in her father's garden. The message brought to her by Saint Catherine, Saint Margaret and the Archangel Michael was so beautiful that she cried when it came to an end. By nineteen she was dead.

Bernadette of Lourdes had fared a bit better. *On February 11, 1858, Bernadette Soubirous (fourteen years of age) had a vision while gathering sticks along the banks of a river. It was there, in a small grotto near the water's edge, that she first saw a lady dressed in white with a long veil covering her head and a perfect rose on each foot. This began a fortnight of visitations by a being who would later identify herself as the Immaculate Conception.* At first, Bernadette's mother thought it was a trick of the Devil. Many people in the girl's village demanded she be put away in an asylum. In the end, the Lady promised Bernadette she'd make her happy "not in this life, but the next." Bernadette was sent to a convent where she spent the rest of her days embroidering altar cloths and vestments. "The Virgin used me as a broom to remove the dust. When the work is done, the broom is put behind the door again," she was supposed to have said. She died at thirty-five.

Even Brooklyn could boast its own "enigma," a young woman who never left her room and lived mostly on air. *Mollie Fancher, "the Fasting Girl," fell victim to a terrible accident in 1865 when she was seventeen years of age. After being dragged behind a streetcar, she lost the ability to see, touch, taste and smell, but thereafter was able to go for long periods of time without food or drink.* According to several reports, Mollie had also gained the power to read without seeing and to predict future events. Was she still lying in her bed after all these years? Did anyone bother to visit her anymore?

The spirits Beatrice had seen hadn't been angels, and she had no idea as to whether or not her "gift" had come from God. Was it temporary or long-lasting? Was she right to pursue it or should she let it go? She supposed there were many instances where people chose to ignore the frightening, curious or miraculous events that'd occurred in their lives, thinking, *Who would believe me if I told them?* Beatrice wondered what her aunt might advise if she confessed her experiences. She guessed Lydia would say just what she'd always said whenever she'd gone to her with something perplexing. "Let's be practical about this, Beatrice. Do you know all there is to know about the matter? If not, then perhaps you should take the time to find out."

That's just what Beatrice intended to do. Tying a ribbon around the end of her braid she made a wish: *May this day hold more answers than questions.*

Adelaide pinned a spray of pheasant feathers to the hat she planned to wear to accompany Beatrice to Dr. Brody's house. Setting the velvet bonnet high atop her curls, she turned her head to appraise her work. Not too bold. Not too sweet. Just right. She was anxious to see how Beatrice would perform, pleased to be spending time with Quinn, again. When she'd gone to his house, he'd invited her to call him by his first name. Was that how she should address him today? With Beatrice along she figured she'd better stick with "Dr. Brody." Inspecting her face in the mirror, she patted the slightest bit of rouge onto her lips. Then she mouthed the words, "You're looking well today, Dr. Brody."

What a brilliant creature he was! With such lovely eyes! Just thinking of him made Adelaide cross her ankles and tighten her thighs. He was endearingly shy, yet she knew he was hungry for her: he had a habit of biting his lip whenever his eyes dropped to her mouth. (Perhaps a little more rouge was in order?) No, today was to be about Beatrice.

She couldn't help but think that the something she'd been feeling was about to happen had already begun and it had everything to do with the girl. When the dumb supper was over and their blood oath made, she'd snuck up to her room with what remained of the pear, and carefully plucked the seeds from its core. Then she'd placed the seeds one by one inside a small, slender phial and hung it by a chain around her neck. She'd worn the thing every day since, keeping the seeds close to her heart as if they were a religious relic. From time to time she'd shake the phial so she could hear the seeds rattle. To her, their tiny sounds were like the rumble of thunder, testifying that everything she'd seen, heard, smelled, touched and tasted that night was real. Was this what it was like to be spiritually transformed? If so, then she'd become a True Believer.

Although she didn't profess to understand every device Quinn had shown her in his study, she'd learned quite a lot about the nature of his research, including his hopes of finding a medium who could get his father's spiritoscope to work. In light of all she'd experienced during the dumb supper, it'd all seemed tremendously compelling and meant to be.

Too bad Eleanor wasn't going to come with them for today's visit, but she'd said an outright no. "You go. I'll stay. Beatrice doesn't need an audience watching her every move." Adelaide had felt the sting of Eleanor's disapproval, but she was convinced she was in the right. She'd been careful not to push or cajole Beatrice in any way. She was simply opening doors and allowing magic to blossom in an effort to help the girl discover her own path. Although her methods might not be ones that Eleanor preferred, Adelaide had to be true to herself, didn't she? She had to use her own gifts in her own way, get back to her old self, as it were. Wasn't that what Madame St. Clair had compelled her to do? Whenever she stopped to consider Beatrice, everything came clear. She could see what the girl needed, sense where she was headed.

Today could prove to be the way forward, for everyone. Great things were on the horizon!

Beatrice came downstairs with Adelaide trailing close behind.

"Your hat's a little crooked," Adelaide said when they reached the bottom. "Shall I make it right?"

"Yes, please," Beatrice replied, holding still while Adelaide deftly straightened it.

"There," Adelaide said, adjusting a hatpin to keep the bonnet in its proper place. Lightly tugging Beatrice's braid, she coaxed it into lying flat and inspected the ribbon that was tied to its end. "I've a wider ribbon in grosgrain that would look quite lovely with your dress. I'm happy to fetch it if you like."

"I'm happy enough with this one. I wouldn't want to make us late."

"Nonsense," Adelaide said. "Dr. Brody is sending a carriage for us, and the driver will wait. I know just where the ribbon is. I'll be back in two shakes."

Eleanor watched the pair with amazement. If someone had told her the week before that Adelaide would be so accommodating towards a shop girl (or to anyone for that matter), she wouldn't have believed them. *Miracles never cease.* Leaning towards Beatrice she lowered her voice and said, "If you're doing this just to impress her, please know you don't have to."

"No, I want to," Beatrice insisted. "I'd like to hear what Dr. Brody has to say."

"All right then," Eleanor replied, "but don't let her bully you into anything."

Taking her witch's pouch from her pocket, Beatrice dangled it in the air. "No worries," she said. "I'm prepared."

Perdu squawked from his perch near the window. A carriage had stopped in front of the door. Its driver sat hunched, hat tipped, collar turned against the rain.

"I believe that's us," Adelaide said, as she came back down the stairs brandishing the ribbon. Taking Beatrice's arm, she said, "We'll change it on the way."

"Take care," Eleanor said, giving Beatrice a little wave. Staring at Adelaide she added, "Be good."

"Be good," said Perdu, his eye on something no one else could see.

> The aura of a medium which thus enables an immortal spirit to do within its scope things which it cannot do otherwise, appears to vary with the human being resorted to; so that only a few are so endowed with this aura as to be competent as media. Moreover, in those who are so constituted as to be competent instruments of spiritual actuation, this competency is various. There is a gradation of competency, by which the nature of the instrumentality varies from that which empowers violent loud knocking and the moving of ponderable bodies without actual contact, to the grade which confers power to make intellectual communication of the higher order without that of audible knocking. Further, the power to employ these grades of mediumship varies as the sphere of the spirit varies.
>
> —Professor Robert Hare, *Experimental Investigation of the Spirit Manifestations*

Study.

Dr. Brody watched the skies as he waited for Adelaide and Beatrice to arrive. He'd thought he might escort the women on a walk if the weather had been agreeable, but he was glad he'd chosen to send a carriage instead, since it seemed yet another deluge was threatening to pour forth from the slate-coloured sky.

On this particularly dreary Saturday, the sidewalk in front of Dr. Brody's house was mostly bare, the traffic on the street slow. Even the smoke coming from the chimney pots along the rooftops seemed to be dragging its heels, eking its way into the sky in stubborn, reluctant puffs. A few sleepy-faced gentlemen strolled past, clearly on their way home after spending the night down on Sisters' Row. The exclusive bordellos were situated on the other side of the street in seven adjacent townhouses, each one managed by a different sister from the same family. Descended from prominent New England stock, they required all of their gentlemen callers to wear formal evening attire and come bearing chocolates and flowers. The eldest sister, Miss Julia Hapgood, had knocked on Quinn's door from time to time to deliver engraved invitations for their private parties. EVENING DRESS. INVITATION ONLY. ALL PROCEEDS GOING TO THE ORPHANED CHILDREN'S FUND. Although he'd never set foot in any of their houses, he respected the sisters' attention to detail and discipline. Theirs were the loveliest-looking houses on the street by far.

In an effort to put his own house in order, Dr. Brody had asked Mrs. Stutt to sort out the rooms he thought the ladies might see during their visit (the front foyer, the study, the downstairs water closet). For his part, he'd gone to the florist in search of something to brighten the house and walked away with a gaudy bouquet of chrysanthemums, marigolds and carnations in shades of yellow, orange and pink. On his way home he'd crossed paths with a desperate-looking flower girl at the corner of Fifth Avenue and Broadway, and had purchased the last blossoms from her basket—six wilted roses in a striking scarlet—in hopes that the poor child could get off the streets for the day. Once home, he'd inserted the roses one by one into the florist's arrangement, battling their urge to droop by propping their heads on the sturdier stems. The scarlet of the blooms reminded him of the suit Miss Thom had worn when they'd first met. She, like the colour of the roses, was not for the faint of heart. Although they'd only crossed paths twice, she had already proved herself to be a woman of rare intelligence and wit. And, he had to admit, incredibly alluring—from her delicate hands to her soulful gaze, from her pouty lips to the unabashed way she spoke her mind.

"Dr. Brody," Mrs. Stutt said, entering the study. "Would you like me to prepare tea now, or wait until your guests arrive?"

"Let's wait," the doctor answered, half lost in his thoughts.

"And will you be wanting luncheon as well?"

He pondered the housekeeper's question, wishing he'd thought of it himself. If the meeting went as he hoped, then his guests might well be in need of refreshment. "Perhaps," he said.

"Where will it be served?" Against her wishes, he'd asked her to leave the dining room in its perpetual state of messiness. He hadn't the heart to remove his father's experiments from the table just yet.

"If it comes to that, we'll take lunch in the study," Dr. Brody replied.

"And will it?" Mrs. Stutt pressed.

"I suppose it might."

"I'll assume it will."

"Very well then," Dr. Brody said, checking his watch for the time.

Mrs. Stutt cocked her head in thought. "It's two for tea?" she asked, as if she'd forgotten.

"Two," Dr. Brody answered with a nod.

"Two, besides you, correct?"

"Yes. Three altogether."

"Two gents, two ladies, or one of each?" Mrs. Stutt fished.

"Two ladies," Dr. Brody answered, wondering what the word for "subtle" was in the German language. His housekeeper wasn't. "Miss Thom, who you've already met, and her companion, Miss Dunn."

Plucking a bruised petal off one of the roses before it could fall, Mrs. Stutt grumbled, "Miss Thom."

"Is there anything else?" Dr. Brody asked, feeling as if he'd already provided her with more than enough information.

"*Nein*," Mrs. Stutt said, stuffing the rose petal into her pocket. "Just ring when you'd like your tea."

When the carriage arrived, Dr. Brody went out to meet his guests at the curb. Umbrella in hand, he greeted them both then ushered Adelaide and Beatrice up the steps and into the house.

Once they were in the study, Beatrice found it difficult to know where to look first. Every book and object that lined the shelves was of immense interest. It was all she could do not to pick each one up for closer inspection. When she came across an old bottle with a scroll of paper inside, she paused to peer at it. Covered in dust and sealed with wax, the bottle looked as though it might've been used to conceal a pirate's treasure map. As she reached to touch it, the scroll began to spin. When she withdrew her hand, the scroll went still.

Glancing over her shoulder to make sure neither Adelaide nor the doctor had noticed, she decided she'd better leave well enough alone for now.

Dr. Brody was seated at his desk on the other side of the room, arranging pen and paper. Meeting Beatrice's eyes, he tried a little small talk. "Miss Thom says you're new to the city?"

Adelaide, who was gracefully reclining on a nearby couch, gave Beatrice a supportive smile.

"Yes and no," Beatrice answered. "I spent much of my youth in Stony Point, but made occasional trips to Manhattan with my aunt. This is the first time that I've chosen to stay."

"I thought we might begin with a few questions," Dr. Brody said, picking up his pen.

"Should I sit or stand?" Beatrice asked, her mouth suddenly dry.

"Whichever you find most comfortable," Adelaide offered.

"Yes, of course," Dr. Brody agreed. "Do as you please."

"Then I'd just as soon stand. If you don't mind." She preferred to stay where she was, near the bookshelves, comforted by the musty scent of old books and leather bindings.

"Why don't we start with something simple," Dr. Brody suggested. "If you wouldn't mind, please state your age."

"Seventeen," Beatrice replied, gazing at the gilding that graced the books' spines.

"Place of birth?"

"Albany, New York."

"Have you suffered any grave illnesses in your lifetime?"

"No."

"Any mental deficiencies diagnosed in yourself or your family?"

"No, and not that I know of."

"Any tragedies or traumas to yourself or those close to you? Accidents? Fire? Thievery? Near drownings or the like?"

Beatrice thought of her mother and father, pale and sickly, lying in their beds as she stood in the doorway with tears streaming down her face. Where had her parents' spirits gone after they'd passed? Why hadn't they appeared to her yet? Was there any chance she'd see them again? "My parents died when I was ten."

"What caused their passing?"

"Smallpox."

"Is that when you started encountering spirits?"

"No, not then."

"You had no visions of your parents, heard no voices after their deaths?"

Beatrice shook her head.

"When did you have your first experience with the spirit world?"

"A little over a week ago—the day I arrived in New York."

"The day you communicated with Mrs. Dashley's deceased son?"

"No, I saw a different ghost the day before Billy appeared, a woman dressed in Gypsy garb. She was sitting at a table in the back of the teashop."

A chill went up Adelaide's spine.

"She seemed quite real to me at first, but then I saw she wasn't made of flesh. She turned into a ghoulish spectre right before my eyes. I thought she meant to kill me."

Head down, Dr. Brody penned line after line. "Did you believe in ghosts before that day?"

"I suppose I did," Beatrice said, pulling a book from the shelf. *Experimental Investigation of the Spirit Manifestations.* "At least I hoped they were real."

"Had you ever tried to communicate with spirits, say, through pendulum or planchette?"

"No, I've never done anything like that."

"Ever attend a table-tipping or séance?"

"No."

"Ever heard knockings or rappings that might be construed as ghostly transmissions?"

"No," Beatrice said, "but I know Mr. Morse's code for communicating by telegraph."

"How resourceful!" Dr. Brody said with a chuckle. "May I ask how you came to learn it?"

Thumbing through the book's pages Beatrice replied, "I'm self-taught. I thought I might find employment as a telegrapher, but Miss St. Clair and Miss Thom took me on, so I didn't pursue it."

Adelaide gave the girl an encouraging nod.

"How many times have you made contact with a spirit?"

"Just twice," Beatrice answered, careful not to mention the dumb supper. Closing her eyes, she hoped he wouldn't press further. She'd never been good at lying.

"And how did the spirits make contact with you?"

"Mostly through my mind."

"In a familiar language, I take it?"

"Yes, although it was more thought than conversation. As if a sense of knowing suddenly sprang up between me and them."

After a few minutes of hasty scribbling, Dr. Brody laid down his pen. "Thank you, Miss Dunn, this has been most enlightening."

"Are we finished?" she asked, still clutching the book.

"Not quite," he answered. "I was hoping you might be willing to submit to a test using the spiritoscope?"

Beatrice looked at Adelaide.

"It's the device I mentioned to you," Adelaide said. "It translates messages as they pass from a spirit through your hands. You'll be acting much like a telegraph operator does when she sends messages over the wires."

Reassured, Beatrice turned to Dr. Brody. "Do you have a particular ghost you wish to contact?"

Thinking of his father, the doctor glanced towards the bottle on the shelf. He'd fetched it from the attic earlier that morning. He'd purposely not mentioned it to Adelaide so there'd be no chance she could tell Beatrice what it was (either on purpose or by mistake). "I'd rather not say," Dr. Brody replied. "I wouldn't want to taint the experiment with my expectations."

Adelaide went to the spiritoscope, pulled out the chair behind it and gently urged Beatrice to sit. "I imagine you'll find it a more reliable and pleasant form of communication with the spirit world than you've experienced thus far. If it doesn't feel right, then just say the word. Nothing ventured, nothing gained."

"All right," Beatrice said. "I'll try."

Once she was comfortably seated, Dr. Brody explained the procedure she was to follow while using the machine. "Place your fingertips ever so lightly on the transmitter board and wait for a spirit to guide your hands. You'll be blindfolded for the duration of the test so as to lessen any chance of distraction. I ask that you not speak while the test is in progress, unless you feel it's absolutely necessary. Miss Thom and I will be nearby, recording any activity on the dial, and observing your progress."

Adelaide placed a reassuring hand on Beatrice's shoulder.

"Thank you," Beatrice said with a smile.

"Are you ready, then?" Dr. Brody asked, holding a silk scarf in his hands.

Beatrice nodded.

After securing the scarf over Beatrice's eyes, Dr. Brody motioned for Adelaide to sit at his desk. "If you'd be so kind, I'd like you to record whatever the needle dictates so I can be free to observe both the machine and Miss Dunn."

"I'd be happy to," Adelaide said, settling behind the desk.

"Miss Dunn," Dr. Brody said, "please place your hands on the board."

Beatrice nodded. No sooner had her fingertips touched the wood than she felt a ghostly pair of hands gently come to rest on hers. Although she was blindfolded, she could see the hands in her mind's eye—spotted, wrinkled, twisted by time, unmistakably masculine. Any fear she had was soon replaced by an overwhelming sense of wonder. With a gentle push, the board began to glide and move across the table.

I A-M T-O-B-I-A-S B-R-O-D-Y.

I T-E-L-L N-O L-I-E-S.

I B-R-I-N-G Y-O-U A M-E-S-S-A-G-E F-R-O-M T-H-E O-T-H-E-R S-I-D-E.

As the needle nervously edged around the dial, it paused and hovered over each letter Mr. Brody's spirit wished to indicate.

Dr. Brody shook his head in disbelief.

Adelaide did her best to keep her amazement in check as she faithfully transcribed each letter of the message.

Beatrice swayed forward and back with the board's movement, as if she were a child on a swing, being pushed ever higher into the air.

W-H-A-T Y-O-U S-E-E-K

Y-O-U S-H-A-L-L F-I-N-D

I-F Y-O-U U-S-E Y-O-U-R W-I-T.

E-V-E-R-Y P-R-O-B-L-E-M

C-A-N B-E S-O-L-V-E-D

I-F Y-O-U D-W-E-L-L W-I-T-H-I-N I-T.

After several minutes of this ethereal push and pull, Beatrice felt the spirit's hands come to a stop. "Is that all you wish to say?" she whispered under her breath, waiting for the ghost to respond.

Y-E-S, the spirit replied before leaving the needle to rest on the phrase "MUST GO."

With that, Mr. Brody's bottle tumbled from the shelf and shattered on the floor.

Plucking the scroll from the broken glass, Dr. Brody pulled loose the ribbon with his teeth and broke the wax seal. "The messages are the same," he said, clutching the paper like a prize. "Word for word."

Adelaide rushed to his side to see for herself.

Beatrice was still seated at the spiritoscope. As she listened to their exclamations of wonder, she felt another presence draw near. A second pair of hands placed themselves on hers—feminine and familiar, thumbnails marked by little moons, a wedding band shining on a ring finger. The board tentatively danced and floated beneath their touch, a mother guiding her daughter in a message that was long overdue.

Sadly, no one saw it.

HOW *a* WITCH SAVED *our* DREAMS

Long ago, the First Witch came face to face with a Demon who meant to do the World great harm. This Demon, whose name we shall not mention (because to do so would cause him to feel flattered and smug), wished to rid the World of all dreams, good and bad. He knew, as all witches know, that dreams are the surest way for beings of flesh and blood to discover the Mysteries of Life. This knowledge made him terribly jealous, because Demons cannot dream.

The Demon was further upset, in his boorish way, over the way dreams provide hope to people in troubled times. (Something else that Demons cannot abide.)

To destroy this precious boon of mankind, the Demon knew he would need to rid the World of the source of all dreams—a race of otherworldly beings whose sole responsibility is to make and deliver dreams to humans as they sleep. Throughout the ages they have been called by various names—angels, memunim, oneiroi, sandmen, Dearlies—but their true name is known only to themselves, a precious secret keenly guarded and strictly kept, for if a human were to utter it, they would never be allowed to dream again. (Perhaps you might be tempted to cry, "How sad, how unjust, how unfair!" but I beg you to hold your tongue. It is the prerogative of the Fay to do as they see fit. If there were no consequences for misbehaviour in our dealings with them, there could be no magic between us. We witches do not question their punishments, so long as they do not question our curses.)

The Demon, wishing to discover the Dearlies' secret name, hid in the branches of a Hemlock tree on the edge of their sacred grove at Twilight on the night of their Great Gathering. What he didn't know was that the First Witch had also come to the outskirts of the grove, her ears plugged with cotton flowers and dandelion fluff. She'd come there to leave an offering of thanks for the Dearlies, a few trinkets she'd gathered together in hopes of adding to their delight—a thimble filled with salt, nine buttons made from brass, a spool of silver thread, and a needle dipped in gold.

In years past, the Witch had never dared stay to watch the Dearlies frolic for she'd feared their merriment might prove too riotous for her senses, leaving her deaf, dumb and blind. This year, as the sun fell below the horizon, she drank a potion made of toadstools and harebells so she might disguise herself as a rabbit in the tall grass near their fairy ring.

The rite was lit by foxfire and lightning bugs, their dances accompanied by beautiful odes depicting their illustrious past. Once the Demon heard what he was after, he snuck into the shadows. As he went, he heard the chance snap of a twig, alerting him to the Witch's presence.

Overpowered by hunger (as such monsters often are), the Demon seized the rabbit by her legs and held her in the air, ready to devour her whole. Struggling to break free, the Witch cried out in fear, her spell broken by her distress. The fairies, alerted to the intruders, threw a net of spider's silk over the pair and dragged them through the glen. Discovering the offerings the Witch had left for them, they blew salt in the Demon's eyes and set the Witch free. Taking the Witch's thread in hand, they guided it through the needle, then pierced the skin of the Demon's lips to sew his mouth shut. As they worked, they tied each of the buttons to the thread to secure their knots. No sooner had they finished than the thread turned to molten lead, searing the Demon's flesh and removing their true name from his tongue. Rather than doing away with the beast, they sentenced him to live, mute and anguished, with only brimstone smoke and the scent of rotting flesh to nourish him.

To thank the Witch for her kind deed, the Dearlies invited her into their circle to share an elixir made of Bog Myrtle and Mugwort, and to teach her the Language of Dreams. In three years' time (which seemed like three minutes to her), she returned to her village to live out her days as an interpreter of Dreams.

In these times, because so many have forgotten the Dearlies and their gifts (men are far more inclined to attribute their dreams to indigestion than magic), these marvellous creatures cling less frequently to our bedposts, and are more likely to be found in places they inhabited in the distant past. (If you've ever wondered why some locations—sunny meadows, mossy grottos, lonely castle towers—generate the most spectacular visions, you now know the reason.) But be not dismayed, the Dearlies will come whenever and wherever they're needed, so long as they are kindly coaxed and treated with respect. Demons of all stripes may try to thwart them, but the Dearlies stand invincible because of the kindness of the First Witch.

And that, my darling girl, is why witches' dreams are the best of all, and should never be dismissed.

Close your eyes and get some rest. We gain new worlds when we sleep.

—*From the grimoire of Eleanor St. Clair*
(as told to her by her mother).

Divinations and Dreams.

BEATRICE DID NOT mention her mother's visitation. The spirit's presence had been brief—there for but a moment, then gone. What could be done about it now? Nothing. Thus far, her encounters with spirits had been varied and strange, and she wasn't sure whether that was due to the nature of ghosts or the newness of her gift.

But during the carriage ride back to the teashop, Adelaide sensed something was amiss. "You're keeping something to yourself," she said. "And you might as well tell me because I'll keep my eye on you until I discover it myself."

Beatrice stared at a cascade of raindrops flowing down the edge of the carriage window. "I'm not sure I should," she said. "It won't do anyone any good."

Adelaide watched as the girl nervously tugged at one of the buttons on her glove. It was a sure sign something was troubling her from the past. If she was haunted in her mind and heart, it followed that she might also be haunted in the truest sense. "Did another ghost visit you while we were at Dr. Brody's?" she asked, wondering if her mother's spirit had attempted to make more dark mischief.

Eyes wet, Beatrice nodded, clutching at the folds of her dress as a child holds fast to her mother's skirts.

"It was someone you knew? Someone you loved?"

Caught in Adelaide's gaze, Beatrice surrendered. No matter what she chose to say she'd already been found out. Eleanor had mentioned that Adelaide's ability to peer into others' souls was beyond compare, but Beatrice hadn't felt the total weight of it until now. "It was my mother," she confessed.

"You're sure?" Adelaide asked. "It couldn't have been anyone else?"

"Quite sure," Beatrice replied. "I didn't see the whole of her, but I saw and felt her hands on mine, much the same as I did with Dr. Brody's father. She guided my hands to move the board but I'm afraid I don't know what she meant to say."

Adelaide bit her lip. The fault lay with her. "I didn't see the needle move around the dial."

"You were caught up with Dr. Brody's excitement over his father's message. I completely understand."

Adelaide shook her head. "I should have stayed where I was while you were at the board and kept my eye on the needle."

"You couldn't have known," Beatrice said.

Adelaide stared out the carriage window. *I would've if I'd been paying attention*, she thought. The situation with Beatrice was too important to be so inattentive. She'd already started to think about what should come next—a meeting with Judith and Marietta, a note to Quinn to arrange another round of experiments, a talk with Eleanor to convince her all was well. How could she have been so careless with the girl?

"It's all right," Beatrice said, "truly it is."

"No, it's not." Adelaide was touched that Beatrice would try to give her comfort when it should've been the other way around. Taking the girl's hand, she added, "Unless of course, you didn't wish to hear from her in the first place?" There was always a chance Beatrice's feelings might be akin to her own when it came to mothers.

"Why wouldn't I?" Beatrice asked, perplexed. "Wouldn't you, if you were in my shoes?"

"Have you forgotten that you've met my mother? In my case, I'd have to say no."

"I hadn't considered that." The girl looked even more distressed.

Adelaide gave Beatrice's hand a squeeze. "Count yourself lucky that you had the kind of mother who didn't require doubt, and that you've lived a life where embracing joy wasn't a dangerous endeavour. Missed messages aside, what did you think of the experience overall?"

"It was all very interesting," Beatrice replied, "the books and the scientific instruments were fascinating, and I liked Dr. Brody too. He's gentlemanly and so smart."

"I agree," Adelaide said, her cheeks turning warm.

Beatrice gave Adelaide a slight nudge with her elbow. "I believe Dr. Brody thinks quite highly of you too."

Nudging back, Adelaide said, "So you've taken up reading minds, have you?"

Beatrice laughed. "I suppose I should add that I quite enjoyed using the spiritoscope. The mechanics of it caused me to feel as though I was leaving less to chance, which leads me to wonder if the ghosts might feel the same? Mr. Brody's communication was so steady and sure, but then, of course, I have to take into account that he built the contraption himself." Thinking of her mother, she wondered if today might've been her only chance to receive a message from her spirit. In her heart, she hoped not.

"Does that mean you'd like to try it again?"

"I think so," Beatrice replied. "Yes."

"Excellent," Adelaide said. "I'll let Dr. Brody know."

As the carriage wheels ground to a stop, Adelaide picked up her skirts, but before she could exit the cab, Beatrice caught her by the arm. "Would you mind terribly if I spoke to Miss St. Clair about it first? I'd like to hear her opinion on the matter. It's been so hard for me to know how best to proceed with my new abilities, and she's been awfully kind about helping me find my way. Sometimes I wish I could gaze into a crystal ball and see exactly what's coming, but Eleanor says that's not how they work."

Adelaide wished she had two eyes so she could roll them both. "Yes, of course you should speak with Eleanor, about everything we've discussed and more. As far as looking into the future goes, I believe I can help with that. I imagine you're getting rather tired of feeling so unsure."

Walking through the shop door, Adelaide took Beatrice by the hand and led her back to her table for a consultation.

Miss Beatrice Dunn. Inquisitive, bright, full of promise. Unbearably lovely in every way.

Her question: What does my future hold?

Her cards: Prudence. Fortune. Hope.

Adelaide's answer: Heavens! I don't believe I've ever seen a more fortuitous spread.

"Is that good?" Beatrice asked, carefully inspecting the cards that Adelaide had placed in front of her. Each one held the image of a formidable-looking woman, more goddess than human in dress and stature. Prudence was dressed in Roman garb, a mirror in one hand, a spear with a large snake wrapped around it in the other. Fortune stood naked except for a scant piece of cloth draped across her middle and a length of cloth wrapped over her eyes. Wheel at her back, she was holding two purses fat with lucre. Hope, dressed demurely in a long flowing gown, was standing in the crook of an anchor. Her face was calm despite the stormy seas that raged beneath her feet.

"You see who those fine ladies are, don't you?" Adelaide asked. "Each one stands for someone you know. She who stands at the crossroads of decision, giving insight, wisdom and forethought; she who spins the wheel on behalf of those who seek her, never allowing despair to get the best of her, for she knows good luck is bound to come around again in time; and she who serves as an anchor for our souls, a refuge for our hearts, the last thing left in Pandora's box."

Pointing to each card, Beatrice assigned each of the goddesses a human counterpart. "Prudence is Miss St. Clair, Fortune is you, and Hope, I suppose, is myself?"

Adelaide gave a wide smile. "How perceptive of you. Well done."

Beatrice shook her head. "But I'm not quite clear on what it all means."

"I'd say it means we're good company for each other," Adelaide replied. "We're better together than apart. This bodes well for everyone's future—yours, mine and Eleanor's."

Out of the corner of her eye, Beatrice saw Perdu waddling towards her with a stray card pinched in his beak. "Is that for me?" she asked, as the raven drew near.

"What's that he's got?" Adelaide asked.

"One of your cards," Beatrice replied, showing it to her. The image on the card was that of a young woman, face to face with a snarling lion, her hand inside the beast's mouth. The girl's expression was serene even though the lion was clearly untamed. Thinking that the frightful-looking token had appeared by magic rather than chance, Beatrice asked, "What do you suppose it means?"

Courage. You will face an unexpected challenge that requires fearlessness and great strength.

Since the day she'd received the cards, Adelaide had never had one get away from her like that. Perhaps it had escaped to serve as a reminder of Beatrice's current situation? *Yes*, Adelaide thought, *let's leave it at that*.

Plucking the card from Beatrice's hand she swiftly shuffled it into the deck. As she turned her head, her vision went cloudy and off-kilter. Before her sat two Beatrices—one, lovely and inquisitive, just as she'd always been; the other, a pale, trembling wreck of a girl in great distress. Head bowed, Adelaide willed the vision to fade. When she looked at Beatrice again, the frightful image was gone. With a nervous laugh, she said, "It means I should pay better attention to what I'm doing."

Evening came and Adelaide left for dinner at the hotel with Judith Dashley and Marietta Stevens. She'd invited Beatrice to join her, but Beatrice chose to stay behind to wash dishes and discuss the day's events with Eleanor.

"Do you think I should try using the spiritoscope again?" Beatrice asked, drying a teapot.

Eleanor replied, "So long as you're mindful in what you're doing, I don't think it could hurt."

"But you can't say for certain?"

Eleanor furrowed her brow, placed the pot on the shelf. "Communication with the spirit world can be something like baking a soufflé. You can use all the best ingredients, follow the instructions to the letter, and still wind up with a confusing mess—oftentimes because of something silly, like heavy footsteps or a slammed door. Although I can't say for certain how things will go the next time around, I can promise you this—I'll be right by your side should you choose to pursue it."

"I'd like that," Beatrice said. Swirling a tea towel inside another pot she asked, "What does it take to be a witch?"

Washing the pot's lid, Eleanor said, "Curiosity, attention, tenacity, courage and an unshakable belief in things unseen. What did it take to be Beatrice Dunn before all this began?"

"Much the same, I suppose," Beatrice said with a shrug. Thinking of the card that'd escaped from Adelaide's deck she added, "Excepting, perhaps, courage."

Eleanor frowned. "I don't believe that, not for a minute. Think of what brought you here in the first place. I dare you to say courage had no part in it."

Beatrice, embarrassed, smiled at her.

"My mother was right to say the world has need of more witches," Eleanor explained. "She worked diligently to help the many women who came to her for assistance. She healed their bodies, minds and hearts as best she could. Still, she felt she had to hide. I suppose in a sense I've been hiding here, too, albeit in plain sight. I often worry what might happen if certain people were to discover what I do. Throughout the ages witches have been hunted and put to death. I'm sure you've read the tales, heard the stories?"

"Yes," Beatrice answered. "But the witches in those tales were bad. They deserved what was coming to them."

"Ah-ha!" Eleanor said, wagging her finger. "That's exactly what the storytellers want you to believe. I guess you haven't come across 'The Princess Who Wished to Be a Witch.' The grimoire will show it to you should you wish to read it. Imagine what the world would be like if all mothers told that tale to their daughters."

"Do you believe everything your mother said about me during the dumb supper?"

"Yes."

"But why me? Why now?" Beatrice asked. "What good does it do me, or anyone else, if I'm a witch?"

"You've barely gotten started and you're already working magic. Think back to your encounter with Judith Dashley. She's been changed by your words, her heart healed."

"Is that what I'm supposed to do then?" she asked. "Spend the rest of my life talking to spirits?"

"Among other things," Eleanor said. "But I believe there's far more ahead for you than that. My mother's words indicated several gifts—the Wisdom of the Mothers, the Language of Dreams . . ."

"Do you believe in the Dearlies?" Beatrice asked. She'd read of them in the grimoire and found the notion of them intriguing. "Or is that just another tale? Sometimes it's difficult to tell the tales from the truth."

"The grimoire doesn't lie," Eleanor replied. "Its wisdom takes many forms within its pages—recipes, spells, sagas . . . and yes, even fairy tales. Every word within it holds truth. As fanciful as it might sound, the Dearlies are real. Have you had any dreams since you arrived?"

"No," Beatrice said, "at least not any that I can remember. It's no wonder, though. I've had a dreadful time getting any rest, because of, well, everything, I guess. When I sat with Mrs. Dashley she mentioned a tea you'd given her to help her sleep. Do you think it might help me?"

Fetching a large canister from behind the counter Eleanor said, "Let's find out, shall we?"

The tea was made from mugwort, peppermint, chamomile, rose petals, valerian root, burdock, yarrow and bog myrtle, and as the canister said, *the perfect tonic to ready the body for sleep and the mind for dreaming.*

Beatrice watched as Eleanor measured the mixture into a teapot then added hot water so it could steep.

"There are a few things you can do to entice the Dearlies, too," Eleanor said. "You must let them know they're needed. Here is how you go about it."

Listening intently, Beatrice took down Eleanor's instructions in her notebook. *Place a drop of honey on top of each bedpost. Tie a sprig of lavender above your head. Fill a muslin pouch with anise seeds and tuck it inside your pillow. Sprinkle marigold petals on the floor beneath your bed.*

"Last but not least," Eleanor said, "the Dearlies adore anything that shines, like raindrops on holly leaves, or morning dew on spider webs. If you've anything that sparkles and glints—a ring, a hair comb, a ribbon with silver thread—wear it to bed."

"I've just the thing," Beatrice said, remembering her mother's glass brooch with the wren's feather inside it. "Should I be worried about nightmares, though?"

"Some witches believe you should always guard against them, but I only do so if they make pests of themselves, returning again and again, refusing to leave me alone. Nightmares are like the rest of our dreams, they come to us for a reason. The Dearlies make them with your exact dimensions in mind. A dream always fits."

Pouring herself some tea, Beatrice hoped Eleanor was right.

"If you wake in the night," Eleanor said, "come tell me your dreams. It's been a while since I've made sense of them for someone else, but I'm happy to try. As my mother used to say, 'An uninterpreted dream is like an unopened letter.' The more you pay attention to them, the more they repay your attention. At the very least, write down every detail you can remember, whether it's at midnight or first light."

"I will," Beatrice said, suddenly feeling quite tired. She hadn't even taken her first sip of the tea, but the scent spiralling from her cup was already working its magic. "Who listens to your dreams?" she asked, stifling a yawn.

"My mother did, when I was young," Eleanor replied, "and there's always been Perdu."

"Not Miss Thom?" Beatrice asked, thinking she would've been a more likely choice.

Eleanor laughed. "Attempting to wake Adelaide from sleep is like trying to wake the dead. Who knows, someday soon, I might tell my dreams to you."

Notebook tucked under her arm, cup and saucer in hand, Beatrice bid Eleanor goodnight. "Thank you for the tea," she said, "and the advice."

"Goodnight, dear Beatrice," Eleanor replied. "May your dreams be all you need them to be."

Bright sat on the edge of Beatrice's saucer staring at Twitch. "Is she asleep?" she asked, impatiently tapping her foot. Twitch had insisted on singing to the girl each night, mostly lullabies in the languages of the Fay. "We don't have time for a serenade," she complained. "There's work to be done, at last!"

"My, she smells heavenly!" Twitch swooned, hovering over the girl, sniffing her hair, her cheeks, her lips.

"That's just the mugwort on her breath," Bright said, arms folded. "Don't let yourself get incapacitated by her glamour. It grows more powerful every day." Walking along the rim of Beatrice's cup, she peered into its bowl to take stock of how much tea the girl had consumed. "It's still half full," she observed. "We'll need to work fast."

Twitch crouched near the brooch Beatrice had pinned to the neck of her nightdress. Clouding the pretty trinket with his breath, he polished the glass with his coat sleeve until it shone bright. He was more excited about Beatrice's dream than he'd been about anything in his entire life. He and

Bright had been planning it for days, constructing the details, bit by precious bit. He'd thought of it each night as he'd sung to her in her sleep, each day as he'd trailed around her room, sharpening her pencils with the edge of a rose thorn, re-mending the hem of her dress with fairy silk. Gently blowing her a kiss, he whispered in her ear, "Sweet dreams, dear Beatrice."

She was flying through the air, high above the city, over rooftops and trees in a cloudless, moonlit sky. She was surrounded by hundreds of witches, careening about on broomsticks, robes trailing in the wind, hair loose, eyes wild. She was not afraid. To her, they were the most beautiful creatures she'd ever seen—powerful, intelligent—free from all care. She followed wherever they led. This was where she belonged.

Their destination was half familiar, half strange—Madison Square Park transformed into a witches' lair. The footpaths glowed with enchantment, the tree branches were strewn with bells, bones and poppets. The flames of Lady Liberty's torch were no longer made of glass, but fire. It raged and hissed and shot overhead as the witches danced around it dressed in veils that trailed to the ground. They were singing in a language she'd never heard but somehow understood. They spoke of the Land of Dreams, the Realm of the Dead, the Wonders of the Otherworld. They called to Hecate, to Circe, to the Morai "to open our minds, to strengthen our spells, to bless our works."

When their rite was finished, they turned and looked upon Beatrice, blessings and secrets flowing from their mouths like a thousand babbling brooks. As she marvelled at the sight, one witch stepped forward. Pulling the veil from her face, she revealed herself to be Adelaide Thom.

"Look!" Adelaide commanded, pointing to the scarred hollow above her cheek.

Beatrice did, and was startled to find that Billy Dashley's precious toy, his shining blue marble, had replaced Adelaide's missing eye. As she stared at the glowing orb twinkling in the firelight, she was transported to an endless corridor lined with chandeliers and mirrors. Ghostly figures flitted all around her, their reflections appearing more as wisps of smoke than flesh. Most of them were unknown to her, but there were a few she recognized—Dr. Brody's father holding the dial of the spiritoscope; Adelaide's mother wearing her tattered silk scarf; Billy Dashley clutching his bag of peanuts, giving her a toothy smile; and her own beloved mother extending a lonely, empty hand. As Beatrice reached for her, the ghost changed into the spirit of Madame St. Clair. "Be still," the witch ordered, reaching through the looking glass and placing a crooked finger on Beatrice's mouth.

Beatrice blinked and Madame St. Clair disappeared, her own reflection taking the witch's place. Her eyes were lined with charcoal and she wore a crown of gold on her head as if she were a queen, or a priestess, or perhaps even a goddess. "This is who you are," Madame St. Clair's voice announced.

No sooner were the words spoken than the corridor went black as pitch. Lost and afraid, Beatrice clung to the wall, hoping to find her way out. The glassy surface beneath her fingers turned to stone, cold and damp and covered with glyphs like those that were carved into the obelisk. In the darkness, she heard a creature draw near, growling and snarling and gnashing its teeth.

“This way!” Eleanor’s voice called from the right.

“Follow me!” Adelaide’s voice called from the left.

Not knowing which way to turn, Beatrice tore a string from the hem of her dress and began tying knots along the length of it. “By knot of one, my spell’s begun. By knot of two, it will come true. By knot of three, so may it be. By knot of four, this power I store. By knot of five, my spell is alive.”

With the fifth knot, a door appeared in front of her, fitted with a forbidding iron lock.

“By knot of six, this spell I fix. By knot of seven, the future I’ll leaven. By knot of eight, my will be fate. By knot of nine, what’s done is mine!”

With that, a key appeared around her neck, hot to the touch, as if it’d been freshly pulled from the forge and quenched in oil.

Putting the key in the lock, Beatrice made to turn it, but was shaken from her dream by the sound of breaking glass.

Perdu squawked and spat and sounded an alarm. “Fiend!” he cried. “Fiend, fiend, fiend!”

Twitch tugged at Bright’s arm. “Your cheeks . . .” he whispered, watching them turn blue.

“I know,” Bright replied, hands to her face as she helplessly watched Beatrice rise from her bed.

Hearing Eleanor and Adelaide tramping down the stairs, Beatrice threw on a wrap and followed them. The three women huddled together near the door, bathed in the dim glow of lantern light. A rock had come through a windowpane and settled amongst a scattering of glass shards. They might've thought it simple vandalism had there not been a message attached.

Eleanor picked up the rock and examined the crude note.

"What does it say?" Adelaide asked.

Peering over Eleanor's shoulder Beatrice read the words aloud, "I know what you are."

Late, late, yestreen
I saw the Old Moon in the New Moon's arms.
I fear, I fear, my Master dear,
That we shall come to great harm.

—The Ballad of Sir Patrick Spens

> The Sibyl, with frenzied mouth uttering things not to be laughed at, unadorned and unperfumed, yet reaches to a thousand years with her voice by the aid of the god.
>
> —Heraclitus

Into the Fire.

The witches were seated around a table in the teashop, enjoying a quiet dinner of brown bread and onion soup. They could've been dining at Delmonico's (Judith Dashley had offered to treat them), but Beatrice had declined the woman's invitation in favour of having supper in, just the three of them. She'd wanted to be surrounded by peace and quiet and familiar faces before they made their way to the Fifth Avenue Hotel where she'd agreed to perform a demonstration with Dr. Brody's spiritoscope for Mr. and Mrs. Dashley, and Marietta Stevens.

Sopping up the last of her soup with a piece of crust, Adelaide glanced at the clock to check the time—quarter past seven. They were expected at the hotel for eight. "I'm going on ahead," she announced. "I'd like to make sure everything's in order."

"We'll be along shortly," Eleanor said, speaking on Beatrice's behalf. "I thought Beatrice might like to have a cup of tea to sort her thoughts."

Beatrice gave Eleanor a grateful nod.

It was just the kind of response Adelaide had expected from Eleanor. In fact, she was surprised her partner hadn't found some excuse for them to call the whole thing off. Since that rock had come crashing through the window, Eleanor had been jittery, on edge. Mr. Withrow, the landlord, had spotted the broken pane before she could get the glazer in to fix it.

"You'll have the repair done and paid for before the next rent is due," he'd grumbled, "or else you'll be out on your ears. I don't know why I even agreed to rent to a pair of petticoats."

Adelaide had tried to calm Eleanor by saying, "As soon as it's fixed, Withrow will forget it ever happened." Shaking her head, Eleanor had replied, "I doubt it."

And she was not wild about the idea of the demonstration at the hotel. "Participating in a few supervised experiments at Dr. Brody's home is one thing, but getting pulled into his search for ghosts is quite another. Can't he conduct that sort of research without Beatrice? And why must the hotel's owner and the Dashleys be present? It's looking for trouble, especially when Beatrice still has so much to learn about her gifts."

"How horribly maternal of you," Adelaide had retorted. "It's Beatrice's choice. Who are we to ask her to wait when the stars are so magnificently aligned? The signs, as you would say, couldn't be clearer. Everything—from Beatrice's arrival, to Dr. Brody's research, to the sudden influx of ghosts—points in this direction. Oh Great Witch of the Bronx River, how many portents do you require?"

Arms crossed, Eleanor had said, "I haven't even met this Dr. Brody of yours. How can you be certain he's not playing Beatrice and you for fools?"

"Have you forgotten I, too, have gifts? Or aren't they worth trusting anymore? If anyone should be worried about getting hoodwinked, it's Dr. Brody. This city is rife with false prophets and seers who'd happily pull the wool over his eyes. And he's not *my* anything. He's a decent man with an open mind."

"You're saying that because you fancy him," Eleanor had accused.

"I make it a practice not to fancy anyone: it's a horrid way to live."

"I have eyes," Eleanor had countered. "Your cheeks turn crimson at each mention of his name. But what does Dr. Brody know of magic? Just because he has an interest in all things supernatural, that doesn't mean he respects Beatrice's gifts."

"Before you condemn the man, you should take the trouble to get to know him," Adelaide said stiffly.

"Very well then," Eleanor had relented. "I'll defer my judgement until I see the good doctor's work for myself. That is, if I'm allowed to attend this grand affair?"

Dr. Brody was standing with Mr. Dashley in a private salon on the second floor of the Fifth Avenue Hotel. The room, richly appointed with Persian rugs, rosewood panelling, crystal chandeliers, overstuffed chairs and a half-dozen porcelain vases filled with palm fronds and tuberoses, was generally reserved for lectures and meetings held by the hotel's elite clientele. Mrs. Stevens had been kind enough to lend it to them for the evening, so long as she was allowed to witness the proceedings. Quinn would've happily continued his experiments at home, but Adelaide had suggested they try their luck at the hotel instead, since the place was supposed to be crawling with ghosts. So there he was, at half past seven on a Saturday night, preparing to help a young woman talk with spirits. Who would've imagined it?

"Is the table where you'd like it?" Mr. Dashley asked. "I can call the porter if you'd like it moved."

"It's fine where it is," Quinn answered. He'd spent the last hour adjusting the various components of the spiritoscope in relation to its position on the table. Moving the table would mean he'd have to go through the entire process again. As he checked the angle of the machine's dial one last time, the powerful scent of tuberoses filled his nose and caused him to sneeze. Fiddling in his pocket for his handkerchief, he stared down the offending flowers. "What the porter can do," he said, pointing to the many vases around the room, "is get rid of those." Mr. Dashley called the porter and one by one the vases disappeared, whisked off to some other part of the hotel to spread their overwhelming scent.

"Better, eh?" Quinn said, looking pleased.

"Much," Mr. Dashley replied, then hoped he hadn't just quashed some act of generosity by his wife. Judith hadn't mentioned she was going to send flowers, but he wouldn't put it past her. Short, stout and balding, Dashley was a veritable giant when it came to intellect, but never certain of himself when it came to his wife. He found it difficult to express feelings, although he, too, had been hit hard by their son's death, so entrenched in sorrow that he'd feared it couldn't be lifted up without a system of fortified levers and wedges. Many men in his position might've drunk themselves into oblivion or thrown themselves into their work, but Alden Dashley had never had much of a taste for drink, and he didn't have to work in any true sense of the word. Judith's family's fortune was the engine that pulled the train of their financial success. He was just the conductor, keeping things on track—legal matters, real estate, business investments and such. In the wake of their son's death, Judith had found distraction and solace in her quest to make contact with the spirit realm. While he'd supported her efforts, he'd found he'd needed to take a different tack. To that end, he'd joined several benevolent societies and lodges including the Freemasons and the Odd Fellows. But it wasn't until he'd gone into Mr. Brody's shop in search of a new magnifying glass that he'd finally found the sort of camaraderie he'd been looking for. Joining the Fraternal Order of the Unknown Philosophers had been a welcome balm for his weary heart. And now he had grown very fond of the late Mr. Brody's only son.

"Thank you for agreeing to attend this evening's proceedings," Quinn said, resisting the urge to tinker with the spiritoscope any further.

"I'm always happy to come to the aid of a fellow Philosopher," Mr. Dashley replied. "Besides, Judith has been going on about Miss Dunn ever since they met. I'd be in hot water if I passed up the opportunity to make her acquaintance. I'm quite curious to see what all the fuss is about. With you involved, I dare say I'm even hopeful something miraculous might transpire." His tone at the end was wistful, his gaze far off.

Dr. Brody recalled just then, with some embarrassment, mind that the ghost child Beatrice had seen in the teashop was Mr. Dashley's son.

When Adelaide arrived, she surveyed the room to see if there was anything left to be done. She couldn't shake the feeling that something was missing. "Flowers," she muttered at last. She'd left the task to Judith, who was keen to be helpful with anything involving the young Miss Dunn, telling her that something understated, yet elegant, would be best. "Leave it with me," Judith had said. "I'll find just the right blooms to create the perfect ambience."

Approaching the porter, Adelaide asked, "Has there been any mention of flowers for the room?"

"Yes, miss," the young man answered. "They arrived this afternoon."

"Then where have they got to? I don't suppose they walked off by themselves."

"No, miss," the porter replied. "The gentleman sent them away."

Adelaide checked the time. It was too late to go chasing after the flowers (and where was Beatrice? It was a quarter to eight already). Just as she tried to think of a plausible excuse for the missing bouquets, Marietta and Judith entered the room. Mrs. Stevens was dressed in her usual black on black on black, several strands of jet beads around her neck. Adelaide admired the way the woman could make her perpetual mourning look fashionable, when so many widows became invisible, swallowed up by endless yards of crepe. Judith had chosen to wear a mustard-coloured dress with a perky bustle and matching hat. The felt topper was trimmed with velvet ribbons and a stuffed goldfinch with glass eyes that stared inquisitively from the brim as if it were a sailor on a ship's prow. Six well-pressed housemaids trailed behind her, each one carrying a large vase filled with the banished tuberose bouquets. "Two on the mantel, two on the floor and two on that table over there," Judith directed, as her husband regarded her with wry affection. Shaking her head she turned to Marietta. "Thank heavens I spotted them in the lobby or they might never have made it upstairs."

As a pair of maids headed to the table that held the spiritoscope, Quinn intervened. Hands up, he politely suggested, "Perhaps those could go on the hallway table outside the door, instead?"

The maids looked at Judith.

"Do as the good doctor wishes," Judith said, giving Quinn a friendly nod. Then turning to Adelaide she breathlessly asked, "Where is our Beatrice?"

"She'll be here soon," Adelaide assured her. "She and Eleanor decided some tea was in order, to calm the nerves and clear the mind."

"Of course," Judith said. "Miss Dunn is remarkably wise for her age."

Adelaide wasn't sure if Judith's unwavering admiration for the girl was good or bad. Beatrice was an unbelievably forthright creature, but she knew nothing of managing expectations or brokering respect. If she wanted to make headway in this town, especially with the likes of Marietta Stevens, she'd have to temper her goodness with confidence and savvy. In Adelaide's opinion, it was the only way to survive.

Strolling around the salon, the women appraised their surroundings, with Judith glancing frequently at the door for sign of Beatrice.

Marietta soon turned her attention to the spiritoscope. "Is this the contraption the girl is to use? It looks like an outdated telegraph machine."

"What an astute observation," Adelaide said, motioning for Quinn to join them.

"Indeed," he chimed in. "That's exactly what inspired it. I'd be happy to explain how it works."

"Don't trouble yourself," Marietta replied. "I expect all to be revealed in the doing."

"If all goes according to plan," Quinn replied.

Adelaide kept quiet, thinking it might be best to let Marietta's remarks go unchallenged. She'd warned Quinn that Mrs. Stevens wasn't driven by emotion, but rather a constant state of waiting to be impressed.

But Judith couldn't leave well enough alone. "I, for one, think it's rather ingenious."

Mr. Dashley slipped his arm around his wife and gave her a quick affectionate squeeze.

Seeing this small act of kindness pass between the pair inspired Adelaide to stick up for Quinn. Tucking her arm through his she declared, "As do I."

Eleanor and Beatrice entered the hotel lobby at ten to eight. Taking in the extravagant decor, from the marble floors to the fluted columns to the gilded mirrors that lined the corridors, Beatrice now understood why her old classmate Joseph Wheeler had said the place made him nervous. All the same, she was eager to try her hand at the spiritoscope again. She hoped this time her mother's spirit might stay a while longer. Based on what she could remember of her dream (thus far, very little), she felt it might be possible, even probable. From time to time brief flashes of what she'd seen were triggered by mundane things—the sound of Eleanor or Adelaide's voice speaking a certain word, or the scent of woodsmoke in the air when the wind was from the west. Among the foggy images in her brain, she'd seen her mother's face, tender, yet fleeting. Clinging to that memory she'd made up her mind to do whatever it took to see her mother again. If it meant she had to endure a thousand experiments and meet a thousand ghosts, then so be it.

"This way," Eleanor said, motioning to the front desk.

As Beatrice followed, she was overcome by the feeling that she was being watched. The scents of furniture oil and lye soap stuck in the back of her throat. The sound of a young woman's laughter rang in her ears. When she turned to try to find the source, she spotted a pair of scrubber girls nearby, pointing at her and whispering. She watched with amazement as they passed in front of her, their bodies effortlessly gliding through a wall of solid marble.

A gentleman in an ill-fitting suit was at the desk in front of them. Waiting for the night manager to assist him, he swayed side to side, softly, almost imperceptibly, talking to himself.

Thinking he, too, might be a ghost, Beatrice reached out and touched the sleeve of his coat. Finding it real, she drew her hand back and looked to see if Eleanor had noticed her indiscretion. Happily, she hadn't.

At last, the manager looked up from a ledger on the desk and addressed the gentleman. "I'm sorry, Mr. Guiteau. Senator Conkling is unable to meet you tonight."

"It's important I speak with him," the man insisted. "Election Day is just a month away."

"Perhaps you can come back tomorrow? I'm afraid there's nothing more I can do for you today."

Disgruntled, Mr. Guiteau left the desk, swearing under his breath.

Beatrice watched him as he skulked away. One by one, shadowy figures came up from the floor beneath his feet and wrapped themselves around him. He seemed completely unaware of their presence, and they seemed frightfully determined to stay put. Unsettled, she quickly looked away.

"Who's next?" the night manager asked, eyes on Eleanor, silently judging her attire. Verdict, *unimpressed.*

"Miss Dunn and Miss St. Clair for Mrs. Stevens, please," Eleanor replied.

Licking the end of his thumb, he turned the page of the ledger and scanned it for their names. "Ah yes, there you are," he said with a surprised smile. "Just one moment and I'll get a bellhop to accompany you to the salon." Ducking back to a small office behind the desk he pulled the cord on a distant bell.

Suddenly feeling dizzy and sick, Beatrice reached for Eleanor's hand to steady herself.

"Are you all right?" Eleanor asked.

"I think so," Beatrice answered, hoping her queasiness would soon pass.

"You don't have to do this," Eleanor said. "We can send our regrets. No one will think any less of you, especially if you're unwell."

"I'm fine now. Really," Beatrice said, standing straight and smoothing her skirts.

Eleanor could see that Beatrice was struggling, but didn't quite know how to help her through it. Her thoughts turned to Lucy Newland standing on the balcony at Liberty's torch and the helpless feeling that'd come over her when Lucy had insisted she could take care of things on her own. That feeling had become far too familiar as of late.

A bellhop in a red wool jacket and cap appeared beside the desk. "Follow me," he said.

Beatrice spotted the table holding the spiritoscope as soon as she entered the room. It was just as it'd been in Dr. Brody's study, only now there were several chairs facing it, as if she were expected to put on a show. Adelaide had told her ahead of time who would be in attendance, but she hadn't met either Mr. Dashley or the formidable Marietta Stevens before, and her nerves flared again. Then Judith Dashley rushed across the room to greet her, taking her by the arm. "You look lovely this evening," she said, "and quite sophisticated too. It's so nice to see you again."

"Thank you, Mrs. Dashley," Beatrice said, not feeling sophisticated at all. She was wearing a dress in a beautiful shade of blue, borrowed from Adelaide. It had required a fair bit of corset tightening to fit her into it and it made her feel like an imposter rather than fashionable. Eleanor had tried to veto the gown, but Beatrice had decided it was best to give in to Adelaide's kindness. She didn't want her to think she was ungrateful.

"Come meet my husband," Judith said, leading Beatrice across the room. "Alden, dear," she called to Mr. Dashley, "here is our darling Miss Dunn."

Beatrice nodded and smiled and tried to look serene.

"Mr. Dashley is here tonight as a representative of the Unknown Philosophers," Judith explained. "But he also has a great interest in hearing from our darling boy."

"Of course," Beatrice said, wishing she could promise them Billy would appear. She, too, hoped for his return. She'd liked his sweet face. “He favours you,” she said to Alden, without considering how strange her words might sound.

“Pardon?” Mr. Dashley said.

“He has your eyes,” Beatrice said. “I saw his face quite clearly during his visitation.”

Mr. Dashley stammered, “What a nice sentiment.”

“And so true!” Judith exclaimed. “I can’t tell you how many times I made the same observation when Billy was alive.”

Next came Mrs. Stevens. Adelaide had described her as “a discerning woman who could dictate the course of our future” but had neglected to mention her formidable stature and intimidating stare. Thankfully the introduction was a brief affair, a simple exchange of names then a cut to the chase.

“Shall we dispense with small talk, Miss Dunn, and get things underway?”

Adelaide ushered Beatrice to the table where Dr. Brody was waiting to help her settle into her chair. “You’ve nothing to worry about,” she said. “Everyone here wishes you well.”

Eleanor, who’d been staying out of the way, now came to Beatrice’s side and whispered in her ear, “Don’t hesitate to bring things to a halt should anything give you pause. If you need my help, I’ll be here.”

“Thank you,” Beatrice said with a nervous smile.

Handing Adelaide the silk blind to tie over Beatrice’s eyes, Dr. Brody gave the girl a few final instructions. “We’ll proceed the same as we did before. After I blindfold you, we’ll take our seats. Adelaide will record any movement of the needle and I’ll keep my eyes on the board. You may disengage from the spiritoscope at any time. All clear?”

"Yes, Dr. Brody."

Adelaide gently draped the silk scarf over Beatrice's eyes, pulled it taut and tied it in place.

"Are you ready, Miss Dunn?" Dr. Brody asked, taking his seat.

"Yes," Beatrice answered, taking a deep breath.

"You may place your hands on the board whenever you'd like to begin," Brody said.

Fingertips to the wood, Beatrice waited for a spirit to approach. From what she'd witnessed in the lobby, there were indeed a few ghosts lurking about the hotel. But several seconds passed and nothing moved, nothing came near. A minute on, she and the board remained still.

She heard a stray cough from Mr. Dashley, an impatient sigh from Mrs. Stevens, the restless tap of Adelaide's foot. She could also feel all eyes upon her, from Eleanor's warm, supportive gaze to Judith's pleading stare.

Should she say something? she wondered. Extend an invitation? "Hello?" she faintly whispered. "Are you here?"

Just as she was about to give up, she felt a tug at her skirt beneath the table.

"Hello, Billy," she said. "I'm glad you've come." Even blindfolded, she could see the boy in her mind's eye.

Judith reached for Alden's hand and excitedly whispered, "That's him. Our boy is here."

Alden responded with a measured nod.

Marietta rolled her eyes in disbelief and shifted in her seat.

Quinn looked concerned. Clearly there was a spirit present. Why wasn't it using the spiritoscope to communicate?

Adelaide glanced at Eleanor.

Eleanor mouthed the word, "Wait."

"Why don't you come out and see my new toy?" Beatrice suggested. "We can play a little game."

Billy frowned and shook his head.

"It's easy," Beatrice urged. "All you have to do is place your hands on mine, then make the needle spin to spell the things you wish to say."

"I can't," Billy insisted.

"Why not?" Beatrice asked.

"I can't make words," Billy replied.

Beatrice thought for a moment. "You mean you can't spell?"

Everyone laughed, except Mrs. Stevens.

Dr. Brody hurriedly wrote, *In future, must consider likelihood of spirit's ability to spell.*

Caring more for Billy's feelings than for making the machine work, Beatrice tried to coax the boy out of hiding. "Why don't you come out from there and give me a proper hello."

Once again, Billy shook his head.

"What's the matter?" Beatrice asked. "Can't you see who's here?"

Pulling his cap over his eyes he said, "Don't tell them where I am."

"Don't tell who where you are?" Beatrice asked, thinking the boy would surely want to see his parents.

"The Marys," Billy whispered, then disappeared.

With that, the same laughter Beatrice had heard in the lobby sounded again, this time ringing loudly in her ears. The overpowering smell of lye soap filled the air. The two scrubber girls were there, with several more by their side. Circling around Beatrice they flew up to the ceiling to hide in the chandeliers. The crystal fobs that hung off the lights tinkled and chimed in sympathy with their flight.

"What's happening?" Judith whispered to Adelaide, eyes wide.

"Shh," Adelaide replied, finger to her lips.

The board under Beatrice's hands grew hot to the touch, so hot she thought her fingertips might burn. Snatching her hands off the board, she felt a violent push against her shoulders. She smelled smoke, felt the searing heat of a fire at her back. Darkness surrounded her. There was no escape.

"Beatrice?" Eleanor softly called. "Are you all right?"

As she opened her mouth to speak, a scrubber girl clasped her hand around her throat, forcing words to come forth that weren't hers. "I am not she," a raspy voice sounded, that of a young woman with an Irish lilt. "I am one of many. Mrs. Stevens knows who I am. She saw me in life. She gazed upon me in death. She knows the secret my body kept. She alone can make it right. She must set in stone what should've been in life."

While everyone else sat stunned at these developments, Eleanor quickly moved to Beatrice's side. She feared for the girl's well-being should the spirit persist. None was so still as Marietta Stevens.

Head bowed, shoulders slumped, Beatrice began to sing.

The Marys have gone rotten,
Dead and forgotten.
Lying in their beds
With their eyes wide open.

The chill hand of death,
Stole them in the night,
As they danced in a fire
That burned too bright.

The chair Beatrice was sitting on began to teeter and shake.

"Beatrice," Eleanor called, trying to steady the girl, "can you hear me?"

Dr. Brody leapt to his feet and came to her aid.

"We can't leave!" Beatrice cried, the voice inhabiting her body now changed to a chorus of desperate wails. "We can't get out!"

Taking a silver charm from her pocket, Eleanor pressed it into Beatrice's hand. "Joan of Arc, Maid of Orleans, Witch of Domrémy, come to our aid, defend this girl."

"Help us!" Beatrice whimpered, her skin turning red, hair singeing at the ends. "We can't breathe!"

The smell of smoke filled the room. The chandeliers began to chime and sway.

Not knowing what else to do, Alden took his wife's hand.

The pear seeds in the phial around Adelaide's neck began to rattle.

Marietta put her hand to her mouth and shook her head.

"Send your angels to protect her," Eleanor implored, "guide her soul to the fore."

Falling into Eleanor's arms, Beatrice gasped for air.

"Beatrice," Eleanor cried, pulling the blindfold loose. "Are you with us?"

Adelaide abandoned her post and rushed to Beatrice's side. Together they held the girl's hands, waiting for her to reply.

"Beatrice," Adelaide whispered, "are you here?"

Eyelids fluttering, Beatrice answered, "I never left."

With that, the needle on the spiritoscope began to move.

Mrs. Stevens watched with astonishment as it spelled out the words M-A-R-Y D-O-N-N-E-L-L-Y A-N-D C-H-I-L-D.

There is a sort of Witchcrafts in those things, whereto the Temptations of the Devil would inveigle us. To worship the Devil is Witchcraft, and under that notion was our Lord urged unto sin. We are told in 1 Samuel 15:23, "Rebellion is as the sin of Witchcraft." When the Devil would have us to sin, he would have us to do the things which the forlorn Witches use to do. Perhaps there are few persons, ever allured by the Devil unto an Explicit Covenant with himself. If any among ourselves be so, my counsel is, that you hunt the Devil from you, with such words as the Psalmist had, "Be gone, Depart from me, ye evil doers, for I will keep the commandments of my God."

—Rev. Cotton Mather, *On Witchcraft*

The Preacher's Confession.

REVEREND FRANCIS TOWNSEND was crouched in front of the fireplace in his study, stirring hot coals with an iron poker. He'd hoped the mundane chore might help stir his thoughts as well, but the mesmerizing glow of the fire had the opposite effect. Taking his pipe from his pocket, he tapped a clump of ash from its bowl onto the hearth, then proceeded to fill it with a pinch of fresh tobacco. Perhaps a few hearty draws on the pipe's stem would clear his mind. Sticking a straw in the fire until it caught light, he brought its glowing end to the bowl and puffed hard.

Checking his watch he saw that it was half past eight. He was supposed to have his weekly sermon written by nine so he could hand the pages over to Sister Piddock. She, in turn, would then choose the appropriate hymns and readings for the Sunday service. That was the arrangement they'd made when he'd first taken the post at the Church of the Good Shepherd just over a year ago, and he'd grudgingly stuck to it. It was that, or choose the hymns himself and take the chance that Sister Piddock, who was also the church organist, might hit a string of sour notes leading up to his homily. Better safe than sorry. The music set the tone for his words, and his words set the stage for the salvation of his flock. Although he was sure the congregation could afford a more accomplished musician, he couldn't afford to lose Sister Piddock's support. Her appearance might be plain, to put it kindly, but her convictions were unshakable. She was obedient to her husband, strong in her faith, and quick to eschew anything that was meant to tempt the weaker sex away from home and family. She especially abhorred the current fashion for ladies to congregate in cafés and teahouses, indulging in idleness and gossip. Childless, she spent her days in the service of the Lord and the Reverend—looking after his vestments, polishing the offering plates, and keeping him informed of those members of the congregation who were in need of his special guidance.

It'd been at Sister Piddock's urging that Townsend had been offered his current position. After hearing him preach at her father's meetinghouse in Utica, she'd asked her husband and several upstanding members of the congregation to consider bringing him to New York. He'd delivered one sermon, "Fidelity to the Word, the Only Shield against the Devil's Malignity," and they'd offered him the job. "We've been praying for a true leader," Sister Piddock had cried, "and clearly God has answered our pleas by delivering you to us." (The previous pastor had been released from his duties after it was discovered he'd taken up the habit of visiting various gambling dens on Saturday nights.)

Reverend Townsend had felt it was the hand of divine Providence, as if he had been called to play a part in some grand holy plan. His grandfather, the Reverend Deodat Townsend, had always insisted that Francis was destined for great things, even when, for a short time in his youth, he'd been drawn to fisticuffs and rum. It was his grandfather who'd advised his father to send him to the seminary in Andover, and it was there Francis had learned not only of theology but of his family's storied past.

He came from a long line of God-fearing men going back to the famed preachers of Massachusetts Bay, who'd lived there when the colony was rife with witchcraft. It'd been his ancestors, in the years after the trials, who'd continued to be watchful for the Devil's workings within God's people. They, along with a few faithful followers, had formed a group called the Brethren, religious folk who wished to practice the strong faith of those who first settled the land. Carrying on the traditions of his forefathers, Reverend Deodat Townsend had become a travelling preacher, moving across the Frontier to spread the Gospel. He quickly gained a reputation for having a beautiful singing voice, knowing the Bible by heart, and having the ability to "put evil to flight." There'd been plenty to distract the people—preachers who peddled false miracles, salesmen of all stripes (hawking brushes, pots, scissors, knives and patent medicines), tawdry circus folk in gaudy tents (bearded ladies, legless men, snake charmers and fortune tellers)—but Deodat had something to offer that no one else had. Upon hearing stories of the magic and witchery that existed in the wilderness of the West, Deodat Townsend guaranteed, hand to God, that he could take care of whatever witchery might be troubling a place with no questions asked.

Francis had inherited his grandfather's personal effects after he had passed—a Bible worn and faded from much use, a small collection of relics from his days on the frontier, and a parcel of writings passed down from the Brethren (sermons, mostly, pertaining to the wages of sin). When Francis's mother had cleared out the room where his grandfather had died, she took all the bedding from the mattress and stripped the pillows of their linens. The pillow on which the old preacher had rested his head felt oddly cold to the touch. Slicing the ticking open, she'd discovered a wreath of feathers buried within the stuffing, large enough to fit on a man's head. She'd cradled the thing to her breast and called it a glorious sign—a feather crown made by the angels to show her that Deodat had made his way to Heaven. His father, thinking it evil, had thrown the crown into the fire. "It's a sign of dark magic," he'd said. "Proof that the witches who've plagued this family cursed him to die."

The one thing that Francis had gained from his grandfather that no one could cast aside was his fervent desire to banish evil. Yes, he knew that it was only by God's will that evil existed, but he also knew that the reason it was there was so that men of God could expose and destroy it. Only by such shining examples could the most rebellious naysayers be brought into the fold. Sometimes his intolerance for sin was so great, he became overwhelmed with a longing for stocks and thumbscrews, pressings and hangings. Choking on his impulses, he'd cried to Heaven with clenched fists, "Dear Lord, what would you have me do when the world allows so little punishment for sin?"

He was glad of the faith of his new congregation and the way they clung to his every word, but no amount of Temperance meetings or weekly Bible study could stop the storm of iniquity that was brewing outside the chapel doors. What would his grandfather think of the times in which he lived? Of this city, so rampant with sin? Surely he would say that it was filled with opportunities for righteous men to carry out the work of the Lord. Francis prayed every night for the chance to stand up to be led to the dwelling places of evil so he might cast it out.

Mr. Beadle's housemaid Lena McLeod had been one answer to that prayer. So had the little Gyspy girl he'd met in the park. The waif had been more a challenge to him than the maid, sent to him as a test. He'd been fooled into thinking that because she was a child there was still goodness inside her, but it hadn't taken him long to discover that was not the case. When he'd asked her to recite the first Bible verse that came to her mind, she'd spat at him and spoken a string of foul words instead. She'd acted sweet then insolent, repentant then wicked. When none of that had succeeded in breaking the Reverend's resolve, she'd pressed herself against him and tried to seduce him. She turned out to be a devil in a child's dress. Perhaps she'd been sent to torment him by Mr. Beadle's maid or some other deceased witch. His father had always warned that a witch's curse couldn't be undone just by killing the witch who spoke it. "Their words stay alive long after the fact. Sometimes gaining more power after death," he'd instructed his son. The Gypsy girl had come at him, eyes filled with fire, cursing and taking the Lord's name in vain. He'd struck her with the back of his hand and she'd fallen in a heap on the floor. Her scalp had blossomed red with blood as her eyes rolled back in her head.

Remembering the words of the two men in black suits who'd come to his door after Mr. Beadle's maid had died, he'd retreated to his bedchamber and prayed until dawn, hoping that they might return and do as they had done before. At first light he'd gone down to the cellar to discover that the little girl was gone, no trace of her to be found. Falling on his knees he'd said a prayer of thanksgiving, praising God for releasing him from the foul little devil. The Lord does indeed work in mysterious ways.

Checking his watch again, Reverend Townsend saw that it was nearly nine. Although he was tempted to leave the parsonage in search of greater challenges, he knew he should get on with composing his sermon. Walking to the bookcase, he pulled out his grandfather's Bible and read the inscription: *Let this book be the Light that guides you through the Storm.* In recent weeks, when he'd been at a loss for inspiration, he'd taken to the practice of Bible dipping to assist him in his work. Last Saturday, after letting the Bible fall open on its own, his finger had landed on 1 Timothy 2:12: *But I suffer not a woman to teach, nor to usurp authority over the man, but to be in silence.* The words had then flown from his pen to the page as if guided by providence of angels. He'd titled the sermon, "Against Intuition."

> Women often say they have a "knowing," a "feeling," that something is right or wrong. They'll claim they've seen the answer to a great dilemma in a dream. Who are they

to claim the gift of prophecy? What force compels them to speak such lies? More often than not their words are merely a ploy to get others to do their bidding. When caught, they say it was nothing but a silly, foolish game. They insist no one got hurt. But this sort of deceit is no laughing matter. It is a terrible crafty tool of women, especially when used upon trusting men—a tool of Satan himself. I say to all gentlemen, do not be fooled by women's talk of intuition. I say to all women, do not be used by Devils as a mouthpiece for Satan's foul words. The only special knowledge he'll afford to you is misery. The only thing you'll gain is regret.

Taking the Bible in hand, Francis set it on its spine. Closing his eyes, he prayed for the Lord to lend divine assistance. "Not my will, Lord, but Thine." As the book fell open and he placed his finger on the page, he discovered something he was sure he'd never seen before. Sticking up between the Bible's pages was a small unbound leaflet, written in a stranger's hand.

"An Attempt to Cure Witchcraft"

For, though it be Folly to impute every dubious Accident or unwanted Effect of Providence to Witchcraft, yet there are some things which cannot be ascribed otherwise. That the following Account will afford to him that shall read with Observation, a further clear confirmation, that, there is both a God and a Devil and Witchcraft.

Early in the year 1693, Reverend M. travelled from Boston to Salem. He had it in his mind that he might deliver a sermon to the good people there and also gather an accurate accounting of what had taken place during The Great Storm of Witchcraft. Upon his arrival he'd found that in the months since the witchcraft tryals, things had gone considerably quiet, especially when it came to Apparitions and Accusations. By and large, people spoke as if the thing had never happened, or at least as if they had no real knowledge of it. When pressed, no one could even point to the exact location of the hangings on Gallows Hill. "You must ask so-and-so," one man would say. "I know nothing," another would profess. "Perhaps Mr. D— can be of help, he has the longest memory of anyone in the Neighbourhood." These cries of ignorance went on and on from farm to farm and house to house, but Reverend M. would not be dissuaded. He was determined to stir the pot as it were, knowing that the Devil could not so easily be put to rest.

During his visit, two odd things occurred to further convince him that witchcraft in this Country was alive and well.

One: The leafs his sermon had been written upon were lost and the only explanation he could find was that they'd been stolen away by spectres. (This was later confirmed by yet another strange occurrence.) "These notes were before the Sabbath stolen from me, with such Circumstances that I am somewhat satisfied, the Spectres or Agents in the Invisible World were the Robbers."

Two: He held discourse with a Mrs. Carver (assumed to be an honest, God-fearing woman), who had been strangely visited with some shining Spirits, which were good Angels, in her opinion of them. "She intimated several things unto me, whereof some were to be kept secret. She also told me that a New Storm of Witchcraft would fall upon the Country, to chastise the Iniquity that was used in the willful Smothering and Covering of the Last; and that many fierce Opposites to the Discovery of that Witchcraft would be thereby convinced."

Not long after the good Reverend returned to Boston, he was called to minister to a young servant girl named Mercy Wylde who had fallen into fits one Sunday after church. Seeing that the girl (just seventeen years of age) was clearly afflicted in the manner of the Damsels of Salem, the Reverend determined that he should retire with her to a nearby house to assess her condition.

In the course of his examinations he began to suspect that the girl had been bewitched. Some time before, at the height of The Great Storm, Mercy Wylde, on her way home from market, had come across one Sarah Gowan who was chained to the wall of the prison. Sister Gowan, since hanged at Salem for witchcraft, called to the girl and begged for tobacco. Fearful of the woman, Mercy had refused and thrown sawdust in her face. The woman, revealing her true nature, cursed the girl to suffer for her unkindness.

In Reverend M.'s words: "I had many Entertainments from the Invisible World in the Circumstances of a Young Woman horribly possessed with Devils. The Damsel was cast into my cares by the singular Providence of God; and accordingly I kept Three Successive Dayes of Prayer with Fasting on her behalf, and then I saw her

Delivered. (For which I kept a Time of solemn Thanksgiving.) But after a while, her Tormentors returned, and her Miseries renewed; and I did alone in my Study fast and pray for her Deliverance. And unto my Amazement, when I had kept my third Day for her, she was finally and forever delivered from the hand of evil Angels; and I had afterwards the satisfaction of seeing not only her so brought home unto the Lord that she was admitted unto our Church, but also many others, even some scores of young people, awakened by the Picture of Hell exhibited in her sufferings, to flee from the Wrath to come."

The following is an account of the trials and tribulations of Mercy Wylde.

Reverend Townsend was taken away from the page by the insistent ringing of a bell. Sister Piddock had arrived to collect the Sunday sermon.

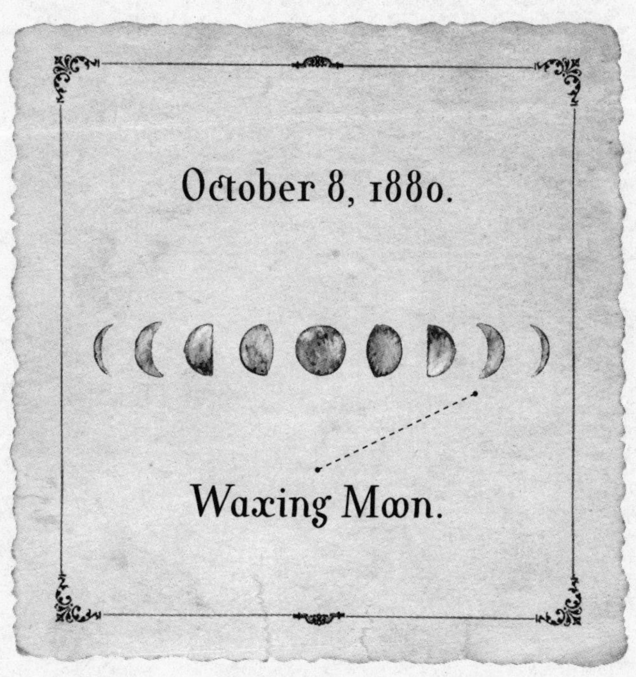
October 8, 1880.
Waxing Moon.

FRIDAY, OCTOBER 8, 1880 *The Evening Star*

Freemasons to Assemble

Tomorrow, October 9th, at approximately three o'clock, a grand parade will take place along Fifth Avenue from Madison Square to Central Park. Some nine thousand Freemasons from within the city and without will assemble to march through the streets to Greywacke Knoll. This momentous gathering is to mark the dedication ceremony for the pedestal on which the Great Obelisk will one day sit.

Although the obelisk has only recently made landfall, the marble pedestal on which it once stood was transported through the city to Central Park in early August. While its journey was far simpler than the Needle's, it was still quite a feat to move it, requiring thirty-two horses in sixteen pairs to pull it to its destination. Since that time, the pedestal has been waiting for preparations at Greywacke Knoll to be completed, so it might be set in place and properly dedicated prior to the obelisk's arrival.

October 8, 1880

Dear Aunt Lydia,

What would you say if I told you I've been visited by ghosts? Regularly and often! I would've mentioned it sooner, but I wanted to be certain that I wasn't suffering from a passing illness that'd put me temporarily out of my head. Lest you think me mad, and I wouldn't blame you if you did, I can assure you that what I've been experiencing is quite real and true. The spirits talk to me and I with them just as naturally as I used to do with you while sitting at the dining room table.

As you might imagine, this has stirred up a fair bit of excitement at the teashop. Happily, Miss Thom and Miss St. Clair are inclined to be understanding of such things, due to their ongoing interest in the unseen world.

I hesitate to describe how it all works because to do so would surely take several more pages, and even then I'm not sure I could do it justice. Suffice to say it's all happened rather suddenly. Perhaps one day soon you'll come for a visit so I can demonstrate my new abilities for you in person.

Your loving niece,
Beatrice

An Unsent Letter.

Beatrice folded the note, tucked it inside an envelope, then threw it into the fire. She'd write a less revealing, more reassuring missive to replace it, later, one that still extended an invitation for Lydia to visit. One that included the parade but not the ghosts.

Settling herself on the floor of her room in front of a small parlour stove, she propped the stove's door open to gaze at the fire's dancing flames. She'd recently learned the practice of scrying from Eleanor, and found it to be a fitting way to end the day. It helped her push unimportant thoughts aside and focus her mind.

"Hold a question in your thoughts and let your sight go slack," Eleanor had instructed. "Watch carefully. Be patient. Eventually a vision will appear within the flames. Give whatever comes to your attention measured thought and consideration. Scrying allows us to see with sight beyond our own."

"How will I know when I've seen what I'm meant to see?" Beatrice had asked. "Surely there must be some sign of assurance that comes along with the visions? Gooseflesh, flushed cheeks, a whisper of affirmation?"

Shaking her head, Eleanor had replied, "That's something you'll have to discover for yourself."

Although Eleanor had described several ways to scry—staring into a bowl of water, gazing upon a darkened mirror, keeping watch on the night sky—Beatrice found she preferred the fire. She'd always appreciated the warmth and comfort a fire could provide, always felt a certain reverence for its potential for destruction. The idea that flames could also hold insights meant only for her was tremendously appealing.

Since the night of her demonstration at the hotel she'd felt the urgent need to learn all she could about the art of witchcraft, as quickly as she could. Everyone who'd been in the salon that evening, including Adelaide and Eleanor, had been concerned that what'd transpired with the scrubber girls' spirits had taken a terrible toll on her. Instead, it had firmed her resolve to embrace her destiny wherever it might lead.

As she watched the fire consume what was left of the letter, she thought of how she'd felt while under the influence of the maids' spirits. Even when the ghosts of the scrubber girls had been speaking through her, she'd never felt frightened or consumed by their presence. Her soul hadn't been possessed, as everyone had feared, but rather she had felt as if she was acting on the girls' behalf. Given the depth of their sorrow and anger, allowing them to speak through her had seemed the best way for her to properly convey their message. Not that she'd thought through any of that in the moment, but she'd always been fully aware of what was taking place and she'd been willing (even glad) to be the ghosts' vehicle.

Predictably, Adelaide and Eleanor had landed on opposite sides of the fence when it came to advising her on what to do next. Eleanor wished to err on the side of caution. "I'm fearful of what might happen if you move too soon, too fast. Don't be afraid to take your time with things. There's no need to rush." Adelaide had been absolutely giddy over the prospect of her undertaking regular communications with spirit. "Perhaps you could hold consultations here at the shop. Enlist one or more of your ghostly companions to look into situations on 'the other side' on behalf of the living."

"That's not how it works," Eleanor had protested.

Though encouraged by Adelaide's enthusiasm, Beatrice had sided with Eleanor on that point. She couldn't just call forth spirits with a snap of her fingers or get them to do her bidding as if they were ponies in a circus. Spirits, of all sorts, shapes and stripes, were everywhere, all the time (unless otherwise banished from a place), and prone to make themselves known to her however and whenever they liked. Eleanor had done an excellent job of keeping them out of the teashop, but whenever Beatrice set foot outside the door, she was confronted with a deluge of the dearly departed. It was confusing and alarming each time it happened, and she'd soon gone to Eleanor for more advice. "Is there anything that can be done to make them less . . . eager?"

"Don't feel you have to talk to each and every one that vies for your attention, or you'll surely go mad," Eleanor had said. "They're fully aware that your gifts are taking hold. They see them in you as clearly as I see the freckles on your nose. You must foster the power to open and close yourself to their supplications as you see fit."

"How do I do that?"

"Through strong will and practice. It's not dissimilar to throwing off unwanted advances from a gentleman. Be confident as you make your way through the world. Hold your head high. Don't be afraid to cast an uninterested eye on those you wish to repel, be they living or dead. Wave them off, speak your peace, shout if you must. Be direct. There's no need to be polite. Even then, some may pester and persist. In such cases, you'll need to resort to more extreme measures."

"Like what?" Beatrice had asked, intrigued, but also frightened.

"There are incantations, charms and spells in the grimoire. Look them up. Learn them well. There are even a few potions for pests of flesh and blood, but remember, no matter what magic you choose to practice, the most effective way to deter any being from your presence, ghostly or otherwise, is to let them know who you are."

"What do they care?" Beatrice had asked, puzzled by the notion. "Who am I to them?"

At that point, Adelaide had sauntered over from her table in the back of the shop. "You are Beatrice Dunn," she'd said. "You're a witch. You're not to be trifled with." At least she and Eleanor had seen eye to eye on that.

She was glad for their advice, especially since tomorrow she'd be retuning to the hotel to assist Dr. Brody with his evening lecture for the Unknown Philosophers' Symposium, "Communication with the Afterlife: a Scientific Approach." The plan was for Dr. Brody to inform the audience of his research and for her to demonstrate the spiritoscope (hopefully with the scrubber girls' cooperation). The latter seemed quite possible now that the maids had become more docile and predictable in their communications.

The change in them had come about after Mrs. Stevens had hired a stone carver to go to the cemetery and make things right on Mary Donnelly's tombstone. "Thank heavens," Mrs. Stevens had exclaimed upon hearing news of the ghosts' new-found spirit of cooperation. "And thank heavens for men who think more of my money than of archaic rules about who should be buried where."

To show their appreciation, the Marys had ushered Mr. Paran Stevens' ghost into the salon to deliver a message to his wife.

T-H-E-R-E I-S N-O O-N-E S-O D-E-A-R A-S M-Y D-A-R-L-I-N-G M-A-R-I-E-T-T-A.

The spiritoscope had stayed put there since Beatrice's first encounter with the maids. Adelaide had escorted her each day to the hotel to meet with Dr. Brody, the trio working diligently to document Beatrice's connection with spirit. Several tests had been conducted, with the spiritoscope and without, and the results of their efforts had been quite encouraging.

Impressed with their efforts (and her husband's recent communication), Mrs. Stevens had insisted on providing them with whatever they needed to further the work. She sent delicious meals from the kitchens: roast chicken with pearl onions in cream sauce, leg of lamb with honeyed carrots and mint jelly. A porter was placed on call to cater to their every request; and, after Marietta had conducted a lengthy consultation with Adelaide, a gorgeous gown was brought to the room for Beatrice to try on. The latter had come shortly after Adelaide had suggested to Beatrice that she might wish to perform under an alias, at least for this particular engagement. "Something to pique the audience's interest. Something exotic and alluring." Although Beatrice hadn't cared much about being seen as exotic or alluring, she'd thought the idea practical, as it would preserve her true identity and eliminate the chance that word of her performance would get back to Stony Point. In the end they'd settled on the Egyptian Sibyl, in honour of her brief encounter with the Great Obelisk.

The gown was a beautiful creation made of layer upon layer of black crepe de chine, decorated top to bottom with gold embroidery depicting various Egyptian figures and glyphs. It came with a matching headdress bearing sphinx-like sidepieces striped in black and gold. The costume had once been worn by Mrs. Stevens' daughter, Minnie, who'd attended the Delmonico fancy dress ball of 1875 as Cleopatra. "Are you sure she won't mind?" Beatrice had asked, worried something awful might happen to the dress while she was wearing it. "Heavens no," Marietta had answered. "Now that she's become Lady Paget and moved to Belgrave Square, her ball gowns all come from Paris, encrusted with gems and jewels."

Detecting a hint of sadness in Mrs. Stevens' voice, Beatrice had gratefully accepted the woman's kind offer, but insisted the dress stay at the hotel for safekeeping until the night of the symposium.

Under Adelaide's direction, the evening was shaping up to be more spectacle than demonstration. She'd been especially excited when she'd discovered that the symposium was to fall on the same date as the Masons' parade, figuring it might well boost the size of their audience. "If all goes well," she'd enthused, "who knows what might come next?"

That was the question on Beatrice's mind as she watched the fire spark and crack. Like the stray bursts of flame that occasionally sprang forth from the dying embers, odd surges of magic had been occurring now and again in her daily life. Along with her encounters with spirits, other strange things had happened, some of her own making, some completely unexpected. She'd managed to execute a number of simple spells from Eleanor's grimoire—making a candle's flame increase or diminish with her mind, calling creatures to her side as she sat on a bench in the park (birds, bees, the odd squirrel, a stray dog), willing Perdu to say specific words without her speaking them aloud—but she'd also woken up in the middle of the night speaking a second language as if it were her mother tongue. It was unlike anything she'd ever heard, and although the meanings hadn't stuck in her mind, she couldn't shake the feeling that one day, with a bit of patience, they would.

She'd written a few of the words on scraps of paper, spelling them as they had sounded. Then she'd pinned them to the wall alongside several newspaper clippings she'd collected since she'd arrived in the city. Like her room in Stony Point, the walls of her garret had quickly become papered with strange and curious ephemera.

Haunted by Dead Wife: Husband Dies of Shock after the Ghost's Visits. A House to Let.

Faith in Ghosts: Mrs. Stymus Sues Mr. Howell for the Rent of her Haunted House.

Is it a Resort for Ghosts? Some Things That Have Excited the Residents of a Staten Island Village.

Woman Accuses Neighbour of Witchcraft.

The Brooklyn Ghost—The Proprietor of the Ghostelrey Determines That it is Old Nick.

Mrs. Lahey's Dreams of a Stranger's Death. Her Premonitions Are Proved True.

A Considerate Ghost Throws Stones About a House for a Year but Injures No One.

Children Witness Their Delancey Street Teacher Face her Doppelgänger at School.

Sorting through the stories day after day, she'd begun to wonder if she should do more than just collect them, but investigate their meaning. Perhaps one day she'd make a *Census of Astonishments*, much like Mr. Pratchett's *Compendium of Miracles.*

Gazing into the fire, she held that thought in her mind, not as a question but as a desire. Such things would have to wait, though. She'd have to get through tomorrow first. She could hardly believe the symposium was only one sleep away. Eyes heavy, she watched the fire's flames undulate amongst the hot embers in waves of blue, orange and gold. Perhaps she was too tired for her scrying to prove fruitful tonight.

Just as she was about to shut the door on the stove, the coals shifted and hissed. From between them, a glowing face looked out, more beast than man. It wore a twisted smirk, its lips ragged at the edges.

"Who are you?" Beatrice asked in a frightened whisper.

Staring at her, the beast refused to answer.

"Be gone!" she ordered, thrusting an iron poker into the stove to stir the coals.

With a burst of sparks the fire surged, and the face disappeared.

God is therefore pleased to suffer Devils sometimes to do such things in the World as shall test the mettle of His followers. Evil is therefore placed in the paths of the faithful so that we might overcome it. It is to His glory that these Devils be cast out by the hands of the righteous.

—from *An Attempt to Cure Witchcraft: The Story of Mercy Wylde*

The Devils Also Believe and Tremble.

THREE PROSTITUTES IN frilly skirts stood under a street lamp near Madison Square Park. Teasing each other and every man who walked by, the trio traded puffs on a cigarillo and passed a half-empty bottle of schnapps hand to hand to hand. Their reedy laughter bounced off the brick buildings behind them while the tacky remains of stale beer stuck to the sidewalk beneath their boots.

A few feet away, a gang of guttersnipes occupied themselves with tossing dice against the curb.

"Double sixes!" one boy exclaimed, bull's eye lantern dangling from his grimy hand.

"Again?" another boy groused.

"Them dice is for sure loaded," a third complained.

The youngest whore, Jenny Greene, rubbed the rabbit's foot that was hanging around her neck, then stuck her hand in her pocket and counted the coins sunk deep within it. Ten quarters, six dimes and an assortment of nickels and pennies. It'd been a good night so far, but ooh-boy that bottle of schnapps was almost empty and she sure could use more booze.

"Hey there, sweetie-pie," she called to one of the boys, "if you fetch me a growler, I'll let you keep the change." Even if he made off with what she gave him, or drank down half the bottle before handing it over, she still wouldn't have lost as much as she stood to lose by missing out on the next john if she went for the booze herself. She was next in the pecking order. It was her turn to score. She considered herself quite smart when it came to the arithmetic of want.

"Shut your trap, you dirty slut," the boy hollered as his gang mates showered him with elbow jabs and guffaws.

"Stubby-fingered little pecker," Jenny grumbled, flicking a stone to the street with the toe of her boot. Once upon a time, any beast with a cock between its legs—man, boy, dog, horse—would prance at her slightest look. With a haughty shrug and a fuck-you chin, she withdrew her offer. These boys were uppity. The boys downtown might be rougher around the edges, but at least they understood the value of tit for tat.

Jenny usually spent her evenings trolling for johns by the docks on the East River, but she'd heard from a reliable source that the saloons surrounding the square would be crawling with out-of-town gentlemen who were there to march in a big parade in honour of a new monument or statue or some such nonsense. So many things got "erected" these days—bronze giants with wreaths on their heads, tall steeples on stone churches, towering buildings with flags flying at attention on sturdy poles. How could she be expected to keep track of it all? She didn't give a hang why the men were coming, only that their pockets would be jangling with silver and their heads muddled with drink. Tying her lucky rabbit's foot around her neck, she'd convened a meeting with the two other girls who boarded in the house where she lived to see if they might be interested in trying their luck at the park.

"Who's up for cruising Madison Square?" she'd asked. "I heard tell the place will be crawling with johns."

"I'm in," Elsie Trew had replied while cleaning her teeth with an orange stick.

"Me too," Mae Blum had chimed in, pinning her hat atop her head.

When Jenny had first met them, she'd thought the two were sisters. In low light, they could easily be mistaken for twins. "We get that a lot," they'd confessed. "And we don't mind it a bit. It has its advantages in certain situations." They weren't exactly fast friends of Jenny's, but more friendly competitors who were willing to loan her a couple of dollars when she was short on rent. In fact, she was currently in debt to Elsie, and she hoped that by inviting her along for the evening some of what she owed might be forgiven. She'd grown tired of the way the girl stared at her during suppers at the boarding house, as if every morsel she put in her mouth had been stolen off someone else's plate. She'd also figured if there were as many men around the park as she'd been told there'd be, she wouldn't be out anything by having them come along. (She certainly couldn't service them all, now could she?) Besides, there was safety in numbers. It'd be a mighty long trek back to the boarding house if she had to walk alone.

Swigging the last of the schnapps from the bottle, Jenny spotted a gentleman walking towards them. Sizing him up, she announced to her companions, "He's mine."

"I say we let the gent choose for himself," Mae announced.

"I thought we agreed to take turns."

Elsie shook her head. "And I thought you were good for your rent money, but seeing as how it's getting late and you still haven't made right on your debt, I'd say he's fair game."

Jenny didn't want to bicker. She guessed if the man heard them arguing, he'd just as soon move along. He was only a few blocks from the Tenderloin where he could get anything he wanted. She had to seem easy, right and ready, if she wanted him to bite.

Squinting in the man's direction Mae sneered, "He looks like a preacher."

"How can you tell?" Jenny asked.

"The wide-brimmed hat, the long frock coat, the cross hanging around his neck, the arrogant, uptight gait."

Elsie gave an indifferent shrug. "You can have him, then."

Mae smiled and teased: "I'd like to see her try."

Spurred by the dare, Jenny pulled up the hem of her skirts to reveal a good portion of her leg as the man drew near. "A quarter for a suck, two for a fuck," she teased. Why should she be coy? Preachers had cocks too.

The man stopped in front of her.

Sidling closer, Jenny flashed a flirtatious smile, working hard to turn his disdain to desire. She'd fried much bigger fish when she was still a child. Back then, she'd had a place in a house that specialized in providing "fresh maids" for its clients, and her favourite caller had been a young priest named Father Whitby. He'd especially liked it when she'd fluttered her lashes and said, "Forgive me Father, for I have sinned." She'd especially liked it when he'd called her his angel and referred to her quim as his "holy vessel." Those were the days!

Too bad the woman who ran the place had decided it was time for her to move on. She missed the wine that'd flowed freely there and the feather bed where she'd slept each night. Perhaps if this gent was truly a man of God he'd pity her enough to take her home with him. Perhaps he had a feather bed just waiting for her to slink between its covers. Rubbing her shoulder against his she whispered, "It won't take long. You'll be glad for it, I promise."

With a nod he grabbed Jenny by the arm and led her down the street. The large silver cross fastened at his collar glinted in the lamplight.

"You like it rough?" Jenny asked. She wasn't averse to a spanking now and then, but he'd have to pay extra if he wanted it like that. "I'll let you leave a mark for a dollar, so long as it's below the neck." For two, he could have someone else watch, so long as they didn't touch her. For three they could both have a turn. For five, she'd take it in the ass, but she made a point of never offering that up front. The man had to ask. She'd once been told by a very wise whore (who also happened to be her mother), *everything has a price.*

Looking over his shoulder, the man pushed Jenny into a dark alley. Tossing a silver dollar to the grimy cobblestones he said, "Pick it up."

She did as she was told, then shoved the coin between her breasts. Back turned, she stroked her rabbit's foot three times for luck.

Arms folded, the man stared at her, waiting.

Spotting a low stack of wooden crates, Jenny bent over them, bracing herself with one hand while pulling her skirts up with the other. In her experience, men who didn't talk much didn't have a sense of humour, didn't want the trouble of kissing, didn't wish to see her face when they fucked. That was fine by her—she'd already gotten paid.

As she waited for the sudden thrust of his cock, she could hear his ragged, excited breathing behind her. Suddenly, she felt his hand take hold of the hair at the back of her neck. Before she could sense anything was wrong or let out a scream, a blade slashed across her throat. Falling to the ground, she reached for the hem of his coat. With the shudder of her last breath she heard him say, "Depart from me, ye cursed, into everlasting fire, prepared for the Devil and his angels."

Watching the life fade from the whore's face Reverend Townsend thought he might weep for joy.

He'd gone to the park to get some fresh air and to search for whatever foul presences might be lurking about. He'd prayed to the Lord that he might be allowed to see things more clearly, be shown the working of devils, bold and unabashed, and it seemed his prayers had been heard and answered. Sinners, devils, witches walked the crowded streets everywhere he went.

He'd been tempted (ever so briefly) by the whore's pale skin and rouged lips, but after he'd kissed his cross and recited a psalm, he'd seen her for what she was, eyes flashing with brimstone, lips wet and thirsting for blood, cloven hooves peeking out from under her skirts. What else could he have done but put the malignant wretch to rest?

God was testing him. Waiting for him to prove his worth. One day soon he, too, might be tasked to save a soul in the form of his own Mercy Wylde.

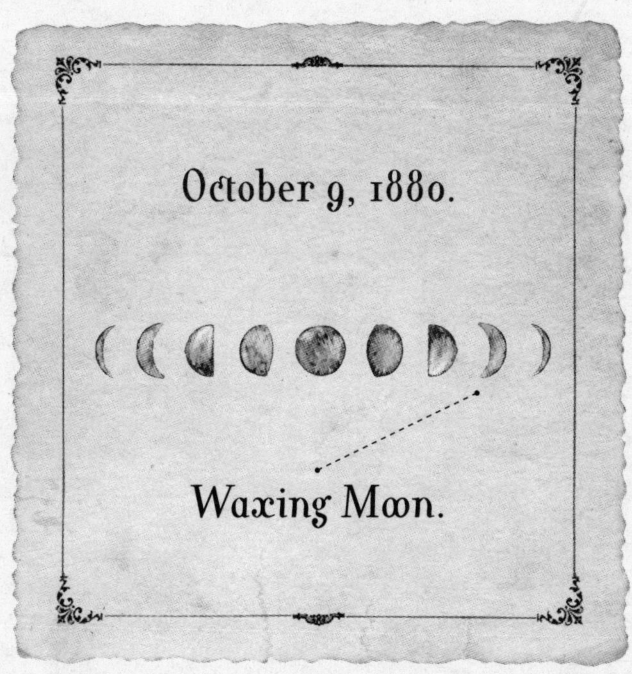
October 9, 1880.
Waxing Moon.

The Final Fitting.

Beatrice was standing, dressed in Minnie Stevens' ball gown, on a low wooden stool in the middle of Judith Dashley's suite. She held her body still and straight while a nimble-fingered seamstress circled her, pins stuck in a cushion strapped to her wrist, a half-dozen more pinched between her lips. Although Beatrice appreciated the woman's efforts, she wished she'd finish the job so she could be free to go downstairs to the hotel lobby and take in the lectures and displays on offer at the symposium.

Earlier that morning, Alden Dashley had delivered a stack of programmes to the teashop and it hadn't taken Beatrice long to find several things that piqued her interest. Pencil in hand, she'd starred the items that most appealed to her—a lecture titled "Women as Inventors"; a presentation by a group called the Followers of the Obelisk; and a travelling bookseller touting an outstanding selection of antiquarian tomes dealing with the occult. Eleanor had chosen to stay behind and mind the shop. Adelaide was taking care of any and all last-minute preparations for their evening presentation. Beatrice had agreed to meet her at the base of Lady Liberty's torch at three o'clock so they could distribute notices for the lecture to interested bystanders who were waiting for the Masons' grand parade. Until then, she was free to do as she pleased, so long as Judith approved of the dress's fit.

As the seamstress put the final touches on the dress's embroidered sleeves, Beatrice kept her eye on the curtains on the other side of the room. The damask panels were moving to and fro, much as they would if a cat were weaving in and out between them. The only trouble was, the Dashleys didn't own a cat.

Judith, noticing Beatrice's distracted state, asked, "Is that my Billy? Is he here?"

Trying her best to keep still, Beatrice whispered yes.

The seamstress let out an impatient cough.

"I knew I sensed him," Judith said. "Ever since that day with you in the teashop I've become increasingly attuned to his presence. I can feel him come and go—sometimes he gives a little tug on my skirt, or rolls a pen out of Alden's reach. I don't know why I never noticed it before. Do you think it might be due to my keeping company with you? Is it possible I've been touched by magic? Sympathetically, of course."

Beatrice just smiled and held her breath as the seamstress slid several pins through a length of lace at the nape of her neck.

Judith's mouth turned down. "You don't suppose *they're* here, too, do you?"

"Who?" Beatrice asked as soon as the seamstress moved on to the dress's hem.

"The scrubber girls." Judith gave a shudder.

The seamstress winced as she pricked her thumb with a pin. Saying a silent prayer she sucked the blood from its fleshy tip. *God protect me from the things I cannot see.* She'd heard tales from the night porter of the unhappy spirits that haunted the hotel corridors.

Shaking her head, Beatrice replied, "They're not here, at least not in your suite. Nor do I think they ever will be. They're much happier now that they're at ease with their fate."

"Thank you for entertaining such questions," Judith said, flushing. "I don't mean to impose on you."

"It's the least I can do," Beatrice said. "You and Alden have been incredibly kind."

Holding out her hand, the seamstress motioned for Beatrice to step down from the stool. "All finished," she announced as she waited for Judith's approval.

Eyes gleaming, Judith clapped her hands. "It's simply ravishing!"

Sewing basket in hand, the seamstress took a bow, then took her leave.

Judith rushed to fetch a small box that was sitting on a nearby table. "While I have you here," she said, "I'd like to present you with a little gift."

"Oh, Mrs. Dashley," Beatrice protested, "you shouldn't do such things."

"It's just a trifle," Judith said. "A small thank-you from me and Alden and the rest of the Philosophers."

Beatrice took the box from her and gently opened its lid. Nestled in a bed of green silk was a little doll with a card that read: "Miss Fortuna." The plaything had dark curls under a pointed velvet hat and was dressed in a long red gown with moons, owls, bats and snakes embroidered on the skirt, like the Gypsy fortune tellers in children's books and European romances. She held a crystal ball in one hand and a tambourine in the other. Her legs were stiff and affixed to the base of a wooden top. Under her skirt, Miss Fortuna held a secret, or more precisely hundreds of them—page upon page of coloured paper shaped, stitched, folded and inscribed to form a never-ending book of tiny prophecies.

"You spin her around to find your fortune," Judith had said, demonstrating how the toy worked. "Wherever the pages fall open is where your luck lies. The fortunes are written inside."

Giving the doll a playful turn, Beatrice tried it for herself.

Pages fluttering, the toy spun around several times then wobbled to a stop.

Hand to her heart, Beatrice read her fortune.

Courage always. Without it there is no hope.

Dr. Brody sat in the hotel reading room, cup of coffee in hand, programme for the symposium laid out before him on the table. He was glad to have a few moments to himself. He enjoyed eavesdropping on the hum of ideas, boasts and complaints that got bandied about the place. Brody found comfort in the predictable din (so long as he wasn't required to participate in it).

"Hello there, St. Nick," a familiar voice sounded, accompanied by the clap of a hand on his shoulder.

"Andersen," Brody replied, turning to greet his old acquaintance. The burly army hero didn't look half so well as he had the last time they'd met. His skin was pale, his eyes dark, his suit rumpled and smelling stale. "How have you been?" Brody asked, wondering if the poor fellow might be suffering from a lingering illness, or was simply down on his luck.

Andersen pulled up a chair. Wiping sweat from his brow, he tugged at his tie to loosen it. "Never better," he said with a tired smile. Leaning close he added, "I'm glad I've run into you. I'm in need of your professional opinion."

Brody shook his head. "If it's medical advice you're after, you might be better served by a full-time practitioner. My work these days centres more on the mind and less on physical ailments."

"And that's exactly why you're the right man for the job," Andersen insisted. "I need a doc who's well-versed in the business of examining brains."

"Yours?" Brody asked, thinking the stress of the war might've finally proved too much after all these years.

"No," Andersen replied. "There's a girl I've come to fancy out on Blackwell's Island."

"At the asylum?" Brody asked.

"She's one in a million," Andersen boasted. "A diamond in the rough. As lovely and witty as any woman I've ever known. And far saner compared to most. For the life of me I can't figure why she's not been let out."

"There must be some reason she's there," Brody said, hoping to bring Andersen to his senses. Still he knew all too well that it was possible (and regrettably easy) for a perfectly sane woman to get put away against her will.

With a laugh Andersen said, "Would you believe she got locked up for witchcraft? Some scuttlebutt about practicing it . . . or was it believing in it? Either way it's a bunch of nonsense."

"I see," Brody said, torn between wanting to learn more and wishing he hadn't asked.

"Come out with me tonight and meet her for yourself," Andersen suggested. "No doubt you'll come to the same conclusion as I have, that it was all a big mistake."

"I'm afraid I can't," Brody replied. "I have another engagement."

"Right," Andersen said, looking dejected. "Maybe another time, then? Perhaps you could talk some sense into the staff there. Put in a good word as to the strength of my character. The opinion of a doctor such as yourself, a respectable society gent, could go a long way towards springing my girl from that hellhole."

Brody knew the asylum, like many public madhouses, was overcrowded and poorly maintained. He also knew that if someone of note had been the one to send the girl there, the chances of her getting out were slim. Without studying the woman's case at length, he wasn't sure he could make an informed plea. But clearly Andersen was desperate. "I'll consider it," he said at last.

"Thank you," Andersen said. "Do you think you could make it sometime soon? Else I might just have to break her out by other means."

Brody could see he wasn't joking. The spell the girl had cast on him was strong and fast. "We'll talk soon," he said, excusing himself from the table. "Be well, Andersen."

"Take care, St. Nick."

Brody found a quiet corner and read over his notes for the evening lecture. It was still hours before he and Beatrice would take the stage, but he wanted to be sure his thoughts were in order. He'd left the minor details of the evening's presentation to Adelaide. Her eagerness to engage in spectacle went far beyond his practical nature, but he could see that it was all in an effort to show how much she respected his work. She had faith in his methods (and, dare he think it, in him), which was something he'd never felt before from a woman. As much as he'd loved his wife, she'd never shown any interest in his profession. He'd been a medical student, on his way to becoming a surgeon, and she'd forbidden him to mention anything related to medicine in her presence. He'd respected her squeamishness, but that didn't mean he hadn't felt let down by her lack of interest. Adelaide, despite her bold, impulsive nature, was a welcome companion and a true equal. If the night turned out to be a success, he planned to express exactly those sentiments to her, put his cards on the table, as it were.

He also planned to suggest they resume their research in his study rather than carry on at the hotel. He hoped to coax his father's ghost into a longer conversation so he might ask him a few pressing questions.

What are your surroundings like on the other side?

What of time? Is it measured? If so, how do you keep track of it?

What of the senses that your body used in life? Do you see, hear, smell, touch?

What is your relationship to the physical world? Why do some spirits move objects, while others do not?

How do you travel from one place to another? Is distance of no consequence?

What, if anything, is beyond where you are now?

He thought if he could gain the answers he sought, he might publish them in a short book. It would, no doubt, be a risky endeavour, but wasn't that the sort of risk that every scientist had to be willing to take? To profess truth despite the looming spectre of ridicule.

And there was another subject he'd like to explore in the privacy of his study. Hearing Andersen speak of his girl and her plight, he'd remembered the card Adelaide had given him the day they'd met. "Miss Adelaide Thom. Mind Reader. Seeress. Witch." She'd mentioned the word a few times since, seemingly in jest, and once, he'd heard Beatrice speak it with shy seriousness. *Witchcraft.* Could their abilities be attributed to some greater mystical force or were they just bandying the word about for effect? Incredible as it seemed, it would explain much of what he'd witnessed while in their presence. There'd been talk of witchcraft at the Salpêtrière—some inmates claiming they were born into it, others threatening to use it to curse the place—but Charcot had dismissed it, saying their claims of sorcery were merely archaic explanations for hysteria. He had been incredibly dismissive, and the procedures he'd used to prove his theories, to document and cure hysteria, had been damaging and dangerous—no better than the trials put to women during the witch hunts of old. The women were treated as if they were criminals and kept like animals in cages. Spirits broken, they'd spent their days crying for mercy and freedom.

If Adelaide, Beatrice and Eleanor (who he suspected was of the same magical persuasion) wished to confess their practices to him, he would surely listen. If they were good enough to allow him into their world, he'd do whatever he could to protect them.

Much like Dr. Brody, Eleanor had decided not to interfere with Adelaide's plans. She'd chosen instead to stand patiently on guard until she was needed. Beatrice was bright and observant and determined, and that would go a long way towards keeping her from falling too far under Adelaide's spell.

"She seems so strong, so unafraid," Beatrice had said once to Eleanor in private. "Has she always been that confident?"

Eleanor had tried to set the record straight. "Adelaide isn't strong because she's confident. She's strong because she's always afraid."

The sooner Beatrice realized that Adelaide had weaknesses, the better. She didn't want the girl to be too eager to follow her every whim. Dr. Brody seemed to have already fallen into that trap, but she figured a man who'd lost an arm in battle could probably take care of himself.

She didn't blame Beatrice for being enthralled with Adelaide or even for wanting to be like her. She'd suffered from that same cycle of admiration-envy-infatuation when she'd cared for Adelaide after the attack. It's what had led her to agree to go into business with her and to suspect that Adelaide had powers that were yet to be made manifest. But it wasn't Adelaide's charm that'd led Eleanor to become her friend. It was discovering the parts of Adelaide that Beatrice had yet to see—her vulnerability, her tender heart, her fear of love. She hoped that Adelaide might reveal those things to Beatrice sooner rather than later, for all their sakes. Who knew what wondrous things might occur when that took place? Adelaide had said it herself, and she'd claimed she'd seen it in Beatrice's cards: "We're better for knowing each other, we're stronger together."

The words her mother had spoken at the dumb supper still lingered in Eleanor's mind, and she'd been struggling to see any signs that might guide her in instructing Beatrice. Everyday rituals that'd been foolproof when she'd lived on the river now felt cumbersome and meaningless. The rhythms of the city intruded on her senses as if they had messages of their own to give, but more often than not, she felt caught between two places, belonging to neither.

Since the rock crashed through the window, she hadn't seen any more signs of trouble. But that didn't mean the person who'd thrown it wasn't lurking about, waiting to strike. She'd been checking her tea leaves, observing the bees, waiting for a dream to be delivered . . . If a sign had been given to point the way, she'd missed it. Beatrice's powers were increasing each day. Was she losing hers in the inverse proportion? Surely her mother would've mentioned that, if it was to be her fate.

Perdu waddled to Eleanor's teacup and tapped his beak on its rim.

Eleanor looked at the cup and discovered a tiny stalk stuck to the edge of the bowl. *A single stalk means a message is on its way. Press it to your palm, and clap your hands together. If the stalk stays put, the message will be fair. If it switches hands, it will be fickle. If it falls to the floor, it will be foul.*

Pinching the stalk between her fingers, Eleanor placed it on the palm of her right hand. She clapped her hands once then looked to see where the stalk had landed. It clung to her left palm for a moment before floating to the floor.

The bells on the shop door jangled and a young man came into the store. "Telegram for Miss St. Clair," he announced, handing an envelope to Eleanor.

"Thank you," she said, motioning for Perdu to give the lad a tip.

Perdu dipped his beak into the change jar and fished out a dime.

The boy laughed as he shoved the coin in his pocket. "Thanks much," he said, tipping his cap.

TO: MISS ELEANOR ST. CLAIR
FROM: MRS. CECIL NEWLAND
I REQUEST YOUR COMPANY AT MY HOME TONIGHT.
7 O'CLOCK.
URGENT.

I have seen wonderful Snares laid for Curious People, by the Mouths of Damsels possessed with a Spirit of Divination.

—Rev. Cotton Mather

Parade.

The weather that afternoon was terrifically inviting. A cloudless blue sky and a high yellow sun made every bit of brass, copper, silver and gold (from buttons to buckles, from medals to sword hilts) shine that much brighter. Scores of Masons rushed here and there decked in their regalia—stewards, deacons, wardens, knights, sword bearers, worshipful masters—greeting one another with secret handshakes and sacred phrases, their sashes pressed flat, their feathered chapeaux set straight, their fringed aprons flapping.

Two gentlemen, decidedly ignoring the proceedings, played checkers under a poplar tree in Madison Square Park. They knew the place would soon fill with noisy parade goers, that Fifth Avenue would turn into a bustling boulevard of pomp and brass bands and horseshit, but they didn't feel the need to concern themselves with any of it. They'd come there every Saturday for the past thirty years, since before the Fifth Avenue Hotel was even thought of, and they weren't about to let a rowdy gathering of nine thousand Freemasons in their ridiculous garb ruin their long-standing tradition.

"Nice weather we're having," one of the gents said, scratching his head beneath his cap. His checkers were black.

"Indeed," his friend replied. His checkers were white. Moving one of his pieces to the end of the board, he crowned it king. "Warm for October, wouldn't you say?"

Mr. Black turned his head sideways, as if changing his perspective would change the game. "I suppose," he replied, hesitating over his turn.

"What's there to suppose about?" Mr. White asked. "It's positively balmy. I was tempted to fling my coat over my shoulder and walk in my shirt sleeves all the way here." Pointing to one of his pieces he said, "There's your move—you have to take it."

"Humpf," Mr. Black snorted, seeing he'd fallen into a trap. "This weather's nothing out of the ordinary, you know. There's been a warm spell in Manhattan every October since 1792."

After Mr. Black made the move he'd been waiting for, Mr. White took three of his friend's checkers and crowned one of his own, king. "You don't say."

"It likely started long before that, though the records of the *Old Farmer's Almanac* only go back so far." Making the only move he could, Mr. Black saw he was going to lose the game. At least he'd been right about the weather.

"Funny how folks forget," Mr. White observed, taking the last of Mr. Black's pieces off the board.

Tossing a nickel into the old tin cup they used for a kitty, Mr. Black nodded and said, "Good game." There was plenty of daylight ahead, plenty of time to plot and scheme. They wouldn't play their final round until sunset, winner take all.

Mr. White set his pieces on the board one by one. No need to ask if Mr. Black wanted another go. "Then why do you suppose we're so quick to say, 'How warm! How strange!' when it's not unusual at all?"

Mr. Black also readied his men for battle. "People like the feeling they get when they think they've stumbled upon something miraculous. It's a proven fact."

Adelaide arrived at the park with a stack of notices tucked under her arm. She'd decided to get there early so she could claim a spot near Lady Liberty's torch and size up the crowd. It was only two o'clock, yet the square was already crowded with politicians, preachers and protesters, as well as a variety of vendors selling everything from roasted peanuts and steamed oysters to a multitude of obelisk-related souvenirs. One enterprising confectioner had even set up shop near the fountain, selling chocolate-covered dates in obelisk-shaped boxes complete with gold-leaf glyphs.

As Adelaide perused the wares in a nearby cart—bracelet charms made from Egyptian coins, figures of Anubis, Osiris and Horus cast in coloured wax—she thought how glad she was that she'd seized upon the idea of Beatrice becoming the Egyptian Sibyl. The city was abuzz with Egyptomania. Why shouldn't they make the most of it? The crowd filling the sidewalks to watch the parade was growing by the minute. She couldn't remember seeing such a crowd in her life, except for the day President Lincoln's funeral procession had passed through the streets. Back then she was nothing but a curly-headed imp at her mother's hip, but the sombre affair had made an indelible impression. She hoped today would turn out to be equally unforgettable, yet in a far more festive way.

"How much for this?" Adelaide asked the woman who owned the cart, pointing to a silver propelling pencil shaped like the obelisk. It was mechanical, practical, novel. She thought she might give it to Quinn as a gift, if the price was right.

"Four dollars," the woman answered with a squint.

"That's too much." Adelaide shook her head.

"It's a steal," the woman argued. "I'm practically giving it to you. It's an exact replica. Look close and you'll see it's accurate down to the last glyph."

Adelaide had no way of knowing if the markings were authentic or mere chicken scratches. "Two dollars," she countered.

"Three dollars and I'll throw in a programme from the big to-do they're having at the Fifth Avenue Hotel. I hear they've got a girl on tonight who calls herself the ''Gyptian Sorceress' or some such. Should be something to see."

"You don't say," Adelaide said, handing over the asking price. Her enthusiasm alone was worth the extra dollar. "I'll take them both."

Gift in hand, Adelaide turned to leave.

"Wait, wait, wait, miss," the woman called. "Would you like to see something really special? I'll bring it out, only for you."

"All right," Adelaide said, "let's have a look."

The woman bent behind her cart then reappeared with a lacklustre piece of stone the size of a lump of coal. "It's from Cleopatra's Needle," she whispered. "The genuine article. The only one I got."

Guessing that the sad little piece of rubble probably came from a stonecutter's trash heap, Adelaide waved it away. She knew a gaff when she saw one. No doubt the woman had at least a dozen more such "relics" hidden behind her cart. "Good luck to you," she said. "All the best."

"Hurry back if you change your mind," the woman called after her. "I'll try to hold on to it, but I can't say how long it will last."

Making her way to the base of the torch, Adelaide passed between two groups of women who were clearly at odds with each other.

Several members of the National Woman Suffrage Association had gathered near the fountain with their colourful VOTES FOR WOMEN banners prominently on display. Distributing the latest issue of the *Ballot Box* they chanted, "Men, their rights and nothing more. Women, their rights and nothing less!" Across from them, the Ladies' Bible League from the Church of the Good Shepherd countered the suffragists' efforts by handing out literature of their own titled, "Votes for Women: Against God's Order."

One of the women from the Bible League waved a tract at Adelaide. "Repent, dear sister, and change your sinful ways!"

Adelaide recognized her by her sour expression. Over the past few weeks the woman had taken up the habit of standing outside the teashop and peering through the window. Only once had she bothered to come through the door, and, sadly, Adelaide hadn't been there to greet her. She'd scared poor Beatrice half to death when she'd accused her of serving Satan and leading women astray.

"Repent, I say!" the woman cried in Adelaide's face. "Repent and be saved!"

Grabbing the tract and tossing it to the ground, Adelaide lifted her veil, faced the woman and snarled until she backed away. This was indeed turning out to be a memorable day.

"Pretzels! Get yer fresh pretzels!" a boy's voice rang out above the crowd. "One for a nickel! Three for a dime!" Isaac Markowitz, son of the man who ran the bakery next door to the teashop, was coming down the path with a basket of salty treats strapped to his front, a sign for his father's store hanging down his back. "Pretzels! Fresh pretzels!" he shouted again, as he came towards Adelaide.

"I'll take one," she called to the boy.

"Here you go, Miss Thom," Isaac said, sliding her pretzel into a small paper sack.

Tucking a quarter in Isaac's front pocket Adelaide said, "Keep the change."

"Thank *you*, Miss Thom," Isaac said, smiling broadly.

Settling on a bench at the foot of the torch, Adelaide bit off a hunk of the pretzel as she waited for Beatrice. There were plenty of society folk out and about, gentlemen reading *Frank Leslie's Illustrated*, ladies promenading with parasols on their shoulders. The people that held Adelaide's interest, however, were those whom the rest of the crowd mostly chose to ignore—the young pickpocket lifting a watch from a distracted sap, the flower girl admiring a rich girl's smart dress, the Bird Lady singing songs to herself one after another. Just as Adelaide was about to take the last bite of her pretzel, a stray dog came towards her through the maze of skirts and suits. Black and tan with blazes of white on its muzzle and chest, it reminded her of the pair of Swissys that'd pulled the rag lady's cart through the neighbourhood where she'd lived when she'd served as a lady's maid. The woman had owned next to nothing but she'd always made sure her dogs were well fed. Each hound had a collar decked with bells that jingled as they walked. This poor dog didn't have a collar, its ribs showed every which way, and it had the hunch and tremble of a creature that had been beaten. Taking pity on the hound, Adelaide tossed the remaining hunk of pretzel to the ground at her feet. She understood what it was like to have loyalty rewarded with a kick in the ass.

Tail between its legs, the dog snatched the bread and wolfed it down.

Pointing towards Isaac, Adelaide told the dog, "Follow that boy."

The dog obeyed and slunk away.

Adelaide hoped that's not what she'd become, a pitiful used-up stray trailing after Beatrice and Quinn in hopes of licking up their scraps. She truly had an interest in what they were trying to accomplish and was more than happy to play a part, but what would happen once they figured out they didn't need her? She'd hardly spent any time alone with Quinn; whenever they'd had a few spare moments to themselves they'd spent them talking about Beatrice. *What might Beatrice become? What should we do to encourage her, educate her, protect her?* Admittedly, much of Quinn's obsession with Beatrice was of her own making, she'd pushed so hard to shine the light squarely on the girl. Until now it'd seemed the best course of action, one that would inevitably lead to recognition, perhaps even fame and fortune. That was the path she'd always taken—choosing limelight over lamplight, lust over love.

Why couldn't she read Quinn better? Was she losing her touch? Maybe the trouble was she'd come to care too much for him. (If that was the case, she really had to put a stop to it.) She could see the interest in his face, so why didn't he see fit to act on it? Was it her disfigurement? Was he planning to cut her loose "out of respect" once he'd had his fill of Beatrice's abilities? Men frequently used that word as an excuse to shy away from topics they didn't want to discuss. Plenty of women had come into the shop weeping over a gentleman's respect. "He broke it off with me, out of respect." "He respected me too much to let it go on any longer." "He said he couldn't respect himself if he held me back from something greater." Bollocks. If Quinn didn't act on his attraction to her soon, she'd be the one to end it. Not out of respect, but because she had no room in her life for games of the heart.

Perhaps he'd decided he'd rather have Beatrice. She wouldn't blame him. The girl had lots she couldn't offer—beauty, cheerfulness, naïveté, and an unparalleled rapport with ghosts. (Though she hadn't seen any signs that Quinn was drawn to Beatrice so far.) Oh how she hated herself for feeling jealous! Was jealousy also destined to go hand in hand with love? If so, she didn't want any part of either. She'd seen where love could lead by watching her mother stand on the porch of a boarding house cursing at a young whore to give her back her husband. If her mother had ever held any witchery in her blood, the pathetic wretch had lost the better part of it the moment her heart had been broken by a man. She'd given whatever power she'd had away—to love, to drink, to laudanum and, eventually, to the river.

Pulled forth by her daughter's thoughts, the spirit of Adelaide's mother rose from the bubbling waters of the park fountain. After shaking a penny loose from her ear, she took her skirts between her hands and attempted to wring them dry. *Chrissakes*, she was sore and damp and groggy from being stuck in the fountain's rusty bladder. *What time is it? What day is it?* Noticing the bustling crowds she wondered whether another president had died. Or was she stuck in a ghostly dream, sent back in time to Lincoln's funeral procession?

It was that damn fairy's fault, she was sure of it. Everything had been a jumbled mess since she'd been tricked into leaving the teashop. She wasn't sure what the foul pixie had done, but she knew it wasn't good. Dizzy and confused, she hadn't been able to make her way back to where she'd been. It was as if the teashop had up and disappeared. Every time she flew down the block, the sign, the door, the whole storefront went missing. She couldn't remember the number of the building. The confusion she felt was akin to waking up after a night of drinking and fucking to find spunk stuck between her legs and her head filled with nothing.

Spitting out three snails, a handful of watery worms and a plug nickel, her memories began to stir, but not in any particular order. Last week, last month, last year, some time ago, she'd gone to the park in search of her daughter. In a strange turn she'd seen not one Adelaide, but two. One was the young woman her daughter had become—the nattily dressed one-eyed seer who called herself Adelaide Thom. The other was the child she had abandoned—the slim, shining, smart-mouthed waif her lost husband had named Moth. She'd chosen to follow the little one through the confines of the park. Over the course of the next while (minutes, hours, days, weeks), she'd trailed after the child, who had a terrible habit of hiding in places even ghosts couldn't see. Was she real? Was she a memory? Was she a spirit, like her? She'd seen the girl fall prey to a terrible man, a man who meant to harm her, and even though she'd tried everything in her power to warn her, the girl wouldn't listen. She'd shouted in the Bird Lady's ear, but the die had already been cast. Some dark force below the pavers had been determined to hold her there, not allowing her to follow the child to her fate. Where was she now? Where was her daughter?

As she searched the park for the little girl, she spotted Adelaide. She's here! Safe and sound! All grown up again. Hovering to Adelaide's right, she swooned over her daughter's beauty. *Look here! That's my girl! So elegant and lovely!* Circling to Adelaide's left, she cringed. *How hideous! How sickening! What's happened to her? Look at my child, the poor, pathetic wretch!*

Rising high above the crowd, she spotted the man who'd led the sweet little girl away. "Watch out!" she cried. "He's here! He means to catch a witch!"

Beatrice rushed across the avenue from the hotel to the park. It was almost three o'clock: she was nearly late. She'd been held up by the session put on by the Followers of the Needle, enthralled by one of the members' accounts of having her rheumatism cured after visiting the obelisk aboard the *Dessoug*. The woman spoke so fervently about her miraculous healing, it'd been all Beatrice could do to hold herself back and not share her experience with the room. But remembering Adelaide's strict instructions not to speak of her connection to the Needle until the symposium, she'd kept her thoughts to herself.

Moving towards the spot where she and Adelaide had agreed to meet, she began to feel uncomfortable amongst the crush of strangers, overwhelmed by the persistent shouts of vendors, the startling racket of gunshots and the swell of brass bands as the parade marched ever closer. She was sad the obelisk itself wasn't going to be part of the celebrations, but the latest report in the papers had said that Mr. Gorringe was now predicting that it might take until the New Year for it to reach Central Park. She supposed the man she'd met the day the Needle came ashore wouldn't be attending today's festivities, either. He'd seemed to take his guardianship of the stone quite seriously and she couldn't imagine him leaving his post.

Beatrice could sense a contingent of spirits drawing near. The sound of drums in the distance, the sea of uniformed men, the clomp of horses' hooves had brought a ghostly parade of soldiers (five Union, two Confederate) to her side. The scent of gunpowder filled her nose while the strains of a melancholy tune rang in her ear. *Me, oh my, I love her so. Broke my heart I had to go. Only time will heal my woe. Johnny has gone for a soldier.* "Move along," she whispered, waving the ghosts away. "I can't speak with you now." Thankfully, they relented, and no one among the living had noticed her odd behaviour.

Ahead of her, she spotted a young woman who looked for all the world like Joan of Arc. Dressed in armour from the waist up, with her chestnut hair and scarlet skirts flowing, she appeared more vision than human, shrouded by the invisible waves of heat that were rising from the stone path. Could this out-of-place Joan be a spectre too? Tracking the young woman with her eyes, Beatrice hastened after her. She needed to find out for herself whether or not the girl was real.

When she finally caught up to her, she discovered it was all a good-natured ruse. Joan, sword strapped to her side, was standing with the suffragists, cigarette holder in one hand, the standard of the NWSA in the other. "Blazing hot today," she exclaimed as she chatted with her sisters.

"Better than being on the stake," one of the women teased.

"I get enough of that," Joan retorted, "eight shows a week."

Beatrice guessed she must be the actress who was starring in *Joan's Lament* on Broadway near Union Square. She'd seen broadsheets for the play plastered on brick walls around the square. Although she was flesh and blood, she was still a wonder to behold. She hoped Adelaide had gotten a chance to see the girl. No doubt she'd approve of the suffragist's flair for the dramatic.

Thinking she might send some of the NWSA literature to Lydia, she started to approach the women to ask for a copy of their paper.

Before she could reach them, a man drew near. "Miss?" he said, his voice hoarse, his dark imperial beard nearly hiding his mouth. "Might I trouble you for a moment?" From the tailored cut of his suit to the gaudy signet ring that glinted on his finger, it was clear he was a man of considerable wealth. Even the handle of his walking stick was a cut above, a silver ram's head with two gleaming emeralds for eyes.

Not wishing to be rude, Beatrice stopped to hear what he had to say.

"I am Mr. Gideon Palsham," the man said, giving Beatrice a polite bow.

"Miss Dunn," Beatrice replied with a wary nod.

"Lovely to make your acquaintance, Miss Dunn."

"Likewise," Beatrice replied, wishing she knew where Adelaide was and how long this might take. The torch was just up ahead, but they'd stepped off the path, close to a group of women who were standing in a circle reciting psalms.

"Correct me if I'm wrong," Mr. Palsham said, "but didn't I see you at the hotel a short while ago, at the meeting of the Followers of the Needle?"

"Yes, I was there," Beatrice answered.

"I knew it!" Mr. Palsham exclaimed, placing his hand on Beatrice's arm. "I was seated in the same row, only a few seats over."

Not liking the thought that he'd taken notice of her, Beatrice flashed a nervous smile. "I'm afraid I really must go."

Gripping her arm so she couldn't leave, he smiled and spoke with pleasant ease. "I hope you'll forgive me for being forward, but I couldn't help but notice your reaction when that lovely woman told her remarkable tale of her miraculous recovery after being in the presence of the Needle. The expression on your face was simply sublime. Angelic. Transcendent."

Beatrice held her breath, not knowing what to do or say.

"Something tells me that you have a tale of your own to tell. I can only assume that perhaps you've had a similar experience? Have you also been in the presence of the Needle?"

"Yes," Beatrice admitted, immediately regretting her answer. "I mean, no," she said, shaking her head, as she tried again to pull away from Mr. Palsham. His gaze was uncomfortably intense, his grip powerful, unyielding. For a moment she swore his eyes glowed bright, as if there was fire within them. Her belly lurched. She thought she might be sick.

"Which is it, Miss Dunn?" Mr. Palsham pressed. "Yes or no?"

The bells from a nearby church tolled the hour, *one, two, three.* Dogs barked from all corners of the square as the parade came closer.

"I have to go," Beatrice insisted, looking around for help.

"You seem confused," Mr. Palsham said, grabbing her around the waist. Lips pressed against her ear he hissed, "I saw you the day the obelisk crossed the tracks. I saw you touch it."

Suddenly, someone loomed tall at her back. "Unhand her," Reverend Townsend commanded, his voice ringing in the air.

Mr. Palsham let loose of Beatrice. Briefly looking at the preacher, he gave a polite nod as if he was handing off a dance partner in the middle of a waltz. Without a word, he slipped into the crowd.

"Are you all right?" Reverend Townsend asked, now standing at Beatrice's side.

"I think so," she answered, still queasy and shaken. Just as she was about to thank him for intervening, Adelaide appeared.

"There you are," she said to Beatrice while giving Reverend Townsend a suspicious stare. "I was starting to think you weren't coming." Handing the preacher a notice for the lecture she said, "If you want to see more of her, you'll have to come to the hotel tonight."

Beatrice linked arms with Adelaide as they walked towards the torch. She'd never been so happy to see anyone in all her life.

The Bird Lady trailed after them, picking notices from the ground whenever they dropped from Adelaide's hand. Cloudy eyes shining, she rattled a string of stinking oyster shells tied to her wrist. "He's here!" she sang. "He's here! He means to catch a witch!"

The speedy gleams the darkness swallo'd;
Loud, deep, and long the thunder bellow'd;
That night a child might understand
The devil had business on his hand.

—Robert Burns

The Coming Storm.

Rather than wait for Sister Piddock to come knocking on his door, Reverend Townsend planned to go to hers. He hadn't begun composing his sermon, yet he felt sure that the message he'd deliver the next morning would be nothing short of inspired.

This evening, there was more important work at hand.

He'd saved that poor girl (the angelic maid with the lovely eyes) from certain danger in the arms of a foul gentleman, only to have her fall into the hands of a witch! That one-eyed wretch, that horrible woman, was by far the greater threat. He was sure he'd smelled sulphur when she was near.

He'd spotted her earlier in the day when she'd turned her grotesque visage towards Sister Piddock and scared the dear lady half to death. It'd been all he could do not to seize the hag and slit her throat then and there. He was sure, of course, that's what she'd wanted—to beguile him into taking a course of action that would leave him looking like he, rather than she, was in league with the Devil.

The evil sorceress clearly had the maid bewitched. What

else could explain the docile way in which the damsel had responded to her touch, her words, her commands? No one but a foul temptress could get so perfect a creature to do her bidding. Nothing but witchcraft could place so firm and convincing a hold on the unblemished.

Ah, but his God was a clever God! Just when the Reverend had thought the girl lost to him forever, the witch herself had provided him with the means to find her again. Now all he needed to do was to get to her before she fell further under her tormentor's spell. The Lord's Providence had put her in his path and he wasn't about to abandon her in her time of need. Hers was a soul in distress waiting to be freed from the Devil's grasp. Only then could she become the full measure of her God-given self and serve as a shining example to others. He could feel the Lord's reason moving through him, making his blood run hot with divine guidance. He could see himself standing at the pulpit with the girl at his side—reformed, refined, reborn. What better way to increase the faithfulness of his fold than by having her stand before the congregation and testify of her woes? What better way to neuter a witch? If he got rid of the witch first, there was a good chance whatever curses she'd cast would live on, but to have one whom she'd afflicted rise up against her would surely break the spell. Once the damsel was saved—once he had his Mercy Wylde—and the witch's evil confirmed, he'd set his sights on the witch herself.

"Oh Lord," he cried, falling to his knees, "I will not shrink away from this calling! I will follow your path to the end of your choosing. I am prepared for whatever you would have me do—to save the girl in her innocence, or save the world from her if she be innocent no more. I believe that devils and witches still roam the earth just as I believe in your goodness. No matter what becomes of me, I will rest easy in the knowledge that I have followed your will.

"Bless me that I might be successful in my efforts, give me the strength, courage and resolve I need to execute your wishes. To Thee I will give thanksgiving, I will sing hymns of praise. Not my will, but Thine shall be done."

After kissing his grandfather's Bible three times along the spine, he tucked a small chemist's bottle in his pocket wrapped in a cotton handkerchief, slid his knife into its sheath, and tied a cross of hazel wood around his neck. His goal was clear, his faith keen, his blade sharp.

Standing at Sister Piddock's door, he handed her a slip of paper.

Psalm 73:27
For, lo, they that are far from thee shall perish:
Thou hast destroyed all them that go a whoring from thee.

"Is this all there is?" she asked, confused as to how she was supposed to choose the Sunday hymns from such an unsavoury verse.

"The scripture is all we need," Reverend Townsend answered, heart pounding, anxious to get on his way. "I trust the Lord to guide me. I suggest you do the same."

Yes, of course, Sister Piddock thought. *The Reverend's given me a test of faith.* "Our God is a knowing God," she said with a solemn nod. "I will pray and find a way."

"He will provide," Reverend Townsend said, tipping his hat.

"Amen."

"Amen."

Eleanor sensed a storm was on the way the minute she left the teashop—the hairs on the back of her neck pricked to attention as the melancholy scent of turning leaves hung heavy in the evening air. There was no sign of lightning yet, but she had no doubt it would arrive soon.

She'd always adored autumn storms—from the quiet that came before the rain when the birds and bugs went silent, to the raucous cracks and grumbles that echoed between the clouds, rife with the possibility of goblins and ghosts. Dancing on the porch of their cottage her mother had often sung an ominous little tune as the first raindrops hit the slate roof, a reminder of the dangers of getting caught in a tempest.

Beware the oak, it draws the stroke. Avoid the ash, it prompts the flash. Creep under the thorn, it saves you from harm.

Madame St. Clair believed that any trees that got burned or struck by lightning should be treated with great respect and that whatever wood remained, be it barely scorched or charred black, contained magical powers. Amongst her most prized possessions was a spoon made from the branch of an ash tree that'd been severed from its trunk by a blinding, terrible strike. She'd used the spoon every day to make soups and sauces, potions and brews. Whenever she got called to visit a house where trouble was stirring, she'd carried the spoon along with her and used it to knock on the door to dispel any anger or hard feelings. Halfway to the Newland residence Eleanor wondered if perhaps she should've stuck the worn relic inside her satchel along with the other items she'd packed for her visit with Lucy.

She hadn't heard from Lucy since their conversation in the park and the last time her aunt had visited the shop, she'd claimed she hadn't spoken to her niece in quite some time. "I suppose our Lucy is fine," Mrs. Scrope had said, shaking her head in dismay, "but I wouldn't know. Just last Monday I stopped by the house unannounced and the maid turned me away. 'Mrs. Newland doesn't wish to be disturbed,' she'd said, arms folded, barring the door. I suppose Lucy has every right to refuse visitors, especially during her confinement, but I'm her family for heaven's sake!"

Tucking a small packet of hibiscus tea in Mrs. Scrope's bag, Eleanor had given the woman a sympathetic nod. "I'm sure it was a maid's mistake. Please wish Lucy well for me next time you see her?"

With a troubled sigh Mrs. Scrope had replied, "I'll tell her you asked after her."

Reaching the Newlands' door now, Eleanor wondered if she should bother. While it was possible that Lucy needed to see her, it was equally as possible that she might've called her there as part of some twisted game. Eleanor was prepared for the latter, but she was also prepared to help the young woman if she truly needed her. She'd brought a host of remedies along—ginger root for morning sickness, raspberry leaf to strengthen her womb, oarweed and a long slender hook if she wanted to turn things the other way and let the child go. She hoped it wouldn't come to that, and she hoped she wouldn't have to stay long. She'd promised Beatrice she'd come to the lecture and she didn't want to be late. After ringing the doorbell, she kissed the brass key tied around her neck, and made a silent wish that her mother be on her shoulder should anything go wrong.

"This way, ma'am," the maid said, showing Eleanor into the Newlands' drawing room.

To Eleanor's surprise, the only person there was Lucy's husband. Dressed in a silk smoking jacket, Cecil Newland was sitting by the fire, a decanter of whiskey and a half-empty glass at his side—the perfect picture of a man of wealth taking his leisure. "Care for a drink?" he asked, pouring more whiskey in his glass. The strong scent of alcohol blossomed in the room.

"No, thank you," Eleanor replied. Looking to the clock on the mantel she wondered where Lucy might be. It was already quarter past seven. Where was she?

"Care to sit?" Mr. Newland asked, gesturing to the chair next to his.

"I'll stand until Lucy arrives."

Mr. Newland threw back his drink. "She's not here," he said, wiping his mouth with his sleeve. Eleanor suspected he'd started drinking long before she'd arrived.

"I'll leave you to it then," she said.

Eyebrow arched, Mr. Newland asked, "You didn't know she'd gone?"

"No," Eleanor replied. "In fact I'm more than a little confused. She sent me a telegram this morning asking I meet her here at seven."

"I sent the telegram," Mr. Newland said. "So I suppose this means she's up and left us both. Such a pity. She seemed so fond of you." Fumbling, he reached for a small book on the table next to his chair. Turning to a page marked with a white ribbon he began to read aloud.

"'June first. Saint C. has a devilishly delicate touch with her tongue! So playful. So masterful. So completely disarming. I tremble whenever I recall our last tryst. I'm counting the hours until I can be with her again. I need to have her naked body next to mine, feel her lips on my flesh. There is no better joy or complete pleasure. Nothing in this world compares to it . . .'" Peering up at Eleanor, he asked, "Shall I go on?"

Her face flushed hot. When she didn't respond, Newland slammed the book shut and tossed it on the table. The decanter took the brunt of his anger, wobbling to and fro, and nearly toppling.

Eleanor tried her best to stay calm. "I assure you, Mr. Newland, I have never been and never will be a threat to your marriage."

Mr. Newland sneered at her. "I believe it's too late for such assurances."

Perhaps it was, Eleanor thought, but her conscience was clear. The fate of his marriage was between him and his wife.

Pouring more whiskey in his glass Mr. Newland asked, "Do you know why men drink?"

Eleanor shrugged. "I haven't the faintest."

"We drink to celebrate. We drink to gain courage. We drink to the beauty, good nature and fidelity of our wives." Tossing the glass at the fire he shouted, "I can't do that tonight!"

Eleanor flinched as the glass shattered and the fire flared. Backing away from him, she said, "Why have you called me here?"

Reaching into the pocket of his smoking jacket, Mr. Newland pulled out a small pistol. "I wanted to see you face to face. That's what gentlemen do in these sorts of situations.

We face our enemies, our rivals. A gentleman never slinks around like a coward behind another man's back."

Stay still, she thought. *No sudden movements*. "Is that what you think I am, a coward and a rival?"

"I think you're abhorrent. I think you're a freakish ghoul who wishes she were a man."

Eleanor calculated how many steps it would take to get to the door. "Trust me when I tell you that's the last thing I wish. I've no interest in being anything other than what I am."

Mr. Newland stroked the barrel of his pistol, toyed with the hammer. "It's a shame duelling has gone out of fashion here in the East. These days, dishonest men die such ignominious deaths. They get shot in the back in stairwells or alleyways, sometimes in the best parts of town. They never see it coming. Where is the romance, the honour in that? Tell me, Miss St. Clair, what do women do when they wish to punish their enemies? Sharpen their scissors? Pick a poison? Cast a spell?"

She felt threatened, but his head was muddled, his hands shaky. His aim would be poor. "Do you intend to shoot me, Mr. Newland?" she asked.

Tucking his pistol back in his pocket, he pointed his fingers at her instead. Squinting one eye, he took aim and pulled an imaginary trigger. "Satisfying as it would be," he said, "it'd leave too big a mess. The cleanup alone would take hours. Not to mention that the scandal that'd follow would be incredibly appalling. Tedious. Boring. I favour more elegant means of revenge."

Now he was toying with her, behaving as if he were holding the winning hand. She realized whatever he had planned wasn't going to play out here. "If you're not going to shoot me, then I really must be on my way," she said. "I'm expected elsewhere."

Newland glanced at the clock and smiled. "By all means," he said waving Eleanor out of the room. "Leave my house, you cunt. Enjoy your evening."

Beatrice was sequestered in a small room adjoining the hotel's Grand Ballroom. The space was usually reserved for the storage of music stands and other paraphernalia used by the house orchestra, but Adelaide, with Mrs. Stevens' blessing, had commandeered it for use as a dressing room. After the room's original contents had been moved elsewhere, other items were shuttled in one by one to accommodate Beatrice's needs—a full-length mirror, a clothing rack, a folding modesty screen, a table for accoutrements, two slipper chairs and a large, overstuffed fainting couch. Beatrice would've been happy to dress in Judith's suite and make her way to the ballroom from there, but Adelaide had insisted she take the room, saying, "The mystery dissolves the minute you're seen off the stage."

Staring at a porcelain vase that was overflowing with yellow roses, Beatrice picked up the card that'd accompanied them. WITH BEST WISHES AND HIGH REGARD. JUDITH AND ALDEN DASHLEY. The flowers were beautiful and perfect and smelled divine and it'd been awfully kind of Judith and her husband to send them, but their presence made Beatrice feel as if she were an ingénue on opening night rather than a participant in a scientific presentation. She only hoped she could live up to everyone's expectations.

She, Adelaide and Dr. Brody had finished their preparations a good hour before the event was supposed to start. The stage was set, the spiritoscope was in good order, but she hadn't been able to stop herself from asking, "What will we do if no spirits come forth?"

"Don't say such a thing!" Adelaide had exclaimed, making a sudden gesture as if she were spitting something foul from her mouth. Her Gypsy roots were showing.

Dr. Brody had responded in a more practical fashion. "You can tell them of the supernatural experiences you've had in the past couple of weeks. I've no doubt the audience would find it highly informative."

"Pish!" Adelaide had said. "Isn't there something we can do to assure at least one ghost will show up? Surely there's some way you can entice them to appear?"

Beatrice had forced a smile and said, "I'll try."

The answer she'd really wanted to give was the one she imagined Eleanor would have offered. *It doesn't work that way.* Why had she even brought up the possibility of there not being any ghosts? The scrubber girls were here, there and everywhere—in the water closets, in the dining hall, in the corridors—one of them was bound to make an appearance. She guessed she was nervous, and unsettled by the frightening run-in she'd had with Mr. Palsham in the park. The full weight of what had happened was only now sinking in. What if he'd not let go of her? Had he meant to do her harm? Was his the face she'd seen last night in the fire? She decided it was best not to mention it to Adelaide, at least not until the lecture was over.

Adelaide had taken her hand and led her to the little room so she could get dressed at her leisure and settle her nerves.

But once she had cinched, buttoned and pinned Beatrice into Minnie Stevens' ball gown, she'd been quick to take her leave. Had Beatrice somehow offended her? Was Adelaide tired of her company? Sometimes she wished she could trade places with Adelaide as she was sure she was better equipped to handle this sort of thing. She was growing tired of constantly wondering if she was out of her depth.

The room had no clock and Beatrice didn't own a watch, so every few minutes she'd poke her head out the door that led to the wings behind the ballroom's stage to ask Adelaide for the time. The last time she'd done it, Adelaide had impatiently stalked to the door and announced, "It's seven thirty." Her tone was decidedly frosty. "The audience will be arriving soon. I don't want there to be any chance of anyone seeing you until the lecture begins. Not even the slightest glimpse between these curtains. Don't be such a child. Get back in there and close the door. I'll come get you when it's time."

She tried to do as Adelaide said, but when she couldn't get the elaborate headdress to sit correctly on her head, she decided it was best to fetch Adelaide to help. Slowly opening the door to the wings, she looked to see if Adelaide was close by. It was then she caught a glimpse of Adelaide and Dr. Brody entwined in an intimate embrace. She'd known they were fond of each other, but to see them kissing with their bodies pressed together was a blush-inducing shock nonetheless. Thinking better of interrupting the pair, she wondered where Eleanor might be. She'd promised she'd be there before the event started, to recite a spell of good fortune on her behalf. Why hadn't she arrived yet? Pulling her wrap over her dress Beatrice snuck out of the room and down the long corridor that led to the lobby. She figured so long as she was covered up, no one would guess that she was the Egyptian Sibyl.

Hiding behind a marble column in the entrance, she searched for Eleanor. The place was filling fast, ladies fanning themselves in the hot, close air; men clutching their programmes with their hands behind their backs. A porter rang a shiny gong suspended from a stand. "Five minutes until seating begins!" he called. "Five minutes!" By the clock in the lobby it was seven forty.

Beatrice spotted several familiar faces in the crowd, including Judith and Alden Dashley, who were holding court with several members of the Fraternal Order of the Unknown Philosophers. Mr. Guiteau was back again (along with his attendant shadows), passionately informing the receptionist of his urgent need to speak with Senator Conkling. Billy Dashley and a pair of scrubber girls darted here and there among the living, playing hide-and-go-seek. As she watched them have their fun, Beatrice thought she caught sight of Mr. Palsham, the man who'd frightened her so terribly in the park. Standing on tiptoe, she tried to get a better look at the gentleman, but before she could confirm it was him, he was gone. Across the room, the preacher who'd come to her aid was looking straight towards her. She pulled the hood of her wrap over her head. There was no sign of Eleanor.

Hands clammy, Beatrice headed out the ladies' entrance to the street, hoping to meet Eleanor at the door. A cool breeze was stirring, rustling the fading leaves that clung to the tops of the trees. A few stray drops of rain fell as lightning flashed in the distance behind a wall of clouds. Beatrice began to count, *one Mississippi, two Mississippi, three Mississippi, four*

Mississippi . . . A grumble of thunder brought her count to a halt. The centre of the storm was about a mile off.

Where was Eleanor? How could she have missed her? Was she still at the shop?

Walking down the street, Beatrice thought, *I won't go far. Just a few steps down the block, and I'll turn right back.* Staring up at the magic lantern show just off the park, she saw the notice for their lecture in letters three storeys high: IT MUST BE SEEN TO BE BELIEVED.

What have I gotten myself into? She could run to the shop, leave the dress on the bed and find her way to the train station. If the trains travelling north along the Hudson didn't run this late on Saturdays, she could always go to Joseph Wheeler's cousin's saloon in the Bowery. It wasn't ideal, but surely they'd give her a place to lay her head until morning. Then it'd be back to Aunt Lydia and Stony Point and her reliable yet unremarkable life.

Crossing the street, she came upon a stretch of sidewalk where a new building was being erected. Rickety-looking scaffolds stretched high above her head. A dark figure was perched on one of the boards leaning against the brick. A mason who'd fallen asleep on the job? A man without a home? To her recollection, the building hadn't even been started when she'd walked to the hotel that morning, but that was the way of the city, she supposed. In the short time she'd been in New York, the city had been constantly changing, one man's idea of what was tremendous elbowing out another's for something taller, newer, better, like bullies who stepped on sand castles on the beach.

The wind picked up and the rain along with it. Drivers perched on their carriages turned up their collars and tipped their hats over their eyes. Lightning spread in wiry fingers between the clouds—brighter, sharper. *One Mississippi, two Mississippi, three Mississippi.* Thunder echoed between the buildings—louder, closer. Does the lightning choose the tree, or does the tree call to the lightning? Eleanor had told Beatrice that it was her deep desire to discover if magic existed in the world that had allowed magic to find her. Beatrice couldn't help but wonder if she was strong enough to withstand its attentions. One by one, several street lamps in front of her sputtered out, leaving her in a long stretch of darkness. It began to pour. She was almost to the shop. If she turned around, she could make it back to the hotel just in time.

What should she do?

Footsteps sounded behind her, gaining fast.

Before she could quicken her own pace, she was grabbed by the waist. Putting a gloved hand over her mouth, the man in black didn't give her the chance to decide.

Lost and Found.

Eleanor arrived at the hotel dripping wet. She'd trudged through the rain, completely shaken by her conversation with Mr. Newland, wondering where Lucy had run to and if there was anything she could do about her husband's veiled threats. For now, she'd simply have to be on the lookout for whatever he might have planned. It was one thing to protect the shop from wayward ghosts, it was quite another to safeguard herself from physical harm. Cecil Newland was used to getting whatever he wanted, whenever he wanted it, without a care for the consequences. If he wished to hurt her, she was sure he'd find a way to do it and come out unscathed.

Shrugging off her wrap, she hurried to the Grand Ballroom knowing she was late. The clock in the lobby had just struck eight, its bells fading out of earshot as Eleanor snuck to the side of the stage. The room was stifling, the audience impatient for the lecture to begin. At least she could take some comfort in the fact that events like these never started on time.

"Where's Beatrice?" she asked when she'd found Adelaide standing with Dr. Brody, heads bent together in deep discussion.

Adelaide looked up, worried, irritated, frantic. "I was hoping she was with you. I thought she might've gone back to the shop for something she'd forgotten."

"I wasn't at the shop." Now wasn't the time to explain where she'd been. "When did you notice Beatrice was missing?"

"No one's seen her for the past half-hour," Adelaide said. "She was in her dressing room, ready to go at half past seven. The next time I checked on her she was gone."

It wasn't like Beatrice to up and disappear—and it wasn't like Adelaide to be so anxious. "Can you think of any reason as to why she might've slipped out? It's awfully hot in here. Perhaps she took a stroll down one of the back hallways and lost track of time."

Adelaide bit her lip.

"The hotel staff has searched high and low but so far they've had no luck," Brody said. Putting his hand on Adelaide's forearm he added, "That's not to say they won't, though. I'm sure she'll turn up."

Mrs. Stevens strode to the doctor's side clutching a black lace fan. "Eight o'clock has come and gone, Dr. Brody. We can't delay much longer."

"Five minutes more?" Adelaide suggested, trying to hide her panic. "We'll still be on the proper side of fashionably late."

"Five minutes it is," Marietta said, her eyes doubtful. "In the meantime I'll make an announcement to pacify the masses. People are already talking of leaving."

As Mrs. Stevens took to the stage, Dr. Brody pulled Adelaide and Eleanor aside. "If Beatrice doesn't show before our five minutes are up, then I'll do the presentation without her."

"How will that work?" Adelaide said shaking her head. "What will you say?"

Looking out at the fidgeting crowd Dr. Brody replied, "I'll say she's taken ill. People will be understanding about that, won't they? Or at least the thinking members of the audience will."

Eleanor gave Dr. Brody a supportive nod. "I think it's a wise solution."

"People won't understand," Adelaide protested. "They're here for a show, to see a sensation. You'll get booed, you'll get heckled, they'll head for the door and leave you talking to empty chairs. This was to be your big night. What of your research, your career?"

"My research will be the same tomorrow as it is today," Brody said. "What's important is that Beatrice is found, safe and sound."

"He's right," Eleanor said. "I'll go to the shop to see if she's there."

Taking hold of Adelaide's hand, Dr. Brody said, "You should go with her. I'll be fine on my own."

Adelaide frowned at him, hesitant.

"When you find her," Dr. Brody added, "please let her know that she's under no obligation to come back. If she shows, I'll count it as a happy surprise. If she doesn't, I've no hard feelings."

Adelaide leaned up and kissed his cheek. "Good luck out there."

As the two women made their way to the lobby, Eleanor whispered to Adelaide, "I'm not placing the blame on you, but I can see that you feel guilty. At some point I fully expect you to tell me what you think you did to make her run off." Holding her breath she waited for Adelaide to rail against her words, to storm off without her, but that moment never came. They walked arm in arm from hotel to home in silence.

The lights were out in the shop and the windows upstairs

were dark. Putting her key in the door, Eleanor found the lock had already been tripped. "Beatrice?" she called moving to turn up the gaslights.

"I'll look upstairs," Adelaide said, twisting the wick key on an oil lamp and striking a match to light it. After turning the flame down so it burned low and steady, she settled the lamp's glass chimney in place and took the light in hand.

Eleanor followed her as she climbed the stairs.

"Beatrice?"

"Are you here?"

Silence. Adelaide briefly cast the light into their own rooms before heading to the garret.

"Hello?"

"Beatrice?"

"Are you all right?"

"Are you unwell?"

Adelaide took the lamp into Beatrice's room but the girl wasn't there. "Where do you suppose she's gotten to?"

"I don't know," Eleanor answered, lighting a second lamp so they could search the room for clues. She'd been up here several times since Beatrice had arrived, but she'd never stayed long enough to take stock of how the girl had made the space her own. It was an endearing sight. Books were piled by the bed. Notes, spells and news clippings covered the walls. The witch's ladder she'd brought with her from Stony Point was safely coiled inside a bottle that rested on the window ledge. Spotting a notebook that was lying open on the bed, Eleanor picked it up to inspect it. It was turned to the last page, which was blank except for the words *Census of Astonishments* written in large, flowery script. The rest of the book was filled with observations and musings, but nothing out of the ordinary for a young witch. Placing the book where she'd found it, Eleanor felt a pang of remorse for having snooped, but what else was she to do?

Adelaide sat on the floor rummaging through the trunk the girl's aunt had sent to Beatrice. "All her dresses are here, except for one," she announced. "The red calico is missing, but she was wearing it today until she changed into the gown for the lecture. It's still in the dressing room."

"She'd never run off in that gown," Eleanor said, fear creeping up her spine.

Clutching a length of striped grosgrain ribbon in her hand, Adelaide replied, "You're right. She wouldn't." She'd gifted the ribbon to Beatrice after she'd let her borrow it for their first visit together to Dr. Brody's house. Beatrice had tried her best to return it, saying, "I can't, it's yours, I'm afraid I'll ruin it." Smoothing the ribbon between her fingers, Adelaide bowed her head, overcome with guilt.

Eleanor took one last look at the clippings on the wall. "It doesn't look like anything's missing."

"Nothing except her," Adelaide said, sitting on the edge of Beatrice's bed, a single tear rolling down her cheek.

"Oh Adelaide," Eleanor said moving to comfort her. She knew how rare a thing it was for her to cry.

Trembling, Adelaide confessed, "I was short with her when I had no good reason to be. She was nervous about the presentation, and I called her a child and left her alone instead of staying with her and making her feel at ease. You've been right all along. All I've ever done is push her, trying to turn her into something I wanted her to be."

"Hush now. You mustn't talk like that. I'm sure she didn't see it that way, any of it. Beatrice adores you. I don't know how many times she's told me she wished she could be more like you."

Wiping her cheek, Adelaide said, "But that's the thing, isn't it? She's not like me, nor should she wish to be. What was she thinking, going out alone in the city at night? She doesn't belong out there."

"She's stronger than you think."

Adelaide thought of the tragic tales she'd grown up with—young women being seduced, raped, battered, stabbed, murdered, and then tossed in back alleys or steamer trunks and left to rot. She'd known many girls, herself included, who'd been used up and discarded as ruined goods. They were girls who wished (maybe once, fleetingly, or maybe hour upon hour) that they were dead. When they'd cried for help, no one listened. When it was over (and over and over and over) they were told, "There are worse fates than this. You deserve what you got." Looking at Eleanor she said, "You don't know what it's like."

"I know your story and I believe every word. And you forget that I came to know the city on my own before I met you."

Adelaide stood and straightened her skirts. Chin up she said, "I'm going out."

"Please don't," Eleanor begged. "It's late. It's raining. You'll catch your death . . ."

"I'm no good here," Adelaide said. "If I stay, I'll go mad. I know where to look, who to talk to. Don't fight me on this."

Taking Adelaide's hand in hers, Eleanor spat in her friend's palm and then traced a star on her skin. Closing her eyes she whispered, "Light before, light behind, light above, light below. May you stay safe wherever you shall roam."

"I'll be back soon," Adelaide said. "Wait up for me?"

"Always," Eleanor replied.

Eleanor saw Adelaide to the door. For the first time since she'd returned to the shop she wondered where Perdu was. He hadn't greeted them when they'd arrived and he wasn't sleeping on his perch. "Perdu?" she called. "Where are you?"

A faint chortle sounded from beneath the counter.

"Come out here," she coaxed. "Come on out. It's all right."

The raven flapped to the top of the counter and began pacing back and forth along the length of it, craning his neck and crying, "Fiend! Fiend! Fiend!"

"Perdu, what's wrong? What's happened?"

The bird quivered and shook as Eleanor gently looked him over from beak to tail. No feathers were missing and there were no signs of injury. Still, it was clear that something had happened to frighten the poor pet.

"Fiend!" he cried again, breaking loose from Eleanor's touch.

She remembered the open door. Had she forgotten to lock it before she'd left for Lucy's or had someone broken in? Had this fiend taken Beatrice? Moving through the shop she looked for missing items, broken glass, drops of blood. But nothing seemed amiss. The teacups were hanging from their hooks on the wall, their saucers evenly spaced on the plate rail behind them. The honey pots, sugar bowls and creamers sat innocently waiting to be filled. There was no evidence of a burglary, no signs of struggle.

"Fiend!" the bird bellowed as if he were sounding an alarm. Ruffling his feathers, Perdu lit on the top shelf behind the counter and began pecking his beak against a glass jar. *Ting, ting, ting,* he tapped. *Ting, ting, ting,* three times more.

Seeing what the bird was pecking at, Eleanor let out a gasp. "*Merde*," she said putting her hand to her mouth.

The jar that Perdu was focused upon wasn't one of Eleanor's. Cobalt blue with a cork stopper, it was fitted with a label that bore a skull and crossbones. Bringing the container down to the counter, Eleanor removed the cork and inspected it with care. "Arsenic," she said, eyes wide with fear. Staring at the many tins and jars that lined the shelves, she had the chilling thought that perhaps everything in the tearoom, every jar of honey, every tin of tea, every container of sugar had been opened and tampered with. Slumping on a stool, she put her head in her hands. This was just the sort of treachery Cecil Newland would exact.

Flapping back to the shelf, Perdu chose a jar of hibiscus tea and began to peck at it, *ting, ting, ting . . . ting, ting, ting.* Chortling, low in his throat, the bird said, "Who's a good boy?"

Knot in her belly, Eleanor replied, "You are."

Shaking his head, Perdu tapped the jar again, *ting, ting, ting . . . ting, ting, ting,* then he repeated his throaty, ghoulish question, "Who's a good boy?"

"You are?" Eleanor asked, wondering if there might be method in the raven's madness.

Ting, ting, ting . . . ting, ting, ting.

Taking the second jar from the shelf, Eleanor opened it and discovered a ring of white powder stuck to the rim. Clearly the bird knew all that'd happened. With any luck she'd soon know too.

Thinking there might be a way to assist the raven with his task, Eleanor grabbed her broom from the closet and pointed the end of the handle at the next jar on the shelf. *Ting, ting, ting,* she lightly tapped the glass and waited for Perdu's response.

The bird stared at her with a gleaming, curious eye.

Ting, ting, ting, she tapped again, looking to the jar. "Safe?" she asked, hoping he'd cotton on.

"Safe!" he croaked, vigorously nodding yes.

Eleanor moved on to the next jar.

After Perdu had declared five jars in a row to be safe, Eleanor gently ran the broom along the rest of her stock as if she were a child running a stick along a picket fence. "All safe?" she asked, praying he'd confirm her hunch.

"Safe!" he crowed, nodding and flapping his wings. "Who's a good bird?"

"You are," she declared.

Sitting in the front window, Eleanor kept watch for Adelaide and Beatrice and anyone who might bring her news. Pulling apart a loaf of Mr. Markowitz's black rye, she tossed a hunk to Perdu then took a piece for herself. The chewy loaf tasted of molasses and malt, and helped to settle her churning belly. She had no doubt that Cecil Newland had ordered someone to do the dirty business with the arsenic, but had he ordered them to take Beatrice too? She didn't think he would dare such a crime—it carried too much risk—but she needed to rule out the possibility. Running to the counter she fetched an egg from a wire basket. "Who wants a treat?" she asked Perdu.

The raven cocked his head. "Perdu," he answered, sidling onto Eleanor's shoulder. "Perdu, do."

Cradling the egg in her hands, Eleanor said, "Tell me who was in the shop tonight?"

"Perdu?" the bird replied, before emitting a series of bubbling coos. Anticipating the slither of yolk down his throat made him hopeful, eager.

"Yes," Eleanor said, with a supportive nod, "and was Beatrice here too?"

The raven shook his head.

"She wasn't?"

"No," he said, clucking his tongue.

"Then who else was in the shop?" Eleanor said, continuing to tempt Perdu with the egg. "I know you weren't alone."

Staring out the shop window, Perdu pecked at the glass. He puffed up his feathers until he was twice his normal size. "Fiend," he said in a low, menacing whisper.

With that, Eleanor cracked the egg on the edge of a saucer and gave up her interrogation. If the bird had recognized the intruder, he would've said so.

As Perdu scooped runny egg into his beak, Eleanor hid the arsenic and the hibiscus tea in the broom closet. Adelaide came through the shop door just as she'd closed the cupboard. Looking at Perdu, Eleanor put her finger to her lips. The bird flew to his perch and tucked his head under a wing.

"Any luck?" Eleanor asked as a dejected Adelaide settled into the window seat.

"None," Adelaide said.

"Tea?"

"Yes, please."

Turning to the shelves, Eleanor chose a jar marked "sweet ease," and went about brewing a pot to calm their nerves. As the water came to a boil, Eleanor whispered a few words over the leaves, first in French then in English. "*Ne laissez aucun mal à s'abattre sur nous.* Let no evil befall us." She trusted Perdu, of course, but a few good words couldn't hurt. She wondered how long she'd feel the need to bless every tea leaf, sugar cube and drop of honey in the place.

Settling across from Adelaide, she made sure she took her first sip of tea before Adelaide took hers. The bright notes of the herbs within—lavender, lemon balm, spearmint and passionflower—were the only tastes she sensed on her tongue. Closing her eyes, she thanked Heaven for Perdu.

Before long the shop's bell rang, startling both women to their feet.

Adelaide rushed to the door.

Dr. Brody was there, cheeks flushed, beer on his breath. Beatrice wasn't with him.

"How did it go?" Adelaide asked, inviting him into the shop. She wasn't quite ready to break the bad news.

Eleanor stood close by, waiting for the penny to drop.

"It was splendid," Dr. Brody said, teetering into the room. "Well actually, it was horrid at first. Most of the crowd left, except of course for the Philosophers and all but one of the North Orange Diviners, and several members of the Followers of the Needle. Mrs. Stevens was just glad there wasn't a riot. After I gave a brief lecture of my findings, and Judith Dashley gave a stunning account of Beatrice's abilities, we adjourned for the evening. I would've been here sooner but the Philosophers insisted we make a toast or ten to my dear father." Squinting, Dr. Brody looked around the room. "How's our girl? Is she faring any better?"

Adelaide guided him to a chair. "I think you'd better sit," she said, staring helplessly at Eleanor.

Eleanor scurried behind the counter. "I'll put on the kettle for more tea."

Upstairs, Twitch was face down, sobbing into Beatrice's pillow.

"Don't worry," Bright said trying to comfort him. "She's a strong, resilient girl."

"How could this have happened?" he whimpered. "We gave her the right dream. I touched all her garments with magic . . ."

Bright placed her hand on the small of his back. "We did all we could do. It isn't up to us."

When the Devil with his confederate and concomitant Spectres came unto this poor girl, it was their custom to cast her into such horrible Darkness that she imagined herself in a desolate cellar, where Day or Night could not be distinguished. Her eyes were open, moving to and fro after the Hellish Harpies that fluttered about her and she was little able to see anything else.

—from *An Attempt to Cure Witchcraft: The Story of Mercy Wylde*

Taken.

Beatrice was huddled on a straw mattress in the corner of a cold, dark cellar, head down, knees hugged to her chest. Shivering, she tried to remember how she'd gotten here but her aching head couldn't muster the answer. Every part of her was sore, from her leaden limbs to her face, and the harder she worked to make sense of things, the more she felt her memory slipping, falling off the edge of reason. Touching the nape of her neck to explore why it hurt, she realized all that remained of her hair was a mess of choppy ends. It had been cut close to the base of her skull. She couldn't remember the mincing of shears or how Minnie Stevens' ball gown had been taken from her, leaving her in nothing but her thin cotton shift. Whenever she swallowed, blood seeped from a gash inside her bottom lip and there was a mass of tender, swollen skin around her mouth. There was an odd smell in her nose, a strange taste in her mouth, medicinal yet sweet.

As her eyes adjusted to the darkness she noticed scant traces of light from between the floorboards above her head and the narrow gap under the door. The walls were stone, the floor dirt. There was no washbasin, no mirror, no way for her to tend to her wounds. Aside from the mattress there was a wooden bucket in the corner, a few pebbles in the dirt, and a large wooden support beam standing at attention in the middle of the room. The air was damp and musty except for an occasional waft of pipe smoke that met her nose, perhaps from the rooms upstairs. Hauling herself up she went to the door, where she discovered there was no knob or latch to loose. She leaned against its wide wooden planks, but it wouldn't budge. She was starting to wonder if she hadn't been thrown into the Tombs. But what for? Hearing the sound of a fly buzzing, she turned her attention to the bucket on the other side of the cellar. The pail was half full of vomit. Holding her breath against the stench, she wondered if the bucket's contents were hers, as if the ownership of such muck mattered. Trembling, she couldn't help the tears that now streamed down her face.

"Help!" she cried.

Instantly she heard footsteps above her—heavy pacing at a steady, even gait. Occasionally a loose board would creak and complain under the weight—it had to be a man. Remembering Mr. Palsham's determined grip on her arm, she wondered if it might be him. She was sure she'd spotted him in the lobby of the hotel. If he'd seen her the day she'd touched the obelisk, had he been following her ever since? As she strained to listen for other sounds that might tell her where she was, she heard the man speak. Although she couldn't quite make out what he was saying, his words had a cadence, like prayer or madness or song. Unlike Mr. Palsham's raspy voice, though, this man's had a pleasant tone and rhythm. Dare she call out again? Perhaps whoever it was would take pity on her and come to her aid.

"Help me!" she wailed. "Please, let me out!" She shouted until her throat was raw. When her voice failed she pounded on the door.

The light above her went out. The footsteps faded, but she was not alone.

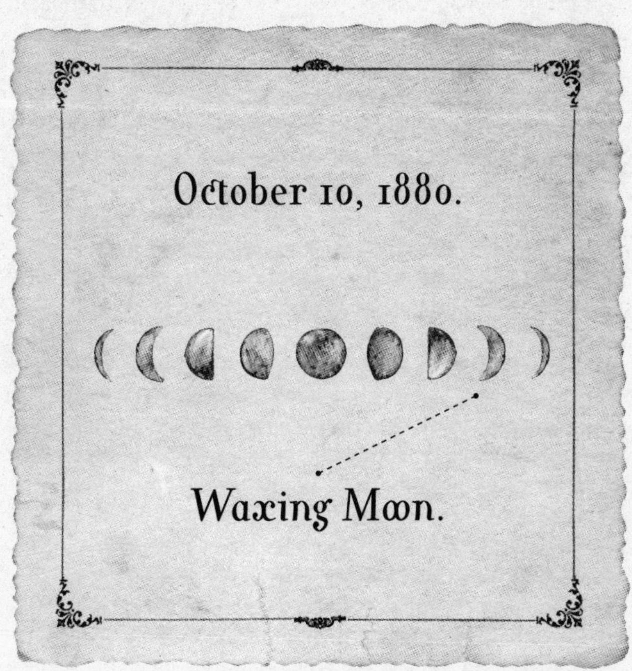
October 10, 1880.
Waxing Moon.

Forerunner, or foretelling. Among the signs and portents that make themselves manifest in the daily world is the forerunner or foretelling. These mystical signals occur in anticipation of, or at the time of, someone's death. There have been many such signs recorded over the ages in various places around the world. The most prevalent include: three knocks on the door when no one's there; a dog howling in its sleep; a bird flying into a house through an open door; a favourite picture falling off the wall; the dream of a loved one bidding goodbye; the sound of church bells ringing in the middle of the night.

—*From the grimoire of Eleanor St. Clair*

Church Bells and Seekers.

Adelaide, Eleanor and Dr. Brody kept vigil at the teashop through the night. On Dr. Brody's recommendation, the three put together a plan of action for the following day: Dr. Brody would speak with the hotel detective and make the rounds among the staff; Adelaide would meet with Mrs. Stevens and the Dashleys to tell them of Beatrice's disappearance and to enlist their help; Eleanor would visit Police headquarters to file a report at the Office of Missing Persons. As their minds grew muddled from constant worry and their bodies weary from lack of sleep, Brody suggested they take turns keeping watch so each might get some much-needed rest.

Eleanor was the last to take her turn. During her watch, she thumbed through her grimoire looking for spells that might aid them in their search. Pausing on the page that addressed forerunners she thanked Heaven that any such signs had been absent thus far. Stopping on an entry titled, "Eye of Illumination," she remembered her mother practicing the spell whenever she'd feared someone might've used magic against her.

In the wake of evil, take a sharp needle and prick the shape of an eye into the palm of your left hand. While guiding that hand over any item, person or space you fear may have been touched by wickedness, close your eyes and repeat the following words: "May my blood sense what my eyes can't see." If dark magic has been cast upon you, the eye will glow and burn. Further steps must then be taken to protect yourself from harm.

Eleanor took a needle from her sewing kit and carefully pricked her palm. Slowly making her way around the shop she held her hand over every inch of the place as she recited the chant over and over again. Although she was certain she and Perdu had uncovered the extent of what must have been Cecil Newland's mischief, she worried something else might be afoot. Upon completing the spell, she stood in the centre of the shop and heaved a great sigh, relieved to find that there were no traces of dark magic to be found there. She was more confused than ever as to what had happened to Beatrice.

At sunrise she took a pencil in hand and made a list of other steps she might take to help find the girl. She had a feeling it was going to take more than keen minds and good will.

1. Ask Maman.

2. Ask the bees.

3. Ask Perdu (again).

4. Ask the Dearlies.

5. Read the Leaves.

6. Look to the mirror.

7. Consult the "Book and Key"

Dr. Brody rose shortly after dawn, shrugging into his jacket and rubbing his stubbled chin.

"Tea?" Eleanor asked, setting a kettle on the stove.

"Please," Dr. Brody replied, though what he really wanted was a cup of the coffee he'd lived on in the army: hot black sludgy fuel that could wake the dead.

"How'd you sleep?" Eleanor asked, dumping three generous spoonfuls of the strongest tea she had into the pot.

"Fitfully, and you?"

"The same."

"No sign of her?"

"None."

Then a flustered Adelaide came downstairs. "What's that racket?"

"Hmm?" Eleanor said, fetching another cup.

Holding up a finger for silence, Adelaide paused to listen. "There," she said. "There it goes again. Don't you hear it?"

"Hear what?" Dr. Brody asked with a shrug.

"I think it's a dog," Adelaide answered. "It's been yowling for the past hour."

Eleanor bit her lip. "Howling?"

Adelaide shook her head. "No, not howling. It's more like whining." Getting nothing but blank stares she headed for the door. "I'm going to see if I can't find it."

Eleanor kept on with the tea.

Quinn looked out the window after Adelaide.

The stray dog Adelaide had fed scraps to in the park was standing on the stoop of Markowitz's Bakery whining and scratching at the door.

The shop was closed for the day, but peering through the window, Adelaide spotted the portly baker. She knocked on the door.

"Miss Thom!" Mr. Markowitz exclaimed as he opened the door with a friendly smile. "How are you this fine morning?"

The dog cowered behind Adelaide's skirts.

"Tired," Adelaide grumbled. "I'm usually not up this early."

The baker waggled his eyebrows. "Late night?"

"Yes," Adelaide confessed, "but not nearly as much fun as I'd like it to have been."

"So sorry to hear that," Mr. Markowitz said looking genuinely concerned. He liked people to be happy, especially the women next door. "Would a basket of turnovers help cheer you up?"

Adelaide wasn't one to refuse the baker's kindness. "That would be lovely," she said, stepping inside the shop and closing the door behind her. "If it's not any trouble."

"No trouble at all. I just took a batch out of the oven."

The dog resumed its frantic bid to get inside the bakery.

"You didn't happen to see Beatrice last evening, did you?" Adelaide asked.

"Can't say that I did," Mr. Markowitz replied. "But you know me . . . early to bed, early to rise."

Adelaide nodded. "How about this morning then? You're usually up before dawn?"

Flipping the turnovers one by one out from their baking tins he replied, "Yes I am, but I haven't seen her. I can't keep track of you young ladies. So many pretty faces running willy-nilly all over the city with rouge on their lips and minds of their own. Where I come from, all three of you dear girls would've been married and holding babes in your arms by now." Turning, he caught the look on Adelaide's face, and the smile dropped off his. "Is Miss Dunn in some sort of trouble?"

The previous night she had searched for Beatrice in the park and along the streets near the hotel, stopping to give her card to every rough, nighthawk, carriage driver and whore she encountered. "Something like that," she said. She didn't want to worry the man too much. "If you see her, could you feed her some turnovers and send her home?" His golden treats were enough to soften even the most stubborn heart.

"I will," he said, handing the basket of baked goods to Adelaide. "My treat. No charge."

"Thank you," Adelaide said. "You're very kind."

As she opened the door to leave, Mr. Markowitz's son Isaac shot from the back room and outside before her. "Cleo!" he exclaimed, wrapping his arms around the dog's neck.

Mr. Markowitz raised a rolling pin in the air and bellowed, "That mangy hound's not to set a single muddy paw inside my shop!"

"But Papa," Isaac protested, "she's got no home."

Mr. Markowitz stared the boy down. "No."

"Please," Isaac begged.

Grumbling, the baker stomped back to his work.

"How about Cleo comes to stay with me?" Adelaide proposed, taking pity on dog and boy.

Cleo cocked her ears, wagged her tail.

"And I can come visit her at your place?" Isaac asked. His eyes were as hopeful as the dog's.

Adelaide nodded. "Any time you like."

"Isaac!" Mr. Markowitz shouted from the back of the shop.

"Coming, Papa!" Isaac shouted back.

Giving the boy a little wave, Adelaide hung the basket from her arm. "Come on Cleo, let's go."

Dog at her side, Adelaide entered the teashop and waited for Eleanor's reaction. She was half certain she'd get the same response as Isaac had gotten from his father.

Setting a saucer of raw stew meat on the floor for Perdu, Eleanor looked up at her friend and then at the dog.

Head low, tail wagging, nose catching the scent of the meat, Cleo slowly approached the raven.

Feathers ruffled, Perdu hissed and defended his breakfast.

Giving a sharp bark, Cleo ran between Dr. Brody's legs.

"Who's this?" Dr. Brody asked, scratching the dog behind its ears.

The dog's tail wildly thumped on the floor.

"Cleo," Adelaide answered, watching the pair with some astonishment. If Eleanor didn't fold, perhaps he'd take the pup.

"Nice name," Dr. Brody said, still scratching.

Taking another saucer from the shelf Eleanor grudgingly asked, "Is she staying?"

Adelaide smiled. "I suppose she is."

Eleanor put several pieces of meat on the saucer and placed

it on the floor. "Come on then," she said to the dog, "eat up before Perdu decides it's his."

Adelaide, Eleanor and Brody stood in silence watching the dog eat, each hoping that their kindness towards the stray might somehow hasten Beatrice's return.

She underwent a sort of plague, which I don't remember that I ever observed in more than one or two bewitched persons besides her. Her tortures were turned into frolics, and she became as extravagant as a wildcat. Her imagination strangely disordered, she was always excessively witty in talk; never downright profane, but yet sufficiently insolent and abusive. Knowing it was not her true self she was displaying, I had no hesitation in putting a stop to it.

—from *An Attempt to Cure Witchcraft: The Story of Mercy Wylde*

Witch's Mark.

THE GHOST OF Lena McLeod hovered in the cell where Beatrice slept. Although her body had been promptly fetched after she'd hung herself, the men who'd collected it couldn't keep her spirit from returning to the parsonage.

Staring at Beatrice she laughed, she swooned, she wept. Would this girl pay attention to her? The other one hadn't listened to a thing she'd said.

"Wake up," she called to Beatrice. "Wake up!"

Beatrice stirred, exhausted and hungry, her throat aching with thirst. Squinting across the room she noticed a bright light eking its way through a crack in the wall. Within the glow was a spirit, or was it an angel? As it drew near, she realized it was no heavenly being.

Head listing, the ghost stared at her, an angry red ring showing around her neck, face mottled in the colours of a nasty bruise—yellow, purple, blue.

"Who are you?" Beatrice asked, unsure but not afraid.

"Who are you?" Lena repeated, touching the tip of her finger to Beatrice's forehead.

Adelaide's voice sounded in Beatrice's head. *You are Beatrice Dunn. You are a witch. You're no one to be trifled with.* "I'm Beatrice," she answered, "Beatrice Dunn."

"Are you a witch, Beatrice?"

She paused to think. Would a witch have gotten herself into such a mess? Was that why she was there? Were Adelaide and Eleanor looking for her? Were they in any danger? Maybe she was better off just being a girl from Stony Point.

"Well are you a witch, or aren't you?" the ghost demanded. "I don't imagine you'd be here unless he thought you were."

"Who?" Beatrice asked.

"The Reverend."

Beatrice wondered what a reverend could possibly want with her.

"He's terrible," Lena said, frowning.

The taste of blood blossomed in Beatrice's mouth. Her head throbbed.

Tugging on the hair at the back of Beatrice's neck, Lena said, "You don't know the half of it."

"Where am I?" Beatrice asked.

"The parsonage," Lena replied.

"How long have you been here?"

"Nearly a month, I think. Three days alive, the rest dead."

"Did he kill you?" Beatrice asked wondering how many days she might have.

Laughing, Lena answered, "He thought he might, but I didn't let him. I beat him to it! He couldn't kill me and they couldn't catch my ghost."

"They?"

"The Collectors. A pair of ghouls dressed in black suits and gentlemen's skins. They snatch up witches' bodies once they're dead."

Beatrice swallowed hard. "They work for him, this Reverend?"

"No, they work for someone much worse. I don't dare say his name, but I'll spell it for ye."

A pebble rolled across the floor to Beatrice's feet.

As Lena spelled the name, "P-A-L-S-H-A-M," the pebble etched a series of letters into the dirt. *M-A-L-P-H-A-S.*

A chill travelled up Beatrice's spine. "Is that who put me here?"

Footsteps sounded on the stairs leading to the cellar.

"Hush!" Lena cried as she disappeared into the crack. "He's coming!"

Beatrice used her foot to erase the markings from the dirt.

The door opened with a jolt and a tall, dour-faced man entered the room, tin pail in one hand, lantern in the other, a thick wooden rod slung at his hip. The heels of his patent leather boots thudded on the dirt floor. His dress was more like that of a military man than a man of God, his trousers tucked into his boots, his coat decorated with braided stitching, his lapel adorned with a shining medal that bore a silver cross. An engraving in the centre of the medallion read, *To give light to those that live in darkness.* Hair slick with oil, dark moustache neatly trimmed, he had an intense, greedy look in his eyes that led Beatrice to think he expected her to be impressed by him.

Stepping back, she put distance between them and tried to quell her fears.

"My child," he said. "Don't be afraid. I'm Reverend Townsend, the pastor of the Church of the Good Shepherd."

Looking him in the eye she asked, "Why am I here?"

"I saved you," he said, setting the lantern and pail on the floor. The pail contained a crusty hunk of bread and a small canteen. "Don't you remember?"

She recognized him now. "You scared off that man, yesterday, in the park."

Smiling he said, "And I saved you again last night, outside the hotel."

Could the ghost have been wrong? Beatrice wondered. Maybe he didn't wish to do her harm after all. Then again, if he'd meant to save her, why had he brought her here?

Inspecting the wooden bucket in the corner, Reverend Townsend frowned with disgust.

"I'd like to go home now," Beatrice said moving towards the door.

"Not yet," he said, blocking her way.

"Am I not free to leave?"

Gripping the wooden rod at his side, his eyes narrowed. "Not now."

The rod was a formidable weapon, fitted with a leather grip and sporting an iron tip. Beatrice knew he'd use it to stop her if she tried to flee. "If you let me go, I'll not tell a soul," she begged. "I swear it."

"Don't try to trick me. That's the Devil talking through you, and I'll not hear it."

"Please," Beatrice begged, "let me go home."

Grabbing her by the shoulders, Reverend Townsend shook her hard. “That foul woman has bewitched you! She’s got you under the influence of devils and demons.”

A series of memories flashed in Beatrice’s mind. The cruel hateful look the Reverend had given Adelaide in the park. Her muffled screams as a moist rag covered her mouth. The sound of his voice in her ear before everything went dark.

“Let me go!” she demanded, struggling to break free.

Holding her fast he hissed, “Fight all you want. Say whatever the Devil tells you, but do not think that you can hide it.” Turning her loose for a moment, he snatched the hunk of bread from the pail, then seized her again. “Eat this,” he said holding the bread in her face, “if you wish to prove me wrong.”

Although her belly was churning with hunger, the bread smelled foul, like urine. Lips tight, she turned her head, repulsed.

Lena McLeod’s ghost flew out of hiding and whispered in her ear. “Gobble it down, my dear! Keep it in your belly for as long as you can.”

Beatrice closed her eyes and opened her mouth to accept the Reverend’s challenge. Taking the bread on her tongue she did her best to swallow it, but besides having a terrible odour it was sickeningly thick with salt. “I can’t,” she whimpered in apology to the ghost, before gagging the thing up and spitting it out.

Reverend Townsend began to pray. “Thank you Lord for exposing the evil that dwells within the afflicted. May she be cleansed by your might so she might walk the path to righteousness.”

Breaking from his grasp, Beatrice dropped to her knees and grabbed at the canteen.

Pulling it out of her hands before she could drink from it, he held it over her head.

"Please," Beatrice hoarsely pleaded, "I need water."

Reverend Townsend uncorked the vessel and put it to her lips. Grasping her by her hair, he let her briefly drink. "That's enough," he said. "We mustn't indulge your appetites, not while that witch still has a hold on you."

Beatrice slumped to the floor. It was clear the Reverend was a madman. She wished he would leave her alone so she could think. She needed to survive long enough to go free.

Reverend Townsend used the cold iron tip of his rod to lift the hem of Beatrice's shift. She wasn't sure if he was toying with her or searching for something.

"Where are my clothes?" she asked, scared that he intended to violate her, worried that he already had. "Where's the dress I was wearing last night?"

"That witch's garb?" he sneered. "It's been done away with. Turned to ash." Smacking the side of the rod against the palm of his hand Reverend Townsend said, "Disrobe."

"No," Beatrice said, shrinking away from him, clutching at the thin white fabric of her gown.

"Disrobe!" he ordered again, this time grabbing her by the arm.

She tried to scream but her voice was gone. Wild with fright, she kicked his shins, scratched at his face, bit his hand so hard it bled.

Reverend Townsend cracked his stick against the side of Beatrice's head.

She fell to the floor in a heap.

Head aching, Beatrice opened her eyes to find she'd been stripped naked. Her hands and feet were bound with rope, and she was gagged. The scent of smouldering coal filled the air, coming from a scuttle near the door. Reverend Townsend was circling around her, lantern in hand, chanting a strange rhyme.

By lamplight and fire's spark,
Help me find the witch's mark . . .
By God's will and grace divine,
Help me spot the Devil's sign . . .

He went once, twice, three times around before he found the thing he was searching for. "There!" he exclaimed, shining his lamp on the pale freckled skin of Beatrice's left thigh. "I've found it."

She knew exactly what he'd spotted. The dark red stain on the tender curve of her leg had been there since her birth.

Crouching next to her, he placed his hand on her leg, then circled the mark with his finger. "She's touched you," he said, his voice soft with indignant wonder. "She's poisoned your body as well as your mind. She's marked you as her own." Taking his rod to the other side of the room, he knelt and muttered a secret prayer. When he returned to Beatrice's side, the iron end of the stick was smoking and hot, the emblem of a double V on its tip glowing red.

She flinched at the sight of it, fearing what was to come.

"Be still," he said holding her fast with a steady hand. "It will soon be gone."

Turning her head she closed her eyes as he came at her with the heated brand. A fettered wail caught in her throat as her flesh sizzled and burned.

The Office of Missing Persons.

ELEANOR WAS SITTING on a bench at Police Headquarters waiting to speak with the men who ran the Office of Missing Persons.

She'd been there for three hours, staring at the two doddering gentlemen, Mr. Osmund and Mr. Kimball, as they went about their work. Although she was seated only a short distance away, the waist-high partition that separated her from their twinned desks might as well have been a brick wall, fifty feet long and five storeys high. With long grey beards tucked inside their waistcoats and white hair flowing past their shoulders, they were impassively hunched over a vast collection of ledgers in which they recorded the particulars of the city's vanished souls. Every so often they looked up from their desks to stare longingly into the distance as if they were a pair of apes caged within the menagerie at Central Park.

"Excuse me," Eleanor said, as she'd done every quarter hour since she'd arrived. "Could you spare a moment?"

Both men looked at her and then at each other.

"Mr. Kimball?" Eleanor said to the gentleman on the right.

"Osmund," the man corrected her. Pointing to his companion he added, "He's Kimball."

Eleanor swore the last time she interrupted the pair it was the other way around. Thank heavens they can tell each other apart, she thought, because surely no one else can.

"Mr. Osmund," she tried again, weary with waiting. "I've a missing person to report."

"Ah, yes!" he said with sudden enthusiasm. "We are aware that you're still here. Mr. Kimball will address your concerns."

Mr. Kimball scowled at his companion, then went back to his work.

Adjusting her skirt, Eleanor settled in for the next quarter hour. She hoped Adelaide and Dr. Brody were having better luck than she was.

Taking up a newspaper that'd been abandoned on the bench, Eleanor saw that it'd been folded open to the missing persons section.

Our lynx-eyed detective police need some widely spread organ to aid in their searches. Our illustrated paper is the only organ in America which combines immense circulation with amplest artistic resources. Perfectly reliable portraits pronounced by friends to be correct. Faithful facsimiles, striking likenesses, official information. Provided by G. Davis, exclusively for *Frank Leslie's Illustrated Newspaper.*

The listings of vanished persons were sandwiched between several notices for lost jewellery and missing dogs. Transcribed from police reports or placed by concerned individuals, they were meant to entice readers to take up the search. A few of them were accompanied by finely drawn illustrations.

Eleanor caught her breath as she counted how many women were on the list. Sixteen out of twenty this week alone, all under thirty years of age.

MISSING: GRETTA BUSKIRK: Twenty-two years old. Short. Thickset. Full features, pug nose, coarse voice. Has a small slit on right ear. Black hair, dark complexion and eyes, and speaks with a slight German accent. Last seen October 3rd at Broadway and Bowery. REWARD OFFERED, alive or deceased.

MISSING: BONNIE FLANNIGAN: Nineteen years of age. Light complexion, light brown hair. Green eyes. Petite. Last seen at Union Square on October 1st wearing blue calico dress. Last known words were to her sister, Polly. "Don't wait up for me tonight." Loved by family. Unaccountably absent. Dear Bonnie, please do not forsake us.

MISSING: LENA MCLEOD: Twenty-five years old. Tall. Thin. Long brown hair. Blue eyes. Last known residence, Vinegar Hill, Staten Island. Was employed as a housekeeper at the Beadle residence. Brother from Scotland wishes to find her. He can be reached at the Seafarer's Mission in Fulton Landing.

Heart filled with dread, Eleanor couldn't bring herself to read any further. "Excuse me," she said, "Mr. Kimball, Mr. Osmund?"

As she waited for their response, another woman walked through the door. Lean and confident, she wore a dark tweed suit, a Phrygian cap, and carried a worn leather satchel at her side. Settling on the bench next to Eleanor she asked, "Been here long?"

"A few hours now," she replied. "I'd advise you make yourself comfortable. You may be in for a wait."

Wiping her hand on her skirt, the young woman held it out to Eleanor. Her fingers were smudged with charcoal and stained with ink. "Georgina Davis," she said. "*Leslie's Illustrated.* Pleased to meet you."

Eleanor accepted Georgina's hand. "Eleanor St. Clair, and likewise."

Getting up from the bench, Georgina whispered, "Let's see if we can't move things along." Taking a small wax-paper sack from her satchel she held it in the air and gave it a hearty shake.

The clerks turned in unison, their eyes lit with childish curiosity.

"Georgie," Mr. Osmund said. "Good to see you!"

"Are those lemon drops?" Mr. Kimball asked. "For me?"

Georgina took aim and tossed the crumpled bag so it landed in the centre of the line where the men's desks were butted together. Smiling she teased, "Be good, boys . . . share and share alike."

Before long the two men were smiling and puckering while licking sugar from their fingers.

"I suppose you've come to gather names for the vanished persons column?" Mr. Osmund finally asked.

"That I have," Georgina replied. "But I believe the fine lady over there was here first."

Motioning for Eleanor to approach, the two men took up their pens, ready to assist her.

"I'll be damned," Eleanor muttered, shaking her head. "What witchery is this?"

Georgina gave her a wink.

Taking turns the men asked Eleanor a series of questions—first Mr. Osmund, then Mr. Kimball (and so on and so forth).

"Name?"

"Eleanor St. Clair."

"Not *your* name," Georgina whispered. "The name of the missing."

"Oh, sorry," Eleanor said. "Beatrice Dunn."

"Age?"

"Seventeen."

"Seventeen, you say?"

"Have you checked the theatres?"

"Or the Tenderloin?"

"Or the East River?"

Eleanor scowled and crossed her arms.

"Nationality?"

"American."

"Height?"

"Five foot and a bit."

"Say, five foot one?" Mr. Kimball asked.

"One and a half?" urged Mr. Osmund.

"Two?" offered Kimball.

Eleanor stood and pointed to a height just below her own.

"Five foot three," Georgina declared with a confident nod.

"Weight?"

Eleanor held out her hands to indicate the size of Beatrice's waist, then compared it to her own.

"One hundred and ten pounds," Georgina said. "Approximately. Hair colour?"

"Red."

"Clothes last worn?"

"A party gown of black silk crepe de chine, embroidered with Egyptian glyphs in gold."

"Sounds fancy," Mr. Kimball said, eyebrow raised.

Sighing, Eleanor brought out a carte-de-visite of Minnie Stevens wearing the gown, and placed it on the man's desk. "That's not her, but it's the same dress."

Mr. Kimball took the photograph and stared at it for a moment before handing it to Mr. Osmund. The two men looked at each other and rolled their eyes.

"Date and time gone missing?" Georgina asked, prompting the men to stay on task.

"Saturday, October ninth, between seven thirty and eight o'clock."

"In the evening?"

"Yes."

"Place last seen?"

"The Fifth Avenue Hotel."

"Oh, I see," Mr. Kimball said, as if that had explained it all.

"Hmmm," Mr. Osmund added, taking a similar tone.

"Is something wrong?" Eleanor asked.

The men exchanged knowing looks but refused to answer.

"To what would you attribute Miss Dunn's disappearance?" Mr. Kimball asked.

"I've no idea," Eleanor said. "That's why I'm here."

"If you had to guess?"

"She had no enemies, no troubles that couldn't be solved, at least not that I know of." Eleanor didn't want to complicate matters by mentioning the girl's involvement with ghosts. The pair of codgers would have a high old time with that.

"When it comes to girls of a certain age," Mr. Osmund explained, "we generally find they tend to follow certain paths . . ."

"Lunacy," Mr. Kimball offered.

"Or suicide," Mr. Osmund said.

"Abduction."

"Or seduction."

"Or succumbing to the drink."

"Or a wily madam."

"Or religious fervour."

"Or some other nefarious scheme."

"Did she have cause to run away from her family?"

"Or a bad situation?"

"Do any of these things ring a bell?"

Eleanor glared at them both and shook her head.

"The police need to know what they're looking for, my dear," Mr. Kimball pressed.

"A slobbery fool."

"A degenerate girl."

"A dead body."

"Any guess as to whether or not she was in her right mind?"

"When?" Eleanor asked.

"At the time of her disappearance?"

"Or any time for that matter."

Eleanor took a deep breath, trying to hang on to her temper.

Georgina placed a supportive hand on her arm.

"It's important to get the details right," Mr. Osmund chided.

"For our records," Mr. Kimball said.

"And these cards," Mr. Osmund added, taking a stack of small notecards from atop a tall crooked pile, one of several that sat precariously on a shelf near his desk. "They're used to alert police and press." Handing the stack to Georgina he said, "Here's this week's missing, Georgie. I put the best ones on top."

Briefly thumbing through them, Georgina handed them back. "These are last week's."

Scratching his head, Mr. Osmund looked them over himself. "So they are," he said, exchanging them for a different, larger stack. "My mistake."

With a shrug Mr. Kimball offered an excuse. "A ship went down in the harbour last Friday. We had twenty missing husbands in one night alone."

Mr. Osmund lifted the left leg of his trouser to reveal a wooden peg. Pounding the end of his false limb on the floor he teased, "Missing . . . my foot!"

Eleanor stood. She'd had enough. Handing Mr. Kimball one of the teashop's cards, she said, "Please contact me at this address should any news come to light. Thank you for your time."

"Don't forget your picture," Mr. Osmund said, waving Minnie Stevens' photograph in the air.

Teary-eyed, Eleanor snatched it from his hand and rushed out of the office.

Georgina followed. "Wait," she called. "I think I can help."

"How?" Eleanor asked, stopping short, her voice sharp with hurt.

Guiding Eleanor to an empty bench in the hallway, Georgina sat beside her and pulled a sketchbook from her bag. "I'd like to include Beatrice in this week's column. I'll include a drawing of her if you'd like."

Eleanor was grateful for the offer, but confused as to how it might work. "I don't have a photograph of Beatrice. How can you draw her if you've never seen her face?"

Georgina opened her sketchbook to a blank page. "I don't necessarily need a photo, in fact I prefer not to rely on them exclusively. Most are just fantasies anyhow, created by a photographer working in a room filled with painted clouds and stuffed peacocks. I'm guessing that you have a picture of Beatrice in your mind that's truer than any carte-de-visite. If you share the details of it with me, I can put it on the page, and that just might be enough."

Down the hall, a couple of roughs were harassing a prostitute. "I was minding my own business!" she yelled. "Why can't you mind yours?" A group of sad-looking beggars filed past and out the door. They were returning to the streets after spending the night on the police station floor.

"All right," Eleanor said, "what do you need to know?"

Head down, pencil in hand, Georgina began the process of piecing together Beatrice's likeness. "What would you say is the shape of her face? Round, oval, square, heart-shaped?"

"Somewhat round," Eleanor said, looking over Georgina's shoulder. "But not full like a child's. Apple cheeked, yet ladylike."

"What about the length of her hair? Or its style?"

"It's quite long," Eleanor answered. "Down to her waist. But I think she planned to wear it up last night. She was supposed to wear that headdress that's pictured with the gown, but it got left behind."

"And this was the gown she was wearing?" Georgina asked, pointing to the card.

"Yes," Eleanor answered, holding it steady as Georgina continued her work.

"And what about her eyes," Georgina asked. "Are they round, narrow . . . close together, wide apart?"

"They're quite large and round and blue."

Bit by bit, the image began to take shape.

"Are her brows heavy or thin, flat or arched?"

"Heavy, but arched."

"Her nose?"

"Narrow. Slightly upturned."

"Is her chin rounded, pointed, dimpled?"

"Round, but firm."

Georgina paused and tapped the end of her pencil against her lips. "You mentioned she has red hair . . . is she freckled as well?"

Eleanor smiled. "Her skin is speckled everywhere, like a bird's egg."

"Was she wearing the necklace that's pictured in the photo? Any rings on her fingers, earrings perhaps?"

"No," Eleanor replied. "She didn't want to borrow Miss Stevens' jewels for fear she'd lose them."

"Did she have anything else of value that might have been taken from her person?"

"Not that I know of."

Making a few notes beneath the sketch, Georgina asked, "What was her business at the hotel?"

Eleanor bit her lip. "You won't believe me if I tell you."

"Try me," Georgina said.

"She was there to demonstrate her ability to speak with ghosts."

Underlining the word "ghosts" three times, Georgina asked, "Truly?"

"Cross my heart," Eleanor replied.

"That's good, actually," Georgina said with a thoughtful nod.

"It is?"

"People love stories about ghosts."

Eleanor gave a tired smile.

"We're almost done," Georgina assured her. "Just a couple more questions. Does she have a sweetheart?"

"No."

"Do you know of any unusual circumstances surrounding her disappearance? Was she acting out of character? Did she leave anything behind?"

"No and no," Eleanor answered. "I have nothing that could serve as a clue."

"What would you say is the most common expression she wears on her face? Quizzical, coy, shy?"

Closing her eyes, Eleanor thought of Beatrice standing at her side in the shop, always asking questions, always keen to learn. "Curious," she said, "but determined."

"That's excellent," Georgina said as she put a few final touches on the sketch. "One last question. Can you offer a reward?"

Wringing her hands Eleanor paused to think. She supposed she could count on Judith to contribute. "Yes, I think so," Eleanor answered. "Would five hundred dollars be enough?" It was the first number that came to mind.

Georgina whistled through her teeth. "That should do it." Turning her sketchbook towards Eleanor she said, "What do you think?"

"That's her," Eleanor said, shocked by the likeness. "That's Beatrice." A wave of worry suddenly came over her. All the questions she'd been keeping in check nagged at her heart. Where was the dear girl? Had she taken ill? Fallen into the wrong hands? Was she whole? Was she safe? "When will the notice appear in the paper?" she asked.

"Not until Saturday, I'm afraid," Georgina replied.

"I see," Eleanor said, disappointed.

Noticing Eleanor's dismay, Georgina said, "But I can go to the press and print up some handbills in advance so you can post them at the hotel and any place else you like."

"How soon can you have them finished?" Eleanor asked, fishing in her pocket for something to offer as an enticement. "I'm willing to pay."

Georgina waved the offer away. "No need for that," she said. "You'll have them by tomorrow."

> You must know, Achilles, that Prayers are the Daughters of Jupiter. They are crippled by frequent Kneeling, have their faces full of Cares and Wrinkles, and their Eyes are always cast towards Heaven.
>
> —Joseph Addison, *Essays, Moral and Humorous: Also Essays on Imagination and Taste*

Prayers Are the Daughters of Jupiter.

After a long day of searching for Beatrice, Dr. Brody went home and retired to his study. He'd informed Mr. Pryor, the hotel detective, of the girl's disappearance, then talked to every maid, porter and attendant he could find. After walking the streets for hours visiting every place he'd thought she might go, he'd decided it best to call it a day. He wasn't sure what else he could offer Eleanor and Adelaide short of what steps to take should Beatrice's body be found. That was advice he hoped he wouldn't have to give.

Sitting at his father's desk he contemplated taking out his opium pipe. Having dabbled without becoming addicted, he'd managed to stay away from it for some time now, but in his current state of mind, the allure of the poppy was strong. Mrs. Stutt had gone to bed and he had no other plans for the night. The pipe and the glow of its attendant oil lamp seemed better company than sitting alone with his guilt—for he didn't count himself blameless in this terrible mess. On the contrary, he felt he'd been the worst offender. Eleanor had always been the voice of reason; Adelaide, even in her overwrought enthusiasm, had been honest about her intentions; and he'd . . . well, he'd held back from taking too firm a stance on any of it, never willing to admit his hopes for where things might be headed, fearing it might make him seem arrogant, presumptuous, unfairly ambitious. Perhaps if he'd spoken up, laid out a plan for the future, Beatrice wouldn't have felt the need to run.

As he tripped the lock of the desk's hidden compartment, a knock sounded at the front door. Quinn found Alden Dashley standing on his stoop.

"Dashley," he said. "Do come in. Have you news to share?"

Alden stepped inside and removed his hat and overcoat. "No news, I'm afraid, but I thought I might remind you of a possible diversion. Heaven knows I could use one while we're waiting for Miss Dunn's safe return. Judith took to bed early, exhausted from pacing the floor, so I thought I'd take a walk and wound up here. The skies are clear and both Jupiter and Saturn are in the southeast sky. I was wondering if I might nip up to your father's observatory to have a look."

"Of course," Dr. Brody said, thankful for Alden's company. He couldn't think of a better interruption unless it was Beatrice herself. "I think that's an excellent plan."

They climbed the spiral staircase to the tower Tobias Brody had built atop his house, and stood side by side in the modest cupola.

Alden waited patiently as Quinn cleaned the lenses on the telescope in preparation for viewing the planets. "According to the *Clipper Annual* tonight's the best night to see Jupiter's bands," Alden remarked.

"Is that so?" Quinn asked, adjusting the scope's height, angle and focus.

"It's in Pisces," Alden directed, "with Saturn below to the left."

Squinting through the eyepiece, Quinn soon announced, "I've got it." Taking a step back he motioned to Alden. "Here, have a look."

Alden peered through the telescope. "Isn't that something!" he exclaimed. "The mighty Jupiter and its four moons as well."

"I Explore God's Creation," Quinn recited under his breath—a saying his father had taught him to help him remember the order of the Galilean moons.

"The sight that Galileo saw that changed the World," Alden mused. "Would you like to have a go?" he asked, stepping back from the instrument.

Quinn took his place. Staring into the heavens, he thought of the Romans who'd named the heavenly object, and how they'd seen it as something brilliant and mighty, worthy of bearing the name of their greatest god. How wondrous and strange it seemed to him, that men, himself among them, could now view the planet with such clarity and discernment, and yet still understand so little about it. Through his father's telescope, this overgrown spyglass, the mighty Jupiter appeared inconsistent—wobbling, flawed, wounded. A fitting sight for this night, he supposed. Men strove so hard to become godlike, forgetting that the world, God's world, would never allow them to be anything but less than perfect. Did that mean that they should stop their striving? No, but perhaps it meant that he should've paused to remember his place, to consider not just Jupiter, but its moons too. Fixed and faithful, Io was closest, then Europa and Ganymede fell into line, and this night, at this moment, poor Calisto was far on the opposite side, lonely and distant and seeming terribly out of reach.

The teashop was quiet except for Twitch, who was regaling Cleo with talk of Beatrice's goodness and beauty, and Eleanor, who was reciting an incantation to bring about her safe return.

Upon the wind,
Within the air,
I send my thoughts to Beatrice Dunn.

I prick my thumb,
I draw my blood,
I send my heart to Beatrice Dunn.

As above
So below
Let all kindly spirits know
By foot and flight they now must go
To find our Beatrice Dunn.

Perdu stood guard, perched over the door, ready to alert his mistress to any change, any news, any danger.

Adelaide had chosen to walk past the hotel and through the park one last time before giving up for the night. Spotting the

Bird Lady sitting alone near the fountain, she'd settled next to her to keep her company.

The ragged-looking old woman was silent as Adelaide confessed her guilt, her worries and her fears. Extending her hand, she took Adelaide's in hers and gently stroked it, but never said a word.

Taking her last calling card from her pocket, Adelaide tucked it under the ribbon that ran around the Bird Lady's hat. It seemed the safest place to put it. "If you see her, or if you hear anything about her, come find me at this address."

On the streets surrounding the park, word got passed from guttersnipes to whores, from roughs to carriage drivers.

"Did you hear about that girl gone lost?"

"The girl from the teashop?"

"The one-eyed soothsayer?"

"No, the pretty young one. The ginger."

In the corridors of the Fifth Avenue Hotel, word got passed from scrubber girls to bootblacks, from chambermaids to porters.

"Do you suppose she's run off with a dandy?"

"Do you suppose she's met her death?"

"Do you suppose they'll offer a reward for the one who finds her?"

"Anything's possible, I guess."

In the basement below *Frank Leslie's Illustrated News*, Georgina Davis was tucked away in the back corner of a cavernous cellar, treadle pumping, flywheel spinning as she lost herself to the give and take of the platen on an old Franklin press. She'd spent the evening sitting at a bench, working to carve Beatrice Dunn's image out of a square piece of boxwood, curled shavings piling around her, clinging to her skirt. She'd set the finished engraving, along with several rows of type, in the press's bed, making a wish as she went, that her work might conjure up the girl whom Miss St. Clair had lost. The creaky *tick* and *ping* of the machine seemed to sing to her as it churned. "You may delay, but time will not."

Beatrice was still bound and gagged and lying on the floor of the parsonage cellar. Reverend Townsend had come and gone several times throughout the day to chastise her, to pray over her, to make certain her bonds were secure. There was never any mention of food or drink or kindness. There was much talk of God and sin and judgement. No indication he ever planned to let her go.

The ghost of Lena McLeod had come and gone as well. The lonely spirit had hovered near, to tell Beatrice tales of her own plight and to give her advice. "Deny all, but believe in your heart."

With what little strength she had, she tried to wriggle free from the ropes, but her attempts only managed to make her wrists raw and bloody. The cold damp of the cellar seeped into her bones, causing her to shiver and shake. Upon Reverend

Townsend's last visit for the night, she looked to him with pleading eyes and thought the word, *mercy*.

Lantern in hand, he'd turned from her and left her in darkness.

He who knows the Daughters of Jupiter, when they draw near to him, receives great Benefit from them; but as for him who rejects them, they entreat their Father to give his Orders to the Goddess to punish him for his Hardness of Heart.

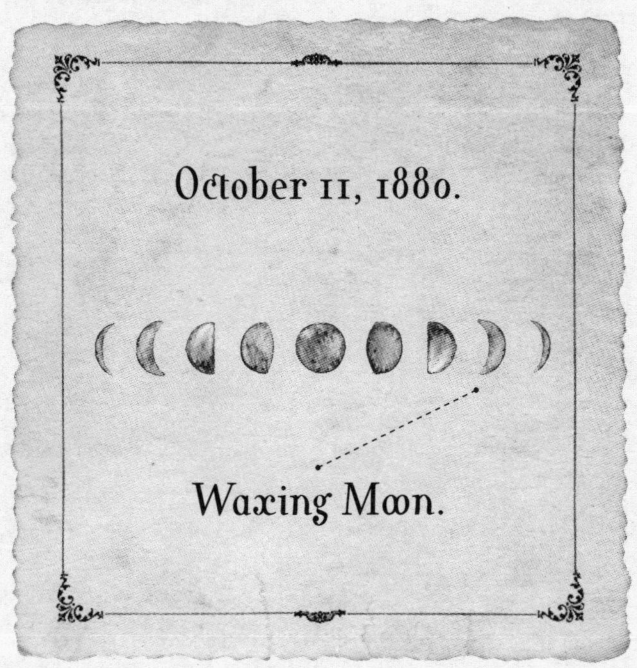
October 11, 1880.
Waxing Moon.

NOTICE TO VACATE.

The Landlord of this property hereby gives notice of intent to raze the structure hereupon.

The tenants of said dwelling, namely the owners of the business St. Clair and Thom are advised to vacate the premises by november 1st, 1880.

As of that date, any possessions, goods or effects remaining on said premises shall be confiscated and disposed of according to the landlord's discretion.

Let this notice serve as an official, binding document.

It shall not be removed from view.

Issued this day, october 11, 1880

Cecil Newland

signed: Mr. Cecil Newland, landlord.

E. M. Withrow

witnessed: Mr. E. M. Withrow.

Come, the Croaking Raven Doth Bellow for Revenge.

On Monday morning, three sharp raps sounded at the teashop door. Eleanor held her breath as she went to answer it.

Mr. Withrow was there, hammer in hand.

"What's this?" Eleanor asked, of the notice now tacked to the door.

"It's your walking papers," Mr. Withrow answered with a smirk.

"If this is about the window . . . it's all fixed."

"Not my circus, not my monkeys," Mr. Withrow said, pointing to Cecil Newland's signature. "Mr. Newland's the proud new owner of this dump and he can do with it however he sees fit." With that he tipped his hat and walked away.

A sweet-faced waif stood in the shadow of the stoop, chewing on a stale piece of Mr. Markowitz's pumpernickel.

"Of course," Eleanor muttered, resisting the urge to tear down the notice. "Of course . . ."

The little girl looked up at Eleanor with sad eyes.

Eleanor dug a few coins out of her pocket and gave them to the girl. "Save some crumbs for me," she half-heartedly teased. "Soon I won't have a home either."

"Good luck to you, ma'am," the girl said before wandering away.

Inside the shop Eleanor paced the floor—bewildered and angry. "What will we do?" she said. "Where will we go? Why do men like Cecil Newland always manage to get what they want instead of what they deserve?"

Only Perdu and Cleo were there to hear her. The raven let out a cranky squawk of commiseration. The dog lay down at Eleanor's feet and rolled over.

Eleanor sat on the floor next to the pup and gave its belly a rub.

Adelaide had gone with Dr. Brody to Bellevue hospital and the City Morgue. They intended to check the medical wards, then visit the found persons gallery to see if Beatrice was among the unidentified dead. Eleanor had barely been able to stand the conversation that'd led up to their departure.

"I'm not saying she'll be there," Adelaide had said. "I just think it'd be wise to check."

"It doesn't seem right," Eleanor had argued. "Aren't there other things we should be doing than trolling through the morgue? Better ways to spend our time?"

"If you think of something, let me know. Until then, this is all I've got."

Dr. Brody had weighed in then, in an attempt to calm the waters. "Ruling certain things out can't hurt. In fact, it might serve to bring a little peace of mind."

But Eleanor couldn't shake the feeling that the morgue wouldn't hold any answers. Short of telling them not to go, what else could she say? She certainly didn't wish to argue with them. Since Beatrice had gone missing, the two had become a pair—she could hear it in the give and take of their conversations, see it in the way their bodies touched here and there. It was new, fragile, and despite all their worries, sweet. She didn't resent it for a minute, but with Beatrice gone it was difficult to see happiness as anything but out of place. Still, she couldn't deny that Brody seemed to be holding everything together, most especially Adelaide. There'd been moments when she'd felt that her friend was terribly close to running away, she was so guilty over Beatrice's disappearance. She just hoped Adelaide understood she didn't place any blame on her.

She needed Adelaide to be present, here with her, rather than running off every evening to the hotel or park. Where was the Adelaide who'd appeared after the dumb supper? The one who'd kept saying, "We're better together than apart." Eleanor was running out of magic she could perform alone.

But she wasn't ready to think the worst, not yet. That's why Adelaide's talk of the morgue had bothered her so. The very thought of Beatrice's body lying on a marble slab was like giving up. Eleanor had to believe that Beatrice was alive.

That morning she'd woken up feeling brittle and raw, yet hopeful. She'd turned the shop sign to OPEN, thinking someone might come through the door with good news, or that Beatrice herself would come skipping across the threshold as if nothing had happened. How long could this go on? How long before they learned the truth? Instead of answers they'd received an eviction notice.

Leaning over Cleo she put her head to the dog's heart, listening to the comforting throb and tick of it. She'd said yes to taking in the stray, thinking its appearance might be a sign—perhaps Cleo might be a benevolent spirit in changed form, come to guide the way. As she mused, the shop door opened, bells jangling.

"Hello," Georgina Davis called, "special delivery for Miss St. Clair."

"Over here," Eleanor replied, standing up, shaking her skirts.

"Everything all right?" Georgina asked. "I couldn't help but see the notice."

Eleanor let out a weary laugh. "When it rains, it pours."

"Sorry to hear that," Georgina said, setting a parcel on the counter. "Here are the broadsheets I promised. I thought you should have them as soon as possible. Any news?"

Shaking her head Eleanor said, "Thank you, and no." Georgina looked something like an overgrown pixie with her wiry limbs, inky fingers, and red felt cap askew. Another messenger sent by magical forces, perhaps. Unwrapping the parcel, she stared at Beatrice's image, blinking back tears. "You must've stayed up all night to get these done."

Georgina shrugged. "The sooner these notices get passed around town, the sooner someone might come forward with information. In my experience, the first hours and days are crucial to finding someone who's lost."

Eleanor nodded. "How long have you been working in the newspaper trade?"

"One year for the missing persons' column, three altogether for Mr. Leslie's papers. Mostly the ladies' beat—roller-skating clubs, women's societies, charitable organizations and such. If you need help distributing the notices, I'm happy to volunteer."

"I can't ask you to do that."

"Please," Georgina said, touching Eleanor's hand. "I'd like to."

"All right then," Eleanor said, turning the sign on the door to CLOSED. "Let's go."

Sister Piddock, making her morning rounds, stopped outside the teashop. She grinned ear to ear as she read the notice nailed to the door. "Our God is a wonderful God!" she exclaimed, clasping her hands together. "My prayers have been answered."

Reverend Townsend was coming up the sidewalk, contemplating Beatrice's fate in the brisk morning air.

"Good morning, Reverend," Sister Piddock said, giving him a wave. Noticing his hand was dressed with a bandage, she asked, "Have you injured yourself in some way?"

"A bite," Townsend replied, too distracted to lie.

"From a dog?" Sister Piddock asked, brow furrowed.

Reverend Townsend ignored the question. Let her think what she liked.

Cleo stood behind the door, crouched. Eleanor had left the dog and raven with strict orders: "No demons allowed in, no magic allowed out." Sniffing at the threshold the dog gave a low growl.

Taking a step away from the door, Sister Piddock said, "I wanted you to know that I thought your sermon yesterday was especially powerful. That story you told of the poor girl who'd been bewitched was very compelling. Will you visit her again? Do you believe she can be saved?"

"I will do all I can," the Reverend answered. "She suffers greatly. Much fasting and prayer is required."

"I shall remember her in my prayers, along with my prayers of thanksgiving," Sister Piddock said. Pointing to the notice, she smiled. "God has seen fit to remove mine enemy."

Reverend Townsend stepped forward and looked through the teashop window.

Cleo began to bark.

"The women who run this place are engaged in the Devil's work," Sister Piddock boasted. "One of them was even so bold as to set herself upon me the other day in the park. But now they will be put out."

"Was it Saturday?" the Reverend asked, remembering the one-eyed witch.

"Indeed it was," Sister Piddock answered. "But the Lord intervened and caused her to turn tail."

As Cleo continued to bark, Perdu hopped onto his perch in the window and peered out to the sidewalk. No sooner had he spotted the preacher than a terrible darkness came over his eyes. Within that darkness was a faint glimmer, and within that glimmer a faint noise—the sound of Beatrice crying. "Mercy," he croaked, causing the dog to fall silent. "Mercy . . ."

"Our God is a wonderful God," Reverend Townsend said, pleased with what he'd just learned. "He will provide."

"Amen," Sister Piddock said.

This Is the Place Where Death Delights to Help the Living.

A CROWD WAS gathered along a tiled hallway that skirted the west side of the City Morgue. Mothers, fathers, brothers, sisters, lovers, workmen, preachers, missionaries, roughs, prostitutes, paperboys and tourists—all were there to participate in the daily viewing of the unclaimed dead. Feet shuffling, elbows touching, voices hushed, the anxious onlookers waited at the gallery windows for the day's corpses to be revealed.

What drama would unfold today? What sadness, what ugliness, what evidence of brutality might they see? Some were there to search for loved ones, others only to satisfy their curiosity.

A curtain of glass and iron separated them from the dead. A patent lamp hung from the ceiling, its flame constantly burning, its flue set to draw out foul smells and bad air. Even with the hygienic contraption dangling above them, the men in the corridor cleared their throats loudly and often, while the women held handkerchiefs to their noses or sucked on candies flavoured with clove and mint. Consumed with thoughts of putrefaction, they were unaware that the soiled state and exhalations of their neighbours posed more of a threat to their well-being than the dead.

A pair of prostitutes, Elsie Trew in red velvet, Mae Blum in gaudy flounced skirts, held the railing at the far end of the viewing windows. They looked so much alike they could be sisters (but they weren't).

"I hope we don't see Jenny," Elsie said.

"I'm pretty sure we will," Mae replied as the spray of feathers in her hat drooped in the morgue's damp air. Their housemate, Jenny Greene, had disappeared from Madison Square and they hadn't seen her since.

"You think she's dead, or just hope she is?" Elsie asked.

"Oh, I know she is," Mae replied. "For a fact."

"That so?"

"I seen her tiptoeing across the telegraph lines and chimney pots last night. God strike me dead if I'm lying."

"I wish you hadn't said that."

"Why? 'Cause she's your friend?"

"No, because she still owes me two dollars for rent."

As the first body arrived behind the glass, the crowd leaned in for a better look. With deliberate care the coroner and his assistant lifted the cadaver from a wheeled stretcher and placed it on one of the marble tables that graced the gallery. This specimen was male, a gentleman of middle age, returned to the window for a second day of viewing. (Like the rest of the nameless bodies that came this way, he'd be displayed for three days before being carted off to a pauper's pit on Hart's Island. The only record of his having been in the gallery would be a portrait taken by the morgue's photographer and a breadbox-sized selection of his personal effects sent to gather dust in an out-of-the-way closet.) Naked, except for the length of gauze neatly covering his manhood, it was plain to see that whatever life he'd lived hadn't been easy.

His most notable disadvantage was his lack of legs. Both ended in stumps at the knees. A less pronounced but ragged scar that cut across his right shoulder possessed a similar sheen, all injuries sustained long ago. Among the tattered pieces of clothing the coroner had chosen to display with the corpse was a worn soldier's cap issued by the Union Army.

The coroner's description for the *Roll of Found Persons* read:

> FOUND, October 10 at Pitt and Delancey Streets, male, approximately 40 years of age. Both legs missing from a previous injury. This unfortunate soul is thought to have been a veteran of the War Between the States, as the underside of the brim of his kepi is marked: *T.D.F. 13th N.Y.* Cause of death, consumption.

It wasn't unusual for the coroner to indulge in modest speculations about the deceased. Corpses that stirred his sympathy were often given captions in death. "Pretty blonde girl." "Portly matron with weary face." "Swarthy scar-faced gent." The sight of a clean liver on his examination table would lead the coroner to note, "The deceased was a temperate soul." A young lady found to be *virgo intacta* was described as "innocent and full of promise."

A gruff-looking man who was watching the proceedings clutched a torn-out page from *Leslie's Illustrated*. The entry for Gretta Buskirk was underlined and the words "reward offered" were circled with grease pencil. Hat cocked and eyes squinted, the man looked as if he were waiting for a racehorse to come into view around the clubhouse turn.

Sadly for him, the second body of the day belonged to a woman around fifty years of age, her dull brown hair streaked with grey, her belly bloated and veined, her sickly yellow skin mottled with angry purple bruises. Long scratches appeared along her thighs, some of them open and starting to rot. After today, her seventy-two hours would be up. The coroner had awarded her a single line in the *Roll of Found Persons*.

FOUND: October 9. Chrystie Street. Woman, grey hair, missing teeth, died from the drink.

The final cadaver to be brought to the gallery was another disappointment to the reward seeker: she, too, was not Gretta Buskirk.

FOUND: October 11, near Madison Square Park. Female, approximately twenty years of age. Hair, auburn. Eyes, blue. Cause of death: knife wound to throat.

Though kept as cool as the morgue could manage, the corpse was already showing signs of decay. It was clear she had been discovered days after she'd died, with the blue tinge to her skin and bites on her toes and fingers where rats had nibbled. Lips turned dark, gash in her throat stitched, wet hair swept back from her face: she looked more ghoul than girl. At the sight of her, a whisper went through the crowd: *murder*. The coroner folded the shroud down from the top, then up from the bottom, arranging it in such a way that the girl's remains were covered from her breasts to her thighs, but enough of her could be seen for someone who had been close to her to make an identification. He then arranged the girl's hair and turned her head slightly so something of her profile showed. He placed her hands on top of the shroud, one over the other, as if she were a sleeping princess waiting to be kissed awake.

Moving behind the marble slab, he hung the girl's garments one by one from an iron rod that ran the length of the back wall. Her undergarments were factory made and common, so he placed them together on one hook. Her dress was also shop-bought, nondescript, so it went up next. Her corset was by far the costliest item in the lot. Made from pink satin, heavily embroidered, and with silver clasps, he hung it against the dress's dark wool, making a backdrop for the young woman's prized possession. Lastly, he took up her mantle and boots, and a well-worn rabbit's foot strung on a piece of ribbon, and hung them side by side by side on three separate hooks.

On the other side of the glass two gentlemen dressed in black stared at the rabbit's foot, then bent their heads in consultation.

"Mr. Palsham isn't interested in her body," the one said. "Just the object."

"You're sure she's no witch, then?"

"There's nothing to her. The only thing that's been touched by magic is the charm."

"How do you propose we go about getting it?"

"When no one claims her, we will."

"And if someone does?"

"We'll offer to pay for the rabbit's foot."

"What if they refuse?"

"We'll persuade them otherwise."

Just then, Adelaide and Dr. Brody entered the gallery, Quinn finding the clearest path to the viewing windows. "Here," he said, taking Adelaide's arm, "this way." He wanted to get them in and out of the place as quickly as possible, for her sake. They fell in behind the two men in black, who blocked their view; they'd have to wait their turn. Resting her hand in the crook of Quinn's good arm, Adelaide lifted her veil, went up on tiptoes and craned in an attempt to see past the men.

Shaking, she came down off her toes, and clutched at Quinn's coat. "There's a girl . . . I can't see all of her but I think her hair is red."

Dr. Brody snuck a look between the men. "More auburn than red," he replied, but not the least bit convinced it wasn't Beatrice.

Adelaide assumed the worst. How would she break the news to Eleanor? "Please," she said, edging close to one of the gentlemen in front of her. "Make room for me."

The man turned and stared, then gave a slight tug on his companion's sleeve, who also turned to look down on her. Neither moved.

Adelaide assumed they were just another pair of insensitive souls gawking at the tangle of scars on her face. "Surely what's behind the glass is more interesting than this," she said, hoping to shame them into taking their leave.

"Let the lady have a look," Dr. Brody said. "You've had your chance."

Muttering one to the other, the men shoved past them.

Shaking off their rudeness, Adelaide stepped forward with Quinn and they took the men's spot at the window. It wasn't Beatrice. Blinking back tears, Adelaide found she couldn't see straight. She wiped her eye with a handkerchief, and it was as if the sight in her lost eye had been restored. When she looked again through the glass, she saw a dark figure standing over the young woman's corpse with a bloody knife in hand. She watched in horror as the corpse changed into a trembling, terrified Beatrice. Adelaide gripped the brass rail that ran along the length of the glass and closed her eye, a wave of dizziness causing her to feel as if she might faint.

"Adelaide," Quinn said, his arm circling her shoulders. "Are you all right?"

"It's not her," Adelaide said shaking her head. "It's not her."

"We've seen enough," Quinn said. "Let's get you home."

The ghost of Jenny Greene floated to the window and watched Adelaide leave. Then slipping behind the marble slab she stared at her cold dead body. Although she'd died days ago, she'd only been brought to the morgue early that morning. The coroner had cleaned her, stitched her up like a treasured rag doll. Then she'd been rolled into another building so a photographer could take her picture. The kindly gent had talked to her as he'd gone about his work, his friendly voice chattering away from behind his boxy camera. He'd said he was sorry no one had found her sooner. She'd shouted at him over and over, "I know who done it. I'll take you to him," but the photographer hadn't heard her. Once he'd finished his task, he'd disappeared to the darkroom to sniff away the wretched stench of her remains with an ether-soaked rag.

Looking at the other people lined up to see the dead, Jenny recognized the two girls she boarded with.

"I'm here!" she cried, as they came towards her body.

"I think that's her," Elsie said, putting her hand to her mouth. "I think it's Jenny."

"I'm not so sure," Mae said. "It's hard to tell, the body is so rotten."

Elsie pointed to the clothes hanging on the rod. "That's her corset there, the one she'd never let me borrow."

"Lots of girls have corsets like that."

"But do them same girls carry around a rabbit's foot on a ribbon?"

"Well so what if it is Jenny?" said Mae. "We can't claim her. We've got no money to bury the body."

"We could at least tell them her name."

"And run the risk that the coppers might think we done her in? No, thank you, ma'am. Let's get out of here."

Elsie took one last look at the body before they turned to go.

Nose pressed to the window, Jenny waved goodbye.

Once the pair was out on the sidewalk, Elsie asked, "You think it might be that preacher who did it? Who slit Jenny's throat?"

"Even if it was," Mae replied, "there's a tale no one would believe, especially not from a pair of whores."

"Ain't you scared?"

"Of what?"

"That it might happen to you?"

"I just won't go to Madison Square no more, and neither should you."

"Guess that rabbit's foot weren't so lucky after all."

In as much as the devilish workings of the witch persisted upon the girl (for they could be seen in the damsel's eyes) I continued to visit the haunted chamber in which she was kept. Through experiments and prayer I endeavoured to put a stop to the Invisible Furies rising within her and to turn her heart by whatever means God saw fit.

It is a dark dispensation of Divine Providence that such an innocent should be under the influence of the Fiends of Darkness. Although I could not see or hear the evil that entertained her (and I hope I never shall) it was made known to me by various means, most prominently by the words uttered from her mouth when a course of Godly questions were put to her. Oh how she begged to learn how she might thwart the temptations of that diabolical witch! For some time I carried on with the questioning, followed by much prayer and fasting. No exercise of religion gave so much vexation unto the evils that beset her as the singing of Psalms.

As the third night of her seclusion approached, the afflicted girl was finally and forever delivered. Prayers poured forth from her mouth, unbidden.

—from *An Attempt to Cure Witchcraft: The Story of Mercy Wylde*

A Brand Pluck'd Out of the Burning.

AFTER RECITING A lengthy prayer of thanksgiving, Reverend Townsend rose from his knees and turned to his desk. Among the books and papers that littered its surface was a shallow brass bowl containing the coiled length of Beatrice's hair. The edge of the bowl was inscribed with the words, GOD LOVETH THE CHEERFUL GIVER. Taking the long red lock in hand, he admired its sheen, its softness, its fiery colour. He'd hated taking it from her, but he'd known that it had to be done. Vanity was generally the first weakness witches seized upon in the young women they wished to control. *They first used a thousand Flatteries and Allurements to induce her unto a compliance with the Desire of the Devil. They showed her very splendid garments, and thence proceeded onto greater glories, which they promised her if she would sign away her soul.* Did he need any more proof? How crushed the girl had looked when he'd told her he'd destroyed her dress, that terrible, whorish gown given to her by that witch. Tonight he would burn her hair as well, to cast out any dark workings that might dwell within its strands.

Although his path had been quite difficult, he felt progress had been made. Late last night he'd entered the damsel's cell to find her docile, the evil within her stayed. The witch's mark hadn't returned, and the brand that'd replaced it was flushed and bright with blood. To test the power of God's touch upon her, he'd loosened her bonds. She'd remained quiet and still, only groaning softly. Amen! Glory to God! And glory to Him for revealing the witch's dwelling to him through Sister Piddock. The good news that the foul women were being cast out onto the street was more proof that his prayers were working. *But there is cause to fear that she who afflicted Mercy is as dangerous and damnable a witch as ever was in the world. If only the words of this young woman were enough to prove it so.*

Beatrice woke from a fitful sleep, somehow returned to the straw mattress and dressed again in her shift. She would've thought she was back to where she'd started, but the painful, angry burn on her thigh and the aching lump at the side of her head told her different. She rose, gingerly, and made her way to the bucket in the corner of the cell. It had been emptied. Squatting over it, she urinated, then stoically wiped herself with the hem of her shift.

In front of her she spied a stray lump of ashen coal that'd escaped the scuttle the preacher had used to heat his brand. Picking it up she found a discreet spot on the wall, behind the mattress, and scraped two dark marks onto the stone, one for each night she'd been here. She tucked the coal inside a hole in the mattress to save it for future days, how few or many there might be. It felt remarkably good to make those two small marks: proof that she was here. Oh how she missed paper and pen and the flow of ink as her thoughts turned to words on a page. She'd never thought of writing as an act of defiance, but those two marks proved it to be so. Her need to leave something of herself was overwhelming. If she was to die here, she wouldn't let him forget she'd lived.

What kind of ghost would she be? Would she be carried off to some happy plane where her mother and father resided? Or would she be stuck in this dank cellar, sad and confused, like Lena McLeod?

Sitting back down on the mattress, she brought her mother's face to mind, loving, gentle, kind. Then she spent a good long while composing a letter to Lydia. She pictured her hand moving across the page, saw the words falling in line, one after another. *What wonders the city holds! How happy I am to be here! There are so many marvellous sights to see, so many opportunities ahead! If I don't see you before, I'll visit you for Christmas. I wouldn't miss your plum pudding for the world!*

Plum pudding. Eggnog. Roast turkey. Giblet gravy. Cherry cordial. Her hunger was its own animal, growling in her belly, pawing at her brain. To tame it she thought of Eleanor's dream tea, hoping the mere memory of the scents of lavender, mugwort and lemon balm would ease her mind. She thought of Eleanor's wise and patient teaching and Adelaide's style, and her sharp wit. She thought of Dr. Brody's dedication to finding the truth, Perdu's shining, curious eyes, Judith Dashley's kindness. Were they looking for her? She hoped they weren't in danger.

She thought of the ghosts who'd crossed her path, and all the strange, wonderful things she'd learned since she'd come to New York. Why had she walked away from the hotel? All she wanted now was to be back at the teashop, curled up on her bed. Closing her eyes she pictured the walls of her room lined with pages of newsprint and the notes she'd made from

Eleanor's grimoire. She saw the bottle on the windowsill that held her witch's ladder.

It was the one spell she knew by heart. She felt as if it lived inside her. She could do it now, make it here. She tore the hem of her shift and worked to unravel some threads. She had no feathers to tie to it and the hair on her head wasn't long enough to braid along the ladder's length, but she hoped that what Eleanor had said was true—*the more you strive to make magic, the more likely it is to find you*. If so, then it was worth trying to cast the spell.

Just then Lena's ghost appeared at her side, brought forth by the sound of ripping cloth. "Are you planning to do away with yourself?"

Beatrice replied, "Why would you think that?"

Sticking out her tongue, the lonely spirit tugged at an imaginary rope around her neck. "That's what I did." Looking around she said, "Though I'm not quite sure how you might go about it. There used to be a window over there with bars across it, but after I did the deed, a man came with a trowel and bricked it over."

"That's *not* what I mean to do."

"But what *are* you doing?" Lena begged. "Maybe I can help."

Finally freeing a long piece of thread from her shift Beatrice said, "I'm making a witch's ladder."

"To curse him!" Lena clapped her hands. "I've heard of such charms, but I never saw one. They say you can cause great illness that way, even death. I wish I'd known how to make one, I would've cursed him myself."

Beatrice wound the thread around her finger, thinking, then said, "I'm afraid I don't know anything about curses. I've only made one witch's ladder before, and it was to make a wish."

Grinning, Lena whispered, "A curse is just a wish turned on its head."

"All I want is to be free from this place," Beatrice said. "What do you care how it happens?"

Tying a knot in the end of the thread Beatrice began to recite the spell. "By knot of one, my spell's begun . . ."

Lena reverently repeated the words.

The sound of Reverend Townsend's boots echoed on the stairs.

"He's coming!" Lena whispered. "You're done for if he finds the charm!"

Beatrice tucked the thread in the mattress alongside the piece of coal.

Reverend Townsend entered the cell, wooden rod at his hip, prayer book in one hand, a low stool in the other. Pipe clenched between his teeth, he shut the door and sat himself down on the stool. Opening the book, he brought out a notice that'd been folded and stuck between its pages.

Smoothing the paper flat, Reverend Townsend cleared his throat. "You are Beatrice Dunn?"

You are a witch. No one to be trifled with.

From where she sat, Beatrice could make out the word MISSING across the top of the page and what seemed to be a likeness of her face. "Yes," she said, incredibly relieved that people were searching for her. Maybe it would scare the preacher into letting her go.

He stared at her with great concern. "She means to find you."

"Who?" Beatrice asked. Did he know of Eleanor and Adelaide?

"The woman who bewitched you."

Lena tapped on Beatrice's shoulder and hissed in her ear, "Deny everything, or else he'll kill you."

Beatrice shook her head. "I'm not bewitched."

"That's what she wishes you to think."

"Who?"

"The witch."

"How am I to know her if she doesn't have a name?"

Lena laughed.

Reverend Townsend scowled. "Do you believe in witches?"

"Deny it!" Lena urged.

Beatrice tried to keep a clear head, but Lena was so close she wasn't sure which thoughts were hers or the ghost's. "I don't know what a witch is."

"How can you be sure you've not been bewitched if you don't know what a witch is?" the Reverend pressed.

Beatrice brushed the spirit away. "If I were to come across any such person as you imagine, I should think I would know it."

"How?"

"By God's grace."

"Who is your god?"

"The god that made me."

The preacher smiled at her. "Do you believe in the Devil?"

"I do," Beatrice answered, staring him straight in the eyes.

"Have you ever seen him?"

"Only in the evil deeds of men."

"Have you ever seen strange creatures lurking about?"

"What sort of creatures?"

"Those not of this earth."

"Goblins or fairies?"

"If you like," Reverend Townsend replied.

"No. Never."

"Do you ever hear voices when no one's there?"

Lena flew in front of Beatrice's face and shook her head. "You must deny it!"

With innocent eyes, Beatrice said, "Only those who bid me to do what's right."

Reverend Townsend shifted forward on his stool. "As in angels?"

"If you like."

Closing his eyes the preacher paused for a moment of contemplation. Then looking at Beatrice, he said, "If you expect mercy from God, you must look for it in confession."

"I've nothing to confess."

"I beg you, dear girl, give glory to God and confess the name of your oppressor to me or all will be lost."

Beatrice couldn't bear the thought of Adelaide or Eleanor suffering, especially not because of her. She would not give this man their names. "If you wish to think me a witch, so be it. If you wish to kill me, then do so."

"I've said nothing of death," Reverend Townsend stammered. Gripping the handle of his rod, his eyes narrowed. "Who spoke to you of such things?"

"Nobody," Beatrice insisted.

"Is someone whispering in your ear? Tell me what they say—I demand it."

Lena frantically whispered in Beatrice's ear. "If you know the Lord's Prayer, recite it now."

Beatrice bowed her head and began to pray.

Our Father, which art in Heaven,
Hallowed be Thy name.

Thy kingdom come, Thy will be done,
On Earth as it is in Heaven.
Give us this day our daily bread,
And forgive us our trespasses, as we forgive them
that trespass against us.
And lead us not into temptation, but deliver us
from evil.
For thine is the kingdom, the power and the glory,
for ever and ever.
Amen.

Heart softened, the preacher knelt in front of Beatrice. “Amen!” he exclaimed. “Praise God.”

As he sang a psalm of thanks, Lena McLeod’s ghost plucked a long red hair from the sleeve of his jacket. “Take this,” she said and handed it to Beatrice. “Use it wisely.”

My dear Beatrice,

I was glad to receive your most recent letter and to find that you are happy in your work and life in the city. Life here in Stony Point is uneventful, as ever. Just the way I like it.

With that in mind, I've decided to decline your invitation to visit for now. Autumn is here, winter not far behind and I would much prefer to make the trip in spring, thus giving you more time to get to know the place so you might give me a tour of <u>your</u> New York. Please understand that delaying my visit doesn't mean you're not welcome home anytime. Would you consider coming to Stony Point for Christmas? Miss St. Clair and Miss Thom are welcome to join you, of course.

I read about the grand parade put on by the Masons in honour of the obelisk's journey to Central Park. It seems as if you and your teashop were right in the middle of the celebrations! I hope it wasn't too noisy and taxing for a country-raised girl. Not that you haven't taken up and mastered every challenge that's ever been handed you. I know I rarely say it, since sentimentality isn't my forte, but I'm proud of your stick-to-itiveness and your pioneering spirit. I like to think perhaps I've even had a bit to do with it.

Be curious, smart, and safe, as I know you always are.

With affection,
Lydia

St. Clair and Thom.

Eleanor measured rose petals, hawthorn berries, St. John's wort, lemon balm and lavender into a waiting pot—a blend of buds and roots meant to soothe a broken heart. Catching a glimpse of Adelaide's face across the room, she added a second dose into the pot, thinking she'd better make enough for two.

Adelaide had returned from the morgue tired and shaken. Taking Eleanor aside, Dr. Brody had said, "I've an errand to run, but I'll be back this evening. I imagine it might be good for you two to spend some time together." The more Eleanor got to know him, the more she realized just how lovely he was. "Thank you," she'd said. "We'll see you tonight."

The two women sat at the table by the front window sipping their tea in silence. They'd agreed not to talk of the eviction notice, at least not for the time being. Since Beatrice had disappeared, every minute felt like an hour, every hour, a day. The end of the month seemed a lifetime away.

Eleanor retrieved Lydia's letter from the pocket of her apron and passed it to Adelaide. "This came in the post today."

Adelaide scanned it, then set it on the table. "I don't know what to say."

"Should we write to the woman? She'll be expecting a letter from Beatrice in return."

Adelaide shook her head. "She wrote the letter before Beatrice went missing. Maybe the girl is back in Stony Point, safe and sound. If we send a frantic note about not knowing where she is, whatever tale Beatrice has spun for her aunt will be torn to shreds."

"I have to believe if Beatrice was back home, she would've sent word by now. Even a telegram."

Adelaide poured more tea into her cup. "How long do we search for her?"

Eleanor crossed her arms. "How can you ask that?"

"I'm as worried as you are," Adelaide insisted. "But I also wish to be practical, for both our sakes. How long before we decide it's more likely she's dead than alive? What do we do when we've run out of places to look? Haunt the same spots, day after day, eventually becoming ghosts of ourselves?"

"She's only been missing for two days."

"It feels like a hundred."

Adelaide took inventory of Eleanor's facial expression, her body language, her posture: worried, fidgety, tightly wound. She decided to change the subject. "Did any customers come in today?"

Pointing to a stack of the notices Georgina had printed, Eleanor replied, "I kept the shop open for awhile, but then I went out to hand those around."

There was no escaping it. Not even for a minute.

Just then the bell on the door rang and Judith Dashley came bursting in, clutching the afternoon paper. "Tell me it's not her," she said, trembling as she spread a page of wrinkled newsprint on the table in front of them.

Special to The Evening Star. Police were alerted to a murder scene in the early hours of Monday morning when the body of a young woman was discovered in an alleyway near Madison Square Park. Her identity is unknown. The Head Coroner of the City Morgue estimates the deceased is approximately twenty years of age. Her hair is light auburn. Her eyes, blue. Cause of death: knife wound to the throat. Anyone with information concerning the victim or the crime is asked to contact Police Headquarters immediately. The body and the woman's personal effects will remain on display at the morgue until Wednesday.

Eleanor reached for Judith's hand. "It's not her, I promise."

"But how can you be sure?"

Adelaide made room for Judith to sit next to her. "I went to the morgue today. It's not her."

Judith gasped, eyes teary. "How horrible!"

Eleanor went to fetch more tea.

Judith attempted to calm herself. "I came by earlier to see how I might help, but I missed you both. Alden says I shouldn't be a pest, but I can't help it. And when I saw the notice on the door, I saw red. I went straight away to Mr. Newland's office to argue on your behalf."

Nearly dropping the fresh pot of tea, Eleanor exclaimed, "Oh Judith, you shouldn't have."

Judith sighed. "I had to try. Sadly, he wouldn't hear me out. He said 'business is business' and showed me to the door.

What a scoundrel Mr. Newland is! How dare he toss you out on the street!"

Adelaide poured for Judith. "Thank you for trying. Clearly Mr. Newland didn't know who he was dealing with."

After adding a dollop of honey, Judith picked up her spoon and gave it a vigorous stir. "You're not to worry. I'll take you in myself. You can move into the rooms next to mine. I don't care what Marietta Stevens thinks."

"Why would it bother her?" Adelaide asked.

Judith bit her lip. "She's worried about Beatrice, of course, as we all are . . . in fact, she's got the hotel detective on the case and her entire staff on their toes. She's even mentioned hiring a Pinkerton . . ."

"But . . ." Adelaide prompted.

Keeping her eyes on her teacup, Judith said, "Just don't expect her to openly show her support."

Eleanor shrugged.

Adelaide shook her head. "If she's upset about her daughter's precious gown, then she can go to hell."

"No, it's not that." Picking up one of the missing person's notices, she pointed at the text. "It's this."

LAST SEEN AT THE FIFTH AVENUE HOTEL.

"Beatrice is missing, and that's what she's most concerned with?" Adelaide sounded more resigned than angry. "Nothing like a scandal to show who your true friends are."

Judith gave Adelaide's hand a pat. Taking a sip of her tea, she turned to Eleanor, hoping that they could all think of something else for at least one moment. "I must tell you of the dream I had last night. Maybe you can make something of it."

"Of course," Eleanor said.

"It's the main reason I tried to find you this morning," Judith said. "Beatrice was in it, her face as plain as day."

Adelaide leaned forward.

"We were sitting at a table . . . you two, Beatrice and me. It wasn't here at the shop, though—it was in a place I've never been. The room was rustic—pot boiling over a fire, a broom leaning against the mantel, a long sturdy table set in the centre of the floor—the kind of place you imagine when you read a tale about a country cottage where fairies dwell. There were flower garlands woven through the rafters. We were laughing, and drinking tea."

"It sounds lovely," Eleanor said, thinking it sounded an awful lot like her childhood home. Wondering if it was a sign somehow sent by her mother, she asked, "What kind of flowers?"

"Forget-me-nots," Judith replied. "I remember because it's not something you'd ever see here in the city."

Adelaide asked, "What kind of tea?"

Sniffling the air as if it held the memory of her dream, Judith said, "Rosehip. Yes, I'm almost certain it was rosehip."

"Was that the whole dream?"

"Yes," Judith replied. "What do you think it means?"

Tears in her eyes, Eleanor said, "It means we shouldn't stop searching."

Judith nodded. "That's what I thought. What more can I do? I want to help. I've a NWSA meeting tomorrow. We can distribute some of those notices, if you can spare them."

Handing part of the stack to Judith, Adelaide said, "Yes, that would be good."

Eleanor moved behind the counter where she scooped several spoonfuls of tea into a jar. Tightening the lid, she gave the jar to Judith. "Tonight after dark, make a cup of this tea, then tuck yourself into bed and try to dream. If you see Beatrice again, come tell me. Who knows where it might lead."

Judith kissed both witches on their cheeks and scurried out the door.

As they watched her move off down the sidewalk, Adelaide thought of the vision she'd had at the morgue that morning. The picture of Beatrice she'd been shown wasn't nearly so lovely as the one Judith had seen. She'd thought of telling Eleanor but couldn't bring herself to do it. Turning to her friend she asked, "Do you think there might be something to Judith's dream?"

"I hope so," Eleanor said, thinking, *Hope is all we've got.*

The Witch of Blackwell's Island.

RAIN OR SHINE, snow or swelter, spring, summer, fall and winter, the women of Blackwell's Lunatic Asylum were led outside for a daily walk, or as the inmates called it, being put "on the rope." One by one the women were fitted with wide leather belts, then tethered by shackle, lock and chain to a thick, greasy line—two by two along the length of it, twenty-two women in all. A pair of nurses kept watch over them, one regularly shouting, "Hands to yourself!" the other crossly commanding, "Keep off the grass!" Nervously, the patients snaked their way along the gravel path. Some dragged their feet, others took to kicking stones. One tiny, meek woman, grateful to feel the warmth of the sun, turned her face to the sky as she shuffled along.

These were the first faces Dr. Brody encountered as he approached the asylum after his ferry ride across the East River from Manhattan. Surveying them, he thought, *Who knew that Hell was so close by?* He was glad he hadn't told Adelaide of his plans. She'd witnessed enough horror for one day.

He figured his chances of finding Beatrice here were slim, but he'd figured he should try. One of his acquaintances from medical school, Dr. Leonard Pitkin, had recently accepted a position at the place, so he'd sent a telegram announcing his intention to visit. He hoped Pitkin might allow him to search the recent asylum records for Beatrice's name. And while he was at it, he'd ask after Bart Andersen's girl, Sophie.

The main building was much larger than he'd imagined. The stone edifice was grand and gleaming, consisting of two long wings that stretched out in the shape of an L, providing two sides of the large courtyard. An octagonal tower rose from the centre, the ornate dome of its rotunda three storeys high, as if to house a band of distraught princesses being kept against their will. The rest of the yard was bounded by a thick wooden fence so tall one could only make out the tops of the masts and sails of the ships in the nearby harbour. Stepping through the main entrance, he was met with one of the great architectural wonders of New York, a grand interior staircase that spiralled to the roof of the rotunda like the twisted tail of a mythical serpent. Sunlight streamed from the dome above. To those visitors who went no further, there was nothing but reassurance to be found in both the grand space and the motto that graced the wide stone arch above the main door: WHILE I LIVE I HOPE. If the place was anything like the Salpêtrière, Brody thought, the corridors beyond were filled with Gothic nightmares and dark horrors. Making his way to the reception kiosk, he rang a bell to get the attention of the nurse on duty. "Excuse me," he said to the matronly woman who sat behind the desk, "I'm here to see Dr. Pitkin."

The round-faced nurse pushed back from her desk, causing the casters on her chair to squawk in protest. "Do you have an appointment?" she asked, her voice flat.

"No," Brody replied, "but I believe he's expecting me."

"Your name?"

"Dr. Quinn Brody."

The nurse sighed and rolled her eyes, then rose from her chair. "I'll see if he's available."

Dr. Pitkin seemed glad to see him. "Brody," he said with a kind smile, extending his hand before pulling it back with some embarrassment. "What brings you out to the island?" He was cheerful and well-pressed and Quinn wondered how long both would last.

"I'm here to inquire about a young woman who's gone missing," he said. "She's been gone since Saturday with no word to family or friends. I don't imagine she's here, but one never knows. She could've suffered a bump on the head or a terrible shock that might've rendered her senseless or dumb. Some well-meaning police officer could've brought her here, not knowing what else to do. I'm sure you've heard of such cases?"

Dr. Pitkin nodded. "Sadly, it's not uncommon for troubled girls to get brought out here, by police or even neighbours who make their own diagnoses of hysteria, brain fever or mania. Sometimes I think the coppers would rather leave them with me than deal with them on the streets."

"I can assure you this girl is of sound mind," Dr. Brody interjected, "but if something knocked her for a loop . . ."

Dr. Pitkin smiled and raised a finger. "Say nothing more. Would you like to check the list of recent arrivals to see if she's on it?"

"If it's not any trouble," Dr. Brody said with a nod.

Dr. Pitkin looked to the nurse behind the reception desk.

"Happy to," she cheerfully replied, her attitude completely changed in Dr. Pitkin's presence. Clearly, she fancied him. Opening a large ledger, she asked, "What's her name?"

"Beatrice Dunn. She's been missing since Saturday night."

Licking her thumb, the nurse turned the pages of the register until she found the proper date. Running her finger down the page, she checked each entry, line by line. After several minutes, she finally looked up at Brody and said, "I don't see her name listed."

"Thank you for checking," Dr. Brody said.

Dr. Pitkin leaned across the desk and touched the nurse's hand. "Thank you, Nurse Brewster."

As the two men made to walk away, she called after them. "Wait. I see here that we had two unidentified girls come in on Saturday night. One couldn't speak, the other said she was Marie Antoinette."

Checking his watch, Dr. Pitkin turned to Dr. Brody and said, "They should be in the courtyard right about now with the rest of the inmates. Shall we go see if one of them might be her?"

In his walk from the ferry, Dr. Brody hadn't thought that any of the women tethered to the rope had resembled Beatrice, but it was worth taking a second look. "Yes," he said. "Please."

The doctors caught up with the women as the nurses were escorting them back into the building. Moving down the line, Dr. Brody looked each one of them in the eyes. They greeted him with scowls, laughter, smiles, winks and blank stares. One woman growled, then licked her lips.

An aged woman in the middle of the bunch flapped her arms and repeatedly moaned, "Oh dear . . . oh no . . . I'm going to soil myself!"

"Keep your pie and shit holes shut," the woman next to her groused.

Reaching the end of the line, Dr. Brody said to Pitkin, "She's not here."

"Sorry I couldn't be more help," the doctor said. "I'll look out for her."

Dr. Brody was about to take his leave, when he remembered Bart Andersen's desperate plea. "If I can trouble you for one more moment, Doctor, there's a patient I'd like to inquire about on behalf of a friend. He visits her quite regularly and seems to feel there might be grounds for her release."

"What's her name?" Dr. Pitkin asked.

"Sophie Miles," Brody answered.

"I know the case well."

"Would I be able to look at her file?"

"I'll get it for you."

Dr. Pitkin settled him in his office, and before long returned with a large brown envelope. Handing it over, he sat in the chair behind his desk and said, "Terrible crime she committed. But since she was completely out of her head, the court saw fit to send her here instead of the Tombs. I've seen some improvement in her since I've arrived and there are days when she seems quite recovered, but I'm not sure she'll ever be fit to leave."

Dr. Brody took the records from the envelope and scanned the page that detailed her admission to the asylum.

> SOPHIE MILES. Aged 28. Found guilty of throwing vitriol in a woman's face resulting in grievous physical harm. The victim suffered the loss of her right eye and extensive facial scarring. The patient mentioned specific delusions

and an outright belief in witchcraft. Her answers were presented in a manner that showed mental instability, violent excitability and a strong disrespect for authority. There is a deep concern for the safety of all those who might come into contact with her. All measures should be taken to subdue the patient at the first sign of agitation.

"She's not so unstable these days," Dr. Pitkin remarked. "She spends most of her time on the third floor, in the small parlour just off the fresh air pavilion. She has a fondness for sewing rag dolls. Would you like to meet her?"

Dr. Brody was shocked and unnerved by what he'd read. "I'm grateful, but not today. I should be getting back to the city."

Sophie Miles was, indeed, seated in a rocking chair in the corner of the parlour, sewing basket at her side. She was giving her attention to a small rag doll in her lap, the one she'd made in the likeness of Bartholomew Andersen, right down to his plaid suit, jaunty hat and peg leg. Holding the doll by its tiny hands she kissed its face, made it dance. "Why is it taking so long?" she asked. "Why haven't you gotten me out of here yet?"

Not an hour before, she could've sworn she'd received a sign of her impending release when she'd performed the little daily ritual she used to detect her future. Cupping her thimble to her ear she'd listened for the prophetic voice that lived inside it. Most days it spoke of simple things she could do to get ahead—"steal that fork," "trip that inmate," "pretend to like Dr. Pitkin"—but today she'd distinctly heard a man's voice within, speaking her name as his footsteps drew near.

The other women in the room were engaged in embroidery, cross-stitch, watercolours. One of them left her work to come close to Sophie and whisper, "Witch." Then another woman did the same, and another, and another. Slyly avoiding the eyes and ears of the room's attendant, they came at her, chanting under their breath, "Witch, witch, she's a witch . . ." not so regularly that they'd get caught, but often enough to drive her mad.

Sophie did her best to ignore their taunts. Putting her thimble to her ear again, she listened closely, but sadly the footsteps had vanished. The usual voice that spoke to her sighed and said, "He's gone away and it's all because of that evil bitch." Seeing the soothsayer's face in her mind's eye, Sophie muttered under her breath, "I'll not let her win." She tied a small noose out of red embroidery floss loosely around the poppet's neck. "Someday soon, love," she whispered to the doll. "Or else."

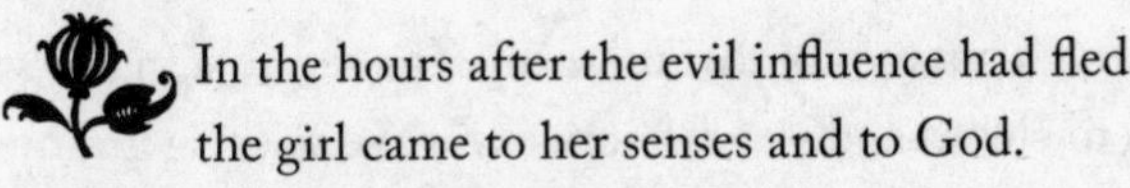

In the hours after the evil influence had fled, the girl came to her senses and to God. I prayed heartily through these precarious moments and observed her with great care.

Weak and trembling she suffered from the vapours, distressed by a final troubling thought from her oppressor: "You shan't be the last."

Still, I did rejoice that she had been saved! She no longer wished to engage in forbidden curiosities. Milk touched by her hands was no longer sour on my lips.

—from *An Attempt to Cure Witchcraft: The Story of Mercy Wylde*

The Third Night.

REVEREND TOWNSEND STOOD over his desk, puffing his pipe and inspecting a lacquered tray he'd filled with bread, oysters, apples, grapes and a pitcher of milk. After spending a good hour or two praying with Beatrice, he'd felt that all evil had fled the haunted chamber at last. Like Mercy Wylde had done, she'd shown all the signs of a damsel newly freed from her oppressor, from her weakened voice to her trembling limbs. When she'd begged for nourishment, he'd decided the girl's fast could end. What better way to show confidence in his faith and in the Lord?

He'd gone shopping for her meal himself. Walking home with his groceries, he'd passed by the teashop Sister Piddock had pointed out to him that morning. The store's sign was still turned to closed and several notices for the missing girl hung in the front window. How he'd rejoiced when he'd seen them! Let the whole city search for her. Let everyone know her name. Let them think she was taken, trapped, even dead. Then, when she came to stand before his congregation to tell her story of being enslaved by that foul witch, how much greater the tale would seem. When she spoke of her deliverance from the evil witch who seduced her heart, how much sweeter God's glory would be . . . how many more sinners would come to believe!

Setting his pipe on a saucer he'd tucked alongside a succulent cluster of grapes, he prepared to give thanks. As he knelt, his rod nagged against his leg, and he removed it from its loop and set it aside. Another act of faith. Hands clasped, he sang a psalm, then uttered a prayer.

> *But I will sing of thy power; yea, I will sing aloud of thy mercy in the morning: for thou hast been my defence and refuge in the day of my trouble.*
>
> *Unto thee, O my strength, will I sing: for God is my defence and the God of my mercy. Psalm 59: 16–17*

While the Reverend was singing, Beatrice was sleeping.

It'd taken all her strength to keep her wits about her through his questions, his accusations, his manic declarations of victory. By the time he'd left her, she was as certain of his madness as he was of her new faith. Hoping that things might turn her way, she'd taken up the thread she'd hidden in her bed and woven a single hair around it to complete the witch's ladder and its spell. "Freedom" was what she'd wished for, the final word she'd spoken before she'd tied the last knot. One could hope, one could pray, one could wish.

The Reverend had promised to bring her food when he came back tonight and perhaps fresh clothes and a warm bed tomorrow, if all continued to go "according to plan." She didn't know what his plan was, and she'd been too weak, too exhausted, too afraid to ask. She'd thought if she could eat something to get her strength up and then just make it through the night, then maybe she could come up with an escape plan of her own. She'd tried her best to stay awake, but once she lay down, her eyes had soon closed.

"Wake up," Lena called to Beatrice. "He's coming soon!"

Wiping the sleep from her eyes, Beatrice looked about the gloomy cellar and was met with a sight that made her think she was still dreaming. A great circle had been dug into the dirt in the middle of the floor, with a five-pointed star scratched inside it. A string of strange words was etched across the stone wall in black: *Titan gan eire ort.*

Lena whispered in Beatrice's ear, "'May you fall without rising.' It's a curse!"

"Why did you do this?" Beatrice hissed, fearing how Reverend Townsend would react.

"You cast your spell," Lena said. "I cast mine."

Hearing heavy footsteps on the stairs, she scrambled on hands and knees to wipe the circle and the star from the dirt.

The Reverend came through the door singing, carrying a tray of food. As soon as he caught sight of the wall, the floor and Beatrice, he threw the tray—plates clattering, oysters tumbling into the muck. The pitcher broke where it landed, spidery fingers of milk streaming forth, filling the points of the star. "You foul creature!" he shouted at Beatrice. "How dare you deceive me!"

Beatrice crept forward to grab the edge of his coat. "I swear I didn't do this. I woke to find it here. I was trying to get rid of it."

The preacher knocked her sprawling. "All I see is the Devil's work and a girl with the heart of a harlot."

Beatrice backed out of his reach, afraid he'd strike her again. "This isn't what it seems, and you don't know my heart."

He came at her, forcing her against the wall.

"Please," she begged. "I've done nothing wrong."

Seething, he kicked her shins. Then, as she crumpled to the floor, the small of her back, her gut.

"Mercy . . ." she whimpered, hugging herself. "Have mercy on me."

He began pacing as if he was the one who was trapped, muttering to himself and his Maker. "I thought she was the one. I thought she'd seen the light. Guide me, oh Lord, in what you would have me do . . ."

Beatrice shut her eyes, trying to keep from sobbing.

Kicking the tray across the room, Townsend stalked out of the cellar and bolted the door behind him.

Lena flew to Beatrice's side. "He means to kill you! He's gone to get the knife."

"Leave me alone," Beatrice said, crawling to the broken pitcher to upend what little milk was left into her mouth. She hurt everywhere, and yet she was so hungry. Spotting a single, intact oyster, she brought it to her lips and sucked out the meat.

"That shell's sharp, you know," Lena said. "Sharp enough to cut a man's throat."

Running her finger along its edge, Beatrice tried to picture herself attacking the Reverend. "I could never manage it," she admitted to herself as much as Lena, and it was then that she gave way to tears.

"Slit your own, then," Lena urged, "before he can do it. We'd be together, you and me . . . two ghosts against him."

The preacher's voice wafted down from the room above, angrily mumbling, likely praying, making it even harder for Beatrice to think. Among the spoiled food and shards of china sat Reverend Townsend's clay pipe, its bowl full of tobacco still gently glowing. Picking it up, Beatrice looked for a place to hide it. No matter what happened, at least she would've taken something from him.

The Fires of Saint Clarus. Each year, come summer, the people of La Haye-de-Routot, a small village in Normandy, celebrate the famed Saint Clarus by building a great bonfire in his honour. This spectacle takes place among a scattering of ancient yew trees very near where Saint Clarus was beheaded, and where Rollo, the Viking king, chose to abandon his pagan religion for Christianity. The villagers, who consider the rite sacred, gather en masse after dark, some setting chairs here and there around the fire for the comfort of the deceased who wish to attend. The most faithful of the followers have been known to approach the fire to collect glowing embers from its flames. Cradling the embers inside spent oyster shells they carry them home, believing that having a small part of the fire in their possession will bless their lives for the year to come.

—T. D. Pratchett, *A Compendium of Miracles*

Careful What You Wish For.

As a child, poring over Mr. Pratchett's collection of miracles, Beatrice had often imagined herself next to the crackling bonfire trying to pick out the ghosts from the villagers. As she picked up the oyster shells scattered on the cellar floor, it occurred to her that she might be able to make a fire of her own.

Setting the largest shell on the floor, she pulled a scant handful of straw from her mattress and made a little nest of it in the bottom of the shell. Then she collected whatever bits of coal she could find (most of the lump she'd hidden had gone to Lena's curse), and dropped them in. Lastly, she took Reverend Townsend's pipe and tapped what remained of the smouldering tobacco from its bowl into the shell. With soft, steady breaths, she fed the embers until the straw sparked and burned, and the coal cinders began to glow. Then she gently placed a second shell over the first to protect her treasure, leaving just enough space between them so the fire wouldn't go out.

"What've you got there?" Lena asked, circling around her. "What are you doing?"

Head bowed, eyes closed, all Beatrice would say was, "I'm going home."

Eleanor sat across from Adelaide at the centre table in the teashop. Five objects lay before them—Eleanor's grimoire, a porcelain teacup, a white feather quill, a small sheet of parchment and the bone-handled dagger that had once belonged to Madame St. Clair. "Are you sure you want to do this?" Eleanor asked, looking at Adelaide for signs of disbelief, or fear. "If you've any misgivings, then it's better I perform the spell alone. My hope is to use the charm to conjure a guide to take us to Beatrice. I can't say what form the guide might take or if it will lead us into peril."

"No misgivings," Adelaide said, staring at the dagger. "I want to help."

"Good," Eleanor said. "Two witches at the table makes the spell twice as able. Would you like to read it through one last time?"

Adelaide nodded. She desperately wanted the spell to work. She wanted to get it right.

The ESAUE Square.

Magicians, witches and mystics have long understood the power of placing numbers, letters or symbols in sacred combinations within a magic square. This square, described below, holds the potential to grant a heart's desire. This charm should only be used with utmost care and caution, for once its magic has been set in motion it cannot be reversed. Never draw the square in its completed form unless you wish to cast the spell.

At the time of the waxing moon, wound the thumb of your left hand with the blade of a consecrated knife. Draw enough blood to write the spell on a piece of parchment with a quill made from the feather of a white goose. Without speaking, spell out E-S-A-U-E in four directions to make the square. Then place the paper between the palms of your hands as if you are praying, and declare what you desire. To enhance the power of this spell, perform it with another who shares the same wish. Once the spell has come to fruition, destroy the charm by burning it.

"I'm ready," Adelaide said, giving the grimoire a shy, friendly pat.

Perdu perched on the back of an empty chair to act as witness. Bright hid beneath his wing. And Cleo, so far as they all knew only a dog, was sleeping at Adelaide's feet with Twitch tucked in the fold of her ear.

Eleanor reached for Adelaide's hand. This spell felt like something of a last resort. She'd seen her mother use it to great effect, only once having it yield less than ideal results. In that instance, a woman had come to l'Hermitage wanting Madame St. Clair to find her lost husband. The man had indeed been found, but to his wife's dismay, in another woman's bed. "Let that be a lesson to you," her mother had said wagging her finger at her daughter. "Those who use magic to find what they seek, may not always like what they find." Picking up her mother's dagger, Eleanor began the ritual by drawing its blade across the fleshy tip of her thumb. The first drop of her blood welled up in the wound, then shone like a ruby as it dropped to the bottom of the cup. Handing the knife to Adelaide, she bid her to do the same.

Adelaide made her cut quick and deep, then pressed with her forefinger to hasten the flow of her blood. It only took a few moments to collect what they needed for the spell.

Putting her finger to her lips, Eleanor reminded Adelaide that the next step was to be taken in silence. Dipping the quill in the cup, she stirred their blood three times clockwise before putting the tip to the parchment. They took turns writing the sacred word, penning the letters one by one—across, down, reversed, up.

As Adelaide set the quill aside after the last iteration, Eleanor picked up the parchment and blew the blood dry.

Laying it on the palm of her right hand, she waited for Adelaide's palm to meet hers, and then they threaded their fingers together, the charm sandwiched between their hands. Closing their eyes in unison, they chanted the verse:

In this square our wish resides
Please send a soul to be our guide.
The next one through the door to come,
Will lead the way to Beatrice Dunn.

Twitch flew to Perdu's side and burrowed between the raven's feathers. Tapping Bright on the shoulder he asked, "What happens now?"

Bright sighed, then whispered, "We wait."

A little girl stood near the fountain in Madison Square Park—the girl who'd told Adelaide's fortune, the girl Reverend Townsend had taken, the girl who'd survived him, the girl Adelaide's mother had mistaken for her daughter, the girl Eleanor had gifted the last coins from her pocket. She was debating whether or not she should wade into the shallow pool to steal a shiny dime that sparkled in the water. That was what the money was for, wasn't it? The small wooden sign that hung on the fountain's iron railing said so. MAKE A WISH, FEED THE POOR.

When the Bird Lady settled on a nearby bench, the girl chose to leave the dime for the ladies who collected the coins for the charity kitchen. For her it'd been a fairly good day, since her belly was fairly full. Fiddling in her pocket, she discovered the last of the pennies the woman from the teashop had given her that morning. Heaven knew she should probably save it, but for once she thought she'd like to make a wish.

A warm bed? A new family? All the bread she could eat? No, no and no. What she wanted more than anything was to not feel afraid. Ever since the Reverend had tricked her, taken her, beaten her and left her for dead, she'd felt his presence around every corner, heard his breathing whenever she closed her eyes. He'd called her a witch. She hoped he was right. She had a faint memory of someone telling her (had it been her mother? her grandmother? a stranger?) that she had witchery in her blood. Pinching the penny between her fingers, she kissed it, then tossed it into the water. "I wish he was dead."

No sooner had the penny splashed, than the ghost of Adelaide's mother rose up from inside the fountain, called by the girl's voice. It'd been weeks since anyone, including Adelaide, had thought of her, so her place among the living was quickly being lost. Was this strange watery grave to be her home forever? That damn fairy had proved more powerful than she'd imagined. Desperate to be noticed, she came towards the little girl, kicking up a whirlwind of wet leaves as she moved.

Thinking the shadowy figure might be the preacher, the little girl panicked and ran. As she flew past the bench where the Bird Lady sat, the old woman called out to her, "Careful what you wish for!"

The Reverend was still pacing the floor above Beatrice. The sound made her more anxious than ever. She had tied the witch's ladder around her ankle, and was cradling the pair of oyster shells that held her little fire, waiting for the preacher to come down the stairs and step into her plan.

"Here he comes," Lena hissed. "It's time!"

As soon as she heard his foot touch the creaky top stair, Beatrice opened her tiny fire to the air, then tucked it into the hollowed-out corner of her mattress. Feeding it with straw and breath, she willed the fire to catch. With any luck the flames would leap up and distract the preacher before he could kill her, and she could escape. His footsteps stopped midway on the stairs, then turned and retreated, just as the fire took hold in a flash, flames reaching for the rafters.

There was nothing Beatrice could do to stop it.

The frightened little girl ran out of the park and up the street to hide in the window well of Markowitz's bakery. Seeing lights in the teashop, she scrambled up the stoop and pounded on the door. The teashop woman had been good to her that morning, and might take pity on her now. "Please," she cried. "Please let me in!"

With a start, Eleanor let Adelaide's hand go and rushed to the door. No sooner had she flung it open than the girl ran into the shop to hide under the table.

"Mercy!" Perdu squawked when he saw her. "Mercy!"

The Dearlies flew from beneath his wings and took shelter inside a teapot.

Ducking her head beneath the table, Adelaide stared at the girl. "Don't I know you?"

Eleanor crouched down, then sat on the floor. "What's wrong, my dear?" she asked. "What's happened?"

The girl's eyes were panicked. "He's after me again!"

Cleo circled around the child and lay in front of her, keeping close watch on the door.

"Who?" Adelaide asked.

"Mercy!" Perdu cried.

Frantic, the girl stammered, "The awful man who always walks with the church-going ladies through the park. They say he's their preacher but I say he's the Devil. He locked me in his cellar with a ghost! I know he meant to kill me. He said I was a witch."

Eleanor looked at Adelaide as if to say, *This is it.* "But you got away from him?"

"He thought I was dead, but I swear he's after me again."

Adelaide put her hand on the girl's shoulder. "Can you take us to the place he kept you?"

The girl buried her face in Cleo's fur. Her only response was the trembling of her body.

"The dog can come with us," Eleanor offered. "She won't let anything happen to you."

Lifting her eyes to meet Eleanor's, the girl bit her lip, uncertain.

"And neither will I," Adelaide said, and as the girl turned to her, she pointed to the sheath on her boot where she kept her knife.

Beatrice pounded on the door as smoke filled the cellar. "Fire!" she shouted. "Please help! Let me out!" The smoke caused her eyes to sting, her throat to burn. Her skin was turning red from the heat, her blood felt as if it was about to boil. Surely, she thought, the Reverend could see the smoke seeping between the planks of his floor. Had he fled the house and left her here to die?

Suddenly she heard his boots thudding down the stairs. Arm over her nose and mouth, she stepped back from the door, desperate to escape.

No sooner did he come through the door than he lunged at her and seized her by the throat. Grim with anger in the fire's flickering light, he flashed a knife before her eyes. "You will not die by your own hand. That privilege will be mine."

With a swift knee to his groin, Beatrice managed to hurt him enough he let go. She stumbled back, and fell, and before she could get to her feet, he came at her again, this time grabbing her wrist, his fingers digging into the sore, tender flesh rubbed raw by the ropes he'd used to bind her.

Pain shot through her. Tears streamed down her face.

"I've got you now, you witch," the Reverend said attempting to haul her up.

Despite the pain, Beatrice resisted—her lungs tight with the effort, stealing her breath. As she struggled for air, Lena's voice sounded in her ear: "Remember my curse."

Flames flashed behind the Reverend and the rafters began to creak. Focused on handing Beatrice her punishment, he ignored the fire raging at his back.

"Once he falls," Lena cried, "he'll not rise again."

Beatrice fought him, shouting, "You'll not get this witch!" The scabs from her wounds broke open as he pulled, and she started to bleed.

Then, as he raised his knife, clearly meaning to end her, her wrist, wet with blood, slipped out of his grip. He toppled backwards, howling and flailing as his hair and clothes caught fire.

Lena's laughter filled the room as a single rafter gave way and sealed the Reverend's fate.

Beatrice fled for the stairs. As she flew through the door, it slammed shut behind her, and the bolt clanged to. The stairwell was filled with smoke. She could barely see or breathe.

"Beatrice," her mother called from the top of the stairs. "Come to me."

Looking up, she saw the silhouette of a woman on the landing, her hand outstretched. Unsure whether she was making her way to safety or Heaven, Beatrice climbed the stairs. Either way, she was going to be free.

Dr. Brody sat at his father's desk and stared at the dying coals of an evening fire he'd built in his study, debating whether or not to go to the teashop. He'd said he would stop by at the end of the day, but there didn't seem to be much sense in disturbing Eleanor and Adelaide at this hour. He had nothing new to offer, no information, no solutions that might lead to finding Beatrice.

He hadn't really expected to find Beatrice at the asylum, but he'd hoped he might. He certainly hadn't expected to stumble across the perpetrator of the acid attack on Adelaide. He supposed he could've guessed at some of the particulars that had led to the loss of her eye, but to read it on the page was a sobering thing. She'd never volunteered what had happened to her and he hadn't asked. He'd figured she'd tell that story, if and when she was ready.

But he wished he'd told her how beautiful she was the night they'd kissed at the hotel, that he'd professed his love for her then and there. Knowing Adelaide, perhaps she already knew how he felt. But how could he pursue happiness while Beatrice was still lost? All he could do was show his support, take the proper actions and hope that Adelaide could see that everything he did was from the heart.

He ran his finger around the dial of the spiritoscope, which he'd fetched from the hotel, thinking it was better to have it home than sitting in some broom closet. Oh how he longed for a ghost to direct his path! Where were Mr. Dickens' spirits of past, present and future? Was it just wishful thinking to hope they might appear? No. What Beatrice Dunn had shown him had been real. It couldn't be denied. "Father," he said, looking to the heavens, "send me a sign."

With a gentle clacking, the spiritoscope's dial began to turn. One by one it pointed out the letters, V-I-V-I-T.

She lives.

The little girl led the two witches to the parsonage with Cleo at their heels. As they drew closer, church bells began a slow, mournful toll. Eleanor stopped short, a chill up her spine. "Someone will die tonight," she whispered.

A team of horses pulling a fire wagon galloped past, spittle and sweat flying every which way in the cold night air. A half-dozen men clung to the ladders strapped to the truck's sides. A young boy, perched on top, clanged a leather hammer against a tinny gong, sounding the alarm. Adelaide smelled the smoke before she saw the fire. "Over there," she said, pointing to the parsonage as they rounded the corner. The building was falling in on itself, engulfed in a mass of flames.

"That's it!" the girl shouted, her eyes lit with glee. "That's the place." Then she danced away down the street, thankful that her wish had come true.

Eleanor slipped her hand in Adelaide's and made a silent wish that Beatrice had survived.

Cleo circled around them and began to bark.

"Look," Adelaide said, tugging on Eleanor. "I think it's her."

Beatrice, backlit by the fire, walked towards them, dirty and in a tattered shift, tears streaming down her cheeks.

Running to her, Eleanor and Adelaide embraced her as one, and held her tight.

By the time Brody got to the teashop, Beatrice had been fed and washed and was tucked safe in her bed with Eleanor and Adelaide taking turns watching over her. Perdu was perched on the headboard, and Cleo was curled at her feet. Twitch and Bright were snuggled up together on the windowsill contemplating her next dream.

When a knock came at the door, Eleanor went to answer it, wondering who might be calling so late. She and Adelaide had decided to keep the news of Beatrice's return to themselves until morning. What the girl needed tonight was rest.

"I'm sorry to impose," Dr. Brody said as Eleanor opened the door. Shyly stepping inside the shop he said, "I've news. A message from my father."

It was clear to Eleanor that it had taken the doctor a fair bit of resolve to say such a thing. "I see," she said, and smiled at him.

Stammering, he said, "I know it may sound foolish, but I'm sure of what I saw. Long story short, my father let me know that Beatrice is alive."

"She is," Eleanor said, taking his hand in hers. "Come see for yourself." It was all she could do not to laugh at the shock and wonder on Brody's face as she led him up the stairs.

At the door of Beatrice's room, he let out a small gasp, shocked by the sight of her ragged hair, her sunken eyes, the wounds and bruises that encircled her wrists.

Propped on her pillows, Beatrice called to him, her voice hoarse. "I'm sorry, Dr. Brody," she said. "I let you down."

"Dear girl," he said, his voice shaking a little, "you could never do that." Looking at Eleanor and then at Adelaide he said, "None of you could."

What wonderful beings they were, these women he'd come to care for, these women who'd helped him chase his dreams, these women he needed so much more than they needed him—these marvellous, glorious, Witches of New York.

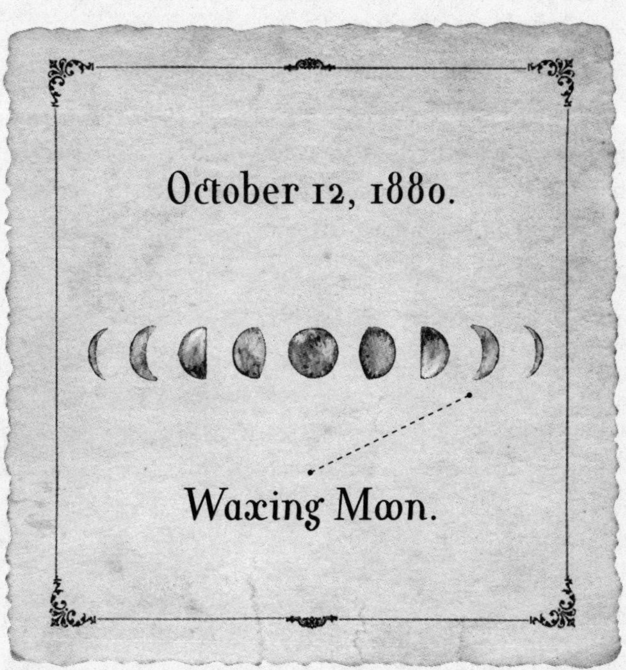
October 12, 1880.
Waxing Moon.

Respected Preacher Dies in Tragic Fire

Last evening at approximately ten o'clock, fire broke out in the parsonage of the Church of the Good Shepherd on Twenty-Third Street. A passerby sounded an alarm after smelling smoke and seeing flames shooting out the first-storey windows of the dwelling. Personnel from the Fire Department responded promptly, but by the time they arrived on the scene the wooden structure was fully engulfed.

The speed and aggressiveness of the fire has been attributed to the house's age and style of construction, which date back to the early 1800s. The building and its contents could not be saved.

As of this morning it has been confirmed that Reverend Francis Townsend, beloved leader of the church's congregation, perished in the fire. His badly burned remains were identified by one of his parishioners, a Mrs. Penelope Piddock. "He was a true soldier of God," she tearfully testified. "May the angels protect him, and Heaven accept him."

Funeral services for the late Reverend Townsend will be held this Friday at two o'clock in the Sanctuary of the Church of the Good Shepherd.

Miraculously, the church, a stone meeting house that dates from the same period as the parsonage, was spared the fire's wrath.

A collection for the poor will be taken in the Reverend's memory this Sunday during regular services.

Mr. Palsham.

The Collectors entered Mr. Palsham's office unannounced. Hands folded at their waists, the pair stood impassively in front of his desk waiting to be addressed.

As was his habit, Mr. Palsham took his time. After sifting through the many papers, plans, schematics and blueprints that littered his blotter, he picked up a silver trowel from a velvet-lined presentation box that sat to one side of his desk. It was a gift from the Masons for his part in bringing the obelisk to New York. Holding the trowel's tip to his finger, he mindlessly spun it around by its wooden handle. Its blade glinted each time it passed through the sunlight streaming through the window, casting a flickering beam on his face. Beneath his bushy beard sat a constellation of scars. If he were ever to allow a barber to shave him clean, his mouth would bear the comical look of a carnival knock-down doll with a smile that had come unstitched. Leaning back in his chair he finally asked, "What brings you here?"

"Reverend Townsend is dead, sir," the first Collector said.

The second Collector gave a nod of confirmation.

"I am aware of it," Mr. Palsham replied. "He was weak. There are others who'll take his place."

The first Collector stared straight ahead. "And the girl is gone as well."

Mr. Palsham winced. The thought of Beatrice Dunn made him uneasy. She was different, special, almost frightening in her naïveté when it came to her power. Her glamour was brighter than any witch he'd ever seen (and he'd seen plenty). He'd made a mistake in thinking that bumbling preacher could do her in. "Perhaps it's for the best."

"You no longer wish to pursue her?" the second Collector asked.

"Only from a distance," Mr. Palsham explained. "It's not her time yet."

"And what of the others?" the first Collector inquired.

Mr. Palsham tapped the trowel on his forehead, thinking. "Leave them be, for now. They're worth more together than apart."

"Very well, sir."

"As you wish."

Setting the tool aside, Mr. Palsham asked, "Did you recover anything from the fire?"

"Only this," the first Collector said, placing Reverend Townsend's pipe on the desk.

"And this," the second replied, placing a blackened oyster shell next to it.

Picking up the shell, Mr. Palsham held it to his nose and sniffed, then ran his finger along its sharp edge. He could feel the magic lingering from where the girl had touched it with her will. In his long existence he'd brought about the demise of many witches merely by encouraging man's hate, man's greed, man's hubris, man's intolerance. These new witches would require careful consideration and planning. A small part of him was glad for the challenge. The hunts in Europe had gone so smoothly. Salem had been far too easy a task.

These women were another matter altogether. There was time yet, though, to observe them, maybe even turn them to his ways. Time was the greatest advantage a demon had.

Waving the Collectors away he said, "You're dismissed."

October 31, 1880.
New Moon,
All Hallows' Eve.

Home.

IN THE DAYS after Beatrice's return, everyone did their part to heal her wounds.

Among her first visitors was Georgina Davis, who'd dropped by the shop to see if anything had come from the notices she'd made. Much to her delight she'd found the girl was no longer lost. "I'll have her name struck from the missing persons list at once."

"Thank you for everything," Eleanor had said with a soft smile. "You've been a tremendous help."

"It's a rare thing to have a happy ending," Georgina had replied. "It's been a pleasure. I do hope we'll remain friends."

Eleanor's cheeks had turned bright pink, much to the surprise of everyone in the room.

Judith Dashley brought bouquets of fresh flowers nearly every day—chrysanthemums, roses, daisies, lilies. "To brighten your room and lift your spirits." Holding Beatrice's hand she'd admitted, "I missed not having you to confide in. You're one of the few people in this world who doesn't look on me with pity. All these years after Billy's death and I still feel the loss wash over me. People mean well, I suppose, but pity is such a dangerous pastime, prone to stir gentle madness in the head and poison the heart. Steer clear of it if you can, my dear. I promise, for my part, I'll never place such a burden on you."

"Thank you, Judith," Beatrice had said. "I couldn't ask for a better gift."

Dr. Brody had come bearing a small trunk filled with books from his father's library—titles covering such subjects as spiritism, psychical research and occult sciences. He'd hoped the girl might find them informative as well as entertaining. "I'll be anxious to hear your thoughts on them when you're up to it," he'd said. "How thoughtful of you," Beatrice had replied, already poring over one of the books.

Taking Brody aside, Adelaide had whispered in his ear, "And I'd like to hear your thoughts on animal magnetism, if you're feeling up to it." She'd made up her mind to not only entertain the notion of love, but to pursue it. This time it was Brody's turn to blush.

For their part, the Dearlies had delivered a handful of lovely dreams to Beatrice to aid in her recovery—visions of hidden rooms filled with gilded books, fairy circles lit with foxfire, secret spells that magically appeared in Eleanor's grimoire. When Bright announced that they needed to give the girl a nightmare, Twitch had protested, saying he refused to participate.

"It has to be done," Bright had insisted. "She needs to remember, not forget."

Curling one of the short strands of what was left of Beatrice's hair around his finger, he'd asked, "Isn't that terrible mark he left on her skin enough of a reminder?"

"It's not him we need her to remember," Bright had explained.

Giving in, Twitch had summoned Cleo to the end of Beatrice's bed so the dog would be there to comfort her when the dream took hold. "All right," he'd said. "Just this once."

Not keen to put the girl through it, either, Bright said, "Hopefully once will be enough."

Beatrice had tossed and turned the whole way through as her dream-self had tried to escape the clutches of Mr. Palsham. Unlike the time he'd caught her by the arm in the park, no one came to her rescue. His hands turned to clawed talons, his face into a ghoulish, horned fright. Fanged teeth glistening, hoarse voice growling he'd said, "Beware the demon's bite." She'd let out a terrible scream, bringing both Adelaide and Eleanor running.

"It's only a dream," Adelaide had said, stroking her arm. "All will be well. You'll be fine."

Taking Madame St. Clair's brass key from around her neck, Eleanor had placed it in Beatrice's hand. "A demon will never outsmart a witch," she'd said. "Remember the princess." Beatrice had worn the key next to her heart every day since.

Eleanor had seen to the girl's care around the clock, bringing her rosehip tea for strength and healing, and dressing her burns and bruises with a salve made from honey, chamomile, lavender and cobwebs. Beatrice had dutifully written down the recipes for each remedy. Eleanor had taken it as a sign Beatrice meant to carry on with them at the shop. "You're welcome to stay with us as long as you like," she'd told the girl. "Although, come November, I can't say for certain where that might be."

Judith had offered countless times to put them up at the hotel, but both Eleanor and Adelaide had turned down her invitations. As October had dwindled away, no solution had been found for their lodging or their business. Cecil Newland's eviction notice had seemingly secured his revenge.

Adelaide had given Beatrice hour after hour of companionship. Knowing what it was like to be bedridden, she'd sat nearby, reading her cards and her palm, and telling tall tales of the days she'd spent in a circus sideshow. Once Beatrice was up and around, they took a stroll every afternoon in the park. It was there that they, along with Dr. Brody, had hatched a plan for what to do next.

"What about *my* house?" Dr. Brody had said with a hopeful smile. "I can't believe I didn't think of it before. There's plenty of room and you can stay as long as you wish."

To Beatrice's surprise, Adelaide hadn't dismissed the idea, only teased, "What will Mrs. Stutt say? Won't she be scandalized?"

"A little scandal might be good for her," Dr. Brody responded. "I'll move into the carriage house out back to keep her from putting up too much of a fuss."

"We can't put you out of your own house," Beatrice had said, though inside she'd been giddy at the thought of having access to Mr. Brody's library at all hours. If it were up to her, she'd live, eat and sleep there for the rest of her life.

"Nonsense. The coach house is perfect for an old bachelor like me. Consider it done."

Slipping her arm through his, Adelaide had said, "But you'll come visit us from time to time, for suppers and entertainments and such?"

Leaning his head to hers he'd whispered, "You could not keep me away."

When they'd put the plan to Eleanor, both Adelaide and Beatrice had done their best to sweeten their proposal with various enticements. "The kitchen is enormous," Adelaide had pointed out. "So well equipped."

"And there's plenty of room out back for beehives and a garden," Beatrice had said.

But it hadn't taken much to convince Eleanor. Time was growing short, and she'd grown quite fond of Dr. Brody. His was a kindness that never felt forced or insincere.

They'd wasted no time, moving Perdu and their personal effects first, and then the contents of the teashop. Adelaide had wanted to find a new space for their business at once, but Eleanor had said she preferred they take their time. If she was going to enter into such a venture again, the place would have to be absolutely right. "I'll know it when I see it," she'd said. She had a picture in her mind of what it should be—more like her mother's cottage than not—and she wasn't sure such a place even existed in New York. Packing her jars, tins, cups and pots in boxes, she'd moved them into a back room at Dr. Brody's.

Mrs. Stutt had adapted to the situation quite well, quickly acquiring a deep affection for Beatrice and a great respect for Eleanor's skills in the kitchen. Adelaide, she learned to tolerate.

When the last day of the month arrived, all that was left in the shop were the bells that hung over the door and Eleanor's hickory broom. After Beatrice fetched the bells from their perch, Adelaide tied them to Cleo's collar.

Eleanor, as witches' tradition dictated, swept the floors back to front, one last time.

As she made her way down the stoop, chasing the dust from each step, she saw Isaac Markowitz staring gloomily in her direction. "Isaac," she called, "come give Cleo a proper send-off."

The boy scurried to the dog's side and wrapped his arms around her. "Don't forget me," he said in her ear.

"You can visit her any time, you know," Adelaide said. "It's only a few blocks."

"That's a world away!"

"Well you'd better get used to making the trip," Eleanor advised. "I've a standing order with your father, every Wednesday, for a loaf of his marble rye."

Beatrice smiled at the boy and he laughed.

Looking up the street, Eleanor asked, "Where do you suppose Judith is today? I thought for sure she'd come say goodbye. I'd gotten used to her moping about, wondering what she'll do without us."

Adelaide shook her head. "Who knows."

Beatrice gave a little shrug.

The pair looked at each other, then away, knowing something that Eleanor didn't.

Seeing the sun was low in the sky, Adelaide checked her watch. "Shall we hire a hansom?" she suggested.

"No," Eleanor said, shaking her head, "it's All Hallows' Eve. Let's walk."

They chose to stroll past the park—Eleanor with her broom on her shoulder, Beatrice and Adelaide on either side of her. Cleo followed behind, bells jangling against her red patent collar.

A group of Fantasticals paraded past them on the street, dressed in patchwork clothes and gaudy masks, carrying turnip lanterns and banging pots and pans. They were going from house to house to beg for pennies and treats. Amongst them was a sprightly little girl dressed in a long black cloak and a tall pointed hat. Running up to Cleo, she gave the dog a pat on the head. "Hello," she said.

Beatrice grinned at the little witch.

With a twirl and a wave she danced away. "Goodbye!"

The witches all laughed.

It was nearly dark when they reached their destination, but before they went inside, Adelaide stole behind Eleanor and covered her eyes with her hands.

"Stop that," Eleanor protested. "What are you up to?"

Beatrice giggled. "That's for us to know and you to find out."

"Unhand me. I insist."

Adelaide whispered in her ear, "That's not how this works."

Running ahead of them up the steps to the building adjacent to the house—the place where Tobias Brody once sold a fine array of philosophical instruments—Beatrice knocked on the door and shouted, "We're here."

With that, a great tarp came down from where Dr. Brody had hung it across the windows, and a beautiful new storefront was revealed. The windows were clean and sparkling with candlelight, the door bore a fresh coat of blue paint. The sign over the door read: THE HERMITAGE.

"What's this?" Eleanor asked, hardly believing her eyes.

"You'll see," Adelaide said, leading her to the door.

Taking Madame St. Clair's key from around her neck, Beatrice handed it to Eleanor and said, "You'll be needing this."

Slipping the key in the door's lock, Eleanor opened it to discover a room that looked for all the world like her mother's kitchen. A long, sturdy table ran down the length of it, set with cups and saucers, pitchers of honey and a plate heaped with teacakes. A fire crackled in a hearth in the back of the room, a cauldron hanging over it, filled with stew. The clock from St. Clair and Thom's graced the mantel. Row upon row of shelves and cupboards lined the walls, filled with the shop's jars and tins, teapots and kettles. Dr. Brody tended the fire as Judith Dashley stood on a stepladder with Alden holding her steady so she could finish stringing tin lanterns and garlands of forget-me-nots from the rafters.

Eleanor shook her head in disbelief. "How did you ever manage it?"

"You're not the only witch around here," Adelaide teased.

Beatrice bit her lip. "Do you like it?"

"Yes," Eleanor said, taking the girl's hand. "It feels like home."

Cleo trotted past her and promptly curled herself up on a rug in front of the fire.

Perdu, who'd been watching from his newly installed perch, flapped to the centre of the table, fished a cake from the top of the pile and gobbled it down.

"What a terrible thief you are," Beatrice teased. "What a silly bird." The raven let out a long, stubborn chortle. Eyeing the girl, he declared, "I am no bird."

That night they celebrated with mulled cider and soul cakes. Alden Dashley brought out a fiddle and much to everyone's delight, Dr. Brody sang while Mr. Dashley played. They laughed and told stories and entertained themselves with the games that witches enjoy most on Hallowe'en: paring apples to find their fortunes, dropping egg whites in hot water, playing round after round of three saucers and book and key.

When the night was over and the Dashleys had gone, and

Dr. Brody went off to his bed, the three women stood together in front of the fire.

"It's almost midnight," Eleanor said, looking at the clock.

"I'm ready," Adelaide replied, taking Eleanor's hand.

"So am I," Beatrice said, holding fast to her sister witches.

As the clock struck twelve they recited a special spell they'd crafted to mark their first All Hallows' Eve together.

By new moon and twinkling stars,
Bless this night and make it ours.
To those who dare to wish us harm,
We cast on them a wicked charm.
To those who aid us in our powers,
We grace their lives with happy hours.
And to ourselves one wish remains,
That we might ne'er be lost again.
Hecate dear, we ask of thee.
So may it be, so may it be, so may it be.

January 21, 1881.
Half Moon.

THE MORNING SUN *Friday, January 21, 1881*

The Great Obelisk to Be Erected

The Egyptian obelisk known as Cleopatra's Needle will be erected on its pedestal tomorrow at noon, on Greywacke Knoll in Central Park. If the attendance during October's dedication of the site is any indication of the public's interest, it should prove to be a crowded and festive affair.

After its arduous months-long journey through the city, the obelisk now waits at the ready atop a great turning structure that in itself is a tribute to man's perseverance and ingenuity. Lt. Commander Gorringe recently remarked, "If all goes accordingly, it will move as easily and deliberately as if it were the minute hand on a lady's watch."

We wish good luck and Godspeed to Gorringe and the good men under his direction.

Cleopatra's Needle.

THE THREE WITCHES spent Christmas with Aunt Lydia in Stony Point. They filled their bellies with crown roast and plum pudding. They admired Lydia's stamp collection. They played many hands of whist. Every night during the week before the New Year, they took turns reading stories to each other in the parlour. One night, after Beatrice had given a particularly lively rendition of *The Cricket on the Hearth*, Lydia, having had one too many glasses of sherry, announced, "I wanted to tell you that I've seen a ghost."

"You have?" Eleanor asked.

"Do tell," Adelaide urged.

Beatrice looked at her aunt with great concern, wondering if perhaps it wasn't good for her to live alone. She still hadn't told Lydia of any of the strange (or terrible) happenings that'd gone on since she'd moved to New York. The time had never seemed right. "It was in October," Lydia said. "Just past mid-month. I remember because it was a full moon. I went out to the porch to sit a spell, and a woman came walking up the road. She was dressed in a long wool cloak with a pointed hood. She came right up to me and asked if I knew a girl with long red hair who wore a wren's feather on her lapel."

Beatrice's eyes went wide.

"Worried some ill might've befallen you, I told her the girl she'd described sounded much like my niece and if she had any news of you she should tell it. With a calm smile and tranquil face she said, 'Beatrice is safe.' Thinking it very queer, I told her I had no reason to think otherwise, then I asked her to leave. In a blink she was gone, no trace of her left. No sign of her in the yard or on the street. If she wasn't a ghost, then what do you suppose she was? And what do you suppose it meant?"

"Who knows . . ." Eleanor said, shaking her head.

"Sounds like a ghost to me," said Adelaide.

Beatrice sat thinking what the other two witches suspected, that Lydia's ghost was Madame St. Clair.

"Well, whatever she was," Lydia said, "I'm sure I never saw the likes of her before, and I suppose I'll never see the likes of her again. What a funny thing to happen, especially in Stony Point. Can you imagine what the ladies at the First United Presbyterian would say if I told them?"

"I wouldn't," Beatrice said.

"Nor would I," added Eleanor.

Shaking her head, Adelaide said, "Better not."

The year got off to a cold and snowy start, one of the worst winters on record. The work on the Dashleys' house got delayed, and then delayed again, so Judith spent much of her time at the Hermitage complaining about the house she couldn't live in and sharing gossip from the hotel. "Marietta's been asking after all of you. She'd like you to know she harbours no hard feelings and that you're welcome any time at the Fifth."

Miss Davis was also a frequent visitor, stopping in to chat with Eleanor, and to invite all three witches to attend the weekly gatherings of the NWSA. When the suffragists lost their regular meeting place, Eleanor had suggested they gather there, any evening except Saturday. (That night was reserved for Dr. Brody and the Unknown Philosophers, many of whom had taken a great liking to Eleanor's tea.) Despite the cold weather, business at the shop was brisk, due in no small part to the ladies of Sisters' Row discovering Eleanor's affinity for making teas, tinctures and powders that met their "specific needs." On any given day the place was full of customers engaged in conversations concerning everything from fortunes to fertility, from tinkering to theosophy.

By day, Beatrice resumed her role as Eleanor's apprentice—helping in the teashop and learning all she could about herbs, potions and the magic of Eleanor's people, the cunning folk. By night, she pored over newspapers and weeklies searching for reports of strange happenings around the city. She'd abandoned the idea of giving public demonstrations in favour of investigating individual sightings of ghosts instead. She'd even wheedled Adelaide and Dr. Brody into visiting several sites around the city, with a few of them turning out to be the real thing. In light of their recent investigations, Beatrice had informed Dr. Brody that she intended to write a book that was akin to Mr. Pratchett's *Compendium*. "But with miracles of the modern age," she'd said. "*A Census of Astonishments*." With that, Adelaide had promptly taken Beatrice to the stationer to have her first calling cards made. After going round and round about what it should say, she'd finally settled on this:

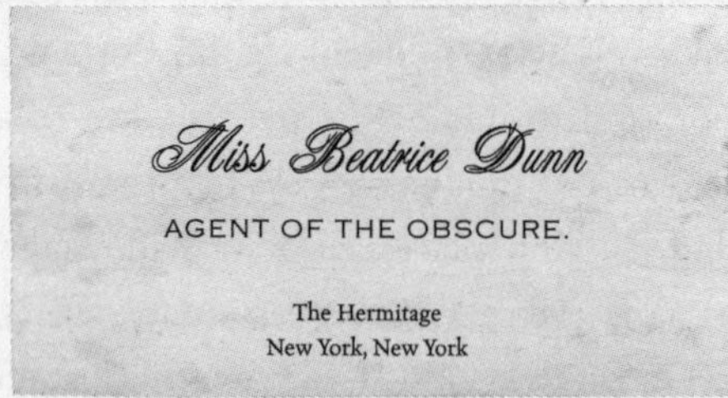

"A far cry from the 'Egyptian Sybil,'" Adelaide had teased.

"I suppose it is," Beatrice had said. "But far nearer to me."

On the evening of January 21, Dr. Brody announced over dinner that he'd arranged for them to take a nighttime sleigh ride through Central Park.

The wind was bitterly cold, but the sleigh driver provided them with blankets, fur pelts and a jug of warm cider. The sound of the sleigh's runners slicing through the snow along with the rhythmic jangle of the bells on the horses' necks cast a charming, happy spell over the cheerful quartet. A few other sleighing parties were out enjoying the evening, and jovial shouts and cheers were often exchanged between them.

It wasn't long before they came to Greywacke Knoll and the site where the obelisk was set to be righted on the morrow. To everyone's surprise except Dr. Brody's, two great bonfires had been lit on either side of the turning mechanism on which the obelisk sat. A small band of men stood between them.

"What's going on?" Eleanor asked, taking hold of Beatrice's hand, worried the sight of the fires might upset her.

"Yes, tell us," Adelaide said, sure that Quinn was keeping something from them. He'd had a terrible twitch in his eyebrow all evening. An endearing tell if she ever saw one.

Dr. Brody asked the driver to stop and to wait for them. Then he leapt from his seat and assisted each of the women down from the sleigh. "Trust me," he said. "You'll want to see this."

As the four of them stood watching, four men went about executing history prematurely. Gorringe, not wanting to leave anything to chance, had called for a dress rehearsal of the obelisk's shining moment. In the glare of the firelight, he stood on a platform and gave the order for the men on the tackles to "haul down, slack away!" Their motions seemed almost inconsequential in comparison with the graceful, effortless movement of the obelisk. Everyone who'd stopped to witness it went silent, struck dumb by the Needle's spell.

When the monument was nearly vertical, Gorringe, satisfied that the contraption could do its job, gave the order to reverse the process. Shouts and cheers rose up when it came to rest, people waving their hats or rising in their sleighs to celebrate the momentous occasion.

Walking to the bonfire that was closest to them, Adelaide, Eleanor, Beatrice and Dr. Brody stood to warm their hands.

"How did you know this was going to happen?" Adelaide asked, in awe of what they'd seen.

"I have my ways," Dr. Brody said with a wink.

"What a sight," Eleanor said, staring up at the Needle. "It truly is magnificent."

Beatrice stood in silence, letting the moment stand.

Before long, her reverie was interrupted by someone tapping her on the shoulder. "Miss," a gentleman's voice said, "remember me?" It was the person who'd bid her to touch the obelisk on her first day in New York.

"Yes," she said, turning to look after the rest of her party, who were making their way back to the sleigh.

"I'm leaving tomorrow," he said, gold tooth glinting in the firelight. "But I've something to give you before I go."

"My friends are leaving."

"I won't let them go without you," he promised. Then reaching his hand into the fire, he pulled out a glowing ember. "Trust me," he said. "Take it."

Closing her eyes, she let him place it in her palm. She felt no burning, no pain.

"Hold it tight," he ordered. "Don't be afraid."

Clutching the ember in her grasp, she felt it turn cold.

When she opened her eyes and her hand, the man was gone. All that remained was a stone scarab sitting in her palm, smooth and sparkling like the granite of the obelisk. She put it in her pocket and ran for the sleigh, planning to keep it to herself for now, or perhaps forever.

That night after everyone had gone to bed, Beatrice sat at her desk staring at the stone scarab. Tomorrow she was to go with Dr. Brody to visit a young telegraph operator who'd reportedly been receiving strange messages after getting a shock from a faulty machine. The *Evening Star* had teasingly asked, "Is she a new witch?" Beatrice wondered what she might say to the girl that would be of any use. Looking through her notes and journals, she searched for a helpful spell Eleanor might've given her, or a bit of worldly wisdom from Adelaide, or some thoughtful saying of Madame St. Clair's. In the end, she chose to pick up her pen.

ADVICE *for* NEW WITCHES.

It starts with an inkling, a twist in the heart. A sigh, a voice without flesh—announcing somewhere between slumber and waking, "Careful what you wish for, lest you receive it."

Next comes the beholding of inexplicable things. A door, shut and locked, opened by forces unseen. A ball of yarn, unravelled in a heap, rolls itself up again. Take note of mysterious happenings—make lists, keep track. See how wonders multiply when magic is not dismissed.

One needn't carry the blood of ancients to be chosen by Fate. No witch's mark, no gap-toothed smile, no dimple in the chin. Only a sense of longing, a restlessness within.

For the time has come, the day has arrived, as the Spinner of Tales once said, when witches the wide world over are no longer born, but made.

By mystery, magic, hopes and dreams. By communing with ghosts in the dark. By ambition, desire, curiosity and need. By tying knots around the wishes of your heart. By charms, enchantments, incantations and schemes. By mixing blood with graveyard dust. By scratching the names of angels on your skin. By struggle, pain, heartbreak and loss.

To all young women who read by foxfire or dance in the crossroads at night—you, darling ladies, are well on your way, nearly ready to take flight. The path lies ahead, daunting and long, so travel it while you are able. Believe in dreams, ghosts and spectres—ignore them at your peril.

And now, you may ask, how will you know when your making's done?

The answer is quite simple, my dear—by the pricking of your thumbs.

The
END

Acknowledgements

My thanks go out to those who kindly lent their expertise and knowledge during both the research and writing phases of this book: the amazing librarians and archivists at both the New York Historical Society and the NYPL; Angie Oriana Jenkins (belly dancing herbalist extraordinaire); and Bree Hyland of BARRE Studio (whose marvellous dream tea kept my imagination flowing).

Of the many books consulted for this work, the following became companions and guides along the way: *Madison Square: The Park and Its Celebrated Landmarks* by Miriam Berman; *America Bewitched: The Story of Witchcraft After Salem* by Owen Davies; *Wonders of the Invisible World* by Cotton Mather; *More Wonders of the Invisible World* by Robert Calef; *Flowers and Flower Lore* by Hilderic Friend; *Ten Days in a Mad-House* by Nellie Bly; *Opium Fiend* by Steven Martin; *Experimental Investigations of the Spirit Manifestations* by Robert Hare; *The History of Last Night's Dream* by Rodger Kamenetz; *Narratives of the Witchcraft Cases: 1648–1706* by George Lincoln Burr; *Egyptian Obelisks* by Henry Honeychurch Gorringe; and *Woman, Church and State* by Matilda Joslyn Gage; as well as the many writings on folk magic, traditions and witchlore by Gerina Dunwich and the late, great Scott Cunningham.

Many thanks go to the Canada Council for the Arts for their generous and vital support during the writing process.

Much gratitude and appreciation goes to the amazing team at Knopf Canada for their enduring dedication to the written word, especially my editor, Anne Collins, whose sublime intuition for finding truth in language always feels like magic.

Thanks also to Claire Wachtel for lunch at Saks, for quoting Frost and for pointing the way; and to Genevieve Pegg at Orion, who saw the heart of the story from the start.

Special thanks to my agent, Helen Heller, for championing my work, and for her archaeological encouragement "to always dig deeper."

Thank you to my friends and family, far and near who have given me such incredible support and love over the years—Skip, Doug and Lori, for cheering me on through scraped knees and spilt milk; Chris O'Neill and Ken Schwartz at the Ross Creek Centre for the Arts and Two Planks and Passion Theatre for your friendship and for building an artistic haven on the mountain; Marta Pelrine-Bacon, Dawn Jones-Graham and Jon Hyneman for late night conversations, cups of tea and witchy consultations.

As always, the most thanks and all my love go to my nearest and dearest: my sons, Ian and Jonah, who have brought more laughter, joy and wonder to my life than I ever imagined possible; and to my beloved husband, Ian, who is my guiding star, my heart and my "yes and" to everything.

Author's Note

While writing this book I stumbled upon a startling fact—my nine times great-aunt Mary Ayer Parker was executed for witchcraft. In the midst of the turmoil that was the Salem witch trials, she and her daughter Sarah were accused and imprisoned. Mary, a fifty-five-year-old widow, was later tried and convicted, and on September 22, 1692, she was hanged at Gallows Hill. Thanks to an edict that put a stop to subsequent hangings, Sarah's life was spared.

As you might imagine, discovering this tragic bit of my family history inevitably shaped the narrative of *The Witches of New York*. So many questions now came to my mind as I wrote—What does the word "witch" truly mean? Had any vestiges of folk magic survived the witch trials? What had happened between the witch hunts (of both Europe and North America) and the constraining, patronizing view of womanhood held in the Victorian era? Surely there were connections to be made.

As a child who loved to play make-believe, I always preferred to pretend to be a witch rather than a princess—specifically, Glinda, the good sorceress of Oz. Not the glitzy film version of Glinda, but the mighty witch that L. Frank Baum originally created for his wonderful series of Oz books. That Glinda was wise and savvy, kind yet firm, and always erred on the side of letting Dorothy find her own way. In hindsight, I suppose I loved her because she reminded me a lot of my own mother, a woman who never failed to encourage me to find magic in the world whenever and wherever I could. My mother, like Glinda, believed in the powers of intellect, tenacity and intuition ("you've always had the power my dear . . . you just had to learn it for yourself"), and taught me that no girl or woman should ever apologize for such gifts.

L. Frank Baum's vision of Glinda (as well as Ozma, the fairy-touched girl who was the rightful ruler of Oz) was inspired by conversations he had with his mother-in-law, Matilda Joslyn Gage, a woman who was a staunch abolitionist, an unapologetic suffragist and a leading voice in the fight for aboriginal rights in the United States. Also a prolific writer, she encouraged her son-in-law to inhabit his Land of Oz with strong female characters so that his four sons might grow up with role models in their fairy tales that would prepare them for a new, enlightened age. In her seminal work, *Women, Church and State*, published in 1893, Matilda boldly addressed the history of witchcraft and the persecution of women accused of it, drawing many parallels to her own time.

> The church degraded woman by destroying her self-respect and teaching her to feel consciousness of guilt in the very fact of her existence.
>
> To this day, an open, confident look upon a woman's face is deprecated as evil.
>
> Death by torture was the method of the church for the repression of woman's intellect, knowledge being held as evil and dangerous in her hands.
>
> The witch was in reality the profoundest thinker, the most advanced scientist of those ages.
>
> The testimony of the ages entirely destroys the assertion sometimes made that witchcraft was merely a species of hysteria.

The treatise was a call to action, a rallying cry to women to reclaim the word "witch." She was tired of female voices being silenced (for being too intelligent, too wise, too feminine, too different). She was tired of seeing women get cast aside—dismissed, ostracized or sent off to asylums. This was the era of Charlotte Perkins Gilman's "The Yellow Wallpaper," and Jean-Martin Charcot's weekly lectures at the Salpêtrière where he paraded his "hysterical" female subjects before the general public. It seemed the hunts hadn't ended, they'd just taken on a more subversive, sinister form.

Sadly, Matilda's work was met with sneers and skepticism, even among a few of her sister suffragists. "Too radical," they said, "too divisive." Yet she persisted, speaking out for the suffragist cause until her death in 1898. I wonder what she'd make of the women's movement today.

I'm guessing she'd say there's still plenty of work to be done. How many times are women still told that their stories, their testimonies, their ideas don't matter? Or that they're only meant for our own gender? How many girls are scolded each day for not smiling? Or shamed for the clothes she chose to wear? Or teased for being too smart? Or refused admittance to school?

Ray Bradbury once wrote, "A witch is born out of the true hungers of her time."

I believe that's true for the witches in this book, for their time as well as mine.

Get ready world, something witchy this way comes.

May 16, 2016,
Scots Bay, NS

AMI MCKAY's debut novel, *The Birth House*, was a #1 bestseller in Canada, winner of three CBA Libris Awards, nominated for the International IMPAC Dublin Literary Award, a finalist for Canada Reads and a book-club favourite around the world. Her second novel, *The Virgin Cure*, also a national bestseller and a Best Book pick across numerous lists, was inspired by the life of her great-great-grandmother, Dr. Sarah Fonda Mackintosh, a female physician in nineteenth-century New York. Born and raised in Indiana, McKay now lives in Nova Scotia.